second edition

food preparation for hotels, restaurants, and cafeterias

ROBERT G. HAINES

*Chef instructor, Norwood Technical School
Norwood, Ohio*

*Member:
American Vocational Association
Ohio Vocational Association
Norwood Teachers Association
Council on Hotel, Restaurant
 and Institutional Education
Iota Lambda Sigma Fraternity
Cincinnati Restaurant Association
Cooks and Pastry Cooks Union
 Local #177*

AMERICAN TECHNICAL PUBLISHERS, INC.
ALSIP, ILLINOIS 60658

preface
to second
edition

Since its first printing, Mr. Haines' excellent book on the art and craft of cooking for commercial food establishments has had immediate and repeated acceptance and acclaim. The 700 and more basic recipes selected for the first edition have been expanded to over 770 recipes, all tested in the kitchen by the author and his students. These recipes are no random selection, but have been carefully organized by the author for specific needs and presented in an easy-to-follow work sequence.

New material introduced in this new Second Edition include recent developments in equipment, the uses and impact of convenience foods in the food service industry, a revised and expanded glossary of culinary terms, and two completely new chapters: Breakfast Preparation (Chapter 7), and Puddings, Ice

Creams, and Specialty Desserts (Chapter 27). Again, Mr. Haines' approach to the ancient and respected art of cooking is fresh and original.

The early chapters of the book (Chapters 1 to 6) deal with the basic fundamentals: equipment, skills, cooking techniques, and products necessary to all areas of food preparation. These chapters should be studied carefully and should also be referred back to whenever the student encounters difficulty with any recipe operation. Specific information and instruction is given on the nomenclature and use of cooks' tools and the operation of kitchen equipment. The basic principles of food preparation and the proper cooking techniques are given, along with the safe methods of work performance and instruction in sanitation and hygiene.

The recipe chapters (Chapters 7 to 27) also provide introductory material to the specific subject covered, suggesting procedures and rules for successful cooking.

The recpies chosen are the basic preparations in common use in most food service establishments. Representative recipes have been chosen in all areas of cooking.

Depending on the complexity and difficulty of the recipe, each recipe has been broken down into a step-by-step series of unit operations. These operations lead, in a logical work sequence, to the finished product. By breaking each recipe into basic performance units or operations, the student can immediately grasp *what* is to be done, *how* it is to be done and *when* to do it. This approach also enables the instructor to more readily check the student's performance and to spot specific operations and manual skills in which more training and guidance are needed.

For the more difficult recipes a short introduction is given outlining how the specific item is prepared and served. Learning objectives, the equipment needed, and precautions and safety measures are also given. The more difficult recipes have their performances broken down into two major areas: (1) the *preparation,* the initial task of bringing all the equipment and ingredients together, and readying the ingredients for cooking; and (2) the *procedure,* the combining or mixing, cooking, and finishing of the preparation. Not only are the food preparation operations given, but also suggestions on portion control, garnishing, and serving. The student is guided from the assembly of ingredients and equipment up to the point where the prepared item is ready to be served to the guest.

If any terms or operations are not understood, the student should consult the glossary at the end of the book, and he should check the text for how-to-do-it instructions and operation information.

In modern food service, quality control in food production is essential. Therefore, each recipe has been standardized so that both quality and quantity control may be attained. To further this end, the text provides the student with information on the accurate weighing and measuring of food ingredients. Instruction in recipe adjustment is also provided—that is, how to calculate the ingredients for a specific number of guests.

To enable the student to better understand food production and the operation of a food service establishment, a chapter on menu making (Chapter 28) has been provided. This will not only give the student an understanding of how to select and write a menu, but also an insight into some of the many problems that must be faced by the managers of food service establishments.

The author, Mr. Haines, is unusually qualified to write a quantity food preparation text. He has worked for over 30 years in the food service industry, and has extensive experience working in commercial kitchens and teaching cooking in the classroom and laboratory. Mr. Haines has also served on various committees over the years for the promotion and development of the food service industry.

The author would like to thank Mr. Elton E. Kistler, Director, Scarlet Oaks Career Development Center, for encouragement, guidance and technical help he provided while the original manuscript was being written. Thanks is also given to all individuals, business firms and organizations who contributed to this book, including Mr. Haines' wife, Dolores; his daughter, Mrs. Connie Kruetzkamp; and his son, Robert M. Haines.

THE PUBLISHERS

contents

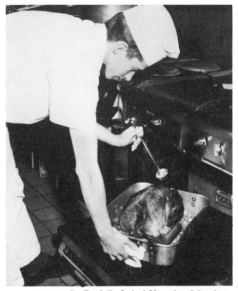

St. Paul Technical Vocational Institute
St. Paul, Minnesota
Photo: F. H. Hofmeister

St. Paul Technical Vocational Institute
St. Paul, Minnesota
Photo: F. H. Hofmeister

Washburn Trade School
Chicago, Illinois

The modern commercial kitchen today needs trained personnel in all areas of food service. *Top left:* Students preparing salads in a cooking class. *Top right:* Student cook basting a roast turkey. *Bottom:* Students learning how to bake rolls in a classroom bake shop.

chapter 1

careers in food service

■ Over the past 15 years many opportunities have arisen in the food service field. This has been due to several reasons: the great population explosion; the decrease in trained European cooks and chefs coming to America to apply their trade; the demand of the American people for finer foods; the establishment of more-and-more restaurants to fulfill the needs of an America on the move; and the fact that more-and-more housewives are working and, consequently, are less willing to prepare the evening meal. Today more people are eating out, and the many restaurants that are springing up need trained food personnel.

Restaurants *small* and *large* through-out the United States are becoming more numerous and are engaged in many different types of operations. De luxe restaurants featuring decor and classical cuisine, cafeterias featuring variety and lower prices, specialty houses featuring extremely popular items, drive-ins offering quick service and popular prices all desire and need good food service personnel. All these different types of operations have created prosperity in the industry and in doing so have made available many opportunities in cooking and managing.

Many of the high school administrators are becoming aware of the opportunities in the food service field today

Food Service Magazine

Undergraduates learn the basics of quantity cooking in classroom laboratory.

and have brought this type of training into their school systems. Most of these commercial cooking courses range in length from two to four years, and across the nation many fine programs have been developed. It would greatly aid the individual aspirant to a food service career to enroll in one of these programs where he can receive a good background in the fundamentals of food preparations, as well as the related information on food cost, food science, and trade conditions. This type of training is necessary to any successful food service man or woman today. Upon completion of his high school training one could further his education in food by attending a junior college or an institute with a food service program.

Further training for the student cook or chef can be provided on the job. Many school systems have programs that work in conjunction with commercial food service establishments. The large hotel and motel kitchens throughout the United States are excellent training grounds for the person who aspires to become a cook or chef. This is true primarily because the large scale production that is carried on in them gives a greater opportunity to see and do.

The food service industry has for many years been a backward industry and has just recently shown indications of modernization and breaking away from the old world methods that have been practiced for years. There are signs of a willingness to pay people wages competitive with other trades, and this is a necessity in order to attract young people. Many people, however, overlook the fact that their meals and clothing are supplied on the job, and this is a big factor in considering overall wages.

Surely the day will come when a pension plan and hospitalization will be offered. In fact, this has already become a reality in some cities.

Food service is a demanding trade or profession but, on the other hand, a very rewarding one. It is required that an employee be willing to work on some holidays, when other people are enjoying a day of leisure, because this is the period when business is at its peak. In some situations, long hours are necessary. This is especially true in the management field: if the manager is conscientious he will *want* to be around to *control* any given situation. Many emergencies arise in a food service operation and someone with authority should be present.

Besides the usual monetary rewards found in most jobs, the many compliments received from the clientele or management when the food or preparation is of excellent quality is extremely rewarding to most individuals. Also, in any food service operation a person can always display and put into practice any artistic or creative ability he may possess. Many people have become famous for original ideas introduced while working as a cook or chef. Most people look upon the outstanding chef as an artist, creating beauty and eye appeal in his preparation and presentation of foods. It is said that beauty enriches goodness and health—desired qualities we all wish to possess.

It is often asked what qualities or talents a person should possess before em-

Display of food preparations in a commercial cooking class. (Note the ice mold in the center of the table.)

barking upon a career in the culinary trade. This question is, of course, a difficult one and most educators and food service operators have varied opinions. The following qualifications are necessary, however, if a person wishes to advance to a position of authority:

1. *Attitude:* Willing to take instructions and criticism.

2. *Dependable:* On the job every day, without fail.

3. *Cooperation with others:* Working at close quarters, in most cases, it is essential that one get along with his fellow workers.

4. *Willingness to work:* When directed to do a task, do it willingly without prodding. Work hard.

5. *Initiative:* Doing a task without being told.

6. *Cleanliness:* The key to good health. Germs spread quickly.

7. *Interest:* One must have some interest in food *production* in order to be successful.

8. *Artistic ability:* A very desirable trait, but not necessarily needed.

9. *Health:* Good physical health is necessary because of the long hours on your feet and, in some cases, heavy lifting.

10. *Stick - to - it - ism:* This word, brought forth in one of Mr. Walt Disney's cartoons, is a must. To accomplish any task requires this quality.

FOOD SERVICE OCCUPATIONS

There are many different positions one might wish to fill in the commercial kitchen, depending on desire and ambition. The following is a list of the jobs and some of the duties that must be performed in carrying out the job.

Manager: He or she conducts and directs all affairs of the operation and oversees food preparation and service. In some cases the manager does the ordering of all equipment and keeps close check on food cost.

Head chef: He is a man of many things and talents. His business is food and food preparation and he is in complete charge of the kitchen. He must organize his employee's work schedule and be able to calculate food and labor cost. He must also be able to make out menus and instruct his personnel in the preparation of foods. He may have any of the following titles: *executive chef, chef steward,* or *working chef.* The title usually depends on the size of the establishment.

The *executive chef* is in charge of the kitchen in large hotels, with sous chefs (first assistants) and a large crew at his command. His duties are mostly devoted to supervising and managing the kitchen. He will plan and write the menus, arrange working schedules, and see that all food is prepared and served according to the standards set by the establishment.

The *chef steward* is a position created by the medium sized hotels. Besides his regular duties as a chef the chef steward also does the purchasing of all food supplies, this responsibility usually requires his absence from the kitchen for a few hours each morning. In his absence, the sous chef or second cook is placed in charge. When the meals for luncheon, dinner and banquets are being served he supervises all activity.

The *working chef* is a position created for the smaller food service establishments as an economy factor. In the small hotels, restaurants and cafeterias the food production is on a smaller scale and the preparation crew must be held to a minimum. Under these conditions the chef besides carrying out his regular duties will assist in production by taking over a work station or assisting where needed. During the hours of service he works as well as supervises.

Sous chef: The head chef's first assistant. He carries out the head chef's orders for each day, instructs the personnel in the preparation of some foods and assists the head chef in directing all kitchen production and service.

Second cook: He is an all around experienced tradesman. He is the top man of the production crew and follows the sous chef in order of authority. He prepares boiled, stewed, braised, sautéed and combination cream dishes, as well as taking care of all special à la carte and chafing dish preparations. The second cook is usually a premium paid employee.

Night chef: He takes complete charge of the kitchen when the executive and sous chef have left for the day. He supervises the preparation and service of the night operation.

Banquet chef: He has complete charge of all the parties. He supervises the preparation of all the party foods. He is under the direct supervision of the executive chef.

Pastry chef: He supervises the pastry department, makes out the dessert menus, schedules all work that is performed in the pastry department and in many cases decorates cakes and special pastries. The pastry chef is under the direct supervision of the executive chef.

Assistant pastry chef: He is under the direct supervision of the pastry chef and is usually in charge of production. He participates in the production of cakes, tarts, cookies, tortes, pies, etc.

Swing cook: He relieves all cooks on all stations on their day off. He usually must cover a different job each day of the week. He must therefore be a highly skilled person with an exceptional amount of experience. The swing cook must adopt to irregular working hours because each day not only is his job dif-

ferent but also the working hours as well. The job of swing cook is an opportunity to acquire additional experience needed to become an exceptionally fine tradesman.

Fry cook: His work is performed around the range and deep fat fryer. He is responsible for the preparation of eggs, fritters, omelettes, crepes (pancakes), potato preparations and all fried items that appear on the menu. The fry cook is also in charge of all vegetable preparation and will direct the work of the vegetable man if one is on the staff.

Roast cook: His work is performed around the ovens and range. He is responsible for the preparation of all roasts and the gravies that may accompany the roast. In smaller establishments the roast cook and broiler cook may be a combination job and the cook who is assigned to the task must be thoroughly trained to do both.

Broiler cook: He prepares all broiled foods such as steaks, fish, chops, chicken, sweetbreads, liver, etc. In some cases, depending on the size of the operation, one man will serve both as broiler cook and roast cook.

Soup cook: He is responsible for the preparation of all soup stocks, consommés, hot and cold soups, etc. He also boils chickens, turkeys and hams taking care to see that the stocks are kept clear for later use in soups. In some establishments this job may be combined with the duties of the second cook.

Cold Meat Man (or the *Garde Manger,* the French term meaning guardian of cold meats). The cold meat department is under the supervision of the garde manager or head cold meat man. His duties are to oversee and help in the preparation of sandwiches, salad dressings and other cold sauces, making seafood and meat salads, breading all meat and fish items, making cold appetizers and canapés, parboiling brains and sweetbreads, cooking shrimp, etc. He is usually a premium-

Photo: Kathryn Adams

A cooking class at Norwood Technical School, Norwood, Ohio, working on salads. In the commercial kitchen side salads are prepared by pantry personnel, but in many cases the entree salads, shown here, are prepared by the cold meat man. An all around cook or chef will possess an extensive knowledge of salad preparation.

Photo: Kathryn Adams

Student cooks working sweet dough under the guidance of the cooking instructor.

paid man and well versed in decorating foods for buffets and smorgasbords.

Breakfast cook: He prepares hot cereals and is responsible for all breakfast orders designated for his station (example: eggs, bacon, ham, potatoes, etc.). He sets up the fry cook station for the luncheon business and in many cases will perform as a fry cook after the breakfast business has been completed.

Butcher: Although referred to as the butcher, he is actually a meat cutter. He is responsible for boning, cutting and preparing all beef, pork, veal and their by-products for cooking. In many establishments today he may also be responsible for cleaning, cutting and preparing fish and poultry for cooking. This would depend on whether the establishment is large enough to hire a fish or poultry butcher. Some of the very large operations will hire butchers for these specific jobs, however this practice is not as common today as it was years ago. It is also of interest to know that many food serv-ice establishments will assign the duties of fish butcher to the cold meat man.

Baker: The head baker bakes all breads, rolls and quickbreads. He is responsible for the operation of the bakery, but is usually under the supervision of the pastry chef.

Baker's helper: He will assist the head baker in most preparations and also perform the task of keeping the bake shop clean and orderly.

Night second cook: He helps serve the lunch, cuts garnishes for the following days preparations and sets up the second cook station for the dinner business.

Night fry cook: He helps serve the lunch then sets up the fry cook station for the dinner business.

Assistant cold meat man: He prepares meat and seafood salad and sandwiches for the luncheon business, assists the head cold meat man in all types of work and sets up for the dinner business.

Vegetable man or cook: He cleans all vegetables and in some cases cooks them under the direction of the fry cook.

Cook's helper: He assists all cooks in preparing and serving food. A few of his specific duties are as follows: (a) cleans shrimp and removes the meat from cooked poultry; (b) cleans and prepares fruits and vegetables; (c) sets up relish trays; (d) helps dish up for parties; and (e) strains soups and stocks. The job of cook's helper presents an excellent opportunity for the ambitious and dependable worker to learn how foods are prepared and served, and in time he will undoubtedly be given the opportunity to become a vegetable or fry cook.

Many of the jobs listed above, depending on the size of the establishment and the amount of preparation carried on in that establishment, are combination jobs performed by one man.

personal hygiene and sanitation

■ When thinking in terms of food preparation, the word *cleanliness* must be given first consideration, for without exercising cleanliness the food service operator is doomed to failure. The public will no longer forgive the establishment that neglects its sanitation responsibilities. In fact, the average customer today will give the food service operator only one chance. If he fails to make good, a potential steady customer is lost. This person will more than likely never return.

It is not only the responsibility of management, but also the responsibility of the entire staff to see to it that good sanitation practices are observed and carried out. Management has the responsibility to see that facilities and equipment are kept clean. The employee has the responsibility to keep himself and his work station clean, as well as to follow the standard rules of everyday personal hygiene.

When using the term *sanitation,* we are speaking of the science of bringing about general, healthful conditions. *Personal hygiene,* on the other hand, refers to the cleanliness practiced by an individual, such as his grooming and other individual habits he may display. Both sanitation and personal hygiene must have top priority in any food service organization today. Everyone should practice them.

PERSONAL HYGIENE

There are many advantages, other than those which are obvious, which the individual may reap by practicing good personal hygiene. We are generally judged by first impressions until, of course, people get to know us better. If those first impressions are poor, people may never take the time or interest to know us better. These first impressions are conveyed largely by appearance. If our appearance is neat, clean, and in good taste, the first impression will be excellent. If the person forming that impression is a prospective employer, he will assume that your work will be neat and clean also. So, from the first, a relationship and association are started that may mature into a profitable partnership for both you and your employer. On many occasions when a well-groomed person enters a room, people will stop whatever they are doing to eye him or her up and down. These well-groomed individuals attract attention and, after all, to a great degree life is a game of selling yourself. Personal hygiene is a way of life. It is a standard that must be set and maintained by any individual who wishes to become successful in the business world today and especially in the food service business. It is an established

PERSONAL GROOMING CHECK LIST

	UNSATISFACTORY	SATISFACTORY
1. HEAD		
(A) HAIR CUT (SHORT FOR FOOD SERVICE) AND COMBED.		
(B) NO DANDRUFF.		
(C) HEAD, NECK, AND EARS CLEAN.		
(D) HAIR SHOULD NOT BE GREASY.		
2. FACE		
(A) CLEAN SHAVEN.		
(B) CLEAN TEETH.		
(C) CLEAR, CLEAN COMPLEXION.		
(D) EYE BROWS TRIMMED IF BUSHY.		
3. HANDS		
(A) CLEAN.		
(B) CLEAN NAILS.		
(C) NAILS TRIMMED FAIRLY CLOSE.		
4. BODY ODOR		
(A) FRESH.		
(B) DON'T USE EXCESSIVE PERFUMES.		
5. POSTURE		
(A) STAND ERECT.		
(B) DO NOT SLOUCH AT ANY TIME.		
(C) HEAD UP AND SHOULDERS BACK.		
6. DRESS		
(A) SHOES SHINED.		
(B) APPROPRIATE CLOTHES WORN CORRECTLY.		
(C) CLOTHES CLEAN.		
(D) CLOTHES FIT PROPERLY.		

fact that a person's appearance is an aid to his personality, and a good personality is another important step in selling yourself.

The *Personal Grooming Checklist* is a list of important factors that must be observed and followed if you desire to become a well-groomed person and be physically attractive. Some of these are absolutely essential to safety in the kitchen. How do you rate?

For safety, the following rules of personal hygiene *must* be observed.

1. Keep your hands and fingernails clean; use soap and water. Be sure to wash your hands after visiting the washroom.
2. Keep your fingers out of food and clean utensils.
3. Never work around food if you have open cuts, sores, etc.
4. Do not cough, spit, sneeze, or smoke near food or food containers. Always cover a cough or sneeze with your handkerchief, and wash your hands after using the handkerchief.
5. Stay at home when you are sick.
6. Wear the proper clothing for your job. Always keep your hair covered.
7. Keep yourself and your clothing clean.
8. Do not allow dirty utensils or equipment to touch food.
9. Keep your work area spotless.

SANITATION

Great responsibility rests on the shoulders of the food service operator and his preparation staff in controlling the harmful bacteria that is found in all foods. Let there be just one case of food poisoning in his establishment, and he can close his doors for good. Food poisoning is the result of eating food that has been contaminated by harmful bacteria or their toxins. This causes the person eating such foods to become extremely ill, and in some cases death may result. To understand food poisoning, it is important to understand bacteria and how they grow and multiply so rapidly. The three main causes of food poisoning are yeast contamination, bacterial growth, and mold. To some degree, the *type* of food will have a direct bearing on just how accessible it will be to these three forms of germs. Orange juice, tomato mixtures, and all acid foods will resist bacterial and mold growth, but are accessible to yeast contamination. Meat will resist yeast contamination but cannot ward off bacterial or mold growth, unless the meat is wiped with some form of acid mixture such as vinegar. Bread is, of course, susceptible to the mold growth.

Regardless of the type of bacteria spoiling the food, they all grow very rapidly under favorable conditions. Bacteria divide once every 20 minutes, so it is possible in a sixteen-hour period for one bacterium to multiply into over seventy trillion. We stated that this could happen under favorable conditions; and favorable conditions to bacteria are *warmth, food,* and *moisture.* Knowing this, the food service personnel must make sure these conditions do not exist when storing or caring for foods. We know that some bacteria and moisture are usually present in all foods, so it stands to reason that our chief weapon against these germs is *temperature control.* Bacteria grow very slowly at temperatures below 40° F, and their growth is stopped completely at 0° F and below. They grow very little at 140° F and they are destroyed at temperatures of 180° F or over. It then becomes the duty of the food service personnel to get foods over the 140° F temperature or below 40° F as soon as possible if they wish to control the growth of these harmful bacteria.

It has also been stated that bacteria

thrive in moisture. Therefore, if all the moisture is extracted from certain foods, the foods will keep indefinitely. This is why powdered eggs and milk, as well as other dehydrated foods, have become so popular.

The following is a list of food-borne diseases and how they may be passed on to the customers.

Food Poisoning: Contaminated food caused by poor refrigeration, unwashed hands, holding the food too long at the danger temperature, food in punctured cans, or food that comes in contact with rodents.

Trichinosis: Undercooked pork. (All pork should be cooked well done.)

Dysentery: Defective plumbing, water contaminated at its source, and food contaminated by flies or unwashed hands.

Typhoid Fever: Milk, water, or shellfish contaminated at their source; food contaminated by flies or unwashed hands.

Diphtheria: Improperly washed dishes or silverware; coughing or sneezing.

To help safeguard from food contamination, it is essential that rats, mice, roaches, and flies, which are carriers of disease and germs, be controlled. Most of these pests live in colonies, and if one is spotted you can be sure there are many more on the premises. There is much that the employee can do to help control the spread of these pests: Check to see that all openings in doors, windows, air vent screens, etc., are sealed; check incoming supplies; and clean up any trash and garbage before it accumulates. However, if these pests become a problem, it is best to retain the services of a professional exterminator and have him check the establishment at least once a month. *Insecticides and poisons are dangerous when in the hands of amateurs.*

Washing

Many problems develop in the sanitation programs of certain food service establishments because of improper dish, silverware, glassware, and pot washing. It is essential to good restaurant management to have these duties under surveillance at all times. Dishes should be scraped and rinsed before placing them in the dish racks. Silverware should be soaked before washing, and glassware should be washed in clear water using a compound recommended for glassware. The procedure for washing, rinsing, and drying these items properly will depend on the kind and size of equipment available and the program set up by management or the sanitation company whose products you may be using. However, you can rest assured that, regardless of the program in operation, the temperature in the wash or rinse water will reach 180° F because in most cities this is a requirement set forth by the Board of Health and, again, it is the temperature that will kill most bacteria. It is also necessary to have employees handle the service ware properly when moving them from one place to another. One of the shortcomings is fingerprints on glass and dish ware. Management must also provide proper storage spaces with closed doors so the equipment will not be contaminated while standing for service.

For proper pot washing, three factors are necessary for good results: hot water, friction, and detergent. Of the three, friction is generally the most neglected. Pots should be scraped clean, placed in hot water containing a good detergent, and scrubbed thoroughly, using a pot brush and that well-known item called "elbow grease." Next, they are passed through a very hot rinse water and left to air dry. Some communities require the use of sanitizing chemicals, such as iodine or chlorine. Local ordinances must be followed in using these chemicals. Caution must be exercised in using steel wool and other types of scouring pads, for too often pieces will come off and be left in the pot to end up in the next day's preparation.

Inspecting steam jacket and steam pressure cookers.

The cook's personal tools are another source of bacteria growth that in many cases is overlooked. Knives are used to cut certain items, and some of the food will cling to the blade. The knife is then stored until the following day when it is used again; this time the knife transfers germs from the blade to the item it is cutting. The same thing happens with the cook's kitchen fork and other personal equipment. Your personal tools must be washed. Otherwise, germs will be spread and your customer's health endangered. At the same time, your own reputation as a chef or cook will be put in jeopardy.

Strict sanitation standards must also be followed in cleaning stationary equipment. All stationary equipment and attachments must be cleansed after use, usually with soap and water. The cutting surface of the meat block, however, should *never* be cleansed with water, as cracks may develop and collect food particles. Use a scraper and wire brush for cleansing meat cutting surfaces.

There are many new products on the market today that will assist management in carrying out a good sanitation program, but in any program the human element must receive priority. It has been stated many times that any cleaning job is 95 percent human element and only 5 percent mechanical. In our fast-moving society, the mechanical element is gaining rapidly. One piece of equipment, for example, that is causing this change is the automatic pot washer, which is faster and does a more thorough job than human labor ever could. If this piece of equipment is ever produced at a lower cost, the job of the pot washer will no longer exist.

Sanitation Rules

For safe food service, the kitchen personnel should put into practice the following rules.

1. Get foods hot as quickly as possible and keep them hot, 140° F or over.
2. Get foods cold as quickly as possible and keep them cold, 40° F or below.
3. Keep foods covered as much as possible; use clean utensils.
4. Purchase inspected meat.
5. Exercise caution when using leftovers.
6. Wash all fresh fruits and vegetables.
7. Purchase pasteurized milk.

8. Do not prepare too much food ahead.
9. Do not expose food to the danger temperatures (40° to 140°F) for more than a three hour period.
10. Do not refreeze thawed meat, fish, or vegetables. (Freezing and refreezing causes cellular breakdown and increases susceptibility to decay.)
11. Make sure bent cans have not been punctured.
12. Check all fish and shellfish for freshness when they arrive. (Fresh fish have firm flesh, bright red gills, and clear eyes.)
13. Cook all pork thoroughly.
14. Dispose of all garbage, rubbish, etc., promptly.
15. If ever in doubt about any food, throw it away.

We have attempted, in this chapter, to impress upon the student the importance of a good sanitation program and the fact that sanitation and personal hygiene is everyone's job. Undoubtedly, the day of the sloppy and unclean cook is at an end. It is hoped that, with the realization that germs multiply rapidly, and with the realization of the harm these spreading creatures can do, the cooks and all food service personnel will not only strive to improve themselves but their surroundings as well.

tools and stationary equipment

chapter 3

■ Learning to become a top journeyman in any field of endeavor requires knowledge and skill in the use of certain tools and other types of equipment associated with the trade. This is especially true of the culinary trade. One of the first requirements for becoming a cook is the knowledge of the proper use of a French knife. The second requirement is to acquire skill and speed with this knife. There are, of course, many other pieces of equipment that the student, aspiring to a career as a cook or chef, must be familiar with and in most cases learn to use properly.

In the commercial kitchen, equipment can be divided into two categories: hand or stationary. Hand tools or equipment are generally small in size and can be found hanging on the equipment rack or stored in drawers or cabinets. They are generally supplied by the establishment; although, in the case of knives and other special tools, most cooks will purchase their own, mark them plainly, and permit no one else to use them. Most cooks take pride in their personal equipment, keeping their knives sharp and their equipment in the best condition at all times. Tools, especially cutlery, will perform better when only one person is using them. Stationary equipment is heavy; it is placed in one definite place and very seldom, if ever, moved. It is *always* purchased by the establishment. In many cases, this type of equipment is essential to a smooth, efficient operation.

HAND TOOLS

The following is a list of equipment the student cook should become familiar with if he wishes to develop in the culinary trade. In many cases, unless he is familiar with certain pieces of this equipment, he will be unable to prepare the recipes presented in this book. A description and an illustration of each piece of equipment are given so the student will learn to recognize it quickly when the time comes for its use.

Cutting implements

Boning knife: A short, thin knife with a pointed blade used to remove bone from raw meat with minimal waste. It may be either stiff or flexible. Popular lengths run 6 to 8 inches.

Boning knife

Butcher knife: A slightly curved, pointed, heavy blade knife used in sectioning raw meat and cutting steaks.

Butcher knife

Butcher's steel: A round steel rod, approximately 1½ feet long with a wooden handle, used to maintain an edge on a knife. It does not sharpen the edge but merely straightens it and breaks off the burrs after sharpening. It is magnetized to remove burrs.

Butcher's steel

Clam knife: A short, flat bladed, round-tipped knife used to open clams.

Clam knife

Cleaver: An extra wide, carbon steel, heavy, square blade knife used to chop bones.

Cleaver

French knife: The most used piece of equipment. Near the handle, the blade is wide and generally a bolster is present; the blade tapers to a point. It is used for slicing, chopping, mincing, and dicing. The most popular blade lengths are 8, 10, and 12 inches.

French knife

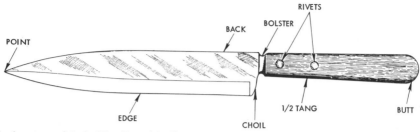

Terminology associated with a French knife.

Ham slicer: A narrow, long, flexible carbon steel blade about 12 inches long, so named because it is used to slice ham.

Ham slicer

Hand meat saw: A thin, fine-toothed blade, attached to a bow-shaped metal frame with a wooden handle, used to saw through bone structure of edible animals. Hand meat saws are available in two or three sizes.

Hand meat saw

Paring knife (vegetable knife): A short, pointed blade knife, 2½ to 3⅓ inches long, used for paring fruits and vegetables. Point is used to remove eyes and blemishes in the fruits and vegetables.

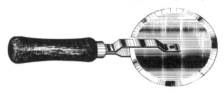

Paring knife

Pastry wheel: A round, stainless steel disc with a cutting edge and mounted handle used to cut all types of pastry.

Pastry wheel

Pie and cake knives: An offset knife with a wide, flat blade tapered to a point, shaped like a wedge of cake or pie, and used to cut and serve pies and cakes without breaking the pieces.

Pie or cake knife

Potato or vegetable peeler: A cutting tool with a metal blade attached to a

Potato or vegetable peeler

metal handle. The blade is in the form of a loop, with sharpened edges, formed over a pin or axis attached to the handle. The blade will shift from side to side, so peeling may be done in two different directions.

Oyster knife: A short, slightly thin, dull-edged knife, with a tapered point. It is used to open oysters.

Oyster knife

Roast beef slicer: A round nosed, long blade knife (14 inches) used to slice any size beef roast.

Roast beef slicer

Food handling implements

Food tongs: Spring-type metal consisting of two limbs shaped like a U with a saw-tooth grip on each end. They are used to pick up and serve foods without using the hands.

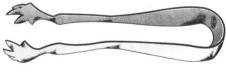

Food tongs

Hot-cake or meat turner: A wide, flat, offset chisel-edged blade with a wooden handle. It is used to slip under and turn hot cakes, hamburgers, and so forth while grilling, broiling, etc.

Hot cake or meat turner

Kitchen fork: A large, two pronged fork used for holding meat while slicing, turning roasts, and broiling steaks.

Kitchen fork

Stirring, serving, scraping, and spreading implements

Ladle: A stainless steel cup, solid or perforated, attached to a long handle used to stir, mix, and dip. It is also used to serve sauces, dressing, and other liquids when portion control is desired. Ladles are available in many sizes. Table I relates ladle size to the approximate weight of the portion in ounces.

Ladles, solid (left) and perforated (right)

TABLE I. LADLE SIZES AND APPROX. WEIGHTS

LADLE SIZE	APPROX. WEIGHT OF PORTION
1/4 CUP	2 OUNCES
1/2 CUP	4 OUNCES
3/4 CUP	6 OUNCES
1 CUP	8 OUNCES

Melon ball or parisienne scoop: A stainless steel blade formed into a round half-ball cup attached to a handle. It is used for cutting various fruits and vegetables into small balls.

Melon ball or parisienne scoop

Pierced kitchen spoon: A large stainless steel spoon, pierced with holes so liquid will run off, used to serve small cut vegetables (for example: diced carrots, peas, or corn).

Pierced kitchen spoon

Plastic scraper: A flexible piece of plastic approximately 4 inches wide and 6 inches long, used to scrape down bowls when mixing batters so that all ingredients will be incorported into the mixture.

Plastic scraper

Scraper or dough cutter: A wide, rectangular metal blade, mounted with a wooden handle, used for scraping meat blocks and cutting doughs.

Scraper or dough cutter

Skimmer: A flat, stainless steel perforated disc, connected to a long handle. It is used to skim grease or food particles from soups, stocks, or sauces.

Skimmer

Slotted kitchen spoon: A large stainless steel spoon with three to four slots cut into the base of the spoon so the liquid will drain off. It is used to serve large, cut vegetables or whole items without its liquid.

Slotted kitchen spoon

Solid kitchen spoon: A large stainless steel spoon, holding about 3 ounces, used to perform the task of folding, stirring, and serving.

Solid kitchen spoon

Spatula or palette knife (the names are used interchangeably): A broad, flexible, flat or offset blade knife with round nose used for mixing, spreading, and sometimes scraping. It comes in lengths from 3⅓ to 12 inches and is semi-flexible to highly flexible. It is used mostly for spreading icing on cakes.

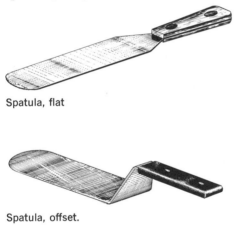

Spatula, flat

Spatula, offset.

Wood or metal paddles: They come in various lengths and sizes and are used to stir foods in deep pots or steam kettles.

Wood paddle

Food preparation implements

Box grater: A metal box with various sized grids used to rub or wear food into small particles.

Box grater

China cap: A pointed, extra strong strainer, shaped like a Chinaman's cap. It has a long handle and hook for hanging on side of pots and is used to strain gravies, soups, sauces, and other liquids or semi-liquids.

China cap

Colander: A bowl-shaped strainer with loop handles, usually made from stainless steel. It is perforated to allow liquids to run off and is used in washing cooked spaghetti and other pastas.

Colander

Strainer: A perforated metal bowl with a fairly long handle and hook for placing across pots. It is used to strain and drain all types of foods.

Strainer

Wire whips: There are two kinds that are in popular use in the commercial kitchen. French whips, which are fairly steady; and piano whips, which are more delicate and flexible. Each serves its purpose, depending on the consistency of the item being whipped. Whips are constructed of wire loops with ends brought together to form a handle. They are used for whipping eggs, cream, gravies, sauces, etc.

Wire whip, French

Wire whip, piano

Hand meat tenderizer: A solid, square block of cast aluminum attached to a wooden handle. The aluminum block is cast with two chopping grids—one coarse, the other fine. It is used to pound and break the muscle fibers of tough cuts of meat, therefore making the meat more tender.

Hand meat tenderizer

Cooking utensils

Bain-marie: A stainless steel food storage container which is round and has high walls. They are available in many sizes from 1¼ quarts to 11 quarts. Also a pan for holding hot water into which other pans, containing food, etc., are put for heating.

Bain-maries

Bake pan: A rectangular, aluminum pan with straight or sloped medium-high walls and loop handles. Bake pans are used for baking apples, macaroni, and certain meat and vegetable items.

Bake pan

Roasting pan: A generally large, rectangular, medium to high-walled metal pan. Roasting pans can be purchased with or without covers and come in various sizes to fit any size oven. They are used for roasting beef, pork, veal, etc.

Roasting pan

Braiser: A shallow-walled, large round pot. It has a large surface that comes in contact with the heat for quicker heating, has loop handles for easy lifting, and is very heavy to resist warping under high heat. It is used for braising, stewing, and searing meats. Braisers are available in sizes from 15 to 28 quarts.

Braiser

Double boiler: Consist of two containers. The bottom part resembles a stock pot and holds the boiling water; the upper section is suspended in the boiling water, thus preventing contact with direct heat. A double boiler is used to prepare items that will scorch quickly if they come in contact with direct heat. Items such as cream pie filling, pudding, etc., are prepared in a double boiler. Double boilers are available in sizes ranging from 8 to 40 quarts.

Double broiler

Frying or sauté pan: A round, sloped, shallow-walled pan with a long handle and a hole in the end for easy hanging. They are generally made of aluminum and range from 7 to 16 inches in the top diameter. Frying or sauté pans are used to sauté vegetables and some meat items.

Frying or sauté pan

Iron skillet: Made of thick, heavy iron. They hold heat well and are used for pan broiling and frying such items as chicken, pork chops, veal cutlets. Iron skillets are available in many sizes, with a top diameter of 6½ to 15¼ inches.

Iron skillet

Sauce pan: A pan similar to the sauce pot, but smaller, shallower, and much lighter. It has only a single long handle with a hole in the end for easy hanging. It is used the same as a sauce pot but for smaller amounts.

Sauce pan

Sauce pot: A fairly large, round, slightly deep pot with loop handles for easy lifting. It is used for cooking on top of the range when stirring and whipping is necessary.

Sauce pot

Sheet pan: A very shallow, rectangular, metal pan used for baking cookies, sweet cakes, and sheet pies. Sheet pans are available in various sizes.

Sheet pan

Skewer: A pin of wood or metal used to hold foods together or in shape while broiling or sautéing them.

Skewer

Steel skillet: Made of steel, light weight with sloping walls. They are used for frying eggs, potatoes, omelets, etc. Steel skillets are available in various sizes, with a top diameter of 6½ to 15⅞ inches.

Steel skillet

Stock pot: A large, round, high-walled pot made of either heavy or light metal. It has loop handles for easy lifting and, in some cases, is equipped with a faucet for drawing off contents. It is used for boiling and simmering items, such as turkeys, bones for stock, ham, and some vegetables. Sizes range from 2½ gallons to 40 gallons.

Stock pot

Baking implements

Bench brush: A long, thin brush with long black or white bristles set in vulcanized rubber with a wooden handle. A bench brush is used to brush excess flour from the bench when working with pastry doughs.

Bench brush

Flour sifter: A round metal container varying in height and diameter, with a sieve or screen stretched across the bottom. A device, such as a paddle wheel, is installed to help work the material be-

ing sifted through the sieve. The purpose of the sifting is to make products light and fluffy.

Flour sifter

Pastry bag: Cone-shaped cloth bag made of duck (water repellent cloth) or other materials used for decorating cakes with icing, plank steaks with duchess potatoes, short cakes with whipped topping, etc.

Pastry bag

Pastry brush: Similar to a paint brush. A narrow shaped implement made of bristles or other material fixed to a plastic, metal or wooden handle. They are used to brush on icing or egg wash (a mixture of egg and milk) when working with certain types of pastry.

Pastry brush

Pastry tubes: A metal canister with metal tips with various shaped openings used to decorate cakes, canapés, cookies, etc.

Pastry tubes: fit to the small end of the pastry bag.

Peel: A fairly long, flat, narrow piece of wood with a handle at one end. It is shaped like a paddle, and it is used to place pizzas in the oven and to remove them.

Peel

Pie and cake marker: A round, heavy wire disc with guide bars for accurate marking of pies or cakes prior to cutting. They come in various diameters and portion sizes.

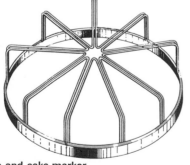

Pie and cake marker

Rolling pin: A roller, made of wood, teflon and other materials, ranging in size from 10½ to 25 inches. Handles are attached on each side of the roller. The rolling pin is used to roll pie dough, sweet dough, biscuit dough, etc.

Rolling pin

Measuring devices

Most recipes are given in weight, however, some are given in measures. The common measures uses are: teaspoon, tablespoon, cup, pint, quart and gallon. These are usually abbreviated in the recipes. Table II gives the common abbreviations used. Table III gives the relationships of the various measures and weights to each other.

The abbreviations given in Table II will be used in recipes throughout this text. Become familiar with them. Table

TABLE II.   ABBREVIATIONS FOR RECIPES

Tsp.	Teaspoon
Tbsp.	Tablespoon
Pt.	Pint
Qt.	Quart
Gal.	Gallon
Oz.	Ounce
Lb.	Pound
Bch.	Bunch

TABLE III. EQUIVALENTS OF MEASURES

1 Pinch	1/8 Teaspoon (approx.)
3 Teaspoons	1 Tablespoon
16 Tablespoons	1 Cup
1 Cup	1/2 Pint
2 Cups	1 Pint
2 Pints	1 Quart
4 Quarts	1 Gallon
16 Ounces	1 Pound
1 Pound (water)	1 Fluid Pint
2 Pounds (water)	1 Fluid Quart

Measuring cup set: A set consists of one-quarter, one-third, one-half and one cup measures. These aluminum cups are used to measure liquids and some dry ingredients.

Measuring cup set

III can be used for converting from one measure to another. For example, if 2 and ½ pounds of water is called for, this may be measured as 1 fluid quart and 1 cup. (Two pounds of water is equivalent to 1 fluid quart. A fluid pint is equivalent to 1 pound of water, but since 1 pint is also equivalent to 2 cups, ½ pound of water would be equivalent to 1 cup of water.) Occasionally a recipe will call for a "pinch" of some ingredient. This would be roughly equivalent to ½ of a teaspoon.

Measures: Metal cups, round, with a slight lip for easy pouring. They have a side handle and are accurately graduated in quarters. They are available in gallons, half gallons, quarts, and pints. They are used to measure liquids and some dry ingredients.

Measures

Scoops (ice cream): A metal bowl of known capacity with an extended handle and thumb-operated lever to release the item it holds. Scoops are used to serve food and also to control the portion. The

Scoop (ice cream)

TABLE IV. SCOOP OR DIPPER SIZES AND APPROX. WEIGHTS

SCOOP OR DIPPER NO.	APPROX. WEIGHT
8	5 ozs.
10	4 ozs.
12	3 ozs.
16	2 to 2 1/2 oz.
20	1 2/3 ozs.
24	1 1/2 ozs.
30	1 1/4 ozs.
40	1 oz.

TABLE V. SCOOP OR DIPPER SIZES AND APPROX. MEASURES

SCOOP OR DIPPER NO.	LEVEL MEASURE
8	1/2 CUP
10	2/5 CUP
12	1/3 CUP
16	1/4 CUP
20	3 1/5 TABLESPOONS
24	2 2/3 TABLESPOONS
30	2 1/5 TABLESPOONS
40	1 3/5 TABLESPOONS

TABLE VI. COMMON CAN SIZES AND APPROX. WEIGHTS AND MEASURES

SIZE	APPROX. CONTENTS	APPROX. MEASURE	PRODUCTS
No. 10	6 1/2 to 7 lbs.	3 qts.	Fruits and Vegetables
No. 5	2 to 3 lbs.	1 qt.	Fruit Juices, Chopped Clams and Soups
No. 2 1/2	1 lb. 12 to 14 ozs.	3 1/2 cups	Fruits and Vegetables
No. 2	1 lb. 4 ozs.	2 1/2 cups	Juices, Soups, Fruits and a few Vegetables
No. 303	1 lb.	1 pt.	Fruit, Vegetables and some Soups
No. 300	14 to 16 ozs.	1 3/4 cups	Cranberry Sauce, Pork and Beans and Blueberries

TABLE VII. SUBSTITUTING ONE CAN SIZE FOR ANOTHER

1 No. 10 Can	4 No. 2 1/2 Cans
1 No. 10 Can	7 No. 303 Cans
1 No. 10 Can	5 No. 2 Cans
1 No. 10 Can	2 No. 5 Cans

various sizes of scoops or dippers are designated by numbers. Table IV relates the numbers to their approximate capacity in ounces. Table V relates the scoop numbers to the approximate content of each scoop size in cups or tablespoons. The numbers which identify scoops or dippers indicate the number of scoopfuls required to make 1 quart. Scoops or dippers are used for portioning muffin batter, meat patties, potatoes, rice, bread dressing, croquette mixtures, some vegetables and salads, etc.

Cans: Many recipes call for the use of food ingredients by can size. Table VI gives the common can sizes and their approximate weight. Table VII shows the substitutions that may be made for the basic can size (no. 10) used in commercial cooking.

STATIONARY EQUIPMENT

Baker's scale: This is the best type of scale or measuring device to use for it will insure accuracy. The baker's scale is a twin platform scale. On the platform to the left is placed a metal scoop, in which the food to be weighed is placed. On the platform to the right is placed a special weight equal to the weight of the scoop. A beam that is graduated in ¼ ounces runs horizontal across the front of the scale. The beam has a weight attached to it. This weight is placed on the number of ounces one wishes to weigh. The beam is graduated in ¼ ounces up to 1 pound. If a larger amount is to be weighed, additional metal weights of 1, 2, and 4 pounds are provided. When using the baker's scale, always balance the scale before setting the weights for a given amount.

To weigh 8 ounces of egg whites, for example, one would place a container large enough to hold the egg whites on the left platform of the twin platform baker's scale and balance the scale.

Penn Scale Manufacturing Co., Inc.
Baker's scale

Move the weight on the beam 8 additional ounces. Add the egg whites until the scale balances again. If one wishes to weigh, let's say, 10¼ ounces of flour, place the metal scoop on one platform and the special balancing weight on the other platform. This will bring the two platforms to a complete balance. The weight on the scaling beam is placed on 10¼ ounces. Flour is placed in the metal scoop until the two platforms balance a second time. For weighing ¼ ounce of salt, however, a piece of paper could be placed on the left platform, and the platforms balanced. Set the balance weight at ¼ ounce, and add salt until the platforms balance again. The baker's scale can be used to weigh up to 8 or 10 pounds.

The student cook will be expected to measure most of his ingredients on this scale. The ingredients of most commercial recipes are given in weights for accuracy. In this text, however, liquids are usually given in liquid measure. It is easier for the beginning student cook to use liquid measure rather than weight. All other ingredients are normally given in weight. The best recipes are those which use weights.

Portion scale: Used for measuring food servings. Has a single square, seamless steel platform on which the food to be weighed is placed. A large dial on front of

Portion scale

Mixing machines: One of the most versatile stationary pieces of equipment in the commercial kitchen. This machine is designed to do many different jobs. With its many attachments, it will whip, grind, shred, slice, and chop foods. It is available in many different sizes. Generally, the size of mixer used in a commercial kitchen will be determined by the amount of production carried on in the establishment.

Mixing machine

scale is graduated from ¼ ounce to 32 ounces. The rotating dial needle determines the weight of the item placed on the platform. This type of scale is used when exact serving portions are required.

Deep fryer: A large, automatic fry kettle used to deep-fry all foods. It will hold from 25 to 50 pounds of shortening depending on the size of the kettle. Temperature controls adjust from 200° to 400°F.

Production unit of three deep fat fryers.

Power dicer attachment for mixer or food cutter.

Attachments for the mixing machine. These attachments are used for mixing dough, slicing vegetables, grinding (chopping) meat, and dicing. When using the meat and food chopper attachment for grinding meat be sure to use the wooden stomper (plunger) for feeding the meat. The coarseness of the ground meat is determined by which plate is used.

Food cutter or chopper with a vegetable slicer attachment being used for shredding fresh coconut.

Food cutter or *chopper:* This is another fairly versatile piece of stationary equipment. It, too, has many attachments and, consequently, can perform such jobs as chopping, grinding, slicing, dicing, and shredding. It has a revolving stainless steel bowl and a revolving knife that will chop foods quickly and efficiently. It can be dangerous to the careless person. *Extreme caution should be exercised when using the food cutter.*

Vertical cutter/mixer: This piece of equipment is designed to cut and mix foods simultaneously for fast volume production. It has only two moveable parts within the bowl: the knife blades, which move at a very high rate of speed, and the mixing baffle which is operated manually to move the product into the cutting knives. The advantage of using a vertical cutter/mixer besides speed of production is that the product being processed is never bruised or mashed because the knife blades, moving at an extremely high rate of speed, slice the product in mid-air. The vertical cutter/mixer is sometimes

called a "snell" cutter after the name of the inventor.

Some of the products that can be prepared in the vertical cutter/mixer are as follows:

67 pounds mayonnaise . . . . 6 minutes
40 pounds frozen beef chuck
    cut into hamburger . . . 40 seconds
43 pounds pie dough
    (mixed) . . . . 20 seconds
24 pounds white cake
    (mixed) . . . . 60 seconds
12 heads lettuce (shredded) 3 seconds
224 portions cole slaw . . . 12 seconds
151 portions meat loaf . . . 45 seconds

Slicing machine: Can be manually or automatically operated. It has a regulator for providing a wide range of slice thicknesses up to ¾ inch and has a feed grip that grips material firmly on top or serves as a pusher plate for slicing small end pieces. All slicing machines have many safety features built in to help protect the user from the very sharp revolving blade. These machines are designed to

Hobart Manufacturing Co.

Vertical cutter/mixer

U.S. Slicing Machine Co.

Slicing machine

be cleaned easily. The slicing machine is not so versatile as the mixer or food chopper but, even so, it can perform more than one job. Besides slicing, it can do an excellent job of shredding lettuce and cabbage.

Convection ovens: These ovens, sometimes referred to as *air-flow* ovens, are unique in that air in them is circulated throughout the interior by means of an electric fan. Because the heat is evenly distributed by forced circulation, the oven can be loaded to capacity while each part or food product receives the same amount of heat. This condition cannot be achieved in the conventional oven.

Convection ovens are available in gas and electric models. Of these, the electric type is more popular. Floor ovens with roll-in dolly, table models, counter models, and stack ovens are manufactured for various uses and capacities.

Use of the convection oven will increase productivity, reduce shrinkage, and cook more uniformly. Cooking cycles are completely automatic, and the same quantity can be cooked in less space and using less fuel than conventional ovens.

Crown-X, Inc.

Automatic steamer

Automatic steamer and boiling unit: These units, designed for really big cooking jobs, have capacities of 158 gallons and are capable of cooking 1500 to 2000 portions of potatoes in one hour. They are ideal for food processors, large hospitals, commissaries, and other institutions.

In addition to boiling potatoes, the automatic steamer and boiling unit gives excellent results when steaming vegetables, chickens, seafood, etc., or boiling pasta products.

Microwave ovens: Ovens of this type, utilizing waves generated by a special vacuum tube called a *magnetron,* have

Crown-X, Inc.

Convection oven

Litton Industries

Microwave oven

been on the market for a number of years. Although they have proved practical for domestic or small-quantity cooking, they have never really been accepted by commercial establishments because of their limited capacity. Their main practicality is for reconstituting convenience foods and reheating cooked foods.

The response of a microwave oven is immediate, with no pre-heating period, and cooking times are controlled by a time-setting device. When this is set by selecting a pushbutton, microwaves are generated by the magnetron and directed into the oven cavity. The food absorbs the energy and almost instantly converts it to heat. Whereas in conventional cooking foods are cooked from the outside in, with microwaves the cooking is reversed —that is, from inside outward to the surface. A necessary caution when cooking in a microwave oven is that foods should be placed on a china, plastic, or paper container, because metallic surfaces reflect microwaves and distort their paths, causing uneven heat.

Tilt fryers: The tilt fryer illustrated here is a fairly new piece of equipment in the United States although it has been in use for many years in Europe. Units of this type are available in gas and electric models.

Although the tilt fryer is a rather expensive piece of equipment, it will pay

for itself in a short time because of its fast operation and versatility. It can be used for frying, braising, stewing, sautéing, simmering, boiling, grilling, and deep-fat frying. In addition to its versatility for different cooking jobs, its main features are the large cooking area, thermostatic heat control, its tilting feature, and the ease with which it can be cleaned and maintained.

Quartz-plate infra-red oven: This equipment combines conventional heating with infra-red rays for fast heating and reconstituting meals previously cooked and refrigerated or frozen. A specially fused silica plate which transmits high intensity infra-red rays is combined with conduction heating to provide a uniform and controllable heating pattern, making it an ideal piece of equipment for preparing convenience foods.

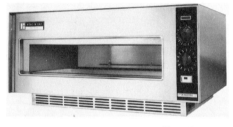

Litton Industries

Infra-red oven

Automatic twin coffee urn: This fully automatic unit has two coffee liners built into a single body section. The urn is unique in that it offers an unlimited flow of hot water for coffee and tea making through its heat exchange system. It is equipped with a spray assembly for spreading the water evenly over the coffee grounds. It has both automatic and manual agitation, a built-in thermostat, and a timer to set for a brewing cycle. This equipment takes all guess-

Crown-X, Inc.

Tilt fryer

Automatic twin coffee urn

work out of coffee making. Each urn has a capacity of 3, 6 or 10 gallons.

Automatic coffee brewer: One of the most convenient coffee brewers using glass bowls simplifiies the operation considerably. Steps required are: (1) pour in cold water, (2) plug in, (3) push button. Coffee is finished in 4 minutes.

There are many more pieces of equipment found in most commercial kitchens and bake shops that you will become familiar with as you gain experience. The ones listed here are the common ones that you will be using more often. It is essential that you learn to handle and operate them properly and safely.

Care should always be exercised in using knives and cutting implements. Many processes involving cutting implements can only be learned through demonstration and practice. This is especially true of the boning knife, French knife and meat cleaver. The instructor will demonstrate some of the more difficult cutting processes; after the demonstration the student, under the guidance of the instructor, can work on his own.

The use of electrical equipment should also only be attempted after demonstration by the instructor. When using electrical equipment always follow the manufacturer's recommended use. Safety information on equipment use is given in the following chapter.

safety

Safety today has become an important phase of every training program. Under the 1970 Federal Occupational Safety and Health Act (OSHA), the employer is required to furnish a place of employment free of known hazards likely to cause death or injury. The employer has the specific duty of complying with safety and health standards as set forth under the 1970 act. At the same time, employees also have the duty to comply with these standards.

■ In the commercial kitchen, safety is everyone's job. It is a responsibility that must be accepted throughout the working day. As stated many times before, accidents are *caused*—they do not just happen. They are caused by not knowing the proper way to do a task or by carelessly performing an operation or job with the attention focused on something else. It is wise to remember that a careless worker not only jeopardizes his own health and well-being but also jeopardizes those around him.

Cooking is considered a fairly safe occupation, but hazards certainly do exist not only in food preparation but in other related tasks as well. The most common accidents that occur in the kitchen are from cuts, burns, falls, and strains. All of these are types of accidents that happen when extreme carelessness or general horseplay is present. Neither carelessness nor horseplay can be justified nor allowed in the commercial kitchen.

Cuts are all too common in commercial kitchens because knives and other cutting implements are constantly in use. It may be reasonable to say that a student cook can plan on being cut a few times while learning the proper use of knives. These cuts, and the seriousness of the cuts, however, can be held to a minimum by the use of ordinary good sense, by attention to the proper safety rules, and by the practice of the proper cutting procedures. Once the skill of using a knife is obtained, accidental cuts should not occur. However, when and if they do occur, they should be treated properly and without delay; for if infection sets in it could result in a more serious consequence and certainly the loss of many working hours. Remember: *Preventive care is always cheaper than advanced treatment.*

Burns that occur in the commercial kitchen can be of two types: minor or serious. The minor burns are caused by popping grease or by handling hot pans with wet or damp towels. Use *dry* towels, pot holders, or gloves to handle hot pans. The more serious burns occur when grease is splashed, when steam escapes or is released too quickly, or when gas is turned on or is released unknowingly. Burns are generally more painful, and certainly take more time to heal, than cuts. If the burn is severe enough to cause a blister, it should be treated promptly by trained medical personnel.

Falls can cause some of the most serious accidents that occur in the commercial kitchen. They may cripple or incapacitate a person for life, thereby taking away his power to earn a living. Falls are caused by extreme carelessness, wet floors and aisles, spilled food or grease, and by torn mats or warped floor boards. All of these pitfalls can, of course, be eliminated by the practice of good safety standards.

Strains are not so serious as the other types of accidents, but they are painful and can cause the loss of many working hours. They can be prevented by not trying to carry loads that are too heavy, by lifting with the leg muscles rather than the back muscles, and by stepping carefully when moving a heavy load from one place to the other. Most strains do not require medical attention, but they do require time and care to heal properly.

SAFETY RULES

The following safety rules should be practiced when performing many of the food service tasks.

Food preparation

1. Use *dry* towels when handling hot skillets, pots, or roasting pans. (Wet cloth conducts heat more readily.)
2. Avoid splashing grease on top of range. Grease will ignite quickly, causing a dangerous fire. Do *not* throw water on a grease or fat fire—smother it. Use a foam fire extinguisher or a wet towel.
3. Remove the lids of pots slowly, lifting the side away from you so the steam will not rush out too quickly causing burns on the hands or face.
4. Always give notice of "HOT STUFF" when moving a hot container from one place to the other.
5. Keep towels used for handling hot foods off the range. Too often, the end of the towel is dangled into or drawn across the fire.
6. Avoid over-filling hot food containers.
7. Never let the long handles of sauce pans or skillets extend into aisles. If they are brushed, hit or bumped the pot may fall off the range.

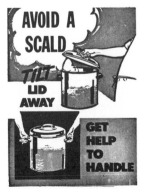

National Safety Council

8. Never turn the handle of any pot toward the fire.
9. When any lifting is required, lift in such a fashion that the strain is absorbed in the legs and arms. Never lift when unbalanced. Lift with the legs not the back.
10. Get help in lifting or moving any heavy pots or containers. If they are heavy, don't gamble — get help.
11. Place a lighted match to gas jets before turning on the gas. Ventilate gas ovens for a few minutes before lighting by leaving the oven door hang open so any gas pockets that might be present can escape.
12. Know the location of fire extinguishers.
13. When placing food in hot grease, always let the item slide *away* from you so the grease will not splash towards you and cause a serious burn.
14. Keep work station clean at all times.
15. At all times have your attention focused on the job at hand.
16. Never have glass near any food, it may break or chip.
17. Never throw any objects in the kitchen. Always pass them from hand to hand.
18. Treat injuries immediately. If minor, see the nurse if one is available. If serious, obtain the services of a doctor.

Hand equipment

1. Use the right knife for the job.
2. Do not grab for falling knives. When a knife starts to fall, jump backward to get out of the way.
3. Always carry a knife with the tip pointing downward and with the cutting edge turned away from your body.
4. Never talk with a knife in your

National Safety Council

hand. If you should start to gesture with the knife, serious consequences could develop.
5. When cutting with any knife, always cut away from your body. The same applies to potato peelers or any implement with a cutting edge.
6. Never place a knife in hot water, as it will cause cracks in the wooden handle. Never reach into soapy water in search of a knife.
7. Use a cutting board at all times. Never cut on metal.
8. Knives should never be placed in drawers. They should always be placed in a knife rack for proper storage.
9. When cleaning or wiping a knife, keep the sharp edge turned away from your body.
10. Always use a sharp knife—it is safer than a dull one. The chances of slipping are not so great, and less pressure has to be applied. Remember: We cut with a back and forth sawing motion — not with downward force. No matter how dull a knife is, it will always cut through human flesh.
11. Use knives for the purpose for which they were designed—not for levers or wedges or for bottle or can openers.

12. Pick up knives by the handle only.
13. Take a firm grip on a knife handle, and keep the handle free of grease or any other slippery substance.
14. When slicing round objects, such as an onion or carrot, cut a flat base so the object will set firmly and will not shift when being cut.
15. Never force a meat saw—it may jump from the bone.
16. When using a cleaver, be sure the item to be chopped is setting solidly.
17. When grating foods, never work the foods too close to the cutting surface.

Stationary equipment

1. Use a wooden stomper (plunger) when feeding meat or other items into a grinder.
2. Before cleaning or adjusting any machine, be sure all electrical switches are in the "OFF" position and pull the plug. This especially applies to the slicing machine.
3. Do not wear rings, wrist watch, or a tie when operating electrical power equipment.
4. Never start a machine until you are sure all parts are in their proper

places. If it is a machine that operates with gears, check gear position.
5. All electrical stationary equipment should be grounded.
6. Keep hands to the front of the revolving bowl when operating the food cutter. This is one of the most dangerous pieces of equipment in use in the commercial kitchen.
7. Never operate any machine unless you have been trained to use it properly. Be familiar with the safety features and the operation of the emergency stop.
8. When using electrical power equipment, always follow manufacturer's instructions and recommendations.

Clothing

1. Wear proper shoes: Rubber heels prevent slipping, proper support provides comfort, and safety toes prevent mashing or crushing. Neatly tied shoe laces may prevent a fall.
2. Wear long sleeves that cling tightly to the arms. They will prevent many burns, especially when frying chicken.
3. Never wear loose fitting clothing. There is always the chance it will get caught in a piece of equipment.
4. Wear aprons at knee length. More protection is provided than with the half-length style.
5. Tuck in all apron strings.
6. Wear the recommended headgear.

China and glassware

1. Discard any chipped or cracked china and glassware.
2. Never use glassware in forming or preparing food (such as for cutting biscuits or ladling liquids).
3. Never force a towel inside a glass to dry it.
4. Never clean up broken china or

The SAFE WAY

USE A PLUNGER

National Safety Council

glassware with the hands. Use a pan and broom.

5. Never place glassware in soapy water, wash them in a dish washer using a compound recommended for glasses.

6. When carrying china and glassware from one place to another, be alert and move cautiously. Keep complete control of the load at all times.

Floors

1. When turning on anything electrical, do not stand on a wet floor.

2. If anything is spilled on the floor, clean it up immediately. If necessary sprinkle salt on the floor to prevent slipping.

3. Never leave any pots, pans, or utensils on the floor.

4. Always walk in the kitchen—never run.

5. When mopping kitchen floors, do only a small area at a time.

6. Using rubber mats behind the range is a good practice; however, mats must be kept in first-class condition by daily cleaning and by replacing them when they begin to wear.

Any new employee who comes into the kitchen or food service area should be advised of all the safety rules and regulations. These rules should then be practiced constantly throughout the working period by all employees. Many commercial kitchens give on-the-job safety training for their employees. Safety in the kitchen, as in all occupations, is of great importance. Safety consciousness is part of the job. It is unfortunate that many employees do not learn just how important safety really is until it is brought to their attention by injury to themselves. With training, with the right attitude, and with alertness to hazardous situations and conditions, accidents can be reduced to a minimum and, in many cases, eliminated.

Clean up Wet or Greasy Spots PROMPTLY!

National Safety Council

chapter 5

basic food items

■ In the commercial kitchen and bakeshop, there are many food products and ingredients used today that would create confusion for the student cook or baker if he attempted to prepare a recipe without a knowledge of their use. In most preparations there always seems to be one item with which the inexperienced person will not be familiar. This often causes unnecessary discouragement.

Not too many years ago it was a simple thing to familiarize yourself with the products used in the culinary trade, but today it is a different story. Each day we find new and, in most cases, better products coming on the market, and it is es-sential for a good tradesman to keep up with the times. If a new product will save time, cut cost, and do just as good a job as the old product, it is time to change.

The following is a list of food products and ingredients the student cook and baker should become familiar with before he attempts to participate in the food preparation of any establishment. The names may be different in various parts of the country but, regardless of the locality, the same or a similar product can be obtained.

Study the descriptions of the food items carefully, most of them will be used in recipes in the following chapters.

VEGETABLES AND VEGETABLE PRODUCTS

Scallions: These are green onions with a very small bulb or, in some cases, no bulb at all. They resemble leeks, but the stems are much smaller and the flavor is much stronger. They are used in salads, as a relish, in soups, and in some cases in sauces.

Shallots: These are of the green onion family but have a bulb that consist of several cloves similar to the garlic bulb. They are very pronounced in flavor and a favorite of many chefs in such preparations as stews and sauces.

Leeks: These are a vegetable of the green onion family. They have long, wide, flat green stems and little or no bulb. The leek has a very delicate flavor that is desired by many chefs in such preparations as stews, soups, and sauces.

Chives: These are small onion-like sprouts that are long, thin, and green in color. They have a mild flavor and are used in salads, soups, entree dishes, and sauces.

Garlic: Garlic is of two types, red garlic and white garlic. The type is denoted by the skins covering the individual cloves: if pink it is called red garlic; if white it is called white garlic. Garlic is of the onion family. It grows in a bulb that consist of many cloves covered with an outer skin. Garlic can be grown in mild or cold climates, but the garlic grown in cold climates is stronger in flavor.

Hominy: Hulled Indian corn; when coarsely ground or broken, called *hominy grits*. It is used as a cereal food.

Tomato purée: This is the cooked down pulp of tomatoes, with all the skins, cores, and seeds removed. It is used in stews, gravies, sauces, and soups.

Tomato sauce: This is the same as tomato purée, but the pulp is cooked down to thicker consistency and it is generally flavored with the basil or bay leaf. It is used in soup, sauces, and stews.

Tomato paste: This is the same as tomato sauce, but the pulp is cooked down to a very heavy consistency, close to a solid.

Lentils: These are small, flat, round beans. Their color is light brown with a touch of green slightly visible. They grow two in a pod and can be used only when they are completely ripe. Lentils are used in soups and are also served as a vegetable.

Bean sprouts: These are the sprouts of the mung bean, a small, round, green bean first developed in China and later brought to the United States. The sprouts are from 1½ to 2 inches long when picked. Bean sprouts are very delicate in flavor and used in chow mein, chop suey, salads, and many oriental preparations.

Bamboo shoots: These are the young tapering shoots of certain species of the bamboo palm. They are about 4 inches thick at the base and about 1½ feet long. The shoots are covered with tough sheaths which are removed before canning. Bamboo shoots are used in the preparation of Chinese dishes.

Okra: This is a fuzzy, tapered, pod vegetable. It is green in color, has from 6 to 12 sides and generally is 2 to 3 inches long when young; it also contains many small seeds. Okra is served as a vegetable and is used in many soup preparations.

Capers: These are the green unopened flower buds of a European plant very similar to the nasturtium plant. The small buds when picked are first dried then placed in a vinegar solution and put up in dark, green bottles which help preserve the flavor. Capers are used in sauces and as a garnish on certain salads.

Gherkins: These are very small sweet or sour pickled cucumbers. They have a prickly skin and are pale-green in color. They are used on relish trays.

Pimientoes: These are large, sweet red peppers, peeled and canned with their stems, core, and seeds removed. They are used in the preparation of many foods and are also an excellent item to use when decorating salads, deviled eggs, canapés, etc.

Stock: The liquid in which meat, fish or vegetables have been cooked. It is used in the preparation of soups, sauces and gravies.

Rough garnish: A rough garnish is a mixture of carrots, onions, and celery, cut rough or coarse and added to an item that is cooking to supply flavor. When the cooking is completed the rough garnish is discarded. A rough garnish is often used in cooking meats.

Food colors: There are of two types: liquid and paste. The liquid food colors are a mixture of water, propylene glycol and U.S. Certified food colors. They are used most often in coloring sauces, potatoes, soups, etc. They can be purchased in an assortment of colors such as red, yellow, green and blue. The paste food colors are a mixture of sugar, glycerine, distilled water, invert sugar and U.S. Certified food colors. They are used most often for coloring icings. They too can be purchased in an assortment of colors such as red, yellow, green, blue, black, etc. All food colorings are harmless in small amounts in which they are generally used.

MEATS AND MEAT PRODUCTS

Meats: Meats (beef, pork, veal, and lamb) are graded by government standards on the basis of (1) *conformation,* form and structure, ratio of meat to bone; (2) *finish,* color and amount of fat to lean (marbling); and (3) *quality,* over-all appearance, judgment of eating qualities. The grades, in order of desirability and quality, are given in Table I.

Lower grades are also available but they are rarely used in the commercial kitchen. Poultry is also graded by the government as Grade A, B, or C. Grade A poultry is full fleshed and meaty, well finished, and has an attractive appearance. Grade B is slightly lacking in fleshing, meatiness and finish; or has some dressing defects. Grade C is not commonly used in commercial kitchens.

Chicken base: This is concentrated chicken mixture used to help provide a rich chicken flavor for various items, such as chicken soup and sauces.

Beef base: This is concentrated beef mixture used to help provide a rich beef flavor for various items, such as beef stock and gravy.

Gelatin: Gelatin is of animal origin, being extracted by heat from the bones, white connective tissues, and skins of food animals. It is odorless and tasteless.

TABLE I. MEAT GRADES

BEEF	PORK	VEAL AND LAMB	MUTTON
Prime	U.S. #1	Prime	Choice
Choice	U.S. #2	Choice	Good
Good	U.S. #3	Good	Commercial
Standard		Commercial	
Commercial			

It can be purchased in three forms: sheet, powdered, or granulated. It is used in cold soups, aspics (meat jelly), and desserts.

Flavored gelatin has flavor and sugar added to the natural unflavored gelatin. It is prepared by dissolving the gelatin mixture in hot water, then adding the cold water. Using this method the gelatin will set up quicker when refrigerated. *Plain or natural gelatin* is natural granulated gelatin, no flavor or sugar added. It must first be soaked in cold water for about 5 minutes before the boiling water is added. This procedure will speed the dissolving action and assure a better dissolution.

Aspic: A clear meat, fish or poultry jelly used for decoration on some preparations.

Crackling: The crisp residue that remains after the grease has been cooked out of meat or fat. Example: bacon crackling.

Suet: The hard fat that lies around the kidneys and loin of beef and mutton. When rendered it is usually used for frying.

Sweetbreads: The thymus glands found on each side of the throat of calves and lamb. They are used as a meat delicacy.

VINEGARS, DRESSINGS, AND SEASONINGS

Cider vinegar: This is made by fermenting apple juice. It has a light to slightly dark-brown color. It is used more often in the commercial kitchen than any other type of vinegar. It is used as a flavoring on salads and in salad dressing, and as a pickling agent.

Distilled or white vinegar: This is made by fermenting diluted distilled alcohol. It is used most often in pickling and when a weaker vinegar is desired.

Tarragon: This is a cider vinegar flavored with the herb tarragon. It has a very pleasing flavor and is generally used in salads or salad dressing. This vinegar can be purchased as tarragon vinegar or it can be made by letting the herb soak in cider vinegar for a couple of days.

Mayonnaise: This is a thick, uncooked emulsion formed by combining salad oil to egg yolks, vinegar, and seasoning. Used in salad dressings, salads, sandwich spreads, etc.

Salad dressing: This is a cooked product with a mayonnaise base. It contains less salad oil than mayonnaise. A filler or stretcher, consisting of water and starch, is whipped into the mayonnaise base until it is smooth and creamy. Salad dressing is much sweeter than mayonnaise and is used in salads, sandwich spreads, and in many of the same items in which mayonnaise is used, but with sweeter results.

Salad oil: This is generally obtained from the small germ portion of the kernel of the common Indian corn or seed of the cotton plant. Both oils are golden in color, bland in taste, and will stand a very high degree of heat without smoking. Salad oil is used in the preparation of mayonnaise and other salad dressings, as well as in frying and sautéing certain items.

Tobasco sauce: This is a very hot, red-colored sauce, made from red peppers, vinegar, and salt. Tobasco sauce is usually put up in small squirt-top bottles and used in flavoring meat sauces, salads, soups, etc.

Worcestershire sauce: This is a very pungent, dark-colored sauce. The formula for making will vary with the different manufacturers. It is used in cooking and for seasoning prepared meats, such as steak.

Soy sauce: This is a very dark-brown sauce, made by mixing mashed soybeans, roasted barley, salt, and water together. A culture is added and the mixture is left to ferment from 6 to 18 months in vats. At the end of the fermentation period this mixture is pressed and strained to produce the soy sauce. Soy sauce is used in the preparation of Oriental dishes.

Chutney: An East Indian pickle relish, prepared from currants, cucumbers, apples, ginger, mustard seed, etc., usually served with curry dishes..

MILK AND MILK PRODUCTS

Homogenized milk: This is whole milk that has been put through a process that breaks up each fat globule into smaller ones and distributes them evenly throughout the body of the milk. The fat particles are so small they never rise to the top of the milk. This process is called homogenization. It creates a product that has a better appearance and tastes richer.

Skim milk: This is milk from which most of the butterfat content has been removed. To be labeled "milk" the butterfat content must be 3½ percent. Anything less than this must be labeled skim milk.

Single or coffee cream: This contains only 18 percent butterfat. It is very seldom if ever whipped and in most cases will not whip. It is used for coffee, cereal, and in some food preparations.

Whipping cream: This contains from 30 to 36 percent butterfat. If the cream is too fresh it will not whip well. If the cream is 24 to 48 hours old the whipping qualities will be improved. For best whipping results the cream, bowl, and wire whip should be cold at time of whipping Over-whipping will result in butter. Whipped cream is used in many desserts and entree items.

Dry milk: This is whole milk with the water content removed. It is more economical to use in baking than liquid milk.

SUGARS AND SWEETENING AGENTS

Granulated sugar: This is a sweet, crystalline substance obtained usually from the sugar cane and beets. This is the most commonly used type of sugar.

Verifine sugar: This is a special type of granulated sugar. It is the same as granulated sugar, but ground or rubbed finer. This sugar is excellent to use when making sugar molds for cake decorations.

Powdered or confectionery sugar: This is obtained by grinding coarse granulated sugar and sifting through a fine silk cloth. Powdered sugar comes in three grades: 4X, 6X, and 10X. The more X's the finer the sugar.

Brown sugar: These sugars are refined in the same way as granulated sugar, except the refining is done at a lower temperature producing a product that contains more molasses and moisture. Dark brown sugar contains more of the molasses and moisture than light brown or yellow sugar because it has not been refined as long.

Sanding sugar: A very coarse sugar used by bakers to garnish sweet rolls, cream rolls or lady locks, etc.

Glucose: This is a heavy corn syrup used in preparing glazes and candy making.

Vanilla extract: This is made by extracting the flavor or oil from the vanilla bean and mixing it with dilute alcohol. Vanilla extract is used to flavor many desserts and baked goods, such as sweet rolls, coffee cakes, cookies, bread pudding, etc.

Chocolate naps: This is bitter chocolate put up in small cakes (about 1 ounce each) of convenient sizes for cooking purposes.

Chocolate shot: This consists of small bits of sweet chocolate used for cake and cookie decorating.

Cocoa: Cocoa is made by pulverizing chocolate after about one half of its butterfat has been extracted. Thus the difference between chocolate and cocoa is a matter of cocoa butter content.

NUTS

Shaved almonds: These are sliced, toasted almonds used to decorate cakes.

Almond paste: This is a cooked mixture consisting of about 56 parts of ground, blanched almonds, 34 parts of sugar, and 10 parts of water and flavoring. Almond paste is used in baking and for making candies, macaroons, and marzipan (a type of candy).

Shredded coconut: This consists of long, thin particles of coconut. Shredded coconut is used for cake decorating and other baking products.

Macaroon coconut: This consists of very small particles of coconut. Macaroon coconut is used in pie fillings and other baking products, and also is used to decorate cakes and tarts.

Pecan pieces: This consists of broken pieces of pecans used for decorating cakes and for pecan pie filling.

Pistachio nuts: This is the kernel of the fruit of the pistachio tree. The nut is shaped like a bean and is covered with a grayish purple skin. It is used in the preparation of certain classical food preparations, such as gelatine of chicken.

BAKING INGREDIENTS

The basic ingredients used in making bread are water, salt, yeast, and flour. (Flour is discussed in the following section.) In addition to the basic ingredients, sugar, shortening (fat), and milk or milk solids are also used. These ingredients give desirable qualities and enrichment to the bread. Baking powder is used for cakes and quick breads.

Yeast: This is a microscopic plant grown in vats containing a warm mash made of ground corn, barley malt, and water. The familiar foil-wrapped cake of fresh yeast contains over twenty-five million such plants, compressed with a small amount of starch. When the yeast plants are mixed with water, sugar and flour into dough, they quickly begin to grow and multiply. In the process of growing they produce the leavening gas (carbon dioxide) which forms the small bubbles which cause the dough to rise. Yeast is used in the preparation of dinner rolls, breads, and sweet doughs.

Sweetex: This is the trade name for an emulsified type of vegetable shortening used in the preparation of high-ratio cakes and icings. A large percentage of sugar may be used with this kind of shortening.

Primex: This is the trade name for a hydrogenated vegetable shortening used in roll dough and for frying. It has a high smoking point.

Glodo: This is a vegetable shortening that has a yellow color. Glodo is used as a roll-in shortening for butter flake and crescent rolls, and is also used in the preparation of sweet doughs.

Baking powder: This is a leavening agent produced by mixing some acid reacting material with common baking soda. Baking powder is used in the preparation of cakes and quick breads, and is also used when the leavening must be quick acting.

Cream of tartar: A chemical compound in the form of a white powder, used in bakery products to retain whiteness. Examples are white cake batter and meringue mixtures.

Puff paste shortening: A special type of shortening developed for use in preparing puff paste dough. It is a firm shortening but has a plastic consistency when worked and a melting point of approx. 113°F.

Ammonium carbonate: A powder leavening ingredient made by combining ammonia and carbonic acid.

FLOURS AND THICKENING AGENTS

Wheat, rye, barley, and corn are commonly milled into flour. Only those flours that contain protein (gluten) can produce a raised bread. Flours that contain little or no gluten, such as rye flour, must have gluten flours mixed with them to produce a raised bread. Flours also contain a small amount of fat, so if stored long under unfavorable conditions they may become rancid. Water must be added to flour in order for the protein to form the gluten which causes the bread to raise. A small amount of salt is also required to slow down the action (fermentation) of the leavening agents and to enhance the flavor. Potato flour is also sometimes used today, mixed with high protein flours, in making some pastries, such as doughnuts. Flours, corn starches, and other agents are used in many recipes as a thickening agent.

Bread flour: This flour is milled from hard wheat and contains protein (gluten), the elastic substance so important in bread and roll making.

Cake flour: This is milled from soft wheat and contains all starch and no gluten.

Pastry flour: This is milled from soft wheat and contains part starch and part gluten, both of which are important when preparing pie dough, cookies, and various pastries.

Rye flour: This is milled from rye grain. The composition is very much like wheat but the protein is quite different. The protein of rye flour, when made into dough with the addition of water, does not produce gluten as is the case when using hard wheat flours. It is necessary, therefore, to use some hard wheat flours with the rye flour to produce a porous, well-raised loaf of bread. If only rye flour is used the loaf will be heavy, soggy, and unpalatable.

All purpose flour: This is a blend of hard and soft wheat flours. It is used mostly by the housewife for all purposes. (In the commercial kitchen or bake shop the kind of preparation dictates the kind of flour used.)

Tapioca flour: This is a flour made from the roots of the tapioca plant. It is used as a thickening agent in pies and glazes.

Arrow-root: This is a starch obtained from the roots of a small tropical plant called arrow-root. This plant resembles to some degree the ginger plant. Arrow-root is used to thicken certain items when a high gloss is desired.

Egg white stabilizer: This is a white powder mixture, consisting of sugar, calcium, sulphate, carragheen and other ingredients, used when beating egg whites to create a stiff meringue.

Corn starch: This is a starch in the form of white flour made from Indian corn. It is used in thickening liquids.

Modified starch: This is a blend of 4 or more starches such as arrow root, corn starches. It is marketed under various trade names. This type of starch is excellent for use in fruit pie fillings and glazes because it will hold a sheen longer than most, even if the item is refrigerated.

Pre-gelatinized starch: This type of starch is blended with sugar and added to a liquid for instant thickening. It reacts quickly without heat because the starch has been pre-cooked and requires no additional heat to enable it to absorb liquid and gelatinize. This is an excellent product to use when speed is required, such as demonstrations of pastries requiring a fruit glaze.

Corn meal: This is the coarsely ground kernels of corn. If yellow corn is ground, we have yellow corn meal. If white corn is ground, we have white corn meal. Corn meal is used in corn bread, corn sticks, mush, and corn muffins.

Breading: To pass an item through seasoned flour, egg wash (4-6 eggs to each qt. of milk), and bread or cracker crumbs.

SEAFOOD PRODUCTS

Anchovy: This is a salted fish fillet of the herring family. It is very small in size and usually canned in olive oil. It is used in the preparation of hors d'oeuvres, canapés and certain salads, such as Caesar salad.

Caviar: This is the prepared and salted roe (egg) of the sturgeon and certain other types of fish.

Sardines: This is a small fish of the herring family. They may be either pilchards, sprats, bristlings or young herrings. They are usually canned packed in olive or cotton seed oil although some of the larger ones are packed in mustard or tomato sauce.

Finnan haddie: This is a salted and smoked haddock fish. It is usually prepared by steaming.

Smoked salmon: This is salmon, such as coho, chinook or chum, that has been smoked, sliced very thin and canned packed in olive or cotton seed oil. It is used in the preparation of hors d'oeuvres or canapés.

(Other information on seafood and seafood products can be found in the chapter on "Fish and Shellfish," Chapter 20.)

CONVENIENCE FOODS

These foods, sometimes referred to as frozen prepared foods (or foods with a high readiness value) have been increasingly accepted by the food service industry in the past few years. In fact, they are starting to cause so much comment in the industry that it is difficult for a food service operator to completely turn his back on this modern emphasis on convenience.

According to some historians, the creation of these convenience foods started with seafood. They pinpoint the start of freezing food to the year 1912, when a young man named Clarence Birdeye journeyed to Labrador to investigate and study the methods used by the Eskimos to preserve seafood by freezing. On his return to the States, Birdeye refined these methods and quickly became such a success in this field that today his name is a household word.

The early success in freezing seafood led to overwhelming successes with frozen French fries and orange juice, which, in turn, started the search for other products and items that could be marketed in a frozen condition. Today this method of preserving food is almost limitless. Presently available on the market are soups, vegetables, appetizers, rolls and bread, potato preparations, desserts and entrees, as well as complete plate combinations that only need to be heated.

Many of the companies in this business, such as Stouffer's and the Kitchens of Sara Lee, not only produce and market a complete line of frozen products but also design complete food systems, including menu writing and design, work flow standards, production and equipment recommendations, cost comparisons, labor standards and cost—in other words, a complete food service package specifically designed to meet an operator's every objective.

From all that has been written on the advantages of convenience foods and food systems the idea may be conveyed that these products and systems will cure all problems of the industry and that cooks, bakers, and food service personnel are no longer needed. This is far from so. Convenience foods and related systems offer another tool to help food management to control labor cost and increase production. They are not the total answer to a successful food service establishment.

The cost of convenience is always high. In any product, the more that is done for the consumer the higher the cost. A successful food establishment must maintain its own identity by preparing and offering foods that are in some way unique and bring the customers back. When dining out, most people are looking for foods they cannot get at home. It is a fact that most of the convenience foods available to the food service is also available to the general public, in the supermarket.

Although many of the convenience foods have been developed to near perfection, some still have shortcomings such as a fibrous texture, starchy taste, and a breakdown of sauces. These, of course, must be avoided. The more acceptable of convenience foods can lend your chef a helping hand in solving his many production problems, but are not the total answer. The items that have proven most successful and have been accepted by the average chef are those which eliminate a great amount of hand work but are still in a raw state, such as chicken Kiev, veal Cordon Blue, and beef Wellington.

We have, of course, just scratched the surface of the food products and ingredients the student cook or baker will come in contact with during his career. However, it was our intention in this chapter to present only the foods that students seem to have the most trouble with. Other food products and ingredients will be introduced and explained in the following chapters.

cooking methods and techniques

■ To cook, is to subject foods to the action of heat in order to make them more digestible. There are various ways of applying heat to foods. The method used depends a great deal on whether the food item is tough or tender. If the item is tough, a lengthy cooking method is selected to make the item more palatable and digestible. If the item is tender, a quick cooking method is selected for the best results.

In this chapter we are going to introduce the student to the various cooking methods he will be required to perform while working in a commercial kitchen. The basic methods and techniques covered in this chapter have been used for centuries, but they have been constantly improved upon. In other words, they have been time-tested, and what was thought to be the perfect, or the only way, ten or twenty years ago is no longer true today.

Equipment for performing these cooking methods has improved a great deal in the last thirty years and will continue to improve for years to come. Most of the new equipment is designed to save time and speed up production. There are many examples of new equipment that has been accepted in commercial kitchens. The fast, deep fry kettles, for example, where the temperature of the grease recovers faster for quicker deep fat frying, are a common sight in most large kitchens. The microwave ovens, which will bake a potato in five minutes and a roast rib of beef in forty-five minutes, are more-and-more being used. The snell cutler, which will prepare a cole slaw in about one or two minutes and mix a meat loaf, using frozen meat, in three or four minutes, is also now common. These are just a few of today's modern changes in equipment. Without a doubt they have helped speed up efficiency and productivity, and have influenced modern thinking about food preparation techniques.

One of the most basic techniques that a student cook must acquire is a thorough knowledge of the *safe preparation* of foods. Meats must often be cut up into smaller pieces before cooking and serv-

ing. How they are to be cut up is usually stated in the recipe. Vegetables too must usually be cut up before being used in a recipe. (The cleaning and peeling is normally done by the vegetable man before the cook uses the vegetables.) The various methods and techniques of preparation for meats and vegetables is given in Table I. The student must familiarize himself in these preparation techniques. Most recipes will require the use of one or more of these methods.

The various cooking methods and techniques are covered under each type of food. The following food types are covered:

Meat Cooking.
Vegetable Cooking.
Baking.

In addition, a section is added to explain

Maisonette Restaurant
Cincinnati, Ohio

A kitchen layout showing a cutting station, sink, steam table, and equipment rack. A microwave oven and a salamander are shown on the shelf (second and third right).

Cutting with the French knife: The French knife is used to perform the tasks of slicing, dicing, mincing, chopping, julienning, and in some cases shredding. The knife should be held with a firm grip with the handle passing between the thumb and index finger. The blade should always be sharp. (A sharp knife is safer than a dull one because it will not so easily slip off the item being cut.) For chopping, mincing, dicing and julienning, the point of the knife should be kept on the table while the blade is rotated rapidly with a forward up and down motion. The cutting is done on the forward stroke. Never lift the point of the knife off the cutting board. For slicing and shredding, the knife is held in the hand in the same manner but the blade is passed across the item being cut with a smooth forward motion. Again the cutting is done on the forward stroke. For all cutting methods the left hand is used to push the food towards the blade and/or to regulate the size of the cut.

TABLE I.   FOOD CUTTING

METHOD	MEANING	TECHNIQUES OF PREPARATION
Slice	A relatively thin, broad piece of food.	Slice by using a slicing machine, French knife or carving knife. Always slice against the grain, moving the blade of the knife in such a way as to cut by a sawing action.
Chop	Cut into uneven bits. May be fine, medium or coarse.	Cut on wood topped table or cutting board. Use a French knife and cut by applying short, sharp blows.
Dice	Cut into cubes. May be small, medium or large.	Dice on wood topped table or cutting board. Use a French knife and cut with slicing motion. An average sized cube cut be dicing would be approximately 1/4 inch.

TABLE I.   CONT'D

METHOD	MEANING	TECHNIQUES OF PREPARATION
Mince	Chop into very fine pieces.	Cut on wood topped table or cutting board. Use a French knife or power food cutter. Cut by applying short, sharp strokes. Meats may be minced by running through a meat grinder.
Purée	Pound or mince fine and force through a sieve.	Same as "mince," but finer.
Julienne	Cut into long thin strips.	Julienne on wood topped table or cutting board. Use a French knife and cut with slicing motion into very thin slices then cut a second time with the grain into very thin strips.
Grind	To crush into fine, medium or coarse particles.	Pass the item through a food grinder, using the fine, medium or coarse chopper plate. Do not force the item into the grinder; feed small amounts at a time.
Grate	Pulverize by rubbing against a rough or indented surface.	Grate by using a box grater. The mesh of the grate will depend upon which surface is used. Grating is also done in a power food cutter.
Shred	Cut into very fine strips.	Shred with the coarse mesh on a box grater, by shaving with forward strokes of a French knife, or by passing the item across the revolving blade of a power slicing machine.
Score	To mark the surface of certain foods with shallow slits.	Cut with a French knife in parallel lines approximately 1/2 inch apart. Cut about 1/8 to 1/4 inch deep.

how recipes are *adjusted* to serve any given number of guests.

MEAT COOKING

Meat cooking, as all other cooking, is done using three different basic methods: (1) dry heat, (2) moist heat, and (3) sautéing or frying. Dry heat is used in roasting, broiling, and panbroiling. Dry heat is used with good results with the more tender cuts of meat. Moist heat is used in braising, steaming, and cooking in liquid. Moist heat is used successfully with the less tender cuts of meat. Sautéing or frying is done by sautéing (pan frying in shallow grease), or by deep fat frying. Regardless of the method of cooking chosen, the purpose of cooking meat is to make it more palatable and digestible.

Roasting: To roast is to surround food with dry, indirect heat in an oven. The roast is not covered. The word "roast" is used interchangeably with the word "bake."

Broiling: The broiling of meat is similar to roasting, but in broiling, direct heat is used—the meat is exposed to the flame.

Panbroiling: Cooking by contact with a heated surface, such as a frying pan,

Range, oven and griddle units: From left to right: a solid plate heating surface, a four unit heating surface, and three griddles. Each unit has a roasting oven below. A stock pot is present on the solid hot plate and sauce pans are on the open flame units.

or sauté pan. No covering, and *no* fat is used.

Braising: Meat is cooked, at a low temperature, in a small amount of liquid (water, stock, thin sauce, or a combination of these) in a covered container until done. Meat is usually browned before cooking.

Steaming: Steaming may be used in conjunction with either braising or cooking in liquid, or it may be used as a method by itself with or without pressure. The steam may be applied directly to foods as would be the case when using a steam pressure cooker.

Cooking in liquid: Meat is put in a container, covered with a liquid (usually water) and then simmered (never boiled) until tender. When simmering the bubbles of the liquid will break below the surface of the liquid, a temperature of 200° F is usually maintained. A rough garnish (onions, carrots and celery, cut rough) may be added to improve the flavor of the meat and liquid. When blanching the item is only partly cooked. The term "scald" is used when a liquid is heated to just below the boiling point.

Sautéing: Cooking by contact with a hot surface, such as a frying pan or sauté pan; no covering and little fat is used. The difference between panbroiling and sautéing is that in panbroiling *no* fat is used, but in sautéing *some* (a small

McGraw-Edison Co.

A versatile kitchen layout. This all electric layout includes, from left to right, a double deck or twin broiler unit for broiling steaks, chops, etc.; a grill for the production of hot cakes, eggs, etc.; a deep fat fryer for frying all types of food; two speed-heat units (one a solid hot plate the other with two open flame units) for bringing liquids to a quick boil; and a double deck oven for roasting and baking meat, fish and poultry items.

amount) is used. To sauté lightly means "to brown." Sautéing is also sometimes called frying or pan frying.

Grilling: To place on a griddle and sauté. The term may also refer to broiling.

Deep fat frying: Cooking with the food completely covered with hot fat. Meat cooked in this manner should be breaded.

In all cases the length of the cooking time will depend on the kind of meat, the oven temperature, the degree of doneness desired, the quality of the meat (prime, choice, good, etc.), and the size and thickness of the meat.

How to roast

Season with salt and pepper: It is best to season the day before roasting. This will give the seasoning a chance to penetrate into the flesh.

Place meat in oven fat side down: This will eliminate adding any excess grease or shortening. If fat side is left up and no grease is added to the roast pan, the roast will stick to the pan.

Brown meat thoroughly: This should be done in a hot, but not overly hot, oven, about 375°F. This will help to develop better flavor for both meat and gravy. Do not sear the meat; contrary to belief searing does not keep in juices.

Add rough garnish: A rough garnish is added when meat is browning to add flavor to both the roast and gravy. The rough garnish consists of onion, celery, and carrots cut rough.

Add water only when it becomes necessary: When roasting at a low or moderate temperature, the drippings should not evaporate. If they should, a small amount of water can be added. One must

Roasting ribs of beef.

Market Forge Co.

How to broil

Turn flame or heat to highest point: How close or how far the item is from the heat will regulate the temperature.

Marinate item in oil and season: The item should be passed through salad oil before placing it in the boiler. This will eliminate sticking and help the appearance of the item. Season with salt and pepper in most cases. When broiling a steak, however, do not add the salt until ready to remove from the broiler. Salt has a tendency to draw out the juice.

Place item on hot broiler: Have broiler hot before placing an item on it. In the case of meats and fish this will create the desired broiler markings. Place meat on the broiler with the fat side facing out.

Broil until top of item is brown: At this point the item should be half done.

Turn item and continue to brown sec-

remember that roasting is cooking by dry heat.

Do not cover roast: When a roast is covered steam is created. This will bring forth a pot roast since the dry heat is eliminated.

Roast at a temperature of 325° to 350°F: A low or moderate temperature reduces shrinkage.

Turn the roast: A rib roast should be turned only once and it should be turned so that it will rest on its natural rack (the arched rib bones) and not lay in bottom of pan. A boneless roast should be turned frequently to prevent dryness. When turning a roast the fork should be used to support the meat when turning; that is, it should be placed under the roast, and with the aid of your free hand and a towel, the meat should be turned. Never stick a fork in the roast for the juices will cook out. Baste the roast often.

Roasting time: The roasting time will depend on four things. Kind of meat, oven temperature, degree to which it is done, and the quality of the meat (prime, choice, good, etc.).

Photo: Kathryn Adams
Student placing ham steaks on a broiler.

ond side: When broiling, the item should be turned only once. In the case of meat, stick fork in fat or tail of steak so juice will not be lost. A pair of tongs may also be used for turning.

Broiling time: This will depend on kind of item, grade, size, degree to which it is done, and the thickness.

How to serve: All broiled items should be served at once and always on hot plates or platters.

How to panbroil

Season meat with salt and pepper: For a better taste season both sides before cooking.

Place meat in sauté pan: No fat is added when panbroiling.

Do not cover: A covering will cause steam to develop.

Brown one side, then turn and brown the other side: This helps develop flavor. Do not pierce meat when turning.

Cook at a moderate temperature: This will prevent too much browning and will make the meat much juicier.

Pour off any fat that appears in sauté pan: If fat is left in pan, this would be sautéing not panbroiling.

Do not add any liquid: This would be braising not panbroiling. Keep pan as dry as possible.

Cooking time: Depends on the cut of meat, kind of meat, thickness, degree to which it is done, and quality of meat.

How to braise

Place meat in braising pot: A braising pot will supply quicker heat because more of the surface of the pot comes in contact with the heating unit.

Season with salt and pepper: Season when starting to cook so seasoning will penetrate into the meat. Herbs and spices may be used if desired.

Brown the meat thoroughly: Browning the meat helps to develop a richer color and a better flavor.

Add liquid: Add just enough liquid to cover the meat; the meat and liquid will then be richer in flavor. The liquid may be water or stock; stock would be the best of the two.

Cover braising pot: This keeps in flavor and allows the meat to cook evenly throughout.

Cook continuously on range or in the oven: Either one will bring forth good results as long as the braiser is kept covered. This will make the meat tender, the flavor more pronounced, and the cooking time shorter.

Cook at a low temperature (about 250°F): The lower the temperature the less shrinkage and the better the flavor.

Cook until the meat is tender: The time required will depend on the size, thickness, grade, and kind of meat used.

How to cook in liquid

Cover the item with liquid: Item should be completely covered with water or stock so it will cook uniformly.

Season with salt and pepper: Seasoning will add flavor to both the item and stock. Additional spices and herbs may be added to enhance the flavor if desired.

Do not cover the pot: If the pot is covered, at any time, the cooking time will be shortened, but the stock will become cloudy and the item will not be as firm when sliced.

Add rough garnish: Add the rough garnish, consisting of carrots, onions, and celery, after you have removed all scum from top of liquid. This will add extra flavor to both the item and the stock.

Simmer item: Do not boil—cook by simmering. The temperature should be about 200°F, just below the boiling point. Using this procedure the item will be firmer, the stock clear, the flavor will be retained.

Cooking time: Will depend on size of the item, quality of item, and kind of item.

How to stew

Cut meat into cubes (large, medium, or small): Cut meat uniformly so it will cook evenly. A boneless stew is more desirable than one with a bone.

Season with salt and pepper: Season when starting to cook for best results. Herbs and spices may be used if desired.

Brown the meat, if desired: A brown stew is more desirable and has more flavor than a white stew; however, if a white stew is desired this step would be eliminated.

Cover the meat with a liquid: The meat should be entirely covered with the liquid so it will cook uniformly. The liquid may be either stock or water.

Cover stewing pot: Pot should be covered to reduce cooking time and to preserve the flavor.

Cook at a low temperature (about 250°F): Cooking at a low temperature will reduce shrinkage and preserve flavor.

Add vegetables: Vegetables should be added when the meat is about three-fourths done so that they will both finish cooking at the same time. Using this method of adding the vegetables, the stew will be more flavorful but will lack in appearance. The alternative method would be to cook each vegetable separately, and when the meat is tender add the cooked, drained vegetables. This last method may be best because each vegetable cooks differently and this way you can be sure each will be tender. This last method also gives the stew a much nicer appearance, and today appearance will help boost sales.

Cooking time: Cook until just tender. A stew that is overcooked lacks appearance and appetite appeal.

How to sauté (pan fry)

Season with salt and pepper: This should be done before cooking so seasoning will penetrate into the flesh.

Pass through flour (if desired): Cover meat thoroughly so it will brown evenly. Dust off the excess flour so that it will not lie in the bottom of the pan and cause the fat to burn.

Do not cover: This will cause steam to form.

Brown meat in small amount of fat on one side: Brown meat quickly on one side at a moderate temperature. To avoid sticking grease should be heated before item is placed in sauté pan.

Turn and brown second side: Meat should be golden brown on both sides. This should be done fairly quick to avoid too much shrinkage. Sautéing is a quick cooking method.

Cook at a moderate temperature: This will make the item more crisp and give it a more eye-appealing appearance.

How to fry in deep fat

Light the fry kettle and set thermostat at 350°F: Very few fried foods need a higher temperature for cooking. One ex-

Photo: Kathryn Adams

Student deep fat frying sweet potato croquettes.

ception would be the second frying of soufflé potatoes which requires a temperature of 400°F. The fat can be used much longer if not overheated, and if it is strained after each day's use.

"Bread" the item: This is done so that the surface of the meat will not be burnt; It also adds to the flavor and appearance of the item. Various breadings may be used, such as flour, corn meal, or bread crumbs. Cover meat thoroughly so it will brown evenly. (French fried potatoes, of course, do not require any breading.)

Shake item when it is placed in fry basket: When the item is placed in the fry basket the excess breading should be shaken off so that it will not settle to the bottom of the grease and burn, thus shortening the life of the grease. Do not overfill the fry basket. Lower the fry basket into the hot fat.

Fry until item is golden brown: Do not overbrown items for they will become dry and tasteless. Some items will float on top of the grease when done.

Drain off excess grease: This is done so item will retain its crispness and be more digestible.

Fat can be clarified: If grease is not too far gone, it can be clarified by placing sliced raw potatoes in the cold fat and heating the fat gradually until the potatoes become brown. Some deep fat fryers are self clarifying.

VEGETABLE COOKING

Vegetables may be cooked using many of the same methods as used for meats, and often the vegetables are cooked along with the meats. Commonly, however, vegetables are cooked by three methods: baking, steaming, and cooking in water. Baking is done using a dry heat in an oven; little or no water is used. Beans and potatoes are examples of vegetables that are baked. In steaming, the vegetables are placed in a perforated kettle

and steam is forced into and through the container. Almost all vegetables may be steamed. Cooking in water is done by first boiling the water then adding the vegetables and bringing the water back to a boil. Little water is used and the vegetables are cooked for only a short time. Most vegetables may be cooked in water. Remember that too much water or overcooking destroys the flavor and causes loss of nutrients. All vegetables should be covered while cooking, except cauliflower, turnips, cabbage, and Brussel sprouts.

These large electric ovens are used for baking vegetables, such as potatoes, and for roasting various kinds of meat.

TABLE II. BAKING FRESH VEGETABLES

VEGETABLE	PREPARATION	OVEN TEMP.	APPROX. BAKING TIME
White Potatoes	Select potatoes that are uniform in size. Wash or scrub well. Potatoes may be wrapped in foil or brushed with oil so they will be soft when baked.	400°F	1 hr. 15 minutes to 1 hr. 30 minutes
Sweet Potatoes	Select potatoes that are uniform in size. Wash or scrub well. They may also be wrapped with foil or brushed with oil the same as white potatoes.	400°F	45 minutes to 1 hr.
Acorn Squash	Wash or scrub well. Cut in half lengthwise, remove all seeds, brush the flesh with melted butter and sprinkle with salt and brown sugar.	375°F	1 hr. 30 minutes (If it becomes too brown cover the surface with foil or oiled brown paper.)
Zucchini Squash	Wash or scrub well. Cut lengthwise, season with salt and pepper, sprinkle with bread crumbs and dot with butter.	350°F	20 to 30 minutes
Tomatoes	Wash thoroughly, remove stem, slice off bottom, rub with salad oil and season.	375°F	30 to 35 minutes

Baking fresh vegetables

1. Prepare the vegetables according to the directions given in Table II.
2. Bake the vegetables, until they are slightly soft, using the suggested temperature given in Table II.
3. The baking time will vary depending on the variety and maturity of the vegetable and its size or the size of the pieces into which it is cut. As a guide see the approximate baking time in Table II.

Boiling fresh vegetables

1. Prepare vegetables according to the directions given in Table III.
2. Cook in amounts not to exceed 10 pounds of prepared raw fresh vegetables.
3. Cook vegetables by simmering until just tender. The exact cooking time will vary depending on the variety and maturity of the vegetable and its size or the size of the pieces into which it is cut. As a guide see the approximate cooking time in Table III.

Boiling frozen vegetables

1. Thaw the tightly frozen vegetables at room temperature or in the refrigerator overnight or until they can be easily separated. The loosely packed frozen vegetables do not need thawing.
2. Cook in amounts no larger than 10 pounds.
3. Add 1 teaspoon of salt for every quart of water used.
4. Add the vegetables to the boiling salt water, bring water back to a boil as quickly as possible. Timing

TABLE III. BOILING FRESH VEGETABLES

VEGETABLE	PREPARATION	BOILING WATER	SALT	APPROX. COOKING TIME
Beans, Green (10 lbs.)	Trim ends, remove strings and wash thoroughly. Cut into desired size pieces.	2 1/2 Qts.	1 Tbsp.	25 to 30 minutes
Beets (10 lb.)	Remove tops, wash thoroughly, remove blemishes.	To cover (approx. 3 Qts.)	None	1 hr. to 1 hr. 30 minutes
Broccoli (10 lbs.)	Cut off tough woody stalk ends and wash. Peel stalks and cut in half lengthwise.	3 Qts.	1 Tbsp.	20 to 25 minutes
Cabbage, cut into wedges (10 lbs.)	Remove blemished outside leaves. Wash, cut into quarters, remove core and cut into wedges.	6 Qts.	2 Tbsp.	1 hr. to 1 hr. 15 minutes
Carrots (10 lbs.)	Scrape or pare, wash, slice or cut as desired.	4 Qts.	1 Tbsp.	20 to 30 minutes
Cauliflower (10 lbs.)	Remove outer leaves and stalks. Separate into flowerets; wash thoroughly.	5 Qts. (plus 1 Qt. milk)	2 Tbsp.	20 to 30 minutes
Celery (10 lbs.)	Trim, cut into desired size pieces.	4 Qts.	1 Tbsp.	20 to 30 minutes
Corn on the cob (10 lbs.)	Husk, remove silk by brushing. Wash thoroughly and drain at once.	4 Qts. (plus 1 Qt. milk)	1 1/2 Tbsp.	10 minutes
Kale (10 lbs.)	Remove blemished leaves, strip leaves from stems. Wash at least 4 times, lifting out of the water each time so dirt will settle to the bottom and not cling to the leaves. When cooking stir occasionally.	4 Qts.	1 Tbsp.	30 to 45 minutes
Kohlrabi (10 lbs.)	Pare, wash and cut into 1 inch cubes or as desired.	4 Qts.	None	20 to 30 minutes
Onions (10 lbs.)	Peel and wash; cut if desired.	6 Qts.	1 1/2 Tbsp.	30 to 40 minutes
Potatoes, White (10 lbs.)	Peel, cut into uniform size, remove all eyes, wash thoroughly.	6 Qts.	2 Tbsp.	45 minutes to 1 hr.
Rutabagas (10 lbs.)	Pare, wash and cut into uniform pieces. (Preferably 1 inch cubes.)	4 Qts.	1 Tbsp.	15 to 30 minutes

TABLE III.   CONT'D

VEGETABLE	PREPARATION	BOILING WATER	SALT	APPROX. COOKING TIME
Spinach (10 lbs.)	Remove blemished leaves and coarse stems. Wash at least 4 times, lifting out of the water each time so dirt will settle to the bottom and not cling to the leaves. When cooking stir occasionally.	4 Qts.	1 Tbsp.	20 to 30 minutes
Squash, Winter (10 lbs.)	Wash and peel: If peel is too hard steam or boil the whole squash for approx. 7 minutes. Cut in half, remove fibers and seeds. Cut into uniform pieces.	5 Qts.	1 1/2 Tbsp.	20 to 30 minutes
Squash, Summer (10 lbs.)	Wash and trim; cut into uniform pieces.	2 Qts.	1 Tbsp.	10 to 20 minutes
Sweet Potatoes (10 lbs.)	Select potatoes that are uniform in size. Wash or scrub well.	5 Qts.	None	45 minutes to 1 hr.
Turnips (10 lbs.)	Pare, wash and cut into uniform pieces.	3 Qts.	None	20 to 30 minutes

TABLE IV.   BOILING FROZEN VEGETABLES

VEGETABLES	BOILING WATER	APPROX. COOKING TIME
Asparagus, Cut or Tips (2 1/2 lb. box)	1 1/2 Qts.	10 to 12 minutes
Beans, Lima, Baby (2 1/2 lb. box)	2 Qts.	15 to 20 minutes
Beans, Lima, Fordhook(2 1/2 lb. box)	2 Qts.	10 to 15 minutes
Beans, Green, Cut (2 1/2 lb. box) or French Cut (2 1/2 lb. box)	1 Qt.	10 to 30 minutes
Broccoli, Cut (2 1/2 lb. box)	1 1/2 Qts.	10 to 20 minutes
Broccoli, Spears (2 lb. box)	1 1/2 Qts.	10 to 15 minutes
Cauliflower (2 lb. box)	1 Qt. (plus 1 Pt. milk)	10 to 15 minutes
Corn, Cut (2 1/2 lb. box)	1 1/2 Qts.	5 to 10 minutes
Kale (3 lb. box)	2 Qts.	20 to 25 minutes
Okra (2 1/2 lb. box)	1 Qt.	5 to 8 minutes
Peas, Green (2 1/2 lb. box)	1 Qt.	5 to 10 minutes
Peas and Carrots (2 1/2 lb. box)	1 Qt.	10 to 12 minutes
Succotash (2 1/2 lb. box)	2 Qts.	10 to 15 minutes
Turnip, Greens (3 lb. box)	2 Qts.	25 to 35 minutes
Vegetables, Mixed (2 1/2 lb. box)	1 Qt.	25 to 30 minutes

should start when the water returns to a boil. Check Table IV for approximate time. The time will vary depending on the quality of the vegetables purchased.

5. After cooking drain off part of the liquid and add 8 to 12 ounces of butter or margarine to each 10 pounds of vegetables.
6. 10 pounds of frozen cooked vegetables will yield approximately 50, 3 ounce servings.

Steaming fresh vegetables at 5 pounds of pressure

1. Prepare vegetables according to the directions given in Table V.
2. The prepared fresh vegetables are placed in a compartment steamer in amounts no larger than 10 pounds. Cook under 5 pounds of pressure until vegetables are just tender. The exact cooking time will vary depending on the variety and maturity

TABLE V. STEAMING FRESH VEGETABLES AT 5 POUNDS PRESSURE

VEGETABLES	PREPARATION	TYPE OF CONTAINER	APPROX. COOKING TIME
Beans, Green (10 lbs.)	Trim ends, remove strings and wash thoroughly. Cut into desired size pieces.	Solid (1/2 full) or perforated (3/4 full)	25 to 35 minutes
Beets (10 lbs.)	Remove tops, wash thoroughly, remove blemishes.	Solid or perforated (full)	1 hr. to 1 hr. 30 minutes
Broccoli (10 lbs.)	Cut off tough woody stalk ends and wash. Peel stalks and cut in half lengthwise.	Bake pan (single layer)	10 to 12 minutes
Cabbage, cut in wedges (10 lbs.)	Remove blemished outside leaves. Wash, cut into quarters, remove core and cut into wedges.	Solid (1/2 full)	20 to 25 minutes
Carrots (10 lbs.)	Scrape or pare, wash, slice or cut as desired.	Solid (1/2 full) or perforated (3/4 full)	25 to 35 minutes 20 to 25 minutes
Cauliflower (10 lbs.)	Remove outer leaves and stalks. Separate into flowerets and wash thoroughly.	Solid (1/2 full) or perforated (1/2 full)	12 to 15 minutes 8 to 12 minutes
Celery (10 lbs.)	Trim, cut into desired size pieces and wash thoroughly.	Solid (1/3 full) or perforated (1/2 full)	15 to 20 minutes 12 to 15 minutes
Corn on the cob (10 lbs.)	Husk, remove silk by brushing. Wash thoroughly and drain at once.	Perforated (1/2 full)	5 to 10 minutes
Kale (10 lbs.)	Remove blemished leaves, strip leaves from stems. Wash at least 4 times, lifting out of the water each time so dirt will settle to the bottom and not cling to the leaves.	Solid (1/4 full)	30 to 35 minutes

TABLE V. CONT'D

VEGETABLES	PREPARATION	TYPE OF CONTAINER	APPROX. COOKING TIME
Kohlrabi (10 lbs.)	Pare, wash and cut into 1 inch cubes or as desired.	Perforated (1/2 full)	15 to 20 minutes
Onions (10 lbs.)	Peel and wash and cut if desired.	Perforated (1/3 full)	25 to 30 minutes
Potatoes, White (10 lbs.)	Peel, cut into uniform size, remove all eyes and wash thoroughly.	Solid (1/2 full) or perforated (3/4 full)	40 to 60 minutes / 30 to 40 minutes
Rutabagas (10 lbs.)	Pare, wash and cut into uniform pieces (preferably 1 inch cubes).	Solid (1/2 full) or perforated (1/2 full)	25 to 35 minutes / 20 to 30 minutes
Spinach (10 lbs.)	Remove blemished leaves and coarse stems. Wash at least 4 times, lifting out of the water each time so dirt will settle to the bottom and not cling to the leaves.	Solid (1/2 full) or perforated (1/2 full)	8 to 10 minutes / 6 to 8 minutes
Squash, Winter (10 lbs.)	Wash and peel: If peel is too hard steam or boil the whole squash for approx. 7 minutes. Cut in half, remove fibers and seeds. Cut into uniform pieces.	Solid (1/2 full) or perforated (1/2 full)	20 to 25 minutes / 15 to 20 minutes
Squash, Summer (10 lbs.)	Wash and trim, cut into uniform pieces.	Solid (1/2 full) or perforated (1/2 full)	20 to 25 minutes / 15 to 20 minutes
Sweet Potatoes (10 lbs.)	Select potatoes that are uniform in size. Wash or scrub well.	Solid (3/4 full) or perforated (3/4 full)	30 to 45 minutes / 25 to 35 minutes
Turnips (10 lbs.)	Pare, wash and cut into uniform pieces.	Perforated (1/2 full)	15 to 20 minutes

of the vegetable and its size or the size of the pieces into which it is cut. As a guide see Table V for approximate cooking time for each vegetable.

3. After cooking drain off part of the liquid and add 8 to 12 ounces of butter or margarine to each 10 pounds of vegetables.

4. Salt may be added to vegetables, if desired, use 1 ounce of salt to each 10 pounds of vegetables.

5. 10 pounds of fresh cooked vegetables will yield approximately 50, 3 ounce servings.

Steaming frozen vegetables at 5 pounds of pressure

1. Thaw the tightly packed frozen vegetables at room temperature or in the refrigerator overnight or until they can be easily separated. The loosely packed frozen vegetables do not need thawing.

Securing the chamber of a steam pressure chamber. Steam pressure can vary from 5 to 15 pounds; steam comes into direct contact with the item being cooked. Either a solid container or a perforated container (to allow more steam in) may be used to hold the item to be cooked.

Market Forge Co.

TABLE VI.   STEAMING FROZEN VEGETABLES AT 5 POUNDS PRESSURE

VEGETABLE	APPROX. COOKING TIME
Asparagus, Cut or Tips (5 lbs.)	6 to 10 minutes
Beans, Lima, Baby (5 lbs.)	12 to 15 minutes
Beans, Lima, Fordhook (5 lbs.)	15 to 20 minutes
Beans, Green, Cut (5 lbs.) or French Cut (5 lbs.)	10 to 15 minutes
Broccoli, Cut (5 lbs.)	12 to 15 minutes
Broccoli, Spears (5 lbs.)	5 to 8 minutes
Cauliflower (5 lbs.)	5 to 10 minutes
Corn, Cut (5 lbs.)	5 to 8 minutes
Kale (5 lbs.)	20 to 30 minutes
Okra (5 lbs.)	4 to 6 minutes
Peas, Green (5 lbs.)	5 to 8 minutes
Peas and Carrots (5 lbs.)	5 to 8 minutes
Succotash (5 lbs.)	12 to 15 minutes
Turnip, Greens (5 lbs.)	15 to 20 minutes
Vegetables Mixed (5 lbs.)	15 to 20 minutes

2. Cook the frozen vegetables in amounts not to exceed 5 pounds by placing them in solid steamer pans and then into a compartment of the steamer.
3. Cook under 5 pounds of pressure until vegetables are just tender. The exact cooking time will depend upon the quality of the vegetables purchased. See Table VI for approximate cooking time.
4. After cooking add 4 to 8 ounces of butter or margarine for each 5 pounds vegetables.
5. Salt may be added to vegetables, if desired use approximately ½ ounce of salt to each 5 pounds of vegetables.
6. 5 pounds of frozen vegetables will yield approximately 25, 3 ounce servings.

BAKING

Baking is the primary cooking method used in preparing breads, quickbreads, cookies, pies, cakes and other pastries. Baking, like the roasting of meats, is cooking by surrounding the item with dry heat in an oven. Baking time will vary depending upon the size of the item, the temperature of the oven, the type of item involved, and the particular ingredients used. Before placing an item in the oven always set the thermostat (an apparatus

Photo: Kathryn Adams

Student removing soft dinner rolls from the bake oven.

for regulating and controlling the oven heat) on the desired temperature. (In some cases it is wise to double check with an oven thermometer to make certain the oven temperature is correct.) Preheat the oven about 30 minutes before using to be sure the correct oven temperature is present when ready to use. It is suggested that the baking instructions given with most recipes be followed very closely, because many failures occur from improper baking. In addition to baking, some pastries, such as doughnuts and fried pies, are cooked in a deep fat fryer. Table VII gives the common baking terms, their meaning and the techniques for their performance. Study and become familiar with these techniques—you will be called upon to perform them.

TABLE VII. COMMON BAKING TERMS

TERM	MEANING	TECHNIQUES FOR PERFORMING
Blend	To mix two or more ingredients thoroughly.	Blending can be done by hand, on the mixing machine, or by using a kitchen spoon.
Cut In	A part blended or rubbed into another.	Usually performed by rubbing the two ingredients together with the palms of the hands.
Dissolved	To cause a dry substance to be absorbed in a liquid.	Use a bowl or bain-marie, when dissolving an item, stir the liquid with a kitchen spoon until fluid.

TABLE VII.   CONT'D

TERM	MEANING	TECHNIQUES FOR PERFORMING
Dust	To sprinkle with flour or sugar.	Dusting may be done with the hand or a flour sifter may be used when dusting with powdered sugar.
Fold	A part doubled over another.	Pass a spoon, skimmer or the hands down through a mixture, run it across the bottom of the container and bring up some of the mixture gently and place it on top.
Ice	To cover a cake or some other item with frosting or icing.	Using a spatula, apply the icing with smooth even strokes; dip the spatula in warm water at intervals for smoother, more even application.
Knead	The manipulation of pressing, folding, stretching the air out of dough.	Knead the dough on a floured bench. Press the dough with heal of the hand while at the same time stretching and fold it in an over and over motion.
Make Up	Method of mixing ingredients or handling when dividing an item into single units.	Each item is usually made up in a different manner, depending on desired results, common practice or creative skill.
Masking	To cover an item completely in order to disguise or protect it.	Masking is usually done with icing or a sauce. The item is placed on a wire rack with a sheet pan underneath. The icing or sauce is poured on in a smooth even flow.
Mix	To merge two or more ingredients into one mass.	Mixing can be done in some cases by hand; however, the most practical way is by using the mixing machine.
Proof	To let yeast dough rise by setting it in a warm, moist place.	Proofing can be done by letting the item set in a warm room; however, for best results use a proofing box. The proofing box is designed to maintain a warm moist temperature of approximately 90°F.
Punch	The method of knocking air out of yeast dough after it reaches right fermentation.	Punching the dough is done by applying sharp blows to the dough using the knuckles of both hands.
Rounding	Shaping of dough pieces to seal ends and prevent bleeding.	Rounding is done on a floured bench. The dough unit is rolled by running the palm of the hand in a forward motion across the base of the dough unit.
Sifting	Passing dry ingredients through a fine screen to make light.	The dry ingredients can be tapped through a fine sieve or passed through a flour sifter.
Tubing	Pressing a substance through a pastry tube.	The substance is placed in a pastry bag with a pastry tube in the small end. Pressure is applied by pressing the top of the bag until the substance flows in a steady stream.
Wash	To apply a liquid to the surface of an unbaked product.	Washing is usually done with a pastry brush. The liquid applied may be egg wash, water, milk or a thin syrup.

ADJUSTING STANDARD RECIPES

Most standard recipes are based on yields of 25, 50, or 100 servings. It is usually necessary to adjust the recipes to the number of expected guests on a given occasion.

Let us assume there are to be 235 guests and that number of servings will be required. The standard recipe yields 100 servings so a working factor will be needed. This factor is obtained by dividing the number of servings needed by 100. In our example this would be 235 ÷ 100 = 2.35, the working factor.

Beef à la Bourguignonne

Approx. yield: 100 servings
    36 lbs. beef tenderloin, cut into 1 in. cubes
    1¼ lbs. shortening
    8 lbs. mushrooms, sliced
    2 lbs. shallots or green onions, minced
    6 ozs. flour
    3 qts. Burgundy wine
    Salt and pepper to taste

For our example it will be necessary to adjust the beef bourguignonne to yield 235 servings. The quantities of beef, shortening, mushrooms, shallots, flour and wine would be as follows.
Beef tenderloin

$$36 \text{ lbs.} \times 2.35 = 84.6 \text{ lbs.}$$

Shortening
$$1.25 \text{ lbs.} \times 2.35 = 2.94 \text{ lbs.}$$

Mushrooms	8 lbs. × 2.35 =	18.8 lbs.
Shallots	2 lbs. × 2.35 =	4.7 lbs.
Flour	6 ozs. × 2.35 =	14.1 ozs.
Wine	3 qts. × 2.35 =	7.05 qts.

The fractional part of a pound represented by the decimal (as 0.6 pounds of beef, 0.94 pounds of shortening, 0.8 pounds of mushrooms, 0.7 pounds of shallots) is converted to ounces by multiplying 16 by the decimal.

16 ozs. × 0.6 lbs. beef =
    9.60 ozs.
16 ozs. × 0.94 lbs. shortening =
    15.04 ozs.
16 ozs. × 0.8 lbs. mushrooms =
    12.80 ozs.
16 ozs. × 0.7 lbs. shallots =
    11.20 ozs.

After the fractional part of a pound has been converted to ounces, as above, use Table VIII to round off the fractional ounces.

Therefore, the 9.60 ounces beef will be rounded to 9¾ ounces. The 15.04 ounces shortening will be 15 ounces; the 12.80 ounces of mushrooms will be 13 ounces; and the 11.20 ounces of shallots will be 11¼ ounces. It will be noticed that the flour is already expressed as 14.1 ounces, so it will only be necessary to round off to 14¼ ounces.

The burgundy wine, being a liquid, has been measured by volume, 7.05 quart. Since there are 32 fluid ounces to a fluid quart, the fractional quart would be converted to ounces by multiplying 32 by the decimal.

32 ozs. × 0.05 qt. = 1.60 ozs.

Using the table to round off the ounces we would have 1¾ ounces of wine.

Considering our calculations the beef bourguignonne recipe for 235 servings would now read:

    84 lbs. 9¾ ozs. beef tenderloin
    2 lbs. 15 ozs. shortening

TABLE VIII. ROUNDING OFF FRACTIONAL OUNCES

0.00 To 0.09	= 0 Oz.
0.10 To 0.29	= 1/4 Oz.
0.30 To 0.59	= 1/2 Oz.
0.60 To 0.79	= 3/4 Oz.
0.80 To 0.99	= 1 Oz.

18 lbs. 13 ozs. mushrooms
4 lbs. 11 ¼ ozs. shallots
14¼ ozs. flour
7 qts. 1¾ ozs. Burgundy wine
Salt and pepper to taste

If the recipe you are using has a yield of 25, or some other number for that matter, the working factor would be found in the same way, 235 ÷ 25 = 9.4. All ingredients would be multiplied by the working factor 9.4 and the fractional parts reduced as already explained.

On occasion the recipe you choose may use *volume* measure rather than weights. If so, the working factor is found as before then multiplied by the cups, tablespoons, teaspoons, etc. Fractional cups would be multiplied by 16, as there are 16 tablespoons in each cup. (See table of equivalent measures in Chapter 3.) Fractional tablespoons are rounded off to the nearest fractional teaspoon.

In converting any recipe by the use of the work factor, there is one ingredient that has not been mentioned. It is *common sense!* This is especially true where the work factor produces a recipe for several hundred servings. In the example given it will be noted that the work factor produced 7 quarts, 1¾ ounces of wine. The application of common sense would tell us that the deletion of 1¾ ounces of wine would in no way affect the taste or quality of 235 servings of beef bourguignonne.

CONVERSION TABLE

Table IX has been provided to aid the student in converting basic foods and ingredients from measures to weights or from weights to measures. The approximate weight needed to make up a tablespoon, cup, pint or quart is given for the common food items. This information is often useful because some recipes are given in weight and some in measures. The most accurate recipes are given in weight. In some cases, however, the student may find it convenient to convert weight to measure. For example, 1 pound of water may be converted to 1 pint. Similarly 1 cup of bread flour may be converted to 5 ounces by weight.

TABLE IX.   APPROX. WEIGHTS AND MEASURES OF COMMON FOODS

FOOD PRODUCT	TBSP.	CUP	PT.		QT.	
Allspice	1/4 oz.	4 ozs.	–	8 ozs.	1 lb.	–
Apples, fresh, diced	1/2 oz.	8 ozs.	1 lb. –		2 lbs.	–
Bacon, raw, diced	1/2 oz.	8 ozs.	1 lb. –		2 lbs.	–
Bacon, cooked, diced	2/3 oz.	10 1/2 ozs.	1 lb. 5 ozs.		2 lbs. 12 ozs.	
Bananas, sliced	1/2 oz.	8 ozs.	1 lb. –		2 lbs.	–
Baking Powder	3/8 oz.	6 ozs.	–	12 ozs.	1 lb.	8 ozs.
Baking Soda	3/8 oz.	6 ozs.		12 ozs.	1 lb. 8 ozs.	
Beef, cooked, diced	3/8 oz.	5 1/2 ozs.	–	11 ozs.	1 lb. 6 ozs.	
Beef, raw, ground	1/2 oz.	8 ozs.	1 lb. –		2 lbs.	–

TABLE IX.   CONT'D

FOOD PRODUCT	TBSP.	CUP	PT.	QT.
Barley	–	8 ozs.	1 lb. –	2 lbs. –
Bread Crumbs, dry	1/4 oz.	4 1/2 ozs.	– 9 ozs.	1 lb. 2 ozs.
Bread crumbs, fresh	1/8 oz.	2 ozs.	– 4 ozs.	– 8 ozs.
Butter	1/2 oz.	8 ozs.	1 lb. –	2 lbs. –
Cabbage, shredded	1/4 oz.	4 ozs.	– 8 ozs.	1 lb. –
Carrots, raw, diced	5/16 oz.	5 ozs.	– 10 ozs.	1 lb. 4 ozs.
Celery, raw, diced	1/4 oz.	4 ozs.	– 8 ozs.	1 lb. –
Cheese, diced	–	5 1/2 ozs.	– 11 ozs.	1 lb. 6 ozs.
Cheese, grated	1/4 oz.	4 ozs.	– 8 ozs.	1 lb. –
Cheese, shredded	1/4 oz.	4 ozs.	– 8 ozs.	1 lb. –
Chocolate, grated	1/4 oz.	4 ozs.	– 8 ozs.	1 lb. –
Chocolate, melted	1/2 oz.	8 ozs.	1 lb. –	2 lbs. –
Cinnamon, ground	1/4 oz.	3 1/2 ozs.	– 7 ozs.	– 14 ozs.
Cloves, ground	1/4 oz.	4 ozs.	– 8 ozs.	1 lb. –
Cloves, whole	3/16 oz.	3 ozs.	– 6 ozs.	– 12 ozs.
Cocoa	3/16 oz.	3 1/2 ozs.	– 7 ozs.	– 14 ozs.
Coconut, shredded, packed	3/16 oz.	3 1/2 ozs.	– 7 ozs.	– 14 ozs.
Coconut, macaroon, packed	3/16 oz.	3 ozs.	– 6 ozs.	– 12 ozs.
Coffee, ground	3/16 oz.	3 ozs.	– 6 ozs.	– 12 ozs.
Cornmeal	5/16 oz.	4 3/4 ozs.	– 9 1/2 ozs.	1 lb. 3 ozs.
Cornstarch	1/3 oz.	5 1/3 ozs.	– 10 1/2 ozs.	1 lb. 5 ozs.
Corn Syrup	3/4 oz.	12 ozs.	1 lb. 8 ozs.	3 lbs. –
Cracker Crumbs	1/4 oz.	4 ozs.	– 8 ozs.	1 lb. –
Cranberries, raw	–	4 ozs.	– 8 ozs.	1 lb. –
Currants, dried	1/3 oz.	5 1/3 ozs.	– 11 ozs.	1 lb. 6 ozs.
Curry Powder	3/16 oz.	3 1/2 ozs.	– –	– –
Dates, pitted	5/16 oz.	5 1/2 ozs.	– 11 ozs.	1 lb. 6 ozs.
Egg Whites	1/2 oz.	8 ozs.	1 lb. –	2 lbs. –
Eggs, whole	1/2 oz.	8 ozs.	1 lb. –	2 lbs. –
Egg Yokes	1/2 oz.	8 ozs.	1 lb. –	2 lbs. –
Eggs, dry (whole)	1/4 oz.	4 ozs.	8 ozs.	1 lb.
Eggs, dry (whole)	1 1/2 cup (6 ozs.) + 1 pt. water = 1 doz. eggs			
Extracts	1/2 oz.	8 ozs.	1 lb. –	2 lbs. –

TABLE IX. CONT'D

FOOD PRODUCT	TBSP.	CUP	PT.		QT.	
Flour, bread	5/16 oz.	5 ozs.	–	10 ozs.	1 lb.	4 ozs.
Flour, pastry	5/16 oz.	5 ozs.	–	10 ozs.	1 lb.	4 ozs.
Flour, cake	1/4 oz.	4 3/4 ozs.	–	9 1/2 ozs.	1 lb.	3 ozs.
Gelatin, flavored	3/8 oz.	6 1/2 ozs.	–	13 ozs.	1 lb.	10 ozs.
Gelatin, plain	5/16 oz.	5 ozs.	–	10 ozs.	1. lb.	4 ozs.
Ginger	3/16 oz.	3 1/4 ozs.	–	6 1/2 ozs.	–	13 ozs.
Glucose	3/4 oz.	12 ozs.	1 lb. 8 ozs.		3 lbs.	–
Green Peppers, diced	1/4 oz.	4 ozs.	–	8 ozs.	1 lb.	–
Ham, cooked, diced	5/16 oz.	5 1/4 ozs.	–	10 1/2 ozs.	1 lb.	5 ozs.
Horseradish, prepared	1/2 oz.	8 ozs.	1 lb. –		2 lbs.	–
Jam	5/8 oz.	10 ozs.	1 lb. 4 ozs.		2 lbs.	8 ozs.
Lemon Juice	1/2 oz.	8 ozs.	1 lb. –		2 lbs.	–
Lemon Rind	1/4 oz.	4 ozs.	–	8 ozs.	1 lb.	–
Mace	1/4 oz.	3 1/4 ozs.	–	6 1/2 ozs.	–	13 ozs.
Mayonnaise	1/2 oz.	8 ozs.	1 lb. –		2 lbs.	–
Milk, liquid	1/2 oz.	8 ozs.	1 lb. –		2 lbs.	–
Milk, powdered	5/16 oz.	4 1/2 ozs.	–	9 ozs.	1 lb.	2 ozs.
Milk, powdered	4 ozs. + 1 qt. water = 1 qt. milk					
Molasses	3/4 oz.	12 ozs.	1 lb. 8 ozs.		3 lbs.	–
Mustard, ground	1/4 oz.	3 1/4 ozs.	–	6 1/2 ozs.	–	13 ozs.
Mustard, prepared	1/4 oz.	4 ozs.	–	8 ozs.	1 lb.	–
Nutmeats	1/4 oz.	4 ozs.	–	8 ozs.	1 lb.	–
Nutmeg, ground	1/4 oz.	4 1/4 ozs.	–	8 1/2 ozs.	1 lb.	1 oz.
Oats, rolled	3/16 oz.	3 ozs.	–	6 ozs.	–	12 ozs.
Oil, salad	1/2 oz.	8 ozs.	1 lb. –		2 lbs.	–
Onions	1/3 oz.	5 1/2 ozs.	–	11 ozs.	1 lb.	6 ozs.
Peaches, canned	1/2 oz.	8 ozs.	1 lb. –		2 lbs.	–
Peas, dry, split	7/16 oz.	7 ozs.	–	14 ozs.	1 lb.	12 ozs.
Pickles, chopped	1/4 oz.	5 1/4 ozs.	–	10 1/2 ozs.	1 lb.	5 ozs.
Pickle Relish	5/16 oz.	5 1/4 ozs.	–	10 1/2 ozs.	1 lb.	5 ozs.
Pineapple, diced	1/2 oz.	8 ozs.	1 lb. –		2 lbs.	–
Pimientas, chopped	1/2 oz.	7 ozs.	–	14 ozs.	1 lb.	12 ozs.

TABLE IX. CONT'D

FOOD PRODUCT	TBSP.	CUP	PT.		QT.	
Potatoes, cooked, diced	–	6 1/2 ozs.	–	13 ozs.	1 lb.	10 ozs.
Prunes, dry	–	5 1/2 ozs.	–	11 ozs.	1 lb.	6 ozs.
Raisins, seedless	1/3 oz.	5 1/3 ozs.	–	10 3/4 ozs.	1 lb.	5 ozs.
Rice, raw	1/2 oz.	8 ozs.	1 lb.	–	2 lbs.	–
Salmon, flaked	1/2 oz.	8 ozs.	1 lb.	–	2 lbs.	–
Sage, ground	1/8 oz.	2 1/4 ozs.	–	–	–	–
Savory	1/8 oz.	2 ozs.	–	–	–	–
Salt	1/2 oz.	8 ozs.	1 lb.	–	2 lbs.	–
Shortening	1/2 oz.	8 ozs.	1 lb.	–	2 lbs.	–
Soda	7/16 oz.	7 ozs.	–	–	–	–
Sugar, brown, packed	1/2 oz.	8 ozs.	1 lb.	–	2 lbs.	–
Sugar, granulated	7/16 oz.	7 1/2 ozs.	–	15 ozs.	1 lb.	14 ozs.
Sugar, powdered	5/16 oz.	4 3/4 ozs.	–	9 1/2 ozs.	1 lb.	3 ozs.
Tapioca, pearl	1/4 oz.	4 ozs.	–	8 ozs.	1 lb.	–
Tea	1/6 oz.	2 1/2 ozs.	–	5 ozs.	–	10 ozs.
Tomatoes	1/2 oz.	8 ozs.	1 lb.	–	2 lbs.	–
Tuna Fish ,flaked	1/2 oz.	8 ozs.	1 lb.	–	2 lbs.	–
Vanilla, imitation	1/2 oz.	8 ozs.	1 lb.	–	2 lbs.	–
Vinegar	1/2 oz.	8 ozs.	1 lb.	–	2 lbs.	–
Water	1/2 oz.	8 ozs.	1 lb.	–	2 lbs.	–

CONVERSION OF ENGLISH TO METRIC UNITS

WEIGHTS:	
1 OUNCE (AVDP)	= 28.35 GRAMS
1 POUND	= 453.6 GRAMS OR 0.4536 KILOGRAM
LIQUID MEASUREMENTS:	
1 (FLUID) OUNCE	= 0.02957 LITER OR 28.35 GRAMS
1 PINT	= 473.2 CU CENTIMETERS
1 QUART	= 0.9463 LITER
1 (US) GALLON	= 3785 CU CENTIMETERS OR 3.785 LITERS
TEMPERATURE MEASUREMENTS:	

TO CONVERT DEGREES FAHRENHEIT TO DEGREES CENTIGRADE, USE THE FOLLOWING FORMULA: DEG C = 5/9 (DEG F - 32)

CONVERSION OF METRIC TO ENGLISH UNITS

WEIGHTS:	
1 GRAM (G)	= 0.03527 OZ (AVDP)
1 KILOGRAM (KG)	= 2.205 LBS
LIQUID MEASUREMENTS:	
1 CU CENTIMETER (CC)	= 0.06102 CU IN.
1 LITER (= 1000 CC)	= 1.057 QUARTS OR 2.113 PINTS OR 61.02 CU INS.
TEMPERATURE MEASUREMENTS:	

TO CONVERT DEGREES CENTIGRADE TO DEGREES FAHRENHEIT , USE THE FOLLOWING FORMULA : DEG F = (DEG C X 9/5) + 32

SOME IMPORTANT FEATURES OF THE CGS SYSTEM ARE:

1 CC OF PURE WATER = 1 GRAM.

PURE WATER FREEZES AT 0 DEGREES C AND BOILS AT 100 DEGREES C.

chapter 7 | # breakfast preparation

■ It is important for the student cook or, for that matter, the journeyman cook to have a thorough knowledge of breakfast preparations, because most commercial establishments have found that the breakfast menu can be profitable if certain conditions such as favorable location, overnight guest accommodations, etc. are present. It is also important because breakfast preparations that include meat, potatoes, eggs, batters, etc. can also be applied to the luncheon menu, and are essential to a finished cook's background.

Many nutrition experts have stated that breakfast is the most important meal of the day and is required by the body to operate at top efficiency through-

out the day. They also point out that breakfast is usually the first food consumed for a period of 12 hours and therefore should be composed of items that are easily digested.

Since this meal is the first of the day and is usually consumed after a long period of inactivity, most people are fussier about breakfast preparations than they are about luncheon or dinner. It is essential, therefore, that all breakfast preparations be presented with the utmost care.

Except for the so-called Continental breakfast, the usual preparations include egg cookery, pancakes, potatoes, waffles, hot cereals, toast (plain, cinnamon, and French), stewed fruit, and meats such as bacon, ham, and sausage. Of these the most important single item is eggs, which may be prepared in a variety of ways. In this chapter we will deal with the most popular egg preparations.

EGGS

Eggs are used to such a great extent in the commercial kitchen that knowledge about them should be acquired before they are used. Knowing the product will lead to better results.

Eggs are a complete protein food, established as one of the very important foods in the daily diet. They are very high in vitamin content and in most cases, when cooked properly, are easy to digest. Besides their importance in breakfast preparations, they are also featured as luncheon and dinner entrees. In fact, eggs, like cheese, is a food that may be used in any part of the menu from appetizer to dessert. A further fact to consider is that eggs are usually inexpensive and can help to hold the food cost in reasonable limits.

In food preparation eggs are very versatile and may be used to perform in various ways:

1. As a thickening or binding agent. *Examples:* meat loaf, custard, pie filling, and croquettes.
2. As an adhesive agent. *Example:* breading.
3. As an emulsifying agent. *Examples:* Mayonnaise and Hollandaise.
4. As a clarifying agent. *Examples:* consomme and aspic.
5. As a lightening agent (incorporating air). *Examples:* soufflés, sponge cakes, and chiffon pies.
6. As an entrée. *Examples:* breakfast preparations, eggs Benedict, and eggs à la goldenrod.

The quality of an egg depends on many factors, the most important of which are appearance and condition of the interior as revealed in the candling process (twirling the egg slowly before an electric light), and, to a lesser degree, the cleanness of the shell. The size of an egg or the color of its shell has no bearing on the quality.

Eggs are graded, first, according to quality. There are four grades. They are Grade AA, also referred to as U.S. Special, a very fancy egg, not very plentiful and seldom found in retail food markets; Grade A, also called U.S. Extra, a very fine egg and usually the top grade found in retail stores; Grade B, also called U.S. Standard, a good quality egg suitable for most purposes; and Grade C, referred to in some quarters as U.S. Trade, suitable for cooking where flavor is not an important factor.

Eggs are also classed according to size. Each of the four grades of eggs are sorted into various sizes. The size is determined by federal standards based on the number of ounces per dozen:

Jumbo	28 oz. per dozen
Extra Large	26 " " "
Large	24 " " "
Medium	21 " " "
Small	17 " " "

In the commercial kitchen fresh eggs are more used than eggs in any other form. This is because in their fresh form they are most versatile. Eggs can be purchased frozen, in 30-lb. cans as whole eggs, egg yolks and egg whites, but these forms are convenient only if the eggs are to be used in other food preparations and in baked products. In this condition they certainly cannot be used as an entrée. Dried eggs may also be purchased, but this product has never been used to any great extent in food service establishments, although it is occasionally used in some bake shops.

Poultry and Egg National Board
Eggs sunny side up with bacon.

Fried eggs

Always fry eggs to order, use high quality eggs, and fry with butter, shortening or margarine. Never fry with bacon grease unless requested to do so by the guest, because bacon and some other greases produce strong characteristic flavors.

Select the correct size skillet. For a single egg the skillet should be four inches in diameter at the bottom. For an order of eggs (2 eggs) the skillet should be 6 inches in diameter. The skillet should have sloped, shallow walls and a long handle.

Place about ⅛ inch of melted butter, shortening or margarine in the bottom of the pan. Heat to a fairly moderate temperature and slide the eggs, which have been previously broken into a soup bowl, into the fat. The hot fat will coagulate the eggs immediately so the whites will not spread.

At this point reduce the heat immediately to avoid a hard, brown surface under or around the edge of the eggs. Proceed to cook the eggs as requested by the guest.

"Sunny side up" eggs are lightly cooked with the yolks unbroken. "Eggs over" are eggs that are flipped over and cooked "easy" (lightly) or hard. Basted eggs are cooked like "sunny side up," but are finished under the broiler by cooking the top of the eggs until the whites are set and a cooked coating appears over the yolk.

Another method of frying eggs is known as "country style." Country style fried eggs are served with ham, bacon, or sausage. The meat is pre-cooked, placed in a greased egg skillet, and heated. The eggs are placed on top of the meat and cooked in the same manner as sunny side up; however, the skillet is covered during the frying period until the whites are set and the yolks are cooked slightly.

Eggs can also be fried on a well greased grill. However, the results are not as attractive as pan fried. The grill must be very clean and well conditioned for best results. When cooking eggs on a grill, maintain a temperature of 300° to 350° F.

Fried egg faults

1. Frying with too much fat. There is danger of burning one's self, and eggs are greasy when served.
2. Using a poorly conditioned pan or grill. Eggs stick to the pan or grill, causing them to burn and break.
3. Frying at too low a temperature. Egg whites spread too rapidly.
4. Frying at too high a temperature. Eggs burn and are usually overcooked.
5. Frying with too little fat. Eggs stick and usually burn.

Scrambled eggs

These are sometimes referred to as "shipwrecked" eggs. Scrambling is the easiest method of preparing eggs and is an excellent method to choose when preparing in quantity. Several ways are possible. Eggs can be scrambled in a well greased pan in the oven, in a steamjacket kettle, in a double boiler, in a steamer, or in a skillet on the range. Except for large quantities, when one of the other methods may prove more efficient, the best method is to scramble in the skillet.

Break the eggs into a stainless steel or china bowl—never aluminum, which will discolor the eggs. Beat slightly with a wire whip or kitchen fork. Add a small amount of milk or cream if desired (about 4 oz. to each pint of eggs). Too much liquid will cause *weeping* (give off water) after they are cooked.

Pour the beaten eggs into a heated greased or buttered skillet so the eggs will start to coagulate immediately. Reduce heat and lift the eggs carefully from the bottom while at the same time stirring gently with a wooden spoon, so the uncooked portion will settle to the bottom and cook.

Scrambled eggs are properly cooked when they are very soft and fluffy. Always undercook them slightly, because they will firm up when held for service. Never let the eggs brown or overcook so they will become dry, hard, and unpalatable. If scrambled eggs are to be held over 5 minutes before serving, add a medium cream sauce (combination of hot milk or cream to roux) using a ratio of 5 to 1. This will extend the holding time. The addition of the cream sauce prevents the eggs from drying and discoloring.

Scrambled egg faults

1. Cooking at too high a temperature. Eggs usually burn and are overcooked.
2. Excessive stirring when cooking. Egg particles become too fine, giving a poor appearance.
3. Holding cooked eggs too long in steam table. The eggs develop off-colors and lose flavors.
4. Scrambling with too much fat in skillet or pan. Eggs become greasy.

5. Scrambling with too little fat in skillet or pan. Eggs stick to pan, become tough and burn.

Boiled or simmered eggs

Although the common term is "boiled eggs," the fact is that eggs should be simmered—never boiled—for best results. Boiling tends to toughen the texture and can form a green coating around the outside of the yolk. Simmering at a temperature of approximately 195° F. is recommended.

Eggs should be at room temperature before they are placed in the hot water, or they may crack. If the eggs are left in the refrigerator until time to cook them, run warm water over them before placing them in the hot water. There are two recommended methods of "boiling" or simmering eggs:

1. Bring water to a boil, 212° F. Place the eggs in the boiling water. Reduce the heat to a simmer by pulling it away from the heat. Cook to desired doneness:
   (A) Soft . . . . 3 to 5 mins.
   (B) Medium . . . 7 to 8 mins.
   (C) Hard . . . . . . 15 to 17 mins.
2. Place the eggs in a pot and cover them with cold water. Place pot on the range and bring the water to a boil, reducing the heat to a simmer by pulling the pot away from the heat. Cook to desired doneness.
   (A) Soft . . . . 1 to 2 mins.
   (B) Medium . . . 3 to 6 mins.
   (C) Hard . . . . . . 8 to 10 mins.

If eggs are simmered for breakfast service they should be plunged immediately into slightly cold water and served in their shells. If the eggs are simmered for hard boiled and held for use in kitchen preparations such as sandwiches, deviled eggs, garnish, etc., they should be cooled in ice cold water, immediately after cooking, for about five minutes.

A boiled egg is peeled by cracking the shell gently on a hard surface or rolling it on a hard surface. Start to peel at the large end of the egg and peel down, keeping the egg submerged in cold water. Holding the egg under cold running water will help loosen the shell.

Place the hard boiled eggs in a bain-marie covered with water, and store in the refrigerator. If the yolk of the egg is exposed do not place it in the water; place it in a bowl and cover it with foil or a damp cloth.

To coddle eggs, for such preparations as Caesar salad, have the eggs at room temperature and place them in a pot. Add boiling water to the pot until the eggs are covered. Put a lid on the pot and let stand, without heating, until the eggs are cooked as desired.

Boiling or simmering faults

1. Cooking at too high a temperature. Eggs become tough and rubbery. A green ring may appear around the yolk.
2. Cooking at too low a temperature. Eggs are usually undercooked.

Note: Very fresh eggs are usually hard to peel. Eggs intended for boiling are preferably about one week old.

Poultry and Egg National Board

Soft boiled eggs.

Poultry and Egg National Board

Poached eggs on toast with bacon.

Poached eggs

While poached eggs are fairly popular on the breakfast menu, they are also used extensively on the luncheon menu in such preparations as eggs a la Florentine, poached eggs on corn beef hash, eggs Benedict, etc.

Fill a fairly shallow pan with enough water to cover the eggs (about 2½ in. deep). Add 1 tbs. of salt and 2 tbs. of distilled vinegar to each gallon of water. The salt and vinegar will cause the white to set firmly around the yolk when the egg is placed in the water, thus retarding the white from spreading. The acetic acid of the vinegar toughens the albumen contained in the egg white, and when the white is set firmly around the yolk a more eye-appealing product is obtained. Acid will not affect the flavor of the egg when used in diluted quantities.

Bring the liquid to a boil, then reduce to a simmer (about 195° to 200° F.) Break eggs into a bowl or saucer and slide the eggs into the simmering liquid. They should slide gently down the side of the pan so the yolk should stay in the center of the white.

Cook as desired; usually three to five minutes is sufficient. Remove with a skimmer, perforated ladle, or slotted spoon. Drain well and serve on buttered toast.

About 12 eggs may be poached in each gallon of liquid. The water may be used for three different batches before it is discarded.

To prepare poached eggs in quantity the above procedure is used, but the eggs are slightly undercooked, placed immediately in cold water to stop further cooking and to hold until ready to serve. To serve, they are reheated in hot salt water. The quantity method is usually for luncheon preparations. For breakfast preparations the eggs are poached to order.

Poached egg faults

1. Too much vinegar added to liquid. This will toughen the eggs and affect their flavor.
2. Cooking at too low a temperature. Eggs will be too tender and difficult to handle when serving.
3. Cooking at too high a temperature. Eggs will become tough and usually are overcooked.

Shirred eggs

When served on the breakfast or luncheon menu shirred eggs present a very attractive dish if they are prepared in a proper manner and are not overcooked, as is too often the case.

The eggs are broken into a bowl or saucer, then placed into a buttered shirred egg dish. Place the shirred egg dish on the range and cook at medium heat until the whites are set. Finish by transferring the dish to the oven or by basting the top of the eggs lightly under the broiler. In either case never cook the eggs hard.

Shirred eggs may be served with a variety of foods. Cooked bacon, ham, sausages, Canadian bacon, kidneys, chicken livers, and cheese are the most popular. The meat or cheese can be

Poultry and Egg National Board

Shirred eggs with corn beef hash. In this case the hash is placed around the eggs after cooking.

placed around the edges of the eggs before or after cooking.

Shirred egg faults

1. Cooking at too high a temperature. Eggs become hard and tough, and usually are burned.
2. Cooking at too low a temperature. Eggs spread and yolk has a tendency to break.

Omelets

Another of the egg preparations that are equally popular on the breakfast and luncheon menus are omelets. There are occasions when omelets can be found on the dinner menu, but this is most unusual. The omelet is a versatile preparation because it blends well with other foods, producing almost limitless variations. When an omelet is served with another item such as bacon, ham, mushroom, or Spanish sauce it takes the name of that accompanying item; for example, Spanish omelet, ham omelet, mushroom omelet, etc.

Omelets should be made to order for best results. If they are held for even a short period of time they lose their tender fluffiness and become tough and rubbery. When preparing an omelet for the breakfast menu, 2 or 3 eggs are usually used. For the luncheon menu 3 eggs are the rule. When an omelet has a sweet accompaniment such as jelly, jam, or marmalade it is usually rolled or folded into the center of the omelet, and when the omelet is completed it is dusted with powdered sugar and scored or branded with a hot metal rod. There are a number of techniques used in preparing omelets, but they usually result in a rolled or folded type with the accompanying food item in the inside.

Rolled type omelet

Break eggs into a bowl and whip slightly with a wire whip or kitchen fork. A small amount of cream may be added if desired, but this practice is not generally recommended.

Place about ⅛ in. of melted margarine or butter, fat or oil in a conditioned egg skillet, and heat to a fairly high temperature. Pour the beaten eggs into the hot grease. As the eggs bubble, tilt the skillet in all directions to spread the eggs to the sides of the skillet so they will cover the surface of the skillet completely. Reduce heat by bringing the skillet to the side of the range, and cook the eggs at a moderate temperature.

As the eggs cook, lift up the cooked portion, using a kitchen fork or palette knife, and letting the uncooked portion run to the bottom and sides of the skillet.

When the eggs are slightly set but still in a very moist condition, tilt the skillet to about a 60° angle and, using a kitchen fork or palette knife, roll the eggs toward you. When the roll is completed place it on a hot plate by grasping the handle of the skillet in the right hand, with fingers and thumb turned up. Bring the hot plate to the lip of the skillet with the left hand. Tilt the skillet over, letting the omelet fall onto the plate. Cover the omelet with a clean cloth to reshape it and also absorb excess grease.

Serve immediately.

Folded type omelet

The same procedure as above is followed until the eggs are set but still in a very moist condition.

Tilt the skillet to a 60° angle and, using a kitchen fork or palette knife, fold in half only. If an accompanying item is to be folded into the omelet it is placed in the center of the eggs before folding. Brown the omelet very lightly and invert onto a hot plate, using the same method as described for the rolled type.

There are many variations of the plain omelet. These are created by the addition of one or more items. A few of these are listed below:

Bacon omelet
Cheese omelet
Ham omelet
Chicken liver omelet
Onion omelet
Western omelet (cooked minced onions, green pepper, and ham)
Spanish or Creole omelet
Jelly omelet
Lobster omelet
Shrimp omelet
Sausage omelet
Fine herb omelet

Extremely fluffy omelets have become popular in some areas, but as a rule the plain or French omelet is mainly featured on most menus. A fluffy omelet is prepared by separating the yolk from the white and beating each to a soft foam. The beaten white and yolk are then folded very gently together until well mixed. In this form the eggs are poured

Fold type plain omelet, served with
fresh blueberry sauce.

into a hot greased skillet and cooked in
the same manner as a rolled or folded
omelet. This type of omelet can also be
finished in a 325° F. oven. When finished
it should be served at once.

Omelet faults

1. Too little fat in pan. Eggs stick
   and burn.
2. Poorly conditioned skillet. Eggs
   stick and omelet will break when
   rolled or folded.
3. Overcooking. Omelet becomes too
   brown and cracks when rolled or
   folded.
4. Too much fat in skillet. Hot grease
   splatters when eggs are added, and
   when rolling or folding excessive
   grease will spill out.
5. Cooking omelet ahead of service.
   Omelet loses its fluffiness, becomes
   tough and rubbery.

PANCAKES

The second most popular breakfast
preparation in most areas are pancakes,
also called "hot cakes" or "griddle
cakes". Reasons for their popularity are
that they are easy to digest, can be
served in a variety of ways, and usually
have a low menu price.

They must always be cooked to order
and served piping hot, on a hot plate or

platter with fresh butter and some type
of jam, jelly, or syrup. Maple syrup is
most popular; however, fruit or fruit-
flavored syrups are also used. Pancakes
cost very little to make and even when
featured with a high-cost accompaniment such as strawberries, cherries,
blueberries, and ice cream still return a
large profit. This is why pancake houses
have become so successful. Pancakes
blend well with meat and when served
for breakfast are usually accompanied
with sausage, ham, or bacon.

There are a number of quality pancake mixes on the market, and most
food service establishments find that
they are more convenient to use than
mixing their own. Convenience, however, depends on the type of mix used.
Some mixes call for just the addition of
milk or water, but most of the better
ones call for the addition of milk, oil,
and eggs. The convenience is then doubt-
ful because with the addition of a few
more ingredients one can prepare his own
mix and save money. The decision of
whether to make the mixes or use a prepared mix is usually made by the food
service operator or the chef, but all cooks
should know some of the basic mixes
and how to prepare them. During one's
career in food service he will find himself
in positions where convenience is not
available, so being prepared for any situation is a good rule to follow.

Plain pancakes.

There are a number of basic pancake mixes, and recipes for the most popular ones are given below.

Buttermilk pancakes

Ingredients: Approx. yield: 1 gal. or 15 orders of 3 cakes to 1 order

         6   whole eggs
         2   qts. cultured buttermilk
         2   lb. all purpose flour
        12   oz. salad oil
         3   tsp. baking soda
         1   oz. baking powder
     2½   oz. granulated sugar
         3   tsp. salt

Procedure

1. Place the eggs in a mixing bowl and mix on the electric mixer at slow speed, using the paddle, for 1 minute.
2. Add the milk and oil, continuing to mix at slow speed for 1 more minute.
3. Combine the remaining dry ingredients, sift 2 times and add gradually to the liquid mixture in the mixing bowl. Mix 1 minute, scrape down bowl if necessary. Remove batter from mixing bowl and place in a bain-marie.
4. Let the batter rest at least 10 minutes.
5. Heat griddle to 375° F., and grease lightly.
6. Using a 3-oz. ladle, spot the batter on the griddle. Cake should spread to 5 inches in diameter.
7. Brown one side until bubbles appear on top and the batter takes on a puffy quality.
8. Turn or flip and brown the second side.
9. Serve 3 cakes to each order with syrup desired.

Plain pancakes or hot cakes

Ingredients: Approx. yield 1 gal. or 15 orders of 3 cakes to 1 order

         8   whole eggs
         2   qts. liquid milk
        12   oz. salad oil
         2   lbs. all purpose flour
         5   oz. granulated sugar
         3   tsp. salt
     1½   oz. baking powder

Procedure

1. Place the eggs in a mixing bowl and mix on the electric mixer at slow speed, using the paddle, for 1 minute.

2. Add the milk and oil, continuing to mix at slow speed for 1 more minute.
3. Combine the remaining dry ingredients, sift 2 times and add gradually to the liquid mixture in the mixing bowl. Mix for approximately 1 minute at slow speed. Scrape down bowl if necessary. Remove batter from mixing bowl and place in a bain-marie.
4. Let the batter rest at least 10 minutes.
5. Heat griddle to 375° F. Grease lightly.
6. Using a 3-oz. ladle, spot the batter on the hot griddle. Cakes should spread to 5 inches in diameter.
7. Brown one side until golden brown, turn or flip and brown second side.
8. Serve 3 cakes to each order with syrup desired.

French pancakes, or crêpes

Ingredients: Approx. yield: 1 gal. or 60 pancakes

         1   qt. milk (liquid)
        10   oz. all purpose flour
         6   whole eggs
      ½   tsp. salt
         3   oz. butter, melted
         3   oz. sugar

Procedure

1. Place the eggs in a mixing bowl and mix by hand, using a piano wire whip, or mix on the electric mixer at medium speed, using the paddle, for approximately 1 minute.
2. Add the milk and continue to mix until incorporated with the eggs.
3. Combine the dry ingredients, sift and add gradually to the liquid mixture. Mix for approximately 1 minute or until all the dry ingredients are incorporated into the liquid mixture.
4. Add the melted butter and mix until blended well.
5. Pour the batter into a bain-marie and place in the refrigerator until ready to use.
6. Using a well conditioned egg skillet or omelet pan (as it is sometimes called), coat with melted butter or shortening and heat slightly.

7. Using a 2-oz. ladle, coat the bottom of the skillet with the crêpe batter. While pouring the batter into the skillet rotate the skillet in a clockwise direction so the batter will spread uniformly over the bottom of the skillet and the coating will remain very thin.
8. Place the skillet on the range and cook one side, then flip or turn by hand and cook second side. Brown the pancakes very lightly.
9. Remove from the skillet and place on sheet pans covered with wax paper. If pancakes are stacked, place a sheet of wax paper between the layers.
10. Spread each pancake (crêpe) with jelly, jam, preserves, marmalade, strawberries, or apple sauce and roll up.
11. Serve 3 rolls to each order, dusted with powdered sugar.

Waffles

Ingredients: Approx. yield: 1 gal.

10	whole eggs
2	qts. milk
2	lb. 10 oz. cake flour
2	oz. baking powder
8	oz. sugar
¼	oz. sugar
1	lb. butter, melted

Procedure

1. Place the eggs in a mixing bowl and mix on the electric mixer at medium speed, using the paddle, for approximately 1 minute.
2. Add the milk and continue to mix until incorporated with the eggs.
3. Combine the dry ingredients, sift three times, and add to the egg-milk mixture. Mix for 1 minute.
4. Add the melted butter and mix until well blended.
5. Pour the batter into a bain-marie and place in the refrigerator until ready to use.
6. Brush the top and bottom of the waffle iron with salad oil. Heat to approximately 375° F.
7. Pour enough batter on the waffle grid to barely cover. The amount used will depend on the size and shape of the waffle iron.

8. Let the waffle cook for about 1 minute before lowering the top of the iron. When the top is lowered cook about 1½ to 2 minutes longer. Exercise caution when cooking, because the top grid is usually hotter than the bottom.
9. Serve 2 waffles for each serving, with jam, jelly, syrup, marmalade, or fruit.

BREAKFAST MEATS

Sausage, bacon, and ham—all pork products—are the popular breakfast meats. Bacon and ham are cured by smoking, whereas the sausage is fresh. These meats are usually pre-cooked and reheated for service when the breakfast volume is large. When the volume is small they are cooked to order. Pre-cooking is done to speed up service, since breakfast must be geared for speed.

Breakfast sausage are of two types: patties and links. The patties may be purchased in this form, in bulk, or prepared in the kitchen from ground fresh pork and spices. If purchased in bulk or prepared in the kitchen they are portioned and formed into 3 or 4 oz. servings by hand. Sausage patties if precooked in anticipation of a large volume of business can be baked on sheet pans in the oven at 350° F., cooked in a skillet on the range, broiled under the broiler, or grilled on a griddle. Whichever method is used, they should only be cooked about three-quarters of the way and finished when ready to serve.

Link sausage, sometimes referred to as "little pigs", average about 12 to the pound, and three or four are considered a good portion for breakfast. They are cooked by separating the links, lining on sheet pans, placing in the oven at 350° F., baking until three-quarters done, draining off excess grease, and finished by browning under the broiler. After cooking they are removed to a hotel pan and held for service. Cook in small amounts because if they are held for the next day's service they become dry.

Bacon may be purchased by the slab and sliced to the thickness desired on the slicing machine after the rind has been removed, or it may be purchased sliced in what is called a hotel slice or pack, meaning there are 20 to 22 slices per pound. Most commercial establishments prefer the hotel pack and are willing to pay a few more cents per pound for convenience.

Bacon is cooked by separating the slices, lining on a sheet pan, fat side down and each slice slightly overlapping the other. The sheet pan is placed in a 350° F. oven and baked until the bacon is three-quarters done. Remove from the oven, pour off the grease, and with a kitchen fork or offset spatula drape the bacon slices over a platter on which vegetable dishes have been inverted. This helps to further drain the bacon and will keep the slices from lying in grease until service. This method of cooking bacon is recommended because it reduces shrinkage and curling, improves appearance, and cooking will be more uniform. Bacon may also be cooked in a skillet on the range, on the broiler, or grilled on a griddle, but the results are not as good.

Ham is usually purchased cooked, in a form that is boneless or boned and rolled, because these forms will give superior shape and the meat is easy to portion into 3 or 4 oz. pieces. Since the meat is already cooked, it is just a matter of heating it on the broiler, griddle, or in a skillet before serving.

Canadian bacon—the boneless, smoked, pressed loin of pork—is popular on breakfast menus if price is not a factor. In recent years the price of Canadian bacon has increased to the point where the average restaurant operator must think of his menu price before using it, because in most establishments breakfast preparations that carry a high price will not sell.

FRIED POTATOES

Fried potatoes are the only kind that have become popular on the breakfast menu. Sometimes they are only served à la carte, at other times they are listed with featured breakfast combinations, such as "Two fried eggs with ham, hash-brown potatoes, toast & beverage $1.45".

Popular breakfast potato preparations are hash brown, home fried, Lyonnaise, and German fried. Refer to Chapter 14 "Potato Preparations".

CEREALS

Ready-to-eat cereal has been big business in the United States for a very long time. The list of the various kinds now offered has become endless; in fact, there are so many on the market today that a retail food market or a commercial restaurant could not begin to handle all of them. Most chefs or food service operators carry the most popular ones such as cornflakes, rice crispies, bran, shredded wheat, etc. The ready-to-eat cereals are purchased in small individual-size boxes. When served, the box is placed before the guest so he can open the container himself. This assures a fresh, crisp cereal. These dry cereals are served with cereal cream, which is usually a blend of half milk and half cream.

Hot cereals are not extremely popular breakfast items, but because they are requested by guests from time to time they must be kept ready. Most establishments keep two kinds on hand: oatmeal and farina ("Cream of Wheat").

Cereals that require cooking are of two kinds: regular and quick-cooking. The regular kind requires a longer cooking period because it is not pre-cooked like the quick-cooking kind. Both kinds are prepared by following the same formula; the difference lies only in the cooking time. Directions for preparation are always given on the box or package.

JUICES

Juices, both fruit and vegetable, are standard breakfast menu items. While these are also served on the luncheon and dinner menus, they are most popular for breakfast because when chilled they perk up tired appetites at an early hour.

Juices may be purchased fresh, frozen, or canned. Frozen juices should be allowed to stand for a while after mixing. Grapefruit juice, orange juice, pineapple juice, tomato juice, cranberry juice, apple juice, V-8 vegetable juice, prune juice, and some mixed or blended juices are the ones most in demand.

Juices are usually served to the guest in a 4-oz. glass.

FRUITS

Fresh, canned, and stewed fruits are excellent for breakfast and are usually good sellers on any breakfast menu. Grapefruit and oranges are the popular citrus fruits and are available on the market and menu in this country the year round. Various melons such as cantaloupe, honeydew, Persian, casaba, and cranshaw are served in halves or wedges, depending on their size. Melons must be ripe and chilled when served.

Canned fruits are served chilled in cocktail glasses just as they come from the can. The most popular canned fruits are pears, peaches, Royal Ann cherries, kadota figs, apricots, and pineapple.

Stewed fruits prepared from dried fruits such as apples, apricots, and prunes have become standard breakfast items. These dried fruits must be cooked slightly in water to restore moisture.

TOAST

Toasted white bread is served with most egg preparations as well as à la carte. The bread may be toasted in an automatic toaster, on a grill, or under the broiler. Usually the bread is toasted on both sides, brushed with melted butter, and served with jelly or jam. Although toasted white bread is the kind most in demand on the breakfast menu, it is not the only kind served. Cinnamon toast and French toast are also fairly popular in many areas.

Cinnamon toast

Ingredients: Approx. yield: 25 servings of 2 slices per serving

75	slices white bread
	melted butter to cover
1	cup sugar
4	tbs. ground cinnamon

Procedure
1. Place the sugar in a shaker, add the ground cinnamon, and blend together.
2. Toast the slices of white bread on both sides, 3 slices per a la carte order.
3. Brush each slice of toast with melted butter on top side.
4. Sprinkle the cinnamon-sugar mixture generously on buttered side of each slice.
5. Place the toast on a sheet pan and place under the broiler until the sugar melts slightly.
6. Remove from the broiler, cut the slices diagonally in halves, and serve.

French toast

Ingredients: Approx. yield: 25 servings of 2 slices per serving

50	slices white bread
20	whole eggs
1	qt. milk or cream
3	oz. sugar
1	tbs. vanilla

Procedure
1. Break the eggs into a stainless steel bowl and beat with a wire whip.
2. Add the milk or cream, sugar, and vanilla, and beat until well blended.
3. Pour the mixture into a hotel pan. Dip each slice of bread into the batter, and coat both sides of the bread.
4. Remove the bread from the batter. Let drain slightly.
5. Brown the bread on both sides by placing it in the deep fat fryer at 350° F., in a greased skillet, or on a hot buttered griddle.

6. Serve two pieces to each order with some type of syrup.

PASTRIES

Certain kinds of pastries are featured on the breakfast menu. The most popular of these are sweet rolls, doughnuts, coffee cakes, and Danish pastry. If possible, it is always best to serve the sweet rolls and Danish warm. Food establishments that have their own bake shop take great pride in producing their own pastries. However, in recent years many operators have found that operating their own bake shop is too costly, so they now purchase these items from commercial bakeries.

CONTINENTAL BREAKFAST

The Continental breakfast that is so popular in European countries is now becoming popular in the United States. It is a light breakfast, usually consisting of fruit or juice, toast or pastry, and coffee. There is no heavy cooking involved when featuring this type of breakfast. While it leaves much to be desired from the standpoint of nutrition, from the standpoint of labor cost it is ideal. Hotels, motels, and resorts using the American plan have popularized the Continental breakfast.

appetizers

■ An appetizer is a small morsel of food generally served as the first course of a meal to stimulate the appetite for more or heavier foods to follow. An appetizer may be served in many different forms, from liquid to solid, as long as it performs its primary function.

The appearance of an appetizer must be eye appealing, colorful, and dainty. In many respects it must possess the same characteristics as a salad. Appetizers are generally classified into six or seven categories.

1. Cocktails
2. Hors d'oeuvres
3. Canapés
4. Relishes
5. Dips
6. Petite Salads
7. Soups and Consommés

Cocktails

Cocktails may be the juice of fruits or vegetables served in a small, well-chilled glass. The juice should be bright in appearance and tangy to the taste. Again, this is for the purpose of perking up the flavor buds. Cocktails may also be of fruit or seafood, usually served well chilled. They must be fresh in appearance and arranged uniformly for attractiveness. The seafood should be cut bite-size to avoid too much chewing.

Cocktail glasses may be plain or fancy but all are constructed in the same manner. A round glass base is attached to a glass stem that stands from 1½ to 3½ inches high. The other end of the glass stem is attached to the glass cup or bowl which holds the item or items being served. The cup or bowl will vary in size depending on the amount one wishes to serve. Cocktail glasses are available in five sizes: 3, 3½, 4, 4½, and 6 ounces.

Hors d'oeuvres

Hor d'oeuvres are small portions of highly seasoned foods formerly used to precede a meal, but today used in many other ways. Served either hot or cold, they may take many forms, such as baked oysters on the half shell, stuffed mushrooms, stuffed celery, stuffed eggs, etc., also hor d'oeuvres may be the chef's own creation. Hor d'oeuvres today have gained much popularity at cocktail parties because they digest well with alcoholic beverages and are to a great degree a "finger food."

Canapés

Canapés are another appetizer used like the hors d'oeuvre as a finger food. They are toasted or plain bread, spread with a rich savory paste or butter, cut into various small shapes and highly decorated to make them eye appealing. Crackers are sometimes used as a base although toasted bread may be more desirable because it will not absorb the moisture of the spread too quickly and one can cut the canapés into more interesting shapes.

When making canapés, variety and imagination are the key to success. Preparing a canapé spread is an excellent way to use up leftovers or small amounts of food that may be accumulating in the refrigerator. There are literally hundreds

Assorted canapés and cold hors d'oeuvres.

of spreads that can be made; and the garnishes one may choose are limitless.

When preparing canapés one should start with eight to ten different spreads and four or five different kinds and colors of bread. For instance, a good selection would be rye bread, white bread, whole wheat bread, red bread, and green bread. The colored bread can be purchased at a local bakery. In some areas blue and yellow bread are available. This will give not only great variety of taste, but also of color. After making spreads and slicing the bread (which should be sliced lengthwise for faster production), you should turn your imagination loose, always keeping in mind, however, good combinations. After the canapés are made the final touch of the garnish is added. This may be a cheese flower, an olive, chopped egg, pimiento, or again, some little edible item that is attractive to the eye.

Hot canapés are made similar to the cold variety, but they are not garnished as highly. Before serving they are heated in the oven or under the broiler and placed before the guest while still warm.

Relishes

Relishes are generally placed before the guest in a slightly, deep, boat-shaped dish. This is covered with crushed ice because all relishes should be served thoroughly chilled. Relishes include celery hearts, radishes, stuffed olives, ripe olives, pickles, vegetable sticks and curls, etc. See Table I.

TABLE I.   RELISH SUGGESTIONS

PREPARATION	INGREDIENT
Curls	Carrots, Celery
Rings	Green Peppers, Onions
Fans	Carrots, Celery, Pickles
Whole	Cherry Tomatoes, Ripe Olives, Green Olives, Stuffed Olives, Gerkins, Green Onions, Pickled Onions, Radishes (roses and accordians), Cauliflower Flowerets
Sticks or Strips	Carrots, Cucumbers, Celery, Green Peppers
Twist	Cucumber Slices, Pickle Slices, Tomato Slices
Slices	Pickles, Tomatoes, Onions

Dips

Dips have become very popular in recent years. When preparing dips always keep in mind that the consistency is all important. Too thick and the cracker or chip will crumble; too thin and the dip will run and be a cause of embarrassment. Most dips are prepared by using a cheese base with various ingredients added to create unusual flavors. They must, therefore, be refrigerated until approximately 30 minutes before serving, at which time they must be removed from the refrigerator and left to stand at room temperature. There are limitless varieties of crackers and chips on the market today that can be served with dips to create different and unusual taste sensations.

Petite salads

Petite salads are so called because they come in very small portions and they usually display the characteristics found in most salads. They are very dainty, artistically arranged, and consist of a base, body and garnish. They differ from the true salad in that they are quite small and are not meant to be filling. Their purpose is to stimulate the appetite for the more filling food that will follow. In so doing they perform the task of an appetizer. Further information on salads is given in Chapter 10, "Salads and Salad Dressings."

Soups and consommés

Soups and consommés are included in the appetizer category because today they are served as this course more than ever before. They will be discussed more thoroughly in the chapter on soups, Chapter 12. (Refer to Chapter 12 for recipes.)

HELPFUL SUGGESTIONS FOR PREPARING AND SERVING APPETIZERS

Cocktails

1. Cut or slice all fruit in an attractive manner; appearance is important.
2. Arrange all ingredients in an attractive fashion, utilizing natural food colors to create eye appeal.
3. Use crisp, clean, fresh lettuce, celery etc., when called for in the recipe.
4. When using shrimp, peel, clean and devein thoroughly.
5. Cut melon balls, using the parisienne scoop, into complete balls anything less will hinder appearance.
6. Select an attractive stem cocktail glass for serving cocktails.
7. Garnish all cocktails with an item that will enhance appearance; and, if possible, improve the flavor.
8. Serve all cocktails well chilled.

Hors D'oeuvres

1. For a smoother, creamier deviled egg mixture, mix the yolk paste in the mixing machine at slow speed, using the paddle.

2. Place the freshly stuffed deviled eggs in the refrigerator to set and become firm before covering with a damp towel.
3. Arrange the pieces of celery to be stuffed on a sheet pan that has been covered with a towel. This will help keep the celery from slipping when filling the crevice with the cheese mixture.
4. When forming meat balls, coat the palm of the hands slightly with salad oil to prevent sticking and to facilitate rolling.
5. When frying clam fritters use two soup spoons; dip both into the hot grease before spooning the batter. If this is done, the batter will release from the spoon quickly making the task simpler.

Canapés

1. Adjust the consistency of all canapé spreads to the point that they can be applied or spread with ease.
2. Select an extra sharp knife for trimming and cutting canapés.
3. Keep all canapé spreads refrigerated until 15 minutes before using.
4. When making canapés, purchase unsliced Pullman style bread (a square load referred to as *sandwich bread*) and slice it lengthwise, using a power meat saw or slicing machine. This will help speed up production.
5. Toast the bread that is to be used for canapés on both sides. This is done by placing it on sheet pans under the broiler. Toasted bread will help prevent a soggy canapé if the spread has a high moisture content.
6. Decorate canapés with an item that will improve appearance and enhance the taste.
7. Keep canapés in the refrigerator covered with a damp cloth until ready to use.

8. Arrange canapés on platters in such a way that they will excite the appetite and display a colorful assortment.
9. Keep butter spreads refrigerated until 15 minutes before using. Let set at room temperature until of spreading consistency.

Relishes

1. Cut or slice vegetable relishes in an attractive manner; appearance is important.
2. Use a sharp French knife or fancy crinkle edge cutter.
3. Keep vegetable relishes refrigerated until ready to serve. Keep items such as radishes, celery and carrots refrigerated and covered with ice water.
4. Serve relishes covered with crushed ice for best results.

Petite salads

1. Use crisp, clean, fresh lettuce as the base for all petite salads.
2. If the recipe calls for chopped hard boiled eggs, chop them on heavy paper applying light blows with a French knife.
3. Set up and garnish all petite salads in such a manner as to create eye appeal.
4. Serve petite salads well chilled.

Points to consider when making sandwiches

1. Prepare fillings just prior to using if practical to do so. Keep them refrigerated until ready to use.
2. Make sandwiches on the day they are to be served. If they must be made ahead, freeze them or keep them in the refrigerator covered with a damp cloth until ready to use.
3. If using lettuce, wash, drain and refrigerate it; keep covered with a damp cloth to insure crispness.

4. Spreading the sandwich bread with butter or margarine is a good practice because it will improve the eating qualities of many sandwiches, and it will also help to keep moist fillings from soaking the bread. Soften the butter or margarine until of good spreading consistency to make the application easier and to keep from tearing the bread.

5. Prepare sandwiches on a wood-topped table or wood cutting board. This will prevent the bread from slipping when being spread and also will provide the proper surface on which all sandwiches should be trimmed and cut.

6. Have the following equipment handy:
   A. Spoon or scoop for portioning certain spreads.
   B. Sharp French knife for trimming and cutting.
   C. Spatula for spreading the butter, margarine and filling mixtures.
   D. Pans for storage, if necessary; wax paper and damp towels.

7. If preparing a fancy sandwich that is to be rolled, place the trimmed bread on a damp towel before spreading. This will keep the bread moist to facilitate rolling.

8. When using toasted bread for a sandwich, use only freshly toasted bread for best results.

Steps to follow when preparing large quantities of sandwiches

1. Arrange all ingredients within easy reach. Place bread supply to the left if the worker is right handed, and to the right if left handed. All spreads or filling ingredients should be directly in front of the worker; tip forward for easy access.

2. Place bread or toast slices in rows directly in front of worker.

Place four rows of bread directly before you.

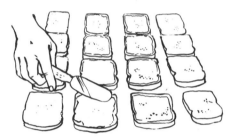

Spread soft filling evenly to edges of bread on two center rows.

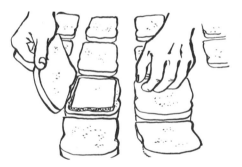

Put meat or cheese filling on inside rows of bread. Turn outside bread slices onto the filling.

3. Spread the slices of bread or toast with soft butter, using a spatula.

4. Portion filling mixture on alternate rows of bread. (If four rows of bread are used, place filling on two center rows.)

5. Spread soft filling evenly, bring filling to the edge of the bread. Arrange meat or cheese slices so the

bread is well covered, but do not let them extend beyond the edge of the bread.

6. Arrange crisp lettuce on the filling, if lettuce is to be used.
7. Place the remaining slices of bread on the slices containing the filling.
8. Trim the crust edges of the bread slightly using a French knife, cut the sandwich in half, in thirds, or fourths depending on preference. (Sandwiches may be stacked so that several may be cut at the same time.)
9. Generally speaking there are five types of sandwiches made in food service establishments. They are as follows:

    A. Closed sandwich
    B. Open-face sandwich
    C. Combination sandwich
    D. Double decker sandwich
    E. Fancy sandwich

The closed sandwich consists of two slices of bread, one on top of the other, with a filling in the center.

The open-face sandwich consists of two slices of bread laid side by side on a plate with the filling exposed on the surface of one or both of the slices.

The combination sandwich is similar to the closed sandwich but instead of just one filling, two are used. The two fillings used must combine well with each other.

The double decker sandwich consists of three pieces of bread or toast and two fillings. The bread and fillings are stacked alternately, starting with a piece of bread and following with a filling. The two fillings used must combine well with one another.

Fancy sandwiches are usually small open-face sandwiches decorated for eye appeal, or roll sandwiches made by cutting the bread lengthwise, removing the crust, spreading with a filling and rolling.

RECIPES: SPECIAL TECHNIQUES AND TERMS TO REMEMBER

Blend: The term blend or blend thoroughly means to mix together two or more ingredients. This should be done manually using a kitchen spoon unless it is stated that a mixing machine is to be used.

Fine chopper plate: A chopper plate is a perforated metal disc that is placed in front of the knife or blade on a food grinder. The grinder comes equipped with a number of chopper plates the holes of which vary in size. The food is first cut by the blade then passes through the chopper plate.

Salad tossing: The term tossing means to lift or throw up quickly. In the kitchen tossing is usually done with the hands. In the dining room, before the guest, tossing is done with two large salad forks. Tossing should be done with a gentle motion so the ingredients, especially the greens, are not bruised.

Grapefruit sections: Grapefruit can be purchased in cans or fresh in jars already sectioned. If the sections are to be removed from a fresh grapefruit, the fruit is peeled and each section is removed by cutting around the inside of the membrane of each grapefruit segment using a grapefruit (scalloped edge knife) or paring knife. The sections are left in their whole state, they are not broken.

Orange sections: Oranges can be purchased in cans or fresh in jars already sectioned. If the fresh fruit is used, the orange is peeled and broken into natural sections and as much of the membrane as possible is scraped off with a paring knife. For some types of cocktails the sections are left whole.

Cheese flowers: To prepare a cheese flower, white cream cheese is worked with a spoon to an elastic consistency. The cheese is colored, as desired, using liquid or paste food colors. To make a rose bud, red is used; for a sweet pea, blue is used; and for leaves, green is used. The colored cheese is placed in a pastry bag with the appropriate type of pastry tube. The flower and leaf are piped onto the item by squeezing the pastry bag with a steady pressure of the hand. Cheese flowers are used to garnish canapés and certain types of hors d'oeuvres.

Butter flowers: A small flower formed by piping a butter spread through a pastry bag and tube. Butter flowers are used to decorate or garnish canapés and certain hors d'oeuvres. Butter flowers are formed in the same manner as cheese flowers; however, the consistency of the butter will require more attention than cream cheese. When forming flowers one should work in a cool place, because butter will break down or melt fairly rapidly.

Egg wash: An egg wash is a mixture of whole eggs and milk (6 eggs to each qt. of milk). The eggs are beaten slightly with a wire whip. The milk is poured into the beaten eggs while stirring with the whip. Egg wash is used for coating items which are to be cooked in hot grease.

Bacon cracklings: The crisp residue that remains after the grease has been cooked out of bacon. The bacon is ground on a food grinder, using the desired chopper plate, placed in a sauce pan, and cooked at a moderate temperature until the grease is cooked out of the bacon and the remaining residue becomes crisp. The cracklings are then drained to remove the grease.

Garnishes: There are many different garnishes that may go with appetizers. Usually the recipe will suggest an appropriate garnish. Examples of common garnishes are: sliced olives, chopped hard boiled eggs, small pieces of pimiento, chopped chives, cheese flowers, paprika, onion rings, anchovies, etc.

APPETIZER RECIPES

The recipes which follow are some of the many popular appetizers. Their successful preparation will enhanace the menu of any food service establishment. The recipes are listed in their order of appearance in the chapter.

**Cocktails
(Pages 91 to 93)**
  Assorted fruit cocktail
  Assorted melon-ball cocktail
  Grape-melon cocktail
  Avocado-grapefruit cocktail
  Pineapple-mint cocktail
  Oyster cocktail
  Shrimp cocktail
  Shrimp-grapefruit cocktail
  Cape Cod cocktail

**Cold hors d'oeuvres
(Pages 93 to 96)**
  Deviled eggs
  Cheese apples
  Cheese and bacon balls
  Stuffed celery
  Stuffed mushrooms
  Salami horns
  Chopped chicken liver mold
  Smoked salmon rolls
  Puff shells
  Bouchées or miniature patty shells

**Hot hors d'oeuvres
(Pages 96 to 100)**
  Cheese puffs
  Sauerkraut balls
  Simple meat balls
  Savory meat balls
  Barbecued wiener tidbits
  Ham and cheese puffs
  Bacon and chicken liver blankets
  Chicken croquette balls
  Clam fritters
  Oysters Rockefeller
  Baked oysters casino
  Shrimp stuffed mushroom caps
  Crabmeat balls
  Salmon nuggets
  Pizza puffs
  Chinese egg rolls

Canapé spreads
(Pages 100 to 103)

Egg spread
Cheddar cheese spread
Bleu cheese spread
Pineapple-cheese spread
Pimiento-cheese spread
Olive-cheese spread
Avocado spread
Chip beef and cheese spread
Deviled ham spread
Bacon-cheese spread
Peanut butter and bacon spread
Chicken-bacon spread
Chicken liver spread
Anchovy spread
Shrimp spread
Crabmeat spread
King crabmeat spread
Lobster spread
Sardine spread
Salmon spread
Tuna fish spread

Butter spreads
(Pages 103 to 104)

Tuna butter
Chive butter
Pimiento butter
Garlic butter
Horseradish butter
Mint butter
Roquefort butter
Onion butter
Shrimp butter
Lobster butter
Anchovy butter
Lemon butter

Relishes
(Pages 104 to 105)

Radish roses
Celery sticks
Carrot sticks
Carrot curls

Dips
(Pages 105 to 106)

Cheddar cheese dip
Roquefort cheese dip
Pineapple-cheese dip
Mint-cheese dip
Onion-cheese dip
Garlic-cheese dip
Avocado dip
Bacon-cheese dip
Clam dip
Shrimp-cheese dip

Petite salads
(Pages 106 to 108)

Eggs à la Russe
Seafood green goddess
Italian antipasto
Chicken liver pâté
Shrimp delight
Deviled lobster or crabmeat
Marinated herring
Tuna fish ravigote

POPULAR COCKTAIL RECIPES

Assorted fruit cocktail

Ingredients: Yield: 1 fruit cocktail
1   slice pineapple, canned
1   peach half, fresh or canned
1   Bartlett pear half, fresh or canned
3   fresh strawberries
2   apple wedges, unpeeled
2   red maraschino cherries
    leaf lettuce
1   mint leaf
Procedure
Dice fruit bite-size and place in a 3 oz. cocktail glass on a base of leaf lettuce or, if desired, use romaine or head lettuce. Garnish with a mint leaf.

Assorted melon-ball cocktail

Ingredients: Yield: 1 cocktail
4   cantaloupe balls
4   watermelon balls
4   honeydew melon balls
1   mint leaf
    leaf lettuce

Procedure

Cut melon balls by using a Parisienne scoop. Place leaf lettuce in a 3 oz. cocktail glass. Arrange melon balls to get best color effect. Garnish with mint and serve chilled.

Grape-melon cocktail

Ingredients: Yield: 1 cocktail
¼ cup seedless grapes
¼ cup honeydew melon, diced
¼ cup cantaloupe, diced
   juice of half a lemon
1 tsp. powdered sugar
1 mint leaf

Procedure

Place all ingredients in a stainless steel mixing container and toss together. Place in a 3½ oz. cocktail glass, garnish with the mint leaf and serve chilled.

Avocado-grapefruit cocktail

Ingredients: Yield: 4 cocktails
1 large, ripe avocado
1 cup, drained, canned grapefruit
½ tsp. tomato catsup
½ tsp. Worcestershire sauce
¾ tsp. lemon juice
¾ cup cream, whipped

Procedure

1. Dice avocado to bite-size. Mix with the drained canned grapefruit and chill.
2. To make the sauce combine the catsup, Worcestershire sauce, lemon juice, and whipped cream. Blend until smooth.
3. Fold half of the sauce into the chilled avocado-grapefruit mixture. Place into 3 oz. cocktail glasses and top with the remaining sauce.

Pineapple-mint cocktail

Ingredients: Yield: 4 cocktails
24 chunks of canned pineapple
16 orange sections (whole, natural sections)
12 candied mints or 6 mint leaves, chopped
½ cup pineapple juice
¼ cup concentrated orange juice
   lettuce leaves

Procedure

Place all ingredients in a mixing container and toss gently. Place leaf lettuce in a 3½ oz. cocktail glass, fill with the tossed mixture, and serve.

Oyster cocktail

Ingredients: Yield: 1 cocktail
4 oysters
1 tsp. celery, diced fine
   leaf lettuce
1 green pepper, minced
1 lemon wedge

Procedure

Place the leaf of lettuce and the finely diced celery in the bottom of a 3 oz. cocktail glass. Add the oysters and top with cocktail sauce and minced green peppers. (Peppers are minced by cutting or chopping very fine with a French knife.) Serve with a wedge of lemon.

National Marketing Service Office
Bureau of Commercial Fisheries
U.S. Dept. of the Interior

Shrimp cocktail

Shrimp cocktail

Ingredients: Yield: 1 cocktail
6 medium shrimp, cooked
¼ cup diced celery
   leaf lettuce

Procedure

In a 3 oz. cocktail glass place the leaf lettuce and the diced celery. Arrange the shrimp on top of the diced celery. Serve with a wedge of lemon and top with cocktail sauce. (See Chapter 15 for sauce.)

Note: Lobster, seafood, and crabmeat cocktails are prepared in the same manner; only the shellfish is changed.

Shrimp-grapefruit cocktail

Ingredients: Yield: 4 cocktails
1   grapefruit, sectioned (whole, natural sections)
12   medium sized shrimp
     shredded head lettuce
     leaf lettuce
½   cup mayonnaise
2   drops Tabasco sauce
½   tsp. horseradish
Procedure
1. Arrange the shrimp and grapefruit sections alternately within a 3 oz. cocktail glass on a base of leaf lettuce and shredded head lettuce.
2. Combine the mayonnaise, Tabasco sauce, and horseradish until well blended.
3. Place the sauce on top of the cocktail and serve well chilled.

Cape Cod cocktail

Ingredients: Yield: 4 cocktails
8   apricot halves, canned, diced
4   bananas, sliced
3   cups whole cranberry sauce
     leaf lettuce
Procedure
Mix together the apricots, bananas, whole cranberry sauce. (Bananas are sliced on a slight bias approximately a half inch thick using a paring knife.) Place in a lettuce lined 6 oz. cocktail glass; top with a spot of whipped topping. Serve well chilled.

POPULAR COLD HORS d'OUEVRES RECIPES

Deviled eggs

Ingredients: Approx. yield: 40 stuffed eggs
20   hard boiled eggs
½   cup mayonnaise (variable)
1   tsp. prepared mustard
½   cup white cream cheese (soft)
¼   tsp. white pepper

2   dashes Worcestershire sauce
2   dashes Tabasco sauce
1   tsp. salt
Procedure
1. Peel and cut the eggs into quarters lengthwise, or cut in half crosswise and after cutting the ends off stand up the egg.
2. Remove the yolks and pass through a fine china cap or sieve.
3. Combine all ingredients and blend thoroughly to a very smooth paste.
4. Place the yolk paste in a pastry bag with a star tube for a decorative effect and refill the egg whites.
5. Decorate the top of each filled egg with a slice of stuffed olive, cheese flower, chopped parsley, paprika, pimiento, black olives, or slice of radish.

Cheese apples (or pears)

Ingredients: Approx. yield: 40 apples
2   lb. Longhorn or Cheddar cheese
     paprika as needed
40   whole cloves
Procedure
1. Grind cheese in food grinder using medium chopper plate.
2. Form ground cheese into balls about the size of an English walnut.
3. Touch each side into the paprika to blush slightly.
4. Stick a clove into the top upside down.

Cheese and bacon balls

Ingredients: Approx. yield: 20 balls
1   lb. sharp Cheddar or Longhorn cheese
⅓   cup mayonnaise
½   lb. bacon
Procedure
1. Fry bacon until it becomes crisp, drain well.
2. Crumble the bacon fine in a food grinder using fine chopper plate; grind cheese on food grinder.
3. Add the mayonnaise to the cheese and blend thoroughly.
4. Form into small balls approximately 1 inch in diameter and roll in the crumbled bacon.
5. Serve on tooth picks.

Stuffed celery

Ingredients: Yield: 20 pieces
20 pieces celery, trimmed and cut about 4 inches long
1 lb. white cream cheese
6 oz. of bleu cheese
2 dashes Tabasco sauce
1 tsp. onions, minced very fine
   juice of half a lemon

Procedure
1. Cut thin strip off the back of each piece of celery so it will lay flat.
2. Blend together the cream cheese, bleu cheese, Tabasco sauce, onions, and lemon juice to a smooth paste.
3. Place in a pastry bag with a star tube and fill the crevice in the celery with the cheese mixture.
4. Refrigerate until cheese is firm, sprinkle with chopped parsley or paprika.

Note: The stuffed celery may also be decorated with cheese or butter flowers.

Stuffed mushrooms

Ingredients: Yield: 20 mushrooms
20 medium mushroom caps
   juice of one lemon
½ cup shortening
¼ cup butter

Procedure
1. Place in sauce pot the shortening and butter. Heat slightly.
2. Add the mushroom caps and sauté until half done. Do not brown.
3. Add the juice of a lemon; continue to cook until mushroom is tender, but still firm; cool.
4. Stuff with crabmeat spread, chicken liver spread, shrimp spread, etc. (See recipes this chapter.)

Salami horns

Ingredients: Approx. yield: 25 salami horns

Stuffed celery varieties

25 slices of hard salami, thin slices
25 tooth picks
1 lb. white cream cheese
2 dashes Tabasco sauce
2 dashes Worcestershire sauce
1 pinch salt

Procedure
1. Cut a slit in each slice of salami by cutting from the center of each slice to the outer edge.
2. Roll the cut slice of salami around the second finger of your hand to form a cornucopia, secure with a tooth pick.
3. Blend the remaining ingredients thoroughly until a smooth paste is acquired. Place in a pastry bag with a star tube.
4. Fill each salami horn with the cheese mixture.
5. Place in refrigerator until cheese becomes firm.

Chopped chicken liver mold

Ingredients: Approx. yield: 12 molds, depending on size
2 lb. chicken livers
2 cups onions, minced
6 hard boiled eggs
3 tbsp. parsley, chopped
5 tbsp. butter
½ cup chicken fat
   pepper to taste
1½ tsp. salt

Procedure
1. Season the chicken livers with salt and pepper. Sauté the livers and onions in the chicken fat until completely done. Let cool.
2. Add the eggs to the liver-onion mixture and put through the fine plate food chopper.
3. Add the chopped parsley and butter, and mix thoroughly.
4. Pack into greased molds and refrigerate.
5. Unmold and serve on a base of leaf and shredded lettuce; garnish with onion rings and lemon.

Smoked salmon rolls

Ingredients: Approx. yield: 30 rolls
1 lb. white cream cheese
¼ lb. butter
1 tbsp. onion, minced
3 tsp. lemon juice

2 lb. smoked salmon, sliced very thin
10 wedges of dill pickle

Procedure
1. Blend together the cream cheese, butter, onions, and lemon juice.
2. Place the thin slices of salmon on a towel and spread each slice with the cheese mixture.
3. Place the dill pickle wedge at one end of the salmon slice and roll up.
4. Wrap in wax paper and refrigerate until firm.
5. Remove from the refrigerator and slice the roll about ½ inch thick.
6. Inject a toothpick into each slice or roll and serve.
Note: Thin slices of square luncheon meat may be substituted for the salmon.

Puff shells

Ingredients: Approx. yield: 60 shells, depending on size
1½ cups pastry flour
½ cup shortening
¼ cup butter
1½ cups water
    pinch of salt
6 whole eggs

Procedure
1. Place the water in a sauce pot and bring to a boil. Add the shortening and butter; place pot to side of range until the shortening and butter melts.
2. Add the flour and salt, stir in thoroughly, cook slowly until flour is cooked and mixture is slightly stiff. Remove from range and let cool. Add unbeaten eggs one at a time, beating thoroughly after each addition. This can be done by hand or on the mixing machine using the paddle at slow speed.
3. Place dough in a pastry bag with a star tube and force out onto sheet pans, covered with silicone paper or dusted with flour, into very small spirals.
4. Bake for about 40 minutes at 400°F or until golden brown, and let cool.
5. Cut the puff half way through the center and fill with any kind of canapé spread.
6. Decorate top of puff with a cheese or butter flower.

Bouchées or miniature patty shells

Ingredients: Approx. yield: 60 shells
1   lb. 4 ozs. bread flour
¼   oz. salt
2   ozs. whole eggs
5   ozs. water, cold
2   ozs. butter
1   lb. 4 ozs. puff paste shortening
Procedure
1. Combine flour, salt, butter, eggs, and cold water; mix into a dough.
2. Remove from mixer, place on flour bench, round into a ball, and allow to stand 15 minutes. Keep covered with a towel.
3. Roll out dough in a long rectangular shape about ½ inch thick. Dot ⅔ of the dough with the shortening. Fold three ways, roll puff paste shortening into dough. Use caution not to let shortening break through. (Puff paste shortening is a trade name given to this special type of shortening manufactured for the use of making puff paste dough. This special shortening is rolled into a basic dough to create layers of fat in the dough so that when heated and baked the dough will expand creating rich flaky layers of extremely tender crust. The shortening is rolled into the dough by using a rolling pin. It is this rolling, folding process that creates the layers of fat that in turn produce the tender flaky layers of crust.)
4. Place dough in the refrigerator for 20 minutes; keep dough covered.
5. Remove dough from refrigerator and repeat the above rolling-folding process. In all, the dough should be rolled and folded (three folds each time) four times; refrigerate between rolls 20 minutes.
6. After the fourth roll, and refrigeration is completed, roll out again and proceed to make up the bouchées as follows: Have dough rolled about ⅛ inch thick; cut out one solid disc using a cutter about 1 inch in diameter. Cut out a second solid disc using a cutter about 1 inch in diameter. Using a ½ inch cutter, cut out the center of this disc and remove the center, leaving the washer shaped dough. (The center that was removed is discarded or baked separately and made up into a special hors d'oeuvre. This type of dough can never be reworked. Any leftover pieces are either discarded or baked and used wherever possible.)
7. Wash the first disc with egg wash (mixture of whole eggs and milk) and place second cut out disc on top.
8. Proceed to make up the remaining dough in this fashion: Place the bouchées on sheet pans with silicone paper, let rest 10 minutes, bake at 360°F with silicone paper on top so the bouchées will not topple over.
9. Bake until golden brown; let cool.
10. Fill the bouchée shells with shrimp spread, crabmeat spread, lobster spread, or chicken spread. (See recipes this chapter.)
11. Decorate top with chopped parsley, chopped hard boiled eggs, or cheese flower.

POPULAR HOT HORS d'OEUVRE RECIPES

Cheese puffs

Ingredients: Approx. yield: 7 doz. puffs
1   lb. Cheddar cheese, shredded
½   cup butter
2   whole eggs
4   cups flour, sifted
½   tsp. salt
3   tsp. baking powder
½   cup milk
Procedure
1. Place the butter and the cheese in a metal bowl and mix with a kitchen spoon until well blended.
2. Add the eggs and beat well.
3. Add the flour which has been sifted with the salt and baking powder; blend well.
4. Add the milk and stir until a crumbly mixture develops.
5. Shape into two long rolls about 1 inch in diameter; chill until firm.
6. Slice the chilled rolls when firm and fry in deep fat at 360°F until golden brown.

Sauerkraut balls

Ingredients: Approx. yield: 12 doz. balls
1   #10 can of sauerkraut, drained
1   lb. onions, peeled

6   ozs. butter
2   tbsp. parsley, chopped
3   ozs. flour
4   whole eggs, beaten
    salt and pepper to taste
Procedure
1. Grind the sauerkraut and onions on the food grinder, using the fine chopper plate.
2. Place the butter in a sauce pot, melt, add the ground onions and sauerkraut, and cook about 8 minutes.
3. Add the flour and blend in to make a thick paste, continue to cook for 8 minutes more, remove from the range.
4. Add the eggs, parsley, and seasoning; let cool.
5. Form into small balls approximately 1 inch in diameter. Bread and fry in deep fat at 360°F until golden brown.

Simple meat balls

Ingredients: Approx. yield: 3 doz. meat balls
1   lb. ground beef chuck
2   tbsp. onions, minced
2   whole eggs, slightly beaten
    salt, pepper to taste
1   cup bread crumbs (moisten with milk)
1   pinch thyme
$\frac{1}{2}$ small clove of garlic, minced
1   tbsp. shortening

Procedure
1. Sauté the onions and garlic in the shortening; let cool.
2. Combine the ingredients and mix together thoroughly.
3. Form into tiny meat balls and place on greased sheet pan.
4. Bake in oven at 350°F until done.
5. Serve in chafing dish in barbecue sauce, curry sauce, or sour cream sauce. (See Chapter 14 for sauce recipes.)

Savory meat balls

Ingredients: Approx. yield: 3 doz. meat balls
1   lb. ground beef chuck
1   whole egg
1   tsp. salt
1   tsp. monosodium glutamate
$\frac{1}{2}$ cup bread crumbs
$\frac{1}{4}$ cup Parmesan cheese, grated
1   tbsp. onions, minced

$\frac{1}{4}$ tsp. oregano
1   pinch of nutmeg
1   pinch dry mustard
2   tbsp. butter
$\frac{1}{2}$ cup chili sauce
    pepper to taste
Procedure
1. Combine all ingredients in a mixing container, except the butter and chili sauce, and mix thoroughly.
2. Form into small meat balls.
3. Heat butter in skillet, add meat balls and cook until slightly brown; remove meat balls.
4. Add the chili sauce to the skillet and bring to a boil.
5. Serve meat balls from a chafing dish using the hot chili sauce as a dip.

Barbecued wiener tidbits

Ingredients: Approx. yield: 72 tidbits
12   wieners
1   qt. barbecue sauce
Procedure
1. Cut each wiener into six pieces.
2. Place the barbecue sauce (see Chap. 14) in a sauce pot, bring to a boil, move pot to side of the range.
3. Add the wiener tidbits to the sauce and simmer for 2 minutes.
4. Serving in chafing dish with picks.

Ham and cheese puffs

Ingredients: Approx. yield: 20, 2 in. disks
HAM MIXTURE
1   cup ham, cooked and ground
2   tsp. prepared mustard
$\frac{1}{2}$ tsp. Worcestershire sauce
$\frac{1}{4}$ cup mayonnaise
1   tsp. onions, minced
1   tsp. baking powder
Procedure
Combine ham, mustard, Worcestershire sauce, mayonnaise, onions, and baking powder; mix well.
CHEESE MIXTURE
$\frac{3}{4}$ cup Cheddar cheese, grated
1   whole egg, beaten
1   tsp. onion, grated
1   tsp. baking powder
Procedure
Combine all ingredients and blend together thoroughly.

Make up: Prepare 20, 2 inch toasted bread rounds, but toast on one side only. Spread untoasted side with the ham mixture. Top with the cheese mixture. Place on sheet pans and broil slowly until topping puffs and becomes golden brown.

Bacon and chicken liver blankets

Ingredients: Yield: 48 blankets
24   chicken livers
24   slices of bacon
Procedure
1. Cut bacon and chicken livers in half.
2. Slightly cook the bacon and wrap around each half of chicken liver, secure with a tooth pick.
3. Place wrapped chicken liver on a sheet pan covered slightly with salad oil. Broil slowly just before serving.

Note: The following items may be substituted for the chicken livers and prepared in the same manner:

Beef tenderloin cubes
Bologna sausage cubes
Cocktail sausage cubes
Scallops
Meat balls
Canned luncheon meat cubes

Chicken croquette balls

Ingredients: Approx. yield: 1 doz. balls
2   cups chicken or turkey, cooked, ground
3   tbsp. onions, minced
1   whole egg, slightly beaten
1½   cups chicken stock
3   tbsp. shortening
½   cup flour
1   tsp. salt
1   pinch nutmeg
½   cup bread crumbs
Procedure
1. Place shortening in sauce pot, add minced onions, and cook without color (do not let brown).
2. Add the flour, making a roux; cook slightly.
3. Add the chicken stock (see Chap. 11) making a thick paste.
4. Add the ground chicken, season with the salt and nutmeg, remove from range, let cool.

5. Add the egg and bread crumbs; mix thoroughly using a kitchen spoon.
6. Form into small balls approximately 1 inch in diameter. Bread and fry in deep fat 350°F until golden brown.
7. Serve in chafing dish with picks.
8. Use cocktail sauce as a dip. (See Chapter 14 for "Cocktail Sauce.")

Clam fritters

Ingredients: Approx. yield: 3 doz. fritters
3   cups flour, sifted
¾   tsp. salt
1½   tsp. sugar
1   tbsp. baking powder
3   eggs beaten
¾   cup milk
¾   cup butter, melted
3   cups canned clams, drained, chopped
Procedure
1. Sift together the flour, salt, sugar, and baking powder; hold.
2. Mix together the eggs, milk, melted butter, and the chopped clams; stir in the above dry mixture; blend well.
3. Drop by spoonfuls, using a soup spoon, into deep fat at 375°F and cook until golden brown. Let drain.
4. Serve in chafing dish with picks.

Oysters Rockefeller

Ingredients: Yield: 24 oysters
24   blue point oysters (on half shell)
⅓   cup butter
1½   cup raw spinach
3   tbsp. onion, minced
¾   cup bread crumbs
½   tsp. salt
1   small pinch nutmeg
Procedure
1. Open oysters and drain; leave the oysters on the deepest half shell.
2. Place the oysters on a pan covered with rock salt.
3. Melt the butter in a sauce pot and add all the remaining ingredients. Cook until ingredients are soft, stirring constantly.
4. Spread the spinach mixture over the oysters.
5. Bake oysters in the oven on the rock salt at a temperature of 400°F for about 10 minutes. Do not overbake.
6. Serve at once.

Baked oysters casino

Ingredients: Yield: 24 oysters
24   blue point oysters (on half shell)
12   slices of bacon, cut in half
½   lb. butter·
1   tbsp. onions, minced
3   tbsp. green pepper, minced
2   tbsp. pimientos, minced
1   tbsp. chives, minced
1   pinch pepper
1   tsp. lemon juice
Procedure
1. Open oysters and drain; leave the oysters on the deepest half shell.
2. Place the oysters on a pan covered with rock salt.
3. Combine all the remaining ingredients, except the bacon, and mix together thoroughly.
4. Dot each oyster with the butter mixture, top with a piece of bacon.
5. Bake in oven at 400°F for about 10 minutes. Serve at once.

Shrimp stuffed mushroom caps

Ingredients: Approx. yield: 25 caps
25   fresh mushroom caps, medium to large
2   cups shrimp, cooked, chopped
2   cups rice, cooked
1½   tbsp. parsley, chopped
1½   tbsp. chutney, chopped
1   tsp. salt
¼   tsp. thyme
½   cup Cheddar cheese, grated
Procedure
1. Wash mushroom caps and dry.
2. Combine remaining ingredients, except the Cheddar cheese, by mixing together in a stainless steel bowl using a kitchen spoon.
3. Press the shrimp mixture firmly and generously into the mushroom caps.
4. Sprinkle the stuffed mushrooms with the grated cheese.
5. Bake at 375°F in the oven for about 10 minutes.
6. Serve hot.

Crabmeat balls

Ingredients: Approx. yield: 1 doz. balls
2   cups king or blue crabmeat
3   tbsp. onions, minced
1   whole egg, beaten
3   tbsp. shortening or butter
1   cup milk or cream
½   cup flour
1   tsp. sherry wine
½   tsp. prepared mustard
1   tsp. salt
1   dash Tabasco sauce
2   dashes Worcestershire sauce
½   cup bread crumbs
Procedure
1. Place shortening or butter in sauce pot and heat.
2. Add the minced onions and cook without color.
3. Add the flour, making a roux; continue to cook slightly.
4. Add the milk or cream, making a thick paste.
5. Add the crabmeat, mustard, salt, Tabasco, wine, Worcestershire; blend thoroughly; remove from the range. Let cool.
6. Add the eggs and bread crumbs; mix thoroughly.
7. Form into small balls approximately 1 inch in diameter. Bread and fry in deep fat at 350°F until golden brown.
8. Serve in chafing dish with picks. Use cocktail sauce as a dip. (See Chapter 14 for "Cocktail Sauce.")

Salmon nuggets

Ingredients: Approx. yield: 48 nuggets
1   16 oz. can of red salmon
½   cup potatoes, mashed
1   tbsp. celery, finely chopped
1   tbsp. onions, grated
1   tbsp. butter, melted
¼   tsp. salt
1½   tsp. Worcestershire sauce
1   whole egg, beaten
¼   lb. Longhorn cheese
½   cup bread crumbs
    pepper to taste
Procedure
1. Drain salmon; flake and remove bones.
2. Add all the other ingredients except the bread crumbs and cheese; mix well.
3. Cut the cheese into 48 cubes approximately ⅜ inch each.
4. Shape the salmon mixture around the cheese cubes to form small balls.
5. Roll in bread crumbs and fry in deep fat at 375°F, until golden brown.

National Marketing Service Office
Bureau of Commercial Fisheries
U.S. Dept. of the Interior

Salmon nuggets arranged on a cauliflower head with olives and pickled onions.

Pizza puffs

Ingredients: Approx. yield: 50 puffs
2	cups mozzarella cheese, shredded
1	cup cracker meal
½	cup cornflake crumbs
½	tsp. oregano
1	clove garlic, minced
¾	tsp. salt
1	pinch basil
2	eggs, separated

Procedure
1. Separate the egg yolks from the whites; whip the whites until stiff; hold.
2. Mix together the remaining ingredients and fold into the stiff egg whites.
3. Shape into balls, roll in additional cracker meal, refrigerate until firm.
4. Fry in deep fat at 350°F until golden brown.

Chinese egg rolls: skins

Ingredients: Approx. yield: 2 doz. skins
2	lb. bread flour
4	eggs, beaten
1½	tsp. salt
1	lb. water, cold

Procedure
1. Sift the flour and salt together, place in the bowl of the mixing machine.
2. Add the eggs and water, using the paddle, mix at slow speed until the dough is firm and smooth.

3. Turn out the dough onto a floured bench, let rest 10 minutes, keep covered with a damp cloth.
4. Using a rolling pin roll out the dough to a thickness of approximately ⅛ inch. Cut into 6 inch squares.
5. Place 1 to 1½ ozs. of filling on each 6 inch square of dough, fold in the two sides, so the filling cannot flow out, roll the filled dough tightly, dampen the end with water and secure.
6. Fry the rolls in deep fat at 350°F until golden brown; drain.
7. Cut each roll into 4 pieces and serve in a chafing dish with picks.

Shrimp filling for egg roll

Ingredients: Approx. yield: 2 doz. fillings
1½	lb. shrimp or crabmeat, cooked, chopped fine
2	tbsp. onions, minced
1	tbsp. scallions, chopped
1	tbsp. bamboo shoots, chopped
3	tbsp. cornstarch
2	whole eggs, well beaten
¼	tsp. soy sauce
	salt and pepper to taste

Procedure
1. Place all ingredients in a round bottom mixing bowl, using a kitchen spoon, mix together until thoroughly incorporated.
2. Refrigerate until ready to use. Add filling to skins (see above).

Note: If variety is desired, the shrimp or crabmeat may be replaced by cooked chicken, lobster, or tuna fish.

POPULAR CANAPE SPREAD RECIPES

Egg spread

Ingredients: Approx. yield: 2 cups
12	egg yolks, hard boiled and strained
2	tsp. horseradish
2	tsp. onions, minced
2	tsp. Worcestershire sauce
1	dash Tabasco sauce
½	cup mayonnaise
½	tsp. salt
⅓	cup white cream cheese

Procedure

Combine all ingredients and blend to a smooth paste of spreading consistency. Refrigerate until ready to use.

Cheddar cheese spread

Ingredients: Approx. yield: 3 cups
1   lb. sharp Cheddar cheese, ground
2   tsp. Worchestershire sauce
2   tsp. onions, minced
1/4   tsp. Tabasco sauce
1   tsp. tarragon vinegar
1/2   tsp. prepared mustard
4   oz. white cream cheese
Procedure

Place all ingredients in mixing bowl. Place on mixing machine, using paddle, and blend to a smooth paste of spreading consistency.

Bleu cheese spread

Ingredients: Approx. yield: 2 cups
1/2   lb. bleu cheese
1   lb. white cream cheese
1/4   lb. butter
1   tbsp. lemon juice, fresh
2   tbsp. fresh dill, chopped
Procedure

Place all ingredients in mixing bowl and blend on mixing machine until of spreading consistency. Refrigerate until ready to use.

Pineapple-cheese spread

Ingredients: Approx. yield: 2 1/2 cups
2   cups white cream cheese
1/2   cup crushed pineapple, drained
      pinch of salt
      yellow color, as desired
Procedure

Place ingredients in mixing container and blend until of spreading consistency.

Pimiento-cheese spread

Ingredients: Approx. yield: 2 cups
1   lb. white cream cheese
2   tbsp. pimientos, drained and chopped
2   drops Tabasco sauce
Procedure

Place all ingredients in mixing container and blend until of spreading consistency. Refrigerate until ready to use.

Olive-cheese spread

Ingredients: Approx. yield: 2 cups
1   lb. white cream cheese
2   tbsp. stuffed olives, chopped fine
2   drops Tabasco sauce
Procedure

Place all ingredients in a mixing container and blend to spreading consistency. Refrigerate until ready to use.

Avocado spread

Ingredients: Approx. yield: 2 cups
2   large ripe avocados, peeled, pitted, and mashed
2   tbsp. onions, minced
1   small clove of garlic, minced
1   tsp. salt
2   tsp. lemon juice
1   tsp. catsup
    pepper to taste
Procedure

Place all ingredients in mixing container and blend to spreading consistency. Refrigerate until ready to use.

Chip beef and cheese spread

Ingredients: Approx. yield: 2 cups
1   lb. white cream cheese
1/2   cup dried chip beef, chopped fine
2   drops Tabasco sauce
Procedure

Place all ingredients in a mixing container and blend to spreading consistency. Refrigerate until ready to use.

Deviled ham spread

Ingredients: Approx. yield: 1 1/2 cups
1   cup ham trimming, packed
2   tbsp. dill pickles
1 1/2   tbsp. onions, peeled, quartered
1   tsp. parsley, chopped
1   tbsp. prepared French mustard
1 1/2   tbsp. mayonnaise
1/2   tsp. Worchestershire Sauce
2   dashes Tabasco sauce
    red food color, as desired
Procedure

Combine the ham, onions, and pickles; put through food grinder. Add remaining ingredients and blend thoroughly. Refrigerate until ready to use.

Bacon-cheese spread

Ingredients: Approx. yield: 2 cups
1 lb. white cream cheese
¼ cup fine bacon cracklings
Procedure
Place ingredients in mixing container and blend until of spreading consistency. Refrigerate until ready to use.

Peanut butter and bacon spread

Ingredients: yield: 4½ cups
3 cups peanut butter
½ cup bacon cracklings
1 cup celery, minced
   sour cream (as needed)
Procedure
Thin the peanut butter to spreading consistency with sour cream. Add the bacon cracklings and minced celery. Mix well. Refrigerate until ready to use.

Chicken-bacon spread

Ingredients: Approx. yield: 2 cups
2 cups boiled chicken, minced
6 slices of bacon, cooked crisp, minced
½ tsp. salt
¾ cup mayonnaise (variable)
½ apple, peeled, minced
Procedure
Place all ingredients in a mixing container and blend to spreading consistency. Refrigerate until ready to use.

Chicken liver spread

Ingredients: Approx. yield: 1½ cups
12 fresh chicken livers
3 tbsp. salad oil
3 tbsp. butter
½ cup onions, minced
1 bay leaf
2 tsp. leaf sage
⅔ cup white wine
1 tsp. chopped parsley
½ tsp. salt
Procedure
1. Sauté the onions and livers in the butter and salad oil until slightly brown.
2. Add the bay leaf, sage, parsley, salt, and wine. Continue to cook until wine is slightly evaporated.
3. Remove from fire, let cool, and remove bay leaf.

4. Put mixture through fine food grinder and blend well.
5. Refrigerate until ready to use.

Anchovy spread

Ingredients: Approx. yield: 1 cup
1 cup soft butter
4 tbsp. anchovies, chopped
1 tbsp. onions, minced
1 tsp. chopped parsley
Procedure
Blend all ingredients together into a smooth paste of spreading consistency.

Shrimp spread

Ingredients: Approx. yield: 2 cups
2 cups peeled, cooked and deveined shrimp
1 tbsp. onions, cut fine
1 tbsp. celery, cut fine
1 tsp. salt
1 tbsp. lemon juice
½ tsp. paprika (Spanish)
1 tsp. Worchestershire sauce
1 tsp. prepared mustard
1 tsp. chopped parsley
3 tbsp. mayonnaise
Procedure
1. Mix together the shrimp, onions, celery, and the lemon juice.
2. Put through the fine grinder.
3. Add the mayonnaise, mustard, parsley, salt, Worchestershire sauce, and paprika; blend together until of spreading consistency.
4. Refrigerate until ready to use.

Crabmeat spread

Ingredients: Approx. yield: 1½ cups
1 lb. back fin lump crabmeat, canned or frozen
2 tbsp. onion, finely cut
4 tbsp. mayonnaise (variable)
1 tbsp. celery
1 tsp. pimientos, chopped fine
½ tsp. lemon juice
2 tbsp. parsley, chopped
½ tsp. salt (variable)
Procedure
1. Mix together the crabmeat, onions, and celery; put through fine food grinder.

2. Add remaining ingredients and blend together until of spreading consistency.
3. Refrigerate until ready to use for crabmeat will spoil quickly.

King crabmeat spread

Ingredients: Approx. yield: 1½ cups
1   lb. frozen king crabmeat
1   tbsp. finely chopped parsley
1   tbsp. celery, cut fine
1   tbsp. onions, cut fine
3   tbsp. mayonnaise (variable)
½   tsp. lemon juice
1   pinch curry powder (if desired)
Procedure
1. Mix together the king crabmeat, the onions, the celery, and the lemon juice; put through the fine food grinder.
2. Add the mayonnaise, chopped parsley, and curry powder. Blend together until of spreading consistency.
3. Refrigerate until ready to use for crabmeat will spoil quickly.

Lobster spread

Ingredients: Approx. yield: 2 cups
2   cups cooked lobster meat
1   tbsp. onions, cut fine
1   tbsp. celery, cut fine
1   tsp. green pepper, cut fine
2   tbsp. mayonnaise (variable)
1   tsp. lemon juice
1   tsp. chopped parsley
Procedure
Mix together the lobster, onions, celery, and green pepper; put through the fine food grinder. Add remaining ingredients and blend together until of spreading consistency. Refrigerate until ready to use.

Sardine spread

Ingredients: Approx. yield: 2 cups
2   cups canned sardines (mashed)
1   tbsp. onions, minced
1   tbsp. lemon juice
1   tsp. parsley, chopped
1   tsp. horseradish
¼   cup mayonnaise
Procedure
Place all ingredients together in a mixing container and blend to a paste of spreading consistency.

Salmon spread

Ingredients: Approx. yield: 2 cups
2   cups canned salmon, drained (remove bones)
1   tbsp. lemon juice
1   tsp. chopped parsley
1   tbsp. onions, finely cut
2   tbsp. mayonnaise (variable)
1   tbsp. dill pickles, finely cut
1   hard boiled egg
½   tsp. salt
Procedure
1. Mix together the salmon, dill pickles, onion, and hard boiled egg.
2. Put through fine food grinder.
3. Add remaining ingredients and blend together until of spreading consistency.
4. Refrigerate until ready to use.

Tuna fish spread

Ingredients: Approx. yield: 2 cups
2   cups, drained, white meat tuna fish
1   tbsp. onions, cut fine
1   tbsp. celery, cut fine
2   tbsp. mayonnaise (variable)
1   tsp. lemon juice
1   tsp. salt
1   hard boiled egg
1   tbsp. pimientos, chopped fine
Procedure
1. Mix together the tuna fish, onions, celery, and hard boiled egg. Put through the fine food grinder.
2. Add the remaining ingredients and blend together until of spreading consistency.
3. Refrigerate until ready to use.

POPULAR BUTTER SPREAD RECIPES

Butter spreads are used in the preparation of canapés not only as a spread, but in many cases as filling or decoration. It is recommended that a high quality butter be used. Before other ingredients are added the butter should be brought to room temperature. This will make it easier to work with when incorporating the other ingredients. All ingredients mixed into the butter should be puréed (pounded or finely minced and forced through a sieve) to make a smooth product that will not clog pastry tubes when using to decorate. (The ingredients may be mixed into the butter by hand using a kitchen spoon; or a mixing machine may be used, in such case use the paddle and mix at slow speed.)

Tuna butter: To 1 lb. of butter add 8 ozs. of puréed canned tuna fish; blend until smooth.

Chive butter: To 1 lb. of butter add 1 small bunch chives chopped fine; blend until smooth.

Pimiento butter: To 1 lb. of butter add 8 ozs. of puréed canned pimientos; blend until smooth.

Garlic butter: To 1 lb. of butter add 1 clove puréed garlic; blend until smooth.

Horseradish butter: To 1 lb. of butter add 4 ozs. of horseradish; blend until smooth.

Mint butter: To 1 lb. of butter add 6 tbsp. of finely chopped mint; blend until smooth.

Roquefort butter: To 1 lb. of butter add 4 ozs. of puréed Roquefort cheese; blend until smooth.

Onion butter: To 1 lb. of butter add 1 small Bermuda or Spanish onion, finely minced; blend until smooth.

Shrimp butter: To 1 lb. of butter add 12 ozs. of puréed cleaned and cooked shrimp; blend until smooth.

Lobster butter: To 1 lb. of butter add 12 ozs. of puréed cooked lobster; blend until smooth.

Anchovy butter: To 1 lb. of butter add 2 ozs. of canned puréed anchovy filets; oil should be drained off the filets; blend until smooth.

Lemon butter: To 1 lb. of butter add 4 tbsp. of fresh lemon juice, strained, and 2 tbsp. of fresh lemon gratings; blend until smooth. (Fresh lemon gratings are made by rubbing the peel of the whole fresh lemon across the medium grid of a box grater. Do not cut too deep into the peel or the gratings may be bitter.)

RELISH RECIPES

Radish roses: Plump, solid radishes are selected. The green stem and leaves are cut off approximately 1 inch from the base of the radish, leaving a 1 inch green stem attached to the radish. The opposite end of the radish is sliced off leaving just a slight part of the white meat visible. Using a paring knife, five very thin vertical slices approximately ½ inch wide are cut into the sides of the radish. The radish is placed in ice water until the slices curl outward.

Celery sticks: Pascal or white celery may be used. The sticks are separated from the stock and cut into fairly uniform pieces approximately 4 inches long and ¼ to ½ inches wide. They are placed in ice water to keep them crisp until they are served.

Carrot sticks: The fresh carrots are peeled, cut into fairly uniform pieces approximately 4 inches long and ¼ to ½ inches wide. They are placed in ice water to keep them crisp until they are served.

Carrot curls: The fresh carrots are peeled, sliced lengthwise paper thin, on the automatic slicing machine. These

Radish roses and accordions, carrot fans and sticks, and celery curls.

very thin slices are then rolled up and secured with a tooth pick, placed in ice water and left to set for approximately 2 hours or longer. When ready to serve the tooth picks are removed. The roll will loosen slightly taking on the appearance of a curl.

POPULAR DIP RECIPES
Cheddar cheese dip

Ingredients: Approx. yield: 2½ cups
- 8 ozs. white cream cheese
- 8 ozs. sharp Cheddar cheese, grated
- 2 tbsp. cider vinegar
- ½ garlic clove, minced
- ½ tsp. salt
- 1 tsp. Worcestershire
- ¼ tsp. prepared mustard
- ½ cup sour cream

Procedure
Place all the ingredients in the bowl of the rotary mixer and mix in second speed using the paddle; blend thoroughly. Use extra coffee cream if necessary to obtain proper consistency.

Roquefort cheese dip

Ingredients: Approx. yield: 3 cups
- 1 lb. white cream cheese
- 5 ozs. Roquefort cheese
- ½ cup sour cream
- 1 tbsp. onion juice
- 1 dash Tabasco sauce
- ½ tsp. salt

Procedure
Place all the ingredients in the bowl of the rotary mixer and mix in second speed using the paddle; blend thoroughly at slow speed. Use extra coffee cream if necessary to obtain proper consistency. (To make onion juice, grind onions in food grinder, place in towel or cloth, and squeeze out the juice.)

Pineapple-cheese dip

Ingredients: Approx. yield: 3 cups
- 1 lb. white cream cheese
- 1 cup sour cream
- ½ cup canned crushed pineapple, drained (reserve juice)
- 3 tbsp. pineapple juice

- ½ tsp. salt
  yellow color as desired
- 1 pinch nutmeg

Procedure
Place all the ingredients in the bowl of the rotary mixer and mix in second speed using the paddle; blend thoroughly. Use extra coffee cream if necessary to obtain proper consistency.

Mint-cheese dip

Ingredients: Approx. yield: 3 cups
- 1 lb. white cream cheese
- 1 cup sour cream
- ¼ cup mint leaves, chopped fine
- 1 tsp. sugar
- 1 tsp. lemon juice
- 1 tsp. salt

Procedure
Place all ingredients in the bowl of the rotary mixer and mix in second speed using the paddle; blend thoroughly. Use extra coffee cream if necessary to obtain proper consistency.

Onion-cheese dip

Ingredients: Approx. yield: 3 cups
- 1 lb. white cream cheese
- 1 cup sour cream
- 2 tbsp. of onion juice
- ½ tsp. salt
- 2 dashes Tabasco sauce
- 1 tbsp. chives, chopped

Procedure
Place all ingredients in the bowl of the rotary mixer and mix in second speed using the paddle; blend thoroughly. (To make onion juice, grind onions in food grinder, place in towel, and squeeze out juice.)

Garlic-cheese dip

Ingredients: Approx. yield: 3 cups
- 1½ cups sour cream
- 1 lb. white cream cheese
- 6 cloves of garlic, puréed
- ½ tsp. salt

Procedure
Place all ingredients in bowl of rotary mixer and mix in second speed using the paddle; blend thoroughly. Use extra coffee cream if necessary to obtain proper consistency.

Avocado dip

Ingredients: Approx. yield: 2 cups
8 ozs. white cream cheese
1 medium-sized avocado, ripe, peeled, pitted, mashed
1 tbsp. lemon juice
½ tsp. salt
½ tsp. onion, minced
3 tbsp. coffee cream
Procedure
Place all ingredients in the bowl of the rotary mixer and mix in second speed using the paddle; blend thoroughly. Use extra coffee cream if necessary to obtain proper consistency.

Bacon-cheese dip

Ingredients: Approx. yield: 3 cups
1 lb. white cream cheese
1 cup sour cream
½ tsp. salt
3 tbsp. bacon grease, slightly warm
⅓ cup bacon crackling, finely crumbled
Procedure
Place all the ingredients in the bowl of the rotary mixer and mix in second speed using the paddle; blend thoroughly. Use extra coffee cream if necessary to obtain proper consistency.

Clam dip

Ingredients: Approx. yield: 3 cups
1 lb. white cream cheese
1 cup minced clams, canned, drained (reserve juice)
3 tsp. lemon juice
2 tsp. Worcestershire
1 dash Tabasco sauce
1 small clove of garlic, minced
¼ cup of the juice from the canned clams
Procedure
Place all ingredients in the bowl of the rotary mixer and mix in second speed using the paddle; blend thoroughly. Use extra clam juice if necessary to obtain proper consistency.

Shrimp-cheese dip

Ingredients: Approx. yield: 3 cups
1 lb. white cream cheese
½ cup chopped, cooked, shrimp

3 tbsp. chili sauce
1 tsp. onions, juice
½ tsp. lemon juice
½ tsp. salt
½ tsp. Worcestershire sauce
1 tsp. horseradish
Procedure
Place all the ingredients in the bowl of the rotary mixer and mix in second speed using the paddle; blend thoroughly. Use extra coffee cream if necessary to obtain proper consistency.

POPULAR PETITE SALAD RECIPES

Eggs à la russe

Ingredients: Approx. yield: 24 servings
12 eggs, hard boiled, cut in half
1 pt. Russian dressing
Procedure
Place a half of hard boiled egg on a 4 inch plate with a base of leaf lettuce and shredded head lettuce. Cover half of the egg with Russian dressing (see Chap. 10.) Top with chopped parsley and serve.

Seafood green goddess

Ingredients: Approx. yield: 20 servings
1 cup shrimp, cooked, deveined, diced
1 cup lobster, cooked, diced
1 cup king or blue crabmeat
2 cups celery, minced
2 tsp. salt (variable)
2 tbsp. onions, minced
1 tsp. lemon juice
2 dashes Tabasco sauce
1 pt. green goddess dressing
20 thick slices of tomatoes
Procedure
Combine the seafood, celery, salt, onions, lemon juice, and Tabasco; toss together gently. Place a slice of tomato on a 4 inch plate with a base of leaf lettuce and shredded head lettuce. Place a mound of the seafood mixture on the tomato. Top with the green goddess dressing. (See Chap. 9 for dressing recipe.) Serve immediately after dressing is applied.

Italian antipasto

Ingredients: Approx. yield: 20 servings
2 cups eggplant, peeled, cut into cubes
½ cup onions, medium diced
½ cup fresh mushrooms, medium diced
2 cloves garlic, minced
½ cup olive or salad oil
1 cup tomato paste
½ cup water
¼ cup wine vinegar
⅓ cup green peppers, medium diced
¼ cup stuffed green olives, sliced
¼ cup ripe olives, pitted, sliced
1½ tsp. sugar
1 tsp. oregano
1 cup cauliflower
1 tsp. salt
   pepper to taste
¼ cup celery, medium diced, precooked
Procedure
1. Place in a braising pot the eggplant, onions, mushrooms, garlic, oil, green peppers, cauliflower, and the precooked celery. Cover and cook gently for about 10 minutes, stirring gently.
2. Add all remaining ingredients, blend well, and continue to cook covered until all ingredients are tender. Remove from fire and let cool.
3. Place in refrigerator overnight for all flavors to blend.
4. Serve on a 4 inch plate with a base of leaf lettuce and shredded head lettuce accompanied by two Brisling sardines and a cornocopia of hard salami. Garnish with parsley or watercress.

Chicken liver pâté

Ingredients: Approx. yield: 12 servings
1 lb. chicken livers
½ cup onions, sliced
½ cup butter
4 eggs, hard boiled
2 tsp. salt
¼ tsp. thyme
¼ tsp. black pepper
1 bay leaf
3 tbsp. white wine
12 onion rings, raw, small
Procedure
1. Place the butter in skillet; heat slightly; add the chicken livers, onions, thyme,

and bay leaf; sauté until brown, stirring frequently. Remove from range, let cool. Remove bay leaf.
2. Add salt, pepper, and 2 of the hard cooked eggs. Grind twice on the food grinder using the fine choppers plate.
3. Add the white wine and blend thoroughly.
4. Refrigerate keeping covered with wax paper.
5. Form mixture into balls the size of a golf ball and serve on a 4 inch plate with a base of leaf lettuce and shredded head lettuce.
6. Garnish with remaining eggs chopped fine, chopped parsley, and a ring of raw onion.

Shrimp delight

Ingredients: Approx. yield: 20 servings
2   lb. shrimp, cooked, cleaned, deveined, chopped
2½ tbsp. anchovy paste
2   tbsp. lemon juice
1½ cups mayonnaise
4   eggs, hard boiled, chopped
2   tbsp. chopped parsley
20 shrimp, whole, cooked, deveined
2   or 3 medium sized avocados, depending on size
Procedure
1. Combine the chopped shrimp, anchovy paste, lemon juice, and mayonnaise together; blend thoroughly.
2. Place a small mound of the mixture on a 4 inch plate with a base of leaf lettuce, shredded head lettuce, and two small wedges of avocado.
3. Top with a spot of mayonnaise, a whole shrimp and the chopped eggs and parsley.

Deviled lobster or crabmeat

Ingredients: Approx. yield: 12 servings
1 lb. lobster or crabmeat, cooked
1 tsp. salt
1 tsp. dry mustard
1 tsp. chopped parsley
3 eggs, hard boiled, chopped
3 tbsp. French dressing
1 tbsp. scallion, minced
1 large cucumber

Procedure

1. Combine the lobster or crabmeat, salt, dry mustard, chopped eggs, parsley, scallions, and French dressing; toss together.
2. Score cucumber with the tines of a fork and slice about ¼ inch thick.
3. Place the cucumber on a 4 inch plate with a base of leaf lettuce and shredded head lettuce.
4. Top the cucumber with the lobster or crabmeat mixture. Garnish with chopped parsley or a piece of pimiento.

Marinated herring

Ingredients: Approx. yield: 12 servings
 1   qt. jar pickled herring, drained
 2   cup sour cream
 1   tsp. salt
 2   tbsp. lemon juice
 ½   tsp. white pepper, ground
 1   med. sized onion, sliced

Procedure

1. Combine all ingredients in a stainless steel mixing container.
2. Refrigerate over night.
3. Serve 4 pieces of herring with onions and some liquid on a 4 inch plate with a base of leaf lettuce and shredded head lettuce.
4. Garnish with a twist of lemon and chopped parsley.

Tuna fish ravigote

Ingredients: Approx. yield: 15 servings
 2   13 oz. cans white meat tuna fish
 2   tbsp. onions, minced

*National Marketing Service Office
Bureau of Commercial Fisheries
U.S. Dept. of the Interior*

Tuna fish ravigote

 1   tsp. lemon juice
 1   cup celery, minced
 1   pt. ravigote sauce

Procedure

1. Combine the tuna fish, onions, lemon juice, and celery; toss together gently so as not to break up the tuna fish too much.
2. Place a small mound of the mixture on a 4 inch plate with a base of romaine lettuce and shredded head lettuce. Top with ravigote sauce (see Chap. 9) and a piece of pimiento.
3. Serve with a wedge of lemon.
   Note: Salmon may be substituted for the tuna fish.

chapter 9

herbs and spices

■ Spices and herbs play a major part in any food preparation because without them most foods would be quite bland. The proper use of spices and herbs is an art that can only be acquired through frequent practice. A knowledgeable use of spices and herbs is not only a means to better flavored foods, but also a way of creating different and more exciting preparations, which is the thing that the general public is searching for today. Many standard food items have become extremely popular in certain food establishments because they have given that old standard new life and individuality by the addition of a special aroma or flavor.

Herbs and spices, like cheese, are as old as civilization. We read about them in the Bible, in history books, and in medical books. If we examine history, we discover that many events might never have happened if men did not have a desire for tastier foods. Would Columbus have discovered America if he had not been searching for a shorter route to the east, which at the time was rich with highly prized spices and herbs? The people of Europe during this period were becoming tired of the bland, tasteless food they were consuming. Once they became aware of the exotic flavors and aromas that could be produced using these exotic spices, they had to find ways of acquiring them. Hence the many voyages of that period.

The difference between herbs and spices generally revolves around the word "pungent." Spices are pungent in aroma and often in flavor. Herbs, on the other hand, are more delicate in both aroma and flavor. There are other differences between the two. Herbs are the leaf, stem or flower of small annual, perennial, or biennial plants which can be grown in any temperate climate. They flourish in most parts of the United States in what is known as herb gardens (small formal gardens created for the beauty they display and the convenience they provide the cook). Spices may be the fruit, berry, root, or leaf of a tree or plant. The true spice is pungent, zesty, and aromatic. Today, for the purpose of buying, spices include other aromatic seeds that are found on the market. All spices are grown in tropical climates where the sun is hot and the rainfall is heavy at certain times of the year.

Cooking techniques

Cooking with herbs and spices, as stated before, is an art. To acquire this art takes patience, practice, and adherence to a few simple rules.

1. Herbs and spices should be used to enhance natural flavor.
2. They should not disguise the flavor of any food.
3. There should be no particular spice or herb apparent when tasting any food. There are exceptions to this, however, such as curry or chili dishes where the character of the preparation depends on a certain spice or herb.
4. Always season in moderation. More can always be added, but none can be taken away.

5. With foods that require a long cooking time, add spices and herbs near the end if the spice is in ground form. If in whole form, add at the start.
6. If the cooking time is short, add the spices and herbs at the start.
7. Before adding herbs to a preparation they should be rubbed in the palm of the hand to release their flavor.
8. When using herbs or spices in soups or gravies, tie them in a cheese cloth bag, or if herbs are fresh, tie them in a bunch. This is done so they can be removed easily after they have served their purpose.
9. In uncooked dishes the spices or herbs should be added hours before serving so the flavor can develop. This is especially true in the case of salad dressings, fruit juices, and marinates.

American Spice Trade Assoc.

Making up a spice bag.

10. Pepper, the most common of all spices, should be used in moderation. Pepper, with its companion salt, may be added at the dinner table to suit the individual taste.

Purchasing

When purchasing herbs and spices, buy in fairly small amounts since they lose their flavor even when stored under proper conditions. The best storage condition is found in a dry and cool place where the heat will not rob their flavor and dampness will not cause them to cake. As soon as a spice is ground it will start to lose its flavor. However, if kept in a tightly closed container, deterioration will be retarded.

Herbs tend to lose their flavor faster than spices if in rubbed or ground form. As a result most users prefer to purchase herbs in whole form because they keep better. Good color, strong flavor, and aroma are the important points to consider when buying both spices and herbs. It is always wise to test these items when they are delivered, for they may have been lying around sometimes before they were delivered.

A good test is to examine the color for a bright, fresh, and rich appearance. In the case of herbs rub a small amount in the palm of the hand and smell. It should be fairly strong and fresh. Use the same test for spices, but, of course, do not rub in the palm of the hand. Just bring slowly to the nostrils and the aromatic aroma should come up to meet you, for fresh spices readily give up their aroma.

It is never to the advantage of a food service operator to purchase imitation spices. Even though he may save a few pennies a pound he will lose in the long run, because they do not really do the job. Imitation spices are weak and cheap because they are made by spraying the oil of the pure spice on a carrier such as ground soya, buckwheat, or cottonseed hulls. The most common imitation spices are pepper, nutmeg, cinnamon, and mace.

Spices are all generally strong in flavor, as stated before, so there is really no reason to classify them into groups. It is different with herbs because a few of them do vary in strength. To make it easier to become familiar with herbs, we shall divide them into three groups: Very strong, fairly strong and delicate.

1. *Very strong herbs:* Sage and Rosemary leaves.
2. *Fairly strong herbs:* Basil, mint, marjoram, tarragon, dill, thyme, etc.
3. *Delicate herbs:* Chives, parsley and chervil.

HERB AND SPICE LIST

The following is a list of the popular herbs and spices used in commercial kitchens throughout the world. The student cook should become familiar with all of these. To help the student achieve this knowledge, we shall state the chief characteristics, where they can be found, and some of the uses of each popular herb and spice.

Allspice: This is the dried, unripened fruit of the small pimiento tree, of the clove tree family, which is grown in the West Indies. Many people think, because of its name, that allspice is a blended spice. This is not true, although this pea shaped spice does possess a flavor that suggests the combined flavors of cinnamon, nutmeg, and cloves. It is because of its flavor, in fact, that it is called "allspice." Allspice is used in both whole and ground form and is used in such preparations as mince meat pie, pumpkin pie, puddings, stews, soups, preserved fruit, boiled fish, relishes, and gravies.

Anise: This is a small annual plant which stems from the parsley family and produces a comma-shaped seed called anise seed. This spice has a licorice flavor. The use of anise dates back to ancient Egypt. Down through the centuries anise has had many uses. It has been used to prevent indigestion, as an antidote for scorpion bite, as a safeguard against evil, and even as a perfume. Today this cherished spice is used in coffee cake, sweet rolls, cookies, sweet pickles, licorice products, candies, cough syrups, and certain fruits. Anise is grown in India, Southern and Northern Europe, Chile, Mexico, and the United States.

Basil or sweet basil: This is one of the most savory and popular herbs because it blends well with so many different foods. It is a native of India where it is considered a holy herb and grown in pots near the Hindu temples. In many countries, such as Italy and Romania, this fragrant herb is considered a token of love. Basil consists of the dried leaves and stems of an annual plant of the same name. It is grown in Europe and the United States and is used to flavor tomato paste products, spaghetti sauces, vegetables, and egg dishes.

Bay or laurel leaf: This spice has always been held in high esteem. Emperors, such as Julius Caesar, Tiberius and Claudius, wore a wreath of laurel. Celebrated scholars and athletes were crowned with a wreath of laurel because it was considered a symbol of the triumphant leader or champion. From this custom has arisen our modern expressions "to rest on his laurels" or "to win one's laurels." The bay or laurel leaves are the thick aromatic leaves of the sweet-day tree grown in Italy, Greece, and other Mediterranean countries. They are used for flavoring soups, roasts, stews, gravies, meats, and pickling.

Allspice

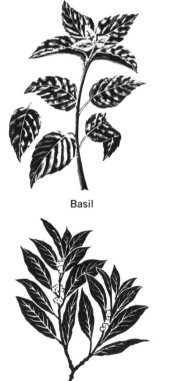

Anise

Basil

American Spice Trade Assoc.

Bay leaves

Caraway seed: This spice is the dark brown dried seeds of the caraway plant, a biennial plant that grows in Holland, Germany, England, and Poland. The Germans use more caraway seed in food preparations than any other nation. They like its flavor not only in rye bread, but also in sauerkraut, pork, and cabbage as well. In the United States we think of caraway seed as "rye seed" because it is always used in the preparation of rye bread. There are, of course, many other delightful uses for this flavorful seed. It can be used in cheese, potatoes, stews, and soups with excellent results. Caraway seed is also one of the major flavoring ingredients in the popular liqueur, Kümmel.

Cardamom: This spice is a member of the ginger family. It is the dried, immature fruit of a tropical bush which grows to a height of about ten feet. The fruit consists of a yellowish colored pod, about the size of a small grape, which holds the dark, aromatic cardamom seeds. Cardamom is considered the world's second most valued spice. Only saffron is considered more valuable. Cardamom is available in whole or ground form and is used in pickling, coffee cake, curries, and Danish pastry. It is grown in Malaya, Ceylon and India (which is considered its native home).

Cassia: This spice is very similar to cinnamon. It takes an expert to distinguish between the two when in ground form. Cassia, like cinnamon, is the bark of a tree; however, cassia bark is thicker and the color is darker. The flavor of cassia is much stronger than cinnamon. Cassia is used in pickling, preserving, and in many of the same preparations as cinnamon. In fact, in many cases, it is used as a substitute for cinnamon. Cassia is grown in Malaya and China.

Cayenne pepper: This spice is the hottest of all peppers. It is ground from the small pods of certain varieties of hot peppers. It is not as bright in color as red pepper, but it is certainly much hotter. Cayenne is grown in South America and Africa, and it is used in cream soups, cream dishes, meats, fish, cheese, and egg dishes. Be sure to use cayenne in moderation—it is very hot.

Celery seed: This spice has little connection with the celery stock that we classify as a vegetable. It does have a similar flavor, but celery seed is actually a wild variety of celery. The seeds are very small and brown in color, and can be purchased whole or in ground form. This spice is grown in France, India, and the United States. It is a delightful seasoning for cole slaw, potato salad, sauces, soups, dressings, and fish and certain meats.

Chervil: This herb has always been admired for its lovely fern-like leaves and its delicate flavor, which is similar to parsley. Chervil is used quite freely in the French kitchens as a substitute for parsley because they consider it more delicate in flavor. It is grown in England, Northern Europe, and the United States. It can be used in salads and soups, and in egg and cheese dishes.

Chili powder: This is a blended spice consisting of cumin, Mexican peppers, oregano, and other spices. It is supposed to have had its origin in Mexico, but today is used throughout the world and especially in the United States. It is used in preparing chili con carne, tamales, stews, Spanish rice, gravies, and appetizers.

Chives: These are one of the two delicate herbs. Chives are small, onion-like sprouts that are long and green and can be grown indoors or out. The chefs of many establishments raise their own chives in small flower pots in their kitchens. Chives add color and flavor to cottage cheese, cream cheese, egg dishes, soups, salads, and potato dishes.

Cinnamon: This spice is the dried, thin inner bark of a medium sized evergreen tree grown mainly in Ceylon, In-

Caraway

Cardamom seed

Celery seed

Chervil

American Spice Trade Assoc.

Cinnamon

donesia, and South Vietnam. The bark is harvested during the rainy season, because the damp atmosphere makes the bark easier to manage. After the bark has been removed from the tree, it is rolled into moderately long quills which are known as cinnamon sticks. Cinnamon can be purchased whole or in ground form. It is used in baking apples, pickling, preserving, pies, cakes, puddings, stewed fruits, custard, and all types of sweet doughs.

Cloves: This spice consists of the dried unopened buds of the clove tree. The tree is very thick and has leaves similar to the laurel leaf. The cloves grown at the end of the twigs in clusters of about twenty. When the buds start to sprout they are white in color, when they are ready to be picked they are red, and when dried they become a dark brown. The clove tree will only grow in mountainous regions and requires a tropical climate to survive. The clove is referred to as the "nail shaped spice" and is thought to possess the most pungent flavor of all the spices. In fact the clove is so rich and pungent in flavor that it is often used in toothache medicines to deaden pain. The clove tree is grown in the East Indies and the islands off the coast of Africa. They are used in pickling and in the preparation of roast pork, corned beef, baked ham, soups, apple sauce, fruit cakes, pumpkin pie, and cakes.

Coriander: This is another of those spices that dates back to the beginning of civilization. Coriander grew in the hanging gardens of Babylon and it was placed in the ancient Egyptian tombs. Coriander is a small seed, light brown in color. To many, the whole seed is similar in appearance to whole white pepper. It has a very pleasant taste that suggests the combined flavors of sage and lemon peel. Coriander is grown in Morocco, and in many of the Mediterranean countries. It is used in candies, pickles, frankfurters, baked goods, meat products, and curry dishes.

Cumin or comino: It was said of the spice cumin that, when it was in the possession of a wife, it would keep the husband from wandering—so most ancient wives kept it handy at all times. Cumin, sometimes called comino, originated in Egypt. It is the dried, aromatic seeds of a plant similar to the caraway plant and grows to a height of about one foot. The spice has a slightly bitter, warm flavor

American Spice Trade Assoc.

Cloves   Coriander seed   Cumin seed and is used quite freely in Italian and Mexican cuisine. Cumin is grown in Morocco, India, Egypt, and South America. It is an essential ingredient in the blending of curry powder and chili powder. This spice is used to flavor chili, soup, hot tamales, rice and cheese dishes.

Curry powder: This blended spice originated in India many years ago, but it has only become popular in America in the past 60 years. It consists of twelve or more spices blended in the proper amounts to create the fabulous flavor that we often associate with the exotic East. The color and to some degree the flavor of curry will vary with different manufacturers. Since India is the home of curry it is only natural that they would excel in curry preparation. There are, however, many different types of curry in use. For instance, the curry dishes served in some regions of India are hot because they like to use generous amounts of red pepper. In other regions, however, they desire a milder curry. Curry powder is used to make curries of meat, fish, chicken and eggs. It is also used to season rice, soups, and some shellfish preparations.

Dill: This is an herb of the parsley family. The small, flat aromatic seeds as well as the dried leaves of the dill plant are used. The seeds, however, are preferred over the dried leaves. Dill is grown throughout the countries of Europe and also in the United States. Dill has become famous because it is used to flavor the very popular dill pickles. Dill is also a welcome addition to such preparations as green beans, potato salad, poached fish, marinated cucumbers, cauliflower, and some lamb dishes.

Fennel seed: This herb consists of the small seed-like fruits of the fennel plant. They are light brown in color and resemble anise seed in flavor and aroma. Fennel is grown chiefly in India and Rumania and is used quite freely in Scandinavian cooking and Italian baking. Fennel seed will also enhance the flavor of roast duck and some chicken preparations.

Garlic: This herb has been used for centuries by the French, Spanish, Italian, and Mexican cooks; however, not until after World War II did the use of garlic become popular in the United States. This popularity was created when the soldiers returned home and began to prepare some of the very desirable dishes

Dill seed

American Spice Trade Assoc.

Fennel seed

they had eaten in the countries of Europe —dishes that required a hint of garlic. Garlic is a potently flavored bulb of the onion family. The bulb contains about a dozen compactly arranged cloves which are covered with a thin skin. If the skin is white, it is known as white garlic; if red, it is known as red garlic. Garlic grown in a warm climate will differ from that grown in a cold climate. Garlic grown in a cold climate is stronger in flavor. Garlic is grown throughout the world and comes in many forms: whole, dehydrated, garlic salt, garlic powder, and instant minced garlic. When using garlic be discreet. A little is very helpful, too much is repulsive. Garlic will help to accent the flavor of sauces, soups, salads, pickles, meat preparations, and salad dressing.

Ginger: It is said that ginger is one of the oldest, if not the oldest, spice known to man. It is an essential ingredient in the preparation of the ever popular gingerbread. The Romans, for example, loved the honey-sweet flavor of gingerbread and carried the recipe throughout their empire. Ginger is the root of a subtropical plant grown in China, India, and on the Island of Jamaica. When the plant is about a year old, the roots are dug up and dried in the sun. Ginger has a very warm, pungent, spicy flavor that adds zest to cakes, cookies, pies, fruits, puddings, and some meat preparations. Ginger is available on the market in whole or ground form.

Mace: This spice is the lacy covering of the nutmeg shell. It lies between the nutmeg shell and the outer covering. It is reddish orange in color when removed from the shell, but turns to a dark yellow when dried. Its flavor resembles to some degree that of the nutmeg, although it is not as pungent as the nutmeg. Mace is the traditional spice for pound cake and sweet doughs. It is also used in doughnuts, cherry pie, chocolate dishes, oyster stew, spinach, and pickling.

Marjoram: This is a perennial herb of the mint family. The herb grows about two feet high and the dried leaves and flowering tops are used to produce the sweet, minty flavor. The marjoram plant originated in regions of Western Asia and has always been a symbol of honor and happiness in many countries of the world. Marjoram is grown in France,

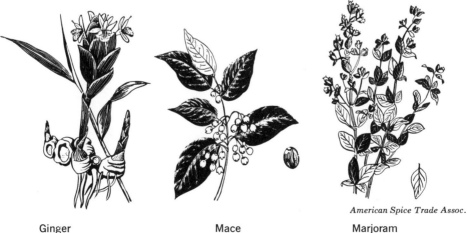

American Spice Trade Assoc.

Ginger   Mace   Marjoram

Chili, Peru, and England. It is used to flavor, soups, stews, sausage, cheese dishes, and all types of lamb preparations.

Mint: Mint is a herb which originally came from the Mediterranean area. It was held in high esteem by the people of the ancient world. Today it is widely known and has become one of the most popular herbs because of its cool, refreshing flavor. It is grown throughout the world and can be found growing in the backyards of city and suburban dwellers. There are many varieties of mint, but only spearmint and peppermint are found on the spice shelf. Mint is used in the preparation of all types of lamb dishes, vegetables, fruit salads, iced tea, fruit drinks, and poached fish.

Mustard seed: These are very small seeds which come in two types: the white or yellow seeds which are mild in flavor, and the dark brown seeds which are more pungent in flavor and are the type most often used in Chinese cuisine. Mustard when in ground form is unique in that its flavor is not released until it is blended with water. After the powdered mustard stands in the liquid for about 10 minutes it is at its best. Mustard can

be purchased in three forms: whole, ground (powdered), and the ever popular prepared mustard which is a blend of ground mustard seed, other spices, and vinegar. Mustard seed is grown in Canada, Denmark, the United Kingdom, the Netherlands, and the United States. It enhances the flavor of pickles, cabbage, beets, sauerkraut, sauces, salad dressings, ham, frankfurters, and cheese.

Nutmeg: This spice is the kernel of the nutmeg fruit. The tree which produces this fruit is bushy and reaches a height of about 40 feet. It is a type of evergreen and grows best in tropical climates near the sea. The tree produces its first fruit when it is 6 or 7 years old and continues to produce for about 60 years. Good production for a nutmeg tree is around 1,000 nutmegs per year. When the nutmeg fruit is ripe, the outer hull splits open, exposing the sister spice *mace,* which partly covers the nutmeg kernel. Nutmeg is grown in the Dutch East Indies and British West Indies. Its sweet, warm, spicy flavor can be used to enhance such preparations as cream soups, doughnuts, puddings, baked goods, potato preparations, custards, cauliflower, sauces, hash, and stews.

Mustard

American Spice Trade Assoc.

Nutmeg

Oregano: The wide use of this herb in the United States today came about with the rise in popularity of the Italian pizza pie. The American soldiers of World War II brought the taste for pizza home with them. It wasn't long after their return that cooks learned to master the use of this new-found herb and the sales of oregano began to sky-rocket. Oregano is obtained from a small plant similar to the marjoram plant. The leaves are slightly curly and small; the flavor is pleasingly pungent and to some degree resembles marjoram. Oregano is native to the Mediterranean Region and is grown extensively in Greece and Italy. In Mexico it grows wild and for this reason is sometimes referred to as Mexican sage. It can be used in all tomato products, in Mexican and Italian dishes, cheese preparations, and, of course, the ever popular pizza pie.

Paprika: This is another of the blended spices and is obtained by grinding and mixing together various sweet red peppers after the seeds and stems have been removed. There are two kinds of paprika used in the commercial kitchen; Spanish and Hungarian. Spanish paprika is slightly mild in flavor and has a bright red color. Hungarian paprika is darker in color and more pungent in flavor. Paprika is grown in Spain, Central Europe and the United States. It is used as a colorful garnish for many foods and in some cases it is used to help brown food. Paprika is a necessary ingredient in such preparations as Hungarian goulash, chicken paprika, newburg sauce, French dressing, and veal paprika.

Parsley: This is one of the two delicate herbs. It has been cultivated for thousands of years, but its origin seems to have been in ancient Greece. Parsley is mentioned in the stories of Hercules; the Romans also used parsley to make crowns for their guests which they thought prevented excessive drinking at banquets. Parsley is a garden plant; the leaves are used as a garnish or to flavor other foods. Parsley is grown throughout the world and is used in soups, salads, stuffing, stews, sauces, potatoes, and vegetable dishes.

Pepper (black and white): This is the most common of all spices. It is a native of the tropics and never grows further than 20 degrees from the equator. There are two kinds of pepper, black and white, and both are produced by the climbing

Oregano

Paprika

American Spice Trade Assoc.

Pepper

vine we know as the pepper plant. Black pepper is the dried, immature berries. They are picked when still slightly green, left to dry in the sun, and either sold whole as peppercorns or they are ground. Black pepper is quite pungent in flavor. White pepper is the mature berry of the pepper plant after the outer covering, which contains most of the hotness, has been removed. It is much milder in flavor than black pepper. It too is sold in either whole or ground form. White pepper is generally more costly than black pepper because the peppercorns used for white pepper are usually more carefully cultivated. Pepper is grown in India, Ceylon, Brazil, and Southeast Sumatra. Pepper is used to some degree in just about every preparation known to man. The rule to follow when seasoning with pepper is: if the item is light in color use white pepper; if dark, use black pepper. Fresh ground pepper will always supply more flavor and aroma than pepper purchased in ground form.

Pickling spice: This is sometimes called a *mixed spice* and is a blend of ten or more whole spices used mainly for pickling purposes. It is also an excellent addition to stocks, soups, relishes,

sauces, and some meat preparations such as pot roast and sauerbraten. In most cases, when pickling spices are used in cooking, they are added in the form of a spice bag. The spice is tied in a piece of cheese cloth, added to the preparation and removed when the desired amount of flavor is acquired.

Poppy seed: Those blue colored, flavoring seeds are the seeds of a specially cultivated poppy plant which grows chiefly in the country of Holland; but it can also be found growing in other parts of the world as well. The poppy seeds are very small and light. It would take about 900,000 of them to make a pound. Poppy seeds are best known for garnishing rolls and bread; however, they can also be used as a topping for cookies and in butter sauces for fish, vegetables, and noodles.

Poppy seed

Sprinkling flavoring seeds and herbs on rolls.

Poultry seasoning: This is one of the more recent blends to be found on the spice shelf. It is a ground mixture of sage, thyme, marjoram, savory, pepper, onion powder, and celery salt. It is most often used in seasoning bread dressing, but has other uses as well. It will also help the flavor of meat loaf and dumplings.

Rosemary: This is the dried, somewhat curved, needle-like leaves of an evergreen plant of the mint family. It is considered to be one of the two very strong herbs. The other is sage. The flavor is fragrant and sweet tasting. Rosemary has been used for centuries as a symbol of fidelity for lovers. In many European countries today, the herb is used to stuff pillows and to supply the fragrance for soap, toilet water and cosmetics. Rosemary is grown in France, Spain and Portugal and is a great asset when used sparingly with lamb, chicken, pork and duck. It also enhances the flavor of tomato and cheese dishes, stuffing, and soups.

Saffron: This is the world's most costly spice, but a little will go a long way. Saffron is the dried, bright red stigmas of a purple, crocus-like flower of the saffron plant. It takes about 225,000 stigmas from over 75,000 flowers to produce one pound of this very desirable spice. There are only three stigmas to each flower and these stigmas are removed by hand. Knowing these facts, it is easy to see why this spice is so expensive. Saffron is grown in Spain and the Mediterranean region. It imparts a very agreeable flavor as well as a rich, deep-yellow color that is desired in such preparations as rice and fine bakery goods. Saffron is used quite freely in Scandinavian and Spanish cuisine. It should be added to any item in the form of saffron tea, made by steeping it in hot water.

Sage: This herb is the greenish-white leaves of the sage plant. It is a low growing, perennial shrub that possesses a minty spiciness. It is considered to be one of the very strong herbs. Sage is grown throughout the world, but the choice sage comes from Yugoslavia. Sage can be purchased either in leaf form or rubbed. It is the perfect seasoning for poultry stuffing. It is also used in the making of sausage and in bean and tomato preparations.

Savory: This is the dried, smooth, slightly narrow leaves of the savory plant, an herb of the mint family. There are two kinds of savory found on the market, summer savory and winter savory. The summer savory is the best because at this time of year the flavor of the leaves are at their peak of quality. Savory is grown in France and Spain and possesses a delicately sweet flavor similar in some respects to thyme. Savory is an important ingredient in flavoring green or dried beans and for this reason is referred to as the "bean herb." It is also used in meat sauces, fish sauces, egg dishes and meat stuffings.

Sesame seed: This is a small, honey-colored seed with a toasted almond flavor and a high oil content. Sesame seeds come from pods that grow on the sesame plant, an herb growing about two feet high. It is native to tropical and semitropical countries. The sesame plant is grown in Central America, Egypt, and the United States. Sesame seeds are baked on rolls, bread, and buns to supply a nut like flavor to the product. The seeds are also toasted and stirred into butter and served over fish, noodles, and vegetables.

Tarragon: This is an herb that is native to the vast waste lands of Siberia. It is a small perennial plant the leaves of which are slightly long and smooth. The herb is best known as a flavoring for vinegar, and the fresh leaves are used quite often to decorate aspic and chaud-froid pieces. Tarragon has a flavor that suggests a touch of licorice similar to the spice, anise. Tarragon blends well with seafood

Rosemary

Saffron

Sage

Sesame seed

American Spice Trade Assoc.

Tarragon

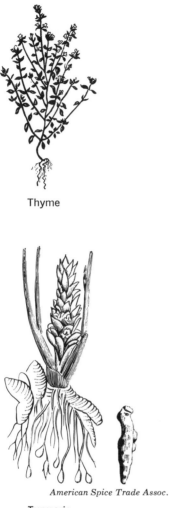

Thyme

American Spice Trade Assoc.

Turmeric

and is a delightful addition to salads and salad dressings. This herb seems to be a favorite of the French chefs and is used more often in French cuisine than any other herb.

Thyme: Thyme has been popular in the United States for many years mainly because it is the finest herb to use with fish and shell fish. Thyme is the leaves and tender stems of a low growing shrub which is a member of the mint family. The leaves and tender stems are picked just before the blossoms start to bloom, then cleaned and dried. Thyme is available in whole or ground form and is a welcome addition to beef stew, clam chowder, oyster stew, meat loaf, poultry seasoning and vegetable preparations. Thyme is grown principally in Southern France and Spain.

Turmeric: This herb is the root of a lily-like plant of the ginger family. It is a native of Asia and is used not only in food preparation, but also in medicine and as a dye. When the turmeric roots are ground a bright yellow powder is produced that has a taste similar to mustard. Turmeric is an important ingredient in blending curry powder and is also used in making some prepared mustards. To some degree, turmeric is associated with the spice saffron because both possess a deep yellow color and are used in much the same way in food preparation. Turmeric is grown in India, Peru, Haiti, Jamaica and wherever ginger thrives.

salads
and
salad
dressings

■ Salads as we know them today are truly American. Although they did not really invent it, Americans have perfected and popularized the salad. America has seldom been given credit for advancing the culinary arts; however, credit must be given for this year round favorite, which has changed the eating habits of people from coast to coast. American women have to a great degree made the salad an American institution. Their luncheons especially have been built around the salad. The reason the American woman has been behind the extreme popularity of the salad is because all salads possess characteristics that appeal to women. They are dainty, colorful, eye-appealing and display an artistic arrangement when properly prepared.

A salad can best be defined as a combination of cold ingredients, served with a dressing. In most cases the ingredients include a salad green. All salads are extremely wholesome regardless of the ingredients used and provide many essential vitamins and minerals necessary for proper nutrition. Salads can generally be found complementing most meals.

Salads may be served as an entree (main course) or as an accompaniment (side salad) to other foods. If the salad is served as a side salad, the rule to follow is always the same: Light salads go with heavy entrees and heavy salads with light entrees. The entree or main course salad can be found on most menus today and is one of the most popular and profitable items featured.

To classify salads is most difficult because they vary greatly. The most common method of classifying is in terms of the ingredients used. Most salads will come under one of the following.

1. Fruit
2. Vegetable
3. Leafy green
4. Meat
5. Seafood
6. Gelatin

There are certain rules that must be followed in the preparation of any salad to achieve the desired results.

1. Use simple colorful combinations.
2. Ingredients should always be fresh and crisp.
3. Balance flavor, texture and color.
4. Use artistic arrangement.
5. Use form in arranging or molding the salad. Flat surfaces are not attractive.

6. Always present a well-chilled salad.
7. Purchase quality ingredients.
8. Keep in mind that salads are a work of art and should always be attractive to the eye.

Parts of a salad

Any successful salad will contain four basic parts: base, body, dressing and garnish. Each part is extremely important when preparing a salad. If just one part is omitted or done poorly, the finished product will be impaired.

Base: The base usually consist of a salad green such as leaf lettuce, romaine, head lettuce or bib. It can be eaten, but in most cases the guest will choose to let it remain on the plate or in the bowl. The main purpose of the base is to keep the plate or bowl from looking bare and to provide contrast in color when the body is added.

Body: The body is the main part of the salad. The type of salad would determine the kind or kinds of ingredients used. It is this part of the salad that should be given the most attention. The body should be prepared by following the rules of good salad preparation.

TABLE I. GARNISH SUGGESTIONS FOR SALADS

Beets, slices or julienne	Green pepper rings or strips
Bonbons—Marshmallows rolled in coconut	Jellies
Carrot curls or sticks	Lemon slices or wedges
Celery curls, celery hearts	Melon balls or wedges
Cheese, American, Swiss—julienne, bar, sliced, shredded	Nuts, whole or chopped
	Olives, green and ripe
Cheese balls or bars rolled in chopped parsley or paprika	Onion rings
	Orange twists or slices
Cherries, canned or maraschino	Paprika, dash of
Coconut, plain or colored	Parsley, sprig or chopped
Cranberry relish	Pickles, all kinds
Croutons	Pimiento, strips or chopped
Cucumber slices or curls	Pineapple fans or fingers
Dates or prunes, stuffed	Poppy seed
Eggs, hard cooked, sliced, quartered, or stuffed	Radishes, plain, roses, accordion, or sliced
Fresh berries or fresh fruit	Strawberries, whole or sliced
Grapes, fresh, sugared	Tomato slices and wedges

Common salad greens

Dressing: A dressing is usually served with all types of salads. It plays many important parts in the overall success of the preparation. It adds flavor, provides food value, helps digestion, improves palatability and in some cases may act as a garnish.

Dressings are explained and recipes given in another section of this chapter.

Garnish: The main purpose of the garnish is to add eye appeal to the finished product, but in some cases it may help to improve the form or increase the taste. The garnish may be a part of the basic salad ingredients or it may be an additional item that will blend with and compliment the body. The garnish should at all times be kept simple. It should attract, not distract, the attention of the diner and help to stimulate his or her appetite. Table I lists some common garnishes.

Salad greens

There are twelve salad greens the student cook should become familiar with if he wishes to excel in salad preparation. A combination of any **four** or more of these greens will make an excellent body for the green salads.

1. Romaine lettuce
2. Belgian endive lettuce
3. Bib or limestone lettuce
4. Boston lettuce
5. Celery cabbage (Chinese)
6. Iceberg or head lettuce
7. Escarole lettuce

8. Spinach
9. Watercress
10. Dandelion greens
11. Chicory lettuce
12. Leaf lettuce

Romaine lettuce: This lettuce is also known as coss lettuce. It has a mild flavor and blends very well with other salad greens. Romaine has an elongated, loosely packed head. The outer leaves are fairly dark green, the inner leaves are usually white or cream colored. This is caused by tying the plant together during growth. Romaine will remain crisp longer than most other kinds of lettuce.

Belgian endive lettuce: This salad green has a bitter taste and creamy-white leaves. It has an elongated, tightly packed head similar in some respects to a bunch of celery. Belgian endive will grow in lengths of 4 to 6 inches and should be split in half lengthwise before it is cleaned. This salad green is generally expensive and served most often by itself with a rich flavorful dressing.

Bib or limestone lettuce: Bib lettuce was perfected by a retired Army major named John Bib. It was first raised in the state of Kentucky. It grows best in soil containing a high percentage of limestone, hence its other name. The name *Bib* is used mostly in the Eastern States and the name *limestone* prevails in the Western States. Bib has a sweet, mild flavor, but will wilt and deteriorate rapidly. It grows into a small loosely packed head with fairly dark green leaves. This lettuce will blend well with other greens or it may be served alone with an appropriate dressing. In almost all cases this lettuce is raised close to market because it does not hold up well when shipped.

Boston lettuce: This lettuce is very tender, fragile, and mild tasting. It has a very loosely packed, round head with leaves that are smooth and easy to separate. It slightly resembles Bib lettuce, but its outer leaves are a lighter green and the inner leaves are light yellow. Boston let-

Burpee Seeds

Celery cabbage

tuce blends well with other salad greens. Because the leaves have a cup shape, it also makes an excellent salad base.

Celery cabbage: Also known as Chinese cabbage, this salad green has an appearance similar to Romaine lettuce, but a taste that resembles cabbage. It grows about a foot long and has tightly fitting pale green leaves on the outside and white inner leaves. Because of the slightly strong cabbage flavor, celery cabbage must be used in moderation when blended with other salad greens.

Iceberg or head lettuce: The most familiar and popular salad green is iceberg or head lettuce. It has a solid compact head, with pale green leaves that are quite mild in flavor. Head lettuce will retain its crispness for a long period of time. Even when bruised with a knife or handled in a careless manner, it will not wilt or blemish rapidly. Head lettuce can be served alone or blended with other salad greens with excellent results.

Escarole lettuce: Also known as broad leaf endive, escarole is similar to chicory lettuce in flavor, but has a broader and thicker leaf. Escarole has a bitter taste and for this reason is very seldom eaten alone. It is almost always blended with milder and sweeter greens. Escarole is grown in places that have slightly mild winters, such as the northern part of Florida and the Texas Panhandle.

Spinach: Although spinach is eaten mostly as a vegetable, the coarse, dark, mild-tasting leaves are also excellent when used as a salad green. The long, tough stem is removed and the leaf is thoroughly washed to eliminate any sand or grit that may be in the ridges of the leaves. Spinach is quite palatable and adds color as well as flavor to any mixture of salad greens. Since spinach is grown in sandy soil it should always be washed two or three times before using.

Watercress: This salad green grows in shallow sandy streams. It has small, round leaves which grow on thin stalks. It has a peppery taste and is quite perishable. It is used more commonly as garnish for salads rather than as a part of the body. Watercress resembles clover to some degree and is purchased in bunches.

Dandelion greens: Dandelion greens grow wild or they may be cultivated. The cultivated greens are more tender and milder in taste. Both are on the market in the early spring. The greens are fairly smooth, but have a slightly rough irregular edge. The wild dandelions are quite tasty until the yellow flower blooms then they become bitter and tough. Dandelion greens can be blended with other salad greens or they may be served alone with a bacon dressing and chopped hard boiled eggs.

Chicory lettuce: Also known as curly endive because of its thin, irregularly twisted leaves, chicory grows in spread out bunches. The leaves are dark green on the outside but white towards the center. It has a bitter taste and is always blended with milder and sweeter greens. Chicory can also be used as a garnish on fruit salads and fruit plates with excellent results.

Leaf lettuce: Leaf lettuce might be referred to as common lettuce because it is almost always used as a base when preparing a salad. It is generally inexpensive

Burpee Seeds

Chicory

Burpee Seeds

Leaf lettuce

and is on the market the year round. The leaves are soft, have a light green color and do not form a head. Leaf lettuce also plays a major part in the preparation of sandwiches.

Serving salads

One should offer a variety of salads to the diner. This may be done by listing a choice of three or four salads on the menu or by allowing the guest to select his side salad from a salad tray. Salads are usually served in small salad bowls. Small salad bowls refer to the small plastic or wood bowls that usually have a diameter of 5½ inches and a depth of 1¾ inch. They will usually hold about 12 ounces and are used for side salads.

Salad preparation by commercial cooking students.

Larger bowls are used if the salad is served as an entree or main course.

SALAD DRESSINGS

A salad may possess all the characteristics of a successful preparation but if the dressing, applied at the time of service, is lacking it will be a complete failure. In most cases the flavor of the dressing is the first flavor or taste the palate will sense. If this first taste sensation is desirable, the preparation will be a complete success. It is important, then, that the dressing be prepared with the finest ingredients available and with the utmost care possible. Table II gives some of the popular salad dressings associated with salads given in this chapter.

There are three basic types of salad dressings: French, mayonnaise, and boiled or cooked.

French dressing may be prepared by forming either a permanent emulsion or a temporary emulsion. When the French dressing is to form a permanent emulsion, the oil is held in suspension by the use of egg yolks or a combination of yolks and whole eggs. This kind of dressing is thicker and will cling to and

TABLE II. SALAD DRESSING COMBINATION SUGGESTIONS*

SALADS	DRESSINGS
Fruit Salads	
Waldorf	Mayonnaise, Boiled Dressing
Diplomat	Mayonnaise, Boiled Dressing
Tossed Fruit	Mayonnaise, Boiled Dressing, French, Sour Cream, Honey Cream, Honey Dressing
Pear and American Cheese	Mayonnaise, Boiled Dressing, French, Sour Cream, Honey Cream, Honey Dressing
Bannana-Pecan	Mayonnaise, Boiled Dressing, Sour Cream
Fruit	Mayonnaise, Boiled Dressing, French, Sour Cream, Honey Cream, Honey Dressing
Belgian Endive and Orange	Mayonnaise, French, Sour Cream, Bleu Cheese, Bleu Cheese–Sour Cream
Orange and Grapefruit	Mayonnaise, French, Boiled Dressing, Sour Cream, Honey Cream, Honey Dressing
Vegetable Salads	
Asparagus and Tomato	Mayonnaise, French, Thousand Island, Louis, Italian, Sour Cream, Vinegar and Oil, Bleu or Roquefort Cheese, Russian, Vinaigrette, Bleu Cheese–Sour Cream, Chiffonade
Tomato and Cucumber	Mayonnaise, French, Thousand Island, Louis, Italian, Sour Cream, Vinegar and Oil, Bleu or Roquefort Cheese, Russian, Vinaigrette, Bleu Cheese–Sour Cream, Chiffonade, Green Goddess , Zippy Italian
Combination	Mayonnaise, French, Thousand Island, Louis, Italian, Sour Cream, Vinegar and Oil, Bleu or Roquefort Cheese, Russian, Vinaigrette, Bleu Cheese–Sour Cream, Chiffonade
Leafy Green Salads	
Mixed Green	French, Thousand Island, Louis, Italian, Sour Cream, Vinegar and Oil, Bleu or Roquefort Cheese, Russian, Vinaigrette, Bleu Cheese–Sour Cream, Chiffonade, Green Goddess
Julienne	French, Thousand Island, Louis, Italian, Sour Cream, Vinegar and Oil, Bleu or Roquefort Cheese, Russian, Vinaigrette, Bleu Cheese–Sour Cream, Chiffonade, Green Goddess
Spring	French, Thousand Island, Louis, Italian, Sour Cream, Vinegar and Oil, Bleu or Roquefort Cheese, Russian, Vinaigrette, Bleu Cheese–Sour Cream, Chiffonade
Garden	French, Thousand Island, Louis, Italian, Sour Cream, Vinegar and Oil, Bleu or Roquefort Cheese, Russian, Vinaigrette, Bleu Cheese–Sour Cream, Chiffonade, Green Goddess , Bacon Bit, Zippy Italian
Western	French, Thousand Island, Louis, Italian, Sour Cream, Vinegar and Oil, Bleu or Roquefort Cheese, Russian, Vinaigrette, Bleu Cheese–Sour Cream, Chiffonade
Italian	Italian, French, Vinegar and Oil, Chiffonade, Bleu Cheese–Sour Cream, Bleu or Roquefort Cheese, Sour Cream, Zippy Italian

TABLE II.   CONT'D

SALADS	DRESSINGS
Chef's	French, Thousand Island, Louis, Italian, Sour Cream, Vinegar and Oil, Bleu or Roquefort Cheese, Russian, Vinaigrette, Bleu Cheese-Sour Cream, Chiffonade

Gelatin Salads

Perfection	Mayonnaise, Sour Cream, French, Boiled Dressing
Spicy Peach Mold	Mayonnaise, Sour Cream, French, Boiled Dressing, Sour Cream, Honey Cream
Cranberry-Orange	Mayonnaise, Boiled Dressing, Sour Cream, Honey Cream
Lime Glow	Mayonnaise, Boiled Dressing, Sour Cream, Honey Cream
Molded Tuna Fish	Mayonnaise, Green Goddess
Cranberry Snow	Mayonnaise, Boiled Dressing, Honey Cream, Sour Cream
Jellied Cole Slaw	Mayonnaise
Molded Spring	Mayonnaise, Thick French, Sour Cream, Boiled Dressing
Jellied Tangy Fruit	Mayonnaise, Boiled Dressing, Honey Cream, Sour Cream
Pineapple-Strawberry Soufflé	Mayonnaise, Boiled Dressing, Honey Cream, Sour Cream
Cranberry Souffle	Mayonnaise, Boiled Dressing, Honey Cream
Cinnamon-Apple	Mayonnaise, Boiled Dressing, Honey Cream
Lime-Pear Aspic	Mayonnaise, Boiled Dressing, Honey Cream
Peach and Raspberry Mold	Mayonnaise, Boiled Dressing
Cinnamon Applesauce Mold	Mayonnaise, Boiled Dressing, Honey Cream
Fruited Cheese Mold	Mayonnaise, Boiled Dressing, Honey Cream
Jellied Diplomat	Mayonnaise, Boiled Dressing, Honey Cream
Tomato Aspic	Mayonnaise, Thick French, Louis, Sour Cream, Chiffonade
Fruited Cranberry	Mayonnaise, Boiled Dressing, Sour Cream, Honey Cream
Green Island	Mayonnaise, Sour Cream, Honey Cream, Boiled Dressing
Cider	Mayonnaise, Boiled Dressing, Sour Cream

coat the salad ingredients better than the temporary kind. When the dressing is to form a temporary emulsion, no eggs are used. The oil is dripped slowly into the vinegar and flavoring ingredients. After it sets a while the oil and acid (vinegar or lemon juice) usually separate. This kind of French dressing must be stirred thoroughly or shaken before serving.

Mayonnaise is a semi-solid dressing prepared by forming an emulsion by dripping salad oil into egg yolks or yolks and whole eggs, depending on how thick you desire the mayonnaise. The quality of the mayonnaise will depend on the quality of the oil used. There are a number of oils available on the market, such as olive oil, cottonseed oil, soybean, peanut and corn oil. Olive oil is the most expensive, but does not make the best mayonnaise because its flavor is of a definite character. A good tasting mayonnaise requires an oil that is more bland in flavor, such as corn or cotton seed oil. If olive oil is used, it is best to blend it with other oils. Mayonnaise is an extremely important dressing because it is the basis for many of the other very popular dressings, such as thousand island, green goddess and bleu cheese. In some cases when mayonnaise is prepared in the commercial kitchen, a stretcher is added. The stretcher is usually prepared by thickening boiling water with diluted cornstarch and tinting it with yellow coloring. A stretcher lessens the cost of the mayonnaise and increases the quantity, but once the stretcher is added the flavor and eating qualities suffer.

Boiled or *cooked dressing* is not used to any great extent in the commercial kitchen. It is used in the preparation of some cole slaws, fruit dressing, and potato salad. Boiled dressing is simple to prepare but care must be taken not to scorch or curdle the mixture.

The following recipes are generally considered the favorites of the dining public. They can be found in restaurants from coast to coast and have satisfied many palates since salads started their climb in popularity. The recipes are listed in their order of appearance in the chapter.

SALAD RECIPES

Side salads, fruits
(Pages 133 to 137)

Waldorf salad

Diplomat salad
Fruited slaw
Pineapple slaw with sour cream
Tossed fruit salad
Pineapple and cottage cheese salad
De luxe Waldorf cheese salad
Pear and American cheese salad
Banana-pecan salad
Pear Saint Charles
Fruit salad
Belgian endive and orange salad
Orange and grapefruit salad
Avocado, grapefruit and orange salad
Cranberry relish salad
Peach and cottage cheese salad

Side salads, vegetables
(Pages 137 to 142)

Asparagus and tomato salad
Green bean and bacon salad
Spanish bean salad
Western garden salad
Carrot cole slaw
Pickled beet salad
Garden cole slaw
Macaroni salad
Kidney bean salad
Potato salad
Cucumber and onion salad
Tomato and cucumber salad
German potato salad
Sour cream cucumber salad
Carrot and raisin salad
Combination salad
Stuffed tomato with cottage cheese

Side salads, leafy green
(Pages 142 to 146)

Mixed green salad
Caesar salad
Julienne salad bowl
Spring salad
Garden salad
Western salad
Italian salad
Chef's salad

SALAD DRESSING RECIPES

FRUIT SIDE SALAD RECIPES

Waldorf salad

Ingredients: Approx. yield: 25 servings
(No. 16 dipper)

4	lbs. eating apples, cored, diced
1	lb. celery, diced
4	ozs. raisins
1/4	cup lemon juice
1	pt. salad dressing
3	ozs. walnuts, chopped
25	lettuce leaves
25	parsley sprigs
	salt and sugar to taste

Procedure

1. Wash, core, and cut apples in half. Do not peel.
2. Dice into 1/2 inch cubes, place in a mixing container.
3. Add diced celery, raisins, lemon juice and salad dressing. Toss gently until thoroughly blended.
4. Season with salt and sugar.
5. Place on a leaf of lettuce. Garnish the top with additional salad dressing. Sprinkle on the chopped nuts and top with a maraschino cherry.
6. Garnish with a sprig of parsley.

Diplomat salad

Ingredients: Approx. yield: 25 servings
(No. 12 dipper)

4	lbs. eating apples, cored, diced
1	lb. celery, diced
1½	lbs. pineapple, tidbits, canned
1/4	cup lemon juice
4	ozs. sugar
3	cups mayonnaise
1	tsp. salt

3 ozs. pecans, chopped
25 lettuce leaves
25 parsley sprigs

Procedure

1. Wash, core, and cut the apples in half. Do not peel.
2. Dice into half inch cubes, place in a mixing container. Add the lemon juice.
3. Dice the celery and pineapple slightly finer than the apples. Place in the mixing container.
4. Add the sugar, mayonnaise and salt. Toss gently until all ingredients are thoroughly blended.
5. Place on a leaf of lettuce. Garnish the top with additional mayonnaise. Sprinkle on the chopped nuts and top with a maraschino cherry.
6. Garnish with a sprig of parsley.

Fruited slaw

Ingredients: Approx. yield: 25 servings (No. 16 dipper)

6 oranges, peeled, diced
4 lbs. cabbage, shredded
5 ozs. raisins, soaked in warm water, drained
16 pineapple slices, diced
1 cup thick French dressing (variable)
1/4 cup orange juice
1/4 cup pineapple juice
3 heads iceberg lettuce, shredded
25 lettuce leaves
1/3 cup chopped parsley

Procedure

1. In a mixing container combine the oranges, cabbage, raisins, and pineapple; toss gently and chill.
2. Blend the pineapple and orange juice into the French dressing.
3. Pour the dressing over the fruit-cabbage mixture and toss gently just before serving.
4. Serve on a base of leaf and shredded head lettuce. Garnish with chopped parsley.

Pineapple slaw with sour cream

Ingredients: Approx. yield: 25 servings (No. 16 dipper)

4 lbs. cabbage, shredded

1 pt. pineapple, canned, drained, medium dice
1 pt. eating apples, medium dice
1 tbsp. onions, minced
1 tbsp. parsley, chopped
1/4 cup salad oil
2 tbsp. lemon juice
1 cup sour cream
1 cup mayonnaise (variable)
salt to taste
25 lettuce leaves
1/3 cup chopped parsley

Procedure

1. In a mixing container combine the cabbage, pineapple, apples and onions, toss gently.
2. Blend together the mayonnaise, sour cream, salad oil and lemon juice. Pour the dressing over the fruit-vegetable mixture and toss gently.
3. Season with salt and serve on a leaf of lettuce garnished with chopped parsley.

Tossed fruit salad

Ingredients: Approx. yield: 25 servings (No. 6 dipper)

1 qt. fresh strawberries, stem removed, washed
1 qt. orange sections
1 qt. grapefruit, sections, cut in half
1 qt. grapes, seeded, washed
1 qt. pineapple, canned, drained, large dice
1/4 cup mint, chopped
1 pt. mayonnaise
1 cup heavy cream, whipped
25 lettuce leaves
3 heads iceberg lettuce, shredded

Procedure

1. Drain all fruits, place in a mixing container and toss together gently.
2. Blend together the mayonnaise and whipped cream.
3. Pour the dressing over the fruit mixture and fold in gently.
4. Serve on a base of leaf and shredded iceberg lettuce, garnish with chopped mint.

Pineapple and cottage cheese salad

Ingredients: Approx. yield: 25 servings (No. 20 dipper)

25 pineapple, slices
3 lbs. cottage cheese

25 lettuce leaves
25 red maraschino cherries, with stem
3 heads iceberg lettuce, shredded
25 parsley sprigs

Procedure
1. Place the leaf lettuce on cold salad plates.
2. Cut the iceberg lettuce into quarters. Shred by cutting into very thin strips using a sharp French knife. Sprinkle the shredded lettuce on the leaf lettuce.
3. Place a slice of pineapple on the shredded iceberg lettuce.
4. Place a scoop of cottage cheese in the center of each pineapple slice.
5. Top with a red maraschino cherry and garnish with a sprig of parsley.

Note: French dressing may be served over this salad if desired.

De luxe Waldorf salad

Ingredients: Approx. yield: 25 servings (No. 12 dipper)
$1\frac{1}{2}$ qts. eating apples, diced medium
1 qt. lean ham, diced medium
$1\frac{1}{2}$ qts. celery, diced medium
3 cups mayonnaise
1 tsp. lemon juice
 salt and white pepper to taste
25 leaves leaf lettuce, washed
3 heads iceberg lettuce, shredded
25 parsley sprigs

Procedure
1. Place the apples, ham, celery and lemon juice in a mixing container.
2. Add the mayonnaise and toss gently until thoroughly mixed.
3. Season with salt and white pepper.
4. Line each cold salad plate with a leaf of lettuce. Sprinkle on the shredded iceberg lettuce.
5. Place a mound of salad in the center of each plate. Top with additional mayonnaise, garnish with a sprig of parsley.

Pear and American cheese salad

Ingredients: Approx. yield: 25 servings
50 small or 25 large pear halves, canned, drained
$1\frac{1}{2}$ lbs. Longhorn cheese, grated coarse
3 heads iceberg lettuce, shredded
25 leaves, leaf lettuce
1 pt. mayonnaise
25 parsley or watercress sprigs

Procedure
1. Line each cold salad plate with a leaf of lettuce. Sprinkle on the shredded iceberg lettuce.
2. Place one or two pear halves on the shredded iceberg lettuce. (Size of pear will determine number to use.)
3. Spot a small amount of mayonnaise in the cavity of each pear and sprinkle the grated cheese over each pear.
4. Garnish with a sprig of parsley or watercress.

Banana-pecan salad

Ingredients: Approx. yield: 25 servings
25 bananas
$\frac{1}{3}$ cup lemon or pineapple juice
10 ozs. pecans, chopped fine
25 maraschino cherries, chopped coarse
3 cups mayonnaise
1 pt. heavy cream, whipped
3 heads iceberg lettuce, shredded
25 leaves, leaf lettuce, washed

Procedure
1. Peel the bananas, cut in half crosswise and dip in the fruit juice.
2. Blend together the mayonnaise and whipped cream.
3. Dip each banana half into the mayonnaise-whipped cream mixture, coat thoroughly.
4. Roll into the finely chopped pecans.
5. Place a leaf of lettuce on cold salad plates. Sprinkle shredded iceberg lettuce on the leaf lettuce.
6. Place the banana halves in the center of each plate and sprinkle on the chopped maraschino cherries.
7. Serve with a small mound of dressing and a sprig of parsley.

Pear Saint Charles

Ingredients: Approx. yield: 25 servings (No. 20 dipper)
50 pear halves, canned, small, drained
3 lbs. cottage cheese
25 red maraschino cherries, with stem
25 leaves of lettuce, washed
3 heads iceberg lettuce, shredded
25 sprigs parsley
 red food coloring

Procedure

1. Place a leaf of lettuce on cold salad plates.
2. Cut the iceberg lettuce into quarters and shred. Sprinkle the shredded lettuce on the leaf lettuce.
3. Place a scoop of cottage cheese in the center of the shredded lettuce.
4. Blush the outside of each pear half with red color and lean two of the halves against the cottage cheese.
5. Place a maraschino cherry on top of the cottage cheese and garnish with a sprig of parsley.

Fruit salad

Ingredients: Approx. yield: 25 servings (No. 12 dipper)

8	oranges, peeled, diced medium
8	slices pineapple canned, diced medium
4	bananas, diced medium
1	canteloupe, seeded, peeled, diced medium
1	lb. grapes, cut in half, seeded
12	pear halves, canned, diced medium
12	peach halves, canned, diced medium
25	fresh strawberries, medium sized
¼	cup lemon juice
1	qt. fruit juice, drained from canned fruit
25	crisp leaves of iceberg lettuce
25	mint leaves

Procedure

1. Combine all the ingredients except the lettuce in a mixing container, toss gently and chill thoroughly.
2. Place a leaf of lettuce on cold salad plates.
3. Portion out the fruit salad and place a mound on each salad plate.
4. Top with honey cream dressing, garnish with mint leaves.

Belgian endive and orange salad

Ingredients: Approx. yield: 26 servings

13	heads Belgian endive lettuce, washed, cut in half lengthwise.
13	oranges, peeled, sliced into cartwheels (6 per orange)
26	leaves, leaf lettuce
26	parsley or watercress sprigs

Procedure

1. Line each cold salad plate with a leaf of

Fruit salad presented in an ice bowl.

lettuce. Place a half head of Belgian endive on the leaf lettuce base.
2. Line 3 cartwheels of oranges on top of the endive, overlapping the cartwheels slightly.
3. Serve with bleu cheese dressing and garnish with a sprig of watercress or parsley.

Orange and grapefruit salad

Ingredients: Approx. yield: 25 servings

10	fresh oranges, sectioned
10	fresh grapefruits, sectioned
3	heads iceberg lettuce, shredded
25	leaves, leaf lettuce or romaine, washed.
25	mint leaves, watercress or parsley sprigs

Procedure

1. Place a leaf of lettuce on cold salad plates. Sprinkle shredded iceberg lettuce on the leaf lettuce.
2. Alternate orange and grapefruit sections on the shredded iceberg lettuce, using 3 orange sections and 3 grapefruit sections.
3. Serve with some kind of fruit or French dressing. Garnish with mint leaves, watercress or a sprig of parsley.

Note: Shredded coconut can be sprinkled on top of the fruit sections to acquire a more interesting affect.

Avocado, grapefruit and orange salad

Ingredients: Approx. yield: 25 servings
8   fresh grapefruits, sectioned
8   fresh oranges, sectioned
4   avocados, ripe
25 leaves, leaf lettuce or romaine, washed
3   heads iceberg lettuce, shredded
¼   cup lemon juice
25 parsley or watercress sprigs
Procedure
1. Cut avocados in half lengthwise. Remove seed and peel. Cut slices crosswise and dip each slice in the lemon juice.
2. Place a leaf of lettuce on cold salad plates. Sprinkle shredded iceberg lettuce on the leaf lettuce.
3. Alternate avocado, orange and grapefruit sections on the shredded lettuce, using 2 orange sections, 2 grapefruit sections and 2 slices of avocado.
4. Serve with French dressing and garnish with a sprig of watercress or parsley.

Cranberry relish salad

Ingredients: Approx. yield: 25 servings (No. 16 dipper)
3   oranges, cut into wedges, do not peel
3   lbs. apples, cored, cut into wedges, do not peel
2   lbs. fresh cranberries, raw
1½ lb. sugar
25 leaves, leaf lettuce
3   heads iceberg lettuce, shredded
25 parsley sprigs
Procedure
1. Grind the apples, oranges and cranberries through the food grinder, using the coarse chopper plate. Mix together thoroughly.
2. Add the sugar and mix.
3. Line each cold salad plate with a leaf of lettuce. Sprinkle on the shredded iceberg lettuce.
4. Drain the juice off the salad and place a mound in the center of each salad plate.
5. Top with a small amount of salad dressing, garnish with a sprig of parsley.

Peach and cottage cheese salad

Ingredients: Approx. yield: 25 servings (No. 20 dipper)

25 large peach halves, canned, cut in half
3   lbs. cottage cheese
25 red maraschino cherries with stem
25 leaves, leaf lettuce
3   heads iceberg lettuce, shredded
25 parsley sprigs
Procedure
1. Line each cold salad plate with a leaf of lettuce. Sprinkle on the shredded iceberg lettuce.
2. Place a scoop of cottage cheese in the center of each salad plate.
3. On each side of the cottage cheese place a wedge of peach.
4. Place a maraschino cherry on top of the cottage cheese, garnish with a sprig of parsley.

VEGETABLE SIDE SALAD RECIPES

Asparagus and tomato salad

Ingredients: Approx. yield: 25 servings
7   fresh tomatoes (4 slices each)
50 asparagus spears, canned or fresh and cooked
3   heads iceberg lettuce, shredded
25 leaves of leaf or romaine lettuce
½   7 oz. can pimientos
25 parsley or watercress sprigs
Procedure
1. Line each cold salad plate with a leaf of lettuce. Sprinkle on the shredded iceberg lettuce.
2. Place a slice of tomato in the center of each salad plate and two asparagus spears on top of the tomato.
3. Cut the pimientos into 25 strips and lay one strip across the asparagus, garnish with a sprig of watercress or parsley.
4. Serve with any type of dressing desired.

Green bean and bacon salad

Ingredients: Approx. yield: 25 servings (No. 16 dipper)
5   lbs. frozen green beans
8   ozs. onions, cut julienne
1   lb. bacon, cut julienne
1   7 oz. can pimientos, cut julienne
1   qt. French dressing
1   tsp. garlic, minced
25 leaves of romaine lettuce

3 heads iceberg lettuce, shredded
⅓ cup chopped parsley
Procedure
1. Cook the frozen green beans in boiling salt water.
2. Drain the beans and let cool thoroughly.
3. Blend together in a mixing container the cooked beans, garlic, onions, pimientos and French dressing. Let set for at least 2 hours.
4. Cook the julienne bacon strips into a crackling, drain and let cool.
5. Line each cold salad plate with a leaf of lettuce. Sprinkle on the shredded iceberg lettuce.
6. Place a mound of the salad in the center of the plate. Sprinkle the bacon crackling over the top.
7. Garnish with chopped parsley.

Spanish bean salad

Ingredients: Approx. yield: 25 servings (No. 16 dipper)

5 cups lima beans, cooked
5 cups garbanzo (chick peas), cooked
5 cups pinto beans, cooked
5 cups kidney beans, cooked
3 cups celery, small dice
1 cup green peppers, diced
2 tbsp. chili powder
1½ tbsp. salt
1 pt. mayonnaise
8 ozs. tomato sauce
25 leaves of iceberg lettuce (lettuce cups)
25 parsley sprigs
Procedure
1. Drain all the beans and place in a mixing container.
2. Add all the remaining ingredients except the lettuce. Mix together thoroughly, cover and let set in the refrigerator overnight so all flavors can blend together.
3. Line each cold plate with an iceberg lettuce cup.
4. Place a mound of salad in the center of the lettuce cups.
5. Garnish each plate with a sprig of parsley.

Western garden slaw

Ingredients: Approx. yield: 25 servings (No. 12 dipper)

4 qts. cabbage, finely shredded
1 qt. celery, diced fine
½ cup green peppers, diced fine
½ cup pimientos, diced fine
½ cup onions, minced
2 tsp. celery seed
1 pt. mayonnaise
1 pt. sour cream
½ cup sugar
½ cup lemon juice
2 tsp. dry mustard
2 tbsp. salt
½ tsp. pepper
25 leaves of leaf or romaine lettuce
⅓ cup chopped parsley
Procedure
1. Blend together in a mixing container the cabbage, celery, green peppers, pimientos and onions.
2. Combine in a separate container the sour cream, celery seed, mayonnaise, sugar, lemon juice, dry mustard, salt and pepper, blend thoroughly.
3. Pour the dressing over the vegetable mixture, toss gently until thoroughly blended.
4. Line each cold salad plate with a leaf of lettuce.
5. Place a mound of the slaw in the center of each plate.
6. Garnish with chopped parsley.

Carrot cole slaw

Ingredients: Approx. yield: 25 servings (No. 12 dipper)

4 lbs. cabbage, shredded
1 lb. carrots, peeled, shredded
2 ozs. onions, minced
1 pt. salad dressing
½ cup vinegar, cider
1 tbsp. salt
½ tsp. white pepper
2 ozs. sugar (variable)
¼ cup chopped parsley
25 leaves of leaf, bib or iceberg lettuce
25 parsley sprigs
Procedure
1. Mix together the cabbage, carrots and onions.
2. Blend together the salad dressing, vinegar, salt, pepper and sugar in a separate container.
3. Pour the dressing over the vegetable mix-

ture and toss gently until thoroughly blended.

4. Place in the refrigerator for at least 2 hours before serving.
5. Line each cold salad plate with a leaf of lettuce.
6. Place a mound of the slaw in the center of each plate.
7. Sprinkle chopped parsley on top of each salad, garnish with a sprig of parsley.

Pickled beet salad

Ingredients: Approx. yield: 25 servings
1	#10 can beets, sliced
12	ozs. onions, small, cut into rings
2	bay leaves
1½	pts. vinegar, cider
1	tbsp. salt
4	whole cloves
1	cup sugar
25	iceberg lettuce cups
⅓	cup chopped parsley

Procedure
1. Place the beets (with juice) and onions in a bain-marie.
2. Blend the vinegar, salt, and sugar together in a separate container, stir until the sugar has dissolved.
3. Pour over the beets and add spices.
4. Cover and place in the refrigerator to marinate overnight.
5. Place a crisp lettuce cup on each cold salad plate.
6. Drain juice from beets and place a serving portion in the center of each lettuce cup.
7. Top with the onion rings, garnish with chopped parsley.

Garden cole slaw

Ingredients: Approx. yield: 25 servings (No. 12 dipper)
4	lbs. cabbage, shredded
1	cup green peppers, chopped fine
½	cup green onions, chopped fine
1	pt. carrots, shredded
1	tbsp. celery seed
1	pt. sour cream
1	pt. mayonnaise
2	tbsp. lemon juice
1	tbsp. vinegar, cider
1	tsp. horseradish
	salt and white pepper to taste

Cole slaw may be quickly prepared in a vertical cutter/mixer. Mixing was done in 12 seconds.

25	iceberg lettuce cups
⅓	cup chopped parsley

Procedure
1. Combine cabbage, green peppers, green onions, carrots and celery seed in a mixing container.
2. Whip the cream slightly and blend in the mayonnaise, lemon juice, vinegar, horseradish and season with salt and pepper.
3. Pour this mixture over the vegetables and blend thoroughly. Cover and place in the refrigerator for at least 2 hours.
4. Place a crisp lettuce cup on each cold salad plate.
5. Place a mound of the slaw in the center of each plate.
6. Garnish with chopped parsley.

Macaroni salad

Ingredients: Approx. yield: 25 servings (No. 12 dipper)
1½	lbs. elbow macaroni
12	ozs. ham, cooked, cut julienne
3	ozs. green onions, minced
3	ozs. green peppers, diced, blanched
1	lb. celery, diced
6	ozs. Longhorn cheese, grated
1	cup sweet relish
3	pts. mayonnaise
3	ozs. pimientos, diced
	salt and white pepper to taste

5 hard boiled eggs, chopped
25 leaves romaine, bib or iceberg lettuce
⅓ cup chopped parsley

Procedure

1. Boil the macaroni in salt water, drain well, let cool and place in a mixing container.
2. Add the remaining ingredients, toss gently until ,thoroughly mixed. Season with salt and pepper.
3. Line each cold salad plate with a leaf of lettuce.
4. Place a mound of the salad in the center of each lettuce leaf.
5. Garnish with chopped hard boiled eggs and parsley.

Kidney bean salad

Ingredients: Approx. yield: 25 servings (No. 16 dipper)

1 #10 can kidney beans, drained
1 pt. sweet relish
1 pt. celery, small dice
⅓ cup green onions, minced
3 ozs. pimientos, small dice
12 eggs, hard boiled, diced
1 pt. mayonnaise
  salt and white pepper to taste
25 iceberg lettuce cups
25 parsley sprigs

Procedure

1. Place the drained kidney beans in a mixing container.
2. Add the relish, celery, onions, pimientos, and half of the hard boiled eggs and mayonnaise. Toss gently.
3. Season with salt and pepper, mix thoroughly.
4. Line each cold salad plate with a lettuce cup.
5. Place a mound of the salad in the center of each lettuce cup. Garnish the top with the remaining chopped eggs and a sprig of parsley.

Potato salad

Ingredients: Approx. yield: 25 servings (No. 12 dipper)

7 lbs. red potatoes, peeled, boiled, cooled
12 ozs. celery, diced

3 ozs. pimientos, diced
3 ozs. onions, minced
4 eggs, hard boiled, chopped medium
1 oz. parsley, chopped
½ cup bacon or ham fat, cracklings, drained
½ cup sweet relish
3 cups mayonnaise
½ cup vinegar, cider
1 tbsp. sugar (variable)
  salt and white pepper to taste
25 iceberg lettuce cups
25 parsley sprigs

Procedure

1. Slice or dice the cold boiled potatoes and place in a mixing container.
2. Add the remaining ingredients, toss gently, so the potatoes will not become broken.
3. Adjust seasoning with salt and pepper.
4. Line each cold salad plate with a crisp iceberg lettuce cup.
5. Place a mound of the salad in the center of each lettuce cup.
6. Serve with a sprig of parsley.

Cucumber and onion salad

Ingredients: Approx. yield: 25 servings

5 lbs. cucumbers, peeled, sliced very thin
1½ lbs. onions, peeled, sliced thin
1 cup water
1 pt. vinegar, cider
1 cup salad oil
2 ozs. sugar
1 tbsp. salt
1 tsp. pepper
¼ cup parsley, chopped
25 iceberg lettuce cups
25 parsley sprigs

Procedure

1. Place the onions and cucumbers in a mixing container.
2. Add the water, salad oil, vinegar, sugar, salt and pepper, blend thoroughly.
3. Cover and let marinate in the refrigerator for at least 2 hours before serving.
4. Line each cold salad plate with a crisp iceberg lettuce cup.
5. Place a mound of the salad in the center of each lettuce cup. Garnish with chopped parsley.
6. Serve with a sprig of parsley.

Scoring a cucumber

Tomato and cucumber salad

Ingredients: Approx. yield: 25 servings
10   fresh tomatoes, medium size
       (5 slices each)
 2   9 inch cucumbers, unpeeled,
25   leaves of leaf or romaine lettuce
 4   heads iceberg lettuce, shredded
25   parsley sprigs

Procedure
1. Score the cucumbers with the tines of a dinner fork and slice on a bias about ⅛ to ¼ inch thick.
2. Line each cold salad plate with a leaf of lettuce, sprinkle on shredded iceberg lettuce.
3. Arrange the cucumbers and tomato slices alternately on the shredded lettuce. Use 2 slices of cucumber and 2 slices of tomatoes for each salad.
4. Garnish with a sprig of parsley, and serve with appropriate dressing.

German potato salad

Ingredients: Approx. yield: 25 servings
(No. 12 dipper)
7   lbs. red potatoes, raw
1   lb. jowl bacon, diced
1   cup vinegar, cider
8   ozs. onions, diced
3   ozs. pimientos, diced
1   pt. ham stock, hot
1   tbsp. sugar (variable)
2   tbsp. parsley, chopped
     salt and pepper to taste

Procedure
1. Boil the potatoes in their jackets, peel and dice or slice thick while still warm.
2. Fry the diced bacon in a sauce pan until crisp (a crackling). Add the diced onions and continue to cook until the onions are slightly tender.
3. Add the stock (see Chap. 11), vinegar, and sugar; bring to a boil. Pour over the potatoes.
4. Add pimientos and chopped parsley, season with salt and pepper and toss gently until all ingredients are blended thoroughly.
5. Check seasoning for desired tart or sweet taste.
6. Serve warm.

Sour cream cucumber salad

Ingredients: Approx. yield: 25 servings
 4   lbs. cucumbers, peeled, sliced thin
1½ lb. onions, peeled, sliced thin
 1   lb. tomatoes, cut julienne
 1   pt. sour cream
 1   pt. vinegar, cider
 1   pt. water
 1   tbsp. salt
 ¼ cup parsley, chopped
 1   cup mayonnaise
25   iceberg lettuce cups
 ⅓ cup chopped parsley
25   parsley sprigs

Procedure
1. Place the cucumbers, onions and tomatoes in a mixing container, toss gently.
2. Add the vinegar, sour cream, water, salt, and mayonnaise. Blend thoroughly.
3. Cover and let marinate in the refrigerator for at least 2 hours before serving.
4. Line each cold salad plate with a crisp iceberg lettuce cup.
5. Place a mound of the salad in the center of each lettuce cup. Garnish with chopped parsley.
6. Serve with a sprig of parsley.

Carrot and raisin salad

Ingredients: Approx. yield: 25 servings
(No. 16 dipper)
5   lbs. carrots, peeled, grated coarse
1   lb. raisins
3   cups water
1   tbsp. sugar

1 tsp. vinegar, cider
1 pt. mayonnaise
1 pt. French dressing
25 iceberg lettuce cups
25 parsley sprigs
Procedure
1. Place the raisins, water, sugar and vinegar in a sauce pan, bring to a boil, remove from the range and let set for 5 minutes, drain thoroughly and let cool.
2. Place the carrots and raisins in a mixing container.
3. Blend together the mayonnaise and French dressing. Pour over the carrot-raisin mixture, toss, until all ingredients are thoroughly blended.
4. Line each cold salad plate with a crisp cup of iceberg lettuce.
5. Place a mound of the salad in the center of each lettuce cup. Garnish with a sprig of parsley.

Combination salad

Ingredients: Approx. yield: 25 servings
4 large heads iceberg lettuce
5 fresh tomatoes, medium size, sliced (5 slices each)
2 9 inch cucumbers, scored, sliced
4 onions, medium size, sliced (6 to 7 slices each)
4 green peppers, seeded, sliced into rings (6 to 7 rings each)
25 leaves, leaf lettuce
25 parsley sprigs
Procedure
1. Clean, core and cut the iceberg lettuce into wedges; 6 to 7 wedges must be cut from each head.
2. Line each cold salad plate with a leaf of lettuce. Place a wedge of head lettuce on top.
3. Lean a slice of tomato and a slice of onion against the wedge of lettuce.
4. Lean two slices of cucumber against the tomato and follow with a ring of green pepper.
5. Garnish with a sprig of parsley and serve with an appropriate dressing.

Stuffed tomato with cottage cheese

Ingredients: Approx. yield: 25 servings
25 fresh tomatoes, medium size, peeled
¼ cup chives, minced

Tomatoes stuffed with cottage cheese.

¼ cup radishes, minced
3 lbs. cottage cheese
4 heads iceberg lettuce, shredded
25 leaves, leaf lettuce
25 parsley or water cress sprigs
Procedure
1. Place the tomatoes in hot water. Allow to set until skin becomes slightly loose. Remove, peel and cut out core of tomato.
2. Cut a slice off the top of each tomato and hollow out the center. Save pulp for use in some other preparation, such as soup or stew.
3. Place the cottage cheese in a mixing container. Add the minced chives and radishes, mix thoroughly.
4. Line each cold salad plate with a leaf of lettuce. Sprinkle on the shredded iceberg lettuce.
5. Place a hollowed out tomato in the center of each plate. Fill the cavity with the cottage cheese mixture.
6. Garnish with a sprig of watercress or parsley.

LEAFY GREEN SIDE SALAD RECIPES

Mixed green salad

Ingredients: Approx. yield: 25 servings (2½ to 3 oz. serving)
3 heads iceberg lettuce
1 head chicory lettuce
1 head escarole lettuce
2 heads bib lettuce
2 heads romaine lettuce
2 bch. watercress

50   tomato wedges
50   hard boiled egg quarters
1   pt. croutons (toasted or fried
      bread cubes)
Procedure
1. Wash all greens thoroughly. Chill in the refrigerator.
2. Cut the greens into bite size pieces, place in a mixing container and toss together gently.
3. Fill small salad bowls and garnish each salad with 2 wedges of tomato, 2 egg quarters and 4 or 5 croutons.
4. Serve with any appropriate salad dressing.

Note: This salad can also be served as an entree or main course salad by increasing the serving portion and serving it in a larger salad bowl.

Caesar salad

Ingredients: Approx. yield: 25 servings
SALAD
3   lb. romaine lettuce
2   lbs. bib or Boston head lettuce
1   lb. bacon, cut into 1 inch squares
50   anchovy filets
1   qt. croutons (toasted or fried bread cubes)
½   cup Parmesan cheese

Caesar salad prepared using chicory and Boston head lettuce.

8   eggs, coddled (simmered in water below boiling point 1 minute)
1   tsp. garlic, minced
DRESSING
3   cups salad oil
¼   cup oil from anchovies
1   tsp. salt
1   pinch black pepper
¼   cup lemon juice
Procedure
1. Wash all greens thoroughly, chill in the refrigerator.
2. Cut the greens into bite size pieces, placing in a mixing container, toss together gently.
3. Cook the bacon squares until slightly crisp. Drain.
4. Break the coddled eggs in a separate container. Beat slightly. Pour over the greens.
5. Add the Parmesan cheese and garlic. Toss gently until thoroughly blended.
6. Blend the salad oil, anchovy oil, salt, pepper and lemon juice together on the mixing machine at medium speed.
7. Fill the small salad bowls with the tossed greens. Refrigerate.
8. To serve ladle the dressing over the salad. Garnish with 2 or 3 crisp squares of bacon, 2 curled anchovies and croutons.

Note: This salad can also be served as an entree or main course salad by increasing the serving portion and serving it in a larger salad bowl. Caesar salad, when served à la carte is prepared and tossed at the diners table.

Julienne salad bowl

Ingredients: Approx. yield: 25 servings
3   heads iceberg lettuce
2   heads romaine lettuce
1   head escarole lettuce
½   lb. spinach
½   bch. celery, peeled, cut julienne
½   bch. carrots, cut julienne
1   bch. radishes, cut julienne
1   4 inch cucumber, cut julienne
1   bch. green onions, cut julienne
1   lb. turkey, white meat, cooked, cut julienne
1   lb. ham, cooked, cut julienne

1   lb. bacon, cooked medium, cut julienne
3   tomatoes, cut julienne
6   hard boiled eggs, chopped coarse
Procedure
1. Wash all greens thoroughly. Chill in the refrigerator.
2. Shred the greens into fairly fine strips, do not bruise. Place in a mixing container and toss together gently.
3. Add the celery, carrots, radishes, cucumber and green onions. Toss together gently a second time.
4. Fill the small salad bowls. Arrange the julienne meat and tomatoes over the greens.
5. Garnish by sprinkling the chopped eggs over the salad.
Note: This salad can also be served as an entree or main course salad by increasing the serving portion and serving it in a larger salad bowl.

Spring salad

Ingredients: Approx. yield: 25 servings
3   heads iceberg lettuce
2   heads romaine lettuce
3   heads bib lettuce
1   bch. watercress
1   head chicory lettuce
6   ozs. dandelion greens
½   bch. celery, diced
1   bch. radishes, sliced
½   bch. carrots, sliced

Procter and Gamble Co.

Spring salad

1   bch. green onions, diced
1   lb. turkey, white meat, cooked, diced
1   lb. ham, cooked, diced
50 tomato wedges
50 hard boiled egg quarters
Procedure
1. Wash all greens thoroughly. Chill in the refrigerator.
2. Cut the greens into bite size pieces, place in a mixing container and toss together gently.
3. Add the celery, radishes, carrots and green onions. Toss together gently a second time.
4. Fill the small salad bowls, arrange the diced ham and turkey over the greens.
5. Garnish with 2 tomato wedges and 2 hard boiled egg quarters.
6. Serve with any appropriate salad dressing.
Note: This salad can also be served as an entree or main course salad by increasing the serving portion and serving it in a larger salad bowl.

Garden salad

Ingredients: Approx. yield: 25 servings
3   heads iceberg lettuce
2   heads romaine lettuce
4   heads bib lettuce
2   bch. watercress
½   bch. carrots, peeled, sliced
1   bch. radishes, sliced
1   cucumber, scored, cut in half lengthwise, sliced
1   bch. green onions, diced
½   bch. celery, diced
1½ lb. ham, cooked, diced
1   lb. Swiss cheese, diced
50 tomato wedges
50 hard boiled egg quarters
Procedure
1. Wash all greens thoroughly. Chill in the refrigerator.
2. Cut the greens into bite size pieces, place in a mixing container and toss together gently.
3. Add the carrots, radishes, cucumber, green onions and celery. Toss gently a second time.
4. Fill the small salad bowls. Arrange the diced ham and cheese over the greens.
5. Garnish with 2 tomato wedges and 2 hard boiled egg quarters.

6. Serve with any appropriate salad dressing.

Note: This salad can also be served as an entree or main course salad by increasing the serving portion and serving it in a larger salad bowl.

Western salad

Ingredients: Approx. yield: 25 servings

3	heads iceberg lettuce
2	heads romaine lettuce
1	head escarole lettuce
½	lb. spinach
2	heads bib lettuce
2	bch. radishes, sliced
1	bch. celery, diced
1½	lbs. beef, cooked, cut into slightly thick strips
1	lb. ham, cooked, cut into slightly thick strips
1	lb. Longhorn cheese, cut into slightly thick strips
50	tomato wedges
50	hard boiled egg quarters

Procedure
1. Wash all greens thoroughly. Chill in the refrigerator.
2. Cut the greens into bite size pieces, place in a mixing container and toss together gently.
3. Add the celery and radishes. Toss gently a second time.
4. Fill the small salad bowls. Arrange the strips of meat and cheese over the greens.
5. Garnish with 2 tomato wedges and 2 hard boiled egg quarters.
6. Serve with any appropriate salad dressing.

Italian salad

Ingredients: Approx. yield: 25 servings

3	heads iceberg lettuce
1	head chicory lettuce
2	heads romaine lettuce
1	lb. spinach
½	bch. celery, diced
1	green pepper, diced
2	bch. radishes, sliced
1	bch. green onions, diced
1	pt. croutons (toasted or fried bread cubes)
1	cup Parmesan cheese
25	red onion slices
50	tomato wedges

50	hard boiled egg quarters
1	lb. salami, cut julienne
1	lb. pepperoni, cut julienne

Procedure
1. Wash all greens thoroughly. Chill in the refrigerator.
2. Cut the greens into bite size pieces, place in a mixing container and toss together gently.
3. Add the radishes, celery, green pepper, green onions and toss gently again.
4. Fill the small salad bowls. Arrange the julienne meat and onion rings over the greens and sprinkle on the Parmesan cheese.
5. Garnish with croutons, 2 tomato wedges and 2 hard boiled egg quarters.
6. Serve with an Italian salad dressing.

Note: This salad can also be served as an entree or main course salad by increasing the serving portion and serving it in a larger salad bowl.

Chef's salad

Ingredients: Approx. yield: 25 servings

3	heads iceberg lettuce
1	head chicory lettuce
1	head escarole lettuce

Procter and Gamble Co.

Chef salad bowl

```
  2   heads bib lettuce
  1   head romaine lettuce
1½   lb. turkey, white meat, cut julienne
1½   lb. ham, cut julienne
1½   lb. Swiss cheese, cut julienne
  ½   bch. carrots, peeled, sliced
  2   bch. radishes, sliced
  1   bch. green onions, diced
  ½   bch. celery, diced
 50   tomato wedges
 50   hard boiled egg quarters
```
Procedure

1. Wash all greens thoroughly. Chill in the refrigerator.
2. Cut the greens into bite size pieces, place in a mixing container and toss together gently.
3. Add the carrots, radishes, onions, and celery. Toss gently again.
4. Fill the small salad bowls. Arrange the julienne cheese and meat over the greens.
5. Garnish each salad with 2 tomato wedges and 2 hard boiled egg quarters.
6. Serve with any appropriate salad dressing.

MEAT SIDE SALAD RECIPES
Chicken salad

Ingredients: Approx. yield: 25 servings (No. 16 dipper)

```
  3   lbs. turkey, cooked, diced into
      ½ inch cubes
1½   lb. celery, diced
  1   pt. mayonnaise (variable)
      juice of 1 lemon
      salt and white pepper to taste
 25   leaves of leaf lettuce
  3   heads iceberg lettuce, shredded
  2   pimientos, cut into 25 small strips
 25   parsley sprigs
```

1. Place the turkey and celery in a mixing container.
2. Add the lemon juice and mayonnaise. Toss gently to blend all ingredients.
3. Season with the salt and white pepper. Toss gently a second time.
4. Line the cold salad plates with a leaf of lettuce. Sprinkle on the shredded iceberg lettuce.
5. Place a mound of the salad in the center of the salad plate. Top with additional mayonnaise and a strip of pimiento.
6. Garnish with a sprig of parsley.

Note: Chicken salad is an extremely popular salad in the commercial kitchen. It can be prepared with all white meat or a combination of white and dark meat. Chicken salad is most popular when served as an entree or main course salad. For a main course salad the serving portion is increased, a salad bowl is used and in most cases it is garnished with tomato wedges and hard boiled egg quarters.

Ham salad

Ingredients: Approx. yield: 25 servings (No. 16 dipper)

```
  3   lbs. ham, cooked, cut julienne
1½   lb. celery, sliced fine diagonal
  1   head iceberg lettuce, shredded
  1   pt. mayonnaise (variable)
  ½   cup sweet relish
      salt to taste
 50   tomato wedges
  5   hard boiled eggs, chopped medium
  ¼   cup parsley, chopped
 25   leaves, romaine lettuce
```
Procedure

1. Place the julienne ham, celery and shredded lettuce in a mixing container. Toss gently.
2. Add the sweet relish and mayonnaise. Toss gently a second time and season with salt.
3. Line the cold salad plates with a leaf of romaine lettuce.
4. Place a mound of ham salad in the center of each plate, top with additional mayonnaise, chopped parsley and chopped eggs.
5. Garnish with 2 wedges of tomato and serve.

Note: Ham salad can be served as an entree or main course. It can be presented in a large salad bowl or on a 9 inch plate. The serving portion is larger and the garnish should be increased enough to enhance the appearance.

Ham and turkey salad

Ingredients: Approx. yield: 25 servings (No. 16 dipper)

```
1½   lbs. turkey, white meat, cooked,
      diced into ½ inch cubes
1½   lbs. ham, cooked, diced into ½
      inch cubes
```

1½ lbs. celery, diced
juice of 1 lemon
1 pt. mayonnaise (variable)
salt and white pepper to taste
50 tomato wedges
50 hard boiled egg quarters
25 leaves of leaf lettuce
3 heads iceberg lettuce, shredded
25 parsley sprigs

Procedure
1. Place the ham, turkey and celery in a mixing container. Toss gently.
2. Squeeze the lemon juice over the ham and turkey mixture.
3. Add the mayonnaise and toss gently a second time. Season with salt and pepper.
4. Line each cold salad plate with a leaf of lettuce. Sprinkle the shredded iceberg lettuce over the leaf lettuce.
5. Place a mound of salad in the center of each plate. Top with additional mayonnaise.
6. Garnish each plate with 2 wedges of tomato and 2 hard boiled egg quarters.
7. Serve with a sprig of parsley.

Note: This salad can be served as an entree or main course salad by serving it in a large salad bowl and increasing the serving portion.

Fruited turkey salad

Ingredients: Approx. yield: 25 servings (No. 12 dipper)
3 lbs. turkey, cooked, diced into ½ inch cubes
1½ lbs. celery, diced
10 ozs. pineapple, canned, drained, diced
8 ozs. red grapes, cut in half, seeded
juice of 1 lemon
1 pt. mayonnaise (variable)
salt to taste
25 red maraschino cherries with stem
25 leaves of leaf or romaine lettuce
3 heads iceberg lettuce, shredded
25 parsley sprigs

Procedure
1. Place the turkey, celery, pineapple and grape halves in a mixing container. Toss gently.
2. Squeeze the lemon juice over the mixture. Add the mayonnaise and toss gen-

tly a second time. Season with salt.
3. Line each cold salad plate with a leaf of lettuce. Sprinkle the shredded iceberg lettuce over the leaf lettuce.
4. Place a mound of salad in the center of each plate, top with additional mayonnaise.
5. Garnish with a maraschino cherry and a sprig of parsley.

Note: This salad may be served as an entree or main course salad by serving it in a large salad bowl and increasing the serving portion and garnish.

Assorted julienne meat salad

Ingredients: Approx. yield: 25 servings (No. 16 dipper)
2 lb. ham sausage, cut julienne
2 lbs. Bologna sausage, cut julienne
2 lbs. Swiss cheese, cut julienne
1 green pepper, whole, sliced paper thin into rings
4 ozs. Bermuda onions, sliced paper thin into rings
⅓ cup parsley, chopped
1 cup salad oil (variable)
⅓ cup vinegar, cider
salt and pepper to taste
25 leaves of leaf or romaine lettuce
3 heads iceberg lettuce, shredded
25 parsley or watercress sprigs

Procedure
1. Place the ham sausage, Bologna sausage, Swiss cheese, green pepper and onion rings in a mixing container. Toss gently.
2. Add the vinegar and salad oil. Toss gently a second time. Season with salt and pepper.
3. Line each cold salad plate with a leaf of lettuce. Sprinkle the shredded iceberg lettuce over the leaf lettuce.
4. Place a mound of salad in the center of each plate. Top with chopped parsley.
5. Serve with a sprig of parsley or watercress.

SEAFOOD SIDE SALAD RECIPES
Tuna fish salad

Ingredients: Approx. yield: 25 servings (No. 12 dipper)
5 lbs. tuna fish canned, drained, flaked

2½ lbs. celery, diced
juice of 2 lemons
⅓ cup onions, minced
1 qt. mayonnaise (variable)
salt and white pepper to taste
3 heads iceberg lettuce, shredded
25 leaves of leaf or romaine lettuce
25 slices or wedges of lemon

Procedure

1. Place the tuna fish and celery in a mixing container. Toss gently.
2. Add the onions, juice of 2 lemons and mayonnaise. Toss gently a second time.
3. Season with salt and white pepper.
4. Line each cold salad plate with a leaf of lettuce. Sprinkle on the shredded iceberg lettuce.
5. Place a mound of the salad in the center of each plate. Top with a small amount of additional mayonnaise.
6. Garnish with a slice or wedge of lemon.

Note: Tuna fish salad can also be served as an entree or main course salad by increasing the serving portion and serving it in a large salad bowl. The garnish generally consists of hard boiled egg slices and slices or wedges of tomato. Tuna fish salad is sometimes prepared by adding sweet relish or chopped hard boiled eggs to the ingredients. Always serve a slice or wedge of lemon with seafood salads.

Shrimp salad

Ingredients: Approx. yield: 25 servings (No. 12 dipper)

5 lbs. shrimp, cooked, peeled, deveined, cut into ½ inch pieces
2½ lbs. celery, diced
juice of 2 lemons
1 qt. mayonnaise (variable)
salt and white pepper to taste
3 heads iceberg lettuce, shredded
25 leaves of leaf or romaine lettuce
25 slices or wedges of lemon

Procedure

1. Place the shrimp and celery in a mixing container, toss gently.
2. Squeeze the lemon juice over the shrimp-celery mixture, add the mayonnaise and toss gently a second time.
3. Season with salt and white pepper.
4. Line each cold salad plate with a leaf of lettuce. Sprinkle on the shredded iceberg lettuce.
5. Place a mound of the salad in the center of each plate. Top with a small amount of additional mayonnaise.
6. Garnish with a slice or wedge of lemon.

Note: Shrimp salad is most popular when served as an entree or main course salad. It is served in a large salad bowl (or on a 9 inch plate); the serving portion is increased and it is garnished with hard boiled egg quarters and tomato slices or wedges. Shrimp salad is also served as a filling in stuffed tomato salads. Always serve a slice or wedge of lemon with seafood.

Lobster salad

Ingredients: Approx. yield: 25 servings (No. 12 dipper)

5 lbs. lobster meat, cooked, cut into ½ inch pieces
2½ lbs. celery, diced
juice of 2 lemons
1 qt. mayonnaise (variable)
salt and white pepper to taste
3 heads iceberg lettuce, shredded
25 leaves of leaf or romaine lettuce
25 slices or wedges of lemon

Procedure

1. Place the lobster and celery in a mixing container. Toss gently.
2. Squeeze the lemon juice over the lobster-celery mixture. Add the mayonnaise and toss gently a second time.
3. Season with salt and white pepper.
4. Line each cold salad plate with a leaf of lettuce. Sprinkle on the shredded iceberg lettuce.
5. Place a mound of the salad in the center of each plate. Top with a small amount of additional mayonnaise.
6. Garnish with a slice or wedge of lemon.

Note: Lobster salad is most popular when served as an entree or main course salad. It is served in a large salad bowl (or on a 9 inch plate); the serving portion is increased and it is garnished with hard boiled egg quarters and tomato slices or wedges. Lobster salad is also presented on the menu in the form of a stuffed tomato salad. Always serve a slice or wedge of lemon with seafood.

King crabmeat salad

Ingredients: Approx. yield: 25 servings (No. 12 dipper)

5	lbs. king crabmeat, cooked, cut into $\frac{1}{2}$ inch pieces
$2\frac{1}{2}$	lbs. celery, diced
	juice of 2 lemons
1	qt. mayonnaise (variable)
	salt and white pepper to taste
3	heads iceberg lettuce, shredded
25	leaves of leaf or romaine lettuce
25	slices or wedges of lemon

Procedure

1. Place the crabmeat and celery in a mixing container, toss gently.
2. Squeeze the lemon juice over the crabmeat-celery mixture, add the mayonnaise and toss gently a second time.
3. Season with salt and white pepper.
4. Line each cold salad plate with a leaf of lettuce. Sprinkle on the shredded iceberg lettuce.
5. Place a mound of the salad in the center of each plate. Top with a small amount of additional mayonnaise.
6. Garnish with a slice or wedge of lemon.

Note: King crabmeat salad is most popular when featured on the menu as an entree or main course salad. It is served in a large salad bowl (or on a 9 inch plate); the serving portion is increased and it is garnished with hard boiled egg quarters and tomato slices or wedges. Crabmeat salad is also presented on the menu in the form of a stuffed tomato salad. Always serve a slice or wedge of lemon with seafood.

Assorted seafood salad

Ingredients: Approx. yield: 25 servings (No. 12 dipper)

1	lb. lobster meat, cooked, cut into $\frac{1}{2}$ inch pieces
2	lbs. shrimp, cooked, deveined, cut into $\frac{1}{2}$ inch pieces
1	lb. tuna fish, canned, drained, flaked
1	lb. king crabmeat, cooked, cut into $\frac{1}{2}$ inch pieces
2	lbs. celery, diced
$\frac{1}{3}$	cup onions, minced
	juice of 2 lemons
1	qt. mayonnaise (variable)
	salt and white pepper to taste
3	heads iceberg lettuce, shredded
25	leaves of leaf or romaine lettuce
25	slices or wedges of lemon

Procedure

1. Place the lobster, shrimp, tuna fish, crabmeat, celery and onion in a mixing container. Toss gently.
2. Add the juice of two lemons and the mayonnaise. Toss gently a second time.
3. Season with salt and white pepper.
4. Line each cold salad plate with a leaf of lettuce. Sprinkle on the shredded iceberg lettuce.
5. Place a mound of salad in the center of each plate. Top with a small amount of additional mayonnaise.
6. Garnish with a slice or wedge of lemon.

Note: Seafood salad can also be served as an entree or main course salad by increasing the serving portion and serving it in a larger salad bowl. The garnish generally consists of hard boiled egg and tomato slices or wedges. Seafood salad can also be presented on the menu in the form of a stuffed tomato salad. Serve a wedge or slice of lemon with all seafood preparations.

Shrimp and tuna fish salad

Ingredients: Approx. yield: 25 servings (No. 12 dipper)

3	lbs. tuna fish, canned, drained, flaked
2	lbs. shrimp cooked, deveined, cut into $\frac{1}{2}$ inch pieces
$2\frac{1}{2}$	lbs. celery, diced
	juice of 2 lemons
$\frac{1}{3}$	cup onions, minced
1	qt. mayonnaise (variable)
	salt and white pepper to taste
3	heads iceberg lettuce, shredded
25	leaves of leaf or romaine lettuce
25	slices or wedges of lemon

Procedure

1. Place the tuna fish, shrimp, celery and onions in a mixing container. Toss gently.
2. Add the juice of two lemons and the mayonnaise. Toss gently a second time.
3. Season with salt and white pepper.
4. Line each cold salad plate with a leaf of lettuce. Sprinkle on the shredded iceberg lettuce.
5. Place a mound of salad in the center of each plate. Top with a small amount of additional mayonnaise.

6. Garnish with a slice or wedge of lemon.

Note: Shrimp and tuna fish salad can also be served as an entree or main course salad by increasing the serving portion and serving it in a large salad bowl. The garnish generally consists of hard boiled egg and tomato slices or wedges. Shrimp and tuna fish salad can also be presented on the menu in the form of a stuffed tomato salad. Serve a wedge or slice of lemon with all seafood preparations.

Salmon salad

Ingredients: Approx. yield: 25 servings (No. 12 dipper)

    5   lbs. red salmon, canned, drained, flaked
    2½ lbs. celery, diced
        juice of 2 lemons
    1   qt. mayonnaise (variable)
    ⅓   cup onions, minced
        salt and white pepper to taste
    3   heads iceberg lettuce, shredded
    25 leaves of leaf or romaine lettuce

Procedure

1. Place the salmon, celery and onions in a mixing container. Toss gently.
2. Add the juice of two lemons and the mayonnaise. Toss gently a second time.
3. Season with salt and white pepper.
4. Line each cold salad plate with a leaf of lettuce. Sprinkle on the shredded iceberg lettuce.
5. Place a mound of salad in the center of each plate. Top with a small amount of additional mayonnaise.
6. Garnish with a slice or wedge of lemon.

Note: Salmon salad can also be served as an entree or main course salad by increasing the serving portion and serving it in a large salad bowl. The garnish generally consists of hard boiled eggs, chopped or quartered and tomato slices or wedges. Salmon salad can also be presented on the menu in the form of a stuffed tomato salad. Serve a wedge or slice of lemon with all seafood preparations.

GELATIN SIDE SALAD RECIPES
Perfection salad

Ingredients: Approx. yield: 25 servings

    ¼   cup chives, chopped

    ½   cup green peppers, chopped
    3   whole pimientos, canned, chopped
    1   qt. cabbage, shredded
    3   cups celery, minced
    ½   cup lemon juice
    1   cup vinegar, cider
    2   tsp. salt
    2   cups sugar
    3   pts. boiling water
    1   cup cold water
    2   ozs. unflavored gelatin

Procedure

1. Soak the unflavored gelatin in the cup of cold water for about 5 minutes.
2. Combine the gelatin, boiling water, salt and sugar in a mixing container. Mix until thoroughly dissolved. Let cool.
3. Add the vinegar and lemon juice, chill until gelatin is partly set, remove from the refrigerator. (Gelatin is partly set when the mixture obtains a jelly-like consistency.)
4. Fold in the remaining ingredients, pour into individual molds, refrigerate until firm.
5. Unmold by dipping the mold in warm water for a few seconds. Invert the mold on to the prepared plate, tap the mold slightly and remove. Serve on chilled greens.

Spicy peach mold

Ingredients: Approx. yield: 25 servings

    1   qt. peaches, canned, sliced, drained
    1   pt. peach syrup
    1   pt. hot water
    1   qt. cold water
    1   cup vinegar
    1½ cup sugar
    1   oz. cinnamon stick
    1   tbsp. whole cloves
    14 ozs. orange gelatin

Procedure

1. Combine the peach syrup, pint of hot water, vinegar, sugar, cinnamon stick and cloves in a sauce pan. Simmer for 15 minutes. Remove from the fire and strain.
2. Add the gelatin to the hot liquid and dissolve thoroughly.
3. Add the cold water and stir.
4. Place a small amount of gelatin in each mold. Chill until firm then remove from the refrigerator.

5. Place the sliced peaches in each mold and cover with the remaining gelatin. Return to the refrigerator and chill until firm.
6. Unmold and serve on crisp salad greens.

Cranberry-orange salad

Ingredients: Approx. yield: 25 servings
12 ozs. orange gelatin
1   pt. boiling water
3   cups cold water
1   cup celery, minced
2   tbsp. sugar
3   cans whole cranberry sauce
2   whole oranges
3   ozs. pecans, chopped
Procedure
1. Dissolve the orange gelatin in the boiling water.
2. Add the cold water, place in a pan and chill until gelatin is partly set. Remove from the refrigerator.
3. Grind the whole oranges on the food grinder, use the medium chopper plate.
4. Blend together the ground oranges, celery, whole cranberry sauce, sugar and pecans.
5. Fold this mixture into the gelatin mixture.
6. Pour into individual molds, refrigerate until firm.
7. Unmold and serve on crisp salad greens.

Lime glow salad

Ingredients: Approx. yield: 25 servings
12 ozs. lime gelatin
1   qt. boiling water
2   cups cold water
1   cup pineapple canned, crushed, drained
2   cups cottage cheese, drained
Procedure
1. Dissolve the gelatin in boiling water.
2. Add the cold water. Stir.
3. Place a small amount of the gelatin about ½ inch deep in each individual mold, refrigerate until **firm.**
4. Combine the pineapple and cottage cheese.
5. Place a small amount in each mold, cover with the remaining gelatin, return to the refrigerator and chill until firm.
6. Unmold and serve on crisp salad greens.

Molded tuna fish salad

Ingredients: Approx. yield: 25 servings
4   cans tuna fish (13 oz. can) white meat, drained, flaked
3½ tbsp. plain granulated gelatin, unflavored
1   cup cold water
1   cup boiling water
1   cup mayonnaise
1   cup catsup
½   cup lemon juice
1   cup celery, minced
½   cup sweet relish
¼   cup onions, minced
    salt to taste
Procedure
1. Soften the gelatin in cold water for about 5 minutes. Add the boiling water and stir until thoroughly dissolved, let cool.
2. Blend together the mayonnaise, lemon juice, catsup and the gelatin mixture.
3. Fold in the tuna fish, sweet relish, onions and celery, season with salt.
4. Pour into individual molds, place in the refrigerator and chill until firm.
5. Unmold and serve on crisp salad greens, topped with additional mayonnaise.

Cranberry snow salad

Ingredients: Approx. yield: 25 servings
1   cup cherry gelatin powder
1   cup lemon gelatin powder
1   qt. boiling water
1   pt. cold water
1   1 lb. can whole cranberry sauce
1   whole orange, ground medium
3   tbsp. plain granulated gelatin, unflavored
1   pt. orange juice
1   pt. mayonnaise
1   pt. sour cream
Procedure
1. Soften the unflavored gelatin in the orange juice. Heat over hot water until gelatin is thoroughly dissolved. Let cool.
2. Blend in the mayonnaise and sour cream.
3. Pour into individual molds until about half full. Refrigerate until firm.
4. Dissolve the cherry and lemon gelatin in the boiling water.
5. Add the cold water and stir.
6. Grind the whole orange on the food

grinder. Use the medium chopper plate. Blend with the whole cranberry sauce.

7. Stir the cranberry-orange mixture into the cherry-lemon gelatin mixture. Blend thoroughly.
8. Pour over the firm gelatin, completing the filling of the molds. Refrigerate until firm.
9. Unmold bottom side up and serve on crisp salad greens.

Jellied cole slaw

Ingredients: Approx. yield: 25 servings

10	ozs. lemon gelatin
1	pt. hot water
1	pt. cold water
5	ozs. vinegar, cider
2	cups mayonnaise
1	tsp. salt
1	pinch white pepper
3	pts. cabbage, shredded very fine
2	tbsp. pimientos, chopped fine
2	tbsp. green pepper, chopped fine
2	tbsp. onions, minced
1/2	tsp. celery seed

Procedure

1. Dissolve the gelatin in hot water. Add the cold water and stir.
2. Place in the refrigerator and chill until it begins to thicken.
3. Place the gelatin in a mixing bowl. Add the vinegar, mayonnaise, salt, pepper and celery seed. Whip until light and fluffy.
4. Combine the remaining ingredients and fold into the whipped gelatin mixture.
5. Pour into individual molds, refrigerate and chill until firm.
6. Unmold and serve on crisp salad greens.

Molded spring salad

Ingredients: Approx. yield: 25 servings

12	ozs. lime gelatin
1	qt. boiling water
1	qt. cold water
1/4	cup vinegar, cider
1/2	oz. salt
1	lb. cucumbers, minced
8	ozs. celery, minced
4	ozs. green onions, minced

Procedure

1. Dissolve the lime gelatin in the boiling water. Add the cold water and stir.
2. Place in refrigerator until gelatin begins to thicken.

Jell-O Gelatin

Molded spring salad

3. Combine the vinegar, salt, cucumbers, onions and celery and fold into the gelatin.
4. Pour into individual molds, refrigerate until firm.
5. Unmold and serve on crisp greens.

Jellied tangy fruit salad

Ingredients: Approx. yield: 25 servings

13	ozs. lemon gelatin
1	qt. boiling water
1	cup cold water
1	cup orange juice
2	cups ginger ale
1	qt. fruit salad, fresh or canned, drained

Procedure

1. Dissolve the gelatin in boiling water, add the cold water, orange juice and ginger ale. Stir.
2. Place in the refrigerator until partly set. Remove.
3. Fold in the drained fruit salad.
4. Pour into individual molds, chill until firm.
5. Unmold and serve on crisp salad greens.

Pineapple-strawberry soufflé salad

Ingredients: Approx. yield: 25 servings

1	oz. plain granulated gelatin, unflavored
1	qt. pineapple juice, boiling
1	pt. pineapple juice, cold
1	cup lemon juice
1/2	cup sugar
2	tsp. salt
1/2	cup mayonnaise

3 cups pineapple, canned, crushed, drained
1 pt. strawberries, fresh, sliced
Procedure
1. Soak the plain gelatin in cold pineapple juice for about 15 minutes. Add the boiling pineapple juice, salt and sugar. Stir until dissolved.
2. Add the lemon juice and chill until the gelatin is partly set. Remove from the refrigerator.
3. Place in mixing bowl, add the mayonnaise and whip at high speed until light and fluffy.
4. Fold in the pineapple and strawberries.
5. Pour into individual molds and refrigerate until firm.
6. Unmold and serve on crisp salad greens.

Cranberry soufflé salad

Ingredients: Approx. yield: 25 servings
1 oz. plain unflavored gelatin
¼ cup sugar
½ tsp. salt
1 cup boiling water
1 cup cold water
1 cup mayonnaise
¼ cup lemon juice
2 tsp. lemon rind, grated
2 1 lb. cans whole cranberry sauce
1 orange, peeled, diced
1 apple, cored, diced
½ cup walnuts, chopped
Procedure
1. Soak gelatin in cold water for 5 minutes, add the boiling water, salt and sugar. Stir until dissolved.
2. Add mayonnaise, lemon juice and rind. Place in mixing bowl and whip until light and fluffy. Refrigerate until partly thickened.
3. Place in mixing bowl and whip until again light and fluffy.
4. Fold in cranberry sauce, oranges, apples and nuts.
5. Pour into individual molds and chill until firm.
6. Unmold and serve on crisp salad greens.

Cinnamon apple salad mold

Ingredients: Approx. yield: 25 servings
12 ozs. cherry gelatin
3 cups apple juice

4 cinnamon sticks
3 lbs. apples, canned, sliced
2 ozs. lemon juice
½ tsp. salt
2 lbs. celery, minced
red color as desired
Procedure
1. Place the apple juice in a sauce pan, add the cinnamon sticks, sliced apples and red color. Bring to a boil then reduce to a simmer and cook for about 5 minutes or until the apples are slightly tender. Remove the cinnamon stick.
2. Add the gelatin and stir until dissolved. Add the salt and lemon juice. Let cool.
3. Stir in the celery gently.
4. Place in individual molds and chill until firm.
5. Unmold and serve on crisp salad greens.

Lime-pear aspic

Ingredients: Approx. yield: 25 servings
12 ozs. lime gelatin
1 qt. hot water
1 qt. cold water or pear juice
25 pear halves, canned, drained
25 maraschino cherries, without stems
Procedure
1. Dissolve the gelatin in hot water. Add the cold water or pear juice. Stir.
2. Cover the bottom (about ¼ inch deep) of a small hotel pan. Refrigerate until it is firm, remove from the refrigerator.
3. Place a cherry in the center of each pear cavity and arrange on the firm layer of gelatin, cut side down.
4. Chill the remaining gelatin until it starts to set. Pour over the pears, being careful not to move them.
5. Refrigerate until firm.
6. To unmold, place pan in warm water until the gelatin pulls away from the sides of the pan. Place a sheet pan on top of mold pan and invert.
7. Cut into serving portions, a half pear per serving and serve on crisp salad greens.

Peach and raspberry mold

Ingredients: Approx. yield: 25 servings
12 ozs. raspberry gelatin
1 qt. hot water
1 qt. cold fruit juice (raspberry and peach)

1 qt. sliced peaches, canned, drained
1 lb. raspberries, frozen, thawed, drained
Procedure
1. Dissolve the gelatin in the hot water. Add the cold fruit juice and stir.
2. Fill individual molds half full of peaches, cover with gelatin, refrigerate until firm.
3. Place the remaining gelatin in a pan. Refrigerate until it begins to thicken. Fold in the raspberries.
4. Pour over the firm peach layer, refrigerate until firm.
5. Unmold and serve on crisp salad greens.

Cinnamon applesauce mold

Ingredients: Approx. yield: 25 servings
12 ozs. lemon gelatin
1 qt. boiling water
1 pt. cold water
½ cup cinnamon candies (Imps)
3 cups applesauce
8 ozs. cream cheese
½ cup single cream
¼ cup salad dressing
Procedure
1. Place the cinnamon candies in the boiling water. Stir until dissolved.
2. Add the gelatin. Stir until dissolved.
3. Add the cold water and applesauce and stir.
4. Place in a pan and chill in the refrigerator until the mixture begins to thicken then remove.
5. Combine the cream cheese, salad dressing and cream. Blend together thoroughly.
6. Pour this mixture over the slightly thickened gelatin mixture and fold in slightly to acquire a marble affect.
7. Pour into individual molds, refrigerate until firm.
8. Unmold and serve on crisp salad greens.

Fruited cheese mold

Ingredients: Approx. yield: 25 servings
6 ozs. lemon flavored gelatin
6 ozs. strawberry flavored gelatin
1 qt. boiling water
1 qt. cold water
½ tsp. salt
3 cups cottage cheese, small curd, drained
3 cups fruit cocktail, canned, drained

¼ cup lemon juice
Procedure
1. Dissolve the lemon gelatin in 1 pt. of the hot water. Add 1 pt. of the cold water and the salt and stir.
2. Refrigerate until it begins to thicken. Fold in the drained cottage cheese.
3. Fill individual molds half full and refrigerate until firm.
4. Dissolve the strawberry gelatin in the remaining pt. of hot water. Add the remaining pt. of cold water and the lemon juice and stir.
5. Refrigerate until it begins to thicken. Fold in the drained fruit cocktail.
6. Pour the fruit mixture over the firm layer in the individual molds.
7. Refrigerate until firm.
8. Unmold and serve on crisp salad greens.

Jellied diplomat salad

Ingredients: Approx. yield: 25 servings
1 cup lemon gelatin
1 pt. hot water
1 cup cold water
12 ozs. mayonnaise
1 lb. 4 ozs. celery, diced
6 ozs. pineapple, diced
1 lb. 6 ozs. apples, unpeeled, diced
½ tsp. salt
2 tbsp. vinegar, cider
Procedure
1. Dissolve the gelatin in the hot water, add the cold water and stir.
2. Chill the gelatin until it begins to thicken.
3. Place the apples, celery, pineapple, mayonnaise, salt and vinegar in a mixing container. Toss until all ingredients are thoroughly blended.
4. Place the slightly thickened gelatin in the mixing bowl. Whip until light and fluffy.
5. Fold the gelatin mixture into the diplomat salad until well blended.
6. Place into individual molds. Refrigerate until firm.
7. Unmold and serve on crisp greens.

Tomato aspic salad

Ingredients: Approx. yield: 25 servings
2 ozs. plain unflavored gelatin
1 pt. cold water
2 qts. tomato juice
½ cup onions, diced

1   bay leaf
½   cup celery, diced
4   whole cloves
1   tsp. mustard, dry
6   ozs. sugar
¼   oz. salt
1   cup lemon juice
Procedure
1. Add the plain gelatin to the cold water and allow to set for 5 minutes.
2. Place the tomato juice, onions, bay leaf, celery, cloves, dry mustard, sugar, and salt in a sauce pan. Bring to a boil, then let simmer for 10 more minutes. Remove and strain.
3. Add the soaked gelatin to the hot tomato liquid and stir until gelatin is thoroughly dissolved.
4. Add the lemon juice and stir.
5. Pour into individual molds, refrigerate until firm.
6. Unmold and serve on crisp salad greens.

Fruited cranberry salad

Ingredients: Approx. yield: 25 servings
9   ozs. cherry gelatin
1   pt. boiling water
1   pt. cold water.
1   cup celery, diced
2   oranges, peeled, diced
1   can (1 lb.) jellied cranberry sauce
1   cup apples, diced
Procedure
1. Dissolve the gelatin in the boiling water, add the cold water and stir.
2. Place in the refrigerator until it begins to thicken then remove.
3. Peel and pit the oranges, grind, peel and dice the pulp. Crush the cranberry sauce slightly, add the celery, apples, orange peel and pulp. Mix thoroughly.
4. Fold cranberry mixture into the slightly thickened gelatin mixture.
5. Pour into individual molds and refrigerate until firm.
6. Unmold and serve on crisp salad greens.

Green island salad

Ingredients: Approx. yield: 25 servings
12   ozs. lime gelatin
3   cups hot water
3   cups pear juice
1   tsp. vinegar, cider

Jell-O Gelatin

Green island salad

½   tsp. salt
1   lb. cream cheese
½   tsp. ginger
1½   lbs. pears, canned, drained, diced
Procedure
1. Dissolve the gelatin in hot water. Add the pear juice, vinegar and salt and stir.
2. Fill individual molds ⅓ full and place in the refrigerator until firm.
3. Chill the remaining gelatin until slightly thickened. Remove from the refrigerator and place in the mixing bowl.
4. Whip at medium speed until light and fluffy.
5. Add the cream cheese and ginger. Continue to whip until the cheese is blended with the gelatin.
6. Remove from the mixer and fold in the diced pears.
7. Spread this mixture over the firm layer of gelatin in the molds. Refrigerate until firm.
8. Unmold and serve on crisp salad greens.

Cider salad

Ingredients: Approx. yield: 25 servings
12   ozs. apple flavored gelatin
3   pts. apple juice or cider
⅓   cup lemon juice
½   tsp. salt
1   cup celery, minced

1 cup carrots, grated
1 cup apples, unpeeled, minced
2 ozs. walnuts, chopped fine
Procedure

1. Heat 2 cups of the cider or apple juice, add the gelatin and dissolve thoroughly.
2. Add the remaining cup of cider or apple juice, lemon juice and salt. Allow to cool.
3. Place in the refrigerator until the gelatin starts to thicken then remove.
4. Fold in all the remaining ingredients, pour into individual molds and refrigerate until firm.
5. Unmold and serve on crisp salad greens.

SALAD DRESSING RECIPES

Mayonnaise

Mayonnaise is a semi-solid dressing prepared by forming an emulsion with eggs and salad oil. This dressing is important in the preparation of other dressings popular in the commercial kitchen.

Equipment

1. Mixing machine and wire whip attachment
2. Baker's scale
3. Qt. measure
4. Cup measure
5. Bain-marie

Ingredients: Approx: yield: 1 gal.

4 egg yolks
4 whole eggs
4 qts. salad oil
$\frac{1}{4}$ oz. mustard, dry
$\frac{1}{3}$ cup vinegar, cider
$\frac{1}{4}$ oz. salt (variable)
4 dashes, hot sauce
$\frac{1}{2}$ cup water
white pepper to taste

Preparation

1. Break the eggs. Separate 4 of the yolks from the whites.

   Method No. 1: Tap the shell on the edge of a bowl until it cracks. Break the shell in half. Holding half the shell in the right hand and half in the left hand pass the yolk back and forth, from one-half shell to the other, until the white runs off. The action of passing the yolk from one shell to the other is done over a bowl so the white can be caught as it runs off.

   Method No. 2: Tap the shell on the edge of a bowl until it cracks. Break the shell in half and let the egg run into your hand. Spread the fingers back and forth slowly letting the white run off the yolk and into a bowl that is placed below the hand.

2. Have all the equipment and ingredients handy.

Procedure

1. Place whole eggs and yolks in a mixing bowl.
2. Add salt, dry mustard, and pepper. Whip slightly.
3. Add $\frac{1}{2}$ of the oil, pouring in a very slow stream with the mixer running at high speed. This will form the emulsion.
4. Add water, vinegar and remaining oil alternately, one-third at a time.
5. Check seasoning, pour into a bain-marie and refrigerate.

Precautions and Safety Measures

1. When adding the oil pour in a very slow stream or the emulsion will not form. After the emulsion has formed, continue to pour slowly because there is still a chance it may break.
2. Have the mixing machine running at high speed throughout the entire operation.
3. When adding the salad oil to the eggs forming an emulsion one must perform the task as instructed (adding the oil in a very slow stream with the mixer running at high speed) or the emulsion may break (return to a liquid). If this should happen one must start over using four more whole eggs and four more yolks.

Note: Most commercial kitchens today have some type of rotary mixer, however, if a school or establishment should not have one, the task of preparing mayonnaise can be done by hand with a French or piano whip. Preparing mayonnaise by hand is a tiresome task and certainly not recommended.

French dressing (thick)

Thick French dressing is prepared by forming an emulsion with eggs and salad oil similar to the mayonnaise preparation, but not as thick.

Equipment

1. Mixing machine and wire whip attachment
2. Qt. measure
3. Bain-marie
4. Spoon measure

Ingredients: Approx. yield: 1 gal.

  2   whole eggs
  1   pt. vinegar, cider
  1/3 cup paprika
  1   tbsp. salt
  1   cup sugar
  1   tbsp. Worcestershire sauce
  1/2 tsp. mustard, dry
  4   qts. salad oil
  1/2 cup catsup
  1   cup lemon juice
  3   dashes hot sauce

Preparation
1. Squeeze juice from lemons.
2. Have all equipment and ingredients handy.

Procedure
1. Blend together the lemon juice, vinegar, paprika, salt, sugar, Worcestershire sauce, hot sauce, catsup and dry mustard.
2. Place the eggs in the mixing bowl. Beat at high speed on rotary mixer.
3. Pour the oil in a very slow stream while continuing to beat at high speed.
4. As the emulsion forms and the mixture thickens, add the above mixture (Step 1) to thin it down. Continue this process until all the ingredients are incorporated.
5. Check seasoning. Pour into a bain-marie and refrigerate.

Precautions and Safety Measures
1. When adding the oil pour in a very slow stream or the emulsion will not form. After the emulsion has formed, continue to pour slowly because there is still a chance it may break.
2. Operate the mixing machine at high speed at least until half of the oil is added.

Thousand Island dressing

Thousand Island dressing is prepared by using mayonnaise as a base. It is a sweet dressing because sweet pickle relish is one of the main ingredients.

Equipment
1. Bain-marie
2. Kitchen spoon
3. Qt. measure
4. French knife
5. Towel

Ingredients: Approx. yield: 1 gal.

  3   qts. mayonnaise
  3   cups chili sauce
  3   hard boiled eggs, chopped
  1   pt. sweet pickle relish, drained
  1/4 cup parsley, chopped
  2   teaspoons paprika

Preparation
1. Boil the eggs, cool, then chop fine.
2. Place the parsley on a cutting board, chop into very fine particles, using a French knife. Place the fine particles in the center of a kitchen towel. Draw up the four corners of the towel to completely envelope the chopped parsley. Holding the towel securely at the top of the enveloped parsley, place under running cold water and wash thoroughly. Twist the towel until all water is wrung from the parsley. Place the chopped parsley in a bowl.
3. Have all equipment and ingredients handy.

Procedure
1. Place the mayonnaise in a bain-marie
2. Add the remaining ingredients and blend thoroughly using a kitchen spoon.

Precautions and Safety Measures
1. Chop the eggs on heavy paper for best results.
2. Drain the sweet relish thoroughly or the dressing will be too runny.

Louis salad dressing

Louis salad dressing is similar in appearance to thousand island, but has a more tart, sharp taste.

Equipment
1. Bain-marie
2. Qt. measure
3. Kitchen spoon
4. Spoon measure
5. French knife

Ingredients: Approx. yield: 1 gal.

  2   qts. mayonnaise
  1/4 cup horseradish
  1   cup dill pickles, chopped
  3   pts. chili sauce
  1   cup celery, chopped fine
  2   tbsps. lemon juice

Preparation
1. Chop the celery very fine.
2. Chop the dill pickles very fine.
3. Squeeze the juice from the lemons.
4. Have all equipment and ingredients handy.

Procedure
1. Place the mayonnaise in a bain-marie.

2. Add the remaining ingredients and blend thoroughly, using a kitchen spoon.
Precautions and Safety Measures
1. Exercise caution when chopping the pickles and celery.

Bacon bit dressing

This is an emulsified dressing with a built-in flavor of hickory smoked bacon. If one desires a bacon flavor this dressing will certainly stimulate the appetite when served with leafy green salads.

Equipment
1. Mixing machine and wire whip attachment
2. Quart measure
3. Bain-marie
4. French knife
5. Spoon measures
6. Baker's scale
7. Food grinder
8. 1-qt. saucepan
9. Kitchen spoon
10. China cap

Ingredients: Approx. yield: 1 gal.

3	whole eggs
3	egg yolks
3	qts. salad oil
6	oz. cider vinegar
1	tbs. salt
$\frac{1}{2}$	tsp. white pepper
1	tbs. Worcestershire sauce
1	tbs. granulated sugar
6	oz. bacon bits
1	tbs. chives

Preparation
1. Using a French knife, mince the fresh chives, frozen or freeze-dried chives.
2. Remove rind from bacon or jowl bacon, using a French knife. Cut into strips, grind on food grinder with medium chopper plate. Place ground bacon in a saucepan. Cook on medium heat until a crackling is formed. Drain in china cap. Save drained grease for use in another preparation.
3. Have all equipment and ingredients handy.

Procedure
1. Place the eggs in the mixing bowl and beat at high speed on rotary mixer, using the wire whip.
2. Pour the oil in a very slow stream while continuing to beat at high speed.
3. As the emulsion forms and the mixture thickens, add the vinegar to thin it down.

Continue this process until all the vinegar and oil have gone into the mixture.
4. Add all the remaining ingredients and blend into the mixture at slow speed until thoroughly blended.
5. Remove from the mixer, place in bain-marie, and refrigerate.
Precautions and safety measures
1. Pour the oil in very slowly.
2. Keep the mixing machine running at high speed until all the oil and vinegar have been added.
3. Exercise caution when mincing the chives and grinding the bacon.
4. If dressing is too thick it can be thinned by adding water.

Italian dressing

Italian dressing is a thin, tart, spicy dressing. It can be served with any leafy green salad. Shake or stir well before using.

Equipment
1. Bain-marie
2. Qt. measure
3. Cup measures
4. Spoon measures
5. Mixing machine and whip attachment
6. Sauce pan
7. China Cap
8. Cheese cloth
9. French knife

Ingredients: Approx. yield: 1 gal.

2	qts. salad oil
$3\frac{1}{2}$	cups catsup
$3\frac{1}{2}$	cups vinegar, cider
4	cloves garlic, minced
$\frac{1}{4}$	cup chives, minced
$\frac{1}{3}$	cup Parmesan cheese, grated
3	tsp. salt
4	tsp. paprika
$\frac{1}{4}$	cup pickling spices
3	tsp. mustard, dry
$\frac{1}{2}$	cup sugar

Preparation
1. Mince the garlic and chives.
2. Have all the equipment and ingredients handy.

Procedure
1. Place the vinegar, pickling spices and garlic in a sauce pan, bring to a boil then reduce to a simmer and cook for 3 more minutes.

2. Remove from the range and allow to cool. Strain through a china cap covered with a cheese cloth.
3. Combine in the mixing bowl the paprika, salt, dry mustard, sugar and Parmesan cheese. Blend in the strained vinegar mixture and mix thoroughly until smooth on the rotary mixer.
4. Pour in the salad oil in a very slow stream while beating briskly.
5. Add the catsup and chives, blend in thoroughly.
6. Remove from the mixer, place in a bain-marie and refrigerate.

Precautions and Safety Measures
1. Pour the oil in very slowly.
2. If the mixture starts to splash when the oil is only half added, reduce the speed of the mixer to number 2 position.

Zippy Italian dressing

This dressing is an emulsified salad dressing with a smooth, creamy texture. Ingredients are added to produce a peppy flavor that will perk up a tired appetite when served with leafy green salads.

Equipment
1. Mixing machine and wire whip attachment
2. Quart measure
3. Bain-marie
4. Spoon measure
5. French knife

Ingredients: Approx. yield: 2 qts.

2	whole eggs
1½	qts. salad oil
1	cup cider vineger
½	tsp. black pepper
1	tbs. garlic, minced
1	tsp. salt
1	tbs. lemon juice
1	tbs. English mustard
4	drops Tabasco sauce
1	tbs. Worcestershire sauce
2	tbs. green onions, chopped
½	tbs. tarragon, chopped
1	tsp. sugar

Preparation
1. Using a French knife, mince the garlic and green onions, chop the tarragon.
2. Squeeze the juice from the 2 lemons.
3. Have all equipment and ingredients handy.

Procedure
1. Place the eggs in the mixing bowl and beat at high speed on rotary mixer, using the wire whip.
2. Pour the oil in a very slow stream while continuing to beat at high speed.
3. As the emulsion forms and the mixture thickens, add the vinegar to thin it down. Continue this process until all the vinegar and oil are blended in.
4. Add all the remaining ingredients, mixing at slow speed, until thoroughly blended.
5. Remove from the mixer, place in bain-marie, and refrigerate.

Precautions and safety measures
1. Pour the oil in very slowly.
2. Keep the mixing machine running at high speed until all the oil and vinegar have been added.
3. Exercise caution when mincing and chopping some of the ingredients.

Sour cream dressing

Sour cream dressing is prepared by blending sour cream, wine vinegar and lemon juice with seasoning. This dressing is excellent when served with most salad greens.

Equipment
1. Bain-marie
2. French knife
3. Wire whip (hand)

Ingredients: Approx. yield: 1 gal.

3	qts. sour cream
1	cup wine vinegar
1	cup lemon juice
2	cups sugar (variable)
1	cup onions, minced
¼	cup mustard, dry
	salt to taste

Preparation
1. Mince the onions
2. Have all the equipment and ingredients handy.

Procedure
1. Place the dry mustard and sugar in a bain-marie, add the vinegar slowly and blend together until smooth.
2. Add the remaining ingredients and whip until thoroughly blended.
3. Season with salt and refrigerate.
4. Serve this dressing very cold.

Precautions and Safety Measures
1. Be sure the dry mustard and sugar are thoroughly dissolved into the vinegar before adding the remaining ingredients.

Green goddess dressing

Green goddess dressing is prepared with a mayonnaise base. It has a flavor of anchovy. The term **green** is used because finely chopped green onion stems flow through the sauce. This sauce is an excellent choice for seafood or leafy green salads.

Equipment
1. Bain-marie
2. French knife
3. Spoon measure
4. Qt. measure
5. Kitchen spoon

Ingredients: Approx. yield: 1 gal.
2 qts. mayonnaise
1 qt. heavy sour cream
1 cup vinegar, tarragon
1 cup scallions, minced
1 cup anchovies, drained, chopped fine
3 cloves garlic, minced
1 tsp. sugar
 salt and white pepper to taste

Preparation
1. Mince the scallions and garlic.
2. Chop the anchovies very fine using a French knife.
3. Have all the ingredients and equipment handy.

Procedure
1. Place all the ingredients in a bain-marie and blend thoroughly.
2. Season with salt and white pepper.
3. Place in the refrigerator.

Precautions and Safety Measures
1. Drain the anchovies before chopping.
2. Exercise caution when chopping with the French knife.

Vinegar and oil dressing

Vinegar and oil dressing is a blend of salad oil and vinegar. Cider vinegar is used most often; however, wine vinegar will also produce excellent results. This type of dressing should be shaken or stirred well before using.

Equipment
1. Cup measure

2. Bain-marie
3. Spoon measure
4. Wire whip (hand)

Ingredients: Approx. yield: 1 qt.
3 cups salad oil
1 cup vinegar, cider
1 tbsp. salt
½ tsp. white pepper
1 tsp. sugar

Preparation
1. Have all equipment and ingredients handy.

Procedure
1. Place all the ingredients in a bain-marie and whip briskly until thoroughly blended.

Precautions and Safety Measures
1. Shake or stir well before serving.

French dressing (thin)

Thin French dressing is prepared by forming a temporary emulsion. This type of dressing will separate soon after mixing so it must be shaken or stirred well before serving.

Equipment
1. Mixing machine and whip attachment
2. Qt. measure
3. French knife
4. Baker's scale
5. Spoon measure
6. Bain-marie

Ingredients: Approx. yield: 1 gal.
2½ qts. salad oil
1 qt. vinegar, cider
2 ozs. paprika
1 tsp. white pepper
¾ ozs. mustard, dry
2½ ozs. salt
2 ozs. sugar
½ oz. garlic, minced
3 cups catsup
2 tbsp. Worcestershire sauce
1 tsp. hot sauce

Preparation
1. Mince the garlic.
2. Have all equipment and ingredients handy.

Procedure
1. Combine all the dry ingredients in the mixing bowl, mix slightly using the wire whip.
2. Add the oil and vinegar alternately, whipping briskly. Reduce speed of mixer.

3. Add the garlic, catsup, Worcestershire sauce and hot sauce. Blend thoroughly.
4. Pour into a bain-marie and refrigerate.

Precautions and Safety Measures
1. Pour oil and vinegar very slowly into the dry ingredients.
2. If the mixture starts to splash when the oil is only half added, reduce the speed of mixer to number 2 position.

Bleu or Roquefort cheese dressing

Bleu or Roquefort cheese dressing is one of the very popular dressings. To prepare this dressing either bleu or Roquefort cheese can be used. Roquefort is a product of France and is superior in taste and quality to the American bleu cheese. The cheese is added to a clear or uncolored French dressing and is excellent when served with leafy green salads.

Equipment
1. Qt. measure
2. Cup measure
3. Spoon measure
4. Bain-marie
5. Mixing machine and whip attachment
6. French knife
7. Kitchen spoon

Ingredients: Approx. yield: 1 gal.

4	whole eggs
3	qts. salad oil
½	cup lemon juice
1	cup vinegar
½	cup sugar
1	tsp. mustard, dry
2	tsp. salt
1	tbsp. Worcestershire sauce
3	drops hot sauce
12	ozs. bleu or Roquefort cheese, chopped

Preparation
1. Chop the bleu or Roquefort cheese into fairly fine chunks with a French knife.
2. Squeeze the juice from the lemons.
3. Break the eggs.
4. Have all equipment and ingredients handy.

Procedure
1. Place the dry mustard, salt, sugar, and lemon juice in the mixing bowl. Whip until thoroughly blended.
2. Add the eggs and continue to whip, using slow speed.

3. Increase the speed of the mixer to the No. 3 position and pour in the oil in a very slow stream to form a permanent emulsion. Add the vinegar at intervals to thin slightly.
4. Reduce the speed of the mixer to the slow position. Add the Worcestershire sauce and hot sauce. Blend in.
5. Remove from the mixer and fold in the bleu or Roquefort cheese.
6. Check the seasoning. Pour into a bain-marie and refrigerate until ready to use.

Precautions and Safety Measures
1. Before attempting to chop the cheese, freeze it, to make the job less difficult.
2. Pour the oil in a very slow stream while the mixer is operated at high speed so there will be no problem forming the emulsion.

Honey cream dressing

Honey cream dressing is a blend of cream cheese, mayonnaise and honey. This dressing is ideal to serve with fruit salads or fruit plates.

Equipment
1. Qt. measure
2. Spoon measure
3. Cup measure
4. Bain-marie
5. Mixing machine and paddle attachment
6. Kitchen spoon

Ingredients: Approx. yield: 1 gal.

2½	qts. mayonnaise
3	cups white cream cheese
¼	cup lemon juice
2	cups honey
¼	cup pineapple juice
1	tsp. salt

Preparation
1. Squeeze the juice from the lemons.
2. Have all the equipment and ingredients handy.

Procedure
1. Place the cream cheese and honey in the mixing bowl. Using the paddle, blend at slow speed until smooth.
2. Add the lemon and pineapple juice. Blend in thoroughly while continuing to mix in slow speed.
3. Add the mayonnaise and salt. Blend in and mix until the mixture is smooth.

4. Place in a bain-marie and refrigerate until ready to use.
Precautions and Safety Measures
1. The entire mixing process should be done in **slow** speed.
2. Do not remove the dressing from the mixer until it is very smooth.

Russian dressing

Russian dressing is similar to thousand island dressing, but caviar is generally added. The caviar may be the **true** caviar, which is the roe (eggs) of the sturgeon fish, or the **imitation** caviar, which is the dyed roe of whitefish. This dressing blends well with most leafy green salads.
Equipment
1. Qt. measure
2. Kitchen spoon
3. Bain-marie
4. Spoon measure
Ingredients: Approx. yield: 1 gal.
3 qts. mayonnaise
3 cups chili sauce
¼ cup paprika
1 cup pimientos, chopped fine
1 cup caviar, if desired
Preparation
1. Chop the pimientos very fine.
2. Have all equipment and ingredients handy.
Procedure
1. Place all the ingredients in a bain-marie and blend together thoroughly, using a kitchen spoon.
2. Place in the refrigerator until ready to use.
Precautions and Safety Measures
1. If imitation caviar is used, drain before blending it.

Vinaigrette dressing

Vinaigrette dressing is prepared by adding finely chopped herbs, pickles, hard boiled eggs, etc., to a vinegar and oil dressing. This dressing is an excellent choice to serve with vegetables and salad greens.
Equipment
1. Qt. measure
2. Spoon measure
3. Kitchen spoon or ladle
4. Bain-marie
5. French knife

Ingredients: Approx. yield: 1 qt.
1 qt. vinegar and oil dressing
1 tbsp. parsley, chopped
1 tbsp. chives, minced
1 tbsp. olives, chopped fine
1 tbsp. capers, chopped fine
1 hard boiled egg, chopped fine
1 tbsp. sweet pickles, chopped fine
1 tbsp. pimientos, chopped fine
Preparation
1. Chop the parsley, chive, olives, caper, hard boiled eggs, sweet pickles and pimientos, very fine.
2. Prepare the vinegar and oil dressing. (See recipe this chapter.)
3. Have all equipment and ingredients handy.
Procedure
1. Place all the ingredients in a bain-marie and blend thoroughly.
2. Place in the refrigerator until ready to use.
Precautions and Safety Measures
1. Chop the hard boiled eggs gently on heavy brown paper for best results.

Honey dressing

Honey dressing is a sweet dressing used exclusively with fruit plates and fruit salads.
Equipment
1. Cup measure
2. Spoon measure
3. Wire whip (hand)
4. Bain-marie
Ingredients: Approx. yield: 1 qt.
1 cup honey
1 cup sugar
2 tsp. salt
2 tsp. paprika
3 tsp. mustard, dry
3 tsp. celery seed
½ tsp. white pepper
1 cup lemon juice
2 cups salad oil
Preparation
1. Squeeze the juice from the lemons.
2. Have all equipment and ingredients handy.
Procedure
1. Place all the ingredients in a bain-marie and whip by hand until all ingredients are thoroughly blended.
2. Refrigerate until ready to use.
Precautions and Safety Measures
1. Stir or shake well before serving.

Bleu cheese sour-cream dressing

Bleu cheese-sour cream dressing is prepared by blending the chopped bleu cheese with a rich sour cream dressing. This dressing is outstanding when served with a leafy green salad.

Equipment
1. Cup measure
2. Spoon measure
3. Bain marie
4. French knife
5. Kitchen spoon
6. Wire whip (hand)

Ingredients: Approx. yield: 1 qt.

1	cup bleu cheese, chopped
1½	cups sour cream
1½	cup mayonnaise
2	tbsp. lemon juice
¼	cup onion, minced
2	tbsp. mustard, dry
2	tbsp. chives, minced

Preparation
1. Chop the bleu cheese with a French knife.
2. Squeeze the juice from the lemons.
3. Mince the onions and chives.
4. Have all equipment and ingredients handy.

Procedure
1. Place the mayonnaise, sour cream, dry mustard, and lemon juice in a bain-marie and whip until smooth.
2. Fold in the onions, chives and bleu cheese.
3. Check the seasoning and place in the refrigerator until ready to use.

Precautions and safety measures
1. Soften the dry mustard in the lemon juice before adding it to the other ingredients.
2. Freeze the bleu cheese before chopping for best results.

Boiled or cooked dressing

Boiled or cooked dressing is used with items that require a certain degree of tartness such as cole slaw, potato salad and some fruit salads.

Equipment
1. Qt. measure
2. Cup measure
3. Spoon measure
4. Double boiler
5. Wire whip (hand)

Ingredients: Approx. yield: 2 qts.

1½	qts. milk
1	cup flour
½	cup sugar
2	tbsp. salt
10	ozs. vinegar, cider
3	tbsp. mustard, dry
10	whole eggs
½	cup butter

Preparation
1. Break the eggs.
2. Have all equipment and ingredients handy.

Procedure
1. Place the eggs in the top of a double boiler.
2. Add the flour, sugar, salt and dry mustard. Blend together.
3. Add the milk and whip until mixture is smooth.
4. Drip the vinegar in very slowly.
5. Cook in the double boiler, whipping constantly, until the mixture is thickened and smooth.
6. Remove from heat and whip in the butter.
7. Pour into a bain-marie, let cool and refrigerate until ready to use.

Precautions and safety measures
1. Whip the mixture constantly while cooking to insure a smooth dressing.

Chiffonade dressing

Chiffonade dressing is prepared by using a thick French dressing as a base and blending in the other ingredients such as the chopped beets, hard boiled eggs etc. This dressing is exceptionally good when served with a leafy green salad.

Equipment
1. Qt. measure
2. French knife
3. Cup measure
4. Bain-marie
5. Kitchen spoon

Ingredients: Approx. yield: 1 gal.

3	qts. thick French dressing
1	pt. beets, canned, drained, chopped very fine
8	hard boiled eggs, chopped fine
¼	cup parsley, chopped fine

1 green pepper, minced
⅓ cup chives, minced
Preparation
1. Chop and wash the parsley.
2. Mince the chives and green pepper.
3. Prepare the thick French dressing. (See recipe this chapter.)
4. Chop the hard boiled eggs fairly fine.
5. Drain and chop the beets fairly fine.
6. Have all equipment and ingredients handy.

Procedure
1. Place all the ingredients in a bain-marie and blend thoroughly, using a kitchen spoon.
2. Place in the refrigerator until ready to use.
Precautions and safety measures
1. Chop the eggs on heavy brown paper for best results.
2. Exercise caution when chopping the vegetables and herbs.

chapter 11

cheese preparation

■ Of all the foods man has created and perfected for his dining pleasure, cheese is the most unusual. Not only is cheese one of the oldest known foods, it is also one of the most diversified. Cheese is the result of fluid milk turning into a solid, it has good keeping qualities and in some cases will keep indefinitely. Of importance to the food service operator is the fact that cheese is the only food that may be used on any part of the menu, from appetizer to the dessert, with good results.

Cheese has had an important role in the history and economics of many nations because it provided the nourish- ment of milk in a solid form so important in the nomadic life of early times. Cheese was such a highly prized food in early days, that it is said to have been the first medium of exchange. The early Greeks considered cheese to be of a divine origin and offered it to their gods. Cheese is also mentioned in the Old Testament. It has been doubted if the Romans would have been so successful in their many conquests without the nourishment provided by cheese. Genghis Kahn, the great war lord, depended on cheese as the basic ration for his soldiers and ever since cheese has been one of the vital foods used by marching men. In World War I Mr.

Kraft perfected process cheese that could be canned and kept for very long periods of time. This helped the army solve one of their very pressing problems. In World War II every package of K-rations contained a can of Cheddar cheese.

Cheese has been described as the wine of food and for good reason. Like wine, cheese is made from another product and has the same association to milk as wine does to grapes. Both cheese and wine are produced in numerous varieties; the many varieties are developed because of the difference in water, climate, temperature, etc. A cheese that is made in one locality can not be exactly reproduced in another, some change always takes place. People have been trying for centuries to produce Roquefort outside of France, Stilton outside of England and Edam outside of Holland, but they have never been able to achieve very good results. They have produced good imitations, and in some cases have even developed a new and exciting product.

No one is sure how cheese making was discovered. The most common of all the legends, however, describes it this way: An ancient traveler set forth on a long hot journey carrying with him some milk in a canteen which had been made from the stomach of a calf or sheep. As the traveler trudged along he became thirsty and stopped to satisfy his thirst with a refreshing drink of milk. As he began to drink he discovered that the milk had turned into a curdy white mass. The liquid that drained from the canteen was thin and watery and did not at all look or taste like the creamy milk that he had placed in the canteen hours before. It is assumed that his curiosity was aroused enough to taste this semi-solid milk product. Finding it to his liking he passed the story on to his friends, who in turn repeated the experiment until it was discovered that the canteen made from the stomach of a sheep or calf was causing the change in the milk. Later, it was discovered that certain enzymes found in a calf or sheep's stomach were the agent that converted milk into curds and wheys. From this curd cheese is made.

Otto Roth and Co., Inc.

American or Cheddar cheese shown in the aging room.

All cheese is made from milk, most of it from cow's milk; however, it is also made from the milk of sheep, buffalo, reindeer, asses, goats, and camels. The chemistry involved in changing the milk to cheese is quite complex and many factors enter into the curing of the cheese to produce the numerous varieties. However, all cheese is begun by the action of the rennet, lactic acid, or some type of culture made from bacteria. This starts the process within the milk which causes the milk to coagulate or curdle.

Cheese has been extensively experimented with throughout the world. The result is the many different textures, flavors, and names that we find in cheese products today.

Popular cheeses

Cheeses are classified into three general groups: hard, semi-hard, and soft. There are also about 18 distinct types and over 400 varieties. In this chapter we would like to familiarize the student with some of the more popular cheeses used in the commercial kitchen today. We are primarily interested in their origin, chief characteristics and uses.

American cheese: This cheese, also known as Cheddar and American Cheddar, is the most commonly used variety in the United States and a great favorite in all English speaking countries. American cheese can be of four different types: American Cheddar, American Colby, American washed curd, and American stirred curd. The difference largely depends on the way the curd is cut and handled and the way the cheese is aged. These cheeses are packed in different styles, such as daisy, longhorn, flat, twin, young American, and Cheddar. American cheese is classified as a hard cheese and is made from cow's milk which may be whole, partly skimmed, or skimmed. This cheese ranges in color from nearly white to dark yellow. It has a smooth solid texture and is mild to sharp in fla-

vor, depending on the length of time it was aged. In the commercial kitchen American cheese is used on grill cheese sandwiches, open face and closed sandwiches, in salad bowls, as a garnish for other items, in Welsh rarebit, cheese sauce, cheese platters, etc. This cheese is very versatile and each day new ways are being found to use it.

Bakers' cheese: Bakers' cheese is a skim-milk cheese very much like cottage cheese, but softer and finer grained. In making bakers' cheese the curd is drained in bags rather than in vats. This cheese is used in making cheese cakes, pies, and certain kinds of pastry.

Blue cheese (bleu): Blue cheese or bleu cheese is a hard cheese of the same type as the French bleu and Roquefort, the Italian Gorgonzola, and the English Stilton. It is made from cow's milk and is characterized by the green-blue mold which flows through the cheese and imparts the fine flavor. Blue cheese is one of the most recent European cheeses to be made successfully in the United States. It was introduced about 1918 when information was made available on the methods of manufacture and curing. Blue cheese is generally produced in wheels weighing about seven pounds. In the commercial kitchen blue cheese is used in making blue cheese dressing, salads, sandwiches, and cheese platters for the buffet tables.

Brick cheese: This cheese is strictly an American development. It was introduced in the mid-nineteenth century and today is made principally in Wisconsin. It is a semi-soft, sweet-cured cheese made from cows milk and has a mild, sweetish flavor and a texture that is firm, yet elastic, with many small, round pin holes. It slices well and does not crumble. Brick cheese got its name because it was originally packaged in brick-shaped sizes, and because bricks were used for weighing the presses. Brick cheese is usually made in four to six pound sizes. Brick cheese

American Dairy Assoc.

Various commercial cheeses.

1. Cheddar
2. Colby
3. Monterey
4. Process
5. Cheese food
6. Cheese spread
7. Cold pack
8. Gouda and Edam
9. Camembert
10. Münster
11. Brick
12. Swiss
13. Limburger
14. Blue
15. Gorgonzola
16. Provolone
17. Romano
18. Parmesan
19. Mozzarella and Acamorze
20. Cottage cheese
21. Cream cheese

is used most often in the commercial kitchen for buffet cheese platters and sandwiches.

Brie cheese: Brie is a soft ripened cheese with a strong odor, a sharp taste, and a creamy white color. It originated in France in the Department of Seine-et-Marne and has been a favorite of the European countries since 1407. Brie is very similar to Camembert cheese, another of the popular French cheeses, but due to variations in manufacturing and ripening there are differences in flavor and aroma. Brie cheese is usually produced in small disks and is known chiefly as a buffet or dessert cheese.

Camembert cheese: Camembert is a soft cheese made from cows' milk. It has a yellowish color and a waxy creamy consistency. The rind is very thin and has the appearance of felt. This cheese is one of the most famous of all the wonderful French cheeses. It became popular during the time of Napoleon. It seems that this cheese was served to Napoleon at one of the local inns. He liked it immediately and requested that Marie Harel, a dairy-maid from the Hamlet of Camembert and the creator of this delicious cheese, be presented to him. At this time the cheese was yet unnamed. Napoleon named it Camembert and Madame Harel became a famous person. Today Camembert-type cheese is made in many countries including the United States. Camembert cheese is served most often as a dessert accompanied with crackers and fruit. For best eating qualities, the cheese should be left at room temperature for at least eight hours before serving.

Cheddar cheese: This cheese is also known as American and American Cheddar. It originated in the village of Cheddar in Somersetshire, England. The date of origin is not known, but Cheddar has been made since the 16th century. The cheddaring process was brought to the United States with the colonists in the 1600's and it is safe to assume that Cheddar was one of the food items that kept the pilgrims alive that first winter in Plymouth. We do not eat the true English Cheddar here in the United States because of import restrictions.

Americans have been producing Cheddar at a rate of 900 million pounds a year, which is about 75 percent of the cheese made in the United States. It is no wonder that we give it the name American Cheddar. Cheddar cheese is used in many ways in the commercial kitchen. It is used in the preparation of Welsh rarebit, golden buck, fondue, souf-

Otto Roth and Co., Inc.

Cheshire cheese from Cheshire, England.

flés, canapé spreads, sandwiches, and that old American favorite, Cheddar cheese with apple pie.

Cheshire cheese: This is the oldest of the many fine cheeses that originated in England. It is classed as a hard cheese and is made from cow's milk. It takes its name from Cheshire county where it originated and where it continues to be produced today. Cheshire cheese is similar to Cheddar cheese, but has a more crumbly texture and is not as compact as Cheddar. It is sold in its natural white color or in deep yellow color. The yellow is the result of adding annatto (a type of dye) to the curd. Cheshire cheese cannot be imitated because of the soil and the kind of grass that grows in England. The grazing lands have rich deposits of salt and this is passed along to the cows, which produce a salty milk. Cheshire cheese is salty, but this salty taste is not so noticeable when consuming this very tasty cheese. Cheshire cheese is used in the same way as Cheddar and makes an excellent Welsh rarebit or fondue.

Cottage cheese: Cottage cheese is a soft cheese and perhaps the simplest of all cheese varieties. It is known by many names which are Dutch cheese, pot cheese, smearcase, and, in some localities, popcorn cheese (because of its large curds). It is marketed in about five different varieties: small curd, large curd, flake curd, home style, and whipped. Actually, however, only two types are produced, plain and creamed. Cottage cheese can be made in the home as well as the factory with fine results. Large quantities of cottage cheese are consumed in the United States today because of its very fine, mild sour taste and because it is an excellent choice for those on reducing diets. In the commercial kitchen cottage cheese is put to many uses. It is used for appetizers, salads, cheesecakes, pies, and also in some cooked dishes. It is very perishable and should always be stored at a low temperature.

Cream cheese: This is a soft cheese, mild and rich in flavor. It is an uncured cheese made from cream or a mixture of cream and milk. It is similar to the unripened French Neufchâtel, but higher in fat content. Cream cheese is one of the most popular cheeses in the United States. There are many brands of cream cheese on the market today and all have good eating qualities; however, they are not necessarily the same. The difference, if any, lies in the use of gum arabic, a stabilizer used to extend the keeping qualities of the cheese. The cream cheese that does not contain gum arabic will have a lighter, more natural texture, although it will not keep as well. Cream cheese is used extensively in the commercial kitchen in the preparation of such items as canapé spreads, sandwiches, salads, salad dressings, and numerous desserts.

Edam cheese: Edam is another cheese that is named after its birthplace, in this case Edam in the province of North Holland, Netherlands. Edam is a hard cheese,

mild in flavor, and is made from cow's milk. It possesses a rather firm and crumbly texture and is usually shaped into what might be described as a flat ball. In the Netherlands the cheese for export is colored red on the outside, rubbed with oil, wrapped, and shipped. The red coating is one of the chief characteristics of the cheese. However, the cheese made for consumption within the country is rubbed with oil, but not colored. Edam cheese made in the United States is covered with a thin coating of red paraffin to give it its characteristic color. It is used most often as a dessert cheese on platters and on buffet tables where its color helps to stimulate the appetite.

Gorganzola cheese: Gorganzola is Italy's contribution to the blue-green veined cheese family. It is the Italian cousin of the French Roquefort, the English Stilton, and the American bleu cheese. It originated in the village of Gorganzola, near Milan; however, very little of the cheese is made there now. Today, it is made chiefly in the regions of Lombardy and Piedmont. The cheese is mottled with the characteristic blue-green veins which are produced by a mold called *penicillium glaucum.* The surface of the cheese was originally protected with a reddish coat made by mixing brick dust, lard, and coloring together and smearing it on the cheese. Today this method has been eliminated and the cheese is protected with tinfoil. Gorganzola cheese is generally cured for a period of six months to a year. Gorganzola is increasing in popularity in the United States where it is used in salads, salad dressings, and as a dessert and buffet cheese.

Gouda cheese: Gouda is very similar to Edam cheese. Like Edam, it is a hard, sweet curd cheese. It also originated in Holland but in a different province. Gouda was first produced in the Dutch province of Gouda and, as is the custom, was named after its place of birth.

The main difference between Edam and Gouda is that Gouda contains more fat. Gouda is usually shaped like a flattened ball or formed into a loaf. Neither Edam or Gouda are especially recommended for cooking. They are intended to be dessert or buffet type cheeses.

Gruyère cheese: Gruyère is a hard cheese similar in many respects to Emmentaler cheese (also known as Swiss cheese). This cheese originated in western Switzerland in the village of Gruyère, which is near the French border. The manufacture of Gruyère cheese is an important industry in France as well as in areas of western Switzerland. In fact there is a slight dispute between the two countries regarding which produces the best Gruyère cheese. To attempt a comparison would be unfair because both are of excellent quality and very satisfying to the palate. Gruyère cheese, as stated before, is much like Emmentaler cheese, but has smaller holes and a sharper taste. It is also manufactured in smaller wheels. Although the Swiss export more Emmentaler than Gruyère, they prefer the Gruyère over the Emmentaler for their own consumption. Gruyère is an excellent cheese to use for cooking. In commercial establishments it is used in such preparations as fondue, veal cordon bleu, sautéed veal chops Gruyère, and many others. Gruyère is also one of the many cheeses used in *process cheese,* but the result is an entirely different product from true Gruyère.

Liederkranz cheese: Liederkranz is a soft, surface-ripened cheese, made from cow's milk and manufactured in the state of Ohio. It is very similar to Limburger cheese in body, flavor, aroma, and method of ripening. Liederkranz, like brick, is strictly American. Liederkranz was discovered by a New York cheese maker in Monroe, New York, in 1882. It was named after Liederkranz Hall in New York where it was first enjoyed by a singing group to which the maker belonged. Liederkranz was made for years in upper-state New York, but in recent years the plant was moved to Van Wert, Ohio. Ohio thus is the largest producer of this cheese. Liederkranz is packaged in small oblong loaves weighing four ounces each and, like Camembert, is never marketed in bulk. Liederkranz cheese will spoil rapidly, so it must be watched closely once it is placed in a store's dairy case. To be enjoyed to its fullest extent, the cheese should be brought to room temperature before serving. This procedure should be followed when serving any cheese. Liederkranz is always served as a dessert or buffet cheese accompanied with crackers and onion.

Limburger cheese: Limburger is a soft, ripened cheese with a characteristic strong aroma and flavor. When thinking of cheeses with a very strong aroma, Limburger is always the first to be mentioned. Limburger cheese is thought to be of German origin, but it was first made in Liege and marketed in Limburg, Belgium. Much of this cheese, however, is made in Germany as well as the United States. Limburger cheese is either made from whole milk or skimmed milk. It has a very creamy texture which is brought about by ripening in a damp atmosphere for a period of two months. Limburger cheese is served most often as a dessert or buffet cheese, always with crackers and onions.

Mozzarella cheese: Mozzarella is a very tender cheese with a soft, plastic curd. It was made originally in southern Italy from buffalo's milk. Today it is also made from cow's milk. Mozzarella cheese is an unripened cheese and when eaten fresh is still dripping with whey. In making Mozzarella cheese the whey is ordinarily drained from the curd and used in making Ricotta cheese. Mozzarella when melted has a very elastic or rubbery consistency and, therefore, is excellent to use in such preparations as pizza pie and lasagna.

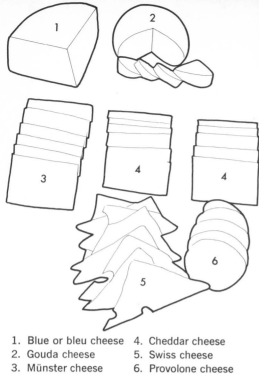

1. Blue or bleu cheese
2. Gouda cheese
3. Münster cheese
4. Cheddar cheese
5. Swiss cheese
6. Provolone cheese

Cheese tray

American Dairy Assoc.

Münster cheese: Münster (or Muenster) cheese is a semi-soft cheese made of cow's milk with a flavor between that of brick and Limburger. It was first produced in the vicinity of Münster, near the western border of Germany. The French also produce a type of Münster but call their product Géromé. The European Münster cheese is unlike the product produced extensively in the United States today because it is much sharper in taste and has a strong aroma. This is mainly due to a longer aging period. Münster is marketed in cylindrical form and is used as a buffet or sandwich cheese.

Neufchâtel cheese: Neufchâtel is very similar to cream cheese, but possesses a higher moisture content and a lower fat content. It is a cheese of French origin and made extensively in the Department of Seine Inférieure, France. Neufchâtel has a very soft texture and a mild flavor. It is made from whole or skim milk or a mixture of milk and cream. Neufchâtel cheese is generally marketed as a fresh cheese although it can be cured. Because of the smooth texture of this cheese it spreads and blends well and is, therefore, used in canapé spreads, salads, salad dressing, and many dessert items.

Parmesan cheese: Parmesan is a hard cheese produced in Italy and is thought of as one of the six best cheeses of the world. It was first made in the vicinity of Parma, in Emilia, hence the name. There are many cheeses of this type made in Italy but Parmesan is certainly the most famous. Parmesan has a granular texture when properly cured and because of this it is classed with a group of Italian cheeses called grana (meaning grain). Parmesan cheese is made in great quantities in the United States and Argentina. This product is not as good as the true Italian product. Parmesan cheese is from time to time rubbed with oil and dark coloring through the aging period. When properly curded, it is very hard and will keep indefinitely. It is sold mostly in grated form, but can be used as a table cheese when still slightly moist. Parmesan could be considered as a seasoning cheese because it is used to season such famous preparations as onion soup, spaghetti and meat balls, macaroni, and lasagna. It is the foundation of true Italian cuisine and is popular with cooks all over the world. Two other Italian cheeses of the grana type, Parmigiano and Reggiano, are very similar to Parmesan and are fairly popular in the United States.

Process cheese: Process cheese or pasteurized cheese is made by combining one or more cheeses of the same variety or by combining two or more varieties, grinding them fine, mixing together by heating and stirring, and adding an emulsifying agent to form an homogeneous plastic mass. To this mass is added vinegar or lactic acid, cream, salt, coloring, and spices as flavoring. The end result is a cheese product that is uniform in body, flavor, and texture and can be packaged in just about any shape or size. For the best process cheese, care must be taken to select cheeses that are fully cured and sharp in flavor.

Process cheese was processed in Germany and Switzerland as early as 1895 but the first patent for process cheese in the United States was not issued until 1916. Today, because of advanced techniques and extensive advertising, it is estimated that at least one-third of all cheeses made in the United States is marketed as process cheese.

There are many pros and cons revolving around process cheese. Some feel that processing adversely affects the cheeses used, or "takes the cheese out of the cheese." The fact remains, however, that process cheese does have certain advantage over "real" cheese. It is more economical, it does not require refrigeration until it is opened, it melts fairly easily and evenly, and it has unusual keeping qualities. Numerous varieties of process cheese are found in the grocer's shelf. Its use in the commercial kitchen is very extensive.

Provolone cheese: Provolone is a hard Italian cheese with a mild to sharp taste and a stringy texture. It was first made in southern Italy but is now made in other parts of Italy as well as Wisconsin and Michigan in the United States. Provolone is light in color and cuts without crumbling. Its most distinguishing characteristic is that it is formed into the shape of a sausage and corded. The cording is done for easy hanging in the smoke room when the cheese is smoked. One of the unusual steps in the making of Provolone is the kneading and stretching of the curd until it is smooth and free of lumps. Provolone is used in the preparation of many Italian dishes, but its most popular use is in pizza pie.

Ricotta cheese: Ricotta is the Italian version of our cottage cheese. Unlike cottage cheese, however, it is not lumpy and is made from the whey of other cheeses instead of milk. It is white and creamy with a bland yet sweetish flavor. Today Ricotta is made in the countries of central Europe and in some parts of southern Europe where the whey of other cheeses is considered too nutritious to be discarded. This cheese is also made in the United States, but here a mixture of whey and whole milk is used in the preparation. Ricotta cheese blends well with the flavor and textures of other foods and for that reason it has become an important ingredient in lasagna and manicotti.

Romano cheese: Romano is another of the famous hard Italian cheeses. It is similar to Parmesan cheese in many respects, but is softer in texture. In Italy it is used both as a grated cheese and a table cheese. It was first made in the vicinity of Rome from ewe's milk. Today it is made in other parts of Italy from cow's and goat's milk, as well as in the United States. Romano cheese has a granular texture, a sharp flavor, and a hard, brittle black rind. The cheese is aged for a period of 5 to 8 months if it is to be used as a table cheese. If it is to be grated it is aged about one year. A longer aging period sharpens the flavor. In the commercial kitchen Romano is used in the same fashion as Parmesan, sometimes as a topping for *au gratin* dishes (browned covering of cheese and/or bread crumbs) and sometimes as a seasoning.

Roquefort cheese: Roquefort is the most famous of the blue-green vein cheeses and the finest of the many French cheeses. It was first made in the Department of Aveyron, France, in the village of Roquefort. It was discovered quite by accident, which has been the case of many popular foods down through the centuries. According to legend a shepherd boy left his cloth pouch of barley bread and new made cheese in one of the many caves to be found in the region around Roquefort. His wandering sheep led him too far away to return for his food. Sometime later he was in this same area and remembering the food he investigated to see if it was still there. His bread was covered with green mold and the cheese was mottled with blue-green veins. Curiosity prompted him to taste this odd appearing cheese, and he found it to be delicious. Word soon spread that a tastier cheese could be developed by using these special caves for curing the cheese. The caves of Roquefort with their unusual air currents and their ideal temperature and humidity are still in use today, although they have been supplemented by man-made curing rooms where conditions are artificially controlled. Roquefort cheese is made from ewe's milk. Although this same type of cheese is made in other countries from cow's milk, they cannot use the word *Roquefort*. A French regulation limits the use of this word in connection with any other cheese product. Roquefort cheese is characteristic by its sharp, tangy flavor and by the blue-green veins that flow through the white curd.

The blue-green veins are created by spreading a type of powdered bread mold over the curd as it is being packed into the hoops. The cheese is cured for a period of 2 to 5 months, depending on the sharpness desired. Roquefort is used principally as a dessert cheese; however, it is also used in salads. Roquefort dressing is famous around the world.

Stilton cheese: Stilton is the English relative of Roquefort. It was first made in the village of Stilton about the middle of the 18th century. It is rich and mellow and has a piquant flavor although it is milder than Roquefort or Gorgonzola. It is made from cow's milk and the curing period is from 4 to 6 months. The distinguishing charactristics are the blue-green veins of mold running through the curd and the wrinkled rind. Stilton, like the other blue veined varieties, has a very crumbly texture. Some Stilton is imported into the United States but not in great quantities. It is used chiefly as a dessert and buffet cheese.

Swiss cheese: Swiss cheese is the fa-

Otto Roth and Co., Inc.

Stilton cheese from England.

mous product of Switzerland. It originated in the country of Switzerland and is known there by the name Emmentaler rather than Swiss. This cheese was first made during the 15th century, and the traditional methods of making it have been handed down from father to son since that time. Swiss cheese is a large, hard, pressed-curd cheese with an elastic body and a mild, sweetish flavor. Its chief characteristic is the large eyes or holes found throughout the body of the cheese. These holes are developed by special gas-producing bacteria released during the ripening period. Swiss cheese has become so famous down through the centuries that it is often referred to as the king of cheeses. A large part of the milk produced in Switzerland is used in the production of this cheese. Swiss cheese was brought to the United States by Swiss imigrants in the year 1850 and since that time has become the second most popular cheese produced in this country. The first, of course, is Cheddar. The curing period for Swiss cheese will vary, depending on where it is made. In the United States it is placed on the market after a curing of 3 to 4 months. In Switzerland the cheese made for export is cured for 6 to 10 months and has a more pronounced flavor. Swiss cheese is used in many preparations in the commercial kitchen, from sandwiches to stuffing veal chops, but the most desirable preparation is the wonderful fondue that can be created using this kind of cheese.

CHEESE RECIPES

The recipes which follow are popular cheese preparations. The student should become familiar with these as he will be called upon to prepare many of them. An outline of the recipes is given in their order of appearance in the chapter.

Cheese soufflé
Macaroni and cheese
Swiss fondue
Welsh rarebit
Cheesecake
Cheese blintzes
Cheese omelet
Cheese biscuits
Cheese Danish pocketbooks
Cheese pizza pie

Cheese soufflé

Cheese soufflé, like any other soufflé item, is very light and puffed up. Success or failure generally lies in the care that is taken when folding the beaten egg whites into the cheese mixture. Cheese soufflé is a specialty item usually served à la carte.

Equipment
1. Thin wire whip
2. Casseroles, 2 qt. size (2)
3. Food grater
4. Cup measure
5. Spoon measure
6. Sauce pot
7. Wooden spoon
8. Mixing machine and whip

Ingredients: Approx. yield: 12 servings

½	cup butter
½	cup flour
3	cups milk
½	tsp. Worcestershire sauce
1	lb. sharp Cheddar cheese, finely grated
10	eggs separated
	salt and white pepper to taste

Preparation
1. Grate the Cheddar cheese fine.
2. Grease the casseroles lightly with butter.
3. Separate the eggs.
4. Heat the milk.
5. Preheat the oven to 375°F.
6. Have all equipment and ingredients handy.

Procedure
1. Place the butter in the sauce pot, melt over low heat, add the flour making a roux; cook slightly.
2. Add the hot milk, stirring vigorously until smooth.
3. Add the Worcestershire sauce, season with salt and pepper. Blend thoroughly. Remove the mixture from the heat and let cool lightly.
4. Add the grated cheese and blend thoroughly until cheese is melted and mixture is smooth.

Cheese soufflé

5. Beat in the egg yolks with the wire whip, one at a time, and let cool.
6. Beat the egg white on the rotary beater until they form soft peaks. Fold the beaten egg whites into the cheese mixture using a very gentle motion.
7. Place the mixture into the greased casseroles and bake for about 35 to 45 minutes in a preheated oven at 375°F until light, puffy, and golden brown.
8. Serve at once.
   Precautions and Safety Measures
1. Do not open oven until the soufflé has been in at least 20 to 25 minutes.
2. Do not overbeat the egg whites. Keep the peaks soft and moist.

Macaroni and cheese

Macaroni and cheese is a very popular item used in many cases as a substitute for potatoes. The pasta (macaroni) is cooked by the boiling method, placed in a thin cream sauce, covered with a good quality Cheddar cheese and baked brown.
   Equipment
1. Bake pans
2. Sauce pot
3. Stock pot
4. Food grater
5. Wire whip
6. Kitchen spoon
7. Collander
8. Baker's scale

Ingredients: Approx. yield: 50 servings
3 lb. macaroni
2 lb. Cheddar cheese, grated
6 ozs. butter or shortening
6 ozs. flour
3 qts. milk
   salt and white pepper to taste
Preparation
1. Grate the Cheddar cheese on coarse grid of food grater.
2. Heat the milk.
3. Preheat oven to 375°F.
4. Have all equipment and ingredients handy.
   Procedure
1. Place water in a stock pot, add salt, and bring to a boil.
2. Add the macaroni, stirring occasionally with a kitchen spoon until the water comes back to a boil. Boil about 7 minutes until the macaroni is tender.
3. Drain in a collander. Wash the cooked macaroni with cold water. Reheat with running hot water, let drain and hold (set aside).
4. Place the butter or shortening in a sauce pot, heat slightly, add the flour and blend it with the wire whip into the shortening. Cook slightly.
5. Add the hot milk, stirring constantly to make a smooth cream sauce.
6. Blend the cream sauce with a kitchen spoon into the cooked macaroni. Season with salt and white pepper.
7. Stir in half the grated cheese, blend thoroughly.
8. Place in bake pans, top with the remaining cheese and paprika.
9. Place in a preheated oven at 375°F until cheese is melted and top is golden brown. Dish up with a 3 oz. solid kitchen spoon.
   Precautions and Safety Measures
1. When boiling the macaroni, stir occasionally to avoid sticking.
2. When mixing the cream sauce with the cooked macaroni, if mixture is too thick, add more warm milk. Mixture should not be too stiff.

Swiss fondue

Swiss fondue is a melted cheese preparation served in a chafing dish as an appetizer. The cheese mixture must be kept warm

Kraft Foods

Swiss fondue

at all times. Special fondue forks are used when served. For proper eating a cube of hard crust bread is speared with a fork and dipped into the fondue.

Equipment
1. Spoon measure
2. Wooden spoon
3. French knife
4. Heavy bottom sauce pot
5. Fondue forks
6. Chafing dish
7. Cup measure
8. Baker's scale
9. Food grater

Ingredients: Approx. yield: 4 servings

1	lb. Switzerland Swiss cheese, shredded
1	tsp. cornstarch
2	cups white wine, dry and light
	salt, pepper, and paprika to taste
2	loaves French bread, cut into bite-sized cubes
3	tbsp. kirsch
1	clove garlic

Preparation
1. Shred the Swiss cheese on course grid of food grater.
2. Cut the French bread into cubes.
3. Have all equipment and ingredients handy.

Procedure
1. Cut the clove of garlic in half and rub the bottom and sides of the heavy bottom sauce pot with the garlic.
2. Add the wine and heat, but do not boil.
3. Add the shredded cheese slowly to the wine stirring constantly with the wooden

spoon, until the cheese has melted and blended with the wine.
4. Dissolve the cornstarch in the kirsch. Add to the cheese mixture, stirring vigorously until mixture starts to bubble.
5. Season with salt and pepper. Add a dash of paprika, remove from the range and place at once in the chafing dish.
6. Serve at once with the cubes of French bread and the fondue forks.

Precautions and Safety Measures
1. Do not let the wine boil.
2. If the fondue is too thick add a little more warm wine.
3. Use caution at all times so as not to scorch the fondue.

Welsh rarebit

Welsh rarebit is a main course cheese preparation. Cheddar cheese is blended with beer and seasoning to create a nippy preparation which is generally served over toast on either the luncheon or à la carte menu.

Equipment
1. Heavy bottom sauce pot
2. Baker's scale
3. Spoon measures
4. Food grater
5. French knife
6. Wooden spoon

Ingredients: Approx. yield: 25 servings

8	lbs. sharp Cheddar cheese
5	bottles (60 ozs.) dark beer
3	tbsp. Worcestershire sauce
2	tbsp. mustard, dry
2	tsp. paprika
½	tsp. Tabasco sauce
1	tbsp. salt
25	slices of sandwich bread

Preparation
1. Grate the Cheddar cheese on the coarse grid of food grater.
2. Toast and trim the bread.
3. Have all equipment and ingredients handy.

Procedure
1. Place the beer in the heavy bottom sauce pot and bring to a boil.
2. Blend, using a wooden spoon, the Worcestershire sauce, dry mustard, paprika, Tabasco and salt to a smooth paste. Add to the beer, blending thoroughly.
3. Add the grated cheese, a little at a time,

until thoroughly blended. Stir constantly with the wooden spoon.

4. Ladle the hot cheese mixture over the toast and serve. Dish up with a 4 oz. ladle.

Variations: Welsh rarebit may be served with a slice of tomato on top of the toast or with tomato and asparagus, tomato and bacon, or just bacon.

Precautions and Safety Measures

1. When the cheese is added to the beer mixture, keep on low heat. If heat is too high the mixture will become rubbery.

2. If the Welsh rarebit is to be held for any length of time, keep warm in a double boiler.

3. Welsh rarebit is at its best when served at once.

Cheesecake

Cheesecake is a tender, tasty cake preparation. It is generally prepared with a graham cracker or cookie crust and always uses the dry bakers' cheese. It is a very popular item on the dessert menu.

Equipment

1. Bakers' scale
2. Mixing bowl
3. 8, 8 in. cake pans
4. Plastic scraper
5. Bun or sheet pans
6. Mixing machine with paddle and whip
7. Skimmer

Kraft Foods

Cheesecake with sour cream topping.

Ingredients: Approx. yield: 8, 8 inch cakes

FILLING

3	lb.	bakers' cheese
3	ozs.	cornstarch
3	ozs.	bread flour
12	ozs.	shortening (Sweetex)
1	lb.	egg yolk
2	lbs.	milk, liquid
½	oz.	vanilla
1	lb.	egg whites
1	lb. 8 ozs.	sugar

GRAHAM CRACKER CRUST

3	lbs.	graham cracker crumbs
10	ozs.	shortening
4	ozs.	whole eggs

Preparation

1. Grease bottom and sides of cake pans heavy with shortening.
2. Prepare graham cracker crumbs.
3. Have all equipment and ingredients handy.

Procedure (filling)

1. Place the cheese in the mixing bowl, mix smooth using paddle.
2. Add cornstarch, flour, and mix smooth with mixer at first speed.
3. Add sweetex shortening, blending to a smooth paste.
4. Add egg yolks gradually while creaming with mixer at second speed.
5. Add milk slowly and mix smooth.
6. Add vanilla. Remove this mixture from the mixer with plastic scraper.
7. Place egg whites in mixer, whip to soft peaks, add sugar gradually.
8. Fold meringue mixture into cheese mixture, using a skimmer. Hold until pans are set up with the graham cracker crust.

Procedure (graham cracker crust)

1. Mix crumbs together by hand with the shortening and eggs, mix thoroughly.
2. Line the heavily greased cake pans with the graham cracker crust mixture.
3. Fill the pans with the cheese cake mixture to about ¼ in. from the top. Set pans in a bun pan with about ½ in. of water.
4. Place in oven and bake at 350°F until filling is set. Remove and let cool.
5. Top cheese cakes with strawberries, blueberries, or sour cream if desired.

Precautions and Safety Measures

1. Use caution when whipping the egg whites.
2. Do not overbake or the top of the cakes will crack and become too brown.

Cheese blintzes

Cheese blintzes are of Jewish and Russian origin and are served most often in restaurants catering to Jewish clientele. Blintzes are thin pancakes with a cheese filling served with sour cream, apple sauce, or some type of jam.

Equipment
1. Small pancake skillets, 6 in.
2. 2 stainless steel mixing bowls
3. Sheet pan
4. Spoon measure
5. Wire whip
6. Flour sifter.

Ingredients: Approx. yield: 10 servings

PANCAKES

    4   whole eggs
    4   egg yolks
    1   cup cake flour
    1   tbsp. sugar
    4   cups milk
    ½   cup butter, melted
    2   tsp. salt

FILLING

    3   lbs. cottage cheese, dry
    1   whole egg, beaten
    1   pinch of nutmeg
        salt to taste

Preparation
1. Melt the butter.
2. Prepare skillets for frying the pancakes.
3. Have all equipment and ingredients handy.

Procedure (pancakes)
1. Beat eggs and egg yolks together slightly with a wire whip.
2. Sift in the flour, sugar, and salt with a flour sifter; blend thoroughly.
3. Add the melted butter and milk, beat well.
4. Heat the pancake skillets. Add enough shortening to coat the bottom and sides of the skillet. Hold the handle of the skillet with your left hand as you pour enough batter into the skillet with your right hand to make a thin layer that will just cover the pan. Turn your left hand back and forth as you are pouring so the pan will be covered quickly and evenly. Place on the heat just enough to let the pancake set. Turn out onto wax paper. Repeat this process until all the pancakes are prepared.

Procedure (filling)
1. Combine all ingredients until thoroughly blended.

2. Place about 2 tablespoons full of the cheese miture on each pancake, cooked side up. Fold up each side to form a square. Turn over and place folded side down on a sheet pan. Repeat this process until all the pancakes are filled and placed on the sheet pan.
3. Sprinkle tops of pancakes with sifted powdered sugar. Glaze lightly under the broiler.
4. Serve 2 to the order with sour cream, cinnamon, apple sauce, or apricot jam.

Precautions and Safety Measures
1. Do not have the skillet too hot when adding the batter.
2. Do not attempt to brown the pancakes.
3. Do not overcook the pancakes.

Cheese omelet

A cheese omelet is a combination of Cheddar or some other high quality cheese and eggs. The eggs are whipped, combined with the cheese and formed into a roll while cooking in a skillet.

Equipment
1. Steel skillet
2. Kitchen fork
3. Mixing bowl
4. Food grater

Ingredients: Approx. yield: 1 serving

    3   eggs
    1   oz. Cheddar cheese, grated
        salt and pepper to taste

Preparation
1. Break eggs into small mixing bowl, whip with a kitchen fork.
2. Grate the cheese on coarse grid of food grater.
3. Clean skillet by rubbing with a cloth.
4. Have all equipment and ingredients handy.

Procedure
1. Place skillet on the range, add a small amount of shortening, heat slightly at a temperature of about 275°F.
2. Pour in the beaten eggs, shaking the pan back and forth with a quick motion to keep the egg mixture turning over in pan.
3. When egg mixture starts to set, but not firm, season with salt and pepper and add the cheese.
4. Using the kitchen fork, start rolling the egg mixture towards you and at the same time giving the pan quick backward snaps until the mixture is completely rolled.

5. Let brown slightly and invert on a warm plate.
6. Serve at once.
   Precautions and Safety Measures
1. Do not overcook the cheese, it will become tough and rubbery.
2. Serve omelet at once. An omelet that is left standing has very poor eating qualities.

Cheese biscuits

Cheese biscuits are a favorite American quick bread with a Cheddar cheese flavor. An excellent choice for either the luncheon or dinner menu when hot breads are desired.

Equipment
1. Mixing container
2. Sheet pans
3. Biscuit cutter
4. Bakers' scale
5. Pt. measure
6. Rolling pin
7. Pastry brush
8. Silicon paper
9. Food grater
10. Wooden spoon
11. Flour sifter

Ingredients: Approx. yield: 7 doz.

1	lb. 8 ozs. cake flour
1	lb. 8 ozs. bread flour
2½	ozs. baking powder
½	oz. salt
1	lb. butter or shortening
6	ozs. sugar
6	egg yolks
1½	pt. cold milk
8	ozs. Cheddar cheese, grated

Preparation
1. Grate the cheese on the coarse grid of the food grater.
2. Preheat oven to 450°F.
3. Place silicon paper on sheet pan.
4. Have all equipment and ingredients handy.

Procedure
1. Place the butter or shortening and sugar in mixing container; cream together using a wooden spoon.
2. Add the egg yolks and blend well by stirring with a wooden spoon.
3. Continue to stir while adding the milk.
4. Combine the flours, baking powder, and salt; using a flour sifter sift into the mixture. Add the grated Cheddar cheese and

blend all ingredients using a gentle motion.
5. Place the dough in the refrigerator to chill for about 45 minutes.
6. Place the dough on a floured bench, roll out with rolling pin to a thickness of about ¾ in. and cut into units with the biscuit cutter.
7. Place the units on the silicon covered sheet pan, fairly close together.
8. Using pastry brush, brush the tops of the biscuits with melted butter or egg wash. Let rest 5 minutes.
9. Place in preheated oven and bake for approximately 15 minutes or until done.

Precautions and Safety Measures
1. At no time should the dough be overworked.
2. When placing the biscuits on the sheet pans, leave just enough space for the heat to penetrate properly.

Cheese Danish pocketbooks

Cheese Danish pocketbooks are a delicious pastry item consisting of Danish pastry with a rich filling of cheese. It is an excellent selection for the dessert menu.

Equipment
1. Rolling pin
2. Bakers' scale
3. Sheet pans
4. Pastry wheel
5. Silicon paper
6. Wire whip
7. Mixing machine and paddle
8. Stainless steel bowl, 1 pt.

Ingredients: Approx. yield: 40 servings

1	qt. of Danish pastry dough
2	lbs. white cream cheese
5	lbs. bakers' cheese
4	egg yolks
6	whole eggs
8	ozs. sugar
	juice of 4 lemons
1	tsp. vanilla
1	pinch of nutmeg

Preparation
1. Prepare 1 qt. of Danish pastry dough. (See Chap. 24.)
2. Separate egg yolks from the whites.
3. Turn on and set oven thermostat at 425°F.
4. Break the whole eggs into a stainless steel bowl and beat slightly with a wire whip.

5. Have all ingredients and equipment handy.
   Procedure
1. Place all the ingredients except the Danish pastry dough and the beaten eggs in the electric mixing bowl; using the paddle, blend thoroughly in mixer at low speed until the cheese mixture is smooth. Place the mixture in the refrigerator overnight for best results.
2. Roll out the Danish pastry dough to a thickness of about 1/4 in.
3. Using pastry wheel divide the dough into 4 in. squares and place approximately 2 to 3 ozs. of the cheese mixture in the center of each square of dough.
4. Brush the edges of the dough with the beaten eggs and fold the four corners of the dough over the cheese filling.

Fold the four corners together.

5. Brush again with the beaten eggs and sprinkle with sliced almonds.
6. Place on a sheet pan covered with silicon paper, proof (let rise) and bake in a preheated oven at 425°F for approximately 30 minutes.
7. Garnish slightly with powdered sugar and serve 1 per order.
   Precautions and Safety Measures
1. Do not overproof the dough; that is, do not let rise too much.
2. Use caution when baking. Do not overbrown.

Cheese pizza pie

Pizza pie is a famous Italian specialty item which has become very popular in America during the past years. It is a combination of a chewy dough, rich and highly seasoned with tomato sauce, and a rubbery textured cheese. It is served generally as a specialty item.

Equipment
1. Rolling pin
2. Food grater
3. Peel
4. Pizza cutter
5. Mixing machine and dough hook
   Ingredients: Approx. yield: 12 pies (Approx. 12 in. in dia.)

DOUGH
   5   lb. bread flour
   3   lb. water (variable)
   3/4 oz. of salt
   3/4 oz. yeast (compressed)
   3   ozs. salad oil
   1/2 oz. sugar

FILLING *(for one pizza)*
   5   ozs. canned pizza sauce
   2   ozs. Mozzarella or Provelone cheese, grated
       Parmesan cheese to taste
   4   drops olive oil
       black pepper, oregano, and basil to taste
   Preparation
1. Preheat oven to a temperature of 550° to 600°F.
2. Grate the Mozzarella or Provolone cheese on coarse grid of food grater.
3. Have all equipment and ingredients handy.
   Procedure
1. Dissolve the yeast in the water.
2. Place all the dough ingredients including the dissolved yeast, in a mixing bowl. Using the dough hook mix on low speed until the dough leaves the side of the bowl and becomes smooth.
3. Turn out dough on a floured bench, knead, and place in a greased container. Place in the refrigerator overnight. Cover the dough with a damp cloth.
4. Next day, remove dough from the refrigerator and knead on a floured bench. Make up into 10 oz. units.
5. Round up the units into balls and let rest 5 minutes.
6. Roll out unit of dough into a circle, stretching the dough as much as possible without creating tears or holes in the surface of the dough.
7. Place the circle of dough on the peel which should be sprinkled with cornmeal to act as a roller.

8. Cover the surface of the dough with the pizza sauce; season with oregano, basil, and black pepper. Sprinkle on the Mozzarella or Provolone cheese and the Parmesan cheese. Dot with olive oil.
9. Slide the pizza off of the peel onto the hearth of the oven. Let bake until dough is slightly brown and crisp. Remove, cut into pie shape wedges with a pizza cutter and serve at once.

Note: For variety, the following items may be added to the pizza: anchovies, pepperoni, green peppers, mushrooms, sausage, salami, etc. The garnishes are limitless.

Precautions and Safety Measures

1. Oven must be cleaned out often or cornmeal will burn. Use a brush or old vacuum cleaner.
2. Be alert when pizza is in the oven. It will brown quickly.

chapter 12

soups
and
stocks

■ Soup is a liquid food consisting mainly of the broth of meat, seafood or vegetables. It was for years thought of as a common food and served as a complete meal. This is still true today in many countries of the world; however, in the United States we have come to regard soup as an appetizer. Soup was accepted as an appetizer when the famous French chefs Careme and Escoffier made it into a culinary delight.

The soups presented under *appetizers* on the menu should be designed to stimulate the appetite for the heavier foods to follow. They should not in any way be filling or consist of food particles that re-

quire much chewing. If a heavy soup is served the portion should be small. The rule to follow when serving soup is: *light entrée, slightly heavy soup; heavy entrée, thin or light soup.*

There are certain standards that should be followed when preparing and serving soup. As with most preparations in the commercial kitchen short cuts can be taken. One can turn out a product in less time and at less cost if he desires to do so; however, it is very difficult to use these hurry-up methods in soup preparation. Generally the first taste will reveal if it is a superior or inferior preparation of soup.

The student should adhere to the following rules when preparing soup:

1. Use a strong, flavorful stock. A soup is only as good as the stock used.
2. Cut the garnish small. A soup should not be filling; the less chewing involved, the less filling.
3. Braise the vegetables slightly when preparing most soups. Braised vegetables will produce a better flavor.
4. Simmer the soup for at least two hours or more. The soup should be the first item placed on the fire in the morning so it can cook fairly long and slow to produce a more pronounced flavor.
5. Season in moderation. More seasoning can always be added and generally is when the guest has salt and pepper available.
6. If flour is added to the vegetables after they are braised, cook the flour for at least 5 minutes. If this is not done the soup will have a raw flour taste.
7. Serve hot soups very hot, cold soups very cold.

To classify soups is a very difficult undertaking because there is little agreement among chefs and cooks on any one classification. Also, there are virtually thousands of soup preparations gracing the menus of food service establishments. To provide the student with a simple method of learning the many different kinds of soup, we will classify all the various soups into four types.

1. Thin soups
2. Thick soups
3. Special soups
4. Cold soups

Thin soups

Thin soups include broths, bouillons, consommé, vegetable soup, and borsch. Most of the thin soups possess a clear, rich liquid and are prepared without the use of a starch.

Bouillons and broths are terms that are used interchangeably and mean practically the same thing. They are liquids in which meat, vegetables or seafood have been simmered. They are stronger in flavor and clearer in body than stocks.

Consommés are clarified bouillons or stocks reduced by simmering to increase their richness. They should be sparkling clear and flavored with a predominating beef or poultry flavor. The word *consommé* comes from the word *consummate* meaning to bring to completion or perfect. In other words consommé is considered the perfect soup.

Vegetable soups are derived from broths and bouillons and contain all types of vegetables. In most cases vegetable soup is prepared without the use of a starch or thickening agent. If one is added, it then becomes a thick soup.

Borsch, a *special soup* of Russian origin, is made mainly from stock, beet juice and lemon juice. It therefore also qualifies in the thin soup classification because it contains no thickening ingredient. Borsch is also sometimes a cold soup and therefore must also be placed in the cold soup category.

Thick soups

Thick soups are soups that derive thickness from products added to the stock: products such as potatoes, rice, barley, macaroni, roux or other items containing starch. Thick soups may also be thickened by puréed vegetables. Included in this group are cream soups, purées, chowders and bisque.

Cream soups are soups that have been thickened with a roux and thinned slightly by the addition of cream or milk. The name of the soup, such as cream of corn, cream of celery or cream of chicken, denotes the predominating ingredient.

Purée soups are thickened by cooking the predominating ingredient such as split peas, tomatoes, potatoes, dried lima beans, etc., into a pulp and straining through a fine sieve. Milk or cream should not be added to a purée soup.

Chowders are prepared from fish, shellfish and, in some cases, vegetables. They are basically a cream-type soup with diced potatoes always added. In fact, the use of diced potatoes is the main difference between a cream soup and a chowder. The most popular of all the chowders is clam chowder.

Bisques are slightly thick cream soups usually prepared from shellfish. They are named according to the kind of shellfish used, such as shrimp bisque, lobster bisque or crab bisque.

Special soups

Special soups include both thick and thin soups and are of great variety. They are soups that originated in a certain locale and will always be associated with that particular place. In some cases these soups have a great tradition, such as Philadelphia pepper pot, which is credited with saving Washington's troops at Valley Forge, and New England clam chowder which helped the early colonists survive many severe winters. A few of the others are as follows: minestrone (Italy), English beef broth (England), onion soup (France), Scotch mutton broth (Scotland), and creole soup (New Orleans).

Cold soups

Cold soups have become so popular in food service establishments in the past decade that a summer menu is not complete unless at least two are listed. These soups may be classed separately, as done here, or they may be classed with the hot soups according to their consistency. Some of the popular cold soups are jellied consommé, jellied chicken broth, cold borsch, jellied tomato madrilene and vichysoisse.

Garnishes

Most soups today are served with some type of garnish to add eye appeal and, in some cases, flavor to the soup. The garnish may be very simple such as croutons, chopped chives or parsley, or more complex such as julienne crepes (pancakes), quenelles (meat dumplings), or egg dumplings. Garnish may be either added to the soup when served, or cooked into the soup before serving.

The vegetable garnish, which is cooked into the soup, is usually cut by the soup cook the day before preparation. This is done because the soup is the first item placed on the range during the morning preparation. It takes a few hours of simmering to create the desired flavor for most soups. Actually the vegetable garnish, which should always be cut small, plays two parts in the soup preparation. It not only adds flavor to the soup, but also color as well. A list of garnishes most commonly used are as follows: vegetables, chopped parsley, minced chives, minced leeks or scallions, croutons (plain or cheese), Parmesan or romano cheese, meats (fine diced or julienne), sour cream, unsweetened whipped cream, egg dumplings, marrow dumplings, pancakes (cut julienne).

Vegetable garnish may be prepared in several ways: *julienne* (cut into long thin strips), *brunoise* (very small dice), *printaniere* (small dice, spring vegetables), and *paysanne* (fine shredded vegetables, in the peasant style).

STOCKS

Stock is a thin liquid which results from boiling meat or meat bones, fish or fish bones, poultry or poultry bones, or vegetables. Stocks are the basis for all soup preparations. In fact, the soup is only as good as the stock used. Stock is without question one of the most important ingredients used in food preparation. It is not only used as a soup base but it is also used in the preparation of gravies.

Years ago the preparation of stocks was a long and tedious process, and most food service establishments had a pot of stock constantly simmering on the fire. The stock was simmered from 12 to 24 hours and in many cases reduced to a demiglacé or glacé de viande (a stock reduced to about one-third its original volume). Today the extremely long cooking periods have been discarded because it has been proven that four to six hours of simmering is usually sufficient time to extract all the strength and flavor from most foods. To reduce the stock to a demi-glacé or glacé de viande has also become obsolete since the development of soup bases. These bases may now be used with fairly good results. The big factor in their favor is that they are time and labor savers, and this is what the food service operator is constantly searching for.

There are a number of different kinds of stocks used in the commercial kitchen from which soups, sauces and gravies are made. Brown stock, beef stock, veal stock, ham stock, chicken stock and fish stock are the popular ones.

SPECIAL TECHNIQUES USED IN THE PRODUCTION OF FINE SOUPS

It is important in the preparation of fine soups that each step of the procedure be performed as skillfully as possible. To aid the student in performing these steps with the utmost efficiency, the following explanations of certain techniques are given.

Cutting the raw vegetable garnish

The raw vegetable garnish required for all soups may be for the purpose of supplying flavor or both flavor and appearance, depending on the type and kind of soup being prepared. If the soup preparation calls for a rough garnish, its purpose is to supply only flavor to the soup and upon completion of the preparation the vegetables are strained off and discarded. A rough garnish usually consists of carrots, onions and celery, or just onions and celery cut in a rough or irregular fashion. Peeling the carrots is not necessary. However, it is wise to peel the onions if the preparation is light in color.

If the soup preparation calls for a diced, minced, or julienne cut garnish, its purpose is twofold. The garnish must supply both flavor and appearance to the soup preparation, and it will remain in the soup upon completion. It is, therefore, important that the vegetable garnish be cut uniform and small in size. If it is cut too large the soup will become filling and defeat its purpose as an appetizer. If the vegetables are cut irregular, they will cook unevenly and the soup will lack appearance. Refer to the *Food Cutting Table* (Table I, Chap. VI) for an explanation of cutting methods.

Cutting and cracking bones

All soup stocks are prepared from animal bones and in most cases these bones are fairly large in size. In order that they will fit into the stock pot and perform their task of providing flavor and strength to the stock more efficiently, it is necessary that they be cut or cracked into fairly uniform, medium-sized pieces. The task of cutting the bones is performed with a hand or power meat saw or a cleaver depending upon the size of the bones. Whatever tool is used, extreme caution must be exercised.

To cut the bones with a hand meat saw it is important that the bones be held firm on a non-slippery surface and the saw should be pushed with a slow, easy motion. If force is used in pushing the saw it may spring or jump onto the hand.

Cutting with a power saw is the most efficient cutting method, but this piece of equipment is not always available in the commercial kitchen. The bones should be held firmly in the hand and moved across the rotating blade with a firm, steady motion. Understand and use all built-in safety features of the saw.

The cleaver should only be used when the other two pieces of equipment are not available. The cleaver can be dangerous in the hands of an unskilled person. The bones should be placed on a solid, non-slippery surface. They are held very firmly with one hand while sharp blows are struck with the cleaver that is held firmly in the other hand. It is extremely important that the bones be placed on a solid surface or the cleaver may jump or spring back rapidly striking some part of the body.

Straining soups and stocks

All stocks require straining, upon completion, to remove undesirable particles that may hinder the appearance and eating qualities of the soup. Some soups, such as cream, purée, broth, bouillon, and consommé, also require straining when completed. The straining is done by pouring the liquid through a china cap or a china cap that has been covered with cheese cloth, depending upon the consistency of the item being strained. The extremely thin or watery liquids such as bouillons, broths, consommés, and most stocks (brown stock is an exception) are strained through a fine hole china cap that is covered with a cheese cloth. This is done so the liquid will be free of all impurities and provide a more satisfactory product whether it is to be served just as it is or converted into a soup or sauce.

The thicker liquids such as cream or purée soups are strained through a china cap upon completion to eliminate the vegetables (rough garnish) or vegetable pulp that must be discarded to make the soup presentable for service. When straining these preparations the vegetables or vegetable pulp is forced down into the tip of the china cap with the bot-

tom part of a ladle to force as much of the flavor as possible into the soup before the vegetables or pulp is discarded. The size of the china cap and sieve will depend upon the size of the pot the liquid is being strained into and the consistency of the liquid.

Sautéing the vegetable garnish

Sautéing the vegetable garnish for most soups is an important step because this action will produce a soup with a superior flavor. The vegetables are added to hot, melted shortening, butter, or grease, depending on preference and the type or kind of soup being prepared. The garnish is sautéed until the onions take on a transparent appearance. The garnish should never be browned or the appearance and flavor of the soup will be impaired. Stir the vegetable garnish with a wooden paddle throughout the sautéing period.

Cracking whole pepper

Whole peppercorns supply a desirable flavor to many soup and stock preparations. Before the peppercorns are added it is suggested that they be cracked. When cracked they will quickly release a more potent flavor. The most efficient way of cracking the peppercorns is to place them on a hard surface and rub across them with the bottom of a sauce pan. Force must be supplied as the bottom of the pan is rubbed across the peppercorns. Peppercorns can also be cracked by placing them in a kitchen towel and tapping them with a wooden mallet.

Skimming fat and scum from the stock

Skimming the fat and scum from the surface of a stock is an essential step in the proper preparation of stocks. The removal of these undesirable particles will produce a clearer stock, which will in turn provide a finer soup or sauce. Skimming can be done with a ladle, or a skimmer may be run across the surface of the liquid removing all the coagulated particles that appear.

Grinding foods

Some recipes call for the grinding of certain ingredients for the purpose of dispersing more flavor particles throughout the body of the soup. Ingredients such as ham fat, cooked giblets, beef and corn kernels are usually processed in this manner. The grinding is accomplished by passing the item through a power food grinder, sometimes called a hamburger grinder. This grinder can be an independent piece of equipment or an attachment of the mixing machine. The grinder is equipped with chopper plates that fit over the front of the grinder and through which the food passes. These plates contain numerous holes that vary in size from very small to very large. The kind of chopper plate used will depend on the soup being prepared and in most cases the hole size is designated in the recipe.

Cooling stocks and soups

Soups and stocks that will not be used immediately should be cooled as rapidly as possible and placed under refrigeration to lessen the chance of souring. The most efficient method of cooling is to place the soup or stock in a tub of ice water and, at intervals, to stir with a kitchen spoon or wooden paddle to speed the cooling action. When the item is completely cooled it should be placed in the coldest part of the refrigerator and left there until ready for use. When it is brought from the refrigerator it must always be brought to a rapid boil before being served or used in the preparation of another item.

STOCK AND SOUP RECIPES

The recipes which follow are popular soup recipes which will be found in food service establishments throughout the country. The stock recipes are given first because they are used as a base for most soup recipes. Both the stocks and soups are listed in their order of appearance in the chapter.

**Stocks
(Pages 189 to 194)**
  Brown stock
  Beef stock
  Veal stock
  Ham stock
  Lamb or mutton stock
  Chicken stock
  Fish stock

**Thin soups
(Pages 194 to 198)**
  French onion soup (also a special
    soup)
  Vegetable soup
  Beef consommé (also a cold soup)
  Tomato madrilène (also a cold soup)
  Petite marmite
  Chicken giblet soup (sometimes a
    thick soup)

**Thick soups
(Pages 198 to 217)**
  Split pea soup
  Purée of tomato soup
  Cream of tomato soup
  Purée of Mongole soup
  Cream of corn soup Washington
  Cream of asparagus soup
  Cream of celery soup
  Potato-leek soup
  Cream of mushroom soup
  Cream of chicken soup à la reine
  Cream of chicken almond soup
  Purée of red bean soup
  Purée of black bean soup
  Bean soup
  Lentil soup
  Corn chowder
  Cheddar cheese soup
  Oxtail soup
  Lobster bisque
  Shrimp bisque
  Oyster or clam bisque

Seafood chowder
Mulligatawny
Mock turtle soup

Special soups
(Pages 217 to 223)
Chicken gumbo soup
Borsch (also a cold or thin soup)
Scotch mutton broth
Philadelphia pepper pot
Spaetzles (Austrian noodles)
English beef broth
New England clam chowder
Manhattan clam chowder
Italian minestrone soup
French onion soup (given under
thin soups)

Cold soups
(Pages 223 to 224)
Cold fruit soup
Vichyssoise
Consommé (given under thin soups)
Tomato madrilene (given under thin
soups)
Borsch (given under special soups)

STOCK RECIPES
Brown stock

Brown stock is prepared by browning, then boiling beef and veal bones. Vegetables and seasoning are added for flavor. Brown stock is used in the preparation of soups, sauces, and gravies.

Objectives
To teach the student:
1. How to cut or saw bones.
2. How to cut garnish.
3. How to blanch meat.
4. How to cook brown stock and remove scum.
5. How to strain brown stock.
6. How to cool brown stock.

Equipment
1. French knife
2. Baker's scale
3. Large stock pot, 10 gal.
4. Spoon measure
5. Wood paddle
6. China cap
7. Ladle or skimmer
8. 5 gal. container (for storing stock)

9. Meat saw
10. Cleaver
11. Roast pan
12. Gal. measure
13. Tub for cooling stock

Ingredients: Approx. yield: 5 gal.

20	lbs.	beef bones
10	lbs.	veal bones
7	gal.	water
2	lbs.	onions, cut rough
1	lb.	celery, cut rough
1	lb.	carrots, cut rough
3		bay leaves
1	tsp.	thyme
1	tsp.	whole black pepper, cracked
4		whole cloves
3		cloves garlic, minced
1	qt.	tomato purée

Preparation
1. Cut the bones with a meat saw or crack with a cleaver into medium sized pieces. Proceed only after demonstration by instructor.
2. Cut the rough garnish (onions, carrots and celery) with a French knife into medium sized pieces.
3. Mince the garlic and crack the pepper.
4. Have all equipment and ingredients handy.

Procedure
1. Place the bones in a large roast pan and brown thoroughly in a 400°F oven.
2. When the bones are brown drain off any grease that may have accumulated in the pan.
3. Add the rough garnish and continue to roast until the garnish is slightly brown.
4. Remove the bones and rough garnish from the pan and place in a large stock pot.
5. Deglaze the roast pan with part of the water. (Deglazing is done by adding water to dissolve crusted juices.)
6. Cover bones with remaining water and liquid from deglazing the pan; bring to a boil.
7. Add all remaining ingredients, reduce heat and simmer for 5 to 6 hours. Stir occasionally with the wooden paddle.
8. Strain through a fine china cap into the 5 gal. container. Cool as quickly as possible in a tub of ice cold water.
9. Refrigerate until ready to use.

1. Exercise extreme caution when cutting or chopping the bones to avoid cutting self.
2. Skim fat and scum from the simmering stock frequently using a ladle or skimmer.
3. Do not let the liquid boil fast. Simmering will produce a more flavorful stock.

Beef stock

Beef stock is prepared by simmering beef or beef bones, vegetables and seasoning in water to extract all strength and flavor. Beef stock is used in the preparation of soups, sauces, and gravies.

Objectives

To teach the student:
1. How to cut or saw beef bones.
2. How to cut garnish.
3. How to blanch meat.
4. How to cook beef stock and remove scum.
5. How to strain beef stock.
6. How to cool beef stock.

Equipment
1. French knife
2. Baker's scale
3. Measuring spoons
4. Large stock pot, 10 gal.
5. China cap
6. Cheese cloth
7. Meat saw
8. Cleaver
9. 5 gal. container for storing stock
10. Gal. measure
11. Tub, for cooling stock
12. Ladle or skimmer

Ingredients: Approx. yield: 5 gal.

15	lbs. beef bones
1	lb. beef, shank
1	lb. onions, cut rough
8	ozs. celery leaves, cut rough
8	ozs. carrots, cut rough
2	bay leaves
1	tsp. whole black pepper, cracked
1	tsp. thyme
6	gal. water
1	oz. parsley stems

Preparation
1. Cut the bones with a meat saw or crack with a cleaver into medium sized pieces.

Proceed only after demonstration by instructor.
2. Cut the rough garnish (onions, carrots and celery) with a French knife into medium sized pieces.
3. Crack the peppercorns.
4. Have all equipment and ingredients handy.

Procedure
1. Blanch the bones and meat in the large stock pot, using a sufficient amount of boiling water to cover them. Drain and wash thoroughly in cold water.
2. Add the 6 gal. of water, bring to quick boil and remove immediately any scum that may appear on the surface. Remove scum with a ladle or skimmer.
3. Add the remaining ingredients and let simmer for 5 to 6 hours.
4. Strain through a china cap, covered with a cheese cloth to remove all foreign particles. Strain into a 5 gal. container and cool as quickly as possible in a tub of ice cold water.
5. Refrigerate until ready to use.

Precautions and Safety Measures
1. Exercise caution when cutting or cracking the bones to avoid cutting self.
2. Do not add the vegetables or seasoning to the stock until all the scum has been removed.
3. Do not let the liquid boil vigorously at any time. Simmering will produce a clearer, more flavorful stock.

Veal stock

Veal stock is prepared by simmering veal or veal bones, vegetables, and seasoning in water to extract all strength and flavor. Veal stock is used in the preparation of soups and sauces.

Objectives

To teach the student:
1. How to cut or saw veal bones.
2. How to cut garnish.
3. How to blanch meat.
4. How to cook veal stock and remove scum.
5. How to strain veal stock.
6. How to cool veal stock.

Equipment
1. French knife
2. Baker's scale
3. Measuring spoons

4. Large stock pot, 10 gal.
5. China cap
6. Cheese cloth
7. Meat saw
8. Cleaver
9. 5 gal. container for storing stock
10. Gal. measure
11. Tub for cooling stock
12. Ladle or skimmer

Ingredients: Approx. yield: 5 gal.

15	lbs. veal bones
1	lb. veal shank
1	lb. onions, cut rough
8	ozs. celery or celery leaves, cut rough
8	ozs. carrots, cut rough
1	bay leaf
1	tsp. thyme
1	tsp. whole black pepper, cracked
6	gal. water
1	oz. parsley stems

Preparation

1. Cut the bones with a meat saw or crack with a cleaver into medium sized pieces. Proceed only after demonstration by instructor.
2. Cut the rough garnish (onions, carrots and celery) with a French knife into medium sized pieces.
3. Crack the peppercorns.
4. Have all the equipment and ingredients handy.

Procedure

1. Blanch the bones and meat in the stock pot, using a sufficient amount of boiling water to cover them. Drain and wash thoroughly in cold water.
2. Add the 6 gal. of water, bring to a boil and remove any scum that may appear on the surface with a ladle or skimmer.
3. Add the remaining ingredients and let simmer for 5 to 6 hours.
4. Strain through a china cap, covered with a cheese cloth to remove all foreign particles. Strain into a 5 gal. container and cool as quickly as possible in a tub of ice cold water.
5. Refrigerate until ready to use.

Precautions and Safety Measures

1. Exercise extreme caution when sawing or cracking the bones.
2. Do not add the vegetables or seasoning to the stock until all the scum has been removed.
3. Do not let the liquid boil vigorously at any time. Simmering will produce a clearer, more flavorful stock.

Ham stock

Ham stock is prepared by simmering ham trimmings and bones, vegetables and seasoning in water to extract all strength and flavor. Ham stock is used in the preparation of soups, vegetables and a few sauces.

Objectives:

To teach the student:

1. How to cut garnish.
2. How to cook ham stock and remove scum.
3. How to strain ham stock.
4. How to cool ham stock.

Equipment

1. Large stock pot, 10 gal.
2. China cap
3. Cheese cloth
4. 5 gal. container for storing stock
5. French knife
6. Baker's scale
7. Gal. measure
8. Ladle
9. Tub for cooling stock

Ingredients: Approx. yield: 5 gal.

16	lbs. ham trimmings and bones
2	lbs. onions, cut rough
1	lb. celery and celery leaves, cut rough
8	ozs. carrots, cut rough
6	gal. water
1	tsp. whole cloves
½	tsp. garlic, minced

Preparation

1. Cut the onions, celery and carrots rough using a French knife.
2. Mince the garlic.
3. Have all equipment and ingredients handy.

Procedure

1. Place the ham bones and trimmings in a large stock pot. Add the water, bring to a quick boil and remove at once any scum that may appear on the surface. Remove the fat and scum with a ladle.
2. Add the remaining ingredients and let simmer for 4 to 5 hours, skimming fat and scum from stock frequently.
3. Strain through a china cap, covered with a cheese cloth to remove all foreign particles. Strain into the 5 gal. container and cool as quickly as possible in a tub of ice cold water.

4. Refrigerate until ready to use.

Precaution and Safety Measures

1. Do not add the vegetables or seasoning to the stock until all the scum has been removed.
2. Do not let the liquid boil vigorously at any time. Simmering will produce a more flavorful stock.

Lamb or mutton stock

Lamb or mutton stock is prepared by simmering lamb or lamb bones, mutton or mutton bones, vegetables, and seasoning in water to extract all strength and flavor. Lamb or mutton stock is not in popular use in most commercial kitchens; however, occasions do arise when it is needed, such as for Scotch mutton broth.

Objectives

To teach the student:

1. How to cut or saw lamb bones.
2. How to cut garnish.
3. How to blanch meat.
4. How to cook lamb stock and remove scum.
5. How to strain lamb stock.
6. How to cool lamb stock.

Equipment

1. French knife
2. Baker's scale
3. Large stock pot, 10 gal.
4. China cap
5. Meat saw
6. Cleaver
7. Measuring spoons
8. Cheese cloth
9. Gal. measure
10. 5 gal. container for storing stock
11. Tub for cooling stock

Ingredients: Approx. yield: 5 gal.

15	lbs. lamb or mutton bones
1	lb. lamb shank
1	lb. onions, cut rough
8	ozs. celery or celery leaves, cut rough
8	ozs. carrots, cut rough
1	bay leaf
2	tbsp. marjoran
1	tsp. whole black pepper, cracked
6	gal. water

Preparation

1. Cut the bones with a meat saw or crack with a cleaver into medium sized pieces.

Proceed only after demonstration by instructor.

2. Cut the rough vegetable garnish (onions, carrots, and celery) with a French knife into medium sized pieces.
3. Crack the peppercorns.
4. Have all equipment and ingredients handy.

Procedure

1. Blanch the bones and meat in the stock pot using a sufficient amount of boiling water to cover them. Drain and wash thoroughly in cold water.
2. Add the 6 gal. of water, bring to a boil and remove any scum that may appear on the surface with a ladle or skimmer.
3. Add the remaining ingredients and let simmer for 5 or 6 hours.
4. Strain through a china cap, covered with a cheese cloth, to remove all foreign particles. Strain into a 5 gal. container. Cool as quickly as possible in a tub of ice cold water.
5. Refrigerate until ready to use.

Precautions and Safety Measures

1. Exercise extreme caution when sawing or cracking the bones.
2. Do not add the vegetables or seasoning to the stock until all the scum has been removed.
3. Do not let the liquid boil vigorously at any time. Simmering will produce a clearer, more flavorful stock.

Chicken stock

Chicken stock is prepared by simmering chicken bones, vegetables and seasoning in water to extract all strength and flavor. Chicken stock is used in the preparation of soups, sauces and gravies.

Objectives

To teach the student:

1. How to cut garnish.
2. How to cook chicken stock and remove scum.
3. How to strain chicken stock.
4. How to cool chicken stock.

Equipment

1. French knife
2. Baker's scale
3. Gal. measure
4. China cap
5. Stock pot, 10 gal.

6. Cheese cloth
7. 5 gal. container for storing stock
8. Ladle or skimmer
9. Tub for cooling stock
   Ingredients: Approx. yield: 5 gal.
   15 lbs. chicken bones, necks or feet
   1   lb. onions, cut rough
   1   lb. celery, cut rough
   2   ozs. concentrated chicken base
   6   gal. water
   ½   tsp. whole black pepper, cracked
   2   ozs. parsley stems
   Preparation
1. Cut the celery and onions rough with a French knife.
2. Crack the peppercorns.
3. Have all the equipment and ingredients handy.
   Procedure
1. Place the chicken bones in a large stock pot add the water, bring to a quick boil and remove at once any scum that may appear on the surface. Remove the scum with a ladle or skimmer.
2. Add the remaining ingredients and let simmer for 5 to 6 hours.
3. Strain through a china cap, covered with a cheese cloth to remove all foreign matter. Strain into a 5 gal. container and cool as quickly as possible in a tub of ice cold water.
4. Refrigerate until ready to use.
   Precautions and Safety measures
1. Do not add the vegetables to the stock until all the scum has been removed.
2. Do not let the liquid boil vigorously at any time. Simmering will produce a clearer and more flavorful stock.

Fish stock

Fish stock is prepared by simmering fish trimmings and bones, vegetables, and seasoning in water to extract all strength and flavor. For best results the trimmings and bones of the lean white meat fish such as cod, haddock, sole or flounder are preferred. Fish stock is used in the preparation of soups and sauces.

Objectives

To teach the student:
1. How to cut garnish.
2. How to cook fish stock and remove scum.
3. How to strain fish stock.

4. How to cool fish stock.
   Equipment
1. French knife
2. Large stock pot, 10 gal.
3. Measuring spoons
4. China cap
5. Cheese cloth
6. 5 gal. container for storing stock
7. Gal. measure
8. Baker's scale
9. Skimmer or ladle
10. Tub, for cooling stock
    Ingredients: Approx. yield: 5 gal.
    16 lbs. of fish trimmings and bones
    2   lbs. onions, cut rough
    1   lb. celery and celery leaves, cut rough
    3   lemons, cut in quarters
    3   bay leaves
    2   ozs. parsley stems
    1   tsp. whole black pepper, cracked
    ½   tsp. dill weed or seeds
    6   gal. water
    Preparation
1. Cut the onions and celery rough using a French knife.
2. Crack the peppercorns and cut the lemons into quarters.
3. Have all the equipment and ingredients handy.
   Procedure
1. Place the fish bones and trimmings in a large stock pot. Add the water, bring to a boil and remove any scum that may appear on the surface. Remove scum with a ladle or skimmer.
2. Add the remaining ingredients and let simmer for 3 to 4 hours. (The extraction of fish stock is more rapid than the extraction of meat.)
3. Strain through a china cap, covered with a cheese cloth to remove all foreign particles. Strain into a 5 gal. container and cool as quickly as possible in a tub of ice cold water.
4. Refrigerate until ready to use.
   Note: White wine may be added to the stock if preferred. Add approximately 4/5 qt. to the 5 gallons of stock, upon completion, for a richer, more flavorful stock.
   Precautions and Safety Measures
1. Do not add the vegetables or seasoning to the stock until all the scum has been removed.

2. Do not let the liquid boil vigorously at any time. Simmering will produce a clearer, more flavorful stock.

THIN SOUP RECIPES

French onion soup

French onion soup is a thin soup which originated in France. It is also a special soup. This soup is extremely popular on the luncheon, dinner and à la carte menu.

Objectives
1. To teach the student the procedure for preparing French onion soup.
2. To teach the student how to cut the onions and serve the soup.

Equipment
1. Stock pot, 5 gal.
2. French knife
3. Qt. measure
4. Baker's scale
5. Wood Paddle
6. 3 gal. container for holding soup
7. Ladle or skimmer

Ingredients: Approx. yield: 3 gal.
  12 ozs. butter
   3 qts. onions, cut julienne
  1½ gal. beef stock or consommé
  1½ gal. chicken stock
   6 ozs. sherry wine (optional)
      salt and pepper to taste

Preparation
1. Prepare the beef stock or consommé. (See recipes this chapter.)
2. Prepare the chicken stock. (See recipe this chapter.)
3. Cut the onions julienne using a French knife.
4. Have all the equipment and ingredients handy.

Procedure
1. Place the butter in a stock pot, heat at a moderate temperature until melted.
2. Add the onions and sauté until they begin to color.
3. Add the hot stocks and stir, using the wooden paddle.
4. Bring back to a boil, reduce heat and simmer for about 1 hour. Remove scum if any appears with a ladle or skimmer.
5. Season with salt and pepper and pour into a 3 gal. container.
6. Add wine if desired and serve with cheese croutons and grated Parmesan cheese.

Precautions and Safety Measures
1. When sautéing the onions do not burn them. A light brown color is desired.
2. Simmer throughout the cooking period so the stocks will not cloud.

Vegetable soup

Vegetable soup is a type of soup consisting of a variety of vegetables. It is served in all commercial kitchens as a *soup du jour* (soup of the day).

Objectives
1. To teach the student the procedure for preparing vegetable soup.
2. To teach the student how to cut the vegetable garnish.

Photo: Kathryn Adams
French onion soup with croutons and julienne cut onions.

Photo: Kathryn Adams
Vegetable soup

Equipment
1. Stock pot, 5 gal.
2. Wood paddle
3. Baker's scale
4. French knife
5. Qt. measure
6. 3 gal. container for holding soup
   Ingredients: Approx. yield: 3 gal.
1	lb. carrots, diced
1	lb. celery, diced
1	lb. onions, diced
½	lb. cabbage, diced
4	ozs. shortening
2½	gal. beef stock
½	gal. crushed tomatoes
2	ozs. salt (variable)
1	oz. minced garlic
1	pinch pepper
1	lb. peas
½	lb. corn
½	lb. lima beans

Preparation
1. Dice carrots, celery, onions and cabbage using a French knife.
2. Prepare beef stock. (See recipe this chapter.)
3. Mince garlic.
4. Have all equipment and ingredients handy.

Procedure
1. Place shortening in stock pot, add diced onions, celery, carrots and garlic. Sauté until vegetables are partly done. Do not brown.
2. Add beef stock, bring to boil, simmer for 1 hour.
3. Add peas, corn, lima beans and cabbage. Continue to simmer until all vegetables are tender.
4. Add crushed tomatoes and continue simmering for 5 minutes.
5. Season with salt and pepper.
6. Pour into 5 gal. container.

Precautions and Safety Measures
1. Use a rich beef stock.
2. Cut vegetable garnish as uniformly as possible.

Beef consommé

Beef consommé is a very clear beef liquid. The name is derived from the word *consummate* meaning the finest or most perfect soup. It is one of the most popular soups served and is listed on the menu of most food service establishments. Beef consommé can be served hot or cold. If serving it cold, unflavored gelatin must be added.

Objectives
1. To teach the student the clarification process.
2. To teach the student the procedure for preparing beef consommé.
3. To teach the student how to serve consommé.

Equipment
1. Stock pot with spigot, 5 gal.
2. Wood paddle
3. Wire whip
4. China cap
5. Cheese cloth
6. Baker's scale
7. Qt. measure
8. 3 gal. container for holding soups
9. Food grinder
   Ingredients: Approx. yield: 3 gal.
3	lbs. beef, shank meat, ground
4	gal. beef stock, cold
2	lbs. onions, cut rough
1	lb. celery, cut rough
8	ozs. carrots, cut rough
	parsley stems from 4 bunches of parsley
½	tsp. thyme
6	cloves
2	bay leaves
2	tsps. black peppercorns, crushed
1	pt. tomato juice
1	pt. whole tomatoes, canned
1	qt. egg whites (save the egg shells and include in the clarification mixture; use yolks for another preparation)

Preparation
1. Prepare the beef stock. Let cool. (See recipe this chapter.)
2. Grind the beef shank meat, using the coarse chopper plate of the food grinder.
3. Cut the rough garnish (onions, carrots and celery) with a French knife.
4. Cut the stems from 4 bunches of parsley.
5. Separate the eggs, the white and shells to be used in the clarification process. Reserve the yolks for use in another preparation.
6. Crack the peppercorns.
7. Have all the equipment and ingredients handy.

Procedure

1. In a large stock pot blend together the rough vegetable garnish, the ground beef, parsley stems, thyme, bay leaves, cloves, peppercorns, egg shells, tomato juice and whole tomatoes. Mix together well.
2. Beat the egg whites slightly with a wire whip and pour into the stock pot.
3. Add the cold beef stock and stir vigorously with a wooden paddle.
4. Place the stock pot on the range and bring to a slow boil, stirring occasionally. Reduce heat to a simmer and allow the coagulated mass to rise to the top of the stock pot forming a raft (floating mass).
5. Continue to simmer for 2 hours. Do not break or disturb the raft.
6. Remove from the range and strain through a china cap covered with a fine cheese cloth into a 3 gal. container.
7. Serve hot or cold. If serving cold add 3½ ozs. of unflavored gelatin to each gallon of liquid. The gelatin should be soaked in cold water and added to the soup during the second step in the procedure. The soaking will insure a complete dissolvement of the gelatin.

Note: To prepare chicken consommé use the same recipe, but substitute chicken stock for beef stock, omit the tomatoes and tomato juice and add a ½ cup of lemon juice.

Consommé is usually served with some sort of *garnish*. The garnishes used are numerous; however, a few of the popular ones are listed below.

Celestine: With julienne French pancakes.

Brunoise: Assorted vegetables cut in a small dice.

Printaniere: Small diced spring vegetables.

Royale: Custard cut in diamond shape.

Xavier: With egg drops.

Beleview: Topped with unsweetened whipped cream and browned under the broiler.

Vermicelli: With small pieces of boiled vermicelli.

Rice: With boiled rice.

Barley: With boiled barley.

Marrow Dumpling: With poached marrow dumplings.

Precautions and Safety Measures

1. Be extremely cautious when grinding the meat.
2. Do not break the raft at anytime during the cooking period or when straining.
3. When straining use the spigot (faucet) on the bottom of the stock pot so the raft will not be broken.
4. Once the raft has set do not let the liquid boil.

Tomato madrilene

Tomato madrilene is a sparkling clear broth with a tomato flavor. It is clarified by using the same process required for preparing consommé. Tomato madrilene can be served hot or cold. If serving it cold, unflavored gelatin must be added.

Objectives

1. To teach the student the clarification process.
2. To teach the student how to cut the vegetable garnish.
3. To teach the student the procedure for preparing tomato madrilene.

Equipment

1. Stock pot, with spigot, 10 gal.
2. French knife
3. Measuring spoons
4. Baker's scale
5. Qt. measure
6. Food grinder
7. China cap
8. Cheese cloth
9. Wood paddle
10. 6 oz. ladle
11. 5 gal. container for holding soup

Ingredients: Approx. yield: 5 gal.

3½	gal. beef or chicken stock, cold
1	#10 can whole tomatoes
1	#10 can tomato juice
2	qts. fresh tomatoes, pieces or over-ripe tomatoes
2	lbs. beef, lean, ground coarse
2	lbs. onions, cut rough
1	lb. celery, cut rough
1	lb. carrots, cut rough
1	pt. parsley or parsley stems
1	tsp. thyme
4	bay leaves
1	tsp. whole cloves
1	tbsp. peppercorns, cracked
1	qt. of egg whites (save the egg shells and include in the clarification mix-

ture; save yolks for another preparation.)

Preparation
1. Prepare the beef or chicken stock. Let cool. (See recipe this chapter.)
2. Grind the lean beef using the coarse chopper plate of the food grinder.
3. Cut the rough garnish (onions, celery and carrots) with a French knife.
4. Separate the eggs, the whites and shells to be used in the clarification process. Reserve the yolks for use in another preparation.
5. Crack the peppercorns.
6. Have all the equipment and ingredients handy.

Procedure
1. To make the clarification mixture, blend together, in a large stock pot, the rough vegetable garnish, the ground beef, fresh tomatoes or pieces, parsley or stems, thyme, bay leaves, cloves, peppercorns, egg shells and whites. Mix together well.
2. Add the remaining ingredients and mix together well.
3. Place the stock pot on the range and bring to a slow boil, stirring occasionally with a wooden paddle. Reduce heat to a simmer and allow the coagulated mass to rise to the top of the stock pot, forming a raft (floating mass).
4. Continue to simmer for 2 hours. Do not break or disturb the raft.
5. Remove from the range and strain into a 5 gal. container through a china cap covered with a fine cheese cloth.
6. Add red color, as desired, because the clarification process destroys most of the tomato color.
7. Serve hot or cold. If serving cold add 3½ ozs. of unflavored gelatin to each gallon of liquid. The gelatin should be soaked in cold water and added to the soup during the second step above.

Note: Hot tomato madrilene is generally served with one of the following garnishes: julienne, brunoise, paysanne or printaniere cut vegetables; rice; egg drops; cooked pasta; dumplings; etc.

Precautions and safety Measures
1. Do not break the raft at anytime during the cooking period or when straining. Discard the raft after straining.
2. When straining, use spigot in the stock pot.

3. Once the raft has set do not let the liquid boil; simmer.

Petite marmite

Petite marmite is a soup that is considered a more fancy preparation in comparison to most other soups. It is a combination of a rich beef consommé and chicken broth, with a garnish of diamond cut vegetables flowing through its rich liquid. *Petite* indicates the vegetables should be cut fairly small. *Marmite* is an earthen pot in which the soup should be served. This soup is a welcomed addition to the à la carte menu or for special menus on holidays or festive occasions.

Objectives
1. To teach the student how to cut the garnish.
2. To teach the student the procedure for preparing petite marmite.
3. To teach the student how to serve the soup.

Equipment
1. Stock pot, 5 gal.
2. French knife
3. 3 gal. container for holding soup

Ingredients: Approx. yield: 3 gal.
- 1½ gal. beef consommé
- 1½ gal. chicken broth or stock
- 2 lbs. cooked beef, cut diamond shape
- 2 lbs. cooked chicken or turkey white meat, cut diamond shape
- 1 lb. carrots, cut diamond shape
- 1 lb. turnips, cut diamond shape
- 8 ozs. celery, cut diamond shape
  salt and white pepper to taste

Preparation
1. Prepare the beef consommé. (Beef consommé recipe is given in this chapter.)
2. Prepare a rich clear chicken broth or stock. (See stock recipe this chapter. Chicken broth is prepared by stewing dressed chicken.)
3. Cut the beef and chicken or turkey diamond shape with a French knife.
4. Cut the vegetables diamond shape with a French knife.
5. Have all the equipment and ingredients handy.

Procedure
1. Combine the beef consommé and chicken broth in a stock pot and bring to a simmer.

2. Add the diamond cut vegetables and continue to simmer until they are tender.
3. Add the diamond cut meat and simmer for 10 more minutes.
4. Season with salt and white pepper and pour into a 3 gal. container.
5. Serve in marmite pots topped with toasted cheese croutons.

Precautions and Safety Measures
1. Do not boil the consommé and chicken broth, it may become cloudy.

Chicken giblet soup

Chicken giblet soup is very similar to chicken gumbo or creole soup, but the okra is replaced by cooked chopped chicken giblets. This is an excellent way to use those giblets that accumulate so rapidly in the freezer and refrigerator. This is a thin soup that is popular on both the luncheon and dinner menus. By the addition of more rice it may be made into a thick soup.

Objectives
1. To teach the student how to cut the vegetable garnish.
2. To teach the student the procedure for preparing chicken giblet soup.

Equipment
1. French knife
2. Stock pot, 5 gal.
3. Baker's scale
4. Qt. measure
5. Wood paddle
6. 3 gal. container for holding soup
7. Food grinder
8. Sauce pan

Ingredients: Approx. yield: 3 gal.

3	gal. chicken stock
3	lbs. onions, diced
2	lbs. celery, diced
1	lb. 8 ozs. green peppers, diced
6	ozs. rice
3	lbs. giblets, cooked, ground coarse
10	ozs. butter or chicken fat
1	oz. chicken base (variable)
3	pt. tomatoes, canned, crushed
	salt and pepper to taste

Preparation
1. Wash the rice thoroughly.
2. Prepare the chicken stock. (See recipe this chapter.)
3. Cook giblets in a separate sauce pan and grind, use the coarse chopper plate of the food grinder.

4. Crush the tomatoes.
5. Dice the onions, celery and green peppers with the French knife.
6. Have all the equipment and ingredients handy.

Procedure
1. Place the butter or chicken fat (rendered) in a stock pot and heat.
2. Add the diced vegetables and sauté, do not brown, until slightly tender.
3. Add the chicken stock, bring to a boil then reduce to a simmer and cook until the celery is slightly tender.
4. Add the rice, ground giblets and crushed tomatoes. Continue to simmer, stirring occasionally with the wooden paddle until the rice is tender.
5. Add the chicken base and season with salt and pepper. Pour into a 3 gal. container.
6. Serve.

Precautions and Safety Measures
1. When sautéing the vegetables do not let them brown.
2. Simmer while cooking to keep the stock clear.

THICK SOUP RECIPES
Split pea soup

Split pea soup is a thick soup, cooked until peas become purée. It is served as a *soup du jour* (soup of the day) in most commercial kitchens.

Objectives
1. To teach the student the procedure for making split pea soup.
2. To teach the student how to cut a rough garnish.
3. To teach the student how to strain the soup.

Equipment
1. 2 stock pots, 5 and 10 gal.
2. China cap
3. Wood paddle
4. French knife
5. 6 oz. ladle
6. Baker's scale
7. Spoon measure
8. Wire whip
9. 5 gal. container for holding soup
10. 1 gal. measure

Ingredients: Approx. yield: 5 gal.

1	lb. of bacon or ham fat

Split pea soup

Photo: Kathryn Adams

8 lbs. split peas
1 lb. flour
5 gal. ham stock
1 lb. ham bones
2 ozs. salt (variable)
2 lbs. carrots
2 lbs. onions
2 lbs. celery
⅛ oz. thyme
1 teaspoon pepper

Preparation
1. Prepare ham stock. (See recipe this chapter.)
2. Cut rough garnish. Cut vegetables into medium sized pieces, using a French knife.
3. Have all equipment and ingredients handy.

Procedure
1. Place peas in 5 gal. stock pot, cover with 3 gal. ham stock, cook by simmering until peas are well done.
2. In 10 gal. stock pot braise vegetables in bacon or ham fat with ham bone until tender.
3. Add flour and mix thoroughly making a roux. Cook slowly without burning for 5 minutes.
4. Add remaining stock to the roux and vegetable mixture and mix well. Stir with wooden paddle until smooth then let simmer.
5. Add cooked split peas, salt, pepper and thyme to the simmering vegetable mixture. Continue to simmer for an additional hour.
6. Strain the soup through a china cap, into a 5 gal. container. Using a ladle, force as much of the vegetable pulp as possible through the china cap.

Precautions and Safety Measures
1. After peas are added to the soup, stir occasionally to avoid sticking.

2. Cook peas until they are puréed.
3. Exercise caution when forcing the vegetable pulp through the china cap.

Purée of tomato soup

Purée of tomato soup is prepared from the pulp and flavor of tomatoes. This soup is quite popular when served as a *soup du jour* (soup of the day). It is usually garnished with small croutons.

Objectives
1. To teach the student how to cut the vegetable garnish and serve the soup.
2. To teach the student the procedure for preparing purée of tomato soup.

Equipment
1. Stock pot, 5 gal.
2. French knife
3. Wood paddle
4. China cap
5. 6 oz. ladle
6. 3 gal. container for holding soup
7. Baker's scale
8. Qt. measure
9. Spoon measure
10. Wire whip

Ingredients: Approx. yield: 3 gal.
2 gal. ham stock
1 #10 can tomato purée
1 lb. onions, cut rough
1 lb. celery, cut rough
8 ozs. carrots, cut rough
8 ozs. bacon grease
6 ozs. flour
2 bay leaves
3 ozs. sugar (variable)
1 tsp. basil
½ tsp. rosemary leaves
salt and white pepper to taste

Photo: Kathryn Adams

Purée of tomato soup

Preparation

1. Prepare the ham stock. (See recipe this chapter.)
2. Cut the rough garnish (onion, carrots and celery) with a French knife.
3. Have all the equipment and ingredients handy.

Procedure

1. Place the bacon grease in a stock pot and heat.
2. Add the rough garnish and sauté until slightly tender.
3. Add the flour, making a roux, and cook for 5 minutes.
4. Add the tomato purée and ham stock, whipping vigorously with a wire whip until thickened and smooth.
5. Add the bay leaves, rosemary leaves, basil and sugar, simmer for approximately 2 hours.
6. Strain through a fine china cap forcing through as much of the vegetable flavor as possible with a ladle.
7. Season with salt and white pepper, pour into a 3 gal. container, and serve garnished with small croutons.

Precautions and Safety Measures

1. When sautéing the vegetables do not let them brown.
2. While the soup is simmering, stir occasionally with a wooden paddle to avoid sticking or scorching.
3. Rub the basil in the palm of your hand to release the flavor before adding it to the soup.

Cream of tomato soup

Cream of tomato soup is prepared by adding a thin cream sauce to a purée of tomato soup. The result is a soup with a smooth creamy consistency. This soup is a popular appetizer on both the luncheon and dinner menu.

Objectives

1. To teach the student the procedure for preparing cream of tomato soup.
2. To teach the student how to cut the garnish and strain the soup.

Equipment

1. Stock pot, 10 gal.
2. China cap
3. Baker's scale
4. Gal. measure

5. 6 oz. ladle
6. French knife
7. Wooden paddle
8. 5 gal. container for holding soup

Ingredients: Approx. yield: 5 gal.

3	gal. ham stock
2	gal. tomato purée
1	lb. celery, cut rough
1	lb. onions, cut rough
1	lb. carrots, cut rough
1	lb. leeks, cut rough
2	lbs. flour
2	lbs. bacon grease, ham fat or shortening
2	cloves garlic, minced
3	ozs. salt
	sugar and pepper to taste
3	bay leaves
1	tbsp. thyme
1	gal. thin cream sauce
2	tsp. baking soda

Preparation

1. Prepare the ham stock. (See recipe this chapter.)
2. Cut the rough garnish (onions, celery, carrots and leeks). Cut into medium sized pieces using a French knife.
3. Mince the garlic.
4. Prepare the thin cream sauce. (See Chap. 14.)
5. Have all the equipment and ingredients handy.

Procedure

1. Place the grease or shortening in a stock pot, add the rough garnish (onions, carrots, celery, leeks and the garlic), and sauté until slightly tender.
2. Add the flour, making a roux. Cook for approximately 5 minutes.
3. Add the hot ham stock and tomato purée, stirring constantly until slightly thickened and smooth.
4. Add the bay leaves, thyme and salt. Simmer for approximately 2 hours.
5. Season with sugar and pepper.
6. Add the baking soda and stir well.
7. Strain the soup through a china cap into a 5 gal. container. Using a ladle, force as much of the vegetable pulp and flavor as possible through the china cap.
8. Blend in the hot cream sauce gradually by stirring gently with the wooden paddle.
9. Adjust seasoning and serve with croutons.

Precautions and Safety Measures

1. When sautéing the rough garnish do not brown the vegetables.
2. The baking soda is added to keep the soup from curdling when the cream sauce is added; however, if the soup is exposed to excessive heat for too long a period it still may curdle.

Purée of Mongole soup

Purée of Mongole soup is prepared by combining purée of split pea soup and purée of tomato soup. Julienne vegetables and cooked peas are added to provide a color contrast. It is served as a *soup du jour* (soup of the day) in the commercial kitchen.

Objectives

1. To teach the student how to prepare purée of Mongole soup.
2. To teach the student how to cut the garnish.

Equipment

1. French knife
2. Stock pot, 5 gal.
3. Sauce pans
4. Wood paddle
5. Qt. measure
6. Kitchen spoon
7. China cap
8. 3 gal. container for holding soup

Ingredients: Approx. yield: 3 gal.

1½	gal. purée of tomato soup
1½	gal. purée of split pea soup
1	pt. carrots, cut julienne
1	pt. onions, cut julienne
1	pt. celery, cut julienne
1	cup leeks, cut julienne
1	pt. frozen peas, cooked, drained
	salt and pepper to taste

Preparation

1. Prepare the purée of split pea soup. (Recipe given in this chapter.)
2. Prepare the purée of tomato soup. (Recipe given in this chapter.)
3. Cut the vegetable julienne using a French knife.
4. Cook the julienne vegetables and peas in water until tender, drain.
5. Have all the equipment and ingredients handy.

Procedure

1. Combine the purée of split pea soup and the purée of tomato soup in a stock pot; bring to a boil.
2. Reduce the heat and simmer for 15 minutes.
3. Add the cooked vegetables and peas, stirring occasionally, using a wood paddle, until the soup returns to a boil.
4. Remove from the range, check seasoning and serve.

Precautions and Safety Measures

1. Stir the soup occasionally, using a wood paddle, throughout the cooking period to avoid scorching.

Cream of corn soup Washington

Cream of corn soup Washington is a rich cream-type soup with the flavor of fresh corn. This soup is generally garnished with small diced pieces of pimiento and whole kernel corn. It is served as a *soup du jour* (soup of the day).

Objectives

1. To teach the student how to cut the garnish vegetable.
2. To teach the student the procedure for preparing cream of corn soup Washington.

Equipment

1. Stock pot, 5 gal.
2. China cap
3. French knife
4. 6 oz. ladle
5. 3 gal. container for holding soup
6. Baker's scale
7. Wire whip
8. Wood paddle
9. Qt. measure
10. Measuring spoons
11. Sauce pans
12. Food grinder

Ingredients: Approx. yield: 3 gal.

2½	gal. milk
6	ozs. onion, diced
1	#10 can corn, cream style
1	lb. corn, whole kernel, frozen
10	ozs. butter
8	ozs. flour
2	qts. cream (single or coffee)
¾	oz. sugar
½	tsp. nutmeg
4	ozs. pimientoes, diced small
	salt to taste

Preparation

1. Dice the onions with a French knife.

2. Heat the milk and cream separately in a sauce pan.
3. Grind the whole kernel corn on the food grinder using the coarse chopper plate.
4. Dice the pimientoes with a French knife.
5. Have all the equipment and ingredients handy.

Procedure
1. Place the butter in a stock pot and heat.
2. Add the onions and sauté until slightly tender.
3. Add the flour, making a roux, and cook for 5 minutes.
4. Add the hot milk, whipping briskly with a wire whip until slightly thickened and smooth.
5. Stir in the cream style corn and sugar with a wooden paddle. Simmer for approximately 45 minutes.
6. Strain through a fine china cap forcing through as much of the onion and corn flavor as possible with a ladle.
7. Stir in the hot cream and nutmeg and blend thoroughly using a wooden paddle.
8. Stir in the ground whole kernel corn and the pimientoes.
9. Season with salt and pour into a 3 gal. container.

Precautions and Safety Measures
1. When heating the butter do not let it burn.
2. When sautéing the onions do not let them brown.
3. While the soup is simmering, stir occasionally with a wooden paddle to avoid sticking or scorching.
4. Do not hold this soup at too high a temperature. It may curdle.

Cream of asparagus soup

Cream of asparagus soup is a rich cream-type soup with an asparagus flavor. The flavor is acquired by simmering fresh asparagus pieces and bottoms in the cream soup. This soup is generally served on the menu as a *soup du jour* (soup of the day).

Objectives
1. To teach the student how to cut the vegetable garnish and strain the soup.
2. To teach the student the procedure for preparing cream of asparagus soup.

Equipment
1. Stock pot, 10 gal.
2. French knife

3. China cap
4. 6 oz. ladle
5. Wood paddle
6. Measuring spoons
7. Baker's scale
8. Gal. measure
9. 5 gal. container for holding soup
10. Wire whip

Ingredients: Approx. yield: 5 gal.
4½	gal. chicken stock
1	gal. milk and cream
2	lbs. shortening or butter
2	lbs. flour
2	lbs. celery, cut rough
2	lbs. onions, cut rough
8	lbs. asparagus, fresh bottoms and pieces, cut medium size
3	bay leaves
½	tsp. thyme
3	cloves
	salt and white pepper to taste
1	tsp. baking soda

Preparation
1. Prepare the chicken stock. (See recipe this chapter.)
2. Cut the asparagus medium size with a French knife.
3. Cut the onions and celery rough with a French knife.
4. Have all the equipment and ingredients handy.

Procedure
1. Place the shortening in a stock pot and heat.
2. Add the rough garnish (onions and celery) and sauté until slightly tender.
3. Add the flour, making a roux, and cook for 5 minutes.
4. Add the hot chicken stock, whipping vigorously with a wire whip until slightly thickened and smooth.
5. Add the bay leaves, thyme, cloves and cut asparagus. Simmer approximately 2 hours or until the asparagus starts to break apart.
6. Strain through a fine hole china cap using a ladle, force through as much of the asparagus pulp as possible.
7. Add the baking soda and pour in the hot milk and cream slowly, stirring gently with a wooden paddle.
8. Season with salt and white pepper and pour into a 3 gal. container.

9. Serve with croutons.

Precautions and Safety Measures
1. Stir the soup occasionally with a wooden paddle to avoid scorching.
2. Exercise caution when straining the soup.
3. The baking soda is added to reduce the possibility of curdling; however, this soup still may curdle if held at a very high temperature for too long a period.

Cream of celery soup

Cream of celery soup is a rich cream-type soup with a strong celery flavor. It is usually served on the menu as a *soup du jour* (soup of the day).

Objectives
1. To teach the student how to cut the vegetable garnish.
2. To teach the student the procedure for preparing cream of celery soup.

Equipment
1. Stock pot, 5 gal.
2. Wood paddle
3. French knife
4. Baker's scale
5. Cup measure
6. Qt. measure
7. Cheese cloth
8. China cap
9. 6 oz. ladle
10. Wire whip
11. 3 gal. container for holding soup
12. 2 sauce pans

Ingredients: Approx. yield: 3 gal.

2	gal. chicken stock
1	gal. milk and cream (½ and ½)
1	lb. butter or shortening
12	ozs. flour
5	lbs. celery, chopped coarse
1	lb. onions, chopped coarse
1	pt. water
¼	cup celery seed
1	bay leaf
	salt and white pepper
½	tsp. baking soda

Preparation
1. Prepare the chicken stock. (See recipe this chapter.)
2. Cut the onions and celery coarse with a French knife.
3. Heat the milk and cream in a sauce pan.
4. Place the celery seed in a sauce pan; add the pt. of water and simmer for 5 minutes.

Strain through a cheese cloth. Reserve liquid to flavor soup.
5. Have all the equipment and ingredients handy.

Procedure
1. Place the butter or shortening in a stock pot and heat.
2. Add the onions and celery and sauté until slightly tender.
3. Add the flour, making a roux and cook for 5 minutes.
4. Add the hot chicken stock, whipping vigorously with a wire whip until slightly thickened and smooth. Simmer for approximately 1½ hours.
5. Strain through a fine china cap into a 3 gal. container. Using a ladle, force as much of the vegetable pulp as possible through the china cap.
6. Add the baking soda and pour in the hot milk and cream, stirring gently with a wooden paddle.
7. Season with salt and white pepper. Adjust the flavor by adding the celery-flavored liquid.
8. Serve garnished with croutons, if desired.

Precautions and Safety Measures
1. When sautéing the onions and celery, do not let them brown.
2. When cooking the roux, do not let it brown.
3. While the soup is simmering stir occasionally with a wooden paddle to avoid sticking or scorching.
4. Do not overheat this soup because it may curdle if held at too hot a temperature.

Potato-leek soup

Potato-leek soup is a rich cream-type soup with a potato-onion flavor. The potatoes are cooked into purée and the pulp is pressed through a china cap to acquire the rich potato flavor. This soup is usually served on the menu as a *soup du jour* (soup of the day).

Objectives
1. To teach the student how to cut the vegetable garnish and strain the soup.
2. To teach the student the procedure for preparing potato-leek soup.

Equipment
1. Stock pot, 5 gal.
2. Wood paddle
3. French knife
4. Baker's scale

5. Gal. measure
6. China cap
7. Sauce pan
8. 3 gal. container for holding soup
9. 6 oz. ladle
10. Wire whip

Ingredients: Approx. yield: 3 gal.

2	gal. chicken stock
1	gal. milk and cream ($\frac{1}{2}$ and $\frac{1}{2}$)
1	lb. onions, cut rough
8	ozs. celery, cut rough
6	lbs. Idaho potatoes, peeled, sliced thin
10	ozs. butter
8	ozs. flour
1	bch. leeks
$\frac{1}{2}$	tsp. baking soda
1	bay leaf
	salt and white pepper to taste

Preparation

1. Prepare the chicken stock. (See recipe this chapter.)
2. Cut the rough garnish (onions and celery) with a French knife.
3. Wash the leeks and dice very small with a French knife.
4. Heat the milk and cream in a sauce pan.
5. Peel and slice the potatoes
6. Have all the equipment and ingredients handy.

Procedure

1. Place the butter in a stock pot and heat.
2. Add the onions and celery and sauté until slightly tender.
3. Add the flour, making a roux, cook for 5 minutes.
4. Add the bay leaf and hot chicken stock; whip briskly with a wire whip until thickened and smooth.
5. Add the potatoes and simmer for approximately 2 hours or until the potatoes cook into mush.
6. Remove from the range and strain through a china cap, forcing as much of the potato pulp through the china cap as possible with a ladle. Return to the range.
7. Add the baking soda and pour in the hot milk and cream slowly, stirring gently with a wooden paddle.
8. Add the fine diced leeks and stir.
9. Season with salt and white pepper and pour into a 3 gal. container.

10. Serve.

Precautions and Safety Measures

1. When sautéing the vegetables, do not let them brown.
2. When cooking the roux, do not let it brown.
3. While the soup is simmering stir frequently with a wooden paddle to avoid sticking and scorching.
4. The baking soda is added to resist curdling; however, if this soup is held at a very high temperature for too long a period, it could still curdle.

Cream of mushroom soup

Cream of mushroom soup is a rich cream-type soup with a mushroom flavor and small diced pieces of mushrooms flowing through is. It is served on the menu as a *soup du jour* (soup of the day).

Objectives

1. To teach the student how to cut the vegetable garnish.
2. To teach the student the procedure for preparing cream of mushroom soup.

Equipment

1. 2 stock pots, 5 gal. each
2. French knife
3. Qt. measure
4. Baker's scale
5. China cap
6. 6 oz. ladle
7. 2 sauce pans, 2 qt. and 3 qt.
8. Kitchen spoon
9. 3 gal. container for holding soup
10. Wire whip

Ingredients: Approx. yield: 3 gal.

$2\frac{1}{2}$	gal. chicken stock
2	qts. cream
1	lb. butter or shortening
1	lb. flour
1	bay leaf
1	lb. onions, cut rough
8	ozs. celery, cut rough
8	ozs. butter
2	lbs. fresh mushrooms, washed and chopped fairly fine
	salt and white pepper to taste
1	tsp. baking soda

Preparation

1. Wash and chop the mushrooms with a French knife.
2. Prepare the chicken stock. (See recipe this chapter.)

3. Cut the onions and celery rough with a French knife.
4. Heat the cream in a sauce pan.
5. Have all equipment and ingredients handy.

Procedure
1. Place the 1 lb. of butter or shortening in a stock pot and heat.
2. Add the onions and celery and sauté until slightly tender.
3. Add the flour, making a roux, and cook for 5 minutes.
4. Add the hot chicken stock, whipping the mixture vigorously with a wire whip until slightly thickened and smooth.
5. Add the bay leaf and simmer until the vegetables are tender (approximately 1 hour).
6. Strain the soup through a fine hole china cap into the second 5 gal. stock pot. Using a ladle, force as much of the vegetable pulp as possible through the china cap. Return to the range.
7. Place the 8 ozs. of butter in a sauce pan and heat.
8. Add the chopped mushrooms and sauté until tender, stirring occasionally with a kitchen spoon. Add to the strained soup and simmer for at least 15 minutes.
9. Add the baking soda and pour in the cream very slowly, while stirring gently with a kitchen spoon.
10. Season with salt and white pepper and pour into a 3 gal. container.

Precautions and Safety Measures
1. When sautéing the vegetables do not let them brown.
2. Whip vigorously with a wire whip when adding the liquid to the roux to avoid lumps.
3. Stir occasionally with a kitchen spoon while the soup is simmering to avoid sticking or scorching.
4. Do not overheat this soup because it may curdle.

Cream of chicken soup à la reine

Cream of chicken soup à la reine is a rich cream-type soup with a strong chicken flavor. The term à la reine means "to the queen's taste" and indicates the presence of puréed white meat of chicken. This soup is featured on the menu as a *soup du jour* (soup of the day).

Objectives
1. To teach the student how to cut the vegetable garnish and mince the chicken.
2. To teach the student the procedure for preparing cream of chicken soup à la reine.

Equipment
1. Stock pot, 5 gal.
2. Baker's scale
3. Qt. measure
4. Measuring spoons
5. French knife
6. China cap
7. Wood paddle
8. 6 oz. ladle
9. Wire whip
10. 3 gal. container for holding soup

Ingredients: Approx. yield: 3 gal.

2	gal. chicken stock
1	gal. milk and cream
1	lb. butter
12	ozs. flour
8	ozs. celery, diced
8	ozs. white meat of chicken or turkey, minced
½	tsp. baking soda
1	lb. onions, diced
1	bay leaf
	salt and white pepper to taste

Preparation
1. Prepare the chicken stock. (See recipe this chapter.)
2. Heat the milk and cream in a sauce pan.
3. Dice the onions and celery with a French knife.
4. Mince the white meat of chicken or turkey with a French knife.
5. Have all the equipment and ingredients handy.

Procedure
1. Place the butter in a stock pot and heat.
2. Add the onions and celery. Sauté until slightly tender.
3. Add the flour, making a roux and cook for 5 minutes.
4. Add the hot chicken stock and bay leaf, whipping vigorously with a wire whip until slightly thickened and smooth. Simmer for approximately 1½ hours.
5. Strain through a fine china cap into a 3 gal. container. Using a ladle, force as much of the vegetable pulp as possible through the china cap.

6. Add the baking soda and pour in the hot milk and cream, stirring gently with a wooden paddle.
7. Stir in the minced white meat of chicken or turkey.
8. Season with salt and white pepper and serve.

Precautions and Safety Measures
1. When sautéing the onions and celery, do not let them brown.
2. When cooking the roux, do not let it brown.
3. While the soup is simmering, stir occasionally with the wooden paddle to avoid sticking or scorching.
4. Do not over-heat this soup because it may curdle if held at too hot a temperature.
5. If the chicken stock is weak, flavor may be added by using a prepared chicken base.

Cream of chicken almond soup

Cream of chicken almond soup is a rich cream-type soup with the essence of chicken and toasted almonds. This soup is not extremely popular in the commercial kitchen because it is a fairly new preparation; however, the demand for it is increasing. This soup can be served on the à la carte menu or as a *soup du jour* (soup of the day).

Objectives
1. To teach the student the procedure for preparing cream of chicken almond soup.
2. To teach the student how to cut the vegetable garnish.
3. To teach the student how to chop and toast the almonds.

Equipment
1. Stock pot, 5 gal.
2. Baker's scale
3. French knife
4. China cap
5. Wood paddle
6. 6 oz. ladle
7. Wire whip
8. Gal. measure
9. 2 sauce pans
10. Small sheet pan
11. 3 gal. container for holding soup

Ingredients: Approx. yield: 3 gal.

2	gal. chicken stock
1	gal. milk and cream (½ and ½)
1	lb. butter
12	ozs. flour
1	lb. onions, diced

8	ozs. celery, diced
4	ozs. almond paste
1	lb. almonds, toasted, chopped fine
½	tsp. baking soda
	salt and white pepper to taste

Preparation
1. Prepare the chicken stock. (See recipe this chapter.)
2. Heat the milk and cream in a sauce pan.
3. Dice the onions and celery with a French knife.
4. Place the bleached almonds in a sauce pan, cover with water and simmer slightly until soft then drain. Chop the almonds very fine with a French knife. Place on a small sheet pan and toast until golden brown in the oven.
5. Have all equipment and ingredients handy.

Procedure
1. Place the butter in a stock pot and heat.
2. Add the onions and celery and sauté until slightly tender.
3. Add the flour, making a roux and cook for 5 minutes.
4. Add the hot chicken stock and almond paste, whipping vigorously with a wire whip until slightly thickened and smooth. Simmer for approximately 1½ hours.
5. Strain through a fine china cap into a 3 gal. container. Using a ladle, force as much of the vegetable pulp as possible through the china cap.
6. Add the baking soda and pour in the hot milk and cream, stirring gently with a wooden paddle.
7. Stir in the chopped toasted almonds.
8. Season with salt and white pepper and serve.

Precautions and Safety Measures
1. When sautéing the onions and celery, do not let them brown.
2. When cooking the roux, do not let it brown.
3. While the soup is simmering, stir occasionally with the wooden paddle to avoid sticking or scorching.
4. Do not over-heat this soup because it may curdle if held at too hot a temperature.
5. Be alert when almonds are toasting in the oven. The time element between a light brown and black (burnt) is very short.

Purée of red bean soup

Purée of red bean soup is prepared by cooking the red beans and seasoning in ham stock until the beans cook apart or become a purée. The soup is then strained through a coarse strainer and served on the luncheon or dinner menu with a garnish of egg and lemon.

Objectives
1. To teach the student how to cut the garnish and strain the soup.
2. To teach the student the procedure for preparing purée of red bean soup.
3. To teach the student how to serve purée of red bean soup.

Equipment
1. Stock pot, 5 gal.
2. French knife
3. China cap
4. 6 oz. ladle
5. Wood paddle
6. Baker's scale
7. Measuring spoons
8. Gal. measure
9. 3 gal. container for holding soup
10. Food grinder

Ingredients: Approx. yield: 3 gal.

5	lbs.	red kidney beans
3	gal.	ham stock
1	pt.	onions, diced
1	pt.	celery, diced
5		cloves of garlic, minced
4		bay leaves
1	tsp.	thyme
8	ozs.	butter
¼	cup	Worcestershire sauce
2	lbs.	ham, ground fine
		salt and pepper to taste
1	pt.	claret wine

Preparation
1. Wash the beans thoroughly, cover with double their amount of water and let soak overnight. Do not refrigerate.
2. Prepare the ham stock. (See recipe this chapter.)
3. Dice the onions and celery, mince the garlic with a French knife.
4. Grind the ham on the food grinder using the fine chopper plate.
5. Have all the equipment and ingredients handy.

Procedure
1. Place the butter in a stock pot. Add the onions, garlic and celery, and sauté until slightly tender.
2. Add the ham stock and the beans, after

draining off the water they were soaked in. Bring to a boil, reduce to a simmer.
3. Add the bay leaves, thyme, and Worcestershire sauce. Simmer for about 3 hours or until the beans become very tender and start to fall apart.
4. Strain through a coarse hole china cap into a 3 gal. container. Using a ladle, force as much of the bean pulp as possible through the china cap.
5. Add the ground ham and the claret wine and stir with a wooden paddle.
6. Season with salt and pepper.
7. Serve hot, garnished with chopped hard boiled eggs and a thin slice of lemon.

Precautions and Safety Measures
1. When sautéing the vegetables do not brown them.
2. When cooking the beans do not boil rapidly. Beans will cook more quickly and more uniform by simmering.
3. When straining the soup force as much of the bean pulp through the china cap as possible.

Purée of black bean soup

Purée of black bean soup is prepared by cooking the beans into a pulp and straining through a slightly coarse china cap to preserve as much of the pulp as possible. This soup is finished by adding Burgundy wine for an exceptional flavor and serving it with a slice of lemon as a garnish.

Objectives
1. To teach the student how to cut the vegetable garnish and serve the soup.
2. To teach the student the procedure for preparing purée of black bean soup.

Equipment
1. Stock pot, 5 gal.
2. French knife
3. China cap
4. 6 oz. ladle
5. 3 gal. container for holding soup
6. Measuring spoons
7. Cup measure
8. Qt. measure
9. Baker's scale
10. Wood paddle

Ingredients: Approx. yield: 3 gal.

4	lbs.	black beans
3	gal.	ham stock
8	ozs.	salt pork

1 lb. onions, small dice
8 ozs. celery, small dice
8 ozs. carrots, small dice
1 qt. Burgundy wine
1 bay leaf
4 cloves, whole
½ tsp. dry mustard
½ tsp. thyme
1 cup flour
salt and pepper to taste

Preparation

1. Wash the beans and remove any foreign matter, place in a pot. Cover three times their amount with water. Let soak overnight.
2. Dice the onions, celery and carrots, small (mirepoix) with a French knife.
3. Prepare the ham stock. (See recipe this chapter.)
4. Dice the salt pork into small pieces with a French knife.
5. Have all the equipment and ingredients handy.

Procedure

1. Place the salt pork in a stock pot and cook until slightly rendered.
2. Add the mirepoix (diced vegetables) and sauté until slightly tender.
3. Add the flour, making a roux, and continue to cook for 5 minutes.
4. Add the hot ham stock and stir vigorously with a wooden paddle until smooth.
5. Add the beans, which have been drained, the bay leaf, thyme, cloves and dry mustard. Simmer for about 3 hours or until the beans are very tender.
6. Strain through a coarse china cap, forcing through as much of the bean pulp as possible with a ladle.
7. Add the Burgundy wine and blend. Pour into a 3 gal. container.
8. Serve with a very thin slice of lemon as a garnish.

Precautions and Safety Measures

1. When sautéing the mirepoix do not let it brown.
2. While the soup is simmering stir occasionally with a wooden paddle.
3. Exercise caution while straining the soup.

Bean soup

Bean soup is a very popular soup in the home as well as in the commercial kitchen.

Bean soup

Photo: Kathryn Adams

In the commercial kitchen it is used as a *soup du jour* (soup of the day).

Objectives

1. To teach the student how to pick and soak the beans.
2. To teach the student how to cut the garnish.
3. To teach the student the procedure for making bean soup.

Equipment

1. 2 stock pots, 10 gal. and 5 gal.
2. Food grinder
3. French knife
4. Wood paddle
5. Baker's scale
6. Qt. measure
7. 5 gal. container for holding soup

Ingredients: Approx. yield: 5 gal.

4 lbs. navy beans
4 gal. ham stock
1 lb. carrots, diced
2 lbs. celery, diced
2 lbs. onions, diced
1 lb. ground ham fat
½ #10 can crushed tomatoes
4 ozs. salt
1 lb. leeks
3 cloves garlic, chopped
1 lb. flour
¼ oz. pepper
⅛ oz. nutmeg

Preparation

1. The day before preparation, pick over the beans, removing all rocks and foreign matter.
2. Wash and soak beans in water overnight. Do not refrigerate.
3. Cut garnish: dice onions, leeks, celery and carrots using a French knife.

4. Grind ham fat in food grinder, chop garlic.
5. Have all equipment and ingredients handy.
6. Prepare ham stock. (See recipe this chapter.)

Procedure
1. Place the beans and the water in which the beans have been soaked, into a 5 gal. pot. Bring to a boiling point, reduce the flame, and let simmer for about 2 hours or until beans are tender and soft.
2. In separate 10 gal. stock pot place the ground ham fat and braise for 5 minutes. Add diced leeks, carrots, celery and onions. Continue to braise until vegetables are partly done. Stir occasionally with a wooden paddle.
3. Add flour to take up the fat and create a roux. Cook with other ingredients for 5 minutes.
4. Add the ham stock which should already be hot.
5. Bring to a boil and simmer until all vegetables are tender.
6. Remove cooked beans from range and add beans and 1 gal. of the liquid in which the beans were cooked.
7. Add the crushed tomatoes and seasoning.
8. Continue to boil until the beans and vegetables are very tender, approximately 30 minutes.
9. Pour into a 5 gal. container.

Precautions and Safety Measures
1. Do not add tomatoes to soup until you are sure beans are thoroughly done.
2. Be thorough when picking the beans. Do not overlook any stones.
3. Be cautious when grinding ham fat.

Lentil soup

Lentil soup is served on the lunch or dinner menu as the *soup du jour* (soup of the day). Lentils are a type of bean, small and flat.

Objectives
1. To teach the student the procedure for making lentil soup.
2. To teach the student how to dice the vegetables.
3. To teach the student how to dish up lentil soup.

Equipment
1. 2 stock pots, 5 gal. and 10 gal.
2. Wood paddle

3. French knife
4. Baker's scale
5. Qt. measure
6. 5 gal. container for holding soup

Ingredients: Approx. yield: 5 gal.
 1 lb. carrots, diced
 2 lbs. onions, diced
 1 lb. celery, diced
 4 lbs. lentils
 5 gal. ham or beef stock
 1 lb. shortening or ham fat
 1 lb. flour
 ½ #10 can crushed tomatoes
    salt and pepper to taste

Preparation
1. Remove all foreign matter from the lentils by picking over them carefully.
2. Wash lentils thoroughly.
3. Have all equipment and ingredients handy.
4. Dice onions, carrots, and celery using a French knife.
5. Prepare ham or beef stock. (See recipe this chapter.)

Procedure
1. In the 5 gal. stock pot cook lentil separately in 4 gal. of the ham or beef stock until tender (approx. 45 min. to 1 hr.).
2. In the 10 gal. stock pot braise vegetables in the shortening. Add flour making a roux, mix well; cook 5 minutes.
3. Add remaining 1 gal. of beef or ham stock to roux. Let boil until vegetables are tender.
4. Add cooked lentils and liquid, lentils were cooked in. Continue to simmer.
5. Add crushed tomatoes.
6. Season with salt and pepper (a dash of nutmeg if desired).
7. Pour into a 5 gal. container.
8. Sliced or diced pieces of wieners or franks may be added if desired.

Precautions and Safety Measures
1. When adding stock, stir until all the roux is dissolved.
2. Pour in the stock slowly.
3. Add tomatoes last. Beans or lentils do not cook well when tomatoes are present.

Corn chowder

Corn chowder is a thick soup with a creamy consistency and a rich corn flavor. The soup contains diced potatoes which characterizes all chowders. Corn chowder is served on the menu as a *soup du jour* (soup of the day).

Objectives
1. To teach the student the procedure for preparing corn chowder.
2. To teach the student how to cut the vegetable garnish.

Equipment
1. Stock pot, 5 gal.
2. French knife
3. Wood paddle
4. 6 oz. ladle
5. China cap
6. Baker's scale
7. Qt. measure
8. Sauce pan
9. 3 gal. container for holding soup

Ingredients: Approx. yield: 3 gal.

2	gal. chicken stock
1	#10 can corn, cream style
1	lb. butter
10	ozs. flour
1	lb. onions, diced
6	ozs. celery, diced
3	lbs. potatoes, diced
3	lbs. corn, fresh, uncooked, cut from cob
2	qts. cream, warm
	salt and white pepper to taste

Preparation
1. Prepare the chicken stock. (See recipe this chapter.)
2. Dice the onions, celery and potatoes with a French knife.
3. Cut the corn off the cob: cut cobs in half crosswise, stand cob on end, and cut with downward stroke of French knife.
4. Heat the cream until it is warm in a sauce pan.
5. Have all the equipment and ingredients handy.

Procedure
1. Place the butter in a stock pot and heat.
2. Add the onions and celery and sauté until partly tender.
3. Add the flour, making a roux, cook 5 minutes.
4. Add the hot chicken stock, stirring constantly with a wooden paddle until slightly thickened and smooth.
5. Add the cream style corn and simmer, stirring occasionally, for approximately

1 hour until the celery becomes very tender.
6. Remove from the fire and strain through a fine china cap, forcing through as much of the corn pulp as possible with a ladle.
7. Return to the range, add the diced potatoes and fresh corn, and simmer until the potatoes are tender.
8. Add the warm cream slowly, stirring constantly, to blend thoroughly.
9. Season with salt and white pepper and pour into a 3 gal. container.
10. Serve.

Precautions and Safety Measures
1. When sautéing the vegetables, do not let them brown.
2. Stir occasionally with a wooden paddle throughout the simmering period to avoid sticking or scorching.
3. Do not hold this soup at too high a temperature for a long period of time because it may curdle.

Cheddar cheese soup

Cheddar cheese soup is a rich cream-type soup with a strong Cheddar cheese flavor. This type of soup is usually served when one wishes to feature a different soup.

Objectives
1. To teach the student how to cut the vegetable garnish.
2. To teach the student how to grate cheese.
3. To teach the student the procedure for preparing Cheddar cheese soup.

Equipment
1. Stock pot, 5 gal.
2. French knife
3. Wire whip
4. Baker's scale
5. Spoon measure
6. Gal. measure
7. 6 oz. ladle
8. China cap
9. Kitchen spoon
10. 3 gal. container for holding soup
11. Metal box grater
12. Sauce pan
13. Wooden paddle

Ingredients: Approx. yield: 3 gal.

2	gal. chicken stock
1	gal. milk and cream (½ and ½)

1 lb. carrots, diced fine
8 ozs. onion, diced fine
8 ozs. celery, diced fine
1 lb. butter
10 ozs. flour
2 lbs. sharp Cheddar cheese, grated
2 tbsp. Worcestershire sauce
1 tbsp. paprika
salt and white pepper to taste

Preparation

1. Prepare the chicken stock. (See recipe this chapter.)
2. Cut the mirepoix (onions, carrots and celery) with a French knife.
3. Grate the cheese by rubbing it on the coarse grid of a metal box grater.
4. Heat the milk and cream in a sauce pan.
5. Have all the equipment and ingredients handy.

Procedure

1. Place the butter in a stock pot and heat.
2. Add the mirepoix and sauté until slightly tender.
3. Add the flour and paprika, making a roux, and cook for 5 minutes.
4. Add the hot chicken stock, whipping vigorously with a wire whip until slightly thickened and smooth.
5. Simmer for approximately 1 hour or until all the vegetables are tender.
6. Strain through a fine china cap forcing through as much of the vegetable flavor as possible using a ladle.
7. Stir in the grated cheese gradually with a wooden paddle.
8. Add the Worcestershire sauce and blend in thoroughly.
9. Add the hot milk and cream and stir in gently with a wooden paddle.
10. Season with salt and white pepper and pour into a 3 gal. container and serve.

Precautions and Safety Measures

1. When sautéing the mirepoix, do not let it brown.
2. While soup is simmering stir occasionally with a wooden paddle to avoid scorching.
3. Do not hold this soup at too high a temperature. It may curdle.

Oxtail soup

Oxtail soup is a thick soup very similar to English beef broth, but with small diced pieces of oxtail meat added. This soup is fairly popular in England, but not as well accepted in the United States. This soup is usually served as a *soup du jour* (soup of the day).

Objectives

1. To teach the student how to cut the vegetable garnish.
2. To teach the student how to cut the oxtail.
3. To teach the student the procedure for preparing oxtail soup.

Equipment

1. 2 stock pots, 5 gal. each
2. Meat saw
3. French knife
4. Wood paddle
5. Baker's scale
6. Qt. measure
7. Sauce pans (2)
8. Roast pan
9. China cap
10. Wire whip
11. Spoon measure
12. 3 gal. container for holding soup

Ingredients: Approx. yield: 3 gal.

2½ gal. beef stock
6 lbs. oxtail, cut into pieces at the joint
6 ozs. barley, uncooked
8 ozs. turnips, diced
2 lbs. onions, diced
4 ozs. leeks, diced
8 ozs. celery, diced
1 lb. carrots, diced
6 ozs. flour
1 pt. tomatoes, canned, crushed
1 cup tomato purée
8 ozs. butter or shortening
2 tbsp. Worcestershire sauce
salt and pepper to taste

Preparation

1. Cut the oxtail into pieces, by cutting through each joint with a French knife and brown them in the oven at 375°F. (Cut the oxtail only after demonstration by instructor.)
2. Prepare the beef stock. (See recipe this chapter.)
3. Place the barley in a sauce pan and wash. Cover with water and simmer for approximately 2 hours or until tender then drain in a china cap and wash with cold water.

4. Dice the onions, leeks, turnips, celery and carrots with a French knife.
5. Crush the tomatoes with your hands.
6. Place the diced turnips in a sauce pan and simmer until tender then drain.
7. Have all the equipment and ingredients handy.

Procedure
1. Place the browned oxtails in a stock pot, cover with the beef stock and simmer until the meat is tender enough to remove from the bone. Strain the stock through a fine china cap and keep hot. Remove the oxtail meat from the bone and dice into small cubes.
2. Place the butter or shortening in a second stock pot and heat.
3. Add the diced onions, leeks, carrots and celery and sauté until slightly tender.
4. Add the flour, making a roux, and cook for 5 minutes.
5. Add the hot beef stock, whipping vigorously with a wire whip until slightly thickened and smooth. Simmer until the vegetables are tender.
6. Add the crushed tomatoes, tomato purée, turnips, barley, diced oxtail meat, and Worcestershire sauce. Simmer for an additional 20 minutes.
7. Season with salt and pepper and pour into a 3 gal. container.
8. Serve.

Precautions and Safety Measures
1. When sautéing the vegetables, do not let them brown.
2. While the soup is simmering stir occasionally with a wooden paddle to avoid sticking or scorching.

Lobster bisque

Lobster bisque is a slightly thick, rich, cream-type soup with small particles of cooked lobster flowing through it to add flavor and color. A small amount of wine is added to enhance the flavor.

Objectives
1. To teach the student how to cook, shuck and dice the lobster.
2. To teach the student the procedure for preparing lobster bisque.

Equipment
1. Stock pot, 5 gal.
2. French knife

3. Baker's scale
4. Sauce pot, 3 gal.
5. Gal. measure
6. 3 gal. container for holding soup
7. China cap
8. Wood paddle
9. Cheese cloth
10. Sauce pan

Ingredients: Approx. yield: 3 gal.

4	lbs. lobster tails, raw, cut into 3 crosswise pieces
2	gal. water
12	ozs. onions, diced
1	lemon, sliced
1	bay leaf
6	ozs. celery, diced
1	lb. 4 ozs. butter
1	lb. flour
1	gal. milk and cream
6	ozs. sherry wine
1	tbsp. paprika
	salt and white pepper to taste

Preparation
1. Place the water, lemon, celery, onion and bay leaf in a sauce pot. Simmer for 30 minutes.
2. Add the lobster tails, which have been cut into 3 pieces, simmer for 10 minutes more, and remove from the fire.
3. Strain the stock through a china cap covered with a fine cheese cloth and hold.
4. Shuck by cracking the lobster shell with the back of a French knife and removing the shell with the hands. Dice the lobster meat with a French knife.
5. Heat the milk and cream in a sauce pan.
6. Have all the equipment and ingredients handy.

Procedure
1. Place the butter in a stock pot and heat.
2. Add the diced lobster and sauté slightly.
3. Add the paprika and flour and cook for approximately 3 minutes.
4. Add the hot stock slowly, stirring continuously with a wooden paddle until slightly thickened and smooth. Simmer for 20 minutes.
5. Pour in the hot milk and cream slowly, stirring gently with a wooden paddle.
6. Add the sherry wine and blend well; pour into a 3 gal. container.
7. Serve.

Precautions and Safety Measures
1. When heating the butter, do not burn.
2. When sautéing the lobster do not brown.
3. Do not hold this soup at too hot a temperature. It may curdle.

Shrimp bisque

Shrimp bisque is a slightly thick, rich, cream-type soup with small particles of cooked shrimp flowing through it, to add flavor and color. A small amount of wine is added to enhance the flavor.

Objectives
1. To teach the student the procedure for preparing shrimp bisque.
2. To teach the student how to cook, peel, devein and dice the shrimp.

Equipment
1. Stock pot, 5 gal.
2. French knife
3. Baker's scale
4. Sauce pot
5. Gal. measure
6. 3 gal. container for holding soup
7. China cap
8. Wood paddle
9. Cheese cloth

Ingredients: Approx. yield: 3 gal.

3	lbs. shrimp, raw
2	gal. water
12	ozs. onion, diced
1	lemon, sliced
1	bay leaf
6	ozs. celery, diced
	stems of 1 bch. parsley
1	lb. 4 ozs. butter
1	gal. milk and cream (½ and ½)
6	ozs. sherry wine
1	lb. flour
1	tbsp. paprika
	salt and white pepper to taste

Preparation
1. Place the water, lemon, celery, onion, bay leaf and parsley stems in a sauce pot. Simmer for 30 minutes.
2. Add the shrimp and continue to simmer for 10 minutes more then remove from the fire.
3. Strain the stock through a china cap covered with a fine cheese cloth and hold.
4. Cool the shrimp in cold water. Remove the shell from the meat by pulling it

*Bureau of Commercial Fisheries
U.S. Dept. of the Interior*

Removing shell from shrimp (top); removing sand vein from shrimp (bottom).

away from the body with your fingers. Devein (remove the sand vein from the back of the shrimp) by taking out the black line with the point of a small knife, a tooth pick, or a beer can opener. Dice the shrimp fine with a French knife.
5. Heat the milk and cream.
6. Have all the equipment and ingredients handy.

Procedure
1. Place the butter in a stock pot and heat.
2. Add the diced shrimp and sauté slightly.
3. Add the paprika and flour and cook for approximately 3 minutes.
4. Add the hot stock slowly, stirring continuously with a wooden paddle until slightly thickened and smooth. Simmer for 20 minutes.
5. Pour in the hot milk and cream slowly, stirring gently with a wooden paddle.
6. Add the sherry wine and blend well. Pour into a 3 gal. container.
7. Serve.

1. When heating the butter, do not burn.
2. When sautéing the shrimp, do not brown.
3. Do not hold this soup at too hot a temperature. It may curdle.

Oyster or clam bisque

Oyster or clam bisque is a slightly thick soup prepared with milk and cream, vegetables and seasoning. Most bisques are prepared from shellfish.

Objectives
1. To teach the student how to mince the onions.
2. To teach the student the procedure for preparing oyster or clam bisque.

Equipment
1. Stock pot, 5 gal.
2. French knife
3. Baker's scale
4. Gal. measure
5. Measuring spoons
6. Wood paddle
7. 3 gal. container for holding soup
8. Sauce pot, 6 qt.
9. China cap
10. Wire whip
11. Sauce pan, 6 qt.

Ingredients: Approx. yield: 3 gal.

3	qts. oysters or clams, shucked, cut into quarters
1	gal. water
1	gal. milk, hot
1	gal. single cream, hot
1	lb. 4 ozs. butter
8	ozs. onions, minced
1	lb. flour
1	bay leaf
1	tsp. paprika
	salt and white pepper to taste

Preparation
1. Cut the oysters or clams into quarters with a French knife. Place in a sauce pot, add the gallon of water and simmer for 10 minutes. Strain the liquid off the cooked oysters or clams by pouring it through a china cap into a separate pan. Chop the oysters or clams very fine and return them to the strained liquid.
2. Mince the onions with a French knife.
3. Heat the milk and cream.
4. Have all the equipment and ingredients handy.

Procedure
1. Place the butter in a stock pot and heat.
2. Add the fine minced onions and sauté until slightly tender. Do not brown.
3. Add the flour and paprika and cook for about 5 minutes.
4. Add the oysters or clams and oyster or clam liquid, milk and cream, whipping vigorously with a wire whip until slightly thickened and smooth.
5. Add the bay leaf and simmer for 30 minutes. Remove the bay leaf. Pour the soup into a 3 gal. container.
6. Season with salt and white pepper and serve.

Precautions and Safety Measures
1. While the bisque is simmering, stir occasionally with a wooden paddle to avoid sticking and scorching.
2. When sautéing the onions do not let them become brown.

Seafood chowder

Seafood chowder is a thick soup similar to clam chowder, but with an assortment of fish and shellfish added instead of just the clams. This soup is an excellent choice for the Friday menu.

Objectives
1. To teach the student how to prepare the seafood.
2. To teach the student how to cut the vegetable garnish.
3. To teach the student the procedure for preparing seafood chowder.

Equipment
1. Stock pot, 5 gal.
2. French knife
3. Qt. measure
4. Baker's scale
5. Wood paddle
6. 3 sauce pans
7. Cheese cloth
8. 3 gal. container for holding soup

Ingredients: Approx. yield: 3 gal.

2½	gal. fish stock
1	qt. milk, hot
1	qt. cream, warm
2	lbs. red snapper, cooked
2	lbs. halibut, cooked
2	lbs. shrimp, peeled, deveined
1	pt. clams, canned, chopped
12	ozs. flour

Lynch Fish Co.

Seafood chowder

1	lb. butter
3	pts. potatoes, diced
1	bay leaf
1	lb. 8 ozs. onions, diced small
8	ozs. celery, diced small
¼	oz. thyme
	salt and white pepper to taste

Preparation

1. Prepare the fish stock. (See recipe this chapter.)
2. Place the red snapper and halibut in a sauce pan, cover with salt water and simmer until the fish is cooked. Break a piece of the fish in half, if the flesh is dull in appearance the fish is done. If it has a slightly glossy appearance, the fish is not fully cooked. When done, drain the liquid from the fish, and allow the fish to cool. Remove all skin and bones, and flake.
3. Peel the raw shrimp: remove the shell from the meat by pulling it away from the body with your fingers. Devein (remove sand vein from the back of the shrimp) by taking out the black line with the point of a small knife, tooth pick or beer can opener. Cut each shrimp into four pieces.
4. Dice the onions, celery and potatoes with a French knife.
5. Simmer the thyme in water, strain through a cheese cloth and reserve juice for seasoning.
6. Have all the equipment and ingredients handy.

Procedure

1. Place the butter in a stock pot and heat.

2. Add the diced vegetables and shrimp and sauté until the vegetables are slightly tender.
3. Add the flour, making a roux, and cook for 5 minutes.
4. Add hot fish stock and bay leaf, stirring vigorously with a wooden paddle until slightly thickened and smooth. Simmer until the vegetables are tender.
5. Add the clams, thyme, liquid, and potatoes. Continue to simmer until the potatoes are tender.
6. Add the cooked red snapper and halibut. Simmer for 5 minutes longer.
7. Pour in the milk and cream slowly, stirring gently with a wooden paddle until well incorporated.
8. Remove the bay leaf and season with salt and pepper, pour into a 3 gal. container.

Precautions and Safety Measures

1. When sautéing the vegetables and shrimp do not let them brown.
2. While the soup is simmering, stir occasionally to avoid sticking or scorching.
3. Before adding the cooked fish to the soup be sure all the bones have been removed.

Mulligatawny

Mulligatawny is a thick soup seasoned with curry powder. It supposedly originated in India where the essence of curry powder is much used. Mulligatawny soup is sometimes placed on the menu as "Mulligatawy à la Indienne" meaning mulligatawny soup prepared in the manner of India. This special soup is usually placed on the menu as a *soup du jour* (soup of the day).

Objectives

1. To teach the student how to cut the vegetable garnish.
2. To teach the student the procedure for preparing mulligatawny soup.

Equipment

1. French knife
2. Stock pot, 5 gal.
3. Wood paddle
4. Sauce pan
5. Baker's scale
6. Qt. measure
7. 3 gal. container for holding soup

Ingredients: Approx. yield: 3 gal.
2½ gal. chicken or veal stock
3 pts. milk and cream (½ and ½)
10 ozs. butter
6 ozs. flour
1 lb. celery, diced fine
1 lb. onions, diced fine
6 ozs. leeks, diced fine
1 lb. green apples diced fine
8 ozs. turkey, white meat, diced fine
8 ozs. rice, raw
1 oz. curry powder
salt and white pepper to taste

Preparation
1. Prepare the chicken or veal stock. (See recipes this chapter.)
2. Heat the milk and cream in a sauce pan.
3. Dice the vegetables, apples and turkey fine with a French knife.
4. Wash the rice.
5. Have all equipment and ingredients handy.

Procedure
1. Place the butter or shortening in a stock pot and heat.
2. Add the vegetables and sauté until partly tender.
3. Add the flour, making a roux, and cook for 5 minutes. Stir in the curry powder.
4. Add the chicken or veal stock slowly, stirring continuously with a wooden paddle until slightly thickened and smooth. Simmer until the vegetables are tender.
5. Add the rice, green apples, and diced turkey. Continue to simmer until the rice is tender.
6. Remove from the fire and stir in the hot milk and cream slowly.
7. Season with salt and white pepper and pour into a 3 gal. container.
8. Serve.

Precautions and Safety Measures
1. When sautéing the vegetables, do not let them brown.
2. While the soup is simmering stir occasionally with a wooden paddle to avoid sticking or scorching.

Mock turtle soup

Mock turtle soups, as the word *mock* indicates, is an imitation turtle soup. It is prepared from a rich brown stock with lemon, chopped hard boiled eggs and sherry wine. This soup is a very popular item in the com-

mercial kitchen and is usually served as a *soup du jour* (soup of the day).

Objectives
1. To teach the student how to cut the vegetable garnish.
2. To teach the student how to chop the eggs and mince the lemons.
3. To teach the student the procedure for preparing mock turtle soup.

Equipment
1. 2 stock pots, 5 gal. each
2. French knife
3. Wood paddle
4. China cap
5. Roast pan
6. Cleaver
7. Boning knife
8. Wire whip
9. Kitchen spoon
10. Baker's scale
11. Qt. measure
12. Measuring spoons
13. 3. gal. container for holding soup

Ingredients: Approx. yield: 3 gal.
6 lbs. calf heads and veal shanks
3 gal. brown stock
12 ozs. shortening
8 ozs. flour
4 lemons, peeled, diced fine
8 ozs. carrots, minced
4 ozs. celery, minced
8 ozs. onions, minced
4 hard boiled eggs, chopped
1 pt. sherry wine
1 bay leaf
½ tsp. thyme
salt and pepper to taste

Preparation
1. Prepare the brown stock. (See recipe this chapter.)
2. Peel the lemons, remove the seeds and membranes and dice very fine with a French knife.
3. Chop the hard boiled eggs fairly fine with a French knife.
4. Mince the onions, celery and carrots with a French knife.
5. The calf heads have most of the flesh removed from the bones when they are received in the kitchen. The eyes are usually left intact. The eyes must be removed from their socket with a boning knife and the head split in half with a cleaver. Pro-

ceed only after demonstration by instructor.

6. Have all the equipment and ingredients handy.

Procedure

1. Place the calf heads and shanks in a roast pan and brown thoroughly in a 400°F oven.
2. Remove from the oven and place in a stock pot, deglaze the pan and add this liquid to the stock pot also.
3. Add the brown stock, bay leaf and thyme, and simmer on the range for 3 hours.
4. Strain the liquid through a china cap and reserve this stock for later use. Pick the meat from the bones and chop fine.
5. In a second stock pot place the shortening and heat.
6. Add the very finely diced vegetables and sauté until slightly tender.
7. Add the flour, making a roux, and cook for 5 minutes.
8. Add the hot brown stock, whip vigorously with a wire whip until slightly thickened and smooth. Simmer until the vegetables are very tender.
9. Add the chopped cooked meat, diced lemons and chopped hard boiled eggs, stir with a kitchen spoon. Return to a simmer.
10. Remove from the range, add the sherry wine and season with salt and pepper; pour into a 3 gal. container.

Precautions and Safety Measures

1. When sautéing the vegetables do not let them brown.
2. While the soup is simmering, stir occasionally with a wooden paddle to avoid sticking or scorching.

SPECIAL SOUP RECIPES
Chicken gumbo soup

Chicken gumbo soup is a creole-type soup, very popular in New Orleans and southern states. It is often served as *soup du jour* (soup of the day) in commercial kitchens.

Objectives

1. To teach the student the procedure for making chicken gumbo soup.
2. To teach the student how to cut the vegetable garnish.

Equipment

1. Large stock pot, 10 gal.

Chicken gumbo soup

Photo: Kathryn Adams

2. French knife
3. Wood paddle
4. Baker's scale
5. Qt. measure
6. 5 gal. container for holding soup

Ingredients: Approx. yield: 5 gal.

2 lbs. celery, diced
1 lb. green peppers, diced
2 lbs. onions, diced
1 lb. shortening or chicken fat
5 gal. chicken stock
1 lb. rice
2 #2 cans okra
1 #10 can tomatoes, crushed
   salt and pepper to taste
   chicken base to taste

Preparation

1. Dice onions, celery and green peppers using a French knife.
2. Prepare chicken stock. (See recipe this chapter.)
3. Crush tomatoes.
4. Wash rice.
5. Have all equipment and ingredients handy.

Procedure

1. Place shortening or fat in stock pot, add diced vegetables and sauté slightly.
2. Add chicken stock and rice. Let cook until rice is done.
3. Add crushed tomatoes and let simmer 5 minutes.
4. Add okra and season with salt and pepper. Add chicken base if stock flavor is lacking.
5. Pour into a 5 gal. container.

Precautions and Safety Measures

1. Do not overcook the okra.
2. Use a rich chicken stock, if possible.

Borscht

Borscht is a thin soup of Russian origin. The main ingredients in the preparation are beets and tomatoes. Borscht can be served hot or cold and is usually garnished with sour cream. It can be served as a *soup du jour* (soup of the day) or as a specialty item.

Objectives

1. To teach the student how to cut the garnish and strain the soup.
2. To teach the student the procedure for preparing borscht.
3. To teach the student how to dish up borscht.

Equipment

1. Qt. measure
2. French knife
3. China cap
4. 6 oz. ladle
5. Measuring spoons
6. Cup measure
7. Pepper mill
8. Stock pot, 5 gal.
9. 3 gal. container for holding soup

Ingredients: Approx. yield: 2½ gal.

1½	qt. beets canned, diced (includes juice)
1	pt. onions, diced
2	qts. tomatoes, canned
1½	gal. beef stock
1	pt. lemon juice
1	tsp. garlic, minced
½	cup parsley stems
2	bay leaves
½	cup sugar
3	tsp. salt
1	tbsp. paprika
	fresh ground pepper to taste
	sour cream as needed

Preparation

1. Prepare the beef stock. (See recipe this chapter.)
2. Dice the onions using a French knife. Squeeze the juice from lemons.
3. Mince the garlic.
4. Have all the equipment and ingredients handy.

Procedure

1. Place the beef stock, tomatoes, onion and garlic in a stock pot and simmer until the onions are partly done.
2. Add the remaining ingredients and simmer for about 1½ hours.

3. Strain the soup through a china cap into a 3 gal. container. Using a ladle, force as much of the vegetable pulp as possible through the china cap.
4. Serve hot with sour cream on top of each serving or let cool, refrigerate, and serve cold with sour cream on top.

Precautions and Safety Measures

1. Exercise caution when straining the soup.

Scotch mutton broth

Scotch mutton broth is a thick soup prepared by combining lamb stock, barley, vegetables and seasoning. This soup supposedly originated in Scotland. It is not a very popular soup in the United States, but can be placed on the menu to create a little variety.

Objectives

1. To teach the student how to cut the vegetable garnish.
2. To teach the student the procedure for preparing Scotch mutton broth.

Equipment

1. French knife
2. Wood paddle
3. Stock pot, 5 gal.
4. Baker's scale
5. Qt. measure
6. Measuring spoons
7. Sauce pan, 3 qt.
8. 3 gal. container for holding soup
9. Sauce pot, 3 gal.
10. China cap

Ingredients: Approx. yield: 3 gal.

2½	gal. lamb or mutton stock
3	lbs. lamb shoulder, cooked by boiling, diced
2	lbs. onions, diced small
1	lb. celery, diced small
1	lb. carrots, diced small
4	oz. leeks, diced small
12	ozs. turnips, diced small
1	tsp. thyme
8	ozs. barley
1	lb. shortening or butter
12	ozs. flour
	salt and white pepper to taste

Preparation

1. Prepare the lamb or mutton stock. (See recipe this chapter.)
2. Boil the barley in a sauce pan with 2 qts. of water until tender (approximately 1½

hours) then drain in a china cap and wash in cold water.
3. Cut the vegetables into a small dice with a French knife.
4. Cook the lamb shoulder in a sauce pot, by covering with water and simmering until tender. Dice the cooked lamb.
5. Have all the equipment and ingredients handy.

Procedure
1. Place the shortening or butter in a stock pot and heat.
2. Add the diced vegetables and sauté until slightly tender. Do not brown.
3. Add the flour, making a roux, and cook for 5 minutes.
4. Add the hot lamb or mutton stock, stirring vigorously with a wooden paddle until slightly thickened and smooth.
5. Add the diced cooked lamb, cooked barley and thyme. Simmer for approximately 1 hour.
6. Season with salt and pepper and pour into a 3 gal. container.

Precautions and Safety Measures
1. When sautéing the vegetables do not let them brown.
2. While the soup is simmering, stir occasionally with a wooden paddle to avoid sticking or scorching.

Philadelphia pepper pot

Philadelphia pepper pot is the soup that reputedly saved Washington's troops at Valley Forge. The soup is highly seasoned with cracked white peppercorns and contains both tripe (beef stomach) and spaetzles (Austrian homemade noodles). Philadelphia pepper pot is usually served as a *soup du jour* (soup of the day).

Objectives
1. To teach the student how to cut the vegetable garnish.
2. To teach the student how to cut the pototoes and tripe.
3. To teach the student the procedure for preparing Philadelphia pepper pot.

Equipment
1. Stock pot, 5 gal.
2. French knife
3. Wood paddle
4. Baker's scale
5. Measuring spoons

6. Qt. measure
7. Sauce pan
8. 3 gal. container for holding soup
9. Wire whip

Ingredients: Approx. yield: 3 gal.

3	lbs. honeycomb tripe, diced
2½	gal. beef or chicken stock
12	ozs. butter
10	ozs. flour
1	lb. onions, diced
8	ozs. celery, diced
12	ozs. green pepper, diced
2	lbs. potatoes, raw, diced
1	tsp. white peppercorns, cracked
1	tsp. majoram
2	qts. spaetzles
	salt to taste

Preparation
1. Prepare the beef or chicken stock. (See recipe this chapter.)
2. Place the tripe in a sauce pan, cover with salt water and simmer until tender. Cool and dice into fairly small cubes with a French knife.
3. Dice the onions, celery and green peppers with a French knife.
4. Crack the white peppercorns.
5. Prepare the spaetzles. See following recipe.
6. Dice the raw potatoes with a French knife.
7. Have all equipment and ingredients handy.

Procedure
1. Place the butter in a stock pot and heat.
2. Add the diced vegetables and sauté, until slightly tender.
3. Add the flour, making a roux, cook for 5 minutes.
4. Add the hot stock, whipping briskly with a wire whip until slightly thickened and smooth.
5. Add the tripe, marjoram and cracked peppercorns. Simmer until the diced vegetables are tender.
6. Add the diced potatoes and spaetzles. (See spatzle recipe following this recipe.) Continue to simmer until the potatoes are tender, pour into a 3 gal. container.
7. Season with salt and serve.

Precautions and Safety Measures
1. When sautéing the vegetables do not let them brown.
2. While the soup is simmering stir occasionally with a wooden paddle to avoid sticking and scorching.

Spaetzles

Spaetzles are a type of noodle that originated in Austria. They are used in preparation of some soups (such as Philadelphia pepper pot) and served as a complement to certain entrees dishes such as goulash, chicken paprika and stuffed cabbage.

Objectives

To teach the student:
1. The procedure for preparing spaetzles.
2. How to cook the spaetzle dough.

Equipment
1. Baker's scale
2. Qt. measure
3. Spoon measures
4. Mixing machine and paddle
5. Large hole collander
6. Stock pot, 5 gal.
7. Wooden paddle

Ingredients: Approx. yield: 1 gal.

12	whole eggs
1	qt. milk
3	lbs. 4 ozs. cake flour
2	tsp. salt
½	tsp. white pepper

Preparation
1. Fill the stock pot half full of water and add additional salt. Bring water to a simmer.
2. Have all equipment and ingredients handy.

Procedure
1. Break the whole eggs into the bowl of the mixing machine. With the paddle, mix slightly at second speed.
2. Add the milk and continue to mix until it is blended with the eggs.
3. Add the cake flour gradually, while mixing at slow speed.
4. Add the salt and pepper and continue to mix until a smooth dough is formed.
5. Place the large hole collander over the simmering water letting the handles of the collander rest on the top edge of the stock pot. The collander will now be suspended over the simmering water.
6. Pour the spaetzle dough into the collander. Rub across the bottom of the collander with the heel of your hand, forcing the dough through the holes of the collander into the simmering water. Continue this action until all the dough has been rubbed through. Remove the collander from the stock pot.

7. Let the spaetzles boil in the salt water for approximately 7 minutes, stirring occasionally with the wooden paddle.
8. Drain the water from the spaetzles by pouring them in a collander. Drain thoroughly and let the spaetzles cool.

Note: If using the spaetzles for soup, they can be cooked in the soup or cooked separately then added to the soup. If they are to be served with an entree dish they must be thoroughly cooled, then sautéed in butter or margarine before serving.

Precautions and Safety Measures
1. When rubbing the dough through the collander the water should be *simmering* to hold the steam to a minimum. Excessive steam will make it impossible to force the dough through the holes of the china cap.

English beef broth

English beef broth is a thick soup with barley as the main ingredient. It is served in most commercial kitchens as a *soup du jour* (soup of the day).

Objectives
1. To teach the student the procedure for preparing English beef broth.
2. To teach the student how to cut the garnish.
3. To teach the student how to cook the barley.

Equipment
1. Large stock pot, 10 gal.
2. French knife
3. Wood paddle
4. Baker's scale
5. Qt. measure
6. 5 gal. container for holding soup
7. Sauce pan

Ingredients: Approx. yield: 5 gal.

2	lbs. carrots, diced
3	lbs. onions, diced
2	lbs. celery, diced
2½	gal. brown stock
1	lb. bacon or ham fat
1	lb. tomato purée
	salt and pepper to taste
1	lb. leeks
2½	gal. ham stock
1	lb. flour
1	lb. 4 ozs. barley

Preparation
1. Wash barley.

2. Dice garnish (carrots, celery and onions) using a French knife.
3. Prepare ham stock. (See recipe this chapter.)
4. Prepare brown stock. (See recipe this chapter.)
5. Have all equipment and ingredients handy.

Procedure
1. Place bacon or ham fat in a stock pot, add the diced onions, carrots, celery and leek. Sauté until partly done (onions will have a transparent appearance).
2. Add flour to take up the fat, making a roux. Cook for 5 minutes.
3. Add ham stock, brown stock and tomato purée and let simmer for 30 minutes.
4. Cook the barley in a separate sauce pan; cover with a ratio of 3 parts water to 1 part barley. Simmer until tender. The barley contains a high percentage of starch and cooking it in the soup will make the soup too thick and starchy.
5. Add cooked barley (after it has been washed) to the soup and continue to simmer until all ingredients are tender (approx. 45 minutes).
6. Season with salt and pepper.
7. Pour into a 5 gal. container.

Precautions and Safety Measures
1. Cook barley separately and wash thoroughly after cooking.
2. While soup is cooking stir occasionally to avoid sticking.
3. After barley is cooked, wash well with water to remove starch before adding it to the soup.

New England clam chowder

New England clam chowder is similar to the Manhattan clam chowder, but the tomatoes are omitted and milk and cream are added. The chowder is prepared by the New England style of cooking which uses no tomatoes in most preparations.

Objectives
1. To teach the student how to cut the vegetable garnish.
2. To teach the student the procedure for preparing New England clam chowder.

Equipment
1. Stock pot, 10 gal.
2. Wood paddle
3. Baker's scale

New England clam chowder

4. Qt. measure
5. French knife
6. Sauce pan, 1 qt.
7. Cheese cloth
8. 5 gal. container for holding soup
9. Sauce pot, 3 gal.

Ingredients: Approx. yield: 5 gal.
3 gal. fish stock and clam juice
2 gal. milk and cream
1 lb. 8 ozs. shortening
1 lb. 8 ozs. flour
2 lbs. onions, diced
2 lbs. celery, diced
1 lb. green pepper, diced
8 ozs. leeks, diced
4 lbs. potatoes, peeled, diced
2 qts. clams, canned, drained, chopped
¼ oz. thyme
1 oz. garlic, minced
   salt and white pepper to taste

Preparation
1. Prepare the fish stock. (See recipe this chapter.)
2. Dice the vegetable garnish (onions, celery, green peppers, potatoes and leeks) with a French knife.
3. Simmer the thyme in water for 5 minutes in a sauce pan. Strain through a cheese cloth and reserve the liquid for seasoning.
4. Heat the milk and cream in a sauce pot.
5. Drain and chop the clams. Mince the garlic.
6. Have all the equipment and ingredients handy.

Procedure
1. Place the shortening in a stock pot, heat.
2. Add the diced vegetables and garlic and sauté until slightly tender, do not brown.
3. Add the flour, making a roux, and cook for 5 minutes.
4. Add the hot stock and clam juice, whip-

ping to make it smooth. Simmer until the vegetables are slightly tender.
5. Add the potatoes, clams and thyme liquid. Continue to simmer until the potatoes are tender.
6. Add the hot milk and cream slowly, stirring gently with a wooden paddle. Bring the soup back to a simmer.
7. Season with salt and pepper; pour into a 5 gal. container.
8. Remove from the range and serve.
   Precautions and Safety Measures
1. Stir the soup occasionally throughout the cooking period to avoid scorching.
2. When sautéing the vegetables do not let them become brown.
3. Remove the soup from the range before the potatoes are over-cooked.

Manhattan clam chowder

Manhattan clam chowder is also called Long Island or Philadelphia clam chowder. This type of chowder differs from the New England type because it contains tomatoes and no milk or cream. A chowder will always contain diced potatoes. This is one of the meatless soups so popular on the Friday menu.
Objectives
1. To teach the student how to cut the vegetable garnish.
2. To teach the student how to prepare Manhattan clam chowder.
Equipment
1. French knife
2. Baker's scale
3. Qt. measure
4. Stock pot, 10 gal.
5. Wooden paddle
6. Sauce pan
7. Cheese cloth
8. 5 gal. container for holding soup
   Ingredients: Approx. yield: 5 gal.
   4½ gal. fish stock and clam juice
   2 qts. clams, canned, drained, chopped
   3 qts. potatoes, peeled, diced
   2 lbs. onions, diced
   2 lbs. celery, diced
   1 lb. green peppers, diced
   1 lb. leeks, diced
   2 lbs. shortening
   ½ oz. thyme

⅛ oz. rosemary leaves
12 ozs. flour
1 oz. garlic, minced
1 #10 can whole tomatoes, crushed
   salt and white pepper to taste
Preparation
1. Prepare the fish stock. (See recipe this chapter.)
2. Dice onions, celery, leeks, potatoes, and green peppers using a French knife.
3. Place the thyme and rosemary leaves in a sauce pan. Simmer in water for a few minutes, strain the liquid through a cheese cloth, and reserve liquid for later use.
4. Mince the garlic and crush the tomatoes.
5. Drain the clams and crop them, if this has not already been done.
6. Have all the equipment and ingredients handy.
Procedure
1. Place the shortening in a large stock pot, heat.
2. Add the diced vegetables and minced garlic, and sauté until the vegetables are slightly tender.
3. Add the flour making a roux, and cook for 5 minutes.
4. Add the hot fish stock and clam juice and cook, stirring vigorously with the wooden paddle until slightly thickened.
5. Continue to simmer until the vegetables are tender.
6. Add the diced potatoes, clams, tomatoes and the thyme and rosemary flavored liquid. Simmer until the potatoes are tender.
7. Remove from the range and season with salt and pepper and place in a 5 gal. container.
8. Serve hot.
   Precautions and Safety Measures
1. When sautéing vegetables do not let them brown.
2. Stir the soup occasionally with the wooden paddle throughout the cooking period to avoid sticking.

Italian minestrone soup

Italian minestrone soup is an Italian vegetable soup which has become quite popular in the United States since the end of World War II. It is served on the menu as a *soup* du jour (soup of the day) or with Italian entrees.

Objectives

1. To teach the student how to cut the vegetable garnish.
2. To teach the student the procedure for preparing Italian minestrone soup.

Equipment

1. Stock pot, 5 gal.
2. Food grinder
3. French knife
4. Wood paddle
5. Baker's scale
6. Measuring spoon
7. Qt. measure
8. Cup measure
9. 3 gal. container for holding soup
10. China cap
11. Sauce pot

Ingredients: Approx. yield: 3 gal.

2½	gal. beef stock
1	cup olive oil
4	ozs. black-eyed beans
4	ozs. red beans
1	small can chick-peas (garbanzos)
1	lb. 8 ozs. onions, minced
1	lb celery, minced
1	lb. carrots, minced
8	ozs. green pepper, minced
6	ozs. cabbage, minced
3	cloves garlic, minced
1	qt. tomatoes, canned, crushed
5	ozs. salt pork, ground
2	tbsp. parsley, chopped
1	tsp. basil
1	tsp. oregano
⅓	cup Parmesan cheese
	salt and pepper to taste

Preparation

1. Prepare the beef stock. (See recipe this chapter.)
2. Wash the black-eyed and red beans. Cover with water and soak them overnight. Drain and place them in a sauce pot, cover with salt water and simmer until tender. Drain a second time through a china cap.
3. Mince onions, celery, green peppers, carrots, cabbage and garlic with French knife.
4. Crush the tomatoes with your hand.
5. Chop the parsley with a French knife.
6. Grind the salt pork on the food grinder, using the very fine chopper plate.
7. Have all the equipment and ingredients handy.

Procedure

1. Place the olive oil in a stock pot and heat.
2. Add the minced vegetables and garlic and sauté until slightly tender.
3. Add the crushed tomatoes, beef stock, basil, and oregano. Simmer for approximately 1 hour or until all the vegetables are tender.
4. Add the black-eyed beans, red beans and chick-peas (garbanzos) and continue to simmer for an additional half hour.
5. Remove from the fire, add the chopped parsley, ground salt pork and Parmesan cheese and blend in thoroughly with a wooden paddle.
6. Season with salt and pepper and pour into a 3 gal. container.
7. Serve by sprinkling Parmesan cheese on top of each serving.

Precautions and Safety Measures

1. When sautéing the vegetables do not let them brown.
2. When adding the basil and oregano, rub them in the palm of your hand to release the flavor of the herbs.

COLD SOUP RECIPES

Cold Fruit Soup

Cold fruit soup is a blend of assorted fruits and their natural juices. This soup is an excellent choice for the summer menu as an appetizer. Cold fruit soup is usually garnished with a mint leaf.

Objectives

1. To teach the student the procedure for preparing cold fruit soup.
2. To teach the student how to serve cold fruit soup.

Equipment

1. Qt. measure
2. French knife
3. Baker's scale
4. Sauce pans (2)
5. 2 gal. bain marie for holding soup
6. Cup measure
7. Wire whip
8. Kitchen spoon
9. Paring knife

Ingredients: Approx. yield: 2 gal.

2	qts. water
1	lb. 4 ozs. sugar, granulated
1	pt. sweet cherries, pitted, drained

½ cup maraschino cherries, drained, cut in half
1 pt. mandarin orange segments and syrup
1 pt. peaches, canned, drained, sliced
4 ozs. raisins, seedless
¼ cup lemon juice
2 qts. orange juice
1 pt. pears, canned, drained, sliced
2½ ozs. cornstarch
1 cup cold water

Preparation

1. Slice the peaches and pears with a French knife.
2. Cut the maraschino cherries in half with a paring knife.
3. Have all the equipment and ingredients handy.

Procedure

1. Combine in a sauce pan the 2 qts. of water and the sugar, bring to a boil and stir with a kitchen spoon until the sugar is dissolved.
2. Add the peaches, pears, both kinds of cherries, mandarin orange sections with syrup, raisins and lemon juice. Bring to a simmer.
3. Place the orange juice in a separate sauce pan and bring to a boil.
4. Dissolve the corn starch in the cup of cold water. Pour slowly into the boiling orange juice, whipping briskly with a wire whip until thickened and smooth.
5. Pour the thickened orange juice mixture slowly into the fruit mixture, stirring gently with a kitchen spoon until thoroughly blended.
6. Bring to a boil and remove from the fire.
7. Pour into a 2 gal. bain marie, cool and refrigerate.
8. Serve in cold bouillon cups garnished with a mint leaf.

Precautions and Safety Measures

1. When adding the thickened orange juice mixture to the fruit mixture, stir very gently so the fruit will not be mashed or broken.

Vichyssoise

Vichyssoise is a rich, creamy, potato soup which is always served cold. It is usually garnished with chopped chives and is an extremely popular appetizer on the warm weather menu.

Objectives

1. To teach the student how to cut the vegetable garnish.
2. To teach the student the procedure for preparing vichyssoise.
3. To teach student how to serve soup.

Equipment

1. Stock pot, 5 gal.
2. Gal. measure
3. Baker's scale
4. French knife
5. Wood paddle
6. 3 gal. container for holding soup
7. Vegetable peeler

Ingredients: Approx. yield: 3 gal.

2 gal. chicken stock
1 gal. light cream
3 lbs. potatoes, raw, peeled and sliced
1 lb. onions, diced
12 ozs. leeks, diced
2 bay leaves
8 ozs. celery, diced
4 white peppercorns
salt and white pepper to taste
chives, minced, for garnish

Preparation

1. Prepare the chicken stock. (See recipe this chapter.)
2. Mince the chives with a French knife.
3. Dice onions and celery with French knife.
4. Peel the potatoes with a vegetable peeler. Wash and slice the potatoes fairly thin.
5. Crack the peppercorns.
6. Have all the equipment and ingredients handy.

Procedure

1. Place the butter in a stock pot and heat.
2. Add the onions, celery, and leeks and sauté until slightly tender.
3. Add the chicken stock, potatoes, bay leaves and peppercorns. Simmer until the potatoes are very well done.
4. Strain the mixture through a fine china cap into a 3 gal. container. Using a ladle, force as much of the potato pulp as possible through china cap. Let mixture cool.
5. Add the cream and blend in thoroughly using a wooden paddle.
6. Season with salt and white pepper.
7. Chill well. Garnish with minced chives and serve ice cold.

Precautions and Safety Measures

1. Stir soup occasionally while simmering.

vegetable preparation

■ Vegetables are a very important part of any meal, but unfortunately the items most neglected. Today the emphasis in most food service establishments is placed on the entree or the dessert. Although these items are of major importance, the vegetables that may accompany the entree are likewise essential. The fact is that many menus give so little importance to the vegetable that it is generally listed as vegetable *du jour* (of the day), rather than specifying the true name of the vegetable or vegetable preparation. Most vegetable preparations lack variety and are frequently overcooked. When observing the vegeta-

ble selection on menus, if such a section is listed, you can readily see that this is the most common weakness among chefs or menu makers. Rather than providing an interesting variety they continually feature the same vegetables, in most cases peas, green beans, lima beans or corn.

VEGETABLE CLASSIFICATIONS

Vegetables are divided into two groups, fresh or dried, depending on their nature when ripe. The fresh vegetables are eaten at the time the plants are ripe, or the ripeness may be preserved to some extent by canning or freezing. The dried vegetables have all their moisture removed and will keep indefinitely. We can further distinguish fresh vegetables by classifying them according to color as green, yellow, red, or white. Dried vegetables are divided into legumes (beans, peas, etc.) and cereals (rice, barley, etc.).

Green vegetables, which include peas, string beans, broccoli, lima beans, etc., obtain their attractive green color from a pigment called chlorophyll. Chlorophyll is easily destroyed by alkalis and acids when heat is applied. It is important that green vegetables be cooked properly to retain their natural green color when they are served. The color of green vegetables becomes extremely bright when cooked in very hard water to which baking soda has been added. We do *not* recommend soda because it destroys much of the vitamin content and the color of the vegetable assumes an artificial appearance. Most green vegetables contain a high percentage of acid. Therefore, they should be cooked slowly and left uncovered so the acid, which would destroy the green color, can escape in the steam.

Yellow vegetables, which include carrots, yellow turnips, corn, rutabagas, squash, etc., are not affected by any change in color when heat is applied unless they are overcooked. If overcooked they become dull in appearance and lose much of their appetite appeal. Most yellow vegetables should be cooked in very little water and covered with a lid to conserve their food value. The only exceptions would be yellow turnips and rutabagas which, since they possess a strong flavor, should always be cooked uncovered.

Red vegetables, such as red cabbage and beets, react in a fashion directly opposite to that of green vegetables when heat is applied. Acids improve the color while alkalies make them fade and turn a bluish gray. To help the natural color of these vegetables when cooking, diluted acids, such as lemon juice, vinegar or cream of tartar should be added. Usually one tablespoon to each quart of water is sufficient. Beets should be cooked with a lid on so they may benefit from the acid content they possess. Red cabbage should be cooked partly uncovered to provide an escape for its sulphur content.

White vegetables, which include white cabbage, white onions, turnips, cauliflower, etc., have a tendency to turn yellow when cooked in hard, alkaline water. They also turn yellow when they are overcooked. To prevent this from occurring, cook such vegetables in just enough water to submerge them. Do not cover them with a lid. Cook until the vegetables are just tender. A small amount of vinegar or lemon juice can be added to counteract the alkalinity that may be present in the cooking water; this will improve the appearance and eating qualities of white vegetables.

Dried legumes include lima beans, lentils, peas, kidney beans, navy beans, great northern beans, etc. This type of vegetable is not used to any great extent in vegetable cookery. They are used more often in soups. When preparing legumes soak them overnight to replace the water lost in ripening and drying. The next day they should be covered with water, using about 1 gallon of water for each pound of legumes, and cooked slowly by simmering until tender. At no time during the cooking should they be subjected to boiling temperatures because boiling tends to toughen legumes. Soaking is not required when preparing split peas and lentils.

Cereals such as rice and barley should be washed, thoroughly covered with water, and simmered until tender. The ratio of water to rice is two to one or 2 quarts of water for each quart of rice. For cooking barley a ratio of three to one is preferred. After boiling, both rice and barley should be washed thoroughly in cold water to eliminate the excess starch. Rice can also be prepared by baking with excellent results. Both of these cereal vegetables are cooked covered.

VEGETABLE MARKET FORMS

On today's market, vegetables may be purchased in the following forms and in most cases the method of proper preparation differs.

1. Fresh vegetables
2. Frozen vegetables
3. Canned vegetables
4. Dried legumes

Fresh vegetables should be thoroughly washed before cooking. This assures cleanliness in vegetables that may be covered with dirt or grit. All blemishes should be removed and the vegetable cut or shaped. Water sufficient to cover the vegetables is brought to a boil separately and poured over the vegetables. Salt is added and the water is again brought to a boil as quickly as possible. When vegetables are slightly tender, but still retain some crispness, they are removed from the heat and placed in another container to cool. A small amount of ice may be placed in the liquid to speed the cooling. The cooked vegetables are reheated and seasoned when they are needed for service. The seasoning will vary with the different kinds of vegetables but generally will consist of salt, pepper, and sugar.

Frozen vegetables are prepared in the same manner as fresh vegetables with the exception of washing. The cooking time is likewise less since all frozen vegetables are blanched (partly cooked) before they are frozen. Frozen vegetables may be cooked in their frozen state, but thawing or partial thawing at refrigerator temperatures (34° to 39°F) will result in more uniform cooking. A few vegetables, such as spinach, kale and other leaf greens, always cook more uniformly when completely thawed. Frozen vegetables are extremely popular in all food service establishments because they are convenient to use. They can be prepared quickly and there is little labor cost involved in their preparation. The finished item always has excellent appearance and taste when prepared properly.

Canned vegetables are fully cooked and require only heating and seasoning before serving. They should be reheated in their own liquid and seasoned with salt, pepper, and sugar. In some cases other items such as butter, bacon grease, onions, ham stock, or fat will improve the taste of the vegetable. Canned vegetables should just be heated, never overcooked. Always prepare them in small quantities. If these rules are not followed much of the food value will be lost.

Dried legumes, as stated before, are peas, lentils, navy beans, great northern beans, lima beans, kidney beans, etc., with all their water content removed. They have excellent keeping qualities because there is no moisture present to breed bacteria. Likewise, they are easy to store. To prepare them soak overnight in water. They should not be refrigerated during the soaking period since they absorb water best at room temperature or at even higher temperatures. It is important to remember that soaking is not required for split peas and lentils. Legumes should simmer not boil when cooking since they toughen when subjected to high cooking temperatures.

VEGETABLE PREPARATION

In most commercial kitchens vegetables are already cleaned and peeled by the vegetable man before the cook works with them. Recipes, therefore, do not normally call for the vegetables to be cleaned or peeled.

In cooking with the already prepared vegetables, there are certain rules that one must follow to turn out a finished product that possesses excellent eating qualities and eye appeal—the two most important factors in vegetable cookery.

Follow the list of *correct* rules when cooking vegetables. Avoid the incorrect procedure.

Rules for proper vegetable cookery

Correct procedures:

1. Use only enough water to cover the vegetable.
2. Use boiling salt water.
3. Cook in small quantities, if practical.
4. Cook only until the vegetable is tender.
5. Cook about 1 hour before serving time, if practical.
6. After cooking cool the vegetables with ice and cold running water if they are not to be used immediately.
7. Save the liquid the vegetables were cooked in for reheating the vegetables for service or for use in stocks and sauces.
8. Season vegetables to taste just before serving.
9. When preparing fresh vegetables, cut them uniformly for proper and even cooking.
10. Clean all fresh vegetables thoroughly and store all vegetables properly for best results. (See storage of vegetables.)

Things to *avoid:*

1. Do *not* let vegetables soak before cooking, except for some dried legumes.
2. Do *not* stir air into the water while cooking.
3. Do *not* use excessive amounts of water: the result will be loss of flavor and food value.
4. Do *not* overcook the vegetables: food value, flavor, and appearance will suffer.
5. Do *not* let the cooked vegetables stand in hot water after cooking. The vegetables will continue to cook, become extremely soft and lose their natural color.
6. Do *not* add baking soda to the green vegetables. The vitamin content will be destroyed and vegetables may become mushy.
7. Do *not* cook in large quantities: food value will be lost and appearance and flavor will suffer.
8. Do *not* mix fresh cooked vegetables with the old: color, texture, and flavor will be different.
9. Do *not* thaw frozen vegetables too far in advance of preparing: food value is lost and the chance of spoiling is present.
10. Do *not* boil vegetables when cooking. Boiling has a tendency to break up and overcook vegetables.

Vegetable storage

Fresh onions and potatoes should be stored in a cool, dry place; however, all other fresh vegetables require refrigeration to preserve their appearance and flavor. Vegetables should be placed in the refrigerator in baskets or containers which are vented so the cold moist air can circulate properly around the vegetables. Peeled and cut vegetables must be refrigerated and sealed from the air by placing them in a plastic bag, covering with water, or treating them with chemical oxidizing agents to prevent discoloration. The method used to seal out the air will depend on the kind of vegetable.

Frozen: All frozen foods should be stored at temperatures of 0° to 10°F. Once frozen vegetables are thawed out they must *never* be refrozen. For best results, frozen vegetables should be thawed at refrigerator temperatures (34° to 39°F).

Dried: Dried vegetables must be stored in a slightly cool (70° to 75°F), dry place. They should be stored in cans or bags and placed on shelves off the floor.

Canned: Canned vegetables must be stored in a cool, dry place where they will not be exposed to sunlight; they should be placed on shelves off the floor.

When storing always move the old stock forward and the new stock to the rear so the old will be used first. If cans are rusted, check contents for spoilage. If there is a puncture the contents will be spoiled. *Remember:* when working with foods, if in doubt, throw it out.

PRESSURE AND STEAM JACKET COOKING

When vegetables are boiled on top the range the highest temperature that can be reached is 212°F. In a *pressure cooker* which operates on 5 to 6 pounds of steam pressure, the temperature is 225 to 230°F, which means the vege- tables can be cooked about 10 percent faster. Since less water is added to the vegetables, pressure cooking will pro- duce a product higher in vital minerals, vitamins, and flavor. Some of the larger pressure cookers operate on 15 pounds of steam pressure which will produce a temperature of approximately 250°F. This means the job can be done 20 per- cent faster than by the ordinary boiling method.

General rules to follow when steam pressure cooking

1. Cut the vegetables into equal size so they will cook uniformly.
2. Place the vegetables in a solid bas-

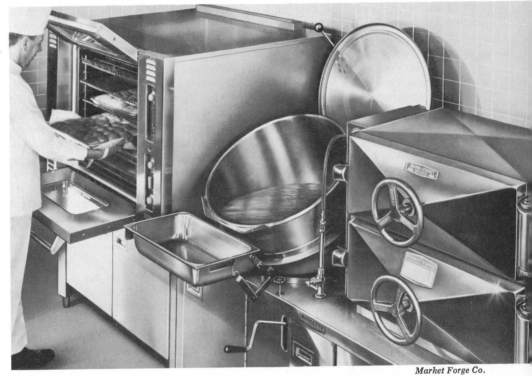

Market Forge Co.

Vegetable cooking: from left to right, baking ovens, steam jacket kettle and twin chamber steam pressure cooker. Vegetables cooked in a steam jacket kettle are surrounded by steam and never come into contact with the steam. In the two chamber steam pressure cooker the items being cooked come in direct contact with the steam. The steam pressure built up in these chambers can vary from 5 to 15 pounds. The advantage of steam cooking is speed of preparation.

ket and add just enough salt water to cover them. If using a perforated basket the water is not necessary.

3. Place the basket in the steam cabinet and lock the door tight.
4. Turn on the steam. A short time must be allowed for the steam to build the cooking pressure (about 5 or 6 pounds).
5. The cooking time will vary with the kind of vegetable being cooked and the amount of pressure being applied.
6. Remove the vegetables when just slightly tender. Season and serve at once; or cool the vegetables by placing them in a bain-marie and placing the container in ice water.

Caution: Do not open the door of a steam pressure cooker until all the steam has dispersed and the pressure gauge is at zero.

Steam jacket cooking is different from steam pressure cooking in that the food is not directly exposed to the steam. The steam flows around the outer jacket of the kettle providing an equal distribution of heat around the sides and bottom. The food is still cooked in the same amount of water as the regular boiling method, and at 212°F, but the boiling point is reached much faster because the kettle is uniformly surrounded by heat. The big advantage of cooking vegetables in a steam jacket is that they get done quicker. This means more minerals, vitamins, and flavor can be preserved.

General rules to follow when cooking in a steam jacket

1. Cut the vegetables into equal size so they will cook uniformly.
2. Place the amount of water needed to cover the vegetables in the kettle. Add salt.
3. Bring the water to a rolling boil.
4. Pour in the vegetables and bring the liquid back to a boil.
5. Reduce the heat and let simmer un-

til the vegetables are slightly tender.
6. Cook the vegetables uncovered to preserve the natural color of the vegetable.
7. Remove the vegetables, and enough liquid to cover them, from the kettle immediately after they are cooked.
8. Season and serve at once, or cool the vegetables by placing the container in ice water.

VEGETABLE RECIPES

Most vegetable preparations are quite simple to prepare if one has a basic knowledge of the product he is working with. For this reason a few pertinent facts on each vegetable is given prior to the recipes. The recipes are presented in a simplified form and all the vegetables popular in food service establishments are included. Serve most of the following vegetable preparations with a 3 ounce kitchen spoon.

Frozen vegetables could be substituted for most of the preparations calling for fresh vegetables and vice versa; however, in most cases the amounts of frozen vegetables used will be less than the fresh. The procedure would also be different in most cases because fresh vegetables are processed and prepared slightly different than the frozen product. The vegetable form used for any recipe is that which should make the most tasty preparation. Actually, any of these preparations can be prepared with fresh, frozen or canned vegetables if one desires.

The vegetable recipes in this chapter are arranged in alphabetical order by the name of the vegetable. Several recipes are given for each of the common vegetables. The following outline lists vegetables and recipes in their order of appearance in the chapter.

Asparagus recipes
(Pages 232 to 233)
    Buttered asparagus
    Creamed asparagus

ASPARAGUS RECIPES

Asparagus has been a highly regarded vegetable for thousands of years. It is a perennial plant of the lily family believed to have originated in Asia. During the days of the Roman empire, asparagus grew wild along the coast of the Mediterranean. The banquet-loving Romans soon learned how to cultivate and cook it. After the Romans, the British discovered this tasty, thistle-like vegetable which they called sparrowgrass. Asparagus is very popular in the United States and grows in many states from coast to coast. It takes about three years to establish an asparagus plant, but, once established, the rate of growth is extremely fast. The plant once mature will produce year after year. Good quality asparagus will possess round, compact tips. The stalks will be straight and brittle.

Buttered asparagus

Ingredients: Approx. yield: 25 servings
10 lbs. asparagus spears, fresh
2 tsp. salt
    water to cover, boiling
8 ozs. butter, melted
Procedure
1. Cut off the tough ends, peel the remaining stalks slightly with a potato peeler.
2. Tie the spears into bundles (12 spears to a bundle).
3. Stand the bundles in a sauce pot. Pour the boiling water over until approximately $\frac{1}{2}$ inch below the tips.
4. Add the salt and simmer uncovered until the butts are tender.
5. Drain and serve with melted butter.
Note: Lemon juice may be added to the butter if desired. Also, frozen asparagus may be substituted for the fresh.

Creamed asparagus

Ingredients: Approx. yield: 25 servings
5 lbs. asparagus, cut, frozen
2 tsp. salt
    water to cover, boiling
2 qts. cream sauce
Procedure
1. Place the cut asparagus in a sauce pan.
2. Add enough boiling water to cover.
3. Add the salt and simmer until the asparagus is tender. Drain thoroughly.
4. Prepare cream sauce. (See Chap. 15.)

5. Add the cream sauce and blend together gently.
6. Check seasoning and serve.

Asparagus au gratin

Ingredients: Approx. yield: 25 servings
5   lbs. asparagus, frozen, cut
2   tsp. salt
    water to cover, boiling
2   qts. cream sauce
3   ozs. Parmesan cheese or 8 ozs. of Cheddar cheese, grated
2   ozs. butter
    paprika, as needed
Procedure
1. Prepare cream sauce. (See Chap. 15.)
2. Place the cut asparagus in a sauce pan.
3. Cover with boiling water and add the salt.
4. Simmer until the asparagus is just tender, then drain.
5. Place in a baking pan; pour the hot cream sauce over.
6. Check seasoning. Sprinkle the grated cheese over the top.
7. Dot the butter over the top and sprinkle slightly with paprika.
8. Bake in a 375°F oven until the cheese melts and the top becomes slightly brown.
9. Serve.

Asparagus Hollandaise

Ingredients: Approx. yield: 25 servings
10   lbs. asparagus spears, fresh
 2   tsp. salt
     water to cover, boiling
 2   qts. Hollandaise sauce
Procedure
1. Prepare Hollandaise sauce. (See Chap. 15.)
2. Cut off the tough ends of the asparagus and peel the remaining stalks slightly with a potato peeler.
3. Place the spears in a baking pan, cover with boiling water and add the salt.
4. Simmer on the range or cook by steam pressure until the stalks are just tender.
5. Serve 3 or 4 spears (depending on size) to each order, half covered with the Hollandaise sauce.
   Note: Frozen asparagus spears may also be used.

Asparagus Maltaise

Ingredients: Approx. yield: 25 servings
10   lbs. asparagus spears, fresh
 2   tsp. salt
     water to cover, boiling
 2   qts. Maltaise sauce
Procedure
1. Prepare Maltaise sauce (See Chap. 15.)
2. Cut off the tough ends. Peel the remaining stalks slightly with a potato peeler.
3. Place the spears in a baking pan, cover with boiling water and add the salt.
4. Simmer on the range or cook by steam pressure until the stalks are just tender.
5. Serve 3 or 4 spears (depending on size) to each order, half covering them with the Maltaise sauce.
   Note: Frozen asparagus spears may also be used.

WAX AND GREEN BEAN RECIPES

Wax beans and green beans (sometimes called snap beans) are the same in both cooking and eating qualities. They differ only in color. Some varieties have round pods while others have flat pods; however, the shape of the beans has no bearing on the flavor or tenderness. Beans that are fresh and tender will snap readily when they are bent.

Green beans chuckwagon style

Ingredients: Approx. yield: 25 servings
 1   #10 can green beans, whole or cut
 ½   #10 can whole tomatoes, slightly crushed
 1   lb. onions, cut julienne
 8   ozs. celery, cut julienne
 1   lb. jowl bacon, cut julienne
 1   pt. ham stock
     salt and pepper to taste
Procedure
1. Prepare ham stock (See Chap. 12.)
2. Place the julienne cut jowl bacon in a sauce pan and cook into a soft crackling.
3. Add the onions and celery, continue to Sauté until slightly tender.
4. Add the ham stock and tomatoes, simmer until the celery is tender.
5. Drain the liquid from the can of green

beans, add the beans to the tomato vegetable mixture, simmer for 5 minutes.

6. Season with salt and pepper.
7. Serve garnished with chopped parsley.

Green beans or wax beans lyonnaise

Ingredients: Approx. yield: 25 servings

1 #10 can green beans or wax beans, whole or cut
8 ozs. onions, cut julienne
6 ozs. butter
  salt and pepper to taste

Procedure

1. Place the butter in a sauce pan, heat.
2. Add the julienne onion and sauté until slightly tender.
3. Add the green beans or wax beans (with liquid). Simmer for 5 minutes.
4. Season with salt and pepper and serve.

Green beans amandine

Ingredients: Approx. yield: 25 servings

2 2½ lb. boxes green beans, frozen, French cut
2 tsp. salt
  water to cover, boiling
8 ozs. butter
6 ozs. almonds, sliced
  salt and pepper to taste

Procedure

1. Place the green beans in a sauce pan.
2. Pour over enough boiling water to cover. Add 2 tsp. salt and simmer until the beans are slightly tender.
3. Place the butter in a separate sauce pan and melt.
4. Add the sliced almonds and brown until golden.
5. Add the butter-almond mixture to the cooked green beans.
6. Season with salt and pepper and serve.

Green beans piquant

Ingredients: Approx. yield: 25 servings

1 #10 can green beans, whole
1 lb. jowl bacon, cut julienne
3 ozs. pimientoes, cut julienne
1 cup wine vinegar
¾ ozs. sugar
½ tsp. dry mustard
3 drops hot sauce
2 ozs. Worcestershire sauce
½ tsp. salt

Procedure

1. Drain the liquid from the canned beans. Place the beans in a sauce pan and hold.
2. Place the bacon in a separate sauce pan and cook until it becomes a light crackling.
3. Add the remaining ingredients and bring to a boil.
4. Pour over the beans and mix well.
5. Bring to a boil. Check seasoning and serve.

Green beans with mushrooms

Ingredients: Approx. yield: 25 servings

1 #10 can green beans, whole
1 lb. mushrooms, fresh, sliced
8 ozs. butter
  salt and pepper to taste

Procedure

1. Place the butter in a sauce pan and heat.
2. Add the mushrooms and sauté until slightly tender.
3. Add the green beans and can liquid. Simmer until mushrooms are completely tender.
4. Season with salt and pepper and serve.

Wax beans with pimientoes

Ingredients: Approx. yield: 25 servings

1 #10 can wax beans
4 ozs. butter
4 ozs. pimientoes, diced small
  salt and pepper to taste

Procedure

1. Place the wax beans (with liquid) and butter in a sauce pan and bring to a simmer.
2. Add the pimientoes and stir in gently.
3. Season with salt and pepper and serve.

BEET RECIPES

Beets are native to the continents of Europe, Africa and Asia. In early times they were raised for their top leaves rather than the root. In fact the roots only achieved popularity when they became larger and more tasty through man's cultivation of the plant. They are now in general cultivation, chiefly for their succulent roots which provide not only a tasty table vegetable, but are also a source of sugar. Beets of good quality are smooth and free from growth cracks and blemishes. Small beets are more desirable than larger ones mainly because they present a better appearance when served.

Rose bud beets in orange juice

Ingredients: Approx. yield: 25 servings
1   #10 can rose bud (small) beets, whole
1   qt. orange juice
2   ozs. sugar
1/4 cup orange peel, grated
2   ozs. cornstarch
1/4 cup vinegar, cider

Procedure
1. Drain the liquid from the beets and place in a sauce pan.
2. Add half of the orange juice, sugar, vinegar and grated orange peel. Bring to a simmer.
3. Dissolve the corn starch in the remaining orange juice. Pour slowly into the hot liquid, stirring constantly, until the mixture becomes slightly thickened and smooth.
4. Add the drained beets, and again bring to a boil.
5. Check seasoning and serve.

Spiced beets

Ingredients: Approx. yield: 25 servings
1   #10 can beets, sliced or diced
3   pts. beef juice and water
1 1/2 pt. vinegar, cider
1   cup sugar
10   whole cloves
4   whole allspice
4   cinnamon sticks
1   tsp. salt

Procedure
1. Place the beet juice and water, the vinegar, salt and sugar in a sauce pan and bring to a boil.
2. Add the cloves, allspice and cinnamon. Simmer for 10 minutes.
3. Strain the hot liquid over the beets and again bring to a boil.
4. Adjust seasoning and serve.

Harvard beets

1   #10 can beets, sliced or diced

1   qt. of beet juice or beet juice and water
3   ozs. cornstarch
1/2 oz. salt
4   whole cloves
1   very small bay leaf
2   ozs. butter
3/4 cup vinegar, cider
6   ozs. sugar

Procedure
1. Place all, but 1/2 cup of the beet juice or beet juice and water in a sauce pan.
2. Add the cloves and bay leaf, simmer 10 minutes, remove the spices.
3. Dissolve the cornstarch in the remaining cup of beet juice. Pour slowly into the boiling liquid, stirring constantly, until thickened and smooth.
4. Add the sugar, salt, vinegar and butter. Blend in thoroughly.
5. Pour the thickened liquid over the beets and blend together gently so the beets will not be broken.
6. Bring back to a boil, adjust the seasoning and serve.

Hot pickled beets

Ingredients: Approx. yield: 25 servings
1   #10 can beets, small whole or sliced, drained
1   qt. beet juice or beet juice and water
8   ozs. onions, sliced into thin rings
1/3 cup salad oil
1   tbsp. salt
8   cloves, whole
1   cup sugar
2   bay leaves
3   cups vinegar, cider

Procedure
1. Place the salad oil in a sauce pan and heat.
2. Add the onions and sauté until slightly tender.
3. Add the beet juice, cloves, bay leaves, salt, sugar and vinegar. Simmer for 15 minutes then remove the spices.
4. Pour the hot liquid over the drained beets and again bring to a boil.
5. Adjust the seasoning and serve.

Buttered beets

Ingredients: Approx. yield: 25 servings
1   #10 can beets, whole, sliced or diced
6   ozs. butter

1 tsp. sugar
   salt and white pepper to taste
Procedure
1. Place the beets and beet juice in a sauce pan and heat.
2. Add the butter and sugar and continue to heat.
3. Season with salt and pepper to taste.
4. Serve.

BROCCOLI RECIPES

Broccoli is a variety of the cabbage species. It is closely related to cauliflower, but has a small green head rather than a firm white head. For many years it was grown only in Europe, but today it has become a very important crop and popular table vegetable in the United States. The broccoli head consists of green leaves and small green flower buds. The entire broccoli, which consists of the stalk, leaves and flower bud clusters, is eaten. There are two types of broccoli: the cauliflower type which forms a head similar to cauliflower and the Italian type which does not form a head. The cauliflower type is the most popular in United States. Broccoli of good quality will possess a compact head with the flower buds unopened. The length of the head and stalk should be about five inches. The color should be a deep green with no yellow showing. (Yellow indicates poor quality.)

Buttered fresh broccoli

Ingredients: Approx. yield: 25 servings
4 bch. broccoli, fresh (approx. 12 lbs.)
   water to cover, boiling
5 tsp. salt
8 ozs. butter
Procedure
1. Remove any poor outer leaves and tough stems from the broccoli. Wash thoroughly in cold salt water. Do not bruise the head.
2. If it is tough or woody, split the stalk in half lengthwise and peel with a vegetable peeler.
3. Place the broccoli in a bake pan (sometimes called a hotel pan) and cover with boiling water. Add the salt and cover the pan with a wet towel to keep the broccoli submerged in the liquid so it will cook uniformly.
4. Simmer on top the range until the stalks become tender. Do not overcook or the heads will come apart.
5. Drain the liquid from the broccoli and serve, dressing each portion with melted butter.
Note: The broccoli may also be cooked by steam pressure. The broccoli is prepared in the same manner for pressure cooking.

Broccoli Hollandaise

Ingredients: Approx. yield: 25 servings
6 lbs. broccoli, frozen, spears
2 tsp. salt
   water to cover, boiling
2 qts. Hollandaise sauce
Procedure
1. Prepare Hollandaise sauce. (See Chap. 15.)
2. Thaw the broccoli spears and place in a hotel pan.
3. Cover with boiling water, add the salt and cover the pan with a wet towel to keep the broccoli submerged in the liquid so it will cook uniformly.
4. Simmer on top of the range until the stalks become tender. Do not overcook or the heads will come apart.

United Fresh Fruit and Vegetable Assoc.
Broccoli Hollandaise

5. Drain the liquid from the broccoli and serve, dressing each portion with a generous amount of Hollandaise sauce.

Note: Fresh broccoli can be used in place of the frozen broccoli. If desired the broccoli may be cooked in the pressure steamer.

Broccoli Polonaise

Ingredients: Approx. yield: 25 servings
4 bch. broccoli, fresh (approx. 12 lbs.)
2 tsp. salt
water to cover, boiling
6 ozs. butter
2 cups bread crumbs, coarse
1/4 cup chopped parsley
1 hard boiled egg, chopped fine
Procedure
1. Remove any poor outer leaves and tough stems from the broccoli. Wash thoroughly in cold salt water. Do not bruise the head.
2. If tough or woody, split the stalk in half lengthwise and peel with a vegetable peeler.
3. Place the broccoli in a hotel pan and cover with boiling water. Add the salt and cover the pan with a wet towel to keep broccoli submerged.
4. Simmer on top the range until the stalks become tender. Do not overcook or the heads will come apart.
5. Remove from the range and hold until the Polonaise is prepared (steps 6, 7 and 8).
6. Place the butter in a sauce pan or skillet and heat.
7. Add the bread crumbs, brown until golden. Remove from the range.
8. Blend in the chopped egg and parsley.
9. Drain the liquid from the broccoli and serve, sprinkling each portion with a generous amount of Polonaise.

Broccoli amandine

Ingredients: Approx. yield: 25 servings
6 lbs. broccoli, frozen, spears
2 tsp. salt
water to cover, boiling
6 ozs. butter
5 ozs. almonds, sliced
Procedure
1. Thaw the broccoli spears and place in a hotel pan.

2. Cover with boiling water, add the salt and cover with a wet towel.
3. Simmer on top the range until the stalks become tender. Do not overcook or the heads will be destroyed.
4. Place the butter in a skillet or sauce pan and heat.
5. Add the sliced almonds and sauté until golden brown.
6. Drain the liquid from the broccoli and serve, sprinkling each portion with the toasted almonds.

Note: Fresh broccoli can be used in place of the frozen broccoli. If desired the broccoli may be cooked in the pressure steamer.

Broccoli with cheese sauce

Ingredients: Approx. yield: 25 servings
4 bch. broccoli, fresh (approx. 12 lbs.)
2 tsp. salt
water to cover, boiling
2 qts. cheese sauce
Procedure
1. Prepare cheese sauce. (See Chap. 15.)
2. Remove any poor outer leaves and tough stems from the broccoli. Wash thoroughly in cold salt water. Do not bruise the head.
3. Split the stalks half way up and peel if tough or woody.
4. Place the broccoli in a hotel pan and cover with boiling water. Add the salt and cover the pan with a wet towel.
5. Simmer on top of the range until the stalks become tender. Do not overcook or the heads will be destroyed.
6. Remove from the range, drain the liquid from the broccoli and serve, dressing each portion with a generous amount of cheese sauce.

Note: Frozen broccoli spears may be used in place of the fresh if desired. The broccoli may be cooked in the pressure steamer if preferred.

BRUSSELS SPROUT RECIPES

Brussels sprouts belong to the cabbage family and look like miniature cabbages. They originated in the country of Belgium, near the city of Brussels from which they took their name. The sprouts grow about one inch in diameter and are attached to the long stalks of the plant that will sometimes grow three feet long. Brussels sprouts are available on the market from October through May. When a sprout is of good quality it will be firm, compact and possess a good green color. The puffy-looking sprouts will provide poor eating qualities. Brussels sprouts are prepared and used in the same manner as cabbage, however, the sprouts possess a superior flavor.

Buttered Brussels sprouts

Ingredients: Approx. yield: 25 servings
6 lbs. Brussels sprouts, fresh (approx. 3 qts.)
2 tbsp. salt
    water to cover, boiling
8 ozs. butter
    salt and pepper to taste
Procedure
1. Remove wilted and discolored outer leaves and trim the stems of the Brussels sprouts.
2. Soak in cold salt water for approximately 30 minutes and drain.
3. Place in a sauce pan, cover with boiling water, add the salt and simmer until tender.
4. Drain off part of the liquid and add the butter.
5. Season with salt and pepper and serve.

United Fresh Fruit and Vegetable Assoc.
Buttered Brussels sprouts garnished with onion rings.

Brussels sprouts in sour cream

Ingredients: Approx. yield: 25 servings
6 lbs. Brussels sprouts, fresh (approx. 3 qts.)
2 tbsp. salt
    water to cover, boiling
4 ozs. onions, minced
4 ozs. butter
2 lbs. sour cream
    salt and white pepper to taste
Procedure
1. Remove wilted and discolored outer leaves and trim the stems of the Brussels sprouts.
2. Soak in cold salt water for approximately 30 minutes then drain.
3. Place in a sauce pan, cover with boiling water, add the 2 tbsp. of salt and simmer until tender.
4. Drain off the liquid and hold.
5. Place the butter in a separate sauce pan and heat.
6. Add the minced onions and sauté, without coloring, until tender.
7. Stir in the sour cream, heat slightly while stirring gently.
8. Pour the sour cream mixture over the cooked Brussels sprouts; fold together gently.
9. Season with salt and white pepper and serve.

Brussels sprouts au gratin

Ingredients: Approx. yield: 25 servings
5 lbs. Brussels sprouts, frozen
2 tsp. salt
    water to cover, boiling
2 qts. cream sauce
8 ozs. American cheese, grated
    salt and white pepper to taste
    paprika as needed
Procedure
1. Prepare cream sauce. (See Chap. 15.)
2. Place the partly thawed sprouts in a sauce pan, cover with boiling water, add the 2 tsp. of salt and simmer until tender.
3. Drain the liquid from the sprouts and pour the hot cream sauce over the sprouts. Stir together gently so the sprouts will not be broken.
4. Season with salt and white pepper.
5. Turn into a baking pan and sprinkle the cheese over the top. Sprinkle the cheese lightly with paprika.

6. Place in a 375°F oven and bake until the cheese melts and becomes slightly brown.
7. Remove and serve.
Note: Fresh Brussels sprouts may be used if desired.

Brussels sprouts Polonaise

Ingredients: Approx. yield: 25 servings
5　lbs. Brussels sprouts, frozen
2　tsp. salt
　　water to cover, boiling
6　ozs. butter
2　cups bread crumbs, coarse
¼　cup chopped parsley
1　hard boiled egg, chopped
Procedure
1. Place the partly thawed sprouts in a sauce pan, cover with boiling water, add the 2 tsp. salt and simmer until tender.
2. Remove from the range and hold until the Polonaise is prepared (steps 3, 4 and 5).
3. Place the butter in a separate sauce pan or skillet and heat.
4. Add the bread crumbs and brown until golden. Remove from the range.
5. Blend in the chopped parsley and hard boiled egg.
6. Drain the liquid from the Brussels sprouts and serve, sprinkling each portion with a generous amount of Polonaise.
Note: Fresh Brussels sprouts may be used if desired.

Brussels sprouts Hollandaise

Ingredients: Approx. yield: 25 servings
6　lbs. Brussels sprouts, fresh (approx. 3 qts.)
2　tbsp. salt
　　water to cover, boiling
2　qts. Hollandaise sauce
Procedure
1. Prepare the Hollandaise sauce. (See Chap. 15.)
2. Remove wilted and discolored outer leaves and trim the stems of the Brussels sprouts.
3. Soak in cold salt water for approximately 30 minutes then drain.
4. Place in a sauce pan, cover with boiling water, add the 2 tbsp. of salt and simmer until tender.
5. Remove from the range and serve, dressing each portion with a generous amount of Hollandaise sauce.

CABBAGE RECIPES

Cabbage, cultivated since prehistoric times, has been developed into many varieties, including the common cabbage, Brussels sprouts, broccoli, kale, etc. In cultivation the common cabbage grows into a head comprised of many leaves. The head may be globular, conical or flat shaped and the leaves may be green or red, wrinkled or smooth depending on the type of cabbage being cultivated. The common cabbage is grouped into five types.

1. *Early cabbage* is also known as pointed cabbage because the head comes to a slight point.
2. *Danish cabbage* has a firm solid head and is grown mainly for winter use.
3. *Domestic cabbage* consists of both early and late varieties. Its head is not as firm and solid as the Danish cabbage.
4. *Red cabbage* has a firm solid head with reddish-purple leaves. The flavor of the red cabbage is much stronger than that of the other types.
5. *Savory* or *curly cabbage* has a very loose head with wrinkled dark green leaves. It has a flavor that is milder than the other types.

In the commercial kitchen, cabbage is not a very popular vegetable because it can produce gases in the stomach. Many people will not choose it as a vegetable unless it is being served with such popular dishes as boiled beef or corn beef.

Buttered cabbage

Ingredients: Approx. yield: 25 servings
10　lbs. cabbage

1 tsp. salt
ham stock to cover, boiling
8 ozs. butter
salt and pepper to taste
Procedure
1. Prepare ham stock. (See Chap. 12.)
2. Remove outer leaves, trim and wash the cabbage.
3. Cut the heads into 25 wedges, do not remove the core unless there is an excessive amount on the wedges.
4. Place the wedges in a braiser or deep baking pan. Cover with the boiling ham stock.
5. Add the salt and simmer uncovered until the cabbage is tender, but still retaining its shape.
6. Drain off a small amount of the liquid. Add the butter.
7. Season with salt and pepper and serve.

Shredded cabbage

Ingredients: Approx. yield: 25 servings
10 lbs. cabbage
water to cover, boiling
2 tbsp. salt
4 ozs. onions, sliced thin
8 ozs. butter (variable)
2 tsp. celery seed
salt and pepper to taste
Procedure
1. Remove outer leaves, trim and wash the cabbage.
2. Cut the heads into six wedges, remove the core and shred coarsely.
3. Place the cabbage in a sauce pot, cover with boiling water. Add the salt and simmer for 10 minutes or until slightly tender. Drain well.
4. Place the butter in a large skillet or braiser until melted.
5. Add the onions and sauté until slightly tender.
6. Add the cooked shredded cabbage and continue to sauté for approximately 5 minutes longer.
7. Add the celery seed and blend in thoroughly.
8. Season with salt and pepper and serve.

Bavarian red cabbage

Ingredients: Approx. yield: 25 servings

8 lbs. red cabbage, trimmed, cored, shredded coarse
1 lb. bacon grease
12 ozs. onions, sliced fine
1 pt. vinegar, cider
6 ozs. sugar
8 ozs. apples, peeled, cored, diced
1 tsp. cloves, ground
1¼ qt. water
salt and pepper to taste
Procedure
1. Place the bacon grease in a sauce pot and heat.
2. Add the onions and sauté until slightly tender.
3. Add the water, vinegar, cloves, and sugar. Simmer for 5 minutes.
4. Add the shredded cabbage and simmer for 15 minutes with a lid on.
5. Add the apples and continue to simmer uncovered until the cabbage is tender.
6. Season with salt and pepper and serve.

Fried cabbage: Chinese style

Ingredients: Approx. yield: 25 servings
10 lbs. cabbage, trimmed, cored, shredded coarse
2 cups chicken stock
¼ cup soy sauce
¾ cup salad oil
2 cloves garlic, minced
1 tbsp. salt
¼ cup sugar
2 tsp. monosodium glutamate
Procedure
1. Prepare chicken stock. (See Chap. 12.)
2. Place the oil and garlic in a braising pot, heat.
3. Add the shredded cabbage and cook for 10 minutes, stirring occasionally.
4. Add the chicken stock, sugar, salt, soy sauce and monosodium glutinate. Simmer until the cabbage is tender.
5. Check seasoning and serve.

CARROT RECIPES

The carrot is a biennial plant that has an orange-yellow tapering root. The early carrot crop produces the most desirable carrots. They are generally small in size, mild in flavor, extremely tender and have a bright color. The late

Buttered carrots garnished with chives.

United Fresh Fruit and Vegetable Assoc.

crop carrots have a more pronounced flavor, a deeper color and a much coarser texture.

Buttered carrots

Ingredients: Approx. yield: 25 servings

6   lbs. carrots, fresh, peeled
1   tsp. salt
    water to cover, boiling
6   ozs. butter
    salt and sugar to taste

Procedure

1. Slice the carrots diagonally. Place in a sauce pan.
2. Cover with boiling water, add 1 tsp. of salt, and simmer until tender.
3. Add the butter and season with sugar and additional salt if needed, then serve.
   Note: 1 #10 can of whole or sliced carrots may be used if desired.

Candied carrots

Ingredients: Approx. yield: 25 servings

6   lbs. carrots, fresh, peeled
1   tbsp. salt
    water to cover, boiling
8   ozs. brown sugar, dark
4   ozs. butter

Procedure

1. Cut the carrots into strips 1 inch long and ½ inch thick.
2. Cover with boiling water, add 1 tbsp. salt and brown sugar and simmer until tender.
3. Add the butter and serve.

Creamed carrots

Ingredients: Approx. yield: 25 servings

6   lbs. carrots, fresh, peeled
1   tsp. salt
    water to cover, boiling
2   qts. cream sauce
2   ozs. butter
    salt and white pepper to taste

Procedure

1. Prepare cream sauce. (See Chap. 15.)
2. Slice or dice the carrots. Place in a sauce pan.
3. Cover with boiling water, add 1 tsp. salt

and simmer until tender. Drain thoroughly.
4. Pour the hot cream sauce over the drained carrots, return to the range and bring to a simmer.
5. Season with salt and white pepper.
6. Add the butter and blend in.
7. Serve.

French fried carrots

Ingredients: Approx. yield: 25 servings
25   medium sized carrots, fresh, peeled
 1   tbsp. salt
     water to cover, boiling
 8   ozs. flour
 1   pt. milk
 4   whole eggs
 1   qt. bread crumbs
Procedure
1. Place the whole, peeled carrots in a sauce pan.
2. Cover with boiling water, add 1 tbsp. salt and simmer until tender. Drain thoroughly and cool.
3. Pass each carrot through the flour, coating thoroughly.
4. Place the eggs in a container, beat slightly and pour in the milk, blending to prepare an egg wash.
5. Place each floured carrot in the egg wash, coating thoroughly.
6. Remove from the egg wash and roll in the bread crumbs.
7. Fry in deep fat at 350°F until golden brown.
8. Serve 1 carrot for each serving.

Carrots vichy

Ingredients: Approx. yield: 25 servings
6   lbs. carrots, fresh, peeled
1   tsp. salt
    water to cover, boiling
8   ozs. butter
1   tbsp. sugar
    salt and white pepper to taste
Procedure
1. Slice the carrots crosswise fairly thin and place in a sauce pan.
2. Cover with boiling water, add 1 tsp. salt and simmer until tender.
3. Add the butter and sugar.
4. Season with salt and white pepper.
5. Serve garnished with chopped parsley.

CAULIFLOWER RECIPES

Cauliflower is a variety of the common cabbage with a white or cream-white head which is the only part prepared for food. Cauliflower of good quality will have a smooth white color, with no blemishes on the surface of the head and is heavy for its size. The outer leaves that protect the delicate head should be green, firm and fresh in appearance. If the leaves should grow up through the head of the cauliflower, this is no sign that the quality is poor. It only hinders the appearance.

Buttered cauliflower

Ingredients: Approx. yield: 25 servings
12   lbs. cauliflower, fresh, trimmed
     water to cover, boiling
 2   tbsp. salt
 1   tsp. lemon juice
 8   ozs. butter
     salt and white pepper to taste
Procedure
1. Place enough boiling water in a sauce pot to cover the cauliflower. Add 2 tbsp. salt and the lemon juice. Bring to a boil.
2. Add the cauliflower and simmer until the base of the head is tender. Drain and break into segments.
3. Serve with a tsp. of melted butter over each serving.

Cauliflower Parmesan

Ingredients: Approx. yield: 25 servings
12   lbs. cauliflower, fresh, trimmed
     water to cover, boiling
 2   tbsp. salt
 1   tsp. lemon juice
 6   ozs. Parmesan cheese
 2   ozs. bread crumbs
 6   egg yolks
 ¼   cup flour
 3   cups milk
     salt and white pepper to taste
Procedure
1. Place enough boiling water in a sauce pot to cover the cauliflower. Add 2 tbsp. salt and the lemon juice. Bring to a boil.
2. Add the cauliflower and simmer until the base of the head is tender then drain thoroughly.

Cauliflower Parmesan served with cubes of ham.

United Fresh Fruit and Vegetable Assoc.

3. Place the cooked cauliflower in a baking pan and break into segments. Combine the Parmesan cheese and bread crumbs and sprinkle over the cauliflower.
4. Break the eggs into a container and beat slightly, blend in the flour and stir until smooth. Add the milk and blend thoroughly.
5. Pour this mixture over the cooked cauliflower and season with salt, white pepper.
6. Place in a 350°F oven for 20 to 30 minutes until the surface becomes golden.
7. Remove from the oven and serve.

Cauliflower au gratin

Ingredients: Approx. yield: 25 servings
- 6 lbs. cauliflower, frozen
- 1 tbsp. salt
- 1 tsp. lemon juice
  water to cover, boiling
- 2 qts. cream sauce
- 10 ozs. Cheddar cheese, grated
  salt and white pepper to taste
- 1 tsp. paprika

Procedure
1. Prepare cream sauce. (See Chap. 15.)
2. Place the partly thawed cauliflower in a sauce pan and cover with boiling water.
3. Add 1 tbsp. salt and the lemon juice, simmer until the base of the cauliflower is tender then drain thoroughly.
4. Place the cooked cauliflower in a baking

pan, pour over the hot cream sauce and season with salt and white pepper.
5. Sprinkle on the grated cheese and top with a sprinkle of paprika.
6. Bake in a 350°F oven until golden brown and serve.

Note: Fresh cauliflower may be used if desired.

Cauliflower creole

Ingredients: Approx. yield: 25 servings
- 6 lbs. cauliflower, fresh, trimmed
- 2 tbsp. salt
- 1 tsp. lemon juice
  water to cover, boiling
- 2 qts. creole sauce
  salt and pepper to taste

Procedure
1. Prepare creole sauce. (See Chap. 15.)
2. Place enough boiling water in a sauce pot to cover the cauliflower. Add 2 tbsp. salt and the lemon juice. Bring to a boil.
3. Add the cauliflower and simmer until the base of the head is tender then drain thoroughly.
4. Break the cooked cauliflower into segments and place in a sauce pan.
5. Pour over the hot creole sauce and bring to a boil.
6. Remove from the range, season with salt and pepper and serve.

Note: Frozen cauliflower may be used if desired.

vegetables **243**

Cauliflower with cheese sauce

Ingredients: Approx. yield: 25 servings
6   lbs. cauliflower, fresh, trimmed
2   tbsp. salt
1   tsp. lemon juice
    water to cover, boiling
2   qts. cheese sauce
Procedure
1. Prepare cheese sauce. (See Chap. 15.)
2. Place enough boiling water in a sauce pot to cover the cauliflower. Add 2 tbsp. salt and the lemon juice. Bring to a boil.
3. Add the cauliflower and simmer until the base of the head is tender then drain thoroughly.
4. Serve, dressing each portion with a generous amount of cheese sauce.
   Note: Frozen cauliflower may be used if desired.

CELERY RECIPES

Celery is a biennial herb of the parsley family and a native of Europe. Today it is grown extensively throughout the world. The cultivated stalks grow to a height of 12 to 30 inches and can be eaten raw or cooked as a vegetable. Celery is marketed in two types, blanched (white) or green. When grown naturally, the stalks are green in color and a touch of bitterness can be detected in the taste. When blanched the stalk is hidden from the sunlight, but the leaves are left exposed. Blanching removes the color of the stalk and eliminates the bitter taste, however, some of the vitamin content is also lost. The best variety of green celery available is called, *pascal celery*. It generally has tender stalks and is high in vitamin content. Celery of good quality will have fairly thick stems, not spread, is free of any blemishes or cracks and is crisp enough to snap when bent.

Braised celery

Ingredients: Approx. yield: 25 servings
8   lbs. celery
6   ozs. butter
4   ozs. flour

2   qts. chicken stock, hot
    salt and pepper to taste
Procedure
1. Prepare chicken stock. (See Chap. 15.)
2. Remove the celery leaves, trim and wash thoroughly. Cut into 1 inch pieces.
3. Place the butter in a braising pot and heat.
4. Add the celery and sauté until slightly tender.
5. Add the flour and blend in thoroughly. Cook for approximately 5 minutes, stirring constantly to avoid scorching.
6. Pour in the hot stock slowly, stirring gradually until thickened and smooth.
7. Bring to a boil, cover and reduce to a simmer.
8. Simmer slowly until the celery is tender and the liquid has reduced.
9. Season with salt and pepper and serve.

Creamed celery

Ingredients: Approx. yield: 25 servings
8   lbs. celery
2   tsp. salt
    water to cover, boiling
2   qts. cream sauce
    salt and white pepper, to taste
Procedure
1. Prepare cream sauce. (See Chap. 15.)
2. Remove the celery leaves, trim and wash, cut into 1 inch pieces.
3. Place the cut celery in a sauce pan, cover with boiling water and add 2 tsp. salt. Simmer until the celery is tender then drain thoroughly.
4. Add the hot cream sauce and bring to a boil.
5. Season with salt and white pepper and serve.

CORN RECIPES

Corn is a cereal grass grown mainly for food and livestock feed. It is a native of both North and South America and was the chief source of food for the American Indians. In the world grain production it ranks behind rice and wheat; however, in the United States it is the chief grain crop. There are two main types of corn on the market: white or sweet corn and yellow corn. Both types are extremely popular in the commercial kitchen, the white corn, however, is generally sweeter and is more tender and superior in flavor to the yellow corn. Corn deteriorates quite rapidly soon after it is picked. The sugar in corn begins to lose its sweetness and converts into starch just as soon as it is picked. This causes a loss in flavor and tenderness. To prepare corn shortly after it has been picked in the field is the ideal way; however, in most cases this is not possible. Immediately upon receipt the corn should be shucked and kept covered with a damp cloth, in the coldest part of the refrigerator.

Corn on the cob

Ingredients: Approx. yield: 25 servings
25   ears of corn (white or yellow)
 2   tbsp. sugar
    water to cover, boiling
 1   qt. milk
    butter, as needed
Procedure
1. Remove the husk and all the corn silk, and trim.
2. Place the milk, sugar and enough boiling water to cover the corn in a sauce or stock pot and bring to a boil.
3. Add the corn and cook slightly, covered, for 4 to 8 minutes or until done. White corn requires less cooking time than yellow corn.
4. Remove from the range and hold the corn in the liquid until ready to serve.
5. Serve 1 ear of corn with corn holders and a generous portion of butter.

Note: If the corn is old, add additional sugar to the water and cook for a longer time. Cook all corn as near to serving time as possible.

Corn Marie (corn and tomatoes)

Ingredients: Approx. yield: 25 servings
2½   lb. box corn, frozen (whole kernel)
    water to cover, boiling
 1   tsp. salt
 1   tsp. sugar
½   #10 can whole tomatoes

 2   tbsp. cornstarch (variable)
 1   tsp. sugar
    salt and white pepper to taste
Procedure
1. Place the corn in a sauce pot and cover with boiling water.
2. Add 1 tsp. of sugar and 1 tsp. salt. Simmer the corn 3 to 5 minutes. Remove from the range and drain thoroughly.
3. Place the tomatoes in a sauce pan, reserving ½ cup of the juice to dissolve the cornstarch, and bring to a boil.
4. Dissolve the cornstarch in the tomato juice and pour slowly into the boiling tomatoes, stirring constantly until slightly thickened and smooth.
5. Add the drained corn and the second 1 tsp. of sugar, and bring to a simmer.
6. Season with salt and white pepper, remove from the range and serve.

Note: The amount of cornstarch used may vary depending on the desired thickness.

Corn O'Brien (Mexican)

Ingredients: Approx. yield: 25 servings
5   lbs. corn, frozen whole kernel
    water to cover, boiling
1   tsp. salt
1   tbsp. sugar
6   ozs. green pepper, diced, small
3   ozs. pimientos, diced, small
4   ozs. butter
Procedure
1. Place the corn in a sauce pot, cover with boiling water.
2. Add the sugar and salt, simmer 3 to 5 minutes, remove from the range.
3. Poach the diced green pepper in a separate sauce pan until just tender. Drain.
4. Add the green peppers and pimientos to the cooked corn.
5. Add the butter, season with additional salt and sugar and serve.

Butter succotash (corn and lima beans)

Ingredients: Approx. yield: 25 servings
2½   lb. corn, frozen (whole kernel)
2½   lb. lima beans, frozen (fordhook)
    water to cover, boiling

2 tsp. salt
1 tsp. sugar
4 ozs. butter
   salt and white pepper, to taste
Procedure
1. Place the corn and lima beans in separate sauce pans. Cover both with boiling water. To the corn add 1 tsp. salt and the sugar; to the lima beans add 1 tsp. salt. Simmer both until tender.
2. Remove both vegetables from the range and combine. Pour off excess liquid.
3. Add the butter, season with salt and white pepper and serve.

Cream corn

Ingredients: Approx. yield: 25 servings
5 lbs. corn, frozen (whole kernel)
   water to cover, boiling
1 tsp. salt
1 tsp. sugar
2 qts. cream sauce
2 ozs. butter
Procedure
1. Prepare cream sauce. (See Chap. 15.)
2. Place the corn in a sauce pot and cover with boiling water.
3. Add the sugar and salt and simmer 3 to 5 minutes. Remove from the range then drain thoroughly.
4. Add the cream sauce and blend together.
5. Add the butter, season with additional salt and sugar and serve.

Corn fritters

Ingredients: Approx. yield: 50 pieces
10 whole eggs, separate yolks
3½ cups whole kernel corn, canned, drained
3 cups cream style corn, canned
1 cup milk
1 lb. 12 ozs. cake flour
2 tbsp. baking powder
½ tsp. salt
Procedure
1. In the mixing bowl place the egg yolks, corn, milk, flour and baking powder. Using the paddle mix at slow speed until a batter is formed.
2. Remove from the mixer and place in a stainless steel bowl. Clean the mixing bowl thoroughly.

3. Place the egg whites in the mixing bowl and whip with a wire whip until dry.
4. Add the salt and continue to whip to a stiff peak.
5. Fold the beaten egg whites gently into the batter with a kitchen spoon.
6. Drop the batter from a No. 24 dipper or scoop into deep fat at 350°F and fry until golden brown.
7. Remove with a skimmer, let drain.
8. Dish up 3 fritters per portion and serve with bacon and maple syrup as a luncheon entree or serve as an accompaniment with other foods or as a side dish.

Corn pudding

Ingredients: Approx. yield: 25 servings
1 #10 can corn, cream style
1 qt. milk
10 whole eggs, beaten
4 ozs. butter
2 ozs. flour, sifted
1 tbsp. sugar
1 pt. bread crumbs
   salt and white pepper to taste
Procedure
1. Place the eggs in a stainless steel container and beat slightly.
2. Blend in the milk and corn.
3. Add the butter and stir.
4. Add the flour, sugar and bread crumbs, blending thoroughly.
5. Season with salt and white pepper.
6. Place in a buttered baking pan and bake at 350°F for approximately 45 minutes or until it becomes slightly solid.
7. Serve 3 ozs. to each portion.

EGGPLANT RECIPES

Eggplant is a pear or egg shaped vegetable that has a watery, grayish pulp and a flavor somewhat similar to that of a cooked oyster. Eggplants of good quality are medium-sized and display a rich purple color, a smooth skin, and are light for their size. Eggplants that are picked just before reaching full growth are the best.

Fried eggplant

Ingredients: Approx. yield: 25 servings
- 6 lbs. eggplant, peeled
- 1 lb. flour
- 5 whole eggs
- 3 cups milk
- 2 lbs. bread crumbs
- 2 tsp. salt
- ½ tsp. pepper

Procedure
1. Cut the eggplant in half lengthwise, slice crosswise ¼ to ½ inch thick.
2. Place the slices in cold salt water to prevent discoloration then drain well.
3. Season the flour with salt and pepper, add the sliced eggplant and coat thoroughly.
4. Beat the eggs slightly, add the milk, making an egg wash. Remove the eggplant from the flour and deposit the slices in the egg wash, coating thoroughly.
5. Remove the slices from the egg wash and place in the bread crumbs. Press crumbs on firmly.
6. Fry in deep fat at 350°F until golden brown.
7. Serve 2 or 3 slices for each portion.

Eggplant sauté

Ingredients: Approx. yield: 25 servings
- 6 lbs. eggplant, peeled
- 2 lbs. flour
- 5 whole eggs
- 3 cups milk
- 1 tbsp. salt
- 1 tsp. pepper

Procedure
1. Cut the eggplant in half lengthwise, slice crosswise ¼ to ½ inches thick.
2. Place the slices in cold salt water to prevent discoloration and drain well.
3. Season the flour with salt and pepper, add the sliced eggplant and coat thoroughly.
4. Beat the eggs slightly, add the milk making an egg wash. Remove the eggplant from the flour and deposit the slices in the egg wash, coat thoroughly.
5. Remove the slices from the egg wash and place back into the flour, press firmly.

6. Fry both sides in shallow grease until golden brown.
7. Serve 2 or 3 slices for each portion.

Eggplant creole

Ingredients: Approx. yield: 25 servings
- 6 lbs. eggplant, peeled
- water to cover, boiling
- 1 tbsp. salt
- 2 qts. creole sauce
- salt and pepper to taste

Procedure
1. Prepare creole sauce. (See Chap. 15.)
2. Cut the eggplant into ½ inch cubes. Place in a sauce pot, covering with boiling water. Add 1 tbsp. salt and simmer for 8 to 10 minutes then drain thoroughly.
3. Pour over the hot creole sauce, return to the range and simmer.
4. Season with salt and pepper and serve.

Scalloped eggplant and tomatoes

Ingredients: Approx. yield: 25 servings
- 4 lbs. eggplant, peeled
- 2 qts. whole tomatoes, canned
- 4 ozs. onions, minced
- 4 ozs. butter
- 2 lbs. bread, cut into ½ inch cubes then toasted
- 1½ ozs. sugar
- 1 tsp. basil
- ¼ cup Parmesan cheese
- salt and pepper to taste

Procedure
1. Cut the eggplant into ½ inch cubes. Simmer in boiling salt water for 8 to 10 minutes drain thoroughly and hold.
2. Place the butter in a sauce pan and heat.
3. Add the onions and sauté until tender.
4. Add the tomatoes, sugar and basil. Simmer for 5 minutes.
5. Stir in the bread cubes and the cooked eggplant. Season with salt and pepper.
6. Pour into a lightly greased hotel pan and sprinkle with Parmesan cheese.
7. Place in a 350°F oven and bake until the top becomes slightly brown and the bread cubes absorb most of the liquid.

KOHLRABI RECIPES

Kohlrabi is a variety of cabbage. But instead the leaves, the swoolen, turnip-like, green or purple stem which grows just above the ground is the edible part. The plant is harvested while the stems are small and tender. If left to mature the stems become woody and strong in flavor. The taste of kohlrabi resembles the combined flavors of turnips and cabbage. The flavor is best when the kohlrabi is young and is pale green in color.

Buttered kohlrabi

Ingredients: Approx. yield: 25 servings
8   lbs. kohlrabi, peeled
     water to cover, boiling
2   tbsp. salt
8   ozs. butter
     salt and pepper to taste
Procedure
1. Cut the peeled kohlrabi into slices, $\frac{1}{4}$ inch thick or dice into $\frac{1}{2}$ inch cubes.
2. Place in a sauce pan and cover with boiling water.
3. Add the salt and simmer approximately 30 minutes or until tender.
4. Drain off any excess liquid and add the butter.
5. Adjust the seasoning with salt and pepper and serve.

Creamed kohlrabi

Ingredients: Approx. yield: 25 servings
8   lbs. kohlrabi, peeled
     water to cover, boiling
2   tbsp. salt
2   qts. cream sauce
2   ozs. butter
     salt and white pepper to taste
Procedure
1. Prepare cream sauce. (See Chap. 15.)
2. Cut the peeled kohlrabi into $\frac{1}{2}$ inch cubes.
3. Place in a sauce pan, cover with boiling water.
4. Add the salt and simmer for 30 minutes or until tender then drain thoroughly.
5. Pour the hot cream sauce over the cooked kohlrabi and fold together gently.
6. Season with salt and white pepper.
7. Blend in the butter and serve.

LIMA BEAN RECIPES

Lima beans originated in the country of Peru and in all probability were named after its principal city, Lima. Francisco Pizarro, Spanish explorer and conqueror of Peru, took the lima bean plant back to Europe from where it spread to its world wide popularity. There are two types of lima beans on the market. The small or baby limas and the large or fordhook limas. The fordhook lima are the most popular in the commercial kitchen. Lima beans of good quality are plump with a tender skin which is green or greenish-white in color.

Buttered lima beans

Ingredients: Approx. yield: 25 servings
5   lbs. lima beans, frozen (fordhook)
     water to cover, boiling
1   tsp. salt
8   ozs. butter
     salt and white pepper to taste
Procedure
1. Place the lima beans in a sauce pan and cover with boiling water.
2. Add the salt and simmer until slightly tender.
3. Drain off any excess liquid and add the butter.
4. Season with salt and white pepper and serve.

Lima beans with bacon

Ingredients: Approx. yield: 25 servings
5   lbs. lima beans, frozen (fordhook)
     water to cover
1   tsp. salt
1   lb. jowl bacon, diced medium
4   ozs. onion, minced
1   tbsp. chopped chives
     salt and white pepper to taste
Procedure
1. Place the lima beans in a sauce pan and cover with boiling water.
2. Add the salt and simmer until slightly tender.
3. Drain off any excess liquid.
4. Place the diced bacon in a separate sauce pan and cook to a light brown crackling.

5. Add the minced onions and sauté until tender. Do not brown.
6. Pour in the cooked limas and the remaining juice.
7. Add the chives and bring to a simmer.
8. Season with salt and white pepper and serve.

Lima beans and mushrooms

Ingredients: Approx. yield: 25 servings
5   lbs. lima beans, frozen (fordhook)
     water to cover, boiling
1   tsp. salt
8   ozs. butter
1   lb. mushrooms, washed, sliced
4   ozs. onion, minced
     salt and white pepper to taste
Procedure
1. Place the lima beans in a sauce pan and cover with boiling water.
2. Add the salt and simmer until slightly tender.
3. Drain off any excess liquid.
4. Place the butter in a separate sauce pan and heat.
5. Add the onions and sauté slightly.
6. Add the mushrooms and continue to sauté until they are tender.
7. Pour in the cooked lima beans and the remaining juice and simmer for 5 minutes.
8. Season with salt and white pepper and serve.

Lima beans and tomatoes

Ingredients: Approx. yield: 25 servings
5   lbs. lima beans, frozen (fordhook)
     water to cover, boiling
1   tsp. salt
2   qts. whole tomatoes, canned
3   ozs. onions, minced
4   ozs. butter
1   tsp. sugar
     salt and white pepper to taste
Procedure
1. Place the lima beans in a sauce pan and cover with boiling water.
2. Add the salt and simmer until slightly tender then drain thoroughly.
3. Place the butter in a separate sauce pan and heat.
4. Add the onions and sauté until slightly tender.

5. Add the tomatoes and sugar and simmer for 5 minutes.
6. Add the drained lima beans and return to a simmer.
7. Season with salt and white pepper.
8. Serve, garnishing each portion with chopped parsley.

Creamed lima beans

Ingredients: Approx. yield: 25 servings
5   lbs. lima beans, frozen (fordhook)
     water to cover, boiling
1   tsp. salt
2   qts. cream sauce
2   ozs. butter
     salt and white pepper to taste
Procedure
1. Prepare cream sauce. (See Chap. 15.)
2. Place the lima beans in a sauce pan and cover with boiling water.
3. Add the salt and simmer until slightly tender. Drain thoroughly.
4. Pour the hot cream sauce over the cooked limas. Stir together gently.
5. Add the butter. Season with salt and white pepper and serve.

OKRA RECIPES

Okra, also known as gumbo plant, is a fuzzy, tapering, many-seeded, pod vegetable. It has from 5 to 12 sides and is about 3 inches long when young. Okra of good quality has a fresh green color, a plump appearance and snaps easily when bent. Okra is extensively cultivated in the Southern States.

Buttered okra

Ingredients: Approx. yield: 25 servings
6   lbs. okra, fresh
     water to cover, boiling
¼   cup vinegar, cider
1   tbsp. salt
8   ozs. butter
     salt and pepper to taste
Procedure
1. Cut off the stems and wash the okra in cold salt water. Cut into ½ inch pieces.
2. Place in a sauce pot and cover with boiling water.

3. Add 1 tbsp. salt and the vinegar. Simmer for approximately 20 minutes or until tender then drain.
4. Add the butter and stir until thoroughly melted.
5. Season with salt and pepper and serve.

Okra and tomatoes

Ingredients: Approx. yield: 25 servings
5   lbs. okra, frozen
4   ozs. butter
2   qts. whole tomatoes, canned
8   ozs. onions, minced
3   tsp. sugar
    salt and pepper to taste
Procedure
1. Place the butter in a sauce pan and heat.
2. Add the onions and sauté until slightly tender. Do not brown.
3. Add the tomatoes and sugar and bring to a boil.
4. Add the okra and simmer until the okra is tender.
5. Season with salt and pepper and serve.

ONION RECIPES

There are three chief kinds of dry onions: yellow, red and white. Each is available in several varieties. Most of the yellow onion varieties produce a mild, sweet flavor. The red onion varieties are generally fairly strong in flavor. The white onion varieties are always quite strong in flavor. Yellow onions, such as Bermuda and Spanish, are best for frying. The red onions are excellent to use in Italian sauce and for cooking. The white onions are best for baking and boiling because they retain their shape after cooking.

Buttered onions

Ingredients: Approx. yield: 25 servings
6   lbs. onions, small, white, peeled
    water to cover, boiling
1   tbsp. salt
8   ozs. butter
    pepper to taste
Procedure
1. Place the peeled onions in a sauce pan and cover with water.

2. Add the salt and simmer for approximately 30 minutes or until tender.
3. Drain off half of the liquid and add the butter.
4. Season with pepper.
5. Serve 2 onions to each portion.

Creamed onions

Ingredients: Approx. yield: 25 servings
1   #10 can onions, small, whole
2   qts. cream sauce
2   ozs. butter
    salt and white pepper
Procedure
1. Prepare cream sauce. (See Chap. 15.)
2. Place the onions and liquid in a sauce pan. Heat then drain thoroughly.
3. Add the hot cream sauce and fold in gently so the onions will not be broken or mashed.
4. Add the butter and season with pepper.
5. Serve 2 or 3 onions to each portion.

French fried onion rings

Ingredients: Approx. yield: 25 servings
5   lbs. onions, Bermuda or Spanish, peeled, cut in 1/4 inch slices, separated into rings
    ice water to cover
1   lb. cake flour
BATTER
5   whole eggs
1   pt. milk
3   tsp. baking powder
1   lb. cake flour, sifted
1   tsp. paprika
1   tsp. salt
Procedure
As soon as the onion rings are sliced, they should be placed in ice water to prevent them from bleeding (losing water). Keep them in the ice water while proceeding to prepare the batter.
1. Break the eggs in a stainless steel container. Beat slightly.
2. Add the milk and blend.
3. Combine the flour, paprika, salt and baking powder and sift.
4. Add the dry ingredient mixture to the milk-egg mixture. Blend together thoroughly, until the batter is smooth.
5. Remove the onion rings from the ice water and drain thoroughly.

6. Place them in the flour then dip into the batter.
7. Fry in deep fat at 350° to 360°F until golden brown.
8. Drain and serve 5 to 8 rings per portion.

Glazed onions

Ingredients: Approx. yield: 25 servings
- 6 lbs. onions, small, white, peeled
  - water to cover, boiling
- 1 tbsp. salt
- 4 ozs. brown sugar, dark
- 4 ozs. butter
- 1½ cups water, hot
- ½ tsp. salt

Procedure
1. Place the peeled onions in a sauce pan and cover with water.
2. Add the salt and simmer for approximately 30 minutes or until tender. Drain thoroughly and place in a baking pan.
3. Place the brown sugar, butter, hot water and salt in a separate sauce pan. Place on the range and simmer for 10 minutes.
4. Pour the syrup over the cooked onions.
5. Bake in a 350°F oven for approximately 40 minutes, basting frequently.
6. Remove and serve 2 onions to each portion.

Broiled onions

Ingredients: Approx. yield: 25 servings
- 10 Bermuda or Spanish onions, peeled, cut into 5 slices each
  - salt as needed
  - sugar as needed
  - paprika as needed

Procedure
1. Place the onion slices on sheet pans, place in the steamer and steam approximately 7 to 10 minutes or until the onions are slightly tender.
2. Remove and sprinkle each onion with salt, sugar and paprika.
3. Place under the broiler and brown.
4. Serve 2 slices to each portion.

PEA RECIPES

Peas are the edible seeds of a pod-bearing vine, cultivated to a considerable extent as a field crop in the northern United States and Canada. The plant will withstand light frosts and is therefore planted very early in spring. There is a great variety of peas on today's market. They vary in size, shape and taste. When using canned peas the variety is generally stated on the label, such as "early June" or "sweet." Frozen peas, which are used most often in the commercial kitchen, are not labeled but are usually uniform in color and size.

Buttered peas

Ingredients: Approx. yield: 25 servings
- 5 lbs. peas, frozen
  - water to cover, boiling
- 1 tbsp. salt
- 4 ozs. butter
- 1 tbsp. sugar

Procedure
1. Thaw, place the peas in a sauce pan and cover with boiling water.
2. Add the salt and simmer until tender.
3. Drain off any excess liquid. Add the butter and sugar and serve.

Creamed peas

Ingredients: Approx. yield: 25 servings
- 5 lbs. peas, frozen
  - water to cover, boiling
- 1 tbsp. salt
- 2 qts. cream sauce

Procedure
1. Prepare cream sauce. (See Chap. 15.)
2. Thaw, place the peas in a sauce pan, cover with boiling water.
3. Add the salt and simmer until tender then drain thoroughly.
4. Blend in the hot cream sauce. Adjust the seasoning and serve.

Peas and mushrooms

Ingredients: Approx. yield: 25 servings
- 5 lbs. peas, frozen
- 1 lb. mushrooms, fresh, diced small
  - water to cover, boiling
- 1 tbsp. salt
- 6 ozs. butter

Procedure
1. Thaw, place the peas in a sauce pan and cover with boiling water.
2. Add the salt and simmer until tender.
3. Drain off any excess liquid.

Peas and mushrooms

Green Giant Co.

4. Place the butter in a separate sauce pan and melt.
5. Add the mushrooms and sauté until tender.
6. Combine the cooked peas and mushrooms.
7. Check seasoning and serve.

Peas and carrots

Ingredients: Approx. yield: 25 servings
5   lbs. peas, frozen
    water to cover, boiling
1   tbsp. salt
1   tbsp. sugar
2   lbs. carrots, fresh, peeled, diced small
    water to cover, boiling
4   ozs. butter
Procedure
1. Place the peas in a sauce pan and cover with boiling water.
2. Add the salt and sugar. Simmer until tender.
3. Place the diced carrots in a separate sauce pan, cover with boiling water and simmer until tender.

4. Combine the cooked peas and carrots. Drain off any excess liquid.
5. Add the butter and adjust the seasoning and serve.

Minted peas

Ingredients: Approx. yield: 25 servings
5   lbs. peas, frozen
    water to cover, boiling
1   tbsp. salt
1   tbsp. sugar
4   ozs. butter
¼   cup chopped mint
Procedure
1. Place the peas in a sauce pan and cover with boiling water.
2. Add the salt and sugar. Simmer until tender.
3. Drain off any excess liquid.
4. Add the butter and chopped mint.
5. Adjust the seasoning and serve.

RICE RECIPES

Common rice, which seems to have originated in Southeast Asia is now grown in all parts of the world where favorable conditions (warm and moist) exist. The seed or grain of the plant, which is the principal food for almost half of the human race, is a white grain enclosed by a layer of bran surrounded by a brown husk. When rice is marketed as white rice, the husk and bran are removed in special machines. The rice kernel is then polished to improve the appearance. When rice is marketed as brown rice, the rice is dried and cleaned with the husk and bran remaining on the kernel. Since most of the vitamins found in rice are contained in the husk, the brown rice is richer in nutritional value. There are three types of rice on the market: long grain, medium grain and short grain. They all contain the same food value but differ in size and texture of the grain, which causes each to require a slightly different cooking time.

Rice pilaf

Ingredients: Approx. yield: 25 servings
1   qt. rice, raw, washed
2   qts. chicken stock, hot
6   ozs. onions, minced
6   ozs. butter
1   small bay leaf
    salt to taste
    yellow color, as needed, if desired
Procedure
1. Prepare chicken stock. (See Chap. 12.)
2. Place the butter in a fairly small braising pot and melt.
3. Add the onions and sauté slightly. Do not brown.
4. Add the rice and continue to sauté for 3 minutes longer.
5. Add the chicken stock and stir.
6. Season with salt, add the bay leaf and yellow color if desired. Stir and bring to a boil.
7. Cover the braising pot and place in a 400°F oven.
8. Bake for approximately 20 minutes or until the rice kernels become slightly tender. (Do not stir the rice during the baking period).

9. Remove from the oven and turn the rice out on a sheet pan. Work in additional butter, remove the bay leaf and check the seasoning.
10. Place in a bain-marie and serve with a No. 12 dipper.
    Note: For rice rissoto add approximately ¼ cup of Parmesan cheese when working in the additional butter.

Rice Valencienne

Ingredients: Approx. yield: 25 servings
1   qt. rice, raw, washed
2   qts. chicken stock, hot
4   ozs. butter
½   cup onions, minced
½   cup ham, lean, minced
3   tomatoes, fresh, peeled, diced
1   small bay leaf
¼   tsp. thyme
    salt and white pepper to taste
Procedure
1. Prepare chicken stock. (See Chap. 12.)
2. Place the butter in a fairly small braising pot and melt.
3. Add the onions and ham and sauté until the onions are slightly tender.
4. Add the rice and continue to sauté for 3 minutes longer.
5. Add the chicken stock, tomatoes, thyme and bay leaf. Stir and bring to a boil.
6. Season with salt and white pepper, cover the braising pot and place in a 400°F oven.
7. Bake for approximately 20 minutes or until the rice kernels become slightly tender. (Do not stir the rice during the baking period).
8. Remove from the oven and turn the rice out on a sheet pan. Work in additional butter, remove the bay leaf and check the seasoning.
9. Place in a bain-marie and serve with a No. 12 dipper.

Spanish rice

Ingredients: Approx. yield: 25 servings
1   lb. rice, raw, washed
½   #10 can whole tomatoes
1½   qts. chicken stock, hot
6   ozs. green peppers, diced small
6   ozs. celery, diced small
8   ozs. onions, diced small

Rice Council

Orange rice garnished with mandarin oranges and sliced sautéed mushrooms. This preparation blends well with the assorted foods shown: bacon, turkey, pork chops, ham, Canadian bacon, lobster tail, shrimp and chicken.

2 ozs. pimientos, diced small
4 ozs. butter
1 bay leaf
1 tbsp. salt
1 tbsp. sugar
pepper to taste

Procedure

1. Prepare chicken stock. (See Chap. 12.)
2. Place the butter in a sauce pan and heat.
3. Add the green peppers, celery and onions and sauté until slightly tender.
4. Add the tomatoes, bay leaf, salt, sugar and chicken stock. Bring to a boil.
5. Add the rice, cover and simmer for ap-

proximately 20 minutes or until the rice is tender.
6. Remove the bay leaf and season with pepper.
7. Serve with a No. 12 dipper.

Orange rice

Ingredients: Approx. yield: 25 servings

1 qt. rice, raw, washed
2 qts. water, hot
1 cup celery, minced
½ cup onions, minced
6 ozs. butter
½ cup frozen orange juice concentrate

½ cup orange peel, cut julienne
1 tbsp. salt
Procedure
1. Place the butter in a fairly small braiser and heat.
2. Add the celery and onion and sauté until slightly tender. Do not brown.
3. Add the orange concentrate, water, salt and orange peel. Bring to a boil.
4. Add the rice, return to a boil, cover and place in a 400°F oven.
5. Bake for 20 minutes or until the rice is tender.
6. Remove from the oven and place in a bain-marie.
7. Serve with a No. 12 dipper.

Curried rice

Ingredients: Approx. yield: 25 servings
1 qt. rice, raw, washed
2 qts. chicken stock, hot
8 ozs. onions, minced
6 ozs. apples, minced
8 ozs. butter
¼ tsp. thyme
2 tsp. curry powder
  salt and white pepper to taste
Procedure
1. Prepare chicken stock. (See Chap. 12.)
2. Place the butter in a fairly small braising pot and melt.
3. Add the onions and sauté until slightly tender.
4. Add the rice, apples and curry powder. Continue to sauté 3 more minutes while stirring constantly.
5. Add the thyme and chicken stock and bring to a boil.
6. Season with salt and white pepper. Cover the braiser and place in a 400°F oven.
7. Bake for approximately 20 minutes or until the rice is tender.
8. Remove from the oven and turn the rice out on a sheet pan. Work in additional butter and place in a bain-marie.
9. Serve with a No. 12 dipper.

RUTABAGA RECIPES

The rutabaga is a turnip-like root that grows partly above and partly below the ground. The flesh of the rutabaga is generally yellow in color although there are some varieties which are white. The rutabaga is similar to the turnip because it contains about ninety percent water; however, the flavor is similar to kohlrabi.

Buttered rutabagas

Ingredients: Approx. yield: 25 servings
6 lbs. rutabagas, peeled
  water to cover, boiling
1 tbsp. salt
6 ozs. butter
1 tsp. sugar
Procedure
1. Cut the rutabagas into ½ inch cubes.
2. Place in a sauce pan, cover with boiling water.
3. Add the salt and sugar, simmer until tender.
4. Drain off any excess liquid, add the butter.
5. Check the seasoning and serve.

Mashed rutabagas

Ingredients: Approx. yield: 25 servings
6 lbs. rutabagas, peeled
  water to cover, boiling
1 tbsp. salt
1 tbsp. sugar
6 ozs. butter
4 ozs. milk or cream, hot
½ tsp. white pepper
Procedure
1. Cut the rutabagas into thin slices.
2. Place in a sauce pan and cover with boiling water.
3. Add the salt, simmer until thoroughly cooked and drain.
4. Place in the bowl of the rotary mixer, using the paddle. Mix at 2nd speed until slightly smooth.
5. Add the butter, hot milk or cream, sugar and pepper. Continue to mix until thoroughly blended and smooth.
6. Remove from mixer, place in a bain-marie and serve with a No. 12 dipper.

SAUERKRAUT RECIPES

Unusual as it may seem, kraut supposedly originated in ancient China during the building of the great wall. It was included in the workers food rations to supplement their diet of rice.

At that time the shredded cabbage was fermented in wine. This method was used until about the 16th century when the people of western Europe found that fermenting cabbage with salt was a far better method. Kraut was introduced to the regions of Germany and northern Europe by the Tartars. It became a favorite of this region and acquired its present name, sauerkraut, which means "sour cabbage," from the Germans.

Sauerkraut Old World style

Ingredients: Approx. yield: 25 servings
- 1 #10 can sauerkraut
  water to cover, boiling
- 2 tsp. salt
- 1 tsp. caraway seed
- 5 ozs. apple sauce
- 10 ozs. onions, julienne
- 1 lb. jowl bacon, julienne
- 6 ozs. raw potatoes, grated
  pepper to taste

Procedure
1. Place the julienne cut jowl bacon in a braising pot and sauté until it becomes a light crackling.
2. Add the onions and continue to sauté until slightly tender.
3. Add the caraway seed, sauerkraut, salt and enough boiling water to cover. Place a lid on the pot.
4. Simmer about 1 hour, until the kraut is tender.
5. Add the apple sauce and grated raw potatoes, continue to simmer for 10 minutes longer.
6. Season with pepper and serve.

Sauerkraut modern style

Ingredients: Approx. yield: 25 servings
- 1 #10 can sauerkraut
  water to cover, boiling
- 2 tsp. salt
- 1 tsp. caraway seed
- 1 lb. ham hocks
- 6 ozs. ham fat or bacon grease
- 12 ozs. onions, julienne
  pepper to taste

Procedure
1. Place the ham fat or bacon grease in a braising pot, heat.
2. Add the onions and sauté until slightly tender.
3. Add the caraway seed, salt, sauerkraut and enough boiling water to cover. Bring to a boil.
4. Add the ham hocks and press into the center of the kraut. Cover the pot and continue to simmer for approximately 1 hour.
5. Season with pepper and serve.

SPINACH RECIPES

Spinach is the edible young leaves of the spinach plant. It is both a favorite vegetable and a salad green. The leaf is broad and thick, dark green in color and smooth or curly, depending on the variety. Spinach is most plentiful during the fall and winter months of the year.

Buttered spinach

Ingredients: Approx. yield: 25 servings
- 10 lbs. spinach, fresh
  water to cover, boiling
- 2 tsp. salt
- 8 ozs. butter
  salt and pepper to taste

Procedure
1. Wash the spinach thoroughly in cold water at least three times. Remove all stems and any discolored leaves. (Note that the curly leaf spinach is more difficult to clean than the smooth leaf and will require more attention.)
2. Place the spinach leaves in a sauce pot. Cover slightly with boiling water.
3. Add the salt and simmer until the leaves are wilted and tender, then drain.
4. Add the butter. Season with salt and pepper and serve.

Spinach à la Ritz

Ingredients: Approx. yield: 25 servings
- 6 lbs. spinach, frozen, leaf or chopped
  water to cover, boiling
- 1 tsp. salt
- 8 ozs. jowl bacon, diced fine
- 4 ozs. onions, minced
- 3 hard boiled eggs, chopped
- ¼ tsp. nutmeg
  salt and pepper to taste

Procedure

1. Place the partly thawed spinach in a sauce pan and cover with boiling water.
2. Add the salt and only simmer until it is tender then drain thoroughly.
3. Place the bacon in a separate sauce pan. Cook until it becomes a crackling.
4. Add the onions and sauté until tender. Do not brown.
5. Add the cooked spinach and nutmeg. Stir gently until all ingredients are thoroughly blended.
6. Season with salt and pepper.
7. Serve, garnishing each portion with the chopped eggs.

Baked spinach Parmesan

Ingredients: Approx. yield: 25 servings

6 lbs. spinach frozen, chopped
water to cover, boiling
1 tsp. salt
4 ozs. butter
4 ozs. onion, minced
1 tsp. Worcestershire sauce
6 whole eggs, slightly beaten
1½ cups cracker crumbs (variable)
⅓ cup Parmesan cheese
salt and pepper to taste

Procedure

1. Place the partly thawed spinach in a sauce pan and cover with boiling water.
2. Add the salt and only simmer until it is tender then drain thoroughly.
3. Place the butter in a separate sauce pan and heat.
4. Add the minced onions and sauté until slightly tender. Do not brown.
5. Add the cooked spinach, Worcestershire sauce and Parmesan cheese. Stir until all ingredients are blended. Remove from range, allow to cool slightly.
6. Add the eggs while stirring constantly.
7. Add the cracker crumbs. The amount may vary, depending on the moisture still present in the spinach. Blend thoroughly.
8. Season with salt and pepper. Place in a buttered baking pan.
9. Bake at 350°F until the mixture binds and becomes firm.
10. Remove from the oven, cut into squares and serve with cream sauce (see Chap.

15), accented with additional Parmesan cheese.

Creamed spinach

Ingredients: Approx. yield: 25 servings

6 lbs. spinach, frozen, chopped
water to cover, boiling
1 tsp. salt
1½ qts. cream sauce
2 ozs. butter
salt and white pepper to taste

Procedure

1. Prepare cream sauce. (See Chap. 15.)
2. Place the partly thawed spinach in a sauce pan and cover with boiling water.
3. Add the salt and only simmer until it is tender then drain thoroughly.
4. Add the hot cream sauce. Stir in gently.
5. Season with salt and white pepper to taste.
6. Add the butter. Blend in and serve.

Spinach country style

Ingredients: Approx. yield: 25 servings

6 lbs. spinach, frozen, chopped
water to cover, boiling
1 tsp. salt
8 ozs. jowl bacon, diced
4 ozs. onion, minced
1 pt. potatoes, raw, diced medium
3 cups ham stock (variable)
¼ tsp. nutmeg
salt and white pepper to taste

Procedure

1. Prepare ham stock. (See Chap. 12.)
2. Place the partly thawed spinach in a sauce pan and cover with boiling water.
3. Add the salt and only simmer until it is tender then drain thoroughly.
4. Place the bacon in a separate sauce pan and cook until it becomes a crackling.
5. Add the onions and sauté until tender. Do not brown.
6. Add the diced potatoes and ham stock. The amount of ham stock may vary, depending on the moisture still present in the spinach. Simmer until the potatoes are tender.
7. Add the spinach and nutmeg, stirring gently so potatoes will not be broken. If mixture is too wet, remove some of the liquid.
8. Season with salt and pepper and serve.

Stuffed acorn squash shown with other common squash varieties.

United Fresh Fruit and Vegetable Assoc.

SQUASH RECIPES

Squash is the edible fruit of a vine type plant belonging to the gourd or cucumber family. The vines, which are similar to the pumpkin vines, produce fruits of widely different shapes and sizes. There are two classes of squash: summer and winter. The summer squashes, including Italian, patty-pan and crookneck, are harvested early before the rind begins to harden. They do not keep well. The winter squashes include, Hubbard, acorn and winter crookneck and have hard rinds and excellent keeping qualities.

Italian squash, also known as zucchini, is one of the most popular squashes used in the commercial kitchen.

It has gained most of its popularity in recent years. It is long and narrow with a dark green skin and somewhat resembles the cucumber. It grows from 3 to 20 inches long although the very young zucchini, 3 to 6 inches long, possess the best eating qualities. Zucchini is generally very tender and mild in flavor and for this reason can be featured on the menu in a variety of ways.

Patty-pan, also known as scalloped squash, is round and flat with scalloped edges. It ranges from 3 to 15 inches in diameter, has a thin, smooth rind and a color that may be yellow or white. The flesh of patty-pan squash is watery.

Crookneck squash, so named because of its curved neck, has a thin, yellow, slightly warted skin. The flesh is very tender with a color that varies from yellow to cream-colored.

Hubbard squash is the most popular of the winter squash. It has a globular shape, and a hard, warted rind that may be orange, green or yellow in color. The green Hubbard is most commonly preferred. The flesh of the Hubbard squash is slightly orange in color, thick and fine grained.

Acorn squash, also known as Danish squash, is shaped somewhat like an acorn. It has a hard, smooth dark green rind and a yellow, sweet-flavored flesh.

Winter crookneck squash is similar in almost all respects to the summer crookneck; however, it has a tougher skin and better keeping qualities.

Baked acorn squash

Ingredients: Approx. yield: 25 servings
12   or 13 acorn squash
       (approx. 1¼ lbs. each)
 8   ozs. butter
 1   tbsp. salt
 6   ozs. brown sugar, dark
       water as needed
Procedure
1. Cut the squash in half lengthwise and remove the seeds.
2. Butter the surface of the flesh lightly. Place on sheet pan skin side down. Add enough water to cover bottom of pan about ¼ inch deep.
3. Place in a 350°F oven and bake for approximately 35 minutes.
4. Brush the surface of the squash with butter a second time. Sprinkle with salt and brown sugar.
5. Return to the oven and continue to bake until golden brown.
6. Serve one half of the squash to each portion.
Note: Baked acorn squash may be stuffed with apples, apple sauce or vegetables if desired.

Mashed Hubbard squash

Ingredients: Approx. yield: 25 servings
10   lbs. Hubbard squash, peeled

 4   ozs. brown sugar, light
 6   ozs. butter
 2   tsp. salt
 4   ozs. cream, warm
Procedure
1. Cut the squash in half, remove the seeds and dice into ½ inch cubes.
2. Place in a baking pan, and sprinkle with the sugar and salt.
3. Dot the top with butter, place in a 350°F oven and bake until very tender.
4. Remove from the oven and place in the bowl of the rotary mixer. Using the paddle, mix at slow speed until fairly smooth.
5. Add the warm cream to obtain proper consistency, while continuing to mix.
6. Adjust seasoning and serve (No. 12 dipper).

Buttered summer crookneck squash

Ingredients: Approx. yield: 25 servings
 8   lbs. summer crookneck squash, washed
       water to cover half way, boiling
 2   tsp. salt
 8   ozs. butter
       salt and white pepper
Procedure
1. Cut off the ends of the squash. Do not peel. Score the squash lengthwise with the tines of a dinner fork.
2. Slice crosswise into ½ inch discs. Place in a braising pot.
3. Cover half way with boiling water, add the salt, cover braiser and simmer until the squash is just tender. Drain off half of the liquid.
4. Add the butter. Adjust the seasoning with salt and white pepper and serve.
Note: Young summer squash, with its characteristic soft rind, need not be peeled.

French fried zucchini

Ingredients: Approx. yield: 25 servings
 6   lbs. zucchini squash, washed
 1   lb. bread flour
 3   cups milk, cold
 5   whole eggs, beaten
 2   lbs. bread crumbs
 2   tsps. salt
 ½   tsp. pepper
Procedure
1. Cut the ends off the zucchini and cut into finger-size pieces (½ in. by 2 in.).

Place in salt water to keep from discoloring.

2. Season the flour with salt and pepper.
3. Drain the pieces of zucchini and pass through the seasoned flour, coating thoroughly.
4. Blend together the beaten eggs and the milk, making an egg wash. Dip the squash into the egg wash and coat.
5. Remove from the egg wash and roll in the bread crumbs, pressing firmly.
6. Shake off excess crumbs and fry in deep fat at 350°F until golden brown.
7. Drain well and serve.

Zucchini squash and tomatoes

Ingredients: Approx. yield: 25 servings
6   lbs. zucchini squash
2   tsp. garlic, minced
½   cup salad oil
1   pt. water
½   #10 can whole tomatoes
    salt and pepper to taste
Procedure
1. Cut the ends off the zucchini and slice into ½ inch discs.
2. Place the salad oil in a sauce pan and heat.
3. Add the garlic and sauté until slightly brown.
4. Add the squash and the water and simmer until almost tender.
5. Add the tomatoes, continuing to simmer until the squash is tender.
6. Season with salt and pepper and serve.

TOMATO RECIPES

It is believed that the tomato originated in the country of Peru and was called *Xitomatles* by the Aztec Indians. This was later modified to the English *tomato*. Tomatoes were first cultivated for their decorative bright red appearance, but were soon found to be edible. There are many varieties of tomatoes and each differs in plant form, fruit shape and size. The color will either be red or yellow. A tomato of good quality will be vine ripened, firm, well formed, free of cracks or blemishes, and with a smooth skin and a rich red color. During the offseason tomatoes are picked green, packed in wooden boxes and shipped to market. They ripen in the box without the benefit of sunshine. Although they are wholesome, they lack the color, texture and flavor of the vine ripened tomato.

Stewed tomatoes

Ingredients: Approx. yield: 25 servings
1   #10 can whole tomatoes
8   ozs. bread, diced, toasted
6   ozs. butter
4   ozs. celery, minced
6   ozs. onions, minced
2   ozs. sugar
    salt and pepper to taste
Procedure
1. Place the butter in a sauce pan and heat.
2. Add the onions and celery and sauté until tender.
3. Add the tomatoes and sugar. Continue to simmer until all ingredients are tender.
4. Remove from the range and add the toasted bread cubes.
5. Season with salt and pepper and serve.

Scalloped tomatoes

Ingredients: Approx. yield: 25 servings
1   #10 can whole tomatoes, solid pack (very little liquid)
6   ozs. onions, minced
1   lb. 8 ozs. bread, diced, toasted
4   ozs. butter
2   ozs. sugar
¼   cup bread crumbs
¼   cup Parmesan cheese
    salt and pepper to taste
Procedure
1. Place the butter in a sauce pan and heat.
2. Add the onions and sauté until tender. Do not brown.
3. Add the tomatoes and sugar. Simmer for 5 minutes then remove from the range.
4. Add the toasted bread cubes and season with salt and pepper.
5. Pour into a lightly greased hotel pan. Top with the bread crumbs and Parmesan cheese.
6. Dot with additional butter and bake in a 350°F oven until the top becomes slightly brown. Serve.

Baked tomatoes Italian

Ingredients: Approx. yield: 25 servings
25 fresh tomatoes, medium size, fairly ripe and solid
1 cup salad oil
2 tsp. sweet basil
1 tsp. oregano
salt and pepper to taste

Procedure
1. Remove the stem of each tomato and slice off the bottom.
2. Place in a baking pan bottom side up.
3. Rub each tomato with salad oil.
4. Rub the sweet basil and oregano together and sprinkle over each tomato.
5. Season with salt and pepper.
6. Bake in a 350°F oven until the tomatoes are just tender.
7. Serve 1 tomato for each portion.

French fried tomatoes

Ingredients: Approx. yield: 25 servings
13 tomatoes, fairly large, half ripe
12 ozs. flour
2 tsp. salt
½ tsp. pepper
5 whole eggs, beaten
3 cups milk
1 lb. bread crumbs (variable)

Procedure
1. Cut each tomato into 4 thick slices.
2. Season the flour with salt and pepper. Pass the tomato slices through the flour, coating thoroughly.
3. Blend the beaten eggs and the milk together, making an egg wash. Dip each tomato slice into the egg wash until thoroughly coated.
4. Remove from the egg wash and place in the bread crumbs, pressing slightly.
5. Fry in deep fat at 360°F until golden brown.
6. Serve 2 slices for each portion.

Baked stuffed tomatoes

Ingredients: Approx. yield: 25 servings
25 fresh tomatoes, medium size, fairly ripe and solid
1 cup salad oil
½ tsp. pepper
1 tsp. salt
2 lbs. cooked peas (or 2 lbs. cooked corn)
8 ozs. butter

Procedure
1. Remove the stem of each tomato and slice off the bottom. Remove a portion of the center to make a cavity, while still leaving a fairly thick tomato wall.
2. Place the tomatoes in a baking pan, cavity facing up, and rub each tomato with salad oil.
3. Season with salt and pepper.
4. Bake in a 350°F oven until the tomatoes are just tender.
5. Fill each cavity with cooked peas or corn.
6. Drip melted butter over each and serve one for each portion.

TURNIP RECIPES

Turnips are a hardy annual or biennial plant belonging to the mustard family and grown for the edible globular, white or yellow root it produces. Turnips are native to Europe and some parts of Asia, but they are also cultivated in temperate regions throughout the world. Turnips of good quality are smooth and firm with very few roots at the base. They are heavy for their size and the tops are green and fresh-looking. The color of the root may be yellow or white, depending on the variety grown. The yellow turnips are stronger in flavor.

Buttered turnips

Ingredients: Approx. yield: 25 servings
8 lbs. turnips, white, peeled
water to cover, boiling
1 tbsp. salt
6 ozs. butter
1 tbsp. sugar
½ tsp. white pepper

Procedure
1. Dice the turnips into ½ inch cubes, place in a sauce pan and cover with boiling water.
2. Add the salt, simmer uncovered until slightly tender then drain off any excess liquid.
3. Add the butter. Sugar and pepper, remove from the range and serve.

Creamed turnips

Ingredients: Approx. yield: 25 servings
6   lbs. turnips, white, peeled
    water to cover, boiling
1   tbsp. salt
2   qts. cream sauce
2   qts. butter
    salt and white pepper to taste
Procedure
1. Prepare the cream sauce. (See Chap. 15.)
2. Dice the turnips into ½ inch cubes, place in a sauce pan and cover with boiling water.
3. Add the salt, simmer uncovered until slightly tender then drain thoroughly.
4. Add the hot cream sauce, stirring gently.
5. Add the butter. Season with salt and white pepper and serve with a No. 12 dipper.

Mashed yellow turnips

Ingredients: Approx. yield: 25 servings
6   lbs. turnips, yellow, peeled
    water to cover, boiling
2   tsp. salt
2   lbs. potatoes, peeled
    water to cover, boiling
1   tsp. salt
2   tbsp. sugar
    salt and white pepper to taste
Procedure
1. Cut the turnips into uniform pieces, place in a sauce pan and cover with boiling water. Add 2 tsp. salt and simmer until tender then drain thoroughly.
2. Cut the potatoes into uniform pieces, place in a sauce pan and cover with boiling water. Add 1 tsp. salt and simmer until tender then drain thoroughly.
3. Place the cooked turnips and potatoes together in the bowl of the rotary mixer. Using the paddle, mix together until smooth.
4. Add the sugar and butter, continuing to mix.
5. Season with salt and pepper and mix.
6. Place in a bain-marie and cover with waxpaper.
7. Serve, using a No. 12 dipper.

potato
preparation

■ It is important that the student cook obtains a knowledge of the popular potato preparations if he intends to advance to the position of journeyman cook or chef. Today, the potato has become the staff of life in America and commands a position similar to bread and rice. In fact, potatoes are the world's second largest food crop, running a close second to rice. The United States is the leading producer of this very popular tuber vegetable. Very few meals are served in America without being accompanied with some kind of potato preparation.

Some people avoid the potato because they believe it is starchy and therefore fattening. This belief has been disproved by nutrition experts. The potato does contain a fairly large percentage of starch, but the starch found in potatoes is much more digestible than other starches. When the potato is properly cooked the starch particles become very tender. If the potato is over or under cooked it becomes hard, watery or soggy and is usually indigestible.

POTATO CLASSIFICATIONS

White meat potatoes are of two types: the *long type,* which become mealy (grain-like and easily broken up) when

United Fresh Fruit and Vegetable Assoc.

Common potatoes used in commercial cooking: from top to bottom, red potatoes, round white (second and third trays from top), long white, and Idaho potatoes.

cooked, and the *round* or *intermediate type,* which is hard and stays more firm when cooked. The long type, such as the Idaho, is therefore the best selection when baking, mashing, or French frying. The round or intermediate type, such as the red or new potato, is the best selection when boiling, sautéing or roasting.

Idaho potatoes are sometimes called the king of potatoes because they have such excellent eating qualities and have a fine white meat. They have a light brown, slightly thin skin and a long shape with shallow eyes. A large percentage of these potatoes are grown in the state of Idaho, hence their name. They are also grown in many other states.

New potatoes or *early crop potatoes* are harvested before they reach full maturity. They have a very thin red skin and contain more water than "old" potatoes. New potatoes are generally small in size and make attractive potato preparations because of their uniformity. New potatoes have poor keeping qualities and cannot be stored for future use as "old" or "late" potatoes can.

Intermediate potatoes, sometimes called *"red" potatoes* because they generally have a redish skin, are very similar to "new" potatoes in appearance but they are larger. They come on the market in September, between the early and late crop potatoes. They are used quite often in the commercial kitchen when the preparation calls for a potato that will hold together. These potatoes have better keeping qualities than "new" potatoes but do not keep as well as the late varieties.

Old or *late potatoes* are the more mature or main crop potatoes. They are harvested in the fall, stored, and used during the year because they have very excellent keeping qualities. They possess a tough brown skin and less water content than the new potato. These potatoes are more of an all-purpose potato because they can be used in many different ways.

Good quality potatoes are firm when pressed in the hand. They will have shallow eyes and be fairly clean. When they are cut they should display a yellow-white color and moisture should appear on the cut side. Occasionally, potatoes are found which are starting to sprout or have a partly green texture. These potatoes should *not* be eaten because they contain a small amount of alkaloid poison. Although alkaloid poison may not be harmful when consummed in small amounts, it renders the potato unpalatable.

Sweet potatoes are different from the white potato because of the color of their flesh and their characteristic sweetish taste. They are strictly American. At the time America was discovered the Indians were already growing this tasty root vegetable. Sweet potatoes are sometimes called "yams." This is an incorrect use of the term which resulted because many people, particularly the people of the South, associated it with the yam. The true yam is similar to but larger in size than the sweet potato. The yam comes from an entirely different plant. Sweet potatoes are quite often used in the commercial kitchen because they can be prepared in many different ways. They bake, mash, fry, and sauté with excellent results. They complement pork and poultry, providing a new taste experience when served with these items.

POTATO MARKET FORMS

Potatoes may be purchased in four market forms: fresh, canned, frozen, or dehydrated. The form to purchase would, of course, depend on the need, time element of preparation, equipment, storage, and cost. Many feel that there is no substitute for the fresh potato, but today the emphasis is placed on speed and labor saving items. More-and-more frequently we find frozen, pre-cooked French fries, dehydrated mashed potatoes, and canned whole cooked potatoes being used. These products have been perfected and are generally good; however, if true quality is desired, one must choose the fresh potato.

POTATO PREPARATIONS

Potato preparations are of two types: simple and complex. The simple preparations can be prepared with little or no training. The complex preparations by their very nature require a considerable amount of skill to prepare.

In presenting the potato recipes in this chapter the amounts of ingredients are given only for the complex preparations. For the simple preparations, only the procedure or method of preparation is given.

Simple potato preparations

American fried potatoes (also called *home fried*): Peel red potatoes and boil until they become tender. Allow to cool overnight in the refrigerator. Slice to a medium thickness and sauté in a steel skillet until golden brown. Serve garnished with chopped parsley. (For home fries it is best to use new potatoes.)

Sauté potatoes: Prepare in the same manner as American fries, but slice the potatoes thicker.

Lyonnaise potatoes: Cut onions julienne style and sauté in butter, using a steel skillet. Prepare the potatoes in the same manner as American fries. When the potatoes are golden brown, add the sautéed julienne onion and continue to sauté until the onions have blended with the potatoes. Serve garnished with chopped parsley.

German fried: Prepare in the same manner as sauté potatoes.

Hash brown potatoes: Peel red potatoes and boil until they become tender. Allow to cool overnight in the refrigerator. Chop or hash the potatoes into slightly small particles, sauté in shallow grease until golden brown. Serve garnished with chopped parsley.

Hash brown O'Brien potatoes: Prepare in the same manner as hash brown, but add small diced pimientos and sautéed small diced green peppers. Serve with chopped parsley.

Hash-in-cream potatoes: Peel red potatoes and boil until they become tender. Allow to cool overnight in the refrigerator. Chop or hash the potatoes into fairly small particles. Prepare a thin cream sauce by adding hot milk to a roux comprised of butter and flour. Add the thin cream sauce to the hashed potatoes. Season with salt and touch of nutmeg. Serve garnished with a touch of paprika. Cream can be used in place of the cream sauce if a richer product is desired.

Delmonico potatoes: Prepare in the same manner as hash-in-cream potatoes, but add diced, blanched green peppers, diced pimientos and coarsely chopped hard boiled eggs. Place this mixture in a bake pan and sprinkle the top with fresh bread crumbs. Dot with butter and bake in a 350°F oven until brown.

Au gratin potatoes: Peel red potatoes and boil until they become tender. Allow to cool overnight in the refrigerator. Chop or hash the potatoes into medium-sized particles. Prepare a thin cream sauce by adding hot milk to a roux comprised of butter and flour. Season with salt and a touch of nutmeg. Place this mixture in a bake pan and sprinkle the top with grated Cheddar cheese and paprika. Bake in a 350°F oven until the cheese is melted and slightly brown.

Baked potato: Select uniform-sized Idaho potatoes. Wash them thoroughly. Lay on a bake sheet or oven rack and bake at a temperature of 375°F until they become slightly soft when squeezed gently. Baked potatoes can also be wrapped in aluminum or gold foil and baked. However, steam is created inside the foil. When wrapped the potato will stay hotter after baking, but it is not, strictly speaking, a baked potato because baking is by dry, not moist heat.

Rissolé or oven brown potatoes: Place shortening in a roast pan and heat in a 375°F oven until hot. Add the potatoes, sprinkle with paprika and season with salt and pepper. Return to the oven and roast, turning occasionally, until potatoes become golden brown and tender.

French fried potatoes: Peel Idaho potatoes, cut with special cutter or French knife about 3 inches long and ½ inch thick. Place in fry baskets and drain thoroughly. Blanch the potatoes in deep fat at a temperature of 325°F until partly done. Do not brown them. Drain and place on sheet pans that have been covered with brown paper and allow to cool. Before serving, fry again in deep fat at a temperature of 350°F until golden brown and crisp. Sprinkle with salt.

Frying long branch potatoes in a
production unit of deep fat fryers.

Long branch potatoes: Follow the method of preparation as for French fries, but cut the potato longer and narrower.

Julienne potatoes: Peel Idaho potatoes and cut into long and very thin strips, using a French knife. Drain off any water that may be present and fry the potatoes in deep fat at a temperature of 350° to 375°F until golden brown and crisp. Sprinkle with salt and serve.

Waffle potatoes: Peel Idaho potatoes and cut with a special waffle cutter. Drain off any water that may be present and fry the potatoes in deep fat at a temperature of 350° to 375°F until golden brown and crisp. Sprinkle with salt and serve.

Shoe string potatoes: Peel Idaho potatoes and cut with a special cutter which cuts the potatoes into a spring or curl shape. Drain thoroughly and fry in deep fat at a temperature of 350° to 375°F

until golden brown and crisp. Sprinkle with salt and serve.

Riced potatoes: Peel Idaho potatoes, boil or steam them until they are very tender then drain thoroughly. Force them through a potato ricer and serve sprinkled with melted butter.

New potatoes in cream: Select uniform new potatoes, peel, and cook by boiling or steaming until they are just tender. Drain thoroughly. Prepare a thin cream sauce by adding hot milk to a roux comprised of melted butter and flour. Add the cooked whole potatoes and season with salt and white pepper. Serve garnished with chopped parsley.

Hash lyonnaise: Mince onions and sauté in butter (about ¼ cup per qt. of potatoes), using a steel skillet, until slightly tender. Do not brown. Prepare the potatoes in the same manner as hash brown; but when the potatoes are golden brown, add the sautéed onions and continue to sauté until the onions have blended with the potatoes. Serve garnished with chopped parsley.

Potatoes fine herbs: Select uniform new potatoes, peel, and cook by boiling or steaming until they are just tender. Drain. Pass them through melted butter, then through fine chopped herbs. The herb mixture is made by combining parsley, chives, and chervil or tarragon.

Polonaise potatoes: Select uniform new potatoes, peel, and cook by boiling or steaming until they are just tender. Drain. Pass them through melted butter, then through Polonaise made by combining bread crumbs browned in butter, chopped parsley, and chopped hard boiled eggs.

Use these ingredients in making the *Polonaise* (approximately enough to cover 50 potatoes):

1½	lbs. butter
2	qts. fresh bread crumbs
4	hard boiled eggs, chopped
3	tbsp. parsley, chopped

French fried sweet potatoes: Peel sweet potatoes, cut with special cutter or French knife about 3 inches long and ½ inch thick. Place in fry baskets and blanch in deep fat at a temperature of 325°F until partly done, drain. Place on sheet pans that have been covered with brown paper. Allow to cool. Before serving, fry again in deep fat at a temperature of 350° to 375°F until golden brown. Serve garnished with powdered sugar.

Swiss potatoes: Peel Idaho potatoes, grate the potatoes using the medium to large cut of a food grater. Place the shreds of potatoes in cold water then drain thoroughly. Place shortening or butter in a steel skillet and heat. Add the potato shreds and sauté until they are golden brown and tender. Season with salt and pepper and serve garnished with chopped parsley.

Chateau potatoes: Select medium sized new potatoes and peel and cut them into the shape of very large Spanish olives. Cook in shortening over a very low flame until they are tender and golden brown. Sprinkle with chopped parsley and serve.

Minute or cabaret potatoes: Peel red potatoes, dice to a medium size, drain thoroughly and blanch in deep fat at 350°F until slightly tender. Finish in a skillet by sautéing them in butter with a small amount of minced garlic.

O'Brien potatoes: Prepare in the same manner as minute potatoes, but omit the garlic and add fine diced green peppers and pimientos.

Mashed potatoes: Peel Idaho potatoes, steam or boil them in salt water until very tender then drain thoroughly. Place in bowl of mixing machine and mix, using whip or paddle, until fairly smooth. Add hot milk until desired consistency is reached.

Parsley potatoes: Select uniform new potatoes, peel and cook by steaming or boiling in salt water until they are just tender then drain thoroughly. Pass them through melted butter and sprinkle with chopped parsley.

Cottage fried potatoes: Select medium sized red potatoes, peel and slice very thin. Dry the slices on a cloth and arrange in circles on the bottom of a steel skillet with the potato slices overlapping one another. Reverse each circle until the bottom of the skillet is covered. Proceed in the same manner with a second layer. Cover the potatoes with melted shortening and place in a 400°F oven until the potatoes become tender. Remove from oven, drain off grease. Brown both sides of potatoes on range top. (Potatoes will adhere together when cooked.) Tilt onto a platter; garnish with chopped parsley.

Anna potatoes: Prepare in the same manner as cottage fried, but when the potatoes are partly browned add Parmesan cheese and continue to brown until golden. Tilt onto a platter and serve garnished with Parmesan cheese.

Parisienne potatoes no. 1: Peel Idaho or red potatoes. Cut out into small round balls, the size of a large marble, using a Parisienne or melon ball scoop. Blanch in the steamer until partly cooked. Finish by browning in deep fat at 350°F until golden brown. Sprinkle with melted butter before serving.

Parisienne potatoes no. 2: Peel Idaho or red potatoes. Cut out into small round balls, the size of a large marble, using a Parisienne or melon ball scoop. Cook in steamer until slightly tender. Sprinkle with melted butter and chopped parsley before serving.

POTATO RECIPES

The more complex potato preparations are given in the following popular recipes. An outline of recipes is given in the order of their appearance in the chapter.

**Fried and sautéed potatoes
(Pages 269 to 272)**

Sweet potato almandine
Potato pancakes
Sweet potato patties with coconut
Sweet potato croquettes à la orange
Croquette potatoes
Barbant potatoes
Lorette potatoes
Dauphine potatoes
Soufflé potatoes

Baked potatoes
(Pages 272 to 276)

Duchess potatoes
Scalloped potatoes
Macaire potatoes
Special baked potatoes
Saucy sweet potatoes
Pommes Elysées
Italian potatoes
Scalloped sweet potatoes and apples
Mushroom potatoes
Suzette potatoes
Mont d'or potatoes
Boulangere potatoes
Cross patch potatoes
Sweet potatoes with cranberries
Sherried sweet potatoes
Sweet potatoes in orange shells

Boiled potatoes
(Pages 276 to 277)

Bouillon potatoes
Hungarian potatoes
Candied sweet potatoes
Kartoffel klosse (potato dumplings)

FRIED AND SAUTEED POTATO RECIPES

Sweet potato amandine

Ingredients: Approx. yield: 25 servings
1 #10 can sweet potatoes, whole
1 tsp. lemon rind, grated
2 tsp. orange rind, grated
½ tsp. cloves, ground
1 tsp. nutmeg
1 tbsp. salt
1½ tsp. cinnamon
6 egg yolks

½ cup brown sugar
1 cup bread crumbs (variable)
1 cup shaved almonds (variable)
Procedure
1. Drain the sweet potatoes thoroughly. Place on a sheet pan and dry out in the oven at 300°F.
2. Place the potatoes, sugar and all seasoning ingredients in a mixing bowl and mix on the electric mixer, using the paddle, until the mixture is fairly smooth and free of lumps.
3. Add the egg yolks and bread crumbs blend well, then remove from the mixing bowl.
4. Form into miniature sweet potatoes about the size of a pullet egg (very small chicken egg).
5. Pass through flour, egg wash (6 eggs to a qt. of milk) and a mixture of bread crumbs and shaved almonds. Press almonds to the potatoes tightly.
6. Fry in deep fat at a temperature of 350°F until golden brown.
7. Serve 2 to each order.

Potato pancakes

Ingredients: Approx. yield: 25 servings
8 lbs. red potatoes, peeled
10 ozs. onions
8 whole eggs
8 ozs. flour, cake (variable)
1 oz. salt
¼ cup parsley, chopped, washed
pepper to taste
Procedure
1. Grate or grind the potatoes and onions and pour off all liquid.
2. Beat the eggs slightly and blend into the potato-onion mixture.
3. Add the remaining ingredients and blend well.
4. Cover the bottom of an iron skillet with ¼ in. of salad oil or shortening and heat. Fill a kitchen spoon (3 oz.) half full of the potato mixture and deposit the mixture in the shallow grease. Repeat this process until the skillet is filled.
5. Brown one side of each pancake, turn and brown the other side.
6. Remove the pancakes from the skillet and allow to drain.
7. Serve 3 pancakes to each order.

Sweet potato patties with coconut

Ingredients: *Approx. yield: 25 servings*
10   lbs. sweet potatoes, fresh
4   ozs. brown sugar
½   cup bread crumbs (variable)
½   oz. salt
1   tbsp. cinnamon
1   tsp. nutmeg
2   tsp. orange rind, grated
2   tsp. lemon rind, grated
1   lb. 8 oz. shredded or grated coconut
5   egg yolks

Procedure
1. Scrub the potatoes until they are clean.
2. Place on sheet pans and bake in a 375°F oven until the potatoes are very tender (time will depend on size of potatoes).
3. Cut potatoes lengthwise, scoop out all the pulp and discard the skin.
4. Place the pulp in bowl of electric mixer. Add the brown sugar, salt, cinnamon, nutmeg, orange rind, lemon rind, egg yolks and bread crumbs (amount will depend on the moisture left in the potatoes after baking). Using the paddle, mix until slightly smooth.
5. Place in a bake pan, cover with wax paper and refrigerate until firm.
6. Portion out 25, 4 oz. balls. Form into round flat patties. Press into the coconut until it adheres to the patties. Place on brown paper on a sheet pan and refrigerate until ready to cook.
7. Sauté each patty in butter until slightly brown on both sides.
8. Arrange on sheet pans and finish in the oven at 350°F for 10 minutes.
9. Serve one 4 oz. patty to each order.

Sweet potato croquette à la orange

Ingredients: *Approx. yield: 25 servings*
12   lbs. sweet potatoes, fresh
2   tsp. salt
½   cup brown sugar
1   tsp. nutmeg
½   tsp. cloves
4   ozs. butter
10   egg yolks
4   oranges, peeled and diced small
1½   tsp. cinnamon
½   cup bread crumbs (variable)

Procedure
1. Scrub the potatoes until they are clean.

2. Place on sheet pans and bake in a 375°F oven until the potatoes are very tender (time will depend on size on potatoes).
3. Cut potatoes lengthwise, scoop out all the pulp and discard the skin.
4. Place the pulp in bowl of electric mixer. Add the salt, sugar, nutmeg, cloves, butter, egg yolks, diced orange pulp, cinnamon and bread crumbs (exact amount will depend on the moisture in the pulp). Using the paddle, mix until all ingredients are well blended.
5. Place in a bake pan, cover with wax paper and refrigerate until firm.
6. Portion into 25 units and form into cone shape croquettes, by hand or by using a cone shaped croquette mold.
7. Bread by passing through flour, egg wash (6 eggs to 1 qt. of milk) and bread crumbs.
8. Fry in deep fat at 350°F until golden brown.
9. Serve 1 croquette on a slice of fresh orange (about ¼ in. thick, crosswise slice).

Croquette potatoes

Ingredients: *Approx. yield: 25 servings*
(3 oz. each)
6   lbs. Idaho potatoes, peeled
½   oz. salt
2   ozs. cornstarch
8   ozs. egg yolks
    pepper to taste
1   pinch of nutmeg if desired
    yellow color to tint if desired

Procedure
1. Steam or boil potatoes and drain thoroughly.
2. Place on sheet pans and dry them out in the oven for about 20 minutes at a low temperature 275° to 300°F.
3. Place the potatoes in the mixing bowl and using the paddle, whip smooth.
4. Add the egg yolks and cornstarch while mixing at slow speed; mix thoroughly.
5. Add the salt, pepper and nutmeg, if desired, and mix in at slow speed.
6. Tint potatoes with yellow color, if desired, and mix in at slow speed.
7. Remove the potato mixture from mixer and mould into 3 oz. portions. Form into desired shape and bread by passing

through flour, egg wash (6 eggs to a qt. of milk) and bread crumbs.

8. Fry in deep fat at a temperature of 340° to 345°F until golden brown. Serve 1 croquette per portion.

Note: If the potato mixture is not stiff or dry enough for successful frying add dehydrated potato flakes to absorb the moisture.

To prepare potato puffs from this same mixture use ¾ croquette mixture to ¼ pâté de choux. (Ingredients for pâté de choux are given with the recipe for Lorette potatoes.) Blend thoroughly and drop one soup spoonful at a time into deep fat at a temperature of 350°F.

To prepare potato cheese puffs, add grated Cheddar cheese to the potato puff mixture and fry the same as for potato puffs.

Barbant potatoes

Ingredients: Approx. yield: 25 servings
- 10 lbs. red potatoes, peeled, boiled
- 2 cups frozen peas, cooked
- 2 cups fresh mushrooms, diced
- 3 cloves garlic, chopped fine
- ¼ cup parsley, chopped
- 8 ozs. butter
  salt and pepper to taste

Procedure

1. Dice the cold, cooked potatoes into medium size cubes.
2. Sauté the potatoes in shortening until golden brown.
3. Sautè the mushrooms and garlic in butter until tender. Add to the sautéed potatoes.
4. Add the boiled or steamed peas and season with salt and pepper. Toss together gently.
5. Sprinkle with chopped parsley and serve a 3 to 4 oz. kitchen spoonful to each portion.

Lorette potatoes

Ingredients: Approx. yield: 25 servings
LORETTE POTATOES
- 8 lbs. duchess potato mixture
- 4 lbs. pâté de choux mixture
  salt and white pepper to taste
PATE DE CHOUX MIXTURE
- 3 cups boiling water

- 1 cup shortening
- ½ cup butter
- 3 cups pastry flour
- ½ tsp. salt
- 12 whole eggs

Procedure: Pâté de choux

1. Sift the flour and salt together.
2. Combine the shortening, butter and boiling water in a sauce pan.
3. Heat over a low flame until the shortening and butter are melted.
4. Add the flour-salt mixture all at once and stir vigorously over low heat until the mixture forms a ball and leaves the sides of the sauce pan. Remove from the heat and allow to cool.
5. Add unbeaten eggs one at a time. Beat gently after each addition until the twelve eggs have all been incorporated into the dough.

Procedure: Lorette potatoes

1. Prepare duchess potato mixture. (See recipe this chapter.)
2. Combine duchess potato mixture and pâté de choux. Blend together thoroughly at slow speed in the mixing machine, using the paddle.
3. With pastry bag and star tube, bag out the mixture onto greased paper into 25 large spiral shaped mounds.
4. Slide potatoes off paper into deep fat 350°F and fry until puffed and golden brown.
5. Drain and serve 1 mound to each serving.

Dauphine potatoes

Ingredients: Approx. yield: 25 servings
- 8 lbs. duchess potato mixture
- 2½ lbs. pâté de choux mixture
  salt and nutmeg to taste

Procedure

1. Prepare the two potato mixtures. (See recipes this chapter. The pâté de choux recipe is given with Lorette potatoes.)
2. Mix together the duchess potatoes and the pâté de choux mixture on slow speed of the mixing machine, using the paddle.
3. Season with salt and a touch of nutmeg.
4. Place mixture in a pan and allow to cool.
5. Mold to the shape of corks. Bread by passing them through flour, egg wash (6 eggs to 1 qt. of milk) and bread crumbs.

6. Fry in deep fat at a temperature of 350°F.
7. Serve 1 potato to each order.

Soufflé potatoes

Ingredients: Approx. yield: 25 servings
  6 lbs. Idaho potatoes, small, peeled
     salt to taste
Procedure
1. Slice the raw potatoes on the slicing machine, lengthwise about ⅛ in. thick.
2. Soak in very cold water about 1 hour, drain and dry thoroughly in a towel.
3. Cook in deep fat at 200°F for about 10 minutes. Remove and cool.
4. Increase temperature of deep fat to 425°F. Add a few potatoes at a time and cook until they puff and become a golden brown. (Keep potatoes moving while they are frying so they will brown uniformly and puff to their fullest extent.)
5. Sprinkle with salt and serve about 2 ozs. of the potatoes to each order.

BAKED POTATO RECIPES

Duchess potatoes

Ingredients: Approx. yield: 25 servings
 10 lbs. Idaho potatoes, peeled
  4 ozs. butter
  8 egg yolks
  1 pinch nutmeg
     salt and white pepper to taste
     yellow color if desired
Procedure
1. Cut the peeled potatoes into uniform pieces. Place in a stock pot, cover with water, add salt and boil until the potatoes are tender. Do not overcook, or potatoes become soggy.
2. Drain the potatoes thoroughly. Place in mixing bowl and mix smooth using the paddle.
3. Add the egg yolk and butter, continuing to mix.
4. Season with a pinch of nutmeg; salt and pepper.
5. Add yellow color if desired.
6. Place the potato mixture in a pastry bag with a star tube and bag out 25 separate cones into a spiral cone shape on sheet pans covered with silicon paper.

7. Brush lightly with egg wash or slightly beaten egg whites.
8. Place in a 400° to 425°F oven and bake until potatoes brown slightly.
9. Remove from the oven and serve 1 cone per portion.

Scalloped potatoes

Ingredients: Approx. yield: 25 servings
  8 lbs. red potatoes, peeled, sliced ⅛ in. thick
  8 ozs. butter
  6 ozs. flour
  3 qts. milk, hot
     salt and pepper to taste
     paprika as needed
Procedure
1. Place the butter in a sauce pan and heat.
2. Add the flour, making a roux, and cook slightly.
3. Add the hot milk, whipping rapidly until cream sauce is slightly thickened and smooth. Season with salt and pepper.
4. Place the sliced potatoes in a baking pan, cover with the cream sauce. Sprinkle paprika lightly over the top.
5. Place in a 350°F oven and bake until potatoes are tender and top is slightly brown.
6. Remove from the oven and serve 4 ozs. per portion. Dish up with a solid kitchen spoon.

Macaire potatoes

Ingredients: Approx. yield: 25 servings
 15 lbs. Idaho potatoes
  2 lbs. butter
     salt and white pepper to taste
Procedure
1. Place the potatoes in a 400°F oven and bake until thoroughly done (soft to the touch). Remove from the oven.
2. Scoop out the pulp of the potatoes onto a sheet pan, discard the skin or shell of the potato.
3. Season the pulp with salt and pepper and work it with a kitchen fork to break it up slightly.
4. Work 1 lb. of the butter into the pulp.
5. Place a very small amount of butter in a small egg skillet and heat.
6. Add a kitchen spoon full of the potato

mixture and brown both sides until golden. Repeat this process until all of the potato pulp has been used up.

7. Dish up 4 ozs. per portion with a solid kitchen spoon. Garnish with chopped parsley.

Special baked potatoes

Ingredients: Approx. yield: 25 servings
25 Idaho potatoes, medium sized
4 ozs. butter
8 ozs. bacon, minced
8 ozs. green pepper, minced
8 ozs. onion, minced
4 ozs. pimientos, minced
1 cup light cream or milk, warm (variable)
salt and white pepper to taste

Procedure

1. Wash potatoes, place on sheet pans and bake in a 375°F oven for about 1½ hrs. or until the potatoes are soft when gently squeezed. Remove from the oven.
2. Cut off the upper portion of the shell lengthwise.
3. Scoop out the pulp of the potato, save the shell. Place the pulp in the mixing bowl and keep hot.
4. Place the bacon in a sauce pan and cook until it becomes light brown.
5. Add the green peppers and onions and continue to cook until they become tender. Do not brown.
6. Remove from the fire and add the pimientos.
7. Mix the potato pulp, on mixing machine, using the paddle, until it becomes smooth.
8. Add the cooked garnish and the butter and continue to mix.
9. Add the warm cream to obtain proper consistency. Mix until thoroughly blended.
10. Season with salt and white pepper and remove from the mixer.
11. Using a pastry bag and star tube refill the potato shells with the mixture.
12. Sprinkle the top with paprika and additional butter.
13. Return potatoes to the oven and bake at 400°F until the potatoes are heated through and the tops become brown.
14. Serve 1 potato to each order.

Note: Instead of restuffing the original potato shells, aluminum potato shells, which are now available, may be used.

Saucy sweet potatoes

Ingredients: Approx. yield: 25 servings
10 lbs. sweet potatoes, boiled until tender, peeled, cut in serving portions (2 to 4 pieces, depending on size)
1 #10 can apple sauce
1 lb. dark brown sugar
2 ozs. lemon juice
8 ozs. butter
10 ozs. chopped walnuts
1 tbsp. mace

Procedure

1. Place the cooked sweet potatoes in a baking pan.
2. Combine the apple sauce, brown sugar, lemon juice and mace. Blend thoroughly and spread over the sweet potatoes.
3. Dot with butter and sprinkle with the coarsely chopped walnuts.
4. Place in the oven and bake at 375°F for 30 minutes.
5. Serve 1 or 2 pieces of potato (depending on how large they were cut) to each order with a small portion of the apple sauce mixture.

Pommes Elysées

Ingredients: Approx. yield: 25 servings
10 lbs. Idaho potatoes, peeled, cut julienne
1 lb. mushrooms, sliced sautéed
1 lb. 8 oz. ham, cooked, cut julienne
1 lb. butter
salt and pepper to taste

Procedure

1. Combine together in a mixing container the julienne potatoes, sliced mushrooms and the julienne ham. Season with salt and pepper.
2. Place butter in a baking pan, coat the bottom and sides well.
3. Pack the potato mixture into the buttered pan, top with pieces of butter and place in a 325°F oven for about 45 minutes or until the potatoes are tender and the top is a golden brown.
4. Dish up 4 to 5 ozs. with a solid kitchen spoon. Garnish with chopped parsley.

Italian potatoes

Ingredients: Approx. yield: 25 servings
8   lbs. red potatoes, cooked, diced into
    ½ in. cubes
1   cup salad oil
2   lbs. onions, sliced thin
1   pt. stuffed olives, sliced thin
    crosswise
1   qt. chili sauce
1   qt. water
    salt and pepper to taste
Procedure
1. Spread half of the salad oil in the bottom of a baking pan. Add the diced potatoes, place in a 450°F oven and bake until brown. Turn occasionally.
2. Place the remaining oil in a sauce pot and heat.
3. Add the sliced onions and sauté until tender.
4. Add the chili sauce, water and sliced olives and simmer for 10 minutes.
5. Pour sauce over the potatoes and mix together gently.
6. Return to the oven and continue to bake for about 15 more minutes or until the potatoes take on a slightly pink color.
7. Dish up 4 ozs. with a solid kitchen spoon. Garnish with minced chives.

Scalloped sweet potatoes and apples

Ingredients: Approx. yield: 25 servings
10 lbs. sweet potatoes
4   lbs. apples, tart
1   lb. brown sugar, dark
5   ozs. butter
½   oz. salt
1   pt. water
Procedure
1. Boil sweet potatoes until slightly tender then drain and peel.
2. Cut into ½ in. slices.
3. Core the apples and cut into ½ in. slices.
4. Arrange potatoes and apples in alternate layers in baking pans.
5. Place the water, brown sugar, salt and butter in a sauce pan. Cook until the sugar is dissolved and mixture is smooth.
6. Pour over the sweet potato and apple slices and place in the oven.
7. Bake at 350°F until apples become tender and serve 3 or 4 ozs. to each portion.

Mushroom potatoes

Ingredients: Approx. yield: 25 servings
25 medium size Idaho potatoes
2   tbsp. salt
1   tsp. white pepper
1   qt. milk (variable), hot
3   cups mushrooms, chopped
2   cups butter
2   tbsp. lemon juice, fresh
50 mushroom caps, small
Procedure
1. Wash the Idaho potatoes, place on sheet pans and bake at a temperature of 375°F until done.
2. Remove from the oven, cut the top off the potatoes lengthwise, and scoop out the pulp. Save the potato shells.
3. Place the pulp in a mixing bowl and keep hot.
4. Sauté the chopped mushrooms in 1 cup of the butter. When almost done add 1 tbsp. of fresh lemon juice and continue to cook until completely tender.
5. Cook the mushroom caps in the same manner as the chopped mushrooms and keep warm.
6. Add the sautéed, chopped mushrooms to the potato pulp in the mixing bowl; salt and pepper. Beat on mixer, using the paddle, until slightly smooth.
7. Add the hot milk to the potato mixture to obtain proper consistency.
8. Place the mixture in a pastry bag with a star tube and refill the potato shells.
9. Top each stuffed potato with 2 caps of cooked mushrooms, spot with melted butter and return to the oven.
10. Bake at 375°F until slightly brown. Serve 1 stuffed potato per portion.
Note: Aluminum potato shells may be used if desired.

Suzette potatoes

Ingredients: Approx. yield: 25 servings
25 medium sized Idaho potatoes
⅓   cup chives, minced
8   ozs. butter
6   egg yolks
1   qt. light cream (variable), hot
    salt and pepper to taste
    Parmesan cheese as needed
Procedure
1. Wash the potatoes, place on sheet pans

and bake at a temperature of 375°F until done.

2. Remove from the oven and cut the top off the potatoes lengthwise. Scoop out the pulp, reserving the shell.
3. Place the pulp in a mixing bowl and beat, using the paddle, until slightly smooth.
4. Add the butter, chives and egg yolks, continuing to mix.
5. Add the hot cream while mixing in slow speed until proper consistency is obtained.
6. Place the mixture in a pastry bag with a star tube and refill the potato shells.
7. Sprinkle Parmesan cheese over the top of each potato.
8. Bake at 375°F until lightly brown. Serve 1 potato per portion.

Note: Aluminum potato shells may be used if desired.

Mont d'or potatoes

Ingredients: Approx. yield: 25 servings
8   lbs. duchess potato mixture
1   lb. 4 ozs. Gruyère cheese, grated
    salt and white pepper to taste
Procedure
1. Prepare duchess potato mixture. (See recipe this chapter.)
2. Place the duchess potato mixture in the mixing bowl. Using the paddle, mix at slow speed while adding the grated cheese. Mix until smooth.
3. Season with salt and white pepper and remove from the mixer.
4. Cover sheet pans with silicon paper and form the potatoes into mounds using a No. 12 ice cream scoop.
5. Sprinkle the tops of each potato with additional grated cheese and bake in a 400°F oven until the cheese is melted and the potatoes are slightly brown. Serve 1 No. 12 dipper or scoop to each portion.

Boulangère potatoes

Ingredients: Approx. yield: 25 servings
10 lbs. red potatoes, peeled, cut boat shape (4 or 6 pieces lengthwise)
12 ozs. carrots, cut julienne
1   lb. onions, cut julienne

⅓   cup parsley, chopped, washed
1   lb. shortening (variable)
    salt and pepper to taste
Procedure
1. Place enough shortening in 2 large steel skillets to cover the bottom of the pans and heat.
2. Add the potatoes cut boat shape and brown slightly. Place in a roast pan or hotel pan. Place in the oven and bake at a temperature of 400°F.
3. Sauté the julienne onions and carrots in shortening until slightly tender. Sprinkle over the potatoes when three-quarters done.
4. Continue to roast until potatoes are completely tender. Remove from the oven and season with salt and pepper.
5. Dish up 4 ozs. per portion with a solid kitchen spoon. Garnish with chopped parsley.

Cross patch potatoes

Ingredients: Approx. yield: 25 servings
25 medium sized Idaho potatoes
8   ozs. butter, melted
    paprika as needed
Procedure
1. Wash the potatoes and cut off the top of the potato lengthwise.
2. Score the top by cutting about ¼ of an inch into the flesh, using a boning knife. Score in both directions.
3. Brush the scored top with melted butter. Sprinkle with paprika.
4. Bake in the oven at 375°F, brush with melted butter at intervals throughout the baking period. Bake until the potatoes are tender and the top golden brown.
5. Serve 1 potato with melted butter.

Sweet potatoes with cranberries

Ingredients: Approx. yield: 25 servings
6   lbs. fresh sweet potatoes, peeled
3   lbs. fresh cranberries
3   lbs. granulated sugar
    butter as needed
1. Cut the potatoes into 1 in. cubes. Place half of them in the bottom of a buttered baking pan.
2. Cover the potatoes with half of the cranberries and sprinkle on half of the sugar.

3. Repeat this process with the remaining ingredients. Cover the pan.
4. Place in the oven at 350°F and bake for approximately 30 minutes, until the cranberries pop open.
5. Remove the cover and bake about 20 minutes longer, until the potatoes are tender.
6. Serve 3 to 4 ozs. per serving. Dish up with a solid kitchen spoon.

Sherried sweet potatoes

Ingredients: Approx. yield: 25 servings
25 medium sized fresh sweet potatoes
1 lb. 8 oz. brown sugar, dark
8 ozs. butter
1 qt. sherry wine
Procedure
1. Boil the potatoes until just slightly tender. Run cold water over them and peel.
2. Place the potatoes in a buttered baking pan. Sprinkle the sugar over them.
3. Dot with butter and pour on the sherry wine.
4. Place in the oven at 350°F and bake for about 30 minutes, until the potatoes are completely tender.
5. Serve 1 potato to each order with a small amount of the remaining liquid.

Sweet potatoes in orange shells

Ingredients: Approx. yield: 25 servings
8 lbs. fresh sweet potatoes
5 egg yolks
¼ cup orange rind, grated
4 ozs. butter
1 tbsp. lemon rind, grated
4 ozs. brown sugar
½ tsp. nutmeg
1 tbsp. cinnamon
½ oz. salt
25 orange skin halves
25 salad marshmallows
Procedure
1. Wash the sweet potatoes, place in the oven and bake at 375°F until the potatoes are tender.
2. Split the potatoes in half lengthwise and scoop out all the pulp.
3. Place the pulp in the mixing bowl of electric mixer, add the sugar, egg yolks, orange rind, lemon rind, salt, cinnamon,

nutmeg and butter. Using the paddle, mix until thoroughly blended and smooth.
4. Place the mixture in a pastry bag with a fairly large star tube.
5. Fill the orange halves with the potato mixture and top with a salad marshmallow.
6. Place in the oven at 350°F until heated through and marshmallow begins to melt. Serve 1 orange half per portion.
Note: To prepare sweet potato pyramid: Prepare the same sweet potato mixture, but pipe the mixture out of the pastry bag onto a ring of pineapple. Top with a salad marshmallow and bake at 350°F until heated thoroughly and marshmallow begins to melt then serve.

BOILED POTATO RECIPES

Bouillon potatoes

Ingredients: Approx. yield: 25 servings
10 lbs. red potatoes, peeled, cut boat shape (4 to 6 pieces lengthwise)
4 qts. chicken or beef stock
8 ozs. butter
12 ozs. onions, cut julienne
8 ozs. carrots, cut julienne
1 oz. parsley, chopped fine
salt and white pepper to taste
Procedure
1. Prepare chicken or beef stock. (See Chap. 12.)
2. Place the butter in a stock pot and melt.
3. Add the julienne onions and carrots and sauté, without color (do not brown) until slightly tender.
4. Add the stock and bring to boil.
5. Add the potatoes and simmer until the potatoes are just tender. Remove from the range.
6. Add the chopped parsley and season with salt and pepper. Hold in a warm place until served.
7. Dish up 4 ozs. per portion with a pierced kitchen spoon.

Hungarian potatoes

Ingredients: Approx. yield: 25 servings
10 lbs. red potatoes, peeled, sliced thick
1 lb. onions, diced fine
8 ozs. butter
2 tbsp. paprika

10 tomatoes, fresh, peeled, diced
2 qts. consommé or beef stock
  salt and pepper to taste
Procedure
1. Prepare consommé (See Chap. 12) or beef stock (See Chap. 12.)
2. Place the butter in a sauce pot, melt.
3. Add the onions and sauté without color.
4. Add the paprika and continue to sauté.
5. Add the tomatoes and the potatoes. Cover with the consommé or beef stock. Simmer until the potatoes are tender and the liquid has become slightly thickened.
6. Season with salt and pepper and serve with chopped parsley. Dish up 5 ozs. per portion with a pierced kitchen spoon.

Candied sweet potatoes

Ingredients: Approx. yield: 25 servings
10 lbs. sweet potatoes
SYRUP
1 pt. water
1 lb. 8 ozs. brown sugar
1 lb. granulated sugar
2 qts. light corn syrup
  juice from 2 lemons
  grating (zest) and juice from
  4 oranges
Procedure: Potatoes
1. Boil or steam the sweet potatoes until just tender (do not cook completely done).
2. Place in cold water and remove the skins.
3. Remove all discolored blemishes and cut into uniform pieces about 2 in. long. Let cool overnight.
4. Remove from the refrigerator and brown slightly in deep fat. Place in a hotel pan and hold until the syrup is prepared.
Procedure: Syrup
1. Bring the water to a boil.
2. Add the sugars, stirring until dissolved.
3. Add the corn syrup, lemon juice, orange grating (zest) and orange juice. Bring to a boil then turn down to simmer for 5 to 10 minutes.
4. Pour the syrup over the sweet potatoes and simmer on the range for 5 minutes.
5. Serve 2 pieces of potatoes (approx. 4 ozs.) to each order. Dish up with a pierced or slotted kitchen spoon.

Kartoffel klosse (potato dumplings)

Ingredients: Approx. yield: 25 servings
8 lbs. red potatoes, peeled, boiled day before
14 whole eggs, beaten slightly
1 lb. cornstarch
⅓ cup parsley, chopped
1 lb. bacon, minced, cooked crisp
1 cup onions, minced, sautéed
10 ozs. flour
1 lb. bread croutons, small cubes
2 lbs. bread crumbs, fresh
1½ lb. butter
  salt and pepper to taste
2 gal. chicken stock (variable)
Procedure
1. Prepare chicken stock. (See Chap. 12.)
2. Dice the potatoes into very small cubes, or chop coarse, and place in a mixing container.
3. Add the eggs, cornstarch, onions, bacon, parsley, bread croutons, salt and pepper and mix by hand until thoroughly blended.
4. Form mixture into balls a little larger than a golf ball. Roll each ball in flour.
5. Place the balls into simmering chicken stock and cook for 10 minutes. Remove using a skimmer.
6. Roll each ball into bread crumbs previously sautéed in butter until golden brown.
7. Serve 1 ball to each order.

sauces and gravies

chapter 15

■ Sauces as we know them today were created by famous European chefs to increase the flavor and palatableness of the poor quality meats generally marketed then. Europeans still place great emphases on a sauce, even though the quality of the meat has improved, because it enhances the flavor, appearance and moistness of nearly any food.

A sauce or gravy is usually a rich flavored, thickened liquid used to complement another dish. The other dish may be meat, vegetable, fish, poultry or dessert. The sauce selected to accompany any dish should heighten the dish's flavor, increase its appearance, and make it easy to digest. The sauce or gravy should flow over the food and provide a thin coating rather than a heavy mass that saturates and disguises the dish.

Since gravies and sauces are similar in most respects they have been placed together in one chapter. The major difference between the two is in the flavor. All gravies contain the flavor of the meat they accompany when being served. The base of any quality gravy is the meat drippings acquired during the roasting period of the meat. Sauces, on the other hand, do not always contain the same flavor as the item it accompanies. In fact a contrast in flavors is often desirable when considering which sauce to serve with a certain dish. For example, mint sauce is often used with roast lamb and raisin sauce with baked ham.

The use of the sauce has declined to some degree in American cookery over the past few years because of the time and cost involved and the lack of skilled cooks. However, when sauces are properly prepared they are very much in demand and certainly contribute to the reputation of any commercial establishment. When more cooks and chefs having the skill to properly prepare sauces are available, there may well be a return to the days when very few items appeared on the menu without being graced with a sauce or gravy.

A cook who has mastered the skill of preparing fine sauces and gravies and presenting them with the proper foods will find his services very much in demand. The student cook should strive to acquire this skill or art to achieve job security and a position of respect among his fellow craftsmen.

SAUCES

The preparation of sauces presents an opportunity to the cook or chef to display his creative or imaginative skills. There are, of course, certain standards that must be met when preparing a sauce, but the person that can adhere to these standards and still create a dish that is different yet tasty is the one that will be remembered whenever good food is discussed.

Sauces vary in name, uses and content, but most all of them can be placed into three major categories: warm sauces, cold sauces, and dessert or sweet sauces. *Warm sauces* consist of two kinds: leading sauces and small sauces. Generally speaking if a person can prepare the five leading sauces, he can also prepare any of the small sauces which are largely variations of the leading

sauces. *Cold sauces* are so named because of their temperature although they may be served with both hot and cold foods. *Dessert* or *sweet sauces* as a rule contain a high percentage of sugar and are usually served with dessert items. There are, of course, some sauces that cannot be placed in a specific category. Sauces such as mint and oriental sweet-sour sauce are in this group.

Warm sauces

The two kinds of warm sauces (leading sauces and small sauces) are the most popular and numerous of the three major sauce categories. They can be served with all types of foods and usually their preparation is not difficult for a person who has mastered the basic skills of food preparation. *Leading sauces,* also referred to as *mother sauces* by the famous French Chef Escoffier, are of extreme importance because they are the basis of all other sauces. Preparing a *small sauce* from a leading sauce is just a matter of changing or adding certain ingredients. Adding chopped hard boiled eggs to béchamel or cream sauce brings forth egg sauce. Adding sautéed onion to brown sauce creates onion sauce. Thus as soon as the student has mastered the preparation of the leading sauces he should be equipped to meet the challenge of any warm sauce preparation.

Most warm sauces are made from stock, which is the backbone of many preparations in the commercial kitchen. The richer the stock is the better the sauce will be. For this reason most stocks used in sauces are reduced or boiled down to a concentrate. The preparation of stocks is explained in Chapter 12, "Soups and Stocks." All warm sauces that are properly prepared should possess the following characteristics:

1. The sauce has a slight sheen.
2. The consistency is flowing, smooth and lump-free.
3. The taste is velvety.

4. The flavor is delicate.
5. The starch is completely cooked.
6. Brown sauces are a rich brown; velouté sauces are a creamy color.

The thickening agent used in the preparation of warm sauces will vary, depending on the kind of sauce and the preference of the cook or chef. In most cases a roux, whitewash or cornstarch will be used. A roux is considered the best thickening agent because it will hold up better under constant heat without breaking back into a liquid. A roux may be of two kinds: a plain roux or a French roux. The difference lies in the kind of shortening used. A plain roux is made by blending together flour and fat of equal portions by weight. Fats such as shortening, margarine, oil or rendered animal fat may be used. A French roux is made in the same manner; however, butter is always used to produce a richer roux. Both rouxs must always be cooked a certain amount of time to eliminate the raw flour taste. The amount of time a roux is cooked will depend on its intended use. A roux that is to be used for a white or light sauce will be cooked only slightly, whereas a roux to be used in a brown sauce will be cooked until it becomes slightly brown in color. When using a roux as a thickening agent always add the hot stock to the roux, stirring constantly to eliminate any lumps and to take full advantage of the thickening powers of the roux. Whitewash is a mixture of equal amounts of cornstarch and flour diluted in water. It is poured slowly into the boiling mass one wishes to thicken (stews, stocks, fricassees, etc.), stirring constantly while pouring. The amount used will depend on the thickness desired and the amount to be thickened. Cornstarch is mixed with cold water or stock and poured into the boiling mass, in the same manner as whitewash, stirring constantly while pouring. Cornstarch not only thickens but also provides a glossy semi-clear finish to a product. It is used extensively in thickening sweet sauces. The amount to use will depend upon the same conditions required for whitewash.

Cold sauces

Cold sauces are blended from many different foods, but the most popular is mayonnaise. There are many cases when it might be more appropriate to call some of the cold sauces *dressings* since they function as a dressing rather than a sauce when served with other foods. It is for this reason that mayonnaise is considered a dressing rather than a cold sauce and therefore will be found in Chapter 10, "Salads and Salad Dressings." Actually the difference between the terms sauce and dressing is very slight. We usually associate the word sauce to thickened liquids that enhance the flavor of meats and vegetables, whereas the word dressing is used when salads are enhanced in the same manner. Also, sauces are usually prepared from rich stocks whereas the bases of a good dressing is usually salad oil. Cold sauces can be served with both hot and cold foods. Although they enhance the flavor and appearance of either they are superior when used with cold foods.

Butter sauces

The butter sauces, although used quite often in the commercial kitchen, have not been mentioned earlier because they are generally simple to prepare. Most butter sauces are fixed by either melting the butter in a sauce pan and adding some other item or items for flavor or by placing the butter in a sauce pan and heating it until it becomes a medium brown color before the flavoring ingredients are added. In either case the butter sauce will increase the flavor and moistness of the dish it is served with, as well as giving the dish a sparkling, fresh-looking sheen.

Dessert or sweet sauces

Dessert or sweet sauces are usually made from fruit, fruit juice, milk or cream. They contain a high percentage of sugar and usually are thickened with cornstarch to give the sauce a sparkling fresh-looking sheen. They are served mostly with dessert items; however, they are also served with items like ham, French toast, pancakes and some poultry. Dessert or sweet sauces can be served with hot or cold food.

Miscellaneous sauces

As mentioned, some sauces do not fit into any of the main categories. These are listed under miscellaneous sauces.

GRAVIES

In a sense gravies are sauces, but a distinction is made because they must possess the same flavor as the meat they accompany when served. They must possess all the characteristic of a sauce, but still maintain their independence in flavor. Gravies of good quality are usually prepared from the drippings of roasting meats. However, the flavor and volume of the drippings can be increased by supplementing it with a brown sauce, prepared by first browning then boiling bones of the same type of animal that is being roasted. Thus when preparing a pork roast, pork bones are used, for a beef roast beef bones are used, etc. This step is sometimes necessary in order to prepare enough gravy for the amount of meat to be served because drippings will evaporate during the roasting period and also some meats (pork and veal) are very delicate in flavor.

SAUCE AND GRAVY RECIPES

Warm sauce:
Brown or espagnole sauces
(Pages 282 to 289)

Brown sauce (leading sauce)
Madeira sauce

Onion sauce
Burgundy sauce
Colbert sauce
Cider sauce
Piquante sauce
Bercy sauce
Chateau sauce
Bordelaise sauce
Mushroom sauce
Chasseur or hunter sauce
Sour cream sauce
Bigarade sauce

Warm sauce:
Cream or béchamel sauces
(Pages 289 to 294)

Cream or béchamel sauce (leading sauce)
Egg sauce
Mustard sauce
Newburg sauce
A la king sauce
Albert sauce
Cheese sauce
Mock Hollandaise sauce
Cardinal sauce
Mornay sauce

Warm sauce:
Velouté or fricassee sauces
(Pages 294 to 299)

Basic velouté sauce (leading sauce)
Horseradish sauce
Homard sauce
Poulette sauce
Caper sauce
Victoria sauce
Duglere sauce
Bonne-femme sauce
Curry sauce

Warm sauce:
Hollandaise sauces
(Pages 299 to 303)

Hollandaise sauce (leading sauce)
Maltaise sauce
Maximillian sauce
Cherburg sauce

Mousseline sauce
Divine sauce
Béarnaise sauce
Choron sauce

Warm sauce:
Tomato sauces
(Pages 303 to 307)

Tomato sauce (leading sauce)
Figaro sauce
Napolitaine sauce
Milanaise sauce
Pizza sauce
Barbecue sauce
Creole sauce
Italian sauce No. I
Italian sauce No. II

Cold sauces
(Pages 307 to 309)

Cocktail sauce
Tarter sauce
Dill sauce
Chaud–froid sauce (white)

Butter sauces
(Pages 309 to 311)

Lemon butter sauce
Anchovy butter sauce
Brown butter sauce
Meuniere sauce

Dessert or sweet sauces
(Pages 311 to 319)

Cinnamon sauce
Plum sauce
Cherry sauce
Orange sauce
Rum sauce
Brown sugar sauce
Butterscotch sauce
Lemon sauce
Custard sauce
Vanilla sauce
Lemon custard sauce
Cranberry raisin sauce
Raisin sauce
Raisin almond sauce
Cumberland sauce
Hard sauce
Melba sauce

Miscellaneous sauces
(Pages 319 to 320)

Oriental sweet sour sauce
Mint sauce

Gravies
(Pages 320 to 323)

Roast beef gravy
Roast veal gravy
Roast pork gravy
Roast lamb gravy
Giblet gravy
Country gravy

BROWN OR ESPAGNOLE SAUCE RECIPES

Brown sauce

Brown sauce is one of the most important leading sauces. It is used in the preparation of gravies, small sauces and certain stews and soups. It is generally prepared in large quantities and kept on hand in the commercial kitchen. Brown sauce is used to supplement natural gravy drippings when preparing gravies and it is also used if additional gravy is needed when preparing beef stew. The important small sauces that use brown sauce are given immediately following this recipe.

Objectives
1. To teach the student the procedure for making brown sauce.
2. To teach the student how to strain the sauce.
3. To teach the student how to use brown sauce.

Equipment
1. Sauce pot, 3 gal.
2. French knife
3. China cap
4. Ladle
5. Wood paddle
6. Baker's scale
7. Spoon measure
8. Qt. or gal. measure

Ingredients: Approx. yield: 2 gal.
2　gal. brown stock, hot
1　lb. 8 ozs. onion, cut rough
1　lb. celery, cut rough
1　lb. carrots, cut rough

1 lb. shortening
1 lb. bread flour
2 bay leaves
2 tsp. thyme
1 cup tomato purée
 salt and pepper to taste
Preparation
1. Cut the vegetabes rough, using a French knife.
2. Prepare the brown stock. (See Chap. 12.)
3. Have all equipment and ingredients handy.
Procedure
1. Place the shortening in the sauce pot and heat. Add the rough garnish (onions, carrots, and celery) and sauté slightly.
2. Add the flour, making a roux, and cook 10 minutes.
3. Add the hot brown stock, tomato purée and seasoning. Bring to a boil, stir with a wooden paddle until thickened and smooth.
4. Continue to simmer for 2 hours, stirring frequently.
5. Strain through a china cap into a stainless steel container. Using a ladle, force as much of the vegetable flavor as possible through the china cap.
6. Use in gravies, beef stews and small sauces as needed.
Precautions and Safety Measures
1. While simmering the sauce be careful so it does not scorch.
2. When sautéing the garnish do not let it brown.
3. Exercise caution when cutting the rough vegetable garnish.

Madeira sauce

Madeira sauce is prepared by adding brown sauce to the rich flavor of Madeira wine. Madeira sauce increases the delicate flavors of ham and veal when served with these entrees.
Objectives
1. To teach the student the procedure for preparing Madeira sauce.
2. To teach the student how to serve Madeira sauce.
Equipment
1. Gal. measure
2. Pt. measure
3. Sauce pot, 6 qt.
4. China cap

5. 1 gal. stainless steel container
 Ingredients: Approx. yield: 1 gal.
 1 gal. brown sauce
 1 pt. Madeira wine
Preparation
1. Prepare brown sauce (see recipe).
2. Have all equipment and ingredients handy.
Procedure
1. Place the prepared brown sauce in sauce pot and simmer until sauce is reduced to about three-fourths its original volume.
2. Add the wine and simmer for 5 minutes more.
3. Check seasoning and strain through a fine china cap into a stainless steel container.
4. Serve 2 ozs. per portion, using a ladle. Serve with baked ham, ham steaks, veal cutlets or veal chops.
Precautions and Safety Measures
1. Use caution so sauce does not scorch while reducing.

Onion sauce

Onion sauce is a combination of fine-cut julienne onions and brown sauce. It is served with items when an onion flavor is desired, such as Salisbury steak or calf liver.
Objectives
1. To teach the student the procedure for preparing onion sauce.
2. To teach the student how to serve the onion sauce.
Equipment
1. Sauce pot, 6 qt.
2. Kitchen spoon
3. French knife
4. Baker's scale
5. Gal. measure
 Ingredients: Approx. yield: 1 gal.
 1 gal. brown sauce
 1 lb. onions, cut julienne
 8 ozs. butter or margarine
 salt and pepper to taste
Preparation
1. Prepare the brown sauce (see recipe).
2. Julienne the onions with a French knife.
3. Have all equipment and ingredients handy.
Procedure
1. Place the butter or margarine in the sauce pot and melt.
2. Add the julienne onions and sauté until tender.
3. Add the brown sauce and simmer for 30

minutes, stir occasionally with a kitchen spoon.

4. Season with salt and pepper.
5. Remove from the range, pour into a stainless steel container.
6. Serve 2 to 2½ ozs. per portion, using a ladle. Serve with calf or beef liver, Salisbury steak, meat loaf, etc.

Precautions and Safety Measures
1. Exercise caution when cutting the onions.
2. Be careful when simmering the sauce so it does not scorch.

Burgundy sauce

Burgundy sauce is a variation of brown sauce. It is served mostly with beef dishes.

Objectives
1. To teach the student the procedure for making Burgundy sauce.
2. To teach the student how to serve Burgundy sauce.

Equipment
1. French knife
2. 1 qt. measure
3. Cup measure
4. Sauce pan, 4 qt.
5. China cap
6. Kitchen spoon
7. 1 gal. stainless steel container

Ingredients: Approx. yield: 2½ qts.
2   qts. brown sauce
1   cup dry red wine, Burgundy
1   cup tomato purée
2   small cloves garlic, minced

Preparation
1. Mince garlic using a French knife.
2. Prepare brown sauce (see recipe).
3. Have all equipment and ingredients handy.

Procedure
1. Place all the ingredients in sauce pan and blend.
2. Let simmer for 30 minutes stirring occasionally with a kitchen spoon then remove from fire and strain through a china cap into a stainless steel container.
3. Serve 2 ozs. per portion, using a ladle. Serve with beef dishes.

Precautions and Safety Measures
1. Do not allow liquid to scorch.
2. Exercise caution when mincing the garlic.

Colbert sauce

Colbert sauce is a brown sauce with claret

wine added to provide a rich flavor that goes well with broiled fish.

Objectives
1. To teach the student the procedure for preparing Colbert sauce.
2. To teach the student how to serve Colbert sauce.

Equipment
1. Sauce pan, 4 qts.
2. French knife
3. Baker's scale
4. Qt. measure
5. Spoon measure
6. Kitchen spoon
7. 1 gal. stainless steel container

Ingredients: Approx. yield: 2 qts.
2   qts. brown sauce
3   tbsp. onions, minced
1   pt. claret wine
4   ozs. lemon juice
2   tbsp. parsley, chopped
3   ozs. butter

Preparation
1. Prepare the brown sauce (see recipe).
2. Chop and wash the parsley.
3. Squeeze the juice from the lemons.
4. Mince the onions using a French knife.
5. Have all the equipment and ingredients handy.

Procedure
1. Place the butter in a sauce pan and heat.
2. Add the minced onions and sauté without color.
3. Add the wine and simmer until the wine is reduced by evaporation to one-half its original amount.
4. Add the brown sauce and lemon juice while stirring with a kitchen spoon. Continue to simmer for 30 minutes.
5. Remove from the range, add the chopped parsley and stir. Pour into a stainless steel container.
6. Serve 2 ozs. per portion, using a ladle, over most kinds of broiled fish.

Precautions and Safety Measures
1. When sautéing do not brown the onions.
2. Exercise caution when chopping the parsley and mincing the onions.

Cider sauce

Cider sauce is a brown sauce that has a slight sweet-sour taste. It is an excellent sauce to serve with ham.

Objectives
1. To teach the student the procedure for preparing cider sauce.
2. To teach the student how to serve cider sauce.

Equipment
1. French knife
2. Sauce pot, 4 qts.
3. China cap
4. Qt. measure
5. 1 gal. stainless steel container

Ingredients: Approx. yield: 2 qts.
1	pt. cider, apple
1	pt. brown sauce
3	shallots, chopped
4	cloves whole
1	bay leaf
	salt and pepper to taste

Preparation
1. Chop shallots using a French knife.
2. Prepare the brown sauce (see recipe).
3. Have all equipment and ingredients handy.

Procedure
1. Place cider in sauce pot and bring to a boil.
2. Add the brown sauce, chopped shallots, cloves and bay leaf.
3. Simmer gently until it is reduced to about half of its volume. Season with salt and pepper to taste.
4. Strain through a china cap into a stainless steel container.
5. Serve 2 ozs. per portion, using a ladle. Serve with baked ham, broiled ham steaks, roast pork, etc.

Precautions and Safety Measures
1. Be sure to strain sauce through china cap. If spices are left in the sauce they continue to disperse flavor.
2. Exercise caution when chopping the shallots.

Piquante sauce

Piquante sauce is a small sauce that possesses a very tangy and sharp taste. It is an excellent choice of sauce to increase the flavor of such foods as pigs feet and corned beef.

Objectives
1. To teach the student the procedure for preparing piquante sauce.
2. To teach the student how to serve piquante sauce.

Equipment
1. Qt. measure
2. French knife
3. Baker's scale
4. Sauce pot, 6 qt.
5. Kitchen spoon
6. Cup measure
7. 1 gal. stainless steel container

Ingredients: Approx. yield: 1 gal.
1	gal. brown sauce
1	pt. vinegar, cider
8	ozs. dill pickles, chopped
8	ozs. butter
1	lb. onions, minced
1/4	cup parsley, chopped

Preparation
1. Chop the dill pickles using a French knife.
2. Chop the parsley.
3. Mince the onions using a French knife.
4. Prepare brown sauce (see recipe).

Procedure
1. Heat the butter in sauce pot, add the onions and sauté. Do not brown.
2. Add the brown sauce and vinegar, let simmer for about 30 minutes.
3. Add the chopped pickles and continue to simmer for 10 minutes more. Stir occasionally with a kitchen spoon.
4. Remove from the range, add the chopped parsley and pour into a stainless steel container.
5. Serve 2 to 2½ ozs. per portion using a ladle. Serve with broiled pig's feet, corned beef, ham and cabbage rolls, etc.

Precautions and Safety Measures
1. When sautéing the onions, do not burn the butter or the onions.
2. Use caution when chopping the pickles and mincing the onions.

Bercy sauce

Bercy sauce is brown sauce that has been flavored with shallots and white wine. Bercy sauce will increase the eating qualities of fish and veal items.

Objectives
1. To teach the student the procedure for preparing Bercy sauce.
2. To teach the student how to serve Bercy sauce.

Equipment
1. French knife
2. Sauce pot, 6 qts.

3. Kitchen spoon
4. Cup measure
5. Spoon measure
6. Gal. measure
7. 1 gal. stainless steel container
Ingredients: Approx. yield: 1 gal.
1 gal. brown sauce
8 ozs. butter
12 ozs. shallots or onions, minced
1 cup white wine
2 tbsp. parsley, chopped
juice of 1 lemon
salt and pepper to taste
Preparation
1. Prepare brown sauce (see recipe).
2. Mince the shallots or onions using a French knife.
3. Chop the parsley and squeeze the juice from lemon.
4. Have all equipment and ingredients handy.
Procedure
1. Place the butter in the sauce pot and melt.
2. Add the minced shallots or onions and sauté without color.
3. Add the white wine and simmer until wine is reduced to half its original amount.
4. Add the brown sauce, and lemon juice, simmer for 20 minutes.
5. Remove from range and add the chopped parsley. Pour into a stainless steel container.
6. Serve 2 ozs. per portion, using a ladle. Serve with sautéed or broiled fish, veal chops or sautéed veal cutlets.
Precautions and Safety Measures
1. Exercise caution to avoid scorching throughout preparation.
2. When sautéing shallots or onion do not let them brown.
3. Exercise caution when mincing the shallots or onions.

Chateau sauce

Chateau sauce is a variation of brown sauce. It can be served with sautéed or broiled meat (beef or veal) or sautéed fish entrees.
Objective
1. To teach the student the procedure for making chateau sauce.
2. To teach the student how to serve chateau sauce.

Equipment
1. French knife
2. Sauce pan, 2 qt.
3. 1 qt. stainless steel container
4. Cheese cloth
5. Baker's scale
6. 1 qt. measure
Ingredients: Approx. yield: 1 qt.
8 ozs. white wine
4 shallots, chopped
2 pinches of thyme
2 bay leaves
1 qt. brown sauce
8 ozs. butter, melted
salt and pepper to taste
Preparation
1. Chop shallots using a French knife.
2. Prepare brown sauce (see recipe).
3. Have all equipment and ingredients handy.
Procedure
1. Place the white wine, chopped shallots, thyme, bay leaves and salt in sauce pan and bring to boil.
2. Continue to boil mixture until it reduces approx. one-half in volume.
3. Add the brown sauce. Continue to boil until mixture reduces at least one-fourth in volume.
4. Strain through fine cheese cloth into a stainless steel container. Add the melted butter.
5. Serve 2 ozs. per portion, using ladle. Serve with broiled beef steaks, sautéed veal steak, broiled veal chops, sautéed Dover sole, etc.
Precautions and Safety Measures
1. When melting butter, do not let it brown or burn.
2. Exercise caution when chopping the shallots.

Bordelaise sauce

Bordelaise sauce is a rich brown sauce; it is served mostly with steaks.
Objective
1. To teach the student the procedure for making bordelaise sauce.
2. To teach the student how to serve bordelaise sauce.
Equipment
1. Sauce pot, 6 qt.
2. Kitchen spoon
3. French knife

4. 1 gal. stainless steel container
   Ingredients: Approx. yield: 1 gal.
   1 lb. minced onions
   1 clove garlic, minced
   1 lb. chopped mushrooms
   1 gal. brown sauce
   1 cup red wine, Burgundy (variable)
   ½ lb. margarine
   salt and pepper to taste
   Preparation
1. Mince onions and garlic and chop mushrooms using a French knife.
2. Prepare brown sauce (see recipe).
3. Have all equipment and ingredients handy.
   Procedure
1. Melt margarine in sauce pot. Add onions, garlic and mushrooms, sauté until just cooked.
2. Add brown sauce and cook for 20 minutes or until vegetables are completely done. Stir occasionally with a kitchen spoon.
3. Remove from fire and pour into a stainless steel container. Add salt, pepper and wine.
4. Serve 2 to 2½ ozs. per portion, using a ladle. Serve with broiled steaks, roast rib and sirloin of beef, meat loaf, etc.
   Precautions and Safety Measures
1. Chop mushrooms fresh. If chopped in advance they will turn black.
2. Use caution when mincing the onions and garlic and chopping the mushrooms.

Mushroom sauce

Mushroom sauce is a brown sauce, rich with the flavor of mushrooms and sherry wine. This sauce is very popular and is generally served with steaks, chops and loafs.
   Objectives
1. To teach the student the procedure for preparing mushroom sauce.
2. To teach the student how to slice the mushrooms.
3. To teach the student how to mince onions and garlic.
4. To teach the student how to serve mushroom sauce.
   Equipment
1. Sauce pot, 6 qt.
2. Kitchen spoon
3. French knife
4. Qt. measure
5. Baker's scale
6. 2 gal. stainless steel container

Ingredients: Approx. yield: 2½ gal.
   2 gal. brown sauce
   1 lb. sliced mushrooms
   1 lb. onions, minced
   1 clove garlic, minced
   1 qt. whole tomatoes, canned, crushed
   8 ozs. butter
   1 cup sherry wine (variable)
   salt and pepper to taste
   Preparation
1. Slice the mushrooms using a French knife.
2. Prepare the brown sauce (see recipe).
3. Mince onions and garlic using a French knife.
4. Crush tomatoes by hand.
5. Have all equipment and ingredients handy.
   Procedure
1. Place butter in sauce pot and melt.
2. Add the minced onions and garlic and sauté slightly without color.
3. Add the sliced mushrooms and continue to sauté until mushrooms are tender.
4. Add the brown sauce and bring to a boil. Stir occasionally with a kitchen spoon.
5. Add the crushed tomatoes, salt and pepper, simmer for 20 minutes.
6. Add sherry wine to obtain desired taste.
7. Remove from fire, check seasoning and pour into a stainless steel container.
8. Serve 2 to 2½ ozs. per portion using a ladle. Serve with beef steaks, veal chops, meat loaf, etc.
   Precautions and Safety Measures
1. Do not brown the onions and garlic while sautéing.
2. Do not use a brown sauce that is too thick.
3. Exercise caution when mincing the onions and garlic.

Chasseur or hunter sauce

Chasseur or hunter sauce is made from brown sauce. It is very similar to mushroom sauce and is best when served with poultry or beef dishes.
   Objectives
1. To teach the student how to prepare chasseur or hunter sauce.
2. To teach the student how to serve chasseur or hunter sauce.
   Equipment
1. French knife
2. Sauce pot, 1 qt.
3. 1 gal. stainless steel container

4. Qt. measure
5. Baker's scale
    Ingredients: Approx. yield: 1 gal.
    1   lb. mushrooms, sliced
    6   ozs. shallots or onions, minced
    ¼   lb. butter
    1   pt. white wine, dry
    1   #2½ can whole tomatoes, crushed
    3   qt. brown sauce
    ½   oz. parsley, chopped
    Preparation
1. Slice mushrooms, mince onions or shallots, using a French knife.
2. Crush tomatoes by squeezing with the hands.
3. Prepare brown sauce (see recipe).
4. Have all ingredients and equipment handy.
    Procedure
1. Place butter in sauce pot and melt.
2. Add mushrooms and onions, sautéing lightly.
3. Add wine and simmer until it evaporates to about half its original volume.
4. Add crushed tomatoes and brown sauce, simmer for 5 minutes.
5. Verify seasoning and add chopped parsley.
6. Pour into a stainless steel container.
7. Serve 2 ozs. per portion, using a ladle. Serve with poultry and beef dishes.
    Precautions and Safety Measures
1. When sautéing onions and mushrooms, do not brown.
2. Exercise caution when slicing the mushrooms and mincing the onions.

Sour cream sauce

Sour cream sauce is a blend of brown sauce and sour cream seasoned mainly with the flavor of bay leaves. It is used mainly with Swedish meat balls and beef stroganoff.

Objective
1. To teach the student the procedure for preparing sour cream sauce.
2. To teach the student how to use sour cream sauce.
    Equipment
1. French knife
2. Sauce pot, 6 qt.
3. Qt. measure
4. Cup measure
5. Spoon measure

6. Wire whip
7. China cap
8. 1 gal. stainless steel container
9. Kitchen spoon
    Ingredients: Approx. yield: 1 gal.
    2   cups butter
    2   cups flour
    3   qts. brown stock
    1   cup tomato purée
    ½   cup vinegar, cider
    1   lb. onions, minced
    1   qt. sour cream
    2   tbsp. salt
    2   bay leaves
    Preparation
1. Prepare brown stock (See Chap. 12.)
2. Mince the onions using a French knife.
3. Have all equipment and ingredients handy.
    Procedure
1. Place butter in sauce pot. Add onions and sauté without color.
2. Add flour, making a roux, and cook for 5 minutes.
3. Add brown stock, tomato purée, vinegar, bay leaves and salt, while whipping constantly with a wire whip. Simmer about 30 minutes.
4. Add the sour cream by folding in gently with a kitchen spoon, bring back to a boil, remove from the range and strain through a china cap into a stainless steel container.
5. Check seasoning and serve with Swedish meat balls, beef stroganoff, veal chop stroganoff, etc.
    Precautions and Safety Measures
1. Avoid scorching while simmering the sauce.
2. When adding the sour cream, fold in gently.
3. After the sour cream is added, bring back to a boil but do not cook for any length of time.

Bigarade sauce

Bigarade sauce is a brown sauce with a fairly high sheen and a slightly sweet-to-tart flavor. This sauce is served most often with roast duckling; however, it can also be featured with wild game and baked ham.

Objectives
1. To teach the student the procedure for preparing bigarade sauce.

2. To teach the student how to serve bigarade sauce.

Equipment
1. 2 sauce pans, 6 qts. and 1 pt.
2. French knife
3. Vegetable peeler
4. Cup measure
5. Spoon measure
6. Qt. measure
7. Wire whip
8. China cap
9. 1 gal. stainless steel container

Ingredients: Approx. yield: 1 gal.

1	cup sugar, granulated
½	cup red currant jelly
¼	cup vinegar, cider
1	gal. brown sauce
2	tsp. brandy
⅓	cup maraschino cherry juice
1	cup orange juice
⅓	cup lemon juice
1	cup orange peel, julienne

Preparation
1. Squeeze juice from oranges and lemons.
2. Skin orange peel using a vegetable peeler. Cut the orange portion of the peel, cut julienne with a French knife, poach in water and drain.
3. Prepare brown sauce (see recipe).
4. Have all equipment and ingredients.

Procedure
1. Place the sugar in a sauce pan and caramelize until light brown.
2. Add the currant jelly and blend into the caramelized sugar using a wire whip.
3. Add the vinegar and brown sauce, whipping constantly with a wire whip, and simmer for 5 minutes.
4. Add the orange juice, lemon juice, brandy, maraschino cherry juice and simmer for 20 minutes more.
5. Strain through a fine china cap into a stainless steel container and add the poached julienne orange peel.
6. Serve 2 to 2½ ozs. per portion, using a ladle. Serve with roast duck, pheasant, cornish hen or baked ham.

Precautions and Safety Measures
1. Caramelize the sugar until it is light brown. Do not let it become dark.
2. Exercise caution when adding the liquid to the caramelized sugar. It will bubble and flair up quickly. Stir with a kitchen spoon to control this action.

CREAM OR BECHAMEL SAUCE RECIPES

Cream or béchamel sauce

Cream sauce is a leading sauce made from a roux and hot milk. The important small sauces that use cream sauce are given immediately following this recipe.

Objectives
1. To teach the student the procedure for making cream sauce.
2. To teach the student how to use cream sauce.

Equipment
1. Sauce pot, 4 qt.
2. Sauce pan, 4 qt.
3. Wire whip
4. China cap
5. Baker's scale
6. Measuring spoons
7. 1 qt. measure
8. 1 gal. stainless steel container

Ingredients: Approx. yield: 2 qts.

THIN

8	ozs. butter or shortening
2	ozs. flour
2	qts. milk
4	tsp. salt

MEDIUM

8	ozs. butter or shortening
4	ozs. flour
2	qts. milk
4	tsp. salt

THICK

1	lb. butter or shortening
8	ozs. flour
2	qts. milk
4	tsp. salt

Preparation
1. Heat the milk in a sauce pan.
2. Have all equipment and ingredients handy.

Procedure
1. Place shortening in sauce pot, melt.
2. Add flour, making a roux, and cook for 5 minutes.
3. Add hot milk whipping constantly with a wire whip until desired consistency is reached.
4. Bring to a boil and season with salt. Remove from fire and strain through a china cap into a stainless steel container.
5. Dot the top of the sauce with butter so it will not form a crust.

1. When cooking shortening and flour be careful not to scorch.
2. Whip constantly when adding the milk to obtain a smooth sauce.

Egg sauce

For egg sauce chopped hard boiled eggs are blended with cream sauce, and chopped pimientos are added for color. This sauce is generally served with croquettes or poached fish.

Objectives
1. To teach the student the procedure for preparing egg sauce.
2. To teach the student how to serve and use egg sauce.

Equipment
1. Sauce pot, 6 qt.
2. French knife
3. Kitchen spoon
4. 1 gal. stainless steel container

Ingredients: Approx. yield: 1 gal.
1   gal. cream sauce
10   hard boiled eggs, chopped
2   pimientos, minced
     salt to taste

Preparation
1. Prepare cream sauce (see recipe).
2. Chop the eggs, gently on paper, using a French knife.
3. Mince the pimientos using a French knife.

Procedure
1. Place the cream sauce in the sauce pot and bring to a simmer.
2. Fold in gently the chopped hard boiled eggs and minced pimientos.
3. Season with salt and tint with yellow color if desired.
4. Serve 3 ozs. per portion with croquettes (ham, seafood or salmon) or poached fish (halibut or Kennebec).

Precautions and Safety Measures
1. Avoid scorching, while simmering the sauce.
2. Do not chop the eggs too fine.
3. Exercise caution when chopping the eggs and mincing the pimientos.

Mustard sauce

Mustard sauce is made by adding prepared mustard to cream sauce to give it a nippy taste. Mustard sauce is most desirable when served with boiled ham, beef, tongue or fish.

Objectives
1. To teach the student the procedure for preparing mustard sauce.
2. To teach the student how to serve mustard sauce.

Equipment
1. Qt. measure
2. Cup measure
3. Sauce pot, 6 qt.
4. Wire whip
5. 1 gal. stainless steel container

Ingredients: Approx. yield: 1 gal.
1   gal. cream sauce
1   pt. prepared mustard
¼   cup vinegar, white
     salt and white pepper to taste

Preparation
1. Prepare the cream sauce (see recipe).
2. Have all equipment and ingredients handy.

Procedure
1. Place the cream sauce in a sauce pot and bring to a simmer.
2. Whip in the vinegar and mustard using a wire whip. Check seasoning and remove from the range. Pour into a stainless steel container.
3. Serve 2 ozs. per portion, using a ladle. Serve over boiled ham, tongue, beef or fish.

Precautions and Safety Measures
1. Stir or whip sauce occasionally, throughout the entire preparation to avoid sticking or scorching.

Newburg sauce

Newburg sauce is a blend of cream sauce, paprika, sherry wine and seasoning. It is used in association with seafood dishes.

Objectives
1. To teach the student the procedure for preparing Newburg sauce.
2. To teach the student how to use Newburg sauce.

Equipment
1. Wire whip
2. Sauce pot, 6 qts.
3. Gal. measure
4. Spoon measure
5. Cup measure
6. Kitchen spoon
7. 1 gal. stainless steel container

Ingredients: Approx. yield: 1 gal.
1 gal. cream sauce
¼ cup butter
2 tbsp. paprika
½ cup sherry wine
    salt and white pepper to taste
Preparation
1. Prepare cream sauce (see recipe).
2. Have all equipment and ingredients handy.
Procedure
1. Place the butter in the sauce pot and melt.
2. Add the paprika and blend it into the butter.
3. Add the sherry wine; bring mixture to a simmer.
4. Add the cream sauce, whipping briskly with a wire whip until all ingredients are thoroughly incorporated. Simmer for 5 minutes. Season with salt & white pepper.
5. Remove from the range and pour into a stainless steel container.
6. Use in the preparation of shrimp, lobster, crabmeat and seafood Newburg.
Precautions and Safety Measures
1. Only blend the paprika into the butter, do not cook.
2. Avoid scorching at all times.

À la king sauce

A la king sauce is a cream sauce containing diced, cooked mushrooms, green peppers and pimientos. This sauce is generally associated with poultry; however, it can also be served with ham or sweetbreads to create variety.
Objectives
1. To teach the student the procedure for preparing à la king sauce.
2. To teach the student how to use à la king sauce.
Equipment
1. Kitchen spoon
2. Sauce pot, 6 qt.
3. French knife
4. Baker's scale
5. Cup measure
6. Gal. measure
7. Sauce pan, 1 pt.
8. China cap
9. 1 gal. stainless steel container

Ingredients: Approx. yield: 1 gal.
1 gal. cream sauce
12 ozs. green peppers, diced
8 ozs. butter
8 ozs. mushrooms, diced
4 ozs. pimientos, diced
½ cup sherry wine
Preparation
1. Prepare the cream sauce (see recipe).
2. Dice the green peppers, mushrooms and pimientos using a French knife.
3. Have all equipment and ingredients handy.
Procedure
1. Place the butter in the sauce pot and melt.
2. Add the mushrooms and sauté until slightly tender.
3. Add the sherry wine and simmer slightly.
4. Add the prepared cream sauce and continue to simmer, stirring occasionally with a kitchen spoon.
5. Place the green peppers in a small sauce pan, cover with water and poach until tender. Drain and add to above mixture.
6. Add the pimientos and check seasoning.
7. Remove from the range and pour into a stainless steel container.
8. Serve 2 to 2½ ozs. per portion, using a ladle. Serve with sautéed sweetbreads and turkey steak. The sauce is used in the preparation of ham, chicken or turkey à la king.
Precautions and Safety Measures
1. Do not brown or over cook the mushrooms when sautéing.
2. After the cream sauce is added stir occasionally to avoid sticking or scorching.
3. Exercise caution when cutting the garnish.

Albert sauce

Albert sauce is similar to horseradish sauce; the difference is the addition of shallots and chopped parsley. Albert sauce is a welcomed addition to boiled beef dishes.
Objectives
1. To teach the student the procedure for preparing Albert sauce.
2. To teach the student how to serve Albert sauce.
Equipment
1. French knife

2. Small sauce pan, 1 pt.
3. Sauce pot, 6 qts.
4. Kitchen spoon
5. 1 gal. stainless steel container
   Ingredients: Approx. yield: 1 gal.
   1 gal. cream sauce, thick
   1 cup horseradish
   ¼ cup shallots, minced
   ⅓ cup vinegar, tarragon
   2 tbsp. parsley, chopped
   Preparation
1. Prepare the cream sauce (see recipe).
2. Mince the shallots using a French knife.
3. Chop the parsley.
4. Have all equipment and ingredients handy.
   Procedure
1. Place the cream sauce in a sauce pot and bring to a simmer.
2. Place the tarragon vinegar and minced shallots in small sauce pan, cook until vinegar reduces slightly and add to the cream sauce.
3. Stir in the chopped parsley and horseradish using a kitchen spoon; blend thoroughly.
4. Bring sauce back to a simmer and pour into a stainless steel container.
5. Serve 2 to 2½ ozs. per portion using a ladle. Serve over boiled short ribs and brisket of beef.
   Precautions and Safety Measures
1. When reducing the vinegar be careful it does not evaporate completely.
2. Exercise caution when chopping the parsley and mincing the shallots.

Cheese sauce

Cheese sauce is prepared by adding Cheddar cheese, and seasoning to cream sauce. This is an excellent sauce to serve with broccoli, asparagus, brussel sprouts, etc.
   Objectives
1. To teach the student the procedure for preparing cheese sauce.
2. To teach the student how to serve cheese sauce.
   Equipment
1. Wire whip
2. Food grinder
3. Measuring spoons
4. Qt. measure
5. Sauce pan, 3 qts.

6. China cap
7. Kitchen spoon
8. 1 gal. stainless steel container
   Ingredients: Approx. yield: 2 qts.
   1 lb. sharp Cheddar cheese, ground
   2 tsp. mustard, dry
   2 tsp. paprika
   ½ cup milk
   1½ tsp. Worcestershire sauce
   1¾ qt. medium cream sauce
   salt to taste
   Preparation
1. Grind Cheddar cheese by passing it through a food grinder and using the medium hole chopper plate.
2. Prepare medium cream sauce (see recipe).
3. Have all equipment and ingredients handy.
   Procedure
1. Place cheese, mustard, paprika and milk in sauce pan, stir with a kitchen spoon.
2. Add 1 cup of the white sauce. Heat until cheese is melted, stirring constantly with a kitchen spoon.
3. Add the remainder of the white sauce, the tobasco sauce, and the Worcestershire sauce. Bring to boil, whipping occasionally with a wire whip.
4. Add salt to taste, if necessary.
5. Strain through a china cap into a stainless steel container.
6. Serve 2 to 2½ ozs. per portion, using a ladle. Serve over broccoli, asparagus, brussel sprouts and cauliflower.
   Precautions and safety measures
1. When melting the cheese and bringing the sauce to a boil, do not scorch.

Mock Hollandaise sauce

Mock Hollandaise sauce is a substitute for the true butter-egg sauce. It is generally used to reduce cost. It is a blend of cream sauce, egg yolks and lemon juice.
   Objectives
1. To teach the student the procedure for preparing mock Hollandaise sauce.
2. To teach the student how to use mock Hollandaise sauce.
   Equipment
1. Qt. measure
2. Baker's scale
3. 2 sauce pans, 4 qts. each

4. Wire whip
5. Stainless steel bowl
6. Cup measure
   Ingredients: Approx. yield: 2 qts.
   2 qts. milk
   8 ozs. butter
   6 ozs. flour
   10 egg yolks
   ¼ cup lemon juice
   salt and white pepper to taste
   yellow color if desired
   Preparation
1. Squeeze juice from lemons.
2. Heat the milk in a sauce pan.
3. Separate the eggs. Reserve the whites for later use.
4. Have all equipment and ingredients handy.
   Procedure
1. Place the butter in a sauce pan, place on the range and heat.
2. Add the flour, making a roux, and cook for 3 minutes.
3. Add the hot milk, whipping vigorously with a wire whip. Allow to simmer for 5 minutes.
4. Place the egg yolks in a stainless steel bowl and beat with a wire whip. Drip in a small amount of the hot cream sauce and blend with the egg yolks. Slowly pour this mixture into the simmering cream sauce, mixing continuously.
5. Add the lemon juice and season with salt and white pepper.
6. Tint with yellow color if desired.
7. Serve the same as the true Hollandaise sauce.
   Precautions and Safety Measures
1. When adding the egg yolks to the hot cream sauce pour very slowly and whip briskly.
2. Exercise caution so not to scorch the sauce.

Cardinal sauce

Cardinal sauce is a small sauce prepared from cream sauce. It contains minced shrimp or lobster and is generally served with seafood.
   Objectives
1. To teach the student how to prepare cardinal sauce.

2. To teach the student how to serve cardinal sauce.
   Equipment
1. Sauce pot, 6 qts.
2. French knife
3. Qt. Measure
4. Cup measure
5. Spoon measure
6. Wire whip
7. Baker's scale
8. Sauce pan, 5 qts.
9. 1 gal. stainless steel container
   Ingredients: Approx. yield: 1 gal.
   1 lb. shrimp or lobster meat cooked, chopped fine
   1 lb. butter
   1 lb. bread flour
   1 tbsp. paprika
   3 qts. milk, hot
   1 qt. single cream
   ¾ cup sauterne wine
   1 tbsp. lemon juice
   salt and white pepper to taste
   Preparation
1. Mince the cooked (poached or steamed) shrimp or lobster using a French knife.
2. Heat the milk and cream in a sauce pan.
3. Have all equipment and ingredients handy.
   Procedure
1. Place the butter in the sauce pot and melt.
2. Add the shrimp or lobster and sauté slightly.
3. Add the flour and paprika, blending thoroughly with the butter to make a roux. Cook slowly for about 5 minutes.
4. Add the hot milk and cream gradually, stirring constantly with a wire whip until thickened and smooth.
5. Add the wine, lemon juice and seasoning.
6. Remove from the range and pour into a stainless steel container.
7. Serve 2 to 2½ ozs. per portion using a ladle. Serve with baked or poached fish.
   Precautions and Safety Measures
1. At no time should the butter or roux be allowed to brown.
2. Be careful that scorching does not occur.

Mornay sauce

Mornay sauce is generally used over items

that are to be glazed, such as lobster thermidor and Florentine items.

Objectives
1. To teach the student how to prepare Mornay sauce.
2. To teach the student how to use Mornay sauce.

Equipment
1. Baker's scale
2. Measuring cups
3. Sauce pot, 1½ to 2 gal.
4. 1 gal. stainless steel container
5. Wire whip
6. Sauce pan, 5 qts.

Ingredients: Approx. yield: 1 gal.
- 1   lb. 4 ozs. bread flour
- 1   lb. 4 ozs. butter, melted
- 4   qts. milk, hot
- 12 egg yolks
- ½   cup light cream
  salt to taste
- 6   ozs. Parmesan cheese
- 8   ozs. butter, cold, broken in small pieces

Preparation
1. Break eggs and separate yolks from whites.
2. Heat the milk in a sauce pan.
3. Have all ingredients and equipment handy.

Procedure
1. Melt the butter in a sauce pot, add flour making a roux and cook for 5 minutes. Do not brown.
2. Add hot milk and stir with a wire whip until slightly thickened and smooth.
3. Beat egg yolks and cream together with a wire whip.
4. Add slowly to above mixture, whipping constantly with a wire whip.
5. Season with salt and cook for 1 minute.
6. Remove from heat and add cheese, pour into stainless steel container.
7. Add cold butter, stirring until blended into the sauce.
8. Serve approximately 2 ozs. over items that are to be glazed. Use a kitchen spoon to apply sauce. Use with lobster thermidor, Florentine items and poached fish.

Precautions and Safety Measures
1. Overheating the sauce may cause it to break and become fluid.

2. When adding egg and cream mixture to sauce, whip small amounts of sauce into it gradually making certain egg will not curdle, then add the mixture to remaining sauce.

VELOUTE OR FRICASSE SAUCE RECIPES

Basic velouté sauce

Basic velouté sauce (or fricassee sauce) is one of the five leading sauces used in the commercial kitchen. The kind of basic velouté sauce prepared will depend upon the kind of stock used. Examples: fish stock-vin blanc, chicken-supreme, or veal or beef stock fricassee. This leading sauce can be converted into many small sauces. (The important small sauce recipes immediately follow this recipe.)

Objective
1. To teach the student the procedure for preparing basic velouté sauce.

Equipment
1. Sauce pan, 5 qt.
2. China cap
3. Cheese cloth
4. Wire whip
5. Baker's scale
6. Qt. measure
7. 1 gal. stainless steel container

Ingredients: Approx. yield: 1 gal.
- 12 ozs. butter or margarine
- 12 ozs. bread flour
- 1   gal. stock (fish, chicken, veal or beef)
  salt and white pepper to taste

Preparation
1. Have all equipment and ingredients handy.
2. Prepare stock to be used and strain through cheese cloth to remove all scum particles. (Stock recipes are given in Chap. 12.)

Procedure
1. Heat butter in sauce pan and add flour. Cook slowly for about 5 minutes, stirring and forming a roux.
2. Add stock slowly, whipping constantly, until thick and smooth.
3. Season and continue to cook for 20 minutes. Adjust to desired consistency. If

too thick add more stock, if too thin add more roux or whitewash.

4. Strain through china cap into gal. container. Reserve for use.
5. Serve 2 to 2½ ozs. per portion using a ladle.

Precautions and Safety Measures

1. When cooking the roux, do not scorch or allow to brown.
2. Whip constantly when adding stock to roux or lumps may form.

Horseradish sauce

Horseradish sauce is served mostly with boiled meats to increase the flavor of the dish. It is a combination of beef fricassee (velouté sauce) and prepared horseradish.

Objectives

1. To teach the student the procedure for preparing horseradish sauce.
2. To teach the student how to serve horseradish sauce.

Equipment

1. Sauce pot, 1½ gal.
2. Wire whip
3. China cap, fine
4. Cheese cloth
5. 1½ or 2 gal. stainless steel container
6. 1 qt. measure
7. Baker's scale

Ingredients: Approx. yield: 1¼ gal.

1	gal. beef stock, hot
10	ozs. flour, bread
10	ozs. shortening or butter
1	pt. horseradish
	salt and pepper to taste
1	dash tobasco sauce

Preparation

1. Prepare beef stock. (See Chap. 12.) Strain through cheese cloth. Reheat when about to use.
2. Have all equipment and ingredients handy.

Procedure

1. Place shortening in sauce pot and heat.
2. Add flour, making a roux, and cook slightly.
3. Add the hot beef stock, stirring constantly with a wire whip.
4. Remove from the fire and strain through a fine china cap into a stainless steel container.

5. Add the horseradish and tobasco sauce.
6. Season with salt and white pepper.
7. Serve 2 to 2½ ozs. per portion using a ladle.

Precautions and Safety Measures

1. Strain stock thoroughly through cheese cloth to eliminate any undesirable scum.
2. When cooking the roux do not let it brown or scorch.
3. Have stock boiling before adding it to the roux.

Homard (lobster) sauce

Homard sauce consists of a combination of fish velouté sauce and diced lobster. This sauce is generally served with fish and shellfish entrees.

Objectives

1. To teach the student the procedure for preparing homard (lobster) sauce.
2. To teach the student how to serve homard sauce.

Equipment

1. French knife
2. Sauce pot, 6 qts.
3. Kitchen spoon
4. Qt. measure
5. 1 gal. stainless steel container

Ingredients: Approx. yield: 1 gal.

1	gal. fish velouté sauce
1	pt. lobster, cooked, diced fairly fine
	salt and white pepper to taste
½	cup butter

Preparation

1. Prepare the fish velouté sauce (see recipe).
2. Cook and dice the lobster meat using a French knife.
3. Have all equipment and ingredients handy.

Procedure

1. Place the butter in a sauce pot and melt.
2. Add the diced lobster and sauté slightly.
3. Add the fish velouté sauce stirring with a kitchen spoon, then simmer for 10 minutes.
4. Remove from the range and pour into a stainless steel container.
5. Serve 3 ozs. per portion, using a ladle. Serve over poached or baked flounder, Kennebec salmon, halibut, etc.

Precautions and Safety Measures
1. Do not brown the butter or lobster when sautéing.
2. When simmering the sauce, stir occasionally with a kitchen spoon to avoid sticking.

Poulette sauce

Poulette sauce is lightly sautéed onions and mushrooms which are added to a chicken velouté sauce. This sauce is used mainly with chicken or turkey.

Objectives
1. To teach the student the procedure for making Poulette sauce.
2. To teach the student how to mince onions and slice mushrooms.
3. To teach the student how to serve Poulette sauce.

Equipment
1. French knife
2. Sauce pan, 5 qt.
3. Stainless steel container
4. Kitchen spoon
5. 1 gal. stainless steel container

Ingredients: Approx. yield: 1 gal.
1 gal. chicken velouté sauce
2 lbs. fresh mushrooms
4 ozs. onions, minced
4 ozs. butter
   yellow color as desired
   salt and white pepper to taste

Preparation
1. Slice mushrooms and mince onions with French knife.
2. Prepare chicken velouté sauce. (See basic velouté sauce recipe.)
3. Have all equipment and ingredients handy.

Procedure
1. Place butter in sauce pan and heat.
2. Add minced onion and sauté slightly. Do not brown.
3. Add the sliced mushrooms and cook until slightly tender.
4. Stir in the chicken velouté sauce. Continue to simmer sauce for 20 minutes, stirring frequently.
5. Season with salt and white pepper. Tint with yellow color.
6. Pour into 1 gal. stainless steel container.
7. Serve, using a ladle, with chicken cro-

quettes, stuffed chicken leg, fried turkey wings, etc.
8. Serve 2 to $2\frac{1}{2}$ ozs. per portion.

Precautions and Safety Measures
1. When simmering sauce take care, do not scorch.
2. Use caution when tinting with yellow color.

Caper sauce

Caper sauce is prepared by adding capers to a fish velouté sauce. Capers are a European flower bud seasoning, very tart to the taste. This sauce frequently accompanies poached fish.

Objectives
1. To teach the student the procedure for preparing caper sauce.
2. To teach the student how to serve caper sauce.

Equipment
1. Gal. measure
2. Cup measure
3. Baker's scale
4. Spoon measure
5. Sauce pan, 6 qts.
6. French knife
7. Kitchen spoon
8. China cap
9. 1 gal. stainless steel container

Ingredients: Approx. yield: 1 gal.
1 gal. fish velouté sauce
4 ozs. butter
$\frac{1}{2}$ cup onions, minced
1 bay leaf
2 tbsp. vinegar, white
6 ozs. capers

Preparation
1. Prepare the fish velouté sauce (see recipe).
2. Mince the onions using a French knife.
3. Have all equipment and ingredients handy.

Procedure
1. Place the butter in a sauce pan and heat.
2. Add the minced onions and sauté without browning.
3. Add the vinegar and bay leaves and simmer.
4. Add the fish velouté sauce, stirring with a kitchen spoon, and continue to simmer for 20 minutes. Strain through a china cap.

5. Add the capers and stir into the sauce gently. Pour into a stainless steel container.
6. Serve 2 to 2½ ozs., using a ladle. Serve over poached fish of the sole or salmon family.

   Precautions and Safety Measures
1. When sautéing the minced onions do not brown.
2. Stir occasionally when sauce is simmering to avoid sticking or scorching.
3. Exercise caution when mincing the onions.

Victoria sauce

Victoria sauce is basically a fish velouté sauce blended with diced mushrooms and lobster and flavored with white wine. Generally served with lobster and shrimp preparations.

Objectives
1. To teach the student the procedure for preparing Victoria sauce.
2. To teach the student how to serve Victoria sauce.

Equipment
1. Qt. measure
2. Cup measure
3. Sauce pan, 6 qts.
4. French knife
5. Kitchen spoon
6. 1 gal. stainless steel container

Ingredients: Approx. yield: 1 gal.

   3 qt. fish velouté sauce
   1 pt. lobster, cooked, diced fine
   1 cup butter
   1 cup white wine (sauterne)
   ⅓ cup shallots, minced
   1 cup mushrooms, diced fine
      salt and white pepper to taste

Preparation
1. Prepare the fish velouté sauce (see recipe).
2. Cook and dice the lobster using a French knife.
3. Dice the mushrooms and mince the shallots, using a French knife.
4. Have all equipment and ingredients handy.

Procedure
1. Place the butter in a sauce pan and melt.
2. Add the shallots and sauté slightly, do not brown.

3. Add the mushrooms and lobster, continuing to sauté.
4. Add the white wine and simmer until it is reduced by evaporation to one-half its original amount.
5. Add the fish velouté sauce while stirring with a kitchen spoon, and continue to simmer for about 10 minutes.
6. Remove from the range and pour into a stainless steel container.
7. Serve 3 ozs. per portion, using a ladle. Serve over sautéed shrimp, lobster, king crabmeat and fish of the sole variety.

   Precautions and Safety Measures
1. When sautéing do not brown any of the ingredients.
2. When simmering stir occasionally to avoid sticking.

Duglère sauce

Duglère sauce is basically a fish velouté sauce with white wine, shallots, mushrooms and crushed tomatoes added. It is served with baked and poached fish entrées.

Objectives
1. To teach the student the procedure for preparing Duglere sauce.
2. To teach the student how to serve Duglere sauce.

Equipment
1. Sauce pot, 6 qt.
2. Qt. measure
3. French knife
4. Cup measure
5. Spoon measure
6. Sauce pan, 1 pt.
7. Kitchen spoon
8. 1 gal. stainless steel container

Ingredients: Approx. yield: 1 gal.

   3 qts. fish velouté
   1 cup white wine (sauterne)
   ½ cup shallots, minced
   ½ cup mushrooms, diced medium
   1 cup tomatoes, crushed
   2 tbsp. parsley, chopped
   ¼ cup butter
      salt and white pepper to taste

Preparation
1. Prepare the fish velouté (see recipe).
2. Mince the shallots and dice the mushrooms using a French knife.
3. Chop and wash the parsley.

4. Crush the tomatoes by squeezing with the hands.
5. Have all equipment and ingredients handy.

Procedure
1. Place the wine in a sauce pot, add the shallots and simmer until the wine is reduced by evaporation to half its original amount.
2. Add the fish velouté sauce and continue to simmer.
3. Place the butter in a small sauce pan, add the diced mushrooms and sauté slightly.
4. Add the mushrooms to the simmering sauce and stir gently with a kitchen spoon.
5. Add the crushed tomatoes and chopped parsley.
6. Season with salt and white pepper and pour into a stainless steel container.
7. Serve 2 to 2½ ozs. per portion, using a ladle. Serve over baked fish entrees.

Precautions and Safety Measures
1. Stir the sauce gently throughout the entire preparation to avoid scorching.

Bonne-femme sauce

Bonne-femme sauce is prepared by adding Hollandaise sauce and whipped cream to a fish velouté sauce. This sauce can also be browned lightly under the broiler.

Objectives
1. To teach the student the procedure for preparing bonne-femme sauce.
2. To teach the student how to serve bonne-femme sauce.

Equipment
1. Qt. measure
2. Cup measure
3. Sauce pan, 6 qts.
4. Mixing machine
5. Kitchen spoon
6. Stainless steel bowl, 1 qt.
7. French knife
8. 1 gal. stainless steel container

Ingredients: Approx. yield: 1 gal.
3 qt. fish velouté sauce
1 cup white wine
½ cup shallots, minced
1 pt. Hollandaise sauce
1 pt. unsweetened, heavy cream, whipped

Preparation
1. Prepare 3 qts. fish velouté sauce (see recipe).
2. Prepare the Hollandaise sauce (see recipe).
3. Whip the cream to a stiff peak on the electric mixing machine.
4. Mince the shallots using a French knife.
5. Have all equipment and ingredients handy.

Procedure
1. Place the wine in a sauce pan, add the shallots and simmer until the wine is reduced by evaporation to half its original amount.
2. Add the prepared fish velouté and continue to simmer.
3. Fold the whipped cream into the Hollandaise sauce.
4. Remove the fish velouté sauce from the range and fold in the whipped cream and Hollandaise mixture. Blend thoroughly using a kitchen spoon.
5. Place the sauce in a stainless steel container.
6. Serve 2 to 2½ ozs. per portion, using a ladle. Serve over poached kennebec salmon, halibut, flounder, etc., and brown lightly under the broiler before serving.

Precautions and Safety Measures
1. Do not overwhip the cream. It will turn to butter.
2. Fold gently when adding the whipped cream to the Hollandaise and when adding the whipped cream—Hollandaise mixture to the fish velouté.

Curry sauce

Curry sauce is a sauce that is associated with the country of India because this is where the curry originated. Curry sauce can be associated with many meats and seafoods, but it is most popular when served with lamb, chicken, shrimp or lobster.

Objectives
1. To teach the student the procedure for preparing curry sauce.
2. To teach the student how to use curry sauce.

Equipment
1. Sauce pot, 6 qts.
2. China cap
3. French knife

4. Baker's scale
5. Ladle
6. Spoon measure
7. Wire whip
8. Kitchen spoon
9. Qt. measure
10. 1 gal. stainless steel container
11. Sauce pan, 2 qts.

Ingredients: Approx. yield: 1 gal.

10 ozs. butter or shortening
8 ozs. flour
3 qts. chicken stock, hot
1 qt. milk, hot
5 ozs. onions, diced
½ tsp. mace
½ tsp. thyme
4 tbsp. curry powder
2 bay leaves
1 banana, peeled, diced
5 ozs. pineapple, diced
5 ozs. apples, diced
   salt to taste

Preparation
1. Prepare chicken stock (See Chap. 12.)
2. Heat the milk in a sauce pan.
3. Dice the fruit with a French knife.
4. Dice the onions with a French knife.
5. Have all equipment and ingredients handy.

Procedure
1. Place the butter in a sauce pot and heat.
2. Add the onions and sauté without browning.
3. Add the flour, making a roux, and cook for 5 minutes.
4. Add the thyme, mace, bay leaves and curry powder and blend into the roux using a kitchen spoon.
5. Add the chicken stock and milk, whipping vigorously with a wire whip to avoid lumps, and bring to a boil.
6. Add fruit, simmer for about 1 hour.
7. Season with salt and strain through a fine china cap into a stainless steel container, using a ladle to force as much of the fruit pulp as possible into the sauce.
8. Use in the preparation of the following entree dishes: shrimp curry, lobster curry, lamb curry, chicken curry, and veal curry.

Precautions and Safety Measures
1. When sautéing the onions do not let them or the butter brown.

2. Stir occasionally while the sauce is simmering to avoid sticking.
3. Exercise caution when dicing the onions and the fruit.

HOLLANDAISE SAUCE RECIPES

Hollandaise sauce

Hollandaise sauce is one of the leading sauces. It is served mostly with vegetables such as asparagus and broccoli. The most important small sauces that use Hollandaise sauce are listed immediately following this recipe.

Objectives
1. To teach the student the procedure for making Hollandaise sauce.
2. To teach the student how to heat the eggs and form an emulsion with the melted butter.
3. To teach the student how to serve the Hollandaise sauce.

Equipment
1. Stainless steel bowl
2. Braiser
3. French whip
4. 1 qt. stainless steel container

Ingredients: Approx. yield: 1 qt.

8 egg yolks
1 lb. butter, melted
   lemon juice from ½ lemon
   salt to taste
   tabasco sauce to taste

Preparation
1. Melt the butter.
2. Break the eggs and separate the whites from the yolks.
3. Squeeze the juice from ½ lemon.
4. Place water in braiser and bring to boil on the stove.

Procedure
1. Put the egg yolks in the stainless steel bowl, add a few drops of water and mix well.
2. Put bowl in hot water temperature 160°F.
3. Beat yolks slowly with a French whip until they foam and tighten.
4. Remove from water and add melted butter very slowly, while whipping continuously with a French whip.
5. When all butter is added, forming the

emulsion, season with salt, tabasco sauce, and lemon juice.

6. Serve with cooked vegetables and poached egg dishes or as a base for small sauces.
7. Serve 2 to 2½ ozs. per portion with a kitchen spoon. The exact amount will depend upon the item it is served with.

Precautions and Safety Measures

1. Be very careful water does not get too hot or eggs will scramble.
2. Whip continuously throughout the entire preparation.

Maltaise sauce

Maltaise sauce is a small sauce to which Hollandaise sauce, orange juice and gratings of orange peel (called zest) are added. This sauce is the finest to serve with asparagus and other select vegetables.

Objectives

1. To teach the student the procedure for preparing Maltaise sauce.
2. To teach the student how to use and serve Maltaise sauce.

Equipment

1. Stainless steel mixing bowl
2. Wire whip
3. Box grater
4. Strainer

Ingredients: Approx. yield: 2 qts.

  2   qts. Hollandaise sauce
  2   small oranges, zest and juice

Preparation

1. Grate the rind of the oranges using the grater.
2. Prepare 2 qts. Hollandaise sauce (see recipe).
3. Squeeze the juice of the two oranges and strain.
4. Have all equipment and ingredients handy.

Procedure

1. Place the prepared Hollandaise sauce in a stainless steel bowl.
2. Blend in the orange juice and grating (zest) using a wire whip.
3. Adjust seasoning.
4. Serve 2 to 2½ ozs. per portion using a kitchen spoon. Serve over cooked asparagus, broccoli, beets, etc.

Precautions and Safety Measures

1. Always place the Hollandaise in a stainless steel container. Aluminum has a bad affect on eggs.
2. When preparing the Hollandaise sauce do not have the water too hot. The eggs will scramble.

Maximillian sauce

Maximillian sauce is prepared by adding anchovy essence to Hollandaise sauce. This sauce is used with poached or baked fish entrees.

Objective

1. To teach the student the procedure for preparing Maximillian sauce.
2. To teach the student how to serve Maximillian sauce.

Equipment

1. 2 qt. stainless steel bowl
2. French knife
3. Qt. measure
4. Wire whip

Ingredients: Approx. yield: 1 qt.

  1   qt. Hollandaise sauce
  2   ozs. anchovies, puréed

Preparation

1. Prepare the Hollandaise sauce (see recipe).
2. Chop the anchovies into a purée with a French knife.
3. Have all equipment and ingredients handy.

Procedure

1. Place the prepared Hollandaise sauce in a stainless steel bowl.
2. Add the puréed anchovies and blend thoroughly with a wire whip.
3. Serve 2 ozs. per portion using a kitchen spoon. Serve over poached and baked fish entrees.

Precautions and Safety Measures

1. Exercise caution when chopping the anchovies.
2. Keep sauce warm. Do not keep hot or it will separate.
3. Serve within two hours of preparation.

Cherburg sauce

Cherburg sauce is a Hollandaise sauce blended with puréed crabmeat to create a sauce that compliments certain shrimp and lobster preparations.

Objectives

1. To teach the student the procedure for preparing Cherburg sauce.

2. To teach the student how to serve Cherburg sauce.
Equipment
1. Qt. measure
2. Cup measure
3. French knife
4. Food grinder
5. Stainless steel mixing container, 2 qts.
6. Kitchen spoon
   Ingredients: Approx. yield: 1 qt.
   1   qt. Hollandaise sauce
   1   pimiento, puréed
   ½   cup crabmeat (king or blue), puréed
Preparation
1. Prepare the Hollandaise sauce (see recipe).
2. Purée the pimiento by chopping with a French knife.
3. Purée the crabmeat by running it through the food grinder.
4. Have all equipment and ingredients handy.
Procedure
1. Place the Hollandaise sauce in the stainless steel mixing container.
2. Blend in the puréed crabmeat and pimiento until thoroughly incorporated, using a kitchen spoon.
3. Serve 3 ozs. over sautéed shrimp, lobster, king crabmeat and flounder.
Precautions and Safety Measures
1. Serve the sauce within two hours after preparation.
2. Keep sauce warm. If kept too hot or too cold it may separate.
3. Exercise caution when using the food chopper.

Mousseline sauce

Mousseline sauce, sometimes called chantilly sauce, is a very light sauce prepared by folding whipped cream into Hollandaise sauce. When served with fish or poultry items the sauce can be glazed under the broiler if desired.
Objectives
1. To teach the student the procedure for preparing Mousseline sauce.
2. To teach the student how to serve Mousseline sauce.
Equipment
1. Stainless steel bowl, 4 qts.
2. Wooden spoon
3. Qt. measure
4. Electric mixer

Ingredients: Approx. yield: 2 qts.
1   qt. Hollandaise sauce
1   pt. heavy cream, whipped, unsweetened
Preparation
1. Whip the heavy cream on the electric mixer until it forms stiff peaks.
2. Prepare the Hollandaise sauce (see recipe).
3. Have all equipment and ingredients handy.
Procedure
1. Place the Hollandaise sauce in the stainless steel bowl.
2. Fold in the whipped cream using a wooden spoon until it is thoroughly blended with the Hollandaise sauce.
3. Serve 2 ozs. per portion, using a kitchen spoon. Serve over poached fish or chicken breast. The sauce can be glazed under the broiler or served without glazing.
Precautions and Safety Measures
1. Do not overwhip the cream. It will turn to butter.

Divine sauce

Divine sauce is prepared by adding the combined flavors of sherry and sauterne wines to Hollandaise sauce. Whipped cream is added to create a smoother consistency and to allow the sauce to brown slightly if desired. Serve this sauce with seafood or poultry dishes.
Objectives
1. To teach the student the procedure for preparing divine sauce.
2. To teach the student how to whip the cream.
3. To teach the student how to serve divine sauce.
Equipment
1. 2 stainless steel mixing bowls
2. Small sauce pan, 1 pt.
3. Cup measure
4. Qt. measure
5. Wire whip
6. Wooden spoon
   Ingredients: Approx. yield: 2 qts.
   2   qts. Hollandaise sauce
   ½   cup heavy cream, whipped
   ¼   cup sherry wine
   ¼   cup sauterne wine
Preparation
1. Prepare Hollandaise sauce (see recipe).
2. Whip the cream. Place the chilled cream in the bowl of a rotary mixer, using the wire

whip, whip at high speed until soft peaks form.

3. Have all equipment and ingredients handy.

Procedure

1. Place the prepared Hollandaise sauce in the stainless steel bowl.

2. Place the wines in sauce pan and boil down to half its original amount. Allow to cool and blend into the Hollandaise sauce using a wire whip.

3. Fold in the whipped cream, using a wooden spoon with a gentle motion.

4. Serve 2 to 2½ ozs. per serving using a kitchen spoon. Serve over poached halibut, Kennebec salmon, king crabmeat, sautéed breast of chicken, etc. The sauce can be glazed under a broiler if desired.

Precautions and Safety Measures

1. Serve this sauce within two hours of preparation.

2. Keep sauce warm, do not overheat it. It will break (become fluid).

3. Wine must be lukewarm or cool before adding it to the Hollandaise sauce.

4. Do not over-whip the cream, it will turn to butter.

Béarnaise

Béarnaise sauce is prepared from the leading sauce, Hollandaise. Béarnaise sauce, however, substitutes a tarragon vinegar mixture for the lemon juice ordinarily used in Hollandaise sauce. Béarnaise sauce is generally served with meats, such as steaks and various types of roast.

Objectives

1. To teach the student the procedure for preparing Béarnaise sauce.

2. To teach the student how to prepare the tarragon vinegar mixture.

3. To teach the student how to serve Béarnaise sauce.

Equipment

1. 2 sauce pans, 1 pt. each
2. Wire whip
3. Cheese cloth
4. 3 qt. stainless steel bowl
5. French knife
6. Measuring cups
7. Measuring spoons
8. Qt. measure

Ingredients: Approx. yield: 2 qts.

4 tbsp. shallots, minced

1 tsp. peppercorns, crushed
1 cup tarragon vinegar; or 1 tbsp. tarragon leaves and 1 cup cider vinegar
2 qts. Hollandaise sauce
1 tsp. tarragon leaves or parsley, chopped fine

Preparation

1. Mince shallots, using a French knife, and crush peppercorns.

2. Have all equipment and ingredients handy.

3. Prepare basic Hollandaise sauce (see recipe) omitting the lemon juice.

4. Chop tarragon leaves or parsley using a French knife.

Procedure

1. Place shallots, peppercorns and tarragon vinegar (or substitute) in small sauce pan. Place on range and boil slowly until mixture is reduced by evaporation to half to three fourths of the original amount. Remove from range and strain reduced liquid through a cheese cloth into another small pan.

2. Add desired amount of reduced liquid to the Hollandaise sauce, whip gently with a wire whip until blended.

3. Add a teaspoon of finely chopped tarragon leaves or parsley to the sauce.

4. Serve 3 ozs. per portion, using a kitchen spoon. Serve with roast rib and sirloin of beef, sautéed veal steak, broiled lamb steak, etc.

Precautions and Safety Measures

1. When reducing liquid do not scorch.

2. Use caution when preparing the Hollandaise sauce so the emulsion will not break.

3. Exercise caution when mincing the shallots and chopping the tarragon leaves or parsley.

Choron sauce

Choron sauce is a tomato-flavored béarnaise sauce. It is a versatile sauce because it can be served with steaks, fish, chicken and eggs with equally good results.

Objectives

1. To teach the student the procedure for preparing Choron sauce.

2. To teach the student how to serve Choron sauce.

Equipment

1. 3 qt. stainless steel container

2. Kitchen spoon
3. Qt. measure
4. Cup measure
   Ingredients: Approx. yield: 2¼ qts.
   2   qt. béarnaise sauce (omit the chopped tarragon or parsley)
   ½   cup tomato paste or ¾ cup tomato purée
       salt to taste
   Preparation
1. Prepare béarnaise sauce, omitting the chopped tarragon or parsley (see recipe).
2. Have all equipment and ingredients handy.
   Procedure
1. Place the béarnaise sauce in a stainless steel container.
2. Pour the tomato paste or purée slowly into the béarnaise sauce while stirring gently with a kitchen spoon.
3. Season with salt.
4. Serve 2 to 3 ozs. per portion, using a kitchen spoon with broiled steaks, poached sole or salmon, poached eggs and sautéed or broiled breast of chicken.
   Precautions and Safety Measures
1. Stir gently when adding the tomato paste or purée to the béarnaise sauce, so it will blend in thoroughly and lessen the chance of the emulsion breaking.

TOMATO SAUCE RECIPES

Tomato sauce

Tomato sauce is a leading sauce used in all commercial kitchens. Served with a number of fried items, such as breaded veal cutlet, breaded pork chops and breaded veal chops. The important small sauces made using tomato sauce immediately follow this recipe.
Objectives
1. To teach the student the procedure for making tomato sauce.
2. To teach the student how to cut rough garnish.
3. To teach the student how to serve tomato sauce.
   Equipment
1. Sause pot, 2 gal.
2. Wire whip
3. China cap
4. French knife

5. Kitchen spoon
6. 2 gal. stainless steel container
   Ingredients: Approx. yield: 1½ gal.
   4   ozs. bacon or ham grease
   6   ozs. onion, cut rough
   6   ozs. celery, cut rough
   6   ozs. carrots, cut rough
   5   ozs. flour
   1   #10 can tomato purée
   ½   gal. ham stock
       salt and sugar to taste
   1   clove garlic
   1   bay leaf
   1   pinch thyme
   Preparation
1. Cut vegetables rough using a French knife.
2. Prepare the ham stock. (See Chap. 12.)
3. Have all ingredients and equipment handy.
   Procedure
1. Place bacon or ham fat in sauce pot, add onions, carrots and celery. Sauté until golden brown.
2. Add bay leaf, thyme and garlic.
3. Add flour, taking up the ham or bacon grease and making a roux. Cook 5 minutes.
4. Add tomato purée and ham stock and bring to a boil, whip occasionally with a wire whip.
5. Let boil until vegetables are completely cooked.
6. Season with salt and sugar.
7. Strain through a china cap and pour into a stainless steel container.
8. Serve 2 ozs. per portion using a ladle. Serve with breaded veal chops, pork chops or pork and veal cutlets.
   Precautions and Safety Measures
1. Do not make your sauce too thick or too heavy with starch.
2. Red color may be added to the sauce to increase appearance.

Figaro sauce

Figaro sauce is a blend of tomato sauce and Hollandaise sauce. It is best when served with poached, steamed or baked fish.
Objectives
1. To teach the student the procedure for preparing Figaro sauce.
2. To teach the student how to use and serve Figaro sauce.
   Equipment
1. Stainless steel mixing bowl

2. Wire whip
3. French knife
4. Qt. measure
5. Kitchen spoon

Ingredients: Approx. yield: 2 qts.
1 qt. tomato sauce
1 qt. Hollandaise sauce
2 tbsp. parsley, chopped

Preparation
1. Prepare tomato sauce (see recipe).
2. Prepare Hollandaise sauce (see recipe).
3. Chop the parsley using a French knife.
4. Have all equipment and ingredients handy.

Procedure
1. Place the prepared tomato sauce in the mixing bowl.
2. Add the Hollandaise sauce slowly, blending thoroughly with a wire whip until the two are incorporated.
3. Add the chopped parsley and blend with a kitchen spoon.
4. Serve 2 ozs. with a kitchen spoon over poached, steamed or baked fish, such as halibut or Kennebec salmon.

Precautions and Safety Measures
1. Tomato sauce must be lukewarm when blending in the Hollandaise.
2. Do not hold this sauce for long periods of time. Serve within 2 hours of preparation.
3. Do not overheat this sauce at any time. It will break (become fluid). Keep warm, but not hot.

Napolitaine sauce

Napolitaine sauce is prepared by adding diced fresh tomatoes, minced ham and parsley to tomato sauce. This sauce should be served chiefly with pork and veal entrees.

Objectives
1. To teach the student the procedure for preparing Napolitaine sauce.
2. To teach the student how to dice the tomatoes and mince the ham.
3. To teach the student how to use and serve Napolitaine sauce.

Equipment
1. Gal. measure
2. Cup measure
3. Sauce pot, 6 qt.
4. Kitchen spoon
5. French knife
6. Paring knife
7. 1 gal. stainless steel container

Ingredients: Approx. yield: 1 gal.
1 gal. tomato sauce
2 small tomatoes, firm, skinned, diced
½ cup ham, lean, minced
1 small clove garlic, minced
¼ cup parsley, chopped
4 ozs. butter

Preparation
1. Prepare the tomato sauce (see recipe).
2. Mince the ham and garlic using a French knife.
3. Peel and dice the tomatoes using a paring knife and chop the parsley.
4. Have all equipment and ingredients handy.

Procedure
1. Place the butter in the sauce pot and melt.
2. Add the garlic and ham and sauté slightly.
3. Add the prepared tomato sauce, bring to a boil then allow to simmer for 10 minutes, stir occasionally with a kitchen spoon.
4. Add the diced tomatoes and simmer for an additional 5 minutes.
5. Remove from the fire and add the chopped parsley.
6. Adjust seasoning and pour into a stainless steel container.
7. Serve 2 to 2½ ozs. per portion using a ladle. Serve with bread fried pork chops, veal cutlets, veal chops, etc.

Precautions and Safety Measures
1. Do not brown when sautéing the garlic and ham.
2. Use caution throughout the entire preparation so scorching does not occur.
3. Exercise caution when dicing the tomatoes and mincing the ham.

Milanaise sauce

Milanaise sauce is made by adding sliced mushrooms, julienne ham and tongue to tomato sauce. This sauce blends exceptionally well with spaghetti and can also be served over sautéed pork and veal items.

Objectives
1. To teach the student the procedure for preparing Milanaise sauce.
2. To teach the student how to serve Milanaise sauce.

Equipment
1. Gal. measure
2. Cup measure
3. Baker's scale
4. Sauce pan, 6 qt.

5. French knife
6. Kitchen spoon
7. 1 gal. stainless steel container
Ingredients: Approx. yield: 1 gal.
 1 gal. tomato sauce
 ½ cup butter
 10 ozs. mushrooms, sliced
 12 ozs. ham, julienne, cooked
 12 ozs. tongue, julienne, cooked
Preparation
1. Julienne the cooked ham and tongue using a French knife.
2. Prepare tomato sauce (see recipe).
3. Slice the mushrooms using a French knife.
4. Have all equipment and ingredients handy.
Procedure
1. Place the butter in a sauce pan and heat.
2. Add mushrooms and sauté until slightly tender.
3. Add the ham, tongue and tomato sauce, then simmer for 10 minutes.
4. Check seasoning and remove from the range. Pour into a stainless steel container.
5. Serve 2 to 3 ozs. per portion, using a ladle. Serve over spaghetti, sautéed pork cutlets or sautéed veal cutlets.
Precautions and Safety Measures
1. Exercise caution when julienning the meat.
2. Stir through the entire preparation to avoid sticking.

Pizza sauce

Pizza sauce is a savory tomato sauce. It is used in the preparation of pizza pie. Many establishments today use canned pizza sauce, but none of these preparations can compare with the homemade sauce.
Objectives
1. To teach the student the procedure for preparing pizza sauce.
2. To teach the student how to use pizza sauce.
Equipment
1. Qt. measure
2. Sauce pot, 6 qts.
3. Spoon measures
4. Cup measure
5. Kitchen spoon
6. French knife
7. 1 gal. stainless steel container
Ingredients: Approx. yield: 1 gal.
 3 qts. tomatoes, canned
 1 qt. tomato paste

 2 cups water
 3 tsp. garlic powder
 3 tsp. onion powder
 3 tsp. salt
 ½ tsp. black pepper
 2 tbsp. basil leaves
 2 tbsp. oregano
 ¼ cup butter
Preparation
1. Strain tomatoes, reserve juice, chop the pulp using a French knife.
2. Have all equipment and ingredients handy.
Procedure
1. In a sauce pot add the tomato pulp, juice, tomato paste and water. Bring to a boil.
2. Add the remaining ingredients and stir with a kitchen spoon. Simmer until mixture reduces slightly and becomes fairly thick.
3. Check seasoning and pour into a stainless steel container.
4. Use in the preparation of pizza pie and serve approx. 2 to 2½ ozs., using a ladle, with veal chop Italienne and sautéed veal steak.
Precautions and Safety Measures
1. Stir occasionally while sauce is simmering to avoid scorching.
2. Exercise caution when chopping the tomato pulp.

Barbecue sauce

Barbecue sauce may be used with any type of barbecue item. It has a tomato base and a very rich, savory taste.
Objective
1. To teach the student how to prepare barbecue sauce.
2. To teach the student how to serve barbecue sauce.
Equipment
1. Measuring cups
2. Measuring spoons
3. Pt. measure
4. French knife
5. Sauce pot, 6 qts.
6. 1 gal. stainless steel container
Ingredients: Approx. yield: 1 gal.
 1 cup shortening or oil
 2½ cups onions, minced
 1½ cups brown sugar
 5 tbsp. mustard, prepared
 3 tsp. salt

5 tbsp. Worcestershire sauce
5 cups catsup
3⅓ cups celery, cut fine
½ cup vinegar
3 pt. water

Preparation

1. Mince onions and celery using a French knife.
2. Have all equipment and ingredients handy.

Procedure

1. Place shortening or oil in sauce pot. Add the minced onions and celery and sauté without browning.
2. Add all other ingredients and simmer slowly for about 30 minutes, stirring occasionally with a kitchen spoon.
3. Remove from fire and pour into a stainless steel container.
4. Serve 2½ to 3 ozs. per portion, using a ladle. Serve with barbecued chicken, spare ribs, pork and beef.

Precautions and Safety Measures

1. When simmering sauce, stir frequently to avoid scorching.
2. Exercise caution when mincing the onions and celery.

Creole sauce

Creole sauce is a sauce suitable for service with many items such as omelets, poached eggs, fish, leftover dishes, meat, poultry and game. Another name for it is "Spanish sauce."

Objectives

1. To teach the student how to cut julienne vegetables.
2. To teach the student the procedure for making creole sauce.
3. To teach the student how to use and serve creole sauce.

Equipment

1. Sauce pot, 6 qt.
2. French knife
3. Kitchen spoon
4. 1 gal. stainless steel container

Ingredients: Approx. yield: 1 gal.

3 lbs. celery, cut julienne
3 lbs. onions, cut julienne
2 lbs. green peppers, cut julienne
1 lb. mushrooms, cut julienne
½ #10 can tomatoes, crushed
½ #10 can tomato purée
2 cloves garlic, chopped

4 ozs. bacon grease or shortening
4 ozs. flour
½ gal. beef stock
1 oz. salt
½ oz. pepper
1 bay leaf

Preparation

1. Prepare the beef stock. (See Chap. 12.)
2. Julienne vegetables and chop garlic using a French knife.
3. Crush tomatoes by squeezing with the hands.
4. Have all equipment and ingredients handy.

Procedure

1. Place bacon grease or shortening in sauce pot, heat.
2. Add onions, green peppers, celery, garlic and mushrooms, sauté slowly, but do not brown.
3. Add flour, stir with a kitchen spoon until smooth and allow to cook for a few minutes.
4. Add tomatoes, tomato purée, stock and seasoning.
5. Cook until vegetables are well done.
6. Verify the seasoning and consistency. Pour into a stainless steel container.
7. Serve 2½ to 3 ozs. per portion, using a ladle. Serve with meat loaf, Salisbury steak, steamed shrimp, baked fish, etc.

Precautions and Safety Measures

1. Do not brown vegetables when sautéing.
2. Do not make sauce too thick.
3. Exercise caution when cutting the vegetables.

Italian sauce No. I

A basic Italian sauce that can be converted into meat sauce or served with meat balls.

Objectives

1. To teach the student how to prepare Italian sauce.
2. To teach the student how to use and serve the sauce.

Equipment

1. Qt. measure
2. Measuring cups
3. Measuring spoons
4. Sauce pot, 2 gal.
5. French knife
6. 2 gal. stainless steel container
7. Kitchen spoon

Ingredients: Approx. yield: 1½ gal.
5 cloves garlic, chopped
1 pt. salad or olive oil
2 #10 cans whole tomatoes, crushed
6 tbsp parsley, chopped
1 tbsp. sweet basil, crushed
4 tsp. salt
2 tsp. black pepper
3 cups tomato paste
1 lb. Parmesan cheese, grated
1 tbsp. oregano, crushed
1 lb. onions, minced
1 qt. tomato purée

Preparation
1. Chop garlic and crush tomatoes.
2. Mince the onions with a French knife.
3. Have all equipment and ingredients handy.

Procedure
1. Place oil in stock pot, add garlic and onions and sauté.
2. Add crushed tomatoes, tomato purée, parsley, basil, salt and pepper, and simmer for 30 minutes, stirring occasionally with a kitchen spoon.
3. Add oregano and tomato paste, continue to cook until thick, then remove from fire.
4. Add cheese and check seasoning. Place in a 2 gal. stainless steel container.
5. Use for meat sauce, meat balls and other Italian dishes.
6. Amount served will depend upon the kind of dish it is used with. Use a ladle for serving.

Precautions and Safety Measures
1. Stir frequently while simmering to avoid scorching.
2. Stir vigorously when adding the cheese to avoid lumps.

Italian sauce No. II

Italian sauce is a basic Italian sauce that has many applications in the preparation of Italian main dishes, such as lasagna, ravioli and spaghetti.

Objectives
1. To teach the student how to prepare the sauce.
2. To teach the student how to use the sauce.

Equipment
1. Baker's scale
2. Pt. measure
3. Measuring spoons
4. French knife
5. Sauce pot, 4 or 5 gal.
6. 3 gal. stainless steel container
7. Kitchen spoon

Ingredients: Approx. yield: 3 gal.
2 lbs. onions, minced
3 tbsp. garlic, chopped fine
1 pt. olive oil
2 #10 cans tomatoes, Italian
2 #10 cans tomato purée
½ cup sugar
4 tbsp. oregano, crushed
4 tbsp. sweet basil, crushed
2 tbsp. salt

Preparation
1. Chop onions and garlic using a French knife.
2. Crush the tomatoes by squeezing with the hands.
3. Have all equipment and ingredients handy.

Procedure
1. Sauté onions and garlic in olive oil for about 5 minutes in sauce pot. Do not brown.
2. Add tomatoes and tomato purée and simmer for 1 hour, stirring occasionally with a kitchen spoon.
3. Add sugar, oregano, sweet basil, and salt. Simmer for an additional 30 minutes, stirring occasionally.
4. Adjust seasoning and pour into a stainless steel container.
5. Serve 3 ozs. per portion using a ladle. Serve over spaghetti, ravioli or other pasta products.

Precautions and Safety Measures
1. Stir occasionally during simmering to avoid scorching.
2. Do not brown onions and garlic when sautéing.

COLD SAUCE RECIPES

Cocktail sauce

Cocktail sauce is a cold tomato sauce. It has a hot, tangy taste and is usually served with hot and cold seafood dishes.

Objectives
1. To teach the student the procedure for preparing cocktail sauce.
2. To teach the student how to serve cocktail sauce.

Equipment
1. 1 gal. stainless steel container
2. Qt. measure
3. Spoon measure
4. Cup measure
5. Kitchen spoon
6. French knife
   Ingredients: Approx. yield: 1 gal.
   2   qts. catsup
   1   qt. chili sauce
   1   pt. tomato purée
   2   tbsp. lemon juice
   1   tbsp. green pepper, minced
   1   cup horseradish
   1   tsp. salt
   2   tbsp. Worcestershire sauce
   1   tsp. tabasco sauce
   2   tbsp. onions, minced
   Preparation
1. Mince onions and green peppers using a French knife.
2. Squeeze juice from lemons.
3. Have all equipment and ingredients handy.
   Procedure
1. Place all the ingredients in a stainless steel container and blend thoroughly using a kitchen spoon.
2. Adjust seasoning if a hotter sauce is desired.
3. Serve 2 to 3 ozs. per portion, in a soufflé cup, with hot or cold seafood items, such as shrimp, oysters and crabmeat.
   Precautions and Safety Measures
1. Exercise caution when mincing the onions and green peppers.

Tartar sauce

Tartar sauce consists of a mayonnaise base with minced dill pickles and onions added. This sauce can be served with meat or seafood, but most often it is associated with seafood.
Objectives
1. To teach the student the procedure for preparing tartar sauce.
2. To teach the student how to serve tartar sauce.
   Equipment
1. 1 gal. stainless steel container
2. Cup measure
3. Qt. measure
4. Kitchen spoon
5. Food chopper or grinder

6. French knife
   Ingredients: Approx. yield: 2½ qts.
   2   qts. mayonnaise
   1   pt. dill pickles, chopped
   ¼   cup parsley, chopped
   1   cup onions, chopped
   Preparation
1. Prepare the mayonnaise (See recipe Chap. 10.)
2. Chop the parsley with a French knife and wash.
3. Grind or chop the dill pickles very fine and drain.
4. Grind or chop the onions very fine and drain.
5. Have all equipment and ingredients handy.
   Procedure
1. Place all the ingredients in a stainless steel container and blend thoroughly using a kitchen spoon.
2. Adjust seasoning and serve 2 to 2½ ozs. per portion, in a soufflé cup, with fried seafood or in some cases with meat, such as hamburger.
   Precautions and Safety Measures
1. Drain the chopped onions and pickles fairly dry before adding to the mayonnaise or the sauce will have a fluid consistency.

Dill sauce

Dill sauce is a tangy type of cold sauce that stimulates the flavor buds when served with cold poached salmon and other seafood items.
Objectives
1. To teach the student the procedure for preparing dill sauce.
2. To teach the student how to use and serve dill sauce.
   Equipment
1. French knife
2. Spoon measures
3. Cup measures
4. Qt. measure
5. 2 qt. mixing bowl
6. Kitchen spoon
7. 2 qt. stainless steel container
   Ingredients: Approx. yield: 1½ qts.
   1   qt. sour cream
   1   cup salad dressing
   1   tbsp. mustard, dry
   1   small onion, minced
   1   tbsp. light brown sugar

2   tbsp. dill seed
¾   cup white vinegar
2   cups cucumbers, chopped fine
    salt and white pepper to taste
Preparation
1. Mince the onions using a French knife.
2. Chop the cucumbers fine using a French knife.
3. Have all equipment and ingredients handy.
Procedure
1. Place all the ingredients at one time in mixing bowl and blend thoroughly using a kitchen spoon.
2. Adjust seasoning and pour into a stainless steel container.
3. Serve 2 ozs. per portion in a soufflé cup or ladled over the item. Serve with cold poached salmon, fried shrimp or scallops, deviled crabs, etc.
Precautions and Safety Measures
1. Exercise caution when mincing the onions and chopping the cucumbers.

Chaud-froid sauce (white)

Chaud-froid sauce is made by adding unflavored gelatin and cream to a velouté sauce. The velouté sauce can be made from chicken or fish stock depending on what the chaud-froid sauce will be used to cover. Chaud-froid, a French term meaning hot-cold, is a jellied sauce used to decorate poultry, fish and ham for buffet display.
Objectives
1. To teach the student the procedure for preparing chaud-froid sauce.
2. To teach the student the uses of chaud-froid sauce.
Equipment
1. Sauce pot, 6 qts.
2. Wire whip
3. Metal bowl, 1 qt.
4. 2 gal. stainless steel container
5. Kitchen spoon
6. Qt. measure
7. Baker's scale
Ingredients: Approx. yield: 1½ gal.
1   gal. velouté sauce
1   qt. coffee cream
1   pt. hot water
12 ozs. unflavored, granulated gelatin
    salt and white pepper to taste

Preparation
1. Prepare the velouté sauce (see recipe).
2. Dissolve the gelatin in the hot water. Place the water in a metal bowl and stir, with a kitchen spoon, while pouring the gelatin in slowly.
3. Have all equipment and ingredients handy.
Procedure
1. Place the velouté sauce in a sauce pot and heat.
2. Whip in the dissolved gelatin, using a wire whip. Remove from the heat.
3. Add the cream slowly, while whipping continuously with a wire whip.
4. Season with salt and white pepper and pour into a stainless steel container, let cool.
5. The sauce may be colored with various food colors if desired.
6. Use chaud-froid to cover poultry, ham and fish when decorating these items for buffet display. When applying the chaud-froid sauce, the item being covered should be cold. The sauce should be chilled to the point where it is ready to jell, but still has a flowing consistency. The work should be done in a walk-in refrigerator so the sauce will jell and adhere, upon contact, to the item being coated. Apply the sauce with a 4 to 6 oz. ladle.
Note: When covering fish with chaud-froid sauce, mayonnaise may be substituted for the velouté sauce, the gelatin reduced to 9 ozs. and the cream omitted.
Precautions and Safety Measures
1. Be alert when chilling the sauce. If the sauce is too warm it will not adhere to the item being covered. If too cold it will jell before contact is made. Chill to the point where the sauce will flow, but not run.
2. Dissolve the gelatin thoroughly before adding it to the mayonnaise or velouté sauce.

BUTTER SAUCE RECIPES

Lemon butter sauce

Lemon butter sauce is a blend of melted butter, lemon juice and chopped parsley. It is usually served with sautéed or broiled seafood.

Objectives
1. To teach the student the procedure for preparing lemon butter sauce.
2. To teach the student how to serve lemon butter sauce.

Equipment
1. Sauce pan, 1 qt.
2. French knife
3. Kitchen spoon
4. 1 qt. stainless steel container

Ingredients: Approx. yield: 1 pt.
1 lb. butter
¼ cup lemon juice
2 tbsp. parsley, chopped

Preparation
1. Chop the parsley with a French knife and wash.
2. Have all equipment and ingredients handy.
3. Squeeze the juice from lemons.

Procedure
1. Place the butter in a sauce pan and melt.
2. Add the lemon juice and chopped parsley and stir. Pour into a stainless steel container.
3. Serve 1 oz. per serving, using a ladle, over broiled or sautéed seafood.

Precautions and Safety Measures
1. Exercise caution when chopping the parsley.
2. Do not brown the butter.

Anchovy butter

Anchovy butter is a blend of melted butter and chopped anchovies. The sauce is usually served with broiled or sautéed seafood.

Objectives
1. To teach the student the procedure for preparing anchovy butter.
2. To teach the student how to serve anchovy butter.

Equipment
1. French knife
2. Sauce pan
3. Kitchen spoon

Ingredients: Approx. yield: 1 pt.
1 lb. butter, melted
⅓ cup anchovies, chopped
2 tbsp. parsley, chopped

Preparation
1. Chop the anchovies into a paste.
2. Chop and wash the parsley.
3. Have all equipment and ingredients handy.

Procedure
1. Place the butter in a sauce pan and melt.
2. Add the chopped anchovies and parsley and stir.
3. Serve over broiled or sautéed seafood.

Precautions and Safety Measures
1. Exercise caution when chopping the parsley.
2. Do not brown the butter.

Brown butter sauce

Brown butter sauce adds taste and color to many broiled meats, such as broiled pork chops, liver, veal chops, etc.
1. To teach the student the procedure for making brown butter sauce.
2. To teach the student the uses for brown butter sauce.

Equipment
1. Sauce pan, 2 qt.
2. Kitchen spoon
3. 1 pt. stainless steel container

Ingredients: Approx. yield: 1 qt.
1 lb. butter
1 cup brown gravy
2 cups consommé

Preparation
1. Prepare consommé. (See Chap. 12.)
2. Prepare brown gravy (See recipe).
3. Have all equipment and ingredients handy.

Procedure
1. Place butter in sauce pan and brown on range (nut brown).
2. Add brown gravy.
3. Thin with consommé while stirring with a kitchen spoon. Pour into a stainless steel container.
4. Serve 1 oz. per portion, using a ladle, with broiled meats.

Precautions and Safety Measures
1. Do not overbrown butter.

Meunière sauce

Meunière sauce is the most popular of the butter sauces. The butter is browned until light brown. Lemon juice and chopped parsley are added and then it is served over sautéed seafood.

Objectives
1. To teach the student the procedure for preparing meuniere sauce.
2. To teach the student how to serve meuniere sauce.

Equipment
1. Cup measure
2. Baker's scale
3. Sauce pan, 1 qt.
4. French knife
5. 1 qt. stainless steel container
6. Kitchen spoon

Ingredients: Approx. yield: 1 pt.
1   lb. butter
2   ozs. lemon juice
¼   cup parsley, chopped

Preparation
1. Chop the parsley with a French knife.
2. Squeeze the juice from lemons.
3. Have all equipment and ingredients handy.

Procedure
1. Place the butter in a sauce pan and brown slightly.
2. Add the lemon juice and stir with a kitchen spoon.
3. Add the chopped parsley.
4. Serve over sautéed seafood.

Precautions and Safety Measures
1. Do not overbrown or burn the butter.
2. The butter will boil up when the juice is added. Stir continuously to avoid boiling over.
3. Exercise caution when chopping the parsley.

DESSERT OR SWEET SAUCE RECIPES

Cinnamon sauce

Cinnamon sauce is a red, cinnamon-flavored dessert sauce. This sauce can be served with any dessert item that is complemented with a cinnamon flavor.

Objectives
1. To teach the student the procedure for preparing cinnamon sauce.
2. To teach the student how to serve cinnamon sauce.

Equipment
1. Sauce pan, 2 qts.
2. Kitchen spoon
3. Cup measure
4. Food grater
5. 1 qt. stainless steel container

Ingredients: Approx. yield: 1 qt.
3   cups water
2   cups sugar
¼   cup cornstarch
2   lemons, grating and juice
½   cup red cinnamon candies (Imps)

Preparation
1. Grate the lemon peel and squeeze the juice from lemons.
2. Have all equipment and ingredients handy.

Procedure
1. Blend the sugar and cornstarch together in a sauce pan.
2. Pour in the water slowly, blending thoroughly with a kitchen spoon. Bring to a boil on the range.
3. Add the lemon rind and juice and cinnamon candies.
4. Cook, stirring constantly, until the sauce thickens and clears.
5. Serve 2 ozs. per portion, using a ladle, over desserts that are complemented with a cinnamon flavor, such as apple cobbler and apple crisp.

Precautions and Safety Measures
1. Stir sauce occasionally while cooking to avoid scorching.

Plum sauce

Plum sauce is a dessert sauce that can be served hot or cold with such items as ice cream, cake, snow pudding or cheese cake.

Objectives
1. To teach the student the procedure for preparing plum sauce.
2. To teach the student how to serve plum sauce.

Equipment
1. Sauce pan, 4 qts.
2. Cup measure
3. Wire whip
4. Spoon measure
5. Stainless steel bowl, 1 qt.
6. 1 gal. stainless steel container

Ingredients: Approx. yield: 2 qts.
2   qts. syrup from canned plums

½ cup cornstarch
1 tsp. salt
¼ cup lemon juice
½ tsp. almond extract
red color

Preparation

1. Squeeze juice from lemons.
2. Drain juice from plums and save plums for another use.
3. Have all equipment and ingredients handy.

Procedure

1. Place the cornstarch and salt in a stainless steel mixing bowl and mix with a small amount of the cold canned syrup. Blend well.
2. Place the remaining plum syrup in a sauce pan and bring to a boil.
3. Add the cornstarch mixture, whipping rapidly with a wire whip, and simmer for 10 minutes until slightly thick and smooth.
4. Add the lemon juice and almond extract. Pour into a stainless steel container.
5. Serve 2 ozs. per portion, using a ladle, over ice cream, snow pudding or cheese cake.

Precautions and Safety Measures

1. Stir occasionally while the sauce is cooking to avoid scorching.

Cherry sauce

Cherry sauce is a dessert sauce that can be served hot or cold. It blends itself well with puddings and cake items.

Objectives

1. To teach the student the procedure for preparing cherry sauce.
2. To teach the student how to serve cherry sauce.

Equipment

1. Sauce pan, 4 qts.
2. Kitchen spoon
3. Baker's scale
4. Cup measure
5. Qt. measure
6. Spoon measure
7. Small stainless steel bowl
8. Wire whip
9. 1 gal. stainless steel container
10. Strainer

Ingredients: Approx. yield: 2 qts.

1 qt. cherry juice

1 cup water
3 cups cherries, drained
1½ lbs. sugar
½ tsp. salt
1 tsp. lemon juice
¼ cup butter
¼ cup cornstarch

Preparation

1. Drain juice from the cherries using a strainer.
2. Squeeze juice from lemons.
3. Have all equipment and ingredients handy.

Procedure

1. Place the cherry juice in a sauce pan and bring to a boil.
2. Dissolve the cornstarch in the water in a small stainless steel bowl. Pour slowly into the boiling juice, whipping vigorously with a wire whip. Simmer until slightly thickened and clear.
3. Add the sugar, salt and lemon juice and return to a simmer.
4. Add the cherries and butter and blend thoroughly with a kitchen spoon.
5. Remove from the range and pour into a stainless steel bowl.
6. Serve 2 ozs. per portion, using a ladle, over cake, bread pudding, French toast, etc.

Precautions and Safety Measures

1. After the starch is added to the liquid, stir occasionally to avoid scorching.
2. Fold the cherries gently into the sauce to avoid breaking them up.

Orange sauce

Orange sauce is a dessert sauce that is served hot. It can be served with any dessert that is complemented with orange flavor.

Objectives

1. To teach the student the procedure for preparing orange sauce.
2. To teach the student how to serve orange sauce.

Equipment

1. Pt. measure
2. Sauce pan, 2 qts.
3. Cup measure
4. Spoon measure
5. Wire whip
6. Stainless steel bowl, 1 qt.

7. Kitchen spoon
8. Food grater
9. 1 qt. stainless steel container
   Ingredients: Approx. yield: 1 qt.
   1   pt. water
   1   pt. orange juice
   2   cups sugar, granulated
   ½   tsp. salt
   2   tbsp. cornstarch
   3   tsp. grated orange rind (zest)
   3   tbsp. lemon juice
   3   tbsp. butter
   Preparation
1. Grate the orange rind on a food grater.
2. Squeeze juice from oranges and lemons.
3. Have all equipment and ingredients handy.
   Procedure
1. Place the water and orange juice in a sauce pan and bring to a boil.
2. Mix the sugar, salt and cornstarch together with a little of the above water-juice mixture. Mix with a kitchen spoon. Pour slowly into the boiling water mixture, whipping constantly with a wire whip. Cook until slightly thickened and clear, then remove from the range.
3. Blend in the orange rind, lemon juice and butter. Pour into a stainless steel container.
4. Serve 2 ozs. per portion, using a ladle. Serve with items that are complemented with an orange flavor, such as cake, banana turnovers, etc.
   Precautions and Safety Measures
1. Once the starch is added, stir occasionally to avoid scorching.

Rum sauce

Rum sauce is a dessert sauce that has a thin consistency and a slightly glossy appearance. It is served hot with any dessert that can be complemented with a rum flavor, such as mince meat pie.
   Objectives
1. To teach the student the procedure for preparing rum sauce.
2. To teach the student how to serve rum auce.
   Equipment
1. Sauce pan, 2 qt.
2. Baker's scale
3. Kitchen spoon

4. Qt. measure
5. 1 qt. stainless steel container
   Ingredients: Approx. yield: 2 qts.
   2   qts. water
   4   lbs. 8 ozs. sugar, granulated
   4   ozs. butter
   8   ozs. glucose
   ¼   oz. cream of tartar
        rum flavor to taste
   Preparation
1. Have all equipment and ingredients handy.
   Procedure
1. Place all the ingredients in a sauce pan and bring to a boil. Reduce heat and simmer for 10 minutes. Stir occasionally with a kitchen spoon.
2. Remove from the range and pour into a stainless steel container.
3. Serve 2 ozs. per portion, using a ladle. Serve over desserts that can be helped by the addition of a rum flavor, such as mince meat pie and baba au rhum cake.
   Precautions and Safety Measures
1. Wet the spoon or hand when weighing the glucose, it is very sticky.

Brown sugar sauce

Brown sugar sauce is a dessert sauce that is always served hot. It is an excellent choice when served with such items as rice and bread pudding.
   Objectives
1. To teach the student the procedure for preparing brown sugar sauce.
2. To teach the student how to serve brown sugar sauce.
   Equipment
1. Qt. measure
2. Sauce pan, 6 qt.
3. Spoon measure
4. Kitchen spoon
5. Wire whip
6. 1 gal. stainless steel container
   Ingredients: Approx. yield: 1 gal.
   3   pt. water
   1   qt. light brown sugar
   1   qt. dark brown sugar
   1   pt. white corn syrup
   4   tbsp. cornstarch
   1   lb. butter
   1   tsp. salt
   2   tsp. vanilla

2 tsp. vinegar, cider
Preparation
1. Have all equipment and ingredients handy.
Procedure
1. Place the water and corn syrup in a sauce pan and bring to a boil.
2. Mix the brown sugar and cornstarch together and add to the boiling mixture, whipping constantly with a wire whip. Cook for 10 minutes.
3. Add the butter and blend thoroughly with a kitchen spoon.
4. Remove the mixture from the fire and blend in the vanilla and vinegar. Pour into a stainless steel container.
5. Serve 2 ozs. per portion, using a ladle, with rice and bread pudding.
Precautions and Safety Measures
1. When adding the starch whip constantly or lumps may form.

Butterscotch sauce

Butterscotch sauce is a dessert sauce that is always served hot. It can be served with cake, bread pudding or cottage pudding.
Objectives
1. To teach the student the procedure for preparing butterscotch sauce.
2. To teach the student how to serve butterscotch sauce.
Equipment
1. Sauce pan, 4 qt.
2. Baker's scale
3. Wire whip
4. 1 gal. stainless steel container
Ingredients: Approx. yield: 2 qts.
2 lbs. dark brown sugar
1 lb. water
8 ozs. light corn syrup
8 ozs. butter
2 lbs. heavy cream
Preparation
1. Have all equipment and ingredients handy.
Procedure
1. Place the water, corn syrup and brown sugar in a sauce pan and boil until the temperature reaches 320°F.
2. Add the butter and blend thoroughly using a wire whip.
3. Add the heavy cream, whipping continuously until it is blended into the sauce.

Remove from the fire. Pour into a stainless steel container.
4. Serve 2 ozs. per portion, using a ladle, over cake, bread pudding and cottage pudding.
Precautions and Safety Measures
1. Add the cream slowly to the hot sauce and whip constantly for best results.

Lemon sauce

Lemon sauce is a dessert sauce that is served hot over items that blend well with the flavor of lemon, such as fruit cobblers.
Objectives
1. To teach the student the procedure for preparing lemon sauce.
2. To teach the student how to serve lemon sauce.
Equipment
1. Sauce pan, 4 qts.
2. Wire whip
3. Baker's scale
4. Spoon measure
5. Qt. measure
6. Cup measure
7. Stainless steel bowl, 1 qt.
8. Kitchen spoon
9. Food grater
10. 1 gal. stainless steel container steel container
Ingredients: Approx. yield: 2 qts.
2 qts. water
2 lbs. sugar, granulated
4 ozs. cornstarch
1 tsp. salt
3 ozs. egg yolks
1 cup lemon juice
1 tbsp. grated lemon rind
8 ozs. butter
Preparation
1. Separate eggs, save the whites for use in another preparation.
2. Grate the rind of the lemon on a food grater. Extract the juice.
3. Have all the equipment and ingredients handy.
Procedure
1. Place the water in a sauce pan and bring to a boil.
2. Mix together the sugar, cornstarch and salt in a stainless steel bowl. Dissolve this mixture with a small amount of the boiling water. Pour slowly into the re-

maining boiling water whipping gently with a wire whip. Cook until thickened and clear.

3. Beat together the egg yolks and lemon juice in a stainless steel bowl. Add slowly to the thickened mixtures, whipping constantly.

4. Remove from the range, add the grated lemon rind and butter and blend thoroughly. Pour into a stainless steel container.

5. Serve hot over any kind of fruit cobbler, allowing 2 ozs. per portion. Serve with a ladle.

Precautions and Safety Measures

1. Whip continuously when adding the egg yolk mixture to the hot liquid.

2. Keep hot only the amount of sauce needed. If this sauce is kept hot for a very long period of time it will thin out.

Custard sauce

Custard sauce is a dessert sauce consisting mainly of milk, eggs and sugar. It is served hot or cold to compliment such dessert items as rice pudding and bread pudding.

Objectives

1. To teach the student the procedure for preparing custard sauce.

2. To teach the student how to serve custard sauce.

Equipment

1. Sauce pan, 4 qts.
2. Wire whip
3. Qt. measure
4. Cup measure
5. Spoon measure
6. Stainless steel bowl, 1 qt.
7. Kitchen spoon
8. 1 gal. stainless steel container

Ingredients: Approx. yield: 2 qts.

2	qts. milk
1	cup sugar, granulated (1st amount)
½	cup sugar, granulated (2nd amount)
1½	tsp. salt
¾	cup cornstarch
6	egg yolks
½	cup butter
	vanilla to taste

Preparation

1. Separate eggs, saving the whites for use in another preparation.

2. Have all equipment and ingredients handy.

Procedure

1. Combine the milk and 1st. amount of sugar in a sauce pan and bring to a boil on the range.

2. In the stainless steel bowl mix together the 2nd. amount of sugar, salt and cornstarch with a little of the above mixture using a kitchen spoon to form a smooth paste. Add the egg yolks and mix smooth. Pour this mixture slowly into the hot sugar-milk mixture, whipping vigorously with a wire whip and cook until slightly thickened and smooth.

3. Whip in the butter and vanilla. If the color is too pale, adjust by adding yellow color. Pour into a stainless steel container.

4. Serve 2 ozs. per portion, using a ladle, with rice pudding, snow pudding or bread pudding.

Precautions and Safety Measures

1. Be alert and stir the milk-sugar mixture while it is on the range or it will boil over.

2. Stir the mixture at all times through the cooking period to avoid scorching.

3. Pour the cornstarch-egg mixture very slowly and whip vigorously when adding it to the hot milk-sugar mixture.

Vanilla sauce

Vanilla sauce is a dessert sauce that is generally served with cakes or cobblers.

Objectives

1. To teach the student the procedure for preparing vanilla sauce.

2. To teach the student how to serve vanilla sauce.

Equipment

1. 2 sauce pans, 4 qts. each
2. Wire whip
3. Qt. measure
4. Baker's scale
5. Spoon measure
6. 1 gal. stainless steel container
7. Kitchen spoon
8. 1 qt. stainless steel bowl

Ingredients: Approx. yield: 2 qts.

2	qts. water, boiling
3	ozs. cornstarch
2	lbs. 8 ozs. sugar, granulated

3   ozs. egg yolks
10   ozs. butter
1   tsp. salt
      vanilla to taste
Preparation
1. Boil the water in a sauce pan.
2. Separate the eggs. Save whites for use in another preparation.
3. Have all equipment and ingredients handy.
Procedure
1. Place the cornstarch, salt and half the sugar in sauce pan. Mix together thoroughly with a kitchen spoon.
2. Add the boiling water while whipping with a wire whip. Cook for about 10 minutes.
3. Beat the egg yolks with a wire whip in a stainless steel bowl. Blend in the remaining sugar, pour slowly into the thickened mixture whipping constantly. Cook 2 minutes.
4. Remove from the range and whip in the butter and vanilla. Pour into a stainless steel container.
5. Serve 2 ozs. per portion, using a ladle, over cake, bread pudding, brown betty or fruit cobblers.
Precautions and Safety Measures
1. Whip rapidly when adding the egg yolk mixture.
2. Use this sauce within two hours of preparation.

Lemon custard sauce

Lemon custard sauce is a rich creamy dessert sauce. It can be served with any dessert that can be complemented with a lemon flavor. This sauce can be converted into an orange custard sauce by substituting orange for the lemon.
Objectives
1. To teach the student the procedure for preparing lemon custard sauce.
2. To teach the student how to serve lemon custard sauce.
Equipment
1. Sauce pan, 6 qts.
2. Wire whip
3. Food grater
4. Baker's scale
5. 1 gal. stainless steel container
6. 1 qt. stainless steel bowl

Ingredients: Approx. yield: 1 gal.
6   lbs. water
12   ozs. sugar, granulated (1st amount)
12   ozs. egg yolks
2   ozs. cornstarch
12   ozs. sugar, granulated (2nd amount)
12   ozs. lemon juice
      rind from 6 lemons (zest), grated
Preparation
1. Grate the rind of the lemons on a food grater.
2. Separate the eggs. Save whites for use in another preparation.
3. Extract the juice from the lemons.
4. Have all equipment and ingredients handy.
Procedure
1. Place the water and first amount of sugar in a sauce pan and bring to a boil.
2. Beat together the egg yolks, cornstarch and sugar (2nd. amount) with a wire whip in a stainless steel bowl. Pour slowly into the above mixture (step 1) whipping constantly with a wire whip until slightly thick. Simmer for about 2 minutes and remove from the range.
3. Stir in the lemon juice and rind. Pour into a stainless steel container.
4. Serve 2 ozs. per portion, using a ladle, over cake or fruit cobblers.
Precautions and Safety Measures
1. Add the egg yolk mixture to the boiling liquid slowly and whip fairly vigorously.
2. Stir while simmering to avoid scorching.

Cranberry raisin sauce

Cranberry raisin sauce is a blend of cranberry juice and raisins. It is a very desirable sauce when served with ham or ham products.
Objectives
1. To teach the student the procedure for preparing cranberry raisin sauce.
2. To teach the student how to serve cranberry raisin sauce.
Equipment
1. Sauce pot or pan, 3 or 4 qt.
2. Measuring spoons
3. Qt. measure
4. Cup measure
5. Kitchen spoon
6. 1 gal. stainless steel container

Ingredients: Approx. yield: 2 qts.

- 2 qts. cranberry juice cocktail
- ½ tsp. allspice, ground
- 1 cup raisins
- 2 cups light brown sugar
- ¾ cup cornstarch
-   salt to taste

Preparation

1. Have all equipment and ingredients handy.

Procedure

1. Place the cranberry juice cocktail in a sauce pan, reserving 1 pt. to dissolve cornstarch, and bring to a boil.
2. Add the salt, allspice, brown sugar and raisins. Bring again to a boil then simmer for 5 minutes.
3. Dissolve the cornstarch in the remaining pt. of cranberry juice. Pour slowly into the boiling mixture, stirring constantly with a kitchen spoon until clear and thickened. Simmer for 5 minutes.
4. Remove from range and pour into a stainless steel container.
5. Serve 2 to 2½ ozs. per portion using a ladle. Serve with baked ham, ham and chicken croquettes, ham or turkey steaks, etc.

Precautions and Safety Measures

1. Stir constantly and gently when adding the cornstarch to avoid lumps and tearing the raisins.

Raisin sauce

Raisin sauce consists of plump raisins flowing through sweet, thick liquid. It is an ideal sauce to serve with ham and ham products.

Objective

1. To teach the student the procedure for preparing raisin sauce.

Equipment

1. Baker's scale
2. Sauce pot, 6 qts.
3. Kitchen spoon
4. Cup measure
5. Spoon measure
6. Small mixing bowl
7. 1 gal. stainless steel container

Ingredients: Approx. yield: 1 gal.

- 10 ozs. raisins
- 3 qts. of water

- 4 ozs. cornstarch
- ⅓ cup orange juice
- ¼ cup lemon juice
- 1 tsp. salt
- 12 ozs. dark brown sugar or granulated sugar
- ¼ cup vinegar, cider
- 1 pt. water

Preparation

1. Squeeze juice from the oranges and lemons.
2. Have all equipment and ingredients handy.

Procedure

1. Combine the raisins and 3 qts. of water in a sauce pot. Simmer until the raisins are slightly soft.
2. Add the orange juice, lemon juice and salt, continuing to simmer.
3. Dissolve the cornstarch in the pt. of water in a small mixing bowl and add slowly to the above mixture, stirring constantly with a kitchen spoon, until slightly thickened and smooth.
4. Stir in the brown sugar and vinegar. Return to a boil and remove from the range.
5. Pour into a stainless steel container.
6. Serve 2 ozs. per portion, using a ladle. Serve with baked and broiled ham and ham products.

Precautions and Safety Measures

1. Dissolve starch thoroughly before adding to the boiling liquid.
2. Do not overcook the raisins because they will break up in the sauce.

Raisin almond sauce

Raisin almond sauce is a combination of raisins and almonds with a slight flavoring of sherry wine. It is very pleasing to the palate when served with ham and ham products.

Objectives

1. To teach the student the procedure for preparing raisin almond sauce.
2. To teach the student how to serve raisin almond sauce.

Equipment

1. Cup measure
2. French knife
3. Baker's scale

4. Spoon measure
5. Sauce pan, 4 qts.
6. Kitchen spoon
7. 1 gal. stainless steel container

Ingredients: Approx. yield: 2 qts.

6	cups apple juice
8	ozs. butter
5	ozs. flour
10	ozs. raisins
1	pt. sherry wine
1	tsp. cloves, ground
2	tbsp. lemon juice
8	ozs. currant jelly
10	ozs. almonds, blanched, chopped
	salt to taste

Preparation
1. Chop the blanched almonds using a French knife.
2. Have all equipment and ingredients handy.

Procedure
1. Place the butter in the sauce pan and melt.
2. Add flour, making a roux and cook 3 minutes.
3. Add apple juice, raisins, cloves, wine, lemon juice and jelly. Cook, stirring constantly with a kitchen spoon, until thickened and smooth.
4. Stir in the almonds. Check seasoning and pour into a stainless steel container.
5. Serve 2 to 2½ ozs. per portion, using a ladle. Serve with baked ham, ham croquettes and cutlets.

Precautions and Safety Measures
1. Do not allow the roux to brown.
2. Avoid scorching the sauce; stir constantly.
3. Exercise caution when chopping the almonds

Cumberland sauce

Cumberland sauce is a partly sweet sauce, although a slight tartness can be detected. It compliments such items as baked ham, roast venison and roast cornish hen.

Objectives
1. To teach the student the procedure for preparing Cumberland sauce.
2. To teach the student how to serve Cumberland sauce.

Equipment
1. Gal. measure

2. Baker's scale
3. Cup measure
4. Sauce pot, 6 qts.
5. French knife
6. Kitchen spoon
7. Vegetable peeler
8. 1 gal. stainless steel container
9. Small bowl

Ingredients: Approx. yield: 1 gal.

1	gal. water
10	ozs. currants
2	oranges
2	lemons
4	ozs. cornstarch
1	cup water
10	ozs. brown sugar, dark
3	ozs. red currant jelly
4	ozs. red port wine

Preparation
1. Peel very thin layers of skin from the oranges and lemons (zest) using a vegetable peeler. The skin should be free of all membrane. Cut these layers of skin julienne using a French knife. Cover with water and poach for 10 minutes. Drain and discard water.
2. Squeeze the juice from the oranges and lemons.
3. Have all equipment and ingredients handy.

Procedure
1. Place the currants and 1 gal. of water in a sauce pot. Simmer slowly until the currants are slightly soft.
2. Dissolve the cornstarch in 1 cup of water in a small bowl. Pour it slowly into the boiling currant mixture, stirring constantly with a kitchen spoon until slightly thickened and clear.
3. Add the brown sugar, orange and lemon juice and blend into the simmering sauce.
4. Blend in the jelly, wine and poached julienne peel. Check seasoning and remove from the range. Pour into a stainless steel container.
5. Serve 2 to 2½ ozs. per portion, using a ladle. Serve with baked ham, roast cornish hen or roast venison.

Precautions and Safety Measures
1. Do not overcook the currants.
2. Stir constantly when adding the cornstarch.

Hard Sauce

This sauce is a blend of creamed butter and powdered sugar. Vanilla, brandy or rum is often added for flavor. Usually served with hot pudding and other hot desserts.

Objectives
1. To teach the student the procedure for preparing hard sauce.
2. To teach the student how to serve hard sauce.

Equipment
1. Small electric mixer and paddle
2. Cup measure

Ingredients: Approx. yield: 1 qt.
1 cup butter
3 cups powdered sugar
  brandy, rum, or vanilla, to taste

Preparation
1. Have all equipment and ingredients handy.

Procedure
1. Place the butter in the electric mixer bowl and, using the paddle, cream the butter at slow speed until light.
2. Add the powdered sugar gradually while mixing at slow speed.
3. When sugar is all added, increase the speed to second position and beat until mixture is smooth.
4. Add the vanilla or liqueur and chill before serving with hot puddings and other hot desserts.

Note: The sauce can be rolled in 8 oz. pieces, in waxed paper, sealed and refrigerated until ready to use. To serve, unwrap and slice as needed.

Precautions and safety measures
1. When mixing, do not let the paddle come in contact with the metal of the bowl. This would give a metallic taste and discolor the hard sauce.

Melba Sauce

This is a raspberry-flavored dessert sauce. It can be served either hot or cold with such popular items as crepes, coupes, and parfaits.

Objectives
1. To teach the student the procedure for preparing Melba sauce.
2. To teach the student how to serve Melba sauce.

Equipment
1. Sauce pot, 2-qt.
2. Baker's scale
3. Small stainless steel bowl
4. Wooden spoon
5. 1-qt. stainless steel container

Ingredients: Approx. yield: 1 qt.
2 lb. fresh raspberries
1 lb. currant jelly
1 lb. sugar
4 oz. water
2 oz. cornstarch or clear jel
4 oz. water

Preparation
1. Clean the fresh raspberries, removing any stems and washing berries thoroughly in cold water.
2. Have all equipment and ingredients handy.

Procedure
1. Place the raspberries, currant jelly, sugar, and first amount of water in a sauce pot. Place on the range and bring to a boil.
2. Place the starch in a small stainless steel bowl, add the second amount of water, and stir with a wooden spoon until thoroughly dissolved.
3. Pour the dissolved starch into the boiling mixture while stirring rapidly with a wooden spoon.
4. Bring the mixture back to a boil, and pour into a stainless steel container.
5. Serve 2 oz. per portion, using a ladle, over crepes, coupes, and parfaits.

Precautions and safety measures
1. After the starch is added to the liquid stir occasionally to avoid scorching.

MISCELLANEOUS SAUCE RECIPES

Oriental sweet-sour sauce

Oriental sweet-sour sauce is a tangy, sweet-sour sauce now closely associated with Oriental cuisine. It is an excellent sauce to serve with sautéed shrimp or with strips of pork.

Objective
1. To teach the student the procedure for preparing Oriental sweet-sour sauce.
2. To teach the student how to serve Oriental sweet-sour sauce.

Equipment
1. Qt. measure
2. Cup measure
3. Sauce pan, 2 qt.
4. Wire whip
5. Kitchen spoon
6. 2 qt. stainless steel container
7. Small bowl
   Ingredients: Approx. yield: 1 qt.
   1 qt. water
   1 pt. sugar
   1 cup vinegar, cider
   1 tbsp. soy sauce
   1 cup sweet pickle relish
   ¼ cup cornstarch
Preparation
1. Have all ingredients and equipment handy.
Procedure
1. In a sauce pan place the vinegar, sugar and all but one cup of the water and bring to a boil.
2. Dissolve the cornstarch in the remaining cup of water in a small bowl and add slowly to the boiling mixture, whipping constantly with a wire whip. Cook until smooth and fairly thick.
3. Add the sweet relish and soy sauce and simmer, stirring occasionally with a kitchen spoon.
4. Remove from the range and pour into a stainless steel container.
5. Serve 2 to 2½ ozs. per portion, using a ladle. Serve with sautéed shrimp, scallops or strips of pork.
Precautions and Safety Measure
1. Stir occasionally after the starch is added to avoid scorching.

Mint sauce

Mint sauce is a liquid with a fresh mint flavor served almost exclusively with roast lamb.
Objectives
1. To teach the student the procedure for preparing mint sauce.
2. To teach the student how to serve mint sauce.
Equipment
1. Sauce pan, 5 qt.
2. Kitchen spoon
3. 1 qt. measure
4. Baker's scale
5. 1 gal. stainless steel container
   Ingredients: Approx. yield: 1 gal.
   1 gal. water
   ½ pt. cider vinegar
   6 ozs. sugar
   12 oz. fresh mint leaves, chopped
Preparation
1. Chop mint leaves very fine with a French knife.
2. Have all equipment and ingredients handy.
Procedure
1. Place the water in the sauce pan and bring to a boil.
2. Add the remaining ingredients, simmer for 25 minutes and remove from range. Pour into a stainless steel container.
3. Serve 2 ozs. per portion, either hot or cold, in a soufflé cup, with roast or potted lamb.
Precautions and Safety Measures
1. Use caution when chopping the mint.

GRAVY RECIPES

Roast beef gravy

Roast beef gravy is a brown gravy with the flavor of roast beef. The flavor is acquired by using the drippings left in the roast pan after the beef is done.
Objectives
1. To teach the student the procedure for preparing roast beef gravy.
2. To teach the student how to serve roast beef gravy.
Equipment
1. Sauce pot, 6 qts.
2. Wire whip
3. Qt. measure
4. Baker's scale
5. China cap
6. 1 gal. stainless steel container
   Ingredients: Approx. yield: 1 gal.
   1 gal. beef or brown stock
   12 ozs. fat (from roast pan) or shortening
   10 ozs. flour
   ½ cup tomato purée
   caramel color if desired
   salt and pepper to taste

Preparation
1. Prepare beef or brown stock (See Chap. 12.)
2. Pour dripping from roast pan in stainless steel container and deglaze the pan with the stock.
3. Have all equipment and ingredients handy.

Procedure
1. Place the fat (from roast pan) or shortening in a sauce pot and heat.
2. Add the flour, making a roux, and cook until it is slightly brown.
3. Add the hot stock, whipping rapidly with a wire whip until slightly thickened and smooth.
4. Add the tomato purée and simmer for 20 minutes.
5. Season with salt and pepper. Strain through a china cap into a stainless steel container.
6. Serve 2 to 2½ ozs. per portion, using a ladle, over each order of roast beef.

Precautions and Safety Measures
1. Stir occasionally while the gravy is simmering to avoid sticking.

Roast veal gravy

Roast veal gravy is a brown gravy with the flavor of roast veal. The flavor is acquired by using the drippings left in the roast pan after the veal is done.

Objectives
1. To teach the student the procedure for preparing roast veal gravy.

Equipment
1. Sauce pot, 6 qt.
2. Wire whip
3. Qt. measure
4. Baker's scale
5. China cap
6. 1 gal. stainless steel container

Ingredients: Approx. yield: 1 gal.

1	gal. veal or brown veal stock
12	ozs. fat (from roast pan) or shortening
10	ozs. flour
½	cup tomato purée
	caramel if desired
	salt and pepper to taste

Preparation
1. Prepare veal or brown veal stock (See Chap. 12.)
2. Pour drippings from roast pan into a stainless steel container and deglaze the pan with the stock.
3. Have all equipment and ingredients handy.

Procedure
1. Place the fat (from roast pan) or shortening in a sauce pot and heat.
2. Add the flour, making a roux, and cook until it is slightly brown.
3. Add the hot stock, whipping rapidly with a wire whip until slightly thickened and smooth.
4. Add the tomato purée and simmer for 20 minutes.
5. Season with salt and pepper. Strain through a china cap.
6. Serve 2 to 2½ ozs. per portion, using a ladle, over each order of roast veal.

Precautions and Safety Measures
1. Stir occasionally while the gravy is simmering to avoid sticking.

Roast pork gravy

Roast pork gravy is a brown gravy containing the flavor of the roast pork. The flavor is obtained by deglazing the pan after the pork roast is done.

Objectives
1. To teach the student the procedure for preparing roast pork gravy.
2. To teach the student how to serve the roast pork gravy.

Equipment
1. Kitchen spoon
2. Sauce pot, 6 qts.
3. Baker's scale
4. China cap
5. 1 gal. stainless steel container
6. Gal. measure
7. Wire whip
8. Cup measure

Ingredients: Approx. yield: 1 gal.

12	ozs. fat (from roast pan) or shortening
10	ozs. flour
1	gal. brown pork stock
½	cup tomato purée
	salt and pepper to taste
	caramel color if desired

Preparation

1. Prepare the brown pork stock (See Chap. 12.)
2. After the roast is done deglaze the roast pan with the hot stock.
3. Have all equipment and ingredients handy.

Procedure

1. Place the fat in sauce pot and heat.
2. Add the flour, making a roux, and cook until flour is slightly brown.
3. Add the hot stock, whipping vigorously with a wire whip until slightly thick and smooth.
4. Add the tomato purée and simmer for 20 minutes.
5. Season with salt and pepper. If gravy is too light, adjust color by adding a small amount of caramel color.
6. Strain through a china cap into a stainless steel container.
7. Serve 2 to 2½ ozs. per portion, using a ladle, over each order of roast pork.

Precautions and Safety Measures

1. Stock must be hot before adding it to the roux.
2. Stir occasionally while the gravy is simmering to avoid scorching.

Roast lamb gravy

Roast lamb gravy is a brown gravy with the flavor of the roast lamb. This flavor is acquired by using the drippings left in the roast pan after the roast is done.

Objectives

1. To teach the student the procedure for preparing roast lamb gravy.
2. To teach the student how to serve roast lamb gravy.

Equipment

1. Sauce pot, 6 qts.
2. Baker's scale
3. Spoon measure
4. Wire whip
5. China cap
6. 1 gal. stainless steel container

Ingredients: Approx. yield: 1 gal.

12	ozs. fat (from roast pan)
10	ozs. flour
1	gal. brown lamb or mutton stock
2	tbsp. marjoram
	salt and pepper to taste

Preparation

1. Prepare brown lamb or mutton stock. (See Chap. 12.)
2. When the lamb roast is done, pour the stock into the roast pan and bring to a boil on the range. By deglazing the pan in this way all the flavor can be utilized.
3. Have all equipment and ingredients handy.

Procedure

1. Place the fat in a sauce pot and heat.
2. Add the flour, making a roux, and cook until flour browns slightly.
3. Add the hot stock, whipping vigorously with a wire whip until gravy is slightly thick and smooth.
4. Add the marjoram and simmer for 30 minutes.
5. Season with salt and pepper. Strain through a china cap into a stainless steel container.
6. Serve 2 to 2½ ozs. per portion, using a ladle, over each order of roast lamb.

Precautions and Safety Measures

1. Stock must be hot before adding it to the roux.
2. Stir occasionally while the gravy is simmering to avoid scorching.

Giblet gravy

Giblet gravy can be prepared in two different ways. The cooked, chopped giblets can be added either to a *brown* or to a *light* turkey gravy. Both kinds are excellent to serve with roast turkey. It is just a matter of preference. (If a *light* gravy is desired, omit the purée and caramel color. If a *plain* light or brown gravy is desired, omit the giblets.)

Objectives

1. To teach the student the procedure for preparing giblet gravy.
2. To teach the student how to serve giblet gravy.

Equipment

1. Sauce pot, 6 qts.
2. Baker's scale
3. Gal. measure
4. Cup measure
5. Wire whip
6. China cap
7. Kitchen spoon

8. 1 gal. stainless steel container
9. Food grinder

Ingredients: Approx. yield: 1 gal.
12 ozs. chicken or turkey fat
10 ozs. flour
6 lbs. giblets, cooked, ground
1 gal. chicken or turkey stock
(include pan drippings from roast chicken or turkey)
salt and pepper to taste
½ cup tomato purée (for brown gravy only)
caramel color as desired (for brown gravy only)

Preparation
1. Prepare chicken or turkey stock (See Chap. 12.)
2. Boil the giblets and grind on a food grinder using the medium chopper plate.
3. Have all equipment and ingredients handy.

Procedure
1. Place the fat in a sauce pot and heat.
2. Add the flour, making a roux, and cook until light brown.
3. Add the stock, whipping vigorously with a wire whip until slightly thick and smooth.
4. If preparing a *light* turkey gravy, season and strain through a china cap into a stainless steel container and then add the ground giblets. If making a *brown* turkey gravy, add the tomato purée and caramel color and continue to simmer for 15 minutes. Season and strain through a china cap into a stainless steel container. Add the ground giblets. (NOTE: If a *plain* light or brown gravy is desired, the ground giblets are omitted.)
5. Serve 2 to 2½ ozs. per portion. Serve this sauce with roast chicken or turkey.

Precautions and Safety Measures
1. Be extremely cautious when using the food grinder.
2. When adding the stock to the roux, be sure the stock is hot. Whip vigorously to eliminate lumps.
3. Exercise caution when adding the caramel color because a little goes a long way.

4. Be sure to include any drippings that are left in the roast pan. Also deglaze the roast pan to utilize all flavor.

Country gravy

Country gravy, also known as pan gravy, is made with milk and is light brown in color. This gravy is most frequently served with fried chicken and pork chops.

Objective
1. To teach the student the procedure for preparing country gravy.
2. To teach the student how to serve country gravy.

Equipment
1. Baker's scale
2. Qt. measure
3. Sauce pot, 6 qts.
4. China cap
5. Sauce pan, 4 qts.
6. Kitchen spoon
7. Wire whip
8. 1 gal. stainless steel container

Ingredients: Approx. yield: 1 gal.
1 lb. chicken, pork fat or butter
1 lb. flour
2 qts. milk
2 qts. chicken or brown pork stock
salt and pepper to taste

Preparation
1. Prepare chicken or brown pork stock (See Chap. 12.)
2. Heat the milk in a sauce pan.
3. Have all equipment and ingredients handy.

Procedure
1. Place the fat or butter in a sauce pot and heat.
2. Add the flour, making a roux, and cook until light brown.
3. Add the hot stock and milk, whipping vigorously with a wire whip until thick and slightly smooth.
4. Season with salt and pepper.
5. Strain through a china cap into a stainless steel container.
6. Serve 2 to 2½ ozs. per portion, using a ladle, with fried chicken or pork chops.

Precautions and Safety Measures
1. Brown the roux slightly, but do not let burn.
2. Exercise caution when straining the gravy.

beef preparation

■ Beef is the most popular of all the edible meats. There is more beef consumed in the United States each year than any other kind of meat. The average commercial establishment spends approximately 25 percent of its food dollar for meat. Since beef is so popular it is important that the kitchen personnel have some knowledge of this product.

Beef is the flesh of steers, heifers, cows, bulls and stags. Since the age and the sex has such a great influence on the taste and quality of the meat, it is important that we have an understanding of the five age and sex classes of the beef animal. This will help explain the variations in

the eating qualities of the carcass and the difference in price.

CLASSES OF THE BEEF ANIMAL

Steers: A steer is a young male that has been castrated when still a calf. These animals produce the best beef because they are superior in conformation, finish and quality. These are the important factors when grading meat. Most steers are about two and a half to three years old when they are marketed. They weigh about 650 to 1250 pounds, producing sides ranging in weight from 200 to 400 pounds. Most steers are grain fed which has a great bearing on the quality. Grain-fed animals are superior to grass-fed animals. Most steers are graded *prime* or *choice* (see *Beef Grading* this page).

Heifers: A heifer is a young female that has not borne a calf. They are a very compact animal and second only to the steer in conformation, finish and quality. Like the steer they are generally marketed when between two and a half to three years old. Heifers will mature and fatten faster than the steer, but steers are preferred because longer grain feeding will produce a better finish of outside fat. Most heifers are graded prime or choice —the two highest grades.

Cows: A cow is a female which has borne one or more calves. Cow meat generally has an uneven fat distribution, which is generally yellow in color. Slightly poor conformation and quality is also evident in cow meat. This meat is generally graded good, commercial or standard. Since cows are kept as long as they produce calves or milk, cow meat is only placed on the market when the animal's age is slightly advanced. Age, of course, influences grading of carcasses.

Stags: A stag is a male castrated after it has become sexually mature. Its meat is generally of poor quality, lacking finish, quality and conformation, and very little ever reaches the kitchens of the commercial establishment. Stags are generally graded commercial, utility, cutter and canner. A big percentage of this beef is used in canned meat products and dried beef.

Bulls: A bull is a male that is sexually mature and uncastrated. Bull meat shows a greater proportion of lean to fat and the flesh itself is very dark red which is one of the chief characteristics of any older animal. The meat has very poor finish, conformation, and quality so consequently it is graded low. Most bull meat is used in the making of sausage and dried beef.

BEEF GRADING

Meat grading is done to provide the purchaser with certain standards to follow when purchasing beef or other meats. Grading and inspection is done by the federal government if the packing house is engaged in interstate commerce. If not, this responsibility falls to the city, municipality or state in which the plant is located.

There are many stamps that appear on a side of beef. This sometimes creates confusion on the part of the purchaser or cook unless he is familiar with them. The largest, most important stamp is the federal inspection stamp, the round and purple one: *U.S. Insp'd & P'S'D.* This indicates the meat is U.S. inspected and passed. It has met minimum government standards and is fit for human consumption. It is stamped with a purple vegetable dye, which is harmless and does not have to be removed before cooking. The stamp also carries an identifying number which is the number assigned to the packing plant where the meat was processed.

The *grading stamp* on meat designates the quality of the meat. These stamps are also placed on the carcasses with the use of the harmless, purple vegetable dye. The grading is done by the federal meat inspector who represents the U.S. Dept. of Agriculture. He is a well-trained person with ready knowledge of the qualifications each beef grade must possess. The grading is based on three factors: finish, conformation and quality. *Finish* refers to the amount and color of fat on the outside and inside of the beef carcass. *Conformation* refers to the general build, shape and proportion of meat on the beef carcass. *Quality* refers to the color and texture of meat and bones and the marblization (mixture of fat and lean within the meat).

There are eight federal beef grades. These are, in their order of desirability: prime, choice, good, standard, commercial, utility, cutter and canner. Of these only four are pertinent to the food service establishment: prime, choice, good and commercial.

U.S. prime: This is the best beef available and comes mostly from prize steers and heifers. Of all the beef marketed in the United States only 4 percent is graded *prime*. Prime beef has a very high fat content which makes it extremely wasteful when it is trimmed for cooking. It is generally used in commercial establishments that have an expensive menu.

U.S. choice: This grade is the most popular and is produced in abundance. It has very good fat covering and good marblization of fat in the lean meat. It is the preference of most commercial establishments because there is not as much waste as in prime beef.

U.S. good: This grade is called the economical beef because one can hold down the menu price and still serve a fairly good product if it is cooked with care. Most beef graded *good* comes from grass-fed steers and heifers. In some cases corn-fed cows are graded *good*. This beef has a soft fat covering which is generally yellow in color. There is just a slight marblization of fat in the lean meat.

U.S. standard: This grade was created by the U.S. Dept. of Agriculture in 1959 and is between the good and commercial grades. Most *standard* beef is from young steers, heifers and cows. It has very poor conformation and little fat covering, depending on the age of the animal. It is not handled by many meat purveyors because it is not suitable for use in commercial food service establishments. It is sold mostly in retail outlets.

U.S. commercial: This grade comes mostly from older cows. It is tough meat and must be cooked by a lengthy cooking method, or treated with a meat tenderizer, for best results. Very little of it is used in the commercial kitchen. *Commercial* meat has poor conformation and although in some cases the fat covering is fair, it is yellow in color indicating an older animal.

U.S. utility: This grade comes mostly from stags, bulls and older cows. This grade is seldom, if ever, used in the commercial kitchen. It is tough meat and, like the commercial grade, must be cooked for a lengthy period of time or treated with a tenderizer. Some retail stores will carry it as block beef, but generally it is not a very popular grade.

U.S. cutter and *U.S. canner:* These grades of beef are very inferior and very tough. All cutter and canner beef comes from bulls and stags. It is largely used in canned meat products. The color of cutter and canner beef is dark red to a light brown and the flesh is soft and watery.

COMMERCIAL CUTS

Beef can be purchased in five different forms: by the side, quarter, wholesale or primal cuts, fabricated and retail. Retail cutting is of very little interest here because the method of cutting beef into units for the local supermarkets or meat markets is considerably different than the way it is prepared in a commercial kitchen. The main difference is that in preparing the meat for retail outlets the meat cutter leaves the undesirable fat and bone on the cut. In the commercial kitchen the meat cutter prepares the meat for immediate cooking and, for the convenience of the guest, he discards most of the unnecessary fat and bone.

The meat form best suited for the food service operator to purchase will, of course, depend on many things. The following are a few examples of the things that must be taken into consideration before the purchase is made.

1. Meat cutting skill of personnel.
2. Meat cutting equipment available.
3. Working space available.
4. Meat storage space available.
5. Utility of all cuts purchased.
6. Meat preparations served.
7. Overall economy of purchasing meat in a particular form.

A *side of beef* is a half of the complete carcass. It will range in weight from 225 to 450 pounds, the average weighing around 300 pounds. It can be purchased at a cheaper cost per pound than any of the market forms, but one must take into consideration many factors before purchasing beef in this form. Are facilities, equipment and people with know how available to block it out into individual units? Can all the cuts be utilized and made into desirable entrée dishes that will sell? Can fat or suet be rendered and used for frying and can bones be used for stock? Only the purchaser can decide whether or not purchasing beef by the side is economical. Each food service establishment necessarily differs, so what is best for one may not be right for the other. A number of years ago a large percentage of the food service establishments purchased their beef by the side. Today, that is no longer true. Apparently two big reasons for the change are: (1) lack of trained personnel for blocking out a side of beef, and (2) emphasis of speed that is put on all departments of the food service establishment today.

A *quarter of beef* is a side divided into two parts. The front or forepart is called the forequarter, the back or hind part

is called the hindquarter. The side is divided into quarters by cutting between the 12th and 13th ribs, leaving 12 ribs on the forequarter and 1 rib on the hind quarter. The hindquarter contains the most desirable meat and, therefore, the cuts are more in demand and the price is higher. On the other hand, since the forequarter contains the less desirable cuts, the price is generally lower. It is more economical for the food service operator to create desirable entrees using meat of the forequarter.

The *forequarter* of beef when blocked out consists of five wholesale or primal cuts: the rib, chuck or shoulder clod, brisket, shank, and short plate or naval. Of these the rib cut is the best because it comes from the part of the animal where the muscles are used the least. The *hindquarters* consist of four wholesale or primal cuts: the round, flank, rump, and sirloin (sirloin and short loin). Of these the sirloin, which is sometimes cut in half and called the sirloin and short loin, is the best. Again it comes from that part of the animal where the muscles are used the least. The sirloin is the steak meat and is always very much in demand. Before the food service operator decides to purchase his beef in this form he must take into consideration the same factors that would govern his decision for purchasing by the side.

The *wholesale or primal cuts* are parts of the forequarter and hindquarter of beef. There are, as stated before, five wholesale cuts in the forequarter and four in the hindquarters. This is a very popular way of purchasing beef today because it will reduce labor cost, save time, require less refrigeration space, and less expensive equipment will be needed. One must also consider the availability of adequate cutting space and properly trained personnel to cut the wholesale cuts into desired units for cooking with the least amount of waste.

Fabricated cuts are prepared espe-

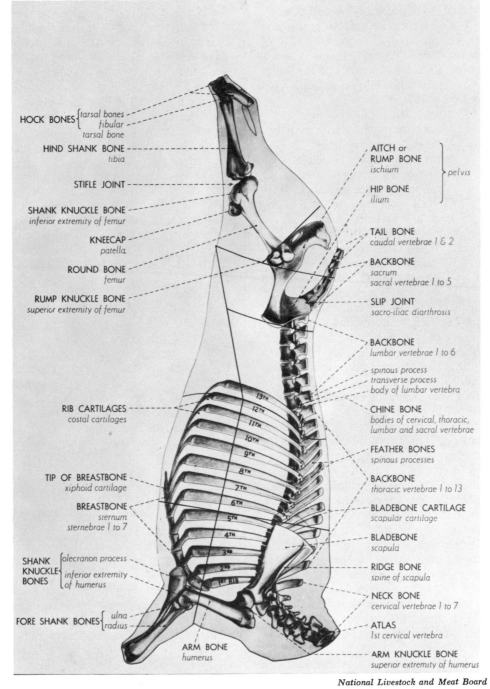

HOCK BONES { tarsal bones / fibular tarsal bone

HIND SHANK BONE — tibia

STIFLE JOINT

SHANK KNUCKLE BONE — inferior extremity of femur

KNEECAP — patella

ROUND BONE — femur

RUMP KNUCKLE BONE — superior extremity of femur

RIB CARTILAGES — costal cartilages

TIP OF BREASTBONE — xiphoid cartilage

BREASTBONE — sternum / sternebrae 1 to 7

SHANK KNUCKLE BONES { olecranon process / inferior extremity / of humerus

FORE SHANK BONES { ulna / radius

ARM BONE — humerus

AITCH or RUMP BONE — ischium } pelvis

HIP BONE — ilium

TAIL BONE — caudal vertebrae 1 & 2

BACKBONE — sacrum / sacral vertebrae 1 to 5

SLIP JOINT — sacro-iliac diarthrosis

BACKBONE — lumbar vertebrae 1 to 6

spinous process / transverse process / body of lumbar vertebra

CHINE BONE — bodies of cervical, thoracic, lumbar and sacral vertebrae

FEATHER BONES — spinous processes

BACKBONE — thoracic vertebrae 1 to 13

BLADEBONE CARTILAGE — scapular cartilage

BLADEBONE — scapula

RIDGE BONE — spine of scapula

NECK BONE — cervical vertebrae 1 to 7

ATLAS — 1st cervical vertebra

ARM KNUCKLE BONE — superior extremity of humerus

National Livestock and Meat Board

Beef skeleton: Location, structure and names of bones.

Retail Cuts

Wholesale Cuts

Retail Cuts

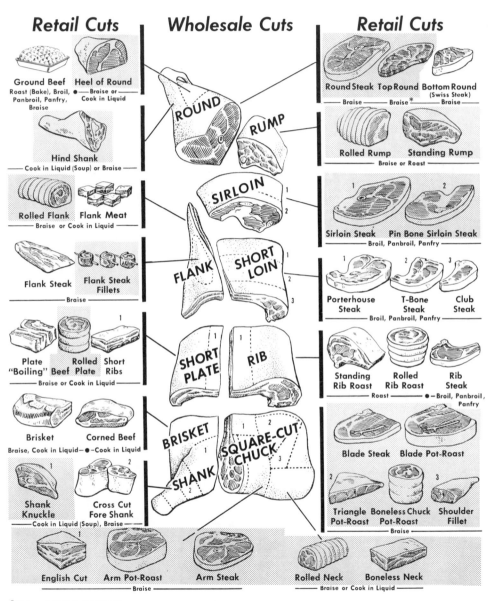

Ground Beef
Roast (Bake), Broil, ●—Braise or
Panbroil, Panfry,   Cook in Liquid
Braise

Heel of Round
—Braise or
Cook in Liquid—

Hind Shank
— Cook in Liquid (Soup) or Braise —

Rolled Flank   Flank Meat
— Braise or Cook in Liquid —

Flank Steak   Flank Steak Fillets
—————— Braise ——————

Plate   Rolled   Short
"Boiling" **Beef Plate** **Ribs**
——— Braise or Cook in Liquid ———

Brisket   Corned Beef
Braise, Cook in Liquid—●—Cook in Liquid

Shank Knuckle   Cross Cut Fore Shank
—Cook in Liquid (Soup), Braise—

English Cut   Arm Pot-Roast   Arm Steak
————————— Braise —————————

ROUND

RUMP

SIRLOIN

FLANK   SHORT LOIN

SHORT PLATE   RIB

BRISKET   SQUARE-CUT CHUCK

SHANK

Round Steak   Top Round   Bottom Round
(Swiss Steak)
— Braise — — Braise* — — Braise —

Rolled Rump   Standing Rump
— Braise or Roast —

Sirloin Steak   Pin Bone Sirloin Steak
— Broil, Panbroil, Panfry —

Porterhouse   T-Bone   Club
Steak   Steak   Steak
— Broil, Panbroil, Panfry —

Standing   Rolled   Rib
Rib Roast   Rib Roast   Steak
— Roast — ●—Broil, Panbroil, Panfry

Blade Steak   Blade Pot-Roast

Triangle   Boneless Chuck   Shoulder
Pot-Roast   Pot-Roast   Fillet
————— Braise —————

Rolled Neck   Boneless Neck
——— Braise or Cook in Liquid ———

*Prime and choice grades may be
broiled, panbroiled or panfried

National Livestock and Meat Board

Beef Chart: Meat cuts and common cooking methods. Cuts shown in grey are not commonly used in the commercial kitchen in the form shown.

cially for the food service operator. They are ready-to-cook meats cut or packaged to certain specifications of quality, size, and weight. This is the most convenient and popular way of purchasing meat today because it eliminates trimming waste, provides uniform portions, controls the cost, eliminates the need of expensive cutting equipment and, most importantly, cuts labor cost. However, before deciding to purchase fabricated cuts the price per pound must be given a great deal of consideration. It will be comparatively high.

WHOLESALE CUTS: COOKING METHODS

The following is a list of the nine wholesale cuts of beef, their chief characteristics and the best cooking methods to use when preparing them in the commercial kitchen. They will be listed in the order of their importance and popularity in food service establishments.

Sirloin: The best cut on a side of beef. It is sometimes cut into two sections called the sirloin and short loin. The sirloin contains two different kinds of meat: sirloin on the outside and tenderloin on the inside. For this reason the Europeans contend that the meat should be separated into its two parts so each cut will have only one kind of meat. When cut by the European method one will have such steaks as strip sirloin, New York sirloin, Filet Mignon, Chateaubriand, minute steak, and tenderloin steaks. The American method of cutting the loin is to leave the T-bone and tenderloin on the sirloin. Cutting cross sections, starting from the end close to the rib cut, one would acquire club steaks, T-bone steaks and porterhouse steaks. The club steaks are the first three cuts from the sirloin and contain little or no tenderloin. The T-bone contains both sirloin and tenderloin meats and the porterhouse contains sirloin and the largest amount of tenderloin. Porterhouse is the best of the steaks cut by the American method.

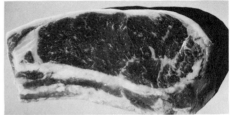

National Livestock and Meat Board

Club steak

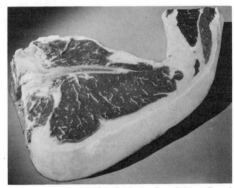

National Livestock and Meat Board

T-Bone steak

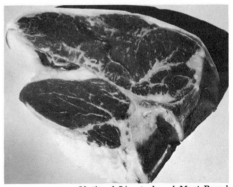

National Livestock and Meat Board

Porterhouse steak

The whole sirloin cut comes from a section of the animal where the muscles are used the least and it is, therefore, very tender meat and must be cooked by a quick cooking method such as broiling or sautéing. The sirloin in many cases is also roasted. (The tenderloin when removed from the underside of the whole sirloin cut may also be roasted.) Sirloins graded prime and choice have excellent fat covering and good marblization, which supplies juices to the meat when cooked. The sirloin cut can be improved by *aging*. Aging is a term applied to meats that are held at a temperature of 34° to 36°F for a certain period of time (time depends on kind and cut of meat) to improve tenderness.

Beef steaks are prepared by the broiling method. (See Chapter 6 for the proper procedure of how to broil.) The following steaks are cooked by broiling: Chateaubriand, Filet Mignon, T-bone steak, porterhouse steak, tenderloin steak, club steak, Delmonico or rib steak, and flank steak.

Rib: The best cut from the forequarter of beef and the only cut from the forequarter that can be improved by aging. The rib contains 7 of the 13 rib bones found on a side. These 7 ribs help make the rib cut the best beef cut for roasting because they form a natural rack. The rib can be easily identified, not only because of the 7 ribs, but also because of the large muscle of meat called the "rib eye" which is a continuation of the sirloin. Ribs graded prime, choice, and good generally have excellent fat covering and extremely good marblization which are the characteristics needed to make an excellent roast. The average weight of a rib is 20 to 25 pounds and, although there is some waste in trimming for cooking, about 75 to 80 percent of this cut is usable. In commercial kitchens the rib is generally roasted and is one of the most popular items to appear on the dinner menu. However, one can also cut steaks from the smaller ribs. These are called Delmonico or rib steaks and in recent years have been increasing in popularity. Short ribs are also extracted from the rib cut when the rib is trimmed for roasting. They make excellent short ribs since there is generally a sizeable portion of lean meat on them. Another preparation is to remove the 7 rib bones, roll up the meat and secure it with butcher twine. This roast is called a rolled rib. Although this type of roast is used in the commercial kitchen, it is not ordinarily a popular item.

Round and rump: This is the hind leg of the beef and when blocked out as a

National Livestock and Meat Board
Standing rib roast

National Livestock and Meat Board
Rolled rib roast

commercial cut it includes the rump. When the round cut is boned completely it will consist of five pieces: rump, top round, bottom round, knuckle or tip, and shank meat. When trimmed for cooking about 70 to 75 percent of this cut is usable. This cut has proven to be very versatile in the commercial kitchen and is used in such preparations as Swiss steak, pot roast, sauerbraten, beef rouladen, etc. It is a fairly tough cut of beef because it comes from a section of the animal where the muscles were used extensively and, for this reason, must be cooked by a lengthy cooking method, such as roasting, braising, stewing, or cooking in water. The round with the shank and rump removed also makes a fine roast for buffets and smorgasbords. This type of roast is referred to as a Chicago round or steamship round roast.

Chuck: This is sometimes referred to as the shoulder clod chuck; it includes that section of the forequarter which contains the first 5 rib bones. It is a fairly tough cut of beef but is fairly lean and possesses excellent flavor. When trimmed for cooking it will produce about 75 to 85 percent usable meat. The chuck like the round has become a very versatile piece of meat in the commercial kitchen. It is used for the preparation of such profitable items as meat loaf, beef stew, Salisbury steak, goulash and ragout. Because the meat is slightly tough it must be cooked at some length or used in items which call for ground beef.

Brisket: This cut contains layers of both lean and fat. It is a thin section of meat with breast bones and short sections of the rib bone present. It has long muscle fibers which run in several directions thus making it difficult to slice. The brisket is a tough cut of beef but excellent in flavor when cooked by a lengthy cooking method. In a commercial kitchen the brisket is used in the preparation of pot roast, sauerbraten, corn beef, and boiled beef.

National Livestock and Meat Board

Beef brisket

Shank: This cut is the lower foreleg of the side of beef and contains a big percentage of bone but little meat. It is seldom purchased for use in the commercial kitchen. It is possible to use it as ground beef or in beef stew, but the chuck is far superior for these preparations.

Flank: This section of the hindquarters is thin and flat. It has long coarse fibers and a larger percentage of fat to lean. It contains one flank steak which, after the fat covering is removed, is a fairly desirable piece of meat. The steak is oval shaped, thin, boneless, and has long muscle fibers running through it and weighs about 1½ pounds. It should be scored or cubed before cooking. Besides the flank steak, very little flank is ever used in commercial kitchens.

Short plate: This is sometimes referred to as the navel, it is a thin portion of the forequarter which lies opposite the rib cut. The bones of this cut are the remaining sections of the rib bones. It consists of layers of both fat and lean and is a very undesirable cut of beef. In the commercial kitchen short plate is sometimes used in the preparation of short ribs, but the short ribs cut from the end of the rib cut are far superior because they contain more lean meat. The average housewife would use this type of beef for soup meat.

VARIETY MEATS

There are other edible parts of beef beside the wholesale or primal cuts. These are known by various names, among which are variety meats, meat specialties, meat sundries, and glandular meats. They include brains, liver, tripe, heart, sweetbreads, tongue, kidney and oxtail. These items have been regarded as delicacies for a long time, but only in recent years have they captured the fancy of the average person and achieved an important place on today's menu.

Liver: Beef liver is the largest and least tender of all the edible livers. It is covered with a very thin membrane which should be removed before slicing. For best results, liver should be partly frozen when it is sliced. Cut at a 45° angle for larger and nicer slices. Beef liver is best when broiled or sautéed and should always be cooked medium unless otherwise specified by the guest.

Tongues: Beef tongues are the most popular of all the edible tongues. They may be purchased smoked, pickled, fresh and corned, but smoked is generally the most popular. Cooking in water is the method by which tongue is always prepared. Feel the tip to test the tenderness of a tongue while boiling. When it is soft the tongue is done. After it is cooked it is cooled in cold water, skinned and stored in the refrigerator. While it is under refrigeration it is covered with water. After the tongue is cooked and skinned it is served cold or reheated and served hot.

Tripe: This is the muscular inner lining of the stomach of meat animals. The most desirable tripe is known as honeycomb tripe. It is the lining of the second stomach of beef. Tripe may be purchased pickled, fresh or canned. The fresh tripe is generally cooked at the packing house before it is sold. However, before serving by other methods, it should be further cooked by simmering in water for about one hour. Tripe may be fried, creamed, served cold with vinaigrette dressing or used as an ingredient in Philadelphia pepper pot soup.

Sweetbread: Beef sweetbreads are the thymus glands of the beef. There are two kind of sweetbreads in a beef animal: the heart sweetbreads, which are the best, and the throat sweetbreads. Sweetbreads come from calves, veal and young beef because as the beef animal matures the thymus gland will disappear. The usual procedure for the preparation of sweetbreads is to blanch them as soon as they are received. The blanching should be done by simmering in a mixture of water, salt, and lemon juice or vinegar for about 10 minutes. The presence of lemon juice or vinegar will keep the sweetbreads white and firm. After blanching all membranes should be removed and the sweetbreads kept in water under refrigeration. When the sweetbreads are blanched, they may be prepared for service by utilizing other cooking methods such as sautéing, braising, broiling, or frying.

Brains: These are much like sweetbreads in tenderness and texture. They do not keep well so they should be used as soon as possible after purchasing. When brains are delivered to the commercial kitchen they are first placed in a solution of cold water, salt, and lemon juice or vinegar then left to soak awhile (approximately 1 hour). This is done so it will be easier to remove the outer membrane. After the membrane is removed, the brains are parboiled for about 15 minutes in another solution of water, vinegar or lemon and salt. The presence of acid in the solution keeps the brains white and firm. After the brains are processed in this manner they may then be breaded and fried or floured and sautéed for a more attractive appearance.

Heart: The heart, like the tongue, is tough because it has received quite a bit of exercise. It is the toughest of all the variety meats. The heart should be washed thoroughly in warm water and some of the arteries and veins cut away before cooking. Soaking the heart in vinegar will improve its tenderness. The heart can be made delicious and tender by slow moist cooking. Simmering or braising are the normal cooking methods with a time element of about 3½ hours for proper tenderness. The heart is very seldom used in the commercial kitchen and hardly, if ever, found on the menu of a food service establishment.

Oxtail: This is sometimes called ox-joint or beef joint; it is the tail of the beef animal. It has considerable bone but also possesses a good portion of meat and a very fine and rich flavor. Oxtail is most popular when used in stew. The thin end of the tail can be used in oxtail soup. When cutting the tail into sections for cooking, use a French knife and cut at the joints. Do not splinter bone by using a cleaver.

Kidneys: Beef kidneys are distinguished by the many irregular lobes divided by deep cracks. Their average weight is about 1 pound. Before cooking, all suet and urinary canals must be carefully removed. Beef kidneys are the toughest of the edible animal kidneys and therefore should be cooked by moist heat. Braising or cooking in water are the recommended methods. Kidneys are highly prized by many chefs and several kidney entrees, such as kidney stew, pie and steak have become famous.

BEEF TERMINOLOGY

There are certain terms associated with beef purchasing that have come into being over the years. An understanding of these terms can be helpful to a student preparing for a career in the food service trade because part of his responsibility may be purchasing beef.

Grain-fed beef is obtained from cattle that were grain-fed for a period of ninety days to a year. The best grades of beef, U.S. Prime, and U.S. Choice, are grain fed in drylots (feeding pens). Most grain fed beef animals are marketed in April and May.

Grass-fed beef is obtained from cattle that were raised on grass with little or no special feed. Most of the grass-fed animals are marketed during the fall months of the year. This type of beef is generally graded U.S. Good or U.S. Standard.

Baby beef is a term applied to beef cattle less than eighteen months of age. The baby beef carcasses will weigh about 400 to 550 pounds. This type of beef is tender, but lacks the pronounced flavor of mature beef.

Calf carcasses and beef dressed veal are from animals too large to be sold as veal, but not eligible for carcass beef. These carcasses will weigh from 150 to 375 pounds.

Branded beef is beef with a trade mark or trade name that is used by some packers to indicate their own grades. These brands are sometimes placed on a product by some packers even though they were already graded by the U.S. Dept. of Agriculture.

Aging is a term applied to meat that is held at a temperature of 34° to 36°F to develop certain factors of palatability, particularly tenderness and flavor. To be suitable for aging, the meat must have a thick fat covering to prevent shrinkage and discoloration of the lean meat. Only the higher grades of beef, lamb, and mutton have a sufficient amount of fat covering to withstand the aging period. Aging does not improve pork and veal. Usually only the loins and ribs of beef are aged.

BEEF RECIPES

The recipes which follow are popular beef and beef variety meat recipes. These are generally popular in every food service establishment over the nation. If the student has a knowledge of these preparations the possibility of success in the culinary trade will be enhanced.

Roasted or baked beef
(Pages 335 to 342)

Roast sirloin of beef
Roast rib or standing rib of beef
Roast round of beef
Meat loaf
Stuffed green peppers
Stuffed cabbage
Italian meat balls

Braised and stewed beef
(Pages 342 to 356)

Beef pot pie
Beef stroganoff
Hungarian goulash
Swiss steak
Beef ragout
Sauerbraten
Pot roast of beef
Chinese pepper steak
Oxtail stew
Spanish steak
Beef à la Deutsch
Braised short ribs of beef
Sautéed beef tenderloin tips in mushroom sauce
Beef Bourguignonne
Beef mandarin
Beef rouladen
English beef stew
Swiss steak in sour cream

Broiled beef
(Pages 356 to 357)

Cheddar steak
Beef tenderloin en brochette
Salisbury steak

Boiled beef
(Pages 358 to 359)

Boiled fresh brisket of beef
Roast beef hash

Beef variety meats
(Pages 359 to 362)

Braised sweetbreads (and variations)
Sautéed beef liver
Braised kidneys
Tripe creole
Fried brains

ROASTED OR BAKED BEEF RECIPES

Roast sirloin of beef

Roast sirloin of beef, the sirloin with the tenderloin and all bones removed, makes an excellent roast for parties or buffets or for use on the dinner menu. The meat can be roasted in a short time, is easy to carve and contains a large portion of lean meat. It is one of the most tender beef cuts available.

Objectives
1. To teach the student how to prepare the sirloin for roasting.
2. To teach the student how to roast the sirloin.
3. To teach the student how to carve and dish up the sirloin.

Equipment
1. Roasting pan
2. Kitchen fork
3. French knife
4. Ladle
5. Hotel pan
6. Baker's scale
7. Bake pan

Ingredients: Approx. yield: 50 servings

25	lbs. sirloin of beef, boneless
1½	lbs. onions, cut rough
½	lb. carrots, cut rough
½	lb. celery, cut rough
1	gal. beef stock, hot
	salt and pepper to taste

Preparation
1. Cut onions, carrots and celery rough with a French knife.
2. Trim sirloin and prepare meat for roasting. Proceed only after demonstration by instructor.
3. Season sirloin the day before roasting with salt and pepper. Season lean side.
4. Preheat oven to 400°F.
5. Prepare the beef stock. (See Chap. 12.)
6. Have all equipment and ingredients handy.

Procedure

1. Place sirloin in roast pan, fat side down.
2. Place in the oven at a temperature of 400°F until thoroughly brown.
3. Reduce temperature to 350°F. Turn the meat over with a kitchen fork. Add rough garnish and continue to roast until desired degree of cooking is obtained: rare, medium or well done.
4. When the sirloin is cooked, remove to a clean bake pan and hold in a warm place. Roast should set at least ½ hour before slicing to order with a French knife.
5. Pour fat off drippings in the roast pan. Add the hot beef stock and simmer gently for about 20 minutes.
6. Strain the natural meat juice (au jus) through a china cap and cheese cloth into a stainless steel container. Adjust seasoning and skim off any excess grease with a ladle before serving.
7. Roast sirloin of beef is sliced with a French knife as ordered. It may be served with other sauces besides the au jus, for example, bordelaise, béarnaise, mushroom, Burgundy and Bercy would be excellent choices.

Precautions and Safety Measures

1. If drippings evaporate during roasting, add a small amount of water.
2. Exercise caution when handling the knife.

Roast rib or standing rib of beef

The length of time required to roast a rib or standing rib of beef depends upon the weight of the roast, the quality of the beef, and the way the roast is to be finished: rare, medium or well done. Scientific research proves that low temperature roasting reduces shrinkage and therefore yields more portions. The average weight of a rib of beef is 20 to 25 pounds and takes from three to three and a half hours to roast, medium rare in the center and medium towards each end. There are always two outside and a few inside well done cuts. Although several acceptable theories on how to roast a rib of beef exist, the following is the one most commonly used in the commercial kitchen.

Objectives

1. To teach the student the procedure for roasting a rib of beef.

Armour and Co.

Roast rib of beef

2. To teach the student how to remove a rib of beef from the roast pan.
3. To teach the student how to stand a rib of beef for the purpose of carving.
4. To teach the student the use of the roasted bones and the beef drippings.

Equipment

1. Roast pan
2. Kitchen fork
3. French knife
4. Heavy towel
5. Bake pan, med. size
6. Butcher's twine
7. Boning knife
8. 1 gal. stainless steel container
9. Cheese cloth
10. Sauce pot, 4 qts.
11. Ladle
12. Baker's scale
13. Meat saw
14. Spoon measure
15. Pt. measure

Ingredients: Approx. yield: 30 servings

20	lbs. rib of beef
8	ozs. onions, cut rough
8	ozs. celery, cut rough
8	ozs. carrots, cut rough
1	pt. water (variable)
	salt and pepper to taste

Preparation

1. Prepare the rib of beef for roasting. Cut off short ribs, remove blade bone, separate the feather bones from the rib

bones (do not remove bones), and tie the rib with butcher's twine. The boning is to be done by the student cook only after the instructor's demonstration.

2. Cut the onions, carrots and celery rough with a French knife.

3. Preheat the oven to a temperature of 350°F.

4. Have all equipment and ingredients handy.

Procedure

1. Place the roast in a roasting pan rib side up.

2. Sprinkle salt and pepper over the ribs and place in the oven at 350°F. Roast until the complete surface of the roast is brown (approximately one hour).

3. Remove the roast pan from the oven. With a kitchen fork and heavy towel lift the rib of beef from the roasting pan. Pour off the rendered fat that has collected in the roast pan; discard.

4. Place the rib of beef back into the roast pan, rib side down, and return to the oven.

5. Add the rough garnish (onions carrots and celery cut rough) and continue roasting until the garnish becomes light brown.

6. Add approximately 1 pt. of water to keep vegetables from getting dry and natural drippings from burning.

7. Reduce oven temperature to 325°F and continue to roast until rare, medium or done as desired. Total roast time will vary from 3 to 3½ hours.

8. Remove the roast from the roasting pan, by using the same method explained in Step No. 3. Place the roast in a bake pan, set in a warm place for 1 hour.

9. Pour the drippings and vegetable garnish into a gal. container. Deglaze the roast pan by adding approximately one-half gal. of water to the pan and bringing it to a boil on the range to dissolve crusted juices that have dried on the bottom and sides of the pan. Pour this flavorful liquid into the same container as the drippings and save for the preparation of au jus (natural juice) which usually accompanies each order of roast rib of beef.

10. Using a French knife remove the butcher

twine and feather bones from the roast, save the bones.

11. Stand the roast in the steam table by placing the largest end of the roast down and the small end up. The beef is now ready to be carved; however, the carving should only be done by a student cook after the instructors demonstration.

Note: The au jus or au natural liquid which is usually served with each order of roast rib of beef is prepared as follows: Place the liquid and vegetables, saved from the roast pan, and all the bones removed from the roast into a sauce pot. Add one tablespoon of Worcestershire sauce and salt to taste. Simmer for 15 minutes. Skim off all fat using a ladle and strain through a china cap covered with a cheese cloth into a stainless steel container. Serve 1½ oz., using a ladle, with each portion of beef.

Precautions and Safety Measures

1. Low roasting temperature reduces shrinkage.

2. Add water only if drippings evaporate and vegetable garnish becomes dry.

3. Tie the rib before roasting, so it will hold shape while cooking.

4. Exercise caution when removing the roast from the pan and pouring the grease and drippings.

Roast round of beef

Roast round of beef is one of the most popular meat entrees to be found in restaurants today. It is the roasted hind leg of the beef animal. It produces lean servings and a very rich and flavorful gravy. It is an excellent choice for both luncheon and dinner menus.

Objectives

1. To teach the student how to cut and tie the roast.

2. To teach the student how to roast the round.

3. To teach the student how to slice and dish up the roast round.

4. To teach the student how to prepare the gravy.

Equipment

1. Baker's scale

2. Qt. measure

3. French knife

4. Sauce pot, 2 gal.

5. Wire whip
6. Kitchen fork
7. China cap
8. Ladle
9. 2 gal. stainless steel container

Ingredients: Approx. yield: 50 servings

25	lbs. boneless beef round, cut into 4 or 5 lb. pieces.
1	lb. onions, cut rough
½	lb. celery, cut rough
½	lb. carrots, cut rough
1	lb. shortening
12	ozs. flour
1½	gal. beef or brown stock
1	cup tomato purée
	salt and pepper to taste

Preparation

1. Cut round into 4 or 5 lb. individual roasts, tie with butcher's twine. Proceed only after demonstration by instructor.
2. Cut the vegetables rough with a French knife.
3. Prepare the beef or brown stock. (See Chap. 12.)
4. Season the meat with salt and pepper the day before roasting.
5. Preheat the oven to 375°F.
6. Have all equipment and ingredients handy.

Procedure

1. Place the meat in the roast pan, put into the oven and roast at a temperature of 375°F until meat is thoroughly brown. Turn occasionally with a kitchen fork.
2. Add the rough garnish (onions, carrots and celery) continue to roast until vegetables are slightly brown. Reduce the oven temperature to 325° to 350°F.
3. Add a small amount of beef or brown stock, continue to roast until the meat is done. Approximate time is 2½ to 3 hours, depending on size of roast and degree of doneness.
4. Remove the meat from the roast pan and place in a steam table pan. Keep in a warm place. Add the beef or brown stock to the roast pan to deglaze the pan. Pour into a stainless steel container and hold.
5. Place the shortening in a sauce pot and heat. Add the flour, making a roux, and cook slightly.
6. Add the hot stock and tomato purée, whipping vigorously with a wire whip un-

til slightly thick and smooth. Cook for 15 minutes. Strain through a fine china cap back into the stainless steel container.
7. Slice meat with a French knife or on a slicing machine across the grain. Serve 4 to 5 ozs. per portion covered with gravy.

Precautions and Safety Measures

1. Turn roast frequently, while roasting, with a kitchen fork.
2. When adding the stock to the roux, whip vigorously with a wire whip to avoid lumping.
3. Use caution when handling the knife.

Meat loaf

Meat loaf is ground beef bound together by the use of soaked bread and eggs. It is an item in which a tough cut of beef can be used and is an excellent item for the luncheon menu.

Objectives

1. To teach the student how to mix the meat loaf.
2. To teach the student how to bake and dish up the meat loaf.

Equipment

1. French knife
2. Baker's scale
3. Pt. measure
4. Pans for baking
5. Mixing machine with grinder attachment
5. Skillet
6. 4 gal. mixing container or stainless steel dish pan
7. Full steam table pan

Ingredients: Approx. yield: 50 servings

13	lbs. boned beef, chuck
½	oz. salt
8	whole eggs
1	pt. milk
1	lb. 8 oz. bread, trimmed
8	oz. salad oil
1	lb. celery, minced
3	lbs. onions, minced
¼	oz. thyme
¼	oz. fresh ground black pepper

Preparation

1. Grind boned beef chuck on a food grinder, using a medium chopper plate.
2. Mince onions and celery with a French knife.
3. Light oven, preheat at 350°F.

Oscar Mayer and Co.

Meat loaf

4. Have all equipment and ingredients handy.

Procedure

1. Sauté onions and celery in a skillet in oil until tender and let cool.
2. Place bread in large mixing bowl and add milk. Mix thoroughly with the hands until smooth.
3. Add eggs, sautéed celery and onions and seasoning.
4. Add ground beef and mix thoroughly with the hands. If mixture is too moist, adjust consistency by adding bread or cracker crumbs.
5. Form into 3 lb. loaves and place in greased pans, lightly oiling the outside of the loaves.
6. Bake at 350°F for about 1½ hours. Remove from oven, let cool and place in the refrigerator overnight.
7. Slice the cold meat loaf with a French knife into 5 or 6 oz. portions, place in a steam table pan. Reheat in steamer or on the steam table. Serve with an appropriate sauce.

Precautions and Safety Measures

1. Bake meat loaf the day before serving since it slices better when cold.
2. Pack the meat mixture solidly in the pans.
3. Exercise caution when handling the knife.

Stuffed green peppers

Stuffed green peppers are excellent for the luncheon menu and also profitable when green peppers are in season. Slightly poached green pepper halves, stuffed with meat-rice mixture and baked in the oven, are used. They are generally served with creole or tomato sauce.

Objectives

1. To teach the student the procedure for making stuffed green peppers.
2. To teach the student how to clean, blanch and stuff green peppers.
3. To teach the student how to bake and dish up stuffed green peppers.

Equipment

1. French knife
2. Large braising pot and cover
3. Food grinder
4. Large kitchen spoon
5. Roast pans
6. Baker's scale
7. Measuring spoons
8. Collander
9. Bake pan
10. 2 full steam table pans

Ingredients: Approx. yield: 50 servings

25	green peppers
11	lbs. cooked beef or cooked beef and ham (boiled or baked leftovers may be used)
3	cloves garlic, minced
3	lbs. onions, minced
1	#10 can tomatoes, crushed
1	qt. tomato purée
2	tbsp. chili powder
3	tbsp. paprika
1	qt. water
	salt and pepper to taste
1½	cups salad oil
2½	lbs. rice, raw

Preparation

1. Grind the cooked meat on a food grinder using the coarse chopper plate.
2. Mince onions and garlic using a French knife.
3. Crush tomatoes by hand.
4. Cut, clean and blanch the green peppers as follows: Cut each pepper in half with a French knife, remove all seeds, being careful not to break the pepper cup. Place the peppers in a sauce pot. Cover with water and cook by simmering until the peppers are partly cooked. Remove from the heat and drain in a collander; let cool.

5. Preheat oven to 375°F.
6. Have all equipment and ingredients handy.
   Procedure
1. Place salad oil in braising pot. Add the minced onions and garlic and sauté without browning.
2. Add the crushed tomatoes, tomato purée and the water. Allow to boil until the onions are tender. Stir occasionally with a kitchen spoon.
3. Add the chili powder and paprika and continue to boil.
4. Add the cooked beef or ham and beef and bring back to a boil.
5. Add the raw rice and season with salt and pepper.
6. Cover the pot and place in the preheated oven. Bake until the rice absorbs the liquid and is tender (approximately 45 minutes).
7. Remove from oven and check seasoning. Place in a bake pan to cool overnight in refrigerator.
8. Remove meat-rice mixture from refrigerator. Stuff green pepper halves, which have been cleaned and blanched, and place in roast pans meat side up.
9. Place a small amount of water in roast pan and bake at 375°F until tops become slightly brown. Remove from oven and place the peppers in a steam table pan.
10. Serve one-half pepper per portion with tomato or creole sauce.
   Precautions and Safety Measures
1. Exercise caution when mincing the onions and garlic, grinding the meat, and cutting the peppers.
2. When blanching the green peppers do not overcook or they will be difficult to stuff and bake.
3. Let the meat-rice mixture cool before placing in the refrigerator.

Stuffed cabbage

Stuffed cabbage is excellent for the luncheon menu. For this item slightly poached cabbage leaves are filled with a meat-rice mixture. The meat-rice mixture is made from cooked meat and, therefore, is an excellent item to serve when using cooked meat leftovers.

Objectives
1. To teach the student the procedure for making stuffed cabbage.
2. To teach the student how to poach and stuff the cabbage.
3. To teach the student how to bake and dish up the stuffed cabbage.
   Equipment
1. Roast pan
2. French knife
3. Large braising pot and cover
4. Kitchen spoon
5. Baker's scale
6. Measuring spoons
7. Food grinder
8. 5 gal. stock pot
9. Large bake pan
10. 2 full steam table pans
    Ingredients: Approx. yield: 50 servings

6	large heads of cabbage
11	lbs. cooked beef or cooked beef and ham (boiled or baked leftovers may be used)
3	lbs. onions, minced
3	cloves garlic, minced
1	#10 can tomatoes, crushed
1	qt. tomato purée
2½	lb. rice, raw
2	tbsp. chili powder
2	gal. brown gravy
3	tbsp. paprika
1	qt. water
1½	cups salad oil
	salt and pepper to taste

    Preparation
1. Remove cores from cabbage heads and place cabbage in a stock pot; cook in boiling water until slightly tender or until leaves can be removed from the head easily. Cook cabbages on the day they are to be used.
2. Mince onions and garlic with a French knife.
3. Crush tomatoes by hand.
4. Grind cooked meat on food grinder using a coarse chopper plate.
5. Prepare brown gravy. (See Chap. 15.)
6. Preheat oven to 375°F.
7. Have all equipment and ingredients handy.
   Procedure
1. Place salad oil in braising pot. Add the minced onions and garlic sauté without browning.

2. Add the crushed tomatoes, tomator purée and the water; let boil until the onions are tender. Stir occasionally with a kitchen spoon.
3. Add the chili powder and paprika and continue to boil.
4. Add the cooked beef or ham and beef and bring back to a boil.
5. Add the raw rice and season with salt and pepper.
6. Cover pot and place in preheated oven and bake until the rice absorbs the liquid and is tender (approximately 45 minutes).
7. Remove from oven and check seasoning. Place in a bake pan to cool. Refrigerate overnight.
8. Remove meat-rice mixture from the refrigerator, place cabbage leaves (about 2 or 3 leaves for each ball) on a kitchen towel, place a ball of the meat-rice mixture on the cabbage leaves and draw the towel tight. Repeat this process until all the cabbage leaves and meat-rice mixture are used up.
9. Place stuffed cabbage in roast pan. Place in oven and bake at 375°F for about 20 minutes. Baste with half the brown gravy. Continue to bake for 30 minutes more. Remove from oven. Place in steam table pans.
10. Serve one ball per portion with remaining brown gravy.

Precautions and Safety Measures
1. When poaching (boiling) the cabbage, do not overcook.
2. Exercise caution when mincing the onions and garlic and grinding the meat.
3. Let meat-rice mixture cool before placing in the refrigerator.

Italian meat balls

Italian meat balls are a ground beef product. They are highly seasoned and are bound by eggs and softened bread. They are most often served with some sort of Italian pasta and sauce.

Objectives
1. To teach the student how to prepare the meat ball mixture.
2. To teach the student how to form and bake the meat balls.

Equipment
1. Baker's scale
2. French knife
3. Cup measure
4. Spoon measure
5. Meat grinder
6. Mixing container, approx. 5 gal.
7. Sheet pans
8. Kitchen spoon
9. Skillet

Ingredients: Approx. yield: 50 servings

12	lbs. beef chuck, boneless
3	lbs. onions, minced
2	tbsp. garlic, minced
1	cup salad oil
1½	lb. bread, cubed
2	cups milk
8	whole eggs, slightly beaten
½	cup parsley, chopped
1	cup Parmesan cheese, grated
1	tbsp. oregano
1	tsp. basil
	salt and pepper to taste

Preparation
1. Cut the beef chuck into pieces that will pass through the food grinder. Use a French knife.
2. Mince onions and garlic with a French knife.
3. Cut bread into cubes with a French knife.
4. Chop the parsley with a French knife.
5. Preheat oven to 350°F.
6. Have all equipment and ingredients handy.

Procedure
1. Sauté the garlic and onion in the salad oil in a skillet.
2. Combine the bread and milk in mixing container and blend well by stirring with a kitchen spoon.
3. Add the sautéed onions and garlic, the pieces of beef, Parmesan cheese, oregano, basil, salt and pepper and blend thoroughly by hand.
4. Pass the mixture through the food grinder twice, using the medium hole chopper plate.
5. Add the parsley and beaten whole eggs, blend thoroughly. Check seasoning.
6. Form into balls by hand and place on greased sheet pans.
7. Bake in a preheated 350°F oven until done. Serve on top of pasta covered with a rich Italian sauce. The number of balls

to a serving will depend on the size. Size may range from 1 in. to 2 in. in diameter.

Precautions and Safety Measures
1. When forming the balls rub hands with a small amount of salad oil for best results.
2. Do not let the onions and garlic brown when sautéing.
3. After grinding, add bread crumbs to take up the moisture if mixture is too wet or loose.
4. Exercise caution when using the knife.

BRAISED AND STEWED BEEF RECIPES

Beef pot pie

Beef pot pie is very similar to beef stew, but it is served with a flaky pie crust topping. This is an excellent entree for the luncheon menu.

Objectives
1. To teach the student how to cut the meat and vegetables.
2. To teach the student how to prepare beef pot pie.
3. To teach the student how to dish up beef pot pie.

Equipment
1. Braising pot and cover
2. French knife
3. Sauce pans, (2) 4 qt. and (1) 2 qt.
4. Kitchen spoon
5. Baker's scale
6. Qt. measures
7. China cap
8. Deep steam table pan
9. Rolling pin
10. Sheet pans

Ingredients: Approx. yield: 50 servings

15	lb. beef round or chuck cut into 1 in. cubes
2	gal. brown stock, hot
1	pt. salad oil
1	lb. flour
1	qt. tomato purée
3	lbs. carrots, medium dice
½	#10 can, small whole onions, drained
1	#10 can small whole potatoes, drained
2½	lb. peas, frozen
2	lb. celery, medium dice
1	tsp. ground thyme
2	bay leaves
	salt and pepper to taste
50	baked pastry cut outs

Preparation
1. Cut the beef round or chuck with a French knife into 1 in. cubes. Proceed only after demonstration by instructor.
2. Cut carrots and celery with a French knife into medium size dice (½ in. by ½ in.).
3. Drain canned onions and potatoes.
4. Preheat oven to 350°F.
5. Prepare brown stock. (See Chap. 12.)
6. Prepare pastry cut outs, using pie dough. (See Chap. 25.) Roll out dough with a rolling pin to a thickness of ⅛ in. Cut out disc large enough to cover the top of serving casserole. Bake cut outs on sheet pans.
7. Have all equipment and ingredients handy.

Procedure
1. Place a small amount of salad oil in the braising pot and heat. Add the cubes of meat and brown thoroughly.
2. Add the remaining salad oil and flour, blend well with a kitchen spoon making a roux and cook slightly.
3. Add the hot brown stock, tomato purée, bay leaves and thyme. Stir with a kitchen spoon. Cook until thickened and smooth.
4. Place in oven at 350°F, cover and cook for about 2 to 2½ hours until meat is tender.
5. Boil all raw vegetables in separate sauce pans in salt water until tender. Drain through a china cap.
6. When the meat is tender, remove from oven. Remove bay leaves and add all the drained cooked vegetables except the peas.
7. Check seasoning and place in a deep steam table pan.
8. Dish up in deep casseroles with a 6 to 8 oz. ladle. Sprinkle cooked peas over each portion and top with a baked pastry cut out.

Precautions and Safety Measures
1. Do not overcook the meat, it will crumble when served.
2. When the flour is added to make the roux, be sure to cook roux slightly or the pot pie will have a raw flour taste.
3. Use caution when handling the knife.
4. Exercise caution when removing the lid from the braising pot, steam will escape.

Beef stroganoff

A braised beef preparation made with sour cream. It is popular on the dinner menu.

Objectives
1. To teach the student the procedure for making beef stroganoff.
2. To teach the student how to sauté the meat.
3. To teach the student how to dish up beef stroganoff.

Equipment
1. Braising pot
2. French knife
3. Skillet
4. Baker's scale
5. Measuring cup
6. Qt. measure
7. Kitchen spoon
8. 1 full steam table pan

Ingredients: Approx. yield: 50 servings

10	lbs. beef tenderloin tips or thin strips of beef (round)
1	lb. minced onions
½	cup shortening
2	cups flour
3	qts. beef stock
1	qt. sour cream
1	cup tomato purée
	salt and pepper to taste
2	bay leaves
2	lbs. sliced mushrooms
½	cup cider vinegar

Preparation
1. Cut beef round or tenderloin into thin slices (approx. 2 in. by 2 in.).
2. Mince onions and slice mushrooms with a French knife.
3. Have all equipment and ingredients handy.

Procedure
1. Place shortening in skillet and heat. Add beef and sauté until brown.
2. Add minced onions and continue to sauté.
3. Place beef and onions in braising pot, add flour taking up the liquid, and cook for 5 minutes.
4. Add beef stock, bay leaves, tomato purée and vinegar; cover and cook until the meat is tender.
5. Sauté sliced mushrooms in a separate skillet, with additional shortening, until tender and add to the cooked beef.
6. Stir in the sour cream, with a kitchen spoon, until thoroughly incorporated.
7. Season with salt and pepper. Remove bay leaves.
8. Bring mixture to a simmer and remove from the range. Place in a steam table pan.
9. Dish up with a ladle, placing a 4 to 5 oz. portion in a shallow casserole with buttered noodles.

Precautions and Safety Measures
1. When sautéing onions, do not over-brown.
2. Add sour cream to hot liquid slowly, stirring constantly.
3. When using tenderloin, cooking time is greatly reduced.
4. Exercise caution when handling the knife.

Hungarian goulash

Hungarian goulash is a type of stew, served mostly on the luncheon menu. It is highly seasoned with paprika to give it the characteristic flavor we associate with Hungarian dishes.

Objectives
1. To teach the student the procedure for making Hungarian goulash.
2. To teach the student how to cut the meat.
3. To teach the student how to mince the onions and garlic.
4. To teach the student how to dish up Hungarian goulash.

Equipment
1. Roast pan or braising pot
2. French knife
3. Kitchen spoon
4. Cover, for braising pot
5. Baker's scale
6. 1 full steam table pan

Ingredients: Approx. yield: 50 servings

18	lbs. beef chuck or shoulder
1	oz. minced garlic
8	ozs. flour (variable)
¾	ozs. chili powder
5	ozs. paprika
1	lb. tomato purée
8	lb. or 4 qt. water or brown stock
	salt and pepper to taste
2	bay leaves
½	oz. caraway seed
2	lb. minced onions

Preparation
1. Dice beef in 1 inch squares using a French knife. Proceed only after demonstration by instructor.

2. Mince onions and garlic using a French knife.
3. Prepare brown stock, if to be used. (See Chap. 12.)
4. Have all equipment and ingredients handy.

Procedure
1. Place diced beef in roast pan or braising pot, whichever is preferred, and brown in oven.
2. Add minced onions and garlic and continue to brown for 5 minutes.
3. Add flour by sprinkling over the beef and stir with a kitchen spoon until flour is incorporated with the beef.
4. Add paprika and chili powder in the same manner as the flour was added. Cook 5 minutes.
5. Add tomato purée and water or brown stock.
6. Season with salt, pepper, bay leaves and carraway seed.
7. Return to oven and cook until meat is very tender.
8. Remove from the oven. Remove bay leaves and place in a steam table pan.
9. Dish up with a ladle, placing 6 ozs. in an individual casserole with buttered spaetzles or noodles. (The recipe for spaetzles is given in Chapter 12.)

Precautions and Safety Measures
1. While beef is cooking, if too much liquid should disappear, add more brown stock or water.
2. While beef is cooking stir occasionally.
3. Exercise caution when handling the knife.

Swiss steak

Swiss steak is served on both luncheon and dinner menus. Since a tougher cut of beef is generally used, Swiss steak is cooked in its own gravy to make it tender.

Objectives
1. To teach the student the procedure for making Swiss steak.
2. To teach the student how to cut Swiss steaks.
3. To teach the student how to dish up Swiss steak.

Equipment
1. Roast pan with cover
2. Skillet
3. French knife
4. Butcher knife

5. Kitchen spoon
6. 2 gal. sauce pot
7. Wire whip
8. Full steam table pans

Ingredients: Approx. yield: 50 servings
50 round steaks, cut ½ in. thick (6 ozs.)
1 lb. onions, minced
2 cloves garlic, minced
12 ozs. tomato purée
6 qts. water or brown stock
3 cups salad oil
12 ozs. bread flour (variable)
    salt and pepper to taste

Preparation
1. Cut steaks with a butcher knife. Proceed only after demonstration by instructor.
2. Mince onions and garlic using a French knife.
3. Prepare brown stock, if to be used. (See Chap. 12.)
4. Preheat oven to 350°F.
5. Have all other equipment and ingredients handy.

Procedure
1. Heat oil in fry pan or skillet and brown steaks on both sides.
2. Place browned steaks in braiser or roast pan and hold.
3. Place minced onions and garlic in skillets where steaks were browned and sauté.
4. Add flour, mixing a roux, and stir with a kitchen spoon until flour is well blended and lightly browned. Remove this mixture to a sauce pot.
5. Add hot brown stock (or water) and tomato purée while whipping with a wire whip. Cook until sauce is slightly thickened.
6. Season with salt and pepper.
7. Pour sauce over steaks. Cover and bake in 350°F oven for about 2 hours or until steaks are tender.
8. Remove from the oven and place in steam table pans. Serve one steak to each order with 2½ to 3 ozs of sauce.

Precautions and Safety Measures
1. Exercise caution when handling the knife.
2. When sautéing onions and garlic do not let them over-brown.
3. When testing steaks when they are in the oven, remove cover with caution to avoid steam.
4. Do not overcook the steaks or they will fall apart when served.

Beef ragout

Beef ragout is a thick, highly seasoned, brown stew served mostly on the luncheon menu.

Objectives

1. To teach the student the procedure for making beef ragout.
2. To teach the student how to cut the beef.
3. To teach the student how to cut the vegetables.
4. To teach the student how to dish up beef ragout.

Equipment

1. French knife
2. Qt. measure
3. Measuring cups
4. Braising pot
5. Baker's scale
6. 3 sauce pans, 4 qt. each
7. 1 sauce pan, 2 qt.
8. 2 deep steam table pans

Ingredients: Approx. yield: 50 servings

20	lbs. beef chuck or shoulder, lean, cut into 1 in. cubes
4	cups salad oil
1	lb. onions, large dice
1	lb. celery, large dice
1½	lb. flour
2	gal. brown or beef stock, hot
1	pt. tomato purée
100	½ in. cubes of carrots
100	½ in. cubes of rutabaga
100	½ in. cubes of potatoes
50	small onions
2½	lb. box green peas, frozen
3	#2½ cans Italian tomatoes, drained salt and pepper to taste

Preparations

1. Cut beef into cubes with a French knife. Proceed only after demonstration by instructor.
2. Cut carrots, rutabaga and potatoes into ½ in. cubes with a French knife.
3. Dice celery and onions with a French knife.
4. Prepare brown or beef stock. (See Chap. 12.)
5. Cook thawed peas in salt water in a sauce pan.
6. Preheat oven to 400°F.
7. Have all equipment and ingredients handy.

Procedure

1. Place salad oil in braiser and heat. Add the beef cubes and sauté until brown.
2. Add the celery and onions and continue to sauté until slightly tender.
3. Add the flour, making a roux, and cook for 5 minutes.
4. Add the hot stock and stir with a kitchen spoon until thick and smooth.
5. Add the tomato purée, cover braiser, place in a 400°F oven and cook until meat cubes are tender.
6. Cook remaining vegetables separately, except tomatoes, in sauce pans until just tender then drain.
7. When meat is tender remove from oven and add the tomatoes and drained vegetables, except green peas, to the ragout. Season with salt and pepper to taste.
8. Return to oven for half an hour. Remove and place in deep steam table pans.
9. Dish up in deep casseroles with a 6 to 8 oz. ladle. Garnish each portion with the cooked green peas.

Precautions and Safety Measures

1. Do not overcook the meat or vegetables.
2. Cut vegetables as uniformly as possible, so they will cook evenly.
3. Use caution in handling the knife.

Sauerbraten

Sauerbraten is a sour beef dish which originated in Germany. It is always found on the menu of establishments featuring German cuisine. To be prepared properly, the beef must be marinated in a souring solution for a period of 3 to 5 days.

Objectives

1. To teach the student the procedure for preparing sauerbraten.
2. To teach the student how to marinate the beef.
3. To teach the student how to slice and dish up sauerbraten.

Equipment

1. Large crock or wooden barrel
2. French knife
3. Kitchen spoon
4. Braising pot and cover
5. Sauce pot, 3 gal.
6. Kitchen fork
7. China cap
8. Wire whip
9. Rolling pin
10. Bake pan
11. Baker's scale

12. Qt. measure
13. Butcher's twine

Ingredients: Approx. yield: 50 servings

25	lbs. beef, round or beef brisket
6	qts. water, cold
2	qts. red wine vinegar
2	lbs. onions, cut rough
1	lb. carrots, cut rough
½	lb. celery, cut rough
½	lb. brown sugar
4	cloves garlic, chopped
2	ozs. salt
6	bay leaves
1	tsp. peppercorns, crushed
15	ginger snaps, crushed
	shortening and flour for roux as needed

Preparation

1. Cut and tie the round of beef into separate roast or, if using brisket, cut into medium sized pieces and trim. Proceed only after demonstration by instructor.
2. Cut onions, carrots and celery rough with a French knife.
3. Clean out crock or barrel.
4. Crush ginger snaps with a rolling pin.
5. On the day of preparation preheat oven to 400°F.
6. Have all equipment and ingredients handy.

Procedure

1. Place the meat in a large crock or barrel.
2. Cover with a solution made by combining the water and red wine.
3. Add the garlic, rough garnish, salt, bay leaves, peppercorns and brown sugar.
4. Let the meat marinate in this solution from 3 to 5 days in the refrigerator.
5. Remove the meat from the marinade the night before using. Strain marinade through a china cap, saving both liquid and vegetable garnish.
6. Place the meat in a braising pot and brown thoroughly in the oven at 400°F.
7. Add the drained vegetable garnish and continue to roast for about 15 minutes or until vegetable garnish becomes slightly brown.
8. Add the marinade liquid, cover and continue to cook until meat is tender.
9. Remove meat from the liquid with a kitchen fork. Place in a hotel pan, cover with a damp cloth and keep warm.
10. In a separate sauce pot place the short-ening, add flour, making a roux (1 lb. shortening, ½ lb. flour for each gal. of liquid). Cook roux slightly.
11. Add the liquid the meat was cooked in to the roux, whipping constantly with a wire whip until slightly thick and smooth.
12. Add the crushed ginger snaps and simmer for about 10 minutes. Check seasoning, strain through a fine china cap into a stainless steel container and hold for service.
13. Slice the beef across the grain with a French knife or on the electric slicing machine.
14. Serve 3 ozs. per portion with the prepared sauce, accompanied with potato pancakes, potato dumplings, buttered noodles or spaetzles.

Precautions and Safety Measures

1. Do not overcook the meat, if overcooked there will be too much crumbling when it is sliced.
2. Always slice meat across the grain.
3. Keep the cooked meat covered at all times with a damp cloth. Air dries the meat out quickly.
4. The desired sweet or sour flavor of the sauce can be controlled by varying the amount of the vinegar and brown sugar.
5. If a dark sauce is desired, some brown flour may be added when preparing the roux. Brown the flour in the oven.
6. Use caution when handling the knife.

Pot roast of beef

Pot roast of beef is cooked by the braising method. A tougher cut of beef can be used and made tender by this lengthy cooking method. Since the browned beef is cooked in its own gravy, most of the flavor is in the sauce or gravy.

Objective

1. To teach the student how to prepare pot roast.
2. To teach the student how to slice and dish up the cooked meat.

Equipment

1. Baker's scale
2. Measuring cups
3. French knife
4. Qt. measure
5. Measuring spoons
6. Large skillet or frying pans

7. China cap
8. Braiser or heavy pot
9. Sauce pot
10. Kitchen spoon
11. Kitchen fork
12. 2 gal. stainless steel container
13. Full steam table pans

Ingredients: Approx. yield: 50 servings

25	lbs. beef brisket or round
2	cups salad oil
1	lb. onions, cut rough
$\frac{1}{2}$	lb. celery, cut rough
$\frac{1}{2}$	lb. carrots, cut rough
1	lb. bread flour (all purpose can be used)
5	qts. beef or brown stock, hot
1	#2$\frac{1}{2}$ can tomatoes, crushed
1	bay leaf
$\frac{1}{2}$	tsp. thyme, ground

Preparation

1. Trim meat. If using round, cut into individual 5 lb. roasts and tie. Proceed only after demonstration by instructor.
2. Cut the onions, carrots and celery rough with a French knife.
3. Prepare the beef or brown stock. (See Chap. 12.)
4. Preheat oven to 400°F.
5. Have all ingredients and equipment handy.

Procedure

1. Place oil and meat in braising pot. Place in the oven and brown meat on all sides at 400°F.
2. Add onions, celery and carrots and continue to cook for an additional 15 minutes.
3. Blend in flour and cook 10 minutes. If roux is too thick, add more oil.
4. Add hot stock and stir with a kitchen spoon until thickened and smooth.
5. Add tomatoes, juice and seasoning and mix well.
6. Cover and cook at 400°F for about 2$\frac{1}{2}$ hours or until meat is tender. Remove from the oven.
7. Remove the meat from the gravy with a kitchen fork and let the meat cool. Strain the gravy through a china cap into a stainless steel container. Adjust seasoning.
8. Slice the meat against the grain with a French knife or on the electric slicing machine. Place in a steam table pan and reheat on the steam table or in the steamer.

9. When dishing up serve approximately 3 ozs. of meat with 2$\frac{1}{2}$ ozs. of gravy. A jardiniere vegetable garnish (carrots, celery and turnips cut 1 in. long and $\frac{1}{4}$ in. thick) is usually served with each order of pot roast.

Precautions and Safety Measures

1. Exercise caution when cutting the vegetables.
2. Simmer the meat rather than boil so that the meat will be firmer and easier to slice.
3. Use care when straining the gravy to avoid getting burned.
4. Slice the meat only after a demonstration by the instructor.

Chinese pepper steak

Chinese pepper steak is an American-Chinese preparation. The thin slices of beef are cooked in a sauce highly flavored with green peppers and soy sauce.

Objectives

1. To teach the student how to slice the meat.
2. To teach the student how to cut the vegetables.
3. To teach the student how to prepare and dish up Chinese pepper steak.

Equipment

1. Baker's scale
2. French knife
3. Braising pot
4. Kitchen spoon
5. Qt. measure
6. Deep steam table pan

Ingredients: Approx. yield: 50 servings

12	lb. beef round, cut into thin slices
6	ozs. shortening
5	lbs. green peppers, cut julienne
3	lbs. onions, cut julienne
3	lbs. celery, cut julienne
6	ozs. pimientos, cut julienne
3	qts. beef stock
4	ozs. soy sauce
3	ozs. cornstarch (variable)
	salt and pepper to taste

Preparation

1. Slice the beef round on the bias (slanting slices against the grain of the meat) into thin slices. Proceed only after demonstration by the instructor.
2. Prepare the beef stock. (See Chap. 12.)
3. Cut julienne the green peppers, onions, celery and pimientos using a French knife.

4. Have all equipment and ingredients handy.

Procedure

1. Place the shortening in the braiser and heat. Add the sliced beef and brown.
2. Add the onion, celery and green peppers; continue to cook until vegetables are slightly done.
3. Add the beef stock and bring to a boil. Continue to cook until the celery and beef are tender.
4. Add the soy sauce to the cornstarch and dissolve. Pour into the boiling mixture, stirring constantly with a kitchen spoon until thick. Simmer for 5 minutes.
5. Add the pimientos and season with salt and pepper. Remove from the range and pour into a deep steam table pan.
6. Dish up in shallow casseroles with a 6 to 8 oz. ladle. Serve with baked or steamed rice.

Precautions and Safety Measures

1. Before adding the cornstarch be sure celery and beef are tender.
2. Add the dissolved cornstarch to the boiling mixture slowly while stirring constantly.
3. Exercise caution when using the knife.

Oxtail stew

Oxtail stew is a type of stew made from the tails of beef animals. It is similar to other stews in that it is a mixture of meat and vegetables; however, it is undesirable to some people because of the presence of the tail bones. It possesses an excellent flavor and is a fairly popular luncheon item.

Objectives

1. To teach the student how to prepare oxtail stew.
2. To teach the student how to cut the oxtail into sections.
3. To teach the student how to cut the jardiniere garnish.
4. To teach the student how to dish up oxtail stew.

Equipment

1. French knife
2. Baker's scale
3. Qt. measure
4. Braising pot and cover
5. Kitchen spoon
6. Skimmer
7. 4 sauce pans, (3) 4 qt. and (1) 2 qt.

8. Skillet
9. Deep steam table pan
10. Ladle

Ingredients: Approx. yield: 50 servings

30	lbs. oxtail, cut into sections
1	lb. shortening
1	lb. 4 ozs. flour
2	gal. beef or brown stock
1	qt. tomato purée
4	4 cloves garlic, minced
2	lbs. onions, minced
50	whole, canned small onions
3	lbs. carrots, cut jardiniere
2	lbs. celery, cut jardiniere
3	lbs. turnips, cut jardiniere
2	bay leaves
3	tbsp. salt
1	tsp black pepper
2½	lbs. box frozen peas

Preparation

1. Cut oxtail at the joints into serving pieces with a French knife. Proceed only after demonstration by instructor. Wash pieces thoroughly and dry.
2. Cut celery, carrots and turnips jardiniere (1 in. long and ¼ in. thick) using a French knife.
3. Mince onions and garlic with a French knife.
4. Prepare beef or brown stock. (See Chap. 12.)
5. Preheat oven to 400°F.
6. Have all other equipment and ingredients handy.

Procedure

1. Put the shortening in the braiser, place in oven at 400°F and heat. When the shortening is hot add the cut sections of oxtail. Season with salt and pepper and brown thoroughly. Turn oxtail with the skimmer.
2. Sprinkle the flour over the brown oxtails and blend thoroughly with a kitchen spoon. Continue to cook for 5 minutes.
3. Add the minced onions and garlic and cook slightly.
4. Add the beef or brown stock, tomato purée, thyme and bay leaves. Cover braiser and cook until oxtail is tender and the sauce is slightly thick. Remove the bay leaves.
5. In separate sauce pans, cook the carrots, celery, peas and turnips in boiling water until tender. Drain and add all to the stew except the peas.

6. Sauté the whole canned onions in a skillet with a small amount of additional butter or shortening. Add to the stew.
7. Remove the stew from the oven and place in a deep steam table pan.
8. Dish up in deep casserole with an 8 oz. ladle. Garnish each serving with the cooked peas.

Precautions and Safety Measures
1. After the oxtail are washed, be sure they are dried thoroughly before browning.
2. When cutting the oxtail use a French knife and cut at the joints. Do not use a cleaver or the bones will splinter. It is all right, however, to use a power saw if one is available.
3. When adding vegetables to the stew, stir gently with a kitchen spoon. Do not break up the vegetables.
4. While oxtails are cooking skim off the grease frequently with a ladle.

Spanish steak

Spanish steak is an individual 4 oz. steak, cut from a fairly tough cut of beef, but baked in a rich tomato, green pepper mixture until it becomes tender. This item is best for luncheon service.

Objectives
1. To teach the student how to cut the steaks.
2. To teach the student the procedure for preparing Spanish steak.
3. To teach the student how to dish up Spanish steak.

Equipment
1. French knife
2. Qt. measure
3. Baker's scale
4. Cup measure
5. Braising pot
6. Large fry pan
7. Sauce pot, 1 gal.
8. Cleaver

Ingredients: Approx. yield: 50 servings

14	lbs.	beef round, cut into 4 oz. steaks
6	ozs.	bread flour (variable)
3	cups	salad oil
2	qts.	beef stock
1		#10 can tomatoes, crushed
½		#10 can tomato purée
2	lbs.	onions, minced
1	lb.	celery, minced

10	ozs.	green peppers, minced
2		bay leaves
		salt and pepper to taste

Preparation
1. Cut the beef round into 4 oz. steaks with a French or butcher knife, flatten with a cleaver. Proceed only after demonstration by instructor.
2. Prepare the beef stock. (See Chap. 12.)
3. Mince the onions, celery and green peppers with a French knife. Crush the tomatoes by hand.
4. Preheat the oven to 350°F.
5. Have all equipment and ingredients handy.

Procedure
1. Place about ⅛ in. of oil in a large fry pan and heat. Add the steaks and brown thoroughly.
2. Place the browned steaks in a large braiser.
3. Sauté the onion, celery and green peppers in the remaining salad oil in a sauce pot. Do not brown.
4. Add the flour, making a roux.
5. Add the beef stock, tomatoes and tomato purée, stirring constantly with a kitchen spoon until thickened.
6. Pour the sauce over the steaks. Add the bay leaves and season with salt and pepper.
7. Place in preheated oven and bake at 350°F for about 2 hours or until steaks are tender.
8. Remove from the oven, remove bay leaves and place steaks and sauce in steam table pan.
9. Serve one steak per portion covered with the sauce and garnished with chopped parsley.

Precautions and Safety Measures
1. Do not overcook the steaks or they will crumble when served.
2. When the liquid is added to the roux, stir constantly.
3. Exercise caution when using the knife.

Beef à la Deutsch

Beef à la Deutsch is an excellent item to feature on the luncheon or dinner menu to use up left over tenderloin tips. These tips are left over when tenderloin or filet mignon steaks are cut. The sautéed tips are poached in a very tasty sauce.

Objectives

1. To teach the student how to slice the tenderloin tips.
2. To teach the student how to prepare beef à la Deutsch.
3. To teach the student how to dish up beef à la Deutsch.

Equipment

1. Qt. & pt. measure
2. Cup measures
3. Baker's scale
4. French knife
5. Sauce pot
6. Skillet

Ingredients: Approx. yield: 25 servings

7	lbs. beef tenderloin tips
1	cup salad oil (variable)
3	cups mushrooms, sliced thick
1½	cup green peppers, cut julienne
1	cup claret wine
2	cups onions, cut julienne
2	cups celery, cut julienne
5	shallots, minced
¾	tsp. garlic, minced
3	qts. rich brown gravy
1	pt. crushed canned tomatoes
	salt and pepper to taste
2	bay leaves

Preparation

1. Slice the tenderloin tips on the bias (slanting) about ¼ in. thick with a French knife. Proceed only after demonstration by instructor.
2. Prepare a brown gravy. (See Chap. 15.)
3. Crush the canned tomatoes by hand.
4. Mince shallots and garlic with a French knife.
5. Julienne the green peppers, celery and onions with a French knife.
7. Have all equipment and ingredients handy.

Procedure

1. Place about ½ cup of the salad oil in a sauce pot. Add the onions, shallots, garlic, green pepper, celery, and mushrooms. Sauté until slightly tender, but do not brown.
2. Add the claret wine and simmer for about 15 minutes. Add the bay leaves.
3. Add the brown gravy and continue to cook until the celery is tender, then remove the bay leaves.
4. Add the crushed tomatoes, continue to simmer.

5. Sauté the tenderloin tips in a skillet in the remaining oil until slightly brown, then add to the sauce and cook until the meat is very tender.
6. Season with salt and pepper, remove from the range and place in a steam table pan.
7. Dish up into shallow casseroles with a 6 to 8 oz. ladle, accompany with a scoop of baked rice.

Precautions and Safety Measures

1. Do not overcook the tenderloin, the meat will break apart.
2. Use caution when cutting the beef and vegetable garnish.

Braised short ribs of beef

Braised short ribs of beef is an excellent luncheon item. The best short ribs are cut from the end of the rib roast. Short ribs are a tough, but flavorful cut of beef. They are made tender by using the braising method of cooking.

Objectives

1. To teach the student how to cut and tie the short ribs.
2. To teach the student the procedure for preparing braised short ribs of beef.
3. To teach the student how to dish up braised short ribs of beef.

Equipment

1. French knife
2. Butcher twine
3. Braising pot
4. China cap
5. Ladle
6. Kitchen fork
7. Baker's scale
8. Qt. measure
9. Spoon measures
10. Cup measures
11. 1 qt. sauce pan
12. 2 full size steam table pans
13. 2 gal. stainless steel container

Ingredients: Approx. yield: 50 servings

50	short ribs (10 ozs. each)
1½	lbs. onions, minced
3	cloves garlic, minced
1	tsp. thyme
1	tsp. sweet basil
6	qts. beef stock, hot
1	pt. tomato purée
2	cups salad oil
1	lb. bread flour (variable)

salt and pepper to taste

Preparations

1. Trim ribs, remove fat and tie with butcher twine. Proceed only after demonstration by instructor.
2. Mince the onions and garlic with a French knife.
3. Prepare the beef stock. (See Chap. 12)
4. Preheat oven to 400°F.
5. Have all equipment and ingredients handy.

Procedure

1. Place the short ribs in braising pot, pour 1 cup of the salad oil over the short ribs. Place in a preheated oven at 400°F and brown thoroughly.
2. Sauté the minced onions and garlic in a sauce pan with cup of salad oil, spread evenly over the browned short ribs and continue to cook for 10 minutes more.
3. Sprinkle the flour over the short ribs using a kitchen spoon and blend well with the oil. Cook for 10 minutes.
4. Add the hot beef stock, stirring with a kitchen spoon until slightly thickened.
5. Add salt, pepper, thyme, basil and tomato purée and blend well.
6. Cover braising pot and continue to cook until short ribs are tender, about 2½ hours; turn meat occasionally with a kitchen fork.
7. Remove the cooked ribs to steam table pans, cover with a damp cloth. Strain the gravy through a fine china cap into a stainless steel container.
8. Adjust the seasoning and thickening. Remove excess grease with a ladle. Hold for service.
9. When dishing up remove butcher twine from short ribs and cover with gravy and a vegetable garnish cut in the jardiniere style (cut 1 in. long, ¼ in. thick).

Precautions and Safety Measures

1. Do not overcook the ribs.
2. Be sure that the gravy is not too thick. If it is too thick, thin by adding water or beef stock.
3. Exercise caution when removing cover from braising pot. Steam will escape.
4. When adding the herbs to the liquid, rub them in the palm of your hand to release the flavor.
5. Use caution when cutting with the French knife.

Sautéed beef tenderloin tips in mushroom sauce

Sautéed beef tenderloin tips in mushroom sauce is an item that can be prepared very quickly so it is generally prepared to order. It is an excellent item for the dinner or à la carte menu. The tenderloin tips require very little cooking.

Objectives

1. To teach the student how to slice the tenderloin tips.
2. To teach the student the procedure for preparing sautéed beef tenderloin tips in mushroom sauce.
3. To teach the student how to dish up sautéed beef tenderloin tips in mushroom sauce.

Equipment

1. Baker's scale
2. Qt. measure
3. French knife
4. Frying pan
5. Braising pot
6. Skillet
7. Full sized steam table pan

Ingredients: Approx. yield: 50 servings

18	lbs. beef tenderloin tips
4	lbs. mushrooms, sliced thick
4	ozs. butter
2	gal. brown sauce, thickened and hot
1	pt. Burgundy wine
1	pt. salad oil (variable)

Preparation

1. Slice the beef tenderloin tips on the bias (slanting) about ¼ in. thick with a French knife. Proceed only after demonstration by instructor.
2. Wash the mushrooms and slice fairly thick with a French knife.
3. Prepare the rich brown sauce. (See Chap. 15.) Thicken with a roux (equal parts shortening and flour).
4. Have all equipment and ingredients handy.

Procedure

1. Place the butter in a skillet, heat. Add the mushrooms and sauté until tender.
2. Place the brown sauce in braiser and bring to a boil.
3. Add the sautéed mushrooms and the Burgundy wine. Simmer slowly.
4. Place the salad oil in a large frying pan and heat. Add the tenderloin tips and brown quickly. Drain off all oil.

5. Add the brown tips to the mushroom sauce, bring to a boil and remove from the heat. Place in a steam table pan.
6. Dish up into a shallow casserole with a 6 to 8 oz. ladle. Garnish with chopped parsley.

Precautions and Safety Measures
1. When washing the mushrooms, lift the mushrooms out of the water, rather than pouring the water off. All dirt will be removed using this method.
2. When sautéing the tenderloin tip do not overcook. They should be medium done.
3. Exercise caution when using the knife.

Beef à la Bourguignonne

Beef à la Bourguignonne is a French preparation. It is cubes of beef tenderloin cooked in Burgundy wine. This item would be an excellent choice for the dinner menu.

Objectives
1. To teach the student how to cut the beef.
2. To teach the student the procedure for preparing beef à la Bourguignonne.

Equipment
1. Baker's scale
2. French knife
3. Qt. measure
4. Braising pot
5. Kitchen spoon
6. Sauce pot, 3 qts.
7. Full sized steam table pan

Ingredients: Approx. yield: 50 servings

18	lbs. beef tenderloin, cut into 1 inch cubes
10	ozs. shortening
4	lbs. mushrooms, sliced thick
1	lb. shallots or green onions, minced
3	ozs. flour
1½	qts. Burgundy wine
	salt and pepper to taste

Preparation
1. Wash and slice the mushrooms fairly thick with a French knife.
2. Mince the shallots or green onions with a French knife.
3. Trim and cut the beef tenderloin into 1 in. cubes with a French knife. Proceed only after demonstration by instructor.
4. Have all equipment and ingredients handy.

Procedure
1. Place ⅔ of the shortening in the braiser and heat. Add the cubes of beef and brown thoroughly.
2. Place the remaining shortening in a sauce pot and heat. Add the mushrooms and shallots and sauté until tender then hold for later use.
3. Add the flour to the brown beef cubes and blend in thoroughly with a kitchen spoon. Cook for 5 minutes.
4. Add the wine and the sautéed shallots and mushrooms, blend thoroughly, and simmer for about 30 minutes or until all ingredients are tender.
5. Season with salt and pepper and remove from the range. Place in a steam table pan.
6. Dish up into a shallow casserole with a 6 to 8 oz. ladle. Serve with yellow or wild rice.

Precautions and Safety Measures
1. Do not overcook the beef tenderloin or it will fall apart when served. Test for doneness by removing a piece of beef with a pierced spoon and pressing with the finger.
2. Exercise caution when using the knife.

Beef mandarin

Beef mandarin is an American dish prepared in the Chinese fashion using crisp vegetables, water chestnuts and bean sprouts. This is an excellent item to feature on the luncheon menu.

Objectives
1. To teach the student how to cut the meat and vegetables.
2. To teach the student how to prepare beef mandarin.
3. To teach the student how to dish up beef mandarin.

Equipment
1. Measuring cups
2. Qt. measure
3. French knife
4. Stock pot, 5 gal.
5. Baker's scale
6. Wooden paddle
7. Deep steam table pan

Ingredients: Approx. yield: 50 servings

15	lb. boneless beef chuck
½	cup salad oil
5	lbs. celery, cut med. dice
4	lbs. onions, cut med. dice

2 cans water chestnuts, drained and sliced
14 ozs. cornstarch
12 ozs. water
½ cup soy sauce
6 qts. beef stock
5 whole pimientoes, canned, cut med. dice
1 cup tomato purée
2 bay leaves
salt and pepper to taste
1 #10 can bean sprouts, drained

Preparation

1. Slice beef chuck with a French knife or on a slicing machine into thin strips approximately 1 in. by 1 in. by ¼ in. Proceed only after demonstration by instructor.
2. Dice celery, onions and pimientoes with a French knife.
3. Slice the water chestnuts very thin with a French knife. Hold firm with the finger tips while slicing.
4. Prepare the beef stock. (See Chap. 12.)
5. Have all other equipment and ingredients handy.

Procedure

1. Place the salad oil in a stock pot, add the sliced beef and sauté until meat is brown. Stir frequently with a wooden paddle.
2. Add the celery, onions and water chestnuts. Continue to sauté for 10 minutes.
3. Add the beef stock, tomato purée, bay leaves, and soy sauce. Boil until beef is tender.
4. Place the cornstarch in a bowl, add water and dilute. Add mixture slowly to the boiling beef, stirring constantly with a wooden paddle.
5. Remove from the fire. Remove bay leaves and add the pimientoes and bean sprouts.
6. Season with salt and pepper. Remove from the range and place in a deep steam table pan.
7. Dish up with a 6 to 8 oz. ladle. Serve with rice and fried Chinese noodles.

Precautions and Safety Measures

1. Pour the diluted starch into the boiling liquid slowly while stirring constantly to avoid lumps.
2. Bean sprouts must be added upon completion of cooking so they will remain crisp.
3. Be sure beef is tender before adding the starch.
4. Exercise caution when using the knife.

Beef rouladen

Beef rouladen consists of thin slices of beef round, flattened and spread with a filling; a piece of pickle is added, then it is rolled and baked in the oven. Beef rouladen is an excellent dinner item.

Objectives

1. To teach the student the procedure for making beef rouladen.
2. To teach the student how to flatten, fill and roll the beef rouladen.
3. To teach the student how to bake and dish up beef rouladen.

Equipment

1. Cleaver
2. Food grinder
3. Mixing container, 2 gal.
4. Roast pan
5. French butcher knife
6. Steel skillet
7. Wire whip
8. Baker's scale
9. Qt. measure
10. Cup and spoon measures
11. China cap
12. Qt. bowl
13. Stainless steel container
14. Kitchen spoon

Ingredients: Approx. yield: 50 servings

10 lb. beef round, trimmed
1 lb. bacon, ground
1 lb. ham scraps, lean, raw, ground
1 lb. hamburger, raw
½ cup onions, minced
6 eggs, beaten
1 qt. bread crumbs, fine, dry
2 tbsp. parsley, chopped
50 strips sweet or dill pickles
1 gal. Burgundy sauce

Preparation

1. Trim beef round, slice beef with a French or butcher knife into 2½ to 3 oz. square pieces and flatten until very thin with the side of a cleaver. Proceed only after demonstration by instructor.
2. Combine the bacon and ham scraps. Grind on the food grinder using the medium chopper plate.
3. Chop the parsley with a French knife, wash after chopping.
4. Mince onions with a French knife and sauté in a skillet with additional shortening.

5. Preheat oven to 375°F.
6. Prepare Burgundy sauce. (See Chap. 15.)
7. Break eggs in a bowl and beat slightly with a wire whip.
8. Have all equipment and ingredients handy.

Procedure
1. Place the bacon, ham, onions, eggs, bread crumbs, hamburger and parsley in a mixing container. Mix thoroughly by hand.
2. Spread filling and place a strip of dill or sweet pickle on each piece of meat. Roll up and secure with twine or toothpicks. Place in roast pan.
3. Place meat rolls in 375°F oven. Allow to brown, then remove excess grease. Discard grease.
4. Add Burgundy sauce and continue to bake until meat rolls are tender. Remove from oven.
5. Place meat rolls in a steam table pan. Strain sauce through a china cap into a stainless steel container.
6. Dish up 1 roll covered with Burgundy sauce for each portion.

Precautions and Safety Measures
1. When placing meat rolls in roast pan, place open side down and keep them close together.
2. When baking the meat rolls, baste frequently with the sauce using a kitchen spoon.
3. When slicing the beef have beef slightly frozen for best results.
4. Exercise caution when handling the knife.

English beef stew

English beef stew is a brown stew. This type of stew is superior in flavor to a white stew. It is a mixture of about ⅔ cooked beef and ⅓ cooked vegetables. It is served mostly as a luncheon entrée.

Objectives
1. To teach the student how to cut the meat and vegetables.
2. To teach the student how to prepare English beef stew.
3. To teach the student how to dish up a beef stew.

Equipment
1. French knife
2. Braising pot and cover

3. Sauce pans, (2) 6 qt. and (1) 4 qt.
4. Baker's scale
5. Qt. measure
6. China cap

Ingredients: Approx. yield: 50 servings

15	lbs. boneless beef chuck, cut into 1 in. cubes
2	gal. beef stock
1	lb. beef fat (suet) minced or 1 pt. salad oil
1	qt. tomato purée
½	oz. garlic, minced
1	lb. flour
3	lbs. carrots, large dice
3	lbs. celery, large dice
½	#10 can whole small onions, drained
2½	lb. peas, frozen
½	#10 can cut green beans, drained
¼	oz. thyme, ground
2	bay leaves
3	ozs. salt (variable)
	pepper to taste

Preparation
1. Cut the beef chuck into 1 in. cubes with a French knife. Proceed only after demonstration by instructor.
2. Dice the carrots and celery with a French knife.
3. Mince the garlic and suet with a French knife.
4. Preheat oven to 375°F.
5. Prepare the beef stock. (See Chap. 12.)
6. Have all equipment and ingredients handy.

Procedure
1. Place the suet in the braising pot and render on top of range until the suet starts to become crisp.
2. Add the cubes of beef and brown thoroughly.
3. Add the flour, blend thoroughly with a kitchen spoon, making a roux, and cook slightly.
4. Add the hot beef stock, tomato purée, minced garlic, thyme and bay leaves. Stir with a kitchen spoon. Cover braiser, place in oven 375°F and cook for about 2 to 2½ hours until the beef is tender.
5. Boil all vegetables in separate sauce pans in salt water until tender; drain.
6. When the meat is tender, take from the oven. Remove bay leaves and add all the

drained cooked vegetables except the peas.

7. Check seasoning and place in deep steam table pans.
8. Dish up into deep casseroles with a 6 to 8 oz. ladle. Garnish the top of each portion with green peas.

Precautions and Safety Measures

1. Do not overcook the beef, it will crumble when dishing up.
2. When adding the flour to make the roux, be sure to cook the roux slightly or stew will have a raw flour taste.
3. Exercise caution when handling the knife.

Swiss steak in sour cream

Swiss steak in sour cream is a preparation utilizing a tougher cut of beef, but baking in its own sauce makes it tender. Sour cream and Parmesan cheese are added to give it an unusual flavor and appearance.

Objectives

1. To teach the student how to cut the steaks from the beef round.
2. To teach the student how to prepare Swiss steaks in sour cream.
3. To teach the student how to dish up Swiss steak in sour cream.

Equipment

1. French or butcher knife
2. Qt. measure
3. Cup and spoon measures
4. Baker's scale
5. Skillet
6. Braising pot and cover
7. Kitchen spoon
8. China cap
9. Wire whip
10. Sauce pot, 2 gal.
11. Full size steam table pan
12. 2 gal. stainless steel container

Ingredients: Approx. yield: 50 servings

50	beef round steaks, 6 oz. portions
1	qt. salad oil
3	lbs. onions, minced
1	cup Parmesan cheese
4	ozs. Worcestershire sauce
6	qt. brown stock
3	tbsp. paprika
2	bay leaves
1	lb. bread flour
1	qt. sour cream
	salt and pepper to taste

Preparation

1. Cut the beef round into 6 oz. steaks with a French or butcher knife, and flatten slightly with a cleaver. Proceed only after demonstration by instructor.
2. Mince onions with a French knife.
3. Prepare brown stock. (See Chap. 12.)
4. Preheat oven to 350°F.
5. Have all equipment and ingredients handy.

Procedure

1. Cover the bottom of a skillet with the salad oil and heat.
2. Place the steaks in the hot oil and brown both sides. Repeat this process until all steaks are browned. Place the browned steaks in a braising pot. Add 1 qt. of brown stock to skillet. Deglaze and save liquid.
3. Place the remaining oil in a sauce pot and heat. Add the minced onions and sauté until tender. Do not brown.
4. Add paprika and flour, blending well with a wire whip, cook slightly.
5. Add the brown stock, whipping constantly with a wire whip until slightly thick and smooth.
6. Add Worcestershire sauce, Parmesan cheese, bay leaves and salt and pepper.
7. Pour this sauce over the browned steaks in the braising pot.
8. Place in oven, cover braising pot and bake for about 2 to 2½ hours at a temperature of 350°F or until the steaks are tender.
9. Remove steaks from the sauce with a kitchen fork and place in steam table pan. Keep steaks covered with a wet towel.
10. Strain the sauce through a china cap into a sauce pan, cool slightly. Stir the sour cream gently into the sauce with a kitchen spoon; heat and remove from the range.
11. Check the seasoning and pour the sauce into a stainless steel container.
12. Dish up a steak per portion. Cover with 2 to 2½ ozs. of sauce.

Precautions and Safety Measures

1. Do not overcook the steaks, they will break when dishing up.
2. When sautéing the onions do not let them brown.

3. Make certain that the liquid the steaks were cooked in is slightly cooled before adding the sour cream.
4. Exercise caution when handling the knife.

BROILED BEEF RECIPES

Cheddar steak

Cheddar steak is a piece of beef, made tender by cubing or chipping, which is broiled to the desired degree of doneness and served with a rich Cheddar cheese sauce. It is generally served on the luncheon menu.

Objectives
1. To teach the student how to prepare Cheddar steak.
2. To teach the student how to dish up Cheddar steak.

Equipment
1. Broiler
2. Qt. measure
3. Kitchen fork
4. Spoon measure
5. Baker's scale
6. Box grater
7. 2 qt. stainless steel container
8. Kitchen spoon
9. Sauce pan, 2 qts.
10. 2 bake pans
11. Mixing bowl

Ingredients: Approx. yield: 50 servings
50   4 oz. cube or chip steaks (purchase ready to cook)
 1   pt. salad oil
 1   tbsp. Worcestershire sauce
 1   tsp. mustard, dry
 1   tsp. paprika
 8   drops Tabasco
 1   qt. tomato juice
 2   lbs. Cheddar cheese, sharp, grated
    salt and pepper to taste

Preparation
1. Grate the Cheddar cheese on the coarse grid of a box grater.
2. Preheat broiler.
3. Have all equipment and ingredients handy.

Procedure
1. Place the salad oil in a bake pan.
2. Season the steaks with salt and pepper, place in the salad oil.

3. Pat off excess oil and place the steaks on a hot broiler. Broil until medium done and remove from the broiler with a kitchen fork. Place in a bake pan and hold in a warm place.
4. In a mixing bowl, mix the Worcestershire sauce, Tabasco sauce, dry mustard and paprika into a paste.
5. Place the tomato juice in a sauce pan, add the paste mixture, and bring to a boil. Stir occasionally with a kitchen spoon.
6. Add the grated Cheddar cheese and cook until smooth, stirring frequently. Remove from the range and pour into a stainless steel container.
7. Serve steak on a hot plate covered with the rich Cheddar sauce.

Precautions and Safety Measures
1. Cook steaks medium for best results.
2. Exercise caution when grating the cheese.

Beef tenderloin en brochette

Beef tenderloin en brochette is an unusual as well as a very attractive entrée. The cubes of beef are alternated with the vegetables on a skewer (metal pin) and cooked as one. It is an excellent dinner item.

Objectives
1. To teach the student how to cut the beef.
2. To teach the student how to set up the beef tenderloin en brochette.
3. To teach the student how to broil beef tenderloin en brochette.
4. To teach the student how to dish up beef tenderloin en brochette.

Equipment
1. Baker's scale
2. 24 skewers (metal pins)
3. French knife
4. Sauce pan, 1 pt.
5. Pastry brush
6. Bake pan

Ingredients: Approx. yield: 24 servings
 7   lbs. beef tenderloin
24   small tomatoes, quartered
96   mushroom caps
96   small onions
 8   ozs. butter, melted
 4   cloves garlic
    salt and pepper to taste

Preparation
1. Trim tenderloin and cut into 1 in. cubes

with a French knife. Proceed only after demonstration by instructor.
2. Cut tomatoes into quarters with a French knife.
3. Preheat broiler.
4. Have all equipment and ingredients handy.

Procedure
1. Arrange 4 each of 1 in. steak cubes, mushroom caps, onions and tomatoes alternately on the skewers.
2. Place the butter in a sauce pan and heat. Add the garlic and cook slightly. Remove from the range and hold for later use.
3. Place the oil in a bake pan and marinate the skewered items in the salad oil. Place on preheated broiler and cook slowly until all items are tender. Turn frequently.
4. Brush on the butter-garlic mixture just before removing from the broiler.
5. Dish up at once on toast, plain or wild rice. Remove skewer before serving.

Precautions and Safety Measures
1. Exercise caution when using the knife.
2. When broiling turn the skewered tenderloin every 3 minutes so it will brown more evenly.
3. Marinate the item in oil before broiling. It will not stick to the broiler and will have a more eye-appealing appearance.

Salisbury steak

Salisbury steak is a ground beef product. The ground beef is highly seasoned then pressed into steak form, broiled or sautéed, and served with a flavorful sauce.

Objectives
1. To teach the student how to grind the beef.
2. To teach the student how to mix and form the Salisbury steak.
3. To teach the student how to cook the Salisbury steak.
4. To teach the student how to dish up a Salisbury steak.

Equipment
1. Baker's scale
2. Cup and spoon measure
3. French knife
4. Sauce pan, 1 qt.
5. Mixing container, approx. 5 gal.
6. Wire whip
7. 1 qt. bowl

8. Kitchen spoon
9. Full size steam table pan
10. Food grinder

Ingredients: Approx. yield: 50 servings

14	lbs. boneless beef chuck
3	lbs. onions, minced
1	tsp. garlic, minced
½	cup salad oil
8	whole eggs
2	lbs. bread, cubed
1½	pt. milk
	salt and fresh ground pepper to taste

Preparation
1. Cut the beef chuck with a French knife into pieces that will pass through the food grinder. Proceed only after demonstration by instructor.
2. Mince the onions and garlic with a French knife.
3. Cut the bread into cubes with a French knife.
4. Break the eggs into a bowl and beat slightly with a wire whip.
5. Have equipment and ingredients handy.

Procedure
1. Place the oil in the sauce pan and heat. Add the onions and garlic and sauté until tender. Do not brown.
2. Place the bread in the mixing container, add the milk and mix thoroughly with a kitchen spoon.
3. Add the sautéed vegetables, beef chuck, salt and pepper and mix together thoroughly by hand.
4. Pass this mixture through the food grinder twice, using the medium hole chopper plate.
5. Add the beaten whole eggs, blend thoroughly. Check seasoning.
6. Form into 5 oz. steaks. Pass through salad oil and broil or sauté. Place in a steam table pan.
7. Dish up one steak per portion and serve with an appropriate sauce.

Precautions and Safety Measures
1. If the mixture is too moist, adjust consistency by adding bread crumbs.
2. When forming the steaks, rub hands with a small amount of salad oil to prevent meat from sticking to the hands.
3. When sautéing the onions and garlic, do not brown.
4. Exercise caution when using the knife.

BOILED BEEF RECIPES

Boiled fresh brisket of beef

Boiled fresh brisket of beef is an excellent entrée for either the luncheon or dinner menu. It is served best with horseradish sauce, boiled cabbage and boiled potatoes.

Objectives
1. To teach the student the procedure for boiling beef.
2. To teach the student how to slice boiled beef.
3. To teach the student how to dish up boiled beef.

Equipment
1. Stock pot, 10 gal.
2. French knife
3. Kitchen fork
4. Ladle
5. Steam table pan

Ingredients: Approx. yield: 50 servings

17	lbs. brisket beef
	water, enough to cover beef
	salt, to taste
1	tbsp. pickling spices
1	lb. onions, cut rough
½	lb. celery, cut rough
½	lb. carrots, cut rough

Preparation
1. If meat has excess fat, trim slightly with a French knife.
2. Cut vegetables rough with a French knife.
3. Have equipment and ingredients handy.

Procedure
1. Place brisket of beef in stock pot and cover with cold water.
2. Bring to a boil and remove any scum that may appear on the surface with a ladle.
3. Add rough garnish (onions, celery and carrots) for flavor. Reduce heat until liquid simmers.
4. Add salt and spices and continue to simmer until meat is tender. Remove the meat from the stock, let cook slightly.
5. Slice the meat against the grain with a French knife. Place in a steam table pan and reheat in the steam table or steamer.
6. Serve 3 to 4 ozs. per portion with horseradish sauce.

Note: Save the beef stock for use in the preparation of horseradish sauce or other sauces or soups.

Precautions and Safety Measures
1. Exercise caution when cutting the vegetables.
2. Do not let the liquid boil too fast or the stock will become cloudy.
3. Slice the meat only after a demonstration by the instructor.

Roast beef hash, Southern style

Roast beef hash Southern style is a profitable item. By putting it on the luncheon menu you can use up all the beef or veal left overs and still put out an attractive dish.

Objectives
1. To teach the student the procedure for making roast beef hash Southern style.
2. To teach the student how to cut the garnish for roast beef hash Southern style.
3. To teach the student how to dish up roast beef hash Southern style.

Equipment
1. Large braiser pot
2. French knife
3. Deep steam table pan
4. Wood paddle
5. Baker's scale

Ingredients: Approx. yield: 50 servings

1	lb. green peppers, diced
2	lbs. 10 ozs. onions, diced
8	ozs. diced pimientos
12	lbs. cooked beef, diced (roasted or boiled leftovers)
9	lbs. raw potatoes, diced
2	lbs. 8 ozs. tomato purée
12	ozs. salad oil
1	gal. beef stock or brown stock
	salt, pepper to taste
1½	tsp. nutmeg

Preparation
1. Dice cooked beef into small cubes with a French knife.
2. Dice onions, green peppers, pimientos and potatoes into small cubes with a French knife.
3. Prepare brown stock or beef stock. (See Chap. 12.)
4. Have all other ingredients handy.

Procedure
1. In braiser place shortening, diced onions and diced green peppers and sauté until partly done.
2. Add brown stock or beef stock.

3. Add tomato purée and diced raw potatoes and cook until potatoes are half done.
4. Add diced beef and diced pimientos and cook until potatoes are completely done. Stir occasionally with a wooden paddle.
5. Season with salt, pepper and nutmeg. Remove from the fire and place in a deep steam table pan.
6. Dish up in shallow casseroles with a 6 to 8 oz. ladle and serve with fried mush or corn fritters.

Precautions and Safety Measures
1. Do not overcook the potatoes.
2. Use caution in handling the knife while dicing the garnish.

BEEF VARIETY MEAT RECIPES

Braised sweetbreads

Braised sweetbreads is a favorite of many gourmets. The sweetbreads are first blanched then braised with a mirepoix garnish (small diced vegetables). The vegetable mirepoix garnish increases the flavor of this popular variety meat.

Objective
1. To teach the student how to blanch the sweetbreads.
2. To teach the student how to prepare braised sweetbreads.
3. To teach the student how to dish up braised sweetbreads.

Equipment
1. French knife
2. Baker's scale
3. Qt. measure
4. Sauce pot, 3 gal.
5. Braising pot
6. China cap
7. Collander
8. Kitchen spoon
9. 1 gal. stainless steel container

Ingredients: Approx. yield: 25 servings
25 pairs of heart sweetbreads
1 lb. of margarine or fat
1 lb. carrots, small dice
1 lb. onions, small dice
12 ozs. celery, small dice
2 bay leaves
4 cloves garlic, minced

2 qts. brown sauce
salt and pepper to taste

Preparation
1. Place the sweetbreads in a sauce pot, cover with water and add salt and lemon juice or vinegar. Place on the range and simmer until partly cooked (approximately 10 to 15 minutes). Drain in a collander and let cool. Remove membranes.
2. Dice the carrots, onions and celery into very small cubes with a French knife. This is the mirepoix. Mince garlic.
3. Prepare the brown sauce. (See Chap. 15.)
4. Preheat the oven to 375°F.
5. Have all equipment and ingredients handy.

Procedure
1. Place the butter in braising pot and melt.
2. Add the mirepoix (small diced vegetables) and spices. Place the sweetbreads over the vegetables. Put in oven at 375°F and cook until vegetables are slightly brown.
3. Add the brown sauce. Reduce the oven temperature to 350°F and continue to braise for 35 minutes, basting frequently using a kitchen spoon.
4. Remove from the oven, strain the juice through a china cap into a stainless steel container.
5. Slice the sweetbreads with a French knife, about one-half inch thick on the bias.
6. Dish up a pair of sweetbreads per portion in a shallow casserole with 2 ozs. of the strained liquid.

Precautions and Safety Measures
1. Use caution when handling the French knife.
2. Do not let the mirepoix burn during cooking.
3. Use caution when slicing the sweetbreads, they will crumble easily.

VARIATIONS
Sauteed sweetbreads: Poach sweetbreads, slice in two then pass through seasoned flour. Sauté in shortening or butter until golden brown on both sides. Serve with a mushroom, brown, bordelaise, brown butter, or Bercy sauce. (See Chap. 15 for sauces.)
Broiled sweetbreads: Poach sweetbreads, slice in two and pass through salad oil. Season with salt and pepper and paprika. Place on the broiler and brown one side then turn

and brown the other side. Serve with a butter sauce. (See Chap. 15.)

Sweetbreads Carolina: Poach sweetbreads, slice in two then pass through seasoned flour. Sauté in butter or shortening, garnish with julienne ham, browned almonds and sautéed mushroom caps. Serve topped with a thin sherry wine cream sauce. (Add small amount of sherry to cream sauce recipe, Chap. 15.)

Sweetbread chasseur: Poach sweetbreads, slice in two then pass through seasoned flour. Sauté in butter or shortening and remove from skillet, let drain and place in sauce pot. Cover with mushroom sauce. (See Chap. 15.) Garnish with julienne ham, turkey and chopped parsley and serve in a casserole.

Sautéed beef liver

Sautéed beef liver is one of the popular variety meats. The liver is sliced, passed through flour and cooked in shallow grease until golden brown.

Objectives
1. To teach the student how to skin and slice the liver.
2. To teach the student the procedure for sautéing beef liver.
3. To teach the student how to dish up sautéed beef liver.

Equipment
1. Butcher or French knife
2. Frying pan
3. Bake pan
4. Kitchen fork
5. Baker's scale

Ingredients: Approx. yield: 50 servings
16 lbs. beef liver
1 qt. salad oil or melted shortening (variable)
3 lbs. bread flour
salt and pepper to taste

Preparation
1. Skin the beef liver by hand, chill or partly freeze the liver, and slice on the bias (slant) into uniform, fairly thin slices. Proceed only after demonstration by instructor.
2. Place the flour in a bake pan and season with salt and pepper.
3. Have all equipment and ingredients handy.

Procedure
1. Place about ¼ in. of oil or shortening in the frying pan and heat.
2. Pass the slices of liver through the seasoned flour.
3. Place the liver in the hot oil or shortening. Brown one side, turn with a kitchen fork and brown the other side.
4. Remove from fry pan and let drain.
5. Serve 2 or 3 slices per portion with a butter sauce accompanied with cooked onions.

Precautions and Safety Measures
1. Sauté liver at a medium temperature or a hard crust will form on the liver.
2. Liver should be cooked medium for best eating qualities.
3. Liver should always be cooked only when ordered.

Note: Liver may also be broiled with excellent results. If broiled, do not pass through flour. Pass the liver through salad oil before placing it on the broiler.

Braised kidneys

Braised kidneys are not a very popular menu item, but they are sometimes used on the luncheon menu for variety. The kidneys are browned and cooked by the braising method until tender.

Objective
1. To teach the student how to prepare the kidneys for cooking.

Custom Food Products, Inc.

Sautéed beef liver

2. To teach the student the procedure for preparing braised kidneys.
3. To teach the student how to dish up braised kidneys.

Equipment
1. Collander
2. French knife
3. Braising pot and cover
4. Baker's scale
5. Qt. measure
6. Spoon measure
7. Stock pot, 5 gal.
8. Kitchen spoon
9. Steam table pan

Ingredients: Approx. yield: 50 servings
20 lbs. beef kidneys
1 lb. shortening
3 lbs. onions, cut julienne
1 gal. brown sauce
3 tbsp. Worcestershire sauce
salt and pepper to taste

Preparation
1. Place the kidneys in stock pot, cover with water, add salt and simmer for 5 minutes. Change water and repeat the simmering. Drain in a collander, remove skin, and slice the kidneys in half lengthwise using a French knife. Remove white centers, fat and tubes.
2. Cut onions julienne with a French knife.
3. Prepare brown sauce. (See Chap. 15.)
4. Have all equipment and ingredients handy.

Procedure
1. Place the shortening in braising pot, melt, add the onions and kidneys, and brown.
2. Add the Worcestershire sauce, brown sauce, and salt and pepper. Cover and cook until the kidneys are tender.
3. Remove from the range and place in a steam table pan.
4. Dish up 2 or 3 pieces of kidney for each portion in a shallow casserole with onions and natural liquid.

Precautions and Safety Measures
1. Use caution when slicing the kidneys and onions.
2. When browning the kidneys, do not burn the onions.
3. Avoid escaping steam when removing cover from braising pot.

Tripe creole

Tripe creole is a mixture of julienne honey-comb tripe and creole sauce. This is an excellent luncheon item and is generally served in a casserole.

Objectives
1. To teach the student how to cut the tripe.
2. To teach the student how to prepare tripe creole.
3. To teach the student how to dish up tripe creole.

Equipment
1. Sauce pot, 5 gal.
2. Stock pot, 5 gal.
3. French knife
4. Braising pot
5. Qt. measure
6. Kitchen spoon
7. Deep steam table pan

Ingredients: Approx. yield: 50 servings
14 lbs. honeycomb tripe, cut julienne
2 gal. creole sauce
1 lb. margarine
3 cloves garlic, minced
salt and pepper to taste

Preparation
1. Mince the garlic with a French knife.
2. Wash the tripe in cold water, remove loose skin.
3. Cut the tripe julienne with a French knife.
4. Prepare creole sauce. (See Chap. 15.)

Procedure
1. Place the tripe in a stock pot. Cover with water and simmer for about 1½ hours or until the tripe is slightly tender then drain off liquid.
2. Place the margarine in a braiser and melt.
3. Add the garlic and the cooked tripe, cook for about 20 minutes, stirring frequently with a kitchen spoon.
4. Add the prepared creole sauce and simmer for about 15 minutes.
5. Season with salt and pepper. Pour into a deep steam table pan.
6. Dish up into shallow casserole with a 6 to 8 oz. ladle. Serve with a scoop of baked rice.

Precautions and Safety Measures
1. When sautéing the tripe in the margarine, do not let the tripe brown or stick to the pan.
2. Use caution when cutting the tripe.

Fried brains

Fried brains is an item that is sometimes served on the luncheon menu although it is not very popular. The brains must first be poached before the frying method can be performed.

Objectives
1. To teach the student how to poach and skin the brains.
2. To teach the student how to bread and fry the brains.
3. To teach the student how to dish up the brains.

Equipment
1. Sauce pot
2. Spoon measure
3. Baker's scale
4. Qt. measure
5. 3 small bake pans
6. 2 qt. stainless steel container
7. Wire whip

Ingredients: Approx. yield: 25 servings

5	lbs. brains
2	ozs. cider vinegar
1½	qts. water
4	tsp. salt
8	ozs. flour
½	tsp. pepper
1	lb. bread crumbs
1	qt. egg wash (4 eggs to 1 qt. of milk)

Preparation
1. Soak the brains in cold water for one hour.
2. Prepare egg wash. Place eggs in a stainless steel container, beat with a wire whip, add the milk and beat again.
3. Have all equipment and ingredients handy.

Procedure
1. Combine the water, vinegar, and salt in a large sauce pot. Add the brains and simmer for 15 minutes. Drain and with fingers remove skin and membrane.
2. Place the flour, egg wash and bread crumbs in separate bake pans. Season the brains with the salt and pepper. First pass them through the flour, then the egg wash and lastly the bread crumbs.
3. Pat off the excess bread crumbs, place in fry baskets and deep fry at a temperature of 350°F.
4. Serve 2 or 3 pieces on top of tomato or cream sauce.

Precautions and Safety Measures
1. Do not over-poach the brains or they will fall apart.
2. At all times handle the brains with care because they are very tender.
3. Be sure all skin and membrane is removed from the brains before breading.
4. When frying do not overbrown the brains.

Note: The same method of preparation is used when sautéing the brains. Instead of breading the brains are passed through flour seasoned with salt and pepper and cooked in shallow grease until golden brown. Sautéed brains can be served with brown butter, or tomato or cream sauce. (See Chap. 15 for sauces.)

veal preparation

■ Veal is the meat of milk-fed calves not over 12 weeks of age. It has very little fat covering and a high moisture content. Consequently, it will dry out very quickly if left to hang in the refrigerator too long or if cooked too long or at too high a temperature. Veal carcasses will average in weight from 60 to 160 pounds, but the best veal is slaughtered when between 6 to 8 weeks old and weighs about 125 pounds.

Veal flesh contains a very delicate flavor and for this reason blends very well with other foods and savory sauces. The European chefs have created many favorite and famous veal dishes. Veal is al-

ways tender, it will cook quickly and it displays a fine appearance when served. Above all, it will blend with many of the popular sauces.

In recent years the consumption of veal has been on the decline in the United States mainly because less has been available in the market. The farmer is reluctant to market his young cattle when he is attempting to increase his herd. Also, in most cases, letting the animal develop into beef proves to be more profitable. However, when the price of grain and corn is high he may be forced to market the calves to reduce his feed bill.

Veal is the first stage in the development of the beef animal. From birth to about 8 weeks old the calf is fed its mother's milk. At this stage it is truly veal. The fat is clear, firm and white. The flesh is light pink in color and there is no marbling of fat in the lean. At this point the animal is turned out to pasture and fed grass, meal or hay. The color of the fat then turns slightly yellow and the flesh becomes darker in color. The animal at this stage becomes a calf. When the animal is wholly fed on grass or grain and is about 14 to 16 weeks old, the flesh becomes firmer and loses its high moisture content, as well as getting darker in color. The fat takes on a more yellow appearance and the bones grow larger and more white. The animal is now developing into beef. The stages of development from veal, to calf, to beef are brought about by natural maturation and the type of feed. Although there is a great difference between calf and veal carcasses they are both referred to as veal when placed on the market.

VEAL GRADING

Veal is graded like beef with the evaluation based on the same three factors: conformation, finish, and quality. The grader considers *conformation* (which refers to the build, form and shape of the animal) before judging finish or quality. *Finish* refers to color, amount and distribution of fat covering the shoulders, rump and kidney. For veal to receive a high rating it is necessary that the fat surrounding the kidney be thick and of high grade. *Quality* refers to the color and texture of the meat and the color and hardness of the bones. This is the most important factor in the grading of any animal. If the meat is firm and has a very smooth surface when cut, it is generally of high quality. If, on the other hand, it is soft and has a rough surface, it is usually judged of poor quality. Hard,

white bones are also an indication that the quality is poor.

There are six federal veal grades. These are, in their order of desirability: prime, choice, good, commercial, utility, and cull. Of these, only the first four are pertinent to the food service operator: prime, choice, good, and commercial.

U.S. prime: This is veal of the highest quality. To be graded prime the animal must be rated superior in the three grading factors. These animals are generally exhibited and therefore very little veal graded *prime* can be found on the market.

U.S. choice: This is the most popular grade used in commercial establishments. It is veal of high quality. Veal graded *choice* is derived from very compact, thick-fleshed and fairly plump animals. They possess small bones in proportion to their overall size, and the flesh is fine textured and moist.

U.S. good: This could be considered the economical grade of veal. It is not the highest quality but can be used with good results in some preparations. The veal carcass graded *good* is thin-fleshed and somewhat slender in appearance. The flesh is slightly soft to the touch, and the cut surface will display some roughness. The bones are large in proportion to the size of the animal.

U.S. commercial: This grade of veal is generally of poor quality. It is seldom used in the commercial kitchen except, in some cases, when the preparation is being stewed or braised. Veal carcasses of this grade are thin-fleshed, rough and sunken in appearance. The flesh is soft and the surface of the flesh is rough when cut. All the bones appear large in proportion to the overall size of the animal.

U.S. utility: This grade of veal is poor quality. It is very seldom if ever used in the commercial kitchen. The veal carcass of this grade is rough, thin and sunken in appearance. It has little fat covering and the flesh is very soft and watery. All bones are large in proportion to the weight and size of the animal.

U.S. cull: This is a grade that is never used in the commercial establishment because it is extremely poor in quality. The veal carcass graded *cull* is extremely rough, sunken and thin-fleshed and generally poor in overall appearance. There is very little fat covering and the flesh is extremely soft and watery. All the bones are extremely large in proportion to the size of the animal.

COMMERCIAL CUTS

Veal can be purchased in six market forms: by the carcass, side, quarter, wholesale or primal cuts, fabricated and retail. Retail cutting will not be discussed in this chapter because it will be of little use to the commercial cooking student.

The cutting of meats for preparation in the commercial kitchen is done much differently than in a retail meat market. The meat form best suited for the food service operator to purchase will, of course, depend on many things. The following are a few examples of the things that must be taken into consideration before the purchase is made.

1. Meat cutting skill of personnel.
2. Meat cutting equipment available.
3. Working space available.
4. Meat storage space available.
5. Utility of all cuts purchased.
6. Meat preparations served.
7. Overall economy of purchasing meat in a particular form.

Carcass: This is the complete animal with the head, hide, and entrails removed. It will average in weight from 60 to 250 lbs, depending on whether it is true veal or calf. The carcass can be purchased at a cheaper cost per pound, but many things must first be considered. Most important is the utility of all cuts after the carcass is blocked out.

Side: A side of veal consists of half the carcass split by cutting lengthwise through the spine bone. There are, of course, two sides to each carcass, a right side and a left side. Each side will average in weight from 30 to 125 pounds, depending on the kind of animal. The side can generally be purchased at a saving to the food service operator, but again one must consider whether all the cuts can be utilized after the veal has been blocked out.

Quarter: The quarter of veal is a side divided into 2 parts. The fore part is known as the forequarter and the hind part as the hindquarter. The side is divided into the two quarters by cutting through the 12th and 13th ribs, the 13th rib remaining on the hindquarter. The hindquarter contains the most desirable cuts and therefore the purchase price is generally high. The forequarter contains less desirable cuts so the price is usually lower. If the food service operator can place tasty and eye appealing entrees on his menu utilizing the cuts of the forequarter, it will certainly be to his advantage and will result in a lower food cost at the end of the month.

Wholesale or primal cuts: These are parts of the fore and the hind quarter of the veal. There are four wholesale cuts in the forequarter and two in the hindquarter. The cuts of the forequarter are the rib, shoulder, shank and breast. The cuts of the hindquarter are the loin and leg. A few years ago this was the most popular way to purchase veal; however, today the trend seems to be to purchase in fabricated (ready to cook) form.

Fabricated: These cuts are purchased ready to cook. This is the most convenient way for the food service operator to purchase veal. The meat can be ordered cut to any desired specification of size and weight. To purchase meat in this form is the most expensive, but when all factors are considered, it may prove to be the most economical.

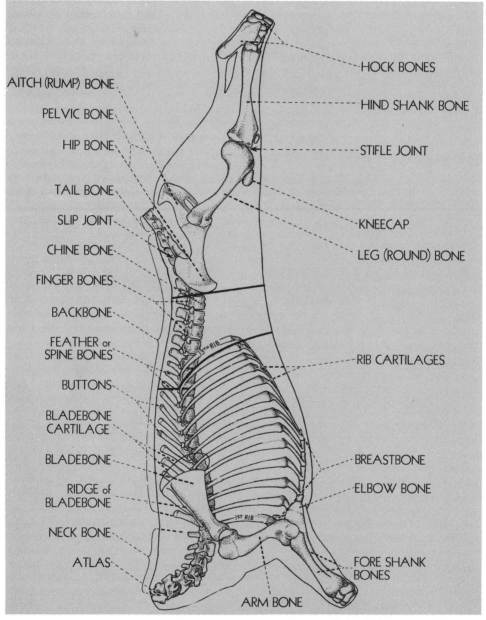

AITCH (RUMP) BONE

PELVIC BONE

HIP BONE

TAIL BONE

SLIP JOINT

CHINE BONE

FINGER BONES

BACKBONE

FEATHER or
SPINE BONES

BUTTONS

BLADEBONE
CARTILAGE

BLADEBONE

RIDGE of
BLADEBONE

NECK BONE

ATLAS

ARM BONE

HOCK BONES

HIND SHANK BONE

STIFLE JOINT

KNEECAP

LEG (ROUND) BONE

RIB CARTILAGES

BREASTBONE

ELBOW BONE

FORE SHANK
BONES

5TH RIB

1ST RIB

National Livestock and Meat Board

Veal skeleton: Location, structure and names of bones.

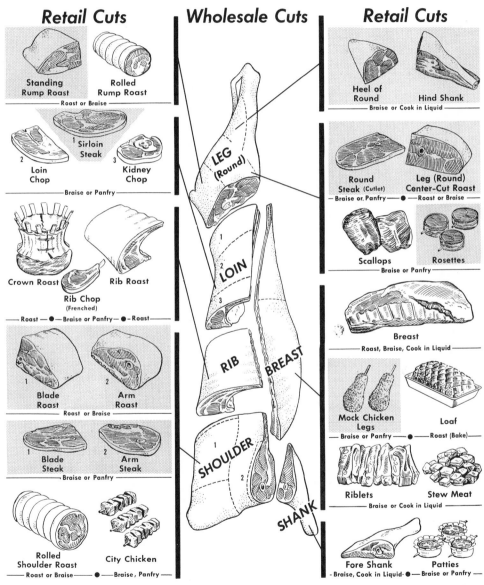

Retail Cuts

Standing Rump Roast **Rolled Rump Roast**
— Roast or Braise —

2 **Loin Chop**   1 **Sirloin Steak**   3 **Kidney Chop**
— Braise or Panfry —

Crown Roast   **Rib Roast**
Rib Chop (Frenched)
— Roast — ● — Braise or Panfry — ● — Roast —

1 **Blade Roast**   2 **Arm Roast**
— Roast or Braise —

1 **Blade Steak**   2 **Arm Steak**
— Braise or Panfry —

Rolled Shoulder Roast   **City Chicken**
— Roast or Braise — ● — Braise, Panfry —

Wholesale Cuts

LEG (Round)

LOIN

RIB   BREAST

SHOULDER

SHANK

Retail Cuts

Heel of Round   **Hind Shank**
— Braise or Cook in Liquid —

Round Steak (Cutlet)   **Leg (Round) Center-Cut Roast**
— Braise or, Panfry — ● — Roast or Braise —

Scallops   **Rosettes**
— Braise or Panfry —

Breast
— Roast, Braise, Cook in Liquid —

Mock Chicken Legs   **Loaf**
— Braise or Panfry — ● — Roast (Bake) —

Riblets   **Stew Meat**
— Braise or Cook in Liquid —

Fore Shank   **Patties**
- Braise, Cook in Liquid- ● — Braise or Panfry —

National Livestock and Meat Board

Veal Chart: Meat cuts and common cooking methods. Cuts shown in grey are not commonly used in the commercial kitchen in the form shown.

WHOLESALE CUTS: COOKING METHODS

The following is a list of the six wholesale or primal cuts of veal, their chief characteristics, and the best cooking method to use when converting them into entrees. They are listed in the order of their popularity.

Leg: The leg is the most desirable of all the veal cuts because of the solid, lean, fine textured meat it contains. The leg should always be boned by following the muscle structure of the meat so that pieces of equal tenderness and with less muscle fiber can be removed. The fleshest and most desired legs come from veal weighing about 100 to 150 pounds. Animals of this size will provide legs weighing about 20 pounds. The leg is good for roasting or for veal steaks, cutlets or scalloping. (Always remember when cooking veal not to cook too long or at too high a temperature.)

Loin or saddle: This cut of veal corresponds to the sirloin of beef. It contains hip and back bones. The flesh consists of loin eye, tenderloin, and some flank meat which is generally removed when the loin is trimmed for preparation. Veal loins are sometimes roasted in the commercial kitchen, but in most cases they are converted into veal chops. When a complete loin from the whole veal carcass is unsplit, it is referred to as a *saddle of veal.*

Rib or rack: This cut corresponds to the standing rib roast of beef. It contains 7 ribs and a rib eye which is a solid section of meat. When the complete rib from the veal carcass is unsplit it is referred to as a *rack of veal.* From this rack, a crown roast of veal is generally prepared by forming the ribs into a crown and Frenching (removing meat and fat from the bones). The rib cut is sometimes roasted in the commercial kitchen, but in most cases it is converted into veal rib chops which are best prepared by frying or sautéing.

Shoulder: This is the fore section of the veal animal, containing the blade bone, neck bone and 5 rib bones. It produces a fairly high percentage of lean meat. This cut is an excellent choice for preparing such items as veal stew, veal loaf, veal goulash, veal paprika or city chicken. The shoulder meat displays the best results when it is stewed or braised.

Breast: This is a thin, flat cut containing breast bone and rib ends. It is not a very desirable cut of meat because it shows very little lean and some layers of fat. The best way to utilize the breast in the commercial kitchen is to braise or stuff it with a forcemeat (meat stuffing) and bake.

Shank: The shank is another of the undesirable veal cuts. It contains a high percentage of bone and connective tissue with a small amount of lean. The full shank is sometimes braised if it is not too large, but in most cases this meat is used in stew or ground meat items.

VARIETY MEATS

The *veal variety meats,* which are the edible parts other than the wholesale cuts, are highly prized by the restaurant operator. They include the sweetbreads, liver, kidneys, brains and tongue. The veal sweetbreads are the finest available. They are white, extremely tender and are prepared the same as beef sweetbreads. The calf or veal liver is also of the finest quality and very much in demand because it possesses a tender texture and an extremely fine flavor. Calf and veal livers are processed and prepared in the same manner as beef liver. Veal kidneys resemble beef kidneys in appearance, but are much more tender. Because of this they can be broiled with excellent results, whereas the tougher kidneys such as beef must be cooked by moist heat. Veal brains are similar to the brains of the other edible animals and can therefore be prepared in the same manner. Although veal tongue is not as tough as the beef tongue, it is not as popular. It can be purchased on the market but is very seldom used in the commercial kitchen.

VEAL TERMINOLOGY

There are certain terms associated with veal that the student cook should familiarize himself with. They will no doubt be used from time to time in the establishment in which he is working or being trained.

Veal: Flesh of calves not over 8 weeks of age, fatted on cow's milk.

Calf: Flesh of calves 12 to 14 weeks old, fatted on grass, meal and hay.

Rack: A complete rib from the whole carcass, containing two unsplit ribs.

Saddle: A complete loin from the whole carcass, containing two unsplit loins.

Cutlet: A thin, boneless slice of meat.

Scallopine: Small thin slices of veal, generally leg meat, about equal to a silver dollar in size.

Wiener schnitzel: A Viennese veal steak; a slice of boneless veal that is breaded and fried. It is the same as a veal cutlet.

Baby T-bone steak: A 6 to 8 ounce steak cut from the loin of veal. It contains loin meat on one side of the small T-bone and tenderloin on the other side. It is similar to the beef T-bone or porterhouse steak, but much smaller.

VEAL RECIPES

Veal entrées are popular on most restaurant menus because they can generally be prepared with a minimum amount of time. They also present the chef with an opportunity to display his skill with sauces since veal is seldom served without a rich, tasty sauce. Veal gives the guest a chance to enjoy a little variety and choose something besides pork and beef. The following veal recipes are preparations that have remained the favorites of the dining public for many years.

Roasted and baked veal
(Pages 369 to 374)

Roast leg of veal
City chicken
Stuffed breast of veal
Veal chops stroganoff
Veal birds

Fried and sautéed veal
(Pages 374 to 378)

Veal chop sauté Italienne
Sautéed veal steak
Veal cutlet cordon bleu
Fried breaded veal cutlet
Sautéed veal chops
Breaded veal cutlet, sautéed Gruyère

Braised and stewed veal
(Pages 378 to 385)

Fricassee of veal
Veal chasseur
Scallopine of veal Marsala
Veal ragout
Hungarian veal goulash
Veal stew
Osso bucco
Veal scallopine with mushrooms

Broiled veal
(Page 385)

Broiled veal loin chops

Boiled veal
(Pages 385 to 386)

Veal paprika with sauerkraut

Veal variety meats
(Pages 386 to 387)

Veal kidney and brandy stew

ROASTED AND BAKED VEAL RECIPES

Roast Leg of veal

For roast leg of veal the leg is boned by following the muscle seams of the meat. Each section of meat is tied and then roasted in the oven until tender. Roast veal is a good choice for the luncheon or dinner menu.

Roast leg of veal served with stuffed baked tomatoes.

Objectives

1. To teach the student how to bone and tie the meat.
2. To teach the student the procedure for roasting a leg of veal.
3. To teach the student how to slice and dish the roast veal.

Equipment

1. Boning knife
2. French knife
3. Butcher twine
4. Roast pan
5. Kitchen fork
6. China cap
7. Wire whip
8. Fullsize steam table pan
9. Sauce pot, 2 gal.
10. Baker's scale
11. Qt. measure
12. Stainless steel containers

Ingredients: Approx. yield: 50 servings

25	lbs. veal leg
6	ozs. carrots, cut rough
8	ozs. celery, cut rough
1	lb. onions, cut rough
1	lb. shortening
1	cup salad oil
12	ozs. flour
1½	gal. beef or brown stock
1	cup tomato purée
	salt and pepper to taste

Preparation

1. Bone the leg of veal by following the muscle seams of the meat with a boning knife. Tie each section of meat with butcher twine so it will hold its shape during the roasting period. Proceed only after demonstration by instructor.
2. Cut onions, carrots and celery rough with a French knife.
3. Prepare beef or brown stock. (See Chap. 12.)
4. Season the meat the day before roasting with salt and pepper.
5. Preheat the oven to 375°F.
6. Have all equipment and ingredients handy.

Procedure

1. Place the meat in the roast pan, pour on salad oil, put in the oven and roast at a temperature of 375°F until the meat is thoroughly brown.
2. Add the rough garnish (onions, carrots and celery). Continue to roast until the vegetables become slightly brown. Reduce the oven temperature to 325° to 350°F.
3. Add a small amount of the beef or brown stock, continue to roast until the meat is done, about 2½ to 3 hours depending on the size of the roast.
4. Remove the meat from the roast pan with a kitchen fork, place in a steam table pan and keep warm. Add the stock to the roast pan to deglaze. Pour into a container and hold.
5. Place the shortening in a sauce pot and heat. Add the flour, making a roux. Cook for about 5 minutes.
6. Add the hot stock and tomato purée, whip-

ping vigorously with a wire whip until slightly thick and smooth. Simmer for 15 minutes.

7. Strain through a fine china cap into a stainless steel container. Check seasoning and color. If color is too light add caramel color.

8. Slice the meat against the grain on a slicing machine or with a French knife. Serve 3 to 4 ozs. per portion covered with gravy.

Precautions and Safety Measures

1. Exercise caution when handling the knife.
2. Turn the roast frequently with a kitchen fork while roasting.
3. When adding the stock to the roux be sure the stock is hot and whip vigorously to avoid lumps.

City chicken

City chicken is a mock chicken drum stick prepared by placing cubes of veal or alternating cubes of pork and veal on a wooden skewer. The item is then breaded, fried and baked until it is tender.

Objectives

1. To teach the student the procedure for preparing city chicken.
2. To teach the student how to cut the meat and place it on the skewer.
3. To teach the student how to fry and bake city chicken.
4. To teach the student how to dish up city chicken.

Equipment

1. 50 wooden skewers
2. French knife
3. Qt. measure
4. Baker's scale
5. Bake pans (5)
6. Qt. bowl
7. Wire whip
8. Full size steam table pan

Ingredients: Approx. yield: 50 servings

10	lbs. boneless veal shoulder, cut into 1 in. cubes
7	lbs. pork, Boston butt, cut into 1 in. cubes
12	eggs, whole
2	qts. milk
3	lbs. bread crumbs, dry
3	lbs. flour
	salt and pepper to taste

Preparation

1. Cut the boneless veal and pork with a French knife into 1 in. cubes. Proceed only after demonstration by instructor.
2. Alternate the veal and pork cubes on wooden skewers. Use 3 cubes of veal and 2 cubes of pork.
3. Place the flour in a bake pan and season with salt and pepper.
4. Prepare the egg wash. Break eggs into a bowl, whip slightly with a wire whip, pour in the milk while continuing to whip. Place in a bake pan.
5. Place bread crumbs in a bake pan.
6. Preheat deep fry to 325°F and oven to 300°F.
7. Have all equipment and ingredients handy.

Procedure

1. Pass each city chicken through the flour, egg wash and bread crumbs, press the bread crumbs on firmly.
2. Brown lightly in deep fat at 325°F. Place in a bake pan.
3. Place in a 300°F oven and bake very slowly for about 1½ hours until each cube is very tender. Remove from oven and place in a steam table pan.
4. Dish up 1 city chicken per portion. Serve plain or with brown gravy.

Precautions and Safety Measures

1. Exercise caution when handling the knife.
2. Do not overbrown when frying the city chicken in the deep fat.
3. Watch carefully while the city chicken is baking in the oven so they do not overbrown or stick to the pan. If they stick to the pan, add a very small amount of water.

Stuffed breast of veal

For stuffed breast of veal the breast, which contains little meat and many breast bones, is stuffed with a forcemeat and braised to create a very desirable, entree out of a slightly undesirable cut of veal.

Objectives

1. To teach the student the procedure for preparing stuffed breast of veal.
2. To teach the student how to trim, cut and stuff the breast.
3. To teach the student how to slice and dish up the stuffed breast of veal.

Equipment

1. Boning knife

2. Meat saw
3. French knife
4. Butcher twine
5. Large eye needle
6. Baker's scale
7. Qt. measure
8. Kitchen fork
9. Skillet
10. Mixing container
11. Roast pan
12. Meat grinder

Ingredients: Approx. yield: 25 servings

3	5 lb. sections (15 lbs.) of veal breast, trimmed
3	lbs. boneless veal shoulder, cut into strips
3	lbs. fresh pork shoulder, boneless, cut into strips
1½	lbs. dry bread cubes
1	qt. milk (variable)
8	ozs. onions, minced
6	ozs. celery, minced
8	ozs. bread crumbs (variable)
6	egg yolks
8	ozs. butter
¼	oz. sage
2	qts. brown gravy
	salt and pepper to taste

Preparation

1. Trim the three veal breasts with a French knife to remove the excess fat and bones. Cut a pocket in the breast by slicing with a boning knife between the flesh and the breast bones. Make the opening as large as possible but do not cut through the flesh at any point. Proceed only after demonstration by instructor.
2. Prepare the brown gravy. (See Chap. 15.)
3. Mince the celery and onions with a French knife.
4. Cut the pork and veal with a French knife into strips that will fit in the grinder.
5. Separate the eggs and beat the yokes slightly. Save the whites for another preparation.
6. Preheat oven to 350°F.
7. Have all equipment and ingredients handy.

Procedure

1. In a mixing container place the dry bread cubes and the milk. Let soak.
2. Sauté the onions and celery in a skillet in the butter and add to above mixture.
3. Add the pork, veal, and sage, mix thoroughly with the hands.

4. Grind this mixture twice, using the fine chopper plate.
5. Add the slightly beaten egg yolks, season with salt and pepper. Mix thoroughly. If mixture is too wet add bread crumbs as needed; if too dry add more milk.
6. Stuff the forcemeat mixture into the pockets cut into the veal breast. Pack it in fairly solid.
7. Using a large eye needle and butcher twine sew up the opening between the layer of meat and the breast bones. Secure properly so the forcemeat will not come out during the roasting period.
8. Season the stuffed breast with salt and pepper and place in a 350°F oven.
9. Roast until the breasts are thoroughly brown. Turn occasionally with a kitchen fork. Pour the brown gravy over the breasts and continue to braise until the breasts are tender and the forcemeat has become solid.
10. Remove from the oven, place in a steam table pan and let set in a warm place for 45 minutes.
11. Slice between the ribs with a French knife. Cut into 8 to 10 oz. portions. Serve covered with brown gravy and accompanied with buttered noodles.

Precautions and Safety Measures

1. Exercise caution when handling the knives.
2. Do not break through the flesh when cutting the pocket.
3. Do not stick a fork into the meat during the roasting period.
4. Use a sharp French knife and apply very little pressure when slicing each order of the veal breast.

Veal chops stroganoff

Veal chops stroganoff are sautéed veal chops, cut from the rib or loin, and baked in a sour cream sauce until tender. This item is a little different and is a good choice for the luncheon or dinner menu.

Objectives

1. To teach the student the procedure for preparing veal chops stroganoff.
2. To teach the student how to cut and sauté the veal chops.
3. To teach the student how to dish up veal chops stroganoff.

Equipment

1. French or butcher knife

2. Baker's scale
3. Cleaver
4. Iron skillet
5. Bake pan
6. Sauce pot, 6 qts.
7. Kitchen fork
8. Wire whip
9. Braising pot and cover
10. Stainless steel container
11. China cap
12. Full size steam table pan

Ingredients: Approx. yield: 25 servings

25	5 to 6 oz. veal chops, cut from the rib or the loin
1	lb. flour, bread
1	lb. 8 ozs. shortening
1	pt. butter, melted
1	pt. flour, bread
3	qts. brown stock
1	cup tomato purée
½	cup vinegar
1	lb. onions, minced
1	qt. sour cream
1	bay leaf
	salt and pepper to taste

Preparation

1. Cut the veal chops with a French or butcher knife from the rib or loin of the veal. Cut 5 to 6 ozs. each depending on the size desired. Proceed only after demonstration by instructor.
2. Prepare the brown stock. (See Chap. 12.)
3. Mince the onions with a French knife.
4. Place the first amount of flour in a bake pan and season with salt and pepper.
5. Preheat oven to 325°F.
6. Have all the equipment and ingredients handy.

Procedure

1. Place enough shortening in an iron skillet to cover the bottom ¼ in. and heat.
2. Pass each veal chop through the seasoned flour, pat off excess. Place in the hot shortening and sauté until golden brown. Turn with a kitchen fork and brown second side. Remove, let drain and line up in a braiser.
3. Place the butter in a sauce pot, heat.
4. Add the minced onions and sauté without color.
5. Add the second amount of flour making a roux and cook for 5 minutes.
6. Add the hot brown stock, tomato purée, vinegar and bay leaf, whipping vigorously with a wire whip until slightly thick and smooth. Let simmer for 30 minutes.
7. Add the sour cream, bring back to a boil. Remove from the range. Remove the bay leaf, check seasoning and pour the sauce over the sautéed chops. Cover the braiser.
8. Place in a 325°F oven and bake for about 1 to 1½ hours until each chop is tender. Remove from the oven.
9. Remove the chops from the sauce and place in a steam table pan. Strain the sauce through a fine china cap into a stainless steel container.
10. Dish up 1 chop per portion covered with sauce.

Precautions and Safety Measures

1. Exercise caution when handling the knife.
2. When sautéing the chops do not over-brown.
3. When sautéing the onions do not brown.
4. Baste the chops frequently with the sauce while baking.

Veal birds

Veal birds are thin slices of veal leg covered with a forcemeat mixture, rolled and secured with a tooth pick. They are browned in hot grease and baked in the oven until tender. This is an excellent choice for the luncheon menu.

Objectives

1. To teach the student the procedure for preparing veal birds.
2. To teach the student how to cut and flatten the thin veal slices.
3. To teach the student how to form the veal birds.
4. To teach the student how to dish up the veal birds.

Equipment

1. 50 round tooth picks
2. Boning knife
3. French knife
4. Cleaver
5. Sauce pan, 1 qt.
6. Kitchen spoon
7. Ladle
8. Meat grinder
9. Mixing container, 3 gal.
10. Wire whip
11. Qt. bowl
12. Roast pan
13. Steam table pan

Ingredients: Approx. yield: 50 servings

50	4 oz. thin slices of veal leg
3	lbs. boneless veal shoulder, cut into strips
2	lb. pork shoulder, boneless, cut into strips
1	lb. dry bread cubes
1½	pts. milk (variable)
6	ozs. onions, minced, sautéed
6	ozs. celery, minced, sautéed
8	ozs. bread crumbs (variable)
4	egg yolks
6	ozs. butter
¼	oz. sage
	salt and pepper to taste
2	qts. brown stock

Preparation

1. Cut the thin slices of veal from sections of a boned leg. Cut with a French or butcher knife, against the grain, about ¼ in. thick on a bias (slanting). Flatten with the side of a cleaver. Proceed only after demonstration by instructor.
2. Mince onions and celery with a French Knife. Sauté in a sauce pan in the 6 ozs. of butter.
3. Prepare the brown stock. (See Chap. 12.)
4. Cut the boneless pork and veal with a French knife into strips that will fit in the food grinder.
5. Separate the yolk from the white of the eggs. Place in a bowl and beat slightly with a wire whip.
6. Cut the bread into cubes with the French knife.
7. Preheat oven to 375°F.
8. Have all equipment and ingredients handy.

Procedure

1. In a mixing container place the bread cubes and the milk, mix with a kitchen spoon until the bread has absorbed the milk.
2. Add the sautéed onions and celery, pork, veal and the sage. Mix thoroughly with the hands.
3. Grind this mixture twice on the food grinder, using the fine chopper plate.
4. Add the slightly beaten egg yolks, season with salt and pepper. Mix thoroughly with the hands. If mixture is too wet (collapses when formed into a roll) add bread crumbs as needed. If too dry (will not hold together) add more milk.
5. Place about 2 to 3 ozs. of the stuffing on each flattened thin slice of veal, roll up and secure the ends with a tooth pick.
6. Place the veal birds in a roast pan and bake in a 375°F oven until golden brown.
7. Reduce the oven temperature to 325°F. Pour the brown stock over the birds and continue to bake for 1 more hour or until the birds are tender. Remove from oven and place in a steam table pan. Remove tooth picks.
8. Dish up 1 bird per portion with 2 ozs. of sauce. Serve accompanied with buttered noodles.

Precautions and Safety Measures

1. Exercise caution when slicing and flattening the veal slices.
2. Secure the veal rolls well, if they come unrolled during the baking period they are not fit to serve.

FRIED AND SAUTEED VEAL RECIPES

Veal Chop Sauté Italienne

For veal chop sauté Italienne the chops are cut from the rib of the veal. A pocket is cut into the meaty side so ham and Swiss cheese can be inserted. The chop is then passed through flour seasoned with Italian herbs and sautéed to a golden brown.

Objectives

1. To teach the student the procedure for preparing veal chop sauté Italienne.
2. To teach the student how to cut and process the veal chops.
3. To teach the student how to stuff and sauté the chops.
4. To teach the student how to dish up veal chop sauté Italienne.

Equipment

1. French or butcher knife
2. Cleaver
3. Boning knife
4. Bake pans, approx. 4
5. Iron skillet
6. Kitchen fork
7. Baker's scale
8. Spoon measures
9. Boning knife
10. Full size steam table pan
11. Qt. measure
12. Slicing machine

Ingredients: Approx. yield: 50 servings
50   6 to 8 oz. veal chops, cut from the rib of the veal
50   1 to 1½ oz. slices of ham
50   1 oz. slices of Swiss cheese
3   lbs. flour (variable)
1   tbsp. oregano
1   tbsp. basil
     salt and pepper to taste
2   qts. milk
12   eggs, whole, beaten slightly
1   qt. salad oil or melted shortening (variable)

Preparation
1. Cut the veal chops from trimmed veal ribs. Cut with a French or butcher knife, against the grain, ¾ to 1 in. thick. Cut a deep pocket into the meaty side of each chop with a boning knife. Proceed only after demonstration by instructor.
2. Slice the ham and Swiss cheese on a slicing machine about ⅛ in. thick.
3. Prepare an egg wash by combining the slightly beaten eggs and the milk. Place the eggs in a bowl, beat with a wire whip, pour in the milk while continuing to whip. Pour into a bake pan.
4. Place the flour in a bake pan and season with the basil, oregano, salt and pepper.
5. Preheat oven to 300°F.
6. Have all equipment and ingredients handy.

Procedure
1. Wrap the ham around each slice of Swiss cheese and insert it into the pocket that was cut into each veal chop.
2. Dredge each chop in the seasoned flour, press firmly with hand to flatten. Dip them into the egg wash and then back into the seasoned flour mixture for the second time. Again press firmly.
3. Place enough salad oil in the skillet to cover the bottom ¼ in., heat.
4. Add the chops and brown both sides slightly. Turn with a kitchen fork. Remove from skillet and drain.
5. Place the chops in a bake pan flesh side up.
6. Place in a 300°F oven and bake for about 1½ hours or until the chops are tender. Remove to a steam table pan.
7. Dish up 1 chop per portion. Place each portion on top of Italian or tomato sauce.

Precautions and Safety Measures
1. Exercise caution when handling the knives.

2. When dredging the chops, press the flour on firmly.
3. Let chops fall away from you when placing them in the hot oil or shortening to avoid splashing.
4. Exercise caution while baking so the chops will not become too brown.

Sautéed veal steak

Sautéed veal steaks are similar to the cutlet, but they are cut slightly thicker and not flattened as much. They are passed through seasoned flour and cooked to a golden brown in shallow grease.

Objectives
1. To teach the student the procedure for preparing sautéed veal steaks.
2. To teach the student how to cut and flatten the veal steaks.
3. To teach the student how to sauté and dish up the veal steaks.

Equipment
1. Butcher or French knife
2. Full size steam table pan
3. Baker's scale
4. Bake pan
5. Iron skillet
6. Cleaver

Ingredients: Approx. yield: 50 servings
50   6 to 8 oz. veal steaks, cut from the leg
3   lbs. flour
     salt and pepper to taste
     shortening as needed

Preparation
1. Cut the 6 to 8 oz. steaks from the boneless sections of the leg. Cut with a butcher or French knife about ¼ in. thick against the grain of the meat. Flatten slightly with the side of a cleaver. Proceed only after demonstration by instructor.
2. Place flour in a bake pan and season with salt and pepper.
3. Have all equipment and ingredients handy.

Procedure
1. Pass each veal steak through the seasoned flour. Dust off excess.
2. Place the steaks in the hot shortening, brown one side, turn with a kitchen fork and brown the other side. Remove and let drain. Place in a steam table pan.

3. Dish up 1 steak per portion covered with Bercy, mushroom, bordelaise or Madeira sauce.

Precautions and Safety Measures
1. Exercise caution when handling the knife and cleaver.
2. Sauté at a moderate temperature.
3. When placing the steaks in the hot grease, let them fall away from you so the grease will not splash towards you.

Veal cutlet cordon bleu

Veal is a delicately flavored meat so it blends well with other foods. In this case the veal is blended with ham and Swiss cheese. This combination has caught the fancy of the dining public and it has become quite a popular menu item.

Objectives
1. To teach the student the procedure for preparing veal cutlet cordon bleu.
2. To teach the student how to cut and process the veal cutlets.
3. To teach the student how to bread the veal cutlets.
4. To teach the student how to dish up a veal cutlet cordon bleu.

Equipment
1. French or butcher knife
2. Cleaver
3. Iron skillet, large
4. Kitchen fork
5. Bake pans (3)
6. 1 qt. bowl
7. Wire whip
8. Wooden mallet
9. Full size steam table pan
10. Slicing machine

Ingredients: Approx. yield: 25 servings

50	3 or 4 oz. very thin cutlets
25	1 oz. slices of Swiss cheese
25	1 oz. slices of ham, boiled
1	lb. butter
1	lb. shortening
8	whole eggs
1	qt. milk
2	lbs. bread flour
2	lbs. bread crumbs
	salt and pepper to taste

Preparation
1. Cut the veal cutlets from sections of a boned leg. Slice the veal thin against the grain with a French or butcher knife, and flatten with the side of a cleaver. Proceed only after demonstration by instructor.
2. Slice the ham and cheese approximately ⅛ in. thick on a slicing machine.
3. Place the flour in a bake pan, season with salt and pepper.
4. Prepare egg wash. Break eggs into a bowl, whip slightly with a wire whip, pour in the milk while continuing to whip. Place in a bake pan.
5. Place the bread crumbs in a bake pan.
6. Have all equipment and ingredients handy.

Procedure
1. Place one slice of cheese and one slice of ham on 25 of the cutlets. Cover with the remaining 25 cutlets. Pound the edges of the two cutlets together with a wooden mallet until they adhere to each other.
2. Bread by passing them through seasoned flour, egg wash, and bread crumbs.
3. Place half butter and half shortening in a skillet and heat. Sauté the cutlets until golden brown on each side. Turn with a kitchen fork. When done, remove and let drain. Place in a steam table pan.
4. Dish up 1 cutlet per portion. Top with melted butter.

Precautions and Safety Measures
1. Exercise caution when handling the knife and cleaver.
2. When flattening the cutlets, do not break the fibers of the meat completely. Tears will develop that will distract appearance.
3. Breading will brown and burn quickly. Exercise caution when sautéing. Sauté at a moderate temperature.
4. Press firmly when passing the cutlets through the bread crumbs so they will adhere tightly.

Fried breaded veal cutlet

Fried breaded veal cutlet is a thin, flattened slice off the leg of the veal. It is breaded by passing through flour, egg wash and bread crumbs and fried to a golden brown.

Objectives
1. To teach the student the procedure for preparing fried breaded veal cutlet.
2. To teach the student how to cut and flatten the veal slices.

3. To teach the student how to fry and dish up the breaded veal cutlet.
   Equipment
1. Full size steam table pan
2. Butcher or French knife
3. Qt. measure
4. Baker's scale
5. Bake pans (3)
6. Kitchen fork
7. Iron skillet
8. Cleaver
9. Wire whip
   Ingredients: Approx. yield: 50 servings
   50 4 or 5 oz. veal cutlets cut from the leg
     3 lbs. bread flour
   12 eggs, whole
     2 qts. milk
     3 lbs. bread crumbs
        shortening as needed
        salt and pepper to taste
   Preparation
1. Cut the veal cutlet from sections of a boned leg. Slice the veal thin against the grain with a French or butcher knife and flatten with the side of a cleaver. Proceed only after demonstration by instructor.
2. Place the flour in a bake pan and season with salt and pepper.
3. Prepare the egg wash. Break eggs into a bowl, whip slightly with a wire whip, pour in the milk while continuing to whip. Place in a bake pan.
4. Place the bread crumbs in a bake pan.
5. Have all equipment and ingredients handy.
   Procedure
1. Bread the cutlets by passing them through flour, egg wash and bread crumbs.
2. Place the shortening in the skillet, cover the bottom about 1/4 in. deep and heat.
3. Add the cutlets and fry until golden brown. Turn with a kitchen fork and brown the other side.
4. Remove from the skillet, let drain. Place in a steam table pan.
5. Dish up 1 cutlet per portion on top of tomato or some other appropriate sauce.
   Precautions and Safety Measures
1. Exercise caution when using the knife and cleaver.
2. Press firmly when passing the cutlets through the bread crumbs so they will adhere tightly.

3. When placing the breaded cutlets in the hot shortening, let them fall away from you so the grease will not splash towards you.
4. Fry at a moderate temperature. Breading will brown and burn quickly.

Sautéed veal chops

The veal chops, cut from the loin or rib, are passed through seasoned flour and cooked in shallow grease until golden brown.
Objectives
1. To teach the student how to cut veal chops from the loin and rib.
2. To teach the student the procedure for sautéing veal chops.
3. To teach the student how to dish up sautéed veal chops.
   Equipment
1. Large iron skillet
2. 2 bake pans
3. Butcher knife
4. Full size steam table pan
5. Kitchen fork
6. Baker's scale
   Ingredients: Approx. yield: 50 servings
   50 6 or 8 oz. veal chops
     2 lbs. shortening (variable)
     3 lbs. flour
        salt and pepper to taste
   Preparation
1. Cut the veal chops from trimmed loins or ribs of veal with a butcher knife or power saw. Proceed only after demonstration by instructor.
2. Place the flour in a bake pan and season with salt and pepper.
3. Have all equipment and ingredients handy.
   Procedure
1. Place shortening in the skillet, enough to cover the bottom about 1/4 inch deep, and heat.
2. Pass each chop through the seasoned flour. Dust off excess and place in the hot shortening, letting the chop fall away from you.
3. Sauté one side until golden brown, turn with a kitchen fork and sauté the other side.
4. Remove the chops from the skillet and let drain. Place in a steam table pan.
5. Dish up by placing one chop on top of

country gravy, brown sauce or Bercy sauce.

Precautions and Safety Measures
1. Exercise caution when cutting the chops.
2. Exercise caution when placing the chops in the shortening. Let them fall away from you so grease will not splash towards you.
3. Use caution when turning the chops. Keep the grease from splashing.
4. Do not overbrown the chops.

Breaded veal cutlet, Sauté Gruyère

Breaded veal cutlet, sautéed Gruyère is an excellent item to serve on either the luncheon or dinner menu. The breaded veal cutlet is sautéed, covered with a slice of tomato and Gruyère cheese and browned under the broiler.

Objectives
1. To teach the student the procedure for preparing breaded veal cutlet, sautéed Gruyère.
2. To teach the student how to cut the veal cutlets.
3. To teach the student how to dish up a breaded veal cutlet, sautéed Gruyère.

Equipment
1. Iron skillet, large
2. Boning knife
3. Butcher knife
4. Cleaver
5. French knife
6. Baker's scale
7. Bake pans (3)
8. Kitchen fork
9. 1 qt. bowl
10. Wire whip
11. 50 shallow casseroles
12. Slicing machine

Ingredients
50	4 or 5 oz. cutlets, cut from the leg of veal
100	thin slices of fresh tomatoes
50	slices of Gruyère or Swiss cheese paprika as needed
1	gal. tomato sauce
3	lbs. shortening (variable)
12	whole eggs
2	qts. milk
2	lbs. flour
3	lbs. bread crumbs salt and pepper to taste

Preparation
1. Cut the veal cutlets from sections of a boned leg of veal. Slice the veal thin, against the grain, with a French or butcher knife and flatten with the side of a cleaver. Proceed only after demonstration by instructor.
2. Prepare egg wash: Break the eggs into a bowl, whip slightly with a wire whip; pour in the milk while continuing to whip.
3. Bread the veal cutlets: Place the egg wash, flour and bread crumbs into separate bake pans. Season the flour with salt and pepper. Pass each cutlet through the flour, egg wash and bread crumbs. Press crumbs on firmly with the palm of the hand.
4. Slice the fresh tomatoes with a French knife.
5. Prepare the tomato sauce. (See Chap. 15.)
6. Slice the Gruyère or Swiss cheese almost ⅛ in. thick on a slicing machine.
7. Preheat broiler.
8. Have all equipment and ingredients handy.

Procedure
1. Place shortening in the iron skillet about ¼ inch deep and heat.
2. Add the veal cutlets and sauté until golden brown on both sides. Turn with a kitchen fork. Place each cutlet in a shallow casserole.
3. Place two thin slices of tomato on top of the sautéed cutlets.
4. On top of the tomato slices place a slice of Gruyère or Swiss cheese. Sprinkle with paprika and place under the broiler until the cheese melts.
5. Serve at once by placing a small amount of tomato sauce in the casserole.

Precautions and Safety Measures
1. Do not overbrown the cheese.
2. Exercise caution when slicing the cutlets, cheese and tomatoes.

BRAISED AND STEWED VEAL RECIPES

Fricassee of veal

Fricassee of veal is a type of stew consisting of meat and sauce. It is generally served on the luncheon menu with either noodles or baked rice.

Objectives
1. To teach the student the procedure for preparing veal fricassee.
2. To teach the student how to cut the veal.
3. To teach the student how to dish up veal fricassee.

Equipment
1. Stock pots (2), 5 gal. each
2. French knife
3. Wire whip
4. China cap
5. Cheese cloth
6. Full size steam table pan
7. Ladle
8. 3 gal. stainless steel container

Ingredients: Approx. yield: 50 servings

18	lbs. veal, shoulder, cut into 1 in. cubes
3	gal. water
2	lbs. shortening or butter
1½	lbs. flour
	yellow color as desired
	salt and white pepper to taste

Preparation
1. Cut the boneless veal shoulder with a French knife into 1 in. cubes. Proceed only after demonstration by instructor.
2. Have all other ingredients and equipment handy.

Procedure
1. Place the cubes of veal in stock pot and cover with water.
2. Bring to a boil and remove any scum that may appear with a ladle. Continue to simmer until veal is tender.
3. Remove from the fire and strain off the veal stock through a china cap covered with cheese cloth into a stainless steel container.
4. In a separate stock pot make a roux (flour and shortening or butter). Cook for 5 minutes, do not brown.
5. Add the strained veal stock, whipping vigorously with a wire whip to make a fricassee sauce. Tint sauce with yellow color and season with salt and white pepper.
6. Add the cooked veal to the sauce. Place in a steam table pan.
7. Dish up with a 6 to 8 oz. ladle. Accompany each portion with buttered noodles or baked rice.

Precautions and Safety Measures
1. Exercise caution when handling the knife.
2. Do not make sauce too thin.
3. Do not overcook the veal, it will fall apart when served.
4. When adding the veal stock to the roux, whip vigorously.

Veal chasseur

Veal chasseur consists of thin slices of veal leg sautéed, then simmered in a rich chasseur sauce until tender.

Objectives
1. To teach the student the procedure for preparing veal chasseur.
2. To teach the student how to slice the veal.
3. To teach the student how to dish up veal chasseur.

Equipment
1. French knife
2. Heavy skillet
3. Cup measure
4. Kitchen spoon
5. Qt. measure
6. Baker's scale
7. Braising pot
8. Bake pan
9. Skimmer
10. Full size steam table pan

Ingredients: Approx. yield: 25 servings

10	lbs. veal leg, boneless, sliced ¼ in. thick and 1 in. square
1	lb. butter
3	cloves garlic, minced
½	cup onions, minced
2	lbs. mushrooms, sliced
1	pt. dry white wine
⅓	cup parsley, chopped
3	qts. brown sauce
	salt and fresh ground pepper to taste
8	ozs. flour

Preparation
1. Slice the boneless leg of veal against the grain with a French knife. Cut into pieces ¼ in. thick and 1 in. square. Proceed only after demonstration by instructor.
2. Mince the onions and garlic with a French knife.
3. Chop and wash the parsley. Chop with a French knife and wash in a kitchen towel.
4. Slice the mushrooms with a French knife.

5. Prepare the brown sauce. (See Chap. 12.)
6. Have all equipment and ingredients handy.

Procedure

1. Place the butter in a skillet, heat slightly.
2. Add the slices of veal and sauté until golden brown. Remove from the skillet with a skimmer. Place in a bake pan and keep hot.
3. Sauté the onions, garlic and mushrooms in the butter remaining in the skillet. Sauté until they are tender. Remove to braising pot.
4. Add the flour and cook slightly.
5. Add the wine and brown sauce and stir with a kitchen spoon. Simmer gently until slightly thick and smooth.
6. Add the parsley and season with salt and pepper to taste.
7. Add the sautéed veal and simmer gently for about 10 minutes or until meat is tender. Place in a steam table pan.
8. Dish up in shallow casseroles with a 6 to 8 oz. ladle. Serve with noodles or baked rice.

Precautions and Safety Measures

1. Exercise caution when handling the knife.
2. When sautéing in the butter do not let the butter burn or become too brown.
3. Do not overcook the squares of veal or item will not appear appetizing when served.

Scallopine of veal Marsala

Scallopine of veal Marsala consists of thin slices of veal cut from the leg which are sautéed and poached in Marsala wine to increase the delicate flavor of the veal. This preparation is truly Italian.

Objectives

1. To teach the student the procedure for preparing scallopine of veal Marsala.
2. To teach the student how to cut the scallopines of veal.
3. To teach the student how to sauté scallopine of veal Marsala.
4. To teach the student how to dish up scallopine of veal Marsala.

Equipment

1. French or butcher knife
2. Baker's scale
3. Qt. measure

4. Iron skillet
5. Cleaver
6. Kitchen fork
7. China cap
8. Bake pan
9. Full size steam table pan
10. 2 qt. stainless steel container

Ingredients: Approx. yield: 25 servings

50	2 oz. thin slices of veal leg
1	lb. flour (variable)
1	lb. butter
1	pt. Marsala wine
1	qt. brown sauce
8	ozs. onions, minced
	salt and pepper to taste

Preparation

1. Slice the veal scallopines from boned sections of veal leg with a French or butcher knife. Slice fairly thin, against the grain, approximately 3 in. by 3 in. in size. Flatten slightly with the side of a cleaver. Proceed only after a demonstration by instructor.
2. Mince the onions with a French knife and sauté in a skillet in additional butter as necessary.
3. Prepare the brown sauce. (See Chap. 12.)
4. Place the flour in a bake pan and season with salt and pepper.
5. Have all equipment and ingredients handy.

Procedure

1. Press each scallopine into the seasoned flour.
2. Melt the butter in the skillet. When slightly hot add the scallopines and brown both sides thoroughly.
3. Pour the wine over the scallopines and simmer gently for about 10 minutes. Remove the meat with a kitchen fork and place in a steam table pan.
4. Add the sautéed onions and brown sauce to the wine still in the skillet. Simmer for 10 minutes. Strain through a china cap into a stainless steel container. Check the seasoning.
5. Dish up 2, 2 oz. scallopines covered with sauce to each portion.

Precautions and Safety Measures

1. Exercise caution when handling the knife and cleaver.
2. Exercise caution when pouring the wine over the meat, the liquid may flare up.
3. Do not overbrown the meat.

Veal ragout

Veal ragout is a thick, highly seasoned, brown stew consisting of a combination of vegetables and tender cubes of veal shoulder. It is served most often on the luncheon menu.

Objectives
1. To teach the student the procedure for preparing veal ragout.
2. To teach the student how to cut the meat and vegetables.
3. To teach the student how to dish up veal ragout.

Equipment
1. French knife
2. Braising pot
3. Qt. measure
4. Kitchen spoon
5. Baker's scale
6. 2 sauce pans, 6 qt. each
7. China cap
8. Full size steam table pan

Ingredients: Approx. yield: 50 servings

20	lbs. veal shoulder, boneless, cut into 1 inch cubes
1	qt. salad oil
2	cloves garlic, minced
1½	lbs. flour
100	½ in. cubes of carrots
100	½ in. cubes of celery
1	lb. onions, med. diced
2	gal. brown stock, hot
1	pt. tomato purée
2½	lb. box frozen peas
½	#10 can whole onions
2	bay leaves
2	tsp. basil
	salt and pepper to taste

Preparation
1. Cut the boneless veal shoulder with a French knife into 1 in. cubes. Proceed only after demonstration by instructor.
2. Mince the garlic and dice the onions with a French knife.
3. Cube the carrots and celery with a French knife.
4. Cook the frozen peas. (See Chap. 13.)
5. Prepare the brown stock. (See Chap. 12.)
6. Preheat the oven to 375°F.
7. Have all equipment and ingredients handy.

Procedure
1. Place the salad oil in braiser, heat. Add the veal cubes and sauté until brown.
2. Add the onion and garlic, continue to sauté until slightly tender.
3. Add the flour, making a roux, cook for 5 minutes.
4. Add the hot brown stock, stir with a kitchen spoon until thick and smooth.
5. Add the bay leaves, basil and tomato purée, cover braiser, place in a 375°F oven and cook until the veal cubes are tender (about 1 to 1½ hours).
6. Cook the celery and carrots in separate sauce pans with salt water until tender, drain.
7. When the meat is tender remove from the oven. Remove the two bay leaves. Add all the drained vegetables, except the peas. Season with salt and pepper.
8. Bring to a boil on the range. Remove from the range and place in a steam table pan.
9. Dish up into deep casseroles with a 6 to 8 oz. ladle. Sprinkle the cooked peas over the top of each portion.

Precautions and Safety Measures
1. Exercise caution when using the knife.
2. Cut the vegetables as uniform as possible, so they will cook evenly.
3. Do not overcook the meat or vegetables. Appearance will be lacking when served.

Hungarian veal goulash

Hungarian veal goulash is a type of stew, very similar to beef goulash. The difference is that veal is used and it is generally served with sour cream. An excellent luncheon item.

Objectives
1. To teach the student the procedure for making Hungarian veal goulash.
2. To teach the student how to cut the meat for cooking.
3. To teach the student how to dish up Hungarian veal goulash.

Equipment
1. French knife
2. Baker's scale
3. Cup measures
4. Qt. measure
5. Measuring spoons
6. Braising pot and cover
7. Kitchen spoon or wood paddle
8. Steel skillet
9. Steam table pan

Ingredients: Approx. yield: 50 servings

18   lbs. veal shoulder, cut into 1 in. cubes
3   cups salad oil
1   lb. flour
½   cup paprika
2   tsp. caraway seed
2   gal. brown stock, hot
1   pt. tomato purée
6   lbs. onions, sliced thin
1   qt. sour cream
     salt and fresh ground pepper to taste

Preparation

1. Cut boneless veal shoulder with a French knife into 1 in. cubes. Proceed only after demonstration by instructor.
2. Prepare brown stock. (See Chap. 12.)
3. Slice onions thin with a French knife.
4. Preheat oven to 350°F.
5. Have all equipment and ingredients handy.

Procedure

1. Place oil in braising pot, add the diced veal and brown meat.
2. Add the flour, paprika and caraway seed, continue to cook for about 5 minutes, stirring frequently with a kitchen spoon.
3. Add the hot brown stock and tomato purée, stir until thick and smooth.
4. Cover braiser, place in oven at a temperature of 350°F and bake for 1 hour.
5. While meat is cooking in the oven, sauté the onions in a skillet in additional oil until tender.
6. After the veal has cooked 1 hour, add the sautéed onions and continue to cook for an additional hour or until meat is tender.
7. Season with salt and pepper. Remove from the oven and place in a steam table pan.
8. Dish up into a casserole with a 6 to 8 oz. ladle. Top each portion with a spoonful of sour cream.

Precautions and Safety Measures

1. Exercise caution when handling the knife.
2. Veal is a tender meat. Check frequently while cooking so it is not overcooked.
3. When sautéing onions do not burn.

Veal stew

Veal stew is a combination of diced veal and vegetables cooked together. The brown stew is superior in flavor to the white or boiled stew. It is served most often on the luncheon menu.

Objectives

1. To teach the student how to cut the meat and vegetables.
2. To teach the student the procedure for preparing veal stew.
3. To teach the student how to dish up veal stew.

Equipment

1. French knife
2. Braising pot and cover
3. 3 sauce pans, (2) 4 qt. and (1) 2 qt.
4. Baker's scale
5. Kitchen spoon
6. Spoon measure
7. Qt. measure
8. China cap

Ingredients: Approx. yield: 50 servings

18   lbs. veal shoulder, boneless, cut into 1 in. cubes
2   gal. beef or brown stock
1   pt. salad oil
½   #10 can whole tomatoes, crushed
½   oz. garlic, minced
1   lb. flour
3   lbs. carrots, large dice
3   lbs. celery, large dice
½   #10 can whole small onions, drained
2½   lb. box frozen peas
½   #10 can cut green beans, drained
8   ozs. onions, minced
1   bay leaf
1   tbsp. thyme
      salt and pepper to taste

Armour and Co.

Veal stew

Preparation

1. Cut the boneless veal shoulder into 1 in. cubes with a French knife. Proceed only after demonstration by instructor.
2. Dice the carrots and celery, large with a French knife.
3. Mince the garlic and onions with a French knife.
4. Crush the canned tomatoes by hand.
5. Prepare the beef or brown stock. (See Chap. 12.)
6. Preheat oven to 375°F.
7. Have all equipment and ingredients handy.

Procedure

1. Place the salad oil in a braising pot, heat.
2. Add the cubes of veal and brown thoroughly.
3. Add the minced onions and garlic and continue to cook for 5 minutes.
4. Add the flour, blend thoroughly with a kitchen spoon, making a roux, cook slightly.
5. Add the hot beef or brown stock, thyme, and bay leaf. Stir with a kitchen spoon. Cover braiser and cook in a 375°F oven for about 1½ hours or until the veal cubes are tender.
6. Boil all the raw vegetables in separate sauce pans in salt water until tender. Drain in a china cap.
7. When the veal has become tender, remove from the oven, remove bay leaf and add the crushed tomatoes and all the drained cooked vegetables, except the peas.
8. Bring stew to a boil, check seasoning and consistency. Place in a steam table pan.
9. Dish up in casseroles with a 6 to 8 oz. ladle. Top with green peas.

Precautions and Safety Measures

1. Exercise caution when handling the knife.
2. Do not overcook the cubes of veal.
3. Drain all vegetables thoroughly before adding to the stew.
4. When adding the flour to make the roux be sure to cook slightly or the stew will have a raw flour taste.

Osso bucco

Osso bucco is a preparation of cross-cut sections of veal shank cooked by the braising method. This is a luncheon preparation.

Objectives

1. To teach the student how to cut the shank.
2. To teach the student the procedure for preparing osso bucco.
3. To teach the student how to dish up osso bucco.

Equipment

1. Meat saw
2. French knife
3. Qt. measure
4. Baker's scale
5. Grater
6. Braiser and cover
7. Wire whip
8. Kitchen spoon
9. Kitchen fork
10. Iron skillet, large
11. Sauce pot, 2 gal.
12. Full size steam table pan

Ingredients: Approx. yield: 50 servings

50	cross cut sections of meaty veal shank, 4 in. long
1	qt. salad oil (variable)
10	ozs. flour (variable)
1	cup white wine
8	ozs. tomato purée
1½	gal. brown stock
3	cloves garlic, minced
1	lb. onions, minced
	gratings of 2 lemons
	salt and pepper to taste

Preparation

1. Prepare the brown stock. (See Chap. 12.)
2. Mince the onions and garlic with a French knife.
3. Grate the 2 lemons on fine grid of box food grater.
4. Cut the veal shank into 4 in. thick cross-cut sections by cutting across the veal shank, against the grain of the meat, with a French knife and meat saw or power saw. Proceed only after demonstration by instructor.
5. Preheat oven to 350°F.
6. Have all equipment and ingredients handy.

Procedure

1. Place salad oil in skillet, cover the bottom about ⅛ in. deep and heat.
2. Add the veal shank and brown both sides. Turn with a kitchen fork.

3. Remove shank to braiser and season with salt and pepper.
4. Sauté the onions and garlic in the same oil used to brown the shanks. (Caution: Do not overbrown the onions.)
5. Add the flour, making a roux, and cook for about 5 minutes. Stir frequently with a kitchen spoon. Place this mixture in a sauce pot.
6. Add the brown stock, tomato purée and white wine, whipping vigorously with a wire whip until slightly thickened and smooth. Simmer 10 minutes.
7. Pour the sauce over the veal shanks, cover braiser and place in a 350°F oven for 1 hour, or until veal shanks are tender.
8. Remove from the oven. Add the grated lemon peel and stir gently with a kitchen spoon. Check seasoning. Place in a steam table pan.
9. Dish up one cross-cut veal shank per portion with a generous amount of sauce.

Precautions and Safety Measures
1. Exercise caution when handling the knife and saw.
2. Do not overbrown the onions.
3. Do not overcook the veal. The meat will fall from the bone.

Veal scallopine with mushrooms

Veal scallopine with mushrooms is of Italian origin as are all scallopine items. The small, thin scallopines are sautéed and then baked with the mushrooms and the rich Marsala wine sauce.

Objectives
1. To teach the student how to cut the scallopines.
2. To teach the student the procedure for preparing veal scallopine with mushrooms.
3. To teach the student how to dish up veal scallopine with mushrooms.

Equipment
1. Boning knife
2. Cleaver
3. French or butcher knife
4. Skillet, large
5. Bake pans
6. Kitchen fork
7. Kitchen spoon
8. Braising pot, large
9. Qt. measure
10. Baker's scale
11. Sauce pot, 2 gal.
12. Full size steam table pan
13. Wire whip

Ingredients: Approx. yield: 50 servings

100	2 oz. scallopines of veal, cut from the leg of veal
3	lbs. flour
1	qt. salad oil (variable)
2	lbs. fresh mushrooms, sliced thin
3	cloves garlic, minced
8	ozs. flour (variable)
6	qts. brown stock
1	pt. Marsala wine
	salt and pepper to taste

Preparation
1. Cut the 2 oz. scallopines from sections of a boned leg of veal. Slice the veal thin against the grain with a French or butcher knife and flatten with the side of a cleaver. Proceed only after demonstration.
2. Slice the mushrooms thin with a French knife and sauté in a sauce pan with part of the salad oil.
3. Mince the garlic with a French knife.
4. Prepare the brown stock and keep hot. (See Chap. 12.)
5. Place the first amount of flour in a bake pan and season with salt and pepper.
6. Have all equipment and ingredients handy.

Procedure
1. Place salad oil in skillet, covering the bottom about ⅛ in. deep, and heat.
2. Dredge (coat with flour) the scallopines in the seasoned flour and shake off excess. Place in the hot oil and sauté until both sides are slightly brown. Turn with a kitchen fork.
3. Remove from skillet and place, overlapping, in a braiser.
4. Sauté the garlic in the same skillet in the remaining salad oil.
5. Add the second amount of flour, making a roux, and cook slightly. Place the roux in a sauce pot.
6. Add the hot brown stock, whipping continuously with a wire whip until slightly thickened and smooth.
7. Add the sautéed mushrooms, the wine, and season with salt and pepper. Simmer for 10 minutes.
8. Pour the sauce over the sautéed scallopines and place in a 350°F oven for about 20 minutes. Remove from the oven and place in a steam table pan.

9. Dish up 2 scallopines per portion with a generous amount of sauce. Accompany each portion with a scoop of rice pilof or rice rissoto.

Precautions and Safety Measures
1. When adding the brown stock, whip vigorously so lumps will not form.
2. When placing the scallopines in the hot oil, let them fall away from you so grease will not splash towards you.
3. Do not overcook the veal. It will fall apart when served.
4. Exercise caution when handling the knife and cleaver.

BROILED VEAL RECIPES

Broiled veal loin chops

Broiled veal loin chops are cut from the loin of the veal. They contain both loin and tenderloin meat and are similar to a beef T-bone or porterhouse steak, but, of course, smaller in size. The veal loin chop is sometimes referred to as a baby T-bone. The chop is passed through salad oil, to help appearance and cooked on the broiler until golden brown. This is an excellent luncheon or dinner item.

Objectives
1. To teach the student the procedure for broiling veal loin chops.
2. To teach the student how to cut veal loin chops.

Armour and Co.

Broiled veal loin chops served on buttered noodles

3. To teach the student how to dish up veal loin chops.

Equipment
1. Cleaver
2. French knife
3. Bake pan
4. Baker's scale
5. Kitchen fork

Ingredients: Approx. yield: 25 servings
  25 6 to 8 oz. veal loin chops
    1 pt. salad oil (variable)
      salt and pepper to taste

Preparation
1. Cut the veal chops with a French or butcher knife or with a power saw against the grain of the meat. Cut from the loin of the veal in 6 to 8 oz. chops depending on size desired. Proceed only after demonstration by instructor.
2. Preheat broiler.
3. Have all equipment and ingredients handy.

Procedure
1. Place the salad oil in a bake pan and pass the chops through the oil. Shake off excess.
2. Place on a hot broiler fat side out.
3. Season with salt and pepper.
4. Brown one side, turn, sticking the fork in the tail of the chop, brown second side.
5. Remove from broiler and serve at once.
6. Dish up 1 chop per portion. Cover with brown butter sauce and garnish with watercress.

Precautions and Safety Measures
1. Exercise caution when handling the knife.
2. Be careful not to burn the fat on the chop. It will hinder the appearance when served.
3. Let the excess oil drain from the chop before placing it on the broiler.

BOILED VEAL RECIPES

Veal paprika with sauerkraut

Veal paprika with sauerkraut is a type of stew. A combination of veal cubes cooked in sauerkraut and served with sour cream, it is an excellent item for the luncheon menu.

Objectives
1. To teach the student the procedure for making veal paprika with sauerkraut.
2. To teach the student how to process the meat before cooking.

3. To teach the student how to dish up veal paprika with sauerkraut.
Equipment
1. French knife
2. Baker's scale
3. Measuring spoons
4. Qt. measure
5. Braising pot and cover
6. Kitchen spoon
7. Full size steam table pan
Ingredients: Approx. yield: 50 servings
15 lbs. veal shoulder, cut into 1 in cubes
1 lb. butter
6 lbs. onions, sliced thin
10 lbs. sauerkraut with juice
3 tbsp. salt
5 tbsp. paprika
1 tbsp. pepper, fresh ground
1 qt. sour cream, thick
3 cloves garlic, minced
Preparation
1. Cut the boneless shoulder veal into 1 in. cubes with a French knife. Proceed only after demonstration by instructor.
2. Slice the onions and mince the garlic with a French knife.
3. Have all equipment and ingredients handy.
Procedure
1. Place butter in braising pot. Add the onions and garlic and cook slowly until tender.
2. Add the diced veal and cook until meat is slightly brown. Stir occasionally with a kitchen spoon.
3. Add sauerkraut, paprika and seasoning. Cover and simmer gently until meat is tender. Remove from range and place in a steam table pan.
4. Dish up in casseroles with a 6 to 8 oz. ladle. Top each portion with a spoon of thick sour cream.
Precautions and Safety Measures
1. Exercise caution when handling the knife.
2. Stir frequently while cooking to avoid scorching.

VEAL VARIETY MEAT RECIPES

Veal kidney and brandy stew

Veal kidney and brandy stew consists of veal kidneys cooked by the stewing method in a rich sauce highly flavored with brandy.

Objectives
1. To teach the student the procedure for preparing veal kidney and brandy stew.
2. To teach the student how to clean and cut the kidneys.
3. To teach the student how to dish up veal kidney and brandy stew.
Equipment
1. French knife
2. Braising pot
3. Cup measure
4. Kitchen spoon
5. Scissors
6. Full size steam table pan
7. Qt. measure
Ingredients: Approx. yield: 25 servings
25 veal kidneys, diced fairly large
1 cup brandy
1 cup onions, minced
1½ cups butter
2 lbs. mushrooms, sliced
1 cup flour
1 cup dry white wine
1 qt. brown stock
⅓ cup parsley, chopped
salt and fresh ground pepper to taste
Preparation
1. Wash kidneys and remove membranes. Dice into ½ in. cubes with a French knife. Remove fat and tubes with a scissors. Proceed only after demonstration by instructor.
2. Slice the mushrooms with a French knife.
3. Prepare the brown stock. (See Chap. 12.)
4. Mince the onions with a French knife.
5. Chop the parsley with a French knife.
6. Have all equipment and ingredients handy.
Procedure
1. Place the butter in the braising pot, melt.
2. Add the kidneys and sauté until slightly brown.
3. Add the onions and mushrooms and continue to sauté until tender, stir frequently with a kitchen spoon.
4. Add the flour, blend in thoroughly. Cook for 5 minutes.
5. Add the wine and brown stock and cook, stirring frequently with a kitchen spoon until thickened.
6. Add the brandy and chopped parsley, simmer until the kidneys are tender. Remove from the range.

7. Season with salt and freshly ground pepper. Place in a steam table pan.
8. Dish up in a shallow casserole or shirred egg dish with a 6 to 8 oz. ladle accompanied with rice rissoto or pilof.

Precautions and Safety Measures

1. Exercise caution when handling the knife.
2. If the kidneys have a strong odor, soak in salt water for 45 minutes before cutting.
3. Stir the mixture gently when adding the flour and the liquid so the mushrooms will not be broken.

pork preparation

■ Pork is the meat of hogs, usually less than 12 months of age. The best pork on the market comes from hogs 6 to 8 months of age. Pork ranks second to beef in total meat consumption in the United States. The average consumption for each person is about 60 to 65 pounds of pork each year. With this much consumption it becomes obvious that pork is extremely popular and must be placed on the menu in one form or another.

Since hogs are raised solely for the edible meat they will produce and are always marketed at an early age, all pork is generally tender. A sow produces her first litter when she is a year old, so she can still be marketed at a young age. This is not possible with other edible meat animals such as beef or lamb. Since the majority of the hogs reach the market at such an early age, their sexual characteristics have not developed enough to make a difference in the meat.

Pork has a very high fat content. Since fat supplies heat for the body, pork is thus considered a winter meat and is extremely popular during that time of the year. Another reason for this seasonal popularity is price. Most hogs are marketed during the fall and winter months and this causes the prices to be lower at that time. Certain pork cuts, though, such as bacon, spare ribs and ham are popular the year round. Since many of these cuts are excellent for back-yard grilling, they will be more expensive in the summer months.

PORK GRADING

There are three grades of pork in use today, in order of desirability: U.S. 1, U.S. 2 and U.S. 3. The grade of pork, however, is not as important as the grading of other animals since all pork is from young animals and is, therefore, tender.

Barrows (male hogs castrated when young) and gilts (immature female hogs) are graded U.S. 1. Fairly young sows are as a rule, graded U.S. 2; old sows, which have soft fat and oily carcasses, are generally graded U.S. 3. The grading is based on three factors: *conformation,* that is, the form of the animal and its wholesale cuts; *finish,* color and amount of fat covering; and *quality,* the color of bones, marbling of fat and lean, and smoothness and fineness of the grain of the lean meat.

COMMERCIAL CUTS

Practically all pork is marketed as cuts rather than by the quarter, side or carcass. This is done for a number of reasons. If pork were sold by the side or carcass, the butcher or restaurant operator would have a very difficult time either reselling or converting all these fresh cuts into desirable menu items since all fresh pork cuts are not popular. Only one-third of all the pork marketed is sold as fresh pork. The majority of the pork cuts are cured or smoked. In fact, every pork cut can be processed by these two methods. Many pork cuts are more desirable when cured or smoked. Another reason pork is marketed by cuts is the fact that pork meat will spoil much more rapidly than other edible meats. Too much surplus on

hand could be very costly for the butcher or restaurant operator.

Pork is a light-colored meat and, therefore, very delicate in flavor. When it is served on the restaurant menu it is usually accompanied with apples in some form to help bring forth a more pronounced flavor. Pork is always cooked well done in order to develop the delicate flavor to its fullest extent. Also, if pork is not cooked well done, a disease called trichinosis might be passed on to the customer.

WHOLESALE CUTS: COOKING METHODS

When the hog's carcass is blocked out or divided for wholesale, eleven different cuts are created. They range from very desirable cuts to less desirable and, of course, the demand dictates the selling price. The following is a list of the wholesale pork cuts, their chief characteristic, and the best method of preparation when placing them on the menu of a food service establishment.

Loin: The pork loin consists of three parts: rib end, loin end and tenderloin. The cut extends along the greater part of the backbone from about the 3rd rib, through the rib and loin area. It is considered one of the leanest and most popular pork cuts and, because of its varied structure, it can be used in a variety of ways on the menu. Pork loins under 15 pounds are considered the best because they are generally more flavorful and tender. In the commercial kitchen the tenderloin, the tenderest of all pork cuts, is taken from the underside of the loin. It is a fairly long, tapered, narrow strip of lean meat and weighs about 8 to 12 ounces. They are generally saved until a quantity sufficient to place them on the menu accumulates. They can be broiled, sautéed, braised, roasted or fried and served in a variety of ways. The loin is generally separated into the rib end and

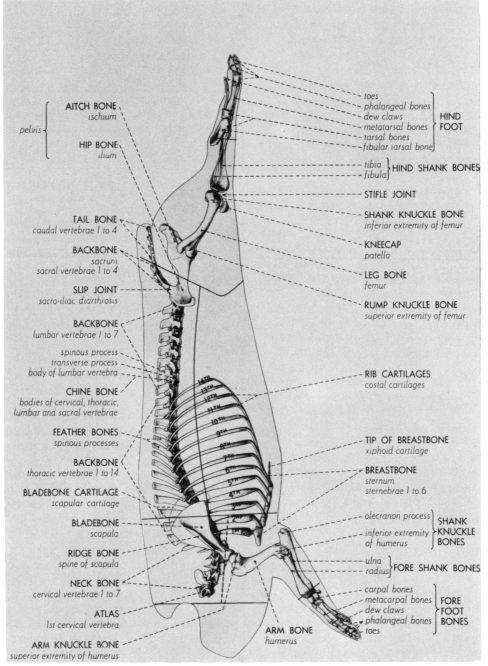

AITCH BONE
ischium

HIP BONE
ilium

pelvis

toes
phalangeal bones
dew claws
metatarsal bones
tarsal bones
fibular tarsal bone

HIND
FOOT

tibia
fibula

HIND SHANK BONES

STIFLE JOINT

SHANK KNUCKLE BONE
inferior extremity of femur

TAIL BONE
caudal vertebrae 1 to 4

KNEECAP
patella

BACKBONE
sacrum
sacral vertebrae 1 to 4

LEG BONE
femur

SLIP JOINT
sacro-iliac diarthrosis

RUMP KNUCKLE BONE
superior extremity of femur

BACKBONE
lumbar vertebrae 1 to 7

spinous process
transverse process
body of lumbar vertebra

RIB CARTILAGES
costal cartilages

CHINE BONE
*bodies of cervical, thoracic,
lumbar and sacral vertebrae*

FEATHER BONES
spinous processes

TIP OF BREASTBONE
xiphoid cartilage

BACKBONE
thoracic vertebrae 1 to 14

BREASTBONE
sternum
sternebrae 1 to 6

BLADEBONE CARTILAGE
scapular cartilage

BLADEBONE
scapula

olecranon process
inferior extremity
of humerus

SHANK
KNUCKLE
BONES

RIDGE BONE
spine of scapula

ulna
radius

FORE SHANK BONES

NECK BONE
cervical vertebrae 1 to 7

carpal bones
metacarpal bones
dew claws
phalangeal bones
toes

FORE
FOOT
BONES

ATLAS
1st cervical vertebra

ARM KNUCKLE BONE
superior extremity of humerus

ARM BONE
humerus

Pork skeleton: Location, structure and names of bones.

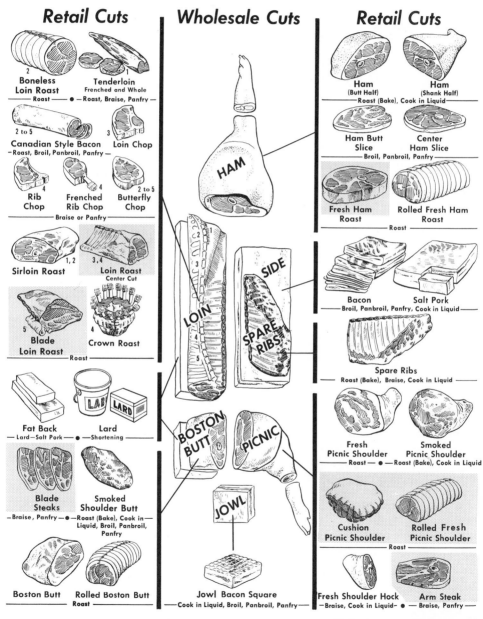

Retail Cuts   Wholesale Cuts   Retail Cuts

2
Boneless Loin Roast
Tenderloin Frenched and Whole
— Roast — ● — Roast, Braise, Panfry —

2 to 5
Canadian Style Bacon
— Roast, Broil, Panbroil, Panfry —
3
Loin Chop

4
Rib Chop
4
Frenched Rib Chop
2 to 5
Butterfly Chop
— Braise or Panfry —

1, 2
Sirloin Roast
3, 4
Loin Roast Center Cut

5
Blade Loin Roast
4
Crown Roast
— Roast —

Fat Back
— Lard—Salt Pork — ● — Shortening —
LAB LARD
Lard

Blade Steaks
— Braise, Panfry — ●
Smoked Shoulder Butt
— Roast (Bake), Cook in Liquid, Broil, Panbroil, Panfry —

Boston Butt
Rolled Boston Butt
— Roast —

HAM

LOIN

SIDE

SPARE RIBS

BOSTON BUTT

PICNIC

JOWL

Jowl Bacon Square
— Cook in Liquid, Broil, Panbroil, Panfry —

Ham (Butt Half)
Ham (Shank Half)
— Roast (Bake), Cook in Liquid —

Ham Butt Slice
Center Ham Slice
— Broil, Panbroil, Panfry —

Fresh Ham Roast
Rolled Fresh Ham Roast
— Roast —

Bacon
Salt Pork
— Broil, Panbroil, Panfry, Cook in Liquid —

Spare Ribs
— Roast (Bake), Braise, Cook in Liquid —

Fresh Picnic Shoulder
Smoked Picnic Shoulder
— Roast — ● — Roast (Bake), Cook in Liquid —

Cushion Picnic Shoulder
Rolled Fresh Picnic Shoulder
— Roast —

Fresh Shoulder Hock
— Braise, Cook in Liquid — ●
Arm Steak
— Braise, Panfry —

National Livestock and Meat Board

Pork Chart: Meat cuts and common cooking methods. Cuts shown in grey are not commonly used in the commercial kitchen in the form shown.

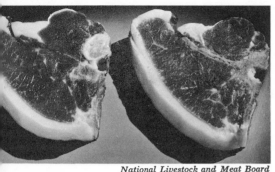

Pork loin chops

Shank half of ham

loin end by cutting through the last two ribs. This leaves one rib on the loin end. All bones are then removed from the cuts except the rib bones which are left on the rib end mainly for appearance when the cut is served. These two cuts are generally placed on the menu as roast loin of pork, broiled or sautéed pork chops, pork cutlets or noisette. They can be served in many different ways.

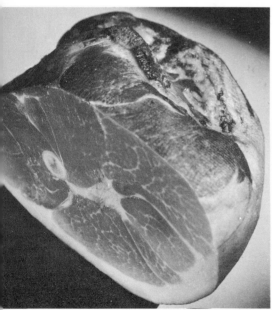

Smoked ham, butt half

Ham: This is the thigh and buttock of the hog. It contains more lean meat and is marketed in two forms: smoked and cured, and fresh. The most popular form is to first cure the ham in a solution of salt, sugar and sodium nitrate and then smoke it. The skin may be left on or removed. Some hams, such as Virginia and country hams, are cured but not smoked. Hams are marketed in a variety of forms, such as partly cooked, cooked, raw smoked, canned, boneless, tenderized and shankless. The best kind to use varies with the specific needs of the food service establishment. In the commercial kitchen hams are baked, cut into steaks and broiled or pan broiled, boiled, sliced and used for sandwiches, etc. In fact, ham is a very versatile item and the ways of serving it are limitless.

Bacon: This is the cured and smoked belly of the hog. The size of the belly will denote the quality of the bacon. Fairly small bellies from very young hogs are the most desirable. High quality bacon should contain about 40 to 45 percent fat and 5 percent rind. In the commercial kitchen bacon is an extremely popular and versatile item. It is used for sandwiches, garnishes, appetizers and entrée dishes. The bacon grease that is extracted when the bacon is cooked is very desirable in seasoning and sautéing certain food items because it is one animal fat that is almost completely digestible.

Pork spareribs

Spare ribs: These are the whole rib section removed from the belly (side) of the hog carcass. They lie right on top of the bacon section. There is little meat on the spare ribs but what there is contains an excellent flavor and is very tender. The best quality spare ribs weigh about 3 pounds or under. Spare ribs may be purchased fresh or smoked but the fresh form is the most popular. On the restaurant menu spare ribs are popular boiled, barbecued, broiled and baked. They can be served as an appetizer or as an entrée.

Boston butt: This is a square cut of shoulder located just above the lower half of the shoulder (picnic or callie). It contains the blade bone and a large portion of lean. It weighs about 6 to 10 pounds and contains meat that has a long fiber and a coarse grain. Boston butt is usually sold fresh when the bone is left in. When boneless the top section is usually cured by smoking and sold as cottage ham. The Boston butt is an excellent cut to choose when a preparation calls for a solid piece of meat that is reasonably priced. The Boston butt can be roasted, boiled, or cut into cutlets and sautéed or fried.

Picnic or callie: This is the lower half of the shoulder of the hog carcass. It resembles the ham in shape, but is smaller and contains more bone and less lean meat. It is marketed in two forms: fresh and smoked. This cut can generally be purchased at a very low cost per pound, but one must remember that he is buying

Boston butt

Smoked picnic shoulder

a big percentage of bone. Fresh picnics are a good choice when preparing such items as chop suey, pork patties, and country sausage. Smoked picnics are a good choice for creamed ham, deviled ham, and ham salad. The average weight of a picnic is 3 to 6 pounds.

Jowls: These, also referred to as *jowl bacon,* are the cured and smoked cheek meat of the large hogs. They are cured and smoked in the same manner as regular bacon and possess a similar flavor, although the eating qualities are much poorer. The jowl weighs about 2 to 4 pounds and is used for bacon crackling, seasoning, or for flavoring such items as baked beans and string beans. Jowl can be purchased at a very reasonable price.

Feet: The *feet* are the cut below the shank. Both front and hind feet are marketed unless they are too coarse. They will average from ¾ to 1½ pounds and are usually sold in a pickled form, although they may also be purchased fresh and smoked. Pigs feet may appear on the restaurant menu as broiled pigs feet, or they may be made boneless and served on a cold plate.

Hock: This is the knee joint of the hog. Hocks are removed from both the front and hind legs. There is not very much meat on the hock, but they contain good flavor and, therefore, are popular when cooked with sauerkraut. Hocks are purchased fresh or smoked.

Fat back and clear plate: These two cuts are very similar, except in some cases the clear plate may contain a few more strips of lean meat running through it. They are both fairly solid, rectangular slabs of fat extracted from the surface of the hog's carcass. Lard is usually rendered from these cuts, but in some cases, when there is lean present, they are cured in salt and marketed as salt pork. In the commercial kitchen salt pork is used in many preparations as a flavoring ingredient or it is inserted to add juice. This is the case when an item such as beef

tenderloin is larded. To lard an item the salt pork is cut into thin strips and drawn, by use of a larding needle, through the meat to increase the juiciness when it is roasted.

Few of the *pork variety meats* are placed on the market. Most of them are used in the preparation of various types of sausage. However, liver, brains and pig tails are marketed. Although they are fairly popular items in the domestic kitchen, they are not very popular in the commercial kitchen where beef and veal variety meats are more desired.

PORK TERMINOLOGY

Chitterlings are the large and small intestines of the hog. They are emptied and thoroughly rinsed before frying.

Canadian bacon is the trimmed, pressed and smoked boneless loin of pork. The average weight of Canadian bacon is 4 to 6 pounds. It can be cooked by baking, sautéing or broiling.

Cottage ham is the smoked, boneless meat extracted from the blade section of the Boston butt. Blade section refers to the section of meat that lies above the flat blade bone. This section is usually compact and fairly lean. Cottage ham weighs about 1½ to 4 pounds. For the best results it should be boiled or steamed.

Head cheese is the jellied, spiced, pressed meat from hog's head. It is covered with a natural casing and sold as a luncheon meat.

Loin backs are the rib bones that are removed from the loin. In some cases loin backs will be used in place of spare ribs because they contain more meat.

Salt pork is fat back or clear plate that has been cured in salt.

Fresh ham is the unsmoked ham cut from the hind leg of the hog.

Suckling pig is a baby pig 4 to 6 weeks old and weighs from 20 to 35 pounds dressed. They are purchased with the head on and are priced per pig rather than by the pound. They are roasted whole and are used for ornamental purposes as well as for providing a tender, delicate flavored meat.

Curing is the salting of an item to retard the action of bacteria and to preserve the meat.

Virginia ham is a ham that is cured in salt for a period of about seven weeks. It is rubbed with a mixture of molasses, brown sugar, saltpeter and pepper, and is cured for two weeks more. The ham is then hung hock down for a period of 30 days to a year. This ham is not smoked and must be scrubbed and soaked for at least a day before cooking.

Proscuitto ham originated in Italy. It is very dry and hard. It comes ready to eat and is usually sliced very thin and used in the making of hors d'oeuvres and appetizers.

PORK RECIPES

The following recipes are for pork items that are popular in the commercial kitchen. A knowledge of these should be extremely helpful to the student or apprentice cook.

Roasted and baked pork
(Pages 395 to 407)

Roast pork loin
Roast fresh ham or picnic
Ham loaf
Barbecued spareribs
Baked sugar cured ham
Sweet-sour ham balls
Baked stuffed pork chops
Apple stuffed pork chops
Stuffed spare ribs
Stuffed fresh cottage ham
Swedish meat balls in sour cream
  sauce
Ham and cabbage rolls

Fried and sautéed pork
(Pages 407 to 410)

Sautéed pork chops or cutlets

Breaded pork chops or cutlets
Ham croquettes
Ham turnovers

Braised pork
(Pages 410 to 415)

Pork chops creole
Barbecued pork chops
Pork chops Jonathan
Pork chops Hawaiian
Pork chops, honey style
Hawaiian pork
Braised pork tenderloin de luxe

Broiled pork
(Pages 415 to 417)

Broiled pork sausage patties
Broiled ham steak Hawaiian
Broiled pig feet
Ham and asparagus rolls Mornay

Boiled pork
(Pages 417 to 420)

Diced ham and lima beans
Boiled smoked cottage ham
Ham à la king
Pork chop suey

ROASTED OR BAKED PORK RECIPES

Roast pork loin

Roast pork loin is usually served during the winter months of the year because of its high fat content. An order consists of two slices: one with rib and one with loin. Roast pork can be served on either the luncheon or dinner menu with or without bread dressing.

Objectives
1. To teach the student how to trim the pork loin for roasting.
2. To teach the student the procedure for roasting a pork loin.
3. To teach the student how to slice and dish up roast pork loin.

Equipment
1. Wire whip
2. Roast pan
3. Qt. measure
4. China cap

Roast loin of pork garnished with baked apples.

5. Kitchen fork
6. French knife
7. Cup measure
8. Kitchen spoon
9. Baker's scale
10. Boning knife
11. 2 gal. stainless steel container
12. 2 gal. sauce pot
13. Full size steam table pan

Ingredients: Approx. yield: 50 servings

35	lbs. pork loin
1	lb. onions, cut rough
½	lb. celery, cut rough
½	lb. carrots, cut rough
10	ozs. bread flour (variable)
5	qts. brown pork stock
1	tsp. whole cloves
	salt and pepper to taste
⅓	cup tomato purée

Preparation

1. Trim the pork loin by separating the rib end from the loin end. Remove the tenderloin with a boning knife. (Save the tenderloin for use in another preparation.) Remove all but the rib bones from both the loin end and the rib end with a boning knife. Proceed only after demonstration by instructor.

2. Season the loin with salt, pepper and sprinkle on whole cloves.
3. Cut the rough garnish (onions, celery and carrots) with a French knife.
4. Preheat oven to 400°F.
5. Prepare the brown pork stock. (See Chap. 12.)
6. Have all equipment and ingredients handy.

Procedure

1. Place the seasoned pork loin in a roast pan, fat side down. Put in a preheated oven at 400°F.
2. Roast until meat becomes brown, remove excess fat from the pan and save for later use in making the gravy. Reduce oven heat to 325°F.
3. Add the rough garnish and continue to roast until vegetables become light brown. Turn meat occasionally with a kitchen fork.
4. Add just enough water to cover the bottom of the roast pan. Continue to roast until meat is well done.
5. Remove meat from the roast pan and place in a steam table pan. Keep covered in a warm place until ready to slice. Pour dripping left in the roast

pan into a stainless steel container. Deglaze roast pan by adding the brown pork stock and bringing it to a boil on the range. Pour this liquid into the stainless steel container also.

6. Place fat that was removed from the pork roast in a sauce pot. Place on the range and heat.
7. Add the flour to the pork fat, making a roux, and cook for 5 minutes. Stir occasionally with a kitchen spoon.
8. Add the hot stock that was placed in the stainless steel container and whip vigorously with a wire whip until slightly thick and smooth. Add the tomato purée and let simmer for about 30 minutes.
9. Check color and seasoning. If gravy is too light in color, add caramel coloring to darken. Strain through a china cap back into the stainless steel container.
10. Slice the pork roast with a French knife. Dish up 2 slices per portion (1 rib and 1 loin). Serve with or without bread dressing; cover with pork gravy.

Precautions and Safety Measures
1. Exercise caution when handling the knives to avoid cutting self.
2. Be sure the pork loin is well done before it is removed from the oven. Test by inserting a kitchen fork into the meat; the fork should penetrate easily.
3. Do not overcook the pork loin; it will crumble when sliced.
4. Use caution when straining the gravy through the china cap; it may splash.

Roast fresh ham or picnic

Fresh ham makes an excellent roast because it contains a large portion of lean meat and enough fat covering to bring forth a juicy piece of meat.

Objectives
1. To teach the student how to bone and tie the fresh ham or fresh picnic.
2. To teach the student the procedure for roasting fresh ham or picnic.
3. To teach the student how to slice and dish up fresh ham or picnic.

Equipment
1. Roasting pan
2. French knife
3. Boning knife
4. Cup measures
5. Qt. measure
6. Baker's scale
7. Wire whip
8. China cap
9. Kitchen fork
10. Kitchen spoon
11. 2 gal. stainless steel container
12. Sauce pot, 2 gal.
13. Butcher twine
14. Full size steam table pan

Ingredients: Approx. yield: 50 servings

30	lbs.	fresh picnic or ham
1	lb.	onions, cut rough
½	lb.	celery, cut rough
½	lb.	carrots, cut rough
1	lb.	bread flour (variable)
5	qts.	brown pork stock
1	tsp.	whole cloves
⅓	cup	tomato purée
		salt and pepper to taste
2	lbs.	pork fat

Preparation
1. Remove all the bones from the fresh ham or picnic with a boning knife. Trim off excess fat and tie the meat with butcher twine. Proceed only after demonstration by instructor.
2. Cut the rough vegetable garnish (onions, celery and carrots) with a French knife.
3. Preheat oven to 375°F.
4. Prepare brown pork stock. (See Chap. 12.)
5. Have all equipment and ingredients handy.

Procedure
1. Place tied roast in roasting pan, fat side down, season with salt and pepper and add whole cloves.
2. Place in the preheated oven at 375°F and brown thoroughly. Remove excess fat and save.
3. Reduce the oven heat to 325°F and add the rough garnish. Continue to roast until garnish is slightly brown. Turn roast occasionally with a kitchen fork.
4. Add a small amount of water to cover bottom of roasting pan.
5. Continue to roast until the meat is done, approximately 3 hours, depending on the size of the roast. Remove meat from the roast pan and place in a steam table pan. Cover and keep warm.
6. Pour the drippings left in the roast pan into a stainless steel container. Deglaze the roast pan by adding brown pork and

bringing it to a boil on the range. Pour into the stainless steel container.

7. Place pork fat in a sauce pot and heat.
8. Add the flour to the pork fat, making a roux, and cook for about 5 minutes. Stir occasionally with a kitchen spoon.
9. Add the hot brown pork stock and whip vigorously with a wire whip until the gravy is slightly thick and smooth. Add the tomato purée and let simmer for about 30 minutes.
10. Check the color and seasoning. If the color is light, darken with caramel coloring. Strain through a fine china cap back into the stainless steel container.
11. Remove the butcher twine and slice with a French knife or on the slicing machine. Serve 3 to 4 ozs. per portion with the pork gravy.

Precautions and Safety Measures
1. Use caution when cutting the meat and vegetable garnish to avoid cutting yourself.
2. Be sure the fresh ham is well done before removing it from the oven.
3. Do not overcook the roast or the meat will crumble when sliced.

4. Use caution when straining the gravy, it may splash.
5. If grease forms on the surface of the gravy, dip it off with a ladle before serving.

Ham loaf

Ham loaf is a ground meat entrée. The ground cured ham is mixed with ground fresh pork to help it bind better when baked. This entree is a luncheon item and is generally served with a fruit or tomato sauce.

Objectives
1. To teach the student the procedure for preparing ham loaf.
2. To teach the student how to bake a ham loaf.
3. To teach the student how to dish up the ham loaf.

Equipment
1. Baker's scale
2. 5 loaf pans, 4x9 inch
3. 2 roast pans
4. Qt. measure
5. Spoon measure
6. Meat grinder

Oscar Mayer and Co.

Ham loaves may be baked in individual molds as shown here or in larger loaf pans.

7. Wire whip
8. Mixing container
9. 1 gal. stainless steel container
10. Kitchen spoon
11. Full size steam table pan

Ingredients: Approx. yield: 50 servings

5	lb. picnic, lean, fresh
8	lbs. ham, cured, smoked
1	lb. 8 oz. bread crumbs
1	qt. milk
14	whole eggs, beaten
1	tsp. pepper

Preparation

1. Cut the fresh pork and cured ham with a French knife into pieces that will pass through the meat grinder.
2. Grind the meat in a meat grinder using the medium chopper plate.
3. Break the eggs into a stainless steel container and beat with a wire whip.
4. Preheat oven to 350°F.
5. Coat the inside of the loaf pans with salad oil.
6. Have all equipment and ingredients handy.

Procedure

1. Place the bread crumbs, milk, beaten eggs and pepper in a mixing container. Blend thoroughly with a kitchen spoon and let set until the crumbs absorb the liquid.
2. Add the ground meat and mix thoroughly by hand.
3. Pack into the oiled loaf pans, then set loaf pans in roast pans which contain about an inch of water and place in oven.
4. Bake at 350°F for about 2 hours or until the loaf is baked through and is firm.
5. Remove from the oven when done. Let cool and remove to bake pans, then place in refrigerator overnight.
6. Slice with a French knife or on a slicing machine into 5 to 6 oz. portions. Reheat in a steam table pan.
7. Dish up 1 slice per portion and serve with fruit, tomato, or raisin sauce.

Precautions and Safety Measures

1. Exercise caution when handling the knife to avoid cutting self.
2. Always bake the loaf the day before serving. It will be firmer for slicing and dishing up.
3. Pack the ham mixture firmly into the loaf pans. The loaf will bake more solid.

4. Be gentle when handling the slices and reheating them, they may break.

Barbecued spareribs

This is the most popular method of preparing spareribs. The tangy barbecue sauce is a welcomed addition to the delicate flavor of the spareribs. A popular item in the commercial kitchen as well as the back yard grill, it is served both as an appetizer and entrée.

Objectives

1. To teach the student the procedure for preparing barbecued spareribs.
2. To teach the student how to dish up barbecued spareribs.

Equipment

1. French knife
2. Qt. measure
3. Portion scale
4. Sheet pans
5. Stock pot, 10 gal.
6. Kitchen fork

Ingredients: Approx. yield: 50 servings

50	pork spareribs, fresh 12 oz. pieces
1	pt. salad oil (variable)
2	gal. barbecue sauce
	paprika, as needed

Preparation

1. Weigh each sparerib section on a portion scale. Cut the trimmed spareribs with a French knife into 12 oz. pieces. Proceed only after demonstration by instructor.
2. Prepare barbecue sauce. (See Chap. 15.)
3. Preheat oven to 350°F.
4. Have all equipment and ingredients handy.

Procedure

1. Place ribs in stock pot, cover with water and bring to a boil.
2. Reduce heat by bringing stock pot to the side of the range. Let ribs simmer for about 30 minutes.
3. Remove ribs from stock and place on sheet pans.
4. Brush oil over each rib and sprinkle with paprika.
5. Brown each side slightly under the broiler. Turn with a kitchen fork. Place in roast pans with the outside of ribs turned upward.
6. Cover each rib with the barbecue sauce.

Place in 350°F oven and bake for about 1 hour or until all ribs are tender.

7. Remove ribs from oven. Cut between every other rib and place in a steam table pan.
8. Dish up 4 or 5 ribs per portion if serving as an entree. Two ribs if serving as an appetizer. Accompany each serving with barbecue sauce.

Precautions and Safety Measures
1. Exercise caution when handling the knife.
2. When boiling the ribs do not overcook. Serving portions will be lost and ribs will be difficult to handle.
3. When baking the ribs, baste at least twice during the baking period.

Baked sugar cured ham

Baked sugar cured ham has long been a favorite on both the luncheon and dinner menu. The ham is first boiled then baked with a covering of honey and sugar to give it that characteristic sweet taste.

Objectives
1. To teach the student the procedure for baking ham.
2. To teach the student how to slice and dish up the ham.

Equipment
1. Stock pot, 10 gal.
2. Roast pans
3. Kitchen fork
4. Boning knife
5. French knife

Ingredients: Approx. yield: 50 servings

30	lbs. ham, smoked, sugar cured
1	qt. honey
1	lb. brown sugar
2	tsp. ground cloves

Preparation
1. Preheat oven to 350°F.
2. Have all equipment and ingredients handy.

Procedure
1. Place hams in stock pot. Cover with hot water, place on range bring to a boil and let simmer for approximately 2 hours.
2. Remove the hams from the water with a kitchen fork. Take off the rind and remove the aitch bone which lies across the upper part of the ham. Use a boning knife.

3. Trim off some of the excess fat for even shaping and score with a French knife.
4. Place hams in roast pans and spread the honey over each ham.
5. Mix the ground cloves with the brown sugar and sprinkle over the ham. Add a small amount of water to the bottom of the roast pan, about 1/4 in. will be sufficient, and place in a 350°F oven.
6. Bake until ham is golden brown. Remove and let cool slightly.
7. Place in ham rack and carve to order; or bone, slice and keep warm in a steam table pan.
8. Dish up 3 to 4 ozs. per portion and serve with cider, raisin, raisin-cranberry or fruit sauce.

Precautions and Safety Measures
1. There are many styles of hams on the market today. Check to be sure that the ham is sugar cured before boiling.
2. Use caution when handling the knives to avoid cutting self.
3. Do not overcook the ham while boiling; remove from the stock when the shank bone becomes loose. If the ham is overcooked, it will be difficult to handle, slice and serve. Overcooking will also result in loss of serving portions.
4. Be alert when ham is baking in the oven. A burnt ham is very undesirable.

Sweet-sour ham balls

Sweet-sour ham balls are a luncheon item. The balls are baked in a sweet-sour sauce to give them a very desirable taste.

Objectives
1. To teach the student the procedure for preparing sweet-sour ham balls.
2. To teach the student how to form the ham balls.
3. To teach the student how to dish up the sweet-sour ham balls.

Equipment
1. Bake pans
2. Qt. measure
3. Baker's scale
4. French knife
5. Cup measure
6. Spoon measure
7. Mixing container
8. Sauce pan, 4 qt.
9. Kitchen spoon
10. Food grinder

11. No. 12 ice cream scoop
12. Wire whip

Ingredients: Approx. yield: 50 servings

5	lbs. ham, smoked, uncooked
8	lbs. picnic, fresh, boneless
2	qts. bread crumbs (variable)
10	whole eggs
1	qt. milk
2	lbs. 8 ozs. dark brown sugar
1	cup onions, minced
1	cup celery, minced
1	cup butter
1	qt. water
1	qt. vinegar, cider
½	cup dry mustard

Preparation

1. Mince the onions and celery with a French knife.
2. Cut the ham and pork into thin strips that will pass through the food grinder.
3. Beat the whole eggs slightly with a wire whip.
4. Preheat the oven to 325°F.
5. Have all equipment and ingredients handy.

Procedure

1. Place the bread crumbs in a mixing container. Add the milk and let soak until the crumbs absorb the liquid.
2. Add the ham and pork and mix thoroughly by hand.
3. Grind the mixture twice on the food grinder using the medium chopper plate. Add the beaten eggs and mix thoroughly by hand.
4. Apportion the mixture using a no. 12 ice cream scoop. Form into balls and place in the bake pans.
5. Place the butter in the sauce pan and heat. Add the onions and celery and sauté until slightly tender.
6. Add the water, vinegar and dry mustard and bring to a boil, stirring occasionally with a kitchen spoon.
7. Pour the liquid mixture over the ham balls. Place in a 325°F oven and bake until the meat is well done. Baste the balls frequently while baking.
8. Dish up 2 balls per portion topped with the sweet-sour sauce the balls were baked in. Accompany each order with sautéed apples, noodles or apple sauce.

Precautions and Safety Measures

1. Use caution when mincing the onions and celery.

2. When sautéing the onions and celery, do not brown.
3. Cook the ham balls well done.

Baked stuffed pork chops

Baked stuffed pork chops are thick chops cut from the rib or loin end of the pork loin. A pocket is cut into the side of the chop and it is stuffed with a forcemeat mixture. The stuffing adds to the delectability of this entree.

Objectives

1. To teach the student how to cut the pork chops.
2. To teach the student how to cut the pocket into the chop.
3. To teach the student the procedure for preparing stuffed pork chops.
4. To teach the student how to dish up the stuffed pork chops.

Equipment

1. Boning knife
2. French or butcher knife
3. Large iron skillet
4. 3 gal. stainless steel container
5. Roast pan
6. Food grinder
7. Cup measure
8. Baker's scale
9. Kitchen fork
10. Sauce pan, 2 qt.
11. Ladle
12. China cap
13. Mixing container
14. Wire whip
15. Bake pan
16. Steam table pan

Ingredients: Approx. yield: 50 servings

50	pork chops, cut thick
3	lbs. pork picnic, fresh, cut in strips
2	lbs. veal shoulder, cut in strips
¾	oz. salt
¼	oz. pepper
¼	oz. sage
1	lb. bread, fresh or dried
3	cups milk
⅓	cup parsley, chopped
8	ozs. onions, minced
6	ozs. celery, minced
6	ozs. shortening or butter
8	ozs. bread crumbs
4	egg yolks, beaten

2 gal. brown sauce
3 lbs. flour
   salt and pepper to taste
Preparation
1. Cut the pork chops from trimmed pork loins. Cut about 1 in. thick with a French or butcher knife. Slit the side and cut a pocket in the flesh of each chop with a boning knife. Make the pocket as large as possible without cutting through the flesh on either side of the pocket. Proceed only after demonstration by instructor.
2. Mince the onions and celery with a French knife.
3. Prepare the 2 gal. of brown sauce. (See Chap. 14.)
4. Separate the eggs and beat the yolks slightly with a wire whip. (Save the whites for use in another preparation.)
5. Crumble the fresh or dried bread by hand.
6. Cut the picnic and veal shoulder into strips with a French or butcher knife so they will pass through the food grinder.
7. Chop the parsley with a French knife and wash.
8. Put the flour in a bake pan and season with salt and pepper.
9. Preheat oven to 350°F.
10. Have all equipment and ingredients handy.
Procedure
1. Place the shortening or butter in the sauce pan and heat. Add the onions and celery and sauté until slightly tender. Remove from the range and let cool.
2. Soak the crumpled bread in the milk until the milk is absorbed.
3. Place the pork, veal, salt, pepper, sage, soaked bread, sautéed onions and celery in a mixing container and mix thoroughly with the hands.
4. Grind this mixture twice in the food grinder using the fine chopper plate.
5. Add the slightly beaten egg yolks, bread crumbs and parsley and mix thoroughly with the hands. Check seasoning.
6. Stuff this forcemeat mixture into the pocket which was cut into the side of each chop.
7. Pass each chop through the seasoned flour; pat off the excess.

8. Place salad oil or shortening in the iron skillet and heat. Add the chops and brown slightly on both sides. Turn with a kitchen fork.
9. Line the sautéed chops, cut edge up, in a roast pan.
10. Ladle the hot brown sauce over the chops, place in a 350°F oven, and bake for approximately 1½ hours or until the chops are tender and well done.
11. Remove from the oven and place the chops in a steam table pan. Strain the sauce in the roast pan into a stainless steel container.
12. Dish up 1 chop per portion with a generous amount of sauce over the top.
Precautions and Safety Measures
1. Use caution when cutting chops and mincing vegetables to avoid cutting self.
2. When sautéing chops use caution so the forcemeat will not come out of the chops.
3. When baking, baste the chops with the sauce frequently.

Apple stuffed pork chops

For apple stuffed pork chops the chops are cut from the rib end of the loin. A pocket is cut into the meaty side of each chop and stuffed with an apple mixture. The apple flavor increases the delicate flavor of the pork meat.
Objectives
1. To teach the student the procedure for preparing apple stuffed pork chops.
2. To teach the student how to cut the chops and process them for stuffing.
3. To teach the student how to dish up the stuffed chops.
Equipment
1. Boning knife
2. French or butcher knife
3. Mixing container
4. Iron skillet
5. Spoon and cup measure
6. Qt. measure
7. Bake pans
8. Sauce pans, 1 qt.
9. Collander
10. Kitchen fork
11. Steam table pan
Ingredients: Approx. yield: 50 servings
   50   pork chops, cut from rib end of loin, 1 in. thick

1 cup onions, minced
1 cup celery, minced
6 tbsp. bacon grease
1½ qts. soft bread crumbs
1 #10 can sliced apples, drained
and chopped
1 cup seedless raisins
2 tsp. poultry seasoning
1 tsp. salt
¼ tsp. pepper
1 qt. salad oil or melted
shortening (variable)

Preparation
1. Cut the chops 1 in. thick from the trimmed rib end of a pork loin with a French or butcher knife. Cut a pocket in the meaty side of each chop with a boning knife. Proceed only after demonstration by instructor.
2. Prepare the soft bread crumbs by rubbing fresh bread, with the hand, across the bottom of a collander.
3. Mince the onions and celery with a French knife.
4. Preheat the oven to 350°F.
5. Drain and chop the apples with a French knife.
6. Have all equipment and ingredients handy.

Procedure
1. Place bacon grease in a sauce pan and heat. Add the minced onions and celery and sauté until slightly tender.
2. Place in a mixing container and add the bread crumbs, apples, raisins, poultry seasoning, and salt and pepper. Toss with the hands gently until thoroughly mixed.
3. Place about ¼ cup of stuffing in the pocket of each chop.
4. Brown the chops lightly on both sides in the iron skillet in oil or shortening. Using a kitchen fork place the chops in bake pans, meaty side up.
5. Bake in a 350°F oven for about 40 minutes, or until chops are well done and tender. Remove from the oven and place in a steam table pan.
6. Dish up 1 chop per portion and serve with brown sauce.

Precautions and Safety Measures
1. Exercise caution when handling the knives to avoid cutting self.
2. When sautéing chops, do not overbrown.

3. Handle chops with care when sautéing so the stuffing will not come out.

Stuffed spare ribs

Stuffed spare ribs are spare ribs cracked across the middle, stuffed with forcemeat, tied and baked. It is a new method of serving spare ribs on the luncheon menu.

Objective
1. To teach the student the procedure for preparing stuffed spare ribs.
2. To teach the student how to stuff and bake the spare ribs.
3. To teach the student how to dish up the stuffed spare ribs.

Equipment
1. French knife
2. Baker's scale
3. Qt. measures
4. Wire whip
5. Butcher twine
6. Roasting pans
7. Sauce pan, 1 qt.
8. Kitchen fork
9. Meat grinder
10. Full size steam table pan

Ingredients: Approx. yield: 50 servings
30 lbs. spare ribs
4 lbs. pork picnic, fresh, lean
2 lbs. bread, fresh or dried
1½ qts. milk (variable)
8 ozs. onions, minced
8 ozs. celery, minced
8 ozs. butter
⅓ cup parsley, chopped
¼ oz. sage
salt and pepper to taste
4 egg yolks, beaten
bread crumbs as needed

Preparation
1. Mince the onions and celery with a French knife.
2. Soak the bread in the milk until all the milk is absorbed.
3. Cut the fresh picnic into strips for grinding. Use a French knife.
4. Crack all the spare ribs with a cleaver, lengthwise down the center of each spare rib. Proceed only after demonstration by instructor.
5. Preheat oven to 375°F.
6. Separate eggs and beat yolks slightly with

a wire whip. (Save the whites for another preparation.)

7. Have all equipment and ingredients handy.

Procedure

1. Place the butter in the sauce pan and heat. Add the onions and celery and sauté until slightly tender.
2. Place the onions, celery, soaked bread, pork picnic, sage and salt and pepper into a mixing container. Mix thoroughly by hand.
3. Grind this mixture on the meat grinder twice, using the medium chopper plate.
4. Add the beaten egg yolks and chopped parsley and mix thoroughly by hand. If mixture is too wet, add bread crumbs as needed; if too dry, add more milk.
5. Place the stuffing on one half of the cracked rib section of each spare rib. Fold over the other half and tie the ribs with butcher twine to hold in the force-meat stuffing.
6. Cover the bottom of the roast pans with about ¼ in. of water. Place the ribs on a rack in the roast pans. Roast at 375°F until the ribs become brown on both sides. Turn ribs frequently while roasting with a kitchen fork.
7. Remove from the roast pans and place in a steam table pan.
8. Cut the ribs with a French knife into 50 equal units.
9. Dish up 1 unit per portion and serve accompanied with apple sauce.

Precautions and Safety Measures

1. Use caution when mincing the onions and cracking the ribs.
2. Tie ribs securely so stuffing will not come out during the roasting. Be gentle when turning the ribs.

Stuffed fresh cottage ham

Stuffed fresh cottage ham is fresh cottage ham sliced butterfly style, flattened, spread with a forcemeat mixture, rolled and roasted. It is another profitable addition to the luncheon menu.

Objectives

1. To teach the student the procedure for preparing stuffed fresh cottage ham.
2. To teach the student how to cut and flatten the meat.

3. To teach the student how to dish up stuffed fresh cottage ham.

Equipment

1. French knife
2. Cleaver
3. Roast pan
4. Sauce pan, 1 qt.
5. Mixing container
6. Meat grinder
7. Wire whip
8. Ladle
9. Baker's scale
10. Cup measures
11. Full size steam table pan
12. No. 12 dipper

Ingredients: Approx. yield: 50 servings

16	lbs. fresh cottage ham cut into 50 portions, butterfly style
3	lbs. fresh pork picnic, boneless, cut into strips
2	lbs. veal shoulder, boneless, cut into strips
1	lb. bread, fresh or dried
3	cups milk
6	ozs. onions, minced
6	ozs. celery, minced
4	egg yolks, beaten
8	ozs. bread crumbs (variable)
6	ozs. butter
⅓	cup parsley, chopped
¼	oz. sage
	salt and pepper to taste
2	gal. thin brown sauce

Preparation

1. Slice the fresh cottage ham into 50 units, butterfly style. Cut one thin slice against the grain with a French knife only three-quarters of the way through. Cut the following thin slice all the way through. This results in the butterfly style cut: two slices joined at the bottom. Spread out the joined slices on a cutting board and flatten with the side of a cleaver. Proceed only after demonstration by instructor.
2. Mince the onions and celery with a French knife.
3. Chop the parsley with a French knife and wash.
4. Cut the pork picnic and veal shoulder into strips that will fit in the grinder.
5. Separate eggs and beat the yolks slightly with a wire whip. (Save the whites for use in another preparation.)

6. Soak the bread in the milk until all the milk is absorbed.
7. Preheat the oven to 350°F.
8. Prepare brown sauce. (See Chap. 14.) Keep hot.
9. Have all equipment and ingredients handy.

Procedure

1. Place the butter in the sauce pan and heat. Add the onions and celery and sauté until slightly tender.
2. Place the onions, celery, soaked bread, pork, veal, sage and pepper into a mixing container. Mix thoroughly by hand.
3. Grind this mixture twice in a meat grinder using the fine chopper plate.
4. Add the beaten egg yolks and chopped parsley and mix thoroughly by hand. If mixture is too wet, add bread crumbs as needed; if too dry, add more milk.
5. Place the stuffing (meat mixture) on each flattened butterfly slice. Use about 4 ozs. or a No. 12 dipper full. Roll up each butterfly slice. Place close together in roast pans with the end of each roll on the bottom.
6. Place in the oven and roast at 350°F until each roll is golden brown. Pour off accumulated grease in bottom of roast pan.
7. Ladle the hot brown sauce over each roll, return to the oven and continue roasting until the meat is tender and well done. Remove from the oven and place in a steam table pan.
8. Dish up 1 meat roll per portion covered with brown sauce. Accompany with a half baked apple or a canned spiced apple.

Precautions and Safety Measures

1. Exercise caution when cutting and flattening the pork.
2. When flattening the butterfly slices of ham, do not hit or pound too hard or the meat will separate along the muscle fibers.
3. When the pork rolls are covered with the brown gravy, watch them closely through the remainder of the baking period. They will overbrown quickly.

Swedish meat balls in sour cream sauce

Swedish meat balls are a combination of small (7 or 8 per portion) meat balls and a rich, sour cream sauce. The meat balls are light in color and delicate in flavor because they are made from a combination of pork and veal meats. This is a profitable luncheon item and is generally accompanied with buttered noodles.

Objectives

1. To teach the student the procedure for preparing Swedish meat balls in sour cream sauce.
2. To teach the student how to form and bake the meat balls.
3. To teach the student how to dish up the Swedish meat balls in sour cream sauce.

Equipment

1. French knife
2. Qt. measure
3. Baker's scale
4. Meat grinder
5. Sheet pans
6. Meat turner
7. Mixing container
8. Wire whip
9. Sauce pan, 1 qt.
10. Full sized steam table pan

Ingredients:

Approx. yield: 50 servings

9	lb. fresh pork picnic, boneless, lean
9	lb. veal shoulder, boneless
8	eggs
10	oz. milk
1¼	qts. bread crumbs
½	pt. celery, minced
½	pt. onions, minced
8	oz. shortening
	salt, pepper and nutmeg to taste
2	gal. sour cream sauce

Preparation

1. Cut the pork and veal into strips that will fit the meat grinder.
2. Mince the onions and celery with a French knife.
3. Grease the sheet pans with salad oil.
4. Prepare 2 gal. sour cream sauce. (See Chap. 15.)
5. Preheat oven to 350°F.
6. Have all equipment and ingredients handy.

Procedure

1. Beat the eggs in the mixing container with a wire whip.
2. Add milk and bread crumbs. Let mixture stand until all the milk is absorbed into the bread crumbs.
3. Place the shortening in the sauce pan and

heat. Add the onion and celery, sauté and let cool.

4. To the bread crumb mixture add the pork, veal, seasoning and sautéed onions and celery. Mix thoroughly by hand.

5. Grind the mixture twice, using the fine chopper plate, then mix thoroughly again and check seasoning.

6. Form into small balls by hand, place on greased sheet pans and bake in the oven at 350°F until light brown and firm when touched.

7. Remove from the oven, pour off grease, add water to cover the bottom of sheet pan and loosen meat balls from bottom of pan.

8. Using meat turner remove meat balls from sheet pan and place in steam table pan to keep warm.

9. Dish up 7 or 8 meat balls per portion in a flat casserole. Serve covered with the sour cream sauce and accompanied with buttered noodles.

Precautions and Safety Measures

1. Exercise caution when handling the knife and grinding the meat mixture.

2. If meat sticks to the hands when forming the balls, rub a little salad oil on the hands.

3. Do not overbake the meat balls. They will become too brown and too firm and will lack appearance when served.

4. Before serving, do not place the meat balls in the sauce. They break up easily.

Ham and cabbage rolls

Ham and cabbage rolls are a profitable addition to the luncheon menu because this is an item where accumulated ham trimmings can be utilized. The rolls consist of partly cooked cabbage leaves rolled around the ham-rice filling.

Objectives

1. To teach the student the procedure for preparing ham and cabbage rolls.

2. To teach the student how to cook the cabbage leaves.

3. To teach the student how to form, bake and dish up the ham and cabbage rolls.

Equipment

1. Large braising pot and cover
2. Bake pans
3. Stock pot, 10 gal.

4. French knife
5. Baker's scale
6. Qt. measure
7. Spoon and cup measure
8. Boning knife
9. Meat grinder
10. Sauce pot, 6 qts.
11. Kitchen spoon
12. Full size steam table pans

Ingredients: Approx. yield: 50 servings

6	large heads of cabbage
12	lbs. ham, cooked, ground
2	lbs. onions, minced
2	cloves garlic, minced
1	#10 can tomatoes, crushed
1	qt. tomato purée
2	lbs. 8 ozs. rice, raw
2	tbsp. chili powder
3	tbsp. paprika
1	qt. water
1	cup salad oil
2	qts. chicken stock
1	qt. catsup
2	qts. canned tomatoes, crushed
	salt and pepper to taste

Preparation

1. Remove cores from the cabbage heads with a boning knife. Place in the stock pot, cover with salted water and boil until the leaves can be removed from the heads easily.

2. Mince the onions and garlic with a French knife.

3. Crush the tomatoes by hand at the time of use.

4. With a French knife cut the ham into pieces that will pass through the meat grinder.

5. Grind the ham in the meat grinder using the coarse chopper plate.

6. Preheat the oven to 400°F.

7. Prepare the chicken stock. (See Chap. 12.)

8. Have all equipment and ingredients handy.

Procedure

1. Place salad oil in braiser and heat. Add the onion and garlic and sauté without browning.

2. Add the first amount of crushed tomatoes (No. 10 can), tomato purée and water and simmer until the onions are tender. Stir occasionally with a kitchen spoon.

3. Add chili powder and paprika and continue to simmer.

4. Add the ham and rice. Bring back to a boil.

5. Season with salt and pepper, cover braiser and place in a 400°F oven. Bake until the rice absorbs the liquid and is tender.
6. Remove from the oven and check seasoning. Place in a bake pan to cool, then refrigerate overnight.
7. Remove ham-rice mixture from the refrigerator. Place cabbage leaves (about 2 leaves for each roll) on a kitchen towel, place a 2½ ounce ball of the ham-rice mixture on the leaves and roll up. Repeat this process until all the cabbage leaves and ham-rice mixture is used. Place the rolls in bake pans.
8. Combine in a sauce pot the second amount of crushed tomatoes, catsup and chicken stock, blend thoroughly with a kitchen spoon and pour over the cabbage rolls.
9. Place in a 350°F oven and bake for 45 minutes. Remove from the oven and place in steam table pans.
10. Dish up 2 rolls per portion topped with the tomato liquid.

Precautions and Safety Measures
1. Exercise caution when grinding the ham and mincing the onions and garlic to avoid hurting self.
2. When baking the ham-rice mixture be cautious in removing the lid to avoid burning self.
3. Baste the ham and cabbage rolls frequently when baking.

FRIED AND SAUTEED PORK RECIPES

Sautéed pork chops or cutlets

For sautéed pork chops or cutlets the pork chops cut from the rib end or the loin end of the pork loin are passed through seasoned flour and cooked in shallow grease until golden brown. This item is an excellent choice for the luncheon, dinner or à la carte menu. The cutlet is a thin, boneless, slice of pork loin or Boston butt and is prepared and served in the same manner.

Objectives
1. To teach the student how to cut the pork chops or cutlets.
2. To teach the student the procedure for preparing sautéed pork chops or cutlets.

3. To teach the student how to dish up sautéed pork chops or cutlets.

Equipment
1. French or butcher knife
2. Cleaver
3. Bake pan
4. Kitchen fork
5. Iron or steel skillets
6. Qt. measure
7. Spoon measure
8. Full size steam table pan

Ingredients: Approx. yield: 50 servings

50	5 oz. pork chops *or* 50 5 oz. pork cutlets
3	tbsp. salt
2	tsp. pepper
3	lb. all purpose flour
2	qts. salad oil or melted shortening (variable)

Preparation
1. Cut the pork chops or cutlets with a French or butcher knife. Flatten them slightly with the side of a cleaver. Proceed only after demonstration by instructor.
2. Place the flour in a bake pan and season with salt and pepper.
3. Have all equipment and ingredients handy.

Procedure
1. Place enough shortening or salad oil in the skillet to cover the bottom at a depth of ¼ in. Place on the range and heat.
2. Pass each pork chop or cutlet through the seasoned flour and pat off excess.
3. Place the chops or cutlets in skillet and brown both sides, while maintaining a moderate temperature. Turn the meat with a kitchen fork. Cook them well done.
4. Remove from skillet and let drain. Place in a steam table pan.
5. Dish up 1 chop or cutlet per portion. Serve with country gravy.

Precautions and Safety Measures
1. Exercise caution when cutting the pork chops or cutlets.
2. Do not overbrown the chops or cutlets while sautéing.
3. Do not let grease in skillet get too hot.
4. Always pat off the excess flour before placing in the grease or it will lie on the bottom of the skillet and burn causing the item to have poor appearance when served.

Breaded pork chops or cutlets

Breaded pork chops or cutlets are cut from

the trimmed loin end or rib end of the full loin of pork. The cutlets are thin, flattened, boneless slices of the loin. Cutlets can also be cut from fresh, boneless Boston butt in the same manner as those cut from the loin. These cuts are coated with a bread or cracker crumb coating and fried to a golden brown. This is a most desirable luncheon entree when served with tomato or cream sauce.

Objectives
1. To teach the student the procedure for preparing breaded pork chops or cutlets.
2. To teach the student how to cut, fry and dish up the chops and cutlets.

Equipment
1. Baker's scale
2. Qt. measure
3. Spoon measure
4. Full size steam table pan
5. French or butcher knife
6. Cleaver
7. Bake pans (3)
8. Iron skillet
9. 4 qt. metal bowl
10. Kitchen fork
11. Wire whip

Ingredients: Approx. yield: 50 servings
50 4 or 5 oz. pork chops or cutlets
1 lb. flour
2 tbsp. salt
1 tsp. pepper
6 whole eggs, beaten
2 qts. milk
2 qts. bread or cracker crumbs
2 lbs. shortening (variable)

Preparation
1. Cut the pork chops or cutlets with a French or butcher knife. Flatten them slightly with the side of a cleaver. Proceed only after demonstration by instructor.
2. Beat eggs with a wire whip. Prepare egg wash by combining the beaten eggs and milk.
3. Place the flour in a bake pan and season with salt and pepper.
4. Place the bread or cracker crumbs in a bake pan.
5. Have all equipment and ingredients handy.

Procedure
1. Pass each chop or cutlet through the seasoned flour coating them completely.
2. Place them in the egg wash, then into the bread or cracker crumbs. Press them firmly and shake off excess crumbs.

3. Place the shortening in iron skillet and heat.
4. Add the chops or cutlets, brown one side then turn with a kitchen fork and brown the other. Remove when done golden brown. Let drain and place in a steam table pan.
5. Dish up 1 chop or cutlet per portion and serve on top of tomato or cream sauce.

Precautions and Safety Measures
1. Use caution when cutting the chops and cutlets.
2. When placing the chops or cutlets in the hot grease, let them fall away from you so that grease will not splash towards you.
3. Fry the chops or cutlets slowly so the meat will be well done when the breading is golden brown. An overly high temperature will brown the breading too rapidly.

Ham croquettes

Ham croquettes are a profitable item when served on the luncheon menu with some type of cream sauce. This is an excellent way to work off ham trimming or scraps.

Objectives
1. To teach the student the procedure for making ham croquettes.
2. To teach the student how to bread, fry and dish up ham croquettes.

Equipment
1. Braiser
2. Baking pans (4)
3. Wire whip
4. Deep fat fryer
5. Meat grinder
6. Kitchen spoon
7. Ice cream scoop, no. 20
8. Cup measures
9. Qt. measure
10. Baker's scale
11. French knife
12. Stainless steel bowls, 8 qt. and 3 qt.
13. Oiled brown paper

Ingredients: Approx. yield: 50 servings
8 lbs. ham, boiled, ground
1 lb. celery, minced
1 lb. onions, minced
1½ lbs. butter or shortening, melted
1½ lbs. bread flour
2 qts. milk, hot, or ham stock
¼ cup mustard, prepared
2 tbsp. mustard, dry

1 cup parsley, chopped
2 qts. milk
12 whole eggs
2 lbs. bread flour
3 lbs. bread crumbs

Preparation
1. Cut the ham with a French knife into strips that will fit into the meat grinder. Grind the ham in the meat grinder using the coarse chopper plate.
2. Mince the onions and celery with a French knife.
3. Chop the parsley with a French knife and wash.
4. Preheat the oven to 350°F.
5. Prepare the ham stock if used. (See Chap. 12.)
6. Prepare egg wash: Place eggs in a stainless steel bowl, beat with a wire whip, and pour in the 2 qts. of milk while continuing to whip. On the day to be used, place in a bake pan.
7. Place the flour and bread crumbs in separate bake pans.
8. Have all equipment and ingredients handy.

Procedure
1. Place celery and onions in the braiser and sauté until tender.
2. Add flour to make a roux and cook 8 to 10 minutes. Stir occasionally with a kitchen spoon.
3. Add hot milk or stock and stir until thick and smooth.
4. Blend dry mustard with prepared mustard and add to ham and parsley in stainless steel bowl.
5. Combine all ingredients, mixing thoroughly with a kitchen spoon in the braiser.
6. Put mixture in greased baking pan and cover with sheet of oiled brown paper.
7. Bake in 350°F oven for 45 minutes.
8. Remove from oven and let cool. Place in the refrigerator overnight.
9. Portion each croquette with level no. 20 ice cream scoop.
10. Shape in cones of uniform size.
11. Bread croquettes by passing them through flour, egg wash and bread crumbs.
12. Fry in deep fat at 350°F until golden brown and place in steam table pans.

13. Dish up 2 croquettes per portion. Serve with cream or tomato sauce.
Precautions and Safety Measures
1. Exercise caution when handling the knife and grinding the meat.
2. When sautéing the vegetables in butter, be careful not to burn them.
3. When breading use a fairly rich egg wash so the croquettes will hold together better when fried.

Ham turnovers

Ham turnovers involve two mixtures, a dough mixture and a ham filling mixture. When the turnovers are prepared the filling is placed inside the dough and the item is deep fried to a golden brown. Many different fillings may be substituted for the ham when preparing this type of item, but ham or chicken seems to be the most popular. This item should always be served with an appropriate sauce.

Objectives
1. To teach the student the procedure for preparing ham turnovers.
2. To teach the student how to roll the dough and form the turnovers.
3. To teach the student how to fry and dish up the turnovers.

Equipment
1. Baker's scale
2. Deep fryer
3. Rolling pin
4. Turnover cutter or 5" round cutter
5. Sauce pot, 6 qt.
6. Cup and spoon measure
7. Kitchen spoon
8. #16 ice cream dipper
9. French knife
10. Stainless dish pan
11. Dinner fork
12. Qt. measure
13. Full size steam table pan.

Ingredients: Approx. yield: 50 servings
HAM FILLING
1 cup Primex shortening
½ cup onions, minced
1 qt. ham stock
2 qts. smoked ham, cooked and minced
2 cups bread flour
1 cup bread crumbs
½ tsp. nutmeg

2 tsp. salt
1 tsp. paprika
½ tsp. pepper
DEEP FRYING DOUGH
7 lbs. 8 ozs. pastry flour
3 lbs. Primex shortening
3¾ ozs. salt
3 lbs. water
Preparation
1. Mince the onions and ham with a French knife.
2. Preheat deep fry kettle to 375°F.
3. Prepare ham stock. (See Chap. 12.)
4. Have all equipment and ingredients handy.
Procedure
DEEP FRYING DOUGH
1. Place the flour and shortening in the stainless steel dish pan, cut the shortening into the flour (by rubbing together with the palms of the hands) until very small lumps are formed.
2. Dissolve the salt in the water by stirring with a kitchen spoon, add to the above, and mix into a dough. Cover with a damp towel and refrigerate for later use.
HAM FILLING
1. Place the shortening in the sauce pot and heat. Add the onions and sauté without color.
2. Add flour making a roux and stir with a kitchen spoon. Cook until well blended.
3. Add the hot ham stock gradually, stirring constantly. Cook for about 3 minutes.
4. Add the ham, crumbs, nutmeg, salt, paprika and pepper to the above and mix thoroughly with a kitchen spoon. Return to the heat, stir until thoroughly heated and mixed, and then let cool.
5. Roll out the dough with a rolling pin on a floured bench to about ⅛ in. thickness or thinner if desired. Cut out with 5 in. round cutter.
6. Dip out the ham mixture with a no. 16 ice cream scoop, roll and shape mixture slightly. Place mixture in center of cut out dough.
7. Wash edges of dough with cold water and fold the circle of dough in half to form a turnover. Seal edges completely with the tines of a dinner fork.
8. Pierce top once or twice with a dinner fork.
9. Deep fry in deep fat at 375°F for 5 to 7 minutes or until golden brown, then drain. Place in a steam table pan.
10. Dish up 1 turnover per portion. Place on top of cream sauce, raisin sauce or some type of fruit sauce.
Precautions and Safety Measures
1. Exercise caution when mincing the ham and onions to avoid cutting self.
2. Do not make up turnovers until filling is cool and dough has been chilled.
3. Dust bench slightly heavy with pastry flour when rolling the dough.
4. Secure the edges of the dough tightly with the tines of a dinner fork before frying.
5. Exercise caution when frying the turnovers to avoid burning self or burning the turnovers.

BRAISED PORK RECIPES

Pork chops creole

Pork chops creole are sautéed pork chops baked in a rich creole or Spanish sauce. This is an excellent choice for the luncheon menu.
Objectives
1. To teach the student how to cut the pork chops.
2. To teach the student the procedure for preparing pork chops creole.
Equipment
1. French or butcher knife
2. Kitchen fork
3. Bake pans
4. Iron skillet
5. Baker's scale
6. Qt. measure
Ingredients: Approx. yield: 50 servings
50 5 oz. pork chops.
2 gal. creole sauce
3 lbs. flour
salt and pepper to taste
1 qt. salad oil or melted shortening (variable)
Preparation
1. Cut the 5 oz. pork chops from trimmed pork loin. Cut with a French or butcher knife. Proceed only after demonstration by instructor.
2. Prepare the creole sauce. (See Chap. 15.)
3. Place the flour in a bake pan and season with salt and pepper.
4. Preheat oven to 350°F.

5. Have all equipment and ingredients handy.
Procedure
1. Place the salad oil or shortening in the iron skillet and heat.
2. Pass each chop through the seasoned flour, pat off excess flour and place in the hot shortening.
3. Brown one side, turn with a kitchen fork and brown the other. Remove from skillet and drain.
4. Place in a bake pan and cover with the creole sauce. Place in a 350°F oven and bake until chops are tender.
5. Dish up 1 chop per portion topped with the creole sauce and accompanied with a mound of rice.
Precautions and Safety Measures
1. Exercise caution when handling the knife to avoid cutting self.
2. Do not overbrown or overcook the chops while sautéing.
3. Do not place the chops too close together in the hotel pan. They will not bake evenly.
4. Use caution when sautéing the chops to avoid burning them.

Barbecued pork chops

Barbecued pork chops are sautéed and baked in a rich barbecue sauce. They are an excellent selection for the luncheon menu.
Objective
1. To teach the student how to cut the pork chops.
2. To teach the student the procedure for preparing barbecued pork chops.
Equipment
1. Boning knife
2. Baker's scale
3. French or butcher knife
4. Qt. measure
5. Iron skillet
6. Bake pans
7. Kitchen fork
Ingredients: Approx. yield: 50 servings
50   5 oz. pork chops
 3   lbs. flour
 1   qt. salad oil or melted shortening (variable)
 2   gal. barbecue sauce
     salt and pepper to taste
Preparation
1. Cut the 5 oz. pork chops from trimmed

pork loin. Cut with a French or butcher knife. Proceed only after demonstration by instructor.
2. Prepare the barbecue sauce. (See Chap. 15.)
3. Place the flour in a bake pan and season with salt and pepper.
4. Preheat oven to 350°F.
5. Have all equipment and ingredients handy.
Procedure
1. Place the salad oil or shortening in the iron skillet and heat.
2. Pass each chop through the seasoned flour, pat off excess flour and place in the hot shortening.
3. Brown one side, turn with a kitchen fork and brown the other. Remove from the skillet and let drain.
4. Place in a bake pan and cover with the barbecue sauce. Place in the oven at 350°F and bake until tender and well done.
5. Dish up 1 chop per portion topped with the barbecue sauce.
Precautions and Safety Measures
1. Exercise caution when handling the knife to avoid cutting self.
2. Use caution when sautéing the chops to avoid burning self.
3. Do not overbrown or overcook the chops while sautéing.
4. Do not place the chops too close together in the bake pan. They will not bake evenly.

Pork chops Jonathan

Pork chops Jonathan are thick chops cut from the pork loin and baked with apples and apple juice. Apples help increase the delicate flavor of pork. This is an excellent choice for the luncheon menu.
Objectives
1. To teach the student the procedure for preparing pork chops Jonathan.
2. To teach the student how to cut the pork chops.
3. To teach the student how to dish up the pork chops.
Equipment
1. Iron skillet
2. Qt. measure
3. French or butcher knife
4. Kitchen fork
5. Kitchen spoon
6. Large braiser and cover

7. Stainless steel bowl, 1 pt.
8. Stainless steel container, 2 gal.

Ingredients: Approx. yield: 50 servings

50	pork chops, cut thick
1	#10 can sliced apples
2	qts. apple juice
½	cup lemon juice
½	tsp. Tabasco sauce
1	tsp. ground cloves
½	cup cornstarch
1	cup cold water
1	pt. salad oil (variable)

Preparation

1. Cut the pork chops from trimmed pork loins, about 1 in. thick, with a French or butcher knife.
2. Preheat oven to 350°F.
3. Have all equipment and ingredients handy.

Procedure

1. Place the salad oil in the iron skillet and heat. Add the pork chops and brown on both sides. Turn with a kitchen fork.
2. Place the chops in the braiser. Pour off the oil left in the skillet and deglaze the skillet by adding the apple juice and bringing to a boil. Pour this liquid over the pork chops.
3. Cover the pork chops with the sliced apples. Add the cloves, Tabasco and lemon juice.
4. Cover braiser and place in a 350°F oven. Bake until the chops are tender and well done. Remove the chops from the braiser and place in a steam table pan. Cover the chops and keep warm. Place the braiser on the range and bring the apple mixture to a boil.
5. In a stainless steel bowl dissolve the cornstarch in the cold water. Pour the starch into the boiling mixture while stirring constantly with a kitchen spoon. Cook until mixture is thickened and clear.
6. Check the seasoning and place the thickened apple mixture in a stainless steel container.
7. Dish up 1 chop per portion and serve on top of a small portion of the apple mixture.

Precautions and Safety Measures

1. Use caution when cutting the chops to avoid cutting self.
2. When adding the diluted cornstarch to the apple mixture, stir constantly until the mixture comes back to a boil. This will avoid lumps.

Pork chops Hawaiian

Because of its delicate flavor pork blends well with many fruits. The chops are extremely tasty when baked with pineapple. This is an excellent luncheon item.

Objectives

1. To teach the student the procedure for preparing pork chops Hawaiian.
2. To teach the student how to cut the pork chops.
3. To teach the student how to dish up pork chops Hawaiian.

Equipment

1. Iron skillet
2. French or butcher knife
3. Bake pans (2 or 3)
4. Qt. measure
5. Spoon measures
6. Wire whip
7. Sauce pan, 4 qt.
8. Boning knife
9. Butcher knife
10. Kitchen spoon
11. Kitchen fork
12. Stainless steel bowl, 1 pt.
13. Steam table pan

Ingredients: Approx. yield: 50 servings

50	pork chops, cut thick
50	slices pineapple
2	qts. pineapple juice
2	bay leaves
1	qt. celery, minced
2	tsp. ground cloves
2	cloves garlic, minced
	salt and pepper to taste
1	pt. salad oil (variable)
⅓	cup cornstarch
½	cup water, cold

Preparation

1. Cut the pork chops about 1 in. thick, with a French or butcher knife, from trimmed pork loins. Proceed only after demonstration by instructor.
2. Mince the onions and celery with a French knife.
3. Preheat oven to 350°F.
4. Have all equipment and ingredients handy.

Procedure

1. Place the salad oil in the iron skillet and heat. Add the pork chops, after seasoning them with salt and pepper, and brown on both sides. Turn with a kitchen fork.
2. Remove the chops from the skillet and

place them in the bake pans. Pour off the oil left in the skillet.

3. Add the pineapple juice to the skillet and bring to a boil to deglaze the skillet. Pour the liquid over the pork chops.
4. Place a slice of pineapple on top of each chop.
5. Add all remaining ingredients except the cornstarch and water and bake in the oven at 350°F until the chops are well done. Remove from the oven.
6. Pour the juice off the baked chops into a sauce pan. Place the chops in a steam table pan and bring the juice to a boil on the range.
7. In a stainless steel bowl dissolve the cornstarch in the cold water. Pour the starch into the boiling juice while whipping vigorously with a wire whip. Cook until juice is thickened and clear.
8. Pour the thickened juice over the chops in the steam table pan.

Precautions and Safety Measures

1. Use caution when cutting the pork chops and celery to avoid cutting self.
2. When adding the diluted cornstarch to the liquid, stir vigorously to avoid lumps.

Pork chops, honey style

Pork chops honey style are chops sautéed lightly, placed in a pan, covered with the honey glaze and baked until golden and tender. The honey glaze increases the appearance and delicate flavor of the chops.

Objectives

1. To teach the student the procedure for preparing pork chops honey style.
2. To teach the student how to cut the pork chops.
3. To teach the student how to dish up the pork chops honey style.

Equipment

1. French or butcher knife
2. Iron skillet
3. Sauce pan, 2 qts.
4. Wire whip
5. Kitchen fork
6. Kitchen spoon
7. Pt. measure
8. Baker's scale
9. Cleaver
10. Bake pans
11. Steam table pans

Ingredients: Approx. yield: 50 servings

50	5 oz. pork chops
1	pt. soy sauce
1	pt. apple sauce
8	ozs. honey
4	ozs. sugar
1	oz. salt
2	lbs. shortening (variable)

Preparation

1. Cut the 5 oz. pork chops from the pork loin. Trim pork chops with a French or butcher knife and flatten each chop gently with a cleaver. Proceed only after demonstration by instructor.
2. Preheat oven to 350°F.
3. Have all equipment and ingredients handy.

Procedure

1. Place shortening in an iron skillet and heat. Add the pork chops and brown slightly on both sides. Place in bake pans with a kitchen fork.
2. Combine remaining ingredients, place in a sauce pan and bring to a gentle boil, whipping slightly with a wire whip.
3. Pour this mixture over the sautéed pork chops. Place in a 350°F oven and bake for about 30 to 45 minutes or until the chops are well done and tender. Remove from the oven and place in steam table pans.
4. Dish up 1 chop per portion and serve with the honey sauce.

Precautions and Safety Measures

1. Use caution when cutting and trimming the chops to avoid cutting self.
2. While the chops are baking, turn and brush them often with the honey mixture.

Hawaiian pork

Hawaiian pork is a type of stew. The pork is cut into strips and cooked with pineapple chunks in a sweet-sour sauce. This item is more suited for the luncheon menu.

Objectives

1. To teach the student the procedure for preparing Hawaiian pork.
2. To teach the student how to cut the pork strips.
3. To teach the student how to dish up Hawaiian pork.

Equipment

1. Boning knife
2. Medium size braising pot
3. French knife

4. Cup and spoon measure
5. Qt. measure
6. Scale
7. Sauce pan, 2 qt.
8. Kitchen spoon
9. Full size steam table pan

Ingredients: Approx. yield: 50 servings

8	lbs. pork shoulder, boiled
½	cup bacon grease
1	cup water
½	cup cornstarch
1	tbsp. salt
1	cup dark brown sugar
1	cup cider vinegar
1	qt. pineapple juice
½	cup soy sauce
1	pt. green pepper, cut julienne
1	cup onion, cut julienne
1	#10 can pineapple chunks

Preparation

1. Remove the bones from the pork shoulder with a boning knife. Proceed only after demonstration by instructor. Boil and refrigerate overnight.
2. Cut the cooked pork with a French knife into strips about 3 in. long and ½ in. square.
3. Julienne the green peppers and onions with a French knife.
4. Have all equipment and ingredients handy.

Procedure

1. Place the bacon grease in the braiser, heat, add the pork strips and brown.
2. Add the water and simmer slowly for about 5 minutes.
3. Dissolve the cornstarch in the pineapple juice. Add the salt, brown sugar, vinegar and soy sauce and blend thoroughly with a kitchen spoon. Add this mixture to the above, stirring constantly until thick and smooth.
4. Add the onions and pineapple chunks. Cook 10 minutes or until the onions are tender.
5. Place the green peppers in sauce pan, cover with water and poach until tender. Drain and add to the pork mixture.
6. Check seasoning and place in a steam table pan.
7. Dish up with a 4 oz. ladle and serve on a mound of baked rice.

Precautions and Safety Measures

1. Stir the mixture gently when adding the pineapple chunks so they will not break up.
2. Use caution when cutting the pork and the vegetables.

Braised pork tenderloin de luxe

Braised pork tenderloin are pork tenderloins which average from 1 to 2 pounds; they are first browned in hot shortening then cooked in a rich liquid until well done.

Objective

1. To teach the student the procedure for preparing braised pork tenderloin.
2. To teach the student how to dish up braised pork tenderloin.

Equipment

1. Baker's scale
2. Qt. measure
3. Spoon measure
4. Cup measure
5. Boning knife
6. French knife
7. Iron or steel skillet
8. Large braising pot and cover
9. Sauce pot, 2 gal.
10. Kitchen spoon
11. Kitchen fork
12. Full size steam table pan
13. 1 gal. stainless steel container
14. China cap

Ingredients: Approx. yield: 50 servings

25	whole pork tenderloins, trimmed
1	pt. salad oil (variable)
½	cup onions, minced
10	ozs. butter
8	ozs. flour
4	tbsp. mustard, dry
¼	tsp. black pepper
4	qt. brown stock, hot
¼	cup lemon juice
8	ozs. Burgundy wine
2	tbsp. sugar
	salt to taste

Preparation

1. Trim the pork tenderloin with a boning knife. Remove any membrane or fat. Proceed only after demonstration by instructor.
2. Mince the onions with a French knife.
3. Preheat oven to 350°F.
4. Prepare the brown stock (See Chap. 12.)
5. Have all equipment and ingredients handy.

Procedure

1. Brown each tenderloin in a skillet in salad oil. Place them in the braiser using a kitchen fork.
2. Place the butter into the sauce pot and heat. Add the minced onions and sauté without color.
3. Add flour and dry mustard and cook for about 5 minutes.
4. Add the brown stock, lemon juice, sugar, salt and wine. Cook, stirring gently with a kitchen spoon, until thick and smooth.
5. Pour the sauce over the tenderloins in the braiser, cover and place in a 350°F oven for approximately 1 hour or until the tenderloins are well done.
6. Remove tenderloins and place in a steam table pan. Keep covered with a damp cloth.
7. Strain the sauce through a china cap into a stainless steel container. Adjust seasoning and consistency.
8. Slice the pork tenderloin on the bias (slanting) with a French knife and dish up one-half of a tenderloin per portion topped with the rich sauce.

Precautions and Safety Measures

1. Use caution when trimming and slicing the tenderloins.
2. Do not overbrown the tenderloins when sautéing.

BROILED PORK RECIPES

Broiled pork sausage patties

For broiled pork sausage patties boneless pork picnic is ground and highly seasoned, then formed into patties and cooked by the broiling method. Two patties are served to the order on the luncheon menu.

Objectives

1. To teach the student the procedure for preparing broiled pork sausage patties.
2. To teach the student how to broil and dish up the patties.

Equipment

1. French knife
2. Meat or pancake turner
3. Mixing container
4. Meat grinder
5. Sheet pans
6. Baker's scale
7. Spoon measure

Armour and Co.

Broiled pork sausage patties served on buttered noodles.

8. Boning knife
9. Full size steam table pan

Ingredients: Approx. yield: 50 servings

14	lbs. pork picnic, fresh, boneless
1¾	oz. salt
¾	oz. granulated sugar
1	tbsp. pepper, fresh ground
1½	tsp. summer savory, ground
1	tsp. ginger
1	tsp. nutmeg
1	tsp. marjoram
2	tbsp. sage, rubbed

Preparation

1. Bone the fresh picnic with a boning knife. Using a French knife cut into strips that will pass through the grinder. Proceed only after demonstration by instructor.
2. Coat sheet pans with salad oil.
3. Preheat broiler.
4. Have all equipment and ingredients handy.

Procedure

1. Place all ingredients in a mixing container and blend thoroughly.
2. Grind twice in the meat grinder using the medium chopper plate. Check seasoning.
3. Form into 2 oz. patties. Place on the greased sheet pans and broil. Brown one side, then turn with a meat turner and brown the other.
4. Dish up 2 patties to each order accom-

panied with apple sauce or some other form of apple preparation.

Precautions and Safety Measures
1. Exercise caution when boning the fresh picnic to avoid cutting self.
2. If meat sticks to hands when forming patties, coat hands slightly with salad oil.

Broiled ham steak Hawaiian

Broiled ham steak Hawaiian is a cross cut section of the ham. The center cuts are best. It is broiled and served with a slice of glazed pineapple and a cherry center.

Objectives
1. To teach the student how to cut ham steaks.
2. To teach the student the procedure for broiling a ham steak.
3. To teach the student how to glaze pineapple.

Equipment
1. French knife
2. Mixing bowl, small
3. Kitchen fork
4. Cup and spoon measures
5. Sheet pan
6. Bake pan
7. Meat saw

Ingredients: Approx. yield: 50 servings
50   4 or 5 oz. ham steaks
50   pineapple slices
50   maraschino cherries, red
  1   cup granulated sugar
 ½   cup brown sugar
  1   tsp. cinnamon
  1   pt. salad oil (variable)

Preparation
1. Cut the 4 or 5 oz. ham steaks with a French knife and hand saw or power saw. Cut approximately ½ in. thick across the complete width of the ham. Proceed only after demonstration by instructor.
2. Light the broiler and turn to the highest point.
3. Have all equipment and ingredients handy.

Procedure
1. Place the salad oil in a bake pan, marinate each steak in the salad oil and place, fat side out, on the hot broiler.
2. Broil one side 2 to 3 minutes, turn with a kitchen fork and broil the other side. Remove from the broiler when done and keep hot.

3. Combine the sugars and cinnamon in a small mixing bowl.
4. Place the pineapple rings on a sheet pan and sprinkle with the sugar-cinnamon mixture.
5. Place pineapple rings under the broiler and glaze.
6. Dish up 1 ham steak per portion with a pineapple slice on top. Garnish the center with a red maraschino cherry and top with brown butter sauce.

Precautions and Safety Measures
1. Use caution when cutting the steaks to avoid cutting self.
2. When broiling the steaks, do not burn the fat.

Broiled pigs' feet

For broiled pigs' feet the feet are split lengthwise, poached, and left to cool. They are then passed through salad oil and bread crumbs and browned under the broiler. This item is served on the luncheon menu with a tart piquant sauce.

Objectives
1. To teach the student the procedure for preparing broiled pigs' feet.
2. To teach the student how to split the pigs' feet.
3. To teach the student how to dish up the broiled pigs' feet.

Equipment
1. Bake pans (2)
2. Stock pot, 10 gal.
3. Power meat saw
4. Sheet pans (3)

Ingredients: Approx. yield: 50 servings
50   pigs' feet, split in half lengthwise
      water, as needed
  2   tbsp. pickling spices
  1   gal. piquant sauce
  1   qt. salad oil (variable)
  3   lbs. bread crumbs (variable)

Preparation
1. Split the pigs' feet lengthwise using a power saw. Proceed only after demonstration by instructor.
2. Prepare piquant sauce. (See Chap. 15.)
3. Coat the sheet pans with salad oil.
4. Place the bread crumbs in a bake pan.
5. Preheat the broiler.
6. Have all equipment and ingredients handy.

Procedure

1. Place the split pigs' feet in the stock pot, add the pickling spices, cover with water and simmer until tender, about 2 to 2½ hours.
2. Remove from the range, let cool and refrigerate overnight, leaving the feet in the stock.
3. Remove the split feet from the jellied stock. The stock will jell when cold because of the natural gelatine in the pork bones. Place feet in a bake pan with salad oil.
4. Pass the feet through the salad oil then into a pan containing the bread crumbs. Coat thoroughly, pressing firmly, and shake off excess.
5. Place the feet on the oiled sheet pan. Put under a low broiler until brown.
6. Dish up 2 halves per portion topped with piquant sauce.

Precautions and Safety Measures

1. Watch fingers when splitting the feet with the power saw.
2. Exercise caution when browning the feet under the broiler. They sometimes pop, spraying hot liquid.

Ham and asparagus rolls Mornay

Ham and asparagus rolls Mornay are a combination of ham and two asparagus spears rolled up in the ham. These rolls are covered with a Mornay sauce and glazed under the broiler.

Objectives

1. To teach the student the procedure for preparing ham and asparagus rolls Mornay.
2. To teach the student how to slice and roll the ham.
3. To teach the student how to set up and serve the ham and asparagus rolls Mornay.

Equipment

1. Boning knife
2. Broiler
3. 50 casserole dishes
4. Ladle
5. Stainless steel container
6. Bake pans
7. Slicing machine
8. Qt. measure

Ingredients: Approx. yield: 50 servings
100 horseshoe slices of cooked ham
200 asparagus spears, cooked

2 gal. Mornay sauce
2 qts. ham stock

Preparation

1. Prepare ham stock (See Chap. 12.)
2. Bone a cooked ham with a boning knife. Slice the horseshoe side of the ham on a slicing machine approximately ⅛ in. thick. Proceed only after demonstration by instructor. Heat the ham slices in the ham stock.
3. Cook asparagus spears if using frozen or fresh asparagus. (See Chap. 13.) If using canned asparagus, open and heat.
4. Prepare the Mornay sauce. (See Chap. 15.)

Procedure

1. Place two asparagus spears on each slice of ham, roll up and place two rolls in each shallow casserole.
2. Top the rolls with Mornay sauce, using a ladle and glaze under the broiler until light brown.
3. Serve at once, 2 rolls per serving.

Precautions and Safety Measures

1. Use caution when boning and slicing the ham to avoid cutting self.
2. When glazing the ham rolls do not over-brown or item will lack appearance.

BOILED PORK RECIPES

Diced ham and lima beans

This item is a combination of cooked dried lima beans and diced cooked ham. It is suited for cafeteria service. If served on the regular luncheon, it should be served in a casserole.

Objectives

1. To teach the student the procedure for preparing diced ham and lima beans.
2. To teach the student how to process and soak the dried lima beans.
3. To teach the student how to dice the ham.

Equipment

1. French knife
2. Stock pot, 10 gal.
3. Baker's scale
4. Kitchen spoon
5. 1 gal. measure
6. Wooden paddle
7. Sauce pan, 1 qt.
8. Deep steam table pan

Ingredients: Approx. yield: 50 servings
8 lbs. lima beans, dried

10 lbs. boiled ham, diced
1 lb. 8 ozs. onions, minced
1 lb. salt pork or jowl bacon, diced small
3 gal. ham stock or 6 ozs. ham base in 3 gal. water
salt and pepper to taste

Preparation
1. Dice the cooked ham into ½ inch cubes with a French knife.
2. Prepare the ham stock. (See Chap. 12.)
3. Clean and soak the beans in the ham stock overnight. Do not refrigerate.
4. Mince the onions and dice the salt pork or jowl bacon with a French knife.
5. Have all equipment and ingredients handy.

Procedure
1. Place the stock pot containing the soaked lima beans and ham stock on the range and bring to a boil. Bring to side of range away from the heat and continue to simmer.
2. Place the salt pork or jowl bacon in a sauce pan and cook until bacon or pork becomes a light brown crackling. Stir occasionally with a kitchen spoon.
3. Add the minced onions and cook until tender. Add to the boiling beans, continuing to simmer until beans are tender. Total cooking time is about 2 hours.
4. Add the diced ham and check seasoning, stir with a wooden paddle. Place in a deep steam table pan.
5. Dish up with 6 to 8 ozs. per portion with a ladle into casseroles. Accompany with a slice of Boston brown bread.

Precautions and Safety Measures
1. Use caution when dicing the ham and mincing the onions.
2. Do not overcook the beans. They will become too mushy and appearance will be lacking.
3. When sautéing the onions, do not brown.

Boiled smoked cottage ham

Boiled smoked cottage ham are cottage hams, about 2 to 2½ pounds each, covered with water, boiled, sliced and generally served with cabbage. This item is more popular on the luncheon menu than the dinner menu.

Objectives
1. To teach the student the procedure for preparing boiled smoked cottage ham.
2. To teach the student how to slice and dish up boiled smoked cottage ham.

Equipment
1. Stock pot, 10 gal.
2. China cap
3. French knife
4. Kitchen fork
5. 2, 3 gal. stainless steel containers
6. Steam table pan

Ingredients: Approx. yield: 50 servings
25 lbs. smoked cottage ham
50 wedges of cabbage, boiled
water as needed

Preparation
1. Cut cabbage into wedges with a French knife and boil. (See Chap. 13.)
2. Have all equipment and ingredients handy.

Procedure
1. Place the cottage hams in the stock pot. Cover with water and bring to a boil on the range.
2. Bring the stock pot to the side of the range so the temperature will reduce and liquid will simmer. Simmer until the meat is tender, about 2 to 2½ hours. Remove meat with a kitchen fork. Place in a steam table pan and keep covered.
3. Strain stock through a china cap into stainless steel containers. Let cool and save for later use in the preparation of soup.
4. Slice the smoked cottage ham and dish up two nice slices on a wedge of boiled cabbage. If a sauce is desired, horseradish sauce would be an excellent choice.

Precautions and Safety Measures
1. Do not overcook the ham or the meat will crumble when sliced, and serving portions will be lost.
2. Use caution when slicing the ham to avoid cutting self.

Ham à la king

Ham à la king is a type of stew where the cooked plump cubes of ham are placed in a rich à la king sauce. Ham à la king is generally served on the luncheon or à la carte menu.

Objectives

1. To teach the student the procedure for preparing ham à la king.
2. To teach the student how to dice the ham and the garnish.
3. To teach the student how to dish up ham à la king.

Equipment

1. French knife
2. Baker's scale
3. Stock pot, 5 gal.
4. Kitchen spoon
5. Deep steam table pan
6. Sauce pan, 1 qt.
7. Wire whip
8. Qt. measure
9. Sauce pot, 2 gal.

Ingredients: Approx. yield: 50 servings

10	lbs. ham, boiled and diced in ½ in. cubes
1	lb. mushrooms, diced in ½ in. size
2	lbs. butter, melted
1½	lbs. flour
7	qts. milk, hot
1	lb. green pepper, diced in ½ in. size
6	whole canned pimientos, diced in ½ in. size.
6	ozs. sherry wine
	salt and white pepper to taste

Preparation

1. Dice the cooked ham with a French knife.
2. Dice the green peppers, pimientos and mushrooms with a French knife.
3. Heat the milk in a sauce pot.
4. Have all equipment and ingredients handy.

Procedure

1. Place the butter in a stock pot and melt. Sauté the mushrooms in the butter until slightly tender.
2. Add flour, making a roux, and cook for 10 minutes. Stir frequently with a kitchen spoon.
3. Add the hot milk, whipping constantly with a wire whip until thick and smooth.
4. Place the green peppers in the sauce pan, cover with water, add salt and boil for 5 minutes.
5. Drain the peppers and add to the above sauce.
6. Add the diced ham, pimientos and sherry wine, and bring back to a boil.

7. Adjust seasoning and place in a deep steam table pan.
8. Dish up with a 6 to 8 oz. ladle and serve on a patty shell, toast or bread cup.

Precautions and Safety Measures

1. Use caution when dicing the ham and vegetables to avoid cutting self.
2. When cooking the flour with the butter, do not brown.

Pork chop suey

Chop suey is a Chinese-American dish and is served in practically every commercial kitchen. It is a very profitable item and can be served on either the luncheon or dinner menu.

Objectives

1. To teach the student the procedure for making chop suey.
2. To teach the student how to cut the vegetables.
3. To teach the student how to dish up chop suey.

Equipment

1. French knife
2. Wood paddle
3. Stock pot, 5 gal.
4. Small container
5. Deep steam table pan
6. Qt. measure
7. Measuring cups
8. Small braiser
9. Kitchen spoon

Ingredients: Approx. yield: 4 gal. or 50 servings

4	qts. fresh pork picnic, cooked and diced
3	qts. celery, cut julienne
2½	qts. onions, cut julienne
1	pt. mushrooms, sliced thin
1	cup salad oil
½	#10 can bean sprouts
½	cup Chinese soy sauce
2½	cups corn starch
2	cans bamboo shoots, sliced thin
2	cans water chestnuts, sliced thin
3	qts. water or chicken stock
1	pt. water
	salt and pepper to taste

Preparation

1. Dice the fresh pork into 1 in. cubes with a French knife. Proceed only after demonstration by instructor.
2. Place the cubes of pork in a braiser and

brown on the range. Add a small amount of water and cook until tender.

3. Julienne the onions and celery with a French knife.
4. Slice the mushrooms fairly thin with a French knife.
5. Slice the bamboo shoots and water chestnuts thin with a French knife.
6. Prepare the chicken stock if to be used. (See Chap. 12.)
7. Have all equipment and ingredients handy.

Procedure

1. Place salad oil in a stock pot and heat.
2. Add the julienne onions and celery and the sliced mushrooms. Sauté until they are tender.
3. Add water or stock and the braised pork. Let boil until the vegetables are done but still crisp.
4. Add the Chinese soy sauce, bamboo shoots and water chestnuts. Continue to boil.
5. In a separate container dilute the cornstarch in water, stir with a kitchen spoon and add to the chop suey. Stir constantly with a wooden paddle. Cook for 5 minutes and remove from the fire.
6. Add the bean sprouts. Stir with a wooden paddle.
7. Season with salt and pepper and place in a deep steam table pan.
8. Dish up with a 6 to 8 oz. ladle and serve each portion with baked rice and fried Chinese noodles.

Note: Water chestnuts and bamboo shoots may be omitted if desired.

Precautions and Safety Measures

1. Exercise caution when handling the knife.
2. Vegetables should be crisp.
3. Discontinue cooking when the bean sprouts are added.

chapter 19

lamb and mutton

■ Lamb is the flesh of immature sheep, both male or female, approximately 12 months old. Mutton is the flesh of mature sheep, both male or female, approximately 20 months or older. There is a great deal of difference between the eating qualities of the two. Lamb is more tender and delicate in flavor. Mutton is slightly tough, depending on its age, and quite strong in flavor. Mutton is mentioned in this chapter only because it is sometimes substituted for lamb in such items as lamb stew and lamb fricassee. Generally, however, mutton is used very little in the commercial kitchen. Mutton has gained very little popularity as an edible meat mainly because of the strong aroma it gives off while cooking and because of the strong flavor. Proof of this is shown by the statistics which state that about 93 percent of all sheep marketed in the United States is marketed as lambs and yearling and about 7 percent as mutton.

There are three types of lambs available on the market: genuine spring lamb, spring lamb, and yearling lamb. *Genuine spring lamb* comes on the market from April to July and is considered the best type of lamb. They are marketed when only 3 to 5 months old and are fattened chiefly on their mother's milk. They are also known as milk lambs and in some quarters as Easter lambs. *Spring lamb* is marketed during the fall and winter months and is fattened chiefly on grass and grain. They are usually 5 to 10 months old when slaughtered and shipped to market. *Yearling lamb* is about 12 to 20 months old when marketed. It is generally too young to be sold as mutton and too old to be sold as lamb. It is considered the most economical type of lamb to use, but in using it one must consider the fact that he is serving an inferior product.

When a lamb is born it feeds on its mother's milk until it is about 5 months old. It is at this point that it will produce the finest eating qualities. The flesh is a pale pink and has a smooth grain. The bones are soft, porous, and have a reddish tinge; and the fat is firm. After the 5 month period the animal is sent out to pasture. Here he feeds on grass and grain and starts to mature. These factors create changes in the character, color and consistency of the flesh, bones and fat of the animal. As the changes take place the animal passes from lamb to yearling to mutton. The flesh becomes darker, the bones whiter and harder, and the fat becomes soft and slightly greasy. When the animal reaches the yearling and mutton stage the edible flesh is dry and strong in flavor.

LAMB GRADING

Lamb is graded on the same basis as beef. The grading is based on conformation, finish, and quality. Conformation refers to the general build of the lamb; finish to the color and firmness of interior and exterior fat; and quality to the color of the flesh and bones. There are five grades of lamb. These are, in their order of desirability: prime, choice, good, utility, and cull. Only the first three are important to the food service operator.

U.S. prime: This is the highest quality of lamb. To be stamped *prime* the animal must be about 3 to 5 months old and must be still feeding on its mother's milk. The body will be compact and have plump legs; the back will be wide and thick and the neck short and thick. The interior will display pale pink flesh with a smooth grain, bones will be soft and porous, and the fat around the kidneys will be white and firm.

U.S. choice: This is the most popular grade used in commercial establishments. It is high quality lamb and will produce excellent eating qualities. To be graded *choice* a lamb carcass must possess a slightly compact body, the legs must be short and plump, the back slightly wide and thick, and the neck slightly short and thick. The interior of the animal will display a pink flesh that is just slightly darker than the prime grade. The grain will be smooth, the bones soft and porous, and there will be a fairly generous amount of white fat around the kidney.

U.S. good: This is the economical grade of lamb. It is not of the highest quality, but can be used in some preparations with good results. The lamb carcass graded *good* is slightly rangy and bony; it has slightly thin legs; a fairly narrow, thin back; and a slightly long, narrow neck. The interior of the carcass will show a dark pink flesh, with a slightly rough grain; the bones will be just slightly hard and on the white side with little or no pink tinge visible; and fat will be on the lean side with the fat around the kidney not too abundant and the kidney may be slightly exposed.

U.S. utility: This grade of lamb is of poor quality and is very seldom, if ever, used in the commercial kitchen. The lamb carcass graded utility is very rangy and bony with thin, moderately tapered legs; it has a narrow, slightly sunken back; and has a long, thin neck. The interior of the carcass will display a dark red flesh with a fairly rough grain and little or no fat will be present except a small amount slightly covering the kidney.

U.S. cull: The poorest grade of lamb. It is never used in the commercial kitchen. The lamb carcass of this grade is extremely rangy and bony. The legs are extremely thin, the back very sunken and thin, and the neck is extremely thin and long. There is no evidence of interior fat and the flesh is a dark red in color with a soft, watery texture.

COMMERCIAL CUTS

Lamb may be purchased by the restaurant operator in four market forms. He may purchase the whole carcasses, saddle (foresaddle and hindsaddle), wholesale or primal cuts, or fabricated. The form best suited for the individual operator to purchase will depend on many factors. The following is a list of some of those factors that must be given a great deal of consideration before the purchase is made.

1. Meat cutting skill of personnel.
2. Meat cutting equipment available.
3. Working space available.
4. Meat storage space available.
5. Utility of all cuts purchased.
6. Meat preparations served.
7. Overall economy of purchasing meat in a particular form.

Carcass: This is the complete animal with head, hide, and entrails removed. It will average from 30 to 75 pounds with the majority being 35 to 45 pounds. The carcass can be purchased at a cheaper cost per pound because there has been less handling involved. This has been the most popular form of lamb to purchase over the years; however, today, with a shortage of skilled personnel and so much emphasis on speed and

production and standardization of all products, more and more the food service operator is turning to fabricated cuts in the commercial kitchen.

Saddle: Lamb carcasses are not converted into sides like beef by splitting or sawing lengthwise through the spine of the animal. They are separated into saddles by cutting across the complete carcass between the 12th and 13th ribs. The fore part of the lamb is then known as the *foresaddle,* the hind portion as the *hindsaddle.* The foresaddle will include the 1st through the 12th ribs, the 13th rib will remain on the hindsaddle. The hindsaddle, which includes the loin and leg cuts, is generally more in demand although the rib cut which is part of the foresaddle is the most popular lamb cut. The other parts of the foresaddle, however, are not so highly prized. Purchasing lamb by the saddle is not as popular today as in former years.

Wholesale or primal cuts: These are parts of the foresaddle and hindsaddle of the lamb carcass. There are six lamb cuts, they include the shoulder, shank, rib, loin, breast and leg. The cuts of the foresaddle include the shoulder, rib, shank, and breast. The cuts of the hindsaddle include the loin and leg. Purchasing lamb by the wholesale cut is still a popular practice although, as mentioned previously, the fabricated form is gaining in popularity.

Fabricated cuts: These are purchased ready to cook. They are cut to specification and are always uniform in weight. They are easy to store and will certainly cut down on labor cost. However, as with most convenient foods, they are expensive so one must consider all the advantages and disadvantages before purchasing. The trend today definitely seems to be favoring this form of purchasing. If the trend continues it will certainly dominate purchasing in the future.

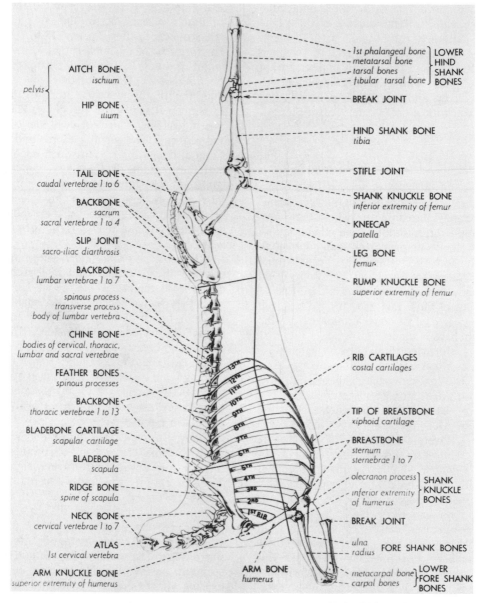

AITCH BONE
ischium

pelvis

HIP BONE
ilium

1st phalangeal bone ⎤ LOWER
metatarsal bone ⎥ HIND
tarsal bones ⎥ SHANK
fibular tarsal bone ⎦ BONES

BREAK JOINT

HIND SHANK BONE
tibia

TAIL BONE
caudal vertebrae 1 to 6

BACKBONE
sacrum
sacral vertebrae 1 to 4

SLIP JOINT
sacro-iliac diarthrosis

BACKBONE
lumbar vertebrae 1 to 7

spinous process
transverse process
body of lumbar vertebra

CHINE BONE
bodies of cervical, thoracic,
lumbar and sacral vertebrae

FEATHER BONES
spinous processes

BACKBONE
thoracic vertebrae 1 to 13

BLADEBONE CARTILAGE
scapular cartilage

BLADEBONE
scapula

RIDGE BONE
spine of scapula

NECK BONE
cervical vertebrae 1 to 7

ATLAS
1st cervical vertebra

ARM KNUCKLE BONE
superior extremity of humerus

STIFLE JOINT

SHANK KNUCKLE BONE
inferior extremity of femur

KNEECAP
patella

LEG BONE
femur

RUMP KNUCKLE BONE
superior extremity of femur

RIB CARTILAGES
costal cartilages

TIP OF BREASTBONE
xiphoid cartilage

BREASTBONE
sternum
sternebrae 1 to 7

olecranon process ⎤ SHANK
⎥ KNUCKLE
inferior extremity ⎥ BONES
of humerus ⎦

BREAK JOINT

ulna ⎤ FORE SHANK BONES
radius ⎦

metacarpal bone ⎤ LOWER
carpal bones ⎦ FORE SHANK
BONES

ARM BONE
humerus

13TH
12TH
11TH
10TH
9TH
8TH
7TH
6TH
5TH
4TH
3RD
2ND
1ST RIB

National Livestock and Meat Board

Lamb skeleton: Location, structure and names of bones.

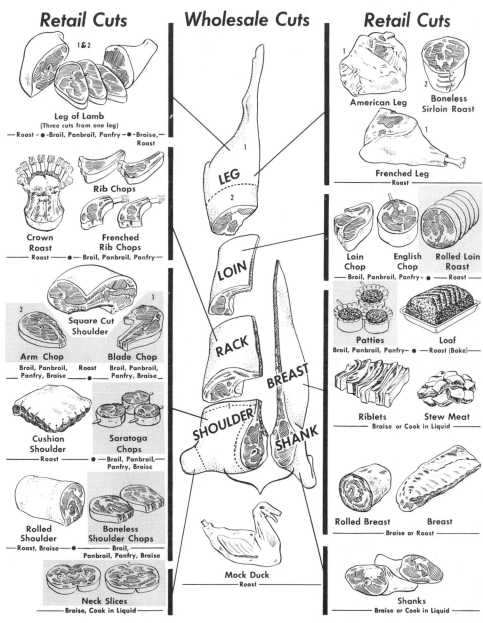

Retail Cuts

Leg of Lamb
(Three cuts from one leg)
—Roast - ●-Broil, Panbroil, Panfry –●-Braise,—
Roast

Rib Chops

Crown Roast
— Roast —

Frenched Rib Chops
● Broil, Panbroil, Panfry —

Square Cut Shoulder

Arm Chop
Broil, Panbroil, Panfry, Braise —

Blade Chop
Broil, Panbroil, Panfry, Braise
●

Cushion Shoulder
— Roast —

Saratoga Chops
● —Broil, Panbroil,—
Panfry, Braise

Rolled Shoulder
— Roast, Braise—●

Boneless Shoulder Chops
—Broil,
Panbroil, Panfry, Braise

Neck Slices
— Braise, Cook in Liquid —

Wholesale Cuts

LEG

LOIN

RACK

BREAST

SHOULDER

SHANK

Mock Duck
— Roast —

Retail Cuts

American Leg

Boneless Sirloin Roast

Frenched Leg
— Roast —

Loin Chop

English Chop
— Broil, Panbroil, Panfry - ●

Rolled Loin Roast
— Roast —

Patties
Broil, Panbroil, Panfry– ●

Loaf
—Roast (Bake)—

Riblets

Stew Meat
— Braise or Cook in Liquid —

Rolled Breast

Breast
— Braise or Roast —

Shanks
— Braise or Cook in Liquid —

National Livestock and Meat Board

Lamb Chart: Meat cuts and common cooking methods. Cuts shown in grey are not commonly used in the commercial kitchen in the form shown.

WHOLESALE CUTS: COOKING METHODS

The six wholesale or primal lamb cuts play an important part in certain preparations prepared in the commercial kitchen. It is important, therefore, that the cooking student acquire a knowledge of their chief characteristics and proper uses. They will be listed according to popularity.

Rib or rack: This is the most popular of all the lamb cuts. It contains 7 ribs and a rib eye muscle of solid lean meat. This cut lies between the shoulder and the loin. It gained its popularity through the fine chops it provides. When two ribs are joined together or unsplit they are referred to as a rack of lamb. From this rack is generally prepared the very popular menu item, roast crown of lamb. The rib of lamb is sometimes roasted in the commercial kitchen but in most cases it is cut into chops.

Loin or saddle: This cut lies between the rib and leg cuts. It contains a loin eye, a small T-shaped bone, a tenderloin, and a small amount of flank meat which is removed when the loin is trimmed. When a complete loin from the whole lamb carcass is unsplit, the cut is referred to as a saddle of lamb. It is from the saddle that English lamb chops are cut. English lamb chops are

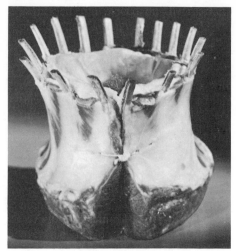

National Livestock and Meat Board
Crown roast

National Livestock and Meat Board
Loin chops

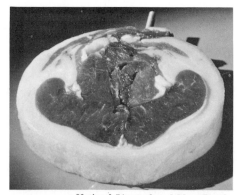

National Livestock and Meat Board
English chops

National Livestock and Meat Board
Rib chops

two inch thick cuts taken along the entire length of the unsplit loin. The loin is roasted on certain occasions in the commercial kitchen, but in most cases it is converted into chops or English lamb chops.

Leg: This is the hind leg of the lamb. It contains a shank bone and aitch bone. (The aitch bone is the buttock or rump bone and lies at the top of the leg.) The flesh is solid, lean, and fine textured. The leg will average about 4 to 9 pounds. It is popular in the commercial kitchen when cut into lamb steaks or when boned and roasted.

Shoulder: This is the largest and thickest part of the foresaddle. It contains 5 rib bones and a fairly high percentage of lean meat. It is used in the commercial kitchen in the preparation of lamb stew, patties, fricassee and curry.

Breast: This is a thin, flat cut containing breastbone and the tips of 12 ribs. It has alternating layers of fat and lean. It is not a very popular cut of lamb, but is used in the commercial kitchen for such preparations as stuffed breast of lamb and lamb riblets.

Shank: The fore legs of the animal. It contains a large portion of bone and connective tissue with little lean meat. To be utilized in the commercial kitchen the shanks are generally braised and served with jardiniere cut vegetables. The shank meat is sometimes ground and formed into lamb patties.

VARIETY MEATS

The lamb variety meats include kidneys, liver, brains, sweetbreads, and tongue. They are not nearly as popular as the variety meats of the other edible animals. The kidneys, liver, brains and sweetbreads are all processed and prepared in the same manner as those of beef, veal, and pork. The lamb tongue, if not utilized in some kind of sausage, is pickled and placed on the market as pickled lamb's tongue.

LAMB TERMINOLOGY

There are certain terms used within the culinary trade pertaining to lamb that the student cook should become familiar with in order to excel in his field of endeavor.

Lamb: The flesh of immature sheep.

Mutton: The flesh of mature sheep.

Yearling: The flesh of lamb 12 to 20 months old.

Fell: The thin, paper-like covering over the outside of a lamb's carcass.

English lamb chop: Several two-inch thick cuts taken along the entire length of the unsplit lamb loin.

Frenched: Generally applied to chops. It means the meat and fat is removed from the end of the rib bones. The ribs of a crown roast are frenched and sometimes the leg bone of a roast leg of lamb is frenched.

Cull: The poorest grade of lamb.

Crown roast: Prepared from the unsplit rack. The rib ends are Frenched and the ribs are formed into a crown.

Riblets: Rectangular strips of meat each containing part of a rib bone. They are cut from the breast.

Hotel rack: Refers to the unsplit rib section of the carcass.

Mock duck: Made from shoulder and

National Livestock and Meat Board

Mock duck

shank cuts, shaped like a duck and roasted.

Hothouse lamb: Lamb produced under artificial conditions. It is available on the market from January to March, but supplies are small. Hothouse lamb is generally graded choice or good.

Double lamb chop: One rib chop cut to a thickness that is equal to two rib chops.

LAMB RECIPES

Americans consume about 7 pounds of lamb per person each year. This is a very low consumption when compared to the other edible meats. It is for this reason that lamb entrées do not appear too often on the menus of the food service establishments. With the exceptions of lamb chops and roast lamb, which have been favorites down through the centuries, chefs and managers are not too eager to gamble with lamb entrées. This could be a mistake on their part because there are many tasty and desirable main dishes that can prove to be a welcome and profitable addition to any luncheon or dinner menu. The following recipes are just a few of these main dishes.

Roasted lamb
(Pages 428 to 429)

Roast leg of lamb

Braised or stewed lamb
(Pages 429 to 441)

Braised stuffed breast of lamb
French lamb stew
Braised breast of lamb
Barbecued lamb riblets
Sour cream lamb stew
Braised lamb shanks jardiniere
Potted leg of lamb
Curried lamb
Navarin of lamb
Irish stew
Lamb stew Dublin style
Lamb à la Indienne
Fricassee of lamb

Broiled lamb
(Pages 441 to 445)

Lamb chop mix grill
Broiled lamb chops
Lamb and mushroom en brochette
Broiled lamb steak
Broiled lamb patties
Shish kebob

Boiled lamb
(Pages 445 to 446)

Boiled lamb with dill sauce

ROASTED LAMB RECIPES
Roast leg of lamb

For roast leg of lamb the leg is boned and roasted at a moderate temperature. It is sliced and served with its natural gravy and mint sauce. An excellent entrée for the dinner menu.

Objectives
1. To teach the student the procedure for preparing roast leg of lamb.
2. To teach the student how to bone and tie the roast.
3. To teach the student how to slice and dish up roast leg of lamb.

Equipment
1. Baker's scale
2. Boning knife
3. Roast pan
4. Sauce pot, 2 gal.
5. French knife
6. Butcher twine
7. Kitchen fork
8. Bake pan
9. Wire whip
10. 2 gal. stainless steel container
11. China cap
12. Spoon measure
13. Cup measure

Ingredients: Approx. yield: 50 servings

5	legs of lamb (5 to 6 lbs. each), boned and tied
12	ozs. onions, cut rough
8	ozs. carrots, cut rough
8	ozs. celery, cut rough
½	tsp. garlic, minced

½ cup salad oil
1 tsp. rosemary leaves
1 tbsp. marjoram
1 lb. shortening
10 ozs. flour
1½ gal. brown stock
1 cup tomato purée
caramel as needed
salt and pepper to taste

Preparation
1. Bone the leg of lamb by removing the aitch, leg and shank bones with a boning knife. Roll the boneless meat and tie with butcher twine. Proceed only after demonstration by instructor.
2. Mince the garlic with a French knife.
3. Cut the vegetables rough with a French knife.
4. Prepare the brown stock. (See Chap. 12.)
5. Preheat oven to 375°F.
6. Have all equipment and ingredients handy.

Procedure
1. Place the tied, boneless legs of lamb in the roast pan. Rub the lamb with salad oil and season with salt, pepper and marjoram.
2. Roast in a preheated oven at 375°F until the roasts become brown. Add the garlic and rough garnish (onion, carrots and celery). Reduce oven temperature to 325°F and continue to roast until the meat is done. (Approx. total time 2 to 2½ hours.)
3. Remove the lamb from the roast pan with a kitchen fork. Place in a bake pan remove twine and hold. Keep warm.
4. Pour the brown stock into the roast pan and bring to a boil on the range to deglaze the roast pan.
5. Pour the liquid from the roast pan into a stainless steel container and keep hot.
6. Place the shortening in a sauce pot, heat.
7. Add the flour, making a roux, cook for 5 minutes. Add the hot brown stock and tomato purée, whipping vigorously with a wire whip until slightly thickened and smooth. Let simmer for 15 to 20 minutes.
8. Check seasoning and if too light add caramel color to darken. Strain through a china cap back into the stainless steel container.

9. Slice the roast lamb against the grain on a slicing machine or with a French knife. Dish up 2½ to 3 ozs. per portion, covered with the brown gravy and accompanied with a soufflé cup of mint sauce or mint jelly.

Precautions and Safety Measures
1. Exercise caution when handling the knives to avoid cutting self.
2. Do not overcook the meat. It will be difficult to slice and will lack appearance when served.
3. While the gravy is simmering, stir occasionally to avoid scorching.
4. If gravy needs to be darkened, add caramel coloring with caution.

BRAISED OR STEWED LAMB RECIPES

Braised stuffed breast of lamb

The breast is a slightly undesirable cut of lamb since it contains only thin layers of lean meat and many breast bones. It is transformed into a desirable menu item by stuffing with a forcemeat mixture and braising in the oven.

Objectives
1. To teach the student the procedure for preparing braised stuffed breast of lamb.
2. To teach the student how to trim and stuff the breast of lamb.
3. To teach the student how to serve braised stuffed breast of lamb.

Equipment
1. Boning knife
2. Full size steam table pan
3. French knife
4. Butcher twine
5. Large eye needle
6. Baker's scale
7. Qt. measure
8. Kitchen fork
9. Kitchen spoon
10. Skillet
11. Wire whip
12. China cap
13. Mixing container, 3 gal. size
14. Roast pan
15. Meat grinder
16. Sauce pot, 1 gal.
17. 1 gal. stainless steel container

Ingredients: Approx. yield: 24 servings

    4   5 lb. breasts of lamb (20 lbs.),
        trimmed
    5   lbs. boneless lamb shoulder,
        cut into strips
 1½   lbs. dry bread cubes
    1   qt. milk (variable)
    8   ozs. onions, minced
    6   ozs. celery, minced
    8   ozs. bread crumbs (variable)
    6   egg yolks
    8   ozs. butter
   ¼   oz. sage
    6   ozs. shortening
    4   ozs. flour
    2   qts. brown stock
        salt and pepper to taste

Preparation

1. Trim the 4 lamb breasts of excess fat and cartilage with a French and boning knife. Cut a pocket in each breast by slicing with a boning knife between the flesh and the breast bones. Make the opening as large as possible but do not cut through the flesh at any point. Proceed only after demonstration by instructor.
2. Prepare the brown stock. (See Chap. 12.)
3. Mince the onions and celery with a French knife.
4. Cut the lamb shoulder into strips that will fit into the grinder. Cut with a French knife.
5. Separate the eggs and beat the yolks slightly with a wire whip. Save the whites for use in another preparation.
6. Preheat oven to 350°F.
7. Have all equipment and ingredients handy.

Procedure

1. In a mixing container place the dry bread cubes and the milk, mix with a kitchen spoon until the bread has absorbed the milk.
2. Sauté the onions and celery in a skillet in butter. Add to above mixture.
3. Add the strips of lamb shoulder and sage, mix thoroughly by hand.
4. Grind this mixture twice in a meat grinder, using the fine chopper plate.
5. Add the slightly beaten egg yolks, season with salt and pepper, mix thoroughly. If the mixture is too wet add the bread crumbs as needed. If too dry add more milk.
6. Stuff the forcemeat mixture into the pock-

ets cut into the lamb breast. Pack it in fairly solid.

7. Using a large eye needle and butcher twine sew up the opening between the layer of meat and the breast bones. Secure properly so the forcemeat will not come out during the roasting period.
8. Season the stuffed breasts with salt and pepper and place in a roast pan, brown thoroughly in the oven at 350°F. Turn occasionally with a kitchen fork.
9. Pour the brown stock over the breasts and continue to braise until the breasts are tender and the forcemeat has become solid.
10. Remove from the oven, place in a steam table pan and let set in a warm place for 45 minutes.
11. Place the shortening in a sauce pot and heat.
12. Add the flour, making a roux; cook for 5 minutes.
13. Add the brown stock the breasts were braised in, whipping vigorously with a wire whip until thickened and smooth. Strain through a fine china cap into a stainless steel container.
14. Slice the stuffed breasts to order with a French knife. Cut 6 portions from each breast. Serve on top of brown sauce accompanied with buttered noodles.

Precautions and Safety Measures

1. Exercise caution when handling the knives to avoid cutting self.
2. Do not break through the flesh when cutting the pocket.
3. Do not stick a fork into the meat during the roasting period.
4. Use a sharp French knife and apply very little pressure when slicing each order of the lamb breast.

French lamb stew

French lamb stew is a brown stew. The meat is browned before it is stewed to bring out a very rich flavor. The vegetables are cooked separately and blended into the stew when the lamb becomes tender. Like most stews it is more desirable on the luncheon rather than the dinner menu.

Objectives

1. To teach the student the procedure for preparing French lamb stew.

2. To teach the student how to cut the meat.
3. To teach the student how to dish up French lamb stew.

Equipment
1. French knife
2. Large braising pot and cover
3. Sauce pans, (2) 4 qt. and (1) 2 qt.
4. Baker's scale
5. Kitchen spoon
6. Spoon measure
7. Qt. measure
8. China cap
9. Steam table pan

Ingredients: Approx. yield: 50 servings

18	lbs. lamb shoulder, cut into 1 in. cubes
2½	gal. brown stock
3	cups salad oil
½	#10 can whole tomatoes, crushed
2	cloves garlic, minced
1	lb. 4 ozs. flour
3	lbs. carrots, large dice
2	lbs. celery, cut ½ in. wide on a bias (slanting)
½	#10 can whole small onions
2½	lb. box frozen peas
½	#10 can cut green beans
8	ozs. onions, minced
1	bay leaf
1	tbsp. marjoram
	salt and pepper to taste

Preparation
1. Cut the boneless lamb shoulder into 1 in. cubes with a French knife. Proceed only after demonstration by instructor.
2. Dice the carrots with a French knife.
3. Cut the celery ½ in. wide on a bias (slanting) with a French knife.
4. Mince the onions and garlic with a French knife.
5. Crush the tomatoes by hand.
6. Preheat oven to 375°F.
7. Prepare the brown stock. (See Chap. 12.)
8. Have all equipment and ingredients handy.

Procedure
1. Place the salad oil in a braising pot and heat.
2. Add the cubes of lamb and brown thoroughly. Stir with a kitchen spoon.
3. Add the minced onions and garlic and continue to cook for 5 minutes.
4. Add the flour and blend thoroughly with a kitchen spoon, making a roux; cook for 5 minutes more.

Armour and Co.

French lamb stew

5. Add the brown stock, marjoram and bay leaf. Stir. Cover braiser and cook in a 375°F oven for about 1½ hours or until the lamb cubes are tender.
6. Boil all the raw vegetables in separate sauce pans in salt water until tender. Drain through a china cap.
7. When the lamb has become tender, remove from the oven. Remove the bay leaf and add the crushed tomatoes and all the drained, cooked vegetables, except the peas.
8. Bring stew to a boil, check seasoning and consistency. Place in a steam table pan.
9. Dish up in casseroles with a 6 to 8 oz. ladle. Serve each portion topped with the green peas.

Precautions and Safety Measures
1. Exercise caution when handling the knife to avoid cutting self.
2. Do not overcook the cubes of lamb.
3. When adding the flour to make the roux be sure to cook slightly or the stew will have a raw flour taste.
4. Drain all the vegetables thoroughly before adding to the stew.

Braised breast of lamb

For braised breast of lamb the breasts are trimmed and cooked by the braising method until tender. This item is generally served with jardiniere or julienne cut vegetables on the luncheon menu.

1. To teach the student the procedure for preparing braised breast of lamb.
2. To teach the student how to trim the breast for braising.
3. To teach the student how to slice and dish up braised breast of lamb.

Equipment
1. Boning knife
2. Qt. measure
3. Baker's scale
4. Braising pot and cover
5. Spoon measure
6. French knife
7. Wire whip
8. Sauce pot, 2 gal.
9. China cap
10. 2 gal. stainless steel container
11. Full size steam table pan

Ingredients: Approx. yield: 24 servings
4   5 lb. breasts of lamb (20 lbs.)
½   cup salad oil
8   ozs. carrots, cut rough
12   ozs. onions, cut rough
6   ozs. celery, cut rough
1   small bay leaf
1   tsp. marjoram
1   gal. brown stock
8   ozs. shortening
6   ozs. flour
½   cup tomato purée
    salt and pepper to taste

Preparation
1. Trim excess fat and cartilage from the breast with a French and boning knife. Proceed only after demonstration by instructor.
2. Cut the carrots, onions and celery rough (rough garnish) with a French knife.
3. Prepare the brown stock. (See Chap. 12.)
4. Preheat oven to 400°F.
5. Have all equipment and ingredients handy.

Procedure
1. Place the breasts in a large braising pot, rub with the salad oil and season with salt and pepper.
2. Place in the 400°F oven and roast until the breasts are thoroughly brown. Do not cover the pot.
3. Add the rough garnish (onions, carrots and celery), marjoram and bay leaf. Continue to roast until garnish becomes slightly brown.
4. Add the tomato purée and brown stock,

cover the braising pot and reduce oven temperature to 350°F. Braise the breasts until tender.
5. Place the shortening in a sauce pot, heat.
6. Add the flour and blend thoroughly into the shortening with a kitchen spoon, making a roux. Cook 5 minutes.
7. Remove the braised breasts from the liquid and place in a steam table pan. Keep warm.
8. Pour the liquid into the roux, whipping vigorously with a wire whip until thickened.
9. Strain gravy through a fine china cap into a stainless steel container.
10. Cut each breast into 6 equal portions with a French knife, cover each portion with the gravy and serve garnished with julienne or jardiniere cut vegetables.

Precautions and Safety Measures
1. Exercise caution when handling the knives to avoid cutting self.
2. When browning the rough garnish with the breasts, do not let the garnish burn.
3. Exercise caution when lifting the lid of the braising pot to avoid the escaping steam.
4. Do not overcook the breasts.

Barbecued lamb riblets

The riblets are similar to the short ribs of beef. They are cut from the breast of lamb, browned in the oven and baked until tender in a rich, tasty barbecue sauce.

Objectives
1. To teach the student the procedure for preparing barbecued lamb riblets.
2. To teach the student how to cut the riblets.
3. To teach the student how to dish up the riblets.

Equipment
1. Large braising pot and cover
2. Kitchen fork
3. Qt. measure
4. Kitchen spoon
5. Baker's scale
6. Steam table pan
7. Hand meat saw or power saw

Ingredients: Approx. yield: 25 servings
14   lbs. lamb breast, cut into riblets
1   cup salad oil
2   gal. barbecue sauce
    salt and pepper to taste

National Livestock and Meat Board

Lamb riblets

Preparation

1. Cut the lamb breast into riblets. Cut length-wise with a hand meat saw or power saw about 1½ to 2 in. wide the full length of the breast. Then cut crosswise into 3 in. lengths. Proceed only after demonstration by instructor.
2. Prepare the barbecue sauce. (See Chap. 15.)
3. Preheat oven to 375°F.
4. Have all equipment and ingredients handy.

Procedure

1. Place the salad oil in the braiser and heat.
2. Add the riblets and brown thoroughly. Turn occasionally with a kitchen fork.
3. Pour the prepared barbecue sauce over the riblets. Cover braiser and place in a 375°F oven.
4. Bake until the riblets are tender. Remove from the oven and check the seasoning. Place in a steam table pan.
5. Dish up 2 riblets per portion. Accompany with baked rice.

Precautions and Safety Measures

1. Exercise caution when handling the hand meat saw or power saw.
2. While baking the riblets in the sauce, stir frequently with a kitchen spoon to avoid scorching or sticking.
3. Do not overcook the riblets. They will be lacking in appearance when served.

Sour cream lamb stew

For sour cream lamb stew cubes of lamb shoulder are gently browned and then baked in a sour cream sauce with mushrooms. This item is similar to stroganoff preparations and is a welcome addition to the luncheon menu when served with buttered noodles or baked rice.

Objectives

1. To teach the student the procedure for preparing sour cream lamb stew.
2. To teach the student how to cut the meat.
3. To teach the student how to dish up the lamb stew.

Equipment

1. French knife
2. Baker's scale
3. Qt. measure
4. Large braising pot and cover
5. Kitchen spoon
6. Sauce pot, 5 gal.
7. Cup measure
8. Deep steam table pan

Ingredients: Approx. yield: 50 servings

18	lbs. lamb shoulder, boneless, cut into 1 in. cubes
2½	gal. brown stock
2	lbs. shortening
1	lb. 8 ozs. flour
1	cup tomato purée
1	cup vinegar
2	lbs. onions, minced
2	cloves garlic, minced
2	bay leaves
½	cup chives, chopped
1	lb. mushrooms, sliced thick
1½	qts. sour cream
1	pt. salad oil
	salt and pepper to taste

Preparation

1. Cut the boneless lamb shoulder into 1 in. cubes with a French knife. Proceed only after demonstration by instructor.
2. Prepare the brown stock. (See Chap. 12.)
3. Mince the onions and garlic with a French knife.
4. Slice the mushrooms thick and chop the chives with a French knife.
5. Preheat oven to 350°F.
6. Have all equipment and ingredients handy.

Procedure

1. Place the salad oil in a large braising pot and heat.
2. Add the cubes of lamb and brown thoroughly. Stir occasionally with a kitchen spoon.
3. Add the minced onions and garlic, continue to cook for 5 minutes more. Remove from the range and hold.
4. Place the shortening in a sauce pot, heat.
5. Add the mushrooms and sauté slightly.

6. Add the flour, making a roux, and cook for 5 minutes.
7. Add the hot brown stock, tomato purée, vinegar and bay leaves, stir gently with a kitchen spoon until sauce becomes slightly thick and smooth.
8. Pour the sauce over the browned cubes of meat, cover braiser and place in a 350°F oven until the meat becomes tender.
9. Remove from the oven and remove the bay leaves. Stir in the sour cream with a kitchen spoon and season with salt and pepper.
10. Add the chives and blend in thoroughly. Place in a deep steam table pan.
11. Dish up into casseroles with a 6 to 8 oz. ladle. Serve accompanied with buttered noodles and baked rice.

Precautions and Safety Measures
1. Exercise caution when handling the knife.
2. When adding the liquid to the roux, stir gently so the mushrooms will not be broken.
3. When the stew is cooking in the oven stir occasionally.
4. Exercise caution when removing the cover from the braiser, steam will escape.
5. Do not overcook the cubes of lamb. They will lack appearance when served.

Braised lamb shanks jardiniere

Braised lamb shanks jardiniere consist of small lamb shanks cooked by the braising method and served with jardiniere vegetables. One whole lamb shank is served to each order. This is a fairly popular luncheon item.

Objectives
1. To teach the student the procedure for preparing braised lamb shanks jardiniere.
2. To teach the student how to prepare the shanks for cooking.
3. To teach the student how to dish up braised lamb shanks jardiniere.

Equipment
1. Braising pot, large, and cover
2. Kitchen fork
3. Wire whip
4. French knife
5. Sauce pans, (2) 4 qt. and (2) 2 qt.
6. Baker's scale
7. Sauce pot, 2 gal.
8. Qt. measure

9. Cup measure
10. Boning knife
11. Deep steam table pan
12. China cap

Ingredients: Approx. yield: 25 servings

25	lamb shanks
1½	gal. brown stock
1	lb. shortening
12	ozs. flour
3	lbs. carrots, cut jardiniere
2	lbs. turnips, cut jardiniere
1	lb. celery, sliced on a bias (slanting)
1	cup tomato purée
2½	lb. box frozen peas
1	tsp. marjoram
1	bay leaf
½	#10 can whole onions
1	cup salad oil
1	cup onion, minced
2	cloves garlic, minced
	salt and pepper to taste

Preparation
1. Trim the lamb shanks with a boning knife. Use the section of meat between the first and second joints. Proceed only after demonstration by instructor.
2. Prepare the brown stock. (See Chap. 12.)
3. Cut the carrots and turnips jardiniere style (1 in. by ¼ in.) with a French knife.
4. Slice the celery on the bias (slanting) about ¼ in. thick with a French knife
5. Cook the frozen peas in a sauce pan in boiling salt water.
6. Heat the canned onions, drain.
7. Mince the onions and garlic with a French knife.
8. Preheat oven to 375°F.
9. Have all equipment and ingredients handy.

Procedure
1. Place the lamb shanks in a large braising pot; pour the salad oil over them and brown thoroughly in a 375°F oven.
2. Sprinkle the minced onion and garlic over the shanks and continue to roast for 10 minutes more. Turn occasionally with a kitchen fork.
3. Add the brown stock, tomato purée, bay leaf and marjoram. Cover braiser and reduce oven temperature to 350°F. Continue to cook until the shanks are tender. Remove from the oven.
4. Boil the carrots, celery and turnips in separate sauce pans in salt water. Drain and hold.

5. Remove the shanks from the braising pot and place in a deep steam table pan. Cover and keep warm.
6. Place the shortening in a sauce pot and heat.
7. Add flour, making a roux, and cook for 5 minutes.
8. Add the hot brown stock in which the shanks were cooked, whipping vigorously with a wire whip until slightly thickened. Simmer for 15 minutes. Strain through a china cap back over the shanks.
9. Dish up 1 shank per portion topped with gravy, jardiniere vegetables and peas.

Precautions and Safety Measures
1. Exercise caution when trimming the shanks and cutting the vegetables.
2. Do not overcook the shanks, the meat will fall away from the bone.
3. Stir occasionally while the sauce is simmering to avoid scorching.

Potted leg of lamb

Potted leg of lamb is cooked by the braising method. The leg is browned thoroughly in the oven, placed in a stock pot, covered with a liquid and simmered until tender. This is an excellent luncheon or dinner entree.

Objective
1. To teach the student the procedure for preparing potted leg of lamb.
2. To teach the student how to prepare the leg for cooking.
3. To teach the student how to dish up potted leg of lamb.

Equipment
1. Butcher twine
2. French knife
3. Boning knife
4. Roast pan
5. Stock pot, 10 gal.
6. Wire whip
7. China cap
8. Sauce pot, 5 gal.
9. 2 gal. stainless steel container
10. Bake pan
11. Kitchen fork
12. Baker's scale

Ingredients: Approx. yield: 50 servings

5	legs of lamb (5 to 6 lbs. each), boned and tied
1	lb. onions, cut rough
½	lb. carrots, cut rough
½	lb. celery, cut rough
2	gal. brown stock
1	lb. 4 ozs. shortening
1	lb. flour
1	cup tomato purée
1	tsp. thyme
1	tsp. marjoram
1	bay leaf
	salt and pepper to taste

Preparation
1. Bone the leg of lamb by removing the aitch, leg and shank bones with a boning knife. Roll the boneless meat and tie with butcher twine. Proceed only after demonstration by instructor.
2. Cut the celery, carrots and onions rough with a French knife.
3. Prepare the brown stock. (See Chap. 12.)
4. Preheat oven to 375°F.
5. Have all equipment and ingredients handy.

Procedure
1. Place the boned, tied legs of lamb in a roast pan. Brown in the oven at 375°F.
2. Add the rough garnish (onions, carrots and celery). Continue to roast until garnish is slightly brown.
3. Remove meat from the oven and place in a stock pot. Deglaze the roast pan with the brown stock. Pour over the meat.
4. Add the tomato purée, marjoram, thyme and bay leaf. Place on the range and let simmer until the meat is tender. Remove the meat from the liquid with a kitchen fork, place in a bake pan and cover with a wet towel and keep warm.
5. Place the shortening in the sauce pot, heat.
6. Add the flour making a roux, cook 10 minutes.
7. Pour the brown stock into the roux, whipping constantly with a wire whip until thickened and smooth.
8. Simmer the gravy for 15 minutes and strain through a china cap into a stainless steel container.
9. Slice the potted lamb across the grain on a slicing machine or with a French knife. Dish up 2½ to 3 ozs. per portion with the rich gravy. Mint sauce or mint jelly should accompany each portion.

Precautions and Safety Measures
1. Exercise caution when boning the leg of lamb to avoid cutting self.
2. Do not overcook the lamb.

Curried lamb

Curried lamb is a type of stew. The cooked cubes of lamb are blended into a rich curry sauce and generally served with rice and chutney. An excellent choice for the luncheon or dinner menu.

Objectives
1. To teach the student the procedure for preparing curried lamb.
2. To teach the student how to cut the lamb shoulder.
3. To teach the student how to dish up curried lamb.

Equipment
1. French knife
2. Wire whip
3. Sauce pot, 5 gal.
4. Stock pot, 5 gal.
5. Kitchen spoon
6. China cap
7. Deep steam table pan
8. Cheese cloth
9. Bake pan
10. 3 gal. stainless steel container
11. Qt. measure
12. Baker's scale
13. Wooden paddle
14. Skimmer

Ingredients: Approx. yield: 50 servings

18	lbs. lamb shoulder, boneless, cut into 1 in. cubes
2½	gal. water
2	lbs. butter or shortening
1	lb. 8 oz. flour
⅓	cup curry powder
2	qts. tart apples, diced
2	lbs. onions, diced
½	tsp. ground cloves
½	tsp. nutmeg
2	bay leaves
1	tsp. marjoram
	salt and white pepper to taste

Preparation
1. Cut the boneless lamb shoulder into 1 in. cubes with a French knife. Proceed only after demonstration by instructor.
2. Dice the tart apples and onions small with a French knife.
3. Have all equipment and ingredients handy.

Procedure
1. Place the meat in a stock pot, cover with the water and bring to a boil. Remove any scum that may appear on the surface with a skimmer.
2. Add the bay leaves and marjoram, let simmer until the cubes of lamb are tender. Remove from the fire.
3. Strain the stock through a china cap covered with a cheese cloth into a stainless steel container. Keep hot. Place the cooked cubes of meat in a pan, cover with a wet towel, keep warm.
4. Place the butter in a large sauce pot, melt.
5. Add the onions and sauté until slightly tender. Add the flour and curry powder, blend in thoroughly with a kitchen spoon and cook for 10 minutes more.
6. Add the hot stock, whipping vigorously with a wire whip until thickened and slightly smooth.
7. Add the apples, nutmeg and cloves, simmer for about 20 to 30 minutes, stirring constantly.
8. Strain through a china cap into the stock pot. Add the cooked cubes of lamb and blend into the sauce with a wooden paddle.
9. Check the seasoning and consistency. Place in a deep steam table pan.
10. Dish up into shallow casseroles with a 6 to 8 oz. ladle. Serve with baked rice and chutney.

Precautions and Safety Measures
1. Exercise caution when handling the knife to avoid cutting self.
2. Do not overcook the lamb cubes or appearance will be lacking when served.
3. Keep the cooked lamb cubes covered with a damp towel at all times or they will dry out and discolor.
4. When sautéing the onions do not let them brown.

Navarin of lamb

Navarin of lamb is a brown lamb stew. When the meat for a stew is browned and then cooked it will produce a richer tasting stew. The vegetables for this type of stew are cut jardiniere to improve appearance when served. This is an excellent choice for the luncheon menu.

Objectives
1. To teach the student the procedure for preparing Navarin of lamb.

2. To teach the student how to cut the meat and vegetables.
3. To teach the student how to dish up Navarin of lamb.

Equipment
1. French knife
2. Braising pot, large
3. Spoon measures
4. 4 sauce pans, (3) 4 qt. and (1) 2 qt.
5. Kitchen spoon
6. Qt. measure
7. Baker's scale
8. China cap

Ingredients: Approx. yield: 50 servings

18	lbs. lamb shoulder, boneless, cut into 1 in. cubes
3/4	qt. salad oil
1	lb. flour
3	lbs. carrots, cut jardiniere
3	lbs. white turnips, cut jardiniere
2	lbs. celery, sliced
1	#10 can tomatoes, drained
2	gal. brown stock
2½	lb. box frozen peas
½	#10 can whole onions, drained
2	bay leaves
1	tbsp. marjoram
	salt and pepper to taste

Preparation
1. Cut the carrots and turnips jardiniere (1 in. by ¼ in.) with a French knife.
2. Slice the celery on a bias (slanting) against the grain with a French knife.
3. Cut the boneless lamb shoulder into 1 in. cubes with a French knife. Proceed only after demonstration by instructor.
4. Drain the tomatoes and onions. Save the tomato juice for use in another preparation.
5. Cook the frozen peas in a sauce pan in boiling salt water.
6. Prepare the brown stock. (See Chap. 12.)
7. Preheat oven to 375°F.
8. Have all equipment and ingredients handy.

Procedure
1. Pour the oil into a large braising pot, heat.
2. Add the cubes of lamb and brown thoroughly.
3. Add the flour and blend in thoroughly with a kitchen spoon, making a roux. Cook for 5 minutes.
4. Add the brown stock stirring constantly with a kitchen spoon until liquid becomes thick and slightly smooth.

5. Add the bay leaves and marjoram, cover and place in the oven at a temperature of 375°F until the cubes of meat become tender.
6. Boil the carrots, celery and turnips in separate sauce pans in boiling salt water until slightly tender. Drain through a china cap.
7. When the lamb becomes tender, remove from the oven, remove the bay leaves and add the tomatoes and all the drained cooked vegetables, except the peas.
8. Bring stew to a boil, check seasoning and consistency. Remove from the range and place in a deep steam table pan.
9. Dish up into casseroles with a 6 to 8 oz. ladle. Garnish each portion with the cooked peas.

Precautions and Safety Measures
1. Exercise caution when handling the knife to avoid cutting self.
2. When adding the flour to make the roux be sure to cook slightly or the stew will have a raw flour taste.
3. Do not overcook the cubes of lamb. Appearance will be lacking when served.
4. Drain all vegetables thoroughly before adding to the stew.
5. When adding the jardiniere cut vegetables to the stew, stir in gently so vegetables will not be broken.

Irish stew

Irish stew is a white or boiled stew. All the ingredients are boiled which makes it easy to digest. Irish stew is generally served with dumplings and is a welcomed addition to any luncheon menu.

Objectives
1. To teach the student the procedure for preparing Irish stew.
2. To teach the student how to cut the meat and vegetables.
3. To teach the student how to dish up Irish stew.

Equipment
1. French knife
2. Stock pot, 5 gal.
3. Skimmer
4. 3 sauce pans, 3 qts. each
5. China cap
6. Cheese cloth
7. Wire whip
8. Wood paddle

9. Baker's scale
10. Sauce pot, 5 gal.
11. Full size steam table pan
    Ingredients: Approx. yield: 50 servings
    - 18 lbs. lamb shoulder, boneless, cut into 1 in. cubes
    - 2½ gal. water
    - ½ #10 can whole onions, drained
    - 2 qts. whole potatoes, canned, drained
    - 1 qt. turnips, cut large dice
    - 1 qt. carrots, cut large dice
    - 1 lb. 8 ozs. butter or shortening
    - 1 lb. 4 ozs. flour
    - ½ cup leeks, minced
    - 1 tbsp. marjoram
    - 2½ lb. box frozen peas
      salt and white pepper to taste

Preparation

1. Cut the boneless lamb shoulder into 1 in. cubes with a French knife. Proceed only after demonstration by instructor.
2. Mince the leeks with a French knife.
3. Dice the turnips and carrots with a French knife into large cubes ½ in. square.
4. Cook the peas in boiling salt water in a sauce pan.
5. Have all equipment and ingredients handy.

Procedure

1. Place the cubes of lamb in a stock pot, cover with the water and bring to a boil. Skim off any scum that may appear on the surface with a skimmer.
2. Add the marjoram, reduce the heat and simmer until the lamb is slightly tender.
3. Cook the carrots and turnips in separate sauce pans in boiling salt water, drain, and add the liquid from the carrots to the stock the meat is cooking in. Discard the liquid the turnips were cooked in.
4. Place the butter or shortening in a sauce pot, heat.
5. Add flour, stir with a wire whip, making a roux; cook slightly but do not brown.
6. When the meat is cooked strain the stock through a china cap covered with a cheese cloth into the roux, whipping vigorously with a wire whip until thickened and smooth.
7. Add the cooked cubes of lamb, potatoes, leeks, carrots, onions and turnips, simmer for 5 to 10 minutes stirring occasionally with a wooden paddle.
8. Season with salt and white pepper. Re-

move from the range and place in a deep steam table pan.

9. Dish up in a slightly deep casserole with a 6 to 8 oz ladle. Serve with dumplings and garnish with the cooked peas.

Precautions and Safety Measures

1. Exercise caution when handling the knife.
2. When thickened sauce is simmering stir occasionally to avoid scorching or sticking.
3. Do not let the roux brown while cooking.
4. Do not overcook the lamb or vegetables. Appearance will be lacking when served.

Lamb stew Dublin style

Lamb stew Dublin style is a white lamb stew with all the items boiled. This is the type of stew one would find in the famous city of Dublin.

Objectives

1. To teach the student the procedure for preparing lamb stew Dublin style.
2. To teach the student how to cut the ingredients.
3. To teach the student how to dish up lamb stew Dublin style.

Equipment

1. French knife
2. Stock pot, 5 gal.
3. Sauce pot, 5 gal.
4. Skimmer
5. Wire whip
6. 3 gal. stainless steel container
7. China cap
8. Cheese cloth
9. Baker's scale
10. Gal. measure
11. Spoon measure
12. Deep steam table pan
    Ingredients: Approx. yield: 50 servings
    - 18 lbs. boneless lamb shoulder, cut into 1 in. cubes
    - 10 lbs. new potatoes, sliced thick
    - 6 lbs. onions, cut julienne
    - 3 bunches leeks, cut julienne
    - 2½ gal. water
    - 2 ozs. salt
    - 1 lb. 4 ozs. butter
    - 10 ozs. flour
    - 1 tbsp. marjoram
    - 2 bay leaves
      salt and pepper to taste

Preparation

1. Cut the boneless shoulder of lamb into 1

in. cubes with a French knife. Proceed only after demonstration by instructor.

2. Slice the new potatoes slightly thick with a French knife.
3. Julienne the onions and leeks with a French knife.
4. Have all equipment and ingredients handy.

Procedure

1. Place the lamb cubes in the stock pot and cover with water. Bring to a boil and skim off any scum that may appear with a skimmer. Add the salt, marjoram and bay leaves.
2. Reduce to a simmer and cook until meat just starts to become tender. Remove from the range and strain the stock through a china cap covered with a cheese cloth into a stainless steel container. Keep both meat and stock warm.
3. Melt the butter in a sauce pot, add the onions, sauté, without color, until slightly tender.
4. Stir in the flour with a wire whip, making a roux; cook slightly.
5. Add the hot stock, whipping vigorously with a wire whip until slightly thick.
6. Add the potatoes and leeks, simmer until the potatoes start to become tender.
7. Add the cooked cubes of lamb and continue to simmer for about 10 minutes more.
8. Season with salt and pepper. Remove from the range and place in a deep steam table pan.
9. Dish up with a 6 to 8 oz. ladle into a casserole. Garnish with dumplings and chopped parsley.

Precautions and Safety Measures

1. Exercise caution when handling the knife.
2. Do not overcook the lamb or the sliced potatoes. The stew will lack appearance when served.
3. When sautéing the onion do not let them brown.
4. When holding the cooked cubes of meat for later use, keep covered with a wet towel.

Lamb à la Indienne

Lamb à la Indienne is a type of lamb stew highly seasoned with curry powder. The term Indienne generally means that the item is served with curried rice; however, it can also mean served in the style or fashion of India. This entree dish is an excellent choice for both the luncheon and dinner menu.

Objectives

1. To teach the student the procedure for preparing lamb à la Indienne.
2. To teach the student how to cut the meat into cubes.
3. To teach the student how to dish up lamb à la Indienne.

Equipment

1. Baker's scale
2. French knife
3. Gal. measure
4. China cap
5. Cheese cloth
6. Stock pot, 5 gal.
7. Sauce pot, 5 gal.
8. Spoon measures
9. Wire whip
10. Wood paddle
11. Ladle
12. Pt. measure
13. 3 gal. stainless steel container
14. 4 qt. sauce pan
15. Deep steam table pan
16. Skimmer

Ingredients: Approx. yield: 50 servings

15	lbs. boneless lamb shoulder, cut into 1 in. cubes
2½	gal. chicken stock
2	ozs. salt
2	cloves garlic, minced
2	bay leaves
1	tbsp. thyme
1	lb. 4 ozs. butter
12	ozs. flour
4	tbsp. curry powder
1	tsp. dry mustard
¼	cup Worcestershire sauce
1	pt. whole tomatoes, canned, crushed
6	ozs. smoked ham, minced
2	qts. apples, fresh, minced
2	qts. cream
3	lbs. onions, minced

Preparation

1. Trim and cut the shoulders of lamb into 1 in. cubes with a French knife. Proceed only after demonstration by instructor.
2. Crush the tomatoes by hand.
3. Prepare the chicken stock. (See Chap. 12.)
4. Mince the onions and garlic with a French knife.

5. Mince the ham and apples with a French knife.
6. Warm the cream in a sauce pan.
7. Have all ingredients and equipment handy.

Procedure

1. Place the cubes of lamb in the stock pot. Pour over the chicken stock, add the salt, bay leaves and thyme. Bring to a boil and skim off any scum that may appear on the surface with a ladle.
2. Reduce to a simmer and cook until the lamb cubes are tender.
3. Strain the stock from the cooked lamb through a china cap covered with cheese cloth into a stainless steel container. Hold meat and stock, keeping both in a warm place.
4. Melt the butter in a sauce pot, add the garlic and onion, sauté without color until slightly tender.
5. Stir in the flour with a wire whip, making a roux; cook slightly.
6. Add the curry powder and mustard, blend into the roux.
7. Add the hot stock, whipping vigorously with a wire whip until thickened and fairly smooth.
8. Add the apples, ham, Worcestershire sauce, and tomatoes; let sauce simmer for approximately 20 minutes.
9. Add the cooked cubes of lamb and continue to simmer for 10 minutes more. Stir occasionally with a wooden paddle. Remove from the range and adjust seasoning.
10. Stir in the warm cream with a wooden paddle. Place in a deep steam table pan.
11. Dish up with a 6 to 8 oz. ladle. Serve with rice and chutney.

Precautions and Safety Measures

1. Exercise caution when handling the knife to avoid cutting self.
2. Do not overcook the cubes of lamb.
3. When holding the cooked cubes of meat, cover with a wet towel to keep them from drying out.
4. When the sauce is simmering, stir occasionally to avoid sticking.

Fricassee of lamb

Fricassee of lamb is a type of stew consisting of boiled cubes of lamb and fricassee sauce. It is generally served on the luncheon menu, with buttered noodles or baked rice.

Objectives

1. To teach the student the procedure for preparing lamb fricassee.
2. To teach the student how to cut the meat.
3. To teach the student how to dish up lamb fricassee.

Equipment

1. Stock pots, 5 gal.
2. French knife
3. Wire whip
4. China cap
5. Cheese cloth
6. Sauce pot, 5 gal.
7. Kitchen spoon
8. Baker's scale
9. Skimmer
10. 3 gal. stainless steel container
11. Bake pan
12. Deep steam table pan

Ingredients: Approx. yield: 50 servings

17	lbs. lamb shoulder, boneless, cut into 1 in. cubes
2½	gal. water
2	lbs. shortening or butter
1½	lbs. flour
	yellow color as desired
	salt and white pepper to taste
⅓	cup fresh mint, chopped

Preparation

1. Cut the boneless shoulder into 1 in. cubes with a French knife. Proceed only after demonstration by instructor.
2. Chop the mint with a French knife.
3. Have all equipment and ingredients handy.

Procedure

1. Place the cubes of lamb in a stock pot and cover with water.
2. Bring to a boil and remove any scum that may appear on the surface with a skimmer. Continue to simmer until the lamb cubes are tender.
3. Remove from the fire and strain the lamb stock through a china cap covered with cheese cloth into a stainless container. Keep hot. Place the cooked lamb in a bake pan and cover with a wet towel.
4. In a separate sauce pot make a roux (2 lbs. shortening or butter and 1½ lbs. flour). Cook 5 minutes.
5. Add the strained lamb stock, whipping vigorously with a wire whip until thickened and smooth.

6. Tint the sauce with yellow color and season with salt and white pepper.
7. Add the cooked lamb cubes and the chopped mint to the sauce. Stir with a kitchen spoon. Place in a deep steam table pan.
8. Dish up into casseroles with a 6 to 8 oz. ladle. Serve with buttered noodles or baked rice.

Precautions and Safety Measures
1. Exercise caution when handling the knife.
2. Do not overcook the cubes of lamb.
3. Do not make the sauce too thin.
4. Do not add too much yellow coloring.

BROILED LAMB RECIPES

Lamb chop mix grill

Lamb chop mix grill is a very popular dinner entrée. It is a combination of 1 broiled *Frenched* lamb chop and 5 other items that combine well with lamb, for example, bacon, grilled tomato, sautéed mushroom cap, link sausage and toast.

Objectives
1. To teach the student the procedure for preparing lamb chop mix grill.
2. To teach the student how to cut and French the lamb chop.
3. To teach the student how to prepare the accompanying items.
4. To teach the student how to dish up lamb chop mix grill.

Equipment
1. Boning knife
2. French or butcher knife
3. Sheet pans
4. Bake pans (2)
5. Kitchen fork
6. Qt. measure
7. Skillet

Ingredients: Approx. yield: 25 servings

25	5 or 6 oz. lamb chops, cut from the rib and Frenched
50	little pig sausages
50	slices of bacon
25	mushroom caps, large
25	pieces of toast, cut triangle style
25	halves of fresh tomatoes
1	cup bread crumbs
1	qt. salad oil (variable)
	salt, pepper and basil to taste

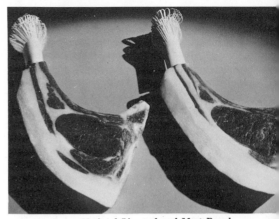

Frenched chops

Preparation
1. Cut the lamb chops from trimmed ribs with a French or butcher knife. Cut against the grain of the meat, between the rib bones. French by cutting away all meat and fat from the end of the rib bones with a boning knife. Proceed only after demonstration by instructor.
2. Preheat oven to 350°F.
3. Line the little pig sausages on a sheet pan. Place in a 350°F oven and bake until done, let drain and keep warm.
4. Line the bacon slices on a sheet pan, overlapping slightly. Place in a 350°F oven and bake until medium. Remove and let drain. Keep slightly warm.
5. Sauté the mushrooms in a skillet in butter or salad oil. Drain and keep warm.
6. Preheat broiler.
7. Wash the tomatoes, remove the stem. Cut the tomato in half crosswise with a French knife and place in bake pan, cut side up. Rub each tomato with salad oil and season with salt, pepper and basil. Sprinkle bread crumbs on the top of each tomato and brown slightly under the broiler. Finish by baking in the oven at 325°F until the tomato slices are fairly soft.
8. Place remaining salad oil in a bake pan.
9. Toast the bread and cut into triangles with a French knife.

10. Have all equipment and ingredients handy.

Procedure

1. Pass each lamb chop through the salad oil, shake off excess oil and place on a hot broiler with the Frenched rib turned away from the heat. Season with salt and pepper.
2. Brown one side, turn, sticking the fork into the fat, and brown the second side.
3. Remove from the broiler when the desired degree of doneness is obtained.
4. Dish up on a hot plate with the chop placed on top of the toast and surrounded with a half broiled tomato, 2 little pig sausages. 2 slices of bacon and a cooked mushroom cap. Drip melted butter over the chop, place a paper frill on the end of each Frenched chop and garnish with parsley or watercress.

Precautions and Safety Measures

1. Exercise caution when handling the knife.
2. At all times protect the Frenched rib from the fire. The exposed rib will burn quickly.
3. During the broiling period turn the fire to the highest point. Adjust cooking temperature by moving the rack towards or away from the fire.
3. Do not overcook the sausage, bacon or tomato.
4. Do not burn the chop.

Broiled loin chops served with pineapple and sausage links.

Broiled lamb chops

Broiled lamb chops are an extremely popular entree on the dinner menu. The chops can be cut from the rib or the loin, but those cut from the rib are more popular because they can be *Frenched* (the meat and fat is cut away from the end of the rib bone) and thus present a more desirable appearance when served.

Objectives

1. To teach the student the procedure for preparing broiled lamb chops.
2. To teach the student how to cut the lamb chops.
3. To teach the student how to dish up the lamb chops.

Equipment

1. French or butcher knife
2. Boning knife
3. Kitchen fork
4. Bake pan
5. Cleaver

Ingredients: Approx. yield: 25 servings

50   5 oz. lamb chops, cut from the rib or loin
1   pt. salad oil (variable)
    salt and pepper to taste

Preparation

1. Cut the 5 oz. lamb chops from trimmed loin or ribs with a French or butcher knife. Cut against the grain of the meat. If using ribs, cut between the rib bones. If using loins, cut until the knife blade hits bone, then chop with a cleaver. Chops may also be cut on a power saw. Rib chops may be *Frenched* by cutting away all meat and fat from the rib bones with a boning knife. Proceed only after demonstration by instructor.
2. Pour the salad oil in a bake pan.
3. Preheat the broiler.
4. Have all equipment and ingredients handy.

Procedure

1. Pass each chop through the salad oil. Place on a hot broiler with the Frenched rib turned away from the heat. Season with salt and pepper.
2. Brown one side, turn, sticking the fork into the fat, and brown the second side.
3. Remove from the broiler when the desired degree of doneness is obtained.
4. Dish up 2 chops per portion. Serve at once with a paper frill on the end of each

Frenched chop. Accompany with mint jelly and garnish with watercress.

Precautions and Safety Measures
1. Exercise caution when handling the knife and cleaver to avoid cutting self.
2. During the broiling period turn the fire to the highest point. Adjust cooking temperature by moving the rack towards or away from the fire.
3. At all times protect the Frenched rib from the fire. The exposed rib will burn quickly.
4. Do not burn the chops.

Lamb and mushrooms en brochette

Lamb and mushrooms en brochette are cubes of lamb shoulder, mushrooms and bacon alternated on a skewer. They are cooked by the broiling method and served with rice.

Objectives
1. To teach the student the procedure for preparing lamb and mushrooms en brochette.
2. To teach the student how to cut the lamb and place the items on the skewer.
3. To teach the student how to dish up lamb and mushrooms en brochette.

Equipment
1. 25 metal skewers
2. French knife
3. Bake pan
4. Kitchen fork
5. Slicing machine

Ingredients: Approx. yield: 25 servings

12	lbs. lamb shoulder, boneless, cut into 1 in. cubes
2	lbs. bacon, slice slightly thick, cut into 1 in. pieces
75	mushroom caps
1	qt. salad oil (variable)
	salt and pepper to taste

Preparation
1. Cut the boneless lamb shoulder into 1 in. cubes with a French knife. Proceed only after demonstration by instructor.
2. Slice the bacon slightly thick on a slicing machine and cut into 1 in. pieces with a French knife.
3. Pick stems from the mushroom caps.
4. Place the salad oil in a bake pan.
5. Have all equipment and ingredients handy.

Procedure
1. Place on the skewer, alternately, 4 cubes of lamb, 3 mushroom caps and 3 pieces of bacon.

2. Place the brochettes in salad oil and season with salt and pepper.
3. Place on the broiler and broil slowly for about 15 minutes, until the cubes of meat are done, turning occasionally with a kitchen fork.
4. Dish up at once with mint jelly and garnish with watercress and a twisted slice of orange.

Precautions and Safety Measures
1. Exercise caution when handling the knife and slicing machine.
2. Broil slowly and turn occasionally to prevent burning.
3. Keep broiler flame slightly low while broiling.
4. Be careful when turning. The metal skewers get quite hot.

Broiled lamb steak

The steaks are cross cut sections of the leg of lamb with the leg bone left in. Approximately 10, 6 to 8 oz. steaks can be cut from the average leg. The steaks are passed through salad oil, seasoned and broiled.

Objectives
1. To teach the student the procedure for preparing broiled lamb steaks.
2. To teach the student how to cut the lamb steaks.
3. To teach the student how to dish up broiled lamb steaks.

Equipment
1. Butcher knife
2. Boning knife
3. Bake pan
4. Kitchen fork
5. Meat saw

Ingredients: Approx. yield: 25 servings

25	6 to 8 oz. lamb steaks
1	qt. salad oil (variable)
	salt and pepper to taste

Preparation
1. Remove tail and aich bones from the legs of lamb with a boning knife. Cut the leg across the grain into steaks with a butcher knife and a hand meat saw or power saw. Proceed only after demonstration by instructor.
2. Place the salad oil in a bake pan.
3. Preheat the broiler.
4. Have all equipment and ingredients handy.

Procedure

1. Pass each steak through the salad oil, shake off excess.
2. Place steaks on a hot broiler, fat side out, season with salt and pepper.
3. Brown one side, turn with a kitchen fork and brown second side.
4. Dish up 1 steak per portion at once with mint jelly. Garnish with watercress.

Precautions and Safety Measures

1. Exercise caution when handling the knife and saw to avoid cutting self.
2. If meat sticks to the broiler, loosen gently so it will not tear.
3. Do not burn the outside fat.

Broiled lamb patties

Broiled lamb patties are a ground meat item served on the luncheon menu. The lamb shoulder is ground, seasoned and formed into 5 oz. patties. Bacon is wrapped around each patty to add juice and flavor when broiled.

Objectives

1. To teach the student the procedure for preparing broiled lamb patties.
2. To teach the student how to cut, grind and form the meat.
3. To teach the student how to broil and dish up the lamb patties.

Equipment

1. Food grinder
2. French knife
3. Sauce pan, 2 qts.
4. Sheet pans (3)
5. Tooth picks
6. Mixing container, approx. 5 gal.
7. Baker's scale
8. Spoon measure
9. Pt. measure
10. Kitchen spoon

National Livestock and Meat Board

Lamb patties

Ingredients: Approx. yield: 50 servings

14	lbs. lamb shoulder, boneless, cut into strips
1	pt. onions, minced
1	cup celery, minced
1	tsp. marjoram
1	tsp. oregano
1	pt. fresh bread, cubes
1	cup salad oil
10	whole eggs
1	pt. milk
½	cup parsley, chopped
	salt and fresh ground pepper to taste
50	slices bacon

Preparation

1. Cut the boneless lamb shoulder with a French knife into strips that will fit in the food grinder. Proceed only after demonstration by instructor.
2. Mince the onions and celery with a French knife.
3. Cut the bread into cubes with a French knife.
4. Chop the parsley with a French knife and wash.
5. Preheat the broiler.
6. Preheat oven to 375°F.
7. Have all equipment and ingredients handy.

Procedure

1. Place the salad oil in a sauce pan, heat.
2. Add the onions and celery, sauté until slightly tender.
3. Mix together in a large mixing container the bread cubes and milk, blend thoroughly with a kitchen spoon.
4. Add the strips of lamb shoulder, the sautéed onions and celery, marjoram and oregano. Mix thoroughly by hand.
5. Put this mixture through the food grinder using medium chopper plate.
6. Blend in the eggs and chopped parsley, season with salt and freshly ground pepper. Mix thoroughly by hand.
7. Form into 5 oz. patties, wrap each with a slice of bacon and secure with a tooth pick.
8. Place the patties on a lightly greased baking sheet pan and place under the broiler.
9. Keep flame low, brown on one side then the other. Finish in 375°F oven.
10. Remove tooth picks and dish up 1 patty per portion. Cover with brown or mint sauce.

Precautions and Safety Measures
1. Exercise caution when handling the knife to avoid cutting self.
2. Exercise caution when grinding the meat.
3. After grinding if the mixture is too wet add bread crumbs as needed.
4. Broil patties very slowly or bacon will burn.

Shish kebob

Shish kebob is combination of lamb cubes and three or four vegetables placed on a skewer alternately, cooked by the broiling method, and served on rice. A popular and unusual item for the dinner menu.

Objectives
1. To teach the student the procedure for preparing shish kebob.
2. To teach the student how to place the items on the skewer.
3. To teach the student how to dish up shish kebob.

Equipment
1. French knife
2. 25 metal skewers
3. 1 gal. stainless steel container
4. Hotel pans
5. Qt. measure
6. Spoon measures
7. Boning knife
8. Kitchen spoon
9. Pastry brush

Ingredients: Approx. yield: 25 servings
SHISH KEBOB

8	lbs. lamb leg, boned, cut into 1 in. cubes.
50	pieces, small tomatoes, cut ¾ in. thick
50	mushroom caps, canned
50	pieces, small whole onions, canned

MARINADE

1	qt. salad oil
1	pt. olive oil
1	cup wine vinegar
5	tbsp. lemon juice
2	cloves garlic, minced
2	tsp. pepper, fresh ground
2	tbsp. salt
½	tsp. thyme
½	tsp. marjoram
½	tsp. basil
½	tsp. oregano

Preparation
1. Bone the legs of lamb with a boning knife and cut into 1 in. cubes with a French knife. Proceed only after demonstration by instructor.
2. Mince the garlic with a French knife.
3. Squeeze the juice from the lemons.
4. Blend all the marinade ingredients together with a kitchen spoon in a stainless steel container. Add the lamb cubes and let marinate overnight.
5. Preheat broiler.
6. Cut the thick slices of tomato with a French knife just before using.
7. Have all equipment and ingredients handy.

Procedure
1. Place the items on the metal skewers alternately, including 2 slices of tomatoes, 2 mushroom cups, 2 whole onions and 5 cubes of lamb.
2. Place the shish kebobs in a bake pan. Pour the marinade over them and marinate until ready to broil.
3. Drain the shish kebob thoroughly.
4. Place under the broiler and broil for approximately 15 minutes under a low fire. Brush frequently with the marinade, turning as needed.
5. Dish up immediately on a bed of baked rice or pineapple rice.

Precautions and Safety Measures
1. Exercise caution when handling the knives to avoid cutting self.
2. Cook the shish kebobs medium unless requested otherwise.
3. Avoid burning the shish kebobs while broiling. Turn frequently.
4. Be careful when turning the broiling shish kebob. The metal skewers get quite hot.

BOILED LAMB RECIPES

Boiled lamb with dill sauce

For boiled lamb with dill sauce the lamb shoulder is cut into cubes boiled and served in a rich dill sauce. The sauce is prepared by using the stock in which the lamb was boiled. This is a fine selection for the luncheon menu.

Objectives
1. French knife
2. Sauce pots (2), 5 gal. each
3. Wire whip
4. China cap

5. Cup measure
6. Baker's scale
7. Cheese cloth
8. 3 gal. stainless steel container
9. Bake pan
10. Kitchen spoon
11. Deep steam table pan
12. Skimmer

Ingredients: Approx. yield: 25 servings

12	lbs. lamb shoulder, boneless, cut into 1 in. cubes
2	gal. water
1	lb. 4 ozs. butter
1	lb. flour
1/4	cup sugar
1/3	cup vinegar
8	white peppercorns
1/2	cup dill seed
8	ozs. onion, cut rough
	salt and white pepper to taste

Preparation

1. Cut the boneless lamb shoulder into 1 in. cubes with a French knife. Proceed only after demonstration by instructor.
2. Cut onions rough with a French knife.
3. Have all equipment and ingredients handy.

Procedure

1. Place the cubes of lamb in a large sauce pot. Cover with water add a small amount of salt and bring to a boil.

2. Remove any scum that may appear on the surface of the liquid with a skimmer. Add the sugar, vinegar, peppercorns, onions and dill seed. Simmer until the meat is tender, about 1 to 1½ hours.
3. In a separate sauce pot melt the butter, add the flour and blend thoroughly to form a roux. Cook for 5 minutes.
4. Strain the stock the lamb was cooked in through a china cap covered with a cheese cloth. Strain into a stainless steel container. Wash the meat cubes in warm water and place in a bake pan. Cover with a damp towel and keep warm.
5. Pour the stock into the roux, whipping vigorously with a wire whip until thickened and smooth. Let simmer 10 minutes. Strain through a fine china cap a second time. Add the cooked meat cubes, stir with a kitchen spoon and place in a deep steam table pan.
6. Dish up into casseroles with a 6 to 8 oz. ladle. Serve with buttered noodles or baked rice.

Precautions and Safety Measures

1. Exercise caution when handling the knife to avoid cutting self.
2. Do not overcook the cubes of lamb. Appearance will be lacking.
3. Stir frequently while the sauce is simmering to avoid scorching.

chapter 20

poultry and game

■ The term *poultry* refers to all domestic edible birds that are placed on the market for human consumption. (The term *fowl,* which is sometimes incorrectly used to refer to poultry, refers to full-grown hens.) *Game birds* are wild birds that are hunted for sport and for their fine edible meat. The following list shows the birds in each group.

Poultry
1. Turkeys
2. Chickens
3. Ducks
4. Squabs
5. Cornish hens
6. Geese
7. Guineas

Game birds
1. Wild ducks
2. Pheasants
3. Partridges
4. Quail
5. Grouse

POULTRY

Turkeys
These birds are truly American, having been found in the forest of New England by our first settlers. This handsome bird was given the honor of being

the main meat course at the first Thanksgiving and since that time has been an important source of meat supply.

Not until recent years has the turkey become a year-round item. It used to be that it was only a traditional treat and would appear on the tables at Christmas and Thanksgiving. With the innovation of freezing and the development of the modern meat-type turkey by the turkey breeders, this tasty bird is now giving beef and chicken competition as one of the most popular items.

Turkeys are bred as lightweight birds and heavyweight birds. The lightweight breeds are bred for fast growth and to produce a size that is more acceptable to the average family. The heavyweight birds are bred for the larger sized turkeys that are used mostly in food service establishments. The larger turkeys produce more meat in proportion to bone and sell at a lower cost per pound. Turkeys are classed as follows.

Baby turkeys: Very young turkeys under 16 weeks old, they are of the lightweight breed, and are very tender with a soft flexible skin. Baby turkeys can be roasted, fried or broiled and average in weight from 4 to 8 pounds.

Young hens: A young female turkey usually less than a year old with a soft tender meat and a flexible skin and breast bone. Young hens of the lightweight breed average in weight from 6 to 10 pounds. The heavyweight breed will average 12 to 16 pounds. This type of turkey is best when roasted or boiled.

Old hens: A mature female turkey over a year old with flesh and skin that has become slightly tough and a hardened breast bone. (On poultry, the harder the breast bone the older the bird.) Old hens of the lightweight variety average in weight from 6 to 10 pounds. The heavyweight breed average 12 to 16 pounds. When cooking it is best to boil this type of bird until it becomes tender.

Young toms: A young male turkey, usually less than a year old with tender meat, a flexible skin and breastbone. Young toms of the lightweight breed average in weight from 12 to 16 pounds. The heavyweight breed average 18 to 30 pounds. This type of turkey is usually roasted; however, the breast meat can also be cut into steaks and sautéed or broiled. The young tom can also be boiled and used for sandwiches, salads and entrée items. This turkey is the most popular one used in the food service establishments.

Old toms: A mature male turkey over a year old with toughened flesh and a hardened breastbone. Old toms of the lightweight breed average in weight from 12 to 16 pounds. The heavyweight breed average 18 to 30 pounds. It is best to boil heavy turkey so the meat can be made tender enough to be consumed in such preparations as chicken hash, pot pies, fricassee and tetrazzini.

Chickens

Fryers and broilers: Very young chickens of either sex and under 16 weeks of age. They have a very tender flesh and a flexible skin. The fryers will average in weight from 2 to 3½ pounds. The weight of a broiler usually is between 1½ to 2 pounds.

Roasters: Young chickens of either sex and averaging in age from 5 to 9 months old. They have a tender meat and a flexible skin. The roaster will average in weight from 3 to 5 pounds.

Hens (fowl): Sometimes referred to as stewing chickens. They are mature female chickens that have laid eggs for one or more seasons and are usually over 10 months of age. The flesh and skin are quite tough and they are usually cooked by moist heat in order to make the meat tender enough to use in such preparations as chicken à la king, salad and other dishes. Hens average in weight from 4 to 6 pounds. They are an excellent source of rich chicken stock, and the fat derived from the hen is highly prized and used in many preparations.

Stags: Mature male chickens with a fairly tough meat and skin. They are usually over 10 months old and weigh about 2 to 6 pounds. This kind of bird is very seldom used in quality food operations, but if the occasion should arise it must be cooked by moist heat for a long period of time in order to make the flesh tender.

Cocks or old roosters: These birds are seldom found on today's market. They are mature male chickens over a year old with a coarse skin and a tough dark flesh. They average in weight from 2 to 6 pounds.

Capons and caponettes: Castrated young male chickens 8 to 10 months old. They are unsexed when they are about 6 weeks old and specially fattened to produce a large well formed breast with flesh that is more tender and better flavored than the average chicken. Once the bird is castrated the tenderness of the flesh is affected very little as the bird ages. The average weight of a capon is 5 to 8 pounds. Caponettes are marketed at lighter weights. The word capon refers to chickens unsexed by physical means, while caponette refers to those unsexed by chemical means.

Ducks

The meat of the duck is all dark and provides less meat in proportion to bone than the other poultry birds. The terms "Long Island" and "Western" which are usually associated with the marketing of ducklings refer to the way they were grown and fattened. The Long Island ducklings are specially fattened young ducks grown on Long Island duck farms. They are force-fed on special grain and marketed when they weigh from 4 to 6 pounds. Ducks of this style are now being produced in various parts of the country, but still carry the Long Island name. The Western ducklings are young ducks that are not force fed or specially fattened. Their meat is not as tender and desirable as that of the Long Island style. Ducks are classed as follows.

Broilers or fryers: These are young ducks of either sex usually less than 8 weeks of age. They have a tender meat, a soft bill and soft windpipe. They weigh about 3 pounds and when broiled or fried present a very delicious entree.

Roaster ducklings: These are young ducks of either sex, usually less than 16 weeks of age. They possess a tender meat, and a bill and windpipe that is just starting to harden. They weigh about 4 pounds and when roasted produces an excellent menu item.

Mature or old ducks: A mature duck of either sex, usually over 6 months of age. The flesh is fairly tough and the bill and windpipe have hardened. The average weight of the mature or old ducks is 4 pounds.

Squabs

Squabs are very young pigeons of either sex that have never flown. They are specially fed to produce a meat that is extra tender and light in color. Squabs are marketed when they are 3 to 4 weeks old and weighing from 6 to 14 ounces. They are quite expensive and are found only on the higher priced menus. Squabs are most popular when prepared by the roasting method; however, they can also be sautéed or broiled.

Cornish hens

Cornish hens resemble the chicken in appearance, but have all white meat and are considered to be a glamour bird. They are fairly new to the poultry family, but are gaining quite rapidly in popularity. They are small in size and usually a whole bird will supply only one or 2 servings. The breast is chubby and the flesh is fine-grained and extremely tender. Although the cornish hen is somewhat expensive it affords the menu maker with the opportunity to add variety to the menu.

Geese

Geese, like the duck, contains all dark meat, but unlike the duck contains a very high percentage of fat. Geese are considered as light when weighing less than 11 pounds, and heavy when weighing over 12 pounds. They are classed into two groups: young, and mature or old geese.

Young geese: These are young geese, of either sex, usually less than 6 months old. They have a tender flesh and a windpipe that is easily dented. They weigh about 4 to 10 pounds and when roasted produces a product with excellent eating qualities.

Mature or old geese: These are mature or old geese, of either sex, over 6 months old. They have a less tender flesh and a hardened windpipe. Mature geese average in weight from 10 to 18 pounds and are very seldom if ever used in quality food establishments.

Guineas

These birds are related to the pheasant and have been domesticated in most parts of the world. They are an agile and extremely colorful bird with a flesh that is darker than that of the chicken and a flavor that is considered to be similar to the flavor of wild game. Guineas are divided into two groups: young, and mature or old guineas.

Young guineas: These are young guineas of either sex and have a tender flesh. They average in weight from 1 to 1½ pounds and are best when roasted. The breast meat of the guineas is the most desirable.

Mature or old guineas: These are mature or old guineas of either sex and have a less tender flesh. They average

in weight from 1 to 2 pounds and because of their tough flesh are never used in quality food operations.

GAME BIRDS

The serving of wild game in public food service establishments is not a popular practice today mainly because these items are high priced, fairly scarce, and the laws of some states prohibit the practice. Game is still served, however, in many of the private clubs, but the possibility of a student cook acquiring a position where he would be required to know game cookery is not too likely. It is because of this that we will treat the subject of game rather lightly in this chapter. We will attempt in a limited way to familiarize the student with some of the game birds and the best methods of preparation.

Wild ducks

Duck hunting has been a favorite American sport for many years because the prize provides an excellent dinner for the hunter and his guest. This is true regardless of the kind of wild duck one may wish to hunt. The black duck is confined mainly to the Eastern States, the blue-winged teal is abundant in the Middle West and the mallard in the West. The canvas-back duck is the most famous of American waterfowl and has such an exceptional game flavor that it is called a king's morsel. The many kinds of wild duck all possess a rich, dark, gamy tasting meat that is best when roasted and served rare. After the duck has been prepared for roasting it is usually placed in a very hot oven 450°F for the first 10 minutes of the roasting period. Then the temperature reduced to 350°F and roasting continued for an additional 15 minutes. Throughout the roasting period the duck should be basted frequently. When cooking wild game it is advisable to lard it, that is, inject or cover the lean meat with fat, usually salt pork or bacon fat. Larding will protect the bird from the intensity of the heat and will also enhance the flavor.

Pheasants

This regal bird is a native of Asia and was first introduced into the United States from China in 1881. It is now found in nearly every state and once it is established in a region it needs only slight protection to assure preservation because they are naturally hardy and reproduce rapidly. The pheasant is a fairly large, long tailed bird that has a dark, rich, gamy tasting meat that is highly prized by gourmets. It can be prepared by roasting or braising; however, the most popular method of preparation is to stuff the bird with wild rice, roast and serve while still rare. To produce the best eating qualities a pheasant should be left to hang and ripen slightly before it is plucked and cooked.

Partridges

This bird is smaller than the pheasant and will usually provide only enough meat to serve two people. It has a short, strong bill that is bent down at the tip, short wings and tail, fairly colorful feathers and legs that may be red or gray depending on the breed. The meat is white and must be cooked slightly on the done side to develop its succulent gamy flavor which is highly prized by gourmet and sportsmen alike. Partridge can be broiled or sautéed, but like the pheasant the most popular way is roasting.

Quail

The quail is similar to the partridge in that they are stout birds with short legs and neck, but a distinguishing difference is found in their bills, longer wings, shorter tails and the presence of a red patch above the eyes. Even with these many differences the quail is still called a partridge in many southern states. The quail is a multiple-colored bird with colors that blend well with the bird's natural habitat. This provides it with a natural protection from its enemies. The quail lives mainly on land in regions that are covered with high grass and bushes. There are many species of quail, but the most common species that inhabit the United States is the bobwhite, so called because of its characteristic call. The quail has a white meat and should be prepared in the same manner as partridge. The meat of most game birds is best when cooked slightly rare; however, the white-meated birds seem to develop a more desirable flavor when cooked slightly longer.

Grouse

Grouse resemble small domestic fowl in appearance but they have thicker and stronger legs which are extremely useful when the bird wishes to spring into a hurried flight. The grouse has thick, soft and ruffled feathers that in most species are a speckled brown and black color. There are over forty species of grouse found in North America. The most important of which are the ruffed grouse, the sage grouse, and the blue or dusty grouse. All species have a fairly long feathered tail, a medium sized wing spread and a short thick bill. The grouse has a dark meat that is universally recognized by gourmets and connoisseurs as one of the finest. It can be prepared by different methods of preparation; however, the large grouse are best when roasted, while the smaller ones may be sautéed to produce their best eating qualities. The flesh of the female bird is usually superior in flavor to that of the male.

Game birds are prepared like domestic poultry, but require, before they are cooked, a slightly different treatment to help preserve the true game flavor. They are usually aged or ripened for a short period of time in the open air. The term *high* is used to refer to birds that have been ripened for 1 or 2 weeks. Game birds lack a sufficient amount of fat covering for longer aging periods. When a bird is *high* the tail feathers pull out easily.

POULTRY GRADING

The U. S. inspection stamp, which all ready-to-cook or cooked poultry products must wear if intended for interstate commerce, is a guarantee by the United States Dept. of Agriculture that the meat is wholesome, that it was processed under proper sanitary conditions, and inspected by trained personnel to make sure that it is fit for human consumption.

In addition to the inspection stamp a U. S. grading stamp may also be stamped or clipped on the poultry or packaging material to provide a guide to the quality of the bird. Grading is based on shape, distribution of fat, condition of the skin and general appearance of the bird. The

U.S. Government grades include U.S. Grade A, U.S. Grade B and U.S. Grade C. Poultry is also graded and inspected by some states to give further assurance that the meat is wholesome. Most food service establishments use Grade A birds because they will yield a slightly greater amount of meat per purchase pound than the other grades.

MARKET FORMS

Poultry can be purchased in two forms: whole or cut up. The whole form is the form usually selected by food service operators. The feathers, head, neck and feet are removed and the bird is eviscerated (the entrails and viscera are removed). The bird may be in a fresh or frozen state depending upon preference. The usual practice is to purchase in the fresh state if it is available. Generally speaking, poultry purchased in the whole form is ready to cook when it arrives in the kitchen. Additional washing may be necessary if all traces of blood are not removed. Cut-up poultry are birds that have been cut into several pieces. They

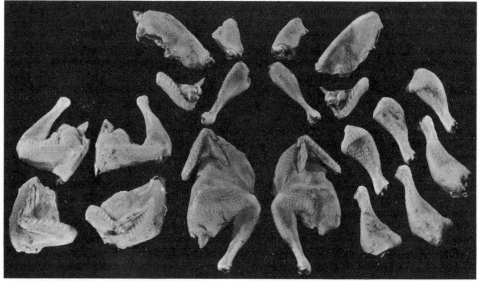

Poultry and Egg National Board

Common ways of cutting up frying chickens.

are usually divided into eight pieces which include 2 breasts, 2 wings, 2 legs and 2 thighs. Chickens are popular when marketed in this form; however, purchasing in this form is more popular in the retail markets rather than in food service operations.

The *giblets* are the heart, gizzard and liver of the poultry. They are the edible internal parts that are utilized in some form or another in the commercial kitchen. They are usually found wrapped in paper inside the butt or neck cavity of the dressed (trimmed and cleaned) bird. One might refer to the giblets as a bonus received when purchasing poultry. The most desirable giblet is the liver. It has excellent eating qualities and can be prepared in a variety of ways. Chicken livers are a very popular menu item. The gizzard and heart can be utilized in soups, gravies and luncheon entrees. Regardless of how they are used, just be sure they are put to some use because utilizing items such as these is the key to successful economy.

STORING POULTRY

All poultry will perish quite rapidly. Spoiled poultry develops an odor that will be immediately recognized as unsafe. Fresh poultry should be refrigerated as soon as it is received and if possible should be packed in crushed ice when it is placed in the coldest part of the refrigerator. Frozen poultry, such as turkey, should be kept frozen until a day or two before using. It should be thawed in the refrigerator or in cold running water. Too many times cooks or chefs will attempt to save poultry that is starting to spoil. This is an unsafe practice and may result in a serious case of food poisoning. As stated before in this text: *when in doubt throw it out*. A safe practice is to purchase fresh poultry the day before using, this will eliminate a long holding period and the chance of spoiling is null.

COOKING POULTRY

In general the cooking procedures for poultry are the same as those used for other meats. The old or tough birds are cooked by lengthy cooking methods and the younger ones by the quicker methods. This means that the older birds will produce best results if cooked by moist heat while the younger birds are more succulent when cooked by dry heat. Regardless of the cooking method, poultry should always be cooked well done except in the case of some wild game. It is further recommended that the larger poultry birds be cooked slowly to reduce shrinkage and retain moisture, while the smaller ones be cooked at temperatures of 375°F or 400°F to prevent them from drying out while cooking. In the commercial kitchen it is a practice to stuff the small birds, such as the cornish hen and squab, but not the larger birds. If stuffing is to be served with the large birds it is prepared and baked separately. This is done to save time and to make serving easier. It also leaves the carcasses in a better condition for use in making stock.

POULTRY RECIPES

There are numerous poultry preparation appearing on menus throughcut the country. This is due to the fact that, although poultry is high on the list of popular meats, people still like variety. Since the list of popular poultry recipes are endless, it is important that the student have a solid background in different types of poultry preparations. It would be impossible to include them all in this chapter so we shall select the ones that are used most often. The following recipes are just a few of the popular poultry dishes. The outline of recipes is arranged in their order of appearance in the chapter. Become familiar with the recipes— you will use them in the kitchen.

Roasted and baked poultry
(Pages 454 to 458)

Roast turkey
Roast chicken
Roast breast of chicken Virginia
Roast duck
Baked stuffed chicken leg

Fried and sautéed poultry
(Pages 459 to 468)

Chicken Maryland
Chicken à la Kiev
Chicken croquettes
Fried boneless turkey wings
Fried chicken country style
Chicken cacciatore
Chicken paprika
Chicken Marengo
Chicken livers chasseur
Coq au vin

Broiled poultry
(Pages 468 to 471)

Chicken livers en brochette
Broiled chicken
Chickenburgers
Chicken divan

Boiled or stewed poultry
(Pages 471 to 475)

Curried chicken
Chicken fricassee family style
Chicken à la king
Chicken chow mein
Chicken pot pie
Chicken tetrazzini

Dressings
(Pages 475 to 476)

Bread dressing

ROASTED AND BAKED POULTRY RECIPES

Roast turkey

Roast turkey is an American tradition dating back to the first Thanksgiving. In recent years this holiday treat has become a year round favorite. The bird is roasted to a golden done-ness, carved and served with a bread dressing and giblet gravy.

Objectives
1. To teach the student the procedure for preparing roast turkey.
2. To teach the student how to prepare the bird for roasting.
3. To teach the student how to dish up roast turkey.

Equipment
1. Roast pan
2. Kitchen fork
3. Kitchen spoon
4. French knife
5. Baker's scale
6. 1 gal. stainless steel container
7. China cap

Ingredients: Approx. yield: 50 servings
25 lbs. turkey, dressed
12 ozs. onions, cut rough
8 ozs. celery, cut rough
6 ozs. carrots, cut rough
10 ozs. ham or bacon grease
salt and pepper to taste

Preparation
1. Lock the turkey's wings by bending under the body and season the inside of the bird with salt and pepper.
2. Cut the rough garnish (onions, carrots and celery cut into medium sized pieces) with a French knife.
3. Preheat oven to 325°F.
4. Have all equipment and ingredients handy.

Procedure
1. Rub the ham or bacon fat over the surface of the turkey. Place it in a roast pan breast up.
2. Place in a 325°F oven and brown the complete surface of the bird by occasionally turning it from side to side using a kitchen fork. When the bird is completely browned turn to original position, breast up.
3. Roast, basting frequently using a kitchen spoon, for approximately 1½ hours. Add the rough garnish to the pan and continue roasting for 2 hours more or until the bird is done.
4. Remove from the oven and place turkey in a clean pan. Strain drippings through a china cap into a stainless steel container. Deglaze the roast pan and pour this liquid into the container.
5. Prepare the giblet gravy. (See Chap. 15.)

Armour and Co.

Roast turkey

6. Prepare the bread dressing. (See recipe this chapter.)
7. To dish up roast turkey a dipper of bread dressing is placed on the plate, dark meat is arranged on top of the dressing, and 2 slices of white meat are placed over the dark meat. Each portion is covered with giblet gravy and served.

Note: To test the turkey for doneness a 'fork can be inserted into the thigh and twisted slightly to cause liquid to flow. If the liquid is white the turkey is done, if red or pink more cooking is required. This part of the bird is selected for testing because it is usually the part that requires the longest cooking.

Note: In most food service establishments turkeys are usually roasted the day before serving, sliced cold, lined in pans with dark meat on one side, white meat on the other, reheated, portioned and served.

Precautions and Safety Measures
1. Exercise caution when handling the knife to avoid cutting self.
2. Even though the turkey is greased before heat is applied, it still may stick to the pan if not turned occasionally during the first hour of the roasting period.
3. If the turkey drippings evaporate during the roasting period a small amount of water may be added to the pan.
4. During the roasting period if the bird begins to overbrown, cover with oiled brown paper or aluminum foil. However, do not cover too completely or steam will be created—proper roasting is by dry heat.

Roast chicken

Roast chicken uses select young tender birds weighing 3 to 5 pounds and under 9 months of age. The roasting is done at a fairly high temperature to improve surface browning. The chicken is roasted on a bed of mirepoix (small diced vegetables) to improve the flavor of both the chicken and the drippings. A half of chicken is usually served to each order on either the luncheon or dinner menu.

Objectives
1. To teach the student the procedure for preparing roast chicken.
2. To teach the student how to cut the mirepoix and prepare the chicken for roasting.

3. To teach the student how to dish up roast chicken.
Equipment
1. French knife
2. Roast pan
3. Baker's scale
4. Kitchen fork
5. Sauce pan
6. Full size steam table pan
7. China cap
Ingredients: Approx. yield: 24 servings
12   3 lb. roasting chickens
10   ozs. onions, diced small
8   ozs. celery, diced small
6   ozs. carrots, diced small
10   ozs. butter or shortening, melted (variable)
salt and pepper to taste
Preparation
1. Season the inside of each chicken with salt and pepper and lock the wings by bending under the body.
2. Cut the mirepoix (small diced onions, carrots and celery).
3. Preheat oven to 375°F.
4. Have all equipment and ingredients handy.
Procedure
1. Place the mirepoix in the bottom of the roast pan.
2. Rub or brush the surface of each chicken with melted butter or shortening, place in the roast pan, breast up.
3. Place in a 375°F oven, roast for a period of approximately 1 hour or until done, turning the birds with a kitchen fork from side to side during the roasting period for more uniform roasting and browning.
4. Remove from the oven and place the chickens in a steam table pan. Keep warm.
5. Strain drippings through a china cap. Deglaze pan and save both liquids for use in the gravy.
6. Prepare the giblet gravy. (See Chap. 15.)
7. Disjoint the chickens with a French knife. When properly disjointed a whole chicken will yield 8 pieces: 2 wings, 2 breasts, 2 legs and 2 thighs. Remove the breast bones by hand.
8. Dish up ½ chicken per portion with a scoop of bread dressing, covered with giblet gravy. (The bread dressing recipe is given at the end of the chapter.)
Precautions and Safety Measures
1. Exercise caution when handling the knife.

2. During the roasting period, check the mirepoix occasionally to prevent burning. If necessary a small amount of water may be added.
3. Do not overcook the chickens, appearance will be lacking.
4. Turn the chicken occasionally during the roasting period with a kitchen fork.

Roast breast of chicken Virginia

For roast breast of chicken Virginia the whole chicken breast is roasted and separated into 2 bone free halves. Each half is placed on top of Virginia or regular smoked ham and served with a rich chicken sauce. This item is popular on the dinner menu.
Objectives
1. To teach the student the procedure for preparing roast breast of chicken Virginia.
2. To teach the student how to bone the cooked breast.
3. To teach the student how to dish up roast breast of chicken Virginia.
Equipment
1. Roast pan
2. French knife
3. Qt. measure
4. Kitchen fork
5. 2 sheet pans
6. Slicing machine
7. Boning knife
Ingredients: Approx. yield: 24 servings
12   whole chicken breasts
1   cup salad oil
24   slices Virginia or smoked ham, cooked
2   qts. chicken velouté sauce
salt and pepper to taste
Preparation
1. Cut the wings off the breast by cutting through the second joint with a French knife, leaving on the section of wing bone that is attached to the breast.
2. Slice the ham fairly thick on a slicing machine. Place on sheet pans and heat in the oven or under the broiler.
3. Prepare the chicken velouté sauce. (See Chap. 15.)
4. Preheat the oven to 375°F.
5. Have all equipment and ingredients handy.
Procedure
1. Season the inside of each whole chicken breast with salt and pepper.

2. Rub each breast with salad oil and oil the roast pan slightly.
3. Place the whole chicken breasts in the roast pan, sitting so the neck cavity is facing up.
4. Place in the preheated oven and roast for approximately 1 to 1½ hours or until done. Remove with a kitchen fork and let cool slightly.
5. Cut the joint at the base of the wing bone, on each side of the breast with a boning knife. Free the meat from the rib cage by working the hands along the rib cage, separating the whole breast into two boneless halves. Proceed only after demonstration by instructor.
6. Place each boneless half on a hot slice of Virginia or smoked ham. Ladle over the chicken velouté sauce and serve.

Precautions and Safety Measures
1. Exercise caution when using the French knife and the boning knife.
2. Do not overcook the breast.
3. If it is too thick, the chicken velouté sauce may be thinned slightly by adding a small amount of hot cream or chicken stock.

Roast duck

For roast duck the duck is roasted at a fairly high temperature to extract excessive fat from the bird and to improve surface crispness. It is roasted on a bed of small diced vegetables called "mirepoix." This improves the flavor of both the duck and its drippings. Roast duck is a favorite when placed on the dinner menu.

Objectives
1. To teach the student the procedure for preparing roast duck.
2. To teach the student how to cut the mirepoix and prepare the duck for roasting.
3. To teach the student how to cut and dish up roast duck.
4. To teach the student how to prepare the sauce that is served with each order of roast duck.

Equipment
1. Roast pan
2. French knife
3. China cap
4. Kitchen fork
5. Bake pan
6. Sauce pot, 6 qts.
7. Wire whip
8. Stainless steel container
9. Qt. measure
10. Baker's scale

Ingredients: Approx. yield: 24 servings
6 4 to 6 lb. ducklings
6 ozs. carrots, small dice
4 ozs. celery, small dice
8 ozs. onions, small dice
8 ozs. duck fat
6 ozs. flour
3 qts. brown stock
1 cup orange juice
   salt and pepper as needed

Preparation
1. Wash and clean the ducks, season the inside with salt and pepper.
2. Dice the onions, carrots and celery small with a French knife.
3. Prepare the brown stock. (See Chap. 12.)
4. Preheat the oven to 375°F.
5. Have all equipment and ingredients handy.

Procedure
1. Place the mirepoix on the bottom of a roast pan.
2. Place the ducks on top of the mirepoix, breast up.
3. Place in the oven at 375°F. Roast for a period of approximately 2 hours or until done. Pour off excess grease and turn the duck at intervals with a kitchen fork. (Save the excess grease.)
4. Remove from the oven, place the ducks in a clean pan, set in a warm place and hold.
5. Pour the duck grease in the sauce pot and heat. Add the flour, making a roux, and cook for 5 minutes.
6. Pour the brown stock in the roast pan, place on the range, bring to a boil to deglaze the pan and capture all possible flavor.
7. Pour the stock from the roast pan into the roux, whipping vigorously with a wire whip until slightly thickened.
8. Season with salt and pepper and strain through a fine china cap, into a stainless steel container.
9. Add the orange juice, stir to blend.
10. Cut each duck into 8 equal pieces and serve a piece of breast and a piece of leg per portion. Garnish with a slice or twist of orange.

1. Exercise caution when handling the knife.
2. Turn the duck occasionally with a kitchen fork during the roasting period for thorough browning and even cooking.
3. Pour off excess grease during the roasting period.

Baked stuffed chicken leg

For baked stuffed chicken leg all bones are removed from the chicken leg, it is stuffed with forcemeat (ground meat mixture) and baked in the oven until tender. Baked stuffed chicken leg is served with an appropriate sauce on the luncheon menu.

Objectives
1. To teach the student the procedure for preparing baked stuffed chicken leg.
2. To teach the student how to bone the chicken leg.
3. To teach the student how to prepare the forcemeat and stuff the leg.
4. To teach the student how to bake and dish up the stuffed chicken leg.

Equipment
1. French knife
2. 25 aluminum potato shells
3. Food grinder
4. Kitchen fork
5. Full size steam table pan
6. Baker's scale
7. Cup measure
8. Wooden mallet
9. Skillet
10. Mixing container
11. (2) sheet pans
12. Pastry brush
13. Boning knife
14. Towel

Ingredients: Approx. yield: 25 servings
25 chicken legs, boneless
1 lb. 8 ozs. fresh pork picnic, boneless, cut into strips
1 lb. veal shoulder, boneless, cut into strips
1 lb. bread, fresh or dried
3 cups milk
6 ozs. onions, minced, sautéed
6 ozs. celery, minced, sautéed
4 egg yolks
8 ozs. bread crumbs, dried
6 ozs. butter
⅓ cup parsley, chopped
¼ oz. sage
½ cup salad oil
salt and pepper to taste

Preparation
1. Remove all bones from the chicken legs with a boning knife. Using a mallet flatten the boneless legs slightly with the skin side down. Proceed only after demonstration by instructor.
2. Cut the boneless pork and veal into strips that will fit into the food grinder with a French knife.
3. Soak the bread in the milk.
4. Mince the onions and celery; sauté in the butter in a skillet.
5. Separate the eggs, save the whites for use in another preparation.
6. Chop the parsley with a French knife. Wash in a towel and wring dry.
7. Preheat the oven to 350°F.
8. Have all equipment and ingredients handy.

Procedure
1. In a mixing container place the pork, veal, softened bread, sautéed onion and celery, and the sage. Mix thoroughly by hand.
2. Grind twice on the food grinder using the fine chopper plate.
3. Add the egg yolks, chopped parsley and bread crumbs. Mix thoroughly by hand until well blended.
4. Season with salt and pepper, mix again.
5. Place a fairly generous amount of this forcemeat mixture on the meat side of each boned chicken leg, roll up and place each leg in an aluminum potato shell with the end of the roll facing down.
6. Place on sheet pans, brush each stuffed leg with salad oil.
7. Place in the preheated oven and bake until the tops are slightly brown and the meat is completely done (approximately 1½ hours, depending on the size of the legs being used.
8. Take from the oven and remove from aluminum shells. Place the legs in a steam table pan.
9. Dish up 1 stuffed leg portion, covered with poulette or barbecue sauce. (See Chap. 15 for sauce recipes.)

Precautions and Safety Measures
1. Exercise caution when handling the knives to avoid cutting self.

FRIED AND SAUTEED POULTRY RECIPES

Chicken Maryland

For this item the chicken is prepared in the style or fashion that originated in the state of Maryland. The chicken is disjointed, breaded and fried in deep fat until golden brown. It is served on cream sauce, topped with two strips of bacon and complimented with two golden brown corn fritters. Chicken Maryland is an excellent choice for the dinner menu.

Objectives
1. To teach the student the procedure for preparing chicken Maryland.
2. To teach the student how to disjoint and bread the chicken.
3. To teach the student how to fry and dish up chicken Maryland.

Equipment
1. French knife
2. Stainless steel bowl
3. Wire whip
4. Qt. measure
5. Baker's scale
6. Bake pans
7. Ladle
8. Deep fat fryer
9. 2 sheet pans
10. Full size steam table pan

Ingredients: Approx. yield: 24 servings

12	2½ lb. chickens, disjointed
1	lb. bread flour
	egg wash (1 qt. milk and 6 eggs)
2	lbs. bread crumbs (variable)
2	qts. cream sauce
48	bacon slices, cooked slightly crisp
44	corn fritters
	salt and pepper as needed

Preparation
1. Clean and disjoint the chickens with a French knife. When properly disjointed a whole chicken will yield 2 wings, 2 breasts, 2 thighs and 2 legs. Proceed only after demonstration by instructor.
2. Prepare the egg wash. Whip together 6 eggs and 1 qt. of milk with a wire whip.
3. Place the flour and bread crumbs in bake pans. Season the flour with salt and pepper.
4. Cook the strips of bacon on sheet pans in the oven until fairly crisp.
5. Prepare the corn fritters. (See Chap. 13.)

Procter and Gamble Co.

The chicken is first passed through seasoned flour and then each piece is dipped into an egg wash.

Procter and Gamble Co.

The chicken is removed from the egg wash and passed through dried bread crumbs.

Procter and Gamble Co.

Place chicken pieces in fry baskets carefully. Shake off excess crumbs and avoid overcrowding. Lower basket into deep fat in the fry kettle and fry until chicken pieces are golden brown.

6. Prepare the cream sauce. (See Chap. 14.)
7. Preheat deep fat fryer to 325°F.
8. Have all equipment and ingredients handy.

Procedure
1. Bread the disjointed chickens by passing them through flour, egg wash and bread crumbs. Pat off excess crumbs.
2. Place the chickens in fry baskets and fry in deep fat at 325°F until golden brown and completely done, remove and let drain. Place in a steam table pan.
3. To dish up: ladle cream sauce on a plate, place a half chicken on top of the sauce, criss-cross two strips of bacon over the chicken and add two corn fritters. Garnish with a sprig of parsley.

Precautions and Safety Measures
1. Exercise caution when disjointing the chicken to avoid cutting self.
2. Press the bread crumbs on firmly so they will not come off when fried.
3. Fry the chicken slowly or the breading will brown before the chicken is done.

Chicken à la Kiev

For chicken à la Kiev the chicken breast is completely boned and an herb flavored butter is rolled into the center of each. The breast is breaded and fried to a golden brown. The herb flavored butter adds an unforgettable flavor to the meat. Chicken à la Kiev is featured on the dinner menu.

Objectives
1. To teach the student the procedure for preparing chicken à la Kiev.

Poultry and Egg National Board

Chicken à la Kiev

2. To teach the student how to bone the breast.
3. To teach the student how to prepare the herb butter filling and stuff the boneless breast.
4. To teach the student how to bread and fry chicken à la Kiev.
5. To teach the student how to dish up chicken à la Kiev.

Equipment
1. Boning knife
2. Mixing machine
3. Baker's scale
4. French knife
5. Pepper mill
6. 3 bake pans
7. Stainless bowl
8. Wire whip
9. Wooden mallet
10. Qt. measure
11. Iron skillet
12. Kitchen fork
13. Full size steam table pan

Ingredients: Approx. yield: 25 servings
25   chicken breasts (halves) from 3 to 3½ lb. chickens, boneless
3   lbs. butter
2   cloves garlic, minced
½   oz. chives, minced
¼   oz. marjoram
    salt and fresh ground pepper to taste
1   lb. flour
    egg wash, rich (8 eggs and a qt. of milk)
1   lb. 8 ozs. bread crumbs (variable)
3   lbs. shortening for frying (variable)

Preparation
1. Cut off the wing tips of each chicken breast, leaving the small wing bone attached to the breast to act as a handle. Starting at the joint where the wing is connected to the breast, follow the breast bones, using the tip of a boning knife, until the breast is boned. Proceed only after demonstration by instructor.
2. Mince the garlic and chives with a French knife.
3. Grind 6 peppercorns in the pepper mill.
4. Prepare the rich egg wash. Whip 8 eggs and 1 qt. of milk together with a wire whip. Place in a bake pan.
5. Place the flour and bread crumbs in separate bake pans.
6. Have all equipment and ingredients handy.

Procedure

1. Place the butter in the mixing machine; using the paddle mix at slow speed until the butter obtains a plastic consistency.
2. Add the minced garlic and chives, rub in the marjoram by hand and season with salt and fresh ground pepper. Mix until well blended.
3. Remove the butter mixture from the mixer, place in the refrigerator until it becomes slightly firm.
4. Flatten the boneless chicken breast, skin side down, using a mallet.
5. In the center of each breast place a finger of rolled cold herb butter. Roll up and fold in the end. Place in the freezer until butter is very firm.
6. Bread each breast by passing it through flour, egg wash and bread crumbs. Pat off excess crumbs.
7. Fry in an iron skillet in fairly deep fat until golden brown and breast is completely cooked.
8. Remove from the skillet with a kitchen fork and let drain. Place in a steam table pan.
9. Dish up 1 breast per portion. Place a paper frill (stocking) on wing bone, serve with a poulette or velouté sauce. (See Chap. 14 for sauce recipes.)

Precautions and Safety Measures

1. Exercise caution when handling the boning knife and French knife to avoid cutting self.
2. Hit gently when flattening the boneless breast. The tender white meat will flatten easily.
3. Do not overmix the butter mixture, it will become too soft and therefore difficult to work with.
4. Before frying the breast it is wise to chill them in the freezer for a short period of time so the butter mixture will become hard.
5. Exercise caution when frying, do not over-brown the breast.

Chicken croquettes

Chicken croquettes are a ground meat preparation. It is an item in which chicken and turkey trimmings can be utilized. Chicken croquettes are shaped into cones, breaded, fried in deep fat and served with an appropriate sauce.

Objectives

1. To teach the student the procedure for preparing chicken croquettes.
2. To teach the student how to form and bread chicken croquettes.
3. To teach the student how to fry and dish up chicken croquettes.

Equipment

1. Large braising pot
2. French knife
3. Deep fat fryer
4. 4 bake pans
5. Wood paddle
6. Baker's scale
7. Food grinder
8. Wire whip
9. Stainless steel bowl
10. Cup and spoon measures
11. Full size steam table pan

Ingredients: Approx. yield: 50 servings

9	lbs. boiled turkey or chicken, ground
1	lb. 8 ozs. shortening or chicken fat
1	lb. 4 ozs. flour
1	lb. onions, minced
2	qts. chicken stock, hot
½	cup parsley, chopped
6	whole eggs
1	tsp. nutmeg
	salt and pepper to taste
	bread crumbs as needed
12	whole eggs
2	qts. milk
3	lbs. flour
3	lbs. bread crumbs

Preparation

1. Grind the chicken or turkey on the food grinder, using the medium chopper plate.
2. Prepare the chicken stock. (See Chap. 12.)
3. Mince the onions and chop the parsley with a French knife.
4. Break the 6 eggs into a container and beat slightly with a wire whip.
5. Place the 3 lbs. of flour and the 3 lbs. of bread crumbs in separate bake pans.
6. Prepare the egg wash. Place the 12 eggs in a stainless steel bowl and beat with a wire whip. Add the 2 qts. of milk while continuing to beat. Place egg wash in a bake pan.
7. Have all equipment and ingredients handy.

Procedure

1. In a braising pot place the shortening or chicken fat and heat.
2. Add onions and sauté without browning.

3. Add the flour, making a roux. Cook for approximately 5 minutes, stirring occasionally with a wooden paddle.
4. Add the chicken stock, whipping vigorously with a wire whip until thickened and smooth. Cook slightly.
5. Add the ground chicken or turkey, nutmeg and chopped parsley. Mix thoroughly with a wooden paddle.
6. Season with salt and pepper and remove from the fire.
7. Stir in the 6 beaten eggs and check consistency. If mixture is too wet, add bread crumbs to absorb some of the moisture.
8. Turn the mixture out into a bake pan and let cool. Refrigerate overnight.
9. Remove from the refrigerator. Form into 100, 2 oz. croquettes. Bread each croquette by passing them through flour, egg wash, and bread crumbs.
10. Fry in deep fat at 350°F until golden brown. Place in a steam table pan.
11. Dish up 2 croquettes per portion, accompanied with cream, poulette or fricassee sauce. (See Chap. 15 for sauce recipes.)

Precautions and Safety Measures
1. Exercise caution when handling the knife to avoid cutting self.
2. Cook the roux to avoid a raw flour taste in the croquette mixture.
3. When adding the 6 beaten eggs to the hot mixture, work the mixture vigorously with a wooden paddle to avoid scrambling the eggs.
4. Exercise caution when cooking the croquette mixture, it will scorch easily.

Fried boneless turkey wings

For fried boneless turkey wings the turkey wings are saved until enough have accumulated to place them on the luncheon menu. The wings are simmered until they are tender, the two wing bones removed and the boneless wings left to cool in the refrigerator overnight. The next day they are breaded, fried to a golden brown in deep fat and served with poulette or chicken velouté sauce.

Objectives
1. To teach the student the procedure for preparing fried boneless turkey wings.
2. To teach the student how to remove the wing bones.

3. To teach the student how to bread and deep fry the boneless wings.
4. To teach the student how to dish up fried boneless turkey wings.

Equipment
1. Cleaver
2. 3 bake pans
3. Deep fat fryer
4. French knife
5. Stock pot, 10 gal.
6. Stainless steel container
7. Wire whip
8. Baker's scale
9. Skimmer
10. China cap

Ingredients: Approx. yield: 25 servings

50	turkey wings
	water, as needed to cover wings
8	ozs. onions, cut rough
4	ozs. carrots, cut rough
4	ozs. celery, cut rough
	egg wash (9 eggs to 1½ qts. of milk)
2	lbs. flour
3	lbs. bread crumbs, dry
	salt and pepper as needed

Preparation
1. Trim excess skin off the sides of the turkey wings with a French knife. Chop off the bone tips on the wing ends with a cleaver.
2. Cut the rough garnish (onions, carrots and celery) with a French knife.
3. Preheat the deep fat fryer to 350°F.
4. Prepare the egg wash. Whip together 9 eggs and 1½ qts. of milk with a wire whip and place in a bake pan.
5. Place the flour in a bake pan and season with salt and pepper.
6. Place the bread crumbs in a bake pan.
7. Have all equipment and ingredients handy.

Procedure
1. Place the turkey wings in a stock pot and cover with water, bring to a boil and skim off any scum that may appear on the surface with a skimmer.
2. Add the rough vegetable garnish and simmer until the wings are tender.
3. Strain off the stock through a china cap and save for use in another preparation. Pull bones from wings, leaving the meat in one piece. Let them cool and place in the refrigerator overnight.

4. Remove from the refrigerator and bread each wing by passing it through flour, egg wash and bread crumbs.
5. Pat off excess bread crumbs and fry in deep fat at 350°F until golden brown.
6. Dish up 2 wings per portion with poulette of velouté sauce. (See Chap. 15 for sauce recipes.)

Precautions and Safety Measures
1. Exercise caution when handling the knife.
2. Do not overcook the wings, they will not hold together when bones are removed.
3. When pulling the bones from the wings, pull gently so the meat will stay in one piece.
4. Exercise caution while frying the wings, do not overbrown.

Fried chicken country style

Fried chicken is the most popular method of preparing chicken. There are many different methods used to fry chicken, but the country style method seems to be the most popular. The chicken is passed through a mixture of seasoned flour and fried to a golden brown in fairly shallow grease. It is served with country gravy and can be featured on any type of menu with assured results.

Objectives
1. To teach the student the procedure for preparing fried chicken country style.
2. To teach the student how to cut, fry and dish up the chicken.

Equipment
1. French knife
2. Iron skillet
3. Kitchen fork
4. Bake pan
5. Baker's scale
6. Full size steam table pan.

Ingredients: Approx. yield: 24 servings

12	2½ lb. chickens, fryers	
1	lb. flour (variable)	
	salt and pepper, as needed	
2	lbs. shortening (variable)	

Preparation
1. Clean and disjoint the chickens with a French knife. When properly disjointed a whole chicken will yield 8 pieces: 2 wings, 2 breasts, 2 thighs and 2 legs. Proceed only after demonstration by instructor.
2. Place the flour in a bake pan and season with salt and pepper.

Procter and Gamble Co.

Fried chicken

3. Have all equipment and ingredients handy.

Procedure
1. Place enough shortening in the iron skillet to cover the bottom ½ in. deep, heat.
2. Place the pieces of chicken in the seasoned flour and dredge (coat with flour).
3. Shake off excess flour and place the chicken pieces in the hot grease, letting the pieces fall away from you as they are placed in the grease.
4. Brown one side to a golden brown, turn with a kitchen fork and brown the other. It will take approximately 20 minutes to fry a chicken.
5. When the chicken is done remove from the grease, let drain. Place in a steam table pan.
6. Dish up ½ chicken consisting of 1 wing, 1 breast, 1 thigh and 1 leg per portion. Accompany each order with country gravy. (See Chap. 15 for country gravy recipe.)

Precautions and Safety Measures
1. Exercise caution when disjointing the chickens to avoid cutting self.
2. While the chickens are frying be alert for popping grease caused when moisture under the skin comes in contact with the grease.

3. Fry to a golden brown, do not overbrown or burn.
4. A lid may be placed on the skillet when starting to fry to speed up the cooking time.

Chicken cacciatore

For chicken cacciatore the chicken is sautéed to a golden brown, placed in a baking pan, covered with a rich Italian type tomato sauce and baked until tender. This Italian dish is popular on both the luncheon and dinner menu.

Objectives
1. To teach the student the procedure for preparing chicken cacciatore.
2. To teach the student how to cut the chickens and the vegetables.
3. To teach the student how to dish up chicken cacciatore.

Equipment
1. French knife
2. Large braising pot and cover
3. Kitchen fork
4. Bake pan
5. Iron skillets
6. Baker's scale
7. Kitchen spoon
8. Qt. measure
9. Sauce pot, 3 gal.
10. Spoon measure
11. Deep steam table pan

Ingredients: Approx. yield: 50 servings

25	2½ lb. chickens, disjointed
2	lbs. flour, season with salt and pepper
1½	qts. salad oil (variable)
2	lbs. 8 ozs. mushrooms, cut into a med. dice
2	lbs. onions, minced
6	cloves garlic, minced
5	qts. whole tomatoes and juice, canned, crushed
2	qts. tomato purée
1	pt. Marsala wine
2	tsp. basil, crushed
2	tsp. oregano, crushed
¼	oz. chives, minced
	salt and pepper to taste

Preparation
1. Clean and disjoint the chicken with a French knife. When properly disjointed a whole chicken will yield 8 pieces. Remove the rib bones from the breast. Proceed only after demonstration by instructor.
2. Place the flour in a bake pan and season with salt and pepper.
3. Cut the mushrooms into a medium size dice with a French knife.
4. Mince the onions, garlic and chives with a French knife.
5. Crush the tomatoes by squeezing with the hand.
6. Preheat oven to 325°F.
7. Have all equipment and ingredients handy.

Procedure
1. Place enough salad oil in an iron skillet to cover the bottom by approximately ¼ in. deep.
2. Pass each piece of chicken through the seasoned flour, shake off excess. Place in the hot oil and sauté until golden brown. Remove with a kitchen fork and let the pieces drain.
3. Line the sautéed chicken in a large braising pot, hold.
4. Cover the bottom of a sauce pot with the oil used to sauté the chickens.
5. Add the onions, mushrooms and garlic, and sauté until slightly tender. Do not brown them. Stir occasionally with a kitchen spoon.
6. Add the wine and simmer for 5 minutes.
7. Add the tomatoes and juice, tomato puré, oregano, basil, chives and season with salt and pepper. Simmer for 5 minutes, stirring constantly with a kitchen spoon.
8. Pour the sauce over the sautéed chicken, cover the braising pot, place in the oven at 325°F.
9. Bake for approximately 45 minutes or until the chicken is tender. Remove from the oven, check seasoning. Place in a deep steam table pan.
10. Dish up ½ chicken per portion. An order should include a breast, wing, thigh and leg. Cover with the sauce and garnish each portion with chopped parsley.

Precautions and Safety Measures
1. Exercise caution when disjointing the chickens to avoid cutting self.
2. When sautéing the vegetables do not let them brown.
3. Do not overbake the chicken or it will fall away from the bone.

Chicken paprika

For chicken paprika disjointed chicken is sautéed to a golden brown and baked in a rich paprika sauce. This item is most popular when served with rice on the luncheon menu.

Objectives
1. To teach the student the procedure for preparing chicken paprika.
2. To teach the student how to disjoint the chickens and cut the vegetables.
3. To teach the student how to sauté and bake the chicken.
4. To teach the student how to dish up chicken paprika.

Equipment
1. French knife
2. Iron skillet, large
3. Large braising pot and cover
4. Baker's scale
5. Kitchen fork
6. Qt. measure
7. Bake pan
8. Kitchen spoon
9. Full size steam table pan

Ingredients: Approx. yield: 24 servings

12	2½ lb. chickens, disjointed
1	lb. flour
1	qt. salad oil (variable)
12	ozs. onions, minced
1	clove garlic, minced
1½	ozs. paprika
4	ozs. green peppers, minced
2	qts. chicken stock
6	ozs. tomato paste
3	ozs. flour
	salt and pepper to taste

Preparation
1. Clean and disjoint the chickens with a French knife. When properly disjointed a whole chicken will yield 2 wings, 2 breasts, 2 thighs and 2 legs.
2. Mince the onions, garlic and green peppers with a French knife.
3. Prepare the chicken stock. (See Chap. 12.)
4. Preheat the oven to 375°F.
5. Place the 1 lb. of flour in a bake pan and season with salt and pepper.
6. Have all equipment and ingredients handy.

Procedure
1. Dredge (coat with flour) the chicken in the seasoned flour.
2. Place the oil in an iron skillet, heat.
3. Add the pieces of chicken and sauté un-

til golden brown on both sides. Turn with a kitchen fork.
4. Remove the chicken from the skillet and place in the braising pot.
5. Pour most of the oil from the skillet, leaving only enough to sauté the vegetables.
6. Add the onions, garlic and green pepper, sauté until slightly tender.
7. Add the 3 ozs. of flour, stir with a kitchen spoon into the sautéed vegetables and cook slightly.
8. Add the paprika, stir until thoroughly blended.
9. Add the hot chicken stock and tomato paste, stirring constantly with a kitchen spoon until the mixture comes to a boil. Season with salt and pepper.
10. Simmer for 5 minutes and pour over the sautéed chicken in the braising pot. Cover the pot and place in the preheated oven at 375°F.
11. Bake for approximately 20 to 30 minutes or until the chicken is tender.
12. Remove from the oven and place in a steam table pan.
13. Dish up ½ chicken per portion and serve with a generous amount of sauce. Accompany each order with baked rice or spaetzles (Austrian type noodle). (The recipe for spaetzles is given in Chapter 12.)

Precautions and Safety Measures
1. Exercise caution when handling the knife to avoid cutting self.
2. When sautéing the chicken do not over-brown.
3. When sautéing the vegetables do not let them become brown.
3. Do not overcook the chickens or the meat will fall from the bones.

Chicken Marengo

For chicken Marengo, sautéed, disjointed chicken is baked in a rich sauce with mushrooms and served with sliced ripe and green olives. Chicken Marengo is usually served on the dinner menu.

Objectives
1. To teach the student the procedure for preparing chicken Marengo.
2. To teach the student how to disjoint and sauté the chicken.

3. To teach the student how to slice the mushrooms and olives.
4. To teach the student how to bake and dish up chicken Marengo.

Equipment
1. French knife
2. Kitchen fork
3. Iron skillet
4. Med. size braising pot and cover
5. Olive pitter
6. Qt. measure
7. Baker's scale
8. Full size steam table pan

Ingredients: Approx. yield: 24 servings

12	2½ lb. chickens, disjointed
1	qt. salad oil (variable)
1	gal. brown sauce
1	pt. sherry wine
1	clove garlic, minced
6	ozs. onion, minced
2	lbs. mushrooms, sliced thick
1	pt. whole tomatoes, canned, crushed
3	ozs. ripe olives, pitted, sliced thin
3	ozs. green olives, pitted, sliced thin
	salt and pepper to taste

Preparation
1. Clean and disjoint the chickens with a French knife. When properly disjointed a whole chicken will yield 2 wings, 2 breasts, 2 thighs and 2 legs. Proceed only after demonstration by instructor.
2. Prepare the brown sauce. (See Chap. 15.)
3. Mince the onions and garlic with a French knife.
4. Slice the mushrooms fairly thick with a French knife.
5. Crush the tomatoes by squeezing in the palm of the hand.
6. Pit the olives with an olive pitter. Slice thin with a French knife.
7. Preheat the oven to 350°F.
8. Have all equipment and ingredients handy.

Procedure
1. Season the disjointed chicken with salt and pepper.
2. Place the oil in an iron skillet, heat.
3. Add the pieces of chicken and sauté until golden brown on both sides. Turn with a kitchen fork.
4. Remove from the skillet and place in the braising pot.
5. Pour most of the oil from the skillet, leaving only enough to sauté the vegetables.

6. Add the onions, mushrooms and garlic; sauté in the oil until slightly tender.
7. Add the crushed tomatoes and sherry wine, bring to a boil and pour this mixture over the sautéed chicken.
8. Add the brown sauce. Cover the braising pot, place in the preheated oven and bake until the chickens are tender. (approximately 30 to 40 minutes.)
9. Remove from the oven, add the sliced olives, season with salt and pepper. Place is a steam table pan.
10. Serve ½ chicken per portion with a generous portion of the sauce the chicken was baked in.

Precautions and Safety Measures
1. Exercise caution when disjointing the chicken to avoid cutting self.
2. Do not overbake the chicken, the meat will fall from the bone.

Chicken livers chasseur

For chicken livers chasseur the livers are sautéed and then poached slightly in a rich chasseur sauce. This item is usually served in a casserole on either the luncheon or dinner menu.

Objectives
1. To teach the student the procedure for preparing chicken livers chasseur.
2. To teach the student how to sauté the chicken livers and how to prepare the chasseur sauce.
3. To teach the student how to dish up chicken livers chasseur.

Equipment
1. Iron skillet
2. Sauce pot, 3 gal.
3. Kitchen fork
4. Kitchen spoon
5. Bake pan
6. French knife
7. 25 individual casseroles
8. Qt. measure
9. Baker's scale
10. Steam table pan

Ingredients: Approx. yield: 25 servings

150	whole chicken livers, cut in half
2	lbs. flour (variable)
	salt and pepper to taste
1½	gal. chasseur sauce
	shortening, as needed

1. Clean the chicken livers, cut them in half with a French knife.
2. Place the flour in a bake pan and season with salt and pepper.
3. Prepare the chasseur sauce. (See Chap. 15.)
4. Have all equipment and ingredients handy.

Procedure
1. Place enough shortening in an iron skillet to cover the bottom approximately ½ in. deep, heat.
2. Dredge (coat with flour) the chicken livers in the seasoned flour, dust off excess.
3. Place the chicken livers in the hot grease and fry until slightly brown. Remove from the skillet with a kitchen fork and let drain.
4. Place the chasseur sauce in a sauce pot, heat.
5. Add the chicken livers and simmer for approximately 10 minutes. Stir occasionally with a kitchen spoon.
6. Remove from the range and place in a steam table pan.
7. Dish up 6 whole livers per portion in a shallow casserole and serve with a generous amount of sauce.

Precautions and Safety Measures
1. Exercise caution when handling the knife to avoid cutting self.
2. Exercise caution when frying the chicken livers. The grease will pop if moisture is present in the livers.
3. Shake off excess flour or it will settle in the bottom of the skillet and burn.

Coq au vin

Coq au vin consists of sautéed chicken cooked in a red Burgundy wine with mushrooms, salt pork and onions. Coq au vin is popular in establishments featuring French cuisine.

Objectives
1. To teach the student the procedure for preparing coq au vin.
2. To teach the student how to disjoint and sauté the chicken.
3. To teach the student how to dish up coq au vin.

Equipment
1. Iron skillet
2. Pt. measure
3. Baker's scale
4. French knife
5. Kitchen spoon
6. Med. size braising pot and cover
7. Paring knife
8. Bake pan
9. Kitchen fork
10. Full size steam table pan

Ingredients: Approx. yield: 12 servings

6	2½ lb. chickens, disjointed
12	ozs. salt pork, cut into ½ in. cubes
2	cloves garlic
1½	pts. red Burgundy wine
1½	lbs. mushroom caps
1	pt. chicken stock
24	pearl onions, raw, peeled
1	bay leaf
½	tsp. thyme
12	ozs. flour
	salt and pepper to taste

Preparations and Safety Measures
1. Clean and disjoint the chickens with a French knife each chicken will yield 8 pieces when properly disjointed. Proceed only after demonstration by instructor.
2. Peel the pearl onions with a paring knife.
3. Place the flour in a bake pan and season with salt and pepper.
4. Prepare chicken stock. (See Chap. 12.)
5. Cut the salt pork into ½ in. with a French knife.
6. Have all equipment and ingredients handy.

Procedure
1. In a braising pot place the cubes of salt pork, cook until they are partly rendered. Remove the salt pork cracklings and save.
2. Add the garlic cloves, cook slightly and remove them from the pot with a kitchen spoon. Discard.
3. Pass each piece of chicken through the seasoned flour, pat off excess. Place in the braising pot and sauté until the chicken pieces are brown on both sides, turn with a kitchen fork. Remove them from the pot, keep warm and hold.
4. Add the onions to the braising pot, brown slightly.
5. Add the mushrooms, cook slightly.
6. Pour in the wine and chicken stock, bring to a boil. Stir occasionally with a kitchen spoon.
7. Return the sautéed chicken and pork cracklings to the pot, add the thyme and bay leaf. Cover the pot and bring to a simmer.

8. Simmer for approximately ½ hour or until the chicken is tender. Remove the bay leaf and adjust seasoning. Place in a steam table pan.

9. Dish up ½ chicken, consisting of 1 wing, 1 thigh, 1 leg and 1 breast. Serve with 2 pearl onions, mushrooms and sauce.

Precautions and Safety Measures

1. Exercise caution when handling the knife to avoid cutting self.

2. When cooking the salt pork do not let it become too brown or crisp. Cook just enough to render out most of the fat.

3. Do not cook the garlic in the fat for too long a period, just enough to draw out part of its flavor.

4. Do not overcook the chickens or the meat will fall away from the bones.

BROILED POULTRY RECIPES

Chicken livers en brochette

For chicken livers en brochette chicken livers, bacon and mushroom caps that have been partly cooked are alternated on a skewer. This is passed through salad oil and placed under the broiler to complete the cooking. Chicken livers en brochette are usually served on toast, covered with a butter sauce. They are featured on the dinner or à la carte menu.

Objectives

1. To teach the student the procedure for preparing chicken livers en brochette.

2. To teach the student how to partly cook each item.

3. To teach the student how to arrange each item on the skewer.

4. To teach the student how to broil and serve chicken livers en brochette.

Equipment

1. 25 metal skewers
2. French knife
3. Bake pan
4. Sheet pans (2)
5. Broiler
6. 2 skillets
7. Kitchen fork
8. Pt. measure

Ingredients: Approx. yield: 25 servings

100	whole chicken livers
100	mushroom caps
50	strips of bacon
1	pt. salad oil (variable)
8	ozs. butter
25	pieces of toasted bread

Preparation

1. Clean the chicken livers, sauté in part of the salad oil in a skillet until they are half done.

2. Clean and sauté the mushroom caps in a skillet in butter until partly done.

3. Line the strips of bacon on a sheet pan, overlaping slightly. Place in the oven and cook until medium, remove and cool, cut in half with a French knife.

4. Preheat the broiler, adjust flame until fairly low.

5. Toast the bread, cut into triangular halves.

6. Place the remaining salad oil in a bake pan.

7. Have all equipment and ingredients handy.

Procedure

1. Alternate chicken livers, half strips of bacon and mushrooms on skewers. Use 4 of each.

2. Marinate (soak in) salad oil, then place on sheet pans.

3. Place the sheet pan under the broiler, approximately 6 in. from the low flame. Cook until all items are completely done, turn the chicken livers occasionally with a kitchen fork.

4. Place the skewered items across 2 half pieces of toast, remove the skewer and serve with a small amount of melted butter ladled over each portion. Serve at once.

Precautions and Safety Measures

1. Exercise caution when sautéing the chicken livers, the oil may pop if moisture is present in the livers.

2. Do not overcook any of the items. They should just be partly cooked.

3. Broil the skewered items slowly.

4. Be careful in turning the skewers. The metal becomes hot.

Broiled chicken

Broiled chicken uses young, tender chickens weighing from 1½ to 2 pounds, selected for broiling. They are split in half, passed through salad oil to prevent sticking and improve appearance, placed in a wire hand broiler rack and broiled under a low flame until golden brown.

Poultry and Egg National Board

Broiled half chicken

Objectives

1. To teach the student the procedure for preparing broiled chicken.
2. To teach the student how to cut the chicken.
3. To teach the student how to broil the chicken.
4. To teach the student how to serve the chicken.

Equipment

1. French knife
2. Pastry brush
3. Wire hand broiler
4. Bake pans (2)
5. Kitchen fork
6. Wire hand broiler racks
7. Sauce pan, 1 pt.
8. Cup measure

Ingredients: Approx. yield: 24 servings

12	1½ to 2 lb. chickens, milk-fed broilers
1	cup salad oil
	salt and pepper to taste
8	ozs. butter, melted

Preparation

1. Clean the chickens and split them in half with a French knife. Proceed only after demonstration by instructor.
2. Place the salad oil in a bake pan.
3. Preheat the broiler and oven, set the oven temperature at 325°F.
4. Melt the butter in a sauce pan.
5. Have all equipment and ingredients handy.

Procedure

1. Place the chicken halves in the salad oil and coat thoroughly. Season with salt and pepper.
2. Place in the wire hand broiler racks and place the chickens (in hand broiler racks) under the broiler, skin side down. Adjust broiler rack to the low position and have the broiler flame fairly low.
3. Cook until the surface of the chicken is brown, turn over, skin side up and cook until the second side is golden brown.
4. Remove the chicken halves from the hand broiler racks and place in a second bake pan.
5. Place in the oven and bake until done. When chicken is properly cooked the drum stick joint will move freely and the thigh will feel soft to the touch.
6. Dish up ½ chicken per portion, brushed with melted butter and accompanied with a peach half, spiced apple or some other kind of fruit.

Note: The tip of the leg bone is sometimes removed and a frill or "stocking" is attached to the end of the leg bone. This adds to the appearance of each portion when served.

Precautions and Safety Measures

1. Exercise caution when handling the knife.
2. Do not let the skin of the chicken burn during the broiling period. It will lack appearance when served.
3. Do not overcook the chicken, it will lack appearance when served.
4. Exercise caution when removing the chickens from the hot hand broiler racks to avoid burning self.

Chickenburgers

Chickenburgers consist of a ground meat patty prepared from chicken or turkey meat and pork. This is an excellent item to select when wishing to utilize the dark meat of chickens or turkeys.

Objectives

1. To teach the student the procedure for making chickenburgers.
2. To teach the student how to form and cook chickenburgers.
3. To teach the student how to dish up chickenburgers.

Equipment

1. French knife
2. Food grinder
3. Baker's scale
4. Pt. measure
5. Skillets, iron and steel

6. Mixing container
7. Sheet pans
8. Steam table pan

Ingredients: Approx. yield: 50 servings
12 lbs. chicken or turkey meat, raw
4 lbs. fresh pork, slightly sautéed
1 lb. 8 oz. celery, minced
1 lb. onions, minced
8 oz. chicken fat
8 whole eggs
½ pt. heavy cream
 salt and pepper to taste
¼ cup parsley, chopped

Preparation
1. Cut chicken or turkey with a French knife into strips that will pass through the food grinder.
2. Cut pork with a French knife into strips that will pass through the food grinder. Sauté in a skillet until partly done.
3. Mince the onions and celery with a French knife.
4. Chop the parsley with a French knife and wash.
5. Coat the sheet pans with salad oil.
6. Preheat broiler.
7. Have all equipment and ingredients handy.

Procedure
1. Place chicken fat in steel skillet and heat. Add the celery and onions and sauté until slightly tender. Do not burn.
2. Place the chicken or turkey, pork, sautéed vegetables, salt and pepper in a mixing container and mix thoroughly by hand, then pass through the food grinder, using the medium chopper plate.
3. Add the eggs, cream and parsley, and mix again.
4. Scale 5 oz. portions. Shape into patties
5. Place on oiled sheet pans and cook under the broiler until done. Place in a steam table pan.
6. Dish up 1 patty per portion. Serve with country gravy, or cream or poulette sauce. (See Chap. 15 for gravy and sauce recipes.)

Precautions and Safety Measures
1. Exercise caution when handling the knife to avoid cutting self.
2. When sautéing the pork, do not overcook. Sauté until the pinkness in the meat disappears.
3. Mix the chickenburger mixture thoroughly before and after grinding.
4. Coat hands with salad oil when forming

patties so the meat will not stick to the hands.

Chicken divan

Chicken divan consists of sliced white meat of turkey or chicken placed over cooked broccoli, covered with a rich, creamy sauce, sprinkled with Parmesan cheese and browned slightly under the broiler. Chicken divan can add variety to the entrées featured on the dinner menu.

Objectives
1. To teach the student the procedure for preparing chicken divan
2. To teach the student how to slice the breast meat and prepare the sauce.
3. To teach the student how to set up and serve chicken divan.

Equipment
1. French knife
2. Sauce pot
3. Baker's scale
4. Qt. measure
5. Wire whip
6. Braising pot
7. 25 individual flat casseroles
8. Stainless steel bowl
9. Kitchen spoon

Ingredients: Approx. yield: 25 servings
6 lbs. boiled breast of turkey or chicken, sliced
6 lbs. broccoli spears, frozen, cooked
1 lb. butter or margarine
12 ozs. flour
1 gal. chicken stock
½ cup sherry wine
1 pt. whipping cream
4 ozs. Parmesan cheese
 salt and white pepper to taste

Preparation
1. Boil, cool, and slice the turkey or chicken breast fairly thin with a French knife. Proceed only after demonstration by instructor.
2. Cook the broccoli in boiling salt water, using a braising pot.
3. Prepare the chicken stock. (See Chap. 12.)
4. Whip the cream in a stainless steel bowl with a wire whip.
5. Have all equipment and ingredients handy.

Procedure
1. In a sauce pot place the butter or margarine, melt.

2. Add the flour, making a roux, cook slightly. Stir with a kitchen spoon.
3. Add the hot chicken stock, whipping vigorously with a wire whip until thickened and smooth.
4. Add the sherry wine, continue to whip.
5. Remove the sauce from the range and fold in the whipped cream with a kitchen spoon until it is thoroughly blended with the sauce.
6. Season with salt and white pepper.
7. Place cooked broccoli in each casserole.
8. Cover the broccoli with approximately 4 ozs. of sliced turkey or chicken.
9. Cover generously with the hot sauce, sprinkle with Parmesan cheese and a dash of paprika.
10. Place each order under the broiler and brown slightly.
11. Serve at once.

Precautions and Safety Measures
1. Exercise caution when slicing the turkey or chicken to avoid cutting self.
2. Fold the whipped cream into the sauce very gently with a kitchen spoon.
3. Do not overcook the broccoli, it will be hard to handle.
4. Exercise caution when browning the individual casseroles under the broiler.

BOILED OR STEWED POULTRY RECIPES

Curried chicken

Curried chicken consists of cubes of cooked chicken or turkey meat placed in a rich creamy curry sauce and served in a casserole usually accompanied with rice or chutney. Curried chicken can be featured on either the luncheon or dinner menu.

Objectives
1. To teach the student the procedure for preparing curried chicken.
2. To teach the student how to cut the chicken or turkey meat.
3. To teach the student how to dish up curried chicken.

Equipment
1. French knife
2. Sauce pots (2), 3 gal.
3. Wire whip
4. Baker's scale
5. Qt. measure
6. Kitchen spoon
7. Sauce pan, 2 qt.
8. Deep steam table pan
9. China cap

Ingredients: Approx. yield: 25 servings

6	lbs. boiled chicken or turkey meat, diced into 1 in. cubes
12	lbs. onions, ½ in. dice
8	ozs. apples, ½ in. dice
12	ozs. butter
10	ozs. flour
1	oz. curry powder
3	qts. chicken stock, hot
1	qt. cream (single), hot
	salt to taste

Preparation
1. Boil, cool and dice the chicken or turkey meat with a French knife into ½ in. cubes.
2. Prepare the chicken stock, keep hot. (See Chap. 12.)
3. Heat the cream in a sauce pan.
4. Have all equipment and ingredients handy.

Procedure
1. Place butter in a sauce pot, add the onions and sauté until they are slightly tender. Do not brown.
2. Add the flour, making a roux, cook for 5 minutes. Stir occasionally with a kitchen spoon.
3. Add the curry powder, blend into the roux.
4. Add the hot stock and cream gradually, whipping vigorously with a wire whip until thickened and smooth.
5. Add the apples and let the sauce simmer until the apples are thoroughly cooked.
6. Strain the sauce through a fine china cap into another sauce pot.
7. Heat the chicken or turkey meat, add to the sauce and stir in gently with a spoon.
8. Season with salt and place in a deep steam table pan.
9. Dish up with a 6 to 8 oz. ladle. Serve with baked rice and chutney (relish).

Precautions and Safety Measures
1. Exercise caution when handling the knife.
2. Stir the sauce occasionally, while it is simmering, to avoid scorching.
3. Stir the cooked meat into the sauce gently to avoid breaking.

Chicken fricassee family style

Chicken fricassee family style is a type of

chicken stew. The chunks of cooked chicken or turkey and the colorful assortment of vegetables flow through a rich, tasty chicken sauce. This item is an excellent choice for the luncheon menu.

Objectives

1. To teach the student the procedure for preparing chicken fricassee family style.
2. To teach the student how to cut the cooked turkey or chicken and the vegetables.
3. To teach the student how to dish up chicken fricassee family style.

Equipment

1. Sauce pot, 5 gal.
2. Wire whip
3. French knife
4. China cap
5. 3 sauce pans, (2) 4 qt. and (1) 1 qt.
6. Baker's scale
7. Qt. or gal. measure
8. Kitchen spoon
9. 50 individual casseroles
10. Deep steam table pan

Ingredients: Approx. yield: 50 servings

12	lbs. boiled chicken or turkey, diced into 1 in. cubes
3	lbs. carrots, ¾ in. dice
3	lbs. celery, ¾ in. diagonal cut
2	lbs. whole onions, canned, drained
2	lbs. shortening or butter
1	lb. 10 ozs. flour
2	gal. chicken stock
2½	lbs. box peas, frozen
	yellow color, as desired

Preparation

1. Boil the chicken or turkey and let cool. Dice into 1 in. cubes with a French knife and heat.
2. Cut the carrots into ¾ in. dice and the celery into ¾ in. diagonal cut with a French knife. Cook in separate sauce pans in boiling salt water until tender. Drain through a china cap.
3. Drain the canned onions.
4. Prepare the chicken stock, keep hot. (See Chap. 12.)
5. Cook the peas in a sauce pan in boiling water, keep warm.
6. Have all equipment and ingredients handy.

Procedure

1. Place the shortening or butter in the sauce pot, heat.
2. Add the flour making a roux, cook for 5 minutes. Stir with a kitchen spoon.

3. Add the hot chicken stock, whipping vigorously with a wire whip until thickened and smooth.
4. Tint the sauce with yellow color as desired.
5. Add the hot chicken or turkey, the drained carrots, onions and celery. Stir carefully to blend all ingredients.
6. Season with salt and place in a deep steam table pan.
7. Dish up with a 6 to 8 oz. ladle into deep casseroles. Garnish the top of each portion with cooked peas.

Precautions and Safety Measures

1. Cook the roux for at least 5 minutes to avoid a raw flour taste in the sauce.
2. When combining the cooked meat and vegetables to the sauce, blend together very gently to prevent the pieces from breaking.
3. Exercise extreme caution when adding the yellow color. Remember more can always be added.

Chicken à la king

Chicken à la king is a colorful entree consisting of chunks of cooked chicken or turkey, green peppers, pimientoes and mushrooms flowing through a rich, flavorful cream sauce. Chicken à la king is an appropriate item for the luncheon or dinner menu, as well as the à la carte menu or buffet.

Objectives

1. To teach the student how to cut the garnish (green peppers, pimientoes and mushrooms).
2. To teach the student the procedure for preparing chicken à la king.
3. To teach the student how to dish up chicken à la king.

Equipment

1. Sauce pot, 5 gal.
2. French knife
3. Kitchen spoon
4. Wire whip
5. 4 sauce pans, (1) 4 qt. and (3) 2 qt.
6. Qt. measure
7. Baker's scale
8. China cap
9. Deep steam table pan

Ingredients: Approx. yield: 50 servings

10	lbs. boiled chicken or turkey, 1 in. dice
1	lb. green peppers, ½ in. dice
8	ozs. pimientoes, ½ in. dice

2 lbs. mushrooms, $\frac{1}{2}$ in. dice
2 lbs. shortening or butter
1 lb. 10 ozs. flour
3 qts. chicken stock
3 qts. milk
1 qt. light cream
1 pt. sherry wine
  salt to taste
  yellow color, as desired

Preparation

1. Boil the chicken or turkey and let cool. Dice into 1 in. cubes with French knife; heat.
2. Dice the green peppers, mushrooms, and pimientoes into $\frac{1}{2}$ in. dice with a French knife.
3. Cook the diced green peppers in a sauce pan in salt water until tender. Drain through a china cap and hold.
4. Sauté the mushrooms in a sauce pan in additional butter until slightly tender.
5. Prepare the chicken stock. (See Chap. 12.)
6. Heat the milk and cream in sauce pans.
7. Have all equipment and ingredients handy.

Procedure

1. Place the shortening or butter in the sauce pot and heat.
2. Add the flour making a roux, cook for 5 minutes. Stir with a kitchen spoon.
3. Add the hot chicken stock, whipping vigorously with a wire whip until thickened and smooth.
4. Add the hot milk and cream, continuing to whip until the sauce is smooth.
5. Add the sherry wine and tint the sauce if desired with yellow color.
6. Add the cooked green peppers, mushrooms, pimientoes and turkey or chicken. Stir carefully with kitchen spoon to blend.
7. Dish up with a 6 to 8 oz. ladle. Serve over toast or patty shell. For the buffet serve in a chafing dish.

Precautions and Safety Measures

1. Exercise caution when handling the knife to avoid cutting self.
2. Cook the roux for at least 5 minutes to avoid a raw flour taste in the sauce.
3. When combining the cooked meat and the vegetable garnish to the sauce, blend together very gently with a kitchen spoon to prevent the pieces from breaking up in the sauce.
4. Exercise extreme caution when adding the yellow color. Remember more can always be added.

Chicken chow mein

Chicken chow mein is a Chinese-American dish that has become quite popular. It appears quite frequently on the luncheon menu of the average food service establishment. It is a mixture of crisp Chinese vegetables and cooked chicken or turkey blended together in a rich, thickened, highly seasoned sauce.

Objectives

1. To teach the student the procedure for preparing chicken chow mein.
2. To teach the student how to cut the meat and vegetables.
3. To teach the student how to dish up chicken chow mein.

Equipment

1. Stock pot, 10 gal.
2. French knife
3. Wood paddle
4. Stainless steel container
5. Deep steam table pan
6. Baker's scale
7. Qt. measure
8. 50 individual casseroles
9. China cap

Ingredients: Approx. yield: 50 servings

8 lbs. boiled chicken or turkey meat, $\frac{1}{2}$ in. diagonal cut
1 pt. salad oil (variable)
6 lbs. onions, cut julienne
6 lbs. celery, cut in thin slices on a bias (slanting)
2 lbs. mushrooms, sliced thick
1 #$2\frac{1}{2}$ can water chestnuts, sliced thin
1 #$2\frac{1}{2}$ can bamboo shoots, sliced thin
1 gal. chicken stock
4 ozs. soy sauce
3 qts. bean sprouts, canned, drained
14 ozs. corn starch (variable)
1 pt. cold water
  salt and pepper to taste

Preparation

1. Boil, remove bones by hand and cut the chicken or turkey into $\frac{1}{2}$ in. diagonal pieces with a French knife.
2. Cut the onions and celery with a French knife.
3. Slice the mushrooms, bamboo shoots and water chestnuts with a French knife.
4. Prepare a rich chicken stock. (See Chap. 12.)
5. Drain the bean sprouts in a china cap.
6. Have all equipment and ingredients handy.

Procedure

1. Place the salad oil in the stock pot, heat.
2. Add the onions and celery, sauté for 5 minutes. Stir with a wooden paddle.
3. Add the mushrooms, continue to sauté until vegetables are partly done.
4. Add the bamboo shoots, water chestnuts, soy sauce and chicken stock, simmer until the celery is done, but still retaining a crisp texture.
5. Dilute the cornstarch in the cold water, add to the simmering mixture stirring vigorously with a wooden paddle until it is thickened and smooth.
6. Add the turkey and stir in gently, remove from the range.
7. Add the bean sprouts and stir in gently, season with salt and pepper. Place in a deep steam table pan.
8. Dish up into casseroles with a 6 to 8 oz. ladle. Serve with baked rice or fried noodles or both.

Precautions and Safety Measures

1. Exercise caution when handling the knife.
2. Add the bean sprouts after all cooking is completed or they will lose their crispness.
3. Stir constantly and vigorously when adding the cornstarch.
4. Do not overcook the vegetables, attempt to retain a slight crispness.

Chicken pot pie

Chicken pot pie consists of fairly large chunks of chicken and cooked, assorted vegetables. These are placed in deep individual casseroles, covered with chicken velouté sauce, topped with a prebaked pie crust disc and served on the luncheon menu.

Objectives

1. To teach the student the procedure for preparing chicken pot pie.
2. To teach the student how to cut the cooked chicken and the raw vegetables.
3. To teach the student how to set up a chicken pot pie.

Equipment

1. French knife
2. 3 sauce pans, (2) 4 qt. and (1) 2 qt.
3. Baker's scale
4. 25 individual deep casseroles
5. Steel skillet
6. Ladle
7. Bake pans

Ingredients: Approx. yield: 25 servings

6	lbs. chicken or turkey meat, boiled, cut in a large dice
25	small onions, canned, drained
50	carrot pieces, medium diced
50	small potatoes, canned, drained
50	celery pieces, medium diced
25	mushroom caps
1	gal. chicken velouté sauce
25	pie crust discs
6	ozs. butter or margarine
1½	lbs. frozen peas

Preparation

1. Dice the boiled turkey meat fairly large with a French knife.
2. Prepare the chicken velouté sauce. (See Chap. 15.)
3. Sauté the mushrooms in the butter.
4. Cut the raw vegetables with a French knife.
5. Cook the raw vegetables in separate sauce pans in boiling salt water until tender, drain.
6. Prepare the pie crust disc, cutting each disc the same shape, but slightly larger than the top of the casserole. The disc will shrink slightly when baked. (See Chap. 25.)
7. Have all equipment and ingredients handy.

Procedure

1. In each individual casserole place approximately 3 to 4 ozs. of chicken meat, 2 carrot pieces, 2 celery pieces, 2 potatoes, 1 onion, 1 mushroom cap and some peas.
2. Ladle the velouté sauce over the meat and vegetables in each casserole, top with a prebaked pie crust disc.
3. Place the casserole in bake pans and add enough water to surround the bottom half of the casseroles with water.
4. Place the bake pans on the side of the range and keep hot until ready to serve.

Precautions and Safety Measures

1. Exercise caution when handling the knife to avoid cutting self.
2. Handle the baked pie dough discs gently, they break easily.
3. Exercise caution when ladling the sauce over the meat and vegetables to avoid burning self. Ladle with a smooth, easy motion.

Chicken tetrazzini

Chicken tetrazzini is a combination of

cream chicken and mushrooms, placed over cooked spaghetti, sprinkled with Parmesan cheese and browned gently under the broiler. It was supposedly a favorite of the famous Italian opera singer Luisa Tetrazzini and was named in her honor.

Objectives

1. To teach the student the procedure for preparing chicken tetrazzini.
2. To teach the student how to cut the cooked meat and mushrooms.
3. To teach the student how to set up a portion of chicken tetrazzini.

Equipment

1. French knife
2. Kitchen spoon
3. Sauce pot (2), 3 gal.
4. Sauce pans
5. Collander
6. Baker's scale
7. Qt. measure
8. 25 individual casseroles
9. Wire whip

Ingredients: Approx. yield: 25 servings

6	lbs. boiled chicken or turkey meat, cut into strips
2	lbs. mushrooms, sliced thick
1	lb. shortening or butter
12	ozs. flour
1	gal. chicken stock
1	pt. cream
½	cup sherry wine
1	gal. thin spaghetti, cooked (variable)
1	pt. Parmesan cheese
	salt and white pepper to taste

Preparation

1. Boil the chicken or turkey until tender, let cool, remove meat from bones and cut into strips (2 in. by ½ in. by ¼ in.) with French knife.
2. Boil the spaghetti in a sauce pot in salt water. Drain in a collander and rinse in cold water, then reheat in warm water. Season lightly with salt and white pepper and hold.
3. Prepare chicken stock. (See Chap. 12.)
4. Warm the cream in a sauce pan.
5. Slice the mushrooms and sauté slightly in additional butter in a sauce pan.
6. Preheat broiler.
7. Have all equipment and ingredients handy.

Procedure

1. In a sauce pot place the butter or shortening, heat.

2. Add the flour, making a roux, cook for 5 minutes. Stir with a kitchen spoon.
3. Add the hot chicken stock, whipping vigorously with a wire whip until thickened and smooth.
4. Whip in the warm cream and sherry wine.
5. Add the cooked strips of chicken or turkey and the cooked mushrooms, stir in gently with a kitchen spoon so the meat will not be broken.
6. Season with salt and white pepper.
7. Arrange spaghetti in the bottom of each casserole. Place the chicken mixture over the spaghetti, cover completely. Sprinkle with grated Parmesan cheese and brown slightly under the broiler.
8. Serve at once.

Precautions and Safety Measures

1. Exercise caution when handling the knife.
2. When adding the liquid to the roux whip vigorously to produce a smooth sauce.
3. Add the cream slowly to the sauce, while whipping briskly.
4. Be alert when browning each order under the broiler.

DRESSING RECIPE

Bread stuffing

Bread stuffing is a highly seasoned bread mixture that is used extensively with poultry preparations. Through the years it has become more associated with roast turkey than the other poultry birds. There are many variations of this basic bread stuffing such as oyster, raisin, giblet, shrimp and chicken liver stuffing, just to name a few.

Objectives

1. To teach the student the procedure for preparing bread stuffing.
2. To teach the student how to cut and sauté the vegetables and fruit ingredients.
3. To teach the student how to mix and bake the stuffing.

Equipment

1. Baker's scale
2. French knife
3. Skillet
4. Larger round bottom bowl
5. Spoon measures
6. Braising pot or roast pan

7. Sheet pans
8. Apple corer

*Ingredients: Approx. yield: 50 servings
(No. 16 dipper)*

  8 lbs. dry bread (2 days old) cut into cubes
  1 lb. celery, diced fine
  3 lbs. onions, minced
  1 lb. fresh apples, sliced thin
  1 lb. margarine or bacon grease
  4 tbsp. sage
  3 tbsp. poultry seasoning
  ½ cup parsley, chopped
  2 gal. chicken stock (variable)
     salt and pepper to taste

Preparation

1. Cut the bread into cubes, place on sheet pans and toast in the oven.
2. Dice the celery fine and mince the onions with a French knife.
3. Core with apple corer and slice the apples into fairly small pieces with a French knife.
4. Chop the parsley with a French knife.
5. Prepare a rich chicken stock (See Chap. 12) or combine approximately 2 to 3 ozs. of chicken base to 1 gal. of water.
6. Grease a large braising pot or roast pan.
7. Preheat oven to 375°F.
8. Have all equipment and ingredients handy.

Procedure

1. Place the margarine or bacon grease in a skillet, heat.
2. Add the celery and onions, sauté until slightly tender.
3. Add the apples and continue to sauté until tender, remove from the heat and cool slightly.
4. Place the toasted bread, parsley, sautéed onions, celery and apples, chicken stock,

sage and poultry seasonng in the large round bottom bowl, mix together thoroughly, using the hands. The mixture should be soft and slightly wet. If it is stiff and dry add more stock.
5. Season with salt and pepper, place in the greased braiser or roast pan.
6. Place in the oven and bake for approximately 1½ to 2 hours until the stuffing is hot throughout and golden brown on the surface.
7. Serve with poultry and other meats.

Note: Variations, add ingredients before baking:

    1. For raisin stuffing add 1 lb. of raisins that have been soaked in warm water and drained.

    2. For giblet stuffing add 2 lbs. boiled, chopped giblets.

    3. For oyster stuffing add 1 to 1½ qts. of oysters that have been sautéed slightly in butter.

    4. For shrimp stuffing add 2 lbs. of cooked, diced shrimp.

    5. For chicken liver stuffing add 3 lbs. of diced chicken livers that have been sautéed in butter.

Precautions and Safety Measures

1. Exercise caution when handling the knife to avoid cutting self.
2. Exercise caution when toasting the bread cubes to avoid burning
3. Blend all ingredients together thoroughly before placing the stuffing in the prepared pan.
4. Bake the dressing thoroughly. If a cold center should remain after baking fermentation could start.

| chapter 21 | # fish
and
shellfish |

■ Fish and shellfish have been an important source of food for mankind since prehistoric times. The Bible, for example, refers to the importance of fish during that period in history. The Greeks and Romans recognized the value of fish and shellfish as a food, and developed their taste for seafood to such an extent that they were able to tell from the taste just where the fish was caught. Today, fish and shellfish still provide an important source of food. With our modern advancement in catching, processing and preparing this tasty food its popularity is increasing to such an extent that most food service establishments feature three or four choices on their menus. Fish and shellfish have also become the basis for many gourmet dishes because they are always tender, can be prepared by a variety of cooking methods, and blend well with delicate gourmet sauces.

Fish are classed into two categories: fresh water fish and salt water fish. In general, fresh water fish are considered to be superior in flavor to salt water fish. The natural habits of a fish also have a bearing on the quality of the edible flesh. If the fish is active, like brook trout, and comes from a running stream it will possess a superior flavor to fish which come from a less active body of water.

The amount of fat a fish may contain also causes a difference in flavor. The so-called *fat* fish are superior in flavor to the *lean* fish. In other words, fat fish like fat meat produces superior quality.

Table I gives the common salt water and fresh water fish with a notation of their fatness or leanness.

The fat content of fishery products will vary with the kind of fish and season of the year. Certain lean fish will contain as little as 0.5 percent fat, while some fat fish will contain as much as 20 percent or more. The fat in fishery products is such that it is very easy to digest and usually this fat content will determine the method of preparation. As a rule fat fish such as mackerel and salmon will produce superior eating qualities if baked or broiled because their natural fat will keep them from drying during the cooking period. Lean fish, such as haddock and cod, are usually best when steamed or poached—their flesh is firm and will hold together during the cooking period. Both fat and lean fish can be sautéed or fried with excellent results.

There are exceptions to these rules of preparation if allowances are made for the fat content. For example, lean fish

TABLE I. GUIDE TO COMMON FISH AND SHELLFISH

Species	Fat or lean	Usual market range of round fish	Usual market forms
SALT-WATER FISH			
Bluefish	Lean	1 to 7 pounds	Whole and drawn
Butterfish	Fat	1/4 to 1 pound	Whole and dressed
Codfish	Lean	3 to 20 pounds	Drawn, dressed, steaks and fillets
Croaker	Lean	1/2 to 2 1/2 pounds	Whole, dressed, and fillets
English and Dover Sole	Lean	1 to 4 pounds	Whole, drawn, dressed and fillets
Flounder	Lean	1/4 to 5 pounds	Whole, dressed and fillets
Haddock	Lean	1 1/2 to 7 pounds	Drawn and fillets
Hake	Lean	2 to 5 pounds	Whole, drawn, dressed and fillets
Halibut	Lean	8 to 75 pounds	Dressed and steaks
Mullet	Lean	1/2 to 3 pounds	Whole
Pomano	Fat	3/4 to 1 1/2 pounds	Whole, drawn, dressed and fillets
Salmon	Fat	3 to 30 pounds	Drawn, dressed, steaks and fillets
Sea bass	Lean	1/4 to 4 pounds	Whole, dressed and fillets
Shad	Fat	1 1/2 to 7 pounds	Whole, drawn and fillets
Snapper, red	Lean	2 to 15 pounds	Drawn, dressed, steaks and fillets
Spanish mackerel	Fat	1 to 4 pounds	Whole, drawn, dressed and fillets
Striped Bass	Lean	1 to 10 pounds	Whole, drawn and dressed
FRESH-WATER FISH			
Brook trout	Fat	1/4 to 1 pound	Whole, dressed and fillets
Catfish	Fat	1 to 10 pounds	Whole, dressed and skinned
Lake trout	Fat	1 1/2 to 10 pounds	Drawn, dressed and fillets
Northern Pike	Lean	2 to 12 pounds	Whole, dressed and fillets
Rainbow trout	Fat	1 1/2 to 2 1/2 pounds	Whole, drawn and dressed
Smelt	Lean	1/3 to 1/2 pound	Whole and drawn
Whitefish	Fat	2 to 6 pounds	Whole, drawn, dressed and fillets
Walleyed Pike	Lean	2 to 5 pounds	Whole, dressed and fillets
Yellow perch	Lean	1/2 to 1 pound	Whole and fillets
SHELLFISH			
Clams	Lean		In the shell, shucked
Crabs	Lean		Live, cooked meat
Lobsters	Lean		Live, cooked meat
Oysters	Lean		In the shell, shucked
Scallops	Lean		Shucked
Shrimp	Lean		Headless, cooked meat

can be baked or broiled if they are basted frequently during the cooking period with butter or margarine. Fat fish may also be steamed or poached if extreme care is exerted when cooking and handling the fish.

Regardless of the method of preparation, one must keep in mind that overcooking will impair the flavor and eating qualities of all fish. Cook just enough to enable the flesh to flake easily from the bones. This will produce a product that will be moist, tender and flavorful.

Shellfish is a general name for all seafood having shells. Shellfish are divided into two classifications: crustacea and mollusks. Crustacea are animals of the sea that have no backbone or spinal column. They have a jointed body, a number of jointed legs and a fairly hard shell. Crustacea include lobsters, shrimp, crayfish and crabs. Mollusks are a division of the animal kingdom which have very soft bodies covered with a hard shell. They include oysters, clams, mussels, snails and scallops.

Most shellfish are extremely popular in the commercial kitchen and are placed on the menu regularly. The exceptions to this would be snails and mussels. Snails are served in establishments that feature French cuisine, but the general public has never accepted them as a favorite. Mussels are fairly popular near the source of supply, but they do not ship well so they have not been given the opportunity to become a universal favorite like their cousins the oyster and clam.

MARKET FORMS

Fish and shellfish may be purchased in various forms. Each form presents certain advantages and disadvantages pertaining to cost, convenience and labor. The more that is done to the fish at the market, the more easy and convenient it is to serve and the higher the cost per pound. The form best suited for any establishment will depend on storage facilities, availability of skilled labor, equipment, kind of seafood desired and type of preparation. Fish may be purchased in seven different forms, shellfish in four different forms. The market forms of fish and shellfish are listed in Table II.

TABLE II. MARKET FORMS:
FISH AND SHELLFISH

Fish	Shellfish
Whole or Round	Alive
Drawn	Shucked
Dressed or Pan Dressed	Headless
Steaks	Cooked Meat
Single Fillets	
Butterfly Fillets	
Sticks	

Fish: Market forms

Whole or round fish are those marketed just as they are taken from the water. Before they are cooked, they must be scaled and eviscerated (entrails removed). The head, tails and fins must be removed and the fish either split and filleted or cut into serving portions. Fish purchased in this form will cost the least per pound, but will involve more labor in preparing it for cooking.

Drawn fish are marketed with only the entrails removed. In preparation for cooking they must be scaled, the head, tail and fins must be removed, and the fish either split and filleted or cut into serving portions, except when preparing the fish in its whole form.

Dressed or pan dressed fish are scaled and eviscerated (entrails removed); the head, tail and fins are also removed. In preparation for cooking the fish has to be either split and filleted or cut into serving portions, except when preparing the fish in its whole form which usually is the case with the smaller fish. This

Scaling: Wash the fish. Place the fish on a cutting board and with one hand hold the fish firmly by the head. Holding a knife almost vertical, scrape off the scales, starting at the tail and scraping toward the head. Be sure to remove all the scales around the fins and head.

Cleaning: With a sharp knife cut the entire length of the belly from the vent to the head. Remove the intestines. Next, cut around the pelvic fins and remove them.

Removing the Head and Tail: Remove the head and the pectoral fins by cutting just back of the collarbone. If the backbone is large, cut down to it on each side of the fish.

Then place the fish on the edge of the cutting board so that the head hangs over and snap the backbone by bending the head down. Cut any remaining flesh that holds the head to the body. Cut off the tail.

Removing the Fins: Next remove the dorsal fin, the large fin on the back of the fish, by cutting along each side of the fin. Then give a quick pull forward toward head and remove the fin with the root bones attached. Remove the ventral fin in the same way. Never trim the fins off with shears or a knife because the root bones at the base of the fins will be left in the fish. Wash the fish thoroughly in cold running water. The fish is now dressed or pan-dressed, depending on its size.

Cutting Steaks: Large size dressed fish may be cut crosswise into steaks, about an inch thick.

Filleting: With a sharp knife cut along the back of the fish from the tail to the head. Then cut down to the backbone just back of the collarbone.

Turn the knife flat and cut the flesh away from the backbone and rib bones.

*Bureau of Commercial Fisheries
U.S. Dept. of the Interior*

Lift off the whole side of the fish or fillet in one piece. Turn the fish over and cut the fillet from the other side.

market form is extremely popular in the commercial kitchen.

Steaks are cross section slices of the larger sizes of dressed fish. They are ready to cook when purchased. Generally the only bone present is a small section of the backbone.

Single fillets are the meaty sides of the fish, cut lengthwise away from the backbone. There are two single fillets to each fish. Fillets are practically boneless and require no preparation for cooking. The skin, with the scales removed, is sometimes left on; in other cases it is removed.

Butterfly fillets are two single fillets held together by the uncut belly of the fish.

Sticks are pieces of fish cut lengthwise or crosswise from single fillets into portions of uniform length and thickness.

Shellfish: Market forms

Alive: Shellfish, such as crabs, lobsters, clams, oysters and mussels should be alive if purchased in the shell.

Shucked: Shellfish which are marketed with their shell removed. Oysters, scallops and clams are marketed in this manner. They may be either fresh or frozen. Some shucked shellfish, such as shrimp and oysters, may be purchased canned.

Headless: This form applies to shrimp and sometimes warm water lobsters, which are marketed with the head and thorax removed. They are marketed frozen. Canned shrimp is also marketed.

PURCHASING FISH

Fresh fish: Most varieties of fish are abundantly fresh during a certain time of each year. When fresh fish are available it is wise to purchase that particular kind. The price will generally be reasonable and they are at their peak in taste and flavor. Your local fish dealer will be glad to advise you when certain fish are in season. When buying fresh fish the five points in Table III should be observed to guarantee freshness.

Fresh fish directly out of the water and into the pan is the desire of all who relish

TABLE III. FISH CONDITION

Desirable	Undesirable
1. Eyes: Bright and Clear	1. Eyes: Dull, Clouded
2. Gills: Bright Red, Free From Slime	2. Gills: Dull Gray or Brown
3. Flesh: Firm, Elastic, Not Separating From Bones	3. Flesh: Soft, Dents When Pressed, Separating From Bones
4. Scales: Bright, Adhere Tightly to the Skin	4. Scales: Lack of Sheen, Loose
5. Odor: Fresh, Free From Objectionable Odors	5. Odor: Strong, Objectionable

seafood; however, this desire is seldom achieved. The next best thing is to preserve as much of this freshness as possible. This can only be achieved through proper storage. Fish deteriorates and decomposes quite rapidly. So if not cooked when it is taken from the water it should be packed in ice immediately and placed in the coldest part of the refrigerator just as soon as possible. The ice will help hold the proper temperature, keep the fish moist, and reduce bruising. It is best to remove the entrails of the fish before storing. Store the fish away from other items in the refrigerator so that its strong odor will not penetrate other food.

The quantity of fresh fish to purchase will depend on three things: number being served, size of portion and market form. The following suggested guide will be extremely helpful.

Sticks, steaks and fillets: Use one-third pound per person.

Dressed fish: Use one-half pound per person.

Drawn fish: Use three-fourth pound per person.

Whole or round fish: Use one pound per person.

Frozen fish: The freezing of fish has been developed to such an extent that most varieties are available the year round. Frozen fish will compare favorably with fresh fish if handled and prepared properly. Do not thaw frozen fish until ready to cook, unless they must be trimmed, cleaned or breaded. Thaw them overnight in the refrigerator at a temperature of 38° to 40°F for best results. If speed is required they may be thawed in cold running water, but never at room temperature. Once frozen fish is thawed *never* refreeze. Frozen fillets and portion cut fish that are breaded and pan ready can be cooked while still frozen, however, the cooking temperature must be reduced considerably and they must be cooked longer.

Frozen fish should always be delivered still in a solid frozen condition. They should be placed in the freezer at 0° to 10°F immediately upon receiving. They must be kept frozen until just prior to using. Any fish placed in the freezer must be wrapped properly with special paper used for freezing. If any part is left exposed it will freeze burn and be unacceptable for use.

In purchasing frozen fish the allowance for each person is the same as for fresh fish, and since frozen fish can not be purchased whole or in the round, one should figure one-third to one-half pound of the edible part per person.

Canned fish: Canned fish is ready to eat as it comes from the can; however, it is not too often used in the commercial kitchen. Canned salmon, tuna fish, anchovies, sardines and in some cases shad roe are fairly popular, but this is usually the extent of their use.

The many developments in the methods of preserving fish products have produced a large variety of specialty items. These include smoked, salted and pickled fish. The popular smoked fish are cod, haddock (also called finnan haddie), salmon, sturgeon and herring. Among the salted fish are cod, mackerel and hake.

Salmon and herring are the most popular pickled fish. These items when used in the commercial kitchen are usually featured on buffets or made into hors d'oeuvres and canapés.

PURCHASING SHELLFISH

Lobsters: Like most shell fish lobsters must be alive until they are ready to be cooked. They are purchased through a local dealer or direct from the source of supply.

Lobsters are shipped by rail or air express in wooden barrels filled with sea weed and ice to create a condition as close to their natural habitat as possible. When they are received they are thoroughly inspected. The ones that are dying, are cooked immediately to save as much meat as possible because when a lobster dies, the meat has such a high moisture content, it will evaporate quickly. Lobsters are graded in four sizes, as shown in Table IV.

Cooked lobster meat is picked from the shell and marketed in frozen and canned form; however, production is so limited that lobster meat is not always available in these forms.

Shrimp: They are always marketed in headless form. The body and thorax are always removed and discarded because the tail is the only edible part. Shrimp are graded and sold according to size. This is based on the number of headless shrimp to the pound. The count or number of shrimp per pound is described in Table V.

Shrimp may be purchased in four general forms: fresh, frozen cooked and canned. Most shrimp used in the commercial kitchen are purchased in the frozen form.

Fresh shrimp are fairly popular near the source of supply, but are practically unheard of inland because like most seafood they spoil rapidly. Fresh shrimp are sold by the pound.

Frozen shrimp are packed mainly in 5 pound blocks for sale to commercial establishments, but recently they have been packaging them in consumer sizes for retail outlets. Frozen shrimp can be bought as green shrimp (uncooked), either peeled or unpeeled; cooked and peeled; or peeled, cleaned and breaded and ready for frying. With all the different ways of

TABLE V. SHRIMP GRADES

Jumbo:	25 or fewer per lb.
Large:	25 to 30 per lb.
Medium:	30 to 42 per lb.
Small:	42 or more per lb.

TABLE IV. LOBSTER GRADES

Chicken:	3/4 To 1 Lb.
Quarters:	1 1/4 Lbs.
Large:	1 1/2 To 2 1/4 Lbs.
Jumbos:	Over 2 1/2 Lbs.

Bureau of Commercial Fisheries
U.S. Dept. of the Interior

How to cook shrimp: Boil in water.

After boiling, remove the shell.

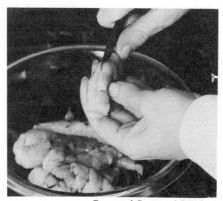

After the shell is removed,
cut out the sand vein.

packaging one must keep in mind that convenience is costly. Frozen shrimp are sold by the pound.

Cooked shrimp may be purchased either peeled and cleaned or in the shell. They are sold by the pound and are fairly popular near the source of supply but not further inland unless they are frozen.

Canned shrimp are available on the market either packed in brine or dry and sold in various size cans. They are not

a very popular item in the commercial kitchen but have become a familiar item on the shelves of the retail store.

Oysters and clams: They may be purchased in three forms: alive in the shell, fresh and frozen shucked, and canned. Oysters and clams in the shell are sold by the dozen, bushel or barrel. They must

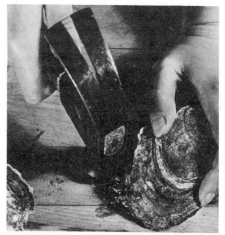

How to shuck oysters: Billing an oyster:
the edge of the shell is broken to allow room
for the knife to be inserted.

Inserting the knife.

Cutting the muscle.

Cutting oyster from the shell.

How to shuck clams: Inserting the knife.

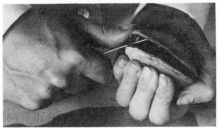

Cutting the muscle.

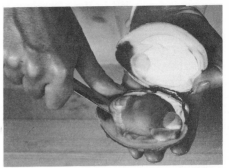

Cutting clam from the shell.

be alive when purchased, this is indicated by a tightly closed shell. If the shell is opened slightly, and does not close when handled, the oyster or clam is dead and no longer fit for human consumption. Shucked oysters and clams which have been removed from their shell are usually packaged fresh in gallon containers. In recent years they have also been freezing these two favorite shellfish in shucked form, with fairly good results. Fresh shucked oysters and clams are packed in metal containers and must be kept refrigerated and packed in ice at all times or they will spoil rapidly. If they are handled in a proper manner they will remain fresh for about one week. Shucked oysters and clams are graded according to size. Clams are graded large, medium and small, but oysters are graded according to federal standards as shown in Table VI. Canned oysters and clams

TABLE VI. OYSTER GRADES

Extra Large or Counts:	160 or less per gal.
Large or Extra Select:	161 to 210 per gal.
Medium or Selects:	211 to 300 per gal.
Small or Standard:	301 to 500 per gal.
Very Small:	Over 500

are very seldom used in the commercial kitchen; however, they are a familiar item in the retail markets.

Crabs: They may be purchased in three forms: alive, cooked meat (fresh or frozen), and canned. In areas close to the sea crabs are sold alive and must be kept alive until they are cooked. This applies to both the hard-shell crab and the soft-shell crab (molting blue crabs). The hard-shell crabs are not sold alive in the inland cities because they do not ship well; however, the soft-shell crabs are packed in sea weed and shipped alive throughout the country. They may be purchased through a local dealer or from the source of supply. Cooked crab meat may be purchased in the shell, fresh or frozen or as fresh cooked meat. The fresh cooked meat is packed in several grades as follows.

Lump meat: Solid lump of white meat from the body of the crab.

Flake meat: Small pieces of white meat from the remaining parts of the body.

Lump and flake meat: A combination of the above two grades.

Claw meat: Meat from the claws, it has a brownish tint. The above grades can also be purchased in frozen form. It is recommended that crab meat be purchased frozen if it is not going to be used right away because the fresh cooked meat is very difficult to keep and will spoil quickly. Fresh cooked crab meat should be kept packed in ice and refrigerated until it is used.

Canned, cooked crab meat is available in various size cans and is fairly popular in commercial kitchens as well as retail outlets. There is little concern for spoilage and it can be used interchangeably with the cooked frozen meat.

There are four principal types of crabs on the market and the meat of each will differ slightly. This will be discussed in another section of this chapter.

Scallops: These are always marketed in shucked form either fresh or frozen. Fresh scallops can be purchased by the gallon or the pound. Frozen scallops are usually purchased in 5 pound blocks.

POPULAR FRESH WATER FISH

Whitefish: This fish is considered the king of the fresh water fish. They are taken from the waters of our northern lakes and in recent years Canada. Whitefish will average in weight from 2 to 6 pounds. The ones weighing 2 to 4 pounds are considered the best. The edible flesh is white, has a flaky grain and a flavor that is highly prized. Whitefish is a member of the salmon family and is on the market the year round. However, the months of May, June, July and August provide the largest catch and consequently at this time the price will be most reasonable. The whitefish is a fatty fish with a black and white skin, a small short head and a deep forked caudal (tail). The fish is very popular in the commercial kitchen and is best when broiled or sautéed. The whitefish has not been as plentiful in recent years because of overfishing and the invasion of the lamprey eel from the ocean when the St. Lawrence seaway was being cut.

Lake trout: This is the largest of all trouts and is taken from the waters of the Great Lakes with the exception of Lake Erie. Lake Michigan provides about 55 percent of the total catch. Lake trout is most plentiful on the market from May to October. The fish has a dark to pale gray skin that is covered with white spots and a fairly large head with strong teeth. The flesh may be red, pink or white depending on which lake it was taken from. The average size of this trout is about 10 pounds; however, the ones weighing 4 to 10 pounds with pink flesh are considered the best. The lake trout is a fatty fish which has a very delicate and desirable flavor that is as highly prized as that of the whitefish. This trout is extremely

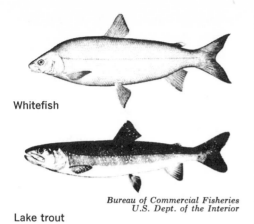

Whitefish

Lake trout

Bureau of Commercial Fisheries
U.S. Dept. of the Interior

popular in the commercial kitchen and is best when broiled or sautéed.

Brook trout: This is considered a medium-fat fish and one of the finest eating fish available, provided it is taken from ice cold water. The fish will thrive in cold water streams. Brook trout has a silver-gray, slightly speckled skin and a square, slightly forked tail. They will average in weight from ¼ to 1 pound. The largest brook trout ever caught weighed 14 pounds 8 ounces; however, 3 and 4 pound brook trouts are very uncommon. A trout weighing 8 to 10 ounces provides a generous serving. In the past ten years the popularity of brook trout in the commercial kitchen has increased greatly. To meet this increased demand they are now producing them on trout farms throughout the United States. In other words, they have become a home grown product and are available the year round.

Rainbow trout: This trout is considered a fresh water fish; however, like the salmon, it passes freely from the ocean to fresh water to spawn. Most trout prefer to remain in one general location but this is not true of the rainbow. It migrates to lakes, streams and ocean; however, they prefer a cold environment such as lakes and streams. The rainbow will vary greatly in color depending on the waters they inhabit. When the trout migrates to salt water his brilliant fresh water color has a tendency to fade. They are generally bluish or olive colored above which shades into a silvery green below; they are spotted generously with small black dots. They have a characteristic marking of a purplish red band that extends along the sides from the head to the tail. It is because of this band the name rainbow was derived. The average weight of a rainbow trout is about 2 pounds but the size of the trout depends to a great degree on the size of the body of water from which it is taken. The larger the body of water the larger the fish. The largest rainbow ever caught weighed 37 pounds. Rainbow trout weighing 5 to 6 pounds are not rare. Rainbow trout are considered a fatty fish and are fairly popular in the commercial kitchen, they are best when sautéed or broiled.

Yellow perch: These are taken from the waters of the Great Lakes and Northern Canada. The name of the fish will vary depending on its size. The small sizes are called lake perch, the larger ones Lake Erie perch, and the extra large ones jumbo or English perch. The skin of the yellow perch is dark olive green on the back merging into a golden yellow on the sides and becoming lighter as it extends to the belly. Its sides are marked with 6 to 8 dark broad vertical bands which run from the back to just above

Bureau of Commercial Fisheries
U.S. Dept. of the Interior

Yellow perch

fish and shellfish   487

the belly. Yellow perch average about 12 inches in length and weigh about 1 pound, the largest on record is a 4 pound yellow perch caught in New Jersey in 1865. This fish is available on the market all year, but is most abundant from April to November. It is a lean fish and is fairly popular in the commercial kitchen. An exceptionally tasty fish when sautéed, fried or broiled.

Walleyed pike: This fish, perhaps better known as jack salmon, is a lean fish and a favorite of sportsmen because of its willingness to strike at any kind of lure. The walleyes inhabit many rivers, lakes and streams in most states except those of the far west and extreme south. The color of the walleye varies with its environment, but it is usually a dark olive green on the back shading into a light yellow on the sides and belly. The name walleye came about because of their exceptionally large shiny eyes. Walleye pike vary considerably in size depending on where they are caught; however, the average weight will be between 2 to 5 pounds. The largest ever caught was 22 pounds. The flesh is slightly fine grained and has an excellent flavor, but many small bones are present. Walleye pike or jack salmon, whichever name may be preferred, is exceptionally popular in food service es-

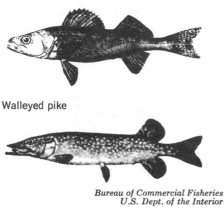

Walleyed pike

Northern pike or pickerel

Bureau of Commercial Fisheries
U.S. Dept. of the Interior

tablishments and are at their best when fried or sautéed.

Northern pike: This fish, sometimes called pickerel, is an enormous eater. It will consume a daily portion of food equal to one-fifth its own weight. Northern pike is very much like the muskellunge, but not as large. It has a long lean body, a long, broad, flat snout and broad bands of sharp teeth on both jaws. It is a lean fish with a very firm, flaky flesh that is dry with many bones present, but has a good flavor. It will average from 2 to 4 pounds, but 10 to 15 pounders are not rare. The record catch is 46 pounds. Northern pike inhabits most of the cold, fresh waters of the world, but in North America it is found mainly in the North Canadian lakes. Lake of the Wood in Canada supplies a large percentage of the catch. Northern pike are available all year but are most plentiful in June. The eating qualities are best during the cold months of the year. Northern pike is a favorite menu item either fried, sautéed, broiled or baked.

Catfish: There are many types of catfish and bullheads. On the market all types are included as catfish or bullhead. Catfish generally have a forked or deeply notched tail, bullheads have a broom shaped, square or slightly notched tail. Both are fat fish and provide a firm, flaky meat with excellent eating qualities. The supply of catfish on the market generally comes from the lakes of Florida, Mississippi River or the Great Lakes. The skin of the catfish will vary in color depending on its environment, but usually it will have a brown or black tone. The catfish or bullhead is without scales and the skin adheres tightly to the flesh making them very difficult to clean. Catfish are most plentiful from March to October and average in size from ¾ to 40 pounds. However in the commercial kitchen the ¾ pound size is preferred and placed on the menu either fried or sautéed.

Smelts: There are two types of smelts,

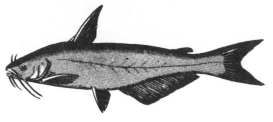

Catfish

Bureau of Commercial Fisheries
U.S. Dept. of the Interior

Smelt

fresh water and salt water. The largest catch of fresh water smelts comes from Lake Michigan. Sea smelts come from the Atlantic Coast from New York to Canada, with Canada producing the largest percentage. Smelts taken from the coldest water are the finest. The smelt is a small, lean fish with a very slender body, a long pointed head, large mouth, a deeply forked tail and a color of olive to dark green along the top blending into a lighter shade with a silver cast along the sides. The belly is silver and the fins are slightly speckled with tiny spots. Smelts are of the salmon family and reach a size of about 10 inches long and weighing as much as 1 pound although most are much smaller. Most smelts used in the commercial kitchen average about 6 to 8 per pound. Smelts are marketed in the round and once the entrails are removed the whole fish is prepared by frying or sautéing. Bone and all may be eaten.

Frog legs: The frog is hatched in the water as a tadpole, but as it matures it can live on land as well. Although it is called an amphibian, the legs, which produce a delicious tasting meat, is classed as a seafood. The best frog legs come from the bull frog which is raised on frog farms and produces a large white meat leg. Only the hind legs of the frog are marketed. The common frog, an uncultivated product, produces a dark meat and the green grass frog, which is very small, produces a very sweet meat leg and is the cheapest to purchase, but its small size prohibits it from becoming popular. Frog-

legs are on the market all year, but are most plentiful from April to October. In the commercial kitchen a big percentage of the froglegs used come from India or Japan. The most desirable legs will average 2 or 3 pair to the pound. Frog legs are best when fried or sautéed.

POPULAR SALT WATER FISH

Haddock: Haddock is very similar to the codfish, but the meat is slightly darker and fibrous; however, it is still considered a white-meated fish and has a firm flesh with an excellent flavor. When the haddock fish is smoked it is called finnan haddie, a product that is quite popular in the commercial kitchen. The most obvious way to distinguish a haddock from the codfish is in the black lateral line and a dusky blotch on each side over the pectoral fin and just below the lateral. These dusky blotches are sometimes referred to as the devil's mark. The average weight of a haddock is 4 pounds, the largest on record is 25 pounds. Haddock is available on the market all year, but reaches its peak in the spring. The largest

Bureau of Commercial Fisheries
U.S. Dept. of the Interior

Haddock

catch of haddock comes from the waters off the New England Coast. The flesh of the haddock is lean and quite dry so it is best to serve this fish with some sort of sauce. Steaming, baking or broiling are the best methods to use when cooking.

Codfish: This is a very well known and important food fish in America. It played a great part in the establishment of the early New England Colonies by becoming a chief source of food. The codfish is very abundant off the coast of Newfoundland and Massachusetts throughout the year, but are seldom caught south of New York. The skin is a brownish gray on the back and upper sides becoming a dirty white on the lower sides and belly. Most of the skin is spotted with brown specks. The young codfish are known as scrod. They average from 1 to 2½ pounds and are very much in demand in the commercial kitchen because of the very tender and agreeable taste. The mature codfish average 10 to 25 pounds. However, 50 to 60 pound cods are not uncommon. The largest on record is 211½ pounds. Codfish for use in the commercial kitchen are usually purchased in fillet form with all skin and bone removed. The meat of the codfish is lean and white with a flaky grain and quite dry. When cooking it is best to poach, steam or bake it. A sauce should always be served with codfish because of its dryness. The scrod is much more moist and is delicious when broiled or sautéed.

Flounder: This fish is of the flat fish family which also includes turbots, sole and halibut. All these flat lean fish are very popular in the commercial kitchen. These flat fish are widely distributed geographically and are comprised of many hundreds of species. The flat fish are very easy to distinguish from other fish because their bodies are quite flat and except in the very young fish the color and both eyes are only on one side of the body. The very young flat fish have eyes and color on both sides but as they start

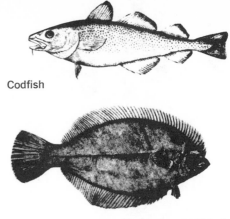

Codfish

Flounder, winter

Bureau of Commercial Fisheries
U.S. Dept. of the Interior

to mature the color leaves one side and it becomes white. The eye on one side will move to a position just above the eye on the other side. The mouth in some species becomes distorted. The fish now leads, so to speak, a onesided life. The largest catch of flounder comes from the waters off the New England Coast. There are five different species sent to market from this region. Many names may be applied to these five species but the most commonly used are winter flounder, sand dab, yellowtail, lemon sole, and gray sole. The *winter flounder,* which is also called common flounder, is noted for its excellent flavor and thick meaty fillets. This flounder will average about 1 pound. *Sand dab,* sometimes called windowpane flounder, is a left handed flounder because its color and eyes are on the left side whereas with most flounders the eyes and color are on the right side. Sand dab is an excellent pan fish, it has bone free fillets and a sweet tasting, oil free meat. The sand dab will weigh from 1 to 2 pounds. *Yellowtail* is so named because its blind side is a lemon yellow rather than the usual white. It has a fairly thin body and because of this it is considered a less desirable food fish; however, it has a good flavor and is marketed in large quantities. *Lemon sole* is also called George's Bank flounder because this is where most of them are caught. Lemon sole is very similar to winter flounder, but large in size, averaging over 2 pounds. It has excellent eating qualities and is highly regarded by gourmets. *Gray sole* is the largest of the winter flounders. It is sometimes called witch flounder and it possesses an excellent flavor. Gray sole will average about 4 pounds. Any of these five species will produce their best eating qualities when sautéed, broiled or fried.

Halibut: Halibut is of the flat fish family and in appearance resembles a giant flounder, it has the usual blind and colored side and both eyes are on the colored side. Halibut can be found in both the Atlantic and Pacific Oceans. The Pacific halibut is more slender than the Atlantic halibut, but otherwise they are alike and both provide a fleshy, lean, fine flavored, white meat. Halibut is on the market all year with the Pacific Ocean producing the largest catch. The halibut is a very large fish and only swordfish, tuna and some sharks reach a greater size. The female halibut is usually larger than the male. The female when full grown will weigh about 100 to 150 pounds whereas the male will average 50 to 150 pounds. The largest halibut catch on record is 720 pounds. The flesh of the halibut has a richer flavor when it weighs under 100 pounds. This is why the halibuts purchased for use in the commercial kitchen will average from 25 to 70 pounds. The very young halibut weighing 4 to 12 pounds is known as chicken halibut and is preferred by many because of its very fine eating qualities. Halibut is one of the most popular fish used in the commercial kitchen because of its versatility. It can be fried, broiled, steamed, poached, sautéed or baked with equally excellent results. Since halibut has a fairly dry texture it should always be served with some type of sauce to add moisture.

Halibut

English and Dover sole: These fish are very similar; they are right sided flounders averaging about 10 inches long with brown to pale brown skin. They are both most plentiful in the Pacific Ocean and have become quite popular in the commercial kitchen. The flesh of the English sole is considered superior to the Dover sole, but both are lean and quite tasty when sautéed, and served à la Meuniere or Almandine.

Sea bass: They are also called black will, blackfish, rock bass, and black bass. They have mottled black skin, interspersed with white markings. They are caught in both the Atlantic and Pacific Oceans; however, the Atlantic sea bass are the leanest and are therefore considered the best. The sea bass is lean and has a white, good flavored meat and averages in size from ¼ to 4 pounds. The largest catch on record is 8 pounds. Sea bass weighing ¾ to 1 pound are considered the best and are usually cleaned and sautéed, broiled or baked whole in commercial kitchens. Sea bass are available on the market the year round, but are most plentiful during the winter months.

Striped bass: This fish is native to the Atlantic Coast, but in the years 1879-1881 they were brought from New Jersey and placed in San Francisco Bay, so today they are sent to market from both oceans. Striped bass are also called rock bass, white bass, striper or rockfish. They are a lean fish and have a skin that

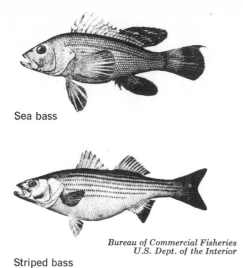

Sea bass

Striped bass

Bureau of Commercial Fisheries
U.S. Dept. of the Interior

is slightly brownish-green on the upper sides, shading to a silver green on the sides and light silver on the belly. The sides are marked with 7 to 8 well defined, fairly dark stripes running from the head to the tail. It is because of these stripes that the most common of its many names is striped bass. The size of the striped bass varies greatly depending on the locality of the catch. An estimated average would be 1 to 10 pounds, but 15 to 25 pounders are not uncommon. The largest catch on record is reported to be 125 pounds. They are quite plentiful on the market during the months of May and June, but are available all year. Striped bass is a popular food fish in the commercial kitchen and are best when sautéed, baked, or broiled.

Red snapper: This is one of the quality fish coming from southern waters. It is a lean fish with a juicy, fine flavored white meat that is held in very high esteem by gourmets. The fish range from the coast of New York to Brazil, but the largest catch is made in the Gulf of Mexico. Red snappers are so named because they have a deep red colored skin and red fins. The red color shades slightly on the belly and

around the throat. It is one of the most attractive colored fish taken from our coastal waters. The red snapper will average about 7 pounds, but 15 to 25 pounders are not uncommon. The largest on record is 55 pounds. The hard tough bones of the red snapper makes it a difficult fish to fillet and one must be extremely cautious for when the flesh is pierced by a red snapper bone and not taken care of properly and immediately, infection sets in quickly. This tasty salt water fish makes a popular menu entree when baked, broiled, steamed or poached.

Bluefish: True to its name this fish has a blue-green color above becoming lighter along the sides and silver on the belly. The edible flesh, which is lean, sweet and delicate in flavor, has a slight blue tone. Blue fish are abundant in the waters of the Atlantic from Florida to Maine. They are available on the market all year, but are most abundant in the New York markets from May to October. The average weight of a bluefish is 2 pounds. The largest catch on record is 24 pounds. Bluefish of finest quality will weigh between 4 to 5 pounds. Generally

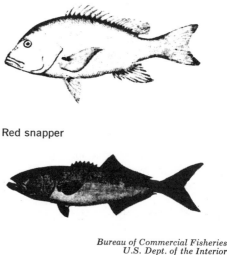

Red snapper

Bluefish

Bureau of Commercial Fisheries
U.S. Dept. of the Interior

speaking the heavier the fish the finer the quality. Bluefish is an excellent eating fish and is best broiled, sautéed or baked.

Pompano: Pompano is regarded as the choicest of all the salt water food fish. It has a firm, flaky white flesh and is usually quite expensive to purchase. Pompano are abundant in the South Atlantic and the Gulf of Mexico. The largest percentage of the catch is brought to the Florida markets. The average size is 2 pounds but the best for use in the commercial kitchen are the ones averaging ¾ to 1½ pounds. Pompano is a fatty fish and has a skin that is covered with very smooth scales and a color that is blue above, but silvery with a slight golden tone below. Pompano will produce the best eating qualities when sautéed, broiled or baked.

Spanish mackerel: Next to the Pompano, Spanish mackerel is considered the best flavored salt water fish. The flesh is firm, slightly dark in color and rich in flavor. The skin is a dark bluish-brown on black with golden spots both above and below the lateral line. The belly is a silver shade. The mackerel is a long streamlined fish, tapering towards the rear. Spanish mackerel is a fatty fish and ranges from Massachusetts to Brazil and is available on the market the year round. It will measure from 14 to 18 inches long and will weigh from 1 to 2½ pounds. The largest catch on record is 15 pounds 9 ounces. Spanish mackerel is a very popular menu item and for best results it should be cooked by broiling or baking.

Shad: Like the salmon the shad is a fat fish and comes in from the sea to ascend fresh water streams to spawn. The shad resembles the whitefish to a degree because it has slightly similar markings and skin color; however, here the resemblance stops. The shad is valuable not only for its edible flesh, but also because of the valuable roe that is re-

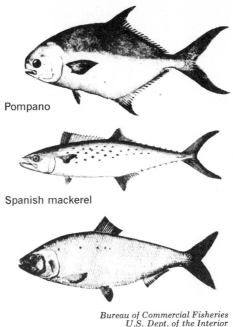

Pompano

Spanish mackerel

Shad

Bureau of Commercial Fisheries
U.S. Dept. of the Interior

moved from the female. The roe is considered a delicacy and is highly prized by gourmets. The shad can be found in both the Atlantic and Pacific Oceans and are most plentiful during the months of March, April and May. Shad will average about 4 pounds but will weigh as much as 12 pounds in some cases. The valuable roe weighs ¼ to 1 pound per pair. Shad fish is best when broiled or sautéed.

Butterfish: This fish, also commonly called dollarfish, is abundant in the middle and north Atlantic during the summer months, but disappear in the fall and winter months. Where they go is unknown, but it is believed they seek deeper waters. The butterfish will average in weight from ¼ to 1 pound and measure approximately 4 inches long; largest on record is 9 inches long. They are a fat fish and contain a high percentage of oil. They are excellent when pan fried and are considered as the best pan fish from the Atlantic waters. They have round firm bodies, a deep forked tail, a single, long thin dorsal (back) fin and a small head. Most of the catch is marketed in whole, drawn or dressed form; however, some is smoked. Butterfish may also be broiled with excellent results.

Croaker: This fish, also called crocus and hardhead, acquired its most common name from the unusual croaking sound made by both the male and female. The croaker is a lean fish and will average in weight from ½ to 2½ pounds; the largest on record is 6 pounds. They are most plentiful during the months of March to October but are available all year. Chesapeake Bay produces the largest catch; however, they are also taken from other areas of the Middle and South Atlantic. The croaker has a brassy color above the lateral line and a lighter color below with irregular, pale, vertical bars running the length of the fish. The upper portion of the fish is spotted with irregular dark brown spots. They have two dorsal fins. The first one is high the second low. The tail is concave and the head is fairly large for the size of the fish. They are marketed whole, dressed or in fillets. Although they are fairly cheap to purchase they have a fairly good eating quality when fried or broiled.

Hake: This fish is of the codfish family, but inferior in food value. The flesh is lean, but darker and more fibrous than the codfish. There are two major species of hake: squirrel hake and white hake; however, they are not separated when marketed. The squirrel will average 1 to 4 pounds in weight and measure approximately 1 to 2 feet long. The white usually run a little larger weighing 2 to 5 pounds and measuring 1½ to 3 feet long. They have a slender body, two sets of dorsal fins the first short, the second long, a forked tail and a pointed snout. The main production areas are the north and middle Atlantic during the months of September and October when the large

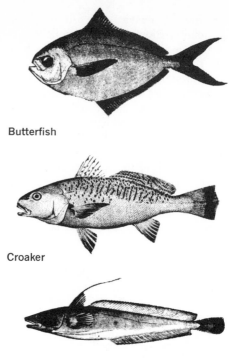

Butterfish

Croaker

Bureau of Commercial Fisheries
U.S. Dept. of the Interior

Hake, white

schools in which they usually travel come in to shore. On the market they can be purchased whole, drawn, dressed, or in fresh or smoked fillets. Sometimes they are substituted for haddock since the flesh and eating qualities are somewhat similar. Although hake is not a popular fish in the commercial kitchen, it can be made desirable if baked or poached and served with an appropriate sauce, such as creole or duglere.

Salmon: There are six varieties of salmon that are of commercial importance. They include the chinook, sockeye, coho, chum, humpback and Atlantic salmon. All salmon are fat fish and are important in one form or another in the commercial kitchen. They may be used in such preparations as salmon croquettes, salmon salad, poached salmon,

Salmon, chinook

broiled salmon steaks, etc. Salmon is graded according to variety and color of the flesh.

Chinook is rated as the finest of the Pacific Coast salmon. It has a deep-red flesh and a superb flavor. It is caught mainly in the Pacific Ocean and like all salmon will come in from the sea and seek fresh water streams to spawn. After the salmon lays its eggs it dies. This is characteristic of all Pacific Coast salmon, but not true of the Atlantic Coast variety. The Chinook is the largest of the Pacific salmon and will average about 20 pounds. The largest ever caught weighed 88 pounds. A large percentage of the Chinook catch is canned.

Sockeye is rated as the second best of the Pacific salmon. Like the Chinook it has a red flesh and excellent eating qualities. It is caught in the Pacific Ocean and rivers draining into the Pacific. Rivers such as the Columbia are an important source for sockeye. The sockeye will average 5 to 8 pounds; however, 12 pounders are not uncommon. Practically the entire catch of sockeye is canned.

Coho which is considered the third best of the Pacific salmon, has a deep pink flesh and a flavor that is rated good. The coho will average from 5 to 10 pounds, but 15 to 20 pounders are not uncommon. This variety of salmon is frequently called silver salmon. The largest percentage of the catch is canned.

Humpback salmon is so named because of a noticeable hump that develops in front of the dorsal fin on the male

salmon during the spawning season. The humpback is the smallest of the Pacific salmon and is rated the fourth best. It has a soft, pink flesh, but a surprisingly good flavor. It will average in weight from 4 to 6 pounds. A small part of the catch is sold fresh and frozen but most of it is canned.

Chum is classed as the poorest of the Pacific Coast salmon. It has pale yellow, soft flesh which contains little oil and has a poor flavor. It is relatively low in price because of its inferior quality. The chum salmon will average in weight from 4 to 8 pounds. A portion of the total catch is sold fresh and frozen, but the bulk is canned.

Atlantic salmon also called Kennebec salmon differs from the Pacific coast varieties in that it rarely dies after spawning. It will return to the sea and live and spawn a second time. The Kennebec comes mainly from the North Atlantic and the rivers and streams along the coast of Maine, Nova Scotia, Quebec, Labrador and New Brunswick. The flesh of the Kennebec is medium pink and the eating qualities are considered to be extremely good. It will average in weight from 10 to 15 pounds; however, salmon weighing over 20 pounds are frequently caught. The largest Atlantic salmon ever caught weighed 79 pounds. A large percentage of the Atlantic salmon catch is marketed fresh and frozen, the remainder is canned.

Salmon has become a popular menu entree from coast to coast. It can be presented on the menu in a variety of ways; however, it is best when prepared by poaching, broiling or baking. Frozen salmon should be used immediately once it is thawed because the flesh will soften quickly and become unpalatable.

POPULAR SHELLFISH

Shrimp: Shrimp is the most popular of the shellfish family. They have a ten-

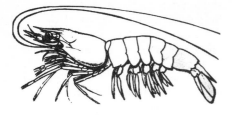

Bureau of Commercial Fisheries
U.S. Dept. of the Interior

Shrimp

der white meat with a distinctive flavor. Shrimp are also known as *prawns* in many quarters and although there may be a very slight difference between the two they are both marketed as shrimp in the United States. Only when our domestic product is shipped to England is the word "prawns" used. There are four kinds of shrimp taken from our coastal waters. The *common* or *white shrimp,* which has a greenish gray color when caught; the *brown* or *Brazilian shrimp,* which is brownish red in color; the *pink* or *coral shrimp,* which have a medium or deep pink color; and the *Alaska* and *California shrimp,* which will vary in color and are small in size. Although these four kinds of shrimp vary in color when caught they differ very little in appearance and flavor when cooked. Only the tail section of the shrimp is edible. The whole shrimp may be sold fresh near the source of supply, but the majority of the catch is processed, by removing the head and the thorax (body), frozen in 5 pound blocks or consumer sized packages, and shipped throughout the country. Shrimp like most seafood will perish rapidly so it must be cooked, frozen or packed in ice and refrigerated immediately after processing. Shrimp are sold according to size or grade. The size or grade of the shrimp is important to the food service operator from the standpoint of time and cost. The jumbo and large shrimp will cost the most, but take less time to peel and clean. The smaller

shrimp will cost less, but take longer to peel and clean because there are more of them. All shrimp have the same distinctive flavor and food value. All uncooked shrimp are referred to as green shrimp. Boiling is the basic method of cooking shrimp, although frying is another extremely popular method. Shrimp are a very versatile item in the commercial kitchen and are featured on the menu in the form of an appetizer, entree or salad.

Lobster: Lobster, often called the king of the shellfish, is the largest of the shellfish group. It has a sweet tasting, white meated flesh that is highly prized as food. There are two types of lobsters available on the market. The cold water lobster, coming mainly from the North Atlantic, and the spiny lobster, which is nearly worldwide in its distribution, coming from the warmer waters of the Atlantic, Pacific and Indian Oceans.

The *cold water lobster* has a dark bluish-green shell, two large heavy claws, a medium size antenna, and four slender legs on each side of the body. The whole lobster is edible except for a small section of membranes located around the eye and, of course, the shell. Cold water lobsters are sold alive and must be kept alive up to the time of cooking. They are available on the market all year; however, they are most plentiful during the summer months when they come closer to shore. Lobsters will vary in size and are graded according to size. It is very seldom that a lobster weighing over 3 pounds can be found in the commercial kitchen; however, some have been trapped weighing as much as 20 pounds. These very large lobsters come from deep waters some distance from shore.

Spiny lobsters, or *rock lobsters* which they are sometimes called, have many prominent spines on its body and legs, a very long slender antenna, no claws and 5 very slender legs on each side of the body. Only the tail section is edible and

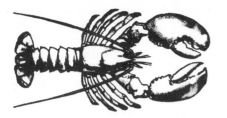

Cold water lobster

the flesh is coarser in texture and not as delicate in flavor as the cold water lobster. The degree of smoothness of the spiny's shell and the way the shell is spotted or marked will depend on the part of the world it comes from. For instance, spiny lobsters from Florida and Cuba have slightly smooth shells with large yellowish spots on the brownish-green colored tail section. South Africa and New Zealand spiny lobsters have rough shells with no spots on the brownish-maroon colored tail sections. When trapped the tail section of the spiny, which will weigh from 4 ounces to 1 pound, is frozen and shipped to market.

The shell of all lobsters will turn red when cooked and it is from this change that the expression "lobster red" was acquired. Lobster, regardless of the type, is an extremely popular item in the commercial kitchen and is placed on the menu in a variety of ways. When preparing lobsters the best cooking methods are broiling, boiling or steaming.

Oysters: Oysters have been a food delicacy for an extremely long time. They have graced the elaborate banquet tables of the Romans and when America was discovered the new settlers realized the richness of the new land when large oysters in great abundance were found.

There are three important species of oysters. The *Eastern Oyster,* which comprises about 89 percent of all the oyster production in the United States, is found along the Atlantic and Gulf Coast from Massachusetts to Texas. The *olympia oyster,* which is quite small is found on the Pacific coast from Washington to Mexico. The *Japanese oyster,* which is quite large, is found on the Pacific coast. This oyster was introduced from Japan in the year 1902 and today is cultivated in fairly large quantities. The West Coast produces only 11 percent of the total oyster catch. Today most oysters are cultivated in beds that require much care and attention if they are to continue to produce. Along the Atlantic Coast, Chesapeake Bay is one of the biggest oyster producing areas. Most states along the Atlantic Seaboard will produce oysters, except the states of Maine and New Hampshire where the oyster beds were destroyed years ago. The United States produces approximately 90 million pounds of oysters a year.

Oysters are at their best from September to April, but they are available the year round. Oysters of good quality are plump, well-shaped and surrounded by a clear jelly-like, semi liquid. Oysters must have a tightly closed shell to be of good quality. If the shell is gaping the oyster is dead and not edible. Oysters have a special appeal to the cooks and chefs in the commercial kitchen, not only because of their delicious flavor, but also because of the ease with which they can be prepared and served. Oysters may be eaten raw or prepared by poaching or frying. Regardless of the cooking method used the secret of proper oyster cooking is to apply just enough heat to heat them through, leaving them plump and tender. Avoid overcooking.

Scallops: This is the large adductor muscle which opens and closes the scallop shell. It is a solid section of cream colored flesh, that is very lean, juicy, and possesses a sweet delicate flavor. There are two types of scallops on the market: bay scallops, and sea scallops. The *bay scallops* are taken from shallow waters and are fairly small. They are considered to have the best flavor and usually are higher in price than the sea scallops. The *sea scallops* come from deep waters, are larger in size and have a coarser texture. Scallops are available on the market all year, but are best during the months of April to October. The Atlantic Coast is the largest producer of scallops with small quantities coming from the Gulf of Mexico. The scallop shell is shaped like a fan and when polished displays many interesting colors that are pleasing to the eye. Many food service operators use the scallop shells as a serving dish when featuring certain seafood appetizers and entrees.

Color is the best way to judge the quality of a scallop. The best quality will have a cream color, if they are white it indicates they have been packed in ice water and the flavor impaired. If they possess a brownish color it indicates they are slightly old. Scallops are a popular seafood in the commercial kitchen and are best when fried or sautéed; however, they may be poached and broiled with fairly good results.

Clams: There are several species of clams that are used for food. The varieties on the market will depend on the source of supply because the varieties of the East Coast differ from those of the West Coast.

The Atlantic Coast produces three important species: the soft clam, hard clam and surf clam. The *soft clam,* also known as the long-neck clam, is taken from the waters of Cape Cod north to the Arctic Ocean. This is the clam that is so popular in the New England area. The *hard clam* is found in abundance south of Cape Cod. Hard clams are sometimes referred to as "quahaug" by the people of New England. This is an old Indian name for the hard shell clams. The small sized hard clams are known as littlenecks and cherrystones and are usually served, in food service establishments, raw on the half shell in the same manner as oysters. The larger hard clams are called chowders and are used mainly in soups and chowders. The hard clam has a stronger flavor than the soft or surf clam. *Surf clams* have a sweet flavor and are not as important or desirable as the other two, mainly because they are usually gritty. They are sometimes used in chowders and soup, but are used mainly for the production of clam juice and broth.

The Pacific coast produces four important species: the butter, razor, littleneck and pismo clams. The *butter clam* is a hard shell clam possessing a very desirable flavor. The *razor clam* is so named because of its sharp razor edge shell. The *Pacific littleneck* is a different species from the Atlantic littleneck and to a degree lacks the flavor of the Atlantic variety. The *pismo clam* comes from a coastal area in California, made famous by these delicious clams, called Pismo Beach.

Clams are presented in many different ways on menus of food service establishments. The most popular of which is clam chowder. The chowder has been and will continue to be the most famous of the many clam preparations. Clams can also be fried and steamed with excellent results.

Crabs: They have become a very popular shellfish because of their tender, juicy, sweet tasting meat that can be converted into many delightful menu items. There are four principal kinds of crabs taken from the waters of the Atlantic and Pacific Oceans that are available on the market: the blue crab, dungeness crab, king crab and rock crab.

The *blue crab* comes from the Atlantic Coast and comprises about three fourths of all the crabs marketed in the United

States. It measures about 5 inches across its shell and weighs approximately 5 ounces. When the blue crab molts (sheds its hard shell) it is marketed as a soft-shell crab. The molting season is in the spring of the year. This is when the soft-shell crab is available on the market. The soft-shell crab is handled and packed with special care so they arrive at their destination alive. Soft-shell crabs must be alive up to the time of cooking, unless, of course, they are cleaned and quick frozen. The hard-shell blue crab is marketed alive within comparatively short distances from the point of capture, but can not be obtained alive at points inland because they do not ship well. The majority of the hard-shell blue crabs are marketed as frozen or canned cooked meat.

Dungeness crabs are found on the Pacific Coast from Alaska to Mexico. It is larger than the blue crab, weighing approximately 1¾ to 4 pounds. The meat has a pinkish tinge and a very desirable sweetest taste. The bulk of the catch is marketed as frozen and canned cooked meat.

King crabs come from the North Pacific off the coast of Alaska. It is the largest of the crab family, weighing from 6 to 20 pounds and measuring as much as 6 feet from the tip of one leg to the tip of the opposite leg. The meat has a pinkish tinge similar to that of the dungeness crab. It is marketed as frozen cooked meat, frozen cooked in shell, and canned cooked meat.

Rock crabs are taken from the coastal waters of California and New England. They are small in size weighing approximately 4 to 8 ounces and measuring about 3 inches across its shell. The meat is brownish in color and considered to be inferior to the white meat of the blue crab. Rock crabs are marketed live, but the bulk of the catch is sold as fresh cooked meat and canned meat.

All kinds of crabmeat are important to the food service industry because this tender, flaky sweet tasting meat is always popular, whether served as an appetizer, salad or entrée. The more versatile the chef can become when placing crabmeat items on his menu the more pleased his discriminating guest will be and in all probability the result will be increased sales.

Dungeness crab

Blue crab

Bureau of Commercial Fisheries
U.S. Dept. of the Interior

King crab

FISH AND SHELLFISH RECIPES

In serving fish and other seafoods, the importance of an attractive and appetizing garnish should not be overlooked. A dash of color or a touch of garnish can turn a plain dish into a highly satisfying one. Some of the common garnishes, with their suggested methods of preparation, are listed in Table VII. The sauces served with seafood preparations also contribute a great deal to the success of the recipe. The method of preparation will determine the kind of sauce to be used. Table VIII is designed to assist the student in making sauce selections for fish and shellfish, depending upon the way they are prepared. Note that some sauces are served to the sides of the prepared item.

The following fish and shellfish recipes are just a few of the time-proven favorites. They do not scratch the surface of the many fish and shellfish preparations found on menus throughout the country; however, they will provide the student with a background upon which to build.

TABLE VII. GARNISHES FOR FISH

Garnishes	Suggested Preparation
Beets	Cooked whole or slices
Carrots	Tops, sticks, curls, or shredded
Celery	Tops, hearts, sticks, or curls
Chives	Chopped
Cucumbers	Slices or sticks
Dill	Sprigs or chopped
Green or red peppers	Sticks or rings
Hard-cooked eggs	Slices, wedges, deviled, or grated yolks
Lemons or limes	Slices, twists, or wedges
Lettuce	Leaves or shredded
Mint	Sprigs or chopped
Nut meats	Toasted whole, halved, slivered, or chopped
Olives	Whole, sliced, or chopped
Oranges	Slices, twists, or wedges
Paprika	Sprinkled sparingly
Parsley	Sprigs or chopped
Pickles	Whole, sliced, or chopped
Radishes	Whole, sliced, or roses
Water cress	Sprigs or chopped

TABLE VIII. SAUCES ASSOCIATED WITH FISH AND SEAFOODS

Sautéd	Broiled	Baked	Poached, Boiled or Steamed	Fried
Meuniere	Lemon butter	Divine	Mornay	Dill
Colbert	Anchovy butter	Maximillian	Mousseline	Cocktail
Bercy	Colbert	Cherburg	Divine	Tartar
Chateau	Bercy	Choron	Maximillian	
Anchovy butter	Chateau	Figaro	Cherburg	
Lemon butter	*Dill	Creole	Mousseline	
Oriental sweet-sour	*Choron	Duglere	Choron	
*Dill	*Cherburg	Homard	Figaro	
*Homard	*Maxmillian	Victoria	Creole	
*Choron	*Divine	Caper	Velouté (vin blanc)	
*Cherburg		Cardinal	Bonne Femme	
		Newburg	Duglere	
		Mustard	Homard	
			Victoria	
			Caper	
			Curry	
			Cardinal	
			Newburg	
			Mustard	
			Egg	
			Dill	

*Denotes sauces that should be served on the side of the prepared item. The sauce may be served in a goose neck container, soufflé cup or other appropriate container. (Sauce recipes are given in Chapter 15. Butter sauce recipes are given in Chapters 8 and 15.)

Fried and sautéed fish
(Pages 501 to 504)

Deep fried fish fillets
Salmon croquettes
Fried seafood platter
Sautéed fish

Broiled and baked fish
(Pages 504 to 508)

Broiled fish
Broiled fillet of sole English style
Baked fish (fillets and steaks)
Baked red snapper creole
Baked seafood casserole au gratin
Stuffed fillet of flounder

Poached fish
(Pages 508 to 509)

Poached fish
Poached halibut duglere

Fried shellfish
(Pages 509 to 512)

Fried soft-shell crabs
Fried oysters or clams
Fried scallops or shrimp
Lobster and shrimp croquettes

Poached or steamed (in sauce) shellfish
(Pages 512 to 517)

Lobster or shrimp curry
Creamed lobster
Coquilles St. Jacques mornay
Lobster thermidor
Scalloped oysters
Lobster, shrimp or crabmeat
    Newburg
Shrimp, lobster or seafood creole
Crabmeat imperial

Baked and broiled shellfish
(Pages 517 to 519)

Deviled crabs
Shrimp pilau
Broiled lobster

FRIED AND SAUTEED FISH RECIPES
Deep fried fish fillets

Most of the lean type fish, such as halibut, haddock and flounders, are best for frying. Fish must be breaded before frying to acquire the crisp golden brown coating. Deep fried fish are most suitable when speed of service and preparation is stressed.

Objectives
1. To teach the student the procedure for preparing deep fried fish.
2. To teach the student how to fry and serve the fish.

Equipment
1. Deep fat fryer
2. Qt. measure
3. French knife
4. Wire whip
5. 3 bake pans
6. 2 qt. stainless steel container
7. Fry baskets
8. Baker's scale

Ingredients: Approx. yield: 25 servings
25 5 oz. fish fillets
 6 whole eggs
 1 qt. liquid milk
 1 lb. flour
 1 lb. 8 ozs. bread crumbs
    salt and pepper to taste

Preparation
1. Cut the fish fillets in 5 oz. portions with a French knife.
2. Prepare an egg wash: break the eggs into a stainless steel container. Beat slightly with a wire whip. Pour in the milk and blend with the eggs.
3. Have all the equipment and ingredients handy.
4. Preheat deep fat fryer to 350°F.

Procedure
1. Place the flour in a bake pan, season with salt and pepper.
2. Add the fish and coat thoroughly.
3. Pour the egg wash into the second bake pan. Remove each portion of fish from the flour and place in the egg wash.
4. Place the bread crumbs in the third bake pan. Dip each piece of fish into the bread crumbs, press on the crumbs thoroughly. Shake off excess.
5. Place in fry basket and fry in deep fat until golden brown and done, let drain.

Fried breaded haddock fillets

6. Serve garnished with a wedge or slice of lemon and tartar or fish sauce. (See Chap. 15 for sauce recipes.)

Precautions and Safety Measures

1. Use caution when handling the knife to avoid cutting self.
2. Do not fry too many orders at one time. The temperature of the fat will reduce too much and the pieces will not cook evenly.
3. Do not overcook. Most fried fish is done when it starts to float on the surface.

Salmon croquettes

For salmon croquettes the drained canned salmon is bound together in a thick cream sauce, cooled and shaped into croquettes. They are breaded and deep fried to a golden brown and served with an appropriate sauce. Salmon croquettes makes an excellent luncheon entree.

Objectives

1. To teach the student the procedure for preparing salmon croquettes.
2. To teach the student how to form, bread and fry the croquettes.
3. To teach the student how to serve salmon croquettes.

Equipment

1. French knife
2. Baker's scale
3. Sauce pot, 2 gal.
4. Deep fat fryer
5. Fry baskets
6. 3 bake pans
7. Kitchen spoon
8. Wire whip
9. 2 qt. stainless steel container
10. 2 qt. sauce pan

Ingredients: Approx. yield: 25 servings

CROQUETTES

4	lbs. salmon, canned, drained
10	ozs. onions, minced
10	ozs. butter or shortening
10	ozs. bread flour
1	qt. milk, hot
½	cup parsley, chopped
	salt and pepper to taste
6	egg yolks

BREADING

1	lb. flour
2	lbs. bread crumbs
1½	qts. egg wash (9 eggs to 1½ qts. of milk)

Preparation

1. Open the canned salmon, drain, and remove the bones.
2. Mince the onions with a French knife.
3. Heat the milk in a pan.
4. Prepare an egg wash. Break the 9 eggs into a stainless steel container, beat with a wire whip, pour in the 1½ qts. of milk, and blend with the eggs.
5. Chop the parsley with a French knife.
6. Preheat the deep fat fryer to 350°F.
7. Have all equipment and ingredients handy.

Procedure

1. Place the butter or shortening in a sauce pot, heat.
2. Add the onions and sauté slightly, do not brown.
3. Add the flour, making a roux, cook slowly for 5 minutes.
4. Add the hot milk, stirring constantly with a kitchen spoon until thickened and smooth, simmer for about 5 minutes.
5. Add the salmon and chopped parsley, blend in thoroughly with a kitchen spoon.
6. Season with salt and pepper. Remove from the range. Let cool slightly.
7. Beat the egg yolks, in a stainless steel container with a wire whip and pour very slowly into the croquette mixture while stirring rapidly with a kitchen spoon.
8. Turn the mixture into a shallow pan cover and refrigerate overnight.
9. Remove the mixture from the refrigerator, shape into uniform croquettes.
10. Bread by following the proper breading procedure of passing each croquette through flour, egg wash and bread crumbs.

11. Fry in deep fat at 350°F until golden brown.
12. Serve 1 or 2 croquettes, depending on desired size, to each order with an appropriate sauce. (See Table VIII for suggested sauces.)

Precautions and Safety Measures
1. Use caution when handling the knife.
2. Stir the mixture occasionally while it is cooking to avoid sticking or scorching.
3. Pour the beaten egg yolks very slowly into the mixture to avoid scrambling.
4. When frying do not overfill the fry baskets. The croquettes will not cook evenly and the temperature of the grease will reduce rapidly.
5. Do not overbrown the croquettes.

Fried seafood platter

This is a combination dish consisting of fish and shellfish which are breaded and deep fried to a crisp golden brown. Fried seafood platters are usually served with tartar or cocktail sauce on the luncheon, dinner or à la carte menu.

Objectives
1. To teach the student the procedure for preparing a fried seafood platter.
2. To teach the student how to fry and dish up a seafood platter.

Equipment
1. French knife
2. 3 bake pans
3. Wire whip
4. Qt. measure
5. Baker's scale
6. Fry baskets
7. 2 qt. stainless steel container

Ingredients: Approx. yield: 10 servings

30	pieces of raw shrimp, peeled and deveined
30	scallops
30	oysters
10	3 oz. sticks fillet of sole (halibut)
9	whole eggs
1½	qts. liquid milk
1	lb. bread flour
2	lbs. bread crumbs (variable)
	salt and pepper to taste

Preparation
1. Cut the fish with a French knife and prepare both the fish and shellfish for bread-ing. Proceed only after demonstration by instructor.
2. Prepare an egg wash: Break eggs into a stainless steel container, beat slightly with a wire whip, pour in the milk and blend with the eggs.
3. Set deep fat fryer at 350°F.
4. Have all equipment and ingredients handy.

Procedure
1. Place the flour in a bake pan, season with salt and pepper.
2. Add the assorted pieces of seafood and coat thoroughly.
3. Pour the egg wash into the second bake pan. Remove the seafood from the flour and place in the egg wash.
4. Place the bread crumbs in the third bake pan. Remove the seafood from the egg wash and place in the bread crumbs, press the crumbs on firmly, shake off the excess.
5. Place in fry baskets and fry until golden brown, let drain.
6. For each portion dish up 3 shrimp, 3 scallops, 3 oysters and 1 fish stick. Serve with tartar or cocktail sauce and a slice or wedge of lemon. (See Chap. 15 for sauce recipes.)

Precautions and Safety Measures
1. Press the breading on firmly so the breading will not fall off while frying.
2. Do not overbrown or the servings will lack appearance.
3. Do not fry too many pieces at one time. The temperature of the fat will reduce too quickly and frying will not be uniform.

Sautéed fish

Small whole fish or fillets are best for sautéing. The fish is seasoned and coated with flour before it is placed in the hot grease. It is cooked until golden brown on both sides. This is an excellent method for preparing fish when speed of service is required.

Objectives
1. To teach the student the procedure for preparing sautéed fish.
2. To teach the student how to serve sautéed fish.

Equipment
1. French knife
2. Qt. measure
3. Spoon measure

4. Skillet
5. Kitchen fork
6. Bake pan

Ingredients: Approx. yield: 25 servings

25 small whole, dressed fish or 5 oz. fillets or steaks
1 qt. flour
2 tsp. paprika
   salt and pepper to taste

Preparation

1. If cutting 5 oz. fillets or steaks, use a French knife.
2. Have all equipment and ingredients handy.

Procedure

1. Place in a bake pan the flour, paprika, salt and pepper and mix by hand.
2. Pass each portion of fish through the flour mixture, press firmly so flour will adhere to the fish.
3. Place enough shortening in the skillet to cover the bottom of the pan about ¼ in. deep, heat.
4. Add fish and sauté until golden brown on each side. Turn with a kitchen fork. Remove and let drain.
5. Serve with meuniere sauce, butter or a sauce of your choice that will compliment the kind of fish being sautéed. Sautéed fish is best when served with a thin light sauce. (See Table VIII for suggested sauces.) Garnish each serving with a wedge or slice of lemon.

Precautions and Safety Measures

1. The fat should be hot before placing the fish in the pan. This will prevent sticking. If skin is left on the fish, place skin side up.
2. Exercise caution when turning the fish in the pan to avoid burning self.
3. Sauté at a moderate temperature. The temperature is regulated by moving the pan towards or away from the fire.

BROILED AND BAKED FISH RECIPES

Broiled fish

Broiling is an excellent method of cooking fish. Fat fish broil the best, but many lean fish are cooked by this method with good results. All fish should be broiled to order. A thin sauce such as butter sauce, lemon butter or anchovy butter is usually served with broiled fish.

Objectives

1. To teach the student the procedure for broiling fish.
2. To teach the student how to serve broiled fish.

Equipment

1. Bake pan
2. Cup measure
3. French knife

Ingredients: Approx. yield: 25 servings

25 5 oz. fish steaks or fillets
1 cup salad oil
¼ cup paprika
   salt and pepper to taste

Preparation

1. Cut 5 oz. steaks or cut fillets into 5 oz. portions with a French knife.
2. Have all equipment and ingredients handy.
3. Light broiler and turn heat to highest point.

Procedure

1. Place the salad oil in a bake pan.
2. Place each piece of fish in the oil.
3. Season with salt and pepper and sprinkle the paprika on the flesh side of the fish.
4. Remove the fish from the oil and place on a hot broiler rack, skin side up if skin is left on.
5. Broil 6 in. from the heat for approx. 5 min. on each side and until the flesh side is slightly brown.
6. Remove and serve with a butter sauce and a wedge or slice of lemon. (See Chapters 8 and 15 for butter sauce recipes.)

Precautions and Safety Measures

1. Use caution when handling the knife to avoid cutting self.
2. Exercise caution when turning the fish on the broiler, some fish will break easily.
3. Do not overcook the fish.

Broiled fillet of sole English style

For broiled fillet of sole English style the halibut fish used is cut into 3 oz. sticks. The sticks are passed through salad oil and bread crumbs and broiled under very low heat. Two sticks are served to each order with a generous amount of butter sauce. A favorite on the luncheon menu.

Objectives
1. To teach the student the procedure for preparing fillet of sole English style.
2. To teach the student how to cut, broil and serve the fish.

Equipment
1. French knife
2. Sheet pans (2)
3. Bake pan
4. Meat turner or kitchen fork
5. Broiler
6. Pt. measure
7. Baker's scale

Ingredients: Approx. yield: 25 servings

9½ lbs. halibut, boned and skinned, cut into 3 oz. sticks
1   pt. salad oil (variable)
2   lbs. bread crumbs
    salt and pepper to taste

Preparation
1. Light the broiler, turn the flame low.
2. Cut the halibut into 3 oz. sticks with a French knife.
3. Have all equipment and ingredients handy.

Procedure
1. Coat the sheet pans quite heavy with salad oil.
2. Roll each piece of fish in the salad oil, coating thoroughly. Season with salt and pepper.
3. Place the bread crumbs in a bake pan. Remove the fish from the salad oil and roll it in the bread crumbs, press the crumbs on the fish firmly.
4. Return the fish to the oil covered pans, rolling each piece in the oil a second time to moisten the crumbs slightly.
5. Place the pans under the broiler and broil very slowly until crumbs become light brown on top.
6. Remove the pans from the broiler and place on top the range for a few minutes to cook the bottom of the fish.
7. Remove from the range and remove fish from the pan with a fork or meat turner.
8. Serve two sticks to each order with a generous amount of butter sauce. (See Chapters 8 and 15 for buttter sauce recipes.) Garnish with a wedge or slice of lemon.

Baked fish (fillets or steaks)

Baking is similar to roasting in that it is a form of dry heat cooking. When baking lean fish some form of liquid or sauce is added to prevent drying; however, if the fish has a high fat content the addition of a liquid or sauce is unnecessary.

Objectives
1. To teach the student the procedure for baking fish.
2. To teach the student how to cut and serve the fish.

Equipment
1. Cup measures
2. French knife
3. 2 bake pans
4. 1 sheet pan

Ingredients: Approx. yield: 25 servings

25   5 oz. fish steaks or fillets
1½ cups salad oil
½   cup lemon juice
¼   cup paprika
     salt and pepper to taste

Preparation
1. Cut 5 oz. steaks or cut fillets into 5 oz. portions with a French knife.
2. Light the oven and preheat to 400°F.
3. Have all equipment and ingredients handy.

Procedure
1. Place the salad oil in a sheet pan.
2. Dip each steak or fillet in the oil, coat thoroughly. Place in a bake pan.
3. Season the fish with salt and pepper
4. Pour the lemon juice over the fish.
5. Sprinkle the paprika on each portion.
6. Place in the oven and bake at 400°F until slightly brown and done.
7. Remove from the oven and serve with creole sauce, duglere sauce (See Chap. 15) or a sauce of your choice that will compliment the kind of fish being baked. (See Table VIII for suggested sauces.)

Precautions and Safety Measures
1. Use caution when handling the knife.
2. Do not overcook or fish will become extremely dry.
3. Exercise caution when serving baked fish as it will break and crumble easily.

Baked red snapper creole

For baked red snapper creole the fillets of red snapper are baked and each portion is served covered with a generous amount of creole sauce. Baked red snapper creole can be served on either the luncheon or dinner menu with excellent results.

Objectives
1. To teach the student the procedure for preparing baked red snapper creole.
2. To teach the student how to bake and serve the red snapper.

Equipment
1. Sheet pan
2. Cup measure
3. French knife
4. Qt. measure
5. Bake pans

Ingredients: Approx. yield: 25 servings

9	lbs. red snapper, fillets, cut into $5\frac{1}{2}$ to 6 oz. portions
$1\frac{1}{2}$	cups salad oil (variable)
$\frac{1}{2}$	cup lemon juice
	paprika as needed
	salt and pepper to taste
2	qts. creole sauce

Preparation
1. Cut the red snapper fillets into $5\frac{1}{2}$ to 6 oz. portions with a French knife.
2. Light the oven and preheat to 400°F.
3. Prepare creole sauce. (See Chap. 15.)
4. Have the equipment and ingredients handy.

Procedure
1. Place the salad oil in a sheet pan.
2. Dip each red snapper fillet in the oil, coat thoroughly. Place in bake pans.
3. Season with salt and pepper.
4. Pour the lemon juice over the fish.
5. Sprinkle the paprika over each fish.
6. Place in the preheated oven and bake at 400°F until slightly brown and done.
7. Remove and serve each portion covered with a generous amount of creole sauce.

Precautions and Safety Measures
1. Use caution when handling the knife.
2. Do not overbake the fish, it will become dry and unappetizing.

Baked seafood casserole au gratin

For baked seafood casserole au gratin the assorted fish and shellfish selected is placed in a rich cream sauce, portioned out into individual casseroles, covered with cheese and baked until golden brown. This eye appealing entree is an ideal selection for the luncheon or dinner menu.

Objectives
1. To teach the student the procedure for preparing a baked seafood casserole au gratin.

2. To teach the student how to set up and serve a baked seafood casserole au gratin.

Equipment
1. Sauce pot, 2 gal.
2. Baker's scale
3. French knife
4. Kitchen spoon
5. Cup measure
6. Pt. measure
7. Spoon measure
8. 25 shallow casseroles
9. Box grater

Ingredients: Approx. yield: 25 servings

3	lbs. shrimp, cooked, peeled, deveined, cut in half
2	lbs. king crabmeat, cooked, thawed, flaked
3	lbs. cod fish, cooked, flaked
4	ozs. butter
1	cup onions, minced
2	small bay leaves
1	lb. mushrooms, diced small
8	oz. sherry wine
$2\frac{1}{2}$	qts. cream sauce, medium consistency
4	tbsp. chives, chopped
1	pt. Parmesan or Cheddar cheese, grated
	salt and white pepper to taste

Preparation
1. Cook, peel and flake, or thaw and cut the fish and shellfish into uniform pieces with a French knife.
2. Prepare the cream sauce. (See Chap. 15.)
3. Mince the onions and chop the chives with a French knife.
4. Dice the mushrooms with a French knife.
5. Grate the cheese on a box grater.
6. Light the broiler and set flame low.
7. Have all equipment and ingredients handy.

Procedure
1. Place the butter in a sauce pot, heat.
2. Add the onions and mushrooms, sauté until slightly tender.
3. Add the bay leaves, shrimp, crabmeat, cod fish and sherry wine. Cover the pot and cook on low heat for 3 minutes.
4. Add the cream sauce and stir with a kitchen spoon. Season with salt and white pepper, and simmer for 5 minutes.
5. Add the chives, blend in thoroughly with a kitchen spoon, simmer for 3 minutes. Remove from the range and remove the bay leaves.

6. Place a 6 to 8 oz. ladled portion in each individual shallow casserole. Sprinkle the Parmesan or Cheddar cheese over the top.
7. Dust the top of each casserole lightly with paprika and cook slowly under the broiler until golden brown.
8. Serve at once garnished with a sprig of parsley.

Precautions and Safety Measures
1. Use caution when handling the knife.
2. Stir in the cream sauce gently so the seafood will not be broken into small pieces.
3. When sautéing the onions and mushrooms do not let them brown.
4. While the mixture is simmering stir occasionally to avoid sticking.

Stuffed fillet of flounder

For stuffed fiillet of flounder the flat flounder fillets are rolled around a crabmeat stuffing, baked and served with a lemon butter sauce. A good selection for adding variety to the seafood choices on the dinner menu.

Objectives
1. To teach the student the procedure for preparing stuffed fillet of flounder.
2. To teach the student how to stuff, bake and serve stuffed fillet of flounder.

Equipment
1. Baker's scale
2. French knife
3. 2 sauce pans, 2 and 4 qts.
4. Kitchen spoon
5. Measuring spoons
6. Qt. measure

National Marketing Service Office
Bureau of Commercial Fisheries
U.S. Dept. of the Interior
Stuffed flounder

7. Bake pan
8. Tooth picks

Ingredients: Approx. yield: 25 servings

9	lbs. fillet of flounder, cut into 5 or 6 oz. pieces
4	lbs. king crabmeat, frozen
12	ozs. celery, minced
12	ozs. onions, minced
6	ozs. green pepper, minced
12	ozs. butter
4	ozs. flour
1	qt. milk, hot
4	tbsp. Worcestershire sauce
1/4	tsp. Tabasco sauce
3	tbsp. prepared mustard
10	ozs. bread crumbs
4	egg yolks
	salt and pepper to taste

Preparation
1. Cut the flounder into 5 or 6 oz. fillets with a French knife.
2. Thaw out the frozen crabmeat.
3. Mince the onions, celery and green pepper with a French knife.
4. Heat the milk in a sauce pan.
5. Separate the eggs, save the whites for use in another preparation.
6. Preheat the oven to 375°F.
7. Have all equipment and ingredients handy.

Procedure
1. Place the butter in a sauce pan and melt.
2. Add the onions, celery and green peppers. Sauté until slightly tender.
3. Add the flour and continue to cook for 5 minutes longer.
4. Add the hot milk and stir constantly with a kitchen spoon until mixture thickens.
5. Add the Worcestershire sauce, Tabasco, mustard and crabmeat. Mix thoroughly with a kitchen spoon. Cook for 5 minutes and remove from the fire.
6. Stir in the egg yolks and the bread crumbs with a kitchen spoon. Season with salt and pepper. Let cool slightly.
7. Place a portion of the stuffing on each flounder fillet, roll up and secure with a tooth pick.
8. Place the rolled fillets in a baking pan. Place in the oven and bake at 350°F for approximately 30 minutes. After the first 10 minutes of the baking period add a small amount of melted butter and water to the pan to prevent sticking.
9. Remove from the oven, remove tooth

picks and serve with lemon butter, cardinal sauce or duglère sauce. (See Chap. 15 for butter sauce recipes.)

Precautions and Safety Measures
1. Use caution when handling the knife.
2. When sautéing the vegetables, do not let them brown.
3. Secure the rolled fillets properly so they will not unroll during the baking period.

POACHED FISH RECIPES

Poached fish

Boiling, poaching and steaming are quite similar. The difference lies in the amount of liquid used and the cooking temperature. Since poaching is done at a simmering temperature (200°F) and slow cooking will produce best results with fish, this method is recommended. Fish should be poached in a liquid that is called *court bouillon*. Court bouillon consists of celery, onions, carrots, water, vinegar or lemon juice, salt and spices if desired. Most poached fish are served with some type of thickened sauce.

Objectives
1. To teach the student the procedure for preparing poached fish.
2. To teach the student how to serve poached fish.

Equipment
1. Qt. measure
2. Baker's scale
3. French knife
4. Deep bake pan
5. Sauce pan
6. China cap

Ingredients: Approx. yield: 25 servings

12	lbs. of dressed fish
3	lemons sliced
12	ozs. celery, diced
8	ozs. onions, diced
10	ozs. carrots, diced
2	ozs. salt
1	gal. water
1	tsp. whole peppercorns
	butter as needed

Preparation
1. Dice the onions, carrots and celery with a French knife.
2. Slice the lemons with a French knife.
3. Have all equipment and ingredients handy.

Procedure
1. Place the water, celery, onions, carrots, salt, peppercorns and lemons in a sauce pan. Simmer for 30 minutes.
2. Strain the liquid through a fine china cap. This is your court bouillon.
3. Grease the bottom and sides of a slightly deep bake pan. Line the fish in the pan. This fish may be whole, steaks or fillets.
4. Pour over the court bouillon, place on the range and continue to poach (simmer) until done.
5. Remove from the range and serve with a sauce prepared from the court bouillon or a sauce of your choice that will compliment the kind of fish being poached. (See Table VIII for suggested sauces.)

Precautions and Safety Measures
1. Use caution when handling the knife to avoid cutting self.
2. For best results start poaching fairly large fish in cold court bouillon. Small ones in hot court bouillon.
3. Always coat the bottom of the poaching pan with butter or oil to prevent sticking.
4. Avoid overcooking or fish will break and become difficult to serve.

Poached halibut duglère

For poached halibut duglère the halibut is poached in a court bouillon and served covered with a generous amount of duglère sauce. This entrée is an excellent choice for either the luncheon or dinner menu.

Objectives
1. To teach the student the procedure for preparing poached halibut duglère.
2. To teach the student how to poach and serve the halibut.

Equipment
1. Deep bake pans
2. French knife
3. China cap
4. Sauce pan, 6 qt.
5. Baker's scale
6. Qt. measure
7. Spoon measure

Ingredients: Approx. yield: 25 servings

9	lbs. halibut, fillets, cut into 5½ to 6 oz. portions
2	lemons, sliced
8	ozs. celery, diced
6	ozs. onions, diced

6 ozs. carrots, diced
1 oz. salt
3 qts. water
½ tsp. peppercorn
butter as needed
3 qts. Duglere sauce

Preparation
1. Dice the onions, carrots and celery with a French knife.
2. Slice the lemons with a French knife.
3. Grease the bake pans with butter.
4. Cut the halibut fillets into 5½ to 6 oz. portions with a French knife.
5. Have all equipment and ingredients handy.
6. Prepare the duglère sauce (See Chap. 15.

Procedure
1. Place the water, celery, onions, carrots, salt, peppercorns and lemons in a sauce pan. Simmer for 30 minutes.
2. Strain the liquid through a china cap. This is the court bouillon in which the fish will be poached.
3. Line the halibut fillets in the greased bake pans, pour over the court bouillon and poach (simmer) on the range until done. (Approximate cooking time 10 minutes.)
4. Remove from the range and serve each halibut fillet with a generous amount of duglere sauce.

Precautions and Safety Measures
1. Use caution when handling the knife.
2. When poaching the fish cook slowly, so the fish will not toughen or break.

FRIED SHELLFISH RECIPES

Fried soft-shell crabs

For fried soft-shell crabs the molting blue crabs with their soft shell are dressed for cooking, breaded and deep fat fried to a crisp golden brown. Fried soft-shell crabs are popular on the luncheon and dinner menu during the spring season. They are usually accompanied with tartar or fish sauce.

Objectives
1. To teach the student the procedure for preparing fried soft-shell crabs.
2. To teach the student how to dress, fry and dish up soft-shell crabs.

Equipment
1. Qt. measure
2. Baker's scale
3. Deep fat fryer
4. Fry baskets
5. 2 qt. stainless steel container
6. Wire whip
7. 3 bake pans

Ingredients: Approx. yield: 10 servings
30 soft-shell crabs, dressed
6 whole eggs
1 qt. liquid milk
1 lb. flour
2 lbs. bread crumbs
salt and pepper to taste

Preparation
1. Prepare an egg wash: break the eggs into a stainless steel container, beat slightly with a wire whip, pour in the milk and blend with the eggs.
2. Set deep fat fryer at 350°F.
3. Dress the crabs by removing the face, just back of the eyes, the apron on the underside of the crab, and the entrail under the pointed tip on each side of the soft shell. Proceed only after demonstration by instructor.
4. Have all equipment and ingredients handy.

Procedure
1. Place the flour in a bake pan, season with salt and pepper.
2. Add the dressed crabs and coat thoroughly.
3. Pour the egg wash into the second bake pan. Remove the crabs from the flour and place in the egg wash.
4. Place the bread crumbs in the third bake pan. Remove each crab from the egg wash and place in the bread crumbs, press the crumbs on firmly, shake off the excess.
5. Place in fry baskets and fry until golden brown, let drain.
6. Dish up 3 soft-shell crabs per portion with a soufflé cup filled with tartar or fish sauce. (See Chap. 15 for sauce recipes.)

Precautions and Safety Measures
1. Press the breading on each crab firmly, so the breading will not fall off while frying the crabs.
2. Handle the crab gently, they are very fragile.
3. Do not overbrown or the servings will lack appearance.
4. Do not fry too many crabs at one time. The temperature of the fat will reduce too quickly and frying will not be uniform.

Fried oysters or clams

These two favorite shellfish are breaded and deep fried to a golden brown. Generally 6 or 8 oysters or clams are served to each order depending on the size. Tartar sauce or cocktail sauce usually accompanies each order.

Objectives
1. To teach the student the procedure for preparing fried oysters or clams.
2. To teach the student how to fry and dish up oysters or clams.

Equipment
1. Baker's scale
2. 3 bake pans
3. Qt. measure
4. Wire whip
5. Deep fat fryer
6. Fry baskets
7. 2 qt. stainless steel container
8. Collander

Ingredients: Approx. yield: 25 servings
150 large oysters or clams
9 whole eggs
1½ qts. liquid milk
1 lb. flour
2 lbs. 8 ozs. bread crumbs

Preparation
1. Prepare an egg wash: Break the eggs into a stainless steel container, beat slightly with a wire whip, pour in the milk and blend with the eggs.
2. Preheat deep fat fryer to 350°F.
3. Place the oysters or clams in a collander and drain thoroughly.
4. Have all equipment and ingredients handy.

Procedure
1. Place the flour and 8 ozs. of the bread crumbs in a bake pan, season with salt and pepper, mix together.
2. Add the oysters or clams and coat thoroughly.
3. Pour the egg wash into the second bake pan. Remove the oysters or clams from the flour-bread crumb mixture and place in the egg wash.
4. Place the remaining bread crumbs in the third bake pan. Dip each oyster or clam in the bread crumbs, press the crumbs on firmly, shake off excess.
5. Place in fry baskets and fry in deep fat until golden brown, let drain.
6. Dish up 6 pieces per portion with tartar or cocktail sauce. (See Chap. 15 for sauce recipes.) Garnish with a wedge or slice of lemon.

Precautions and Safety Measures
1. Press the breading on each oyster or clam firmly, so the breading will not fall off while frying.
2. Do not fry too many pieces at one time. The temperature of the fat will reduce too quickly and frying will not be uniform.
3. Do not overbrown or the servings will lack appearance.

Fried scallops or shrimp

Frying is a popular and quick method of preparing these two favorite shellfish. They should be cooked to order and approximately 6 to 8 pieces served per portion. These crisp, golden brown shellfish are usually served with tartar or fish sauce.

Objectives
1. To teach the student the procedure for preparing fried scallops or shrimp.
2. To teach the student how to fry and dish up fried scallops or shrimp.

Equipment
1. Baker's scale
2. 3 bake pans
3. Qt. measure
4. Wire whip
5. Deep fat fryer
6. Fry baskets
7. 2 qt. stainless steel container
8. Shrimp peeler
9. Paring knife

Ingredients: Approx. yield: 25 servings
150 large shrimp or scallops
9 whole eggs
1½ qts. liquid milk
1 lb. flour
2 lbs. bread crumbs
salt and pepper to taste

Preparation
1. Prepare an egg wash: Break the eggs into a stainless steel container, beat slightly with a wire whip, pour in the milk and blend with the eggs.
2. Preheat deep fat fryer to 350°F.
3. If frying shrimp, peel the raw shrimp by hand or with a plastic shrimp peeler. Remove the mud vein by scraping the back of each shrimp with the tip of a paring knife. Cut half way through each shrimp

Procter and Gamble Co.

Fried shrimp

lengthwise using a paring knife (butterfly style). Flatten the shrimp with the heel of the hand. Proceed only after demonstration by instructor.

4. Have all equipment and ingredients handy.

Procedure

1. Place the flour in a bake pan, season with salt and pepper.
2. Add the shellfish and coat thoroughly.
3. Pour the egg wash into the second bake pan. Remove each piece of shellfish from the flour and place in the egg wash.
4. Place the bread crumbs in the third bake pan. Dip each piece of shellfish in the bread crumbs, press the crumbs on firmly. Shake off excess.
5. Place in fry baskets and fry until golden brown and done, let drain.
6. Dish up 6 pieces per portion; serve with tartar or fish sauce. (See Chap. 15 for sauce recipes.) Garnish with a wedge or slice of lemon.

Precautions and Safety Measures

1. Take care when handling the knife to avoid cutting self.
2. Do not fry too many pieces at one time. The temperature of the fat will reduce too quickly and the pieces will not cook evenly.
3. Do not overbrown or the servings will lack appearance.

Lobster and shrimp croquettes

Lobster and shrimp croquettes are an extremely tasty, but slightly expensive croquette. After the croquettes are formed and breaded, they are deep fried to a golden brown and served on the dinner menu with a rich, tasty sauce.

Objectives

1. To teach the student the procedure for preparing lobster and shrimp croquettes.
2. To teach the student how to form, bread and fry the croquettes.
3. To teach the student how to dish up lobster and shrimp croquettes.

Equipment

1. French knife
2. Baker's scale
3. Cup measure
4. Sauce pot, 2 gal.
5. Deep fat fryer
6. Fry baskets
7. 3 bake pans
8. Kitchen spoon
9. Wire whip
10. Stainless steel container
11. Spoon measures
12. 2 qt. sauce pan

Ingredients: Approx. yield: 25 servings

MIXTURE

3	lbs. shrimp, cooked, peeled and deveined
2	lbs. lobster meat, cooked
6	ozs. butter
6	ozs. flour
1	qt. milk, hot
1/3	cup brandy
1	tbsp. lemon juice
2	tsp. mustard, dry
1	tbsp. chives, chopped
8	egg yolks
	salt and pepper to taste

BREADING

1	lb. flour
2	lbs. bread crumbs
1½	qts. egg wash (9 eggs to 1½ qts. of milk)

Preparation

1. Cook, peel, clean and dice the lobster and shrimp fairly small. Proceed only after demonstration by instructor.
2. Heat the milk in a sauce pan.
3. Chop the chives with a French knife.
4. Separate the eggs. Save the whites for use in another preparation.

5. Prepare an egg wash. Break the eggs into a stainless steel container, beat slightly with a wire whip, pour in the milk and blend with the eggs.
6. Preheat the deep fat fryer to 350°F.
7. Place the flour and the bread crumbs in separate bake pans.
8. Have all equipment and ingredients handy.
   Procedure
   1. Place the butter in a sauce pot, heat.
   2. Add the flour, making a roux, and cook for approximately 5 minutes. Stir with a kitchen spoon.
   3. Pour in the hot milk gradually, whipping briskly with a wire whip until very thick and smooth.
   4. Add the lobster, shrimp, brandy, lemon juice, dry mustard and chives, stir in gently with a kitchen spoon so the seafood will not break.
   5. Season with salt and pepper. Cook over low heat 5 minutes, remove from fire.
   6. Beat the egg yolks with a wire whip in a stainless steel container and pour very slowly into the hot mixture while stirring rapidly with a kitchen spoon.
   7. Turn the mixture into a bake pan, cover and refrigerate overnight.
   8. Remove the mixture from the refrigerator, shape into 50 uniform croquettes.
   9. Bread by following breading procedure of passing each croquette through flour, egg wash and bread crumbs.
   10. Fry in deep fat at 350°F until brown.
   11. Dish up 2 croquettes per portion and serve with an appropriate sauce. (See Table VIII for suggested sauces.)
   Precautions and Safety Measures
1. Use caution when handling the knife.
2. Stir the mixture occasionally to avoid sticking or scorching.
3. Pour the beaten egg yolks very slowly into the hot mixture to avoid scrambling.
4. When frying the croquettes do not over-brown, the serving will lack appearance.

POACHED OR STEAMED (IN SAUCE) SHELLFISH RECIPES

Lobster or shrimp curry

For lobster or shrimp curry the cooked lobster or shrimp is placed in a rich curry sauce and generally served in a casserole accompanied with baked or boiled rice.
   Objectives
1. To teach the student the procedure for preparing lobster or shrimp curry.
2. To teach the student how to dish up lobster or shrimp curry.
   Equipment
1. Sauce pot, 2 gal.
2. Kitchen spoon
3. Baker's scale
4. Qt. measure
5. French knife
   Ingredients: Approx. yield: 25 servings
   8   lbs. steamed or boiled lobster or shrimp
   3   qts. curry sauce
   Preparation
1. Cook by steaming or boiling and remove the shells by hand.
2. Dice the lobster or shrimp into uniform pieces with a French knife.
3. Prepare the curry sauce. (See Chap. 15.)
4. Have all equipment and ingredients handy.
   Procedure
1. Place the prepared curry sauce in a sauce pot, bring to a simmer.
2. Add the cooked lobster or shrimp, blend into the sauce gently with a kitchen spoon and bring back to a simmer. Remove from the fire.
3. Dish up with a 6 oz. ladle into shallow casseroles. Serve with boiled or baked rice.
   Precautions and Safety Measures
1. Use caution when handling the knife.
2. When adding the shellfish to the sauce, stir in gently so the meat will not break.

Creamed lobster

For creamed lobster the cooked pieces of lobster are added to a rich cream sauce and served in a casserole with baked yellow rice. This item is an excellent choice for the luncheon, dinner or à la carte menu.
   Objectives
1. To teach the student the procedure for preparing creamed lobster.
2. To teach the student how to dish up creamed lobster.
   Equipment
1. Sauce pot, 2 gal
2. Kitchen spoon
3. Baker's scale

4. Qt. measure
5. French knife
   Ingredients: Approx. yield: 25 servings
   8 lbs. steamed or boiled lobster meat
   3 qts. cream sauce
      salt and white pepper to taste
   Preparation
1. Cook the whole lobsters or lobster tails in boiling salt water (1 tbsp. per gal. water) until the lobster shell turns red; or steam in steam pressure cooker at 5 lbs. pressure for approximately 10 to 12 minutes or at 15 lbs. pressure for approximately 3 to 5 minutes. The exact time will depend on the size of the whole lobsters or lobster tails.
2. Remove the meat from the shell and dice with a French knife. (To remove the lobster meat from the shell cut through the underside of the shell with a heavy scissors. Insert the fingers between the shell and the lobster meat and push the meat out of the shell.)
3. Prepare a rich cream sauce. (See Chap. 15.)
4. Have all equipment and ingredients handy.
   Procedure
1. Place the prepared cream sauce in a sauce pot and bring to a simmer.
2. Add the cooked lobster and blend into the sauce gently with a kitchen spoon. Bring back to a simmer and season with salt and white pepper. Remove from the fire.
3. Dish up with a 6 oz. ladle into shallow casseroles. Serve with baked yellow rice.
   Precautions and Safety Measures
1. Use caution when handling the knife.
2. When adding the lobster to the sauce, stir in gently so it will not break.

Coquilles St. Jacques mornay

Coquilles St. Jacques mornay is a classical French preparation consisting of a combination of poached scallops and mornay sauce placed in a scallop shell, topped with grated Parmesan cheese and browned lightly under the broiler. Coquilles St. Jacques mornay are popular on the dinner menu.
   Objectives
1. To teach the student the procedure for preparing coquilles St. Jacques mornay.
2. To teach the student how to poach the scallops and set up each order.

3. To teach the student how to serve coquilles St. Jacques mornay.
   Equipment
1. Sauce pot, 1 gal.
2. French knife
3. Kitchen spoon
4. China cap
5. 12 large scallop shells
6. Sheet pan
7. Qt. measure
8. Cup measure
9. Spoon measure
10. Baker's scale
11. Sheet pan
    Ingredients: Approx. yield: 12 servings
    2½ lbs. scallops
        water to cover, boiling
    ½   tsp. salt
    2   bay leaves
    ¼   cup Parmesan cheese, grated
    1   qt. mornay sauce
    Preparation
1. Wash the scallops in lemon juice and water, drain thoroughly through a china cap.
2. Prepare the mornay sauce. (See Chap. 15.)
3. Preheat the broiler.
4. Have all equipment and ingredients handy.
   Procedure
1. Place the scallops in a sauce pot, cover with boiling water, add the salt and bay leaves, simmer for 7 minutes.
2. Remove from the fire and drain thoroughly through a china cap.
3. Slice the scallops approximately ½ in. thick with a French knife.
4. Combine the sliced scallops and the prepared mornay sauce, fold together gently with a kitchen spoon.
5. Fill the scallop shells with a generous amount of the mixture. Sprinkle with grated Parmesan cheese. Place the shells on a sheet pan.
6. Place the sheet pan under the broiler and brown the surface of each filled shell slightly.
7. Serve at once.
   Note: For increased eye appeal a border of duchess potatoes may be piped around the edge of each scallop shell.
   Precautions and Safety Measures
1. Drain the poached scallops thoroughly before adding them to the mornay sauce.

Coquilles St. Jacques mornay

2. Use caution when handling the knife.
3. Exercise caution when browning the preparation under the broiler, if they are over-browned they will lack eye appeal.

Lobster thermidor

For lobster thermidor the northern cold water lobster is boiled in salt water or steamed, cooled and split in half lengthwise. The meat is removed from the shell, diced, placed in a rich sauce and placed back into the lobster shell. It is then covered with a mornay sauce and glazed lightly under the broiler. Lobster thermidor is served on the dinner menu.

Objectives
1. To teach the student the procedure for preparing lobster thermidor.
2. To teach the student how to split the lobster and remove the meat.
3. To teach the student how to set up and serve lobster thermidor.

Equipment
1. Stock pot and cover, 5 gal.
2. Sauce pot, 3 gal.
3. Cup measure
4. Spoon measure
5. Qt. measure
6. Kitchen spoon
7. French knife
8. Sheet pan
9. Mallet

Ingredients: Approx. yield: 12 servings

12   1½ to 2 lbs. northern cold water lobsters, boiled
1   qt. Newburg sauce
2   tbsp. chives, minced
½   cup mushrooms, diced small
4   ozs. butter
1   qt. mornay sauce

Preparation
1. Place the lobsters in boiling salt water (allow 1 tbsp. of salt for each qt. of water). Cover the pot and boil for 20 minutes. Drain and let them cool.
2. Prepare the Newburg sauce. (See Chap. 14.)
3. Mince the chives with a French knife.
4. Dice the mushrooms fairly small with a French knife.
5. Prepare the mornay sauce. (See Chap. 15.)
6. Have all equipment and ingredients handy.

Procedure
1. Place the butter in a sauce pot, melt.
2. Add the diced mushrooms and sauté until slightly tender.
3. Add the Newburg sauce, bring to a simmer.
4. Stir in the chives with a kitchen spoon. Place on the side of the range and hold.
5. Place each lobster on its back and split in half lengthwise using a French knife. Remove the intestines and sac near the head. Remove all the meat from the body, saving the shells. Break the claws, using a mallet, pick out all the meat, discard the shells of the claws. Proceed only after demonstration by instructor.
6. Cut the lobster meat into a fairly small dice, fold into the sauce gently with a kitchen spoon.
7. Refill the lobster shells with a generous amount of the mixture. Cover the top with mornay sauce.
8. Place on sheet pans and glaze slightly under the broiler.
9. Serve 2 lobster halves per portion. Garnish with a wedge of lemon and a sprig of parsley.

Precautions and Safety Measures
1. Exercise caution when splitting the lobsters to avoid cutting self. Learn to hold the hand and knife properly.
2. Do not let the mushrooms brown while sautéing.
3. Cover the top of the filled lobster shells completely with the mornay sauce.

4. Do not burn while glazing the mornay sauce.

Scalloped oysters

Scalloped oysters has been a favorite for many years. This simple, easy to cook preparation is ideal for the luncheon menu. It is a mixture of rich plump oysters and bread or cracker crumbs, baked together with cream.

Objectives
1. To teach the student the procedure for preparing scalloped oysters.
2. To teach the student how to bake and serve scalloped oysters.

Equipment
1. 25 individual casseroles
2. Qt. measure
3. Baker's scale
4. Spoon measures

Ingredients: Approx. yield: 25 servings

150	oysters, shucked, and their liquid
2	qts. cracker or bread crumbs, very coarse
1	qt. light cream (variable)
1	pt. oyster liquid (variable)
12	ozs. butter
2	tbsp. Worcestershire sauce
	salt and white pepper to taste

Preparation
1. Brush melted butter on the bottom and sides of each casserole.
2. Prepare the bread or cracker crumbs.
3. Have all equipment and ingredients handy.
4. Preheat oven to 350°F.

Procedure
1. Place a layer of crumbs in each casserole.
2. Cover the crumbs with 6 oysters.
3. Add more crumbs to slightly cover the oysters.
4. Mix together the cream, oyster liquid and Worcestershire sauce, season with salt and white pepper.
5. Pour enough liquid over each casserole to moisten the crumbs.
6. Dot the top of each casserole with butter.
7. Place in the oven and bake until thoroughly heated and the edges of the oysters ruffle.
8. Remove from the oven and serve at once.

Precautions and Safety Measures
1. Do not overcook the oysters; they will become tough.

Lobster, shrimp or crabmeat Newburg

Lobster, shrimp or crabmeat Newburg is a cream dish colored slightly with paprika and highly seasoned with sherry wine. The Newburg is named according to the seafood used. Newburgs are generally served in a chafing dish or over toast or patty shell.

Objectives
1. To teach the student the procedure for making Newburg.
2. To teach the student how to process the seafood before it is added to the Newburg sauce.
3. To teach the student how to dish up the Newburg.

Equipment
1. French knife
2. Baker's scale
3. Qt. measure
4. Spoon measure
5. Sauce pot, 5 gal.
6. Kitchen spoon

Ingredients: Approx. yield: 50 servings

10	lbs. lobster, shrimp or crabmeat, steamed or boiled
1	lb. butter
2	gal. medium cream sauce
	juice of 1 lemon
6	ozs. dry sherry wine
3	tbsp. monosodium glutamate
5	tbsp. paprika
	salt and white pepper to taste

Preparation
1. Cut shrimp, lobster or crabmeat into ½ in. pieces with a French knife.
2. Prepare cream sauce. (See Chap. 15.)
3. Have all equipment and ingredients handy.

Procedure
1. Place the butter in sauce pan, melt, add paprika and heat slowly.
2. Add the seafood that is being used and heat slowly.
3. Add the cream sauce and blend thoroughly with a kitchen spoon. Bring mixture to a boil.
4. Add the sherry wine, lemon juice, monosodium glutamate; blend with a kitchen spoon.
5. Season to taste with salt and white pepper. Remove from the range.
6. Dish up with a 6 oz. ladle into shallow casseroles; serve with toast points.

1. Use caution when handling the knife to avoid cutting self.
2. When heating paprika in the butter, take care not to burn.
3. When heating the seafood do not break into small pieces when stirring.
4. Use white pepper when seasoning any light or cream dish. Black pepper will ruin the appearance.

Shrimp, lobster or seafood creole

For this preparation the cooked seafood selected is placed in a creole sauce and is generally served in a casserole accompanied with baked rice. Usually a combination of shrimp, fish and crabmeat is used. However, just fish may be used if desired. Any cooked fish can be used in the preparation, but as a rule cooked fish left over from the previous day's menu is used. The preparation is also made with just shrimp or just lobster. This item is an excellent choice for the luncheon, dinner or à la carte menu.

Objectives
1. To teach the student the procedure for preparing shrimp, lobster or seafood creole.
2. To teach the student how to dish up shrimp, lobster or seafood creole.

Equipment
1. Baker's scale
2. Sauce pot, 2 gal.
3. Kitchen spoon
4. Qt. measure

Ingredients: Approx. yield: 25 servings
8 lbs. cooked shrimp, lobster or seafood
3 qts. creole sauce
salt and pepper to taste

Preparation
1. Cook by steaming or boiling and remove shells or skin of the fish or shellfish by hand.
2. Prepare the creole sauce. (See Chap. 15.)
3. Have all equipment and ingredients handy.

Procedure
1. Place the prepared creole sauce in a sauce pot, bring to a simmer.
2. Add the cooked shrimp, lobster or seafood, blend into the sauce gently with a kitchen spoon, and bring back to a simmer. Season with salt and pepper.

3. Dish up with a 6 oz. ladle into shallow casseroles. Serve with baked rice.

Precautions and Safety Measures
1. When adding the shellfish or seafood to the sauce, stir in gently so the meat will not break.

Crabmeat imperial

Imperial usually refers to something of excellence. In the case of this entrée it is certainly well named. The king crabmeat is covered with rich, smooth cream sauce, topped with a mixture of bread crumbs and almonds and browned gently under the broiler. It is best suited for the dinner menu.

Objectives
1. To teach the student the procedure for preparing crabmeat imperial.
2. To teach the student how to set up, brown and serve crabmeat imperial.

Equipment
1. Pt. measure
2. Sauce pan, 4 qts.
3. Sauce pot
4. Shallow casseroles
5. Spoon measures
6. Baker's scale
7. Wire whip
8. Small stainless steel bowl
9. Kitchen spoon

Ingredients: Approx. yield: 25 servings
10 lbs. king crabmeat, cooked, thawed and drained
8 ozs. butter
6 ozs. flour
2 qts. milk, hot
1 qt. cream, hot
1 tsp. Tabasco sauce
12 egg yolks
½ cup lemon juice
1 pt. bread crumbs, dry
1 pt. almonds, chopped
salt and white pepper to taste

Preparation
1. Light the broiler, set flame low.
2. Thaw the cooked frozen crabmeat and cut into uniform pieces with a French knife.
3. Heat the milk and cream in a sauce pan.
4. Separate the eggs, save the whites for use in another preparation.
5. Chop the almonds fairly fine with a French knife.
6. Have all equipment and ingredients handy.

Procedure

1. Place approximately 6 ozs. of crabmeat in each shallow casserole.
2. Place the butter in a sauce pot, melt.
3. Add the flour, making a roux, cook for 5 minutes. Stir with a kitchen spoon.
4. Pour in the hot milk and cream, whipping constantly with a wire whip until thickened and smooth. This is the cream sauce.
5. Add the Tabasco sauce and season with salt and pepper, stir with a kitchen spoon.
6. Place the egg yolks in a stainless steel bowl. Beat slightly with a wire whip. Add the lemon juice and continue to beat until blended.
7. Beat a little of the above hot cream sauce into the egg yolk mixture, then pour gradually into the hot cream sauce, whipping briskly with a wire whip.
8. Return the sauce to the heat and cook until hot. Do not boil.
9. Pour enough hot sauce over the crabmeat to cover.
10. Mix together the almonds and bread crumbs by hand. Sprinkle over each casserole.
11. Place each casserole under the broiler and broil very slowly until the top is golden brown.
12. Serve at once garnished with a sprig of parsley.

Precautions and Safety Measures

1. When melting the butter do not let it brown.
2. Exercise caution when adding the egg yolk mixture to the cream sauce, pour slowly and whip briskly with a wire whip or the eggs may curdle. Heat, but do not boil mixture once the eggs are added.
3. When browning each serving under the broiler be alert, bread crumbs will burn quickly.

BAKED AND BROILED SHELLFISH RECIPES

Deviled crabs

For deviled crabs the rich, sweet tasting blue crabmeat is seasoned and flavored to acquire a slightly tangy taste. It is bound together with the addition of a thick cream sauce, packed into an aluminum crab shell and baked until the mixture becomes slightly brown. Deviled crabs used to be served in their original hard shell until the health department put a stop to this practice. Crabs are placed on the luncheon or dinner menu.

Objectives

1. To teach the student the procedure for preparing deviled crabs.
2. To teach the student how to form and bake deviled crabs.
3. To teach the student how to dish up and serve deviled crabs.

Equipment

1. Sauce pot, 2 gal.
2. Baker's scale
3. French knife
4. 25 aluminum crab shells
5. Kitchen spoon
6. Paring knife
7. Qt. measure
8. Spoon measure
9. Bake pan
10. 2 sheet pans
11. 2 qt. sauce pan

Ingredients: Approx. yield: 25 servings

6	lbs.	crabmeat, blue crabmeat or king crabmeat, steamed or boiled
12	ozs.	butter or shortening
12	ozs.	flour
12	ozs.	onions, minced
1½	qts.	milk, hot
3	tbsp.	prepared mustard
1	tbsp.	Worcestershire sauce
1	tsp.	Tabasco sauce
2	tbsp.	lemon juice
1	cup	sherry wine
		salt and pepper to taste
		paprika as needed

Preparation

1. Mince the onions with a French knife.
2. Heat the milk in a sauce pan.
3. Cook the crabmeat by steaming or boiling, if it is not already cooked. Remove the meat from the shell by hand. Flake the meat by hand.
4. Preheat the oven to 350°F.
5. Have all equipment and ingredients handy.

Procedure

1. Place the butter or shortening in a sauce pot, melt.
2. Add the onions and sauté slightly, do not brown.

3. Add the flour making a roux, cook for 5 minutes. Stir with a kitchen spoon.
4. Add the hot milk, stirring constantly with a kitchen spoon until thickened.
5. Stir in the crabmeat gently with a kitchen spoon.
6. Add the mustard, Tabasco sauce, wine, and Worcestershire sauce, stir to blend thoroughly.
7. Season with salt and pepper, if the mixture is too wet add bread crumbs to stiffen.
8. Pour into a bake pan, cover with oiled brown paper, cool and refrigerate overnight.
9. Remove from the refrigerator. Pack each shell with a generous amount of the crabmeat mixture. Score the top of the mixture in each shell with a paring knife.
10. Sprinkle paprika over the top of each shell and dot slightly with additional melted butter.
11. Place on sheet pans and bake in a 350°F oven until hot and slightly brown.
12. Dish up 1 shell per portion and serve with tartar or fish sauce. (See Chap. 15 for sauce recipes.)

Precautions and Safety Measures
1. Use caution when handling the knife.
2. While the mixture is cooking stir occasionally with a kitchen spoon to avoid sticking or scorching.
3. When sautéing the onions do not let them brown.

Shrimp pilau

Shrimp pilau originated in the Old South, it has long been a favorite south of the Mason Dixon line. It is a casserole type of dish with shrimp, rice and bacon baked together. An excellent choice for the luncheon menu.

Objectives
1. To teach the student the procedure for preparing shrimp pilau.
2. To teach the student how to serve shrimp pilau.

Equipment
1. Baker's scale
2. Qt. measure
3. French knife
4. Sauce pot and lid, 2 gal.
5. Kitchen spoon
6. Paring knife
7. Plastic shrimp peeler

Ingredients: Approx. yield: 25 servings
6 lbs. shrimp, raw, peeled and deveined
1½ qts. rice
2 qts. water
1½ qts. whole tomatoes, canned
1 lb. bacon, sliced, cut into 1 in. pieces
1 qt. onions, sliced
2 cloves garlic, minced
salt and white pepper to taste

Preparation
1. Peel the raw shrimp by hand or with a plastic shrimp peeler. Remove the mud vein by scraping the back of each shrimp with the tip of a paring knife.
2. Slice the onions with a French knife.
3. Mince the garlic with a French knife.
4. Cut the strips of bacon into 1 inch pieces with a French knife.
5. Have all equipment and ingredients handy.

Procedure
1. Place the bacon in a sauce pot and cook until it becomes slightly crisp. Remove the crisp bacon from the pot, leaving the hot grease.
2. Add the rice, onions and garlic, cook very slow until the rice is golden brown.
3. Add the tomatoes and water, stir with a kitchen spoon.
4. Season with salt and pepper, bring mixture to a boil.
5. Add the shrimp, cover the sauce pot and simmer for approximately 20 minutes, or until the shrimp and rice are cooked.
6. Remove from the range and stir in the bacon with a kitchen spoon.
7. Check seasoning and dish up with a 6 oz. ladle into casseroles.

Precautions and Safety Measures
1. Use caution when handling the knife.
2. Do not overbake the rice. It will become mushy.
3. All cooking should be done at a low temperature.

Broiled lobster

Whether cold or warm water lobsters are used this is an extremely popular shellfish entree. It is generally served with melted butter on the dinner or à la carte menu. Broiled lobsters are always cooked to order.

Objectives

1. To teach the student the procedure for broiling lobsters.
2. To teach the student how to prepare the lobster for broiling.
3. To teach the student how to dish up a broiled lobster.

Equipment

1. French knife, heavy
2. Kitchen fork
3. Broiler
4. Bake pan
5. Small container
6. Cup measure
7. Spoon measure

Ingredients: Approx. yield: 1 serving

1	cold water lobster or 2, 3 or 4 oz. spiney lobster tails, raw
½	cup salad oil
	paprika as needed
2	tbsp. bread crumbs, dry
1	tsp. butter, melted

Preparation

1. *COLD WATER LOBSTER:* Using a heavy French knife, chop off the claws and legs. Crack the shell of the claws with the back of the French knife. Save the legs. Insert the blade of the French knife into the back of the lobster shell at the point where the tail section joins the body. Split in half lengthwise, first the tail section then the body section. Remove the stomach that lies just behind the head and the intestinal vein. The cold water lobster is now ready for broiling. Proceed only after demonstration by instructor.
SPINEY LOBSTER TAILS: Using a French knife insert the blade into the back of the lobster shell in the center of the tail. Split in half lengthwise, first the lower section, then turning the knife and tail split the upper section. The spiney lobster tail is now ready for broiling. Proceed only after demonstration by instructor.
2. Melt the butter.
3. Have all equipment and ingredients handy.

Procedure

1. Place the lobster halves (and claws if cold water lobster is used) in a bake pan. Pour the salad oil over the exposed flesh.
2. Season with salt and sprinkle with paprika.
3. In the case of cold water lobster, blend the melted butter into the bread crumbs and fill the cavity caused by removing the stomach with this mixture. Place a few of the legs on top of the stuffing.
4. Place the lobster halves (and claws if cold water lobster is used) on the broiler flesh side up. Broil under a low flame until the flesh side browns slightly and the shell becomes red.
5. Remove the lobster halves (including the claws) with a kitchen fork and place in a shallow pan.
6. Place in the oven or the hot chamber above the broiler until lobster is completely done. The cooking time will depend on the size of the lobster or lobster tail. Total cooking time of 15 to 20 minutes is usually sufficient.
7. Dish up on a platter with a small cup of melted butter and a wedge or slice of lemon.

Precautions and Safety Measures

1. Exercise caution when splitting the lobsters or cracking the claws to avoid cutting self.
2. Broil the lobster slowly, do not overbrown.

quickbread preparation

chapter 22

■ Quickbreads are extremely important to any food service operation because customers desire and expect hot breads. Items such as biscuits, muffins, cornbread and corn sticks can meet this need with quickness and ease. In many cases food service establishments have built their reputation on the quickbreads they feature on their menu. Quickbreads that are placed before the guest, freshly baked and still warm, are a delight to any diner and will certainly call for a return visit.

Quickbreads have acquired their name because they are made with a quick acting leavening agent, such as baking pow-der, instead of the slower acting yeast. They can be prepared in a comparatively short time since the mixture is taken directly from the mixing machine, made up and baked. There is no waiting period of one or more hours for gases to develop to leaven the dough. Since the trend today is to place emphasis on speed, quickbreads will certainly suit that need.

The requirement for turning out successful quickbreads are quite simple: (1) high quality ingredients, (2) good formulas and (3) a fairly skilled cook or baker. Of these the first two are most important. The skillful cook or baker is important, but could be substituted by a fairly intelligent person who can follow directions and has a desire to succeed. There are some pitfalls in the production of quickbreads, but many of these can be eliminated by an understanding of each ingredient and by knowing how to handle and mix these ingredients properly.

BISCUITS

There are many formulas available for making biscuits; however, they will all contain basically the same ingredients, only the amounts and ways of handling will vary. Sugar, baking powder, salt, flour, shortening and milk are the basic ingredients. To these eggs and butter may be added to improve the eating qualities. The flavoring may also vary greatly to create different and unusual products, such as orange biscuits and cheese biscuits.

Basically there are two types of biscuits; the cake type and the flaky type. The difference lies mainly in the mixing. The *cake type* is mixed by developing a fairly smooth dough.

The *flaky type* contains a higher percentage of shortening and is mixed like a pie crust: the shortening is cut into the dry ingredients and the liquid is added slowly and blended in gently until a dough is formed. This type of dough is considered most difficult for the unskilled because overhandling will cause the dough to toughen.

Shortening is considered the most important ingredient in the preparation of biscuits because it supplies the tenderness. Baking powder is the quick acting leavening and causes the dough to rise when liquid is added and heat is applied. Flour supplies body, form and texture to the biscuit. Milk provides moisture, regulates the consistency of the dough, develops the flour and causes the baking powder to generate its gas. Salt brings out the flavor and taste of the other ingredients. Sugar supplies sweetness, helps retain moisture and helps to cause the golden brown color that is so desirable. Knowing the reaction of the basic ingredients is helpful when preparing a biscuit dough. However, proper mixing is more important so follow your formula carefully.

MUFFINS

Muffins are a favorite of any meal and are featured on the breakfast, luncheon and dinner menus of many food service establishments. This round, tender textured, golden brown quickbread can be prepared in many different varieties so it is very unlikely that one would tire of them quickly. Muffins like biscuits should always be placed before the guest fresh from the oven. This can be accomplished with comparative ease since most recipes call for a baking period of only 15 to 20 minutes. In fact, of all the quickbreads, muffins take the least time to prepare.

There are many different formulas that one may select when preparing muffins, the amount of ingredients will vary but the method of mixing will generally be the same. The sugar, shortening and salt is creamed together, the eggs are blended in, the dry ingredients are sifted together and added alternately with the milk. All the mixing is done in slow or second speed with the paddle. The reaction of each ingredient within the batter is similar to that of the biscuit mix. The chief secret of a successful muffin lies in the mixing.

Mixing the batter to a point where the gluten within the flour becomes tough is a common fault. To avoid this pitfall the dry and liquid ingredients should be mixed together in slow speed with the paddle. Mix just enough to moisten, leaving the batter with a slightly rough appearance.

Bake shop layout in the Student Union building, University of Oklahoma.

CORNBREAD AND CORN STICKS

These two items are generally prepared from the same batter although in some cases the consistency of the batter may be a little heavier when preparing cornsticks. This is usually accomplished by eliminating a small amount of the liquid. The formulas for preparing cornbread and corn sticks vary not only in the amounts of ingredients used but in mixing methods as well. A formula may call for a mixing method similar to muffins or for a three-stage method of blending an egg-milk mixture into the dry ingredients and stirring in melted shortening. Whichever method is used the mixing should be done in slow or second speed using the paddle. The liquid must be added slowly because cornmeal does not absorb liquid very quickly and if the liquid is added too fast lumps will form. Mix the batter only until fairly smooth and avoid overmixing.

QUICKBREAD RECIPES

The recipes for quickbreads given on the following pages will produce products of slightly different flavors and textures. The purpose is to expose the student to the different techniques in the production of quickbreads. An outline of the quickbread recipes is given in the order of their appearance in the chapter.

Baking powder biscuits (flaky type)
Biscuits (cake type)
Golden rich biscuits
Buttermilk biscuits
Basic muffin mix I
Basic muffin mix II
Cornmeal muffins or corn sticks
Golden cornbread
Blueberry muffins
Bran muffins
Spicy apple muffins
Southern spoon bread
Popovers

Baking powder biscuits (flaky type)

Ingredients: Approx. yield: 6 doz.

1	lb. 4 ozs. cake flour
1	lb. 4 ozs. bread flour
4	ozs. sugar, granulated
3/4	oz. salt
2 1/4	oz. baking powder

Baking powder biscuits (flaky type).

Biscuits (cake type)

Ingredients: Approx. yield: 6 doz.

8 ozs. granulated sugar
½ oz. salt
5 ozs. dry milk
8 ozs. shortening (hydrogenated) or butter or margarine
2 lbs. cold water
1 lb. cake flour
2 lbs. 4 ozs. bread flour
3 ozs. baking powder

Procedure

1. In a stainless steel dish pan place the sugar, salt, dry milk and shortening, blend with a wooden spoon to a soft paste.
2. Add the cold water and stir with a wooden spoon.
3. Sift together the cake flour, bread flour and baking powder. Add to the above mixture and mix by hand to a smooth dough.
4. Turn the dough out of the mixing container onto a floured bench; cover with a cloth and let rest 10 minutes.
5. Roll the dough out to a ½ in. thickness with a rolling pin.
6. Cut with a small biscuit cutter (2 to 2½ in.) and place on sheet pans covered with silicon paper, or lightly greased. Place fairly close together.
7. Brush the top of each biscuit with a rich egg wash (blend together 2 eggs and 1 cup of milk). Let rest 5 minutes.
8. Bake in a preheated oven at 425°F until golden brown.

1 lb. 8 ozs. liquid milk, skimmed (variable)
1 lb. shortening (Primex)

Procedure

1. In a large stainless steel dish pan place the flours, sugar, salt, and baking powder, blend together by hand.
2. Add the shortening and cut in by hand until a fine crumb (small lumps) is formed.
3. Add the milk and mix gently by hand until all the ingredients are moistened and a dough is formed.
4. Turn the dough out of the mixing container onto a floured bench, cover with a cloth and let rest 10 minutes.
5. Roll the dough out to a ½ in. thickness with a rolling pin.
6. Cut with a small biscuit cutter (2 to 2½ in.) and place on sheet pans covered with silicon paper or lightly greased, place fairly close together.
7. Brush the top of each biscuit with a rich egg wash (blend together 2 eggs and 1 cup of milk). Let rest 10 minutes.
8. Bake in a preheated oven at 425°F until golden brown.

VARIATIONS:

1. *Cheese biscuits:* Add 6 ozs. of grated Cheddar cheese to the above mix.
2. *Raisin biscuits:* Add 1 lb. 4 ozs. of raisins to the above mix.

Golden rich biscuits

Ingredients: Approx. yield: 10 doz.

1 lb. 8 ozs. butter
8 ozs. granulated sugar
8 ozs. egg yolks
2 lbs. 4 ozs. cold milk
2 lbs. 4 ozs. bread flour
2 lbs. 4 ozs. cake flour
1 oz. salt
3¾ ozs. baking powder

Procedure

1. Place the butter and sugar in a mixing container. Cream together with a kitchen spoon until a soft paste is formed.
2. Add the egg yolks, blend in with a kitchen spoon until mixture is slightly smooth.

3. Add the cold milk, stir gently with a kitchen spoon.
4. Sift together the cake flour, bread flour, salt, and baking powder. Add to the above mixture and mix by hand to a slightly smooth dough.
5. Place the dough in the refrigerator until thoroughly chilled (approximately 45 minutes).
6. Turn the dough out on a floured bench, roll out with a rolling pin to a ¾ in. thickness.
7. Cut with a small biscuit cutter (2 to 2½ in.) and place on sheet pans covered with silicon paper or greased and floured.
8. Brush the top of each biscuit with a rich egg wash (blend together 2 eggs and 1 cup of milk).
9. Bake in a preheated oven at 450°F until golden brown.
   VARIATIONS:
   1. *Cheese biscuits:* Add 10 ozs. of grated Cheddar cheese to the above mix.
   2. *Raisin biscuits:* Add 1 lb. 12 ozs. of raisins to the above mix.

Buttermilk biscuits

Ingredients: Approx. yield: 6 doz.

1 lb. 8 ozs. cake flour
1 lb. 8 ozs. bread flour
3½ ozs. baking powder
½ oz. salt
4 ozs. sugar
1 lb. butter
2 lbs. 4 ozs. buttermilk

Procedure

1. Sift together the dry ingredients. Place in a mixing container.
2. Add the butter and cut in by hand until a fine crumb is formed.
3. Stir in the buttermilk gradually with a wooden spoon until all the ingredients are moistened and a dough is formed.
4. Place the dough in the refrigerator until thoroughly chilled (approximately 45 minutes).
5. Turn the dough out on a floured bench, roll out with a rolling pin to a ¾ in. thickness.
6. Cut with a small biscuit cutter (2 to 2½ in.) and place on sheet pans covered with silicon paper or greased and floured.

7. Brush the top of each biscuit with melted butter.
8. Bake in a preheated oven at 425°F until golden brown.

Basic muffin mix I

Ingredients: Approx. yield: 12 doz.

3 lbs. granulated sugar
2 lbs. shortening (Primex)
1½ ozs. salt
2 lbs. whole eggs
3 lbs. 8 ozs. cake flour
1 lb. bread flour
2½ ozs. baking powder
2 lbs. liquid milk, skimmed (variable)

Procedure

1. Place the sugar, shortening and salt in electric mixing bowl. Using the paddle, cream together 3 to 5 minutes on second speed.
2. Add the eggs gradually while continuing to mix in second speed. Mix about 2 minutes.
3. Add the flour, baking powder and about two-thirds of the milk. Mix smooth.
4. Add the remaining milk and mix for 1 minute more, remove from the mixer.
5. Fill greased muffin tins or muffin tins lined with paper baking cups two-thirds full of batter.

Muffins.

6. Place in a preheated oven at 400°F and bake until golden brown.

MUFFIN VARIATIONS: To each pound of muffin mix add the following ingredients for interesting varieties.

1. *Corn muffins:* 4 ozs. yellow cornmeal and 2 ozs. liquid milk, skimmed.
2. *Date and walnut muffins:* 2 ozs. dates, chopped and 2 ozs. walnuts, chopped.
3. *Marmalade muffins:* 4 ozs. marmalade.
4. *All-bran muffins:* 4 ozs. all-bran and 2 ozs. liquid milk, skimmed.
5. *Bacon muffins:* 1 oz. chopped bacon, fried.
6. *Molasses muffins:* 2 ozs. molasses.
7. *Cinnamon-raisin muffins:* 4 ozs. raisins and ½ tsp. cinnamon.
8. *Apricot muffins:* 4 ozs. apricots, chopped.
9. *Honey whole wheat muffins:* 2 ozs. whole wheat flour; 2 ozs. honey; and 2 ozs. liquid milk.
10. *Banana muffins:* 4 ozs. bananas, well chopped.
11. *Pineapple muffins:* 4 ozs. pineapple, chopped.

Basic muffin mix II

Ingredients: Approx. yield: 12 doz.

2	lbs. powdered sugar (10X)
8	ozs. shortening, Primex (hydrogenated)
8	ozs. butter
1	oz. salt
2	lbs. whole eggs
2	lbs. liquid milk
2¼	ozs. baking powder
3	lbs. 8 ozs. cake flour
3	lbs. fruits or nuts

Procedure

1. Place the sugar, shortening, butter and salt in electric mixing bowl. Using the paddle cream together on second speed until smooth.
2. Add the eggs gradually while continuing to mix in second speed.
3. Add the milk, mix until smooth.
4. Sift the flour and baking powder together. Add gradually to the above mixture, mix until smooth.
5. Fold in the fruit or nuts with a kitchen spoon. Remove from the mixer.
6. Fill greased muffin tins or paper baking cups two-thirds full of batter.

7. Place in a preheated oven at 400°F and bake until golden brown.

MUFFIN VARIATIONS: The fruit or nuts called for in the above recipe may be any of the following: blueberries, apricots, pineapple, apples, raisins, pecans or walnuts.

Cornmeal muffins or corn sticks

Ingredients: Approx. yield: 9 doz. muffins or 15 doz. sticks

2	lb. 8 oz. granulated sugar
1½	oz. salt
6	oz. powder milk
1	lb. 8 oz. whole eggs
2	lb. water
3	lb. 12 oz. bread flour
1	lb. 8 oz. corn meal
5	oz. baking powder
1	lb. water
1	lb. 8 oz. salad oil

Procedure

1. Place the sugar, salt, powder milk, and eggs in electric mixing bowl. Using the paddle, mix until smooth, on second speed.
2. Add the first amount of water to the above mixture and continue to mix on second speed until thoroughly absorbed.
3. Add the bread flour, corn meal, and baking powder. Continue to mix until smooth.
4. Reduce the speed of the mixing machine to number one speed and add the second amount of water and salad oil alternately. Mix until smooth.
5. Fill greased muffin tins, muffin tins lined with paper baking cups, or greased and heated corn stick pans, two-thirds full of batter.
6. Bake in preheated over at 400° F. until golden brown.

Golden cornbread

Ingredients: Approx. yield: 10 pans

1	lb. 10 ozs. cornmeal, yellow
1	lb. pastry flour
2	lbs. 12 ozs. bread flour
4½	ozs. baking powder
1½	ozs. salt
2	lbs. 10 ozs. granulated sugar
⅛	oz. nutmeg

Cornbread, corn sticks and corn muffins.

Procter and Gamble Co.

4 lbs. liquid milk, skimmed (variable)
1 lb. 9 ozs. melted shortening
(Primex)
1 lb. whole eggs
Procedure
1. Place the dry ingredients in electric mixing bowl. Using the paddle blend together in slow speed.
2. Add the milk gradually, continuing to mix in slow speed until the mixture is slightly smooth.
3. Add the melted shortening, mix smooth in slow speed.
4. Add the eggs gradually and mix in slow speed until the batter is smooth. Remove from the mixer.
5. Place approximately 24 ozs. of batter into each greased pan (9 in. x 9 in. x 1½ in.).
6. Bake in a preheated oven at 375° to 400°F until golden brown.
Note: This formula is also adaptable to muffins and corn sticks.

Blueberry muffins

Ingredients: Approx. yield: 9 doz.
2 lbs. 8 ozs. cake flour

1 lb. 4 ozs. shortening (Sweetex)
2 lbs. 8 ozs. sugar, granulated
1½ ozs. salt
8 ozs. honey
½ oz. baking soda
½ oz. baking powder
1 lb. 4 ozs. buttermilk
1 lb. 8 ozs. whole eggs
2 lbs. blueberries, fresh or frozen
Procedure
1. Place the flour and shortening in electric mixing bowl, using the paddle mix from 3 to 5 minutes in slow speed. Scrape down the bowl at least once.
2. Add the sugar, salt, honey, baking soda, buttermilk and baking powder. Mix for 3 to 5 minutes in second speed. Scrape down at least once.
3. Add the half of the eggs, mix smooth in second speed. Scrape down and mix smooth again.
4. Add the remaining eggs and continue mixing in second speed for a total of 3 to 5 minutes. Scrape down again to insure a smooth batter.
5. Drain the blueberries thoroughly, sprinkle

them with flour to absorb excess moisture and fold into the batter gently with a kitchen spoon.
6. Fill greased muffin tins or paper baking cups two-thirds full of batter.
7. Bake in a preheated oven at 385°F until golden brown.

Bran muffins

Ingredients: Approx. yield: 10 doz.
1   lb. granulated sugar
¾   oz. salt
6   ozs. powdered milk
10 ozs. shortening, Primex (hydrogenated)
1   lb. 3 ozs. honey and molasses
8   ozs. whole eggs
3   lbs. water
1   oz. baking soda
8   ozs. cake flour
1   lb. 8 ozs. bread flour
1   lb. bran flour
1   oz. baking powder
Procedure
1. Place the sugar, salt, powdered milk, shortening, molasses and honey in electric mixing bowl, using the paddle blend together in second speed until smooth.
2. Add the eggs gradually, continuing to mix in second speed until thoroughly incorporated.
3. Add the water slowly, mix in second speed until thoroughly blended with other ingredients.
4. Sift together the baking soda, bread flour and cake flour. Add the baking powder and bran flour and blend together with kitchen spoon. Add slowly to the above mixture and mix in second speed until batter is smooth. Remove from the mixer.
5. Fill greased muffin tins or paper baking cups two-thirds full of batter.
6. Bake in preheated oven at 400°F until golden brown.
Note: 10 ozs. of raisins, soaked in warm water and drained thoroughly may be added to the batter if desired.

Spicy apple muffins

Ingredients: Approx. yield: 6 doz.
1   lb. 8 ozs. granulated sugar
1   lb. shortening, Primex (hydrogenated)
¾   oz. salt
1   lb. whole eggs
1   lb. 12 ozs. cake flour
8   ozs. bread flour
1½ ozs. baking powder
¼   oz. cinnamon
¼   oz. nutmeg
¼   oz. ginger
¼   oz. mace
1   lb. liquid milk, skimmed (variable)
1   lb. 12 oz. apples, peeled, cored and diced fine.
Procedure
1. Place the sugar, shortening and salt in electric mixing bowl, using the paddle cream together on second speed until smooth.
2. Add the eggs gradually while continuing to mix in second speed. Mix about 2 minutes.
3. Add the flours, baking powder and spices with two-thirds of the milk, mix smooth in second speed.
4. Add the remaining milk and mix smooth a second time in second speed. Remove from the mixer.
5. Fold in the diced apples with a kitchen spoon.
6. Fill greased muffin tins or paper baking cups two-thirds full of batter.
7. Place in a preheated oven at 400°F oven and bake until golden brown.

Southern spoon bread

Ingredients: Approx. yield: 50, 2½ ounce spoonfuls
2   lbs. cornmeal, white
4   lbs. water, boiling
¾   oz. salt
4   lbs. liquid milk
8   ozs. butter
8   ozs. egg yolks
1   oz. baking powder
12 ozs. egg whites
Procedure
1. Place the cornmeal and salt in a mixing container. Pour in the boiling water and mix with a kitchen spoon until smooth. Let set until the mixture cools.
2. Blend in the milk by stirring with a kitchen spoon.
3. Place the egg yolks and butter in the bowl of electric mixing machine, using

the paddle mix on second speed until creamy.

4. Add the above cornmeal mixture gradually, mixing in second speed.
5. Add the baking powder and continue to mix in second speed until a smooth batter is formed. Remove the batter from the mixer.
6. Beat the egg whites separately with a wire whip until they form fairly stiff peaks.
7. Fold the beaten egg whites into the batter with a kitchen spoon.
8. Pour the batter into buttered baking pans, fill the pans about ⅓ full.
9. Bake in a preheated oven at 350°F until the batter sets (approximately 45 minutes).
10. Serve each 3 oz. spoonful with melted butter on top.

Popovers

Ingredients: Approx. yield: 4 doz.

2 ozs. granulated sugar
2 lbs. liquid milk
1 lb. whole eggs
1 oz. salt
1 lb. 8 ozs. bread flour

Procedure

1. Place the sugar, milk, eggs and salt in the electric mixing bowl. Beat with a wire whip in high speed until well blended.
2. Add the flour and mix with the paddle in slow speed, until a smooth batter is formed.
3. Fill greased muffin tins three-fourths full of batter. For best results fill every other cup so the batter will have room to pop over.
4. Bake in a preheated oven at 400°F until golden brown and popped over.

chapter 23 | # cookie preparation

■ Cookies are one of the most profitable items produced in the bakeshop. It is also an important and profitable item in the commercial kitchen. In the local bakeshop cookies are produced for the profit they bring in over-the-counter sales. They are a popular item because they are attractive and tasty looking when on display in the bake case. In other words they have eye appeal, and since people generally buy with their eyes, cookies will always be among the best sellers. In the commercial kitchen cookies play a somewhat different part; they are profitable in a different sense. Cookies are served with ice creams, sherbets, puddings, fruit cups, and on buffet tables. In each case, if properly presented, they add eye appeal and that extra sweet morsel to top off the final course of a delightful meal. This final touch will leave its impression on the diner to the extent that he will look forward to a return visit.

The commercial cooking student should be taught the fundamentals of cookie production because a good journeyman will possess some knowledge of baking as well as cooking. It is also possible that during his career in food service he may wish to specialize in baking, or a situation may arise where he will be required to prepare cookies since food production and baking are closely related.

COOKIE CLASSIFICATIONS

Cookies can be classed into two groups according to their texture: soft cookies and brittle cookies. *Soft cookies* are prepared from dough that contains a fairly high degree of moisture, while *brittle cookies* are prepared from doughs that contain a high percentage of sugar. These two groups of cookies are divided into six different types, depending on preparation: the ice box method, rolled method, bagged method, bar method, sheet method, and drop method.

Ice box method: Prepared from a stiff, fairly dry dough. The dough is scaled into units of 1 to 1½ pounds, rolled into round strips approximately 16 inches long; they are wrapped in wax paper and refrigerated overnight. The next day they are sliced into units approximately ½ inch thick, placed on sheet pans, covered with silicon paper, and baked.

Rolled method: Prepared from a stiff, fairly dry dough. The dough is refrigerated until thoroughly chilled, rolled out on a floured piece of canvas until about ⅛ inch thick. They are cut into desired shapes and sizes with a cookie cutter, placed on sheet pans covered with silicon paper, and baked.

Bagged method: Prepared from a moist, soft dough. The dough is placed in a pastry bag containing a pastry tube of desired shape and size, it is squeezed or pressed onto sheet pans covered with silicon paper, and baked.

Bar method: Prepared from a stiff, fairly dry dough. The dough is scaled into 1 pound units, refrigerated until thoroughly chilled, and rolled out on a floured piece of canvas to the length of a sheet pan. Three strips are placed on each silicon lined pan, leaving a space between each. The strips are flattened by pressing with the hands, brushed with egg wash, baked, and cut into bars.

Sheet method: Prepared from a moist, soft batter. The batter is spread over the surface of a silicon lined sheet pan, brushed with egg wash and sometimes sprinkled with nuts, baked, and cut into square or oblong units.

Drop method: Prepared from a moist, soft batter. The batter should be at room temperature and is dropped by spoonfuls onto silicon covered sheet pans. The amount dropped should be as uniform as possible and about the size of a quarter so they will bake evenly.

MIXING METHODS

Of all the many kinds of cookies on the market, they are all usually mixed by utilizing one of three methods:
1. Single-stage method
2. Creaming method
3. Sponge or whipping method

The *single-stage method* is performed by the simple act of placing all the ingredients in the mixing bowl at one time and mixing until all ingredients are blended to a smooth dough. All mixing is done in slow speed.

The *creaming method* involves creaming together the shortening or butter, sugar, salt and spices until light and fluffy, adding the eggs and liquid, if any is required, and sifting in the flour and leavening agent. All mixing is done in slow speed.

The *sponge or whipping method* is similar to the method used when preparing a sponge cake and therefore is so named. The eggs (whole, whites or yolks) are whipped at high speed with the sugar until either light and fluffy (soft peaks) when whipping egg whites, or until slightly thickened and lemon colored when whipping whole eggs or yolks. The remaining ingredients are usually folded into the beaten egg mixture in a very gentle motion to preserve as many air cells as possible. This method produces a product that has a light and aerated texture.

Regardless of the mixing method used never over-mix a cookie dough or the finished product will become coarse and very hard to handle. It is also recommended that the sides and bottom of the mixing bowl be scraped down with a plastic scraper at least once or twice during the mixing period to insure a lump free batter.

There are, of course, exceptions to most mixing methods but in almost all cases the mixing of a cookie dough or batter will follow very closely one of these three methods.

Rules to follow when preparing cookies

1. Use the highest grade of ingredients for best results.
2. Follow mixing instructions carefully. Overmixing makes the batter tough so they will not spread properly when baked. Undermixing results in too much spreading.
3. Weigh all ingredients carefully, too much or too little of one or the other ingredients will result in a finished product of poor quality. Use recipes that give weights rather than measures. Weights are more exact than measures.
4. Form cookies in uniform size so they will bake evenly.
5. Bake cookies on pans covered with

TABLE I.   DEFECTS AND CAUSES OF FAULTY COOKIES

Defects	Causes
Lack of spread	Too fine a granulation of sugar. Adding all sugar at one time. Excessive mixing, causing toughening of the flour structure or breaking down of sugar crystals or combination of both. Too acid a dough condition. Too hot an oven.
Excess spread	Excessive sugar. Too soft a batter consistency. Excessive pan grease. Too low an oven temperature. Excessive or improper type shortening. Too alkaline a batter.
Fall during baking	Excessive leavening. Too soft a batter. Weak flour. Improper size.
Tough cookies	Insufficient shortening. Overdeveloped batter. Flour too strong.
Sticks to pans	Too soft flour. Excessive egg content. Too slack a batter. Unclean pans. Sugar spots in dough. Improper metal used in pan construction.
Greenish cast or dull dark color	Excess bicarbonate of soda.
Black spots and harsh crumb	Excessive ammonia.
Loss of flavor	Overbaking. Too alkaline a dough.

silicon paper. The old method of greasing, or greasing and flouring, is more time consuming in setting up and cleaning up. It also creates unpleasant kitchen odors.

6. Bake according to recipe instructions but watch the baking progress carefully—adjustments may have to be made. It is difficult to give exact baking time for cookies because much depends on size, thickness of dough, and quality of ingredients.

7. Double pan if cookies are getting too much bottom heat. This can be detected if the edges of the cookies brown rapidly. To double pan an extra sheet pan is placed under the original pan to make a false bottom.

8. Check the baked cookies for possible defects. See Table I for possible causes of defects.

9. Store cookies properly:

A. *Crisp cookies:* Place in a tin container with a loose fitting top. Store in a dry place. Place in a cool oven 225°F for 5 minutes before serving.

B. *Soft cookies:* Place in an airtight tin container with a few slices of fresh apple. The apples must be changed from time to time to insure freshness.

COOKIE RECIPES

The following recipes are some of the popular ones found in the modern bake shop. They are listed in their order of appearance in the chapter.

Single stage method
(Pages 532 to 541)

Chocolate chip cookies (drop or bag method: soft)
Fruit bars (bar method: soft)
Cocoa brownies (sheet method: soft)
Fruit tea cookies (bagged method: soft)
Nut cookies (rolled method: brittle)
Brown sugar cookies (rolled method: brittle)

Ginger cookies (rolled method: brittle)
Oatmeal-raisin cookies (rolled method: brittle)
Chocolate nut wafers (bagged method: brittle)
Sugar cookies (rolled method: brittle)
Fudge cookies (rolled or bag method: brittle)
Ice box cookies (plain) (ice box method: brittle)

Creaming method
(Pages 541 to 546)

Almond toffee bar (sheet method: brittle)
Danish butter cookies (bagged method: brittle)
French macaroons (bagged method: brittle)
Gingerbread cookies (rolled method: brittle)
Short paste cookies (rolled method: brittle)
Vanilla wafers (bagged method: brittle)
Lemon wafers (bagged method: brittle)
Fruit and nut ice box cookies (ice box method: brittle)

Sponge or whipping method
(Pages 546 to 548)

Chocolate brownies (sheet method: soft)
Lady fingers (bagged method: soft)
Nut lady fingers (bagged method: soft)

SINGLE STAGE METHOD RECIPES

Chocolate chip cookies

Chocolate chip cookies are prepared from a soft, moist dough, the chips of chocolate which flow through the batter create eye appeal and supply a rich chocolate flavor to the finished product. The chocolate chips may be purchased in a retail food market or baker's supply house or small broken up pieces of sweet chocolate may be substituted. This cookie is mixed by the single-stage method.

Objectives
1. To teach the student the procedure for preparing chocolate chip cookies.
2. To teach the student how to form and bake the cookies.

Equipment
1. Mixing machine and paddle
2. Sheet pans
3. Silicon paper
4. Plastic scraper
5. Pastry bag and large plain tube
6. Baker's scale
7. French knife

Ingredients: Approx. yield: 13 doz.

1	lb. 8 ozs.	granulated sugar
1	lb.	shortening (Primex)
½	oz.	salt
¼	oz.	soda
1	lb. 8 ozs.	pastry flour
8	ozs.	pecans, chopped
4	ozs.	water (variable)
8	ozs.	whole eggs
		vanilla to taste
1	lb. 8 ozs.	chocolate chips or pieces

Preparation
1. Cover sheet pans with silicon paper.
2. Chop pecans fairly fine with French knife.
3. Have all equipment and ingredients handy.

Procedure
1. Scale all the ingredients in the electric mixing bowl at one time.
2. Mix at medium speed using the paddle, until the dough is smooth. Scrape down sides and bottom of bowl at least once during the mixing period with a plastic scraper.
3. Place the batter in a pastry bag with a large hole plain tube. Squeeze out in quarter sized cookies (approx. 1 in. dia.) onto silicon covered sheet pans.
4. Bake very light in preheated oven at 375°F.
5. Remove from the oven and let cool.

Precautions and Safety Measures
1. Use caution when chopping the pecans to avoid cutting self.
2. Do not overmix the dough.
3. Do not form a cookie larger than the size of a quarter.
4. When baking do not brown the cookies, bake light.

5. Do not remove the cookies from the sheet pan until they are cold.

Fruit bars

Fruit bars are a soft, tender, chewy cookie. They are prepared from a slightly soft dough which can prove difficult to form if the raisins are not dried properly. The dough is mixed by the single-stage method.

Objectives
1. To teach the student the procedure for preparing fruit bars.
2. To teach the student how to form, bake and cut fruit bars.

Equipment
1. Baker's scale
2. Mixing machine and paddle
3. Sheet pans
4. Silicon paper
5. Plastic scraper
6. Sauce pan, 2 qts.
7. Towel
8. French knife
9. Flour sifter

Ingredients: Approx. yield: 20 doz.

2	lbs.	granulated sugar
1	lb.	dark brown sugar
1	lb.	shortening (Primex)
¼	oz.	baking soda
1	lb.	whole eggs
½	oz.	cinnamon
3	lbs.	pastry flour
3	lbs. 8 ozs.	raisins
½	oz.	salt

Preparation
1. Soak the raisins in warm water in a sauce pan for 15 minutes, drain thoroughly, dry in a towel.
2. Line the sheet pans with silicon paper.
3. Have all ingredients and equipment handy.

Procedure
1. Place all the ingredients in the electric mixing bowl at one time.
2. Mix at low speed, using the paddle, until all ingredients are thoroughly incorporated. Scrape down sides and bottom of bowl at least once during the mixing period with a plastic scraper.
3. Scale the dough into 1½ lb. units, refrigerate until thoroughly chilled.
4. Remove one unit at a time from the refrigerator, place on a floured bench and form into a roll.

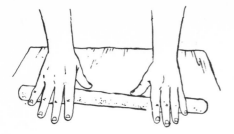

Forming dough strips for fruit bars.

Flattening to desired thickness.

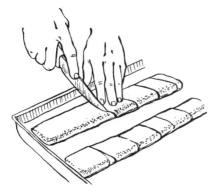

Cutting baked fruit bars.

5. Place 4 rolls across the width of each sheet pan. Flatten each roll with the hands.
6. Brush with egg wash (2 eggs and 1 cup milk blended together) or slightly beaten egg whites.
7. Bake in preheated oven at 360°F until fairly brown, let cool.
8. Cut with a French knife into bars approximately 1 in. by 3 in.
9. Dust with sifted powdered sugar.

Precautions and Safety Measures

1. Do not overmix the dough.
2. Dry the raisins thoroughly before adding to the other ingredients.
3. Do not overbake.
4. Do not attempt to cut the cookies until they have cooled.

Cocoa brownies

Cocoa brownies are very similar to the chocolate brownies but are lighter in color. Since they are mixed by the single-stage method they can be prepared much quicker.

Objectives

1. To teach the student the procedure for preparing cocoa brownies.
2. To teach the student how to bake and cut the brownies.

Equipment

1. Baker's scale
2. Sheet pans
3. Spatula
4. Mixing machine and paddle
5. French knife
6. Plastic scraper
7. Silicon paper

Ingredients: Approx. yield: 8 doz. 2 in. square cookies

2	lbs. 8 ozs. granulated sugar
1	lb. shortening (Primex)
4	ozs. butter
8	ozs. cocoa, sifted
12	ozs. glucose
1	lb. 8 ozs. pastry flour
12	ozs. whole eggs
4	ozs. water
1	lb. pecans, chopped
	vanilla, to taste
1	oz. salt

Preparation

1. Grease the sheet pans (18 in. by 24 in.) lightly or cover with silicon paper.

2. Chop the pecans fairly fine with a French knife.
3. Have all equipment and ingredients handy.
Procedure
1. Place all the ingredients in the electric mixing bowl at one time.
2. Mix at medium speed, using the paddle, until a smooth batter is formed. Scrape down sides and bottom of bowl at least once during the mixing period with a plastic scraper.
3. Remove from the mixer and pour the batter onto the prepared sheet pans. Spread evenly with a spatula.
4. Sprinkle with additional chopped pecans, if desired.
5. Place in a preheated oven at 385°F and bake until slightly firm to the touch.
6. Remove from the oven, let cool, cut with a French knife into 2 in. squares and remove from the pan with a spatula.
Precautions and Safety Measures
1. Do not overbake.
2. Do not attempt to cut the cookies until they have cooled slightly.

Fruit tea cookies

Fruit tea cookies are a type of drop cookie since they are formed by depositing small amounts of batter on sheet pans. Fruit tea cookies are mixed by the single-stage method. The fruit and nuts added to the batter produces a very tasty product.

Objectives
1. To teach the student the procedure for preparing fruit tea cookies.
2. To teach the student how to form and bake the cookies.
Equipment
1. Baker's scale
2. Sheet pans
3. Pastry bag and large plain tube
4. Kitchen spoon
5. Mixing machine and paddle
6. French knife
7. Silicon paper
8. Plastic scraper
Ingredients: Approx. yield: 18 doz.
   1 lb. 6 ozs. shortening (Primex)
   1 lb. 6 ozs. powdered sugar
   2 lbs. 8 ozs. pastry flour
   2 ozs. liquid milk (variable)
   6 ozs. raisins, chopped

Procter and Gamble Co.
Large and small size fruit tea cookies.

   2 ozs. pecans, chopped
   2 ozs. pineapple, chopped
   2 ozs. peaches, chopped
   8 ozs. whole eggs
  $\frac{1}{2}$ oz. salt
  $\frac{1}{4}$ oz. baking soda
      vanilla to taste
Preparation
1. Chop the raisins, pecans, pineapple and peaches fairly fine with a French knife.
2. Cover the sheet pans with silicon paper.
3. Have all equipment and ingredients handy.
Procedure
1. Place all the ingredients in the electric mixing bowl at one time.
2. Mix at medium speed, using the paddle, until a smooth batter is formed. Scrape down the sides and bottom of the bowl at least once during the mixing period with a plastic scraper.
3. Remove from the mixer and, using a kitchen spoon, place the dough into a pastry bag with a large plain tube. Squeeze out in quarter size cookies (approx. 1 in. dia.) onto silicon covered sheet pans.
4. Bake in a preheated oven at 375°F until very light brown.
5. Remove from the oven and let cool.
Precautions and Safety Measures
1. Do not overmix the dough; mix only until dough is smooth.
2. Do not form the cookies much larger than a quarter.

3. Do not overbake the cookies; bake only until light brown.
4. You may have to increase or decrease the moisture slightly, by adding or leaving out milk, to produce a dough best suited to your own use.
5. Do not remove the cookies from the sheet pans until they are cold.

Nut cookies

Nut cookies are prepared from a fairly stiff, dry dough, seasoned with cinnamon and flavored with chopped nuts. Nut cookies are mixed by using the single-stage method.

Objectives
1. To teach the student the procedure for preparing nut cookies.
2. To teach the student how to form and bake cookies.

Equipment
1. Mixing machine and paddle
2. Baker's scale
3. Rolling pin
4. French knife
5. Sheet pans
6. Silicon paper
7. Plastic scraper
8. Cookie cutter

Ingredients: Approx. yield: 20 doz.

14	ozs. granulated sugar
11	ozs. brown sugar
1	lb. 6 ozs. shortening (Primex)
$\frac{1}{2}$	oz. salt
$\frac{1}{4}$	oz. cinnamon
11	ozs. whole eggs
$\frac{1}{8}$	oz. baking soda
6	ozs. pecans or walnuts, chopped
2	lbs. 8 ozs. pastry flour

Preparation
1. Chop the pecans or walnuts with a French knife.
2. Line the sheet pans with silicon paper.
3. Have all equipment and ingredients handy.

Procedure
1. Place all the ingredients in the electric mixing bowl at one time.
2. Mix at medium speed, using the paddle, until a smooth dough is formed. Scrape down sides and bottom of bowl at least once during the mixing period with a plastic scraper.
3. Remove from the mixer and scale the dough into 1 lb. units. Refrigerate until chilled.
4. Remove 1 unit of dough from the refrigerator at a time and roll out to a thickness of approximately $\frac{1}{4}$ in.
5. Using a cookie cutter, cut out the cookies and place on a silicon covered sheet pan.
6. Bake in a preheated oven at 375°F to 400°F until a very light brown.

Precautions and Safety Measures
1. Use caution when chopping the nuts to avoid cutting self.
2. Do not overmix the dough, mix only until dough is smooth.
3. Do not overbake the cookies, bake only until they are slightly brown.
4. Let the cookies cool thoroughly before removing them from the sheet pan.

Brown sugar cookies

Brown sugar cookies are prepared from a fairly stiff, dry dough, with a high percentage of brown sugar present to add flavor and color to the finished product. Brown sugar cookies are mixed by using the single-stage method.

Objectives
1. To teach the student the procedure for preparing brown sugar cookies.
2. To teach the student how to form and bake brown sugar cookies.

Equipment
1. Mixing machine and paddle
2. Plastic scraper
3. Baker's scale
4. Silicon paper
5. Cookie stamp
6. Sheet pans

Ingredients: Approx. yield: 14 doz.

3	lbs. 2 ozs. brown sugar
2	lbs. 4 ozs. shortening (Primex)
1	oz. salt
$\frac{1}{2}$	oz. baking soda
4	lbs. 8 ozs. pastry flour
1	lb. whole eggs
	vanilla, to taste

Preparation
1. Line the sheet pans with silicon paper.
2. Have all equipment and ingredients handy.

Procedure
1. Place all the ingredients in the electric mixing bowl at one time.
2. Mix at medium speed, using the paddle, until a smooth dough is formed (approxi-

mately 2 minutes). Scrape down sides and bottom of bowl at least once during the mixing period with a plastic scraper.
3. Remove from the mixer and scale the dough into 12 oz. pieces (larger if desired). Refrigerate until dough is chilled.
4. Remove 1 unit of dough from the refrigerator at a time and roll by hand into round strips 16 inches long.
5. Cut into 12 equal pieces and place on the prepared sheet pans.
6. Flatten each cookie by hand, use a cookie stamp to produce an embossed effect or cut with a scalloped edge cookie cutter, if desired.
7. Bake in a preheated oven at 375°F until slightly brown.

Precautions and Safety Measures
1. Do not overmix the dough; mix only until dough is smooth.
2. Do not overbake the cookies; bake only until they are slightly brown. If the bottom is getting too much heat, double pan.
3. Let the cookies cool thoroughly before removing them from the sheet pan.

Ginger cookies

Ginger cookies are prepared from a stiff, fairly dry dough which is seasoned with ginger to create a spicy ginger taste. Ginger cookies are mixed by using the single-stage method.

Objectives
1. To teach the student the procedure for preparing ginger cookies.
2. To teach the student how to form and bake the cookies.

Equipment
1. Mixing machine and paddle
2. Plastic scraper
3. Baker's scale
4. Silicon paper
5. Cookie stamp
6. Sheet pans
7. French knife

Ingredients: Approx. yield: 8 doz.

1	lb.	granulated sugar
8	ozs.	brown sugar
8	ozs.	shortening (Primex)
1/4	oz.	baking soda
1/4	oz.	salt
1	lb. 8 ozs.	cake flour
1/4	oz.	ginger

1 1/2	oz.	molasses
8	ozs.	whole eggs
3	ozs.	water

Preparation
1. Line the sheet pans with silicon paper.
2. Have all equipment and ingredients handy.

Procedure
1. Place all the ingredients in the electric mixing bowl at one time.
2. Mix at medium speed, using the paddle, until a smooth dough is formed (approximately 2 minutes). Scrape down sides and bottom of bowl at least once during the mixing period with a plastic scraper.
3. Remove from the mixer and scale the dough into 1 lb. pieces. Refrigerate until dough is chilled.
4. Remove 1 unit of dough from the refrigerator at a time and roll by hand into round strips 16 inches long.
5. Cut with a French knife into 24 equal pieces; place on the prepared sheet pans.
6. Flatten each cookie by hand, use a cookie stamp to produce an embossed effect.
7. Bake in a preheated oven at 375°F until slightly brown.

Precautions and Safety Measures
1. Do not overbake the cookies; bake only until they are slightly brown. Double pan if necessary.
2. Do not overmix the dough; mix only until dough is smooth.
3. Let the cookies cool thoroughly before removing from the sheet pan.

Oatmeal-raisin cookies

Oatmeal-raisin cookies are prepared from a stiff, fairly dry dough with oatmeal and ground raisins being the two main ingredients. Oatmeal-raisin cookies are mixed by using the single-stage method.

Objectives
1. To teach the student the procedure for preparing oatmeal-raisin cookies.
2. To teach the student how to form and bake oatmeal-raisin cookies.

Equipment
1. Sheet pans
2. Mixing machine with paddle and grinder attachments
3. Plastic scraper
4. Silicon paper
5. Cookie stamp

6. Baker's scale
7. French knife

Ingredients: Approx. yield: 12 doz.

1	lb. 12 ozs. granulated sugar
13	ozs. shortening (Primex)
½	oz. baking soda
½	oz. salt
	cinnamon, a pinch
	vanilla, to taste
10	ozs. oatmeal, whole
4	ozs. raisins, ground
1	lb. 10 ozs. cake flour
8	ozs. water (variable)

Preparation
1. Line the sheet pans with silicon paper.
2. Grind the raisins in the food grinder using the medium hole chopper plate.
3. Have all equipment and ingredients handy.

Procedure
1. Place all the ingredients in the mixing bowl at one time.
2. Mix at medium speed, using the paddle, until a smooth dough is formed (approximately 2 minutes). Scrape down sides and bottom of bowl at least once during the mixing period with a plastic scraper.
3. Remove from the mixer and scale the dough into 1 lb. pieces. Refrigerate until the dough is chilled.
4. Remove 1 unit of dough from the refrigerator at a time and roll by hand into round strips 16 inches long.
5. Cut with a French knife into 24 equal pieces; place on the prepared sheet pans.
6. Flatten each cookie by hand, use a cookie stamp to produce an embossed effect if desired.
7. Bake in preheated oven at 350°F until slightly brown.

Precautions and Safety Measures
1. Do not overmix the dough; mix only until dough is smooth.
2. Do not overbake the cookies; bake only until they are slightly brown. Double pan if necessary.
3. Let the cookies cool before removing them from the pan.

Chocolate nut wafers

Chocolate nut wafers are prepared from a soft, moist dough, flavored with chocolate and nuts. Chocolate nut wafers are a drop type cookie and are mixed by using the single-stage method.

Objectives
1. To teach the student the procedure for preparing chocolate nut wafers.
2. To teach the student how to form and bake chocolate nut wafers.

Equipment
1. Sheet pans
2. Mixing machine with paddle and grinding attachments
3. Plastic scraper
4. Silicon paper
5. Pastry bag and large hole tube
6. Small double boiler
7. Kitchen spoon
8. Baker's scale

Ingredients: Approx. yield: 10 doz.

1	lb. granulated sugar
1	lb. shortening (Primex)
12	ozs. pastry flour
½	oz. salt
1	lb. pecans, ground very fine
4	ozs. chocolate, bitter, melted
8	ozs. egg whites
	vanilla to taste

Preparation
1. Line the sheet pans with silicon paper.
2. Grind the pecans very fine in the food grinder using the fine chopper plate.
3. Melt the bitter chocolate in a double boiler.
4. Have all equipment and ingredients handy.

Procedure
1. Place all the ingredients in the electric mixing bowl at one time.
2. Mix at medium speed, using the paddle for approximately 2 minutes, until a smooth, light mixture is obtained. Scrape down sides and bottom of bowl at least once during the mixing period with a plastic scraper.
3. Place the batter in a pastry bag with a large hole tube, using a kitchen spoon.
4. Squeeze out in quarter size cookies (approx. 1 in. dia.) onto silicon covered sheet pans.
5. Bake in preheated oven at 375°F until cookies start to brown.

Precautions and Safety Measures
1. Do not overmix the dough.
2. Form the cookies properly. The size of a quarter is large enough.
3. Bake the cookies on the light side; do not let them become too brown.

Sugar cookies

Sugar cookies are prepared from a fairly stiff, dry dough with a high percentage of sugar present to create a brittle cookie. Sugar cookies are mixed by using the single-stage method.

Objectives
1. To teach the student the procedure for preparing sugar cookies.
2. To teach the student how to form and bake sugar cookies.

Equipment
1. Sheet pans
2. Mixing machine and paddle
3. Plastic scraper
4. Baker's scale
5. Silicon paper
6. Cookie stamp
7. French knife

Ingredients: Approx. yield: 14 doz.

2	lbs. granulated sugar
1	lb. 8 ozs. shortening (Primex)
¾	oz. salt
⅛	oz. mace
2	lbs. 12 ozs. cake flour
1½	oz. baking powder
8	ozs. whole eggs
8	ozs. skim milk (variable)

Preparation
1. Line the sheet pans with silicon paper.
2. Have all equipment and ingredients handy.

Procedure
1. Place all the ingredients in the electric mixing bowl at one time.
2. Mix at medium speed, using the paddle, until a smooth dough is formed (approximately 2 minutes). Scrape down sides and bottom of bowl at least once during the mixing period with a plastic scraper.
3. Remove from the mixer and scale the dough into 1 lb. pieces. Refrigerate until dough is chilled.
4. Remove 1 unit of dough from the refrigerator at a time and roll by hand into round strips 16 inches long.
5. Cut with a French knife into 24 equal pieces and place on the prepared sheet pans.
6. Flatten each cookie by hand, use a cookie stamp to produce an embossed effect.
7. Bake in preheated oven at 375°F until a very light brown.

Precautions and Safety Measures
1. Do not overmix the dough; mix only until dough is smooth.
2. Do not overbake the cookies; bake only until they are slightly brown. If the bottom is getting too much heat, double pan.
3. Let the cookies cool thoroughly before removing them from the sheet pan.

Fudge cookies

Fudge cookies are prepared from a fairly stiff dough that is very rich with chocolate flavor. This dough, when mixed, has a consistency that makes the cookies easy to form by using either the rolled or bagged method. Fudge cookies are mixed by using the single-stage method.

Objectives
1. To teach the student the procedure for preparing fudge cookies.
2. To teach the student how to form and bake fudge cookies.

Equipment
1. Mixing machine and paddle
2. Plastic scraper
3. Baker's scale
4. Sheet pans
5. Silicone paper
6. Pastry bag

Ingredients: Approx. yield 14 doz.

2	lbs. granulated sugar
1	lb. 8 oz. shortening (Primex)
¾	oz. salt
2	lb. 4 oz. cake flour
6	oz. cocoa
1½	oz. baking powder
8	oz. whole eggs
8	oz. liquid skim milk (variable)

Preparation
1. Line the sheet pans with silicone paper.
2. Have all equipment and ingredients handy.

Procedure
1. Place all the ingredients in the electric mixing bowl at one time.
2. Mix at medium speed, using the paddle, until a smooth dough is formed (approxi-

mately 2 mins.). Scrape down sides and bottom of bowl with plastic scraper.

3. Remove from the mixer and scale the dough into 16-oz. pieces. Mold and roll by hand into round strips about 16 in. long.
4. Cut with a French knife into 24 equal pieces and place them on prepared sheet pans.
5. Flatten each cookie by hand and use a cookie stamp to produce an embossed effect. Top with fruit or nuts if desired.
6. Bake in a pre-heated oven at 375° F until cookies start to brown.

Note: these cookies may also be formed by placing the batter in a pastry bag with medium size star or plain tip tube, squeezing out into the prepared sheet pans in pieces about the size of a quarter, then decorating the tops with decorettes and baking.

Precautions and Safety Measures
1. When baking, avoid strong bottom heat.
2. Do not over-bake. Remember that cookies continue to bake when removed from the oven.
3. Form the cookies as uniformly as possible so they will bake evenly.
4. Let the cookies cool thoroughly before removing from the sheet pan.

Ice box cookies (plain)

Ice box cookies are prepared from a stiff, fairly dry dough which is formed into rolls and refrigerated for at least six hours before they are sliced and baked. Fruits, nuts, chocolate, and spices can be added to the dough to create variety. This recipe is mixed by using the single-stage method.

Objectives
1. To teach the student the procedure for preparing ice box cookies.
2. To teach the student how to create variety using the basic mix.
3. To teach the student how to form and bake ice box cookies.

Equipment
1. Baker's scale
2. Sheet pans
3. Silicon paper
4. Mixing machine and paddle
5. French knife

Procter and Gamble Co.
Large and small varieties of ice box cookies.

6. Plastic scraper
7. Wax paper
8. Pastry brush

Ingredients: Approx. yield: 12 doz.
1	lb. 12 ozs. powdered sugar (4x)
1	lb. 8 ozs. shortening (Primex)
¾	oz. salt
2	lbs. pastry flour
8	ozs. whole eggs
	vanilla, to taste

Preparation
1. Line the sheet pans with silicon paper.
2. Have all equipment and ingredients handy.

Procedure
1. Place all the ingredients in the electric mixing bowl at one time.
2. Mix at medium speed, using the paddle, until a smooth dough is formed (approximately 2 minutes). Scrape down sides and bottom of bowl at least once during the mixing period with a plastic scraper.
3. Remove dough from the mixing machine, divide into 1 lb. units, roll into units about 18 inches long. Roll in ground nut meats, macaroon coconut, or colored sugars.
4. Wrap each roll in wax paper, place on sheet pans. Place in the refrigerator for at least 6 hours.
5. Remove from the refrigerator, unwrap and slice each roll into ½ in. slices with a French knife. Place on the prepared cookie sheets.

6. Bake in a preheated oven at 370°F until the cookies become light brown. Avoid too much bottom heat.

Note: Wash the cookies with egg wash before baking or brush with glaze after baking. (*Glaze:* to 2 lbs. of glucose add 1 lb. of water and bring to a boil.) Cookies may also be decorated with icing after baking.

VARIATIONS:

1. *Fruit cookies:* Add 1 lb. of chopped fruits to 6 lbs of cookie dough.
2. *Nut cookies:* Add 1 lb. of chopped nuts to 6 lbs. of cookie dough.
3. *Molasses-spice cookies:* Add 3 ozs. of spice combination, 4 ozs. molasses, and 2 ozs. of flour to 6 lbs. of cookie dough. (*Suggested spice combination:* 8 ozs. cinnamon, 3 ozs. mace, 1 oz. ginger, 1 oz. allspice, 3 ozs. nutmeg. Blend together.)

Precautions and Safety Measures

1. Do not overmix the dough. Mix only until a smooth dough is formed.
2. Do not overbake the cookies. Avoid too much bottom heat.
3. Handle the cookies carefully after baking. Let them cool thoroughly before removing them from the sheet pans.

CREAMING RECIPES

Almond toffee bars

Almond toffee bars are prepared from a soft, moist batter of spreading consistency. The basic dough is spread on sheet pans and baked, then spread with a thin layer of chocolate and topped with nuts. Almond bars are mixed by using the creaming method.

Objectives

1. To teach the student the procedure for preparing almond toffee bars.
2. To teach the student how to bake and cut the bars.

Equipment

1. Sheet pan (12 in. by 18 in.)
2. Baker's scale
3. French knife
4. Plastic scraper
5. Mixing machine
6. Double boiler
7. Spatula

Ingredients: Approx. yield: 54 cookies
2 in. square

1	lb. butter
1	lb. brown sugar
1½	oz. egg yolks
1	lb. 3 ozs. pastry flour
1	lb. semi-sweet chocolate
4	ozs. sliced almonds
	vanilla, to taste

Preparation

1. Grease the bottom and sides of the sheet pan with additional butter.
2. Melt the chocolate in a double boiler.
3. Separate the egg yolks from the whites. Save whites for use in another preparation.
4. Have all equipment and ingredients handy.

Procedure

1. Place the butter in the electric mixing bowl; using the paddle, mix at slow speed until the butter is creamed.
2. Add the brown sugar and continue creaming until the mixture is light and fluffy.
3. Add the egg yolks and vanilla, increase the speed of the machine to high and beat well.
4. Reduce the speed of the mixer to slow, add the flour and mix until well blended. Scrape down bowl at least once, while mixing in this stage, with a plastic scraper.
5. Spread the mixture on the greased sheet pan as evenly as possible with a spatula.
6. Bake in a preheated oven at 325°F for about 20 minutes or until the batter is set.
7. Remove from the oven and spread a thin layer of melted chocolate over the cookie layer with a spatula while it is still warm.
8. Sprinkle with almonds, cut into 2 in. squares while still slightly warm with a French knife.
9. Let cool before removing the cookies.

Precautions and Safety Measures

1. Do not overbake the cookie mixture, bake only until set.
2. Spread the cookie mixture on the sheet pan as evenly as possible, so it will bake uniform.
3. Melt the chocolate in a warm place or in the top of a double boiler.

Danish butter cookies

Danish butter cookies are prepared from a soft, smooth, moist dough which is very rich in butter content. The cookies are formed by using a star tube in a pastry bag. Danish butter cookies are mixed by using the creaming method.

Objectives
1. To teach the student the procedure for preparing Danish butter cookies.
2. To teach the student how to form and bake the cookies.

Equipment
1. Sheet pans
2. Silicon paper
3. Flour sifter
4. Pastry bag and large star tube
5. Baker's scale
6. Plastic scraper
7. Mixing machine and paddle
8. Kitchen spoon

Ingredients: Approx. yield: 16 doz.
1   lb. 8 ozs. granulated sugar
12   ozs. shortening (Primex)
12   ozs. butter
¼   oz. salt
2   lbs. 6 ozs. cake flour
1   oz. milk, dry
⅛   oz. baking powder
5   ozs. whole eggs
4   ozs. water
      vanilla, to taste

Preparation
1. Line the sheet pans with silicon paper.
2. Have all equipment and ingredients handy.

Procedure
1. Place the sugar, shortening, butter, salt, vanilla, and dry milk together in the electric mixing bowl. Using the paddle, cream at slow speed until light and fluffy. Scrape down bowl with plastic scraper.
2. Add the eggs and continue to mix at slow speed until well incorporated (approximately 3 minutes).
3. Add the water and blend in thoroughly still mixing at slow speed.
4. Sift together the baking powder and flour, add to the above mixture and mix at slow speed until a smooth batter is formed. Scrape down bowl with plastic scraper.
5. Remove from the mixer and place the batter in a pastry bag with a fairly large star tube. Use a kitchen spoon to put the batter in the pastry tube.
6. Squeeze out onto the prepared sheet pans.

Form the cookies about the size of a quarter or larger if desired.
7. Bake in preheated oven at 375°F until they start to brown.

Note: These cookies can be decorated with chopped nuts, colored sugars or by placing a cherry, raisin, icing, cinnamon candy or pecan in the center of each cookie.

Precautions and Safety Measures
1. Do not overmix the batter; mix only until smooth.
2. Form the cookies as uniform as possible so they will bake evenly.
3. Do not overbake; remove from the oven when cookies become slightly brown. Avoid too much bottom heat.

French macaroons

French macaroons are prepared from a smooth, medium stiff, rich dough which contains a large percentage of almond paste to provide the characteristic almond flavor. French macaroons are mixed by using the creaming method.

Objectives
1. To teach the student the procedure for preparing French macaroons.
2. To teach the student how to form and bake French macaroons.

Equipment
1. Sheet pans
2. Silicon paper
3. Pastry bag and star tube
4. Baker's scale
5. Mixing machine
6. Plastic scraper
7. Kitchen spoon

Ingredients: Approx. yield: 5 doz.
2   lbs. almond or macaroon paste
1   lb. granulated sugar
8   ozs. powdered sugar
⅛   oz. salt
10   ozs. egg whites (variable)

Preparation
1. Line the sheet pans with silicon paper
2. Have all equipment and ingredients handy.

Procedure
1. Place the almond or macaroon paste, granulated sugar, salt, and powdered sugar in the electric mixing bowl. Using the paddle, mix in slow speed until slightly blended. Scrape down the bowl with a plastic scraper.

2. Add the egg whites gradually while continuing to mix in slow speed until a medium stiff dough is formed. The amount of egg whites added will vary depending on the dryness of the paste.
3. Remove the dough from the mixer, place in a pastry bag with a medium star tube, using a kitchen spoon, and squeeze out onto prepared sheet pans. Form the cookies into various shapes, decorate with fruit or nuts.
4. Place the cookies on a rack and allow them to dry for several hours. This will cause a crust to form which is desirable for this kind of cookie.
5. Bake the cookies in a preheated oven at 375°F until they become light brown. Brush them with a glaze as soon as they are removed from the oven. (Glaze: 1½ lbs. glucose and 8 ozs. water. Combine the two ingredients and bring to a boil, stirring occasionally with a kitchen spoon.)

Precautions and Safety Measures
1. Add the egg whites only until the desired dough consistency is reached.
2. Do not overbake the cookies; bake until they become light brown.
3. When glazing the warm cookies, brush lightly so cookies will not be broken.

Gingerbread cookies

Gingerbread cookies are prepared from a smooth, stiff, fairly soft dough which is highly seasoned with ginger. The dough can be formed into bars or into little ginger men. This type of dough is mixed by using the creaming method.

Objectives
1. To teach the student the procedure for preparing gingerbread cookies.
2. To teach the student how to form and bake gingerbread cookies.

Equipment
1. Sheet pans
2. Silicon paper
3. Baker's scale
4. Mixing machine and paddle
5. French knife or gingerbread man cookie cutter
6. Rolling pin
7. Plastic scraper

Ingredients: Approx. yield: 16 doz. cookies or 24 gingerbread men
1 lb. shortening (Primex)
2 lb. granulated sugar
1 lb. brown sugar
¾ oz. baking soda
3 ozs. molasses, dark
½ oz. salt
1 lb. whole eggs
3 lbs. pastry flour
¼ oz. ginger
¼ oz. cinnamon

Preparation
1. Line the sheet pans with silicon paper.
2. Have all equipment and ingredients handy.

Procedure
1. Place the shortening, granulated sugar, brown sugar, baking soda, salt, and molasses together in the electric mixing bowl. Using the paddle, cream together at slow speed until smooth. Scrape down the bowl with the plastic scraper.
2. Add the eggs, continue to cream at slow speed until light and smooth.
3. Sift together the flour, ginger and cinnamon. Add to the above mixture slowly, mix at slow speed until the dough is very smooth. Scrape down the bowl at least once during this mixing stage with a plastic scraper.
4. Remove the dough from the mixer and divide into 1 lb. 8 oz. units. Refrigerate until chilled.
5. Remove one unit of dough from the refrigerator at a time. Roll out about ¼ in. thick on a floured piece of canvas.
6. Cut into bars with a French knife or cut out with a gingerbread man cookie cutter. If forming gingerbread men use currants for eyes, noses, etc.
7. Place on prepared sheet pans and bake in preheated oven at 400°F until they brown slightly.
8. Remove from the oven, let cool, and decorate the gingerbread men with icing.

Precautions and Safety Measures
1. Chill the dough thoroughly for best results when rolling.
2. Roll the dough on a floured piece of canvas to avoid sticking.
3. Do not overbake; bake until light brown.
4. Let cookies cool before removing them from the sheet pan.

Short paste cookies

Short paste cookies are prepared from a smooth, stiff, fairly dry dough which contains a large percentage of shortening. The finished product is crisp and extremely tender. Short paste cookies are mixed by using the creaming method.

Objectives
1. To teach the student the procedure for preparing short paste cookies.
2. To teach the student how to form and bake the cookies.

Equipment
1. Baker's scale
2. Sheet pans
3. Silicon paper
4. Rolling pin
5. Cookie cutters
6. Plastic scraper
7. Pastry brush
8. Mixing machine and paddle

Ingredients: Approx. yield: 10 doz.
1 lb. shortening (Primex)
8 ozs. butter
1 lb. granulated sugar
½ oz. salt
4 ozs. whole eggs
4 ozs. liquid milk
2 lbs. 8 ozs. pastry flour
vanilla, to taste

Preparation
1. Line sheet pans with silicon paper.
2. Have all equipment and ingredients handy.

Procedure
1. Place the sugar, shortening, butter, and salt in the electric mixing bowl. Using the paddle, cream together at slow speed. Scrape down the bowl with a plastic scraper.
2. Add the eggs gradually, while continuing to mix at slow speed, until thoroughly blended with other ingredients.
3. Add the milk and mix at slow speed until thoroughly blended.
4. Add the vanilla and flour while continuing to mix at slow speed. Mix until dough is smooth (approximately 2 minutes). Scrape down the bowl.
5. Remove the dough from the mixer divide into 1 lb. units. Refrigerate until chilled.

Procter and Gamble Co.

Cookie varieties prepared from short paste cookie dough.

6. Remove one unit of dough from the refrigerator at a time. Roll out about ⅛ inch thick on a floured piece of canvas.
7. Cut out cookies with cookie cutters into various shapes, place on prepared sheet pans. Brush with egg wash and decorate.
8. Bake in a preheated oven at 375°F until light brown.

Precautions and Safety Measures
1. Do not overmix the dough; mix only until smooth.
2. Roll only one unit of dough at a time. Chilled dough is easier to work with.
3. Do not overbake; bake only until cookies are light brown.

Vanilla wafers

Vanilla wafers are prepared from a soft, smooth, moist dough which is flavored with vanilla to supply the characteristic flavor. Vanilla wafers are mixed by using the creaming method.

Objectives
1. To teach the student the procedure for preparing vanilla wafers.
2. To teach the student how to form and bake vanilla wafers.

Equipment
1. Baker's scale
2. Sheet pans
3. Silicon paper
4. Plastic scraper
5. Mixing machine and paddle
6. Pastry bag and plain tube
7. Kitchen spoon

Ingredients: Approx. yield: 10 doz.

- 1 lb. granulated sugar
- 10 ozs. butter
- 6 ozs. shortening (Primex)
- ¼ oz. salt
  vanilla, to taste
- 12 ozs. whole eggs
- 1 lb. 6 ozs. pastry flour

Preparation

1. Line the sheet pans with silicon paper.
2. Have all equipment and ingredients handy.

Procedure

1. Place the sugar, butter, shortening, salt and vanilla in the electric mixing bowl. Using the paddle, cream at slow speed until smooth. Scrape down the bowl with a plastic scraper.
3. Add the flour gradually, mix at slow speed until smooth. Scrape down the bowl again while mixing in this stage.
4. Remove from the mixing machine and place the batter in a pastry bag, with a plain tube, using a kitchen spoon.
5. Squeeze out onto the prepared sheet pans. Form the cookies about the size of a quarter. Leave enough space between drops for spreading.
6. Bake in a preheated oven at 375°F until the edges start to brown.

Precautions and Safety Measures

1. Do not overmix the batter; mix only until smooth.
2. Form the cookies as uniform as possible so they will bake evenly.
3. Do not overbake the cookies; remove from oven when edges start to brown.
4. Let the cookies cool before removing them from the sheet pan.

Lemon wafers

Lemon wafers are prepared from a soft, moist, smooth batter which has a pronounced lemon flavor. These wafers contain a high percentage of sugar which will produce a crisp, brittle cookie. Lemon wafers are mixed by using the creaming method.

Objectives

1. To teach the student the procedure for preparing lemon wafers.
2. To teach the student how to form and bake lemon wafers.

Equipment

1. Sheet pans
2. Silicon paper
3. Plastic scraper
4. Pastry bag and plain tip tube
5. Baker's scale
6. Mixing machine and paddle
7. Box grater
8. Flour sifter
9. Kitchen spoon

Ingredients: Approx. yield: 8 doz.

- 12 ozs. granulated sugar
- ¼ oz. salt
- 8 ozs. shortening (Primex)
- ½ oz. powdered milk
- 2 ozs. whole eggs
- 3½ ozs. water
- ½ oz. lemon flavor
- ⅛ oz. lemon rind, grated
- 1 lb. cake flour
- ¼ oz. baking powder

Preparation

1. Grate the lemon rinds on the medium grid of a box grater.
2. Line the sheet pans with silicon paper.
3. Have all equipment and ingredients handy.

Procedure

1. Place the sugar, salt, shortening, and powdered milk in the electric mixing bowl. Using the paddle, cream together in low speed. Scrape down the bowl with a plastic scraper.
2. Add the eggs and continue to cream at low speed until thoroughly blended.
3. Add the water, lemon flavor, and rind; blend in, continuing to use low speed.
4. Sift together the flour and baking powder, add gradually while continuing to mix at low speed; mix until batter is smooth.
5. Remove the batter from the mixer, place in a pastry bag, with a large plain tip tube, using a kitchen spoon.
6. Squeeze out quarter size cookies (approx. 1 in. dia.) onto the prepared sheet pans. Allow about 1 in. space between each cookie as they will spread slightly.
7. Bake in preheated oven at 375°F until they become light brown.

Precautions and Safety Measures

1. Do not overmix the batter; mix only until smooth.
2. Form the cookies as uniform as possible so they will bake evenly.

3. Do not overbake; bake only until light brown.
4. Let the cookies cool before attempting to remove them from the sheet pans.

Fruit and nut ice box cookie

Fruit and nut ice box cookies are prepared from a stiff, rich, slightly dry dough which is filled with chopped cherries and pecans to improve the eating qualities. This cookie is mixed by using the creaming method.

Objectives
1. To teach the student the procedure for preparing fruit and nut ice box cookies.
2. To teach the student how to form and bake the cookies.

Equipment
1. Sheet pans
2. Baker's scale
3. Silicon paper
4. Mixing machine and paddle
5. Plastic scraper
6. French knife
7. Wax paper

Ingredients: approx. yield: 18 doz.

1	lb.	granulated sugar
1	lb.	shortening (Primex)
1	lb.	butter
1¼	oz.	salt
3	ozs.	egg whites
¼	oz.	vanilla
3	lbs.	pastry flour
1	lb. 8 ozs.	glazed cherries, chopped
6	ozs.	pecans, chopped

Preparation
1. Chop the cherries and pecans fairly coarse with a French knife.
2. Line the sheet pans with silicon paper.
3. Have all equipment and ingredients handy.

Procedure
1. Place the sugar, salt, shortening, and butter together in the electric mixing bowl. Using the paddle, cream together slightly in second speed. Scrape down the bowl with a plastic scraper.
2. Add the egg whites and vanilla gradually; blend in at second speed and scrape down the bowl with the plastic scraper.
3. Add the pastry flour and mix at slow speed until smooth.
4. Add the cherries and pecans; mix at slow speed until the dough is smooth (approximately 1 minute).

5. Remove the dough from the mixer and scale into 12 oz. pieces, roll in ground nutmeats, colored sugar or macaroon coconut to about 20 inches long.
6. Wrap each roll in wax paper. Place on a sheet pan and refrigerate until thoroughly chilled.
7. Remove one roll from the refrigerator at a time, slice crosswise with a French knife about ½ in. thick and place the cookies on the prepared sheet pans.
8. Bake in preheated oven at 370°F until they start to brown slightly.

Precautions and Safety Measures
1. Do not overmix the dough; mix only until smooth.
2. If the dough is too warm, chill slightly before attempting to roll.
3. Use a sharp French knife when slicing the cookies.
4. Do not overbake; bake until they become a very light brown. If too much bottom heat is present, double pan.
5. Let the cookies cool thoroughly before removing them from the sheet pans.

SPONGE AND WHIPPING METHOD RECIPES

Chocolate brownies

Chocolate brownies are a rich, fudgy, sheet type cookie. The batter is moist and smooth with a slightly runny consistency. Nuts are generally added to the batter to enhance the eating qualities. This cookie is similar to a cake and is mixed like a cake (sponge or whipping method) rather then a cookie.

Objectives
1. To teach the student the procedure for preparing chocolate brownies.
2. To teach the student how to bake and cut the brownies.

Equipment
1. Baker's scale
2. Sheet pans
3. Spatula
4. Mixing machine and wire whip attachment
5. French knife
6. Plastic scraper
7. Kitchen spoon
8. 1 qt. sauce pan
9. Wooden spoon

Ingredients: Approx. yield: 8 doz. 2 in.
square cookies

1   lb. 8 ozs. butter
1   lb. chocolate, bittersweet
3   lbs. granulated sugar
1   lb. 4 ozs. whole eggs
1   lb. cake flour, sifted
1   lb. pecans, chopped
    vanilla, to taste

Preparation

1. Chop the pecans fairly fine with a French knife.
2. Melt the chocolate and butter together in a sauce pan.
3. Grease sheet pan slightly.
4. Have all equipment and ingredients handy.

Procedure

1. Place the eggs and sugar in the electric mixing bowl. Using the wire whip, beat for approximately 10 minutes in high speed until the eggs become a lemon color.
2. Reduce the mixing speed to slow and pour in the melted butter-chocolate mixture. Mix until thoroughly incorporated. Scrape down bowl with a plastic scraper.
3. Remove from the mixing machine and fold in the sifted flour with a wooden spoon.
4. Add the vanilla and fold in the chopped pecans with a wooden spoon.
5. Pour the batter onto a greased sheet pan 18 by 24 in., spread even with a spatula.
6. Bake in preheated oven at 350°F until slightly firm to the touch.
7. Remove from the oven, let cool, cut into 2 in. squares with a French knife and remove from the pan with a spatula.

Precautions and Safety Measures

1. Do not overbake.
2. Do not attempt to cut the cookies until they have cooled slightly.

Lady fingers

Lady fingers are prepared from a very light, fluffy, sponge type batter. The secret of a successful preparation lies in beating the eggs and sugar to a proper degree of stiffness and folding the flour in gently so not to break the air cells. Lady fingers are used to decorate or set up special pastry items or as a special cookie. They are mixed by the sponge or whipping method.

Objectives

1. To teach the student the procedure for preparing lady fingers.
2. To teach the student how to form and bake lady fingers.

Equipment

1. Baker's scale
2. Sheet pans
3. Silicon paper
4. Pastry bag and large hole plain tube
5. Mixing machine and wire whip attachment
6. Plastic scraper
7. Wooden spoon
8. Flour sifter

Ingredients: Approx. yield: 110 fingers

12   ozs. whole eggs
12   ozs. egg yolks
1   lb. 8 ozs. granulated sugar
2   ozs. glucose
¼   oz. salt
¼   oz. vanilla
1   lb. 10 oz. pastry flour
     powdered sugar (10X) as needed

Preparation

1. Line the sheet pans with silicon paper.
2. Have all equipment and ingredients handy.

Procedure

1. Place the whole eggs, egg yolks, sugar, salt, and glucose in the electric mixing bowl. Using the wire whip, beat until slightly thick and lemon colored. Scrape down the bowl with a plastic scraper. Remove from the mixer.
2. Add the vanilla, fold in gently using a large wooden spoon.
3. Sift the flour and fold in gently using a large wooden spoon.
4. Place the mixture in a pastry bag with a large whole plain tube, press out strips 2½ in. long and ½ in. wide on the prepared sheet pans.
5. Dust the tops of the lady fingers with sifted powdered sugar. Remove the excess sugar from the sheet pan.
6. Bake in a preheated oven at 400°F until very light brown.
7. Let cool, remove the fingers from the paper, and press two fingers together forming a sandwich.

1. When folding the flour, incorporate thoroughly but do not overmix.
2. After dusting the tops of the fingers with powdered sugar, bake immediately.
3. Do not overbake the fingers; bake only until they start to brown.
4. If a problem develops when removing the fingers from the paper, moisten the back of the paper with water.

Nut finger wafers

Nut finger wafers are prepared from a soft, moist, smooth batter which is formed into finger shape by using a pastry bag and plain tube. They are mixed in the same manner as a cake by using the sponge or whipping method.

Objectives
1. To teach the student the procedure for preparing nut finger wafers.
2. To teach the student how to form and bake nut finger wafers.

Equipment
1. Sheet pans
2. Silicon paper
3. Baker's scale
4. Mixing machine and wire whip
5. Pastry bag and plain tube
6. Plastic scraper
7. Wooden spoon
8. French knife

Ingredients: Approx. yield: 12 doz.

1	lb. 8 ozs. egg whites
1	lb. 8 ozs. granulated sugar
1	lb. 8 ozs. powdered sugar
1	lb. 6 ozs. pecans or walnuts, chopped very fine
4	ozs. cornstarch
1/4	oz. cinnamon

Preparation
1. Chop the pecans or walnuts very fine with a French knife.
2. Line the sheet pans with silicon paper.
3. Have all equipment and ingredients handy.

Procedure
1. Place the egg whites in the electric mixing bowl. Using the wire whip, beat at high speed until they start to foam.
2. Add the granulated sugar gradually while continuing to mix at high speed until the mixture forms a soft peak, remove from the mixer. Scrap bowl with plastic scraper.
3. Blend together the powdered sugar, corn starch, cinnamon, and nuts; fold into the meringue mixture with a wooden spoon.
4. Place the mixture in a pastry bag, with a plain tube, using a wooden spoon. Squeeze out in finger shapes onto the prepared sheet pans.
5. Bake in preheated oven at 275°F until slightly brown.

Precautions and Safety Measures
1. Do not overwhip the meringue; whip only until soft peaks form.
2. Form the cookies as uniformly as possible so they will bake evenly.
3. Do not overbake the cookies, remove from the oven when they start to brown slightly.
4. Let the cookies cool before removing them from the sheet pans.

chapter 24

roll doughs and sweet doughs

■ The purpose of this chapter is to acquaint the student with roll doughs and sweet doughs. The different types of doughs and the variety of products that can be prepared from each are introduced. It is important that the student becomes acquainted with these yeast risen products because they are so common in the food service industry.

The homemade product has always been successful in the food service industry. The homemade pie, soup, or biscuit is usually recognized as a superior product and in many cases an establishment builds its reputation on them. The same can be said for hot rolls and sweet dough products, such as Danish pastry, that are served warm directly from the oven. When products such as these can be featured on the breakfast, luncheon and dinner menus, total sales and customer count is bound to increase.

To produce these products it takes know-how and skill. Both of these essentials can be acquired by the student cook if exposed to these products while in school or on the job. He should become familiar with the ingredients in the dough and their reaction during the mixing, proofing and baking periods. Skill will improve through the constant practice of working with the various units of dough.

DOUGH FORMULAS

Most roll and sweet dough formulas consist of flour (bread or pastry), liquid (dry milk and water or milk), shortening, sugar, eggs, salt and yeast. Sweet dough usually has a spice, such as mace, and a flavor, such as vanilla, added to it. Each one of these ingredients plays an important part in producing successful rolls and sweet dough varieties.

Flour is one of the most important ingredients used in the preparation of roll and sweet dough. Wheat, from which flour is made, is the only cereal that contains fairly equal portions of gluten and gliadin, the two properties that must be present in the flour used for a successful roll or sweet dough. When these two properties are mixed with water they form the rough, rubbery, elastic substance known as gluten. It is the gluten in bread and pastry flour that gives the dough the strength to hold the gases produced by the yeast. Flour performs the following tasks when mixing and baking rolls and sweet doughs:

1. Supplies strength to the dough.
2. Supplies structure to the baked product.
3. Supplies nutritional value.
4. Acts as an absorbing agent.

Milk used in the preparation of roll and sweet doughs may be either in liquid or dry form. If the liquid form is used either whole milk or skim is usually called for in the formula. If dry milk is used it must be reconstituted in water. This can be done before mixing or during the mixing period. Milk performs the following tasks in doughs:

1. Improves the texture of the dough.
2. Supplies moisture.
3. Causes the gluten to form.
4. Adds food value.
5. Improves the flavor.

Shortening used in yeast-dough products is important for the following reasons:

1. Supplies richness and tenderness to the baked product.
2. Improves the eating qualities.
3. Improves the grain and texture of the baked product.
4. Develops the flaky layers in puff and Danish pastry.
5. Improves the keeping qualities of the baked product.

Most yeast dough formulas will call for the standard hydrogenated shortening because it possesses the properties required for best results.

Eggs used in the yeast dough products are generally in whole form, the yolk and whites. They may be either fresh or frozen—both will produce good results. They are important to the finished product for the following reasons:

1. Supplies the dough with added color.
2. Adds flavor to the baked product.
3. Supplies structure to the dough.
4. Increases the volume.
5. Improves the grain and texture of the product.

Sugars in granulated or syrup form are usually used in yeast dough formulas. They are important for the following reasons:

1. Supplies the necessary sweetness.
2. Serves as a form of food to stimulate the growth of the yeast.
3. Supplies color to the baked product.
4. Supplies moisture and helps prolong freshness.
5. Helps provide a good grain and texture to the baked product.

Yeast, the leavening agent used in roll and sweet dough formulas, may be of two types:

1. Compressed yeast.

2. Dry yeast (most moisture is removed).

Whichever type called for in the recipe is the one that should be used. However, occasions may arise where dry yeast will have to be substituted for compressed yeast. In that case only 40% of dry yeast by weight is used. For example if the recipe calls for 1 lb. of compressed yeast or 16 ozs., then 40% of 16 = 6.4 ozs. Use 6.4 ozs. of dry yeast.

(The remaining 60% is made up of water: 60% of 16 = 9.6 ozs.)

If the dry yeast is purchased in the small ¼ oz. package (which equals ⅔ oz. of the compressed yeast), then three packages must be used for every 2 ozs. of compressed yeast called for in the formula.

It is important in the preparation of yeast dough products that the action of the yeast be controled. The amount of salt used in the formula will control the yeast to some degree, but the big controlling factor is the temperature of the dough. Yeast reacts to temperatures as follows:

Storage stage: 30°F to 40°F.
Slow: 60°F to 75°F.
Normal: 80°F to 85°F.
Fast: 90°F to 100°F.
Action stops: 140°F.

The yeast starts to grow when it is mixed with flour, water and sugar. Yeast plants multiply rapidly and produce the carbon dioxide gas which causes the dough to rise. Yeast is important to roll and sweet doughs because it increases the volume, improves the flavor, grain and texture.

DOUGH PRODUCTION

The steps taken in the production of roll and sweet doughs are listed below in the sequence that is usually followed.

1. Have all equipment and ingredients handy.
2. *Scale* all ingredients correctly. A baker's scale is normally used.
3. *Mix* to develop the dough. An electric mixer is normally used.
4. *Knead* the dough: work it smooth and force out all air.
5. *Proof* the dough: Place in a lightly greased container and let rise to double in bulk.
6. *Punch* the dough by pressing it back to its original size; place on a floured bench.
7. *Knead* a second time to remove all air.
8. *Scale* the dough into individual units.
9. *Make up* into desired shapes and sizes.
10. *Pan:* Place the units on prepared pans allowing space for proofing.
11. *Pan proof:* Let each unit rise to double in bulk. This is usually done in a proofing cabinet under proper moisture and temperature conditions (high moisture content and a temperature of 85 to 90°F).
12. *Bake* at required temperatures until golden brown and done.

ROLL AND SWEET DOUGH RECIPES

The roll and sweet dough formulas presented on the following pages will produce a great variety of yeast risen products. The doughs are easy to work with and will possess excellent eating qualities, provided care is taken in each production step. Fillings and toppings for sweet rolls are given at the end of the chapter.

Roll doughs
(Pages 552 to 557)

Soft dinner roll dough no. I
Soft dinner roll dough no. II
Soft rye dough
Hard roll dough
Butter flake roll dough

Sweet doughs
(Pages 557 to 562)
Virginia pastry dough
Sweet dough
Danish pastry dough

Danish and sweet dough fillings and toppings
(Pages 562 to 565)
Almond paste filling
Fruit filling
Cream filling
Honey fruit filling
Orange filling no. I
Almond filling
Filbert filling
Applesauce-pecan filling
Aloho filling
Date nut filling
Orange filling no. II
Confection roll filling
Butter topping
Prep streusel topping
Almond brittle topping or filling
Cinnamon nut topping

ROLL DOUGH RECIPES

Soft dinner roll dough No. I

Soft dinner roll dough (No. I) is a smooth, white-textured dough that is easy to work with and can be used to prepare many different varieties. Soft dinner roll dough produces a baked product with excellent eating qualities.

Objectives
1. To teach the student the procedure for preparing soft dinner roll dough.
2. To teach the student how to scale the ingredients and mix the dough.
3. To teach the student how to proof, make up, and bake the rolls.

Equipment
1. Mixing machine and dough hook
2. Baker's scale
3. Plastic scraper
4. Dough cutter (metal scraper may be used)
5. Stock pot, 5 gal.
6. Sheet pans

1. Making up soft dinner rolls into pocketbooks: Proofing up or forming each unit of dough.

2. Marking or denting each unit of dough with a pie pin.

3. Forming the pocketbooks.

Procter and Gamble Co.

4. Sheet pan of rolls ready for the proofing cabinet.

Procter and Gamble Co.
Soft dinner rolls formed into pocketbooks.

7. Silicon paper
8. Dough thermometer
9. Proofing cabinet
10. Kitchen spoon
11. 1 gal. stainless steel container

Ingredients: Approx. yield: 15½ doz. rolls
1 lb. granulated sugar
1 lb. 4 ozs. hydrogenated shortening
8 ozs. dry milk
2 ozs. salt
6 ozs. whole eggs
6 ozs. compressed yeast
4 lbs. cold water
7 lbs. bread flour

Preparation
1. Prepare an egg wash (4 eggs to a pt. of milk).
2. Cover sheet pans with silicon paper.
3. Light the oven, preheat to 375°F.
4. Grease the inside of a 5 gal. stock pot.
5. Have all equipment and ingredients handy.

Procedure
1. Dissolve the yeast in the water. Place in a stainless steel container and stir with a kitchen spoon.
2. Place all the ingredients, including the dissolved yeast, in the electric mixing bowl. Mix, using the dough hook, at medium speed until the gluten develops and the dough leaves the sides of the bowl and clings to the dough hook. Check the dough temperature with a dough thermometer. Temperature should be approximately 80°F.
3. Remove dough from mixing bowl using a

plastic scraper; place on a floured bench and knead.
4. Place the dough in greased container. Let rise until double in bulk.
5. Turn out on a floured bench, knead a second time. Cut the dough into 1¼ oz. units using a dough cutter.
6. Form into rolls of desired shape, dip in egg wash and sesame or poppy seed if desired. Place the rolls on the silicon covered sheet pans approximately 1 in. apart.
7. Place in the proofing cabinet, proof until double in bulk.
8. Bake at 375°F until golden brown.

Precautions and Safety Measures
1. Have the water fairly cold to control the yeast while mixing.
2. Scale all the ingredients correctly; double check all weights.
3. The dough temperature should be approximately 80°F when it is removed from the mixer for best results.

Soft dinner roll dough No. II

Soft dinner roll dough (No. II) is a smooth, white-textured dough that is easy to work with. It can be used to create a variety of soft roll products that will have excellent eye appeal and eating qualities.

Objectives
1. To teach the student the procedure for preparing soft dinner roll dough.
2. To teach the student how to scale the ingredients and mix the dough.
3. To teach the student how to proof, make up, and bake the rolls.

Equipment
1. Mixing machine and dough hook
2. Baker's scale
3. Plastic scraper
4. Dough cutter (metal scraper may be used)
5. Stock pot, 5 gal.
6. Sheet pans
7. Silicon paper
8. Dough thermometer
9. Proofing cabinet
10. Kitchen spoon
11. 1 gal. stainless steel container

Ingredients: Approx. yield: 16½ doz. rolls
1 lb. 4 ozs. granulated sugar
1 lb. 4 ozs. hydrogenated shortening
2 ozs. salt
6 ozs. dry milk

6 ozs. whole eggs
7 lbs. 8 ozs. bread flour
4 lbs. water
10 ozs. yeast, compressed

Preparation

1. Prepare an egg wash (4 eggs to 1 pt. of milk).
2. Cover sheet pans with silicon paper.
3. Light the oven, preheat to 375°F.
4. Grease the inside of a 5 gal. stock pot.
5. Have all equipment and ingredients handy.

Procedure

1. Dissolve the yeast in the water. Place in a stainless steel container and stir with a kitchen spoon.
2. Place all the ingredients including the dissolved yeast in the electric mixing bowl. Mix using a dough hook at medium speed until the gluten develops and the dough leaves the sides of the bowl and clings to the dough hook. Check the dough temperature with a dough thermometer. Temperature should be approximately 80°F.
3. Remove dough from mixing bowl using a plastic scraper; place on a floured bench and knead.
4. Place the dough in greased container, let rise until double in bulk.
5. Turn out on a floured bench, knead a second time. Cut the dough into 1 1/4 oz. units with a dough cutter.
6. Form into rolls of desired shape, dip in egg wash and sesame or poppy if desired. Place the rolls on the silicon covered sheet pans approximately 1 in. apart.
7. Place in the proofing cabinet, proof until double in bulk.
8. Bake at 375°F until golden brown.

Precautions and Safety Measures

1. Have the water fairly cold to control the yeast while mixing.
2. Scale all ingredients correctly; double check all weights.
3. The dough temperature should be approximately 80°F when it is removed from the mixer for best results.
4. Do not overproof the rolls.

Soft rye dough

Soft rye dough can be used to prepare many different varieties of rolls. The dough is easy to work and the baked product is of excellent quality.

Objectives

1. To teach the student the procedure for preparing soft rye dough.
2. To teach the student how to scale the ingredients and mix the dough.
3. To teach the student how to proof, make up, and bake the rolls.

Equipment

1. Mixing machine and dough hook
2. Baker's scale
3. Plastic scraper
4. Dough cutter (metal scraper may be used)
5. Stock pot, 5 gal.
6. Sheet pans
7. Silicon paper
8. Dough thermometer
9. Proofing cabinet
10. Kitchen spoons
11. 1 gal. stainless steel container

Ingredients: Approx. yield: 12 doz. rolls

6 lbs. 6 ozs. bread flour
1 lb. 4 ozs. rye flour, dark
6 ozs. yeast, compressed
1 3/4 ozs. salt
5 ozs. dry milk
1 lb. Primex shortening (hydrogenated)
1 lb. sugar
1 1/2 ozs. malt
4 lbs. 8 ozs. water (variable)
6 ozs. caraway seed

Preparation

1. Prepare an egg wash (4 eggs to 1 pt. of milk).
2. Cover sheet pans with silicon paper.
3. Light the oven, preheat to 400°F.
4. Grease the inside of a 5 gal stock pot.
5. Have all equipment and ingredients handy.

Procedure

1. Dissolve the yeast in the water. Place in a stainless steel container and stir with a kitchen spoon.
2. Place all the ingredients including the dissolved yeast in the electric mixing bowl. Mix using the dough hook at medium speed until the dough has developed. Check dough temperature with a dough thermometer. Temperature should be approximately 80°F.
3. Remove dough from mixing bowl using a plastic scraper. Place on a floured bench and knead.
4. Place the dough in greased container, fer-

ment for approximately 1½ hours, punch, and allow to rest for 30 minutes.

5. Take to the bench, knead a second time. Scale into 1½ oz. units. Cut the units with a dough cutter.
6. Form into rolls of desired shape, dip in egg wash. Place the rolls on the silicon covered sheet pans.
7. Place in the proofing cabinet, proof until double in bulk.
8. Bake at 400°F until golden brown.

Precautions and Safety Measures
1. Have the water fairly cold to control the yeast while mixing.
2. Scale all ingredients correctly; double check all weights.
3. The dough temperature should be approximately 80°F when it is removed from the mixer for best results.
4. Do not overproof the rolls.

Hard roll dough

Hard roll dough will produce rolls with a crisp, slightly hard crust. In order to produce a hard roll of good quality, steam must be injected into the oven for the first 10 minutes of the baking period.

Objectives
1. To teach the student the procedure for preparing hard roll dough.
2. To teach the student how to scale the ingredients and mix the dough.
3. To teach the student how to proof, make up, and bake hard roll dough.

Equipment
1. Mixing machine and dough hook
2. Baker's scale
3. Sheet pans
4. Plastic scraper
5. Dough cutter (metal scraper may be used)
6. Dough thermometer
7. Proofing cabinet
8. Stock pot, 5 gal.
9. 1 gal. stainless steel container
10. Kitchen spoon

Ingredients: Approx. yield: 11½ doz.

7	lbs. 8 ozs.	bread flour
3	ozs.	salt
3½	ozs.	granulated sugar
3	ozs.	shortening
3	ozs.	egg whites
4	lbs. 8 ozs.	water (variable)
4½	ozs.	yeast, compressed

Preparation
1. Sprinkle corn meal on sheet pans.
2. Preheat the oven to 400°F and inject steam by turning on the steam valve (oven must be equipped to produce steam).
3. Grease the inside of a 5 gal. stock pot.
4. Have all equipment and ingredients handy.

Procedure
1. Dissolve the yeast in the water. Place in a stainless steel container and stir with a kitchen spoon.
2. Place all the ingredients including the dissolved yeast in the electric mixing bowl, mix using a dough hook at medium speed for approximately 12 minutes until the dough is developed. Check dough temperature with a dough thermometer. Temperature should be approximately 80°F.
3. Remove the dough from the mixing bowl, using a plastic scraper; place on a floured bench and knead.
4. Place the dough in a greased container, let rise for approximately 1 hour. Punch down and knead a second time.
5. Cut the dough with a dough cutter into 1½ oz. units. Form into rolls of desired shape. Place the rolls on the prepared sheet pans.
6. Place in the proofing cabinets. Proof until double in bulk.
7. Bake at 400°F until golden brown. Have steam in the oven for the first 10 minutes of the baking period.

Precautions and Safety Measures
1. Take the dough from the mixer at a temperature of 75°F to 80°F for best results.
2. Scale all ingredients correctly; double check all weights.
3. Exercise caution when opening the oven. It can be dangerous with steam present in the oven.
4. Do not overproof the rolls.

Butter flake roll dough

Butter flake roll dough is prepared by mixing a basic dough and rolling in butter or shortening to give the dough a very flaky and tender texture. The dough is given 3 rolls and 3 folds each time it is rolled. The eating qualities of this dough is exceptionally fine. It may be used to form French crescents or butter flake rolls.

Objectives
1. To teach the student the procedure for preparing butter flake roll dough.
2. To teach the student how to scale the ingredients and mix the basic dough.
3. To teach the student how to roll in the shortening, form, proof, and bake the rolls.

Equipment
1. Baker's scale
2. Mixing machine and dough hook
3. Plastic scraper
4. Rolling pin
5. Dough thermometer
6. Pastry wheel
7. Muffin tins or sheet pans
8. Proofing cabinet
9. 1 gal. stainless steel container
10. Wire whip
11. Kitchen spoon

Ingredients: Approx. yield: 8 doz. crescents or rolls

9	ozs. granulated sugar
1¼	oz. salt
8	ozs. glodo shortening
4	ozs. dry milk
10	ozs. egg yolks
4	ozs. yeast, compressed
1	lb. 12 ozs. water 80°F
4	lbs. bread flour (variable)
1	lb. glodo shortening or butter (roll in)

Preparation
1. Grease muffin tins or cover sheet pans with silicon paper. The kind of pan used will depend on the kind of roll being made.
2. Preheat oven to 400°F.
3. Have all equipment and ingredients handy.

Procedure
1. Place the egg yolks in a stainless steel container, beat slightly with a wire whip, add the water, and blend together.
2. Dissolve the yeast in the water-egg yolk mixture by stirring with a kitchen spoon.
3. Place all the dry ingredients including the first amount of glodo shortening in the electric mixing bowl.
4. Add the liquid mixture, while mixing with the dough hook at slow speed, increase mixing speed to medium and mix until a smooth dough is formed. Scrape down the bowl at least once with a plastic scraper during the mixing period.
5. Bring the dough from the mixer at approximately 75°F. Check the temperature with a dough thermometer, place it on a floured bench, knead slightly, and let it rest for 40 minutes.
6. Roll the dough with a rolling pin into an oblong shape ½ in. thick cover two-thirds of the dough with the "roll-in" shortening or butter. Fold the uncovered third of the dough towards the center. Then fold other third over it towards the center.
7. Roll dough again into ½ in. thick oblong shape and fold as before. Repeat this process for a total of 3 rolls, with 3 folds to each roll.
8. Place the dough in a cold retarder or freezer for several hours. Return to the bench and proceed to make up as follows.

French crescents: Roll the dough fairly thin into a rectangular shape. Cut with a pastry wheel into strips about 4 in. wide, then cut into 4 in. squares. Cut the squares into 2 triangular shapes. Wash with a mixture of half egg and half milk, roll or twist the dough, shape into a crescent. Brush the top with the egg wash and sprinkle with poppy or sesame seed. Place on the prepared sheet pans, give a three-fourth proof and bake at 400°F until golden brown. Remove from the oven and brush with melted butter. *Approx. yield: 8 doz.*

Butter flake rolls: Roll the dough fairly thin into a rectangular shape. Brush the surface of the dough with melted butter. Cut with a pastry wheel into strips 1½ in. wide. Stack about 5 or 6 strips high. Cut the strips into units 1½ in. wide. Place in greased muffin tins cut side up. Brush the tops with melted butter. Place in the proofing cabinet give a

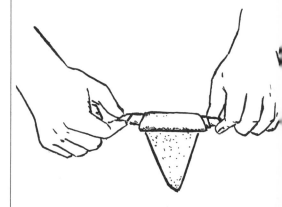

Rolling up French crescents.

three-fourths proof and bake at 400°F until golden brown. Remove from the oven and brush with melted butter again. *Approx. yield: 8 doz.*

Precautions and Safety Measures
1. Bring the dough from the mixer at 75°F. If warm, the action of the yeast will be too fast and an old dough will result (old dough is one that is overproofed).
2. Scale all ingredients correctly; double check all weights.
3. When rolling in the shortening or butter dust off any flour that may be present on the surface of the dough before folding.
4. The shortening or butter to be rolled in must be slightly soft if it is too hard it will break through the dough causing an inferior product.

SWEET DOUGH RECIPES

Virginia pastry dough

Virginia pastry dough is easy to make, easy to work with and easy to sell. It is an unusual yeast dough mixture because it requires very little fermentation. The dough can be mixed, and made up without a period of waiting for gases to react. The dough can be made up into a variety of products that will produce a taste thrill and bring customers back for more.

Objectives
1. To teach the student the procedure for preparing Virginia pastry dough.
2. To teach the student how to scale the ingredients and mix the dough.
3. To teach the student how to make up and bake Virginia pastry dough.

Equipment
1. Baker's scale
2. Mixing machine and sweet dough paddle
3. Plastic scraper
4. Rolling pin
5. Baking pans
6. 1 gal. stainless steel container
7. Wire whip
8. Pastry wheel
9. Proofing cabinet
10. Dough thermometer
11. Kitchen spoon
12. 2 to 2½ in. round cutter
13. Pastry brush
14. Boning knife

Ingredients: Yield depends on product made
1 lb. 8 ozs. pastry flour
12 ozs. bread flour
4 ozs. dry milk
1 lb. 12 ozs. water, cold
1 lb. whole eggs
6 ozs. yeast, compressed
8 ozs. granulated sugar
2 lbs. 8 ozs. Sweetex shortening
1½ oz. salt
mace, to taste
vanilla, to taste
2 lbs. 4 oz. bread flour.

Preparation
1. Prepare the baking pans needed for product selected to be made.
2. Preheat the oven to required temperature.
3. Have all equipment and ingredients handy.

Procedure
1. Place the eggs in a stainless steel container, beat slightly with a wire whip, add the water, and blend together.
2. Dissolve the yeast in the water-egg mixture by stirring with a kitchen spoon and place in the electric mixing bowl.
3. Add the first amount of bread flour, pastry flour, and dry milk. Using the sweet dough paddle. Mix together 2 to 3 minutes at medium speed.
4. Add the sugar, shortening, salt, mace, vanilla and the second amount of bread flour. Mix at low speed for about 2 minutes until all the ingredients are thoroughly blended. Scrape down the bowl at least once with a plastic scraper.
5. Bring the dough from the mixer at 65°F or below. Check temperature with a dough thermometer. Take directly to the bench and make up into the following products:

Breakfast cake: Roll out with a rolling pin an 8 to 10 oz. piece of the dough to cover the bottom of an 8 in. cake pan, building the edges slightly. Place 12 ozs. of desired fruit filling in the center. Proof in a proofing cabinet for about ½ hour. Bake 20 minutes at 380°F. After removing from the oven, cool and wash over the filling with a light glaze if desired. Edges may be iced with roll icing (see chapter 26). Approx. yield; 15 units.

Shortcake biscuits: Roll the dough with a rolling pin to ½ in. thickness. Cut out with 2 to 2½ in. round cutter. Wash the tops with liquid skim milk using a pastry brush and

Procter and Gamble Co.

Fruit crisps.   Turnabouts.   Concertinas.

turn upside down on granulated sugar. Place right side up on bun pans. Proof in a proofing cabinet for ½ hour. Bake approximately 10 minutes at 400°F. Each biscuit should be scaled at 1½ ozs. *Approx. yield: 115 units.*

Fruit crisp: Roll the dough with a rolling pin to about ⅛ in. thick. Cut into 4 in. squares with a pastry wheel. Place a desired fruit filling in the center of each square. Wash edges with liquid skim milk using a pastry brush. Then fold to form either triangles or rectangles, seal the edges. Turn upside down on granulated sugar. Pierce the center of each crisp to permit steam to escape from the filling. Proof about ½ hour, bake for approximately 10 minutes at 380°F to 400°F. If desired a flat or roll icing may be applied on unsugared crisps after baking (see Chapter 26.) *Approx. yield: 80 units.*

Turnabouts: Roll out the dough with a rolling pin to about ¼ in thickness. Cut into 4 in. squares with a pastry wheel. Fold each corner to the center, wash with liquid skim milk using a pastry brush and turn upside down on bun pans. Proof in a proofing cabinet for about ½ hour. Bake at 380°F to 400°F. After baking spot the center of each piece with a good jam. *Approx. yield: 70 units.*

Concertinas: Roll out the dough with a rolling pin to about ⅛ in. thickness. Spread the surface with coffee cake filling and roll up as for cinnamon rolls. Flatten slightly by hand and slice with a boring knife into units 3 to 4 in. in length. Make 3 cuts in each piece about ¾ of the way through. Wash with liquid skim milk using a pastry brush and invert on granulated sugar. Place right side up on bun pans. Proof in a proofing cabinet about ½ hour and bake at 380°F to 400°F. *Approx. yield: 40 units.*

Precautions and Safety Measures
1. The dough will be easier to handle and produce the best results if the temperature of the dough can be kept on the cool side (under 65°F).
2. Do not overmix the dough.

Sweet dough

Sweet dough is a rich, flavorful yeast dough. It has a golden yellow color and can be used to produce such popular baked products as sweet rolls, coffee cakes, pecan rolls, cinnamon buns, etc.

Objectives
1. To teach the student the procedure for preparing sweet dough.
2. To teach the student how to scale the ingredients and mix the dough.
3. To teach the student how to proof, make up, and bake sweet dough products.

Equipment
1. Baker's scale
2. Mixing machine and sweet dough paddle
3. Plastic and metal scraper
4. Rolling pin
5. Baking pans
6. Pastry wheel
7. Stock pot, 5 gal.
8. Proofing cabinet
9. Dough thermometer
10. Wire whip
11. Kitchen spoon
12. 1 gal. stainless steel container
13. Pastry brush

Ingredients: Yield depends on product made

1	lb. granulated sugar
1	lb. glodo shortening
1	oz. salt
3	lbs. bread flour
1	lb. 8 ozs. pastry flour
12	ozs. whole eggs
4	ozs. dry milk
2	lbs. water (variable)
8	ozs. yeast, compressed
	mace, to taste
	vanilla, to taste

Preparation

1. Prepare the baking pans needed for product selected to be made.
2. Preheat the oven to required temperature.
3. Have all equipment and ingredients handy.
4. Grease the 5 gal. stock pot.

Procedure

1. Place all the dry ingredients, including the shortening, in the electric mixing bowl.
2. Place the eggs in a stainless steel container. Beat slightly with a wire whip, add the water, and blend together. Add the yeast and stir with a kitchen spoon until thoroughly dissolved.
3. Using the sweet dough paddle, mix at slow speed while adding the liquid mixture. Increase speed to medium and mix until a smooth dough is formed. Scrape down the bowl at least once during the mixing period with a plastic scraper.
4. Add the vanilla and mix in at slow speed. Check dough temperature with a dough thermometer. Temperature should be approximately 78° to 85°F.
5. Turn the dough out on a floured bench, and knead until all air is worked out and the dough is smooth.
6. Place in a greased container and let proof until double in bulk.
7. Turn out onto a floured bench and knead a second time.
8. Make up into the following units:

Sweet rolls: Roll out 10 ozs. of dough, using a rolling pin, to a thickness of about ⅛ in. and about 8 in. wide. Spread with desired kind of filling or brush dough slightly with water and sprinkle with a mixture of cinnamon and sugar. Roll up the dough and cut with a metal scraper into 1 in. rolls weighing from 1½ to 2 ozs. each. Brush with egg wash, using a pastry brush, and proof in a

1. Making up center twist coffee cakes: Spreading the rolled out sweet dough with the desired filling.

2. Cutting the folded dough into units.

3. Forming the center twist coffee cake.

4. Topping the formed units with pecans and streusel. (This coffee cake can be prepared using either sweet dough or Danish pastry dough.)

roll doughs and sweet doughs **559**

proofing cabinet until double in bulk. Bake in a 375°F preheated oven until golden brown. Remove from oven and brush with a glaze (consisting of 1 lb. glucose and ½ lb. water brought to a boil). Let rolls cool and ice with roll icing (see Chapter 26). *Approx. yield: 80 units.*

Coffee cake: Scale the dough into 10 or 12 oz. units. Roll out with a rolling pin to a thickness of ¼ in. Spread with desired filling, roll up the dough, and form into desired shapes. Proof in proofing cabinet until double in bulk. Bake at 375°F until golden brown. Remove from the oven, brush with a glaze. Let the coffee cakes cool and ice with roll icing (see Chapter 26.) *Approx. yield: 12 to 14 units.*

Pecan rolls: Prepare a caramel pan smear by blending together the following ingredients:

4	lbs. dark brown sugar
1	lb. 8 ozs. prep liquid shortening
½	oz. salt
12	ozs. honey or glucose
8	ozs. milk

Place the pan smear in a pastry bag, cover the bottom of muffin tins about ¼ in. deep with the smear. Sprinkle a few chopped pecans over the pan smear in each tin. Grease the sides of each tin lightly. Scale the sweet dough into 1½ oz. units, proof up by hand, and place the dough in the muffin tins. Place in the proofing cabinet and proof until double in bulk. Bake in a 375°F oven until golden brown. Remove from the oven and turn the pans upside down on a sheet pan. Remove the muffin tins. Let the rolls cool. *Approx. yield: 100 units.*

Cinnamon sugar buns: Scale off enough dough to cover a sheet pan at a thickness of ½ in. Dock the dough by tapping it with a docker or the tines of a dinner fork. Brush the top of the dough slightly with water, sprinkle on a mixture of cinnamon and sugar (1 part cinnamon to 3 parts sugar) proof in the proofing cabinet until double in bulk. Bake at 375°F until golden brown. Remove from the oven, let cool and cut with a pastry cutter into 3 in. squares. *Approx. yield: 80 units.*

Precautions and Safety Measures
1. Bring the dough from the mixer at 78°F to 85°F for best results.
2. In making larger batches of sweet dough if a longer time is required on the bench

you may need to cut down on the amount of yeast used.
3. Do not let the dough overproof.

Danish pastry dough

Danish pastry dough is a rich, tender, flaky dough that produces baked products with exceptional eating qualities. It is prepared by mixing a basic sweet dough and rolling in extra shortening to create the tender flaky layers which are the chief characteristics of a good quality Danish. Danish pastry dough can be used to make a variety of products such as rolls, coffee cakes and specialty items.

Objectives
1. To teach the student the procedure for preparing Danish pastry dough.
2. To teach the student how to scale the ingredients and mix the basic dough.
3. To teach the student how to roll in the shortening, form, proof, and bake the rolls.

Equipment
1. Mixing machine and sweet dough paddle
2. Baker's scale
3. Plastic and metal scraper
4. Rolling pin
5. Dough thermometer
6. Pastry brush
7. Proofing cabinet
8. Baking pans
9. 1 gal. stainless steel container
10. Wire whip
11. Kitchen spoon
12. Bench brush

Ingredients: Yield depends on product made

12	ozs. granulated sugar
12	ozs. glodo shortening
1¾	oz. salt
3	lbs. bread flour
1	lb. 8 ozs. pastry flour
1	lb. whole eggs
4	ozs. dry milk
2	lbs. water (variable)
8	ozs. yeast, compressed flavor to taste
2	lbs. 8 ozs. glodo shortening (roll in)

Preparation
1. Prepare the pans selected for baking.
2. Preheat the oven to 390°F.
3. Have all equipment and ingredients handy.

Procedure

1. Place all the dry ingredients including shortening in the electric mixing bowl.
2. Place the eggs in stainless steel container, beat slightly with a wire whip, add the water, and blend together. Add the yeast and stir with a kitchen spoon until thoroughly dissolved. Add the flavoring.
3. Using the sweet dough paddle, mix at slow speed while adding the liquid mixture, increase speed to medium and mix for approximately 4 to 5 minutes. Scrape down the bowl with a plastic scraper at least once during the mixing period.
3. Bring the dough from the mixer at 70°F to 75°F. Check with a dough thermometer. Place on a sheet pan (roll out with a rolling pin until it fills the pan) and allow it to rest in the refrigerator for approximately 30 minutes.
5. Bring the dough from the refrigerator and place on a floured bench. Roll the dough with a rolling pin into an oblong shape ½ in. thick. Cover two-thirds of the dough with the "roll-in" glodo shortening. Fold the uncovered third of the dough towards the center. Then fold other third over it towards the center. Brush off any excess flour with a bench brush. Roll dough again into ½ in. thick oblong shape and fold as before. Place the dough on a sheet pan and retard in the refrigerator for 20 minutes.
6. Return the dough to the bench, repeat this process for a total of 3 rolls with 3 folds to each roll, let the dough rest in the retarder for 20 minutes between each roll.
7. Return the dough to the bench and proceed to make up as follows:

Danish rolls: Roll out 10 ozs. of dough with a rolling pin to a thickness of about ⅛ in. and about 8 in. wide. Spread with desired kind of filling. Roll up the dough and cut with a metal scraper into 1 in. rolls weighing from 1½ to 2 ozs. each. Brush with egg wash using a pastry brush. Proof until double in bulk, and bake at 390°F until golden brown. Remove from the oven and brush with a glaze (consisting of 1 lb. glucose and ½ lb. water brought to a boil). Let the rolls cool and ice with roll icing (see Chapter 26). *Approx. yield: 100 units.*

Fruit filled coffee cake: Scale the dough

1. Making up fruit filled coffee cakes: Spreading fruit filling on half the dough.

2. Using the pie pin to indent surface.

3. Placing the units into square cake pans.

Procter and Gamble Co.

4. Sprinkling streusel topping on the dough.

into 10 or 12 oz. units. Roll out with a rolling pin to about ⅛ in. thick, 14 in. long and 7 to 8 in. wide. Spread fruit filling on half of dough. Wash edges with water and fold unfilled portion over, seal edges securely. Using a rolling pin, press down to indent surface slightly. Place unit in a square, prepared cake pan. Dock the surface of each unit formed with a docker or with the tines of a fork. Brush with egg wash, top with streusel topping, proof until double in bulk, and bake at 390°F until golden brown. Remove from the oven, let cool, and sprinkle with roll icing (see Chapter 26). *Approx. yield: 16 units.*

Spiral coffee cake: Scale the dough into 10 oz. units, roll with a rolling pin to about ¼ in. thickness, 20 in. long, and 3 in. wide. Spread with the desired kind of filling over half of the dough. Wash edges with water and fold unfilled portion over, seal edges securely. Twist by rolling the dough on the bench with the palms of your hands. Coil the twisted dough strip flat on the bench and seal the outside end. Place coffee cakes on sheet pans covered with silicon paper or in 8 in. prepared cake pans. Brush with egg wash using a pastry brush. Proof in proofing cabinet until double in bulk and bake at 390°F until golden brown. Remove from the oven, brush with a hot corn syrup (1 lb. glucose and ½ lb. of water brought to a boil), and sprinkle with roll icing (see Chapter 26). *Approx. yield: 20 units.*

Fruit cluster coffee cake: Scale the dough into 10 to 12 oz. units. Roll out with a rolling pin to a thickness of about ⅛ in. and about 8 in. wide. Spread on desired fruit filling and roll up as for sweet rolls. Cut rolls with scissors about every inch, spreading cuts in alternate directions. Brush with egg wash, proof in proofing cabinet until double in bulk, and bake at 390°F until golden brown. Remove from the oven, brush with a hot corn syrup glaze (1 lb. glucose and ½ lb. water brought to a boil), and sprinkle with roll icing (see Chapter 26). *Approx. yield: 16 units.*

Honey fruit coffee cake: Scale the dough into 10 to 12 oz. units. Roll out with a rolling pin to a thickness of about ⅛ in. and about 8 in. wide. Spread on honey fruit filling (see recipe this chapter) and roll two sides towards the center until about 1 in. apart. Cut each side of the roll with scissors about 1 in. apart. Fill center with your favorite filling. Brush with egg wash using a pastry brush,

proof until double in bulk, and bake at 390°F until golden brown. Remove from the oven, brush with a hot corn syrup glaze (1 lb. glucose and ½ lb. water brought to a boil), and sprinkle with roll icing (see Chapter 26). *Approx. yield: 16 units.*

Confection roll: Scale the dough into 3 lb. units. Roll out with a rolling pin to about ⅛ in. thickness (thin as possible) and about 12 in. wide. Brush the unit with egg wash using a pastry brush, and spread on confection roll filling (see recipe this chapter). Roll up as for sweet rolls and flatten by hand until about 4 in. wide. Proof in proofing cabinet until double in bulk and bake at 390°F until golden brown. Remove from the oven, brush with a hot corn syrup glaze (1 lb. glucose and ½ lb. of water brought to a boil), and sprinkle with roll icing (see Chapter 26). Cut into serving units. *Approx. yield: 4 rolls.*

Precautions and Safety Measures

1. Bring the dough from the mixer at 70°F to 75°F for best results.
2. Scale all ingredients correctly; double check all weights.
3. When rolling in the shortening dust off any flour that may be present on the surface of the dough before folding.
4. The shortening to be rolled in must be slightly soft. If it is too hard it will break through the dough causing an inferior product.

DANISH AND SWEET DOUGH FILLINGS AND TOPPINGS

ALMOND PASTE FILLING

Ingredients: Approx. yield: 1 qt.

1	lb. almond paste
1	lb. granulated sugar
4	ozs. whole eggs
2	lbs. cake crumbs
1	oz. dry milk
12	ozs. water (variable)
½	oz. salt

Procedure

1. Place the almond paste and sugar in the electric mixing bowl, using the paddle, cream together in slow speed.
2. Add the eggs and continue to cream at slow speed.
3. Add the cake crumbs, dry milk, water and salt; mix together at medium speed until thoroughly blended.

FRUIT FILLING

Ingredients: Approx. yield: 1½ qts.

2 lbs. cake crumbs
1 lb. raisins
8 ozs. chopped pecans
8 ozs. chopped maraschino cherries
1 oz. cinnamon
2 ozs. dry milk
14 ozs. water (variable)

Procedure

1. Place the cake crumbs, raisins, nuts, cherries and cinnamon in the electric mixing bowl, using the paddle mix together at medium speed.
2. Dissolve the dry milk in the water, add to the above mixture to obtain proper consistency.

CREAM FILLING

Ingredients: Approx. yield: 1 qt.

2 lbs. powdered sugar
6 ozs. glodo shortening
6 ozs. prep shortening or butter
8 ozs. whole eggs
14 ozs. cake flour

Procedure

1. Place the powdered sugar, and both shortenings in the electric mixing bowl. Using the paddle cream together until thoroughly blended at slow speed.
2. Add the eggs, slowly and continue to cream at slow speed.
3. Add the flour and mix until smooth at slow speed.

HONEY FRUIT FILLING

Ingredients: Approx. yield: 1½ qts.

1 lb. 8 ozs. brown sugar
1 lb. 8 ozs. glodo shortening
1 lb. honey
1 oz. salt
1 lb. 8 ozs. chopped fruits
8 ozs. cake flour

Procedure

1. Place the brown sugar, shortening, honey and salt in the electric mixing bowl, using the paddle cream together in slow speed until thoroughly blended.
2. Add the chopped fruits, mix at medium speed until mixed in.
3. Add the flour, continue to mix until smooth.

ORANGE FILLING NO. I

Ingredients: Approx. yield: 2 qts.

1 lb. 8 ozs. water
12 ozs. granulated sugar
8 ozs. ground whole oranges
1½ ozs. lemon juice
2 ozs. prep shortening
1 oz. Sweetex shortening
8 ozs. water
4 ozs. cornstarch
6 ozs. egg yolks

Procedure

1. Place the water, sugar, ground whole oranges, lemon juice, prep and Sweetex in in a sauce pot, bring to a rolling boil.
2. Mix together thoroughly the water, cornstarch, and egg yolks. Add slowly to the boiling mixture while stirring constantly with a kitchen spoon.
3. Cook until thick, let cool and use. (Apply by spreading.)

ALMOND FILLING

Ingredients: Approx. yield: 1 qt.

1 lb. ground almonds or almond paste
1 lb. Sweetex shortening
1 lb. granulated sugar
2 ozs. whole eggs
4 ozs. cake flour

Procedure

1. Place all the ingredients in the electric mixing bowl, using the paddle, mix the filling at medium speed until thoroughly blended.

FILBERT FILLING

Ingredients: Approx. yield: 1½ qts.

1 lb. ground filberts, roasted
½ oz. cinnamon
2 lbs. granulated sugar
6 ozs. whole eggs
3 lbs. cake crumbs
2 ozs. dry milk
14 ozs. water

Procedure

1. Place all the ingredients together in the electric mixing bowl, using the paddle, mix at medium speed until thoroughly blended.

APPLESAUCE-PECAN FILLING

Ingredients: Approx. yield: 1½ qts.

1 lb. 8 ozs. chopped pecans
2 lbs. cake crumbs
1 lb. brown sugar
1 lb. applesauce

Procedure

1. Place all the ingredients in the electric mixing bowl, using the paddle, mix the filling at medium speed until thoroughly blended.

ALOHO FILLING

Ingredients: Approx. yield: 1½ gal.

- 6 lbs. 11 ozs. crushed pineapple (#10 can)
- 2 whole oranges, ground
- 2 lbs. water
- 2 lbs. 12 ozs. granulated sugar
- 2 lbs. water
- 8 ozs. modified starch
- ½ oz. salt
- yellow color as desired

Procedure

1. Place the pineapple, ground oranges, water and sugar in a sauce pot. Bring to a boil.
2. Dissolve the starch in the second amount of water. Add slowly to the above mixture, stirring constantly with a kitchen spoon. Cook until thickened and clear.
3. Remove from the heat and blend in the salt and yellow color, let cool before using.

DATE NUT FILLING

Ingredients: Approx. yield: 2 qts.

- 2 lbs. 8 ozs. pitted dates
- 8 ozs. brown sugar
- 1 lb. 8 ozs. water
- 1 lb. chopped pecans

Procedure

1. Place the dates, brown sugar and water in a sauce pot, bring to a boil, continue to cook for 5 minutes.
2. Remove from the fire and stir in the pecans with a kitchen spoon.
3. Let cool before using.

ORANGE FILLING NO. II

Ingredients: Approx. yield: 3 qts.

- 8 ozs. ground whole oranges
- 5 lbs. granulated sugar
- 8 ozs. currants

Procedure

1. Place all the ingredients in the electric mixing machine, using the paddle, mix at slow speed until thoroughly blended. (Apply by sprinkling.)

CONFECTION ROLL FILLING

Ingredients: Approx. yield: 3 qts.

- 2 lbs. 8 ozs. dark brown sugar
- 1 lb. prep shortening
- 2½ ozs. cinnamon
- 2 lbs. 8 ozs. granulated sugar
- 1 lb. 4 ozs. nut meats, ground coarse
- 1 lb. 4 ozs. cake crumbs
- ½ oz. salt

Procedure

1. Place all the ingredients in the electric mixing bowl, using the paddle, mix at medium speed until thoroughly blended.

BUTTER TOPPING

Ingredients: Approx. yield: 3 qts.

- 4 lbs. powdered sugar (4, 6 or 10X)
- 2 lbs. cake crumbs
- 1 lb. butter
- 1 lb. glodo shortening
- 10 ozs. whole eggs
- ½ oz. vanilla

Procedure

1. Place the sugar, cake crumbs, butter and glodo in the electric mixing bowl, using the paddle, mix at medium speed until thoroughly blended.
2. Add the eggs and vanilla and continue mixing until smooth.

PREP STREUSEL TOPPING

Ingredients: Approx. yield: 3 qts.

- 1 lb. 4 ozs. bread flour
- 1 lb. prep shortening
- ½ oz. lemon flavor
- 1 lb. 8 ozs. granulated sugar
- ½ oz. salt
- 1 lb. 4 ozs. bread flour

Procedure

1. In mixing container place the flour, shortening and lemon flavor; blend together by hand.
2. Add the sugar, salt and bread flour; rub

Student cooks rolling, making up and icing coffee cakes and sweet rolls.

by hand to a streusel or medium size crumb.

To make streusel varieties:
1. Cinnamon streusel: Add ½ oz. cinnamon to each lb. of flour.
2. Nut streusel: Add 4 ozs. ground nutmeats to each lb. of flour.
3. Crunch streusel: Add 4 ozs. macaroon crunch to each lb. of flour.
4. Chocolate streusel: Add in the first mixing stage 4 ozs. melted chocolate to each lb. of flour.
5. Orange streusel: add ½ oz. of orange gratings to each lb. of flour.

ALMOND BRITTLE TOPPING OR FILLING
Ingredients: Approx. yield: 1 qt.
2 lbs. granulated sugar
1 lb. water
8 ozs. glucose
12 ozs. chopped almonds
Procedure
1. In a sauce pot place the sugar, water and glucose, boil to 275°F.
2. Add the chopped almonds and boil to 300°F.
3. Pour into bun pans in thin sheets, cool and break up with a rolling pin into fine pieces.

CINNAMON NUT TOPPING
Ingredients: Approx. yield: 1 pt.
1 lb. granulated sugar
1 oz. cinnamon
2 ozs. ground nuts
Procedure
1. Place all the ingredients together in a mixing container and mix by hand until thoroughly blended.

pie doughs and fillings

chapter 25

■ Pie is America's most popular dessert. It is one of the few items in the culinary field that America has been given credit for creating and developing. This popular dessert has won and held its place at the top of the dessert menu and today in the food service establishments throughout the United States more meals are finished with a piece of pie than any other kind of dessert.

Generally speaking there are two types of pies: single crust and double crust. The *single crust pie* consists of just a bottom crust, whereas the *double crust pie* contains both bottom and top crust. In both types of pies the important fea-

ture is a good tender crust. It is the tenderness or toughness of the crust on which the opinion of any pie is based. The filling may be of excellent quality, but if a tough crust is present and is left on the plate it is the customers way of rejecting the complete product. It is important then that the student understands how to prepare pie doughs to produce a crust that is tender and has good eating qualities. To do this he must have some knowledge of the action of the ingredients and must be able to apply that knowledge to obtain the desired results. The basic information for preparing pies is given on the following pages—study it carefully.

PIE DOUGH TYPES

Doughs are all similar in respects to the ingredients used, but differ in the degree of mixing the flour and shortening together and in the amount of water or liquid added to the dough. Pie doughs are classified into three types: mealy, short flake, and long flake. The *mealy crust* will absorb the least amount of liquid because the flour and shortening is rubbed together until the flour is completely covered with shortening. Therefore the flour is unable to absorb a large amount of liquid. The *short flake crust,* which is the most common type used, will absorb a slightly larger amount of water because the flour and shortening is only rubbed until no flour spots are evident. Although the flour is coated with the shortening it has not been coated to the degree of the mealy type. Therefore the flour will be able to absorb a slightly larger amount of liquid. The *long flake crust* will absorb the largest amount of water because the flour and shortening are rubbed together to a lesser degree than in either of the other two types. The flour and shortening are rubbed together very lightly leaving the shortening in fairly large chunks, about the size of the tip of the little finger.

After mixing, the mealy crust and short flake crust are handled the same. They are chilled in the refrigerator until they are firm enough to handle or roll with ease. Usually 45 minutes to one hour is sufficient time for refrigeration. The long flake type must also be refrigerated, but for a longer period of time. Usually several hours or overnight is the required amount of time, otherwise the dough will be soft, making it difficult to roll out or requiring too much flour for dusting.

PIE DOUGH INGREDIENTS

The ingredients used in most pie dough formulas are: flour, shortening, liquid (water or milk), salt and sugar. Each plays an important part in the finished product. The *flour* should not contain too high or too low a gluten content. Too high a gluten content will absorb water too quickly causing the dough to become tough. Too low a gluten content absorbs water too slowly causing the dough to become sticky and wet. A pastry flour, milled from a soft winter wheat, contains the ideal gluten content for pie dough and will produce the best results. The flour should always be sifted when preparing pie dough because the soft pastry flour has a tendency to pack and lump. If not sifted these lumps will not absorb the water as readily as they should and may necessitate overmixing which will result in a tough crust. It is important too that pastry flour be used for dusting the bench when the pie dough is rolled or toughness will develop.

The *shortening* or *fat* used in pie dough may be lard, hydrogenated shortening or butter; lard will produce a good pie dough if the best quality is purchased. A lard that is tough and fibrous will meet the need. However, most lards impart a flavor that is sometimes objectionable and if the filling does not cover up this taste it could prove to be unwise selection. Hydrogenated shortening is used more than any other kind of fat because it has no taste and has a plastic consistency that is an ideal feature when cutting the flour into the fat. If butter is used to improve the flavor of the dough it is suggested that it be blended with hydrogenated shortening, using one-third butter to every two-thirds of shortening. This blend must be chilled in the refrigerator and allowed to harden slightly before it is cut into the flour because in mixing the butter and shortening together the butter will have a tendency to soften. The use of butter will increase the cost of the product and many times the fine flavor provided by the butter is lost because of the flavor of the filling.

The *liquid* used in preparation of pie dough may be water or milk depending on the formula being used. Milk will produce a richer dough and a better colored crust. If powdered milk is used in place of liquid milk it must be dissolved in the water before it is added to the flour-shortening mixture. Regardless of whether water or milk is called for in the formula it must be cold and in extremely warm weather ice water is recommended. This will keep the fat particles fairly hard and prevent the dough from becoming too soft. The amount of liquid called for in the formula will depend on the type of pie dough being prepared. The mealy type will require less liquid and as a rule the more the flour-shortening mixture is worked or rubbed the less liquid required.

Salt is used to bring forth the flavors of all the ingredients used in the dough. The salt must be dissolved in the liquid that is being used to insure better distribution and prevent burnt spots that will appear in the baked crust if it is added in solid form.

Sugar will add sweetness and color to the baked crust. The form used may be granulated, syrup or dextrose depending on what is called for in the formula. The sugar ingredient should be treated in the same manner as the salt—it should be dissolved in the liquid to insure complete distribution.

PIE DOUGH PREPARATION

Most faults in the preparation of pie doughs develop when the dough is being mixed. Proper mixing of pie dough is a two-step procedure that can either be done by hand or by using a mixing machine. For the inexperienced student mixing by hand is recommended because it is a simple matter to overmix when using a mixing machine.

The flour is sifted into a large round bowl and the shortening or fat is added and cut or rubbed into the flour by hand. The degree of rubbing will be determined by the type of dough one wishes to prepare. The salt, sugar and cold liquid are blended together in a bain-marie until the salt and sugar are thoroughly dissolved. The liquid mixture is poured over the flour-shortening mixture. This is the most important step in the preparation for it is at this point that most problems develop. The two mixtures should be mixed *only* until the liquid is absorbed by the flour. Too many times if the dough appears sticky at this point extra flour is added or if the dough appears stiff extra water is added. This practice usually will unbalance the formula and certainly cause overmixing which will result in toughness. This is the most common mistake made when preparing a pie dough. Remember that the amount of liquid added is the most important factor in producing a successful dough. After the dough is mixed it is placed in a pan, covered with a damp cloth and refrigerated until firm enough to be rolled. When the dough has become firm remove from the refrigerator and scale into 8 oz. units. Return the 8 oz. units to the refrigerator to be kept firm until ready to roll. When rolling the dough work with one unit of dough at a time. An 8 oz. unit will provide enough dough for one bottom or one top crust when making an 8 or 9 inch pie. Experienced bakers usually can roll out a bottom or top crust with less dough, for the inexperienced, however, more dough is needed. The rolling is done on a floured bench, and the same pastry flour used in making the dough should be used to dust the bench. The amount of flour used to dust will depend on the consistency of the dough. In some cases, bakers will roll the pie dough on a floured piece of canvas. This is a good practice because it is very seldom that the dough will stick to the canvas. If not properly handled, however, it will stick to the bench. After the dough is rolled and the bottom or top crust formed, any scraps that are left are pressed together and should only be used for the bottom crust. Table I gives some of the possible causes and possible remedies for faulty pies.

PIE FILLINGS

We have emphasized the importance of a good tender pie crust in the preparation of any pie, and while this is of the utmost importance it does not necessarily mean that because the crust is of excellent quality the filling can be poor. The filling must meet the same high standards set for the crust if the pie is to be considered as a successful product. The filling should be thickened to the just right consistency, it should be made from the best ingredients, and it should be flavored and seasoned properly. The appearance of the filling is also important because sight comes before the bite and if a starchy, pasty, heavy filling is sighted the bite may never take place.

The fillings for dessert pies are usually divided into four types:

1. Fruit filling.
2. Cream filling.
3. Chiffon filling.
4. Soft filling.

There are other fillings used such as ice cream and nesselrode (type of fruit filling flavored with rum); however, these pies are considered as specialty pies and are not included in the group that we know as the common pie.

FRUIT FILLINGS

The most popular of the four general types of pie filling is the fruit filling. The fruit used may be fresh, dried, frozen or canned and each must be treated differently when being prepared for a pie fill-

TABLE I.   CAUSES AND REMEDIES FOR FAULTY PIES

Nature of Trouble	Possible Causes	Possible Remedies
Excessive shrinkage of crusts	Not enough shortening Too much water Dough worked too much Flour too strong	Increase the shortening. Cut quantity of water. Do not overmix. Use a weaker flour or increase shortening content.
Crust not flake	Dough mixed too warm Shortening too soft Rubbing flour and fat too much	Have water cold. Have shortening at right temperature. Do not rub too much.
Bottom crust soaks too much juice	Insufficient baking Crust too rich Too cool an oven	Bake longer. Reduce amount of shortening. More bottom heat.
Tough crust	Flour too strong Dough overmixed Overworking the dough Too much water	Increase the shortening. Just incorporate the ingredients. Work dough as little as possible. Reduce amount of water.
Soggy crust	Not enough bottom heat Oven too hot Having filling hot	Regulate oven correctly. Regulate oven correctly. Use only cold fillings.
Fruit boils out	Oven too cold Fruit slightly sour No holes in top crust Crust not properly sealed	Regulate oven temperature. Use more sugar. Have a few openings in top crust. Seal bottom and top crust on edges.
Custard pies curdle	Overbaked	Take out of oven as soon as set.
Blisters on pumpkin pies	Oven too hot Too long baking	Regulate oven temperature. Take out of oven as soon as set.
Bleedings of meringue	Moisture in egg whites Poor egg whites Grease in egg whites	Use a stabilizer in the meringue. Check egg whites for body. Be sure equipment is free from grease.

ing. The formula being used should state which type of fruit is being used.

Fresh fruit is used for pie filling when in season because at this period the fruit is firm and ripe and can be purchased cheaper than at any other time of the year. How the fruit is treated will, of course, depend on the kind of fruit it is, the method being used to prepare the filling, and the condition of the fruit (over-ripe, ripe, slightly green).

Dried fruit such as apricots, apples and raisins are sometimes used for pie filling although they are not extremely popular. Since these fruits have most of their natural liquid removed they must be soaked in water to restore their natural moisture. In some cases the liquid and fruit may be brought to a boil and then, after removing from the range, allowed to soak for a short period. This method not only restores moisture but also causes the fruit to become more soft and plump. After soaking, the liquid is drained from the fruit, thickened and flavored by using one of the standard methods; then it is poured back over the fruit.

Frozen fruit is the type most commonly used in pie fillings today. The fruit has all the advantages of fresh fruit plus the fact that they are usually available the year round. The fruit is frozen as soon as possible after picking, either in raw form or slightly parboiled (partly cooked), and packed in cans with liquid, sugar and in some cases additional color. They are available on the market in 30 lb. tin cans. In some cases smaller amounts (6½ and 10 lb. cans) are made available. Frozen fruit must be completely defrosted before it is used for a pie filling. The best method of defrosting is to place the unopened can in a refrigerator at normal refrigeration temperatures. This usually takes about one day. To speed up defrosting, the opened fruit container can be set in hot water, but one must use caution by constantly stir-ring to be sure the fruit is completely defrosted before using. After defrosting the juice is drained from the fruit, thickened and flavored by using one of the standard methods and poured back over the fruit. At this point if the fruit is not completely defrosted it will bleed (continue to release juice) and cause the filling to separate.

Canned fruit is used very often in pie fillings mainly because it is available the year round and the cans (no. 10) are easy to store. In general, canned fruit can be purchased in two different packs: the solid pack and the water or syrup pack. The water or syrup pack contains less fruit and a higher percentage of juice and sugar than the solid pack. It is advisable to use the solid pack for pie fillings because one is purchasing more fruit and also the solid pack has a lesser sugar content. This permits the addition of more sugar after the juice is thickened. If sugar is added after the juice is thickened, better results can be obtained.

The following are three accepted methods of preparing fruit fillings:

Drained fruit method

1. Drain juice from the fruit and place on the range to boil.
2. Dissolve starch in cold water and pour slowly into the boiling juice while stirring constantly.
3. Bring the juice back to a boil and cook until clear.
4. Add granulated sugar, salt, spices (if used) and lemon juice, stir until thoroughly blended.
5. Add additional color, stir.
6. Pour the thickened syrup over the drained fruit and stir gently so the fruit is not mashed or broken.
7. Cool slightly and pour the filling into unbaked pie shells. This method is recommended when preparing cherry, blueberry, peach, apricot and blackberry pie filling.

Fruit and juice method

1. Place the fruit and juice in a pot with the desired or required spices. Place on the range and bring to a boil.
2. Dissolve starch in cold water and pour slowly into the boiling fruit and juice mixture while stirring constantly.
3. Bring the mixture back to a boil and cook until clear.
4. Add the granulated sugar, salt and color (if desired) and stir until thoroughly blended.
5. Cool slightly and pour the filling into unbaked pie shells.

This method is recommended when preparing pineapple, apple and cranberry-apple pie filling.

Old style method

1. Mix the fruit (generally fresh fruit) with a mixture of flour, spices and granulated sugar.
2. Place this mixture in unbaked pie shells.
3. Dot the top of the fruit mixture with butter.
4. Cover the top of the pie with a sheet or strips of pie dough and bake.

This method can be used best with fresh fruit such as apples, peaches and apricot. However, it is not a popular method because the consistency of the juice cannot be controlled.

CREAM FILLINGS

This filling is quite simple to prepare; however, care must be taken to assure a smooth, rich, full-flavored filling. One of the most common mistakes made in preparing this type of filling is to undercook the flour or starch, thereby causing the finished product to have a raw flour or starch taste. Another shortcoming is not beating vigorously enough once the starch or flour starts to thicken; this causes the filling to become lumpy and lack appetite appeal. The most popular cream pies are chocolate, vanilla, coconut, butterscotch and banana. After the filling is prepared it is placed in a prebaked pie shell and topped with meringue or some other type of cream topping. The usual steps taken in preparing cream filling are listed below.

Cream filling method

1. Place milk in the top of a double boiler, holding back approximately 1 qt. (depending on amount being made) to liquefy the dry ingredients. Heat the milk.
2. Beat the eggs in a separate container, add the sugar, salt and starch or flour. Pour in the remaining milk while stirring constantly until a thin paste forms.
3. Pour the thin paste into the scalding milk, whip constantly until the mixture thickens and becomes smooth.
4. Cook until all traces of starch are removed; remove from the heat.
5. Stir in the flavoring, add required amount of butter or shortening.
6. Pour into prebaked pie shells, let cool.
7. Top with meringue or whipped topping.

CHIFFON FILLINGS

This is an extremely light, airy, fluffy type of filling. It is prepared by folding (blending one mixture over another) together a fruit or cream pie filling with a meringue. In most cases a small amount of plain gelatin is added to the fruit or cream filling to help the chiffon filling set up when cooled. Chiffon pies are quite popular with women because they tend to be less filling than most dessert items. Chiffon pie fillings are usually prepared by the following steps.

Chiffon filling method

1. Prepare a cream filling or a fruit filling using the fruit and juice method, but chopping the fruit instead of leaving it whole.
2. Soak plain gelatin in cold water and add it to the hot cream or fruit filling, stirring until it is thoroughly dissolved. Place the filling in a fairly shallow pan, let cool.
3. Refrigerate until the filling begins to set.
4. Prepare a meringue by whipping egg whites and sugar together; whip to stiff peaks.
5. Fold the meringue into the jellied fruit or cream mixture gently, preserving as many of the air cells as possible.
6. Deposit the chiffon filling in pre-baked pie shells. Refrigerate until set.
7. Top with whip cream or whipped topping.

SOFT FILLINGS

These are fillings that are uncooked and baked in an unbaked pie crust. These are the most difficult pies to make. The difficulty lies in baking the filling and crust to the proper degree without over or under baking one or the other. Soft fillings are used in such popular pies as pumpkin, custard and pecan. To eliminate some of the problems that develop during the baking of soft pies, consideration should be given to the tips listed below. Since there are many different formulas in use it would be difficult to state just what problem may develop when the pie is baked.

1. Rolling the pie dough on graham cracker crumbs instead of flour will help to eliminate the soggy crust that sometimes develops.
2. Use precooked or pregelatinized starch instead of cornstarch to bind the filling. The starches will give the filling more body and eliminate separation.
3. Egg white stabilizer (¼ oz. per. qt. of filling) or tapioca flour (1 oz. per qt. of milk) may also be used to bind the filling and improve the appearance of the finished product.
4. Bake soft pies at a plus 400°F for at least the first 10 to 15 minutes of the baking period. After that the temperature may be reduced. Remove the pie from the oven as soon as the filling is set.
5. Fill the pie shell only half full of the fillings and bake for a few minutes before filling the shell completely. This will, in most cases, produce a more uniformly baked product.

THICKENING AGENTS USED IN PIE FILLINGS

Starches and flours are used to thicken pie fillings. Starches are used more than flour because they produce a better sheen and do not have a tendency to discolor or become heavy. Starches used may be of many types, such as corn, tapioca, rice or a blended product called modified starch. Modified starch is a blend of four or more starches and is available on the market under various trade names. The modified starch is becoming popular in thickening fruit fillings because it will hold a sheen longer when the filling is refrigerated. In most cases, other starches cloud up quickly when the fruit filling is refrigerated.

The amount of starch used in a formula will depend on the jelling quality of the starch and the acidity of the fruit and juice being thickened. The higher the acid quality the more thickener required to thicken and hold the gel of the liquid. Usually 3 to 5 ozs. of starch for each qt. of liquid (water and juice) is the amount required. The flour or starch being added to a filling should be diluted in cold water or juice before it is poured into the boiling liquid. When being added to the boiling liquid the liquid should be whipped vigorously to avoid lumps and scorching.

New starches have deen developed recently which will thicken without cooking. They are known as pregelatinized starch and will thicken when blended with the sugar and added to the liquid. They react quickly without heat because the starch has been pre-cooked and does not require additional heat to enable it to absorb liquid and gelatinize. When using this type of product always follow the manufacturers recommended instructions.

PIE DOUGH AND FILLING RECIPES

The pie dough recipes presented on the following pages vary in types and tenderness. Some are easy to work with others are slightly difficult. It is recommended that the inexperienced student use the short flake type or the sure-fire method pie dough when starting to learn how to roll the dough. When experience is obtained he may attempt to work with a shorter dough. (A *shorter dough* has a higher percentage of shortening and results in a more tender crust.) A few of the most popular pie fillings are given after the pie doughs.

The following outline gives recipes in their order of appearance in the chapter.

Pie doughs
(Pages 573 to 576)

Fruit fillings
(Pages 577 to 584)

Cream fillings
(Pages 584 to 587)

Chiffon fillings
(Pages 587 to 590)

Soft fillings
(Pages 590 to 591)

Fried pie fillings
(Pages 591 to 592)

Meringue toppings
(Pages 592 to 593)

PIE DOUGH RECIPES

Sure-fire method pie dough

Sure-fire method pie dough is prepared slightly differently than most pie doughs. The formula calls for 2 amounts of flour instead of the usual one. The second amount of flour is mixed into the liquid ingredient before it is added to the flour-shortening mixture. This type of formula leaves little chance for failure, hence its name.

Objectives

1. To teach the student the procedure for preparing sure-fire method pie dough.
2. To teach the student how to mix and handle the dough.

Equipment

1. Large round bowl, 5 gal.
2. Plastic scraper
3. Baker's scale
4. 1 gal. stainless steel container
5. Wire whip
6. Sheet pan

Ingredients: Approx. yield: 12, 8 in. double crust pies

5	lbs. pastry flour
4	lbs. 8 ozs. Primex shortening
2½	ozs. salt
1	lb. pastry flour
1	lb. 8 ozs. water, cold

Preparation

1. Chill the water.
2. Have all equipment and ingredients handy.

Procedure

1. Place the first amount of flour in the large round bowl.
2. Add the shortening and rub together by hand until the mixture has formed into small lumps.
3. Place the salt and the second amount of flour in a stainless steel container, add the cold water, and whip with a wire whip until the mixture is smooth.
4. Pour the liquid mixture over the flour-shortening mixture and mix together gently by hand until the liquid is absorbed by the flour.
5. Place dough on a sheet pan, scrape bowl clean with a plastic scraper, and refrigerate the dough for approximately 1 hour until it becomes very firm to the touch.
6. Remove from the refrigerator, scale into 8 oz. units, and refrigerate again until ready to roll.

Precautions and Safety Measures

1. When blending the salt, flour and water together mix until all the ingredients are blended before adding it to the flour-shortening mixture.
2. Do not overmix the dough.
3. Chill the dough thoroughly before using.
4. Scale all ingredients correctly.

Pie dough (short flake type)

Pie dough (short flake type) is the most common type of pie dough made. The shortening is cut or rubbed into the flour until small lumps are formed and no flour spots are evident. This type of dough is very versatile and can be used in any preparation calling for a pie dough or crust.

Objectives

1. To teach the student the procedure for preparing the short flake pie dough.
2. To teach the student how to mix and handle the dough.

Equipment

1. Large round bowl, 5 gal.
2. Plastic scraper
3. Baker's scale
4. 1 gal. stainless steel container
5. Kitchen spoon
6. Sheet pan

Ingredients: Approx. yield: 22, 8 in. double crust pies

10	lbs. pastry flour
7	lbs. 8 ozs. hydrogenated (Primex) shortening
5½	ozs. salt
3	lbs. water, cold
10	ozs. sugar or corn sugar solids

Preparation

1. Chill the water.
2. Have all equipment and ingredients handy.

Procedure

1. Place the flour and shortening in a large round bowl. Rub together by hand until small lumps are formed and no raw flour spots (lumps of dry flour) are evident.
2. Place the water, salt and sugar or corn sugar solids (dextrose mixture in powdered form) in a stainless steel container. Mix with a kitchen spoon until the sugar and salt are dissolved.
3. Pour the liquid mixture over the flour-shortening mixture and mix together gently by hand until the liquid is absorbed by the flour.
4. Place dough on a sheet pan, scrape bowl clean with a plastic scraper, and refrigerate the dough until it becomes very firm to the touch.
5. Remove from the refrigerator, scale into 8 oz. units, and refrigerate again until ready to roll.

Precautions and Safety Measures

1. Scale all the ingredients correctly.

2. When cutting or rubbing the shortening into the flour be sure all the flour is worked in before adding the liquid.
3. Be sure the salt and sugar are thoroughly dissolved in the water before adding it to the flour-shortening mixture.
4. Do not overmix the dough.
5. Chill the dough before using.

Pie dough (mealy type)

To prepare this type of pie dough the flour and shortening are rubbed together more thoroughly than they are when preparing the other two types. All flour particles are thoroughly coated with shortening, thus preventing the flour from absorbing much moisture. It is for this reason that less water is called for in the mealy type formulas. The mealy type dough is usually easy to work with.

Objectives
1. To teach the student the procedure for preparing the mealy type pie dough.
2. To teach the student how to mix and handle the dough.

Equipment
1. Large round bowl, 5 gal.
2. Plastic scraper
3. Baker's scale
4. 1 gal. stainless steel container
5. Kitchen spoon
6. Sheet pan

Ingredients: Approx. yield: 20, 8 in. double crust pies

10	lbs. pastry flour
7	lbs. 8 ozs. hydrogenated (Primex) shortening
5	ozs. salt
2	lbs. 8 ozs. water, cold
10	ozs. sugar or corn sugar solids

Preparation
1. Chill the water.
2. Have all equipment and ingredients handy.

Procedure
1. Place the flour and shortening in a large round bowl. Rub together by hand until the flour is completely covered with shortening and the mixture is mealy.
2. Place the water, salt and sugar or corn sugar solids (dextrose mixture in powdered form) in a stainless steel container. Mix with a kitchen spoon until the sugar and salt are dissolved.

3. Pour the liquid mixture over the flour-shortening mixture and mix together gently by hand until the liquid is absorbed by the flour.
4. Place the dough on a sheet pan, scrape the bowl clean with a plastic scraper, and refrigerate until it becomes firm enough to roll.
5. Remove from the refrigerator, scale into 8 oz. units and refrigerate again until ready to roll.

Precautions and Safety Measures
1. Work the flour and shortening mixture together thoroughly.
2. Work all flour into the shortening, no raw flour should be present.
3. Be sure the salt and sugar are thoroughly dissolved in the water before adding it to the flour-shortening mixture.
4. Do not overmix the dough.
5. Chill the dough before using.

Pie dough (long flake type)

This type of pie dough is usually very tender. Shortening spots are visible throughout the dough and for this reason it should be used only for top crust or prebaked pie shells.

Objectives
1. To teach the student the procedure for preparing the long flake pie dough.
2. To teach the student how to mix and handle the dough.

Equipment
1. Large round bowl, 5 gal.
2. Plastic scraper
3. Baker's scale
4. 1 gal. stainless steel container
5. Kitchen spoon
6. Sheet pan

Ingredients: Approx. yield: 23 double crust pies

10	lbs. pastry flour
7	lbs. 8 ozs. hydrogenated (Primex) shortening
6	ozs. salt
5	lbs. water, cold
10	ozs. sugar or corn sugar solids

Preparation
1. Chill the water.
2. Have all equipment and ingredients handy.

Procedure
1. Place the flour and shortening in a large

round bowl. Rub together lightly by hand leaving the shortening in fairly large chunks, about the size of the tip of the little finger.

2. Place the water, salt and sugar or corn sugar solids (dextrose mixture in powdered form) in a stainless steel container. Mix with a kitchen spoon until the sugar and salt are dissolved.
3. Pour the liquid mixture over the flour-shortening mixture and mix together gently by hand until the liquid is absorbed by the flour.
4. Place the dough on a sheet pan, scrape the bowl clean with a plastic scraper, and refrigerate until it becomes very firm to the touch.
5. Remove from the refrigerator, scale into 8 oz. units, and refrigerate again until ready to roll.

Precautions and Safety Measures
1. Do not overwork the flour and shortening during the rubbing stage or the long flake dough can not be obtained.
2. Work all flour into the shortening, no raw flour should be present.
3. Be sure the salt and sugar are thoroughly dissolved in the water before adding it to the flour shortening mixture.
4. Do not overmix the dough.
5. Chill the dough before using.

Pie dough for frying

Pie dough for frying is prepared the same as the regular pie dough formulas. However, less shortening is used because the dough is fried in deep fat and will absorb fat during the frying period. This dough is used to prepare that old favorite from Dixie Land, Southern fried pies.

Objectives
1. To teach the student the procedure for preparing pie dough for frying.
2. To teach the student how to mix and handle the dough.
3. To teach the student how to prepare Southern fried pies.

Equipment
1. Large round bowl
2. Plastic scraper
3. Baker's scale
4. 1 gal. stainless steel container
5. Kitchen spoon
6. Sheet pan
7. 5½ in. round cutter
8. Deep fat fryer
9. Pastry brush
10. Dinner fork

Ingredients: Approx. yield: 60 pies

5	lbs.	pastry flour
2	lbs.	Primex shortening
2½	ozs.	salt
2	lbs.	water, cold

Preparation
1. Chill the water.
2. Have all equipment and ingredients handy.

Procedure
1. Place the flour and shortening in a large round bowl. Rub together by hand until the flour is completely covered with shortening and no raw flour spots are present.
2. Place the water and salt in a stainless steel container; stir with a kitchen spoon until the salt is dissolved.
3. Pour the salt water over the flour-shortening mixture and mix together gently by hand until the liquid is absorbed by the flour.
4. Place the dough on a sheet pan, scrape the bowl clean with a plastic scraper, and refrigerate until it becomes very firm to the touch.

Make up: Roll out the dough on a floured bench to about ⅛ in. thickness. Cut out with a 5½ in. round cutter (about 2 ozs. dough). Use about 2 ozs. of filling. Place the filling in center of rolled out dough, wash edges with cold water, using a pastry brush and shape to form a turnover (fold the circle in half). Seal the edges securely and pierce top twice with the tines of a dinner fork. Fry in deep fat for 5 to 7 minutes at 375°F. Let drain, cool and ice the fried pies with roll icing. See chapter 26 for roll icing recipe.

Note: Filling for fried pies can be found in the section on pie fillings. (See *Fried Pie Fillings*, pages 591 to 592.)

Precautions and Safety Measures
1. Dissolve the salt in the water thoroughly or small burnt spots will appear on the finished product.
2. Do not overmix the dough.
3. Seal the edges of each turnover completely.

FRUIT FILLING RECIPES

Pineapple pie filling

For pineapple pie filling canned, crushed pineapple and juice are thickened with starch, flavored, and placed into unbaked pie shells. Pineapple pie filling will produce pies with eye and taste appeal that is a welcomed addition to any menu.

Objectives
1. To teach the student the procedure for preparing pineapple pie filling.
2. To teach the student how to thicken the fruit and juice mixture.

Equipment
1. Baker's scale
2. Sauce pot, 2 gal.
3. Kitchen spoon
4. Small stainless steel bowl
5. Qt. measure
6. Collander

Ingredients: Approx. yield: 6, 8 in. pies

6	lbs. 8 ozs. pineapple, crushed, canned (#10 can)
2	lbs. pineapple juice and water
1	lb. 8 ozs. granulated sugar
1/4	oz. salt
8	ozs. water
4 1/2	ozs. modified starch or cornstarch
6	ozs. corn syrup
	yellow color as needed

Preparation
1. Open the no. 10 can and drain the juice from the pineapple through a collander. Save the juice and add water to equal 2 lbs. (1 qt.).
2. Have all equipment and ingredients handy.

Procedure
1. Place the crushed pineapple, sugar, salt and juice in a sauce pot; bring to a boil.
2. Dissolve the starch in the 8 ozs. of water in a stainless steel bowl. Pour slowly into the boiling pineapple mixture stirring constantly with a kitchen spoon until thickened and clear.
3. Simmer the mixture for approximately 2 minutes, remove from the heat.
4. Stir in the corn syrup and tint with yellow color, let the mixture cool.
5. Proceed to fill unbaked pie shells and make up as desired.
6. Bake in a preheated oven at 400° to 425°F.

Precautions and Safety Measures
1. Pour the dissolved starch slowly into the boiling mixture and stir constantly with a kitchen spoon to avoid lumps.
2. When simmering the thickened mixture, stir occasionally to avoid sticking and scorching.
3. Exercise caution when adding the yellow color; a little will enhance the appearance, too much will hinder.

Spiced peach pie filling

For spiced peach pie filling the peach juice is boiled with vinegar and spices to bring forth a pungent spicy flavor. The juice is then thickened and folded into the sliced peaches. This desirable spicy filling is generally used in the preparation of double crust pies.

Objectives
1. To teach the student the procedure for preparing peach pie filling.
2. To teach the student how to thicken the juice and fold in the peaches.

Equipment
1. Baker's scale
2. Sauce pot, 2 gal.
3. China cap
4. Wire whip
5. Collander
6. Small stainless steel bowl
7. Qt. measure
8. Kitchen spoon
9. 1 gal. stainless steel container

Ingredients: Approx. yield: 6, 8 in. pies

6	lbs. 8 ozs. peaches (#10 can) sliced, drained
2	lbs. peach juice and water
1/8	oz. whole cloves
1/4	oz. stick cinnamon
8	ozs. vinegar, cider
8	ozs. water
3 1/2	ozs. modified starch or corn starch
1	lb. 8 ozs. granulated sugar
1/4	oz. salt

Preparation
1. Open the no. 10 can and drain the juice from the peaches by placing the peaches in a collander. Save the juice and add water to equal 2 lbs. (1 qt.).
2. Have all equipment and ingredients handy.

Procedure
1. Place the peach juice, cinnamon stick, cloves and vinegar in a sauce pot, bring to a boil.

Fruit pie varieties.

Procter and Gamble Co.

2. Simmer for approximately 20 minutes, strain through a china cap into a stainless steel container.
3. Return the strained juice to the sauce pot, bring back to a boil.
4. Dissolve the starch in the 8 ozs. of water in a stainless steel bowl. Pour slowly into the boiling liquid while whipping briskly with a wire whip.
5. Bring mixture back to a boil, cook until thickened and clear.
6. Add the sugar and salt, stir with a kitchen spoon until thoroughly dissolved.
7. Add the drained peaches, folding them into the thickened juice gently with a kitchen spoon to avoid breaking the fruit, let the mixture cool.
8. Proceed to fill unbaked pie shells and make up pies as desired.
9. Bake in a preheated oven at 425°F.

Precautions and Safety Measures
1. Pour the dissolved starch slowly into the boiling mixture and whip briskly to avoid lumps.
2. Once the starch is added, stir the mixture continuously to avoid scorching.

Cherry pie filling (canned)

This formula calls for the use of canned cherries which will produce an excellent tasting pie filling, but will lack color. Canned cherries, unlike frozen cherries, do not retain their natural color. Red color must be added to improve the appearance. This filling can be used for making double crust pies or single crust pies with a streusel or whipped cream topping.

Objectives
1. To teach the student the procedure for preparing cherry pie filling.
2. To teach the student how to thicken the juice and fold in the fruit.

Equipment
1. Baker's scale
2. Sauce pot, 2 gal.
3. Wire whip
4. Kitchen spoon
5. Colander
6. Small stainless steel bowl
7. Cup measure
8. Paring knife
9. Qt. measure

Ingredients: Approx. yield: 5 to 6, 8 in. pies

6 lbs. 8 ozs. cherries, canned, drained (#10 can)
2 lbs. cherry juice and water
4 ozs. modified starch or cornstarch
1 lb. 8 ozs. granulated sugar
lemon juice (from 1 lemon)
red color as desired

Preparation

1. Open the no. 10 can and drain the juice from the cherries by placing the cherries in a collander. Save the juice and add enough water to equal 2 lbs. (1 qt.).
2. Cut the lemon in half with a paring knife and squeeze the juice from the lemon by hand.
3. Have all equipment and ingredients handy.

Procedure

1. Place the cherry juice in a sauce pot, reserving 1 cup for dissolving the starch, bring to a boil.
2. In a stainless steel bowl dissolve the starch in the cherry juice held in reserve. Pour slowly into the boiling juice, whipping vigorously with a wire whip.
3. Bring mixture back to a boil, cook until thickened and clear.
4. Add sugar, whip until dissolved.
5. Add the lemon juice and red color, stir with a kitchen spoon until blended into the thickened juice. Remove from the range.
6. Add the drained cherries, folding them into the thickened juice gently with a kitchen spoon to avoid crushing the fruit. Let cool.
7. Proceed to fill unbaked pie shells and make up pies as desired.
8. Bake in a preheated oven at 400° to 425°F.

Precautions and Safety Measures

1. Drain the cherries thoroughly.
2. Pour the dissolved starch slowly into the boiling mixture and whip vigorously to avoid lumps.
3. Once the starch is added, stir the mixture continuously to avoid scorching.

Cherry pie filling (frozen cherries)

This formula calls for the use of frozen cherries which will produce a rich red, natural looking filling. The cherries must be thoroughly thawed before being used. This filling can be used for making double crust pies or single crust pies with a streusel or whipped topping.

Objectives

1. To teach the student the procedure for preparing cherry pie filling.
2. To teach the student how to tighten the juice and fold in the fruit.

Equipment

1. Baker's scale
2. Sauce pot, 2 gal.
3. Wire whip
4. Kitchen spoon
5. Collander
6. Small stainless steel bowl
7. Pt. measure
8. Qt. measure

Ingredients: Approx. yield: 10, 8 in. pies

10 lbs. cherries, frozen, thawed, drained
4 lbs. cherry juice and water
8 ozs. modified starch or cornstarch
2 lbs. granulated sugar
1 lb. corn syrup

Preparation

1. Thaw the frozen cherries.
2. Drain the juice from the cherries by placing them in a collander. Save the juice and add water to the juice, if needed, to equal 4 lbs. (2 qts.).
3. Have all equipment and ingredients handy.

Procedure

1. Place all, but 1 lb. (1 pt.) of the cherry juice in a sauce pot, bring to a boil.
2. In a stainless steel bowl dissolve the starch in the remaining 1 lb. (pt.) of cherry juice, pour slowly into the boiling mixture while whipping vigorously with a wire whip.
3. Bring mixture back to a boil, cook until thickened and clear.
4. Add the corn syrup and stir with a kitchen spoon until thoroughly blended. Remove from the heat.
5. Add the cherries, folding them into the thickened juice gently with a kitchen spoon to avoid breaking or crushing the fruit. Let cool.
6. Proceed to fill unbaked pie shells and make up pies as desired.
7. Bake in preheated oven at 400° to 425°F.

Precautions and Safety Measures

1. Drain the cherries thoroughly.
2. Pour the dissolved starch slowly into the boiling mixture and whip vigorously to avoid lumps.

Blueberry pie filling (frozen)

For blueberry pie filling the blueberry juice is thickened with starch, flavored, and poured over the blueberries. This method is used to avoid crushing the plump tender berries.

Objective
1. To teach the student the procedure for preparing blueberry pie filling.
2. To teach the student how to thicken the juice and fold in the berries.

Equipment
1. Baker's scale
2. Sauce pot, 3 gal.
3. Wire whip
4. Kitchen spoon
5. Collander
6. Small stainless steel bowl
7. Qt. measure
8. Paring knife

Ingredients: Approx. yield: 9, 8 in. pies

9	lbs. blueberries, frozen, thawed, drained
2	lbs. blueberry juice and water
1	lb. granulated sugar
1/4	oz. salt
1/4	oz. cinnamon
8	ozs. water
4 1/2	ozs. modified starch or cornstarch
2	lbs. 8 ozs. granulated sugar
1/2	oz. lemon juice

Preparation
1. Thaw the frozen blueberries
2. Drain the juice from the berries by placing them in a collander. Save the juice and add water to the juice to equal 2 lbs. (1 qt.).
3. Cut the lemon in half with a paring knife and squeeze the juice out by hand.
4. Have all equipment and ingredients handy.

Procedure
1. In a sauce pot place the blueberry juice or the water-juice mixture, the first amount of sugar, cinnamon, and salt. Bring to a boil.
2. In a stainless steel bowl dissolve the starch in the 8 ozs. of water. Pour very slowly into the boiling mixture while whipping briskly with a wire whip.
3. Bring the mixture back to a boil, cook until thickened and clear.
4. Add the second amount of sugar and lemon juice, stir with a kitchen spoon until thoroughly blended. Remove from the heat.
5. Add the blueberries, folding them into the thickened juice gently with a kitchen spoon to avoid crushing. Let the mixture cool.
6. Proceed to fill unbaked pie shells and make up pies as desired.
7. Bake in a preheated oven at 400° to 425°F.

Precautions and Safety Measures
1. Drain the blueberries thoroughly.
2. Pour the dissolved starch slowly into the boiling mixture and whip briskly to avoid lumps.
3. Once the starch is added, stir the mixture continuously to avoid lumps.

Peach pie filling (canned peaches)

For pie filling the peach juice is thickened with starch, flavored, and poured back over the sliced canned peaches. This kind of filling is usually used in the preparation of double crust pies.

Objectives
1. To teach the student the procedure for preparing peach pie filling.
2. To teach the student how to thicken the juice and fold in the peaches.

Equipment
1. Baker's scale
2. Sauce pot, 2 gal.
3. Wire whip
4. Kitchen spoon
5. Collander
6. Small stainless steel bowl
7. Qt. measure

Ingredients: Approx. yield: 6, 8 in. pies

6	lbs. 8 ozs. peaches (1 #10 can) sliced, drained
2	lbs. peach juice and water
12	ozs. granulated sugar
1/4	oz. salt
8	ozs. water
4	ozs. modified starch or cornstarch
1	lb. granulated sugar
	yellow color as needed

Preparation
1. Open the no. 10 can and drain the juice from the peaches by placing them in a collander. Save the juice and add water to the juice to equal 2 lbs. (1 qt.).
2. Have all equipment and ingredients handy.

Procedure
1. Place the peach juice and water, the first amount of sugar, and salt in a sauce pot, bring to a boil.

Armour and Co.

Peach pie with a lattice top.

2. In a stainless steel bowl dissolve the starch in the 8 ozs. of water, pour slowly into the boiling mixture while whipping vigorously with a wire whip.
3. Bring mixture back to a boil, cook until thickened and clear.
4. Add the second amount of sugar, stir with a kitchen spoon until thoroughly dissolved.
5. Add yellow color as needed. Remove from the heat.
6. Add the drained peaches, folding them into the thickened juice gently with a kitchen spoon to avoid breaking or crushing the fruit. Let cool.
7. Proceed to fill unbaked pie shells and make up pies as desired.
8. Bake in a preheated oven at 400° to 425°F.

Precautions and Safety Measures
1. Pour the dissolved starch slowly into the boiling mixture and whip vigorously to avoid lumps.
2. Once the starch is added stir the mixture continuously to avoid scorching.

Apricot pie filling (frozen)

For apricot pie filling frozen apricots are used because they produce a filling that is superior in appearance. Apricot pie filling can be used in preparing both single and double crust pies.

Objectives
1. To teach the student the procedure for preparing apricot pie filling.

2. To teach the student how to thicken the fruit and juice mixture.

Equipment
1. Baker's scale
2. Sauce pot, 3 gal.
3. Wire whip
4. Kitchen spoon
5. Qt. measure
6. Collander
7. Stainless steel bowl

Ingredients: Approx. yield: 7 to 8, 8 in. pies

10	lbs. apricots, frozen, thawed, drained
2	lbs. apricot juice and water
1	lb. 8 ozs. granulated sugar
1/4	oz. salt
8	ozs. water
6	ozs. modified starch or cornstarch
	yellow color as needed

Preparation
1. Thaw the frozen apricots.
2. Drain the juice from the apricots by placing them in a collander. Save the juice. Add water to the juice to equal 2 lbs. (1 qt.).
3. Have all equipment and ingredients handy.

Procedure
1. Place the apricots, sugar, salt, water and juice in a sauce pot; bring to a boil.
2. In a stainless steel bowl dissolve the starch in the 8 ozs. of water. Pour slowly into the boiling mixture, stirring constantly with a kitchen spoon until thickened and clear.
3. Simmer the mixture for approximately 2 minutes. Remove from the heat.
4. Tint as desired with yellow color, stir thoroughly. Let the mixture cool.
5. Proceed to fill unbaked pie shells and make up as desired.
6. Bake in a preheated oven at 400° to 425°F.

Precautions and Safety Measures
1. Pour the dissolved starch slowly into the boiling mixture while stirring gently to avoid crushing the apricots.
2. When simmering the thickened mixture, stir occasionally to avoid sticking or scorching.
3. Exercise caution when adding the yellow color; a little will enhance the appearance, too much will hinder.

Apple pie filling (canned)

For apple pie filling canned apples, which seem to be the most common type used for pie filling, are cooked slightly with water or apple juice, seasoned, and thickened with starch. Apple pies are the all-American favorite and can be made up into single crust or double crust varieties.

Objectives
1. To teach the student the procedure for preparing apple pie filling.
2. To teach the student how to thicken the fruit and juice mixture.

Equipment
1. Baker's scale
2. Sauce pot, 2 gal.
3. Kitchen spoon.
4. Small stainless steel bowl.

Ingredients: Approx. yield: 6 to 7, 8 in. pies

7	lbs.	apples, canned (#10 can)
1	lb. 8 ozs.	water or apple juice
1	lb. 4 ozs.	granulated sugar
$\frac{1}{4}$	oz.	salt
$\frac{1}{4}$	oz.	cinnamon
$\frac{1}{8}$	oz.	nutmeg
3	ozs.	butter
8	ozs.	water
3	ozs.	modified starch or cornstarch

Preparation
1. Have all the equipment and ingredients handy.

Procedure
1. Place the apples, sugar, salt, spices, and the first amount of water or juice in a sauce pot, bring to a boil.
2. In a stainless steel bowl dissolve the starch in the second amount of water. Pour slowly into the boiling mixture, stirring constantly with a kitchen spoon until thickened.
3. Simmer the mixture for approximately 2 minutes. Remove from the heat.
4. Stir in the butter with a kitchen spoon. Let mixture cool.
5. Proceed to fill unbaked pie shells and make up pies as desired.
6. Bake in a preheated oven at 400° to 425°F.

Note: For a Dutch apple filling add 8 ozs. of raisins to step No. 1.

Precautions and Safety Measures
1. When adding the dissolved starch to the boiling mass, stir gently so the fruit will not be broken.
2. When simmering the thickened mixture, stir occasionally to avoid sticking and scorching.

Cranberry-apple pie filling

Cranberry-apple pie filling is a combination that is a sure winner during the fall and winter seasons. The canned apples are seasoned and thickened in the same manner as regular apple pie filling, but at this point the whole canned cranberry sauce is folded into the mixture to create an exciting new type of filling.

Objectives
1. To teach the student the procedure for preparing cranberry-apple pie filling.
2. To teach the student how to thicken the fruit and juice mixture and fold in the whole cranberry sauce.

Equipment
1. Baker's scale
2. Sauce pot, 3 gal.
3. Kitchen spoon
4. Small stainless steel bowl
5. Paring knife

Ingredients: Approx. yield: 7, 8 in. pies

7	lbs.	apples, canned
2	lbs.	water or apple juice
1	lb. 8 ozs.	granulated sugar
$\frac{1}{4}$	oz.	cinnamon
$\frac{1}{8}$	oz.	nutmeg
$\frac{1}{4}$	oz.	salt
4	ozs.	modified starch or cornstarch
6	ozs.	water
2	lbs.	whole cranberry sauce
4	ozs.	corn syrup
		lemon juice (1 lemon)

Preparation
1. Cut the lemon in half with a paring knife and squeeze the lemon juice by hand.
2. Have all equipment and ingredients handy.

Procedure
1. Place the apples, sugar, salt, spices and the first amount of water or juice in a sauce pot, bring to a boil.
2. In a stainless steel bowl dissolve the starch in the second amount of water. Pour slowly into the boiling mixture, stirring constantly with a kitchen spoon until thickened.
3. Simmer the mixture for approximately 2 minutes. Remove from the heat.
4. Stir in the corn syrup and lemon juice.
5. Fold in the whole cranberry sauce gently with a kitchen spoon to avoid crushing the berries, let the mixture cool.
6. Proceed to fill unbaked pie shells and make up as desired.

7. Bake in a preheated oven at 400° to 425°F.

Precautions and Safety Measures
1. When adding the dissolved starch to the boiling mass, stir gently to avoid crushing the fruit.
2. When simmering the thickened mixture, stir occasionally to avoid sticking and scorching.
3. Fold the whole cranberry sauce into the apple mixture with a very gentle motion.

Fresh apple pie filling

For fresh apple pie filling the fresh apples are peeled, cored and sliced. They are placed in unbaked pie shells, sprinkled with a mixture of starch, sugar and seasoning, covered with a thin sheet of pie dough and baked. The juice from the apples thickens during the baking period. This is the old style method of preparing the filling.

Objectives
1. To teach the student the procedure for preparing fresh apple pie filling.
2. To teach the student how to process the apples.
3. To teach the student how to blend the seasoning.

Equipment
1. Apple corer
2. Vegetable peeler
3. Paring knife
4. Baker's scale
5. 2 containers for mixing
6. Pastry brush

Ingredients: Approx. yield: 5 to 6, 8 in. pies

10	lbs. fresh apples, cored, peeled, sliced
1	lb. granulated sugar
2	ozs. lemon juice
1	lb. granulated sugar
⅛	oz. nutmeg
¼	oz. cinnamon
¼	oz. salt
5	ozs. cornstarch
	butter as needed

Preparation
1. Core the apples with an apple corer, peel with a vegetable peeler and slice with a paring knife. Use Winesap or Roman Beauty apples for best results.
2. Squeeze the juice from the lemons.
3. Have all equipment and ingredients handy.

Procedure
1. Place the apples in a fairly large mixing container, add the first amount of sugar and the lemon juice, toss together very gently by hand and let set for approximately 1 hour.
2. Place the second amount of sugar, salt, nutmeg, cinnamon and cornstarch in a separate container. Mix together thoroughly by hand.
3. Sprinkle the seasoning mixture over the bottom of each unbaked pie shell. Fill the shells with the sliced apples and sprinkle a generous amount of the seasoning mixture over the top of the sliced apple.
4. Dot the top of each filled pie with butter, cover the top with pie dough. Secure the top layer of dough to the bottom by fluting (forming grooves) the edges of the pies.
5. Brush the top of each pie with melted butter or egg wash (egg and milk) using a pastry brush.
6. Bake in a preheated oven at 425° to 450°F.

Note: As the pies bake the filling thickens. The juice that cooks out of the apples activates the cornstarch.

Precautions and Safety Measures
1. Exercise caution when coring, peeling and slicing apples to avoid cutting self.
2. Toss the apples with the sugar and lemon juice very gently to avoid breaking the apples.
3. Keep the apples covered during the setting period with a damp cloth. If uncovered they may turn brown.

Fruit glaze

Fresh fruit glaze is a sweet, clear, semi-liquid that is used to cover fresh or canned fruit when preparing tarts (individual type of small pie) or open face pies. The glaze protects the fruit from the air and increases the appearance of the fruit.

Objectives
1. To teach the student the procedure for preparing fresh fruit glaze.
2. To teach the student how to add the starch to the boiling liquid.
3. To teach the student how to color the glaze.

Equipment
1. Sauce pot, 1 gal.

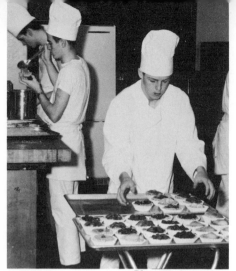

Photo: Kathryn Adams
Preparing fruit tarts in a cooking class.

2. Wire whip
3. Baker's scale
4. Paring knife
5. Strainer
6. Stainless steel bowl
   Ingredients: Approx. yield: 2 qts.
   2   lbs. water
   2   lbs. 8 ozs. granulated sugar
   8   ozs. water
   4   ozs. modified starch
   4   ozs. corn syrup
   1   oz. lemon juice
       food color as desired
   Preparation
1. Cut the lemon in half with a paring knife and squeeze the juice out by hand. Strain in a strainer.
2. Have all equipment and ingredients handy.
   Procedure
1. Place the first amount of water and the sugar in a sauce pot, bring to a boil.
2. In a stainless steel bowl dissolve the starch in the second amount of water. Pour slowly into the boiling liquid, whipping vigorously with a wire whip.
3. Cook until thickened and clear.
4. Add the corn syrup and lemon juice, bring the mixture back to a boil. Remove from the heat.
5. Color as desired, the glaze should be colored to blend with the fruit being used.
6. This glaze can be used to cover fresh or canned fruit.
   Note: To set up a fresh strawberry pie

spread 8 ozs. of glaze on the bottom of an 8 in. prebaked pie shell. Place 12 ozs. of cleaned strawberries over the glaze. Spread another 8 to 10 ozs. of glaze over the strawberries, refrigerate the pie for about 1 hour. Cover the top with whipped cream or topping and serve.
   Precautions and Safety Measures
1. Whip constantly when adding the dissolved starch to the boiling liquid to avoid lumps.
2. Once the starch is added, whip or stir continuously to avoid scorching.
3. Exercise caution when adding the color; a little will enhance, too much will hinder.

CREAM FILLING RECIPES

Vanilla pie filling

This basic vanilla pie filling can be used to prepare many different kinds of pies. It can be used to prepare coconut cream, banana cream and apricot cream pies.
   Objectives
1. To teach the student the procedure for preparing vanilla pie filling.
2. To teach the student how to thicken the milk mixture.
3. To teach the student how to convert the filling into different pie varieties.
   Equipment
1. Baker's scale
2. Double boiler
3. Wire whip
4. Large stainless steel bowl
5. Kitchen spoon
   Ingredients: Approx. yield: 12 to 14, 8 in. pies
   12 lbs. liquid milk
   4   lbs. granulated sugar
   1   lb. cornstarch
   ¼   oz. salt
   2   lbs. whole eggs
   6   ozs. butter
       vanilla to taste
   Preparation
1. Have all equipment and ingredients handy.
   Procedure
1. Place 10 lbs. (5 qts.) of the milk in the top of a double boiler, cover and heat until scalding hot (a film will form on the surface of the milk).
2. In a large stainless steel bowl place the

cornstarch, sugar, salt and eggs, blend together thoroughly with a wire whip.

3. Add the remaining 2 lbs. (1 qt.) of milk, blend until a paste is formed. Pour the paste mixture into the scalding milk, whipping briskly with a wire whip.

4. Continue to cook and whip the mixture until it becomes quite stiff. Remove from the heat.

5. Stir in the butter and vanilla with a kitchen spoon until thoroughly blended.

6. Pour into prebaked pie shells, let cool, top with a meringue and brown in the oven.

For banana cream pie: Cover the bottom of a prebaked pie shell about 1/2 in. deep with vanilla pie filling. Slice one banana crosswise and line the slices on the surface of the pie filling. Cover the banana slices with enough pie filling to fill the pie shell. Let the filling cool, cover with a meringue topping and bake in the oven until the meringue browns.

For apricot cream pie: Add 6 lbs. 8 ozs. (1 no. 10 can) of drained, chopped apricots to the vanilla pie filling. Fold the chopped apricots into the filling and pour into prebaked pie shells. Let the filling cool, cover with a meringue topping and bake in the oven until the meringue browns.

For coconut cream pie: Stir 1 lb. 8 ozs. of macaroon coconut into the vanilla pie filling, pour into prebaked pie shells. Let the filling cool, cover with a meringue topping and bake in the oven until the meringue browns.

Precautions and Safety Measures

1. Whip constantly and briskly when adding the starch mixture to the scalding milk to avoid lumps.

Chocolate macaroon pie filling

For chocolate macaroon pie filling macaroon coconut is blended into a rich chocolate pie filling. This type of pie filling is extremely rich and slightly expensive to prepare, but the eating qualities are outstanding and not soon forgotten.

Objectives

1. To teach the student the procedure for preparing chocolate macaroon pie filling.

2. To teach the student how to thicken the milk mixture and blend in the chocolate and coconut.

Equipment

1. Sauce pot, 3 gal.

2. Baker's scale
3. Wire whip
4. Kitchen spoon
5. 1 pt. sauce pan
6. 1 gal. stainless steel container

Ingredients: Approx. yield: 7 to 8, 8 in. pies

3	lbs. 2 ozs. granulated sugar
1/4	oz. salt
8	ozs. dry milk
3	lbs. 12 ozs. water
1	lb. 4 ozs. water
6 1/2	ozs. modified starch or cornstarch
12	ozs. egg yolks
10	ozs. bitter chocolate, melted
5	ozs. Primex shortening
10	ozs. macaroon coconut
	vanilla to taste

Preparation

1. Place the chocolate in a sauce pan set near the heat or over boiling water and melt.

2. Separate whole eggs to acquire the yolks. Save the whites for a meringue topping.

3. Have all equipment and ingredients handy.

Procedure

1. In a sauce pot place the sugar, salt, dry milk and first amount of water, bring to a boil.

2. In a stainless steel container dissolve the starch in the second amount of water. Blend in the egg yolks using a wire whip. Pour this mixture slowly into the boiling mixture while whipping constantly with a wire whip.

3. Cook until the mixture becomes thick.

4. Stir in the melted chocolate, shortening, macaroon coconut and vanilla with a kitchen spoon. Remove from the heat.

5. Pour into prebaked pie shells, let cool, top with a meringue.

6. Sprinkle additional macaroon coconut over the meringue and brown in the oven.

Note: To prepare a plain chocolate pie omit the macaroon coconut.

Precautions and Safety Measures

1. Exercise caution when bringing the ingredients in the first step to a boil. The mixture will boil over if not properly cared for.

2. Whip constantly while adding the starch and egg mixture.

3. Stir constantly while cooking the filling to avoid scorching.

Lemon pie filling

Lemon pie filling is a rich lemon cream

type filling that can be used in a variety of ways, including the very popular lemon meringue pie.

Objectives
1. To teach the student the procedure for preparing lemon pie filling.
2. To teach the student how to add the thickening mixture to the boiling liquid.

Equipment
1. Baker's scale
2. Food grater
3. Paring knife
4. Wire whip
5. Sauce pot, 3 gal.
6. Stainless steel bowl
7. 1 pt. sauce pan
8. Strainer or china cap
9. Kitchen spoon

Ingredients: Approx yield: 8 to 9, 8 in. pies

4	lbs. water
3	lbs. 6 ozs. granulated sugar
$\frac{1}{2}$	oz. salt
3	ozs. lemon gratings
1	lb. water
8	ozs. cornstarch
12	ozs. egg yolks
1	lb. 6 ozs. lemon juice
4	ozs. butter or shortening, melted yellow color as needed

Preparation
1. Using a food grater, grate the rinds of fresh lemons.
2. Cut the lemons in half with a paring knife and squeeze the juice out by hand. Strain in a strainer or china cap.
3. Separate the egg whites from the yolks by passing the yolk back and forth from one half egg shell to the other until all the white has run off. Save the whites for use in a meringue (beaten egg whites).
4. Place the butter or shortening in a sauce pan and melt.
5. Have all equipment and ingredients handy.

Procedure
1. Place first amount of water, sugar, salt and lemon grating in sauce pot, bring to a boil.
2. In a stainless steel bowl whip the egg yolks slightly with a wire whip. Add the starch and the second amount of water, stir together with a kitchen spoon until the starch is dissolved.
3. Pour the starch-egg mixture slowly into the boiling liquid, whipping vigorously with a wire whip until thickened and clear.

Poultry and Egg National Board
Lemon meringue pie.

4. Add the lemon juice and melted butter or shortening, stir with a kitchen spoon until thoroughly blended, remove from the heat, tint with yellow color if desired.
5. Pour the filling into prebaked pie shells, let cool and top with whipped topping or meringue.

Precautions and Safety Measures
1. When adding the starch mixture to the boiling liquid, whip vigorously to avoid lumps.
2. Once the starch mixture is added, stir or whip constantly to avoid scorching.

Cream filling

Cream filling is a rich, creamy egg-milk filling that can be used in the preparation of many different dessert varieties.

Objectives
1. To teach the student the procedure for preparing cream filling.
2. To teach the student how to add the thickening ingredients to the hot milk.

Equipment
1. Double boiler
2. Wire whip
3. Stainless steel bowl
4. Baker's scale
5. Kitchen spoon
6. Qt. measure
7. 2 gal. stainless steel container

Ingredients: Approx. yield: 5$\frac{1}{2}$ qts.

9	lbs. liquid milk
2	lbs. 6 ozs. granulated sugar
1	lb. cake flour
$\frac{3}{4}$	oz. salt

1   lb. 12 ozs. whole eggs
1   oz. vanilla
    yellow color as needed
Preparation
1. Break the eggs into a stainless steel bowl, beat slightly with a wire whip.
2. Have all equipment and ingredients handy.
3. Place water in the bottom of a double boiler, bring to a boil.
Procedure
1. Place 8 lbs. (4 qts.) of the liquid milk in the top of a double boiler, heat until scalding hot.
2. Combine the dry ingredients and blend with the beaten eggs. Add the remaining milk and stir with a kitchen spoon until a smooth paste is formed.
3. Pour the paste mixture slowly into the scalding milk, whipping vigorously with a wire whip until thickened and smooth.
4. Cook in the double boiler for approximately 15 minutes, whipping constantly.
5. Tint with yellow color, add the vanilla and remove from the heat.
6. Place in a stainless steel container, let cool and refrigerate until ready to use.
Precautions and Safety Measures
1. Whip vigorously and constantly when adding the paste mixture to the scalding milk.
2. Exercise caution when adding the yellow color; a little will enhance the appearance, too much will hinder.

Lemon filling

Lemon filling is a rich creamy lemon flavored filling that can be used in the preparation of many different dessert varieties. Lemon filling blends itself well with fruit preparations.
Objectives
1. To teach the student the procedure for preparing lemon filling.
2. To teach the student how to thicken the liquid mixture.
Equipment
1. Baker's scale
2. Wire whip
3. Stainless steel bowl
4. 1 gal. stainless steel container
5. Sauce pot, 1 gal.
6. Kitchen spoon
Ingredients: Approx. yield: 2½ qts.
4   lbs. water
1   lb. 8 ozs. granulated sugar

½   oz. salt
4   ozs. butter
8   ozs. egg yolks
6   ozs. corn starch
10 ozs. lemon juice
Preparation
1. Cut the lemons in half with a paring knife and squeeze the juice out by hand.
2. Separate the egg yolks from the whites by passing the yolk back and forth from one half egg shell to the other until the white has run off. Save the whites for use in another preparation, keep refrigerated.
3. Have all equipment and ingredients handy.
Procedure
1. Place the water, sugar, salt and butter in a sauce pot, bring to a boil.
2. Place the egg yolks in a stainless steel bowl, beat slightly with a wire whip. Add the lemon juice and blend together.
3. Add the corn starch and stir with a kitchen spoon until thoroughly dissolved in the liquid. Pour slowly into the boiling liquid, whipping briskly with a wire whip until thickened. Remove from the heat.
4. Pour into a stainless steel container, let cool, and refrigerate until ready to use.
5. Use in fruit tarts, cream puffs and Boston cream pies.
Precautions and Safety Measures
1. Whip briskly when adding the starch mixture to the boiling liquid to avoid lumps.
2. When cooling, coat the top of the filling with a thin covering of melted butter to prevent a crust from forming.

CHIFFON FILLING RECIPES

Pumpkin chiffon pie filling

For pumpkin chiffon pie filling beaten egg whites (meringue) are folded into a chilled pumpkin pie filling to create a mixture that is light and fluffy. Chiffon fillings are fairly new, but are rapidly growing in popularity. The filling is poured into prebaked pie shells and refrigerated until they set.
Objectives
1. To teach the student the procedure for preparing pumpkin chiffon pie filling.
2. To teach the student how to prepare a meringue.

3. To teach the student how to fold the meringue into the pumpkin filling.

Equipment

1. Baker's scale
2. Double boiler pot
3. Wire whip
4. Stainless steel bowl, small
5. Kitchen spoon
6. Mixing machine and wire whip
7. Bake pan

Ingredients: Approx. yield: 10 to 12, 8 in. pies

4	lbs. 8 ozs. pumpkin, canned
2	lbs. 8 ozs. light brown sugar
1	lb. 12 ozs. egg yolks
3/4	oz. cinnamon
1/8	oz. ginger
1/8	oz. mace
1/2	oz. salt
8	ozs. water, hot
2	ozs. plain gelatin
1	lb. 12 ozs. egg whites
1	lb. 12 ozs. granulated sugar
1/4	oz. nutmeg

Preparation

1. Separate the egg whites from the yolks by passing the yolk back and forth from one half egg shell to the other until all the white has run off.
2. Have all equipment and ingredients handy.
3. Place water in the bottom of the double boiler, bring to a boil.

Procedure

1. In the top of a double boiler place the pumpkin, brown sugar, egg yolks, spices and salt, cook until the mixture becomes thick, stir constantly with a kitchen spoon.
2. In a small stainless steel bowl soak the gelatin in the water. Stir into the hot mixture with a kitchen spoon until thoroughly dissolved; remove the mixture from the heat.
3. Place the pumpkin mixture in a bake pan, refrigerate until it is cool and starts to thicken. Remove from the refrigerator.
4. Place the egg whites in the electric mixing bowl and whip on the mixing machine at high speed until a meringue starts to form.
5. Add the granulated sugar slowly while continuing to whip at high speed, whip until stiff peaks form.
6. Fold the meringue into the slightly thickened pumpkin mixture with a kitchen spoon using a gentle motion.

7. Pour the filling into prebaked pie shells and cool in the refrigerator until the filling sets and becomes firm.

Precautions and Safety Measures

1. When adding the gelatin to the hot pumpkin mixture, stir continuously until thoroughly dissolved.
2. To whip the meringue, the mixer should be running at high speed throughout the operation and the sugar must be added slowly.
3. Fold the meringue gently into the thickened pumpkin mixture to preserve as many air cells as possible.

Cherry chiffon pie filling

For cherry chiffon pie filling beaten egg whites (meringue) are folded into a cherry pie filling to create a light, fluffy filling. Chiffon fillings are poured into prebaked pie shells and refrigerated until they set.

Objectives

1. To teach the student the procedure for preparing cherry chiffon pie filling.
2. To teach the student how to chop the cherries and thicken the juice.
3. To teach the student how to prepare a meringue.
4. To teach the student how to fold the meringue into the cherry filling.

Equipment

1. Baker's scale
2. French knife
3. Sauce pot, 2 gal.
4. Bake pan
5. Stainless steel bowl
6. Kitchen spoon
7. Mixing machine and wire whip
8. Collander

Ingredients: Approx. yield: 10 to 12, 8 in. pies

6	lbs. 8 ozs. cherries and juice (1 #10 can), chopped
3	lbs. 8 ozs. granulated sugar
1	oz. salt
1	lb. water
8	ozs. cornstarch
8	ozs. water, hot
2	ozs. plain gelatin
2	lbs. egg whites
1	lb. granulated sugar
	red color as needed

Preparation

1. Open the no. 10 can of cherries, place

in a collander to drain, save the juice. Chop the cherries using a French knife. Return the cherries to the juice.

2. Separate the egg whites from the yolks by passing the yolk back and forth from one half egg shell to the other until all the white has run off. Save the yolks for use in another preparation.
3. Have all equipment and ingredients handy.
   Procedure
1. Place the chopped cherries and juice, first amount of sugar and salt in a sauce pot, bring to a boil.
2. In a stainless steel bowl dissolve the cornstarch in the first amount of water. Pour slowly into the boiling cherry mixture stirring rapidly with a kitchen spoon until thickened.
3. Simmer for approximately 2 minutes, remove from the heat. Add desired amount of red color.
4. In a stainless steel bowl dissolve the gelatin in the 8 ozs. of hot water. Stir into the thickened cherry mixture using a kitchen spoon. Pour into a bake pan and refrigerate until the mixture jells slightly.
5. Place the egg whites in the electric mixing bowl and whip on the mixing machine at high speed until a meringue starts to form.
6. Add the second amount of sugar slowly while continuing to whip at high speed, whip until stiff peaks form.
7. Fold the meringue into the partly jellied cherry filling with a kitchen spoon using a gentle motion.
8. Pour the filling into prebaked pie shells and cool in the refrigerator until filling sets.
   Note: To prepare a peach chiffon pie filling, use a no. 10 can of sliced peaches (water or syrup pack) in place of the canned cherries. Use yellow color in place of the red color and reduce the first amount of sugar to 1 lb.
   Precautions and Safety Measures
1. When adding the dissolved starch to the boiling cherry mixture stir rapidly to avoid lumps.
2. Stir the thickened cherry mixture continuously once the starch has been added.
3. To whip the meringue, the mixer should be running at high speed throughout the operation and the sugar must be added slowly.

4. Fold the meringue gently into the jellied cherry mixture to preserve as many air cells as possible.

Lemon chiffon pie filling

For lemon chiffon pie filling beaten egg whites (meringue) are folded into a lemon cream filling to create a light, fluffy filling. Chiffon fillings are poured into prebaked pie shells and refrigerated until they set.
Objectives
1. To teach the student the procedure for preparing lemon chiffon pie filling.
2. To teach the student how to prepare the lemon filling.
3. To teach the student how to prepare a meringue.
4. To teach the student how to fold the meringue into the lemon filling.
   Equipment
1. Baker's scale
2. Food grater
3. Paring knife
4. Sauce pot, 1 gal.
5. Wire whip
6. Stainless steel bowl
7. Kitchen spoon
8. Mixing machine and wire whip
   Ingredients: Approx. yield: 9 to 10, 8 in. pies

3	lbs. water
2	lbs. granulated sugar
¾	oz. salt
2	ozs. lemon grating (rind)
1	lb. egg yolks
1	lb. lemon juice
9	ozs. corn starch
1½	ozs. plain gelatin
1	lb. water, hot
2	lbs. egg whites
1	lb. 8 ozs. granulated sugar
	yellow color as needed

Preparation
1. Using a food grater, grate the rinds of fresh lemons on the medium grid.
2. Cut the lemons in half with a paring knife and squeeze out the juice by hand.
3. Separate the egg whites from the yolks by passing the yolk back and forth from one half egg shell to the other until all the white has run off.
4. Have all equipment and ingredients handy.
   Procedure
1. Place the first amount of water and sugar,

salt and lemon gratings (rind) in a sauce pot. Bring to a boil.

2. In a stainless steel mixing bowl whip the egg yolks slightly with a wire whip. Add the juice and blend together.
3. Add the cornstarch and stir with a kitchen spoon until dissolved, pour this mixture slowly into the boiling mixture, whipping vigorously with a wire whip until thickened and smooth. Remove from the heat.
4. In a stainless steel bowl dissolve the plain gelatin in the hot water and stir into the lemon filling using a kitchen spoon. Improve the appearance by adding yellow color, if desired.
5. Place the egg whites in the electric mixing bowl and whip on the mixing machine at high speed until a meringue starts to form.
6. Add the second amount of sugar slowly while continuing to whip at high speed, whip until stiff peaks form.
7. Fold the meringue into the hot lemon filling with a kitchen spoon using a gentle motion.
8. Pour the filling into prebaked pie shells and cool in the refrigerator until the filling sets.

Note: This filling may be used for orange chiffon pie by using orange grating (rind) in place of the lemon and changing the juice ingredient to 14 ozs. of orange juice and 2 ozs. of lemon juice.

Precautions and Safety Measures
1. When adding the starch mixture to the boiling mixture whip vigorously to avoid lumps.
2. To whip the meringue the mixer should be running at high speed throughout the operation and the sugar must be added slowly.
3. Fold the merigue gently into the lemon filling to preserve as many air cells as possible.

SOFT FILLING RECIPES

Pecan pie filling

Pecan pie filling is one of the popular soft pie fillings. The filling is quite simple to prepare because all ingredients are placed in the mixing bowl at the same time and blended together. The pecans are not added to the filling, they are placed in each individual pie shell so even distribution can be obtained.

Objectives
1. To teach the student the procedure for preparing pecan pie filling.
2. To teach the student how to mix the filling.
3. To teach the student how to set up a pecan pie.

Equipment
1. Baker's scale
2. Mixing machine and wire whip
3. Sauce pan, 1 pt.

Ingredients: Approx. yield: 11 to 12, 8 in. pies

4	ozs. bread flour
6	ozs. Primex shortening, melted
2	ozs. corn meal
1	lb. 8 ozs. whole eggs
8	lbs. light corn syrup
1	lb. granulated sugar
$\frac{1}{2}$	oz. salt
1	oz. vanilla
$\frac{1}{4}$	oz. cinnamon
2	lb.s 4 ozs. pecans (variable)

Preparation
1. Melt the shortening in a sauce pan.
2. Have all equipment and ingredients handy.

Procedure
1. Place all the ingredients, except the pecans, in the bowl of the electric mixing machine. Using the wire whip, whip at medium speed until all ingredients are thoroughly blended, remove from the mixer.
2. Place 3 ozs. of pecans in the bottom of each 8 in. unbaked pie shell. Add approximately 1 lb. 2 ozs. of filling to each shell.
3. Bake in a preheated oven at 350°F until the filling sets.

Precautions and Safety Measures
1. Whip the mixture only until thoroughly blended.
2. Bake filling only until set, do not overbake.

Pumpkin pie filling

For pumpkin pie filling the highly seasoned pumpkin mixture is thickened by the reaction of the cornstarch and eggs when heat is applied. This soft pie filling is extremely popular during the fall and winter months and has become a traditional favorite at Thanksgiving and Christmas time.

1. To teach the student the procedure for preparing pumpkin pie filling.
2. To teach the student how to mix the filling.

Equipment

1. Baker's scale
2. Mixing machine and wire whip
3. Sauce pan, 1 pt.

Ingredients: Approx. yield: 9 to 10, 8 in. pies

2	lbs. 4 ozs. dark brown sugar
2	ozs. salt
1½	ozs. cornstarch
¾	oz. spice mix
1	lb. 8 ozs. whole eggs
4	lbs. 8 ozs. pumpkin, canned
4	lbs. 8 ozs. liquid whole milk
6	ozs. Primex shortening, melted

Preparation

1. Prepare the spice mix by blending together the following spices: ½ oz. cinnamon, ¼ oz. allspice, ¼ oz. ginger, and ¼ oz. mace.
2. Melt the shortening in a sauce pan.
3. Have all equipment and ingredients handy.

Procedure

1. Place the pumpkin, brown sugar, salt, cornstarch and spice mix in the bowl of the electric mixing machine. Using the wire whip, mix together in second speed until thoroughly blended.
2. Add the eggs, continue mixing in second speed.
3. Add the milk, reduce to slow speed, mix until thoroughly blended and smooth, remove from the mixer.
4. Stir in the melted shortening with a kitchen spoon.
5. Pour the filling into unbaked pie shells with fluted (grooved) edges, fill to the top.
6. Bake in a preheated oven at 400°F.

Precautions and Safety Measures

1. For best results let the filling stand for about 1 hour before filling the pie shells. This will give the sugar time to dissolve completely and the spices time to disperse their flavor.

FRIED PIE FILLING RECIPES

Fried pie fillings

The three pie filling recipes listed below are all prepared in the same general manner and are used exclusively in the preparation of fried pies. They differ from conventional pie fillings because more starch is added to develop the thicker consistency which is necessary when the filling is to be used in a fried product.

Objectives

1. To teach the student the procedure for preparing fried pie fillings.
2. To teach the student how to add the starch to the boiling mixture.
3. To teach the student how to cool the mixture.

Equipment

1. Sauce pot, 2 gal.
2. Wire whip
3. Kitchen spoon
4. Stainless steel bowl
5. Collander
6. Baker's scale
7. Bake pan
8. Pt. measure
9. French and paring knife

Preparation

1. Drain the fruit, if necessary, in a collander; save the juice.
2. Chop the fruit, if necessary, with a French knife.
3. Soak and drain the raisins, if they are being used.
4. Cut the lemons with a paring knife and squeeze the lemon juice by hand.
5. Have all equipment and ingredients handy.

APPLE FILLING

Ingredients: Approx. yield: 100 fillings

7	lbs. apples, canned, chopped
1	lb. raisins, soaked, drained
2	lbs. 8 ozs. granulated sugar
1	lb. water
½	oz. salt
¼	oz. cinnamon
1	oz. lemon juice
1	lb. water
7	ozs. modified starch or cornstarch

Procedure

1. Place the first 7 ingredients listed in a sauce pot, bring to a boil, cook until the apples become soft.
2. In a stainless steel bowl dissolve the starch in the second amount of water. Pour slowly into the boiling mixture stirring rapidly with a kitchen spoon until thickened and clear.

3. Remove the mixture from the heat, place in a bake pan, let cool, refrigerate until thoroughly chilled.
4. Remove the apple filling from the refrigerator and make up the turnovers following the directions given in the recipe for fried pie dough. Use approximately 2 ozs. of filling to each turnover.

CHERRY FILLING

Ingredients: Approx. yield: 70 fillings

6 lbs. 8 ozs. cherries (#10 can), drained
2 lbs. cherry juice and water
5 ozs. modified starch or cornstarch.
1 lb. 8 ozs. granulated sugar
  lemon juice (from 1 lemon)
  red color as needed

Procedure

1. Place the cherry juice and water in a sauce pot, reserving 1 pt. for dissolving the starch. Bring to a boil.
2. In a stainless steel container dissolve the starch in the cherry juice held in reserve; pour slowly into the boiling juice, whipping vigorously with a wire whip.
3. Bring mixture back to a boil, cook until thickened and clean.
4. Add sugar, whip with a wire whip until dissolved.
5. Add the lemon juice and red color, stir with a kitchen spoon until blended into the thickened juice. Pour over cherries; blend.
6. Pour into a bake pan, let cool, refrigerate until thoroughly chilled.
7. Remove the cherry filling from the refrigerator and make up the turnovers following the directions given in the recipe for fried pie dough. Use approximately 2 ozs. of filling for each turnover.

PINEAPPLE FILLING

Ingredients: Approx. yield: 85 fillings

6 lbs. 8 ozs. pineapple (1 #10 can), crushed, drained
2 lbs. pineapple juice and water
1 lb. 8 ozs. granulated sugar
¼ oz. salt
5 ozs. modified starch or cornstarch
8 ozs. water
5 ozs. corn syrup
  yellow color as needed

Procedure

1. Place the crushed pineapple, sugar, salt and juice in a sauce pot, bring to a boil.
2. In a stainless steel bowl dissolve the starch in the 8 ozs. of water; pour slowly into the boiling mixture stirring constantly with a kitchen spoon until thickened and clear.
3. Simmer the mixture for approximately 1 minute. Remove from the heat.
4. Stir in the corn syrup and tint with the yellow color.
5. Pour the mixture into a bake pan, let cool, refrigerate until thoroughly chilled.
6. Remove the pineapple filling from the refrigerator and make up the turnovers following the directions given in the recipe for fried pie dough. Use approximately 2 ozs. of filling for each turnover.

Precautions and Safety Measures

1. Pour the dissolved starch slowly into the boiling mixture and stir constantly to avoid lumps.
2. When cooking the thickened fruit mixtures, stir occasionally to avoid sticking and scorching.

MERINGUE TOPPING RECIPES

Meringue toppings

Meringue toppings are prepared by beating egg whites and granulated sugar together until air cells are formed and incorporated into the mix, forming soft, stiff, white peaks. Meringue toppings are used to top a variety of desserts and pies to improve the appearance and taste. Listed below are the three most popular methods of preparing meringues.

Objectives

1. To teach the student the three different methods of preparing meringues.
2. To teach the student how to whip the meringue.
3. To teach the student how to use meringue toppings.

Equipment

1. Baker's scale
2. Plastic scraper
3. Mixing machine and wire whip
4. Sauce pan
5. Kitchen spoon
6. Double boiler
7. Wire whip (hand)

Preparation

1. Separate the egg whites from the yolks by passing the yolk back and forth from one half egg shell to the other until the white has run off. Save the yolks for another

Hobart Manufacturing Co.

Preparing a meringue in an electric
mixing machine.

preparation by covering them with cold
water and placing in the refrigerator.
2. Have all equipment and ingredients handy.

COMMON MERINGUE

*Ingredients: Approx. yield: topings for 6,
8 in. pies; 4, 8 in. cakes; or 4 baked Alaska*

1   lb. egg whites
2   lbs. granulated sugar
2   ozs. tapioca flour

Procedure

1. Place the egg whites in the bowl of the
   electric mixing machine, using the wire
   whip, beat at high speed until the whites
   start to foam.
2. Mix the granulated sugar and tapioca flour
   together and add slowly to the egg whites
   while continuing to whip in high speed.
3. Whip until wet or dry peaks are formed.
   How the meringue is to be used will determine the type of peak needed. This type
   of meringue is used to top pies, cakes and
   baked Alaska.

SWISS MERINGUE

*Ingredients: Approx. yield: toppings for 4
to 5, 8 in. cakes*

1   lb. egg whites
2   lbs. granulated sugar

Procedure

1. Place the sugar and egg whites in the top
   of a double boiler; heat, while whipping
   constantly with a wire whip until sugar is
   dissolved and mixture warms (120°F).
2. Remove from the heat and place in the
   bowl of the electric mixing machine, using
   the wire whip, beat at high speed until desired peaks (wet or dry) are reached. How
   the meringue is to be used will determine
   the type of peak needed. (A wet peak will
   display a shiny appearance; a dry peak, a
   dull appearance. A wet peak is more moist
   and will usually spread better than a dry
   peak, which is stiffer.) This type of meringue is used mainly for making certain
   types of petite fours (small cakes) and for
   frosting cakes.

ITALIAN MERINGUE

*Ingredients: Approx. yield: toppings for 7,
8 in. pies or 5, 8 in. cakes*

1   lb. egg whites
1   lb. 8 ozs. water
1   lb. 12 ozs. granulated sugar
1½   oz. egg white stabilizer
⅛   oz. vanilla

Procedure

1. Place the water, sugar and egg white stabilizer in a sauce pan, place on the range
   and bring to a boil, allow to boil for 3 minutes. Remove from the range.
2. Place the egg whites in the bowl of the
   mixing machine, using wire whip, beat at
   high speed until heavy foam develops.
3. Add the hot liquid slowly to the beaten
   egg whites. Continue to whip until desired
   peaks (wet or dry) are reached. How the
   meringue is to be used will determine the
   type of peak needed. This type of meringue
   is used mainly for frosting cakes, but can
   be used to top pies if desired.

Precautions and Safety Measures

1. Have all utensils clean and free of grease.
2. The egg whites should contain no particles
   of egg yolk.
3. Once the whipping of the whites begins,
   continue whipping without stopping the
   machine until the meringue is completely
   developed.

cakes and icings

chapter 26

■ The commercial cooking student, as stated in a previous chapter, should have some background in baking. Situations will occur during his career where this knowledge will be invaluable. It may develop that after graduating from school he will wish to specialize in baking. Therefore, the purpose of this chapter is to supply the student with the basic knowledge of proper cake and icing production.

If a cake is to be a success it will depend upon five essentials:
1. A good formula.
2. High quality ingredients.
3. Careful weighing.
4. Proper mixing.
5. Proper baking.

If any of these five essentials are neglected the finished product will suffer in some way and, although the cake may be edible, it will lack the qualifications of a successful cake.

CAKE FORMULA

A good formula is one that has a proper balance of the various ingredients and has been tested to prove that it will produce a successful product. Most bakers have a recipe file of successful formulas that they obtain from trade publications, other bakers, or from companies that sell the products used in the bakeshop. These companies usually have research or test kitchens that develop new formulas and improve the old ones. Of the five essentials for preparing a successful cake, this one is the easiest to come by.

CAKE INGREDIENTS

There are usually eight ingredients used in making most cake batters. They are shortening, cake flour, eggs, sugar, baking powder, liquid (milk or water), salt and flavoring. Each one is classified into terms that suggest their function in preparing the cake batter. Some of these ingredients have more than one function to perform to produce a successful finished product. A list of these functions and the ingredients that perform them are as follows:

Tenderizers: Sugar, shortening, egg yolks and baking powder.

Moisteners: Milk or water, syrups, eggs and sugar.

Tougheners: Flour, dry milk solids and egg whites.

Driers: Flour, starches and dry milk solids.

Flavorers: Eggs, butter, vanilla or other flavoring liquid and salt.

High quality ingredients should be purchased for cake production. They will improve the taste, texture, volume and over-all quality of the finished product. *Shortening* may be butter, margarine or any good commercial shortening. If using shortening, a hydrogenated or emulsified shortening will produce the best results. Hydrogenated shortening is vegetable oils that have been hydrogenated to transform them into a solid, white colored fat that has a flexible melting point. (With a flexible melting point the shortening will melt at various temperatures without breaking and still perform the task of tenderizing.) Use of this type of shortening will improve creaming qualities and help trap and hold a greater amount of air. Emulsified shortening is made from hydrogenated vegetable oils and has greater emulsifying powers. It is produced for use in cakes with a high sugar content, sometimes called *high ratio cakes*. This shortening will blend more readily with the liquid ingredients of the cake batter and produce a cake with greater volume and better keeping qualities.

Milk may be whole or skim liquid milk, buttermilk or dry milk. Whole or skim liquid milk and buttermilk should be purchased fresh each day. If using dry milk, purchase one that has a high degree of solubility so it will blend quickly when mixed with water.

Cake flour, which is milled from soft wheat and contains all starch and no gluten, is required to produce a successful cake. Purchase a well-known brand to be sure of quality. A cake flour with good quality will be pure white, have strength, uniform granulation and a high absorption.

Sugar is extremely important in cake production because cake is a sweet dessert. The granulated sugar used in making cakes must be clear, bright and pure white. Most granulated sugar on the market today has a high degree of purity so one is not likely to go astray when the purchase is made.

Eggs are one of the most important of the eight basic ingredients used in making a cake. Therefore it is important that care be taken when they are purchased. Both fresh or frozen eggs will produce a quality cake. Fresh eggs will deteriorate rapidly so they should be purchased to keep pace with production, keeping only enough on hand to last about three days. Purchase fresh eggs that have a firm, clear white and a deep yellow yolk. Eggs laid in the spring are the most desirable. Frozen eggs have been improved to such an extent that they are used in most bake shops today. They can be purchased as whole eggs, whites or yolks. They are usually sold in 30 pound tins and can be stored easily. They are more convenient for the baker to use and the chances of getting spoiled or off flavored eggs are practically nill.

Baking powder, which is usually the leavening agent used to make a batter light and porous, may be purchased in three different types: fast-acting, slow-acting, or double acting. The type used will regulate the speed at which the gas will be released or generated. The double acting type is used most often. Purchase well-known brands for dependable results.

Salt is a minor ingredient in cake making, but does play an important role in bringing out the taste and flavor of the cake so it too should be of good quality. Salt should be a pure white with no bitter taste.

Flavoring is usually an expensive item, so many establishments will cut cost by purchasing lesser grades or imitations. This is false economy because half as much pure flavoring is better than twice as much of the imitation.

CAKE WEIGHING

Careful weighing is a necessity if uniform results are to be obtained when making a cake. Weights are more accurate than measures so use formulas calling for weights. Use scales that balance with weights rather than springs; use scales that will weigh from fractions of ounces up to several pounds. Take care in weighing each ingredient and have a check-off sheet to eliminate guess work as to whether a certain ingredient was added. A check-off sheet listing each ingredient will prove quite valuable if the memory should falter.

CAKE MIXING

Proper mixing and handling of the bat-

ter is of extreme importance for more cake failures occur during this important step than any of the other preparation steps. The cake should always be mixed in accordance with the formula being used, and every step of the mixing instructions must be carefully followed. There are three recognized methods of mixing a cake batter:

1. Creaming method.
2. Sponge or whipping method.
3. Two-stage or blending method.

Creaming method

1. The sugar, butter or shortening, salt and spices are creamed together in the bowl of the electric mixer. During the mixing small air cells are formed and incorporated into the mix. The volume increases and mix becomes softer in consistency.

2. Add the eggs gradually and continue to cream, with the electric mixing machine running at slow speed. During the mixing the eggs will coat the cells formed during the creaming stage and allow them to expand and hold the liquid, when it is added, without curdling.

3. Add the liquid (milk or water) alternately with the sifted baking powder and flour and mix until a smooth batter is formed. During this stage the liquid and the baking powder-flour mixture are added alternately so the batter will not curdle. If all the liquid is added at one time the cells coated by the addition of the eggs will not be able to hold all the moisture and curdling will result.

4. Add the flavoring, blend in thoroughly.

Note: Before mixing, all ingredients should be at room temperature. At intervals throughout the entire mixing process the bowl must be scraped down so all ingredients are incorporated and a smooth batter is obtained. There are some variations to this method of mixing so follow the mixing instructions of each formula carefully.

Sponge or whipping method

1. The eggs and sugar are warmed to about 100°F. This is done over hot water. This softens the egg yolks and slightly dissolves the sugar which allows for quicker whipping and a greater volume. The mixture is then whipped on an electric mixer until the required volume or stiffness is obtained.

2. Add the liquid and flavoring, if called for in the formula, slowly.

3. Fold in the sifted flour gently to insure a smooth and uniform batter.

Note: Before mixing, all the ingredients except the eggs and sugar should be at room temperature. There are variations to this method of mixing so follow the mixing instructions of the formula carefully.

Two-stage or blending method

1. All the dry ingredients, shortening and part of the milk are placed in the mixing bowl together. They are blended together at slow speed for the required period of time.

2. The eggs and the remaining milk are blended together and added to the above mixture at three different intervals to insure a smooth uniform batter.

Note: Before mixing, all ingredients should be at room temperature. At intervals throughout the entire mixing process the bowl must be scraped down so all ingredients are incorporated and a *smooth* batter is obtained.

CAKE BAKING

Whenever possible cakes should be placed in the center of the oven where the heat will distribute evenly. If a number of cakes are being baked at one time, the pans should be placed so they will not touch one another or any part of the oven wall. Always allow the heat to circulate freely around each pan. The oven must be preheated to the required temperature and temperatures should be checked periodically with an oven thermometer.

Generally speaking, the larger the unit being baked and the richer the cake batter the slower it should be heated. If the oven heat is too slow, however, the cake will usually rise and then fall causing a very heavy texture. If the oven heat is too fast the outside of the cake will bake rapidly forming a crust, then when the heat reaches the center causing expansion the surface will burst. The baking time of a cake is divided into four stages of development:

1. The cake is placed in the oven and then it starts to rise. At this stage use the lowest temperature called for in the baking instructions to prevent quick browning and to keep a crust from forming.

2. The cake continues to rise and the top surface starts to brown. Exercise caution in this stage; do not open the oven door. The heat may be increased at this stage if the recipe suggests it.

3. The rising stops and the surface of the cake continues to brown. The oven door can now be opened if it is necessary. The oven heat may be reduced if the cake is browning too fast.

4. The cake starts to shrink, leaving the sides of the pan slightly. It can now be tested for doneness.

Cakes can be tested for doneness by sticking a wire tester, or toothpick into the center of the cake. If the tester comes out dry with no batter adhering to it the cake is done. Another method may be employed for heavier cakes, such as fruit cakes. Press the top surface of the cake with a finger if it feels firm and the impression of the finger does not remain, the cake is done.

When cakes are removed from the oven they should be placed on wire racks or shelves so the air will circulate around the pan; allow it to cool or set approxi-

TABLE I. CAUSES AND REMEDIES FOR FAULTY BATTER CAKES
(CREAMING OR BLENDING METHOD)

Defect	Cause	Remedy
1. Layers uneven	1. Batter spread unevenly 2. Oven racks out of balance 3. Cake tins warped	1. Spread batter evenly. 2. Adjust oven racks. 3. Do not use damaged tins.
2. Cakes peak in center	1. Insufficient shortening 2. Batter too stiff	1. Balance formula. 2. Increase moisture and/or decrease flour content.
3. Cakes sag in center, poor symmetry.	3. Too much oven top heat 1. Excessive sugar in formula 2. Insufficient structure building materials. 3. Too much leavening 4. Cold oven 5. Cakes underbaked	3. Check drafts and burners. 1. Balance formula. 2. Increase egg content and/or flour content. 3. Balance formula. 4. Correct oven temperature. 5. Bake thoroughly.
4. Undersized cakes	1. Unbalanced formula 2. Oven too hot 3. Oven too cool 4. Improper mixing 5. Cake tins too large for amount of batter	1. Correct formula balance. 2. Check oven temperature. 3. Check oven temperature. 4. Exercise care in mixing. 5. Use proper amount of batter.
5. Dark crust color	1. Oven too hot 2. Too much top heat in oven 3. Too much sugar, too much milk solids.	1. Use correct baking temperature. 2. Check oven drafts. 3. Balance formula.
6. Light crust color	1. Oven too cool 2. Unbalanced formula	1. Raise oven temperature. 2. Balance formula.
7. Uneven baking	1. Oven heat not uniform 2. Variation in baking pans	1. Check oven drafts, flues, insulation 2. Use same type tins for entire batch.
8. Tough cakes	1. Insufficient tenderizing 2. Flour content too high 3. Wrong type flour	1. Increase sugar or shortening or both. 2. Balance formula. 3. Use soft wheat flour.
9. Thick, hard crust	1. Oven too hot 2. Cakes baked too long 3. Slab type cake tins not insulated.	1. Reduce oven temperature. 2. Reduce baking time. 3. Use insulation around cake molds.
10. Sticky crust	1. Sugar content too high 2. Improper mixing	1. Balance formula. 2. Use care in mixing.
11. Soggy crust	1. Cakes steam during cooling	1. Remove cakes from tins and allow to cool on rack. Cool cakes before wrapping.
12. Crust cracks	1. Oven too hot 2. Stiff batter	1. Reduce oven temperature. 2. Adjust flour and liquid contents.
13. Poor flavor	1. Inferior materials used 2. Poor flavoring material or wrong combination. 3. Materials improperly stored	1. Care in selecting materials. 2. Use quality pure flavors. Check flavor combinations. 3. Material storage space should be free from foreign odors.
14. Lack of flavor	1. Lack of salt 2. Lack of flavoring materials or weak-flavoring materials.	1. Use correct amount of salt. 2. Use sufficient flavoring and correct types.
15. Heavy cakes	1. Too much sugar 2. Too much shortening 3. Liquid content high 4. Insufficient leavening 5. Too much leavening 6. Cakes underbaked	1. 2. 3. Balance formula. 4. 5. 6. Bake out correctly.
16. Cakes too light and crumbly.	1. Batter overcreamed 2. Leavening content high 3. Shortening content too high	1. Mix properly. 2. Balance formula. 3. Balance formula.
17. Coarse grain	1. Leavening content high 2. Separation of liquids and fats (curdled characteristic in batter).	1. Balance formula. 2. Add liquids at proper temperatures and liquid only as fast as it will emulsify well.
18. Tough-eating cakes	1. Formula low in tenderizing materials, sugar and shortening. 2. Oven too hot	1. Balance formula. 2. Regulate oven temperature.

TABLE II. CAUSES AND REMEDIES FOR FAULTY SPONGE TYPE CAKES

Defect	Cause	Remedy
1. Undersized cakes	1. Overbeating or underbeating 2. Overmixing after flour is added. 3. Sugar content is too high 4. Oven too hot 5. Cakes removed from pans too soon after baking. 6. Cakes underbaked 7. Greased pans or tins	1. Beat egg whites, sugar, salt, and cream of tartar to a wet peak. 2. Fold in just enough to incorporate. 3. Balance formula. 4. Regulate oven temperature. 5. Allow cakes to cool before removing from tins. 6. Bake thoroughly. 7. Do not grease tins for angel food cakes.
2. Light crust color	1. Cakes underbaked 2. Cool oven 3. Overbeaten and overmixed batter.	1. Bake correctly. 2. Regulate oven temperature. 3. Mix properly.
3. Dark crust color	1. Oven too hot 2. Cakes overbaked 3. Excessive sugar content causing cake to have sugar crust.	1. Regulate oven temperature. 2. Give proper bake. 3. Balance formula.
4. Tough crust	1. Oven too hot 2. Sugar content too high 3. Improper mixing	1. Regulate oven temperature. 2. Balance formula. 3. Exercise care in assembling batter.
5. Thick and hard crust	1. Overbaking 2. Cold oven	1. Lessen baking time. 2. Regulate oven temperature.
6. Strong flavor	1. Off-flavored materials 2. Poor flavoring materials 3. Cakes burned or overbaked	1. Check storage space of materials for foreign odors. 2. Use only top-quality flavors. 3. Exercise care in baking.
7. Lack of flavor	1. Insufficient salt in formula 2. Poor flavor combination 3. Poor-quality flavoring materials used.	1. Increase salt content. 2. Use proper flavor blends. 3. Use only top-quality materials
8. Heavy cakes	1. Over or under beaten eggs 2. Overmixing after flour has been added. 3. Too much sugar 4. Too high a baking temperature	1. Beat eggs to wet peak. 2. Fold flour in just enough to incorporate. 3. Balance formula. 4. Regulate oven temperature.
9. Coarse grain	1. Cold oven 2. Overbeaten whites 3. Insufficiently mixed batter	1. Regulate oven temperature. 2. Whip to wet peak. 3. Fold until smooth.
10. Tough cakes	1. Overmixing ingredients 2. Excessive sugar content 3. Bakes too hot 4. Flour content high or wrong type flour used.	1. Mix properly. 2. Balance formula. 3. Regulate oven temperature. 4. Balance formula; use soft wheat flour.
11. Cakes dry	1. Low sugar content 2. Overbaking 3. Eggs overbeaten 4. Flour content too high	1. Balance formula. 2. Lessen baking time. 3. Whip to wet peak. 4. Balance formula.

mately 5 minutes. Invert the pan, remove the cake from the pan. If wax or silicon paper is used on the bottom of the pan remove this also. Place the cake back on the rack and continue to cool throughly.

Tables I and II give some of the defects a baked cake may have and suggests possible causes and remedies. Table I should be used with cakes made by the creaming or blending (two-stage) methods. Table II should be used with cakes prepared by the sponge or whipping method.

The formula used in making a cake must have the ingredients so balanced that each function will perform properly to produce a cake with desirable results.

CAKE BAKING AT HIGH ALTITUDE

Most cake formulas are developed in areas of low altitude. The ingredients are balanced so they will produce good results when the cake is baked at or near sea level. If these formulas are to be used in areas of high altitudes, adjustments will have to be made by reducing the baking powder and sugar and increasing the liquid to a certain degree. These adjustments can be brought about by experimenting with the formula or consulting companies such as General Mills and Procter and Gamble who have made studies and performed tests on high altitude baking.

ICINGS

Icing is a sweet coating or covering of which sugar is the main ingredient. It has from one to three main functions when applied to a baked product:

1. It may form a protective coating around the item to seal in the moisture and flavor.
2. It will improve the taste.
3. It will add eye appeal, which is so important to any baked product.

Icing preparation

Icings are usually quite simple to prepare. However, certain basic rules must be followed if the best results are to be obtained:

1. Use the best products obtainable. This is especially true of the shortening if it is called for in the recipe.
2. Use proper combinations of flavoring.
3. Color icing in pastel shades for a more attractive appearance.
4. Mix most butter cream icings at medium speed. Increase the mixing time to aerate the icing and increase the volume.
5. Obtain proper consistency before applying or using the icing. In most cases the consistency can be controlled by adding or eliminating certain amounts of powdered sugar. The consistency of the icing will depend upon the use.

Icing classification

Icing may be classified into six basic kinds:

1. Cream
2. Flat
3. Boiled
4. Fudge
5. Fondant
6. Royal

Cream icing is one of the most popular kinds. More cream icing is used in the average bake shop than any other kind. This is true mainly because it is simple to prepare, easy to keep, and when applied to cakes and cup cakes adds eye appeal and taste. It is usually made by creaming together shortening or butter, powdered sugar, and in some cases eggs. Cream icings are light and aerated because more air cells can be retained with this method of mixing. Cream icing colors well but remember to use pastel shades for best results.

Flat icing is the simplest of all to prepare. It is usually prepared by blending together water, powdered sugar, corn syrup and flavoring; and heating to approximately $100°F$. It is applied by brush or hand to such items as sweet rolls, doughnuts, Danish pastry, etc. The icing should be heated in a double boiler because direct heat or overheating causes the icing to lose its gloss or shine when it cools.

Boiled icing is prepared by combining sugar, glucose and water; boiling it to approximately $240°F$; and adding the resulting syrup to an egg white meringue while still hot. If a heavy syrup is added to the meringue a heavy icing will be the result, if a thin syrup is added the result will be a thin icing. Boiled icing may be colored slightly and must be applied the same day it is prepared. If held overnight it breaks down. This kind of icing is used on cakes and should be applied in generous amounts so it can be worked into peaks.

Fudge icing is a rich, heavy bodied icing that is usually prepared by adding a hot liquid or syrup to the other ingredients called for in the recipe, while whipping to obtain the smoothness required for this kind of icing. Fudge should be used while still warm; or if left to cool it should be reheated in a double boiler before applying. Fudge icing is generally used to ice layer cakes, loaf cakes, and cup cakes. To store, cover and place in the refrigerator.

Fondant icing is a rich, white, cooked icing that hardens when exposed to the air. It is used mainly on small cakes that are picked up with the fingers to be eaten. It is prepared by cooking glucose, sugar, and water to a temperature of 240°F; letting it cool to 150°F; and then working it (by mixing) until it is creamy and smooth. Fondant is the most difficult and time-consuming icing to prepare and for those reasons most bakers will purchase a ready-made fondant from a bakers supply house. It is usually purchased in a 40 pound tin and keeps well if covered with a damp cloth or a small amount of water to keep it from drying out when stored in a cool place.

When needed for use fondant is heated to about 100°F in a double boiler while stirring constantly. This causes the icing to become thin so it will flow freely over the item to be covered. If the fondant is too heavy after it is heated, it can be thinned down by using a glaze consisting of 1 part glucose to 2 parts water or a regular simple syrup may be used. The fondant may be colored and flavored to suit the need. Exercise caution when heating the fondant. If it is heated over 100°F it loses its gloss or shine and when it hardens the product will have a dull finish. This icing can also be used as a base for other icings.

Royal icing is quite simple to prepare since it is just a matter of blending powdered sugar, egg whites and cream of tartar to the consistency desired. Royal icing will set up and harden when exposed to air so for that reason it must be kept covered with a damp towel when not in use. It is used for decorating, flower making, and for dummy cakes used in window displays.

CAKE, ICING AND FILLING RECIPES

The following cake recipes, icings and fillings are popular in bake shops throughout the country. An outline of recipes is given in the order of their appearance in the chapter.

**Cake: Creaming method
(Pages 602 to 606)**
Sunny orange cake
Brown sugar cake
Apple-nut cake
Spice cake
Fruit cake

**Cake: Whipping or sponge method
(Pages 606 to 609)**
Semi-sponge cake
Jelly roll sponge cake
Banana chiffon cake
Lemon chiffon cake

**Cake: Blending or two-stage method
(Pages 609 to 614)**
White cake
Yellow cake
Devil's food cake
Fudge cake
White pound cake
Honey cake
Christmas candy cake

**Icings
(Pages 614 to 619)**
New York buttercream icing
Butter cream icing

White cream icings
Chocolate malted milk icing
Maple icing
Flat icing
Roll icing
Boiled icing
Chocolate supreme fudge icing
Caramel fudge icing
Bittersweet chocolate icing
Fondant icing
Butterscotch fondant icing
Strawberry fondant icing
Pineapple fondant icing
Orange or lemon fondant icing
Chocolate fondant icing
Royal icing

Fillings
(Page 619)

Strawberry cake filling
Butterscotch cake filling
Fudge cake filling
Orange cake filling

CAKE: CREAMING RECIPES

Sunny orange cake (high-ratio)

Sunny orange cake is a moist tender cake with a refreshing orange flavor. This batter can be used for preparing cup cakes, loaves, layer or ring cakes.

Objectives
1. To teach the student the procedure for preparing sunny orange cake.
2. To teach the student how to scale the ingredients and mix the batter.
3. To teach the student how to bake the cake.

Equipment
1. Mixing machine and paddle
2. Baker's scale
3. Plastic scraper
4. 16, 8 in. diameter cake pans
5. Wire whip
6. 1 gal. stainless steel container
7. Food grinder

Ingredients: Approx. yield: 13 to 16, 8 in. cakes

2   lbs. 8 ozs. cake flour
1   lb. 6 ozs. Sweetex shortening
3   lbs. 8 ozs. granulated sugar
1½ oz. salt
2½ ozs. baking powder
1   lb. liquid skim milk
1   lb. 8 ozs. whole eggs
1   lb. 6 ozs. liquid skim milk
8   ozs. ground whole oranges
    flavor to taste

Preparation
1. Grind the whole oranges in a food grinder using the medium size chopper plate.
2. Prepare 8 in. diameter cake pans: grease the sides and cover the bottom with silicon paper.
3. Preheat the oven to 375°F.
4. Scale off all ingredients carefully using a baker's scale.
5. Have all equipment and ingredients handy.

Procedure
1. Place the flour and shortening in the electric mixing bowl, using the paddle, mix for 3 to 5 minutes at slow speed. Scrape down the bowl and paddle with a plastic scraper at least once in this stage.
2. Add the sugar, salt, baking powder and liquid skim milk. Mix at slow speed from 3 to 5 minutes, scrape down the bowl.
3. In a stainless steel container combine the second amount of milk, eggs and oranges, beat together slightly using a wire whip. Add half of this mixture to the bowl and mix at slow speed until smooth. Scrape down the bowl and mix smooth again.
4. Add the balance of the liquid mixture and continue mixing at slow speed for a total of 3 to 5 minutes in this stage, scraping down again to insure a smooth batter.
5. Scale 12 to 14 ozs. of batter into each prepared 8" diameter cake pan.
6. Bake at 375°F until golden brown. Remove from the oven when done.

Precautions and Safety Measures
1. Scale all ingredients correctly; double check all weights.
2. All mixing should be done at slow speed.
3. Scrape down the bowl at least once during each mixing stage to insure a smooth batter and incorporate all ingredients.
4. Check oven temperature with an oven thermometer.

Brown sugar cake

Brown sugar cake is a dark moist, tender

textured cake with a maple flavor and possessing excellent eating qualities. The batter is mixed by using the creaming method.

Objectives
1. To teach the student the procedure for preparing brown sugar cake.
2. To teach the student how to scale the ingredients and mix the batter.
3. To teach the student how to bake the cake.

Equipment
1. Mixing machine and paddle
2. Baker's scale
3. Plastic scraper
4. 9, 8 in. cake pans
5. Flour sifter
6. 1 gal. stainless steel container
7. Wire whip

Ingredients: Approx. yield: 8 or 9, 8 in. cakes

2	lbs. dark brown sugar
12	ozs. shortening
1/4	oz. vanilla
	maple flavoring to taste
1	lb. whole eggs, beaten
1	lb. 12 ozs. cake flour
1 1/2	oz. baking powder
1/2	oz. salt
1	lb. 8 ozs. liquid milk

Preparation
1. Prepare the 8 in. diameter cake pans: grease the sides and dust slightly with flour, cover the bottom with silicon paper.
2. Preheat the oven to 375°F.
3. Place the eggs in a stainless steel container and beat slightly with a wire whip.
4. Scale off the ingredients carefully using a baker's scale.
5. Have all the equipment and ingredients handy.

Procedure
1. Place the shortening, brown sugar, vanilla and maple flavoring in the electric mixing bowl, using the paddle, cream together at slow speed, until light and fluffy.
2. Add the beaten eggs gradually, continuing to cream at slow speed.
3. Sift together the flour, baking powder, and salt; add alternately with the milk to the creamed mixture, mixing at slow speed until the batter is smooth. Scrape down the bowl with a plastic scraper.
4. Scale 12 to 14 ozs. of batter into each prepared 8 in. cake pan.

5. Bake at 375°F until done. Remove from the oven.

Precautions and Safety Measures
1. Scale all ingredients correctly; double check all weights.
2. Scrape down the bowl at least once in the final mixing stage to insure a smooth batter.
3. Check the oven temperature with an oven thermometer.

Apple-nut cake

Apple-nut cake is a rich, tender, spicy, apple flavored, moist cake that can be formed and baked to produce many different varieties. Apple cake is mixed by using the creaming method. This cake is topped with a pecan mixture before it is baked to produce a sugar nut topping on the finished product.

Objectives
1. To teach the student the procedure for preparing apple-nut cake.
2. To teach the student how to scale the ingredients and mix the cake.
3. To teach the student how to bake the cake.

Equipment
1. Mixing machine and paddle
2. Baker's scale
3. Plastic scraper
4. 10, 8 in. cake pans
5. Apple corer
6. Paring knife
7. French knife
8. Flour sifter
9. Wooden spoon

Ingredients: Approx. yield: 10, 8 in. cakes

2	lbs. 8 ozs. granulated sugar
6	ozs. shortening
6	ozs. butter
1/4	oz. salt
1/8	oz. cinnamon
1/8	oz. mace
8	ozs. whole eggs
1	lb. liquid milk
3/4	oz. baking soda
1	oz. baking powder
2	lbs. 12 ozs. cake flour
2	lbs. 12 ozs. fresh apples, chopped

Preparation
1. Core the apples with an apple corer, peel with a paring knife and chop the apples fine with a French knife.
2. Prepare topping by blending together the following ingredients:

10 ozs. chopped pecans
6 ozs. butter
¼ oz. cinnamon
2 ozs. sugar

3. Preheat the oven to 375°F.
4. Prepare 8 in. cake pans for baking.
5. Scale off all ingredients carefully using a baker's scale.
6. Have all equipment and ingredients handy.

Procedure

1. Place the sugar, shortening, butter, salt, mace and cinnamon in the electric mixing bowl, using the paddle, cream together in low speed.
2. Add the eggs and continue to cream at low speed until thoroughly blended.
3. In a stainless steel container dissolve the baking soda in the milk. Add to the above and mix at low speed until thoroughly blended.
4. Combine the cake flour and baking powder, sift with a flour sifter and add to the mixture, mix at low speed to a smooth batter. Scrape down the bowl with a plastic scraper.
5. Fold in the chopped apples with a wooden spoon until thoroughly blended.
6. Scale 1 lb. of batter into each prepared 8 in. cake pan. Sprinkle a small amount of the pecan mixture on top of the batter.
7. Place in the oven and bake at 375°F until golden brown. Remove from the oven.

Precautions and Safety Measures

1. Scrape down the bowl at intervals during the mixing period to incorporate all ingredients to insure a smooth batter.
2. Scale all ingredients correctly; double check all weights.

Spice cake (high ratio)

Spice cake is a high ratio cake: this means that the enrichening ingredients such as sugar, shortening, eggs and milk are balanced in a formula that will produce a higher quality cake. The shortening used in a high ratio cake must be a special type so a large percentage of sugar may be used in the cake batter. High ratio cakes are mixed in three stages by using the creaming method. The spices in this cake are so blended to produce an unforgetable flavor.

Objectives

1. To teach the student the procedure for preparing a high ratio spice cake.

2. To teach the student how to scale the ingredients and mix the cake.
3. To teach the student how to bake the cake.

Equipment

1. Mixing machine and paddle
2. Baker's scale
3. Plastic scraper
4. Approximately 15, 8 in. cake pans
5. Stainless steel container

Ingredients: Approx. yield: 15, 8 in. cakes

1 lb. 14 ozs. cake flour
1 lb. 6 ozs. Sweetex shortening
3 lbs. 5 ozs. granulated sugar
9 ozs. cake flour
1¼ oz. salt
¾ oz. baking soda
2 ozs. baking powder
1 oz. spice mix
1 lb. 4 ozs. buttermilk
1 lb. 10 ozs. whole eggs
2 lbs. 7 ozs. pumpkin (canned)

Preparation

1. Prepare the spice mix by combining the following:

4 ozs. cinnamon
1½ ozs. mace
½ oz. all spice
1½ ozs. nutmeg
½ oz. ginger

2. Preheat the oven to 375°F.
3. Scale off all ingredients carefully using a baker's scale.
4. Have all equipment and ingredients handy.

Procedure

1. Place the flour and shortening together in an electric mixing bowl, cream together and mix at slow speed using the paddle for 4 minutes. Scrape down the bowl with a plastic scraper at least once in this stage.
2. Add the sugar, second amount of flour, salt, soda, baking powder, spice mix and buttermilk continue to mix in slow speed for 4 minutes, scrape down at least once in this stage.
3. In a stainless steel container blend the pumpkin and eggs together and add approximately half of it to the bowl. Mix at slow speed until smooth, scrape down and mix until smooth again.
4. Add the balance of the egg and pumpkin mixture and continue mixing at slow

speed for a total of 3 to 5 minutes in this stage, scraping down again to insure a smooth batter.

5. Scale 12 to 14 ozs. of batter into each 8 in. diameter cake pan and bake at 375°F until golden brown. Remove from the oven.

Note: This batter may also be used for cup cakes, loaves and rings; however, adjustments must be made in weights and baking temperature.

Precautions and Safety Measures

1. Scrape down the bowl at intervals during the mixing period to incorporate all ingredients and to insure a smooth batter.
2. Scale all ingredients correctly; double check all weights.

Fruit cake

Fruit cake is the traditional yuletide treat enjoyed by people of all ages. The dark, moist, heavy textured cake is full of rich fruit and nuts. The batter is mixed by using the creaming method and can be baked in the form of loaves or rings.

Objectives

1. To teach the student the procedure for preparing fruit cake.
2. To teach the student how to blend the fruit cake mix.
3. To teach the student how to scale the ingredients and mix the batter.
4. To teach the student how to bake the cake.

Equipment

1. Mixing machine and paddle
2. Baker's scale
3. Baking pans as desired
4. Plastic scraper
5. 3 gal. stainless steel container
6. Kitchen spoon
7. Sauce pan, 1 qt.
8. Collander
9. Paring knife
10. French knife
11. 14, 6 in. ring pans or 7⅛ in. by 3¼ in. by 2½ in. loaf pans

Ingredients: Approx. yield: 14, 6 in. ring cakes or loaf cakes

2	lbs.	granulated sugar
1	lb.	bread flour
1½	oz.	salt
⅛	oz.	baking soda

2	lbs.	Sweetex shortening
2	lbs.	whole eggs
1	lb. 8 ozs.	bread flour
8	lbs. 12 ozs.	fruit mix
1	lb. 4 ozs.	water
		brandy flavor to taste
4	ozs.	dark molasses
5	lbs.	raisins
		mace to taste
		cinnamon to taste
1	lb.	black walnuts
1	lb.	pecans

Preparation

1. Prepare pans selected for baking: grease the sides lightly and cover the bottoms with silicon paper.
2. Prepare the fruit mix using the following formula:

2	lbs. 8 ozs.	glazed red cherries
1	lb. 8 ozs.	glazed green cherries
3	lbs. 4 ozs.	glazed pineapple
8	ozs.	citron
8	ozs.	orange peel
8	ozs.	lemon peel

Mix all ingredients together by hand until thoroughly blended.

3. Prepare a glucose wash using the following formula:

2	lbs.	glucose
1	lb.	water

Bring to a boil in a sauce pan. Use this solution warm as a wash.

4. Preheat the oven to the desired temperature, see Table III for baking fruit cake.
5. Wash the fruit mixture thoroughly in a collander and allow it to drain.
6. Cut the washed fruit mix into medium sized pieces with a paring knife. Place in a stainless steel container; add the water, flavoring, raisins, molasses and spices in the amounts called for in the ingredients listed. Place this mixture in the refrigerator, cover and let set overnight. This insures full flavor in the cake.
7. Chop the nuts into medium sized pieces with a French knife.
8. Scale off all ingredients carefully using a baker's scale.
9. Have all the equipment and ingredients handy.

Procedure

1. Place the sugar, soda, Sweetex (shortening) and first amount of bread flour in the electric mixing bowl, cream together,

TABLE III. FRUIT CAKE

Scaling Weight	Pan Size	Baking Temp.	Baking Time
1 lb. 12 ozs.	6" ring pan	340° F — 350° F	Approx. 1 1/2 hrs.
1 lb. 12 ozs.	7 1/8" x 3 1/4" x 2 1/4" loaf pan	340° F — 350° F	Approx. 1 1/2 hrs.

at slow speed, using the paddle until light and smooth.

2. Add the eggs slowly and continue to cream at slow speed.
3. Add the second amount of bread flour, mix for 3 minutes on second of 3 speed machine speed.
4. Remove the flavored fruit mixture from the refrigerator. Add the chopped nuts and mix together thoroughly.
5. Add the fruit-nut mixture to the batter and mix in well at slow speed until it is thoroughly distributed in the batter.
6. Follow Table III for proper scaling and baking.
7. After the cakes are baked wash generously with the glucose wash using a pastry brush.

Precautions and Safety Measures
1. Weigh all ingredients correctly; double check all weights.
2. The cakes should either be covered during baking or baked in an oven containing moisture in order to produce moist cakes and to prevent the tops from becoming too dark.

CAKE: WHIPPING OR SPONGE RECIPES

Semi sponge cake

Semi sponge cake is so named because part of the leavening is provided by eggs and part by baking powder. To be a true sponge cake the eggs should provide all the leavening power. This cake may be used to prepare many different well known dessert items. It may be used for Boston cream pie, strawberry short cake or roll cake.

Objectives
1. To teach the student the procedure for preparing semi sponge cake.
2. To teach the student how to scale the ingredients and mix the batter.
3. To teach the student how to bake the cake.

Equipment
1. Mixing machine and wire whip
2. Plastic scraper
3. Baker's scale
4. 16, 8 in. diameter cake pans

Ingredients: Approx. yield: 16, 8 in. cakes

2	lbs. 8 ozs. cake flour
3	lbs. granulated sugar
1½	oz. salt
2½	ozs. baking powder
¼	oz. baking soda
1	lb. egg yolks
1	lb. whole eggs
8	ozs. water
4	ozs. dry milk
8	ozs. salad oil
1	lb. 4 ozs. water
	vanilla to taste

Preparation
1. Prepare cake pans. Grease the bottom and sides of each pan lightly, cover the bottom with wax paper and grease over the wax paper slightly.
2. Preheat the oven to 375°F.
3. Separate the egg yolks from the whites.
4. Scale off all ingredients carefully using a baker's scale.
5. Have all equipment and ingredients handy.

Procedure
1. Place in the electric mixing bowl the flour, sugar, salt, baking powder, soda, egg yolks, whole eggs, water and dry milk. Using the wire whip, mix on medium speed for 5 to 10 minutes or until mix-

Poultry and Egg National Board

Chocolate roll cake prepared from
chocolate semi-sponge cake.

ture becomes lemon colored. Scrape down
the bowl with a plastic scraper.

2. Add the salad oil, second amount of water
   and the vanilla, mix on low speed for 2 or
   3 minutes or until thoroughly incorporated.

3. Scale approximately 10 ounces of batter
   into each prepared cake pan.

4. Bake at 375°F for 12 to 15 minutes. Remove from the oven.
   Note: To convert this formula to a chocolate semi-sponge cake, add 8 ozs. of cocoa
   in the first stage and increase the first stage
   water from 8 to 12 ozs.
   Precautions and Safety Measures

1. Scale all ingredients correctly; double
   check all weights.

2. Check the oven temperature before baking.

Jelly roll sponge cake

Jelly roll sponge cake is a soft, sponge
textured cake that will roll with ease. This
cake can also be rolled with ice cream, lemon
filling, vanilla filling and pineapple filling. It
is mixed by using the sponge or whipping
method.
   Objectives

1. To teach the student the procedure for preparing jelly roll sponge cake.

2. To teach the student how to scale the ingredients and mix the cake.

3. To teach the student how to bake and roll
   the cake.
   Equipment

1. Mixing machine and whip
2. Baker's scale
3. Plastic scraper
4. 2, 17 in. by 24½ in. sheet pans
5. Sauce pan, 1 pt.
6. Kitchen spoon
7. 1 gal. stainless steel container
8. Wooden spoon
   Ingredients: Approx. yield: 2 sheet cakes

12	ozs. whole eggs
8	ozs. egg yolks
1	lb. 10 ozs. granulated sugar
½	oz. salt
	vanilla to taste
1½	oz. dry milk
12	ozs. water
4	ozs. honey
1	lb. 6 ozs. cake flour
½	oz. baking powder

   Preparation

1. Preheat the oven to 375°F.
2. Prepare the sheet pans, line them with
   wax, silicon or parchment paper.
3. Combine the water and honey, blend together in a sauce pan and heat.
4. Scale off all ingredients carefully using a
   baker's scale.
5. Have all equipment and ingredients handy.
   Procedure

1. Place the whole eggs, egg yolks, sugar,
   salt, vanilla and dry milk in the electric
   mixing bowl. Using the whip, beat at high
   speed for approximately 10 minutes, until
   mixture becomes lemon colored.

2. Pour the warm water-honey mixture into
   the above mixture, while continuing to mix
   at medium speed.

3. Combine the cake flour and baking powder, sift together and fold in to the above
   mixture very gently with a wooden spoon.

4. Pour the batter on two 17 in. x 24½ in.
   prepared sheet pans. Scrape the bowl
   clean with a plastic scraper.

5. Place in the oven and bake at 375°F until
   golden brown (approximately 12 to 15
   minutes).

6. Remove from the oven and turn the cakes
   out onto white cloths sprinkled with granulated sugar or coconut. Spread with jelly

or desired filling and roll. Proceed to roll only after demonstration by instructor.

Note: To prepare a chocolate roll cake use the same mixture, but change Step 3 to:

1	lb. of cake flour
6	ozs. cocoa
½	oz. baking soda
½	oz. baking powder

Proceed as instructed.

Precautions and Safety Measures
1. Scale all ingredients correctly; double check all weights.
2. Bake the cake on the light side.
3. Turn the cake out of the pan just as soon as it is removed from the oven.
4. Spread the batter over the pan evenly before placing it in the oven.

Banana chiffon cake

Banana chiffon cake is a light, fluffy, spongy type cake with a true banana flavor. The secret of a successful chiffon cake lies in proper mixing and folding the egg white mixture into the batter gently so the air cells will not be broken.

Objectives
1. To teach the student the procedure for preparing banana chiffon cake.
2. To teach the student how to scale the ingredients and mix the cake.
3. To teach the student how to bake the cake.

Equipment
1. Mixing machine and paddle
2. Baker's scale
3. Plastic scraper
4. 4 or 5, 10 in. by 4 in. center-tube cake pans
5. French knife
6. Skimmer
7. Flour sifter
8. Wooden spoon

Ingredients: Approx. yield: 4 cakes

1	lb. 12 ozs. cake flour
1	lb. 6 ozs. granulated sugar
1¼	oz. baking powder
½	oz. salt
14	ozs. egg yolks
14	ozs. salad oil
14	ozs. bananas, chopped
8	ozs. water
	banana flavor to taste
1	lb. 12 ozs. egg whites
1	lb. granulated sugar
¼	oz. cream of tartar

Preparation
1. Chop the bananas very fine with a French knife.
2. Separate the eggs by hand.
3. Prepare the 10 by 4 in. center-tube cake pans: grease lightly and then dust with flour, or grease the sides and cover the bottom with silicon paper.
4. Preheat the oven to 350°F.
5. Scale off all ingredients carefully using a baker's scale.
6. Have all equipment and ingredients handy.

Procedure
1. Sift together, into the mixing bowl with a flour sifter the flour, first amount of sugar, baking powder and salt. Scrape down the bowl with a plastic scraper.
2. Using the paddle, mix at second speed, while adding the salad oil, egg yolks, water and banana flavor in several portions, mix until smooth. Remove from the mixer.
3. Blend in the chopped bananas with a wooden spoon.
4. In a separate electric mixing bowl place the egg whites and cream of tartar, beat at high speed using a wire whip, while adding the second amount of sugar gradually until stiff peaks form.
5. Fold the egg white mixture onto the batter using a flat skimmer, until well blended.
6. Scale 1 lb. 14 ozs. of batter into each 10 by 4 in. prepared cake pan.
7. Bake at 350°F until golden brown. Remove from the oven.

Precautions and Safety Measures
1. Use a high-grade salad oil.
2. Scale all ingredients correctly; double check all weights.
3. When adding the egg white mixture (meringue) to the batter fold only enough to blend the two together. (Overworking will break the air cells down.)
4. Bake immediately after mixing the batter.
5. When the cakes are removed from the oven turn upside down immediately to let them cool.

Lemon chiffon cake

Lemon chiffon cake is a light, fluffy, spongy type cake similar to the well known angel food cake. Chiffon cakes are fairly new to the baking industry, but are increasing in popularity quickly.

Objectives

1. To teach the student the procedure for preparing lemon chiffon cake.
2. To teach the student how to scale the ingredients and mix the cake.
3. To teach the student how to bake the cake.

Equipment

1. Mixing machine, paddle and whip
2. Baker's scale
3. Plastic scraper
4. 4, 10 in. by 4 in. center-tube cake pans
5. Box grater
6. Skimmer
7. Flour sifter
8. Wire rack

Ingredients: Approx. yield: 4 cakes

1	lb. 8 ozs. cake flour
2	lb. granulated sugar
1½	ozs. baking powder
12	ozs. salad oil
14	ozs. egg yolks
1	lb. water, cold
½	oz. lemon flavor
1½	oz. lemon rind, grated
1	lb. 4 ozs. egg whites
¼	oz. cream of tartar
½	oz. salt

Preparation

1. Grate the lemons on the medium grid of the box grater.
2. Separate the eggs by hand.
3. Prepare the 10 by 4 in. center-tube cake pans: grease and dust with flour, or grease and dust the sides and cover the bottom with silicon paper.
4. Preheat the oven to 330°F.
5. Scale off all ingredients carefully.
6. Have all equipment and ingredients handy.

Procedure

1. Sift together, into the electric mixing bowl, the flour, sugar and baking powder.
2. Using the paddle, mix at moderate speed, while adding the salad oil, egg yolks, water and lemon flavor in several portions, mix until smooth. Scrape down the bowl with a plastic scraper. Do not overmix.
3. In a separate mixing bowl place the cream of tartar, salt and egg whites. Beat, using the wire whip, until they form very stiff peaks. Remove from the mixer.
4. Fold the egg white mixture into the batter, using a flat skimmer, until well blended.
5. Scale 1 lb. 14 ozs. of batter into each 10 by 4 in. prepared cake pan.

6. Bake at 330°F until golden brown. Remove from the oven.

Precautions and Safety Measures

1. Use a high-grade salad oil.
2. Scale all ingredients correctly; double check all weights.
3. When adding the egg white mixture (meringue) to the batter, fold only enough to blend the two together.
4. Bake immediately after mixing the batter.
5. When the cakes are removed from the oven, turn upside down immediately on a wire rack to let them cool.

CAKE: BLENDING OR TWO-STAGE RECIPES

White cake

White cake is a fine grain and soft white textured cake, with excellent eating qualities. This cake is mixed by the blending or two-stage method. A number of different varieties of cakes can be made from this basic recipe.

Objectives

1. To teach the student the procedure for preparing white cake.

Procter and Gamble Co.

White cake, sheet pan variety.

TABLE IV. CAKE CHART
SCALING AND BAKING FOR HIGH-RATIO CAKES*

VARIETY	SCALING WEIGHT	PAN SIZE	BAKING TEMPERATURE
Layer Cakes	11 – 12 ozs.	8" Diameter	375° F
Bar Cakes	5 – 6 ozs.	2 3/4" x 10"	375° F
Mary Anns	16 – 18 ozs. per doz.	3 1/2" Diameter	375° F
Cup Cakes	13 – 14 ozs. per doz.	2" Diameter	390° F
Loaf Cake	11 – 12 ozs.	3 1/4" x 7 1/8"	375° F
Ring Cake	10 – 11 ozs.	6 1/2" Diameter	375° F
Oval Loaf	6 – 8 ozs.	6 3/4" Long	375° F
Sheet Pan	5 1/2 – 6 Pounds	17" x 25"	375° F
Thick Sheet Pan	8 – 9 Pounds	17" x 25" with 2 3/4" wooden side	360° F

*High-ratio cakes use an emulsified shortening, such as Sweetex, which allows more sugar to be added. Use with these cakes: white cake, yellow cake, devil's food cake, Windsor gold cake, fudge cake, and Christmas candy cake.

2. To teach the student how to scale the ingredients and mix the cake.
3. To teach the student how to bake the cake.
   Equipment
1. Mixing machine and paddle
2. Baker's scale
3. Plastic scraper
4. Cake pans as desired
5. 1 gal. stainless steel container
Ingredients: Weight of mix 11 lbs.
   2 lbs. 8 ozs. cake flour
   1 lb. 12 ozs. Sweetex shortening
   3 lbs. 2 ozs. granulated sugar
   1½ oz. salt
   2½ ozs. baking powder
   14 ozs. water
   2½ ozs. nonfat dry milk
   10 ozs. whole eggs
   1 lb. egg whites
   1 lb. water
      vanilla to taste
   Preparation
1. Preheat the oven to required temperature. See *Cake Chart*, Table IV.
2. Prepare baking pans selected.
3. Scale off all ingredients carefully using a baker's scale.
4. Have all equipment and ingredients handy.
   Procedure
1. Place in the electric mixing bowl the first seven ingredients. Using the paddle, mix for 5 minutes on low speed if a three-speed

machine is used, or second speed on a four-speed machine. Scrape down the bowl and paddle with a plastic scraper at least once in this stage.
2. Scale off eggs, water and flavor together in a stainless steel container and add approximately half of it to the bowl. Mix on slow speed until smooth. Scrape down and mix until smooth again.
3. Add the balance of the liquid ingredients and continue mixing on slow speed for a total of 3 minutes in this stage. Scrape down again to insure a smooth batter.
4. See the *Cake Chart* for scaling and baking instructions.
   Precautions and Safety Measures
1. Scrape down the bowl at intervals during the mixing period to incorporate all ingredients and to insure a smooth batter.
2. Scale all ingredients correctly; double check all weights.

Yellow cake

Yellow cake is a fine grain, soft, yellow textured cake, with excellent eating qualities. This cake is mixed by the blending or two-stage method. Endless varieties of cakes can be made using this basic yellow cake batter.
   Objectives
1. To teach the student the procedure for preparing yellow cake.

2. To teach the student how to scale the ingredients and mix the cake.
3. To teach the student how to bake the cake.
   Equipment
1. Mixing machine and paddle
2. Baker's scale
3. Plastic scraper
4. Cake pans as desired
5. 1 gal. stainless steel container
   Ingredients: Weight of Mix 11 lbs.

2	lbs. 8 ozs.	cake flour
1	lb. 6 ozs.	Sweetex shortening
3	lbs. 2 ozs.	granulated sugar
1	oz.	salt
1¾	oz.	baking powder
4	ozs.	nonfat dry milk
1	lb. 4 ozs.	water
1	lb. 10 ozs.	whole eggs
12	ozs.	water
		vanilla to taste

Preparation
1. Preheat the oven to required temperature. See *Cake Chart*, Table IV.
2. Prepare baking pans selected.
3. Scale off all ingredients carefully using a baker's scale.
4. Have all the equipment and ingredients handy.
   Procedure
1. Place in the electric mixing bowl the first seven ingredients. Using the paddle, mix for 5 minutes on low speed if a three-speed machine is used, or second speed on a four-speed machine. Scrape down the bowl and paddle with a plastic scraper at least once in this stage.
2. Scale off eggs, water and flavor together in a stainless steel container and add approximately half of it to the bowl. Mix on slow speed until smooth. Scrape down and mix smooth again.
3. Add the balance of the liquid ingredients and continue mixing at slow speed for a total of 3 minutes in this stage, scraping down again to insure that a smooth batter is developed.
4. See the *Cake Chart* for scaling and baking instructions.
   Precautions and Safety Measures
1. Scrape down the bowl at intervals during the mixing period to incorporate all ingredients and to insure a smooth batter.
2. Scale all ingredients correctly; double check all weights.

Devil's food cake

Devil's food cake is a soft, tender cake with a rich chocolate flavor. Devil's food cake is mixed by the blending or two-stage method. Many different cake varieties can be made from this batter.

Objectives
1. To teach the student the procedure for preparing devil's food cake.
2. To teach the student how to scale the ingredients and mix the cake.
3. To teach the student how to bake the cake.
   Equipment
1. Mixing machine and paddle
2. Baker's scale
3. Plastic scraper
4. Cake pans as desired
5. 1 gal. stainless steel container
   Ingredients: Weight of mix 13 lbs.

2	lbs. 8 ozs.	cake flour
1	lb. 6 ozs.	Sweetex shortening
3	lbs. 8 ozs.	granulated sugar
8	ozs.	cocoa
1½	oz.	salt
¾	oz.	baking soda
1½	oz.	baking powder
6	ozs.	nonfat dry milk
1	lb. 4 ozs.	water
1	lb. 14 ozs.	whole eggs
1	lb. 9 ozs.	water
		vanilla to taste

Preparation
1. Preheat the oven to required temperature. See *Cake Chart*, Table IV.
2. Prepare baking pans selected.
3. Scale off all ingredients carefully.
4. Have all equipment and ingredients handy.
   Procedure
1. Place in the electric mixing bowl the first nine ingredients. Using the paddle, mix for 5 minutes on low speed if a three-speed machine is used, or second speed on a four-speed machine. Scrape down the bowl and paddle with a plastic scraper at least once in this stage.
2. Scale off eggs, water and flavor together and add approximately half of it to the bowl. Mix at slow speed until smooth, scrape down and mix until smooth again.
3. Add the balance of the liquid ingredients and continue mixing at slow speed for a total of 3 minutes in this stage, scraping down again to insure a smooth batter.

4. See the *Cake Chart* for scaling and baking instructions.
   Precautions and Safety Measures
1. Scrape down the bowl at intervals during the mixing period to incorporate all ingredients and to insure a smooth batter.
2. Scale all ingredients correctly; double check all weights.

Fudge cake

Fudge cake is a rich, flavorful, tender chocolate colored cake. This cake is rich in sugar and eggs and will produce a product with above average eating qualities. Fudge cake is mixed by the blending or two-stage method and can be formed to produce many different fudge cake varieties.

Objectives
1. To teach the student the procedure for preparing fudge cake.
2. To teach the student how to scale the ingredients and mix the cake.
3. To teach the student how to bake the cake.

Equipment
1. Mixing machine and paddle
2. Baker's scale
3. Plastic scraper
4. Cake pans as desired
5. 1 gal. stainless steel container
   Ingredients: Weight of mix 11 lbs. 12 ozs.

2	lbs. 2 ozs. cake flour
6	ozs. cocoa
1	lb. 12 ozs. Sweetex shortening
3	lbs. 2 ozs. granulated sugar
1½	oz. salt
¾	oz. baking soda
1½	oz. baking powder
1	lb. water
3½	ozs. nonfat dry milk
2	lbs. 4 ozs. whole eggs
10½	ozs. water
	flavor to taste

Preparation
1. Preheat the oven to required temperature. See *Cake Chart*, Table IV.
2. Prepare baking pans selected.
3. Scale off all ingredients carefully using a baker's scale.
4. Have all equipment and ingredients handy.

Procedure
1. Place in the electric mixing bowl the first nine ingredients. Using the paddle, mix for 5 minutes on low speed if a three-speed machine is used, or second speed on a four-speed machine. Scrape down the bowl and paddle with a plastic scraper at least once in this stage.
2. In a stainless steel container scale off eggs, water and flavor together and add approximately half of it to the bowl. Mix at slow speed until smooth, scrape down and mix smooth again.
3. Add the balance of the liquid ingredients and continue mixing at slow speed for a total of 3 minutes in this stage, scraping down again to insure a smooth batter.
4. See the *Cake Chart* for scaling and baking instruction.
   Precautions and Safety Measures
1. Scrape down the bowl at intervals during the mixing period to incorporate all ingredients and to insure a smooth batter.
2. Scale all ingredients correctly; double check all weights.

White pound cake

White pound cake is a rich, pure white, very smooth textured cake. This cake is perfect when eaten by itself, with ice cream or fruit. It is mixed using the blending or two-stage method.

Objectives
1. To teach the student the procedure for preparing white pound cake.
2. To teach the student how to scale the ingredients and mix the cake.
3. To teach the student how to bake a pound cake.

Equipment
1. Mixing machine and paddle
2. Baker's scale
3. Plastic scraper
4. Cake pans as desired
5. 1 gal. stainless steel container
   Ingredients: Weight of mix 11 lbs.

2	lbs. 8 ozs. cake flour
1	lb. 10 ozs. Sweetex shortening
3	lbs. 2 ozs. granulated sugar
1½	oz. salt
1¼	oz. baking powder
1	lb. water
4	ozs. nonfat dry milk
1	lb. 10 ozs. egg whites
10½	ozs. water
	vanilla to taste

Preparation
1. Preheat oven to either 350°F (for 1 lb. cakes) or 330°F (for 3 lb. cakes).

2. Prepare the loaf pans selected. Size will be determined by the weight of the cake desired (1 lb. or 3 lbs.) For 1 lb. use 4½" x 8½" x 3" loaf pans; for 3 lb. use 4½" x 13" x 3".

3. Scale off all ingredients carefully with a baker's scale.

4. Have all equipment and ingredients handy.

Procedure

1. Place in the electric mixing bowl the first seven ingredients. Using the paddle mix for 6 to 8 minutes on second speed if a three-speed machine is used, or third speed on a four-speed machine. Scrape down the bowl and paddle with a plastic scraper at least once in this stage.

2. Scale off eggs, water and flavor into a stainless steel container and add approximately half of it to the bowl. Mix at slow speed until smooth, scrape down. Mix until smooth again.

3. Add the balance of the liquid ingredients and continue mixing at slow speed for a total of 5 minutes in this stage, scrape down again to insure a smooth batter.

4. Scale the batter into selected loaf pans.

5. Bake the one pound cakes at 350°F. Bake the three pound cakes at 330°F until golden brown. Remove from the oven.

Note: If a larger volume, more open grain pound cake with a larger crack or split on top is desired, add ¼ to ½ oz. of baking powder or increase mixing time.

Precautions and Safety Measures

1. Scrape down the bowl at intervals during the mixing period to incorporate all ingredients and to insure a smooth batter.

2. Scale all ingredients correctly; double check all weights.

Honey cake (high ratio)

Honey cake is a moist, tender cake with a mellow honey flavor. Honey cake batter can be used for preparing cup cakes, loaves, layer or ring cakes. The batter is mixed by using the blending method, but the mixing is done in three stages rather than the usual two stages.

Objectives

1. To teach the student the procedure for preparing honey cake.

2. To teach the student how to scale the ingredients and mix the batter.

3. To teach the student how to bake the cake.

Equipment

1. Mixing machine and paddle
2. Baker's scale
3. Plastic scraper
4. 15, 8 in. diameter cake pans
5. Wire whip
6. 1 gal. stainless steel container

Ingredients: Approx. yield: 13 to 15, 8 in. cakes

2	lbs. 8 ozs. cake flour
1	lb. 6 ozs. Sweetex shortening
1	lb. 14 ozs. light brown sugar
1	lb. 4 ozs. granulated sugar
1½	oz. salt
2½	ozs. baking powder
6	ozs. honey
1	lb. liquid skim milk
1	lb. 8 ozs. whole eggs
1	lb. 10 ozs. liquid skim milk
	vanilla to taste

Preparation

1. Prepare 8 in. diameter cake pans: grease the sides and cover the bottom with silicon paper.

2. Preheat the oven to 375°F.

3. Scale off all ingredients carefully using a baker's scale.

4. Have all equipment and ingredients handy.

Procedure

1. Place the flour and shortening in the electric mixing bowl, using the paddle, mix for 3 to 5 minutes at slow speed. Scrape down the bowl and paddle with a plastic scraper at least once in this stage.

2. Add the brown sugar, graduated sugar, salt, baking powder, honey and the first amount of milk, mix at slow speed from 3 to 5 minutes, scrape down the bowl.

3. In a stainless steel container combine the eggs, second amount of milk and the vanilla, beat together slightly using a wire whip. Add half of this mixture to the bowl and mix at slow speed until smooth.

4. Add the balance of the liquid mixture and continue mixing at slow speed for a total of 3 to 5 minutes in this stage, scraping down again to insure a smooth batter.

5. Scale 12 to 14 ozs. of batter into each prepared 8 in. diameter cake pan.

6. Bake at 375°F until done. Remove from the oven.

Precautions and Safety Measures

1. Scale all ingredients correctly; double check all weights.

2. All mixing should be done at slow speed.
3. Scrape down the bowl at least once during each mixing stage to insure a smooth batter and incorporate all ingredients.
4. Check oven temperature with an oven thermometer.

Christmas candy cake (high ratio)

Christmas candy cake is a white cake with a tender moist texture and a peppermint flavor. This cake is mixed by the blending method, but three mixing stages rather than the usual two stages are used.

Objectives
1. To teach the student the procedure for preparing Christmas candy cake.
2. To teach the student how to scale the ingredients and mix the batter.
3. To teach the student how to bake the cake.

Equipment
1. Mixing machine and paddle
2. Baker's scale
3. Plastic scraper
4. 14, 8 in. diameter cake pans
5. 1 gal. stainless steel container
6. Kitchen spoon
7. Rolling pin

Ingredients: Approx. yield: 14, 8 in. cakes

2	lbs. 8 ozs. cake flour
1	lb. 6 ozs. Sweetex shortening
2	lbs. 14 ozs. granulated sugar
10	ozs. crushed peppermint candy
1½	oz. salt
½	oz. cream of tartar
2½	ozs. baking powder
1	lb. liquid skim milk
1	lb. 14 ozs. egg whites
1	lb. 6 ozs. liquid skim milk
	peppermint flavor to taste

Preparation
1. Crush the peppermint candy with a rolling pin.
2. Separate the eggs using the whites and saving the yolks for use in another preparation.
3. Prepare the 8 in. diameter cake pans: grease the sides lightly and cover the bottom with silicon paper.
4. Preheat the oven to 375°F.
5. Scale off all ingredients carefully using a baker's scale.
6. Have all the equipment and ingredients handy.

Procedure
1. Place the flour and shortening in the electric mixing bowl, using the paddle, mix 3 to 5 minutes at slow speed. Scrape down the bowl and paddle with a plastic scraper at least once during this stage.
2. Dissolve the peppermint candy in the first amount of milk and add with the salt, cream of tartar, baking powder and granulated sugar to the flour shortening mixture. Mix at slow speed from 3 to 5 minutes, scraping down the bowl at least once.
3. In a stainless steel container combine the egg whites, second amount of milk and the peppermint flavor, blend together by stirring with a kitchen spoon. Add half of this mixture to the bowl and mix at slow speed until smooth, scrape down the bowl and mix until smooth again.
4. Add the balance of the liquid mixture and continue mixing at slow speed for a total of 3 to 5 minutes in this stage, scraping down the bowl again to insure a smooth batter.
5. Scale 12 to 14 ozs. of batter into each prepared 8 in. diameter cake pan.
6. Bake at 375°F until golden brown. Remove when done.

Precautions and Safety Measures
1. Scale all ingredients correctly; double check all weights.
2. All mixing should be done at slow speed.
3. Scrape down the bowl at least once during each mixing stage to insure a smooth batter and incorporate all ingredients.

CAKE ICING RECIPES

New York buttercream icing

Ingredients: Approx. yield: 4 qts.

2	lbs. 8 ozs. Sweetex shortening
1	lb. butter
½	oz. salt
12	ozs. non-fat dry milk
5	lbs. powdered sugar
1	lb. water (110°F)
1	oz. vanilla

Procedure
1. Place all the ingredients in electric mixing bowl. Use paddle and beat at medium speed for 5 minutes, then at high for 2 minutes or to desired lightness.

Procter and Gamble Co.

Applying icing and decorations to a cake.

Butter cream icing for decorating

Ingredients: Approx. yield: 1½ qts.

1   lb. 8 ozs. shortening
2   lbs. 8 ozs. powdered sugar
1   oz. egg whites
2   ozs. corn starch (variable)
    (use corn starch only in hot weather)

Procedure

1. Place all the ingredients in electric mixing bowl. Use paddle and beat at medium speed until smooth.

White cream icings

Ingredients: Approx. yield: 3 qts.

1   lb. 4 ozs. Sweetex shortening
½   oz. salt
5   ozs. non-fat dry milk
14 ozs. water
    vanilla to taste
5   lbs. powdered sugar

Procedure

1. Place all the ingredients in electric mixing bowl. Using the paddle mix on slow speed for about 5 minutes.
2. Whip at medium speed for 10 to 15 minutes to acquire desired lightness.

White cream icing varieties: Add ingredients to 5 lbs. of icing for each of the following:

Nut icing: 8 ozs. chopped nuts.
Raisin icing: 8 ozs. ground raisins.
Cherry icing: 8 ozs. chopped cherries.
Candied fruit icing: 8 ozs. chopped fruit.
Jam or marmalade icing: 8 ozs. jam or marmalade.
Coconut icing: 8 ozs. macaroon coconut.
Fondant icing: 2 lbs. 8 ozs. fondant.
Peppermint candy icing: 4 ozs. crushed peppermint candy.
Cocoa: 5 ozs. cocoa plus 5 ozs. water.
Lady Baltimore filling: 1 lb. of chopped cherries, nuts and raisins.
Fresh fruit icing: 3 ozs. ground citrus or other fresh fruit.

Chocolate malted milk icing

Ingredients: Approx. yield: 3½ qts.

1   lb. 4 ozs. Sweetex shortening
¾   oz. salt
4   ozs. non-fat dry milk
6   ozs. malted milk powder
1   lb. 8 ozs. melted chocolate
1   lb. 8 ozs. water
5   lbs. powdered sugar

Procedure

1. Place the shortening, salt, dry milk and malted milk powder in the electric mixing bowl. Using the paddle, cream together on slow speed until light and smooth.

2. Add the melted chocolate, continue to mix at slow speed.
3. Add the water, mix at slow speed.
4. Add the powdered sugar, mix at slow speed until smooth.

Maple icing

Ingredients: Approx. yield: 3 qts.
2 lbs. 8 ozs. light brown sugar
1 lb. 2 ozs. water
½ oz. salt
1 lb. 4 ozs. Sweetex shortening
5 ozs. non-fat dry milk
maple flavor to taste
3 lbs. 12 ozs. fondant
Procedure
1. Place the brown sugar, water and salt in a sauce pan. Bring to a boil and cool to room temperature.
2. In the electric mixing bowl place the shortening, dry milk and maple flavoring. Whip together at second speed and gradually add the above syrup, continue beating for about 5 minutes.
3. Add the fondant (see recipe) and whip until light (about 10 minutes).

Flat icing

Ingredients: Approx. yield: 1 qt.
2 lbs. 8 ozs. powdered sugar
4 ozs. corn syrup
2 ozs. egg whites
8 ozs. hot water (variable)
Procedure
1. Place the powdered sugar, corn syrup and egg whites in the electric mixing bowl. Using the paddle, mix at slow speed, while adding the hot water.
2. Mix until smooth.
Note: When ready to use, heat the amount of icing needed in a double boiler. Use it on rolls, Danish pastry, coffee cakes, etc.

Roll icing

Ingredients: Approx. yield: 1 qt.
2 lbs. 8 ozs. powdered sugar
4 ozs. salad oil
6 ozs. glucose
¼ oz. salt
4 ozs. hot water (variable)
flavoring to taste
Procedure
1. Place the powdered sugar, salad oil, glu-

cose and salt in the mixing bowl. Using the paddle, mix at slow speed while adding the hot water.
2. Mix until smooth.
3. Stir in the flavoring until thoroughly blended.

Boiled icing

Ingredients: Approx. yield: 1 gal.
1 lb. egg whites
½ oz. salt
2 lbs. granulated sugar
6 ozs. glucose
8 ozs. water
Procedure
1. Place the sugar, glucose and water in a sauce pan, boil to 240°F.
2. Place the egg whites and salt in the electric mixing bowl, beat until soft wet peaks form.
3. Pour in the hot mixture very slowly while continuing to beat.
4. Beat until desired consistency is obtained.

Chocolate supreme fudge icing

Ingredients: Approx. yield: 3 qts.
1 lb. Sweetex shortening
4 ozs. butter
½ oz. salt
12 ozs. cocoa
5 lbs. powdered sugar
4 ozs. honey
14 ozs. hot water (variable)
Procedure
1. In a sauce pan place the shortening and butter, melt, place in the electric mixing bowl.
2. Add the cocoa and salt. Using the paddle mix at slow speed until blended.
3. Add the powdered sugar, mix at slow speed until smooth.
4. Mix the honey in the hot water. Add to the above slowly to prevent lumping, continue at slow speed until smooth.

Caramel fudge icing

Ingredients: Approx. yield: 3½ qts.
1 lb. 12 ozs. light brown sugar
8 ozs. butter
½ oz. salt
¼ oz. cream of tartar
8 ozs. water
5 lbs. powdered sugar

Caramel fudge icing being applied to a yellow cake.

2   ozs. Sweetex shortening
8   ozs. butter
6   ozs. liquid milk (variable)
½   oz. vanilla
Procedure

1. In a sauce pan place the brown sugar, salt, cream of tartar, first amount of butter and the water, boil to 242°F.
2. Place the powdered sugar, shortening, second amount of butter, milk and vanilla in electric mixing bowl. Using the paddle beat high speed until mixture becomes light.
3. Add the hot syrup, while mixing in second speed. Mix until just smooth (approx. 1 to 2 minutes). Do not overmix.

Bittersweet chocolate icing

Ingredients: Approx. yield: 3½ qts.
2   lbs. 8 ozs. melted bitter chocolate
1   lb. 4 ozs. cocoa
3   lbs. 12 ozs. powdered sugar
1   lb. 14 ozs. hot water
Procedure

1. Place the melted chocolate in the electric mixing bowl and add the powdered sugar and cocoa. Blend thoroughly at slow speed, using the paddle.
2. Add the hot water and mix smooth.

3. If adjustment of flavor is desired salt and vanilla may be added.

Fondant icing

Ingredients: Approx. yield: 5 qts.
10   lbs. granulated sugar
1   lb. glucose
4   lbs. water
Procedure

1. Place all the ingredients in a sauce pot, boil to 240°F. Wash the sides of the kettle carefully (keep sides of bowl clean by constantly rubbing the sides with a wooden spoon).
2. Pour the cooked mixture in the electric mixing bowl. Set the bowl in cold water, cool to 150°F.
3. Using the paddle, grain the mixture (smooth or develop the texture) at high speed until it becomes stiff and white in color.
4. Place in a container and cover tightly with a damp cloth.

Butterscotch fondant icing

Ingredients: Approx. yield: 3 qts.
3   lbs. 4 ozs. fondant
1   lb. 6 ozs. butterscotch stock

4　ozs. glucose
1　lb. Sweetex shortening
1　oz. salt
8　ozs. evaporated milk (variable)
Procedure

1. Place the fondant, butterscotch stock and glucose in the electric mixing bowl. Mix slowly using the paddle until smooth.
2. Add the shortening and salt, mix until smooth at low speed. Cream 2 minutes at medium speed.
3. Add evaporated milk; incorporate at low speed. Cream 3 minutes at med. speed.

BUTTERSCOTCH STOCK:
Ingredients: Approx. yield: 1½ qts.
2　lbs. brown sugar
4　ozs. glucose
8　ozs. butter
8　ozs. water
Procedure

1. Place all the ingredients in a sauce pan, boil to 244°F, stirring occasionally with a wooden spoon. Cool before using.

Strawberry fondant icing

Ingredients: Approx. yield: 2½ qts.
3　lbs. 12 ozs. fondant
4　ozs. crushed strawberries
2　lbs. 8 ozs. Sweetex icing base
　　citric acid to taste
Procedure

1. Place all the ingredients in the electric mixing bowl. Using the paddle mix together in second speed to a smooth creamy consistency (about 5 minutes).

SWEETEX ICING BASE:
Ingredients: Approx. yield: 2½ qts.
1　lb. 8 ozs. Sweetex shortening
3　lbs. 2 ozs. powdered sugar
6　ozs. whole eggs
Procedure

1. Place the shortening in the electric mixing bowl. Using the paddle whip at second speed until light.
2. Add the sugar and continue whipping at second speed.
3. Add the eggs and whip at high speed until light (about 5 minutes).

Pineapple fondant icing

Ingredients: Approx. yield: 2½ qts.
4　lbs. 12 ozs. fondant
1　lb. 4 ozs. Sweetex shortening

¼　oz. salt
4　ozs. evaporated milk
6　ozs. crushed pineapple
Procedure

1. Place the fondant, shortening and salt in the electric mixing bowl. Mix slowly at 70°F to 80°F, using the paddle, until smooth. Cream for 2 minutes at medium speed.
2. Add the evaporated milk and mix slowly until smooth. Cream at medium speed for 3 minutes.
3. Drain the pineapple and blend into the icing, cream for 2 minutes at medium speed.

Orange or lemon fondant icing

Ingredients: Approx. yield: 2½ qts.
3　lbs. 12 ozs. fondant
4　ozs. ground whole oranges or 2 ozs. ground whole lemons
2　lbs. 8 ozs. Sweetex icing base
　　citric acid to taste
Procedure

1. Place all the ingredients in the electric mixing bowl. Using the paddle mix together to a smooth consistency (mixing time about 10 min.).

Note: For Sweetex icing base refer to strawberry fondant icing.

Chocolate fondant icing

Ingredients: Approx. yield: 3 qts.
3　lbs. 6 ozs. fondant
4　ozs. glucose
4　ozs. butter
10　ozs. Sweetex shortening
½　oz. salt
1　lb. bitter chocolate, melted
12　ozs. evaporated milk
Procedure

1. Place the fondant, glucose, butter, shortening and salt in the electric mixing bowl. Using the paddle mix at slow speed until smooth. Cream at medium speed for 2 minutes.
2. Add the melted bitter chocolate and mix at slow speed until smooth.
3. Add the evaporated milk, mix slowly until smooth. Cream 3 or 4 minutes at medium speed.

Royal icing

Ingredients: Approx. yield: 1½ qts.
4 lbs. powdered sugar
10 ozs. egg whites (variable)
½ tsp. cream of tartar
Procedure
1. Place the sugar, cream of tartar and half of the egg whites in the mixing bowl. Using the paddle mix at slow speed while adding the remaining egg whites to obtain proper consistency.
2. Mix until icing is smooth.
3. Keep icing covered with a damp cloth.

CAKE FILLING RECIPES

Strawberry cake filling

Ingredients: Approx. yield: 2½ qts.
1 lb. water
1 lb. 8 ozs. sugar
¼ oz. salt
2 lbs. strawberries, fresh or frozen, chopped
6 ozs. modified starch
1 lb. water
½ oz. red color
1 oz. lemon juice
Procedure
1. Place the first amount of water, sugar, salt and strawberries in a sauce pot, bring to a boil.
2. Dissolve the starch in the second amount of water. Add to the boiling mixture while stirring constantly with a kitchen spoon. Cook until thickened.
3. Remove from the heat and add the color and lemon juice.

Butterscotch cake filling

Ingredients: Approx. yield: 3 qts.
1 lb. 4 ozs. dark brown sugar
1 lb. granulated sugar
2 lbs. water
½ oz. salt
8 ozs. glucose
10 ozs. water
8 ozs. cornstarch
2 ozs. butter
¼ oz. maple flavoring
½ oz. vanilla
Procedure
1. Place the brown sugar, granulated sugar, water, salt and glucose in a sauce pot, bring to a boil.
2. Dissolve the starch in the second amount of water, pour into the boiling mixture while stirring constantly with a kitchen spoon. Cook until thickened and clear.
3. Remove from the heat and stir in the butter, maple flavoring and vanilla.

Fudge cake filling

Ingredients: Approx. yield: 2½ qts.
2 lbs. water
2 lbs. 8 ozs. sugar
6 ozs. cocoa
¼ oz. salt
7 ozs. modified starch
1 lb. water
¼ oz. vanilla
2 ozs. Sweetex shortening
Procedure
1. Place the water, sugar, cocoa and salt in a sauce pot, bring to a boil.
2. Dissolve the starch in the second amount of water, pour into boiling mixture while stirring constantly with a kitchen spoon. Cook until thickened and clear.
3. Remove from the heat and stir in the vanilla and shortening until thoroughly blended.

Orange cake filling

Ingredients: Approx. yield: 3½ qts.
3 lbs. water
1 lb. 4 ozs. orange concentrate, frozen
2 lbs. granulated sugar
½ oz. salt
1 lb. 8 ozs. water
10 ozs. modified starch
8 ozs. egg yolks
4 ozs. Sweetex shortening
4 ozs. butter
4 ozs. lemon juice
Procedure
1. Place the water, orange concentrate, sugar and salt in a sauce pot, bring to a boil.
2. Dissolve the starch in the second amount of water. Add egg yolks and mix together with a kitchen spoon. Add to the boiling mixture while stirring constantly with a kitchen spoon. Cook until thickened and clear.
3. Remove from the heat and stir in the shortening, butter and lemon juice until thoroughly blended.

puddings ice creams and specialty desserts

chapter 27

■ Previous chapters have dealt with procedures and recipes for pies and cakes. Next in importance in the repertory of desserts are three general classes covered in this chapter.

The first of these are puddings, which are of several types that are popular in nearly all areas. They are well adapted to quantity production, most of them economical, and they have the advantage that they can be made in advance of ordering.

Ice creams and sherbets, nearly synonymous in most uses, are universally popular and can be purchased in all varieties. Served either plain or with cake, the procedure is so simple it requires no explanation.

At the same time, the ice creams when combined with fruits, fruit sauces, and liqueurs, are used to create eye-appealing parfaits and coupes, and the more spectacular flambés, or flaming desserts, such as jubilees and such masterpieces as baked Alaska.

Flaming desserts and other chafing dish specialties such as crêpe Suzette are strictly à la carte items that must be prepared before guests seated at their tables. These are very demanding but are required where the finest cuisine is more important than price considerations.

Among the most popular and delicious specialty desserts none surpass the light, flaky pastries made from puff paste and choux paste dough. These provide a great variety of attractive forms such as patty shells (filled with fruit, ice cream, or any number of delightful things), cream puffs, and éclairs. These pastries, artistically decorated, are especially appreciated when they are placed before the guest on a silver platter or wheeled in on a cart. This service is a fitting finale to a memorable dinner.

PUDDINGS

Usually puddings are among the simplest of desserts to prepare, although two types—soufflés and steamed puddings—can be somewhat complex. In most cases puddings can be made in advance of serving time, they are usually low in cost, popular, and profitable if made properly and presented to the guest in an eye-appealing manner.

There are five types of puddings in general use in food service establishments. Some, simpler to prepare than others, are more popular. They will be listed in the order of their importance and popularity.

1. *Cream puddings or starch-thickened puddings* are quite simple to prepare. They are made from hot milk, sugar, starch, vanilla, salt, and eggs. The procedure for making them is to heat the milk, reserving a small amount of cold milk to blend with the sugar and cornstarch, then blending this mixture into the hot milk. This preparation is usually done in a double boiler. Puddings of this type can be served warm or chilled; however, chilled is more popular. Included in this type are: chocolate pudding, vanilla pudding, coconut pudding, butterscotch pudding, etc.

2. *Baked puddings or egg-thickened puddings* include such popular desserts as rice pudding, bread pudding, custard, etc. This type of pudding is usually bound together by a baked custard made of eggs and milk or cream. The preparation is generally baked in a water bath (pans containing water) at a temperature of 325° F. to 340° F. until the custard has set but not completely cooked, because custard will continue cooking after it has been removed from the oven. Overcooking will cause a watery condition which is very undesirable.

Custard may be tested by inserting a knife. If the knife comes out clean the custard is done.

Oven temperature is highly important in baking an egg-thickened pudding. If oven temperature is too low a weak product is obtained. If oven temperature is too high the product becomes watery.

Baked puddings are usually served with a warm sauce.

3. *Chilled puddings or gelatin type puddings* are usually very light and fluffy because whipped cream or egg whites are folded into the basic gelatin mixture. In this group are included Bavarian creams, snow pudding, mousses, etc.

4. *Soufflé puddings, usually referred to as soufflés.* The kind of soufflé is always stated on the menu. Examples are: chocolate soufflé, vanilla soufflé, etc. Puddings of this type are practical only on the à la carte menu because they can only be made properly when baked to order. The beaten egg whites must be folded into the basic mix very gently and baked very carefully. Otherwise the soufflé becomes heavy and soggy. Soufflés are difficult to prepare, and even the most experienced chef will have problems with them from time to time.

5. *Steamed puddings or boiled puddings* are usually served during the cold seasons of the year and have become famous as holiday desserts. Generally they are made with a large percentage of fruit, suet (animal fat) as the shortening, flour, eggs and bread crumbs as binders, baking soda if a leavening is used, and brown sugar or molasses as the sweetener. The use of the dark colored sweetener gives this type of pudding its characteristic dark appearance. Also the puddings are highly spiced with

such spices as ginger, mace, nutmeg, and alspice. In most cases rum or brandy, or both, are essential to provide the unforgettable aroma and taste.

This type of pudding can be cooked in large or individual metal containers by steaming in a steam pressure chamber covered with aluminum foil or baked in water baths in a 350° F. oven, covered with a damp cloth, for approximately 2 to 3 hours. Another method of cooking is to place the pudding in a damp muslin cloth which has been dusted with flour, tying the ends of the cloth loosely to allow for expansion, and lowering into simmering water. The bag may also be suspended just above the water and cooked by the steam vapors provided by the water.

Steam puddings have a heavy, tight, and sometimes waxy texture. They are served hot with a hot sauce that complements the pudding's flavor and color. One exception is that hard sauce may be used unheated.

PUDDING RECIPES

Creamed puddings
(Pages 622 to 625)
Vanilla pudding (with variations)
Chocolate pudding
Butterscotch pudding

Baked puddings
(Pages 625 to 627)
Bread pudding
Rice pudding (with variations)
Baked custard (with variations)

Chilled puddings
(Pages 627 to 631)
Rice imperatrice
Chocolate mousse
Vanilla Bavarian cream
 (with variations)
Lemon snow pudding

Soufflé puddings
(Pages 631 to 632)
Basic vanilla soufflé (with variations)

Steamed puddings
(Pages 632 to 633)
Plum pudding

ICE CREAM DESSERT RECIPES
Parfaits
(Page 633)
Parfait crème de menthe
Rainbow parfait
Parfait Melba
Pineapple parfait
Chocolate parfait
Butterscotch parfait

Coupes
(Page 634)
Coupe Melba
Coupe Hélène
Strawberry coupe
Pineapple coupe
Coupe savory

Jubilees
(Pages 634 to 635)
Cherry jubilee
Strawberry jubilee

Baked Alaska
(Pages 635 to 636)

CREPE DESSERT RECIPES
(Pages 636 to 637)
Crêpe Suzette

SPECIALTY PASTRIES RECIPES
(Pages 637 to 642)
Puff paste dough (with variations)
Eclair or choux paste (with variations)

CREAMED PUDDINGS

Vanilla pudding (with variations)
Vanilla pudding, a basic cream pudding, is thickened with both cornstarch and eggs, and although this preparation is similar to the French blanc mange it is richer because of the addition of the eggs. Many variations can be obtained from this preparation by the addition of other ingredients. Banana, cocoa,

coconut, and pineapple puddings are popular variations. If convenience is desired there are excellent pudding mixes on the market. Some are used by adding cold milk, others require cooking in hot milk. For the highest quality there is a good argument for making your own mixes based on the policy that quality will outsell convenience every time.

Objectives
1. To teach the student the procedure for preparing vanilla pudding and variations.
2. To teach the student how to add the cornstarch and eggs.
3. To teach the student how to serve vanilla pudding and its variations.

Equipment
1. Baker's scale
2. Wire Whip
3. Double boiler
4. Quart measure
5. Stainless steel mixing bowl
6. Spoon measures
7. Wooden spoon
   Ingredients: Approx. yield: 25 servings
6	lb. (3 qts.) milk
12	oz. sugar
6	oz. corn starch
8	oz. egg yolks
½	tsp. salt
3	oz. butter
½	tsp. vanilla (variable)

Preparation
1. Separate eggs, hold yolks, store whites in refrigerator or freezer.
2. Have all equipment and ingredients handy.

Procedure
1. Place the milk and half of the sugar in the top of a double boiler, cover and heat until scalding hot. (A film will form on the surface of the milk)
2. In a stainless steel bowl place the remaining sugar, cornstarch, egg yolks, and salt. Add some of the milk from Step 1 gradually, while whipping steadily, until a thin paste is formed.
3. Pour the paste mixture into the scalding milk, whipping briskly with a wire whip.
4. Continue to cook and whip the mixture until it becomes fairly stiff. Remove from the heat.
5. Add the vanilla and butter, stir with a wooden spoon until the butter melts and blends into the pudding.
6. Pour into champagne or cocktail glasses, chill, and serve topped with whipped cream.

Note: It is possible to serve this pudding warm, but it is very seldom done.

Precautions and Safety Measures
1. Work the whip constantly when adding the hot milk to the egg-starch mixture.
2. Whip vigorously when adding the egg-starch mixture to the scalding milk.
3. Exercise caution when whipping the hot mixture. Do not splash.

VARIATIONS:

For *banana pudding*, add 2 lb. of sliced bananas to the cold pudding.

For *coconut pudding*, add 4 lb. of plain or toasted shedded coconut.

For *pineapple pudding*, add 12 oz. drained, crushed pineapple.

For *vanilla nut pudding*, add 4 oz. chopped nuts (peacans, walnuts, or toasted almonds).

For *lemon pudding*, omit the vanilla and add 5 oz. lemon juice.

Chocolate pudding

Chocolate pudding is generally thickened with cornstarch, flour, and eggs. However, if a pudding with a higher sheen is desired, just cornstarch may be used. This dessert is very easy to prepare and serve in quantity. If convenience is desired there are excellent prepared mixtures on the market. Chocolate pudding is usually served topped with whipped cream or topping and garnished with a cherry or some type of fruit.

Objectives
1. To teach the student the procedure for preparing chocolate pudding.
2. To teach the student how to add the diluted starch and egg mixture to the scalding milk.
3. To teach the student how to serve chocolate pudding.

Equipment
1. Baker's scale
2. Wire whip
3. Double boiler

4. Gallon measure
5. Pint measure
6. Stainless steel mixing bowl
7. Measuring spoons
8. Wooden spoon
   Ingredients: Approx. yield: 25 servings
1	gal. milk
4	oz. cornstarch
3	oz. flour (all purpose)
1	lb. 8 oz. sugar
7	oz. cocoa
½	tsp. salt
1	pt. milk
6	whole eggs
1½	oz. butter
1	tsp. vanilla

Preparation
1. Break the eggs into a stainless steel bowl and beat slightly with a wire whip.
2. Have all equipment and ingredients handy.

Procedure
1. Place the milk and half the sugar in the top of a double boiler, cover and heat until scalding hot. (A film will form on the surface of the milk.)
2. In the stainless steel bowl containing the beaten eggs add the pint of milk, remaining sugar, cornstarch, flour, salt, and cocoa. Mix to a smooth paste.
3. Pour the paste mixture into the scalding milk gradually, whipping vigorously with a wire whip.
4. Continue to cook, whipping the mixture at intervals until it becomes smooth and stiff. Remove from the heat.
5. Add the vanilla and butter, stir with a wooden spoon until thoroughly blended in.
6. Pour into champagne or cocktail glasses, chill, and serve topped with whipped cream or topping and garnished with a cherry or some type of fruit.

Precautions and Safety Measures
1. Work the whip vigorously when adding the starch-egg mixture to the scalding milk so lumps will not form.
2. Exercise caution when whipping the hot mixture. Do not splash.

Butterscotch pudding

Butterscotch pudding is usually thickened with cornstarch and eggs and prepared in somewhat the same manner as any of the cream or starch-thickened puddings. Like chocolate pudding, butterscotch pudding is popular in cafeteria service. It can also be purchased in convenient form.

Objectives
1. To teach the student the procedure for preparing butterscotch pudding.
2. To teach the student how to add the cornstarch to the scalding milk.
3. To teach the student how to serve butterscotch pudding.

Equipment
1. Baker's scale
2. Spoon measures
3. Large and small double boilers
4. Gallon measure
5. Pint measure
6. Wire whip
7. Stainless steel mixing bowl
   Ingredients: Approx. yield: 25 servings
1	gal. milk
6	oz. cornstarch
1	pt. water
1	lb. 8 oz. dark brown sugar
10	oz. butter
6	whole eggs
1	tsp. vanilla
1	tsp. maple flavor

Preparation
1. Break the eggs into a stainless steel bowl and beat slightly with a wire whip.
2. Combine the sugar, butter, and salt. Place in the top of the small double boiler and cook until the sugar is melted.
3. Have all equipment and ingredients handy.

Procedure
1. Place the milk in the top of a double boiler, cover and heat until scalding hot. (A film will form on the surface of the milk.)
2. In the stainless steel bowl containing the beaten eggs, add the pint of water and cornstarch. Mix until smooth.
3. Pour the starch-egg mixture into the scalding milk gradually while whipping vigorously with a wire whip, and cook until mixture thickens.
4. Add the melted sugar and butter mixture while continuing to whip vigorously. Continue to cook until thick and smooth.
5. Add the vanilla and maple flavor, blend in thoroughly, using the wire whip.
6. Pour into champagne or cocktail glasses, chill, and serve topped with whipped cream or topping and garnished with a cherry or some type of fruit.

Note: If desired, ¾ cup of chopped walnuts or other nuts may be added for an interesting variation.

Precautions and Safety Measures
1. Work the whip vigorously when adding the starch-egg mixture to the scalding milk so lumps will not form.
2. Exercise caution when whipping the hot mixture. Do not splash.

BAKED PUDDINGS

Bread pudding

Bread pudding is popular, economical and profitable if prepared and served properly. Bread slices are lined up, overlapping in a bake pan. Custard is poured over the bread slices until they are thoroughly saturated. They are then baked in a water bath (one pan sitting in another which contains water) until the custard becomes firm.

Bread pudding is always served with a sauce.

Objectives
1. To teach the student the procedure for preparing bread pudding.
2. To teach the student how to bake bread pudding.
3. To teach the student how to serve bread pudding.

Equipment
1. 2 bake pans
2. Wire whip
3. Baker's scale
4. French knife
5. Stainless steel mixing bowl
6. Measuring spoons
7. Sauce pot

Ingredients: Approx. yield: 25 servings

3	qts. milk
14	whole eggs
½	tsp. salt
1	tsp. vanilla
12	oz. sugar
1	lb. 8 oz. bread, sliced
	nutmeg, to taste
	cinnamon, to taste

Preparation
1. Trim the crust from the bread slices and cut each slice in half, using a French knife. Line the bread slices in a bake pan, slightly overlapping each slice.
2. Break the eggs into a stainless steel mix-

ing bowl and beat slightly with a wire whip.
3. Have all ingredients and equipment handy.

Procedure
1. Place the milk and sugar in a sauce pot and heat until scalding. Remove from the heat.
2. Add the salt and vanilla to the eggs in the mixing bowl. Pour this mixture into the scalding milk and sugar mixture while whipping vigorously with a wire whip.
3. Pour this custard mixture over the bread slices, then sprinkle cinnamon and nutmeg lightly over the surface.
4. Place on a second bake pan containing water (water bath) and bake in the oven at 375° F. until the custard is just set.
5. Remove from the oven and let set until firm. Portion with an ice cream dipper and serve warm with an appropriate sauce such as brown sugar sauce, cherry sauce, lemon sauce, etc.

Note: For raisin bread pudding, sprinkle 10 oz. of raisins over the bread slices before pouring the custard mixture.

Precautions and Safety Measures
1. Whip vigorously and exercise caution when whipping the eggs into the hot liquid.
2. Bake pudding only until custard is just set, because custard will continue to cook after it leaves the oven.
3. Cover all pieces of bread thoroughly with the custard.

Rice pudding (with variations)

Rice pudding is basically a mixture of cooked rice and custard, baked until slightly firm. This dessert should be served warm, with cream or an appropriate sauce. It is an excellent choice when serving a large group.

Objectives
1. To teach the student the procedure for preparing rice pudding.
2. To teach the student how to bake rice pudding.
3. To teach the student how to serve rice pudding.

Equipment
1. 2 bake pans
2. Wire whip
3. Baker's scale
4. Stainless steel mixing bowl
5. Double boiler
6. Wooden spoon

7. Quart measure

   Ingredients: Approx. yield: 25 servings

1	gal. milk
1	lb. rice
1	lb. sugar
1	tsp. salt
10	oz. egg yolks
1	qt. single cream
1	tsp. vanilla
	nutmeg, to taste
	cinnamon, to taste

Preparation

1. Separate the yolks of eggs from the whites. Place the yolks in a stainless steel bowl and beat slightly with a wire whip. Freeze the whites and save for another preparation.
2. Wash the rice in cold water and drain thoroughly.
3. Have all equipment and ingredients handy.

Procedure

1. Place the milk and salt in the top of a double boiler, cover and heat until scalding hot. (A film will form on the surface of the milk.)
2. Add the rice and cook, stirring occasionally with a wooden spoon, until the rice is tender. Remove from the heat.
3. Add the sugar, cream, and vanilla to the bowl containing the egg yolks and sugar.
4. Pour this mixture slowly into the cooked rice while whipping with a fairly rapid motion.
5. Pour rice and custard mixture into a bake pan and sprinkle cinnamon and nutmeg lightly over the surface.
6. Place on a second bake pan containing water (water bath) and bake in the oven at 375° F. until mixture has set.
7. Remove from the oven and let set until firm. Portion into serving dish with an ice cream dipper and serve warm with an appropriate sauce such as brown sugar sauce, cherry sauce, etc.

Precautions and Safety Measures

1. When adding the egg mixture to the cooked rice, whip continuously and exercise caution to avoid splashing.
2. Bake pudding until just set, because cooking will continue after it leaves the oven.

VARIATIONS:

For *raisin rice pudding*, add 8 oz. of raisins to the rice after it has been cooked.

Baked custard (with variations)

Baked custard is a mixture of eggs and milk, with a sweetener and flavoring added. To prepare a successful baked custard a ratio of 10 to 12 oz. of whole eggs to each quart of milk is required, and proper baking is essential. Custard can be baked in a pan or in individual custard cups.

Baked custard can be served plain, garnished with a little cinnamon, nutmeg, or both, or with an appropriate sauce.

Objectives

1. To teach the student the procedure for preparing baked custard.
2. To teach the student how to bake custard.
3. To teach the student how to serve baked custard.

Equipment

1. 25 individual custard cups
2. 2 bake pans
3. Wire whip
4. Quart measure
5. Spoon measures
6. Sauce pot
7. Baker's scale
8. Wooden spoon

Ingredients: Approx. yield: 25 servings

3	qts. milk
2	lb. whole eggs
1½	tsp. vanilla
½	tsp. salt
1	lb. sugar

Preparation

1. Break the eggs into a stainless steel mixing bowl and beat slightly with a wire whip.
2. Butter the inside of each individual custard cup.
3. Have all ingredients and equipment handy.

Procedure

1. Place the milk, salt, and vanilla in a sauce pot. Heat until scalding and remove from the heat.
2. Add the sugar to the mixing bowl containing the eggs. Blend thoroughly, using a wooden spoon, but do not whip.

3. Pour some of the hot milk slowly into the egg-sugar mixture while stirring rapidly with a wooden spoon, then pour this mixture into the remaining hot milk, continuing to stir rapidly.
4. Pour the custard mixture into the buttered custard cups. Place in bake pans approximately two-thirds full of water.
5. Place bake pans in the oven and bake at 375° F. until custard has just set.
6. Remove from the oven and let set until firm and cool.
7. Unmold on a dessert plate and serve topped with cinnamon and nutmeg, whipped cream, or an appropriate sauce such as vanilla, cherry, lemon, etc.

Precautions and Safety Measures
1. Beat the eggs only slightly; overbeating them may prevent a smooth custard.
2. When adding the hot milk to the egg mixture, and again when adding the egg mixture to the remaining hot milk, stir constantly and with a rapid motion.
3. Bake the custard only until it is just set, because custard will continue to cook after it leaves the oven. If the custard is shaky when it is removed from the oven, don't be concerned. It will become firm when cool.

VARIATIONS:

For *coffee custard,* add ½ cup of instant coffee to the hot milk.

For *caramel custard,* boil together 2 lb. granulated sugar and 1 lb. water until a temperature of 330° F. is reached or until the mixture becomes dark. Pour about ¼ inch of this syrup into dry custard cups and proceed as above.

CHILLED PUDDINGS

Rice imperatrice

Rice imperatrice is a chilled dessert that has excellent eye appeal because of its two-tone color. The top of this molded dessert contains red gelatin and the bottom a creamy rice mixture.

Rice imperatrice is served with an appropriate cold sauce.

Objectives
1. To teach the student the procedure for preparing rice imperatrice.
2. To teach the student how to whip cream and fold it into the jellied rice mixture.
3. To teach the student how to unmold and serve rice imperatrice.

Equipment
1. 25 fairly large individual gelatin molds 2½ to 3 inches deep
2. Wooden spoon
3. Skimmer
4. Sauce pot
5. Stainless steel mixing bowls (medium and small)
6. Wire whip
7. Mixing machine and wire whip
8. French knife
9. Quart measure
10. Baker's scale
11. Hotel pan

Ingredients: Approx. yield: 25 servings

8	oz. flavored gelatin: raspberry, cherry, or strawberry
1	pt. hot water
1	pt. cold water
1	qt. milk
1	qt. single cream
1	tsp. vanilla
1	lb. rice
2	oz. plain gelatin (unflavored)
1	pt. cold water
10	egg yolks
1	lb. sugar
1	pt. whipping cream
5	oz. maraschino red cherries, chopped
	or
8	oz. candied fruit, washed and chopped

Preparation
1. Wash the rice and drain thoroughly.
2. Separate the egg yolks from the whites. Place the yolks in the medium size stainless steel mixing bowl. Place the whites in a separate container and hold for use in another preparation.
3. Chop the maraschino red cherries with a French knife, or wash and chop the candied fruit.

4. Heat 1 pt. of water until scalding hot.
5. Place the plain gelatin in the small stainless steel mixing bowl, add the pint of cold water, stir, and let set.
6. Have all equipment and ingredients handy.

Procedure
1. Dissolve the flavored gelatin in the pint of scalding water. Stir until thoroughly dissolved. Add the pint of cold water and stir until blended.
2. Pour the dissolved gelatin into the individual molds until about ½ inch deep.
3. Place molds in the refrigerator until gelatin sets.
4. Place the milk, single cream, and vanilla in a sauce pot and bring to a simmer.
5. Add the washed rice and cook slowly, stirring frequently with a wooden spoon, until rice is tender. Remove from the heat.
6. Add the plain gelatin, which was dissolved in the cold water, stir with a wooden spoon until thoroughly blended.
7. Add the sugar to the egg yolks and whip slightly with a wire whip. Pour slowly into the cooked rice while stirring rapidly with a wire whip.
8. Pour the rice mixture into a hotel pan, place in the refrigerator and let cool until it starts to set.
9. Place the whipping cream in the bowl of an electric mixer, whip until stiff.
10. Remove the rice mixture from the refrigerator when it starts to set. Fold in the whipped cream and chopped fruit, using a skimmer. Blend together thoroughly.
11. Remove the gelatin molds from the refrigerator and complete filling them with the rice mixture.
12. Return molds to the refrigerator and chill until firm.
13. Unmold by dipping each mold in warm water and serve on dessert plate, covering each serving with an appropriate sauce such as vanilla or lemon.

Precautions and Safety Measures
1. Exercise caution when chopping the fruit.
2. Dissolve the flavored gelatin in the scalding water thoroughly or gelatin will not set properly.

3. Always soak plain gelatin in cold water before adding it to a hot mixture. It will dissolve quicker and will not lump.
4. When whipping the cream, the bowl, whip, and cream should all be cold.
5. Use a very gentle motion when folding the whipped cream into the rice mixture.

Chocolate mousse

Chocolate mousse is a very light, delicate dessert. A mousse is always light and fluffy. It is similar in many respects to a Bavarian or chiffon filling because whipped cream, meringue, or both, are folded into the basic mixture to incorporate air and produce a light, delicate texture. A mousse may or may not contain gelatin to help it set up. This would depend on the kind of mousse and the ingredients used. Mousses are especially popular in establishments serving French cuisine.

Objectives
1. To teach the student the procedure for preparing chocolate mousse.
2. To teach the student how to whip egg whites and cream.
3. To teach the student how to fold the egg whites and cream into the chocolate mixture.
4. To teach the student how to serve chocolate mousse.

Equipment
1. Electric mixer and wire whip
2. Baker's scale
3. Pint measure
4. Small double boiler
5. Stainless steel mixing bowls (2 medium)
6. Wooden spoon
7. Skimmer

Ingredients: Approx. yield: 25 servings
2	lb. sweet chocolate, grated
12	oz. water
12	egg yolks
12	egg whites
10	oz. sugar
1	pt. whipping cream

Preparation

1. Separate the egg yolks from the whites, placing in separate medium size stainless steel bowls.
2. Have all equipment and ingredients handy.

Procedure

1. Place the chocolate and water in the top of a small double boiler. Heat until the chocolate melts and blends with the water. Stir occasionally with a wooden spoon.
2. Remove the chocolate from the heat and let cool. Stir occasionally to speed cooling.
3. When the chocolate mixture starts to set, add the slightly beaten egg yolks while whipping briskly with a wire whip. If mixture becomes too stiff add a little milk. Set aside and hold for later use.
4. Place the egg whites in the bowl of the electric mixer and whip at high speed until they start to froth. Add the sugar slowly until a fairly stiff meringue is formed. Place in a stainless steel bowl and hold for later use.
5. Place the whipped cream in the bowl of the electric mixer and whip at high speed until stiff. Remove from the mixer.
6. Fold the whipped cream and meringue alternately into the chocolate mixture, using a skimmer or wooden spoon.
7. Pour the mixture into individual silver cups, cocktail glasses or champagne glasses and chill in the refrigerator until ready to serve.

Precautions and Safety Measures

1. The egg yolk and chocolate mixture should be fairly stiff; however, if it is too stiff problems could develop when folding. The mixture can be made thinner by adding a very small amount of milk.
2. For best results in whipping the cream, have the mixing bowl and whip cold, as well as the cream. Whip only until stiff, but don't over-whip.
3. When preparing the meringue, whip at high speed and add the sugar gradually after the egg whites start to froth. Continue whipping until soft peaks form.

Vanilla Bavarian cream (with variations)

Vanilla Bavarian cream is a light, smooth, and fluffy desert. Whipped cream is folded into a basic gelatin mixture to create a delicate texture that is characteristic of all Bavarians.

Bavarians can be set up and served in individual portions or for group servings. They may be featured in molded form or in a silver cup, cocktail glass, or champagne glass. They may be served with or without a cold sauce.

Objectives

1. To teach the student the procedure for preparing vanilla Bavarian cream and its variations.
2. To teach the student how to whip cream.
3. To teach the student how to fold the whipped cream into the basic gelatin mixture.
4. To teach the student how to serve vanilla Bavarian cream and its variations.

Equipment

1. Electric mixer and wire whip
2. Quart measure
3. Wooden spoon
4. Baker's scale
5. Wire whip
6. Double boiler
7. Skimmer
8. Stainless steel mixing bowls

Ingredients: Approx. yield: 25 servings

1½	qts. milk
2	oz. unflavored gelatin
1	pt. water, cold
16	egg yolks
12	oz. sugar
1	qt. whipping cream
	vanilla, to taste

Preparation

1. Separate the egg yolks from the whites. Place yolks in a stainless steel bowl. Keep whites for use in another preparation.
2. Place unflavored gelatin in stainless steel bowl, add the cold water, and let soak to soften gelatin.
3. Have all equipment and ingredients handy.

Procedure

1. Place the milk in the top of a double boiler and heat. Remove from the double boiler.
2. Add 8 oz. of the sugar to the egg yolks in the stainless steel bowl, whipping gently until the mixture is stiff and smooth.
3. Pour the hot milk gradually into the sugar and egg yolk mixture while whipping briskly with a wire whip.
4. Add the remaining sugar, the vanilla, and water and gelatin mixture. Stir with a

wooden spoon until the gelatin mixture is dissolved and thoroughly incorporated.

5. Place this mixture in the refrigerator to cool until it begins to set.

6. Place the whipping cream in the bowl of the electric mixer and whip at high speed until stiff. Remove from the mixer.

7. Fold the whipped cream into the cold vanilla mixture, using a skimmer or wooden spoon.

8. Pour the mixture into individual or large size molds, silver cups, cocktail glasses or champagne glasses. Serve unmolded with an appropriate cold sauce or leave in cup or glass and garnish the top with whipped cream and candied fruit.

Precautions and Safety Measures

1. When cooling the basic mixture do not let it set too firm. Jelly-like consistency will produce best results.

2. When adding the hot milk to the egg yolk mixture pour the milk slowly and whip briskly to avoid burning the egg yolks.

3. When whipping cream, have the mixing bowl and whip cold, as well as the cream, for best results. Do not over-whip cream after it has become stiff.

4. Fold gently when adding the whipping cream to the vanilla mixture.

VARIATIONS:

For *chocolate Bavarian cream*, add 3 oz. unsweetened and 12 oz. sweet chocolate to the hot milk.

For *mocha Bavarian cream*, add 4 tbs. of instant coffee to the hot milk.

For *walnut Bavarian cream*, add 4 to 6 oz. of finely chopped walnuts to the vanilla Bavarian cream.

Lemon snow pudding

Lemon snow pudding, when served in molded form, resembles a mound of snow. A meringue is folded into a whipped lemon gelatin mixture to create this light, delicate, eye-appealing dessert.

Serve lemon snow pudding on an appropriate cold sauce with a contrasting color.

Objectives

1. To teach the student the procedure for preparing lemon snow pudding.

2. To teach the student how to soak and dissolve unflavored gelatin.

3. To teach the student how to prepare a meringue.

4. To teach the student how to fold the meringue into the lemon gelatin mixture.

5. To teach the student how to serve lemon snow pudding.

Equipment

1. Baker's scale
2. Quart measure
3. Spoon measure
4. Stainless steel bowl
5. Grater
6. Mixing machine and wire whip
7. Sauce pot
8. Hotel pan
9. Wooden spoon
10. Skimmer

Ingredients: Approx. yield: 25 servings

1	qt boiling water
8	oz. cold water
1¼	oz. unflavored gelatin
1	lb. sugar
8	oz. lemon juice
2	tbs. lemon rind, grated
1	pt. egg whites
12	oz. sugar

Preparation

1. Separate the egg yolks from the whites. Save the yolks for another preparation.

2. Place the unflavored gelatin in a stainless steel bowl, add the cold water, and let soak until gelatin is soft.

3. Grate the lemon rind on the fairly fine grid of a box grater.

4. Squeeze the juice from fresh lemons.

5. Have all equipment and ingredients handy.

Procedure

1. Place 1 qt. of water in a sauce pot, place on the range and bring to a boil. Remove from heat.

2. Add the softened gelatin, first amount of sugar, lemon juice and lemon rind. Stir with a wooden spoon until gelatin and sugar are thoroughly dissolved.

3. Pour into a bake pan, place in the refrigerator until the mixture starts to set.

4. Place the egg white in the bowl of the electric mixer and whip at high speed until

the egg whites start to froth. Add the second amount of sugar gradually while continuing to whip at high speed until stiff peaks are formed. Remove from mixer and hold.

5. Remove the lemon gelatin mixture from the refrigerator, place in the bowl of the electric mixer, and whip at high speed until light and fluffy.

6. Fold the meringue into the whipped gelatin mixture gradually, using a skimmer, until thoroughly blended.

7. Pour into large or individual molds and refrigerate until set.

8. Remove from the refrigerator, unmold, and serve on an appropriate cold sauce.

Precautions and Safety Measures

1. To whip the meringue properly, the mixer should be running at high speed throughout the operation and the sugar must be added slowly.

2. Fold the meringue gently into the lemon gelatin mixture to preserve as many air cells as possible.

3. Exercise caution when grating the lemon rind. Avoid scraping fingers.

4. Remove the lemon mixture from the refrigerator as soon as it starts to set.

SOUFFLE PUDDINGS

Basic vanilla soufflé (with variations)

Basic vanilla soufflé will produce many variations by the addition of other ingredients. All soufflés should be prepared to order and served at once, with a sauce. Whipping the egg whites, folding them into the basic mix, and proper baking are all very important steps in producing a successful soufflé.

Objectives

1. To teach the student the procedure for preparing basic vanilla soufflé and its variations.

2. To teach the student how to whip the egg whites.

3. To teach the student how to fold the egg whites into the basic vanilla mixture.

4. To teach the student how to prepare a soufflé baking dish and how to bake the soufflé properly.

5. To teach the student how to serve a basic vanilla soufflé and its variations.

Equipment

1. Small bake pan
2. Electric mixer and wire whip
3. Sauce pot
4. Wire whip
5. Baker's scale
6. Pint measure
7. 2 stainless steel bowls
8. Soufflé cups or dishes (special casseroles)
9. Skimmer

Ingredients: Approx. yield: 12 servings

3	oz. bread flour
3	oz. butter
3	oz. sugar
1	pt. milk
8	egg yolks
10	egg whites
3	oz. sugar
	vanilla, to taste

Preparation

1. Separate the egg yolks from the whites and place in separate stainless steel bowls.

2. Butter soufflé cups or dish and dredge with granulated sugar.

3. Pre-heat the oven to 425° F.

4. Have all equipment and ingredients handy.

Procedure

1. Place the milk and vanilla in a sauce pot. Bring to a boil on the range, and remove from the heat.

2. In a small bake pan place the bread flour, butter, and the first amount of sugar. Rub together, by hand, to form a smooth paste.

3. Add this paste to the hot milk while whipping briskly with a wire whip.

4. Return mixture to the range and cook gently for approximately 2 minutes.

5. Place the hot mixture in a round stainless steel bowl and add the egg yolks, one at a time, while whipping with a wire whip after each addition.

6. Place the egg whites in the bowl of the electric mixer, and whip at high speed until the egg whites start to froth. Add the second amount of sugar gradually while continuing to whip at high speed until soft peaks form.

7. Fold the meringue immediately into the creamy vanilla mixture, using a skimmer. Blend gently.
8. Fill the prepared soufflé cups or dish to within ½ inch of the top. Sprinkle heavily with powdered sugar and bake immediately at 425° F. for approximately 25 minutes (depending on size of cup or dish) until golden brown.
9. Serve immediately with an appropriate sauce.

Precautions and Safety Measures
1. The egg whites should be stiff, but not dry, in order to obtain best results.
2. Fold the meringue carefully into the creamy vanilla mixture. Do not over-mix.
3. Never let the oven temperature exceed 425° F. Check oven with a thermometer.
4. Butter the baking dish or dishes generously with butter and dredge thoroughly with granulated sugar.

VARIATIONS:

For *chocolate soufflé*, add 1½ oz. of sweet chocolate (melted) to the hot vanilla mixture at the same time the egg yolks are added. Increase the egg yolks to 10 and the egg whites to 12.

For *mocha soufflé*, add 2 tbs. of instant coffee to the hot vanilla mixture.

For *orange soufflé*, add 3 oz. of grand marnier liqueur and 2 tbs. of grated orange peel to the hot vanilla mixture.

For *cherry soufflé*, add 2 oz. Kirschwasser and 4 oz. of chopped candied cherries to the hot vanilla mixture.

STEAMED PUDDINGS

Plum pudding

Plum pudding is one of the most popular steamed puddings. This pudding has a very heavy texture because the ratio of fruit to batter is about two to one. It should be served with a hot sauce unless a hard sauce is used. Traditionally plum pudding is most popular during the Christmas season.

Objectives
1. To teach the student the procedure for preparing plum pudding.
2. To teach the student how to steam plum pudding.
3. To teach the student how to serve plum pudding.

Equipment
1. Electric mixer and paddle
2. Baker's scale
3. Steam table pan
4. Stainless steel bowl
5. Wire whip

Ingredients: Approx. yield: 25 servings
8 oz. butter
8 oz. brown sugar
⅛ oz. salt
⅛ oz. allspice
½ oz. ginger
8 oz. whole eggs
8 oz. dark molasses
3 oz. rum
3 oz. brandy
8 oz. bread flour
1 lb. raisins
1 lb. 8 oz. currants
8 oz. citrons
8 oz. orange peel
4 oz. lemon peel
8 oz. bread crumbs

Preparation
1. Break the eggs and place in a stainless steel bowl. Beat slightly with a wire whip.
2. Grease steam table pan lightly with butter and dust with flour.
3. Have all equipment and ingredients handy.

Procedure
1. Place the butter, brown sugar, salt and spices in the bowl of the electric mixer. Cream together at slow speed, using the paddle.
2. Add the slightly beaten eggs while continuing to mix at slow speed. Blend thoroughly.
3. Add the molasses, rum and brandy, continuing to mix at slow speed until mixture is thoroughly blended and smooth.
4. Add the bread flour, raisins, currants, citrons, orange peel and lemon peel, and mix until blended.

5. Add the bread crumbs and mix until thoroughly incorporated.
6. Pack the pudding in prepared steam table pan, filling only 2/3 full to allow for expansion in cooking. Cover the pan with aluminum foil, place in steamer, and steam for 2 hours.
7. Remove from steamer. For each serving place a No. 12 scoop of pudding in a dessert bowl or on a dessert plate and serve with a hard sauce or a hot sauce such as brandy, vanilla, or rum.

Precautions and Safety Measures
1. Exercise extreme caution when removing the pudding from the steamer.
2. Fill the pan only two-thirds full of pudding, because it will expand while in the steamer.

PARFAITS

Parfaits are eye-appealing, tasty and elegant ice cream desserts that are prepared by alternating layers of crushed fruit or syrup and various colored and flavored ice creams. They are topped with whipped cream, chopped nuts and maraschino cherry.

Parfaits may be served immediately after they are made or placed in the freezer and held for service at a later date. The fact that they can be made up ahead of the serving time makes them ideal for serving large parties.

The following are just a few of the many variations of this very attractive and popular dessert.

Parfait crème de menthe
Alternate layers of crème de menthe and vanilla ice cream. Garnish with whipped cream, chopped nuts, and maraschino cherry.

Rainbow parfait
Alternate layers of strawberry sauce and vanilla, strawberry and chocolate ice cream. Garnish with fresh strawberries and chopped nuts.

Parfait Melba
Alternate layers of Melba sauce and vanilla ice cream. Garnish with fresh raspberries and whipped cream.

Pineapple parfait
Alternate layers of crushed pineapple and vanilla ice cream or lemon sherbet. Garnish with whipped cream, chopped nuts and maraschino cherry.

Chocolate parfait
Alternate layers of chocolate syrup and vanilla or chocolate ice cream. Garnish with chocolate shot, whipped cream and maraschino cherry.

Strawberry parfait
Alternate layers of strawberry sauce and vanilla ice cream. Garnish with whipped cream, chopped nuts and fresh strawberries.

Butterscotch parfait
Alternate layers of butterscotch sauce and vanilla ice cream. Garnish with whipped cream, chopped nuts and maraschino cherry.

United Fresh Fruit and Vegetable Association
Parfaits.

COUPES

Coupes are desserts combining ice cream or sherbet, liqueurs, sauces, fruit, and whipped cream. They are arranged in champagne glasses or silver cups in a way that will be attractive and eye-appealing. Coupes are economical and quick to prepare and can in some cases be partially prepared, frozen, and finished at serving time.

The following are just a few of the many variations of this famous dessert created and made popular by master French chefs such as Careme and Escoffier.

Coupe Melba

Vanilla ice cream covered with peach half and topped with Melba sauce, garnished with whipped cream and a sliced peach.

Coupe Hélène

Vanilla ice cream covered with a half of Bartlett pear and topped with chocolate sauce, garnished with whipped cream and a maraschino cherry.

Strawberry coupe

Vanilla ice cream covered with fresh strawberries that have been tossed in curaçao liqueur, garnished with whipped cream and a fresh strawberry.

Pineapple coupe

Vanilla ice cream covered with diced pineapple flavored with Kirschwasser, garnished with whipped cream and a maraschino cherry.

Coupe savory

Assorted diced fresh fruit flavored with anisette liqueur, covered with mocha ice cream and garnished with whipped cream and chopped nuts.

JUBILEES

Jubilees are a combination of ice cream and a flaming fruit sauce that is poured over the ice cream, in front of the guest, while the liqueuer is still aflame. It is the most spectacular of desserts and is unique in that the sauce keeps flaming momentarily when it comes in contact with the cold ice cream.

The flame is extinguished when all the alcohol has been burned out, and the exquisite flavor remains to blend itself with the ice cream that is only slightly melted on the surface.

The most popular jubilee is the cherry jubilee; however, other fruits such as peaches, strawberries, and oranges may also be used to create a variety of jubilees.

Cherry jubilee

Ingredients: Approx. yield: 4 servings
- 1   pt. pitted Bing cherries and juice
- ¼   cup sugar
- ¼   tsp. arrowroot
- 2   oz. Kirschwasser
- 4   large scoops of vanilla ice cream

Procedure
1. Pour the juice from the pint of cherries into the blazer of a chafing dish. Reserve enough juice to dissolve the arrowroot.
2. Place the blazer pan directly over the flame of the chafing dish and bring the juice to a boil.
3. Dissolve the arrowroot in the reserved cherry juice and pour slowly into the boiling juice while stirring constantly. Cook until the juice is slightly thickened.
4. Add the sugar and reduce heat to a simmer.
5. Add the cherries, stirring them into the sauce.
6. Heat the Kirschwasser in a separate pan and pour the warm (not hot) liqueur over the cherry mixture.
7. Ignite the liqueur and pour the flaming cherry mixture over each scoop of ice cream.

Note: The above preparation should be done before the guest.

Strawberry jubilee

Ingredients: Approx. yield: 4 servings
- 1   pt. whole strawberries and juice, frozen
- ½   tsp. arrowroot
- 1   oz. cointreau

2 oz. brandy
4 large scoops vanilla ice cream

Procedure
1. Pour the juice from the thawed berries into the blazer of a chafing dish. Reserve enough juice to dissolve the arrowroot.
2. Place the blazer pan directly over the flame of the chafing dish and bring the juice to a boil.
3. Dissolve the arrowroot in the reserved strawberry juice and pour slowly into the boiling juice, while stirring constantly. Cook until juice is slightly thickened.
4. Add the strawberries and cointreau and stir into the sauce.
5. Heat the brandy in a separate pan and pour the warm (not hot) brandy over the strawberries.
6. Ignite the brandy and pour the flaming strawberry mixture over each scoop of ice cream.

Note: The above preparation should be done before the guest.

BAKED ALASKA

Baked Alaska is a combination of cake, ice cream, and meringue. It is a dessert that will stimulate both appetite and conversation because of its decorative appearance and an element of surprise that has made it world famous. This dessert is unique in that it has an ice cream center and a golden brown outside and it can also be set aflame.

Baked Alaska can be set up for an individual serving or for a number of servings. It can be prepared ahead of service and held in the freezer. The outside meringue covering can then be browned in the oven or with a blow torch just before serving.

Baked Alaska (standard recipe)

Ingredients: Approx. yield: Depends on size set up
    ice cream (vanilla, chocolate, strawberry, etc., in any combination)
    sponge or pound cake (pages 606 and 612)
    meringue, as needed (page 592)

Procedure
1. Place a layer of sponge cake approximately ½ to 1 inch thick on a silver or stainless steel platter. Cut the cake the shape of the platter, leaving a 3-inch margin.
2. Cover the cake with ice cream, using the flavor desired or combination of flavors distributed evenly. Mold the ice cream to a height of approximately 4 inches.
3. Cover the ice cream with very thin sheets of sponge cake, cut about ¼ inch thick. Cover with a cloth and place in the freezer several hours, until the ice cream is quite solid.
4. Remove from the freezer and cover entirely with meringue, using a spatula to produce a smooth surface.
5. Fill a pastry bag with the meringue. Using a star tube in the tip of the bag, decorate the baked Alaska as desired. (The meringue placed in the pastry bag may be tinted a pastel color if a two-tone Alaska is desired.)
6. Dust the baked Alaska entirely with powdered sugar and brown very quickly in a hot oven (450° F.) or brown with a blow torch. Using a torch will eliminate any chance of melting the ice cream.
7. Serve the baked Alaska immediately, with an appropriate sauce, or return it to the freezer for later use. To present a baked Alaska flambé, press half-egg shells into the top, hiding the sides of the shells with meringue. Pour a small amount of warm brandy or rum into the shells, ignite, and carry the flaming baked Alaska into the dining room.

Note: The same preparation can be made with either white or yellow pound cake rather than the more usual sponge cake. Pound cake is preferable because it has better eating qualities and is easier to slice.

Individual baked Alaska

Individual baked Alaska is essentially the same as the standard recipe, differing only in form and certain details of the procedure to be followed.

From sheet of sponge or pound cake sliced about ½ inch thick, cut out rounds approximately 3 inches in diameter and place them on a sheet pan about 3 inches apart.

Place a No. 12 scoop of ice cream on top of each 3-inch cake round. Cover with a cloth and place in the freezer until the ice cream is quite solid.

Fill a pastry bag with meringue and, using a star tube in the tip, cover the ice cream entirely, creating some type of decorative design.

Dust with powdered sugar and brown quickly in a 450° F. oven or with a blow torch.

Serve immediately, plain or flambé. To flame, pour warm brandy or rum over the individual baked Alaska, ignite and serve aflame.

Hawaiian baked Alaska

Ingredients: Approx. yield: 2 servings
1 fresh pineapple, ripe
ice cream (vanilla, chocolate or strawberry, or an assortment of all three), as needed
meringue (page 592), as needed
Procedure
1. Cut the fresh pineapple in half, lengthwise.
2. Scoop the meat out of the center of the pineapple, leaving the wall of the pine-

United Fresh Fruit and Vegetable Association

Hawaiian baked Alaska.

apple about ½ inch thick. Place the scooped-out pineapple half on a platter.
3. Fill the pineapple cavity with the desired type of ice cream and place in the freezer until the ice cream is quite solid.
4. Remove from the freezer. Fill a pastry bag with meringue and, using a star tube in the tip, cover the ice cream entirely, creating some kind of decorative design.
5. Dust with powdered sugar and brown quickly in a 450° F. oven or with a blow torch.
6. Serve immediately, plain or flambé. To flame, pour warm brandy or rum over the Hawaiian baked Alaska, ignite and serve aflame.

CREPE DESSERTS

Crêpe desserts are all prepared by using the thin french pancakes called crêpes. The recipe for their preparation is given in Chapter 7 on "Breakfast Preparations", page 79. Most crêpe desserts will call for 3 crêpes, approximately 5 inches in diameter, for each order.

The crêpes are either rolled or folded in four, with or without a filling, and served with a hot, sweet sauce. Often these desserts are served to the guest while they are aflame. Brandy, rum, or cognac are the liqueurs used most because of their alcohol content and flavor.

A liqueur will burn best if it is approximately 100 proof and slightly warm. Never boil a liqueur, because the alcohol will be boiled off and the liqueur cannot be ignited.

Crêpes are usually prepared ahead of service and stacked on a sheet pan between layers of silacone or wax paper, covered with a damp towel and stored in a cool place until ready to use.

The most famous and popular crêpe dessert is called crêpe Suzette; however there are others of equal merit but less well known.

Crêpe Suzette

Ingredients: Approx. yield: 4 servings
12 French pancakes (crêpes)
4 oz. sugar
1 tbs. orange rind, grated

1 tsp. lemon rind, grated
¼ cup orange juice
1 tbs. lemon juice
3 oz. butter
1 oz. grand marnier
2 oz. cognac

Procedure
1. Sprinkle 3 oz. of the sugar in the blazer pan of a chafing dish and melt over low heat while stirring constantly with wooden spoon.
2. Add the orange and lemon rind, continuing to cook until the sugar is slightly brown.
3. Add the butter, orange and lemon juice, and stir until thoroughly blended. Do not let mixture boil.
4. Place the crêpes, one at a time, into the sauce. Sprinkle the remaining sugar over the crêpes, turn them over at least once, and fold in four, piling them around the sides of the pan.
5. Add warm congnac to the sauce, ignite and let flame while moving the pan back and forth gently.
6. Serve 3 crêpes to each order on a hot plate and pour on flaming sauce.

Note: The above preparation should be done before the guest.

SPECIALTY PASTRIES

Puff paste dough (with variations)

Puff paste dough is an unusual type of dough because it contains no sugar or leavening agent; yet, when heat is applied, it rises to approximately 8 times its original size. This is brought about by rolling and folding alternate layers of fat and dough a total of five times. Much care must be exercised when preparing this type of dough. And, since a minimum of 15 to 20 minutes should be allowed between each of the five rollings and foldings, preparation is time-consuming.

Puff paste dough has a texture that is very tender, flaky, and crisp. A wide variety of baked goods can be prepared by using puff paste.
Objectives
1. To teach the student the procedure for preparing puff paste dough.

Swift and Co.

Assortment of desserts created with puff paste dough.

2. To teach the student how to scale the ingredients and mix the dough.
3. To teach the student how to roll the puff paste shortening into the dough.
4. To teach the student how to roll, fold, make up and bake puff paste dough.
Equipment
1. Mixing machine and dough hook
2. Baker's scale
3. Sheet pans
4. Silicone paper
5. Rolling pin
6. Bench brush
7. Pastry wheel
8. 3-in. and 2-in. round cutter (for patty shells)
9. Yard stick (for turnovers, cream horns, or lady locks)
10. Dough docker or dinner fork

Ingredients: Approx. yield: Determined by the item being prepared
5 lb. bread flour
8 oz. whole eggs
8 oz. butter
1 oz. salt
2 lb. 4 oz. cold water, variable
5 lb. puff paste shortening
Preparation
1. Scale 5 lb. puff paste shortening. Break shortening into fairly small pieces, place on a sheet pan covered with wax paper. Let set

at room temperature. This is done so shortening will have the same consistency as the dough when rolled in. If one is stiffer than the other a poor dough will result.

2. Prepare sheet pans. Cover pans with silicone paper if preparing turnovers, patty shells, lady locks, cream horns, or puff paste stars. If preparing Napoleon slices, dampen sheet pan with cold water.

3. Light the oven and preheat to 375°F.

4. Have all equipment and ingredients handy.

Procedure

1. Place the bread flour, salt, butter, whole eggs, and cold water in the electric mixing bowl. Using the dough hook, mix in slow speed, then second speed, until a very smooth dough is formed.

2. Remove the dough from the mixer, place on a floured bench, and round up into the shape of a smooth ball.

3. Cover the dough with a damp cloth and let rest on the bench for 15 to 20 minutes.

4. Roll the dough into a rectangular shape twice as long as it is wide and approximately ¼ to ½ inch thick.

5. Spot the puff paste shortening evenly over two-thirds of the dough's surface. Do *not* bring the shortening to the edge of the dough; keep it about ½ inch from the edge.

6. Fold over the unspotted third of the dough over one half of the spotted portion. Then fold the remaining spotted one-third of dough over this folded portion, completing a three-fold dough.

7. Brush the dough free of excess flour and give it a half turn, so the former length now becomes the width. Proceed to roll out the dough into a rectangular shape a second time. This rectangle should be twice as long as wide and about ½ inch thick. Again brush off excess flour.

8. Fold both ends of the dough toward the middle, then double again. This is referred to as a *pocketbook fold*. Place the dough on a sheet pan and cover with a damp cloth. Refrigerate for 15 to 20 minutes.

9. Remove the dough from the refrigerator and repeat the rolling and folding process a total of five times, but each time allow the dough to rest in the refrigerator 15 to 20 minutes. The width of the previous roll should be rolled into the length each time.

10. After rolling the dough for the fifth time, the dough should be made up into desired units. Allow the units to stand 30 minutes before baking at 375°F.

Swift and Co.

Puff paste shortening purchased in pressed squares is placed in center of rectangle of dough.

Swift and Co.

The two end pieces of dough that are free of shortening are folded over the shortening and brought together in center.

Swift and Co.

First fold of dough

Three-fold method of rolling and folding described in Step 6 of procedure.

Swift and Co.

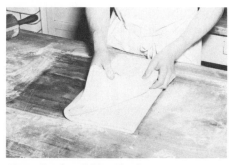

Alternative four-fold method, called the "pocketbook" method.

Swift and Co.

Precautions and Safety Measures

1. The dough and shortening should always be of the same consistency to prevent rupture of the dough walls.
2. Between each rolling allow the dough to rest in a cool place for 15 to 20 mins. This permits the gluten in the dough to relax, making the dough easier to roll.
3. All excess flour should be brushed off before folding over the dough. Excess flour will toughen the dough.
4. Care must be taken that the puff paste shortening is evenly distributed through the dough. All corners and ends should be even when dough is folded.

5. Left-over puff paste will require additional rolling and folding before it can be made into units.

Swift and Co.

Forming patty shells

VARIATIONS:

Patty shells: Roll out a piece of puff paste dough approximately ⅛ inch thick. Cut out rounds three inches in diameter, using a plain or scalloped-edge cutter. Place these rounds on a sheet pan covered with silicone paper.

Take a second piece of puff paste dough and roll it to a thickness of ¼ inch. Using the same size cutter, cut the second piece of dough into 3-inch rounds. Then cut the center out of these thicker rounds by using a 2-inch cutter.

Wash the first rounds with water and place the rings (cut from the second rounds) on top. Continue this procedure until all of the first rounds are covered with the rings. Wash them with egg wash (eggs and milk) and allow to stand at room temperature for 30 minutes.

Place a piece of greased paper over the top of the patty shells so they will not topple over while they are baking. Place them in the oven and bake at 375°F. until they are crisp and dry. They will rise up to approximately 2 to 2½ inches high. Remove from the oven and let cool.

Patty shells can be filled with fruit topped with whipped cream or, if served as an entrée, they can be filled with chicken à la king, shrimp, lobster, seafood Newburg, creamed ham, or cream chicken and mushrooms.

Turnovers: Roll out a piece of puff paste dough to a thickness of approximately ⅛ inch. Cut the dough into 4-inch squares. Dampen the surface of the dough with water.

Spot the center of each square with the desired kind of fruit filling and fold cornerwise to form a triangle. Secure the edges with tines of a dinner fork and puncture the top of the turnover twice with the fork tines.

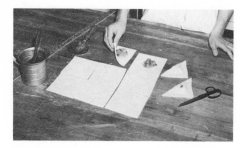

Forming turnovers

Swift and Co.

Forming puff paste pocketbooks

Swift and Co.

Place the turnovers on sheet pans covered with silicone paper. Allow them to stand at room temperature for 30 mins., then bake at 375°F.

Turnovers may be made up and baked without filling. In this case the filling is added after baking by splitting them slightly with a knife and adding the filling with a spoon or pastry bag. Before serving, turnovers may be iced with a roll icing or dusted with powdered sugar.

Lady locks or cream horns: Roll the puff pastry dough into a thin rectangle about 48 inches long and 15 inches wide, about ⅛ inch thick. Cut this sheet of dough into strips approximately 1¼ inches wide, using a pastry wheel. Wash the surface of the dough slightly with water and roll each strip around a lady lock or cream horn tin, starting at the small end of the tin and overlapping the dough strip slightly as you follow a diagonal direction around the tin. Leave about one inch of the tin exposed so it will be easier to remove after baking.

Place the lady locks or cream horns on a sheet pan covered with silicone paper and sprinkled with sanding sugar (very coarse sugar). Allow them to rest about 15 minutes before baking at 375°F. until golden brown.

Remove from the oven, pull the tins out of the horns while they are still hot, and let them cool. After cooling, fill the centers of the baked horns with whipped cream, meringue topping, or cream filling. Dust with powdered sugar and serve.

Puff paste pocketbooks: Roll out the puff paste dough to a thickness of ¼ inch. Cut the dough into 4-inch squares. Turn each of the four corners into the center and secure by pressing the dough with your finger.

Place the pocketbooks on a sheet pan covered with silicone paper, let rest for 30 minutes, and bake at 375°F. until the dough puffs upward and outward and is golden brown.

Remove from the oven, let cool. Poke a hole into the center of each pocketbook and fill with the desired fruit filling. Dust with powdered sugar and serve.

Napoleon slices: Roll out a piece of the puff paste dough quite thin (approximately ⅛ inch thick). Place the thin sheet of dough on a sheet pan and allow to stand for about 30 mins.

Pick the dough with a docker or the tines of a dinner fork all over to prevent blistering while baking.

Bake the dough at 350°F. until dry and crisp, but do not over-brown.

After baking, cut into three equal strips, stack the strips together with a rich cream filling between each layer.

Frost the top with two different colors of fondant icings (for example, white and chocolate), draw the two colors together *before the icing sets*, by using the edge of a spatula. This will create a marbelized effect. When fondant sets, cut into bars about four inches long and two inches wide.

Napoleon slices

Swift and Co.

Cream slices: Roll out the puff paste dough to a thickness of ⅛ inch. Brush the surface of the dough with water, then sprinkle with shaved almonds. Cut the dough into units 2 inches wide and 4 inches long.

Place on a sheet pan covered with silicone paper and allow to stand at room temperature for 30 minutes, then bake at 375°F. until golden brown and crisp. Let cool, then split each unit in two, fill with whipped topping or cream filling, dust with powdered sugar, and serve.

Eclair or choux paste (with variations)

Another unusual type of dough that contains no leavening agent. Yet, when heat is applied steam is created by the moisture in the mix and expansion takes place to form a crisp dough shell with a hollow center. The centers of these crisp shells are filled with various fillings to create interesting and unusual desserts. Cream puffs and éclairs are the most popular desserts made from this type of dough; however, many other variations can be created by exercising the imagination.

One reason why these desserts have maintained their popularity over the years is that they contain an element of surprise when cut into.

Objectives
1. To teach the student the procedure for preparing éclair or choux paste.
2. To teach the student how to form éclairs, cream puffs and other varieties.
3. To teach the student how to bake, cool, and make up éclairs, cream puffs and other varieties.

Equipment
1. Baker's scale
2. Sauce pot
3. Wooden spoon
4. Pastry bag
5. Plain pastry tube
6. Mixing machine and paddle
7. Kitchen spoon
8. Plastic scraper
9. Sheet pans
10. Silicone paper
11. Pint measure

Ingredients: Approx. Yield: Depends on item size

2	lb.	water
1	lb.	hydrogenated shortening
1	lb. 8 oz.	bread flour
2	lb.	whole eggs
¼	oz.	powdered ammonia
6	oz.	milk (variable)

Preparation
1. Place the milk in the pint measure, add the powdered ammonia, and dissolve.
2. Cover sheet pans with silicone paper.
3. Light the oven and preheat to 400°F.
4. Have all ingredients and equipment handy.

Procedure
1. Place the water and shortening in a sauce pot, place on the range, and bring to a rolling boil.
2. Reduce the heat and continue to boil at a less rapid rate until the shortening has completely melted.
3. Add the flour, stirring constantly with a wooden spoon, until the dough pulls away from the sides of the pot.
4. Remove from the range and place the cooked mixture in the mixing bowl.
5. Using the paddle, mix at medium speed (2nd position) for approximately one minute to cool mixture slightly.
6. Add the eggs gradually while continuing to mix at medium speed.
7. When all the eggs have been added, adjust the consistency of the paste by adding the ammonia-milk mixture. The paste should be stiff enough to hold its shape when formed.
8. Remove the paste from the mixing bowl, scrapping out with a plastic scraper.
9. Place the paste in a pastry bag with the plain pastry tube. On a sheet pan, covered with silicone paper, squeeze out to form paste into cream puffs, eclairs, or other desired varieties.
10. Place in the oven and bake at 400°F. until the shell is dry, crisp, and golden brown. Remove from the oven and cool in a warm place.

Note: Cream puffs can also be formed using a star tube or ice cream scoop.

Precautions and Safety Measures
1. Do not add the flour until the shortening has completely dissolved.
2. When adding the flour, stir with a wooden spoon. Never use a metal spoon, because metal rubbed against metal will give a metallic taste to the dough.

3. Keep the consistency of the paste fairly heavy so the items will hold their shape when formed.
4. After the shells (éclairs or cream puffs) are removed from the oven, cool them slowly in a warm place (top of oven). If cooled too quickly the shell may collapse.

VARIATIONS:

Cream puffs: Place the éclair or choux paste in a canvas pastry bag with a No. 8 star or a No. 8 plain pastry tube. Pipe the mixture through the tube onto sheet pans covered with silicone paper, into the shape of a mound approximately 2 inches in diameter at the base. The paste can also be deposited on the sheet pans by using a soup spoon or a No. 16 ice cream dipper.

Place in the oven and bake at 400°F. until the shell is dry, crisp, and golden brown.

Remove from the oven and cool gradually in a warm place. Fill the center of the shell with desired type of filling (such as vanilla pie filling, lemon filling, cream filling, or others) using an éclair filler or a pastry bag with a plain tip tube.

Place the filled cream puffs on a pastry screen and dust with confectionery sugar or drip fondant icing over the top and down the sides.

Frozen cream puffs: After baking the cream puffs, split them in half, crosswise. Fill the bottom half of the shell with ice cream of the desired flavor. Replace the top half of the shell. Place in the freezer until 15 minutes before serving time. Serve with an appropriate sauce.

Proctor and Gamble Co.

Cream puffs and èclairs

Eclairs: Place the éclair or choux paste in a canvas pastry bag with a No. 8 plain tip tube. Pipe the mixture through the tube onto sheet pans covered with silicone paper, into strips approximately 3½ to 4 inches long and 1 inch wide.

Place in the oven and bake at 400°F. until the shell is dry, crisp, and golden brown.

Remove from the oven and cool gradually in a warm place. Fill the shell with desired type of filling (such as vanilla pie filling, lemon filling, cream filling, or others) using an éclair filler or a pastry bag with a plain tip tube.

Dip the top half of the éclairs into a fairly thin fondant chocolate or white icing, set on a screen until the icing hardens.

Frozen eclairs: After baking the éclair shell, split in half lengthwise. Fill the bottom half of the shell with ice cream of the desired flavor. Replace the top half of the shell. Place in the freezer until 15 minutes before serving time. Serve with an appropriate sauce.

chapter 28

menu
making

It is not our purpose in this chapter to make an experienced menu maker out of the student, but to acquaint him with this very important subject that plays such a major part in any food service establishment. The menu is of such importance that it would be very difficult to sell food without it. The menu is the reason for production, and acts as a production sheet in the kitchen and a salesman in the dining room.

A menu is a list of the various dishes served in a food service establishment. It is from this list that the customers make their food selections. The kind of food presented on the menu would depend on whether it is a breakfast, luncheon, dinner or à la carte menu.

Breakfast menu

The *breakfast menu* usually features fruits, juices, cereals, hot cakes, egg dishes, potato preparations and assorted items that digest well at an early hour. It is quite simple in form, but is set up and worded in such a manner that it will do a good selling job. In many cases pictures of the plate combinations will be displayed to show the guest just what they will receive if this certain item is ordered. Presenting pictures on the breakfast menu is an excellent way to merchandise food because people have a habit of buying with their eyes and at this early hour pictures of food look better than at any other time of the day.

Luncheon menu

The *luncheon menu* is geared for speed. The average person has approximately one hour in which to be seated and served, so time is a big factor to him. In other words, the customer sets the pace for your luncheon menu planning. The luncheon menu should be simple to read and easy to select from. Appetizers should be listed first followed by the featured selections. The selections featured should include the entree or main course and all items that will be served with it; this is followed by the price. Example:

1. *Braised Pot Roast Jardiniere*
   Rissole Potatoes
   Cole Slaw
   $1.75

2. *Fried Jack Salmon*
   Tartar Sauce
   Parsley Potatoes
   Sliced Tomato Salad
   $1.65

The featured selections are followed by the desserts and beverages. The appetizer and dessert is usually not included in the luncheon price; if these items are desired they cost extra.

Casserole dishes and items that can be prepared quickly or in advance of service are the key to a successful and profitable luncheon business. It is also important that the luncheon prices be kept as low as possible and the emphasis placed on customer turnover. The luncheon menu should be changed daily.

Dinner menu

The *dinner menu* must set a leisure pace because this is the one meal served each day where the element of time is not a factor. The customer prefers to take his time between each course and enjoy his food to the fullest extent. Dinner menus usually consist of four courses: appetizer, salad, entree with vegetable and potato, and dessert. The beverage may be served with the entree or the dessert, whichever is preferred by the guest. The dinner menu should have a fairly large selection and, if possible and practical, the entree items should be prepared to order. The prices are higher on the dinner menu because the average guest occupies his seat longer and customer turnover is held to a minimum.

A la carte menu

The *à la carte* menu consists of foods individually priced and usually prepared to order. It is a menu that is not changed very often, four times a year is considered sufficient. It has an extensive selection of foods that are generally classified into 13 groups as follows:

1. Appetizers.
2. Soups.
3. Vegetables.
4. Potatoes.
5. Salads.
6. Seafood selections (entrées).
7. Meat and poultry selections (entrées)
8. Cold selections.
9. Desserts.
10. Ice cream.
11. Cheese.
12. Fresh or stewed fruit.
13. Beverages.

The à la carte menu is provided for the guest who does not like the selections offered on the luncheon or dinner menu or who wishes to consume only one or two courses rather than a full course luncheon or dinner. The à la carte menu can be profitable in certain establishments, but unprofitable in others. The difference would lie in the percentage of guests who select the full course luncheon or dinner. The disadvantage of an à la carte menu is that the food must be kept on hand to fill the orders if they should arrive in the kitchen. The more food kept on hand the greater the waste if it is not sold.

MENU TYPES

There are many different types of food service establishments in America and each must present a menu that will give the people what they want, in the way they want it, when they want it or they will not be in business very long. This is why we find a difference in all menus. A successful menu in one establishment may not prove successful in another. Although all menus are different in some respect, they can usually all be divided into four groups:
1. Specialty menu.
2. Limited menu.
3. Standard menu.
4. Extensive menu.

There are advantages and disadvantages to each group. Many factors must be considered before determining the type of menu that would be best to present.

Specialty menus

This is a menu with less than 12 items including desserts and beverages. All the items must be best sellers for this type of menu to be successful. Items which have become famous or extremely popular are sure winners. Examples are Frisch's big boy, Kentucky fried chicken and McDonalds' hamburgers, just to name a few. The specialty house will feature low prices and cater to the middle and low income group. With a small profit, but a large volume of business, fortunes have been made in a comparatively short time. In the past few years the pancake houses and pizza parlors have proved how successful a specialty menu can be if the item is basically popular and prepared in an eye appealing manner. The advantages of this type of menu are: (1) holds labor cost to a minimum, (2) controlled purchasing and waste, (3) no expensive decor needed,

(4) automation production possible, and (5) speed of service.

Limited menus

This is a menu that contains less than 30 items and most of these will be best sellers. This type of menu is ideal when opening a new establishment and also for special occasions when speed of service and production is necessary. The new establishment should start with controled purchasing and production until they are able to determine the factors necessary to prepare a menu just right for their situation. As volume increases, more variety can be added. On certain occasions during the year when one can be sure he is going to be extremely busy, such as Mother's Day, Easter or local festive days, the limited menu will provide an answer to faster service and production. The limited menu will feature foods commonly liked by most people. Beef, poultry, pork and seafood items are usually offered. In most cases a vegetable is not offered. A salad and a popular potato preparation, such as baked, French fries or hash brown, will please everyone. The advantages of this type of menu are: (1) controled purchasing and waste, (2) holds labor cost to a minimum, (3) speed of service, and (4) a higher quality of food. If the limited menu is to be successful, remember that each item must be prepared properly and presented to the guest in an attractive manner.

Standard menus

The standard menu will contain from 50 to 80 items and is the most popular type used in the better hotels, clubs and restaurants. The selection is large enough to satisfy the desires of most guests. The entree selections will feature variety in assortment of foods served and methods of preparation. When featuring the standard menu it is necessary to employ skilled cooks, and usually a larger labor force is necessary because more hard work is involved. The standard menu is most successful in establishments doing a fairly large volume of business. The larger the volume of business the more varied the eating habits will be.

Extensive menus

The extensive menu will have over 100 items listed and will feature an extremely large selection for each course. To feature this type of menu one must be doing a very large volume of business. It is necessary to have more skilled personnel on the preparation crew, to have storage facilities for the many items that must be kept available, and to have an expensive dining room decor with adequate seating capacity. The biggest advantage in offering this type of menu, when it is practical to do so, is the fact that it offers a greater opportunity for working off all leftovers, and the guest can usually satisfy his every desire from such a large selection.

The task of formulating the menu is the duty of management, with the help of the head chef. However, before the actual formulation can take place, they must analyze and weigh many important factors within the two required stages for producing a successful menu: (1) planning the menu, and (2) writing the menu.

PLANNING THE MENU

Planning the menu is time consuming, but extremely important if the finished product is to suit the needs of the establishment and give the people what they want, when they want it, and the way they want it. Before a definite menu plan is decided upon one should consider the following factors:

1. Location of food service establishment.
2. Type of customers.
3. Type of food service establishment.
4. Skill and size of preparation crew.
5. Serving hours.
6. Size of dining room and dining room equipment.
7. Competition.
8. Sales volume.
9. Skill and size of service crew.
10. Kitchen equipment.
11. Seasons of the year.
12. Festive occasions.

1. Location of restaurant

The section of the city or town where the food service establishment is located will dictate to a great degree the type of menu that must be offered. Examples are as follows:

A. *Business section:* One should offer a menu that would be attractive to men and clerical workers, featuring steaks, chops, and slightly heavy dishes with a few items that would appeal to women. Quick service would be essential for the luncheon menu and moderate prices should prevail.

B. *Transportation section:* With people on the move one must cater to a transit trade. Light and heavy dishes of popular preparations would be necessary. An à la carte menu with quick service and moderate prices would satisfy the need.

C. *Department store section:* One must offer a menu that would be appealing to women and featuring child portions, dainty, attractive combinations, sandwiches, quick service and popular prices.

D. *Residential section:* The menu must appeal to families, featuring a moderate variety, plate combinations, simple service and moderate prices.

E. *Theater section:* A standard or limited dinner menu should be featured for pre-theater service and an à la carte menu for after-theater service. Moderate prices should prevail and quick service for the after-theater patrons.

F. *Road side or highway section:* One must cater to the transit trade by featuring an à la carte menu, plate combinations, large portions, quick service, limited variety and low prices.

2. Type of customers

Since the customers set the pace and are the reason for all menu planning, certain facts pertaining to their economic, religious and social background must be learned. Food habits are sometimes formed early in life and are difficult to change. For example, the Italian will usually like pasta in any form; the Southerner, fried chicken; and the New Englander his clam chowder. Answers to the following questions about your customers will help in planning the correct menu.
    A. Type of clientele to please: men, women, teen-agers, families.
    B. Nationality and religion.
    C. Type of work they perform.
    D. Eating habits.
    E. Prices they can afford to pay.

3. Type of food service establishment

This will certainly influence the kind of cuisine to be offered. If it is a German type restaurant, certainly the majority of the selection will be of German origin. This would also be true in a French, Italian or Chinese restaurant. A steak house must offer a number of different kinds of steaks and a seafood house must feature a large selection of seafood. If a restaurant is in operation to do a distinctive type of food business, it is difficult to promote and sell other foods.

4. Skill and size of the Preparation crew

In planning the menu one of the most neglected factors is the preparation crew: who is going to prepare the items presented to the guest is very seldom considered. It is sheer folly to plan an elaborate menu if it is beyond the ability of the cooks to prepare the dishes. If you have a small crew plan a menu with a minimum of hand work; a more elaborate menu can be presented as the size and skill of the crew is increased. Keep in mind all the work stations in the kitchen so all stations are kept busy. Too many times the menu planner will load up one or two stations while the others stand idly by. Plan the menu so the leisure hours of the preparation crew can be utilized.

5. Serving hours

The hours a food service establishment is open will determine the kind of menus needed. Some places will serve breakfast, lunch and dinner. If they continue to stay open after 9:00 p.m. they feature an à la carte menu. Other places may serve only luncheon or dinner so just two menus a day are sufficient. The luncheon is usually the busiest meal of the day; therefore the menu must be streamlined for quick service and the prices should be lower. Dinner is served in a more leisurely manner, so the menu can be dressed up with more elaborate trimming to justify the increased prices. Restaurants that stay open all night should change their menu and the tempo of service four times (breakfast, lunch, dinner and à la carte) during the 24 hour period.

6. Size of dining room and dining room equipment

The size of the dining room and the equipment in the dining room will have an effect on the items featured on the menu. For example, with large floor space and table space more elaborate foods can be served. There are many preparations that require unusual service with many side dishes involved. With limited space it is impossible to do justice to these classical preparations. It takes a fairly large table to do justice to a broiled plank sirloin steak à la bouquetiere, roast pheasant sous cloche (under glass), and filet de sole Marguery. In many cases when serving certain foods a waiter or waitress must work from side stations. If these are not available or are too small one cannot do the task properly. Therefore, if this is the case they should never appear on the menu. It is important that a food service establishment have good balance between its dining space and the size of the kitchen. If the dining space is too small in comparison to the size of the kitchen the food is usually left waiting. The result is cold, dried food and the loss of customers. If the kitchen is too small for the dining space the customers are kept waiting. The result: turnover is reduced and customers lost.

7. Competition

Today the competition in the food service field is very keen and one must be kept constantly informed as to what is going on around him if he wishes to stay in business. The old cliché "it's a good sign when you are too busy to watch your competition" may still have some merit, but the way the trend in eating habits are changing today it would certainly be wise to know what the other fellow is doing. New ideas that may be worked into the menu can be acquired by reading trade magazines, attending food service conventions, and belonging to food service organizations.

8. Sales volume

Your sales volume will be instrumental in determining the type of menu to be used. If you are doing a small volume of business a limited menu should be offered. As the volume of business increases greater variety can be added to satisfy the more varied eating habits. Increased volume will make the menu maker's and the chef's job easier, because it affords the opportunity to work off left-overs and trimmings which normally lie around and spoil. Offering a standard or extensive menu when doing a small volume of business will lead to failure.

9. Skill and size of service crew

This is a factor that the average menu maker will overlook, yet it is extremely important whether the staff is capable of serving certain dishes which call for spe-cial presentation and eloquent service. If the food service crew lacks the knowledge or training required to do the job, it is best to feature only foods that they are capable of serving properly. Whether the staff is comprised of men or women will also have a bearing on the items featured. Men can carry heavier trays than women. Therefore with a staff of waiters, items calling for silver service or side dishes may be offered. With waitresses, service must be simplified to plate combinations with elimination of too many side dishes. The number of staff members on the floor during the service hours will determine whether a limited or standard menu is advisable.

10. Kitchen equipment

To plan a menu without considering the kind of equipment available, its condition, and capacity would produce a menu that would be unworkable. The kitchen is the backbone of any food service establishment, and the equipment in the kitchen produces the finished product when operated by skilled hands. Certain foods make certain pieces of equipment necessary to do the task properly. Mashing potatoes by hand is possible, but usually lumps will be present. A mixing machine will do the job properly, turning out a smooth, fluffy product. To plan a menu calling for 3 or 4 roasted or baked items with only one oven in the kitchen is asking for the impossible. The same would be true if 4 or 5 broiled items were placed on the menu when only one broiler was available. It is also wise for the menu maker to understand that old equipment will not produce as efficiently as new equipment.

11. Seasons of the year

It is wise to change the menu completely at each season of the year. The items featured should be those popular during that season. For example, cold soups and cold entrées during the summer season; pumpkin pie, roast turkey and hot soups during the fall season; roast pork, beef stews and heavy soups during the winter season; and fresh fruit, ham and lamb during the spring season. It is also advisable to feature in-season foods because they are looked for and expected by the guest, and also they are economical to provide.

12. Festive occasions

These provide the menu maker with an opportunity to exercise his imagination and display the creative ability he may possess. All the legal holidays should be noted as well as any local festive occasions and items appropriate for those days should be worked into the menu. Examples are listed below:

A. Washington's Birthday: cherry pie.
B. St. Patricks Day: Irish lamb stew.
C. Lincoln's Birthday: log cake or ice cream.
D. Thanksgiving: roast turkey, pumpkin pie and mince meat pie.
E. Christmas: roast turkey, pumpkin pie and plum pudding.
F. Easter: roast lamb or ham.
G. Independence Day: jellied tomato madrilene or something red.
H. St. Valentine's Day: Heart shaped gelatine salads and cakes.

WRITING THE MENU

The second stage in the construction of the menu is to put the plan into written form. Keep in mind that the menu presented to the guest establishes an impression of the standards set by the operation, and to some degree will reflect the quality of the food served. It should be written in such a way that it will sell food and enable the guest to make quick and pleasing selections. To obtain these desired results the menu maker should consider the following suggestions when writing the menu.

Variety

In the food service business variety is not so much the spice of life, but the key to a successful operation. People do get tired of the same old thing and are constantly on the lookout for new and interesting preparations. Variety can be achieved in four different ways: methods of preparation, ideas for service, kinds of food served, and garnishes. The element of surprise if worked into certain food preparations can increase sales and profit, because surprise will stimulate the appetite and get people talking about your establishment. If the same kind of meat or fish must be placed on the menu two or three days in a row, vary the method of preparation. Creating variety through ideas for service is not as difficult as one may imagine when we consider the many different serving dishes and casseroles available on the market today. Skewered items and foods served in natural shells or ramkins is another possibility. There should be no need for lack of the kinds of food served, because the markets are full of foods that can be featured in interesting and appetizing manners. Garnishes create appetite appeal and can be brought about by the addition of some extra colorful item which will add eye appeal.

Color

This will stimulate and influence the appetite more than anything else. How desirable would a salad, a plate combination, or a buffet table be without the beautiful and natural colors provided by certain foods? The menu maker must take advantage of the natural food colors and utilize them in an interesting and attractive manner just as an artist does in creating an outstanding masterpiece. Without color, eating would just be a necessity, not an adventure and one of the true pleasures in life. When writing the menu always consider color.

Leftovers

Before starting to write the menu, a complete refrigerator inventory should be made in order to work off all leftovers and foods that spoil rapidly. It is better to get some return from your investment than to hold them too long and absorb a heavy loss. The leftovers sometimes present a challenge to the menu maker, but if he can utilize them in desirable preparations that will sell he has contributed greatly to the success of the operation. The following are a few examples of the things that can be done with leftovers:

1. *Soup:* convert consommé to onion soup; convert tomato or split pea soup into purée of Mongole; etc.

2. *Beef trimming:* roast beef hash, barbecue, meat sauce, etc.

3. *Chicken or turkey:* chicken salad, chicken croquettes, chicken hash, etc.

4. *Vegetables:* mixed vegetables, vegetable soup, vegetable salad, etc.

5. *Fruit:* fruit cups, fruit salad, tarts, etc.

6. *Fish:* fish chowder, deviled crabs, seafood Newburg, etc.

Form

Most people can see very little beauty in flat surfaces. It takes hills, valleys, canyons and mountains to bring forth true scenic beauty. This is also true in the preparation and presentation of foods. Items laying flat on a plate are uninteresting and in many cases will cause loss of appetite. It is for this reason that foods must be presented to the guest in various shapes and sizes, trying to eliminate the flat surfaces whenever possible. Examples of food possessing excellent form are as follows:

1. Duchess potatoes.
2. Stuffed chicken leg.
3. Stuffed green peppers.
4. Beef rouladen (roll).
5. Stuffed cabbage.
6. Chicken croquettes.

Consistency

When combining foods to be presented to the guest as a combination, at least one item must be present that the teeth can chew on. A meal of all soft or mushy foods is considered improper and most certainly lacks appeal. An example of *good* consistency: broiled sirloin steak, mashed potatoes, and buttered broccoli. An example of *poor* consistency: seafood Newburg in patty shell, mashed potatoes, and cream style corn.

Food temperatures

Regardless of the weather or seasons of the year, every meal should include at least one hot or cold item. It is thought that slightly varying temperatures will improve digestion. During the summer the menu presented will include many cold items; however, hot items are also present, and even though the guest may consume a majority of cold items the hot coffee, soup or biscuit eaten with those cold items will stimulate the gastric juices and help the food to digest more rapidly. In the winter the reverse is usually true in the presentation of foods, the hot foods prevail; however, the cold ones are very much in evidence especially in the appetizer and dessert choices. It is also wise for the menu maker to keep in mind that all hot foods must be served *hot* and cold foods served *cold*. Facilities should be available for keeping hot foods hot and cold foods cold or they should not be placed on the menu. Many a guest has been displeased and their meal spoiled by being served a cold cup of coffee or soup, a gelatin salad on a slightly warm plate, a warm glass of juice and a cold biscuit or muffin.

On hand supplies

To hold spoilage and waste to a minimum the menu maker should be aware of the supplies he has on hand when writing the menu. It is an established fact that very few foods will improve with age.

We are sometimes led to believe that canned goods will keep indefinitely if the can it not opened; this is a fallacy. (Canned foods will keep for an indefinite period only if they are *always* stored under proper conditions. This, however, is not always done and the can will start to swell, rust or puncture in about 18 months or less.) Control all supplies and keep them turning over so fresh products are always available. Avoid the common mistake of shoving the old products to the rear of the shelf. All perishable foods should be ordered for the day of service and used promptly or they will lose their fresh appearance and taste. Avoid keeping meat hanging in the refrigerator for too long a period of time. Approximately 75 per cent of the meat structure is comprised of moisture, and air will dry the moisture causing shrinkage and loss of profits.

Balance

The menu should be balanced by including the basic seven foods required for proper daily nourishment. Examples of the basic seven are as follows:

1. Citrus fruit, tomatoes or raw cabbage.
2. Green or yellow vegetables.
3. Milk, cheese or ice cream.
4. Butter or margarine.
5. Bread, rolls or quickbreads.
6. Meat, fish, poultry or eggs.
7. Potatoes, rice or macaroni.

By including something from each of the basic seven categories on the menu, those people who know and follow proper dietetic principles can select foods they require and desire. It also makes selection easier for those patrons who may be on some type of special diet.

Flavor

All foods contain some flavor. The flavor may be strong, mild or delicate, depending on the item being served. If the flavor is strong, such as beef entrées, an accompanying sauce or condiment is not necessary to bring forth a more pronounced flavor. If the food has a mild flavor, an accompanying sauce or condiment may be necessary for the item to be enjoyed to its fullest extent. For delicate flavored foods, such as pork and veal items, help in the form of a sauce or condiment is a must. It is for this reason that we usually find the following items so closely associated with each other when they appear on the menu: mint with lamb, apples with pork, onions with liver, cranberries with turkey, lemon with fish and melons.

In-season foods

The wise menu maker will take advantage of in-season foods by offering them on the menu, because when in season they are best and cheapest. Learn new ways of presenting them to the guest and dress up the old favorite recipes to stimulate sales. Most people will look for such items as corn on the cob, strawberry short cake, and fresh peach pie when these items are in season.

Speed of service

If it is necessary for the menu maker to consider speed of service when writing the menu, he must think in terms of pre-finished items and casserole dishes. These preparations may require more time to prepare, but save time when serving because the dishing up is usually done in advance. These items will speed up customer turnover and increase profits. Deep fried items are another answer to speeding up the service, provided the establishment has quick-recovery deep fryers or a number of fryers that can handle the burden of heavy frying and keep hot grease available at all times.

MENU WRITING SUGGESTIONS

There are no precise rules for writing the menu. However, the following tips could prove most helpful:

1. Capitalize all words except explanations and descriptive material.
2. Build the menu around the main dishes.
3. Know your customers and the foods they like to eat.
4. Do not become repetitious when listing foods. That is, for example, do not list apple juice for an appetizer, broiled pork with apple fritters for the entrée and apple pie for dessert.
5. Vary methods of preparing the entrées.
6. Blend the salad to the entrée: heavy salad, light entrée; light salad, heavy meal.
7. Blend the soup to the entrée: heavy entree, light soup; light entrée, heavy soup.
8. Work in the leftovers.
9. Keep up with the trends in eating habits.
10. Offer hot rolls and quickbreads.
11. Create variety and excitement with garnishes.
12. Choose desserts that blend with the season and the entrées.
13. Offer variety with the vegetable selection.
14. Word each item to stimulate the appetite. The choice of words can produce sales. Examples: *farm fresh* eggs, *fresh caught* brook trout, *fresh Florida* fruit cup, *garden fresh* green beans, *vine ripened* tomatoes., etc.

culinary terms

American cuisine is a combination of various foreign preparations brought to America by the immigrant cooks and chefs who for years staffed our commercial kitchens. Because of this we find many foreign terms gracing our menus and being used in our kitchens today. Some of these terms have even become part of our own language. Terms such as filet, omelet, and meringue are examples of this. Listed below are a number of terms. An understanding of these terms will prove quite helpful to the student cook. Many of the terms listed are used throughout this text. Become familiar with these culinary terms.

Aging: A term applied to meat being held at a temperature of 34° to 36°F for the purpose of improving its tenderness.

Agneau: French for "lamb."

A la: With, in the manner or fashion of.

A la bouquetière: Served with a variety of vegetables in season. Usually associated with broiled meat or fish surrounded with a variety of colorful vegetables.

A la bourgeoise: Plain, family style meats, garnished with assorted vegetables, cut fairly large (as for beef stew).

A la broche: Cooked on a skewer.

A la carte: Foods ordered and paid for separately. In most cases the foods are prepared to order.

A la goldenrod: Hard cooked egg whites, chopped coarse, placed in a cream sauce, served on toast, and garnished with grated hard cooked yolks.

A la Holstein: Used with a fried veal cutlet that is served on tomato sauce with a fried egg on top and garnished with lemon, capers, and anchovy.

A la king: Foods served in a white sauce with mushrooms, green pepper and pimientos. Usually flavored with sherry.

A la maison: Specialty of the house.

A la Marengo: Sautéed chicken simmered in a brown sauce with wine, tomatoes, mushrooms and ripe and green olive slices.

A la Maryland: Usually refers to chicken that is disjointed, breaded with bread crumbs, fried in deep fat and served with cream sauce, crisp bacon and corn fritters.

A L'Americaine: In the American style or fashion.

A la Meyerbeer: Applied to eggs that are shirred and served with kidneys. The kidneys are usually sautéed or broiled and placed in a brown sauce.

A la mode: May refer to ice cream served on top of pie or cake, or to beef prepared and served in a special way (example: beef à la mode).

A la Newburg: Cream sauce colored slightly with paprika and flavored with sherry wine. Usually associated with seafood.

A L'Anglaise: In the English style or fashion.

A la reine: To the queen's taste, this expression is usually applied to soup to indicate the presence of finely chopped white meat of chicken or turkey.

A la Provencale: With garlic and oil.

A la Russe: In the Russian style or fashion.

Al dente: Italian expression meaning slightly chewy or tough to the bite, a little toughness or firmness remaining in a cooked product such as vegetables, pasta, etc.

Allemande: White sauce with egg yolks added.

Ambrosia: Assorted fruits with shredded coconut.

Anchois: French for anchovy.

Anchovy: A very small fish of the herring family. They are salted and packed in oil when canned.

Anisette: A cordial flavored with anise seed.

Antipasto: An Italian appetizer (hor d'oeuvres).

Arrowroot: A starch extracted from the roots of a West Indian plant used as a thickening agent in certain soups and sauces. It brings forth a high sheen.

Aspic: A clear meat, fish, or poultry jelly.

Au or **aux:** With, in the manner or fashion of.

Au gratin: Foods covered with a sauce, sprinkled with cheese or bread crumbs or both, and baked to a golden brown.

Au jus: Served with natural juice.

Au lait: With milk.

Au naturel: According to nature, prepared in a plain or simple manner.

Aux croutons: With croutons. Croutons are toasted or fried small cubes of bread. Usually served as a garnish in soups and salads.

Aux cresson: With watercress.

Avocado: A thickened skin, pear shaped tropical fruit with a green buttery flesh. Also known as alligator pear.

Baba au rhum: A small rum flavored cake usually served with a topping of whipped cream.

Baked Alaska: Ice cream on cake, completely covered with meringue and delicately browned in a quick oven.

Barbecue: To cook over the embers of an open fire. Also a highly seasoned tomato base sauce.

Barder: To cover poultry or game with

thin slices of bacon or salt pork when roasting. To inject flavor and juice.

Bar le Duc: A famous jam made from red currants. Imported from France.

Baste: To ladle drippings over a piece of meat that is being cooked as a roast to make juicy and prevent dryness.

Batter: A mixture of flour, sugar, eggs, milk, etc., which can be poured.

Bavarian: A dessert consisting of whipped gelatin and whipped cream folded together. It is placed in a mold and refrigerated until set.

Béarnaise: A sauce, consisting of Hollandaise sauce with a tarragon vinegar mixture added. Used with meat and fish.

Beat: To lift a mixture with a whip for the purpose of injecting air and to make the mixture smooth.

Béchamel: A white sauce, usually made with milk and cream.

Beef à la Stroganoff: Sautéed small thin slices of beef tenderloin, poached in a sour cream sauce.

Bercy: A sauce consisting of brown sauce, shallots, lemon juice and white wine. Usually served with meat or fish.

Beurre: French, meaning "butter."

Beurre noir: Browned butter.

Bigarade: A sweet-sour brown sauce, flavored with orange peel and juice. Usually served with roast duck.

Biscuit: Small round quickbread, made light with baking powder.

Bisque: A thick, rich cream soup, usually made from shellfish (lobster, shrimp, etc.).

Blanc: French, meaning "white."

Blanch: To make white or scald. To partially cook an item.

Blanquette: A stew of chicken, veal or lamb in a white sauce.

Blend: To mix thoroughly two or more ingredients.

Blinis: Russian pancakes, usually served with caviar.

Blue points: Small oysters which are served raw on the half shell.

Boeuf: French, meaning "beef."

Bombe: A molded dessert of two or more ice creams.

Bonne femme: French, meaning "good woman," this term is applied to dishes prepared and served in a simple home style way.

Bordelaise: A brown sauce flavored with red wine. Usually served with beef entrées.

Bordure: An item served with a ring of vegetables, usually duchess potatoes.

Borsch: A Russian beet soup. Made with beef stock, beets, tomatoes, sour cream and seasoning.

Boston cream pie: A sponge layer, cut in half crosswise, filled with a cream filling and topped with icing or fruit.

Bouchée: Very small patty, made of puff paste and filled with creamed meat or fish.

Bouillabaisse: A fish soup or stew. Made with 5 or 6 different fish or shellfish flavored with white wine and seasoned with saffron. It is served in a soup dish with toast.

Bouillon: A liquid similar to a stock, but cleaner and richer in flavor. Usually made of beef unless otherwise specified. Example tomato bouillon, etc.

Bouquet-garni: A bunch of herbs tied together as a bouquet or in a cheese cloth bag for the purpose of cooking with an item to season and for easy removal when its task is completed.

Bourguignonne. Referring to Burgundy; with Burgundy wine.

Braten: A German term meaning "roast."

Brandy: An alcoholic liquor distilled from wine or fruit juices.

Breading: To pass an item through flour, egg wash and bread crumbs.

Brine: A liquid of salt and water or vinegar used for pickling. Saltpeter is added on many occasions to set the red meat color (example: corn beef).

Brioche: A roll made of light sweet dough, originated in France.

Broche: A skewer.

Brochette: Meat or other foods broiled on a skewer.

Broth: A liquid in which meat, fish, poultry or vegetables have been simmered.

Brown betty: A type of pudding with apples, bread or cake crumbs, spices and sugar. Usually served with a vanilla or lemon sauce.

Brunoise: Assorted vegetables, cut into a fine dice (carrots, celery, leeks, etc.) used to garnish soups and consommés.

Brunswick stew: A stew comprised of rabbit, squirrel, veal or chicken, salt pork and assorted vegetables such as corn, onions, potatoes and beans.

Buffet: A display of ready-to-eat hot and cold foods. It is self service, with the exception of the hot foods.

Cacao: Cocoa, chocolate.

Cacciatore: An Italian term applied to sautéed chicken that is baked in a highly seasoned (basil and oregano) tomato sauce with diced mushrooms and chives.

Café: French, meaning "coffee."

Café au lait: A beverage consisting of equal parts hot milk and coffee.

Café noir: Black coffee.

Camembert: A soft full flavored, ripened cheese made in the region of Camembert, France; usually served as a dessert.

Canadian bacon: Trimmed, pressed, smoked loin of pork. May be purchased cooked or uncooked.

Canapé: An appetizer, toasted bread or cracker covered with a savory paste and garnished attractively.

Canard: French word meaning "duck".

Candying: To cook certain fruits and vegetables in a heavy sweetened syrup.

Caper: European flower bud seasoning (nasturtium bud) or garnish. The buds are pickled in vinegar and packed in small green bottles. Used mainly as a tart condiment in sauces for meats and in velouté sauce for poached fish.

Capon: A castrated young male chicken noted for its fine flavored, tender textured meat.

Caramelize: To heat granulated sugar to a golden brown color for the purpose of flavoring and coloring other foods.

Carte: Bill of fare (menu).

Carte du jour: Menu of the day.

Casaba melon: Large oval shaped, yellow skin, white meated melon. A winter melon in season October to April.

Casserole: An earthenware dish or pot in which certain food items are baked and served.

Caviar: The salted eggs or roe of the sturgeon and certain other fish.

Cepes: A type of mushroom, usually canned in a brine.

Chablis: A white, good-bodied wine, sometimes referred to as white Burgandy.

Champignon: French, meaning "mushroom."

Chantilly: Indicates the use of whipped cream.

Chantilly sauce: Hollandaise sauce with unsweetened whipped cream folded in.

Charlotte: A mold lined with ladyfingers, filled with fruit and whipped cream or custard.

Charlotte Russe: A mold lined with ladyfingers and filled with a Bavarian cream.

Chasseur: French, meaning "hunter style."

Châteaubriand: A thick beef tenderloin steak, weighing approximately one pound. It is cooked by the broiling method.

Chaud-froid: Jellied white sauce, used for decorating certain foods that are to be displayed.

Chef: Head of the kitchen.

Cherries Jubilee: Slightly thickened dark sweet cherries and juice with Kirchwasser added, which is poured over ice cream, ignited and served aflame.

Chicory: A salad green of the endive family.

Chiffonade: Finely shredded or chopped vegetables used in soups or salad dressing.

Chives: Small onion-like sprouts that are long, very slender and green. They have a mild flavor and are used mainly in sauces and salads.

Chop: To cut into small pieces using a knife or some type of sharp tool.

Choux paste: A paste consisting of eggs, water, salt, shortening and flour. Used in making éclairs and cream puffs.

Chutney: A spicy relish of fruits and spices. Served with curry dishes.

Citron: A lemon-like fruit, but thicker skinned, larger in size and with less acid.

Clarify: To make clear or transparent, free from impurities as a consommé.

Cloche: A glass bell, used to cover certain foods when served.

Coat: To cover the surface of one food with another.

Cobbler: A deep dish pie, usually made of fruit.

Coddle: To cook or simmer an item just below the boiling point for a short period of time.

Colbert Sauce: A sauce consisting of brown sauce, shallots, claret wine, butter and lemon juice.

Compote: Fruits stewed in a syrup or a mixture of assorted stewed fruit.

Condiment: A seasoning for food, a spicy or pungent relish.

Connoisseur: A critic having trained and competent judgment in art or other matters of taste.

Consommé: A clear, strong flavored soup. Consommé is derived from the word *consummate,* meaning perfect.

Coq au vin: Chicken in wine.

Cottage pudding: Cake served with a warm sweet sauce.

Coupe: A shallow dessert dish; also a popular dessert such as strawberry coupe or pineapple coupe.

Court bouillon: A liquid comprised of water, vinegar or wine, herbs and seasoning in which fish is poached.

Crème: French, meaning "cream."

Creole: To give the appearance of creole type food. Usually a soup or sauce containing tomatoes, onions, green peppers, celery and seasoning.

Crêpe: French, meaning "pancake."

Crêpe suzette: Thin French pancakes, rolled and served aflame with a rich brandy sauce.

Cresson: French, meaning "watercress."

Croissant: A crescent shaped roll.

Croquette: A ground food product, bound together with the addition of a thick cream sauce and eggs, formed into balls or cones, breaded and fried in deep fat.

Croutons: Small cubes of bread browned to a golden color in the oven or deep fat fryer. Usually served with salads or soups.

Cube: To cut into square pieces.

Cuisine: The art of cookery.

Cure: To preserve by pickling, salting or drying.

Curry: East Indian stew or dish containing curry powder, a blended spice.

Cut in: A part blended into another.

Cutlet: A small flattened boneless piece of meat. Usually the term is associated with pork and veal.

Deglaze: Adding water to a pan in which meats have been sautéed or roasted to dissolve crusted juices that have dried on the bottom and sides of the pan.

Demi: French, meaning "half."

Demiglace: A rich brown stock reduced by simmering until it is only half of its original amount.

Demitasse: A small cup of black coffee.

Deviled: An item flavored with hot condiment such as pepper, mustard. Tabasco, etc.

Diable: A term applied to deviled or highly seasoned food.

Diced: To cut into small cubes or squares.

Dissolved: To cause a dry substance to be absorbed into a liquid or become fluid.

Dot: To spot small particles of butter over the surface of an item.

Dough: A thick, soft uncooked mass of moistened flour. Used in association with bread, cookies and rolls.

Drawn butter: Melted butter.

Dredge: To coat an item with dry ingredients, usually flour.

Dress: A term usually associated with poultry and fish, meaning to trim and clean.

Drippings: Fat and natural juice that drips from roasting meats.

Du jour: French, meaning "of the day."

Duchess potatoes: Boiled potatoes whipped with egg yolks and pressed through a pastry tube.

Duglere: With tomatoes; usually the term is associated with a white fish sauce with crushed tomatoes flowing through it.

Dust: To sprinkle an item with flour or sugar.

D'Uxelles: A type of stuffing, consisting of mushrooms, shallots and seasoning. Usually moisture is added to this base in the form of tomatoes or brown sauce before it is used to stuff mushrooms, tomatoes, etc.

Eclair: A fairly long, thin, hollow center shell made from choux paste and filled with cream filling and iced.

Eggplant: A large, dark purple, pear shaped vegetable.

Eggs Benedict: Poached eggs placed on top of a toasted English muffin and ham, covered with Hollandaise sauce and garnished with truffles.

Emulsify: A liquid mixture suspended in another (usually eggs and oil) to prevent separation.

En brochette: To cook on a skewer.

En chemise: With their skin, usually used in association with potatoes.

Enchiladas: A dish of Mexican origin, consisting of tortillas (flat, unleavened corn cake) spread with grated cheese and chopped onions or some other type of filling, and rolled in the manner of an omelet. Usually served with melted cheese on top.

En coquille: Served in a shell.

En tasse: Served in a cup.

Entrée: Main course of a meal.

Epicure: A lover of food and wine.

Epigramme: An entrée of two pieces of meat prepared differently, but usually cooked and served together.

Escallop: To cut into thin slices or to bake in a white sauce, with a topping of crumbs.

Escargot: French, meaning "snail."

Escarole: A salad green of the endive family.

Escoffier: A famous French chef (1846-1939); author of a famous cookbook. Also a trade name for a bottled table sauce.

Espagnole sauce: Literally "Spanish." In cooking terminology a rich brown sauce of meat, vegetables and seasoning.

Essence: That which is the true character or quality of anything. Extract of meat flavors.

Extract: That which has been obtained by pulling or drawing out. Drawing flavors from certain foods, used to flavor other food items.

Farce: French, meaning "stuffing."

Farci: French, meaning "stuffed," such as meats or vegetables.

Farina: The coarsely ground inner portion of hard wheat.

Fermentation: The chemical changes of an organic compound caused by the action of living organisms, such as yeast when added to liquid with sugar will produce carbon dioxide gas.

Filet de sole: Boneless piece of fish belonging to the sole family of fish.

Filet mignon: Filets of beef tenderloin usually free of all fat.

Fine herbs: A mixture of three or four herbs chopped very fine.

Finnan haddie: Smoked haddock fish.

Flambé: Served aflame (example: crêpe suzettes).

Flambeau: To serve on a flaming torch.

Florentine: With spinach.

Foie gras: Fatted goose liver.

Fondant: An icing made by boiling sugar and water to the point of crystallization then whipping to a creamy mass.

Fondue: A warm cheese dip. fine and highly seasoned. Used for stuffing meat and fish. fing meat and fish.

Forcemeat: Meat or fish ground very fine and highly seasoned. Used for stuffing meat and fish.

Française: In the French style or fashion.

Frappé: Frozen or partly frozen to the consistency of mush. Used with dessert items.

Frenched: To scrape meat and fat from the bones of meat, a little distance from the end. This term is usually associated with chops, such as lamb and veal rib chops.

French toast: Bread dipped in a batter of milk and eggs, then fried until golden brown on both sides. Served with some type of syrup.

Fricassée: Pieces of chicken, lamb or veal stewed in a liquid and served in a sauce made from this same liquid.

Fritters: Foods dipped or coated with a batter and fried to a golden brown in deep fat. The fritter is named after the food being fried.

Froid: French, meaning "cold."

Fromage: French, meaning "cheese."

Fry: To cook in oil or fat.

Fumet: A stock of fish, meat or game reduced with wine until concentrated.

Galantine: Poultry, game or meat, boned, stuffed, with forcemeat, boiled, cooled, covered with chaud-froid and aspic and decorated. Usually served sliced on buffets.

Garbanzo: Chick peas; can be purchased dried or canned.

Garde manger: French, meaning guardian of the cold meats. Cold meat department or person in charge of it.

Garnish: To decorate a dish with an item that will improve its appearance.

Garniture: French for "garnish."

Gefülte fish: A favorite Jewish entrée. Fish fillets stuffed with a ground fish mixture and poached.

Gherkin: A small sweet or sour pickled cucumber.

Giblet: Gizzard, heart and liver of poultry.

Glacé: Glazed, iced, frosted to cover with a glossy coating.

Glacé de viande: Reduced meat stock.

Glaze: To coat an item with a glossy coating.

Golden buck: Welsh rarebit topped with a poached egg.

Goulash: A rich, savory, brown stew; the main seasoning is paprika.

Gourmet: A lover of fine foods.

Grate: To rub or wear into small particles, by rubbing on the rough surface of a grater.

Gruyère. A type of Swiss cheese made in France and Switzerland. Has smaller holes than the true Swiss cheese.

Griddle: A large, flat, heavy plate with heat applied from the bottom.

Grill: To cook on a griddle. The term is sometimes used interchangeably with broil.

Grits: Coarsely ground hominy.

Gumbo: A rich creole type soup consisting of chicken broth, onion, celery, green peppers, okra, tomatoes and rice.

Hacher: Meaning to hash or mince.

Hard sauce: A dessert sauce consisting of butter, lemon extract, sugar, and vanilla.

Hasenpfeffer: German rabbit stew.

Head cheese: Jellied, spiced, pressed meat from the hog's head.

Heifer: A young cow that has never borne a calf.

Herbs: Savory leaves such as tarragon, sage, basil, parsley, etc.

Homard: French, meaning "lobster."

Hominy: Hulled Indian corn, coarsely ground or broken, used as a cereal food.

Homogenize: To break up fat globules into very small particles.

Hongroise: In the Hungarian style or fashion.

Hors d'oeuvres: Small portions of food served as a first course of a meal. An appetizer, they may be served in many forms either hot or cold.

Hush puppies: A Southern deep fried food consisting of corn meal, milk, onions, baking powder etc. A fried dough.

Indian pudding: A dessert prepared by combining yellow corn meal, eggs, brown sugar, milk, raisins and seasoning and baking slowly in the oven.

Indienne: Dishes prepared in the style of India and in which curry powder is the main seasoning.

Irish stew: A white lamb stew consisting of lamb, carrots, turnips, potatoes, onions, dumplings and seasoning.

Italienne: In the Italian style or fashion. Usually the preparation contains some type of pasta.

Jambalaya: A combination of rice and meat or seafood, cooked together.

Jambon: French, meaning "ham."

Jardinière: Gardner's style, a garnish for meat entreés, usually consisting of carrots, celery, and turnips cut approximately one inch long and a quarter of an inch thick. Peas are sometimes added to this garnish. (Examples: braised pot roast jardinière, braised short ribs of beef jardinière.)

Julienne: To cut into long very thin strips.

Jus: Natural meat juice.

Karo: A fairly thin, light or dark, corn syrup.

Kartoffel klosse: A German potato dumpling.

Kebob: Small cubes of meat roasted on a skewer.

Kippered: Lightly salted and smoked fish.

Kirschwasser: A liqueur made from cherries; it is frequently used to flame certain dishes.

Kitchen bouquet: Trade name for a bottle seasoning, used to flavor and color gravies.

Knead: The manipulation of pressing, folding,and stretching the air out of dough.

Kohlrabi: Vegetable of the cabbage family with an enlarged edible turnip-like stem.

Kosher: Meat butchered and processed according to prescribed Hebrew religious laws.

Kuchen: German cakes made with sweet yeast dough.

Kümmel: Liqueur flavored with caraway seed.

Kumquat: A small citrus fruit, about the size and shape of an olive. Resembles a very small orange.

Lait: French, meaning "milk."

Lamb fries: Lamb testicles.

Langouste: French for lobster or crawfish.

Larding: To insert strips of salt pork into meat to add flavor and prevent dryness while roasting. Larding is done by attaching the strip of salt pork to a larding needle and drawing it through the meat.

Leek: A plant of the green onion family. It has little or no bulb and has fairly long, broad, mild flavored, green stems.

The green stems are used to season or flavor other foods.

Légumes: Vegetables. Also refers to dried vegetables such as beans, lentils and split peas.

Lentil: A flat edible seed of the pea family; it is used in soup.

Limburger cheese: Soft, rich, odorous, ripened cheese originally made in Belgium.

London broil: A broiled flank steak, sliced on the bias and usually served with a rich mushroom or Bordelaise sauce.

Lyonnaise: To prepare and serve with onions (example: lyonnaise potatoes).

Macédoine: A blended mixture of fruit or vegetables.

Madrilène: A clear consommé with a tomato flavor. It can be served jellied or hot.

Maître d'hôtel: Head of the dining room service.

Maraschino: Cherries preserved in an imitation maraschino liqueur.

Marinade: A brine or pickling solution in which meat is soaked before cooking to change or enrich the flavor.

Marinate: To soak an item in a marinade.

Marmite: An earthenware pot in which soup is heated and served.

Marrow: Soft tissue from the center of beef and veal bones.

Marsala: A semi-dry Italian sherry wine.

Masking: To cover an item completely, usually with a sauce.

Mayonnaise: A rich salad dressing emulsified by whipping together eggs, oil and vinegar.

Melba: Applied to servings of whole fruits with ice cream between and covered with a melba sauce.

Melba toast: Very thin, toasted, slices of white rolls or bread.

Menthe: French, meaning "mint."

Melt: To dissolve or make liquid by the application of heat.

Menu: List of foods served. Bill of fare.

Meringue: Egg whites and sugar beaten together to form a white frothy mass. It is used to top pies and cakes.

Meunière: Pan fried, served with butter freshly browned, lemon juice and chopped parsley.

Mignon: Petite or small pieces, usually of beef tenderloin.

Milanaise: In the style of Italy. Used when some type of pasta is being served. (Example: spaghetti Milanaise).

Minced: To cut very, very fine.

Mincemeat: A blended mixture of finely chopped cooked beef, currants, apples, suet and spices. Used in the preparation of mincemeat pie.

Minestrone: A thick Italian vegetable soup, with some vegetables, dried légumes and Italian pasta. Usually served with Parmesan cheese.

Minute steak: A small, fairly thin, boneless sirloin steak.

Mirepoix: A mixture of fairly fine diced vegetables (carrots, onions and celery).

Mixing: To merge into one mass two or more ingredients.

Mixed grill: A combination of any four broiled or grilled items. Usually lamb chop, bacon, sausage and tomato slices.

Mocha: Coffee flavoring; used for icings.

Mold: A metal form in which certain foods are shaped.

Mongol soup: A combination of tomato and split pea soup, with julienne cut vegetables.

Mornay sauce: A rich cream sauce with eggs and Parmesan cheese added.

Mousse: A frozen dessert made chiefly of whipped cream, sweetening, and flavoring. Also a gelatin entrée of ground poultry, meat or fish lightened by the addition of whipped cream.

Mozarella: A fairly soft Italian type

cheese, originally made from buffalo's milk. It has a rubbery texture and is excellent to use in pizza pies.

Mulligatawny: A thick East Indian soup consisting of chicken stock, rice, vegetables and highly seasoned with curry powder.

Mutton: The flesh of mature sheep.

Napoleons: A French pastry made by separating layers of puff paste with a cream filling and topping with fondant icing.

Navarin: A rich brown mutton stew garnished with carrots and turnips.

Noir: French, meaning "black."

Noisette: Small pieces of loin of lamb or pork (usually the eye of a chop) minus all bone and fat either broiled or sautéed.

Nougat: A confection of pasty consistency, containing sugar, almonds, and pistachio nuts.

O'Brien: With green peppers and pimientos, usually diced small.

Oeuf: French for "egg."

Omelet: Beaten eggs, seasoned, fried with butter or grease in a pan until it starts to puff, then rolled or folded over.

Panache: An expression meaning "of mixed colors"; can be two or more kinds of one item in a dish.

Papaya: A tropical fruit whose juice yields an enzyme used to tenderize certain meats.

Papillote: With paper. Usually the item associated with the word is cooked and served in paper.

Parboil: To partially cook or boil in water.

Parfait: Varicolored ice creams served in a tall parfait glass with syrup and sometimes fruit, garnished with whipped cream, chopped nuts and cherry.

Parisienne: French, meaning a female of Paris, but usually used in reference to potatoes cut into small round balls with a Parisienne scoop.

Parmentière: Served with potatoes. This term is usually used with soup (that is, soups containing potatoes).

Parmesan: A hard Italian cheese, usually sold in grated form.

Parsley: One of the two delicate herbs used mainly to garnish other foods.

Pastry bag: A duck cloth, cone bag with metal tip at the small end. It is used to decorate foods.

Pâté: A paste of ground meat or liver.

Paysanne: Peasant style, usually vegetables diced small or shredded.

Persillade: Garnished with parsley.

Petite: French, meaning "small."

Petite marmite: A strong consommé and chicken broth blended together and served with diamond cut cooked vegetables, beef and chicken.

Petits fours: Small cakes, iced with fondant and decorated.

Pilau or **pilaf:** Rice cooked in chicken stock with minced onions and seasoning.

Pimiento: Sweet red peppers, canned.

Piquant: An item, usually a sauce, that is sharp and tart to the taste.

Pistachio nuts: Small, thin shell, light green tropical nut.

Planked: Meat or fish served on a board or hardwood plank, garnished with duchess potatoes and vegetables.

Poach: To cook in water that bubbles only slightly.

Poisson: French, meaning "fish."

Polonaise: A garnish consisting of bread crumbs freshly browned and mixed with chopped parsley and hard boiled eggs.

Pomme: French, meaning "apple."

Pommes de terre: French, meaning earth apples or apples of the earth, that is *potatoes.*

Popovers: Quick puffed-up hot bread made of milk, sugar, eggs, and flour.

Porter house steak: Cut from the loin by the American method of cutting. Cut with the T-bone left in the loin, contains both sirloin and a large amount of tenderloin.

Potage: A thick soup.

Pot pie: Meat and vegetables in a rich

sauce, served in a casserole covered with a pie crust.

Poulet: French, meaning "chicken."

Printanière: Served with an assortment of small cut spring vegetables.

Proof: To let yeast dough rise by setting it in a warm moist place (85°F).

Purée: Any food cooked to a pulp. Thick soup (pea, tomato, etc.).

Quahog: Indian name for the large Atlantic Coast clams.

Quenelle: A meat dumpling, usually of chicken or veal.

Ragout: A thick, savory brown stew.

Ramekin: A small shallow baking dish in which foods are baked and served.

Rasher: A thin slice of bacon; usually a rasher of bacon calls for 3 slices.

Ravigote: Cold sauce, made with a mayonnaise base, chopped green herb and tarragon vinegar, it has a tart taste.

Ravioli: Small, square noodle dough cases filled with seasoned ground meat and spinach which are poached in chicken stock and served with a meat sauce.

Reduce: To concentrate a liquid by lengthly simmering.

Remoulade sauce: A highly seasoned cold sauce similar to tartar sauce, but with mustard and ground pepper added.

Render: To cook the grease out of animal fat.

Risotto: Rice baked with minced onions and meat stock. After baking, Parmesan cheese is added.

Rissolé: French, meaning "brown." This term is generally used with oven-brown potatoes (example: rissolé potatoes).

Roe: Fish eggs.

Romaine: Long narrow, crisp leaves of salad green. The outer leaves are a fairly dark green, the inter leaves are light in color. It has a mild flavor.

Roquefort: A famous French blue vein cheese.

Rôti: French, meaning "roast."

Rouge: French, meaning "red."

Roulade: Meat roll or rolled meat.

Roux: Equal parts of flour and fat used to thicken liquids when preparing sauces, soup and gravies.

Royale: A mixture of cream and eggs baked into a custard to be used as a garnish for consommé and broth.

Saccharin: A coal tar product used as a substitute for sugar. It has no food value.

Saffron: A seasoning. The dried orange colored stigmas of a purple crocus. It is exteremely expensive.

Salamander: A small broiler-like heating unit with the heat coming from above. Used to brown and glaze individual servings of certain preparations.

Salami: A highly seasoned dried sausage of pork and beef.

Sauerbraten: A sour beef pot roast. The meat is marinated from 3 to 5 days in a vinegar solution to sour the beef. Served with a sour sauce.

Sauté: To fry quickly in shallow grease.

Sautoir: A heavy, flat, copper sauce pan.

Scald: To heat milk or cream just below the boiling point until a scum forms on the surface.

Scallion: A green onion with long thick stem but very small bulb.

Scallop: The muscle of a sea mollusk which operates the opening and closing of the two shells.

Scone: A type of Scottish quick bread similar to a biscuit.

Score: To mark the surface of certain foods with shallow slits to improve appearance or to increase tenderness.

Scrapple: A food made by boiling together seasoned chopped meat, usually pork, and corn meal or flour. Served in fried slices.

Scrod: A young cod or haddock fish.

Sear: To brown the surface of meat by intense heat.

Shad: A salt water fish with markings similar to the whitefish. It is valuable because of its highly prized roe.

Shallots: A small onion-like vegetable allied to the garlic bulb, has a fairly strong onion flavor.

Sherbet: Fruit juices that have been flavored and frozen.

Shirred eggs: Eggs that have been cooked in a shallow casserole with butter.

Shredded: Cut or shaved into thin strips. Shredding is usually done with a French knife or slicing machine.

Sift: To pass dry ingredients through a fine screen to make light.

Simmer: To cook in liquid just below the boiling point (200°F).

Sizzling steak: Steak served on a very hot metal platter so that the juice is still sizzling when the steak is served.

Smörgåsbord: Swedish appetizers, salads, meat balls, etc., displayed for self service as a first course, it is followed by a hot meal.

Smother: To cook in a covered container until tender (example: smothered onions).

Sole: A flat, white meated fish from both the Atlantic and Pacific Oceans. It has a white and black skinned side.

Soufflé: A very light, puffed up item. Usually caused by folding beaten egg whites into a basic batter.

Sous cloche: To serve an item under a glass bell.

Spaetzles: A heavy Austrian noodle prepared by running a heavy batter through a large hole colander into boiling stock.

Spit: A pointed metal rod used for roasting meats over an open fire.

Spoon bread: A southern type of corn bread baked in a casserole and of such consistency that it must be served with a spoon.

Spumone: A fancy Italian ice cream containing fruit and nuts.

Squab: A young pigeon that has never flown.

Steep: To soak in a hot liquid to extract flavor and color.

Steer: A young, castrated, male beef animal.

Stew: To cook meat and vegetables in liquid just below the boiling point.

St. Germain: Containing purée of peas, usually used with split pea soup.

Stir: To blend ingredients using a circular motion.

Stock: The liquid in which meat, poultry, fish or vegetables have been cooked.

Strawberries Romanoff: Strawberries soaked in cointreau or kirsch liqueur and folden into whipped cream.

Stroganoff: Sautéed pieces of beef tenderloin, cooked gently in a sour cream sauce.

Suet: The hard fat around the kidney and loins of mutton and beef animals used in cooking and for making tallow.

Suprême: Rich chicken velouté sauce made with chicken stock and cream; also a way of serving. (Examples: shrimp cocktail or fruit cup on crushed ice may be referred to as "shrimp cocktail suprême.")

Sweetbreads: The thymus gland of calves and lambs.

Swiss chard: A variety of beets, the leaves of which are used as a vegetable and for salad. It is cooked like spinach.

Swiss steak: A fairly tough cut of beef, cut into steak form, browned and baked in its own juice until tender.

Tabasco: A brand name for a red pepper sauce, very hot.

Table d'hôte: A meal of several courses served at a set price. The dinner menu in most restaurants is served table d'hôte.

Tapioca: A starch prepared from the roots of a bitter cassava plant, used in puddings and for thickening some soups. Fine grain tapioca is called "pearl."

Tarragon: A European herb the leaves of which are used in cooking and to flavor vinegar.

Tart: Small individual pies, filled with fruit or fruit and cream, without a top crust.

Tartare steak: Highly seasoned, raw, ground steak, usually served with a raw egg yolk and onions.

Tasse: French for cup.

Tenderloin: A strip of very tender meat lying inside the loin cavity of beef, pork, lamb and veal animals.

Terrapin: Any of several North American fresh-water turtles, prized as a food.

Terrine: An earthenware pot resembling a casserole.

Timbale: A baked drum-shaped mold.

Torte: A fairly small, rich, decorated cake.

Tortilla: Mexican griddle cake, a flat unleavened corn cake, baked on a heated stone or iron.

Tortoni: An ice cream dessert containing chopped almonds or dried ground macaroons.

Toss: To cause a rising and falling action for the purpose of blending certain ingredients together, such as various types of salads.

Tournedos: Small, round, fairly thin slices of beef tenderloin, usually sautéed. or broiled.

Tripe: The edible lining of a beef stomach.

Truffle: A black fungus somewhat similar to the mushroom, grown mainly in France. They grow underground and are rooted out by trained pigs. They are used for seasoning and garnishing.

Truss: To bind or fasten with string or skewers, usually applied to poultry in preparation for roasting.

Tureen: A fairly large deep vessel, usually of silver, in which soup is served.

Variable: Changeable.

Veal birds: Flattened veal fillets rolled around a forcemeat and baked in the oven.

Velouté: French, meaning "velvety"; a smooth, creamy white sauce made by combining stock and roux.

Venison: Deer meat.

Vermicelli: Long fine rods of dried flour paste (pasta), similar to spaghetti but thinner.

Vert: French, meaning "green."

Viande: French, meaning "meat."

Vichyssoise: A cream of potato soup served cold.

Vin: French, meaning "wine."

Vol au vent: A case or shell made of puff pastry which is filled with a meat or poultry mixture and served covered with a lid of puff pastry.

Wellington: Beef tenderloin baked in a rich dough until tenderloin is slightly rare and crust is crisp and golden. A gourmet item.

Welsh rarebit: Melted Cheddar cheese, flavored with beer, mustard and Worcestershire sauce, served very hot over toast.

White wash: A thickening agent consisting of equal parts of flour and cornstarch diluted in cold water.

Whip: To beat rapidly to increase volume and incorporate air.

Wiener Schnitzel: A veal cutlet, breaded and fried and usually served with a slice of lemon and anchovy. It is of Viennese origin.

Wild rice: The brown seed of a tall northern water grass; usually served with wild game.

Yorkshire pudding: A batter of flour, milk, salt, etc., baked with roast rib of beef and served with each order.

Zest: A rind of lemon or orange.

Zucchini: Italian squash resembling the cucumber in appearance.

bibliography

AMENDOLA, JOSEPH. *Bakers' Manual for Quantity Baking and Pastry Making.* New York: Hayden Book Co., 1972.

CRAWFORD, H. W., & McDOWELL, M. C. *Math Workbook, Food Service & Lodging,* Published by: Institutions Volume Feeding Magazine, Chicago, Ill., 1970. Distributed by: Cahners Books, Boston, Mass.

DANIEL, A. R. *The Bakers' Dictionary.* London: Maclaren and Sons, Ltd., 1949.

ESCOFFIER, A. *The Escoffier Cook Book.* New York: Crown Publishers, Inc., 1959.

Establishing and Operating a Restaurant. Washington, D.C.: Government Printing Office, 1957.

FINANCE, CHARLES. *Buffet Catering.* New York: Hayden Book Co., 1958.

Gourmet Cookbook. New York: Gourmet Books, Inc., 1965.

LEFLER, JANET; RUPP, MILDRED and CHIAPPERINE, FELICE. *Canapes, Hors d'oeuvres and Buffet Dishes.* New York: Hayden Book Co., 1963.

LEVIE, ALBERT. *The Meat Handbook.* Westport, Conn.: Avi Publishing Co., 3rd edition, 1970.

The Professional Chef. Chicago: Medalish Publications, 1967.

SHIRCLIFFE, ARNOLD. *Edgewater Beach Salad Book.* Evanston, Ill.: John Willy, Inc., 1965.

SNYDER, RICHARD V. *Decorating Cakes for Fun and Profit.* New York: Exposition Press, Inc., 1953.

STRAUSE, MONROE. *Pie Marches On.* New York: Hayden Book Co., 1954.

SULTAN, WILLIAM J. *Practical Baking,* 2nd edition, 1969. Westport, Conn.: Avi Publishing Co.

TRACY, MARIAN. *The Shellfish Cookbook.* Indianapolis, Ind.: Bobbs-Merrill Co., Inc., 1964.

WENZEL, GEORGE L. *Blueprints for Restaurant Success,* rev. edition, 1970. Austin, Texas: George L. Wenzel, 403 Riley Road.

The Wise Encyclopedia of Cookery. New York: Wm. H. Wise and Co., Inc., 1953.

index

Veal goulash, Hungarian
381-382
Veal gravy 321
Veal kidney and brandy stew
386-387
Veal loin chops, broiled 385
Veal paprika with sauerkraut
385-386
Veal ragout 381
Veal scallopine with mushrooms
384-385
Veal steak, sautéed 375-376
Veal stew 382-383
Veal stock 190-191
Vegetable man, duties of 6
Vegetables peeler 17
Vegetable products 40-41
Vegetable salads 137-142
Vegetable soup 194-195
Vegetables 225-262; baking 58;
boiling 59-61; classifications
225-227; cooking 57-64;
market forms 227; prepara-
tion 227-230; recipes
230-262; steaming 61-64;
storage 228-229
Velouté sauces 294-299
Vertical cutter/mixer 30

Vichyssoise 224
Victoria sauce 297
Vinaigrette dressing 162
Vinegar and oil dressing 160
Vinegars 42
Virginia pastry dough 557-558

W

Waffle potatoes 267
Waffles 80
Waldorf salad 133, 135
Warm sauces 279-280, 282-289
Washing 11-12
Washing (bakery items) 65
Watercress 128
Wax bean recipes 233-234
Wax beans with pimientos 234
Weighing 27-28; adjusting
recipes 66-67; cakes 596;
conversion of weights
67-70; cookies 531; pie
dough 568
Weights, conversion of 67-70
Welsh rarebit 177-178
Western garden slaw 121
Western salad 145
Whipping cookie mixing
530-531, 546-548

Whipping method of cake
mixing 597, 606-609
White cake 609-610
White cream icing 615
White vegetables 226
Whitefish 486
Whitewash, how to make 280
Wholesale cuts, beef 327,
330-333; lamb 423,
405-407; pork 389-394; veal
365, 368-369
Wiener Schnitzel 369
Wiener tidbits, barbecued 97
Wire whips 20
Worcestershire sauce 42
Working chef, duties of 4-5

Y

Yeast 44; how used 550-551
Yellow cake 616-617
Yellow vegetables 226

Z

Zippy Italian dressing 159
Zucchini, French fried 259;
squash and tomatoes 260

Apple Pie

3/4 - 1 C. sugar.

1 tsp. cinn./nut.

6-7 C. apples.

1½ tsp - butter

→ add flour.

425°